# Nutrition and Health in Developing Countries

## Second Edition

# NUTRITION AND HEALTH SERIES

Adrianne Bendich, PhD, FACN, SERIES EDITOR

## *Recent Volumes*

# NUTRITION AND HEALTH IN DEVELOPING COUNTRIES

## Second Edition

**Editors**

**Richard D. Semba, MD, MPH**
Department of Ophthalmology, Johns Hopkins University School of Medicine,
Baltimore, MD
USA

**Martin W. Bloem, MD, PhD**
Nutrition and HIV/AIDS Policy, United Nations World Food Programme, Rome, Italy,
Department of International Health, Johns Hopkins Bloomberg
School of Public Health, Baltimore, MD,
Friedman School of Nutrition Science and Policy, Tufts University, Boston, MA

**Foreword by Peter Piot, MD, PhD**
Executive Director UNAIDS, and Under Secretary-General of the United Nations

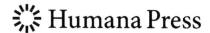 Humana Press

*Editors*
Richard D. Semba, MD, MPH
Department of Ophthalmology, Johns Hopkins
    University School of Medicine,
Baltimore, MD
USA

Martin W. Bloem, MD, PhD
Nutrition and HIV/AIDS Policy,
    United Nations World Food Programme,
    Rome, Italy,
Department of International Health,
Johns Hopkins Bloomberg School of Public
    Health, Baltimore, MD,
Friedman School of Nutrition Science and Policy,
Tufts University, Boston, MA

*Series Editor*
Adrianne Bendich, PhD, FACN
GlaxoSmithKline Consumer Healthcare
Parsippany, NJ
USA

ISBN: 978-1-934115-24-4        e-ISBN: 978-1-59745-464-3
DOI: 10.1007/978-1-59745-464-3

Library of Congress Control Number: 2008922756

Printed on acid-free paper

9 8 7 6 5 4 3 2

springer.com

# Dedication

To our parents, who struggled to bring a better life for the next generation: Hannah Semba and the late Thomas T. Semba, Japanese Americans interned in the Tule Lake and Heart Mountain "relocation" camps, and Alexander and Jacqueline Bloem, Dutch Indonesians and survivors of the Sumatra railway "work camp," the Kramat camp, and the sinking of the *Junyo Maru* by the British submarine *HMS Tradewind* off the west coast of Sumatra.

# Series Editor's Introduction

The Nutrition and Health™ series of books, as an overriding mission, provide health professionals with texts that are considered essential because each includes (1) a synthesis of the state of the science; (2) timely, in-depth reviews by the leading researchers in their respective fields; (3) extensive, up-to-date, fully annotated reference lists; (4) a detailed index; (5) relevant tables and figures; (6) identification of paradigm shifts and the consequences; (7) virtually no overlap of information between chapters, but targeted, inter-chapter referrals; (8) suggestions of areas for future research; and (9) balanced, data-driven answers to patient/health professionals questions, which are based upon the totality of evidence rather than the findings of any single study.

The series volumes are not the outcome of a symposium. Rather, each editor has the potential to examine a chosen area with a broad perspective, both in subject matter as well as in the choice of chapter authors. The international perspective, especially with regard to public health initiatives, is emphasized where appropriate. The editors, whose trainings are both research and practice oriented, have the opportunity to develop a primary objective for their book; define the scope and focus, and then invite the leading authorities from around the world to be part of their initiative. The authors are encouraged to provide an overview of the field, discuss their own research, and relate the research findings to potential human health consequences. Because each book is developed *de novo*, the chapters are coordinated so that the resulting volume imparts greater knowledge than the sum of the information contained in the individual chapters.

A key objective of the series is to develop volumes that reviewers indicate offer great value to the reader. One consequence of the favorable reviews that have followed publication of books in the series to date is the potential for the publishing of updated, second editions, lending further credence to the reviewers' assessments.

*Nutrition and Health in Developing Countries, Second Edition*, edited by Richard D. Semba and Martin W. Bloem, is an excellent example of the development of a second edition based upon the value that readers and reviewers found in the first edition, and thus there is real anticipation of this critically important updated and greatly enhanced second edition. This is the 25th volume to be published as part of the Nutrition and Health series and fully exemplifies the series' goals.

The first volume of *Nutrition and Health in Developing Countries*, edited by Richard D. Semba and Martin W. Bloem, represented the most comprehensive overview of the state of the science in international nutrition available in 2001. The volume reflected the extensive field as well as laboratory bench expertise of both world-renown editors and their in-depth knowledge of the interactions of nutritional status and its impact on global health. The first volume contained outstanding chapters that reviewers praised because of the significant insights into biological as well as public health issues concerning, as examples, food availability, nutrient function, disease consequences, and health policy issues.

*Nutrition and Health in Developing Countries, Second Edition* is especially timely as the first volume was published before the advent of many of the major natural disasters that have severely affected the nutritional status of many populations already documented to be at high risk of under-nutrition. Moreover, new serious diseases have been identified, including severe acute respiratory syndrome (SARS), and these novel infectious organisms, as opportunistic pathogens, cause illness in the weak and malnourished that further debilitates these populations. The second edition is comprised of 34 chapters and contains 12 new chapters that focus on information about the consequences of natural disasters, such as the Indian Ocean tsunami in 2004, where 1.7 million people were displaced and emerging infections, such as SARS and bird flu, that have the potential to be transmitted rapidly from developing nations to the rest of the world. There are also new chapters dealing with nutrition in the elderly, nutritional consequences of tobacco, industrialization of food production and retail sales and impact on health, the effects of multi-micronutrient supplementation programs, nutrition surveillance programs and policy issues, and of great interest, the ethics of clinical nutrition research in developing countries. All of the 22 chapters that were included in the First Edition have been significantly updated and enhanced in the Second Edition. Thus, the benchmark status of the First Edition has been raised to an even higher level and the Second Edition continues to provide clear, objective documentation of the nutritional status of populations and the effects of nutritional interventions on the health and well-being of affected populations in developing countries.

Dr. Richard D. Semba and Dr. Martin W. Bloem, who have edited both the First and Second Editions, are internationally recognized leaders in the fields of clinical nutrition, ophthalmology, and immunology research. Both editors are physicians and each has also completed further advanced degrees. Dr. Semba, MD, MPH, is the W. Richard Green Professor of Ophthalmology at the Wilmer Eye Institute at Johns Hopkins University and is a global leader in nutrition research who has published extensively on the role of vitamin A deficiency in childhood blindness. Dr. Bloem, MD, PhD, is Chief of Nutrition Service, United Nations World Food Program in Rome, Italy, and previously served as the Chief Medical Officer for Helen Keller International. Each has extensive experience in academic medicine as well as in-depth field experiences, and collectively they have over 300 professional publications and numerous awards for their efforts to improve the nutrition of those with the greatest needs around the world.

The Second Edition is organized as a stand-alone text that provides the historic beginnings of public health nutritional interventions in developing nations, assessment of the current nutritional status of the populations across the lifespan, examines the macro as well as the micronutrient intakes of at-risk populations, and discusses the clinical research that has contributed to the acceptance by governments of intervention programs to improve the health of their nations. In addition, recommendations for future research are provided and targeted to those at greatest risk for malnutrition including infants, toddlers, women of childbearing age, pregnant and lactating women, and the elderly. Of importance, the area of obesity in developing countries is also explored as the number of overweight and obese malnourished children has continued to grow over the past decade.

The Second Edition almost doubles the size of the original volume and contains 34 extensive, in-depth chapters covering the most important aspects of the complex interactions between diet, under-nutrition, obesity patterns around the world, infections, immune function, and the mental, physical, as well as the genetic consequences of malnutrition throughout the lifespan. The editors have chosen 44 well-recognized and respected chapter authors from 14 countries who have included complete definitions of terms with the abbreviations fully defined for the reader and who use terms consistently between chapters.

The volume concentrates on the examination of the major health and nutrition-related problems seen in developing countries and the population groups most affected. There are separate chapters on maternal mortality, low birth weight and perinatal mortality, infant mortality and child growth and development, as well as the new chapter that concentrates on the elderly. Other chapters include well-organized, updated information on malaria, tuberculosis, HIV, measles, diarrheal diseases, and acute lower respiratory tract infections and the populations at greatest risk for these adverse health conditions. Separate chapters are devoted to vitamin A, vitamin D, iron, iodine, zinc, multiple micronutrient deficiencies, as well as overall macronutrient under-nutrition. There are critical reviews of the current and future scenarios that include the shifting importance between under- and over-nutrition (obesity), rural to urban shifts in populations, increased exposure to environmental hazards including pollution, food- and water-borne contaminants and pathogens, and others that are affected by changes in socioeconomic factors. Finally, there are critical insights into the relevance of nutritional interventions and ethical considerations in the conduct of studies in developing countries. Relevant chapters include a systematic cost-effectiveness analysis of intervention programs and the difficulties of both implementing as well as then analyzing the effectiveness of nutrition programs. The remaining chapters place in perspective the multifaceted requirements to affect global policies, even in areas of agreement, such as the improvement of the nutritional status of individuals at greatest risk in developing countries. Readers will benefit greatly from the 96 well-organized tables and 125 relevant figures and over 4600 references that are cited in this comprehensive volume.

*Nutrition and Health in Developing Countries, Second Edition* edited by Richard D. Semba and Martin W. Bloem, stands as the most comprehensive reference text in the field, and provides health professionals at all levels of care as well as policy makers and program designers and implementers with balanced, referenced facts and data on which to base sound recommendations. This volume is of equal importance in the education of the next generation of health care professionals interested in improving global health, as nutrition remains the key to success. I applaud the efforts of the editors as they have developed the most authoritative resource published to date. This excellent text is a very welcome addition to the Nutrition and Health Series.

*Adrianne Bendich, PhD, FACN,*
*Series Editor*

# Foreword

With the threat of a global recession and major climate-related disasters looming large in the popular media, society as a whole faces the danger of losing sight of key problems that underlie much of the potential social damage from such crises—problems, such as those relating to nutrition and health in developing countries, that persist and hinder the achievement of the Millennium Development Goals (MDGs).

Global health and nutrition problems can only be solved through a firm understanding of the various levels of causality and the interactions between their various determinants. This second edition of *Nutrition and Health in Developing Countries*, which contains new chapters on humanitarian emergencies, food in humanitarian relief, food policy, the emerging role of supermarkets in developing countries, homestead food production, aging, ethics, and the adverse impact of parental tobacco use, reflects the transitions and increasing complexity in developing countries.

Among the major problems facing the world today is AIDS. As I stated in 2007, the AIDS epidemic is not done yet, but is still expanding and globalizing. It is a disease that was not even known 26 years ago but is now the leading cause of death in Africa and the fifth leading cause of death in the world, after heart diseases, all cancers, strokes, and respiratory illness.

Throughout the world, more women are becoming infected with HIV. Where AIDS has severely affected human and social capital, development has not only stagnated, it has reversed, threatening the very future of vulnerable populations.

While we have gained scientific understanding on the biological and social drivers of the AIDS epidemic, and solutions are available to deal with the disease itself as well as conditions arising from it, there is still a great need for increased investment and focused spending on evidence-informed strategies for HIV prevention and for impact mitigation.

The global problem of AIDS is not just a medical or public health problem any more than climate change is just an environmental problem. Like most of the world's major problems, AIDS presents a social challenge—a problem of how people relate to other people and how these relations have shaped economic, sexual health, and other important individual and collective choices. Accordingly, effective solutions must be developed with a view to addressing all the aspects we now know to be important—access to antiretroviral therapies, gender equality and women's empowerment, poverty alleviation, food and nutrition security, and other key factors that can lead to the eradication of the disease worldwide.

We have also seen how successes in HIV prevention and treatment lead to increased uptake of other health services and therefore improved health and well being. This means greater investments are needed to strengthen health systems and human resources for health as well as the capacity of local communities to respond given that prevention efforts are happening largely outside the health sector.

In this volume, readers will find many of the same authors from the first edition and some new ones. The commonality they share is the diversity of their backgrounds: clinical nutrition, medicine, immunology, infectious disease, epidemiology, public health nutrition, anthropology, health policy, economics, and disaster planning.

The breadth of knowledge and information in this book should stimulate fresh thinking, comprehensive and effective policies and programs, and continued research across disciplines toward the goal of improving health and nutrition in developing countries. This will bring us steps closer to our wider goals of solving major humanitarian crises such as AIDS and achieving the vision of the world set forth in the MDGs.

*Peter Piot, MD, Phd*
*Executive Director, UNAIDS*
*Under Secretary-General of the United Nations*

# Preface

*Nutrition and Health in Developing Countries, Second Edition,* was written with the underlying conviction that global health and nutrition problems can be solved only through a firm understanding of the different levels of causality and the interactions between the various determinants. Although the book focuses on the problems in developing countries, we recognize that as a result of globalization, there is no longer a clear distinction between health and nutrition problems between the developed and the less-developed world. Emerging diseases such as HIV/AIDS, tuberculosis, and obesity show how the world is connected, and that knowledge about health and nutrition problems is also essential for professionals in developed countries. The objective of *Nutrition and Health in Developing Countries, Second Edition,* is to provide policymakers, nutritionists, students, scientists, and professionals with the most recent and up-to-date knowledge regarding major health and nutritional problems in developing countries. This specific knowledge is presented to facilitate an integrated approach to health research, programs, and policy. As such, the approach represents the tension inherent in combining diverse disciplines. This book is meant as a synthesis, and it is not meant as an exhaustive treatise of all infectious diseases or every nutrient deficiency in developing countries as such information is generally accessible in other textbooks.

We have greatly expanded the second edition to 34 chapters and have included new chapters relevant to humanitarian emergencies, including a case study of the Indian Ocean tsunami in 2004, food in humanitarian relief, food policy, the emerging role of supermarkets in developing countries, homestead food production, aging, ethics, and the adverse impact of parental tobacco use on child health in poor families. These new chapters reflect the increasing complexity and changes that are occurring in developing countries. The Millennium Development Goals of the United Nations call for major progress in eradicating extreme poverty and hunger, in reducing child mortality, and in improving maternal health; we hope that these chapters provide insight and solutions that will help to attain these goals.

*Nutrition and Health in Developing Countries, Second Edition,* begins with a historical overview of the idea of nutrition and development, and shows how the concepts of progress and development evolved from the Enlightenment and shaped the basic precepts underlying work in nutrition and public health for the last two centuries. Many people working in public health may be impressed by the conditions often found in developing countries today: high infant mortality, widespread malnutrition, goiter, tuberculosis, and other health problems. However, similar conditions were faced by public health and policy makers in the early 20th century in Europe and the United States. A better understanding of nutrition and implementation of this new knowledge into policy helped to eradicate many nutritional and infectious diseases. An appreciation of these historical examples may help avoid "reinventing the wheel," a phenomenon apparent in some nutrition and health research conducted in developing countries today.

The first section of *Nutrition and Health in Developing Countries, Second Edition*, focuses on the major health indicators in developing countries: maternal mortality, low birth weight, neonatal mortality, infant mortality, and child growth and development. The differences in mortality rates between developing countries and industrialized countries are presented in these chapters and are striking, with the disparity greatest for maternal mortality. In many circumstances, the application of known, effective interventions could reduce the large disparities in mortality between developed and developing countries.

The second section of the book deals with major infectious diseases in which nutrition plays a role: diarrheal diseases, acute lower-respiratory infections, measles, malaria, tuberculosis, and HIV infection. There is a purposeful overlap between these chapters on specific health problems and subsequent chapters on nutritional deficiencies (e.g., the role of zinc in prevention and treatment of diarrheal diseases). This approach was used to emphasize the different perspectives that may be taken either from the standpoint of infectious disease or from a specific nutrient.

In the third section of the book, the general problem of malnutrition and specific deficiencies in vitamin A, vitamin D, zinc, iron, and iodine and multiple-micronutrient deficiencies are presented. Large advances have been made in our understanding of micronutrient malnutrition in the last three decades. Vitamin A deficiency is a major cause of childhood morbidity, mortality, and blindness in developing countries, and it is apparent that many diverse approaches are needed to eliminate this problem. New research shows that zinc deficiency is widespread, and that zinc supplementation can reduce morbidity from diarrheal and respiratory diseases. Iron deficiency remains the most common micronutrient deficiency among women and children worldwide, and its reduction will be a major challenge. The elimination of iodine deficiency disorders through widespread use of iodized salt appears to be an attainable goal in the near future. As micronutrient deficiencies often occur together due to limited consumption of good dietary sources, there is a shift in focus to combating these deficiencies in combination.

The fourth section of the book deals with new emerging issues of countries in an intermediate stage of development, such as the nutrition transition in which many nutritional deficiencies decline and other health problems, such as obesity, diabetes, and cardiovascular disease, become more prominent. Life expectancy is increasing in most developing countries, which raises new concerns about nutrition in older adults. Another pressing problem in developing countries is rapid urbanization, as observed in large cities such as Mexico City, Lagos, Dhaka, and Jakarta, and there are new challenges in achieving food and nutrition security in these settings. Although tobacco control has not usually been considered a problem related to child health and survival, new findings from Bangladesh, India, and Indonesia show that, among poor families, smoking diverts precious resources from food to tobacco, with an adverse impact on quality of diet and an associated higher level of child malnutrition and mortality of infants and children under 5 years old. In many countries, especially in Asia, the prevalence of smoking is 50% to 75%, which has serious implications for child health. Tobacco control is placed front and center as a child survival strategy.

The fifth and final section of *Nutrition and Health in Developing Countries, Second Edition,* deals with special topics such as humanitarian emergencies, the role of food in humanitarian relief, homestead food production, how supermarkets are changing agricultural economics and food security, food policy, benefits of multimicronutrient supplements in children, use of nutritional surveillance data, ethics in public health research, and the Indian Ocean tsunami of 2004 as a case example of emergency relief. The book closes with a broad view on nutrition and health policy, analytical frameworks for public policy analysis, and thoughtful insight into the development and implementation of sound public policy in public health and public nutrition.

During the preparation of this Second Edition, we were deeply saddened by the passing of our friend and colleague, François Delange, the Executive Director of the International Council for Control of Iodine Deficiency Disorders. He was strongly dedicated to the elimination of iodine deficiency disorders, and he will be greatly missed by the international nutrition community.

We wish to thank our lovely series editor, Adrianne Bendich, for the kind support and encouragement that she has been giving us over the last decade. Her enthusiasm and breadth and depth of knowledge regarding the complex field of nutrition has been an inspiration for all of us.

As editors, we are pleased to bring together this group of authors from diverse backgrounds of clinical nutrition, medicine, immunology, infectious disease, epidemiology, public health nutrition, anthropology, health policy, economics, and disaster planning. We hope that this book will stimulate further thought, comprehensive and effective policies and programs, and research across disciplines in the goal of improving health and nutrition in developing countries to reach the Millennium Development Goals by the year 2015.

*Richard D. Semba, MD, MPH*
*Martin W. Bloem, MD, PhD*

# Contents

# Contributors

CORA M. BEST, MSC • *Nutrition Service, World Food Programme, Rome, Italy*

ODILIA I. BERMÚDEZ, PhD, MPH • *Nutritional Epidemiology Program, Jean Mayer USDA Human Nutrition Research Center on Aging, Tufts University, Boston, MA*

ROBERT E. BLACK, MD, MPH • *Department of International Health, Johns Hopkins Bloomberg School of Public Health, Baltimore, MD*

MARTIN W. BLOEM, MD, PhD • *Nutrition Services, United Nations World Food Programme, Rome, Italy, and Department of International Health, Johns Hopkins Bloomberg School of Public Health, Baltimore, MD; and Friedman School of Nutrition Science and Policy, Tufts University, Boston, MA*

MICKEY CHOPRA, BSC, BMED, MSC • *South African Medical Research Council, Cape Town, South Africa*

PARUL CHRISTIAN, DRPH • *Division of Human Nutrition, Department of International Health, Johns Hopkins Bloomberg School of Public Health, Baltimore, MD*

SIMON COLLIN, MSC • *Infectious Diseases Epidemiology Unit, Department of Epidemiology and Population Health, London School of Hygiene and Tropical Medicine, London, UK*

IAN DARNTON-HILL, MD, MPH, MSC • *Nutrition Section, UNICEF; and Institute of Human Nutrition, College of Physicians and Surgeons, Columbia University, New York, NY*

FRANÇOIS DELANGE, MD[†] • *International Council for Control of Iodine Deficiency Disorders, Brussels, Belgium*

MERCEDES DE ONIS, MD, PhD • *Department of Nutrition, World Health Organization, Geneva, Switzerland*

SASKIA DE PEE, PhD • *Nutrition Service, World Food Programme, Rome, Italy; and Friedman School of Nutrition Science and Policy, Tufts University, Boston, MA*

COLLEEN M. DOAK, PhD • *Department of Nutrition and Health, Institute of Health Sciences, Vrije University, Amsterdam, The Netherlands*

TANYA DOHERTY, MSC, MPH, PhD • *South African Medical Research Council, Cape Town, South Africa*

---

[†]*Deceased*

WAFAIE W. FAWZI, MBBS, MPH, DRPH • *Departments of Nutrition and Epidemiology, Harvard School of Public Health, Boston, MA*

VÉRONIQUE FILIPPI, DDG, DISP, PhD • *Infectious Diseases Epidemiology Unit, Department of Epidemiology and Population Health, London School of Hygiene and Tropical Medicine, London, UK*

JAMES L. GARRETT, PhD • *Food Consumption and Nutrition Division, International Food Policy Research Institute, Washington, DC*

LAWRENCE HADDAD, PhD • *Institute of Development Studies, University of Sussex, Brighton, UK*

SUSAN HORTON, PhD • *Wilfrid Laurier University, Waterloo, Ontario, Canada*

SANDRA L. HUFFMAN, SCD • *Consultant, Global Alliance for Improved Nutrition, Geneva, Switzerland*

GREGORY HUSSEY, MB, CHB, FFCH • *Child Health Unit, Department of Pediatrics and Child Health, University of Cape Town, Rondebosche, Cape Town, South Africa*

REINHARD KAISER, MD, MPH • *Nairobi, Kenya*

CLAUDIO F. LANATA, MD, MPH • *Instituto de Investigacion Nutricional, Lima, Peru*

KARIM MANJI, MBBS, MMED, MPH • *Muhimbili University College of Medical Sciences, Dar-es-Salaam, Tanzania*

REGINA MOENCH-PFANNER, MSC, PhD • *Food Fortification Program, Global Alliance for Improved Nutrition, Geneva, Switzerland*

DAVID PELLETIER, PhD • *Division of Nutritional Science, Cornell University, Ithaca, NY*

JOHN M. PETTIFOR, MB, BCH, PhD, FCPAED • *Department of Paediatrics and Medical Research Council Mineral Metabolism Research Unit, University of the Witwatersrand and Chris Hani Baragwanath Hospital, Johannesburg, South Africa*

BARRY M. POPKIN, PhD • *Department of Nutrition, Carolina Population Center, University of North Carolina, Chapel Hill, NC*

USHA RAMAKRISHNAN, PhD • *Department of International Health, Rollins School of Public Health, Emory University, Atlanta, GA*

MARIE T. RUEL, PhD • *Food Consumption and Nutrition Division, International Food Policy Research Institute, Washington, DC*

CARINE RONSMANS, MD, DPH • *London School of Hygiene and Tropical Medicine, Maternal and Child Epidemiology, London, UK*

DIRK G. SCHROEDER, SCD, MPH • *DrTango, Inc., Roswell, GA; and Hubert Department of Global Health, Rollins School of Public Health, Emory University, Atlanta, GA*

RICHARD D. SEMBA, MD, MPH • *Department of Ophthalmology, Johns Hopkins University School of Medicine, Baltimore, MD*

ANURAJ H. SHANKAR, SCD • *World Health Organization, Jakarta, Indonesia*

ROGER SHRIMPTON, PhD • *United Nations Standing Committee on Nutrition, New York, NY; and Institute of Child Health, London, UK*

NOEL W. SOLOMONS, MD • *Center for Studies of Sensory Impairment, Aging and Metabolism (CESSIAM), Guatemala City, Guatemala*

PAUL B. SPIEGEL, MD, MPH • *United Nations High Commissioner for Refugees, Geneva, Switzerland*

AMINUZZAMAN TALUKDER, BSC • *Helen Keller International, Phnom Penh, Cambodia*

C. PETER TIMMER, PhD • *Center for Global Development, Washington, DC*

ANDREW THORNE-LYMAN, MHS • *Nutrition Service, World Food Programme, Rome, Italy*

MONIQUE VAN LETTOW, PhD • *Dignitas International, Zomba, Malawi*

CESAR G. VICTORA, MD, PhD • *Universidade Federal de Pelotas, Pelotas, Brazil*

EDUARDO VILLAMOR, MD, MPH, DRPH • *Departments of Nutrition and Epidemiology, Harvard School of Public Health, Boston, MA*

PATRICK WEBB, PhD • *Friedman School of Nutrition Science and Policy, Tufts University, Boston, MA*

CHRISTOPHER WHALEN, MD • *Department of Epidemiology and Biostatistics, Case Western Reserve University School of Medicine, Cleveland, OH*

KEITH P. WEST, JR., DRPH, MPH • *Division of Human Nutrition, Department of International Health, Bloomberg School of Public Health, Johns Hopkins University, Baltimore, MD*

# 1

## Nutrition and Development: *A Historical Perspective*

*Richard D. Semba*

## 1.1 INTRODUCTION

In the last two centuries, there has been a general improvement in the health of people worldwide that has been attributed largely to changes in nutrition, hygiene, and public health. At the beginning of the 19th century, the burden of morbidity and mortality from infectious diseases such as malaria, cholera, measles, tuberculosis, and diarrheal disease and nutritional deficiency diseases such as pellagra, rickets, and vitamin A deficiency was relatively high in Europe, North America, and much of the rest of world. By the end of the 20th century, these diseases were largely eradicated from industrialized countries, but many of these diseases and their associated morbidity and mortality continue to be major problems in developing countries today. Mortality rates from infectious diseases have generally been declining in industrialized countries over the last 200 years, and improved nutrition and resistance to disease as well as better hygiene and sanitation have been cited as the main factors for a reduction in infectious disease mortality rather than technological advances in medicine [1–4].

The purpose of this chapter is to provide a brief historical overview of major ideas and events that have shaped public health over the last two centuries, with an emphasis on developments related to nutrition and infectious disease. As a concise review, this chapter is limited to selected highlights from the last 200 years; for a more detailed overview, the refer to general texts on the history of public health [5–7], medicine [8], infectious disease [9, 10], and geographical medicine [11] as well as to more specialized sources dealing with protein and energy [12], scurvy [13], pellagra [14], food [15–17], and hunger [18]. Most of this review focuses on developments in Great Britain, the United States, and France as these countries have drawn the most attention of historians of public health and nutrition.

## 1.2 THE IDEA OF PROGRESS IN PUBLIC HEALTH

The idea of progress in public health largely rose during the Enlightenment in France among the philosophes such as Denis Diderot (1713–1784) and Jean le Rond d'Alembert (1717–1783). Earlier antecedents were found in the methods of the French

From: *Nutrition and Health: Nutrition and Health in Developing Countries, Second Edition*
Edited by: R. D. Semba & M. W. Bloem © Humana Press, Totowa, NJ

rationalist philosopher and mathematician René Descartes (1596–1650) [19]. Diderot and d'Alembert edited the monumental *Encyclopédie, ou Dictionnaire raisonné des sciences, des arts et des métiers*, which was published between 1751 and 1772. The *Encyclopédie*, a major work of the Enlightenment, was meant to benefit future generations with a compendium of human knowledge [20], and it included some issues relating to health, such as the duration of life, the health of infants, and growth of population.

One of the greatest Encyclopedists was Marie-Jean-Antoine-Nicolas Caritat, Marquis de Condorcet (1743–1794), a French statesman, philosopher, and mathematician who wrote the *Esquisse d'un tableau historique des progrès de l'esprit humain* (*Sketch for a History of the Progress of the Human Mind*) [21]. A critic of Robespierre and the Jacobins, Condorcet had been accused of treason and was sentenced in absentia to the guillotine. During a period of hiding in Paris in 1792, Condorcet wrote the remarkable *Esquisse,* in which he argued for the infinite perfectability of man. Condorcet predicted that there would be equality between men and women, the abolition of war, the end of colonialism and the slave trade, more equal distribution of wealth, and the eradication of disease through progress in medical science [21]:

> *No one can doubt that, as preventive medicine improves and food and housing become healthier, as a way of life is established that develops our physical powers by exercise without ruining them by excess, as the two most virulent causes of deterioration, misery and excessive wealth, are eliminated, the average length of human life will be increased and a better health and a stronger physical constitution will be ensured. The improvement of medical practice, which will become more efficacious with the progress of reason and of the social order, will mean the end of infectious and hereditary diseases and illnesses brought on by climate, food, or working conditions. It is reasonable to hope that all other diseases may likewise disappear as their distant causes are discovered.* [22].

Condorcet's work was published posthumously in 1795 and became a seminal work in the idea of progress in Western thought [19, 23].

The assumption that "the happiness of the human species is the most desirable object for human science to promote" was expressed by William Godwin (1756–1836) in *An Enquiry Concerning Political Justice, and Its Influence on General Virtue and Happiness* [24]. Godwin noted the vast inequality in property and the role of political institutions in favoring these conditions, and he envisioned a future when intellectual and moral improvement and reform of government would reduce inequality, war, and injustice. According to Godwin, the perfectability of man was intrinsic to the human species, and the political and intellectual state of man was presumed to be in a course of progressive improvement.

Instead of indefinite progress, Thomas Robert Malthus (1766–1834), a British economist, predicted overpopulation, misery, famine, and war, and his views first appeared in an anonymous book, *An Essay on the Principle of Population as It Affects the Future Improvement of Society, with Remarks on the Speculations of Mr. Godwin, M. Condorcet, and Other Writers*, which was published in 1798 [25]. Malthus believed that the population was growing greater than the ability of the earth to provide subsistence. Preventive checks on population included moral restraint, such as the postponement of marriage and avoidance of extramarital relationships. Later, Malthus was to concede that more personal and social action could prevent much of the grim scenario that he had predicted, and the debate about Malthus is frequently revived [26].

A central idea of social medicine—an outgrowth of Enlightenment thought—was that government could use medical knowledge to improve the health of the people. A comprehensive social medicine approach was described by Johann Peter Frank (1745–1821), a German physician, in *System einer vollständigen medicinischen Polizey* (*A System of Complete Medical Police*) [27]. Frank's recommendations for sanitary, social, and economic reforms were broad and based on the idea that medical police, a benevolent form of despotism, could provide for the health and protection of the people from cradle to grave. Frank was director general of public health of Austrian Lombardy and professor of clinical medicine at the University of Padua, and his social concerns were clearly stated in his graduation address, *De populorum miseria: morborum genitrice* (*The People's Misery: Mother of Diseases*) in 1790:

> *Starvation and sickness are pictured on the face of the entire laboring class. You recognize it at first sight. And whoever has seen it will certainly not call any one of these people a free man. The word has become meaningless. Before sunrise, after having eaten a little and always the same unfermented bread that appeases his hunger only half-way, the farmer gets ready for hard work. With emaciated body under the hot rays of the sun he plows a soil that is not his and cultivates a vine that for him alone has no reward. His arms fall down, his dry tongue sticks to the palate, hunger is consuming him. The poor man can look forward to only a few grains of rice and a few beans soaked in water. And to this he can add only very sparingly the condiment with which nature has provided mankind in such a liberal way. ...*
>
> *Scarcity of food, however, and a quality of food that has no nutritional value make the citizens physically unfit for any sustained effort and predispose them for catching any matter of diseases. The weaker the organism and the more exhausted from troubles the human machine is, the sooner miasmas and contagions penetrate it like a dry sponge. Hence famine—sterility of the fields increased under an unfortunate constellation—is immediately followed by epidemics in the provinces.* [28].

Among the myriad recommendations made by Frank in the *System* were that wells and springs used by the public should be examined regularly, and that rivers and ponds be kept clean and protected against sewage, industrial discharges, and refuse. The police were to be responsible for ensuring that an abundant and pure food supply was available, and observations were to be made whether certain kinds of foods eaten by different classes might predispose to serious ills or greater mortality. Frank also emphasized the importance of breast-feeding of infants. Although Frank's work on "medical police" was considered somewhat outmoded by the time it was completely published, it was influential in setting a standard for broad approaches to public health [29].

The underlying theme of this book—nutrition and health in developing countries—implies the prevailing model, which is inextricably tied to the parlance of "developing" and "developed" countries. This model for development implies that knowledge is cumulative and that progress in nutrition and health generally proceeds in a linear fashion in which the world is destined for improved nutrition, better health, more equity, and greater justice. Such precepts are implicit in the mission of large organizations such as the United Nations Children's Fund, the World Health Organization (WHO), the United

States Agency for International Development, the Overseas Development Agency, the World Bank, and the Food and Agricultural Organization (FAO).

## 1.3   THE RISE OF STATISTICS AND PROBABILITY

The importance of keeping statistical records of health problems, including births, deaths, and other statistics relating to population, was emphasized by William Petty (1623–1687), an economist and physician, and John Graunt (1620–1674), a merchant, in England [30, 31]. In this early work on vital statistics, Graunt used detailed parish records to show the major causes of death, that mortality rates were higher in urban than rural areas, that more boys are born than girls, and that death rates varied by season [32]. Early attempts to enumerate all births and deaths and determine total population were undertaken in Sweden in the middle of the 18th century, and other efforts were made in France and Holland [33]. The use of "political arithmetic," or "the art of reasoning by figures upon things relating to government" [34], continued into the 19th century.

By 1836, the registration of births, marriages, and deaths had been made compulsory in England, and William Farr (1807–1883), a physician and compiler of abstracts in the registrar general's office, became an advocate for social reform using statistics. Farr used life tables, an innovation introduced by the English astronomer Edmund Halley (1656–1742) [35], to show the relative health of districts, and infant mortality rates were used as a primary indicator of health [36]. Better statistics would help improve health and assist in the efforts of preventive medicine, and Farr assigned a greater role in public health to physicians [37]:

> It has been shown that external agents have as great an influence on the frequency of sickness as on its fatality; the obvious corollary is, that man has as much power to prevent as to cure disease. That prevention is better than cure, is a proverb; that it is as easy, the facts we had advanced establish. Yet medical men, the guardians of public health, never have their attention called to the prevention of sickness; it forms no part of their education. To promote health is apparently contrary to their interests: the public do not seek the shield of medical art against disease, nor call the surgeon, till the arrows of death already rankle in the veins. This may be corrected by modifying the present system of medical education, and the manner of remunerating medical men.
>
> Public health may be promoted by placing the medical institutions of the country on a liberal scientific basis; by medical societies co-operating to collect statistical observations; and by medical writers renouncing the notion that a science can be founded upon the limited experience of an individual. Practical medicine cannot be taught in books; the science of medicine cannot be acquired in the sick room.

Vital statistics were also examined by Adolphe Quetelet (1796–1874), a Belgian astronomer and mathematician, who showed that the distribution of observations around a mean could be expressed as the distribution of probabilities on a probability curve. In *Sur l'homme et le développement de ses facultés, ou Essai d'une physique sociale* (*On Man and the Development of his Faculties: An Essay on Social Physics*), Quetelet investigated different aspects of "social physics," such as birth and death, height and weight, health and disease. In this work, he elaborated the important concept that the average man, or *l'homme moyen*, could be expressed mathematically [38]. Statistics became the means to study the condition of the population, especially the working classes, and early Victorian Britain saw the formation of the Statistical Society of Manchester in 1833 and the Statistical Society of London in 1834 [39].

Modern mathematical statistics arose largely from biometry in the late 19th century [40]. Francis Galton (1822–1911), an English scientist and explorer of Africa, originated the concepts of regression and correlation, tools that were being developed to study heredity [41]. Karl Pearson (1857–1936), a statistician at University College, London, continued to study the concepts of variation, correlation, and probability, and he introduced the term *standard deviation* in 1893 and defined the correlation coefficient mathematically in 1896 [42]. Other important developments in statistics were the $\chi^2$ test in 1900, and the *t* test and its distribution was defined by W. S. Gosset (Student) in 1908 [43]. Analysis of variance derives from an article by Ronald A. Fisher (1890–1962), a British geneticist and statistician, in 1918. An important development in statistical methods was the integration of statistics with experimental design in *The Design of Experiments* by Fisher, in which the idea of randomization was promoted in experimental design [44]. The idea of alternative hypotheses and two types of error was developed in the late 1920s [45] and was important in the determination of sample size and power calculations for experimental studies. The concepts of randomization, sample size and power, and placebo controls helped to refine the controlled clinical trial as the basis for scientific evaluation of new therapies [46].

## 1.4   EARLY FOUNDATIONS OF PREVENTIVE MEDICINE

The modern movement in preventive medicine and public health largely began in France in the first half of the 19th century, largely inspired by the Enlightenment approach to health and disease [47, 48]. Louis René Villermé (1782–1863) used a numerical approach to show that there was a large gap in health between the rich and poor. Villermé was a former French army surgeon who was familiar with the psychological and social consequences of famine during the war [49]. Shortly after leaving the military, Villermé showed, in a large demographic study of Paris, *Recherches statistiques sur la ville de Paris* (*Statistical Researches in the City of Paris*), that mortality rates were highest in the poorest arrondissements, or districts, and lowest in the wealthy arrondissements [50]. Thus, the differences between the rich and poor clearly extended far beyond financial position into matters of life and death.

Louis François Benoiston de Châteauneuf (1776–1862), a physician and contemporary of Villermé, showed that there were large differences in diet in Paris [51], and the differences in diet became incorporated into sociomedical investigations of mortality [52]. According to Villermé [53], famine was followed by epidemics, and the poor were always hit the hardest by hunger and epidemics. He argued that a high state of civilization reduces epidemics and called for reforms so that people would be protected against the high price of food, which, for the poor, meant the same as famine. Some of Villermé's and Benoiston's work appeared in France's first journal of public health, *Annales d'hygiène publique et de médecine légale*, founded in 1829. In 1840, the appalling health conditions of textile workers were reported by Villermé [54], leading to a law the following year limiting child labor in France.

In the kingdom of Naples, an important early survey was conducted in 1811 by the government of Joachim Murat (1767–1815) that addressed the relationship between nutrition and disease [55, 56]. In 1765, a year after a terrible famine killed thousands in the kingdom of Naples, Antonio Genovesi (1713–1769), a local leader of the Enlightenment, expressed the proto-Malthusian idea that an equilibrium exists between the population of the state and the availability of resources [57]. An attempt was made to address such a relationship in a survey, which showed that there was widespread nutritional deprivation in the kingdom, especially in rural areas. In one area, famine was so common it was said that *"tanto li contadini che li artieri pria degli occhi, aprono la bocca* (upon awakening peasants and workers alike open their mouths before they open their eyes)." This survey was an early analysis of the mutual relationships among environmental, social variables, nutrition, and public health, and nutritional deprivation was identified as a main factor predisposing to disease [56].

## 1.5   THE SANITARY IDEA

During the early industrialization of England, Jeremy Bentham (1748–1832), a writer on jurisprudence and utilitarian ethics, expressed the belief that laws should be socially useful and that actions should support "the happiness of the greatest number"[58]. Edwin Chadwick (1800–1890), a follower of Bentham, became secretary of the Royal Commission to investigate the Elizabethan Poor Laws, legislation from the early 17th century in which relief for the indigent was to be provided by the local parish, and employment of the poor was provided by workhouses.

As the population grew, the problems of urban overcrowding and deterioration of food, sanitation, and housing became a major crisis by the 19th century. In 1842, Chadwick published a report on the *Sanitary Condition of the Labouring Population of Great Britain,* which described the unsanitary living conditions among the poor [59]. As in Villermé's report, higher mortality was shown among the poorer classes than among the wealthy classes. The report recommended that the highest priority be given to practical measures such as drainage, removal of refuse, and improvement in the water supply, and it was emphasized that much disease among the poor could be prevented by public health measures. As Chadwick put it, *"all* smell is disease" [60]. Legislation followed in the wake of the report, including the British Public Health Act (1848), which established a general board of health, and legislation aimed at food adulteration, regulation of slaughterhouses and other trades, water supplies, and sewers.

The sanitary movement in the United States largely echoed the efforts in France and England. In 1850, a major plan for public health, *Report of the Sanitary Commission of Massachusetts,* was presented to the government of Massachusetts state by Lemuel Shattuck (1793–1859), a teacher, bookseller, and genealogist [61]. The report reviewed the sanitary movement abroad and in the United States, reviewed disease in the state of Massachusetts, and made recommendations for promotion of public health through creation of state and local boards of health; conduct of a regular census; better collection of vital statistics; improved sanitation, water, and housing; and other measures. The main basis for the report was that "measures for prevention will effect infinitely more, than remedies for the cure of disease." Although Shattuck was unable to have many of the recommendations enacted into law immediately, the report was a harbinger for a comprehensive public health policy in the United States.

The first census in the United States by the federal government took place in 1790, and a nationwide census was decreed in the constitution to occur every 10 years [62]. In Great Britain, the first nationwide census was undertaken in 1801, and periodic national censuses gained authority in France after 1840 [52]. National registration systems and their vital statistics were used to bring attention to problems in public health in Europe, Great Britain, and the United States, and a greater need for accurate statistics was noted after the arrival of the worldwide cholera pandemics in the mid-19th century [63].

## 1.6   CONTAGION VERSUS MIASMA

By the 19th century, epidemics of plague were gone from Europe, but other epidemic diseases such as scarlet fever, typhoid, typhus, and measles continued in outbreaks. Malaria was present in both Europe and the United States, and yellow fever was present in the south of the United States. Great pandemics of cholera swept large parts of the world in dates approximating 1817–1823, 1826–1837, 1846–1863, 1865–1875 [64], and later. The theory that epidemic disease was caused by miasmas rising from decaying organic matter was a dominant belief in the middle of the 19th century and a strong impetus behind the reforms of the sanitarians [6, 9]. Another major theory of epidemic disease was the contagionist theory, in which an animate organism caused disease and was spread by person-to-person contact [65, 66]. Further credence to the contagionist theory was provided by epidemiological studies of measles, cholera, diphtheria, and typhoid fever.

A measles epidemic affected the Faroe Islands in 1846, and a medical commission was sent by the Danish government to investigate. The commission included two Danish physicians who had just finished medical school, 26-year-old Peter Ludwig Panum (1820–1885) and 25-year-old August Henrik Manicus (1821–1850). In what is considered a classic study in epidemiology [9], Panum described the incubation period of measles and noted that transmission of measles was through person-to-person contact [67]. He noted that measles attacked individuals of all ages, but those with a history of a previous attack of measles from a previous epidemic in 1781 were immune. Manicus observed that mortality was highest in a village that had the greatest poverty and poor diet, and he noted that diarrheal disease was mild among well-to-do islanders but was severe and persistent in the poorer villages [68]. Both Panum and Manicus concluded that measles was contagious and not miasmatic in origin.

Other studies that further may have changed perceptions about the contagiousness of disease were an investigation of cholera in London by John Snow (1813–1858), an English physician and anesthetist [69], and investigations of cholera by William Budd (1811–1880), a physician in Bristol. Budd thought that cholera was caused by a specific living organism that was found in the human intestinal tract and was spread through contaminated drinking water [70]. During the cholera epidemic of 1854 in London, Snow demonstrated that the number of deaths from cholera was related to the amount of pollution from the Thames River among the different private companies supplying drinking water. Nearly all the victims had used water from the Broad Street pump in Soho. Snow concluded that cholera was carried in water contaminated by excreta of cholera patients, and that cholera was transmitted by ingestion of contaminated water and food and not through miasmata. Snow persuaded the local authorities to remove the handle from the Broad Street pump—presumably averting further deaths—but the epidemic was already in decline.

**Fig. 1.1.** A Monster Soup Commonly Called Thames Water, by William Heath (1795–1840), circa 1828. Philadelphia Museum of Art: Gift of Mrs. William Horstmann. Reproduced with permission.

The contamination of the Thames by sewage and industrial waste was acknowledged by a London commission in 1828 and became the subject of satire (Fig. 1.1). The Metropolis Water Act of 1852 required London water companies to draw their water supplies from cleaner nontidal reaches of the Thames and to filter all water supplies for domestic use [71]; the cholera outbreak of 1854 occurred before all companies could comply with the 1852 act. The findings of Snow and Budd regarding the contagious nature of cholera did not lead to a sudden revolution in water science as has been generally believed [72, 73], but these studies gave additional weight to the contagion theory. In the ensuing years, many international experts continued to hang on to the idea that miasmas were the cause of cholera [74]. Other detailed investigations that reinforced the contagion theory of epidemic disease were those of diphtheria by Pierre Fidèle Bretonneau (1778–1862), a physician in Tours, France [75], and of typhoid fever by William Budd [76].

## 1.7  ADVANCES IN MICROBIOLOGY

A further foundation for microbiological investigations was laid by Jacob Henle (1809–1885), a pathologist in Zurich, who thought that conclusive proof for an organism being responsible for a disease required three conditions: constant presence of the parasite, isolation from foreign admixtures, and reproduction of the disease with the isolated parasite [77]. These postulates were further developed by his student, Robert Koch (1843–1910) [78]. Louis Pasteur (1822–1895), a French chemist and microbiologist, further elaborated the germ theory of disease through broad studies that included the fermentation of beer and wine and diseases of silkworms. The last quarter of the 19th century was characterized by a rapid period of microbiological investigations, during which descriptions were made of the organisms responsible for anthrax [79], malaria [80], tuberculosis [81], and cholera [82]. Other organisms, including streptococcus, staphylococcus, *Escherichia coli*, the organisms responsible for leprosy and diphtheria, and *Yersinia* were described, and investigation was facilitated by the development of new staining techniques and culture media [5, 65].

Strategies to control infectious diseases by the turn of the century included reporting of cases, isolation of affected individuals, and disinfection of the premises. Compulsory notification of infectious diseases was enacted in London, Berlin, and Paris within the last quarter of the 19th century [83]. The ways in which diseases could be transmitted through contaminated water, ice, milk, and uncooked food were outlined by William Sedgwick (1855–1921), a biologist [84]. In 1887, the first systematic monitoring of the public water supply in the United States was conducted by Sedgwick for the Massachusetts Board of Health, and his techniques for measurement and filtration of bacteria in the water supply became a standard for the country. In his influential treatise, *The Sources and Modes of Infection* [85], Charles V. Chapin (1856–1941), the superintendent of health in Providence, Rhode Island, emphasized the role of the carrier and further clarified the idea that diseases could be transmitted through lack of hygiene, by direct and indirect contact, by fomites, through the air, in food and drink, and by insects.

## 1.8 NUTRITIONAL SCIENCE IN THE 19TH CENTURY

Modern nutritional science has early roots in experimental physiology in France at the beginning of the 19th century, when ideas surrounding nutrition were subjected to examination by animal experimentation [86]. François Magendie (1783–1855), professor of anatomy at the Collège de France, attempted to differentiate between various kinds of food and made a clear distinction between nitrogenous and nonnitrogenous foods [87]. In an early experiment that hinted at the existence of vitamin A, Magendie found that dogs fed only sugar and distilled water developed corneal ulcers and died [88]. The importance of nitrogenous foods was further recognized by Gerrit Jan Mulder (1802–1880), a Dutch physiological chemist, who coined the term *protein* to describe nitrogenous substances in plants and animal foods [89].

The German chemist Justus von Liebig (1803–1873) considered food to be divided into "plastic" foods (plant and animal proteins) and "respiratory" foods (carbohydrates and fat). Liebig's main doctrine was that protein was used to build up the organism or repair tissues, whereas carbohydrates and fats served as fuels to facilitate the respiratory process [90]. The definition of food was further refined by Carl von Voit (1831–1908), a physiologist in Munich: "The foodstuffs are those substances which bring about the deposition of a substance essential to the composition of the body, or diminish and avert the loss thereof" [91]. A former pupil of Voit's, Wilbur Olin Atwater (1844–1907) conducted investigations into the caloric value of food using a bomb calorimeter and derived food and nutrient composition for an "average diet"; the energy-yielding functions of food were emphasized [92]. By the end of the 19th century, the prevailing notion was that food consisted of proteins, carbohydrates, fats, salts, and water.

Improved nutrition was considered to strengthen resistance to disease, and Germain Sée (1818–1896), a French physician, made dietary recommendations for individuals with specific diseases [93]. The influence of Liebig and Voit could be seen in some approaches; sufficient nourishment was thought to prevent "tissue waste" during a fever. Milk was given paramount importance as a dietary [94]. Modern knowledge of nutrition was used to recommend diets for institutions such as schools, hospitals, prisons, and asylums. Special diets high in milk, whey, and egg yolk were recommended for certain diseases [95]. In the early 20th century, influential textbooks in nutrition put heavy emphasis on the caloric value of food for human health [96, 97].

## 1.9  INFANT MORTALITY AND SOCIAL REFORM

In the late 18th century, infant mortality became the target of social reform in France, England, and the United States [98, 99]. A major cause of infant mortality was diarrheal disease, which often occurred in epidemic proportions during the summer

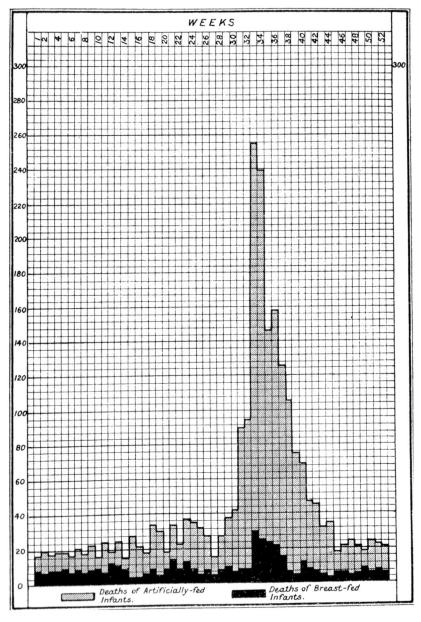

**Fig. 1.2.** Epidemics of diarrheal disease in Paris described by Newman in 1906. Adapted from ref. 100.

in cities of England, Europe, and the United States. Using data from Paris (Fig. 1.2) and Finsbury, a poor area of England's Bedfordshire where he worked as medical officer of health, George Newman (1870–1948), argued that breast-fed infants suffered less from summer diarrhea than infants who were fed artificial formula or cow's milk [100]. The high infant mortality rate was considered to be mainly a problem of motherhood, and he emphasized proper training of mothers and promotion of breast-feeding. Newman argued that the infant mortality rate was gauge of the health of a community, not the general death rate, and he considered it a sign of social degeneration that Great Britain should have a falling overall death rate but little change in the infant mortality rate over the proceeding 50 years. Arthur Newsholme (1857–1943), Newman, and others [101] implicated fecal contamination of food and milk in the epidemics of summer diarrhea [102].

Similar concerns over infant mortality were voiced in Europe and the United States and led to the formation of national and international organizations devoted to the study and prevention of infant mortality, including the Ligue Française contre Mortalité Infantile (1902), the German Union for the Protection of Infants (1908), and the American Association for the Study and Prevention of Infant Mortality (1910). Among the measures sought by these groups were the education of mothers, the promotion of breast-feeding, improved prenatal care, and widespread gathering and compilation of vital statistics [98, 99]. Testing of the milk supply in large cities had revealed high bacterial counts in milk, and reform was aimed at providing a more pure milk supply through pasteurization [98].

## 1.10 THE EMERGENCE OF THE VITAMINS

The late 19th and early 20th centuries were marked by the emergence of the vitamin theory and the characterization of the vitamins. Although descriptions of scurvy, beriberi, night blindness and keratomalacia, and rickets—manifestations of vitamin C, thiamin, vitamin A, and vitamin D deficiencies, respectively—and their empirical treatments are known in the older medical literature, it was not until the last quarter of the 19th century that major progress commenced in the characterization of vitamins and vitamin-deficiency diseases.

In the 19th century, beriberi was widespread in eastern and Southeast Asia, and it was especially a problem for sailors on long voyages. In 1882, a Japanese naval vessel, *Riujo*, sailed from Japan to Honolulu via New Zealand and Chile, and after 272 days of navigation, 60% of the ship's 276 crew members developed beriberi, and 25 died [103]. A Japanese naval surgeon, Kanehiro Takaki (1849–1920) (Fig. 1.3), conducted epidemiological investigations of beriberi on different warships and examined clothing, living quarters, weather records, and rank. Takaki concluded that beriberi was related to the quality of food, particularly an insufficient intake of nitrogenous foods. In 1884, he persuaded the Japanese government to provide additional meat and dry milk on a training ship, *Tsukuba*, which sailed the same route of the ill-fated *Riujo*. When the *Tsukuba* arrived in Japan 287 days later, there were a handful of cases of beriberi and no deaths. After Takaki's dietary reforms were introduced, the cases of beriberi plummeted sharply in the Japanese navy [104, 105].

In 1886, Christiaan Eijkman (1858–1930), a Dutch army physician, was sent to the Dutch East Indies to investigate beriberi, which was generally thought at that time to

**Fig. 1.3.** Vessels involved in Navy research on beri-beri by Kanehiro Takaki in the late 19th century.

be due to an unidentified bacterial infection. Eijkman demonstrated that chickens raised on polished rice alone developed a paralytic disorder similar to human beriberi, and that this disorder could be corrected by a diet of unpolished rice. The bran portion of rice contained a substance that could prevent beriberi, and Eijkman originally thought that the polished rice contained a toxin that was neutralized by a substance in the bran portion [106]. His colleague, Gerrit Grijns (1865–1944) believed that the disease affecting chickens and human beriberi were both due to an absence in the diet of a factor present in the rice polishings [107].

From the time of the early experiments of Magendie, the contributions of several investigators over many decades helped to characterize vitamin A [108, 109]. Nicholai Ivanovich Lunin (1853–1937) (Fig. 1.4), working in the laboratory of Gustav von Bunge (1844–1920) at the University of Dorpat, determined that mice cannot survive on a purified diet of fats, carbohydrates, proteins, and salts alone; however, he noted that mice could survive when milk was added. Lunin concluded "other substances indispensable for nutrition must be present in milk besides casein, fat, lactose, and salts" [110]. Lunin's conclusion was disseminated widely in von Bunge's *Lehrbuch der physiologischen und pathologischen Chemie* [111]. Another student performed experiments with simplified diets in mice and found that there was an unknown substance in egg yolk that was essential for life [112]. At the University of Utrecht, Cornelius Pekelharing (1848–1922) conducted experiments that showed that mice are able to survive on diets in which small quantities of milk are added [113], and Wilhelm Stepp (1882–1964) showed that if the milk supplied to mice was extracted with alcohol-ether (thus removing the fat-soluble substance later known as vitamin A), the mice could not survive [114].

The most explicit statement of the theory regarding the existence of vitamins came in 1906, when Frederick Gowland Hopkins (1861–1947), a biochemist at Cambridge University, who—on the basis of his own unpublished experiments and other observations—expressed the belief that there were "unsuspected dietetic factors" besides proteins, carbohydrates, fats, and minerals that were vital for health [115]. In 1911, Casimir Funk (1884–1967) thought he had isolated the dietary factor involved in beriberi and coined the name *vitamine* for it [116]. Further exposition of the vitamin theory came in 1912, when Funk presented that idea that beriberi, scurvy, and pellagra were all nutritional deficiency diseases [117]. Later, Eijkman and Hopkins jointly received the 1929 Nobel Prize for their early pioneering scientific research on vitamins [118].

In the United States, Thomas Osborne (1859–1929) and Lafayette Mendel (1872–1935), working at Yale University, showed that a fat-soluble substance in butterfat was

**Fig. 1.4.** Nicholai Ivanovich Lunin (1853–1937).

needed to support the growth of rats [119, 120]. After a period of illness, Hopkins published work he undertook in 1906–1907, which showed that mice could not survive on a purified diet without milk. Hopkins postulated the existence of what he called "accessory factors" in foods that were necessary for life [121]. In studies with eggs and butter, Elmer McCollum (1879–1967), a biochemist at the University of Wisconsin, noted that their data "supports the belief that there are certain accessory articles in certain foodstuffs which are essential for normal growth for extended periods" [122]. The accessory factor was later named *fat-soluble A* by McCollum, but it actually contained both vitamins A and D, leading to the initial belief that lack of fat-soluble A was responsible for rickets [123, 124]. In 1922, it was shown that cod-liver oil contained both vitamins A, an antixerophthalmic factor, and vitamin D, an antirachitic factor [125]. Soon the term fat-soluble A was combined with Funk's designation to become *vitamine A* and later *vitamin A*. The molecular structure of vitamin A was deduced in 1931 [126, 127], and vitamin A was eventually crystallized in 1937 [128].

## 1.11   FURTHER RESEARCH ON NUTRITIONAL DEFICIENCY DISEASES

Pellagra, a syndrome characterized by dermatitis, diarrhea, dementia, and death, was described in Europe as early as the 18th century, and it was often ascribed to spoiled maize [129]. With the rise of the germ theory of disease, it was thought that pellagra might also be attributable to an infection [130]. In the early part of the 20th century, pellagra was increasingly recognized in the United States, especially in the South [131], and by 1916, it was second among the causes of death in South Carolina. Outbreaks of pellagra seemed to occur more commonly in asylums, jails, and poorhouses [132]. The Pellagra Commission of the State of Illinois conducted investigations in 1911 and concluded that pellagra was attributable to an infection [133], and another investigation in South Carolina implicated poor sanitation [134]. In 1914, Joseph Goldberger (1874–1929), a physician in the US Public Health Service [135], conducted investigations of pellagra in South Carolina and showed that pellagra could be prevented by supplying milk, butter, and lean meat in the diet [136]. Careful study showed that household ownership of a cow was protective against pellagra. Further investigations among prison volunteers revealed that pellagra could be produced by a restricted, mainly cereal diet [137]. In later animal studies, niacin was implicated as the deficient dietary factor involved in the etiology of pellagra [129].

After World War II, a controversy erupted over whether protein deficiency was a major nutritional problem of developing countries [12]. The syndrome of kwashiorkor—edema, wasting, diarrhea, and peeling of the skin—was described by Cicely Williams (1893—1992), an English physician, among children in the Gold Coast of West Africa [138]. High mortality was noted among these children, and those affected appeared to be mostly 1 to 4 years old, weaned early, and fed entirely on white corn gruel. Initially, it was thought that the condition was related to a deficiency of B complex vitamins, but after the condition failed to respond to vitamins, it was considered a problem of protein deficiency. International efforts were focused on closing the "protein gap" through high-protein sources such as fish, soybeans, and peanuts. Efforts to market an infant formula based on peanut flour ended when it was discovered that under humid, tropical conditions, carcinogenic aflatoxins were produced by fungi growing in the flour [139]. The importance of calories was realized when children with kwashiorkor recovered on eating foods with relatively low protein but high energy content [140], and the term *protein-calorie malnutrition* soon replaced *protein malnutrition* [141]. Concern was raised that the problem of marasmus, which was more common owing to a decline in breast-feeding, was being relatively neglected [142]. It was soon acknowledged that the protein gap was a myth; the chief problem in developing countries lay in a "food gap and an energy gap" or an issue of "quantity rather than quality of food" [143].

## 1.12   NUTRITIONAL IMMUNOLOGY

*Nutritional immunology,* the study of the relationship between nutrition and immunity, was a discipline that arose largely during the early 20th century. Although it had been observed over the centuries that famine would reduce an individual's resistance to epidemic diseases, more specific clues were provided with the advent of animal experimentation using controlled diets. The recognition of specific vitamins and developments in immunology made it possible to study the effects of single or multiple vitamin deficiencies on immune function. By the end of the 19th century, humoral antitoxic antibodies in the serum of immunized animals had been described, and this led to the development of serological tests involved in the diagnosis of infectious disease and measurement of immunological protection [144]. Experimental infections were soon conducted in animals on controlled diets, and serological tests allowed assessment of the effect of dietary deprivation on immunity to infection. By the mid-1930s, animal studies suggested that deficiencies of some of the vitamins reduced resistance to infection [145–147].

## 1.13   VITAMIN A AND REDUCTION OF CHILD MORTALITY

Two Danish physicians, the pediatrician Carl Bloch (1872–1952) and the ophthalmologist Olaf Blegvad (1888–1961), dealt with a large number of children with clinical vitamin A deficiency in Denmark in the period 1910–1920. They noted that children with vitamin A deficiency had greatly increased mortality, and that their mortality could be reduced by providing the children with vitamin A-rich foods such as cod-liver oil, whole milk, cream, and butter [148–151].

In the late 1920s, vitamin A was recognized to have an effect on immunity to infection, and vitamin A became known as the "anti-infective" vitamin [152]. Largely through the influence of Edward Mellanby (1884–1955), a professor of physiology at Sheffield University (Fig. 1.5), vitamin A underwent a period of intense clinical investigation. Between 1920 and 1940, at least 30 trials were conducted to determine whether vitamin A could reduce the morbidity and mortality from infectious diseases, including respiratory disease, measles, puerperal sepsis, and tuberculosis [153]. These trials were conducted prior to the time when many of the innovations known to the modern controlled clinical trial, such as randomization, sample size and power calculations, and placebo controls, were widely known.

By the 1930s, it was firmly established that vitamin A supplementation could reduce morbidity and mortality in young children. In 1932, Joseph Ellison (b. 1898), a physician in London, showed that vitamin supplementation reduced the mortality of vitamin

**Fig. 1.5.** Dr. Edward Mellanby (1884–1955).

A-deficient children with measles [154]. During the 1931–1932 measles epidemic in London, Ellison assigned 600 children with measles at the Grove Fever Hospital to one of two groups of 300 each. One group received vitamin A, and the other group did not receive vitamin A. Overall mortality rates in the vitamin A and control groups were 3.7% and 8.7%, respectively, representing a 58% reduction in mortality with vitamin A treatment. Ellison's study, published in the *British Medical Journal* in 1932, was the first trial to show that vitamin A supplementation reduces mortality in young children with vitamin A deficiency [155].

Vitamin A became a mainstream preventive measure: Cod-liver oil was part of the morning routine for millions of children—a practice promoted by physicians and popularized by the pharmaceutical industry [155]. The US production and importation of cod-liver oil totaled 4,909,622 pounds in 1929 [156]. In the early 1930s in England, the annual consumption of cod-liver oil was 500,000 gallons [157]. Much of the world's supply of cod-liver oil, and hence vitamins A and D, came from the commercial fisheries of New England, Norway, and Newfoundland. As noted in the *British Medical Journal*, "cod-liver oil was in use in almost every working-class household, and local authorities spent considerable sums in purchasing bulk supplies for hospitals and sanitoriums" [158].

In England, a proposal to tax cod-liver oil in the Ottawa Agreements Bill in the House of Commons in 1932 raised protests as there was concern that child mortality would increase if the price of cod-liver oil increased and it became less accessible to poor people. As reported in both *The Lancet* and the *British Medical Journal*, one legislator who supported an amendment to exempt cod-liver oil from the proposed taxation noted that many a child in the north of England "owed its life to being able to obtain cod-liver oil." [157, 159]. Two British physicians also supported the amendment in letters published in *The*

*Lancet* [157]. One expert from the Lister Institute of Preventive Medicine noted: "It is evident that any steps which may raise the price and lower the consumption of cod-liver oil, especially in the winter, would have deleterious effect upon the health of the population, involving particularly the well-being of the children of the poorer classes." [157]. The concerns of physicians and legislators alike that children receive sufficient vitamin A to protect against the well-known morbidity and mortality of vitamin A deficiency were clearly expressed. The discovery of the sulfa antibiotics and their clinical applications soon overshadowed investigations of vitamin A as anti-infective therapy, and there was about a 50-year lull until the late 1980s in clinical investigation of vitamin A as an intervention to reduce morbidity and mortality [160].

In 1950, a joint expert committee on nutrition of the FAO and WHO recommended that studies be made on the relationship of nutritional status to resistance against intestinal parasites. Further observations made in the ensuing decade suggested that many infectious diseases were associated with malnutrition. A WHO Expert Committee on Nutrition and Infection reviewed the issue of the interaction between nutrition and infection in 1965, and a comprehensive monograph, *Interactions of Nutrition and Infection*, by Nevin Scrimshaw, Carl Taylor, and John Gordon appeared in 1968 [161]. The effect of nutritional status on resistance to diarrheal and respiratory disease and viral, parasitic, and other infections was reviewed, and the present state of knowledge regarding the effects of specific micronutrient deficiencies on immune function was presented. The authors concluded:

> *Infections are likely to have more serious consequences among persons with clinical or subclinical malnutrition, and infectious diseases have the capacity to turn borderline nutritional deficiencies into severe malnutrition. In this way, malnutrition and infection can be mutually aggravating and produce more serious consequences for the patient than would be expected from a summation of the independent effects of the two.*

This seminal work served as the foundation for research on nutritional immunology, especially for vitamin A and for zinc research, in the last three decades of the 20th century. An important detailed review of the effects of single nutrients on immunity was made by William Beisel in 1982 [162]. Tremendous advances in nutritional immunology have been made in the last 20 years or so, and many of these recent findings regarding the relationship between micronutrients and immunity to infection are presented elsewhere in this book.

## 1.14   GROWTH IN FOOD PRODUCTION

In England, growth in food production from 1750 to 1880 was not seen not so much as owing to technological innovation as to increasing soil fertility and crop yield through manuring and sowing of legumes [163]. Improved reaping machines appeared in the early 19th century, and cast iron replaced wrought iron and wood in many agricultural implements. Introduction of new fodder crops for winter feeding helped better animal husbandry. In France, railway construction was considered to be a vital factor in improving the agricultural economy in the mid-19th century, and animal breeding, crop rotation, and mechanization contributed to improve agricultural practice [164]. In

England, better road transport increased the market for the dairy producer. Advances in the process by which ammonia could be produced from atmospheric nitrogen allowed more widespread use of fertilizers in the early 20th century [165]. Increased mechanization with tractors, combined harvesters, automatic hay-balers, and seed and fertilizer drills has been noted between 1910 and 1950 in England, and advances in plant breeding brought new cereal and clover varieties [165]. In the United States, technological advances in the plow, reaper, binder, and thresher aided the development of mechanized farming in the 19th century. Industrialized agriculture expanded in the beginning of the 20th century with the development of gasoline-powered tractors.

## 1.15   LONG-TERM TRENDS IN DIET

Available evidence suggests that the majority of the world's population before 1800 consumed a diet below contemporary minimum standards of optimal nutrition [166]. In France, the caloric intake of the average diet increased steadily during the 19th century, but the basic composition of the diet did not appear to change much until after about 1880 [167]. Inspired by the French voluntary *Caisses des Écoles*, which fed hungry schoolchildren, charities were founded to feed children in England. The Victorian working class diet was especially poor in quality and quantity [168]. Near the end of the 19th century, over one in ten children attending London schools were estimated to habitually go hungry [169].

Alarm was raised over the problem of inadequate nutrition when the report of the Inter-Departmental Committee on Physical Deterioration was published in 1904 [170]. The committee showed that 40–60% of young men presenting for military service at the time of the South African War were rejected on medical grounds, and much of this physical inadequacy was attributed to malnutrition. This and other reports led to the Education (Provision of Meals) Act of 1906, which mandated a national policy for feeding needy children at school. The number of London children receiving meals was about 27,000 in 1907 and by 1909 that number had doubled [171]. When the *Report on the Present State of Knowledge Concerning Accessory Food Factors (Vitamines)* appeared in 1919, it helped shape dietary recommendations based on newer knowledge of vitamins [172]. The value of milk was emphasized by the report, and a study showed that provision of supplemental milk each day resulted in better weight and height gain than occurred in those who were not supplemented [173]. By 1945, about 40% of the school population was taking school meals, and 46% were drinking school milk [171].

An association between low socioeconomic level and inadequate diet was known in France [51] and England [174]. In *A Study of the Diet of the Labouring Classes in Edinburgh* (1901), D. Noël Paton and his colleagues showed that many workers did not have the income to obtain a sufficient supply of food and lacked the education to make correct choices of food [175]. A discussion later followed in the *British Medical Journal* [176]:

> *Who is responsible for the conditions which lead to the state of poverty and bad nutrition disclosed by this report? Lies the fault with poor themselves—is it because they are thriftless, because they lack training in cooking and in the economical spending of*

*such income as they possess? Or is it that the actual wages which they can command are so low that it is impossible for them to purchase the actual necessities of life?*

Whether the problem lay with lack of education or inadequate income was unclear, and each side had its adherents [177]. In 1936, John Boyd Orr (1880–1971) published *Food Health and Income: Report on a Survey of the Adequacy of Diet in Relation to Income*; this report created a sensation in England and was widely publicized around the world. This dietary survey suggested that the poorest of the poor, about 4.5 million people, consumed a diet deficient in all dietary constituents examined, and that the next poorest, about 9 million people, had a diet adequate in protein, fat, and carbohydrates but deficient in all vitamins and minerals [178]. Only half the population surveyed had a diet that was adequate in all dietary constituents, including all vitamins and minerals. Although the per capita consumption of fruit, vegetables, and dairy products had greatly increased between 1909 and 1934 in Great Britain, there was clearly more that could be done to improve nutrition [178]. Analysis of household budgets suggests that the average daily intakes of vitamin A, vitamin C, and thiamin were mostly inadequate in 1900 but increased to largely sufficient intakes by 1944 among poor, working class, and middle class families in Great Britain [174]. Long-term analysis of nutritional status show that height grew in the United Kingdom between the mid-19th century and through the years following World War II [179].

In the United States, there have been large dietary changes over the last 200 years [17, 180]. In the early 19th century, many individuals did not consume adequate amounts of fruits, vegetables, and dairy products, and dietary deficiencies were not uncommon among rural and urban dwellers. From about 1830–1870, the mean stature of Americans had a prolonged decline, and this may possibly have been due to increased urbanization and poorer nutrition for urban workers during industrialization [181, 182]; from the 1880s to the present, there has been a steady increase in stature. The apparent per capita consumption of dairy products increased in the United States between 1909 and 1930 [183, 184]. The discovery of the vitamins led to a greater awareness of nutrition, and using a combination of fear, hope, and guilt, the pharmaceutical and food industries promoted their products to mothers [185]. Fortification of baker's bread with thiamin, riboflavin, niacin, iron, and calcium became mandatory in 1943. When federal wartime legislation ended in 1946, many states continued to require the enrichment of bread [180].

When George Newman, one of the primary architects of public health reform in Great Britain, wrote to a colleague in 1939, he reminisced about the "silent revolution" in Great Britain:

*[They] … who say I am an idealist and wild optimist do not know their history. How can one be otherwise who knew England and English medicine in 1895 and know it now? It is the greatest silent revolution in our time. The opportunity and the quality of human life has, as you truly say, been "transformed." They don't know what "malnutrition" means nowadays. Everybody is undernourished in some degree a way, but prevalent malnutrition is rare, whilst it used to be common. [186].*

In *The Building of a Nation's Health* in 1939, Newman identified adequate nutrition as one of the "most powerful instruments" of preventive medicine [187].

## 1.16   THE DECLINE OF MORTALITY

In *The Modern Rise of Population* (1976), Thomas McKeown (1912–1988) showed that population grew in Europe since the mid-18th century, and he attributed the rise in population largely to a reduction in deaths from infectious diseases [1]. The decline of infectious disease mortality was occurring prior to the identification of specific pathogens, the widespread use of immunizations, the development of antibiotics, and the rise of sophisticated, technologically based clinical medicine (Fig. 1.6). Improved nutrition, greater food supplies, purification of water, better sanitation, and improved housing are among the main factors cited in the reduction of infectious disease morbidity and mortality [2]. A close interrelationship among nutrition, infection, and hygiene was acknowledged [2, 3], and McKeown's conclusions were primarily based on observations of infectious disease mortality rates from the late 19th century and later. These views have become orthodox and influential in the debate regarding appropriate strategies for reducing mortality in developing countries, and scientific findings of the last 20 years from developing countries largely support McKeown's contention that nutritional status influences infectious disease morbidity and mortality.

Others have disputed some of McKeown's conclusions, citing evidence that the rise of population from the 16th century may have been primarily caused by an increase in fertility rather than a decline in mortality [188], or that the relationship between nutri-

**Fig. 1.6.** Case fatality rates for measles, 1850–1970. Adopted with permission from McKeown (1).

tion and infection is "controversial" [189]. There is little question that there has been a general decline in mortality in Europe since the middle of the 17th century, but given the close relationship among socioeconomic level, education, housing, food, clean water, sanitation, and hygiene, it has been difficult to separate specific causal factors [190–192]. During the same period, there was a probable reduction in exposure to pathogenic organisms through changes in our environment [4], and over the last 200 years, there has been a near disappearance of deficiency diseases that were once commonly reported in Europe, such as goiter, pellagra, rickets, and xerophthalmia [129, 150, 193]. These deficiency diseases cause significant morbidity and mortality but have been relatively neglected in historical demography.

## 1.17   GRADUATE EDUCATION IN PUBLIC HEALTH

The early sanitary reform efforts in the 19th century were dominated by nonmedical personnel in the United States and Europe as it was often seen as the responsibility of engineers, biologists, and chemists. The appointment of John Simon (1816–1904), a surgeon, to the head of the medical department of the Privy Council in 1854 was a visible sign of change in which the public health system was dominated by the medical profession [194]. New public health legislation created a need for qualified medical practitioners to serve as officers of health, and programs offering a diploma in public health appeared in Dublin, Edinburgh, and Cambridge. In Vienna, the subjects "medical police" and "forensic medicine" were combined under the designation "state medicine" at the Vienna Medical School [195]. At first, medical police was taught largely with emphasis on knowledge of ordinances and sanitary regulations in Austria, which were influenced by Frank's *Medicinische Polizey*, but emphasis slowly changed to scientific investigation and sanitation after cholera and typhoid epidemics struck Vienna.

Courses in public health were taught in some universities in the United States at the turn of the century, but schools of hygiene and public health were not created as a separate entity until the early 20th century. In 1916, the School of Hygiene and Public Health was established at the Johns Hopkins University with William H. Welch as its director [196], and the School of Public Health opened at Harvard University in 1922 [197]. With endowment of the Rockefeller Foundation, the London School of Hygiene and Tropical Medicine opened in 1929. By 1925, the teaching of hygiene varied enormously, with institutes of hygiene established among medical faculty in Germany and Sweden, hygiene taught through bacteriology in France, and new schools of public health at Johns Hopkins, Harvard, and Pennsylvania in the United States [198]. The number of universities with schools or programs of public health continued to grow in the United States, Great Britain, and Europe [199].

## 1.18   INTERNATIONAL ORGANIZATIONS

Among the larger institutions involved in scientific research related to public health were the Institut Pasteur, the Lister Institute, the Rockefeller Institute, and the National Institutes of Health (NIH). The success of Pasteur in microbiological investigations and rabies immunization led to the establishment of the Institut Pasteur in Paris in 1888. The institute was a model for bacteriological research, and within a few years, other Pasteur Institutes were established in more than 40 places around the world. These institutes scattered around the globe were loosely knit and linked by ideology [200]. The Institut Pasteur made major contributions to preventive medicine with new vaccines and therapies for infectious diseases [201]. In 1891, the Lister Institute was established in London, and research on vitamins was a major part of the research program, with notable emphasis on rickets [202].

The Rockefeller Foundation established an International Health Commission in 1913, and the commission grew out of early efforts of the Rockefeller Sanitary Commission to eradicate hookworm in the southern United States [203]. The International Health Division, or Health Commission, of the Rockefeller Foundation, expanded efforts to eradicate hookworm overseas, and during the 1920s the focus expanded to malaria, yellow fever, and tuberculosis [204, 205]. The Rockefeller Foundation helped to transform medical education in the United States and tended to emphasize a technological approach to medicine [206].

The NIH had its early roots in public health with the establishment of the Hygienic Laboratory of the Marine Hospital Service in 1887 [207]. The laboratory was responsible for bacteriological work, including diagnosis of infectious diseases among immigrants. The scope of the laboratory increased with Progressive Era regulations such as the Biologics Control Act of 1902 and the Pure Food and Drugs Act of 1906. In 1912, the service became known as the US Public Health Service, and among its activities were investigations of pellagra by Joseph Goldberger. The National Institute of Health was formally established by the US Congress in 1930, and by 1948 it consisted of several institutes to become the National Institutes of Health (NIH) [208]. Although the NIH had its roots in hygiene and public health, a shift occurred with the creation of the Communicable Disease Center (CDC) in Atlanta, Georgia, in 1946. The CDC soon dealt with epidemics and other public health crises such as influenza outbreaks, polio surveillance, and measles eradication.

International health organizations grew out of efforts to coordinate quarantines and control international epidemics such as those of cholera and plague. In 1907, the Office International d'Hygiène Publique (International Office of Public Health) was established in Rome, and the purpose of the organization was to collect and disseminate epidemiological information about smallpox, plague, cholera, and other diseases. The Health Organization of the League of Nations was created in 1923, and its activities included promotion of health, international standardization of biological tests and products, and control of disease. In 1948, the WHO was created after international ratification, and it assumed the activities of the Health Organization of the League of Nations and other offices. The Pan American Sanitary Bureau became the regional office of the WHO for Latin America in 1949, and in 1958 it changed its name to the Pan American Health Organization (PAHO). Treatment campaigns against yaws, smallpox eradication, oral rehydration therapy, and childhood immunizations are among the many achievements of the WHO since its inception.

The United Nations International Children's Emergency Fund (UNICEF) was created in 1946 by resolution of the United Nations General Assembly, and the purpose of UNICEF was to protect the well-being of children around the world. Early activities of UNICEF included shipments of powdered milk for children in Europe, vaccination efforts, support for vector control, and provision of equipment for maternal and child health centers [209]. Milk powder—which required reconstitution through heating and rapid cooling—reportedly had little impact on nutritional deficiency in rural Africa because it proved too time consuming for women to boil and cool milk in large cauldrons over a wood fire in the face of other work in their fields [209]. Most of UNICEF's assistance in Africa in the 1950s went toward malaria eradication. By 1970, the focus of UNICEF moved away from milk and protein supplementation toward emphasis on improving community water supplies by installation of hand pumps and tube wells and an emphasis on primary health care.

The FAO was founded in 1945 in Quebec, Canada, with the purpose of raising the levels of nutrition and standards of living, securing improvements in the production and distribution of food and agricultural products, and improving the condition of rural populations [210]. The first director general of FAO was John Boyd Orr, who brought attention to the relationship between income and diet in England in the 1930s. The FAO, based in Rome, provides assistance for sustainable agriculture, promotes transfer of skills and technology in field projects, offers advice on agricultural policy and planning, and fosters international cooperation on nutrition, biodiversity, and agricultural commodities.

The World Bank originated with reconstruction efforts after World War II, when delegates from 44 nations met in Bretton Woods, New Hampshire, and drew up articles of agreement for the International Bank for Reconstruction and Development in 1944 [211, 212]. The mission of the World Bank shifted from reconstruction to development, especially for economically developing countries. World Bank loans to poor countries in Africa and Asia increased under the tenure of the World Bank's fifth president, Robert McNamara. McNamara was aware of Alan Berg's work on nutrition and health at the Brookings Institution, which later appeared in *The Nutrition Factor* [212, 213], and a nutrition unit was created at the World Bank in 1972. The role of the bank was to encourage development-oriented work rather than mass food distribution in developing countries, and such projects included identifying populations at high risk for malnutrition; developing food subsidy programs; integrating nutrition assistance with primary care and family planning, nutrition education, and promotion of home gardening; improving water and sanitation; and delivering micronutrient supplements [214].

## 1.18 CONCLUSIONS

Over the last 200 years in most of Europe and the United States, there has been a major reduction in mortality rates, a virtual elimination of many infectious diseases, an improvement in diet, and virtual disappearance of nearly all nutritional deficiency disorders. Many of the so-called tropical diseases, such as malaria, yellow fever, and cholera, were once endemic or epidemic in industrialized countries and have now disappeared (Table 1.1). Case fatality rates for many infectious diseases dropped tremendously during the late 19th and early 20th centuries. New knowledge of nutrition and the characterization of vitamins helped to improve the diet in the early 20th century, and innovations in agricultural practices helped to increase food production. After World War II, international organizations grew in strength and are addressing basic issues of nutrition, hygiene, and control of infectious diseases in developing countries. Nutrition has played a major role among the developments in public health during the last 200 years and is likely to remain as a major foundation for public health.

Table 1.1.
Major Diseases in Europe, Great Britain, and the United
States During the 19th Century

| Infectious diseases | Nutrition deficiency disorder |
| --- | --- |
| Diarrheal disease | Rickets |
| Cholera | Pellagra |
| Malaria | Goiter/cretinism |
| Yellow fever | Nutritional blindness |
| Tuberculosis | |
| Typhoid | |
| Typhus | |
| Measles | |

# REFERENCES

1.  McKeown T. The modern rise of population. London: Arnold, 1976.
2.  McKeown T. The role of medicine: dream, mirage, or nemesis? Princeton, NJ: Princeton University Press, 1979.
3.  Woods R, Woodward J, eds. Urban disease and mortality in nineteenth century England. New York: St. Martin's, 1984.
4.  Riley JC. The eighteenth century campaign to avoid disease. New York: St. Martin's, 1987.
5.  Rosen G. A history of public health. New York: MD Publications, 1958.
6.  Duffy J. The sanitarians: a history of American public health. Urbana: University of Illinois Press, 1990.
7.  Fee E, Acheson RM. A history of education in public health: health that mocks the doctors' rules. Oxford: Oxford University Press, 1991.
8.  Porter R. The greatest benefit to mankind: a medical history of humanity. New York: Norton, 1997.
9.  Winslow CEA. The conquest of epidemic disease: a chapter in the history of ideas. Princeton, NJ: Princeton University Press, 1943.
10. Dowling HF. Fighting infection: conquests of the twentieth century. Cambridge: Harvard University Press, 1977.
11. Ackerknecht EH. History and geography of the most important diseases. New York: Hafner, 1965.
12. Carpenter KJ. Protein and energy: a study of changing ideas in nutrition. Cambridge, UK: Cambridge University Press, 1994.
13. Carpenter KJ. The history of scurvy and vitamin C. Cambridge, UK: Cambridge University Press, 1986.
14. Roe DA. A plague of corn: the social history of pellagra. Ithaca, NY: Cornell University Press, 1973.
15. Drummond JC, Wilbraham A. The Englishman's food: a history of five centuries of English diet. London: Cape, 1939.
16. Tannahill R. Food in history. New York: Stein and Day, 1973.
17. Levenstein HA. Revolution at the table: the transformation of the American diet. New York: Oxford University Press, 1988.
18. Newman LF, ed. Hunger in history: food shortage, poverty, and deprivation. Oxford: Blackwell, 1990.
19. Frankel C. The faith of reason: the idea of progress in the French Enlightenment. New York: King's Crown, Columbia University, 1948.
20. Diderot D, Alembert JLR d', Mouchon P. Encyclopédie, ou dictionnaire raisonné des sciences, des arts et des métiers, par une société de gens de lettres. Paris: Briasson, 1751–1765.
21. Condorcet MJAN Caritat, Marquis de. Esquisse d'un tableau historique des progrès de l'esprit humain. 2nd ed. Paris: Agasses, 1795.

22. Condorcet MJAN, Caritat, Marquis de. Sketch for a historical picture of the progress of the human mind. J. Barraclough, trans. London: Weidenfeld and Nicholson, 1955.

23. Baker K. Condorcet: from natural philosophy to social mathematics. Chicago: University of Chicago Press, 1975.

24. Godwin W. An enquiry concerning political justice, and its influence on general virtue and happiness. London: Robinson, 1793.

25. Malthus TR. An essay on the principle of population as it affects the future improvement of society, with remarks on the speculations of Mr. Godwin, M. Condorcet, and other writers. London: Johnson, 1798.

26. Avery J. Progress, poverty and population: re-reading Condorcet, Godwin and Malthus. London: Cass, 1997.

27. Frank JP. System einer vollständigen medicinischen Polizey. 3rd rev. ed. Wien, 1786–1817.

28. Sigerist HE. The people's misery: mother of diseases, an address delivered in 1790 by Johann Peter Frank, translated from the Latin, with an introduction. Bull Hist Med 1941;9:81–100.

29. Sigerist HE. Landmarks in the history of hygiene. London: Oxford University Press, 1956.

30. Greenwood M. Medical statistics from Graunt to Farr. Cambridge, UK: Cambridge University Press, 1948.

31. Pearson ES, ed. The history of statistics in the seventeeth and eighteenth centuries against the changing background of intellectual, scientific and religious thought: lectures by Karl Pearson given at University College London during the academic sessions 1921–1933. New York: Macmillan, 1978.

32. Graunt J. Natural and political observations mentioned in a following index, and made upon the bills of mortality. London: Martin, Allestry, and Dicas, 1662.

33. Westergaard H. Contributions to the history of statistics. London: King, 1932.

34. Petty W. Several essays in political arithmetic. London: Clavel and Mortlock, 1699.

35. Halley E. An estimate of the degrees of mortality of mankind, drawn from curious tables of the births and funerals of the city of Breslaw, with an attempt to ascertain the price of annuities upon lives. Phil Trans 1693;17:596–610.

36. Eyler JM. Victorian social medicine: the ideas and methods of William Farr. Baltimore, MD: Johns Hopkins University Press, 1979.

37. Farr W. Vital statistics, or the statistics of health, sickness, diseases, and death. In: A statistical account of the British empire: exhibiting its extent, physical capacities, population, industry, and civil and religious institutions. McColloch JR, ed. London: 1837, 2:567–601.

38. Quetelet A. Sur l'homme et le développement de ses facultés, ou Essai de physique sociale. Paris: Bachelier, 1835.

39. Cullen MJ. The statistical movement in early Victorian Britain: the foundations of empirical social research. New York: Barnes and Noble, 1975.

40. Porter TM. The rise of statistical thinking, 1820–1900. Princeton, NJ: Princeton University Press, 1986.

41. Galton F. Natural inheritance. London: Macmillan, 1889.

42. Pearson K. Mathematical contributions to the theory of evolution, III. Regression, heredity and panmixia. Phil Trans Roy Soc London A 1896;187:253–318.

43. Stigler SM. The history of statistics: the measurement of uncertainty before 1900. Cambridge: Harvard University Press, 1986.

44. Fisher RA. The design of experiments. London: Oliver and Boyd, 1935.

45. Neyman J, Pearson ES. On the use and interpretation of certain test criteria for purposes of statistical inference. Biometrika 1928; 20A (part 1):175–240; (part 2):263–294.

46. Marks HM. The progress of experiment: science and therapeutic reform in the United States, 1900–1990. Cambridge, UK: Cambridge University Press, 1997.

47. Ackerknecht EH. Hygiene in France, 1815–1848. Bull Hist Med 1948;22:117–155.

48. La Berge A. Mission and method: the early nineteenth century French public health movement. Cambridge, UK: Cambridge University Press, 1992.

49. Villermé LR. De la famine et ses effets sur la santé dans les lieux qui sont le théâtre de la guerre. J gén méd chir pharm 1818;65:3–24.

50. Villermé LR. Recherches statistiques sur la ville de Paris et le département de la Seine. Bull Soc méd d'emul 1822:1–41.

51. Benoiston de Châteauneuf LF. Recherches sur les consommations de tout genre de la ville de Paris en 1817, comparées à ce qu'elles étaient en 1789. Paris: Author, 1820.

52. Coleman W. Death is a social disease: public health and political economy in early industrial France. Madison: University of Wisconsin Press, 1982.

53. Villermé LR. Des epidémies sous les rapportes de l'hygiène publique, de la statistique médicale et de l'économie politique. Paris, 1833.

54. Villermé LR. Tableau de l'état physique et moral des ouvriers employés dans les manufactures de coton, de laine et de soie. 2 vols. Paris: Renouard, 1840.

55. Napoli Archivio di Stato. Statistica del 1811. Ministero dell'Interno, 1% Inventario, 96:1–65.

56. Constantini AM. Ambiente, alimentazione e salute nell'inchiesta murattiana del 1811. Medicina nei Secoli 1996;8:339–357.

57. Genovesi A. Ragionamento intorno all'agricoltura con applicazione al Regno di Napoli. In Scrittori Classici Italiani di Economia Politica. Parte Moderna, Tomo IX. Milano: De Stefanis, 1803:305–325.

58. Bentham J. Traités de législation civile et pénale. Paris: Bossange, Masson, and Besson, 1802.

59. Chadwick E. Report to Her Majesty's principal secretary of state for the Home Department, from the Poor Law Commissioners, on an inquiry into the sanitary condition of the labouring population of Great Britain. London: Clowes, 1842.

60. Finer SE. The life and times of Sir Edwin Chadwick. London: Methuen, 1952.

61. Shattuck L. Report of a general plan for the promotion of public and personal health, devised, prepared and recommended by the commissioners appointed under a resolve of the legislature of Massachusetts, relating to a sanitary survey of the state. Boston: Dutton and Wentworth, 1850.

62. Cassedy JH. Demography in early America: beginnings of the statistical mind, 1600–1800. Cambridge, MA: Harvard University Press, 1969.

63. Cassedy JH. American medicine and statistical thinking, 1800–1860. Cambridge: Harvard University Press, 1984.

64. Hirsch A. Handbook of geographical and historical pathology. London: New Sydenham Society, 1883–1886.

65. Bulloch W. The history of bacteriology. London: Oxford University Press, 1938.

66. Pelling M. Cholera, fever, and English medicine, 1825–1865. Oxford, UK: Oxford University Press, 1978.

67. Panum PL. Iagttagelser, anstillede under Maeslinge-Epidemien paa Faerøerne i Aaret 1846. Bibliothek f Laeger, 1847;1:270–344.

68. Manicus A. Maeslingerne paa Faeröerne i Sommeren 1846. Ugeskrift for Laeger 1847;6:189–210.

69. Snow J. On the mode of communication of cholera. 2nd ed. London: Churchill, 1855.

70. Budd W. Malignant cholera: its mode of propagation and its prevention. London: Churchill, 1849.

71. Bruce FE. Water-supply. In: A history of technology. Vol. 5. The late nineteenth century, ca. 1850 to ca. 1900. Singer C, Holmyard EJ, Hall AR, Williams TI, eds. New York: Oxford University Press, 1958.

72. Goubert JP. The conquest of water: the advent of health in the industrial age. Princeton, NJ: Princeton University Press, 1986.

73. Hamlin C. The science of impurity: water analysis in nineteenth century Britain. Berkeley: University of California Press, 1990.

74. Girette J. La civilisation et le choléra. Paris: Hachette, 1867.

75. Bretonneau PF. Des inflammations spéciales du tissu muqueux et en particulier de la diphthérite, ou inflammation pelliculaire. Paris: Crevot, 1826.

76. Budd W. Typhoid fever; its nature, mode of spreading, and prevention. London: Longmans, Green, 1873.

77. Henle FGJ. Pathologische Untersuchungen. Berlin: Hirschwald, 1840.

78. Koch R. Untersuchungen über die Aetiologie der Wundinfectionskrankheiten. Leipzig: Vogel, 1878.

79. Koch R. Die Aetiologie der Milzbrand-Krankheit, begründet auf die Entwicklungsgeschichte des Bacillus anthracis. Beitr z Biol d Pflanzen. 1876; Bd. II, Heft 2:277–310.

80. Laveran CLA. Un nouveau parasite trouvé dans le sang plusieurs malades atteints de fièvre palustre. Bull Soc méd Hôp Paris (Mém) 1881;2 sér. 17:158–164.

81. Koch R. Die Aetiologie der Tuberculose. Berlin klin Wchnschr 1882;19:221–230.
82. Koch R. Ueber die Cholerabakterien. Dtsch med Wchnschr 1884;10:725–728.
83. Legge TM. Public health in European capitals: Berlin, Paris, Brussels, Christiania, Stockholm, and Copenhagen. London: Swan Sonnenschein, 1896.
84. Sedgwick WT. Principles of sanitary science and the public health with special reference to the causation and prevention of infectious diseases. New York: Macmillan, 1903.
85. Chapin CV. The sources and modes of infection. 2nd ed. New York: Wiley, 1912.
86. Lesch JE. Science and medicine in France: the emergence of experimental physiology, 1790–1855. Cambridge: Harvard University Press, 1984.
87. Magendie F. Précis élémentaire de physiologie. 2nd ed. Paris: Méquignon-Marvis, 1825.
88. Magendie F. Mémoire sur les propriétés nutritives des substances qui ne contiennent pas d'azote. Bull Sci Socphilomatique Paris 1816;4:137–138.
89. Mulder GJ. Ueber die Zusammensetzung einiger thierischen Substanzen. J prakt Chemie 1839;16: 129–152.
90. Liebig J von. Die Thier-Chemie oder die organische Chemie in ihrer Anwendung auf Physiologie und Pathologie. Braunschweig, 1846.
91. Voit C von. Handbuch der Physiologie des gesammt-Stoffwechsels und der Fortpflanzung. Theil 1. Physiologie des allgemeinen Stoffwechsels und der Ernährung. In: Handbuch der Physiologie, vol. 6. Hermann L, ed. Leipzig: Vogel, 1881:1–575.
92. Atwater WO. Methods and results of investigations on the chemistry and economy of food. Washington,, DC: U.S. Department of Agriculture, Office of Experiment Stations, 1895. Bulletin 21.
93. Sée G. Du régime alimentaire. Traitement hygiénique des malades. Paris: Delahaye and Lescrosnier, 1887.
94. Thompson WG. Practical dietetics with special reference to diet in disease. New York: Appleton, 1896.
95. Friedenwald J, Ruhräh J. Diet in health and disease. 2nd ed. Philadelphia: Saunders, 1906.
96. Lusk G. The elements of the science of nutrition. Philadelphia: Saunders, 1906.
97. Chittenden RH. The nutrition of man. New York: Stokes, 1907.
98. Meckel RA. Save the Babies: American public health reform and the prevention of infant mortality, 1850–1929. Baltimore, MD: Johns Hopkins University Press, 1990.
99. Klaus A. Every child a lion: the origins of maternal infant and health policy in the United States and France, 1890–1920. Ithaca, NY: Cornell University Press, 1993.
100. Newman G. Infant mortality: a social problem. London: Methuen, 1906.
101. Peters OH. Observations upon the natural history of epidemic diarrhoea. Cambridge, UK: Cambridge University Press, 1911.
102. Eyler JM. Sir Arthur Newsholme and state medicine, 1885–1943. Cambridge, UK: Cambridge University Press, 1997.
103. Shimazono N, Katsura E. Review of Japanese literature on beriberi and thiamine. Kyoto: Vitamin B Research Committee of Japan, 1965.
104. Takaki K. Prevention of beriberi in the Japanese Navy. Se-i-kai Med J 1885;4:29–37.
105. Takaki K. Three lectures on the preservation of health amongst the personnel of the Japanese Navy and Army. Lancet 1906;1:1369–1374, 1451–1455, 1520–1523.
106. Eijkman C. Polyneuritis bij hoenderen. Geneesk Tijdschr nederl Indië 1890;30:295–334; 1892;32:353–362; 1896;36:214–269.
107. Grijns G. Over polyneuritis gallinarum. Geneesk Tijdschr nederl. Indië 1901;41:3–110.
108. Steenbock H. A review of certain researches relating to the occurrence and chemical nature of vitamin A. Yale J Biol Med 1932;4:563–578.
109. Wolf G, Carpenter KJ. Early research into the vitamins: the work of Wilhelm Stepp. J Nutr 1997;127:1255–1259.
110. Lunin N. Über die Bedeutung der anorganischen Salze für die Ernährung des Thieres. Zeitschr physiol Chem 1881;5:31–39.
111. Bunge G von. Lehrbuch der physiologischen und pathologischen Chemie. Leipzig: Vogel, 1887.
112. Socin CA. In welcher Form wird das Eisen resorbirt? Zeitschr physiol Chem 1891;15:93–139.
113. Pekelharing CA. Over onze kennis van de waarde der voedingsmiddelen uit chemische fabrieken. Nederlandsch Tijdschr. Geneeskunde 1905;41:111–124.

114. Stepp W. Experimentelle Untersuchungen über die Bedeutung der Lipoide für die Ernährung. Z Biol 1911;57:136–170.

115. Hopkins FG. The analyst and the medical man. Analyst 1906;31:385–404.

116. Funk C. On the chemical nature of the substance which cures polyneuritis in birds induced by a diet of polished rice. J Physiol 1911;43:395–400.

117. Funk C. The etiology of the deficiency diseases. Beri-beri, polyneuritis in birds, epidemic dropsy, scurvy, experimental scurvy in animals, infantile scurvy, ship beri-beri, pellagra. J State Med 1912;20: 341–368.

118. Needham J, Baldwin E, eds. Hopkins and biochemistry, 1861–1947. Cambridge, UK: Hefner, 1949.

119. Osborne TB, Mendel LB. Feeding experiments with isolated food-substances. Washington, DC: Carnegie Institute of Washington, 1911. Publication 156.

120. Osborne TB, Mendel LB. The relationship of growth to the chemical constituents of the diet. J Biol Chem 1913;15:311–326.

121. Hopkins FG. Feeding experiments illustrating the importance of accessory factors in normal dietaries. J Physiol 1912;44:425–460.

122. McCollum EV, Davis M. The necessity of certain lipins in the diet during growth. J Biol Chem 1913;15:167–175.

123. Mellanby E. The part played by an "accessory factor" in the production of experimental rickets. J Physiol 1918–1919;52:xi–xii.

124. Mellanby E. A further demonstration of the part played by accessory food factors in the aetiology of rickets. J Physiol 1918–1919;52:liii–liv.

125. McCollum EV, Simmonds N, Becker JE, Shipley PG. Studies on experimental rickets. 21. An experimental demonstration of the existence of a vitamin which promotes calcium deposition. J Biol Chem 1922;53:293–312.

126. Karrer P, Morf R, Schöpp K. Zur Kenntnis des Vitamins-A aus Fischtranen. Helv Chim Acta 1931;14:1036–1040.

127. Karrer P, Morf R, Schöpp K. Zur Kenntnis des Vitamins-A aus Fischtranen II. Helv Chim Acta 1931;14:1431–1436.

128. Holmes HN, Corbet RE. The isolation of crystalline vitamin A. J Am Chem Soc 1937;59:2042–2047.

129. Carpenter KJ, ed. Pellagra. Benchmark papers in biochemistry, vol. 2. Stroudsburg, PA: Hutchinson Ross, 1981.

130. Sambon LW. Progress report on the investigation of pellagra. J Trop Med Hyg 1910;13:289–300.

131. Etheridge EW. The butterfly caste: a social history of pellagra in the South. Westport, CT: Greenwood, 1972.

132. Searcy GH. An epidemic of acute pellagra. Alabama Med J 1907;20:387–392.

133. Report of the Pellagra Commission of the State of Illinois, November, 1911. Springfield, IL: State Journal, 1912.

134. Siler JF, Garrison PE, MacNeal WJ. The relation of methods of disposal of sewage to the spread of pellagra. Arch Intern Med 1914;14:453–474.

135. Terris M, ed. Goldberger on pellagra. Baton Rouge: Louisiana State University Press, 1964.

136. Goldberger J, Wheeler GA, Sydenstricker E. A study of the diet of nonpellagrous and of pellagrous households in textile mill communities in South Carolina in 1916. J Am Med Assoc 1918;71:944–949.

137. Goldberger J, Wheeler GA. Experimental pellagra in the human subject brought about by a restricted diet. Public Health Rep 1915;30:3336–3339.

138. Williams CD. A nutritional disease of childhood associated with a maize diet. Arch Dis Child 1933;8:423–433.

139. Orr E. The use of protein-rich foods for the relief of malnutrition in developing countries: an analysis of experience. London: Tropical Products Institute, 1972.

140. Pretorius PJ, Smith ZM. The effects of various skimmed milk formulae on the diarrhea, nitrogen retention and initiation of cure in kwashiorkor. J Trop Pediatr 1968;4:50–60.

141. Jelliffe DB. Protein-calorie malnutrition in tropical preschool children. J Pediatr 1959;54:227–256.

142. McLaren DS. The great protein fiasco. Lancet 1974;2:93–96.

143. Waterlow JC, Payne PR. The protein gap. Nature (London) 1975;258:113–117.

144. Silverstein AM. A history of immunology. San Diego, CA: Academic, 1989.
145. Fox FW. Vitamin A and infection: a review of recent work. East Afr Med J 1933;10:190–214.
146. Robertson EC. The vitamins and resistance to infection. Medicine 1934;13:123–206.
147. Clausen SW. The influence of nutrition upon resistance to infection. Physiol Rev 1934;14:309–350.
148. Blegvad O. Xerophthalmia, keratomalacia and xerosis conjunctivae. Am J Ophthalmol 1924;7:89–117.
149. Blegvad O. Om xerophthalmien og dens forekomst i Danmark i aarene 1909–1920. København: Gyldendalske Boghandel, 1923.
150. Bloch CE. Blindness and other diseases in children arising from deficient nutrition (lack of fat-soluble A factor). Am J Dis Child 1924;27:139–148.
151. Bloch CE. Further clinical investigations into the diseases arising in consequence of a deficiency in the fat-soluble A factor. Am J Dis Child 1924;28:659–667.
152. Green HN, Mellanby E. Vitamin A as an anti-infective agent. Br Med J 1929;2:691–696.
153. Semba RD. Vitamin A as "anti-infective" therapy, 1920–1940. J Nutr 1999;129:783–791.
154. Ellison JB. Intensive vitamin therapy in measles. Br Med J 1932;2:708–711.
155. Semba RD. On Joseph Bramhall Ellison's discovery that vitamin A reduces measles mortality. Nutrition 2003;19:390–394.
156. Prescott SC, Proctor BE. Food technology. New York: McGraw-Hill, 1937.
157. Lancet. Parliamentary Intelligence. Ottawa and cod-liver oil. Lancet 1932;2:978–979.
158. British Medical Journal. Medical notes in Parliament. Ottawa Agreements: cod-liver oil. Br Med J 1932;2:661.
159. British Medical Journal. Medical notes in Parliament. Ottawa Agreements: cod-liver oil. Br Med J 1932;2:819.
160. Beaton GH, Martorell R, L'Abbe KA, Edmonston B, McCabe G, Ross AC, Harvey B. Effectiveness of vitamin A supplementation in the control of young child morbidity and mortality in developing countries. New York: United Nations, 1993. ACC/SCN State-of-the-Art Nutrition Policy Discussion Paper No. 13.
161. Scrimshaw NS, Taylor CE, Gordon JE. Interactions of nutrition and infection. Geneva: World Health Organization, 1968.
162. Beisel WR. Single nutrients and immunity. Am J Clin Nutr 1982;35(suppl):417–468.
163. Chambers JD, Mingay GE. The agricultural revolution, 1750–1880. New York: Schocken, 1966.
164. Price R. The modernization of rural France: communications networks and agricultural market structures in nineteenth century France. New York: St. Martin's Press, 1983.
165. Holmes CJ. Science and practice in English arable farming, 1910–1950. In: Diet and health in modern Britain. Oddy DJ, Miller DS, eds. London: Croom Helm, 1985.
166. Aymard M. Toward the history of nutrition: some methodological remarks. In: Food and drink in history. Forster R, Ranum O, eds. Selections from the Annales Economies, Sociétés, Civilisations, vol. 5. Baltimore, MD: Johns Hopkins University Press, 1979:1–16.
167. Toutain JC. La consommation alimentaire en France de 1789 à 1964. Geneva: Droz, 1971.
168. Wohl AS. Endangered lives: public health in Victorian Britain. Cambridge: Harvard University Press, 1983.
169. Buckley ME. The feeding of school children. London: Bell, 1914.
170. Great Britain. Inter-Departmental Committee on Physical Deterioration. Report of the Inter-Departmental Committee on Physical Deterioration. London: Wyman, 1904.
171. Burnett J. The rise and decline of school meals in Britain, 1860–1990. In: The origins and development of food policies in Europe. Burnett J, Oddy DJ, eds. London: Leicester University Press, 1994.
172. Medical Research Committee. Report on the present state of knowledge concerning accessory food factors (vitamines), compiled by a committee appointed jointly by the Lister Institute and Medical Research Committee. London: Her Majesty's Stationery Office, 1919.
173. Mann HCC. Diets for boys during the school age. London: Her Majesty's Stationery Office, 1926. Medical Research Council Special Report Series, No. 105.
174. Nelson M. Social-class trends in British diet, 1860–1980. In: Food, diet and economic change past and present. Geissler C, Oddy DJ, eds. Leicester: Leicester University Press, 1993;101–120.
175. Paton DN, Dunlop JC, Inglis E. A study of the diet of the labouring classes in Edinburgh, carried out under the auspices of the town council of the city of Edinburgh. Edinburgh: Otto Schulze, 1901.

176. Editorial. Diet of the labouring classes. Br Med J 1913;1:647.

177. Smith D, Nicolson M. Nutrition, education, ignorance and income: a twentieth century debate. In: The science and culture of nutrition, 1840–1940. Kamminga H, Cunningham A, eds. Amsterdam: Rodopi, 1995:288–318.

178. Orr JB. Food health and income: report on a survey of the adequacy of diet in relation to income. London: Macmillan, 1936.

179. Floud R, Wachter K, Gregory A. Height, health and history: nutritional status in the United Kingdom, 1750–1980. Cambridge, UK: Cambridge University Press, 1990.

180. McIntosh EN. American food habits in historical perspective. Westport, CT: Praeger, 1995.

181. Fogel RW, Engerman SL, Trussell J. Exploring the uses of data on height. Soc Sci History 1982;6: 401–421.

182. Lindhert PH, Williamson JG. Three centuries of inequality. In: Research in economic history, vol. 1. Sedling P, ed. Greenwich, CT: JAI, 1976:69–123.

183. US Bureau of the Census. Historical statistics of the United States, colonial times to 1970. Washington, DC: US Government Printing Office, 1975.

184. US Department of Agriculture. Consumption of foods in the United States, 1909–1952. Washington, DC: US Government Printing Office, 1953. Agricultural Handbook No. 62.

185. Apple RD. Vitamania: vitamins in american culture. New Brunswick, NJ: Rutgers University Press, 1996.

186. Newman G. Letter to Charles Flemming. July 28, 1939 (collection of the author).

187. Newman G. The building of a nation's health. London: Macmillan, 1939.

188. Wrigley EA, Schofield RS. The population history of England, 1541–1871. Cambridge: Harvard University Press, 1981.

189. Livi-Bacci M. Population and nutrition: an essay on European demographic history. Cambridge, UK: Cambridge University Press, 1986.

190. Tranter NL. Population and society, 1750–1940: contrasts in population growth. London: Longman, 1985.

191. Schofield R, Reher D, Bideau A, eds. The decline of mortality in Europe. Oxford, UK: Clarendon Press, 1991.

192. Corsini CA, Viazzo PP, eds. The decline of infant and child mortality. The European experience: 1750–1990. The Hague: Kluwer Law International, 1997.

193. Hess AF. Rickets including osteomalacia and tetany. Philadelphia: Lea and Febiger, 1929.

194. Fee E, Porter D. Public health, preventive medicine, and professionalization: Britain and the United States in the nineteenth century. In: A history of education in public health. Health that mocks the doctors' rules. Fee E, Acheson RM, eds. Oxford, UK: Oxford University Press, 1991:15–43.

195. Lesky E. The Vienna Medical School of the nineteenth century. Baltimore, MD: Johns Hopkins University Press, 1976.

196. Fee E. Disease and discovery: a history of the Johns Hopkins School of Hygiene and Public Health, 1916–1939. Baltimore, MD: Johns Hopkins University Press, 1987.

197. Curran JA. Founders of the Harvard School of Public Health, with biographical notes, 1909–1946. New York: Macy Foundation, 1970.

198. Flexner A. Medical education: a comparative study. New York: Macmillan, 1925.

199. Cottrell JD. The teaching of public health in Europe. Geneva: World Health Organization, 1969.

200. Moulin AM. The Pasteur Institutes between the two world wars. The transformation of the international sanitary order. In: International health organizations and movements, 1918–1939. Weindling P, ed. Cambridge, UK: Cambridge University Press, 1995:244–265.

201. Delaunay A. L'Institut Pasteur: des origines a aujourd'hui. Paris: Editions France-Empire, 1962.

202. Chick H, Hume M, Macfarlane M. War on disease: a history of the Lister Institute. London: Deutsch, 1971.

203. Ettling J. The germ of laziness: Rockefeller philanthropy and public health in the new South. Cambridge: Harvard University Press, 1981.

204. Farley J. The International Health Division of the Rockefeller Foundation: the Russell years, 1920–1934. In: International health organizations and movements, 1918–1939. Weindling P, ed. Cambridge, UK: Cambridge University Press, 1995:203–221.

205. Cueto M. The cycles of eradication : the Rockefeller Foundation and Latin American public health, 1918–1940. In: International health organizations and movements, 1918–1939. Weindling P, ed. Cambridge, UK: Cambridge University Press, 1995:222–243.

206. Brown ER. Rockefeller medicine men: medicine and capitalism in America. Berkeley: University of California Press, 1979.

207. Williams RC. The United States Public Health Service, 1798–1950. Washington, DC: Commissioned Officers Association of the US Public Health Service, 1951.

208. Harden VA. Inventing the NIH: federal biomedical research policy, 1887–1937. Baltimore, MD: Johns Hopkins University Press, 1986.

209. Black M. The children and the nations: the story of UNICEF. Sydney: P.I.C. for UNICEF, 1986.

210. Phillips RW. FAO: its origins, formation and evolution, 1945–1981. Rome: Food and Agricultural Organization of the United Nations, 1981.

211. Salda ACM. Historical dictionary of the World Bank. Lanham, MD: Scarecrow Press, 1997.

212. Kapur D, Lewis JP, Webb R. The World Bank: its first half century. Washington, DC: Brookings Institution, 1997.

213. Berg A. The nutrition factor: its role in national development. Washington, DC: Brookings Institution, 1973.

214. Berg A. Malnutrition: what can be done? Lessons from World Bank experience. Baltimore, MD: Johns Hopkins University Press, 1987.

# 2

## Maternal Mortality in Developing Countries

### Carine Ronsmans, Simon Collin, and Véronique Filippi

## 2.1  INTRODUCTION

According to the latest estimates of the World Health Organisation (WHO) and the United Nations International Children's Emergency Fund (UNICEF), 529,000 women still die every year from complications of their pregnancy, and nearly 90% of these deaths are in sub-Saharan Africa and Asia [1]. Obstetric complications continue to represent the major cause among women of childbearing age, far ahead of tuberculosis, suicide, sexually transmitted diseases, or AIDS [2]. While developed countries have made enormous progress in bringing down the huge death rates associated with pregnancy, women in developing countries continue to face very high risks of death and disability as a result of pregnancy. The risk of a woman dying as a result of pregnancy or child-birth during her lifetime is about 1 in 6 in the poorest parts of the world compared with about 1 in 30,000 in Sweden [3].

The growing awareness of the continuing high rates of maternal mortality during the early 1980s led to the launch of the Safe Motherhood Initiative in Nairobi in 1987. After this "call for action," governmental and nongovernmental organisations joined forces to reduce the huge burden of maternal mortality in the world. Substantial progress has been made in documenting the extent of maternal ill health, and many of the actors involved have now embraced safer motherhood as among the highest priorities in public health practice. As a result, the reduction of maternal mortality is now one of the major targets promoted within the Millennium Development Goals set up by the United Nations in 2000 [4]. The recent *World Health Report* [2] also marked two decades of attention for Safe Motherhood and highlighted key strategies that may make pregnancy safer.

The aim of this chapter is to review the evidence underlying the strategies proposed to reduce the huge burden of maternal mortality. It starts off by documenting the magnitude of maternal mortality while briefly highlighting the problems associated with its measurement. After a review of the main factors known to contribute to maternal mortality, the strategies that have been proposed to reduce the high levels of maternal mortality in the world are discussed.

From: *Nutrition and Health: Nutrition and Health in Developing Countries, Second Edition*
Edited by: R. D. Semba & M. W. Bloem © Humana Press, Totowa, NJ

This review explicitly focuses on the evidence linking maternal mortality with effective strategies, ignoring the fact that some of these strategies, while perhaps not proven effective to reduce maternal mortality, may have beneficial effects on the health of the unborn child or the woman in general. In doing so, an incomplete picture of intervention strategies to improve perinatal and women's health in developing countries is presented. It is important, however, to separate the different entities to gain a better understanding of what we can hope to achieve in reaching the goal of a reduction in maternal mortality in poor countries.

## 2.2   MAGNITUDE AND CAUSES OF MATERNAL MORTALITY

### 2.2.1   *Measuring Maternal Mortality*

The measurement of maternal mortality is surprisingly complex. The factors that make maternal mortality difficult to measure include (1) the uncertainty about the precise time period during which pregnant women are at higher risk of adverse health effects; (2) the lack of insight into the causes of death that are indirectly attributable to the pregnancy; and (3) the underreporting of pregnancy as a cause of death. In addition, the relative rarity of maternal deaths (in statistical terms) makes interpretation of trends in maternal mortality over time or between geographical areas very difficult.

Traditionally, a death is defined as maternal if it occurs during pregnancy or within 42 days of its termination [5]. The length of the postpartum period at risk has varied substantially, however, and the tenth revision of the *International Classification of Diseases (ICD-10)* now acknowledges the need for an extended time period referring to "late maternal deaths," which occur after 42 days and up to 1 year after delivery [6] (Table 2.1).

Table 2.1
**Definition of maternal mortality** (*International Classification of Diseases, Tenth Edition*)

*Maternal death*: The death of a woman while pregnant or within 42 days of termination of pregnancy, irrespective of the duration and site of the pregnancy, from any cause related to or aggravated by the pregnancy or its management, but not from accidental or incidental causes

*Late maternal death*: The death of a woman from direct or indirect obstetric causes more than 42 days but less than 1 year after termination of pregnancy

*Pregnancy-related death*: The death of a woman while pregnant or within 42 days of termination of pregnancy, irrespective of the cause of death

*Direct obstetric death*: The death of a woman resulting from obstetric complications of the pregnant state (pregnancy, labour, and puerperium); from interventions, omissions, incorrect treatment; or from a chain of events resulting from any of the above; includes conditions such as hypertensive diseases of pregnancy, haemorrhage, dystocia, genital tract sepsis, spontaneous or induced abortion.

*Indirect obstetric death*: The death of a woman resulting from previous existing disease or disease that developed during pregnancy and was not due to direct obstetric causes but was aggravated by physiologic effects of pregnancy

*Source*: Adapted from [6].

Not all deaths during or shortly after pregnancy are due to the pregnancy. Traditionally, deaths from direct and indirect obstetric causes have been included in the maternal mortality statistic, while deaths from accidental and incidental causes have not (Table 2.1). Deaths from direct obstetric causes such as eclampsia, haemorrhage, obstructed labour, or puerperal sepsis are undoubtedly attributable to the pregnancy as such conditions can only occur in pregnant women. Far less certainty exists, however, regarding indirect obstetric causes, particularly those due to infectious diseases. The notion of "diseases aggravated by the pregnancy" is not straightforward, and some diseases may merely coincide with the pregnancy without being aggravated by it. In addition, the verbal autopsy methods on which most cause-of-death ascertainments are based may be unreliable, particularly for indirect causes of maternal death [7]. In settings that rely on verbal autopsy methods, all deaths in pregnant or recently delivered women are commonly included in the maternal mortality statistic (whether or not they are attributable to the pregnancy), except for deaths due to unintentional and intentional injuries [7–9]. However, it is becoming increasingly clear that the burden of indirect causes may have been underestimated, particularly in Africa, where the prevalence of HIV is high [10].

The exclusion of deaths from accidents, homicides, or suicides from the maternal mortality statistic is a matter of controversy, and there is a growing awareness that such deaths may, at least in part, be caused by the pregnancy [11, 12]. In India, deaths due to domestic violence were the second largest cause of death in pregnancy (16%) [13]. In Matlab, Bangladesh, 20% of deaths of pregnant unmarried women were due to suicide compared to 5% for married women, and pregnant girls were nearly three times more likely to die from violent causes than nonpregnant girls [11, 14]. Studies in developed countries suggested that suicide may be precipitated by pregnancy, and that some accidents may be pregnancy related, although a recent study in the United Kingdom did not support these findings [12, 15]. Authors of a recent systematic review of violence and pregnancy-related mortality have called for further research in this area, arguing that very few rigorous epidemiological studies exist [16].

Many pregnancy-related deaths still go unnoticed or unreported, and substantial errors in the estimates of maternal mortality persist [17, 18]. Correctly measuring maternal mortality requires not only a complete registration of deaths in women of reproductive age, which in many countries may be lacking, but also the recognition that the woman was pregnant or recently delivered at the time of her death. Deaths during early pregnancy, such as those due to abortion or ectopic pregnancy, are often not recognised or reported as pregnancy related, and death certificates often omit the notion of pregnancy. The verbal autopsy techniques on which many cause-of-death assignments are based may have poor reliability [7].

Maternal mortality is usually expressed in two different ways: the maternal mortality *rate* and the maternal mortality *ratio*. The rate is expressed as maternal deaths per 100,000 women of reproductive age. The maternal mortality ratio—sometimes erroneously called the maternal mortality rate—refers maternal deaths to the numbers of live births. The maternal mortality rate and ratio measure very different kinds of risks. The ratio measures the risk of death a woman faces with each pregnancy, whereas the rate measures the risks to women, whether or not they are pregnant. The rate is a compound measure of the level of fertility and the risks associated with each pregnancy. Any intervention lowering fertility will automatically lower the maternal mortality rate but not necessarily the ratio. As many assessments of progress in Safe Motherhood aim at separating the effects of lowering fertility from those directly aimed at improving the health of women once they are pregnant, the maternal mortality ratio has now become the preferred statistic [19]. Denominator information for the maternal mortality ratio is also easier to capture routinely, from hospital records or vital registration.

The problems in the measurement of maternal mortality are such that maternal mortality has not always been recommended as an outcome measure against which to assess programme successes. Although hopes were raised that morbidity would be a good alternative measure, it has proven very difficult to measure the prevalence of maternal morbidity at the community level [20, 21]. In fact, very little is known about the incidence of obstetric complications in developing countries. The use of facility-based data has been suggested as an alternative means to study programme effectiveness, and experience so far has been encouraging [9, 22, 23]. Investigation of women who had a near-miss obstetric morbidity, for example, may provide useful insights into the pathways leading to maternal death [24, 25]. Whether the measurement of near-miss or other life-threatening complications can inform programme success at the population level, however, is not known.

### 2.2.2   Medical Causes of Maternal Mortality

In developing countries as a whole, maternal mortality ratios range from 55 per 100,000 live births in eastern Asia to 920 per 100,000 in sub-Saharan Africa (Table 2.2). In many countries of East, Central, and West Africa, maternal mortality exceeds 1,000 deaths per 100,000 live births.

The majority of maternal deaths in developing countries are due to five major direct obstetric complications: haemorrhage, infection, unsafe abortion, hypertensive disorders of pregnancy, and obstructed labour [19] (Fig. 2.1). While huge variations are seen in the relative contribution of each of the direct obstetric causes to mortality, deaths from intra- or postpartum haemorrhage tend to be the leading cause of death, with about one quarter of all deaths attributed to severe bleeding. Estimates for deaths from unsafe abortion have varied substantially, but the consequences of illegal abortions may still be

Table 2.2
**Estimates of maternal mortality by United Nations regions (2000)**

| Region | Maternal mortality ratio (maternal deaths per 100,000 live births) |
|---|---|
| Sub-Saharan Africa | 920 |
| Southern Asia | 540 |
| Oceania | 240 |
| Southeastern Asia | 210 |
| Western Asia | 190 |
| Latin America and the Caribbean | 190 |
| Northern Africa | 130 |
| Commonwealth of Independent States | 68 |
| Eastern Asia | 55 |

Source: From [4].

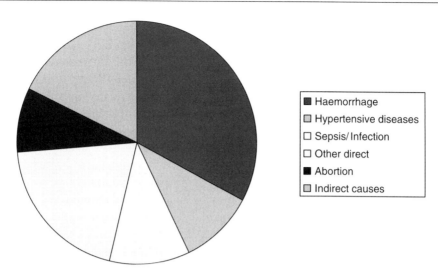

**Fig. 2.1.** Main causes of maternal death. (Adapted from [19].)

underestimated. Some authors have suggested that postpartum sepsis, a condition that carries a huge risk for the mother, may be declining in certain areas [26].

WHO has estimated that approximately 17% of maternal deaths worldwide are due to the so-called indirect obstetric causes, including anemia, cardiovascular diseases, and infections [19]. These figures are based on a small number of studies, however, and in settings with a high prevalence of HIV/AIDS, the contribution of infections may have increased [10, 27]. While there is no doubt that certain chronic diseases such as diabetes or cardiovascular disease or infections such as hepatitis are aggravated by the pregnancy, the common belief that the stresses of pregnancy lead to a breakdown of immune resistance allowing infectious diseases to set in is not always supported by strong epidemiological evidence [28]. The widely acknowledged association between tuberculosis and pregnancy, for example, has been challenged, and the authors concluded that tuberculosis is not associated with pregnancy [29]. Similarly, whether pregnancy accelerates the progression of HIV in HIV-infected women is still uncertain [27, 30], although a study in Uganda suggested that the risk of HIV acquisition may rise during pregnancy [31]. The overall impact of HIV on pregnancy-related mortality remains unclear [27]. Adverse effects of malaria during pregnancy on maternal health have been documented, but the increased prevalence and density of malaria parasitaemia in pregnant women are not necessarily associated with symptoms in the mother [32, 33]. The frequency and severity of malaria are of greater magnitude during pregnancy and the early postpartum period than outside pregnancy [34, 35]. In settings with low malaria transmission, the effects of malaria are particularly severe [36]. Malaria may also increase the risk of maternal death through its effect on maternal anemia [37].

Severe anemia is believed to be an important cause of maternal death in developing countries, although much of the evidence is circumstantial [38]. Mild anemia in pregnancy may go unnoticed, but the potential adverse effects of pregnancy increase as hemoglobin levels fall. Very severe anemia with hemoglobin levels of less than 4 g/dL can lead to heart failure and death from shock [39]. It has also been suggested that anaemic mothers are less able to tolerate blood loss during childbirth, although this has never been empirically verified [40]. Severe anemia in pregnancy has been reported as the main cause of 8–23% of maternal deaths in some hospitals and 11–16% in community-based studies [41–43]. It was also the main cause of near-miss obstetric events in several African hospitals [25]. In Tanzania, symptoms such as severe weakness, pallor, shortness of breath, and peripheral oedema, which may be suggestive of anemia, were present in nearly half of maternal deaths [42]. In a hospital study in western Kenya, reproductive age women with hemoglobin levels below 6 g/dL were eight times more likely to die than women with a hemoglobin level of more than 6 g/dL [44]. In a multivariate analysis, severe anemia and HIV status were significant predictors of mortality, while pregnancy status was not. In other words, severe anemia carries a huge risk of death for women of reproductive age, but pregnancy may not aggravate that risk.

## 2.3   STRATEGIES TO REDUCE MATERNAL MORTALITY

The strategies that have been promoted as potentially effective ways to overcome the high rates of maternal mortality have been multiple [45], and substantial changes have occurred in recent decades. Initial efforts since the 1950s have focused on antenatal clinics and maternal education, followed by an emphasis on family planning [22]. In the 1970s, training and promotion of traditional birth attendants (TBAs) were introduced, while the 1990s were dominated by an emphasis on increased access to and quality of obstetric care. More recently, a new magic bullet has been introduced, namely, the nutritional supplementation of pregnant or reproductive age women.

Relatively few of the strategies proposed in this recent time period have involved the medical profession directly as interventions such as family planning or antenatal care were thought to be deliverable by community health workers. Many of the suggested strategies were modelled after the experience with child survival programmes, and the desire for finding so-called cheap and community-based interventions has left many of the interventions unchallenged for long. Only in 1991, when Maine et al. published their influential work using evidence from the Kasongo study did the emphasis shift to the importance of professional delivery care [46]. Ensuring skilled medical attendance at delivery has now become the leading goal for maternal health programmes [45].

In reviewing the evidence in support of certain strategies, it has to be borne in mind that there is very little *direct* evidence linking maternal health interventions to maternal mortality [45]. The absolute numbers of maternal deaths are generally small, and large populations are needed to investigate the determinants of maternal mortality. For this reason, evidence from randomised controlled trials, the gold standard in health care evaluations, is seldom available to those trying to understand the strategies underlying maternal mortality reductions. Our knowledge so far is largely based on historical precedent in Western countries and on so-called thought experiments [47]. A main priority is the implementation of an effective intrapartum care strategy [45].

## 2.4    SOCIOECONOMIC DEVELOPMENT, WOMEN'S EDUCATION, AND MATERNAL MORTALITY

There is no doubt that the poorest countries suffer the highest burden of maternal mortality. The maternal mortality ratio is often quoted as the statistic that most clearly highlights the huge gap between developed and developing countries. The women's lifetime risk of maternal death is almost 40 times higher in the developing than in the developed world; and the highest maternal mortality ratios of 1,000 per 100,000 live births found in some regions of eastern and western Africa are as much as 100 times higher than those observed in some Western countries [3].

Yet, the relationship between high levels of maternal mortality and poverty is not straightforward. When De Brouwere and colleagues [48] mapped the maternal mortality ratios by gross national product (GNP) per capita for countries with a GNP per capita below US $1,000 in 1993, the estimates ranged from 22 to 1,600 per 100,000 without any clear association with the level of economic development (Fig. 2.2). Countries with a similar GNP per capita such as Vietnam, Uganda, and Burundi (US $170–180), for example, had maternal mortality ratios of 160, 1,200, and 1,300 respectively. Similarly, Loudon [49], in his excellent review of historical trends in maternal mortality in Western countries, could not explain the huge differences in the levels of maternal mortality between the United States, England and Wales, and the Netherlands in the earlier part of 1900s by differences in the social or economic context prevailing at that time in each of these countries (Fig. 2.3). In the 1920s, the United States experienced maternal mortality ratios as high as 689 per 100,000 live births, a figure not unlike many developing countries today. The Netherlands, in contrast, had already reached levels as low as 242 deaths per 100,000 live births, while England and Wales were at an intermediary level of 433. Loudon [49] remarked that, "Maternal mortality, unlike infant mortality, was remarkably insensitive to social and economic factors per se but remarkably sensitive to standards of obstetric care."

In most countries, the better-off are more fully covered by maternal health services than the poorest, and poor–rich differences are greater for higher-level than for primary

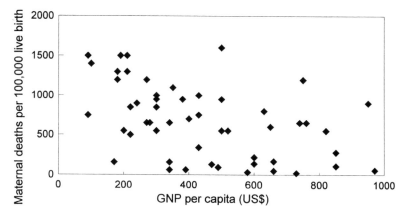

**Fig. 2.2.** Maternal mortality ratios by gross national product (GNP) per capita for countries with GNP <$1000. Adopted with permission from [48].

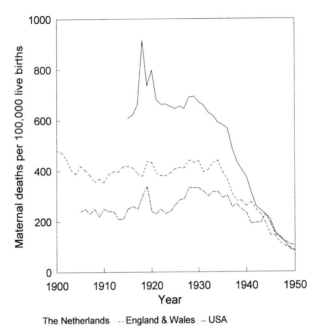

**Fig. 2.3.** Maternal mortality in the Netherlands, England, Wales, and USA, 1900–1950. Adapted with permission from [49].

care [50]. Data on within-country variation in maternal mortality are scarce, although a study suggested strong associations in six countries with demographic and health survey data [51]. In Indonesia, a third of all maternal deaths were in women from the poorest quintile of the population, whereas fewer than 13% of maternal deaths were in women in the richest quintile [51].

The relationship between women's education and maternal mortality is relatively well established. Using data from 11 demographic and health surveys, Graham and colleagues showed a strong association between maternal education and maternal mortality [51]. A cross-country analysis conducted by Shen and Williamson [52] also showed that women's level of education *relative to* men's education was a strong predictor of maternal mortality level, together with two other women's status variables (age at first marriage and reproductive autonomy). Interestingly, others have also shown that while maternal education was not associated with an increased risk of maternal death, a higher level of education in men was protective against maternal mortality [13]. These studies highlight the importance of women's status in safe motherhood.

## 2.5   FAMILY PLANNING AND MATERNAL MORTALITY

During the 1980s, family planning was presented as one of the key strategies for maternal mortality reduction in developing countries [39, 53]. If accepted by a large proportion of the population, and if used continuously for prolonged periods, contraceptive methods should, at least in theory, contribute to lowering the high levels of maternal mortality. Family planning may prevent unwanted pregnancy (and illegal abortion), redistribute births from high- to low-risk categories, reduce the total numbers of births, and have direct benefits from the contraceptive methods themselves [54]. Yet, various reports examining the potential impact of family planning on the reduction of maternal mortality have suggested disappointing effects [54–57].

There is no doubt that widespread use of contraceptives will reduce the total numbers of maternal deaths and hence lower the maternal mortality *rate* as fewer women will be exposed to the risks of pregnancy. However, the effects on the maternal mortality *ratio*, that is, the risk of death once a woman is pregnant, are thought to be minimal [54–56]. The vastly lower mortality ratios in the developed world when compared to developing countries cannot be attributed to changes in the demographic distribution of births [49, 54].

There is considerable evidence that the extremes of maternal age affect the risk of dying in pregnancy, and studies generally also confirmed the excess risk of first births and births of higher order [54, 58]. What is less clear is whether age and parity act independently of one another or whether the effects persist after taking into account the possible confounding effect of socioeconomic status. At very young ages, the growth of the bony pelvis is immature, and childbearing in girls less than 16 years old has been shown to carry huge risks [59]. Experiences from industrialised countries, however, suggest that pregnancies in very young girls may be only marginally more risky than in older women [60–62]. In a review article, Zimicky [58] concluded that, "While the evidence is suggestive rather than conclusive, it seems that ages below 20 and above 30 enhance the simple parity-specific patterns."

The widely held view that short birth intervals affect the risk of maternal death has not been supported by strong empirical evidence [56, 58, 63]. The results of a large study from Matlab, Bangladesh, did not find an association between the preceding birth-to-conception interval and the risk of maternal mortality [63]. In a more recent study in Latin America, very short (<6 months) interpregnancy intervals were associated with higher risks for maternal death, third trimester bleeding, puerperal endometritis, and anemia [64]. Long interpregnancy intervals (longer than 59 months) had significantly increased risks of preeclampsia and eclampsia, however, and these effects may outweigh those of short intervals.

Eliminating births to very young, old, or high-parity women will not have a major impact on the survival chances associated with pregnancy [54, 55]. Although the risks of maternal death tend to be highest in the extremes of reproductive performance, most births, and by consequence maternal deaths, occur in the low-risk groups. Moreover, first births are generally at highest risk, and family planning programmes, by inducing a relative shift from high-parity–high-risk groups to first-birth–high-risk groups, will have little effect on the overall level of maternal mortality.

## 2.6   NUTRITION AND MATERNAL HEALTH

During pregnancy, growth of the foetus and the uterus induces an increase in the demand for energy and many nutrients, including iron, folic acid, calcium, vitamin A, and zinc. In chronically malnourished populations, micronutrient supplementation appears attractive as a potential intervention to reduce maternal and foetal mortality because it is believed to be cheap, safe, and easier than the more fundamental changes in society that may be required [65]. Widespread appeals for the promotion of micronutrient supplementation of pregnant or reproductive age women have been made, and some agencies have incorporated supplementation strategies in their policy agenda [66, 67]. This section analyses the evidence linking energy and micronutrient deficiencies with an increased risk of maternal mortality. As very few studies have been able to explore such direct links, efforts are made to explore the potential for energy and micronutrient deficiencies to reduce life-threatening maternal complications.

### 2.6.1  Direct Effects of Energy or Micronutrient Deficiency on Maternal Mortality

Recent reviews of evidence from randomised controlled trials provided very little support for a direct link between micronutrient deficiencies in the mother and her risks of dying in pregnancy. There is at present no evidence of benefit from routine micronutrient supplementation during pregnancy in reducing the mortality risks associated with pregnancy [68–81]. Few studies were done in communities with micronutrient deficiencies, however, and most trials were not sufficiently large to draw meaningful conclusions regarding effects, beneficial or harmful, on maternal mortality.

Results from a large, randomised, double-blind, placebo-controlled trial of vitamin A and β-carotene in Nepal suggested that vitamin A or β-carotene may be associated with a 40% reduction in maternal mortality [8]. The trial was well conducted and involved the supplementation of more than 40,000 women of reproductive age with weekly doses of placebo, vitamin A (7,000 μg retinol equivalents), or β-carotene (42 mg or 7,000 μg retinol equivalents). Causes of death were ascertained using verbal autopsy methods. The investigators observed a reduction in mortality during pregnancy and within 12 weeks after delivery, from 704 deaths per 100,000 live births in women receiving the placebo to 426 and 361 deaths per 100,000 live births in the vitamin A and β-carotene groups, respectively (Fig. 2.4). The authors suggested that, "Raising the intake of preformed vitamin A or provitamin A carotenoids towards the values recommended for pregnancy or lactation, presumably by supplementation or by dietary means, can complement antenatal and essential obstetric services in lowering maternal mortality in rural South Asia."

An accompanying editorial suggested that further work is needed before putting the findings of this trial into practice [82]. Methodological difficulties (particularly loss to follow-up), the fact that the effect was most pronounced in the group of causes least likely to respond to supplements (deaths from injuries), and the possible teratogenic effects of vitamin A supplementation led the author to conclude that further evaluation of benefits and possible hazards is needed before the findings can be translated into policy. In addition, the study leaves us uncertain whether the appropriate intervention is vitamin A or β-carotene, whether the supplementation should be delivered before conception or antenatally, and whether it is feasible for programmes to administer supplementation weekly [83]. Given these uncertainties, it is rather astonishing that certain agencies have already opted for the supplementation of pregnant women with vitamin A during antenatal care [84]. Two large trials in Ghana and Bangladesh are currently ongoing and may shed some light on the role of vitamin A in the reduction of maternal mortality.

Historical data from Western countries do not provide compelling evidence that the general health status of women affects their risk of dying in childbirth. Loudon [49]

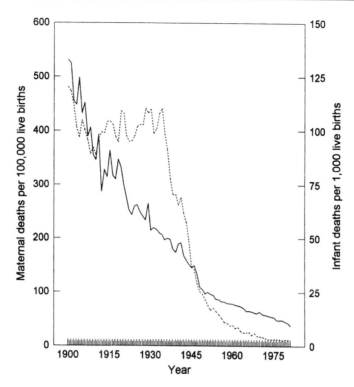

**Fig. 2.4.** Infant and maternal mortality in England and Wales, 1900–1980. Based in part upon [49].

was puzzled by the paucity of evidence showing that an improvement in the health of the mothers reduced maternal mortality in Western countries. Although the standard of living rose throughout Britain after 1880, and although Loudon regarded the health of mothers as a key determinant of the level of maternal mortality, he could find no evidence supporting such an association. The sharp contrast between the trends in infant and maternal mortality between 1900 and 1980 in England and Wales provide very useful insights (Fig. 2.5). Infant mortality rates, which were widely believed to be associated with increased living standards and improved nutrition, declined steadily throughout that period. The maternal mortality ratio, on the other hand, remained high until 1940 and declined sharply thereafter.

Pantin, on the other hand, suggested that the declines in maternal mortality on the Isle of Man before 1911 may have been attributable, at least in part, to improved maternal health [85]. Recent studies that examined the plausibility of adverse effects attributable to micronutrient deficiencies during pregnancy tended to focus on perinatal and neonatal outcomes [86–90].

In the absence of strong evidence of a direct link between nutritional deficiencies and maternal mortality, the next step is to search for evidence of a link between nutritional deficiencies and obstetric complications. The associations that merit attention include (1) malnutrition and obstructed labour; (2) calcium deficiency and preeclampsia;

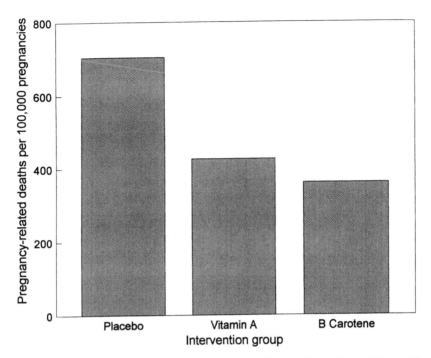

**Fig. 2.5.** Effect of vitamin A or beta-carotene on maternal mortality. Adapted from [8].

(3) iron deficiency and anemia; (4) vitamin A deficiency and anemia or infection; and (5) zinc deficiency and haemorrhage or infection. We also look at evidence for the efficacy of multiple micronutrient supplements in preventing obstetric complications.

### 2.6.2 Malnutrition and the Risk of Obstructed Labour

The association between short stature and an increased risk of cephalo-pelvic disproportion is well established [91, 92]. In a review of 14 studies, the WHO found that women in the lowest quartile of height had a 60% higher risk of assisted delivery than women in the top quartile, and the findings were consistent across study sites [92]. Although assisted delivery does not always equate cephalo-pelvic disproportion, it is probably a good marker for dystocia in settings where caesarean sections are only done in extreme circumstances. The nature of the effect appears to be relative rather than absolute in that, whatever the average height of the population of women, the lowest tenth percentile is always at higher risk [91]. The conventional cutoff for low height of 150 cm, for example, does not hold true in the Bangladeshi population, with half of these women below that cutoff, yet only women shorter than 140 cm are at increased risk of prolonged labour [93].

The WHO meta-analysis did not find evidence for an association between poor anthropometric measurements such as mid-upper-arm circumference, prepregnancy weight or body mass index (BMI), attained weight or BMI during pregnancy and weight gain during pregnancy, and increased risks of assisted delivery [92]. In fact, most of the anthropometric indicators had an inverse relationship with assisted delivery in that thinner women had a lower risk of assisted delivery than their better-nourished peers. This, according to the authors, is plausible "insofar as a low body mass index indicates a thin mother, probably with limited calorie intake, for whom foetal growth is likely to be constrained, thus reducing the likelihood of assisted delivery" [92]. This adaptive mechanism, although adversely affecting foetal survival, may protect the mother.

It has been suggested that the low levels of maternal mortality among Scandinavian women before 1930 could be partly due to the fact that they had a stronger build, had a broader pelvis, and suffered less rickets. This hypothesis was invalidated by the observation that recent Scandinavian immigrants in the United States suffered as many high risks of maternal death as their "native" peers [49]. The high levels of maternal mortality in the United States at that time were in large part attributable to mismanagement of the delivery by doctors [48, 49].

Nutritional advice in pregnancy appears to increase the pregnant woman's energy and protein intake, but the implications for maternal health cannot be judged from the available trials [94]. Kramer and colleagues also stated that, "Given the rather modest health benefits demonstrated with actual protein/energy supplementation, the provision of such advice is unlikely to be of major importance." The assertion that the increased foetal size that may accompany nutritional supplementation may lead to an increased risk of prolonged labour [95] has not been empirically tested. High-energy supplementation of pregnant women in the Gambia led to a significant increase in the head circumference of babies [96]. However, the small size of this increase and the impressive reduction in perinatal mortality suggest that the supplementation was unlikely to have increased the incidence of cephalo-pelvic disproportion.

While certain risk factors, such as a small pelvis in a short woman or in growing teenage girls, generally fall under the broad heading of "nutritional" factors, the strategies to either prevent or treat them are not necessarily nutritional. Stunting caused by early malnutrition cannot be reversed in adulthood. Although nutritional supplementation in childhood may enhance future height [97], it is uncertain what the small gains in average attained height mean in terms of preventing difficult labour. Improved labour management is probably the most appropriate strategy for preventing adverse health effects in stunted women. The low risks associated with pregnancies in very young girls in Western countries do suggest that adequate labour management can ensure a safe delivery in these girls [60–62].

### 2.6.3   Calcium Deficiency and the Risk of Preeclampsia

The association between high calcium intake and a low incidence of hypertensive diseases in pregnancy was first shown in a study among the Mayan Indians in Guatemala in 1980 [98]. The traditional practice of soaking corn in lime before cooking was associated with an unusually high calcium intake and a low incidence of preeclampsia and eclampsia. A similar association between high calcium intake and a low prevalence of preeclampsia has also been reported from Ethiopia and was later confirmed by further epidemiological and clinical studies [68].

Low calcium intake may cause high blood pressure by stimulating parathyroid hormone or renin release and inducing vasoconstriction by increasing intracellular calcium in vascular smooth muscle and intensifying smooth muscle reactivity [99]. Calcium supplementation has been postulated to act on smooth muscle reactivity by reducing parathyroid hormone release and intracellular calcium. By the same mechanism, calcium supplementation has been suggested to reduce uterine smooth muscle reactivity and prevent preterm labour and delivery [100].

Reviews of calcium supplementation trials during pregnancy provide strong support for the supplementation of pregnant women with calcium as a means of preventing pregnancy-induced hypertension and preeclampsia in communities with low calcium intake [68]. Supplementation with 1–2 g calcium daily was associated with a 42% reduction in risk of hypertension with or without proteinuria (10 trials) and a 65% reduction in risk of preeclampsia (11 trials). Among women with low dietary calcium intake, risk of hypertension and preeclampsia was reduced by 62% (five trials) and 71% (six trials), respectively. The absence of an effect of calcium on either the incidence or the severity of preeclampsia in nulliparous low-risk women in the largest study to date [101] does cast doubt on the potential benefits of calcium supplementation in low-risk women with adequate dietary calcium intake. The findings of this study, however, do not call into question the potential role of calcium supplementation in populations whose dietary calcium intake during pregnancy is inadequate [102]. A multicountry trial is being conducted by WHO among 8,500 nulliparous women living in areas of low calcium intake in six middle-income countries. The results of this trial will determine whether calcium supplementation should become recommended policy in such areas.

There is very little evidence linking poor nutritional status (expressed by anthropometric indicators) during pregnancy and preeclampsia [92]. A systematic review of risk factors for preeclampsia found that higher body mass indices were associated with increased risk of preeclampsia [103].

Preeclampsia has also been linked to oxidative stress, and supplementation with antioxidants has been suggested as an effective way to improve vascular endothelial function and prevent preeclampsia. In a pilot study, vitamin C and E supplementation of pregnant women at increased risk of preeclampsia substantially reduced the risk of preeclampsia [104]. The sample size was small, however, and larger trials in different populations, with attention for safety, particularly for the infant, are needed before adopting such a strategy [105].

### 2.6.4   Iron Deficiency and Anemia

During pregnancy, the demands for iron may increase because of the expansion of the red cell mass and the deposition of substantial amounts of iron in the foetus and the placenta [38]. These increased demands are partially offset by the cessation of menses and the increased absorption of iron during pregnancy. During pregnancy, the hemoglobin and serum iron concentrations fall, and the needs for additional iron increase as the pregnancy progresses [38]. Iron supplementation in pregnancy has become routine practice throughout the world.

In developing countries, anemia during pregnancy is very common. WHO [106] estimates that more than half of pregnant women in developing countries may be anaemic (defined as hemoglobin below 11 g/dL). The prevalence of severe anemia (defined as hemoglobin below 8 g/dL) is not well documented, and it is not certain that the prevalence of mild anemia mirrors the prevalence of severe anemia. Stoltzfus [107] summarised data from six different populations on the prevalence of anemia (Table 2.3). While the prevalence of overall anemia was similar in the six sites, the prevalence of moderate-to-severe anemia was markedly different. Rush and Brabin et al. concluded that severe but not moderate anemia was associated with a higher risk of maternal mortality; hence, the prevalence of mild anemia may not be in itself a good marker of risk [108, 109].

There is little doubt that iron supplementation of around 60 mg elemental iron daily in pregnancy improves maternal iron status during pregnancy and immediately after delivery in both industrialised and developing countries [75, 110]. Increases in hemoglobin, haematocrit, serum ferritin, and serum iron are usually apparent within 3 months. Routine iron supplementation results in a substantial reduction in the proportion of women with a hemoglobin level below 10 or 10.5 g/dL in late pregnancy. Some questions remain, though, not least whether iron supplementation reduces the incidence of severe anemia [108, 111]. Most trials exclude severely anaemic women, and the assumption that the supplementation of the entire population of pregnant women would cause a shift in the distribution of anemia such that the prevalence of very severe anemia would decrease has not been empirically tested.

Despite the long-standing universal practice of iron supplementation in pregnancy, it is surprising how little is known about its effects on pregnancy outcome. A review of randomised controlled trials of routine iron supplementation during pregnancy concluded that while the trials demonstrated a positive effect on hemoglobin levels at delivery and at 6 weeks postpartum, there was very little information on a possible effect on maternal or foetal outcomes [75]. A trial of routine versus selective iron supplementation during pregnancy in Finland suggested that caesarean sections and postpartum blood transfusions were more common among the selectively supplemented group, but the authors

Table 2.3
Prevalence of mild, moderate, and severe anaemia in various populations

| Population | Sample size | Anaemic[a](%) | Hb < 10 g/ dL (%) | Hb < 9 g/ dL (%) | Hb < 8 g/ dL (%) | Hb < 7 g/ dL (%) |
|---|---|---|---|---|---|---|
| Nepal, 3 months postpartum | 613 | 81.4 | 28.4 | 13.6 | 6.3 | 2.4 |
| Central Java, 3 months postpartum | 146 | 71.9 | 15.1 | 2.7 | 2.1 | 2.1 |
| Zanzibar, not pregnant | 583 | 71.7 | 26.2 | 13.0 | 8.9 | 5.3 |
| Nepal, pregnant | 1,052 | 69.8 | 40.5 | 20.8 | 9.5 | 4.9 |
| Shanghai, pregnant | 826 | 66.2 | 25.3 | 5.5 | 0.8 | 0.2 |
| Peru, pregnant | 670 | 44.3 | 14.5 | 4.3 | <0.1 | <0.1 |

Source: From [107].

[a]Anaemic = Hb < 11 g/dL in pregnant women and < 12 g/dL in nonpregnant women.

warned that such effects may have been due to reactions of midwives and doctors to low haematocrit values [112]. From the available evidence, no conclusions can be drawn on the effects of iron supplementation during pregnancy on its outcome for the mother.

Limited compliance with iron supplementation is thought to be a major reason for the low effectiveness of anemia prevention programmes in developing countries [113, 114]. Reasons for noncompliance include inadequate program support, insufficient service delivery (particularly unavailability of iron supplements), and patient factors such as fear of side effects [115]. Weekly rather than daily supplementation with iron appears to be promising [116–118].

In developing countries, anemia in pregnancy may only in part be due to iron deficiency. Malaria, HIV, vitamin A deficiency, and intestinal parasites may be equally important causes [119–123]. It has been demonstrated conclusively that drugs given routinely for malaria to low-parity women prevent severe anemia [124]. Intermittent presumptive treatment with antimalarials (and insecticide-treated nets) is recommended for all pregnant women in areas of holoendemic malaria [125, 126].

### 2.6.5   Vitamin A Deficiency and the Risk of Anemia or Infection

In children, vitamin A has been associated with sharp reductions in mortality and the severity of infections. The hypotheses underlying such an association have mainly centred on the immunity-impairing effects of vitamin A deficiency. During pregnancy, four pathways have been suggested through which vitamin A supplementation (or its precursors) may improve the maternal health status [127, 128]. First, vitamin A may decrease the risk of bacterial and viral infections during pregnancy through its beneficial effects on maternal immunity. Second, vitamin A may improve the mother's haematological status. Third, vitamin A may enhance the implantation and development of the placenta. Fourth, vitamin A deficiency has been associated with pregnancy-induced hypertension.

Vitamin A deficiency has not often been shown to be associated with infections during or after pregnancy. Circumstantial evidence suggests that vitamin A or β-carotene deficiency may be associated with puerperal infection, bacteriuria, and vaginal candidosis [129–131]. Christian and colleagues found that Nepali women with night blindness were twice as likely as normal pregnant controls to report symptoms such as lower abdominal pain, painful urination, vaginal discharge, or convulsions or swelling of the face and hands [132]. Women's reports of reproductive ill-health are unreliable, however, and should not be taken to represent medically defined illness [20, 21].

Retinol is known to be decreased by the acute-phase response of infections, even in the presence of adequate liver stores of vitamin A [133]. Therefore, vitamin A serum concentrations may be markers of infection rather than causally related to it. The randomised controlled trial of vitamin A and β-carotene supplementation in women of reproductive age in Nepal failed to find an effect of supplementation on mortality from sepsis or infection [8]. There is so far no direct evidence supporting an association between vitamin A supplementation and the risks of severe infection during or after pregnancy in malnourished populations.

Vitamin A deficiency is thought to contribute to low hemoglobin levels [128]. Vitamin A supplements given to pregnant women in Indonesia reduced the prevalence of nutritional anemia, suggesting a possible causal role of vitamin A, but this finding was not reproduced in two trials in Malawi [134]. Among HIV-positive women in South Africa, supplementation with megadose β-carotene combined with preformed vitamin A had no detectable effect on self-reported pre- or postpartum HIV or pregnancy-related symptoms but did appear to protect against postpartum weight loss, especially among women with low serum retinol or high CD4 counts [135, 136]. In a trial of multivitamin supplementation (with or without megadose β-carotene, 30 mg/day, plus vitamin A) among HIV-positive women in Tanzania, megadose β-carotene plus vitamin A did not contribute to the improved hemoglobin levels attributed to the multivitamins [137].

There is no direct evidence linking vitamin A deficiency to the risk of obstetric haemorrhage or plausible biological pathways underlying a potential association between vitamin A or β-carotene deficiency and uterine atony, the leading cause of postpartum haemorrhage. Vitamin A and its precursors may be essential for the placenta as the placenta has been shown to have higher concentrations of retinol-binding protein and β-carotene than other body tissues [138]. In HIV-1-infected women, supplementation with multivitamins, but not vitamin A, has been shown to increase the weight of the placenta [137]. Sharma et al. reported a significant reduction in serum antioxidants, including β-carotene, in pregnancies complicated by abruptio placentae compared to normal pregnancies [139]. As with infections, however, the low concentrations of vitamin A and β-carotene may be the result of the stress of placental abruption rather than its cause.

A number of observational studies have found a higher prevalence of vitamin A or β-carotene deficiency among women with preeclampsia [140–143]. As mentioned, such observational evidence should not be interpreted as causal as decreased retinol might be a consequence of acute-phase reaction or a decrease in circulating serum protein associated with the preeclampsia. Two randomised controlled trials of fish oil supplementation (which is rich in vitamin A) in pregnant women found no significant effects on preeclampsia [144, 145].

Unlike β-carotene, vitamin A may be highly toxic when taken in high doses, and its teratogenicity is still a subject of debate [82, 146, 147]. In a large cohort study, US women consuming more than 10,000 IU of vitamin A per day were found to have a fivefold increased risk of defects associated with cranial-neural crest tissue than women consuming 5,000 IU or less [147]. However, a large case-control study found no association between periconceptual vitamin A exposure of more than 10,000 IU and malformations [148]. It is now generally accepted that the supplements suggested for malnourished women in developing countries are safe.

The most compelling potential mechanism of action of vitamin A and its precursors is through improvements of the immune and haematological status of the pregnant woman. The Cochrane Review of vitamin A supplementation during pregnancy concluded that, despite positive findings from Nepal and Indonesia, further trials are needed to provide evidence of a beneficial effect on maternal mortality and morbidity and to elucidate the mechanism behind any such effect [135].

### 2.6.6 Zinc Deficiency and the Risk of Haemorrhage or Infection

Zinc supplementation in infants may reduce the incidence of diarrhoea and acute respiratory infections [149, 150], and it has been suggested that zinc may therefore also influence maternal health [19]. Zinc plays an important role in many biological functions, including protein synthesis and nucleic acid metabolism. Certain reports have suggested an association between serum zinc deficiency and dysfunctional labour, placental ablation, and haemorrhage [151–154]. Others have not found such associations [155]. Observational studies have to be interpreted with caution, however, as zinc values vary significantly by gestational age, and zinc deficiency may be a consequence rather than a cause of pregnancy complications [152].

There is no evidence to date supporting a beneficial effect on maternal health of routine zinc supplementation during pregnancy [76]. A well-conducted randomised controlled trial in pregnant women in the United Kingdom found no effect of zinc supplementation on pregnancy complications such as pregnancy-induced hypertension, abnormal labour, postpartum haemorrhage, or postpartum infection [76]. Hunt et al. found a significantly lower risk of pregnancy-induced hypertension among Hispanic women living in the United States who had received zinc supplements during pregnancy but found no effect on infections or bleeding during pregnancy [156].

There are very few trials of zinc supplementation in pregnant women with a poor dietary intake. A study in Peru showed that adding zinc to antenatal iron and folic acid supplements may increase maternal zinc status [157]. Among African American women with relatively low plasma zinc concentrations, daily zinc supplementation increased plasma zinc concentrations and birth weight [158]. The implications of improved maternal zinc status for maternal health, however, are unknown.

### 2.6.7  Multiple Micronutrients

As might be expected given the inconsistent and conflicting evidence described for single micronutrients, trials of multiple micronutrient supplementation during pregnancy have yet to demonstrate a clear benefit for the mother. In Mexico, multiple micronutrients did not improve hemoglobin levels any more than iron only [159]. In Nepal, multiple micronutrients plus vitamin A did not improve hemoglobin levels any more than iron and folic acid plus vitamin A [160].

Different results were obtained in two trials in sub-Saharan Africa. In Tanzania, a daily micronutrient-fortified beverage was associated with a 51% reduction in risk of predelivery anemia compared with iron and folic acid [161]. Among HIV-positive women, also in Tanzania, daily multivitamins (20 mg vitamin $B_1$, 20 mg vitamin $B_2$, 100 mg vitamin $B_3$, 25 mg vitamin $B_6$, 50 µg vitamin $B_{12}$, 500 mg vitamin C, 30 mg vitamin E) with or without megadose (30 mg/day) β-carotene plus vitamin A were associated with increased CD4, CD8, and CD3 counts; increased postpartum hemoglobin levels; and reduced risk of weight loss and low rate of weight gain in the third trimester [137, 162, 163].

Several trials (in Pakistan, Nepal, Bangladesh, Indonesia, and Guinea-Bissau) of routine multiple micronutrient supplementation are being conducted as a collaborative effort overseen by the UNICEF/UNU (United Nations University)/WHO Multiple Micronutrient Supplementation During Pregnancy (MMSDP) Study Team [164]. Members of this team have agreed on a formulation based on the US recommended daily allowance (RDA): 2,664 IU vitamin A, 1.4 mg thiamin, 1.4 mg riboflavin, 18 mg niacin, 1.9 mg vitamin $B_6$, 2.6 µg vitamin $B_{12}$, 70 mg vitamin C, 200 IU vitamin D, 10 mg vitamin E, 0.4 mg folic acid, 30 mg iron, 15 mg zinc, 2 mg copper, 65 µg selenium, and 150 µg iodine [165].

A lower dose of iron than recommended by WHO (60 mg) is justified on the grounds of improved absorption and utilisation when iron is combined with vitamins A, C, and riboflavin and because a 60-mg dose would require a 30-mg dose of zinc to offset a negative effect of iron on absorption of zinc. A lower dose of iron would also improve adherence by reducing side effects; severely anaemic women can be given additional iron supplementation. Calcium was omitted due to concerns over tablet size and reduction in bioavailability of iron and zinc. Magnesium was omitted because there were no strong arguments in favour of its inclusion, and vitamin K was omitted because deficiency is only likely in cases of severe malnutrition. Only one trial (Indonesia) was originally powered to measure an effect on maternal mortality, but this trial has failed to reach the planned sample size.

The Nepal team has reported no difference in hemoglobin levels between the group supplemented with multiple micronutrients and the group supplemented only with iron and folic acid [166]. Unpublished data from the Guinea-Bissau team confirmed this finding even among a group given double the RDA formulation. The MMSDP trials have been designed to permit a meta-analysis of the combined data, an approach that has not been possible with many other micronutrient trials due to heterogeneity in study design, including the type of supplementation given to the control group, selection by hemoglobin status, dosage, compliance, duration of supplementation, gestational age at enrolment, and the prevalence and severity of nutritional deficiencies, anemia, and infections.

## 2.8   ANTENATAL CARE

Antenatal care has long been seen as the backbone of maternal health services. The primary rationale for the widespread introduction of antenatal care has been the belief that if a predominantly healthy population is screened, early signs of, or risk factors for, morbidity and mortality can be detected and intervention implemented [167]. Antenatal care has been widely seen as an intervention that could be introduced at the community level and has been presented as among the most cost-effective strategies to improve women's and children's health [39, 53].

Reviews examining the effectiveness of formal risk assessment in pregnancy have concluded that the risk approach may not be effective in preventing maternal death or in ensuring rational use of resources [19, 46, 167, 168]. The low predictability of some of the major causes of maternal death—postpartum haemorrhage, shock, and sepsis—had been recognised as early as 1932 [169]. Evaluations of the performance of risk-scoring systems in developing countries have also shown that complications such as dystocia and postpartum haemorrhage cannot be adequately predicted [91, 93, 170]. The low predictability of such adverse maternal outcomes has led to a shift in the emphasis of safe motherhood strategies from universal antenatal care to universal access to professional delivery care [19].

The narrow focus on the failure of sociodemographic factors, physical characteristics of women, or clinical signs during pregnancy to adequately predict obstructed labour or postpartum bleeding has led us to overlook the potential wider role of antenatal care. Antenatal care clearly has value for the detection and treatment of pregnancy-related complications (i.e., malaria, severe anemia, urinary infections, hypertensive diseases) and the prevention of potential problems (i.e., HIV, malaria) [168]. A model of antenatal care that emphasises fewer (i.e., five or less) visits and actions that are known to be effective may be as effective as the more standard multivisit model routinely practiced in middle-income countries [171]. In addition, antenatal care offers an opportunity for informing the woman about the risks associated with the pregnancy and about her options for professional care during delivery. Women seeking antenatal care may also be more likely to seek professional care during delivery [93]. Antenatal care may not be an efficient strategy to identify those most in need for obstetric service delivery, but if promoted in concurrence with effective environment of care (EOC), and delivered in skilled hands, it may become an effective instrument for better use of EOC services.

## 2.9    TRAINING OF TRADITIONAL BIRTH ATTENDANTS

It has long been recognised that women should not give birth alone. As it was not deemed feasible to provide access to professional medical care for all women, and as women throughout the developing world were already giving birth in the presence of TBAs, the training of such attendants appeared to be an attractive option. The training of TBAs was also in accordance with empowerment of the community, a growing paradigm during the 1970s and 1980s, and that period saw the emergence of the training of hundreds of thousands of TBAs. TBAs were expected to screen women during antenatal clinics and to provide a clean environment for giving birth. It was also hoped that they could be integrated into the health system and be recognised as official health personnel [48].

Training of TBAs has not proven to be an effective strategy for reducing maternal mortality [45, 48]. In a quasi-experimental study from the Gambia, Greenwood et al. showed that the use of TBAs may have a positive effect, but 3 years after the programme began maternal mortality remained a high as 700 per 100,000 [172]. In Bangladesh, training of TBAs had no effect on maternal mortality [173]. A comprehensive review of the role of TBAs in the reduction of maternal mortality concluded that the impact of their training on maternal mortality is low [174]. Although there has been recent renewed interest in the role of TBAs or other community-based providers in the reduction of maternal mortality, results remain inconclusive [175, 176]. It is now clear that TBAs will have little impact on maternal mortality, and that facilitating access to professional medical care would be a more effective strategy [46, 177, 178].

The reasons for the failure of TBA training are multiple [46]. There is a large variation in the skills and experience of TBAs, and some may have little more skill than holding the woman in their arms, while others master a good number of basic obstetric skills through years of experience. Resources to provide the necessary supervision and support have often been lacking [179]. Traditional knowledge is rooted in the local culture and may be difficult to change. Most important, the content of the training programme has never been clear [46].

## 2.10    ACCESS TO PROFESSIONAL DELIVERY CARE

The past two decades have seen a shift from community-based strategies to reduce maternal mortality to an increasing emphasis on the role of professional care at the time of delivery [45]. Historical data provide the most compelling evidence for the crucial role of obstetric care in the decline of maternal mortality. There can be no doubt that the remarkably steep and sustained decline in maternal mortality in all Western countries from 1935 onwards is due to increased access to high-quality obstetric care compounded by major advances in obstetric techniques [49]. Factors such as the discovery of antibiotics in the 1940s, the use of blood transfusion and ergometrine during the Second World War, and safer methods for caesarean section and induction of labour since the 1950s all contributed to the extraordinary decline in maternal mortality in Western countries [49]. While in the 1920s some Western countries were still at levels of maternal mortality currently seen in developing countries, improved delivery care caused their levels to decline to as low as 20 deaths per 100,000 in a period as short as 30 years. The main obstacles to increasing the expansion of care is the shortage of skilled providers and health care infrastructure, substandard quality of care, and reluctance of women to use maternity care because of high cost and other factors [180, 181].

Support for the crucial role of obstetric care is also provided from a current example in the United States. Members of a religious group who received no antenatal care and who delivered at home without trained attendance had a maternal mortality ratio about 100 times higher than the statewide rates [182]. Although the numbers of maternal deaths were small, the maternal mortality ratio of 872 deaths per 100,000 live births among Faith Assembly members was significantly higher than the ratio of 9 deaths per 100,000 among the remainder of the population. These findings suggest that, even in the United States, absence of skilled obstetric care greatly increased the risk of maternal death.

How to best organise maternity services to ensure that all women have access to highly skilled care for childbirth remains a matter of debate. As shown in the Netherlands, hospital delivery for all women is not necessary to achieve very low levels of maternal mortality. Similarly, the Swedish success in the late 19th century was a result of the training of professional midwives in the systematic use of aseptic techniques, while hospital births were uncommon [183]. Doctors, in fact, have often been shown to be the cause of high levels of maternal mortality [49, 85]. In Egypt, where a large proportion of the women deliver in a hospital, more than half of the maternal deaths have been attributed to inappropriate management by obstetricians (Table 2.4) [184]. Health care systems have been said to contribute to rather than to prevent maternal mortality

Table 2.4
**Avoidable factors for 718 maternal deaths in Egypt (1992–1993)**

| Avoidable factors | Number of deaths (%) |
|---|---|
| No or poor antenatal care | 239 (33) |
| Delay in seeking medical care | 304 (42) |
| Unwanted pregnancy | 36 (5) |
| Substandard care from general practitioner | 87 (12) |
| Substandard care from obstetricians | 334 (47) |
| Substandard care from traditional birth attendant | 84 (12) |
| Lack of drugs, supplies, and equipment | 15 (2) |
| Lack of blood bank | 15 (2) |
| Lack of transportation | 28 (4) |
| No avoidable factors | 54 (8) |

Source: Adapted from [180].

[185]. Encouraging women to give birth in health centres where a team of midwives and midwife assistants provides delivery care is probably the most effective and efficient way of ensuring access to a skilled attendant in poor countries [180].

Direct evidence from developing countries that increased access to obstetric care can reduce maternal mortality is scarce. The few quasi-experimental studies addressing the potential role of professional care in the reduction of maternal mortality in developing countries have not been able to provide conclusive evidence. The findings from a large community-based study in Matlab, Bangladesh, for example, which provided support for professional midwifery care in the community, have been questioned repeatedly [186, 187]. Other studies either had very low sample sizes or were poorly designed [172, 188–192].

The available evidence suggests that low mortality can be achieved with a variety of different models of health care. Rural China, for example, reached low levels of maternal mortality despite nonprofessional attendance at home births, while Malaysia reached low mortality by training a large body of professional midwives to attend home deliveries [178]. Other countries such as Sri Lanka have reached low levels of mortality in the presence of nearly universal institutional delivery rates [19]. What is certain is that all countries that have successfully managed to make motherhood safer have done so within a context of universal financial and geographical access to skilled care and with a backup system of hospital care for those requiring higher-level referral [2, p. 68; 45].

One of the key messages emerging from the Safe Motherhood technical consultation held in Sri Lanka in 1997 was that maternal mortality reduction could not occur in the absence of a change in the political environment around women's health. Reductions in maternal mortality in Western countries would also not have been possible without a political commitment to do so. This commitment involves the necessity to document the magnitude of the problem, the recognition that most maternal deaths are avoidable with the currently available technology, and most importantly, the active mobilisation of qualified health professionals and the community [48]. Without a willingness of decision makers to take up their responsibility and health providers to be held accountable for their actions, the decline could not have taken place. WHO also emphasises that national commitment at a high level and by health care providers will be necessary to ensure that implementation of the actions required by the mother–baby package will be feasible and sustainable.

## 2.11   SUMMARY AND CONCLUSIONS

Maternal mortality is one of the statistics showing the largest degree of disparity between developed and developing countries. Poverty contributes to this disparity but does not explain it completely as countries with similar levels of socioeconomic development have widely ranging levels of maternal mortality.

Historical data from Western countries provide the most compelling evidence regarding which strategies will most likely contribute to the decline of maternal mortality in less-developed countries. Sustained reductions in maternal mortality will be possible if modern high-quality obstetric care will be made available to all women through a system of professional midwifery and referral hospital care in a context of political commitment and accountability of health providers. There is very little evidence from the industrialised world supporting the direct role of strategies involving family planning or nutrition in the improvement of the health of pregnant women.

Nutritional supplementation of pregnant or reproductive age women has been proposed as a new strategy for the reduction of maternal mortality in developing countries. The suggestion for a possible role for nutritional supplementation has largely emanated from the beneficial effects micronutrient supplementation may have on child survival. The evidence so far in support of such a strategy in pregnant women is scant, except for calcium supplementation, which has been convincingly shown to be associated with a reduction in the incidence of preeclampsia. Further research is needed before micronutrient supplementation can be introduced as a complementary strategy to increasing the access to and quality of professional obstetric care for all women.

The adoption of a strategy of intrapartum care in health centres is a top priority needed to reduce maternal mortality by two thirds by 2015, the Millennium Development Goal for maternal health [45, 191]. The goal of reducing maternal mortality is linked with other Millennium Development Goals discussed in other chapters of this book, including poverty reduction, women's empowerment, child survival, and infectious diseases [191].

## REFERENCES

1. World Health Organisation, UNICEF, UN Population Fund. Maternal mortality in 2000: estimates developed by WHO, UNICEF, UNFPA. Geneva: World Health Organization, 2004.
2. World Health Organisation. World health report 2005. Make every mother and child count. Geneva: World Health Organization, 2005.
3. Ronsmans C, Graham WJ, Lancet Maternal Survival Series Steering Group. Maternal mortality: who, when, where, and why. Lancet 2006;368:1189–1200.
4. United Nations. The Millennium Development Goals report. United Nations, 2005. Available at: http://unstats.un.org/unsd/mi/pdf/MDG%20Book.pdf.
5. Campbell OMR, Graham W. Measuring maternal mortality and morbidity: levels and trends. London: London School of Tropical Medicine and Hygiene, 1991. Maternal and Child Epidemiology Unit Publication No. 2.
6. World Health Organisation. Statistical classification of diseases and related health problems. Tenth revision. Geneva: World Health Organization, 1992.
7. Ronsmans C, Vanneste AM, Chakraborty J, Van Ginneken J. A comparison of three verbal autopsy methods to ascertain levels and causes of maternal deaths in Matlab, Bangladesh. Int J Epidemiol 1998;27:660–666.
8. West KP, Katz J, Khatry SK, et al. Double blind cluster randomised trial of low dose supplementation with vitamin A and β carotene on mortality related to pregnancy in Nepal. BMJ 1999;318:570–575.
9. Ronsmans C, Walraven G, Etard JF. Verbal autopsies: learning from reviewing deaths in the community. In: Beyond the numbers. Reviewing maternal deaths and complications to make pregnancy safer. Geneva: World Health Organization, 2004.
10. Fawcus SR, Van Coeverden de Groot HA, Isaacs S. A 50-year audit of maternal mortality in the Peninsula Maternal and Neonatal Service, Cape Town (1953–2002). Br J Obstet Gynaecol 2005;112:1257–2002.
11. Fauveau V, Blanchet T. deaths from injuries and induced abortion among rural Bangladeshi women. Soc Sci Med 1989;9:1121–1127.
12. Fortney J. Measurement and levels of maternal mortality. In: Demographie: analyse et synthèse- causes et conséquences des évolutions démographiques. Actes du séminaire de San Miniato (Pise), 17–19 December 1997, vol. 1. Rome, 1997.
13. Ganatra BR, Goyaji KR, Rao VN. Too far, too little, too late: a community-based case-control study of maternal mortality in rural west Maharashtra, India. Bull World Health Organ 1998;76:591–598.

14. Ronsmans C, Khlat M. Adolescence and risk of violent death during pregnancy in Matlab, Bangladesh. Lancet 1999;354:1448.

15. Ronsmans C, Lewis G, Hurt L, et al. Mortality in pregnant and non-pregnant women in England and Wales 1997–2002: are pregnant women healthier? In: Why mothers die 2000–2002. Confidential enquiry into maternal and child health. Improving the health of mothers, babies and children. Lewis G, ed. London: RCOG, 2004: Chap. 20.

16. Khlat M, Guillaume A. Evolution du concept de mortalité maternelle et émergence de la mortalité violente en relation avec la grossesse. In: Santé de la Reproduction au Nord et au Sud: de la connaissance à l'action. Louvain-la-Neuve: Academia-Bruylant (Collection Chaire Quételet), 2004.

17. Bouvier-Colle MH, Varnoux N, Costes P, et al. Reasons for the underreporting of maternal mortality in France, as indicated by a survey of all deaths among women of childbearing age. Int J Epidemiol 1991;20:717–721.

18. Campbell OMR, and Graham W. Measuring maternal mortality and morbidity: levels and trends. London: London School of Tropical Medicine and Hygiene, 1991. Maternal and Child Epidemiology Unit Publication No. 2.

19. Khan KS, Wojdyla D, Say L, Gulmezoglu AM, Van Look P. WHO systematic review of causes of maternal deaths. Lancet 2006,367:1066–1074.

20. Stewart MK, Stanton CK, Festin M, Jacobson N. Issues in measuring maternal morbidity: lessons from the Philippines Safe Motherhood Survey Project. Stud Fam Plann 1996;27:29–35.

21. Ronsmans C, Achadi E, Cohen S, Zazri A. Women's recall of obstetric complications in South Kalimantan, Indonesia. Stud Fam Plann 1997;28:203–214.

22. De Brouwere V, Van Lerberghe W. Les besoins obstetricaux non-couverts. Paris : L'Harmattan, 1998.

23. United Nations International Children's Emergency Fund, World Health Organisation, and United Nations Fund for Population Activities. Guidelines for monitoring the availability and use of obstetric services. New York: United Nations Fund for Population Activities, 1997.

24. Filippi V, Brugha R, Browne E, et al. How to do (or not to do) … Obstetric audit in resource poor settings: lessons from a multi-country project auditing "near miss" obstetrical emergencies. Health Policy Plan 2004;19:57–66.

25. Filippi V, Ronsmans C, Gohou V, et al. Maternity wards or emergency obstetric rooms? Incidence of near-miss events in African hospitals. Acta Obstet Gynaecol Scand 2005;84:11–16.

26. Groupe MOMA Morbidite maternelle en Afrique de l'Ouest. Resultat d'une enquete en population a Abidjan, Bamako, Niamey, Nouakchott, Ouagadougou, Saint-Louis, Kaolack. INSERM Unite 149. Ministere des affaires etrangeres. Cooperation et Francophonie, 1998.

27. Le Coeur S, Khlat M, Halembokaka G, et al. HIV and the magnitude of pregnancy-related mortality in Pointe Noire, Congo. AIDS 2005;19:69–75.

28. Peckham CS, Marshall WC. Infections in pregnancy. In: Obstetrical gynecology. Barron SL, Thompson AM, eds. New York: Academic Press, 1983.

29. Espinal MA, Reingold AL, Lavandera M. Effect of pregnancy on the risk of developing active tuberculosis. J Infect Dis 1996;173:488–491.

30. Bessinger R, Clark R, Kissinger P, et al. Pregnancy is not associated with the progression of HIV disease in women attending an HIV outpatient program. Am J Epidemiol 1998;147:434–440.

31. Gray RH, Li X, Kigozi G, Serwadda D, Brahmbhatt H, et al. Increased risk of incident HIV during pregnancy in Rakai, Uganda: a prospective study. Lancet 2005;366:1182–1188.

32. Gilbert GL. Infectious diseases in pregnancy and the newborn infant. Paris: Harwood, 1991.

33. Brabin BJ. An analysis of malaria in pregnancy in Africa. Bull World Health Organ 1983;61:1005–1016.

34. Diagne N, Rogier C, Sokhna C, et al. Increased susceptibility to malaria during the early postpartum period. N Engl J Med 2000;343:598–603.

35. Whitty C, Edmonds S, Mutabingwa TK. Malaria in pregnancy. Br J Obstet Gynaecol 2005;112:1189–1195.

36. Luxemburger C, Ricci F, Nosten F, et al. The epidemiology of severe malaria in an area of low transmission in Thailand. Trans R Soc Trop Med Hyg 1997;91:256–262.

37. Shulman C, Graham W, Jilo H, et al. Malaria as an important cause of anaemia in primigravidae: evidence from a district hospital in coastal Kenya. Trans R Soc Trop Med Hyg 1996;90:535–539.

38. Lindsay H. Pregnancy and iron deficiency: unresolved issues. Nutr Rev 1997;55:91–101.
39. Royston E, Armstrong S. Preventing maternal deaths. Geneva: World Health Organization, 1989.
40. Rush D. Nutrition and maternal mortality in the developing world. Am J Clin Nutr 2000;72:212S–240S.
41. Shulman CE, Dorman EK, Cutts F, et al. Intermittent sulphadoxine-pyrimethamine to prevent severe anaemia secondary to malaria in pregnancy: a randomised placebo-controlled trial. Lancet 1999;353:632–636.
42. MacLoed J, Rhode R. Retrospective follow-up of maternal deaths and their associated factors in a rural district of Tanzania. Trop Med Intern Health 1998;3:130–137.
43. Boerma JT, Mati JKG. Identifying maternal mortality through networking: results from coastal Kenya. Stud Fam Plann 1989;20:245–253.
44. Zucker JR, Lackritz EM, Ruebush TK, et al. Anaemia, blood transfusion practices, HIV and mortality among women of reproductive age in western Kenya. Trans R Soc Trop Med Hyg 1994;88:173–176.
45. Campbell OMR, Graham WJ, Lancet Maternal Survival Steering Group. Strategies for reducing maternal mortality: getting on with what works. Lancet 2006;368:1284–1299.
46. Maine D, Rosenfield A, McCarthy J, et al. Safe Motherhood: options and issues. New York: Columbia University, 1991.
47. Campbell O, Filippi V, Koblinsky M, et al. Lessons learnt. A decade of measuring the impact of safe motherhood programmes. London: London School of Hygiene and Tropical Medicine, 1997.
48. De Brouwere V, Tonglet R, Van Lerberghe W. Strategies for reducing maternal mortality in developing countries: what can we learn from the history of the industrialised West? Trop Med Int Health 1998;3:771–782.
49. Loudon I. Death in childbirth. An international study of maternal care and maternal mortality 1800–1950. Oxford: Clarendon, 1992.
50. Gwatkin DR, Bhuiya A, Victora CG. Making health systems more equitable. Lancet 2004;364:1273–1280.
51. Graham WJ, Fitzmaurice AE, Bell JS, Cairns JA. The familial technique for linking maternal death with poverty. Lancet 2004;363:23–27.
52. Shen CE, Williamson JB. Maternal mortality, women's status, and economic dependency in less developed countries: a cross national analysis. Soc Sci Med 1999;49:197–214.
53. Tinker A, Koblinsky M. Making motherhood safe. World Bank discussion papers. Washington, DC: World Bank, 1993.
54. Winikoff B, Sullivan M. Assessing the role of family planning in reducing maternal mortality. Stud Fam Plann 1987,18:128–143.
55. Trussell J, Pebley AR. The potential impact of changes in fertility on infant, child and maternal mortality. Stud Fam Plann 1984;15:267–280.
56. Marston C, Cleland J. The effects of contraception on obstetric outcomes. Geneva: Department of Reproductive Health and Research, WHO, 2004.
57. Fortney J. The importance of family planning in reducing maternal mortality. Commentary. Stud Fam Plann 1987;18:109–114.
58. Zimicky S. The relationship between fertility and maternal mortality. In: Contraceptive use and controlled fertility. Health issues for women and children. Background papers. Parnell AM, ed. Washington, DC: National Academy Press, 1989:1–47.
59. Harrison K. Child bearing, health and social priorities: a survey of 22,774 consecutive hospital births in Zaria, Northern Nigeria. Br J Obstet Gynaecol 1985;92:1S–119S.
60. Sandstrom B. Pregnancy in the young teenage woman. Acta Obstet Gynaecol Scand 1977;66:125S–128S.
61. Bremberg S. Pregnancy in Swedish teenagers. Scand J Soc Med 1977;5:15–19.
62. Smith GC, Pell JP. Teenage pregnancy and risk of adverse perinatal outcomes associated with first and second births: population based retrospective cohort study. BMJ 2001;323:476.
63. Ronsmans C, Campbell OMR. Short birth intervals don't kill women: evidence from Matlab, Bangladesh. Stud Fam Plann 1998;29:282–290.
64. Conde-Agudelo A, Belizan JM. Maternal morbidity and mortality associated with interpregnancy interval: cross sectional study. BMJ 2000;321:1255–1259.

65. Rouse DJ. Potential cost-effectiveness of nutrition interventions to prevent adverse pregnancy outcomes in the developing world. J Nutr 2003;133:1640S–1644S.

66. Zarocostas J. UNICEF calls for efforts to eradicate vitamin deficiency. Lancet 2004;363:378.

67. Aguayo VM, Kone D, Bamba SI, et al. Acceptability of multiple micronutrient supplements by pregnant and lactating women in Mali. Public Health Nutr 2005;8:33–37.

68. Atallah AN, Hofmeyr GJ, Duley L. Calcium supplementation during pregnancy for preventing hypertensive disorders and related problems. Cochrane Database Syst Rev 2002:CD001059.

69. Charles DH, Ness AR, Campbell D, et al. Folic acid supplements in pregnancy and birth outcome: re-analysis of a large randomised controlled trial and update of Cochrane review. Paediatr Perinat Epidemiol 2005;19:112–124.

70. Kramer MS, Kakuma R. Energy and protein intake in pregnancy. Cochrane Database Syst Rev 2003: CD000032.

71. Kramer MS. High protein supplementation in pregnancy. Cochrane Database Syst Rev 2000: CD000105.

72. Kramer MS. Isocaloric balanced protein supplementation in pregnancy. Cochrane Database Syst Rev 2000:CD000118.

73. Mahomed K. Folate supplementation in pregnancy. Cochrane Database Syst Rev 2000:CD000183.

74. Mahomed K. Iron and folate supplementation in pregnancy. Cochrane Database Syst Rev 2000: CD001135.

75. Mahomed K. Iron supplementation in pregnancy. Cochrane Database Syst Rev 2000:CD000117.

76. Mahomed K. Zinc supplementation in pregnancy. Cochrane Database Syst Rev 2000:CD000230.

77. Mahomed K, Gulmezoglu AM. Pyridoxine (vitamin $B_6$) supplementation in pregnancy. Cochrane Database Syst Rev 2000:CD000179.

78. Mahomed K, Gulmezoglu AM. Vitamin D supplementation in pregnancy. Cochrane Database Syst Rev 2000:CD000228.

79. Makrides M, Crowther CA. Magnesium supplementation in pregnancy. Cochrane Database Syst Rev 2001:CD000937.

80. Rumbold A, Crowther CA. Vitamin C supplementation in pregnancy. Cochrane Database Syst Rev 2005:CD004072.

81. Villar J, Merialdi M, Gulmezoglu AM, et al. Nutritional interventions during pregnancy for the prevention or treatment of maternal morbidity and preterm delivery: an overview of randomized controlled trials. J Nutr 2003;133:1606S–1625S.

82. Olsen SF. Effect of vitamin A and β carotene supplements on women's health. BMJ 1999;318:551–552.

83. Ronsmans C, Campbell O and Collumbien M. Slight modifications in definitions could alter interpretation of results. BMJ 1999;319:1201.

84. UNICEF. Vitamin A supplements save pregnant women's lives. In: The state of the world's children 1998. New York: Oxford University Press, 1998:12–13.

85. Pantin CG. A study of maternal mortality and midwifery on the Isle of Man, 1882 to 1961. Med Hist 1996;40:141–172.

86. Goldenberg RL. The plausibility of micronutrient deficiency in relationship to perinatal infection. J Nutr 2003;133:1645S–1648S.

87. Fall CH, Yajnik CS, Rao S, et al. Micronutrients and fetal growth. J Nutr 2003;133:1747S–1756S.

88. Costello AM, Osrin D. Micronutrient status during pregnancy and outcomes for newborn infants in developing countries. J Nutr 2003;133:1757S–1764S.

89. Keen CL, Clegg MS, Hanna LA, et al. The plausibility of micronutrient deficiencies being a significant contributing factor to the occurrence of pregnancy complications. J Nutr 2003;133:1597S–1605S.

90. Neggers Y, Goldenberg RL. Some thoughts on body mass index, micronutrient intakes and pregnancy outcome. J Nutr 2003;133:1737S–1740S.

91. Dujardin B, Van Cutsem R, Lambrechts T. The value of maternal height as a risk factor for dystocia: a meta-analysis. Trop Med Int Health 1996;4:510–521.

92. World Health Organisation. Maternal anthropometry and pregnancy outcomes. A WHO collaborative study. Bull World Health Organ 1995;73:1S–98S.

93. Vanneste AM, Ronsmans C, Chakraborty J, de Francisco A. Prenatal screening in rural Bangladesh: from prediction to care. Health Policy Plan 2000;15(1):1–10.
94. Kramer MS. Nutritional advice in pregnancy. Cochrane Database Syst Rev. 2000;(2):CD000149.
95. Garner P, Kramer M, Chalmers I. Might efforts to increase birth weight in undernourished women do more harm than good? Lancet 1992;340:1021–1023.
96. Ceesay SM, Prentice AM, Cole TJ, et al. Effects on birth weight and perinatal mortality of maternal dietary supplements in rural Gambia: 5 year randomised controlled trial. BMJ 1997;315:786–790.
97. Rivera JA, Martorell R, Ruel MT, et al. Nutritional supplementation during the preschool years influences body size and composition of Guatemalan adolescents. J Nutr 1995;125:1068S–1077S.
98. Belizan JM, Villar J. The relationship between calcium intake and oedema, proteinuria, and hypertension-gestosis: an hypothesis. Am J Clin Nutr 1980;33:2202–2210.
99. Belizan JM, Villar J, Repke J. The relationship between calcium intake and pregnancy-induced hypertension: up-to-date evidence. Am J Obstet Gynecol 1988;158:898–902.
100. Villar J, Repke JI. Calcium supplementation during pregnancy may reduce preterm delivery in high risk populations. Am J Obstet Gynecol 1990;163:1124–1131.
101. Levine RJ, Hauth JC, Curet LB, Sibai BM, Catalano PM, Morris CD, DerSimonian R, Esterlitz JR, Raymond EG, Bild DE, Clemens JD, Cutler JA. Trial of calcium to prevent preeclampsia. N Engl J Med 1997;337:69–76.
102. Prentice A, Laskey MA, Shaw J, et al. The calcium and phosphorus intakes of rural Gambian women during pregnancy and lactation. Br J Nutr 1993;69:885–96.
103. Duckitt K, Harrington D. Risk factors for pre-eclampsia at antenatal booking: systematic review of controlled studies. BMJ 2005;330:565.
104. Chappell LC, Seed PT, Briley AL, et al. Effect of antioxidants on the occurrence of pre-eclampsia in women at increased risk: a randomised trial. Lancet 1999;354:810–816.
105. Roberts JM, Hubel CA. Is oxidative stress the link in the two-stage model of pre-eclampsia? Lancet 1999;354:788–789.
106. World Health Organisation. The prevalence of anemia in women: a tabulation of available information. 2nd ed. Geneva: World Health Organisation, 1992.
107. Stoltzfus RJ. Rethinking anemia surveillance. Lancet 1997;349:1764–1766.
108. Rush D. Nutrition and maternal mortality in the developing world. Am J Clin Nutr 2000;72:212S–240S.
109. Brabin BJ, Hakimi M, Pelletier D. An analysis of anemia and pregnancy-related maternal mortality. J Nutr 2001;131:604S–614S.
110. Allen LH. Anemia and iron deficiency: effects on pregnancy outcome. Am J Clin Nutr 2000;71:1280S–1284S.
111. Sloan NL, Jordan E, Winikoff B. Effects of iron supplementation on maternal hematologic status in pregnancy. Am J Public Health 2002;92:288–293.
112. Hemminki E, Rimpela U. A randomised comparison of routine versus elective supplementation during pregnancy. J Am Coll Nutr 1991;10:3–10.
113. Ekstrom EC, Kavishe FP, Habicht JP, et al. Adherence to iron supplementation during pregnancy in Tanzania: determinants and hematologic consequences. Am J Clin Nutr 1996;64:368–374.
114. Schultink W, van der Ree M, Matulessi P, Gross R. Low compliance with an iron-supplementation program: a study among pregnant women in Jakarta, Indonesia. Am J Clin Nutr 1993;57:135–139.
115. Galloway R, McGuire J. Determinants of compliance with iron supplementation: supplies, side effects, or psychology. Soc Sci Med 1994;39:381–390.
116. Ridwan E, Schultink W, Dillon D, Gross R. Effects of weekly iron supplementation on pregnant women are similar to those of daily supplementation. Am J Clin Nutr 1996;63:884–890.
117. Ekstrom EC, Hyder SM, Chowdhury AM, et al. Efficacy and trial effectiveness of weekly and daily iron supplementation among pregnant women in rural Bangladesh: disentangling the issues. Am J Clin Nutr 2002;76:1392–1400.
118. Pena-Rosas JP, Nesheim MC, Garcia-Casal MN, et al. Intermittent iron supplementation regimens are able to maintain safe maternal hemoglobin concentrations during pregnancy in Venezuela. J Nutr 2004;134:1099–1104.

119. van den Broek NR, White SA, Neilson JP. The relationship between asymptomatic human immunodeficiency virus infection and the prevalence and severity of anemia in pregnant Malawian women. Am J Trop Med Hyg 1998;59:1004–1007.

120. Dreyfuss ML, Stoltzfus RJ, Shrestha JB, et al. Hookworms, malaria and vitamin A deficiency contribute to anemia and iron deficiency among pregnant women in the plains of Nepal. J Nutr 2000;130:2527–2536.

121. Antelman G, Msamanga GI, Spiegelman D, et al. Nutritional factors and infectious disease contribute to anemia among pregnant women with human immunodeficiency virus in Tanzania. J Nutr 2000;130:1950–1957.

122. Guyatt HL, Snow RW. The epidemiology and burden of Plasmodium falciparum-related anemia among pregnant women in sub-Saharan Africa. Am J Trop Med Hyg 2001;64:36–44.

123. Steketee RW. Pregnancy, nutrition and parasitic diseases. J Nutr 2003;133:1661S–1667S.

124. Garner P, Gulmezoglu AM. Drugs for preventing malaria-related illness in pregnant women and death in the newborn. Cochrane Database Syst Rev 2003:CD000169.

125. World Health Organisation. Pregnancy, childbirth, postpartum and newborn care: a guide for essential practice: Geneva: World Health Organisation, 2003.

126. World Health Organisation. A strategic framework for malaria prevention and control during pregnancy in the African region. Geneva: World Health Organisation, 2004.

127. Faisel H, Pittrof R. Vitamin A and causes of maternal mortality: association and biological plausibility. Public Health Nutr 2000;3:321–327.

128. Semba RD, Bloem MW. The anemia of vitamin A deficiency: epidemiology and pathogenesis. Eur J Clin Nutr 2002;56:271–281.

129. Edmund C, Clemmesen SV. On parenteral vitamin A treatment of dysaptatio (nyctalo-hemeralopia) in some pregnant women. Acta Med Scand 1936;89:69–92.

130. McGanity WJ, Cannon RO, Bridgforth EB, et al. The Vanderbilt cooperative study of maternal and infant nutrition. IV. Relationship of obstetric performance to nutrition. Am J Obstet Gynecol 1954;67:501–527.

131. Mikhail MS, Palan PR, Basu J, et al. Decreased B carotene levels in exfoliated vaginal epithelial cells in women with vaginal candidiasis. Am J Reprod Immunol 1994;32:221–225.

132. Christian P, West KP, Khatry SK, et al. Night blindness of pregnancy in rural Nepal - nutritional and health risks. Int J Epidemiol 1998;27:231–237.

133. Filteau SM, Morris SS, Abbott RA, et al. Influence of morbidity on serum retinol of children in a community-based study in northern Ghana. Am J Clin Nutr 1993;58:192–197.

134. van den Broek N, Kulier R, Gulmezoglu AM, Villar J. Vitamin A supplementation during pregnancy. Cochrane Database Syst Rev 2002:CD001996.

135. Kennedy CM, Coutsoudis A, Kuhn L, et al. Randomized controlled trial assessing the effect of vitamin A supplementation on maternal morbidity during pregnancy and postpartum among HIV-infected women. J Acquir Immune Defic Syndr 2000;24:37–44.

136. Kennedy-Oji C, Coutsoudis A, Kuhn L, et al. Effects of vitamin A supplementation during pregnancy and early lactation on body weight of South African HIV-infected women. J Health Pop Nutr 2001;19:167–176.

137. Fawzi WW, Msamanga GI, Spiegelman D, et al. Randomised trial of effects of vitamin supplements on pregnancy outcomes and T cell counts in HIV-1-infected women in Tanzania. Lancet 1998;351:1477–1482.

138. Dimenstein R, Trugo NM, Donangelo CM, et al. Effect of subadequate maternal vitamin A status on placental transfer of retinol and β carotene to the human fetus. Biol Neonate 1996;69:230–234.

139. Sharma SC, Bonnar J, Dostaova L. Comparison of blood levels of vitamin A, β carotene and vitamin E in abruption placentae with normal pregnancy. Int J Vit Nutr Res 1986;56:3–9.

140. Basu RJ, Arulanantham R. A study of serum protein and retinol levels in pregnancy and toxaemia of pregnancy in women of low socio-economic status. Indian J Med Res 1973;61:589–595.

141. Koskinen T, Valtonen P, Lehtovaara I, Tuimal R. Amniotic fluid retinol concentration in late pregnancy. Biol Neonate 1986;49:81–84.

142. Mikhail MS, Anyaegbunam A, Garfinkel D, et al. Preeclampsia and antioxidant nutrients: decreased plasma levels of reduced ascorbic acid, alpha-tocopherol, and β-carotene in women with preeclampsia. Am J Obstet Gynecol 1994;171:150–157.

143. Ziari SA, Mireles VL, Cantu CG, et al. Serum vitamin A, vitamin E, and β carotene levels in pre-eclamptic women in northern Nigeria. Am J Perinatol 1996;13:287–291.

144. Salvig JD, Olsen SF, Secher NJ. Effects of fish oil supplementation in late pregnancy on blood pressure: a randomised controlled trial. Br J Obstetr Gynaecol 1996;103:529–533.

145. Onwude JL, Lilford RJ, Hjartardottie H, et al. A randomised double blind placebo controlled trial of fish oil in high risk pregnancy. Br J Obstet Gynaecol 1995;102:95–100.

146. Hathcock JN, Hattan DG, Jenkins MY, et al. Evaluation of vitamin A toxicity. Am J Clin Nutr 1990;52:183–202.

147. Rothman KJ, Moore LL, Singer MR, et al. Teratogenecity of high vitamin A intake. N Engl J Med 1995;333:1369–1373.

148. Mills JL, Simpson JL, Cunningham GC, et al. Vitamin A and birth defects. Am J Obstet Gynecol 1997;177:31–36.

149. Sazawal S, Black RE, Bhan MK, et al. Efficacy of zinc supplementation in reducing the incidence and prevalence of acute diarrhea—a community-based, double-blind, controlled trial. Am J Clin Nutr 1997;66:413–418.

150. Sazawal S, Black RE, Jalla S, et al. Zinc supplementation reduces the incidence of acute lower respiratory infections in infants and preschool children: a double-blind, controlled trial. Pediatrics 1998;102:1–5.

151. Prema K, Ramalakshmi BA, Neelakumari S. Serum copper and zinc in pregnancy. Indian J Med Res 1980;71:547–553.

152. McMichael AJ, Dreosti IE, Gibson GT, et al. A prospective study of serial maternal serum zinc levels and pregnancy outcome. Early Hum Dev 1982;7:59–69.

153. Jameson S. Zinc and copper in pregnancy, correlations to fetal and maternal complications. Acta Med Scand Suppl 1976;593:5–20.

154. Jameson S. Zinc status in pregnancy: the effect of zinc therapy on perinatal mortality, prematurity, and placental ablation. Ann NY Acad Sci 1993;678:178–192.

155. Cherry FF, Bennett EA, Bazzano GS, et al. Plasma zinc in hypertension/toxemia and other reproductive variables in adolescent pregnancy. Am J Clin Nutr 1981;34:2367–2375.

156. Hunt IF, Murphy NJ, Cleaver AE, et al. Zinc supplementation during pregnancy: effects on selected blood constituents and on progress and outcome of pregnancy in low income women of Mexican descent. Am J Clin Nutr 1984;40:508–521.

157. Caulfield LE, Zavaleta N, Figueroa A. Adding zinc to prenatal iron and folate supplements improves maternal and neonatal zinc status in a Peruvian population. Am J Clin Nutr 1999;69:1257–1263.

158. Goldenberg RL, Tamura T, Neggers Y, et al. The effect of zinc supplementation on pregnancy outcome. JAMA 1995;274:463–468.

159. Ramakrishnan U, Neufeld LM, Gonzalez-Cossio T, et al. Multiple micronutrient supplements during pregnancy do not reduce anemia or improve iron status compared to iron-only supplements in semirural Mexico. J Nutr 2004;134:898–903.

160. Christian P, Shrestha J, LeClerq SC, et al. Supplementation with micronutrients in addition to iron and folic acid does not further improve the hematologic status of pregnant women in rural Nepal. J Nutr 2003;133:3492–3498.

161. Makola D, Ash DM, Tatala SR, Latham MC, Ndossi G, Mehansho H. A micronutrient-fortified beverage prevents iron deficiency, reduces anemia and improves the hemoglobin concentration of pregnant Tanzanian women. J Nutr 2003;133:1339–1346.

162. Villamor E, Msamanga G, Spiegelman D, et al. Effect of multivitamin and vitamin A supplements on weight gain during pregnancy among HIV-1-infected women. Am J Clin Nutr 2002;76:1082–1090.

163. Fawzi WW, Msamanga GI, Spiegelman D, et al. A randomized trial of multivitamin supplements and HIV disease progression and mortality. N Engl J Med 2004;351:23–32.

164. United Nations International Children's Emergency Fund/World Health Organisation/United Nations University. Multiple Micronutrient Supplementation During Pregnancy (MMSDP): efficacy trials. Report of a meeting held on March 4–8, 2002, at the Centre for International Child Health, Institute of Child Health, University College London, London, 2002.

165. United Nations International Children's Emergency Fund/World Health Organisation/United Nations University. Composition of a multi-micronutrient supplement to be used in pilot programmes among

pregnant women in developing countries. Report of a Workshop held at United Nations International Children's Emergency Fund headquarters, New York, July 9, 1999.

166. Osrin D, Vaidya A, Shrestha Y, et al. Effects of antenatal multiple micronutrient supplementation on birthweight and gestational duration in Nepal: double-blind, randomised controlled trial. Lancet 2005;365:955–962.

167. Rooney C. Antenatal care and maternal health: How effective is it? A review of the evidence. Geneva: World Health Organisation, 1992.

168. Carroli G, Rooney C, Villar J. How effective is antenatal care in preventing maternal mortality and serious morbidity? An overview of the evidence. Pediatr Perinat Epidemiol 2001;15:1S–42S.

169. Browne, Aberd. Antenatal care and maternal mortality. Lancet 1932;ii:1–4.

170. Kasongo Project Team. Antenatal screening for fetopelvic dystocias: a cost-effectiveness approach to the choice of simple indicators for use by auxiliary personnel. J Trop Med Hyg 1984;87:173–183.

171. Villar J, Ba'aqeel H, Piaggio G, Lumbiganon P, Belizan JM, et al. WHO antenatal care randomised trial for the evaluation of a new model of routine antenatal care. Lancet 2001;357:1551–1564.

172. Greenwood AM, Bradley AK, Byass P, et al. Evaluation of a primary health care programme in the Gambia. I. The impact of trained traditional birth attendants on the outcome of pregnancy. J Trop Med Hyg 1990;93:58–66.

173. Fauveau V, Chakraborty J. Women's health and maternity care in Matlab. In: Matlab, women, children and health. Fauveau V, ed. Dhaka: International Centre for Diarrhoeal Diseases Research, 1994.

174. Bergstrom S, Goodburn E. The role of traditional birth attendants in the reduction of maternal mortality. Stud Health Serv Organ Policy 2001;17:77–96.

175. Manandhar DS, Osrin D, Shrestha BP, et al. Effect of a participatory intervention with women's groups on birth outcomes in Nepal: cluster-randomised controlled trial. Lancet 2004;364:970–979.

176. Jokhio AH, Winter HR, Cheng KK. An intervention involving traditional birth attendants and perinatal and maternal mortality in Pakistan. N Engl J Med 2005;352:2091–2099.

177. Koblinsky M, Tinker A, Daly P. Programming for safe motherhood: a guide to action. Health Policy Plan 1994;9:252–266.

178. Koblinsky MA, Campbell O, Heichelheim J. Organizing delivery care: what works for safe motherhood? Bull World Health Organ 1999;77:399–406.

179. Sai FT, Measham DM. Safe Motherhood Initiative: getting our priorities straight. Lancet 1992;339: 478–480.

180. Koblinsky M, Matthews Z, Hussein J, Mavalankar D, Mridha MK, Anwar I, et al. Going to scale with professional skilled care. Lancet 2006;368:1377–1386.

181. Borghi J, Ensor T, Somanathan A, Lissner C, Mills A, Lancet Maternal Survival Steering Group. Mobilising financial resources for maternal health. Lancet 2006;368:1457–1465.

182. Kaunitz AM, Spence C, Danielson TS, Rochat RW, Grimes DA. Perinatal and maternal mortality in a religious group avoiding obstetric care. Am J Obstet Gynecol 1984;150:826–831.

183. Hogberg U, Wall S, Brostom G. The impact of early medical technology of maternal mortality in late nineteenth century Sweden. Int J Gynaecol Obstet 1986;24:251–261.

184. Egypt Ministry of Health. National maternal mortality study: Egypt 1992–1993. Findings and conclusions. Cairo: Child Survival Project, 1994.

185. Sundari TK. The untold story: how the health care system in developing countries contribute to maternal mortality. Int J Health Serv 1992;22:513–518.

186. Maine D, Akalin MZ, Chakraborty J, de Francisco A, Strong M. Why did maternal mortality decline in Matlab? Stud Fam Plann 1996;27:179–181.

187. Ronsmans C, Vanneste AM, Chakraborty J, Van Ginneken J. Maternal mortality decline in Matlab, Bangladesh: a cautionary tale. Lancet 1997;350:1810–1814.

188. Lamb WH, Foord FA, Lamb CMB, Whitehead RG. Changes in maternal and child mortality rates in three isolated Gambian villages over ten years. Lancet 1984;2:912–914.

189. Foord F. Gambia: evaluation of mobile health care service in West Kiang district. World Health Stat Q 1995;48:18–22.

190. Zhenxuan X. China: lowering maternal mortality in Miyun county, Beijing. World Health Stat Q 1995;48:11–14.

191. Filippi V, Ronsmans C, Campbell OMR, Graham WJ, Mills A, Borghi J, et al. Maternal health in poor countries: the broader context and a call for action. Lancet 2006;368:1535–1541.

# 3

## Low Birth Weight and Neonatal Mortality

### *Richard D. Semba and Cesar G. Victora*

## 3.1 INTRODUCTION

Worldwide, an estimated 4 million babies die each year during the first 4 weeks of life (the neonatal period), and the proportion of deaths that occur during the neonatal period has been increasing [1]. Of these 4 million deaths, 99% occur in developing countries. Low birth weight (LBW) is an important indicator of fetal and neonatal health, and although LBW babies comprise 14% of all children born, they account for 60–80% of neonatal deaths worldwide [1]. There are also an estimated 4 million stillbirths annually, with the vast majority of cases also occurring in developing countries. Birth weight in particular is strongly associated with fetal, neonatal, and postneonatal mortality, infant and childhood morbidity, long-term growth, development, and some chronic diseases [2–4]. According to the World Bank/World Health Organization (WHO) study of the global burden of disease, LBW and other perinatal causes are a leading cause of death and disability [5]. In the last two decades, less progress has been made in reducing neonatal mortality compared to reducing child mortality among children after the first month of life until 5 years of age [1].

## 3.2 HISTORICAL BACKGROUND

As presented in Chapter 1 in *The Modern Rise of Population*, Thomas McKeown showed how large decreases in case-fatality rates from major infectious disease occurred before the introduction of technological-based medicine [6]. A comparable situation appears to have occurred with declines in neonatal mortality in developed countries prior to the introduction of expensive neonatal intensive care [7]. In Sweden, perinatal mortality declined at the end of the 19th century by 15–32% in those cared for by midwives, who were licensed for home deliveries and trained in aseptic techniques [8]. Midwives were trained to keep the babies warm, give neonatal resuscitation with tactile stimulus, provide daily care of the umbilicus, and promote early breast-feeding [8]. In England from 1940 to 1975, the neonatal mortality rate fell threefold prior to the introduction of expensive neonatal intensive care [7]. These historical examples show that large reductions in neonatal and perinatal mortality are possible without access to high technology.

From: *Nutrition and Health: Nutrition and Health in Developing Countries, Second Edition*
Edited by: R. D. Semba & M. W. Bloem © Humana Press, Totowa, NJ

In developing countries in the 1970s and 1980s, emphasis was placed on primary health care and large-scale training of community health workers and traditional birth attendants, with less focus on skilled care [9]. A recent meta-analysis suggested that there was an 8% decrease in perinatal mortality and 11% reduction in asphyxia-related neonatal mortality among those cared for by traditional birth attendants [10]. By the end of the 1990s, global policy began to focus on the provision of skilled care for childbirth as the training of traditional birth attendants was viewed as ineffective and drawing away resources that could be invested in skilled care [9].

This view is largely supported by research on maternal mortality, for which the potential impact of interventions delivered by traditional birth attendants is small [11]. Evidence from neonatal health interventions, which are summarized in this chapter, suggest that substantial mortality reductions can be achieved through simple measures delivered at high coverage by community-based health workers [9, 12].

## 3.3  DEFINITIONS

### 3.3.1  Neonatal Mortality

The *neonatal period* commences at birth and ends 28 completed days after birth. The *neonatal mortality rate* is defined as the number of deaths per 1,000 live births during the neonatal period [13]. According to WHO, a *live birth* is defined as the complete expulsion or extraction from its mother of a product of conception, irrespective of the duration of the pregnancy, that, after such separation, breathes or shows any other evidence of life (e.g., beating of the heart, pulsation of the umbilical cord, or definite movement of voluntary muscles), whether or not the umbilical cord has been cut or the placenta is attached. Each product of such a birth is considered live born [13].

### 3.3.2  Perinatal Mortality

*Perinatal deaths* include both fetal deaths (i.e., deaths in utero among fetuses born without signs of life) at 20 weeks or more gestational age and deaths among live-born infants occurring in the first week of life (the latter referred to as *early neonatal deaths*). The *perinatal mortality rate* is defined as the number of fetal deaths plus the number of first-week infant deaths divided by total number of births (live births plus fetal deaths) at 20 weeks or more gestational age. Fetal deaths occurring prior to 20 weeks are considered *miscarriages* (*spontaneous abortions*), whereas those occurring at 20 weeks or more are commonly referred to as *stillbirths*. Fetal deaths may occur either antepartum (before the onset of labor) or intrapartum (during labor). Antepartum fetal death is strongly associated with intrauterine growth restriction (IUGR) [14, 15], whereas intrapartum fetal death is usually independent of IUGR. In fact, intrapartum death is more likely to occur in the context of a macrosomic (large) fetus [16, 17]. This is particularly a problem in developing countries when access to emergency obstetric care and caesarean section is problematic [18–20].

Early neonatal death is highly associated with preterm birth [21]. In fact, the majority of deaths occurring in the first week of life in developed countries now occur among extremely preterm infants (<32 weeks). In developing countries, lesser degrees of prematurity also carry a risk of early neonatal death, and IUGR is a more common cause of early neonatal death in developing countries than in developed ones [22–25].

### 3.3.3 Low Birth Weight and Intrauterine Growth Restriction

*Low birth weight* (LBW) is defined by WHO as a birth weight of less than 2,500 g [13]. Birth weight, however, is determined by two processes: the duration of gestation and the rate of fetal growth. Thus, a fetus or newborn infant can have a birth weight below 2,500 g either because the infant is born early (preterm birth) or is born small for gestational age (SGA), a proxy for IUGR [26]. *Preterm birth* is defined as delivery before 37 completed weeks (259 days). Although some SGA infants are merely constitutionally small rather than truly growth restricted, and some growth-restricted infants who would otherwise be constitutionally large do not meet standard criteria for SGA, SGA is often used as a proxy for IUGR. WHO defines SGA as a birth weight below the tenth percentile for gestational age based on the sex-specific reference by Williams and colleagues [27, 28].

LBW is a concept developed and promulgated by epidemiologists and public health practitioners. Its popularity can probably be attributed to two facts: (1) Infant mortality (particularly neonatal mortality) increases exponentially at birth weights below 2,500 g [29], and (2) birth weight (and hence LBW) can be measured with excellent precision. Because of many differences between preterm birth and IUGR, however, the LBW concept has been a major hindrance to progress in perinatal epidemiology in general and to understanding the effects of maternal nutrition in particular. As shown in Fig. 3.1, newborn infants may be growth restricted or preterm without having LBW. For example, the SGA cutoff for males at 40 weeks is 2,944 g, whereas the median birth weight for males at 35 weeks is 2,562 g [28].

From an etiologic perspective, the two different types of LBW are quite heterogeneous. It is now clear that the causal determinants of preterm birth and IUGR differ both qualitatively (i.e., they have different etiologic determinants) and quantitatively (the relative risks are different for common determinants) [26]. Table 3.1 lists the most important determinants of preterm birth and IUGR in developing country settings. The distinction between preterm birth and IUGR is important for understanding the prevalence of LBW, which differs vastly between and within countries. For example, it has been clearly demonstrated that in developing countries where LBW rates are extremely high, most LBW infants are growth restricted rather than preterm [30, 31]. In interracial comparisons within the United States, on the other hand, the increased LBW prevalence among blacks is largely owing to an increase in preterm birth [21, 32, 33].

IUGR and preterm birth also have important differences with respect to prognosis. Preterm infants are at increased risk of infant death; short- and long-term pulmonary,

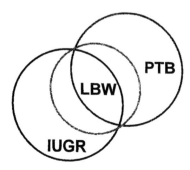

Fig. 3.1. Venn diagram illustrating relationships between low birth weight (LBW), intrauterine growth restriction (IUGR), and preterm birth (PTB).

Table 3.1
Determinants of preterm births and IUGR in rural developing country settings[a]

| Preterm birth | IUGR |
| --- | --- |
| Genital tract infection | Low energy intake/gestational weight gain |
| Multiple birth | Nonwhite racial/ethnic origin |
| Pregnancy-induced hypertension | Low prepregnancy BMI |
| Low prepregnancy BMI | Short stature |
| Incompetent cervix | Malaria[b] |
| Prior preterm birth | Cigarette smoking[c] |
| Abruptio placentae | Primiparity |
| Heavy work | Pregnancy-induced hypertension |
| Cigarette smoking[c] | Congenital anomalies |
|  | Other genetic factors |

*BMI* body mass index, *IUGR* intrauterine growth restriction
[a]Listed in decreasing order of importance.
[b]For primiparae.
[c]Assuming a 10–20% prevalence of maternal smoking during pregnancy.

ophthalmologic, and neurologic morbidity; and delayed psychomotor development [34–36]. In developed countries, preterm birth generates high health care costs, particularly for neonatal intensive care, which is often required for many months for infants born extremely preterm (<32 weeks gestational age) [37]. Severely growth-restricted infants are at increased risk of neonatal death and of significant short-term morbidity from hypoglycemia, hypocalcemia, and polycythemia. Over the longer term, they tend to have small but permanent deficits in growth and neurocognitive development. Recent epidemiologic studies by Barker and colleagues suggested that such infants may be at increased risk of type 2 diabetes, hypertension, and coronary artery disease when they reach middle age many decades later [38].

In developing country settings, the distinction between IUGR and preterm birth has been more difficult to make because of the difficulty in obtaining valid estimates of gestational age. Because of late entry into prenatal care, poor recall of the last normal menstrual period, and absence of routine early ultrasound dating, gestational age is often based on examination of the newborn [39–41] in these settings, although such methods systematically overestimate the gestational age of extremely preterm infants [42–44]. The available evidence, however, indicates that even mildly growth-restricted term infants from developing countries are at increased risk of death [45, 46] and morbidity from both diarrhea and respiratory infections in the first 2 years of life [46, 47].

## 3.4   DESCRIPTIVE EPIDEMIOLOGY

Of the estimated 4 million neonatal deaths annually, the largest absolute numbers of neonatal deaths occur in India, China, Pakistan, Nigeria, Bangladesh, and Ethiopia (Fig. 3.2). The global distribution of neonatal mortality rates by category (>45, 30–45, 15–29, <15 deaths per 1,000 live births) and country are shown in Fig. 3.3. The highest

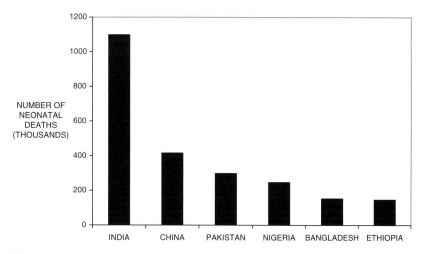

**Fig. 3.2.** The six countries with the highest numbers of neonatal deaths worldwide. (Adapted from [1].)

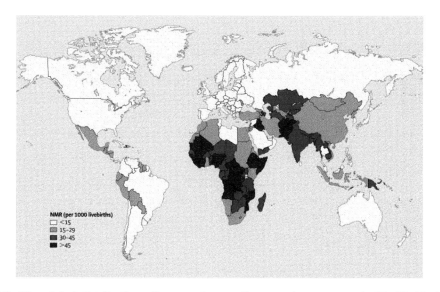

**Fig. 3.3.** The global distribution of neonatal mortality rates by category (>45, 30–45, 15–29, <15 deaths per 1,000 live births) and country. The highest neonatal mortality rates (NMRs) occurred in South Asia and sub-Saharan Africa [1]. [Reproduced from the *Lancet* with permission of Elsevier Inc.]

neonatal mortality rates occur in South Asia and sub-Saharan Africa [1]. During the entire neonatal period, the highest risk of dying occurs in the first 2 days of life and then tapers off steeply (Fig. 3.4) [1]. Three quarters of all neonatal deaths occur in the first week of life, an observation that has obvious programmatic implications.

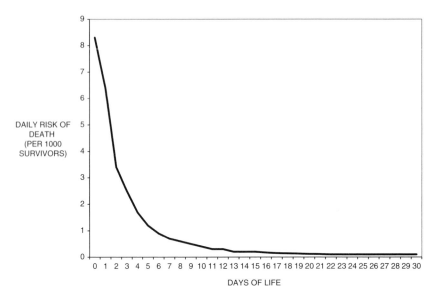

**Fig. 3.4.** General trend in the daily risk of dying during the first month of life in developing countries. (Adapted from [1] with smoothing after removing day preference in data recording.)

The main risk factors identified in population-based studies for neonatal and perinatal death have been categorized as life-cycle, antenatal, and intrapartum factors [1]. Life-cycle risk factors include maternal age less than 18 or more than 35 years, maternal height below 150 cm, prepregnancy weight less than 47 kg, primigravida, parity greater than 6, and a previous history of perinatal death or instrumental delivery. Antenatal risk factors include multiple pregnancy (i.e., twins, triplets, etc.), preeclampsia, eclampsia, bleeding from the vagina after the eighth month, maternal jaundice, maternal anemia, maternal malaria (smear positive), syphilis, and HIV infection. Intrapartum risk factors include breech birth or other malpresentations, obstructed labor/dystocia (difficult delivery), prolonged second stage, maternal fever (>38°C), rupture of membranes for longer than 24 hours, and meconium (green fecal material from the fetal intestines that is discharged at or near the time of birth) staining of liquor [1].

The rates of LBW, IUGR, preterm births, and infant mortality are shown for selected countries in Table 3.2 [48]. LBW rates vary widely among the listed countries, with prevalences of 4–6% of live births in China and some of the most highly developed countries, 10–15% in developing countries in Latin America and Africa, 15–20% in some areas of South Asia, and nearly 30% in India [48]. The data shown in Table 3.2 should be interpreted with caution, however, because the country samples participating in the WHO Collaborative Study may not be generalizable to the entire birth cohorts of the respective countries. Table 3.2 also provides prevalence rates for preterm birth and IUGR, although caution is advised in interpreting the preterm data from developing countries given the aforementioned problems in accurate estimation of gestational age in many such settings. Despite these problems, the data clearly underline the point made, that is, that the main determinant of variation in LBW rates is the IUGR rate, and that the high LBW rates reported in some developing countries are largely attributable to high rates of IUGR.

Table 3.2
Pregnancy outcome among countries participating in WHO Collaborative Study [27]

| | LBW (% of live births) | IUGR (% of live births) | Preterm (% of live births) | Infant mortality 1,000 (per live births) |
|---|---|---|---|---|
| Argentina | 6.3 | 9.7 | 7.2 | 24 |
| China | 4.2 | 9.4 | 7.5 | 38 |
| Colombia | 16.1 | 17.8 | 15.7 | 30 |
| Cuba | 8.1 | 14.7 | 7.2 | 9 |
| Gambia | 12.1 | 13.5 | 13.5 | 80 |
| Guatemala | 12.5 | 25.3 | 15.8 | 49 |
| India (Pune) | 28.2 | 54.2 | 9.7 | 76 |
| Indonesia | 10.5 | 19.8 | 18.5 | 50 |
| Ireland | 5.6 | 6.9 | 6.2 | 6 |
| Malawi | 11.6 | 26.1 | 8.2 | 138 |
| Myanmar | 17.8 | 30.4 | 24.6 | 105 |
| Nepal (rural) | 14.3 | 36.3 | 15.8 | 81 |
| Sri Lanka | 18.4 | 34.0 | 14.0 | 15 |
| Thailand | 9.6 | 17.0 | 21.3 | 27 |
| United Kingdom | 6.2 | 12.3 | 4.6 | 6 |
| U.S./CDC (black) | 10.6 | 11.2 | 16.6 | a |
| U.S./CDC (Hispanic) | 4.8 | 5.8 | 10.2 | a |
| U.S./CDC (white) | 6.0 | 6.9 | 9.3 | a |
| Vietnam | 5.2 | 18.2 | 13.6 | 34 |

CDC Centers for Disease Control and Prevention, IUGR intrauterine growth restriction, LBW low birth weight

[a] For U.S. overall, 8 per 1,000.

United Nations International Children's Emergency Fund (UNICEF) data [48] on infant mortality also vary widely, with rates varying inversely with level of socioeconomic development. Developing countries other than Cuba report generally higher rates of both LBW and infant mortality than developed countries. Table 3.2 also demonstrates several notable exceptions, however. Argentina, China, and Vietnam all report high infant mortality despite low rates of LBW, whereas in Sri Lanka the reverse pattern is seen. These results reflect large differences in birth-weight-specific mortality owing to variations in access to and quality of high-risk obstetric and neonatal care. The extremely high infant mortality reported for Malawi and Myanmar also indicates high birth-weight-specific mortality.

The WHO Collaborative Study demonstrated that maternal height, prepregnancy body mass index (BMI; in kg/m$^2$), and gestational weight gain are considerably lower in developing countries compared with industrialized countries (Table 3.3) [27]. In many respects, the data parallel those shown in Table 3.2 for IUGR, which is concordant with the important effects of these anthropometric factors on fetal growth [26].

Table 3.3
Maternal anthropometric measures (means) among countries participating in WHO
Collaborative Study [27]

| Country | Height (cm) | Prepregnancy BMI | Weight gain (kg) |
|---|---|---|---|
| Argentina | 157 | 22.4 | 10.8 |
| Myanmar | 151 | 19.8 | — |
| China | 160 | 19.5 | 11.7 |
| Colombia | 155 | 23.3 | 10.1 |
| Cuba | 157 | 21.8 | 4.6 |
| Gambia | 157 | 19.7 | 6.5 |
| Guatemala | 148 | 20.8 | 7.1 |
| India (Pune) | 150 | 18.3 | — |
| Indonesia | 149 | 20.2 | — |
| Ireland | 158 | 23.7 | 11.0 |
| Malawi | 155 | 21.0 | 4.7 |
| Nepal (rural) | 150 | 19.5 | — |
| Sri Lanka | 150 | 18.8 | — |
| Thailand | 153 | 20.8 | 8.0 |
| UK | 159 | 22.2 | 11.6 |
| U.S./CDC (black) | 162 | 23.1 | 13.5 |
| U.S./CDC (Hispanic) | 158 | 23.7 | 12.8 |
| U.S./CDC (white) | 163 | 22.6 | 14.4 |
| Vietnam | 152 | 19.6 | 5.6 |

*BMI* body mass index, *CDC* Centers for Disease Control and Prevention

## 3.5  CAUSES OF NEONATAL DEATH

The main causes of neonatal deaths identified in the year 2000 by WHO were preterm birth, severe infections, tetanus, diarrhea, complications of asphyxia, and congenital abnormalities (Fig. 3.3) [1]. Added together, infections accounted for the largest proportion of neonatal deaths (36%), followed by preterm birth (28%), and birth asphyxia (23%), and 60–80% of neonatal deaths occurred among low birth weight babies [1].

## 3.6  INFLUENCE OF MATERNAL FACTORS

From a public health standpoint, the importance of an etiologic determinant is reflected by its etiologic fraction (also called the *population-attributable risk*). The etiologic fraction in turn depends both on the determinant's relative risk for the particular pregnancy outcome and on its prevalence in the population.

### 3.6.1  *Maternal Factors and Intrauterine Growth Restriction*

In developing countries, low gestational weight gain, prepregnancy BMI, and short stature are associated with large etiologic fractions for IUGR [26]. The large etiologic fractions are the consequences not only of the high relative risk for individual women with these anthropometric risk factors but also of their high prevalence in developing country settings. A summary of the relative risks for associations between maternal anthropometric indicators and IUGR is shown in Table 3.4, again based primarily on findings from the WHO Collaborative Study [27].

Table 3.4

Association between low values (lowest quartile) of anthropometric indicators and IUGR and preterm birth, from the WHO Collaborative Study

| Anthropometric indicator | IUGR[a] | Preterm birth[a] |
|---|---|---|
| Short stature | 1.9 (1.8–2.0) | 1.2 (1.1–1.2) |
| Low prepregnancy BMI | 1.8 (1.7–2.0) | 1.3 (1.1–1.4) |
| Weight gain to mo 5 | 1.8 (1.4–2.4) | 0.4 (0.3–0.6) |
| Weight gain to mo 7 | 1.8 (1.5–2.2) | 0.7 (0.6–0.9) |

Source: Adapted from [38].
BMI body mass index, IUGR intrauterine growth restriction
[a]Odds ratios and 95% confidence intervals.

Another important aspect of maternal nutrition concerns work and energy expenditure during pregnancy. This is particularly important in developing countries, where women often work in strenuous agricultural activities, in seeking and carrying water for the family, and in other physically demanding domestic tasks [49]. Although few epidemiologic studies carried out in developing countries have examined the relationship between energy expenditure and pregnancy outcome, it seems reasonable to assume that if energy intake is limited, either by availability or cost, heavy energy expenditure during pregnancy can lead to insufficiently positive (or even negative) maternal energy balance and thereby increase the risk of IUGR. Studies from the Gambia clearly demonstrated that the combination of reduced food availability and heavy agricultural work had a negative impact on both maternal weight gain and fetal growth [50].

### 3.6.2 Maternal Stature and Preterm Birth

Anthropometric factors that appear etiologically important for IUGR are not nearly so important for preterm birth [26, 27]. As shown in Table 3.4, the WHO Collaborative Study found small increases in the relative risk for preterm birth associated with short stature and low prepregnancy BMI. Methodologic problems pervade studies relating gestational weight gain to preterm birth. Preterm pregnancies are associated with a lower total weight gain merely because women have had a shorter period of time in which to gain weight. The evidence concerning the effects on preterm birth of rate of weight gain, or of weight gain in early pregnancy, is conflicting. In fact, the WHO Collaborative Study found that low weight gain was protective against preterm birth [27], although this finding is not consistent with other studies [51].

### 3.6.3 Maternal Nutrition and Fetal Death

In studies of developed countries [52–55] and one study from Brazil [56], antepartum fetal death was associated with high prepregnancy BMI (obesity) rather than with low prepregnancy BMI. Although fetal death has been poorly studied in developing countries, it may be true that the low prepregnancy BMI characteristic of clearly undernourished mothers in such countries would also be associated with an increased risk. Low gestational weight gain is also associated with antepartum fetal death, particularly when it results in a severely growth-restricted fetus. In a randomized trial from the Gambia, balanced energy/protein supplementation resulted in an increase in gestational weight gain and a reduced risk of stillbirth, although the timing of the stillbirths (ante- vs. intrapartum) was not specified [50]. Nonetheless, antepartum fetal death is largely determined by nonnutritional factors, including inadequate prenatal care surveillance and delayed referral when fetal or maternal pathology is detected. These health care system factors are particularly important in some developing country settings, where the training of prenatal care providers and the availability of highly trained specialists may be inadequate [18]. In other developing countries, however, high-risk obstetrics may be all too accessible. Brazil, for example, has recently witnessed an epidemic of caesarean section [57]. In developed countries, prenatal care surveillance, diagnostic procedures, referral, and early intervention (induction or caesarean section) have probably been responsible for the continued fall in antepartum stillbirths.

Intrapartum stillbirths are often associated with obstructed labor. This is more likely to occur in women of short stature and thus constitutes a greater potential risk in women from developing countries [27], particularly when access to emergency obstetric care and caesarean section is a problem [18–20]. Moreover, obesity is becoming more prevalent in many developing countries [58], and it is a known determinant of macrosomia [59–61]. A large fetus can result in a difficult delivery and, again, if emergency obstetric facilities are not readily available, can greatly increase the risk of fetal death [16, 17]. The importance of well-trained birth attendants, and of prompt transfer and transport when problems arise, cannot be overemphasized in this regard.

### 3.6.4   Maternal Factors and Early Neonatal Death

Because most early neonatal deaths in developed countries occur among extremely preterm infants, the etiologic determinants of early neonatal death are similar to those for preterm birth. Severely growth-restricted infants are also at risk for early neonatal death [62], but in most developed countries, such infants, if born alive, are likely to survive and to survive intact. As mentioned, severely growth-restricted infants are known to have an increased risk of hypoglycemia and hypercalcemia and of stroke and other complications owing to polycythemia and high blood viscosity [62]. In the context of modern neonatal intensive care, these complications of IUGR are treatable. Obviously, however, in developing countries where access to such care is difficult or impossible, IUGR is likely to play a more important role in neonatal death, particularly from infection [45–47, 63].

### 3.7   INTERVENTIONS TO IMPROVE NEONATAL SURVIVAL

The *Lancet* Neonatal Survival Steering Team reviewed 46 interventions aimed at improving neonatal survival and identified 16 interventions that had proven efficacy and that could be combined into packages of health care delivery [64]. These 16 interventions are presented separately below. The evaluation of these and other interventions have been reviewed in greater detail by Bhutta and colleagues [12].

### 3.7.1   Folic Acid Supplementation

Folate is a water-soluble B complex vitamin that serves as a coenzyme for single-carbon transfers involved in the metabolism of nucleic acids and amino acids. Maternal folate intake was originally reported by Hibbard in the 1960s to be associated with the occurrence of neural tube defects [65]. Neural tube defects are the most common major congenital malformation of the central nervous system, and these defects include anencephaly (fatal form in which there is partial absence of brain tissue); craniorachis-chisis (fatal form in which the area from brain to spinal cord is dysplastic and lacks covering by dura, muscle, or skin); meningomyelocele (midline defect of the spinal cord characterized by dysplasia of neural tissues and meninges to form a cystic expansion); and meningocele (a meningomyelocele that involves only the meninges). Clinical trials have shown that periconceptual folic acid supplementation has a strong protective effect against neural tube defects [66].

### 3.7.2   Tetanus Toxoid Immunization

Tetanus, an acute and often fatal disease caused by *Clostridium tetani*, may occur in newborn infants who are born without a sufficient level of maternal antibodies to protect their infants against infection. In 2000, neonatal tetanus accounted for an estimated 200,000 deaths worldwide, and over 90% of the neonatal cases of tetanus occurred in developing countries [67]. Neonatal tetanus can be prevented by vaccination of pregnant or nonpregnant women with tetanus toxoid [68]. Two doses of tetanus toxoid are administered as part of antenatal care on the primary care level.

### 3.7.3   Syphilis Screening and Treatment

Congenital syphilis is an infection caused by the spirochete *Treponema pallidum* and passed from mother to infant during the fetal period or birth. It is estimated that there are more than 500,000 fetal deaths a year from congenital syphilis worldwide [69]. Most pregnant women with syphilis are asymptomatic, and syphilis infection must be diagnosed using serological testing, such as a rapid plasma reagin (RPR) test [70]. Penicillin treatment is effective in the treatment of syphilis in pregnancy and the prevention of congenital syphilis, but questions remain regarding the optimal treatment regimens [71]. At the primary care level, pregnant women are screened for syphilis using RPR and if the test is positive, are treated with benzathine penicillin.

### 3.7.4   Preeclampsia and Eclampsia Prevention (Calcium Supplementation)

Preeclampsia is part of the spectrum of conditions known as the hypertensive disorders of pregnancy and affects 2–8% of pregnancies [72]. Preeclampsia is characterized by the development of elevated blood pressure and proteinuria after the 20th week of pregnancy, and its etiology is poorly understood. The complications of preeclampsia include seizures (eclampsia), stroke, blindness, renal cortical and tubular necrosis, pulmonary edema, laryngeal edema, jaundice, blood clotting disorders, placental infarction or abruption, fetal death, preterm birth, and IUGR [72]. Calcium supplementation during pregnancy has been shown to reduce the risk of preeclampsia, especially among those with a low calcium intake [73]. At the level of primary care, pregnant women receive blood pressure measurements, a urine test for proteinuria, and referral if they have preeclampsia or eclampsia.

### 3.7.5   Intermittent Presumptive Treatment for Malaria

Malaria in pregnancy is a leading cause of maternal, fetal, and neonatal morbidity and mortality [74]. Women who were semi-immune to malaria before pregnancy may lose some of their immune protection against malaria when pregnant, and they may develop placental malaria, or the sequestration of large numbers of malarial parasites in the placenta when none can be found in the blood. Thus, a negative blood slide for malaria parasites does not necessarily exclude the diagnosis of malaria among pregnant women in areas holoendemic for malaria. Among pregnant women in malaria endemic areas, treatment for malaria reduces parasitemia, placental malaria, severe maternal anemia, and perinatal mortality and increases birth weight [75].

### 3.7.6  Detection and Treatment of Asymptomatic Bacteriuria

Asymptomatic bacteriuria is a persistent bacterial infection of the urinary tract that has no specific symptoms, and it occurs in 5–10% of all pregnancies [76]. Asymptomatic bacteriuria may contribute to preterm birth, LBW, and pyelonephritis in the mother. The risk of pyelonephritis (kidney infection) may be higher during pregnancy because of obstruction of the urine flow during pregnancy and increased urine stasis. Quantitative culture with the detection of more than 100,000 bacteria/milliliter is considered the definitive diagnostic test, and *Escherichia coli* is the most common pathogen found, followed by other gram-negative bacteria and group B streptococci [76]. Antibiotic treatment is effective in clearing the asymptomatic bacteriuria, reducing the risk of pyelonephritis and reducing the incidence of preterm birth or LBW babies [76]. At the level of primary care, pregnant women are screened for bacteriuria and if the screening is positive, are treated with amoxicillin.

### 3.7.7  Antibiotics for Preterm Premature Rupture of Membranes

Preterm rupture of the fetal membranes (PROM) occurs in 2.0–3.5% of pregnancies and increases the risk of infection for both mother and child and increases the risk of preterm delivery and associated complications of prematurity. PROM that occurs before 37 weeks' gestation is referred to as preterm premature rupture of the membranes (PPROM). PPROM occurs in about 1% of all pregnancies and is an antecedent of 30–40% of preterm deliveries [77]. PPROM is the leading identifiable cause of preterm delivery and its complications, which can include respiratory distress syndrome, neonatal infection, and intraventricular hemorrhage [77]. The etiology of PROM is multifactorial, and infection, inflammation, hormones, apoptosis, and mechanical factors have been implicated [77]. Antibiotic treatment for PPROM is associated with a delay in delivery and a reduction in neonatal and maternal morbidity [78]. Erythromycin is an effective treatment, but amoxicillin/clavulanic acid should be avoided because it can increase the risk of necrotizing enterocolitis (acute inflammation in the intestines of a newborn that can cause necrosis of intestinal tissues) [78].

### 3.7.8  Corticosteroids for Preterm Labor

Respiratory distress syndrome occurs in about 10% of preterm infants and is characterized by lack of lung surfactant, a substance that maintains the structure of air sacs and allows them to inflate with air. In respiratory distress syndrome, the infant develops breathing problems because the air sacs collapse. Complications of respiratory distress syndrome include intraventricular hemorrhage (bleeding into the ventricles of the brain) and pneumothorax (collapse of the lung). Administration of corticosteroids to women expected to give birth preterm is associated with a significant reduction in mortality, respiratory distress syndrome, and intraventricular hemorrhage in preterm infants

[79]. For women with suspected preterm labor, steroids are administered antenatal and intrapartum, and women are followed with inpatient care.

### 3.7.9 Detection and Management of Breech

Breech presentation, the position during labor in which the buttocks or feet appear first, occurs in about 4% of term deliveries [80]. About one quarter to one half of breeches are undiagnosed until after the onset of labor [81]. Breech presentation increases the risk of cord prolapse, fetal hypoxia or asphyxia, and obstructed labor, and breech presentation is among the leading indicators for cesarean section [82]. External cephalic version is a procedure that externally rotates the fetus from a breech presentation to a vertex (head first) presentation [80]. Persistent breech presentation requires a cesarean section in a referral center.

### 3.7.10 Labor Surveillance

The partograph has been used as tool for monitoring labor and to identify women who may develop complications and need obstetrical intervention [83]. A new version of the partograph was introduced in 2000 [84]. Fetal heart rate, amniotic fluid, molding, cervix diameter, contractions per 10 minutes, pulse, blood pressure, temperature, urine chemistry, and use of drugs are recorded in the WHO partograph [84].

### 3.7.11 Clean Delivery Practice

Clean delivery practice for home births consists of hand washing for delivery and newborn care, use of clean instruments for cord cutting, and clean umbilical cord care. The training of traditional birth attendants in clean delivery practice and the provision of clean delivery kits reduce neonatal tetanus, neonatal mortality, and sepsis [12].

### 3.7.12 Resuscitation of Newborn Baby

Birth asphyxia, or failure to establish breathing at birth, is a major cause of neonatal mortality [12]. Approximately 5–10% of newborn infants require some assistance to begin breathing within the first 5 minutes after delivery [85]. Interventions for birth asphyxia include simple resuscitation techniques (mouth-to-mouth resuscitation), and traditional birth attendants and primary care staff are capable of learning and using these techniques.

### 3.7.13 Breast-feeding

Breast-feeding provides the foundation for neonatal health and is greatly protective against neonatal mortality [86] as well as against mortality in infancy and in the second year of life [87]. Breast-feeding helps to prevent hypothermia and hypoglycemia in newborn infants and provides protection against sepsis, acute respiratory tract infections, meningitis, omphalitis (umbilical infection), and diarrhea [86]. Breast milk contains maternal antibodies and other immunological factors that provide both passive and active immunological protection of the neonate. Colostrum is higher in protein and micronutrients than normal milk and helps to facilitate the establishment of normal flora in the digestive tract. Breast-feeding promotion and support by community workers is known to be effective in increasing breast-feeding duration and exclusiveness [12].

### 3.7.14 Prevention and Management of Hypothermia

At birth, infants are exposed to a colder temperature than experienced in utero, and infants are risk of losing heat soon after birth unless measures are taken to prevent this heat loss. In the newborn period, hypothermia has been associated with morbidity such as increased risk of infection, coagulation defects, metabolic abnormalities, hyaline membrane disease, and brain hemorrhage [12, 88]. Early suckling has been shown to protect against low body temperature in the neonate [89]. Skin-to-skin contact of the neonate with the mother, so-called kangaroo mother care (Section 3.7.15) has been emphasized as a low-cost intervention to prevent hypothermia. Other ways to prevent hypothermia include warming the room and immediately drying and wrapping the infant after delivery.

### 3.7.15 Kangaroo Mother Care

Kangaroo mother care is a technique for care of LBW infants that is characterized by skin-to-skin contact between the mother and her newborn, frequent or nearly exclusive breast-feeding, and early discharge from the hospital [90]. Kangaroo mother care has been shown to reduce nosocomial infection, severe illness, and lower respiratory tract disease and to increase infant weight gain [90]. Evidence on mortality reduction is not conclusive, in large part due to the absence of large, well-designed studies, but data on the reduction of severe illness are impressive.

### 3.7.16 Community-Based Pneumonia Case Management

A case management approach has been advocated as a simple and feasible intervention to reduce pneumonia case fatalities, which account for 20% of all child deaths (see Chapter 7). The assumptions of this approach are that a high proportion of potentially fatal bacterial pneumonia is cause by *Haemophilus influenza* and *Streptococcus pneumoniae*, that timely use of antibiotic therapy can reduce pneumonia case fatality, that a simple algorithm based on counting respiratory rates is sensitive and specific enough to identify those children who require antibiotic therapy, and that health care workers can use this algorithm to provide antibiotics to children [91]. A meta-analysis has shown that pneumonia case management reduces pneumonia mortality among neonates by 42% [91].

## 3.8 NUTRITIONAL INTERVENTIONS

The use of folic acid supplementation for prevention of neural tube defects (Section 3.7.1) and calcium supplementation for reducing the risk of preeclampsia (Section 3.7.4) have been described previously. Various nutritional interventions have been evaluated in pregnant women and for neonates and are described next.

### 3.8.1 Protein-Energy Supplementation

Interventions to increase protein-energy intake of pregnant women have included giving dietary advice to pregnant women, providing balanced energy/protein supplements during pregnancy, providing high-protein nutritional supplements during pregnancy, and providing isocaloric protein supplements, as examined in a meta-analysis [92]. For overweight women or those with high weight gain, energy/protein restriction has been evaluated.

Nutritional advice to increase energy and protein intake resulted in increased intake but had no consistent benefit for pregnancy outcomes [92]. Analysis of five trials [93–97] showed mean increases of 105.61 (95% confidence interval [CI] 18.94 to 230.15 kcal/day) for energy intake and 17.99 (95% CI −1.48 to 37.45) g/day for protein [92]. Balanced energy/protein supplementation in a large number of trials [50, 98–109] overall showed an increase in maternal weight gain and mean birth weight and a substantial reduction in SGA birth [92]. Pooled results from these trials showed that balanced energy/protein supplementation resulted in a gestational weight gain of 20.74 (95% CI 1.46 to 40.02) g/week, an increase in mean birth weight of 37.62 (95% CI −0.21 to 75.45) g, and reduction of the incidence of SGA birth (relative risk [RR] 0.68, 95% CI 0.56 to 0.84) [92]. There was no apparent effect on fetal growth in the largest trials of highest methodological quality [92].

High-protein supplementation during pregnancy in two trials [110, 111] showed no apparent benefit for weekly maternal weight gain and a nonsignificant decrease in birth weight of −58.37 (95% CI −146.23 to 29.50) g [92]. Isocaloric protein supplementation in three trials [103, 104, 111] showed a nonsignificant impact on gestational weight gain. The largest trial conducted in Chile showed an increased risk of SGA birth (RR 1.35, 95% CI 1.12 to 1.61) [111]. Energy/protein restriction was associated with a reduction in maternal weight gain in two trials [112, 113] of −254.81 (95% CI −436.56 to −73.06) g/week [92]. In three trials, there was an inconsistent effect on birth weight, but trials were conducted in Scotland [113] and Egypt [114].

### 3.8.2   Maternal Iron Supplementation

Iron deficiency anemia is highly prevalent among pregnant women worldwide, and severe anemia in pregnancy has been associated with increased risk of maternal and perinatal mortality [115]. The amount of dietary iron may be insufficient to meet the needs of increased demands for iron by the mother and growing fetus for a large proportion of women, and in developing countries, low consumption of iron-rich foods, malaria, and helminthic infections may further exacerbate the situation. Meta-analysis of 20 trials of iron supplementation trials for pregnant women showed that supplementation reduced the incidence of low maternal hemoglobin in late pregnancy but had no effect on birth outcomes [116]. In developing countries, iron supplementation has a substantial impact on reducing maternal anemia [117–121]. Current WHO/UNICEF guidelines recommend iron-folate supplementation for pregnant women where anemia is highly prevalent [12].

### 3.8.3   Maternal Iodine Supplementation

Iodine is essential for brain and cognitive development (see Chapter 17), and three trials conducted in developing countries suggested that maternal iodine supplementation or addition of iodine to drinking water supply reduced cretinism and improved child survival [122, 123], increased birth weight [124], and reduced neonatal mortality [125]. Iodine supplementation of pregnant women is not widely practiced, even in areas of endemic iodine deficiency, as universal salt iodization is considered the main intervention to control endemic iodine deficiency. However, iodized salt may not reach some high-risk populations for whom fish sauce is used as the main source of salt, as in the Mekong Delta of Vietnam.

### 3.8.4  Antenatal Vitamin A or β-Carotene Supplementation

Antenatal supplementation with preformed vitamin A, β-carotene, or a combination of the two has been evaluated in clinical trials in Asia and Africa among HIV-infected women [126–128] and among women in lowland Nepal [129]. Among HIV-infected pregnant women in Tanzania, supplementation with megadose β-carotene (30 mg/day) plus 5,000 IU of vitamin A had no effect on fetal growth or fetal loss [126], while the same combination of daily β-carotene and vitamin A significantly reduced preterm delivery but had no impact on fetal mortality among HIV-infected pregnant women in South Africa [127]. In a clinical trial that used preformed vitamin A alone (10,000 IU/day), HIV-infected pregnant women receiving supplementation had a significant reduction in incidence of LBW and an improvement in hemoglobin among their infants [128]. In a large trial in Nepal, weekly antenatal vitamin A or β-carotene supplementation had no impact on fetal loss, neonatal mortality, or prevalence of preterm births [129]. Megadoses of β-carotene of 20–30 mg/day have been associated with increased mortality in humans [130], and adverse effects of megadose β-carotene have been attributed to increased oxidative stress and impairment of mitochondrial function caused by excentric cleavage products of β-carotene [130–132].

### 3.8.5  Antenatal Zinc Supplementation

Zinc is required for normal growth, immunity, and development (see Chapter 15), and animal studies and some human data suggested that there was an association between maternal zinc status and birth outcomes [133, 134]. Antenatal zinc supplementation has been evaluated in many controlled clinical trials, and a meta-analysis showed that maternal zinc supplementation had no impact on birth weight but a small effect on reduction of preterm births [135]. It has been pointed out that many of the zinc supplementation trials took place in developed countries, and it is not conclusive whether zinc supplementation has no benefit for pregnant women in populations with more prevalent malnutrition [12]. However, the overall evidence does not support the use of zinc supplementation alone for pregnant women [12].

### 3.8.6  Multiple Micronutrient Supplementation

Although prenatal multivitamins are standard of care in many developed countries, there have been few controlled clinical trials that examined whether there is any benefit to pregnant women and birth outcomes. Randomized clinical trials of multiple micronutrient supplements are currently being conducted in developing countries such as Nepal, Pakistan, Guinea-Bissau, Bangladesh, and Indonesia.

One trial in Nepal suggested that multiple micronutrient supplementation does not give any additional advantage over iron-folate supplements and may actually increase perinatal and neonatal mortality because of obstructed labor [136–138].

### 3.8.7  Reduction in Childhood Stunting

A long-term intergenerational strategy to improve neonatal morbidity and mortality may be to reduce childhood stunting, such that women have greater stature at the time of childbearing. Improved childhood nutrition, particularly in the first 2 to 3 years, would reduce the prevalence of childhood stunting and of consequent maternal short stature [139, 140]. In the long term, this should help reduce the risks of intrapartum fetal death, IUGR, and (to a lesser degree) preterm birth in developing countries [26, 27].

### 3.8.8  Prevention of Maternal Obesity

Maternal obesity is increasing in many developed countries [141–143] and is even becoming prevalent in some developing ones, especially in Latin America [58] (see Chapters 20 and 21). Given its strong association with both antepartum and intrapartum fetal death, reduction in maternal obesity would help reduce these adverse pregnancy outcomes, although such reduction could theoretically increase the risk of IUGR. Unfortunately, however, data on the efficacy of interventions to prevent or treat obesity are extremely discouraging. New preventive and therapeutic interventions are urgently required in both developed and developing countries to stem this worrisome epidemic.

## 3.9  IMPLEMENTATION OF INTERVENTIONS TO REDUCE LOW BIRTH WEIGHT AND NEONATAL MORTALITY

The Millennium Development goals include a commitment by the international community to reduce mortality in children aged 5 and under by two thirds from 1990 to 2015 [1]. It will not be possible to meet this goal without having a substantial reduction in neonatal mortality since neonatal mortality accounts for a large proportion of mortality in those younger than 5 years [1, 7]. Many effective interventions are known to reduce neonatal mortality, as presented in this chapter, and developing countries will need to scale up the magnitude of these interventions. Scaling up interventions, however, is a complex enterprise that needs to take several dimensions into account [144].

A four-step strategy has been proposed to scale up neonatal health that consists of assessing the situation and creating a policy environment conducive to neonatal health, achieving optimal neonatal care with the constraints of the situation, systematically scaling up neonatal care, and monitoring coverage, effect, and cost [9]. Martines and colleagues have proposed that progress of interventions to improve neonatal survival should be based on the following indicators: (1) neonatal mortality rate, (2) coverage of antenatal care and tetanus toxoid vaccination; (3) skilled care at birth; (4) exclusive breast-feeding, proportion of newborn babies breast-fed within 1 hour of delivery, proportion of infants exclusively breast-fed at 1 and 6 months of age; (5) postnatal care visit within 3 days of birth; and (6) proportion of births registered [7].

## 3.10  CONCLUSIONS

High neonatal and perinatal mortality are a major public health problem in many developing countries. Although high IUGR rates may contribute to this high mortality, it is caused largely by high birth-weight-specific (and gestational age-specific) mortality owing to inadequate access to trained birth attendants, high-risk obstetric care, and neonatal intensive care. The gestational age distribution also plays an important role. Even though data are sparse on prevalence of preterm birth in developing country settings, perinatal mortality is so much higher among preterm infants (particularly those born before 32 weeks) that preterm birth prevention should become a high priority for developing countries as well. The fetal growth (birth weight-for-gestational age) distribution plays a less-important role, although severely growth-restricted infants are at greatly increased risk of perinatal death in developing countries. Because maternal undernutrition is a major contributor to IUGR in developing country settings, it may play an important role in perinatal mortality. The etiologic contribution of IUGR is probably even more important in the suboptimal long-term growth and development of children in such settings. Maternal undernutrition, particularly low prepregnancy BMI, is also likely to increase the risk of preterm birth and therefore of early neonatal death.

One of the challenges for developing countries will be to reduce maternal undernutrition without encouraging a concomitant epidemic of maternal obesity. Maternal overnutrition has been demonstrated to have adverse consequences for both offspring and mother. These consequences may be even more important in settings without ready access to emergency obstetric care and caesarean section. It would be unfortunate indeed if developing countries compounded their problems in perinatal health by experiencing the same epidemic in obesity now plaguing so many developed countries.

Work on neonatal survival [7, 9] showed that it is possible to achieve substantial reductions in early deaths through reaching universal coverage with simple, cost-effective interventions.

## 3.11   RECOMMENDATIONS

- Clinical and public health interventions should focus on reducing perinatal mortality, among both low- and normal-weight infants, rather than on preventing LBW. These interventions include institutional (hospital or clinic) delivery, access to caesarean section and other aspects of emergency obstetric care, and training of local health workers to recognize and treat neonatal sepsis (infection).
- Where universal institutional delivery is still a long way in the future, community-based strategies for providing simplified antenatal care, including tetanus immunization, clean delivery, newborn resuscitation, breast-feeding promotion, and antibiotic treatment of pneumonia and sepsis, will contribute to substantially reduce newborn mortality.
- Where maternal undernutrition is prevalent, universal balanced energy/protein supplementation should be offered.
- Other successful nutritional interventions are likely to be limited to prevention of neural defects through folate fortification of food or periconceptual supplementation.
- Priorities for future research include additional randomized trials of zinc, folate, and calcium supplementation and observational studies of possible interactions between common nutritional deficiencies (iron, zinc, folate, and vitamin A) and the microbial agents causing neonatal sepsis.
- Effectiveness studies using randomized or observational designs are important to assess the impact of interventions when these are rolled out on a large scale.

## REFERENCES

1. Lawn JE, Cousens S, Zupan J, for the Lancet Neonatal Survival Steering Team. Four million neonatal deaths: When? Where? Why? Lancet 2005;365:891–900.
2. McCormick MC. The contribution of low birth weight to infant mortality and childhood morbidity. N Engl J Med 1985;312:82–90.
3. World Health Organization. Physical status: the use and interpretation of anthropometry. Geneva: World Health Organization, 1995. WHO Technical Report Series No. 854.
4. Barker DJ. Fetal origins of coronary heart disease. BMJ 1995;311:171–174.
5. Murray CJL, Lopez AD, eds. The global burden of disease: a comprehensive assessment of mortality and disability from diseases, injuries, and risk factors in 1990. Cambridge: Harvard University Press, 1996.
6. McKeown T. The modern rise of population. London: Arnold, 1976.
7. Martines J, Paul VK, Bhutta ZA, Koblinsky M, Soucat A, Walker N, et al. Neonatal survival: a call for action. Lancet 2005;365:1189–1197.

8.  Andersson T, Högberg U, Bergström S. Community-based prevention of perinatal deaths: lessons from nineteenth century Sweden. Int J Epidemiol 2000;29:542–548.

9.  Knippenberg R, Lawn JE, Darmstadt GL, Begkoyian G, Fogstad H, Walelign N, et al. Systematic scaling up of neonatal care in countries. Lancet 2005;365:1087–1098.

10. Sibley L, Ann ST. What can a meta-analysis tell us about traditional birth attendant training and pregnancy outcomes? Midwifery 2004;20:51–60.

11. De Brouwere V, Tonglet R, Van Lerberghe W. Strategies for reducing maternal mortality in developing countries: what can we learn from the history of the industrialized West? Trop Med Int Health 1998;3:771–782.

12. Bhutta ZA, Darmstadt GL, Hasan BS, Haws RA. Community-based interventions for improving perinatal and neonatal health outcomes in developing countries: a review of the evidence. Pediatrics 2005;115:519–617.

13. World Health Organization. Prevention of perinatal morbidity and mortality. Geneva: World Health Organization, 1970. WHO Technical Report Series No. 457.

14. Gardosi J, Mul T, Mongelli M, Fagan D. Analysis of birthweight and gestational age in antepartum stillbirths. Br J Obstet Gynaecol 1998;105:524–530.

15. Cnattingius S, Haglund B, Kramer MS. Differences in late fetal death rates in association with determinants of small for gestational age fetuses: population based cohort study. BMJ 1998;316:1483–1487.

16. Modanlou, HD, Dorchester WL, Thorosian A, Freeman RK. Macrosomia-maternal, fetal, and neonatal implications. Obstet Gynecol 1980;55:420–424.

17. Boyd, ME, Usher RH, Mclean FH. Fetal macrosomia: prediction, risks, proposed management. Obstet Gynecol 1983;61:715–722.

18. Govindasamy P, Stewart MK, Rutstein SO, Boerma JT, Sommerfelt AE. High-risk births and maternity care. Demographic and health survey. Calverton, MD: DHS, 1993. Comparative Studies No. 8.

19. Ferraz EM, Gray RH. A case-control study of stillbirths in northeast Brazil. Intl J Gynecol Obstet 1990;34:13–19.

20. Escoffery C, Greenwood R, Ashley D, Coard K, Keeling J, Golding J. Deaths associated with intrapartum asphyxia in Jamaica. Paediatr Perinat Epidemiol 1994;8(suppl 1):119–142.

21. Parker JD, Schoendorf KC, Kiely JL. Associations between measures of socioeconomic status and low birth weight, small for gestational age, and premature delivery in the United States. Ann Epidemiol 1994;4:271–278.

22. Perera T, Lwin KM. Perinatal mortality and morbidity including low birthweight: a South-east Asia regional profile. SEARO Regional Health Papers No. 3, 1984.

23. Victora CG, Barros FC, Vaughan PJ, Texeira AMB. Birthweight and infant mortality: a longitudinal study of 5914 Brazilian children. Intl J Epidimiol 1987;16(2):239–245.

24. Samms-Vaughan ME, McCaw-Binns AM, Ashley DC, Foster-Williams K. Neonatal mortality determinants in Jamaica. J Trop Pediatr 1990;36:171–175.

25. Gray RH, Ferraz EM, Amorim MS, De Melo LF. Levels and determinants of early neonatal mortality in natal northeastern Brazil: results of a surveillance and case-control study. Int J Epidemiol 1991;20:467–473.

26. Kramer MS. Determinants of low birth weight: methodological assessment and meta-analysis. Bull World Health Organ 1987;65:663–737.

27. World Health Organization. Maternal anthropometry and pregnancy outcomes: WHO Collaborative Study. Bull World Health Organ 1995;73(suppl):1–98.

28. Williams RL, Creasy RK, Cunningham GC, Hawes WE, Norris FD, Tashiro M. Fetal growth and perinatal viability in California. Obstet Gynecol 1982;59:624–632.

29. Hogue CJR, Buehler JW, Strauss LT, Smith JC. Overview of the National Infant Mortality Surveillance (NIMS) project: design, methods, results. Public Health Rep 1987;102:126–138.

30. Villar J, Belizan JM. The relative contribution of prematurity and fetal growth retardation to low birth weight in developing and developed societies. Am J Obstet Gynecol 1982;143:793–798.

31. de Onis M, Habicht JP. Anthropometric reference data for international use: recommendations from a World Health Organization Expert Committee. Am J Clin Nutr 1996;64:650–658.

32. Blackmore CA, Savitz DA, Edwards LJ, Harlow SD, Bowes WA. Racial differences in the patterns of preterm delivery in central North Carolina, USA. Paediatr Perinat Epidemiol 1995;9:281–295.

33. Goldenberg RL, Cliver SP, Mulvihill FX, Hickey CA, Hoffman HJ, Klerman LV, Johnson MJ. Medical, psychosocial, and behavioral risk factors do not explain the increased risk for low birth weight among black women. Am J Obstet Gynecol 1996;175:1317–1324.
34. McCormick MC. The contribution of low birth weight to infant mortality and childhood morbidity. N Engl J Med 1985;312:82–90.
35. Committee to Study the Prevention of Low Birthweight, Division of Health Promotion and Disease Prevention, Institute of Medicine. Preventing low birthweight. Washington, DC: National Academy, 1985.
36. Dollfus C, Paletta M, Siegel E, Cross AW. Infant mortality: a practical approach to the analysis of the leading causes of death and risk factors. Pediatrics 1990;86:176–183.
37. Morrison JC. Preterm birth: a puzzle worth solving. Obstet Gynecol 1990;76(suppl):5S–12S.
38. Barker DJP. Fetal and infant origins of adult disease. London: BMJ, 1992.
39. Dubowitz LMS, Dubowitz V, Goldberg C. Clinical assessment of gestational age in the newborn infant. J Pediatr 1970;77:1–10.
40. Ballard JL, Novak KK, Driver M. A simplified score for assessment of fetal maturation of newly born infants. J Pediatr 1979;95:769–774.
41. Capurro H, Konichezky S. Fonseca D. Caldeyro-Barcia R. A simplified method for diagnosis of gestational age in the newborn infant. J Pediatr 1978;93:120–122.
42. Spinnato JA, Sibai BM, Shaver DC, Anderson GD. Inaccuracy of Dubowitz gestational age in low birth weight infants. Obstet Gynecol 1984;63:491–495.
43. Alexander GR, de Caunes F, Hulsey TC, Tompkins ME, Allen M. Validity of postnatal assessments of gestational age: comparison of the method of Ballard et al. and early ultrasonography. Am J Obstet Gynecol 1992;166:891–895.
44. Donovan EF, Tyson JE, Ehrenkranz RA, Verter J, Wright LL, Korones SB, et al. for the National Institute of Child Health and Human Development Neonatal Research Network. Inaccuracy of Ballard scores before 28 weeks' gestation. J Pediatr 1999;135:147–152.
45. Balcazar H, Haas J. Classification schemes of small-for-gestational age and type of intrauterine growth retardation and its implications to early neonatal mortality. Early Hum Dev 1990;24:219–230.
46. Ashworth A. Effects of intrauterine growth retardation on mortality and morbidity in infants and young children. Eur J Clin Nutr 1998;52:S34–S42.
47. Barros FC, Hutly SRA, Victora CG, Kirkwood BR, Vaughan JP. Comparison of the causes and consequences of prematurity and intrauterine growth retardation: longitudinal study in southern Brazil. Pediatrics 1992;90:238–244.
48. United Nations International Children's Emergency Fund (UNICEF). State of the World's Children 2008. New York, UNICEF, 2007.
49. Subcommittee on Diet, Physical Activity, and Pregnancy Outcome, Food and Nutrition Board, US Institute of Medicine/National Academy of Sciences. Diet and activity during pregnancy and lactation. In: Nutrition issues in developing countries. Washington, DC: National Academy, 1992.
50. Ceesay SM, Prentice AM, Cole TJ, Foord F, Weaver LT, Poskitt EME, et al. Effects on birth weight and perinatal mortality of maternal dietary supplements in rural Gambia: 5 year randomised controlled trial. BMJ 1997;315:786–790.
51. Carmichael SL, Abrams B. A critical review of the relationship between gestational weight gain and pre-term delivery. Obstet Gynecol 1997;89:865–873.
52. Naeye RL. Maternal body weight and pregnancy outcome. Am J Clin Nutr 1990;52:273–279.
53. Little RE, Weinberg CR. Risk factors for antepartum and intrapartum stillbirth. Am J Epidemiol 1993;137:1177–1189.
54. Lucas A, Morley R, Cole TJ, et al. Maternal fatness and viability of preterm infants. BMJ 1988;296:1495–1497.
55. Cnattingius, S, Bergstrom R, Lipworth L, Kramer MS. Prepregnancy weight and the risk of adverse pregnancy outcomes. N Engl J Med 1998;338:147–152.
56. Barros FC, Victora CG, Vaughan JP, Estanislasu HJ. Perinatal mortality in southern Brazil: a population-based study of 7,392 births. Bull World Health Organ 1987;65:95–104.
57. Barros FC, Vaughan JP, Victora CG, Huttly SRA. An epidemic of caesarean sections in Brazil? The influence of tubal ligations and socioeconomic status. Lancet 1991;338:167–169.

58. World Health Organization. Obesity: preventing and managing the global epidemic. Geneva: World Health Organization, 1998.

59. Udall, JN, Harrison GG, Vaucher Y, Walson PD, Morrow GIII. Interaction of maternal and neonatal obesity. Pediatrics 1978;62:17–21.

60. Ounsted M, Scott A. Associations between maternal weight, height, weight-for-height, weight-gain and birth weight. In: Maternal nutrition in pregnancy: eating for two? Dobbing J, ed. London: Academic, 1981:113–129.

61. Wolfe HM, Zador IE, Gross TL, Martier SS, Sokol RJ. The clinical utility of maternal body mass index in pregnancy. Am J Obstet Gynecol 1991;164:1306–1310.

62. Kramer MS, Olivier M, McLean FH, Willis DM, Usher RH. The impact of intrauterine growth retardation and body proportionality on fetal and neonatal outcome. Pediatrics 1990;85:707–713.

63. Bang AT, Bang RA, Baitule SB, Reddy MH, Deshmukh MD. Effect of home-based neonatal care and management of sepsis on neonatal mortality: field trial in rural India. Lancet 1999;354:1955–1961.

64. Darmstadt GL, Bhutta ZA, Cousens S, Adam T, Walker N, de Bernis L, et al. Evidence-based, cost-effective interventions: how many newborn babies can we save? Lancet 2005;365:977–988.

65. Hibbard BM. The role of folic acid in pregnancy. J Obstet Gynaecol Br Commonw 1964;71:529–542.

66. Lumley J, Watson L, Watson M, Bower C. Periconceptual supplementation with folate and/or multivitamins for preventing neural tube defects. Cochrane Database Syst Rev 2000;(2):CD001056.

67. Vandelaer J, Birmingham M, Gasse F, Kurian M, Shaw C, Garnier S. Tetanus in developing countries: an update on the maternal and neonatal tetanus elimination initiative. Vaccine 2003;21:3442–4335.

68. Demicheli V, Barale V, Rivetti A. Vaccines for women to prevent neonatal tetanus. Cochrane Database Syst Rev 2005;(4):CD002959.

69. Schmid G. Economic and programmatic aspects of congenital syphilis prevention. Bull World Health Organ 2004;82:402–409.

70. Peeling RW, Ye H. Diagnostic tools for preventing and managing maternal and congenital syphilis: an overview. Bull World Health Organ 2004;82:439–446.

71. Walter GJ. Antibiotics for syphilis diagnosed during pregnancy. Cochrane Database Syst Rev 2001;(3):CD001143.

72. Duley L, Meher S, Abalos E. Management of pre-eclampsia. BMJ 2006;332:463–468.

73. Atallah AN, Hofmeyr GJ, Duley L. Calcium supplementation during pregnancy for preventing hypertensive disorders and related problems. Cochrane Database Syst Rev 2000;(3):CD001059.

74. Whitty CJM, Edmonds S, Mutabingwa TK. Malaria in pregnancy. Br J Obstet Gynecol 2005;112:1189–1195.

75. Garner P, Gulmezoglu AM. Drugs for preventing malaria-related illness in pregnant women and death in the newborn. Cochrane Database Syst Rev 2003;(1):CD000169.

76. Smaill F. Antibiotics for asymptomatic bacteriuria in pregnancy. Cochrane Database Syst Rev 2001;(2):CD000490.

77. Parry S, Strauss JF. Premature rupture of the fetal membranes. N Engl J Med 1998;338:663–670.

78. Kenyon S, Boulvain M, Neilson J. Antibiotics for preterm premature rupture of membranes. Cochrane Database Syst Rev 2001;(4):CD001058.

79. Crowley P. Prophylactic corticosteroids for preterm birth. Cochrane Database Syst Rev 1996;(1):CD000065.

80. Coco AS, Silverman SD. External cephalic version. Am Fam Physician 1998;58:731–738, 742–744.

81. Roberts CL, Cameron CA, Nassar N, Raynes-Greenow CH. A simple patient-initiated intervention to increase antenatal detection of breech presentation at term. Paediatr Perinat Epidemiol 2004;18:371–376.

82. Founds SA. Maternal posture for cephalic version of breech presentation: a review of the evidence. Birth 2005;32:137–144.

83. World Health Organization. World Health Organization partograph in management of labour. Lancet 1994;343:1399–1404.

84. World Health Organization. Managing complications in pregnancy and childbirth: a guide for midwives and doctors. IMPAC. Geneva: World Health Organization, 2003. WHO/RHR/00.7.

85. Niermeyer S, Kattwinkel J, van Reempts P, Nadkami V, Philips B, Zideman D, et al. International guidelines for neonatal resuscitation: an excerpt from the Guidelines 2000 for Cardiopulmonary Resuscitation and Emergency Cardiovascular Care: International Consensus on Science. Pediatrics 2000;106:e29.

86. Huffman SL, Zehner ER, Victora C. Can improvements in breast-feeding practices reduce neonatal mortality in developing countries. Midwifery 2001;17:80–92.

87. WHO Collaborative Study Team on the Role of Breastfeeding on the Prevention of Infant Mortality. Effect of breastfeeding on infant and child mortality due to infectious diseases in less developed countries: a pooled analysis. Lancet 2000;355:451–455.

88. World Health Organization. Thermal control of the newborn: a practical guide. Geneva: World Health Organization, 1993.

89. van den Bosch CA, Bullough CH. Effect of early suckling on term neonates' core body temperature. Ann Trop Paediatr 1990;10:347–353.

90. Conde-Agudelo A, Diaz-Rossello JL, Belizan JM. Kangaroo mother care to reduce morbidity and mortality in low birthweight infants. Cochrane Database Syst Rev 2003;(2):CD002771.

91. Sazawal S, Black RE, for the Pneumonia Case Management Trials Group. Effect of pneumonia case management on mortality in neonates, infants, and preschool children: a meta-analysis of community-based trials. Lancet Infect Dis 2003;3:547–556.

92. Kramer MS, Kakuma R. Energy and protein intake in pregnancy (review). Cochrane Database Syst Rev 2003;(4):CD000032.

93. Hankin ME, Symonds EM. Body weight, diet and pre-eclamptic toxaemia of pregnancy. Austr N Z J Obstet Gynenol 1962;4:156–160.

94. Hunt IF, Jacob M, Ostergard NJ, Masri G, Clark VA, Coulson AH. Effect of nutrition education on the nutritional status of low-income pregnant women of Mexican descent. Am J Clin Nutr 1976;29: 675–684.

95. Sweeney C, Smith H, Foster JC, Specht J, Kochenour NK, Prater BM. Effects of a nutrition intervention program during pregnancy: maternal data phases 1 and 2. J Nurse Midwifery 1985;30:149–158.

96. Kafatos AG, Vlachonikolis IG, Codrington CA. Nutrition during pregnancy: the effects of an educational intervention program in Greece. Am J Clin Nutr 1989;50:970–979.

97. Briley C, Flanagan NL, Lewis NM. In-home prenatal nutrition intervention increased dietary iron intakes and reduce low birthweight in low-income African American women. J Am Dietet Assoc 2002;102:984–987.

98. Ross SM, Nel E, Naeye RL. Differing effects of low and high bulk maternal dietary supplements during pregnancy. Early Hum Dev 1985;10:295–302.

99. Blackwell RQ, Chow BF, Chinn KSK, Balckwell BN, Hsu SC. Prospective maternal nutrition study in Taiwan: rationale, study design, feasibility and preliminary findings. Nutr Rep Int 1973;7: 517–532.

100. Mora JO, de Navarro L, Clement J, Wagner M, de Paredes B, Herrera MG. The effect of nutritional supplementation on calorie and protein intake of pregnant women. Nutr Rep Int 1978;17:217–228.

101. Rush D, Stein Z, Susser M. A randomized controlled trial of prenatal nutritional supplementation in New York City. Pediatrics 1980;65:683–697.

102. Elwood PC, Haley TJL, Hughes SJ, Sweetnam PM, Gray OP, Davies DP. Child growth (0–5 years), and the effect of entitlement to a milk supplement. Arch Dis Child 1981;56:831–835.

103. Viegas OAC, Scott PH, Cole TJ, Mansfield HN, Wharton P, Wharton BA. Dietary protein energy supplementation of pregnant Asian mothers at Sorrento, Birmingham. I. Unselective during second the third trimesters. BMJ 1982;285:589–592.

104. Viegas OAC, Scott PH, Cole TJ, Eaton P, Needham PG, Wharton BA. Dietary protein energy supplementation of pregnant Asian mothers at Sorrento, Birmingham. II. Selective during third trimester only. BMJ 1982;285:592–595.

105. Campbell Brown M. Protein energy supplements in primigravid women at risk of low birthweight. In: Nutrition in pregnancy. Proceedings of the Tenth Study Group of the RCOG. Campbell DM, Gillmer MDG, eds. London: RCOG, 1983:85–98.

106. Girija A, Geervani P, Rao GN. Influence of dietary supplementation during pregnancy on lactation performance. J Trop Pediatr 1984;30:79–83.

107. Ross SM, Nel E, Naeye RL. Differing effects of low and high bulk maternal dietary supplements during pregnancy. Early Hum Dev 1985;10:295–302.

108. Kardjati S, Kusin JA, de With C. Energy supplementation in the last trimester of pregnancy in East Java. I. Effect on birthweight. Br J Obstet Gynaecol 1988;95:783–794.

109. Atton C, Watney PJM. Selective supplementation in pregnancy: effect on birth weight. J Hum Nutr Dietet 1990;3:381–392.

110. Iyengar L. Effect of dietary supplements late in pregnancy on the expectant mother and her newborn. Indian J Med Res 1967;55:85–89.

111. Mardones-Santander F, Rosso P, Stekel A, Ahumada E, Llaguno S, Pizzaro F, et al. Effect of a milk-based food supplement on maternal nutritional status and fetal growth in underweight Chilean women. Am J Clin Nutr 1988;47:413–419.

112. Campbell DM, MacGillivray I. The effect of a low calorie diet or a thiazide diuretic on the incidence of pre-eclampsia and on birthweight. Br J Obstet Gynaecol 1975;82:572–577.

113. Campbell DM. Dietary restriction in obesity and its effect on neonatal outcome. In: Nutrition in pregnancy. Proceedings of the Tenth Study Group of the RCOG. Campbell DM, Gillmer MDG, eds. London: RCOG, 1983:243–250.

114. Badrawi H, Hassanein MK, Badroui MHH, Wafa YA, Shawky HA, Badrawi N. Pregnancy outcome in obese pregnant mothers. New Egypt J Med 1993;6:1717–1726.

115. Gallego EB, ed. Severe anemia in pregnancy. Report of a workshop held at the Institute of Child and Mother Health in Dhaka, Bangladesh. Ottawa: International Development Research Centre, 2000.

116. Mahomed K. Iron supplementation in pregnancy. Cochrane Database Syst Rev 2000;(2):CD000117.

117. Agarwal K, Agawal D, Mishra KP. Impact of anaemia prophylaxis in pregnancy on maternal haemoglobin, serum ferritin and birth weight. Indian J Med Res 1991;94:277–280.

118. Suharno D, West KJ, Muhilal C, Karyadi D, Hautvast J. Supplementation with vitamin A and iron for nutritional anaemia in pregnant women in West Java, Indonesia. Lancet 1993;342:1325–1328.

119. Menendez C, Todd J, Alonso P, Francis N, Lulat S, Ceesary S, et al. The effects of iron supplementation during pregnancy, given by traditional birth attendants, on the prevalence of anaemia and malaria. Trans R Soc Trop Med Hyg 1994;88:590–593.

120. Atukorala S, de Silva L, Dechering W, Dassanaeike T, Perera R. Evaluation of effectiveness of iron-folate supplementation and antihelminthic therapy against anemia in pregnancy—a study in the plantation sector of Sri Lanka. Am J Clin Nutr 1994;60:286–282.

121. Preziosi P, Prual A, Galan P, Daouda H, Boureima H, Hercberg S. Effect of iron supplementation on the iron status of pregnant women: consequences for newborns. Am J Clin Nutr 1997;66:1178–1182.

122. Pharaoh P, Buttfield I, Hetzel B. Neurological damage to the fetus resulting from severe iodine deficiency during pregnancy. Lancet 1971;1:308–310.

123. Pharoah P, Connolly K. Effects of maternal iodine supplementation during pregnancy. Arch Dis Child 1991;66:145–147.

124. Thilly C, Delange F, Lagasse R, Bourdoux P, Ramioul L, Berquist H, et al. Fetal hypothyroidism and maternal thyroid stratus in severe endemic goiter. J Clin Endocrinol Metab 1978;47:354–360.

125. De Long GR, Leslie PW, Wang SH, Jiang XM, Zhang ML, Rakeman M, et al. Effect on infant mortality of iodination of irrigation water in a severely iodine-deficient area of China. Lancet 1997;350:771–773.

126. Fawzi WW, Msamanga GI, Spiegelman D, Urassa EJ, McGrath N, Mwakagile D, et al. Randomised trial of effects of vitamin supplements on pregnancy outcomes and T cell counts in HIV-infected women in Tanzania. Lancet 1998;351:1477–1482.

127. Coutsoudis A, Pillay K, Spooner E, Kuhn L, Coovadia HM. Randomized trial testing the effect of vitamin A supplementation on pregnancy outcomes and early mother-to-child HIV-1 transmission in Durban, South Africa. AIDS 1999;13:1517–1524.

128. Kumwenda N, Miotti PG, Taha TE, Broadhead R, Biggar RJ, Jackson JB, et al. Antenatal vitamin A supplementation increases birth weight and decreases anemia among infants born to human immunodeficiency virus-infected women in Malawi. Clin Infect Dis 2002;35:618–624.

129. Katz J, West KP Jr, Khatry SK, Pradhan EK, LeClerq SC, Christian P, et al. Maternal low-dose vitamin A or β-carotene supplementation has no effect on fetal loss and early infant mortality: a randomized cluster trial in Nepal. Am J Clin Nutr 2000;71:1570–1576.

130. Siems W, Wiswedel I, Salerno C, Crifo C, Augustin W, Schild L, et al. β-Carotene breakdown products may impair mitochondrial functions—potential side effects of high-dose β-carotene supplementation. J Nutr Biochem 2005;16:385–397.
131. McGill CR, Green NR, Gropper SS. β-Carotene supplementation decreases leukocyte superoxide dismutase activity and serum glutathione peroxidase concentration in humans. J Nutr Biochem 2003;14:656–662.
132. Palozza P, Serini S, DiNicuolo F, Piccioni E, Calviello G. Prooxidant effects of β-carotene in cultured cells. Mol Aspects Med 2003;24:353–362.
133. King J. Determinants of maternal zinc status during pregnancy. Am J Clin Nutr 2000;71 (suppl 5);1334S–1343S.
134. Keen C, Clegg M, Hanna L, et al. The plausibility of micronutrient deficiencies being a significant contributing factor to the occurrence of pregnancy complications. J Nutr 2003;133:1597S–1605S.
135. Mahomed K. Zinc supplementation in pregnancy. Cochrane Database Syst Rev 2000:CD000230.
136. Christian P, Shrestha I, LeClerq S, et al. Supplementation with micronutrients in addition to iron and folic acid does not further improve the hematologic status of pregnant women in rural Nepal. J Nutr 2003;133:3492–3498.
137. Christian P, Khatry S, Katz J, et al. Effects of alternative maternal micronutrient supplementations on low birth weight in rural Nepal: double blind randomised community trial. BMJ 2003;326:571.
138. Christian P, West KP, Khatry S, et al. Effects of maternal micronutrient supplementation on fetal loss and infant mortality: a cluster-randomized trial in Nepal. Am J Clin Nutr 2003;78:1194–1202.
139. Haas JD, Murdoch S, Rivera J, Martorell R. Early nutrition and later physical work capacity. Nutr Rev 1996;54(2 pt 2):S41–S48.
140. Martorell R, Ramakrishnan U, Schroeder DG, Ruel M. Reproductive performance and nutrition during childhood. Nutr Rev 1996;54(4 pt 2):S15–S21.
141. Subcommittee on Nutritional Status and Weight Gain During Pregnancy, Food and Nutrition Board, US Institute of Medicine/National Academy of Sciences. Nutrition during pregnancy. Washington, DC: National Academy, 1990.
142. Galuska DA, Serdula M, Pamuk E, Siegel PZ, Byers T. Trends in overweight among US adults from 1987 to 1993. Am J Public Health 1996;86:1729–1735.
143. Kuczmarski RJ, Flegal KM, Campbell SM, Johnson CL. Increasing prevalence of overweight among US adults. JAMA 1994;272:205–211.
144. Victora CG, Hanson K, Bryce J, Vaughan JP. Achieving universal coverage with health interventions. Lancet 2004:364:1541–1548.

# 4 Infant Mortality

## Parul Christian

### 4.1 INTRODUCTION

Each year, more than 10 million children under 5 years of age die, with almost 4 million within the first 4 weeks of life [1, 2]. The most recent estimate of the number of infant deaths (deaths under the age of 1 year) is 7.2 million in the developing world compared with about 54,000 who die in the industrialized world [3] (Table 4.1). Thus, a vast majority of child deaths occur in infancy and in developing countries, predominantly those in South Asia and sub-Saharan Africa. It is estimated that six countries account for 50% of the worldwide deaths in children under 5 years and 42 countries for 90% [1]. The same countries are likely to harbor the highest risk of infant mortality rates (IMRs).

One of the eight United Nations Millennium Development Goals (MDGs) is to reduce mortality by two thirds among children under 5 years by 2015 using a 1990 baseline. It is now halfway to this deadline, with less than a decade remaining to achieve this goal. Child and neonatal survival are placed at high priority for action by the global health community, including governments, international organizations, scientists, and programmers. In 2003, the Bellagio Study Group on Child Survival put out a five-article series in the *Lancet* [1, 4–7] that was a call to action for all segments of the public health community to bring to the forefront the continuing high rates and unacceptable disparities of child mortality in the world. This was followed in 2005 by a series [8–11] by the Neonatal Survival Steering Committee that focused attention on the neonate and the burden of morbidity and mortality in this short period of human life after birth.

The child survival group identified four prerequisites for transforming knowledge into action to reduce child mortality: leadership; strong health systems; adequate and targeted resources; awareness and commitment to action [7]. Apart from a strong political will and commitment, it is estimated that an additional US $52.4 billion will be needed to scale up child health interventions to attain full coverage of these in 75 countries with the highest mortality rates [12]. An alternate cost estimate is that of US $5.1 billion required to save the lives of 6 million children who die of preventable and treatable causes in 42 countries in which 90% of child deaths occur [13]. Along these lines, a strong case for a global fund for maternal, neonatal, and child survival was made [14] to coalesce global effort toward preventing maternal and child deaths and for reducing health inequities that persist in the 21st century. This chapter provides an overview of

From: *Nutrition and Health: Nutrition and Health in Developing Countries, Second Edition*
Edited by: R. D. Semba & M. W. Bloem © Humana Press, Totowa, NJ

Table 4.1

Infant mortality rates and number of infant deaths by United Nations International Children's Emergency Fund (UNICEF) region

| Region | Infant mortality rate (per 1,000 births) | Number of deaths (millions) |
|---|---|---|
| Sub-Saharan Africa | 104 | 2.80 |
| Middle East and North Africa | 45 | 0.44 |
| South Asia | 67 | 2.48 |
| East Asia and Pacific | 31 | 0.98 |
| Latin America and Caribbean | 27 | 0.31 |
| CEE/CIS | 34 | 0.18 |
| Industrialized countries | 5 | 0.05 |
| Developing countries | 60 | 7.20 |
| Least-developed countries | 98 | 2.73 |

Source: From [3].
CEE/CIS Central Eastern Europe/Central Independent States

the trends, causes, and risk factors of infant mortality and current evidence on effective interventions for reducing its burden in the developing world.

## 4.2   GLOBAL TRENDS

### 4.2.1   Historical Trends: United States

The dramatic declines in mortality rates, including those in infant mortality, that were achieved in the United States during the late 19th and early 20th centuries had never been recorded in any other period in history. Nearly all the mortality decline was related to those in infectious diseases [15]. While much debate exists regarding the major causes of these improvements, three explanations have been put forth: (1) economic advances and improvement in nutrition; (2) behavior change due to health behavior campaigns leading to improved hygiene; and (3) large-scale public health innovations, including clean water technologies, sanitation, refuse management, milk pasteurization, and meat inspection [16]. Recent analyses suggested that clean water technologies (filtration and chlorination) were associated with nearly halving total mortality and reductions in three quarters of infant and two thirds of child mortality in major US cities [15]. Currently, worldwide, 1.1 billion people lack access to clean water, and 2.4 billion do not have adequate sanitation (http://www.wsp.org). MDG-7 aims to reduce by half the proportion of individuals without access to safe drinking water by 2015.

### 4.2.2   Decline in Infant Mortality in Developing Countries

Global trends suggest that infant mortality is declining [17, 18] in many regions of the developing world, although as indicated in Table 4.2, the rates in many African nations may have reached a plateau. Even in South Asia, the decline appears to have slowed. South Asia contributes to the highest number of child deaths, while sub-Saharan Africa has the highest mortality rates. The declines in IMR are largely attributable to those in postneonatal mortality, with neonatal mortality rates having remained unchanged over the past decade [8]. The high coverage rates achieved by the expanded programs on

Table 4.2
**Infant mortality rates over the past 40 years by region**

| Last update: May 2004 | Infant mortality rate | | | | | | |
|---|---|---|---|---|---|---|---|
| Regional summaries | 1960 | 1970 | 1980 | 1990 | 1995 | 2000 | 2002 |
| Northern Africa | 167 | 142 | 104 | 66 | 50 | 38 | 34 |
| Sub-Saharan Africa | 163 | 141 | 117 | 109 | 109 | 104 | 104 |
| Latin America | 102 | 86 | 61 | 43 | 35 | 30 | 28 |
| Eastern Asia | 147 | 83 | 48 | 37 | 36 | 32 | 30 |
| South Asia | 149 | 130 | 114 | 87 | 77 | 70 | 67 |
| Southeastern Asia | 111 | 87 | 68 | 54 | 45 | 38 | 36 |
| Western Asia | 152 | 128 | 83 | 53 | 55 | 50 | 49 |
| Oceania | 132 | 97 | 72 | 63 | 61 | 59 | 59 |
| Developed regions | 36 | 23 | 14 | 10 | 8 | 6 | 6 |
| EURASIA (countries in CIS) | 51 | 32 | 38 | 34 | 35 | 35 | 35 |
| Developing regions | 142 | 109 | 88 | 71 | 67 | 62 | 61 |
| World | 127 | 96 | 79 | 64 | 61 | 57 | 55 |

*Source*: United Nations International Children's Emergency Fund (UNICEF) monitoring the situation of women and children, http://www.childinfo.org/cmr/revis/db1.htm, accessed February 19, 2006.
*CIS* Central Independent States

immunization and national programs for the control of diarrheal diseases were mainly responsible for the rapid gains in child survival of the 1980s [19–21].

Among five categories of explanatory factors for infant mortality, improvements in the use of health services, environmental conditions, and socioeconomic status (SES) may be more likely to be associated with the declining trends in IMR during the 1990s; fertility behavior and breast-feeding and infant feeding may have played only a small role [22]. The reversal in mortality decline from the 1960s during the 1990s in Africa has long been a cause of much concern and perhaps, but not fully, attributable to the HIV/AIDS epidemic and mother-to-child transmission (MTCT) [23]. A pooled analysis shows that IMR among HIV-infected infants in Africa was 35.2% compared with 4.9% among uninfected ones [24]. By the second year of life, more than half the infected children die, compared to only 7.6% uninfected children. The regional variation between South Asia and sub-Saharan Africa may also in part be explained by malaria, which contributes to 20% of child deaths in Africa [1, 17, 25]. A note of caution regarding the adequacy of sample sizes, derived mostly from Demographic Health Survey (DHS) data for examining increasing (or decreasing) trends, should be made; of all surveys conducted between 1986 and 2002 in Africa, only half of the trends observed in mortality reduction achieved statistical significance [26].

Global inequity in child health and survival is wide, and both geographic differences between rich and poor countries and within country/region inequities between the rich and the poor need urgent attention [6]. Compared to a rate of 6 per 1,000 in affluent countries, 61 per 1,000 live-born infants die in the first year of life. The declines in mortality are also lower in developing countries relative to the richer ones, making the gap wider. A stark example of this is provided in the difference between the IMR in Afghanistan and that in Japan, with the latter having the lowest rate in the world (Fig. 4.1).

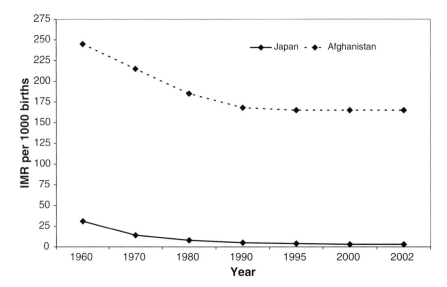

**Fig. 4.1.** Infant mortality trends in Afghanistan and Japan over the past 40 years.

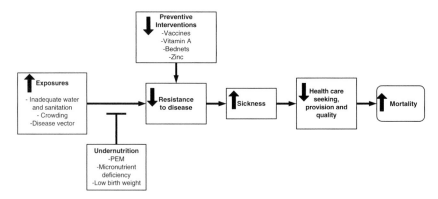

**Fig. 4.2.** This figure illustrates that poorer children are more likely to be exposed to infectious pathogens due to inadequate sanitation and clean water supply, crowding, and higher exposure to disease vectors. This will result in an increased susceptibility to disease exacerbated by undernutrition and increased sickness due to lack of access to preventive interventions. After becoming sick, lower quality of health care can cause increased mortality. (Adapted from [6].) PEM: Protein energy malnutrition

The same situation exists within countries with high levels of inequality between the poorest and richest segments of the population. The causal pathway shown in Fig. 4.2 examines why poor children tend to die at a much higher rate than their richer counterparts [6].

Another differential in infant mortality is seasonal variation observed in many regions of the world. This seasonality may be related to numerous factors, including rainfall; extreme temperatures; harvest and hungry seasons; diseases such as malaria, measles, diarrhea, acute lower respiratory infections, and other infections; and low birth weight [27–36].

## 4.3    DETERMINANTS OF INFANT MORTALITY

An analytic framework for studying the determinants of child survival proposed by Mosley and Chen [37] and recently examined for its cogency to modern times by Hill [38] defines five categories of proximate determinants: maternal factors (age, parity, birth interval); environmental contamination (air, food/water/fingers, skin/soil, inanimate objects, insect vectors); nutrient deficiencies (calories, protein, micronutrients); injury (accidental/intentional); and personal illness control (personal prevention measures, medical treatment). Distal determinants as developed by the United Nations International Children's Emergency Fund (UNICEF) for undernutrition, including human, economic, and organizational resources and the political and ideological system, could also be added to such an analytic framework [39].

### 4.3.1    Macrofactors: Socio-Politico-Economic Dimensions

Both modernization (economic, social, and political) and dependency theories, although seemingly opposing, may influence infant mortality [40]. The former may explain intra-national and the latter international variation in IMRs, although an interaction of the two may provide a more holistic explanation [40]. The economic modernization theory stresses economic growth as the driving force behind development within countries. Economic growth is tied to increases in industrialization and urbanization and thereby

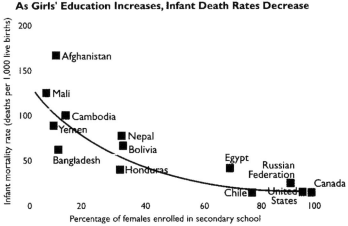

**As Girls' Education Increases, Infant Death Rates Decrease**

This chart shows the intersection between girls' education and infant mortality rates. In countries where a higher percentage of girls is enrolled in secondary education, infant mortality rates are lower. Numerous studies have documented the correlation between educated mothers and healthier babies. In Chile, for example, 78 percent of girls are enrolled in secondary school and nearly all babies (99 percent) survive the first year of life. Compare this to Mali, where only 8 percent of girls are enrolled in secondary school and 1 out of every 8 babies dies before its first birthday.

Sources: IMR – Unicef 2004 (data from 2002). Female secondary enrollment – Population Reference Bureau 2000 NOTE: Trendline based on data from 145 countries. Chart concept adapted from: *Teach a Child, Transform a Nation*, The Basic Education Coalition 2004.

**Fig. 4.3.** Declines in infant mortality rate with increasing levels of girls' education. (From [44]).

increased standards of living and access to medical care, which may lead to decline in mortality. A social modernization perspective stresses the role of education as an intra-national factor in the development process. The often-quoted example of Kerala State in India, where high levels of education among women, among other social factors, has been linked to IMR, is more comparable to that in the developed world [41–43]. Using ecologic data, Fig. 4.3 illustrates the impact of girls' education on infant mortality [44].

Increases in education may lead to increased viability in the labor market, resulting in economic growth [45]. However, decreases in IMR may also be linked to fertility reductions and birth spacing [46], both of which are associated with maternal education. Last, better-educated mothers will be more knowledgeable about health and nutrition, which is likely to result in better infant health and survival. It has long been demonstrated that maternal education induces behavioral changes, which in turn may have an impact on better feeding and child care practices and health service utilization, which in turn may have an impact on child health [47]. Less understood and perhaps examined is the role of education in enhancing maternal self-esteem and status, resulting in higher degrees of control and decision-making power. Women with increased decision-making abilities are known to prioritize expenditures on health and nutrition of their children [48, 49]. Last, the political modernization perspective posits that political democracies that are more responsive to public opinion, interests, and social movements are more likely to promote health-related issues such as infant mortality [40]. Lack of democracy and repressive governments, on the other hand, are less likely to be responsive. Some studies have also shown that increased government spending is associated with lower infant mortality [50].

In contrast to the modernization theory, according to dependency theory the capitalist nations create a global division of labor and trade dependence that destabilizes the economies of developing countries, leading to decreased economic growth and increased income inequality, in turn leading to the poor well-being of the population [40]. A decrease in the state's ability to generate revenue depresses its ability to support funding of health and social service programs. Furthermore, many developing countries are caught in a debt crisis, which may directly affect government spending on programs to reduce infant mortality. There is also evidence to suggest that multinational corporations may foster increased infant mortality [40]. An analysis of 59 developing countries found that intranational political factors interact with international economic forces to have an impact on infant mortality; both multinational corporations and international lending institutions (International Monetary Fund, World Bank) may adversely affect infant mortality [40].

### 4.3.2   Gender

Gender inequality is a factor of global importance in trying to combat infant mortality. Female newborns are at a higher biologic advantage for survival compared to males. In later infancy, behavioral factors and male gender preference result in the reversal of this advantage. In rural Nepal, the adjusted odds ratio for male mortality (relative to female) was 1.39 in the first week of life, 1.22 in the 8- to 28-day period, and 0.73 at 4–24 weeks of life [51]. Indeed, according to modernization theory, economic development affects child mortality, but there may be a gender differential in this impact. At low levels of development, even strong gender bias against females is offset by greater susceptibility to disease and poor nutritional conditions. In contrast to this, in more developed settings, with adequate means to ensure health, male and female risks are equalized. It is at the intermediate levels of development that boy children benefit preferentially from public health measures as a result of cultural biases against female infants [52–54]. Also, total fertility rates show a strong negative relationship with male-to-female IMR, with low total fertility rate associated with higher female survival due to a higher value placed in female children [54]. In Bangladesh, mortality of sons but not daughters was associated with a decrease in both initiation and continuation of contraceptive use [55]. Another finding is related to the impact of gainful employment of females positively influencing female infants due to improved women's status in general [54].

Another differential important to consider is derived from the theory of evolutionary psychology, which proposes that heterogeneous communities with competing racial/ethnic/linguistic groups can override other structural variables, such as gender, resulting in lower female discrimination [54]. A growing concern, however, is the continuing high rate of female infanticide related to strong preference for males in countries such as India and China, which have highly heterogeneous populations. Many reports of "missing girls" due to selective abortions and female infanticide in India are available in the literature. As recently as 1998, using data from the Special Fertility and Mortality Survey, of about 1.3 million births studied, the adjusted sex ratio for the second and third birth when the preceding child was a girl was 759 and 719 per 1,000 males [56]. In contrast, these ratios were about equal (1,102:1,176) if the previous children were boys. This analysis estimated that selective abortion of female fetuses may account for 0.5 million missing female births yearly, with approximately 10 million abortions having occurred in the past two decades.

### 4.3.3  Household Socioeconomic Factors

The SES factors that have been associated with infant mortality include maternal (and paternal) education, household assets, occupation, rural versus urban residence, race/ethnicity, and access and quality of health care and safe water and sanitation. The role of women's education was discussed in the preceding section. Maternal education in many settings has been shown to be associated with a reduction in neonatal and infant mortality [51, 57–62]. Others have found this association to disappear when other explanatory factors, such as income and health services, have been adjusted for in multivariate models [63].

In Norway, using the medical birth registry during 1967 to 1998, data were analyzed to examine maternal education and the risk of infant death [64]. Risk difference for neonatal mortality between high and low maternal education was found to be reduced from 3.5/1,000 in the 1970s to 0.9/1,000 in the 1990s. Conversely, for postneonatal mortality, the risk difference increased from 0.7/1,000 to 2.0/1,000 during this time. The authors inferred that, for neonatal mortality, the influence of socioeconomic factors may have declined, and obstetric and neonatal care services were more likely to play a role. Postneonatal mortality, on the other hand, may be more closely associated with SES. These data are important for the implementation of public health interventions targeted to different periods of risk. Also, note that covariates of infant mortality may be variable and setting-specific and may change over time.

Lower infant mortality has also been linked to household ownership/use of toilets, piped water, and sanitation [65–69]. Distance from the nearest health center and quality of health care services have also been associated with infant mortality [62, 70, 71]. Access to health care can be reduced by removing user fees. A simulation model based on evidence for the impact of key interventions on child mortality calculated that approximately 233,000 deaths of children under 5 years could be prevented annually by abolition of user fees with alternative financing strategies in 20 African countries [72].

### 4.3.4  Maternal Age, Parity, and Birth Spacing

Maternal age has been documented to have an inverse J-shaped relationship with infant mortality; both young and older mothers have an increased risk of infant deaths [73–75]. Because teenage pregnancy may be associated with low SES and other risk factors, adjusting for confounders may lead to an attenuated risk associated with maternal age per se. For example, after adjusting for race, marital status, parity, education, smoking, prenatal care utilization, and poverty status, the risk of postneonatal but not neonatal mortality was significantly associated with younger adolescent age (12–17 years) but not with older adolescents (age 18–19 years) in the United States [76]. First birth, especially at young age, is associated with an increased risk of infant morality. Conversely, high parity may also be a predictor of increased risk, perhaps due to maternal depletion in malnourished settings. Thus, the relationship between parity and infant mortality is also J-shaped, with nulliparity and increasing parity associated with an increased risk of infant mortality [51, 77–83]. Twinning compared to singleton births also increases the risk of infant mortality [84, 85]. Perinatal, neonatal, and 24-week mortality was six to eight times higher among twins than singleton births in rural Nepal [86].

Birth spacing is well recognized as a major risk factor for neonatal and infant mortality. Numerous demographic health survey analyses have demonstrated the benefits of a longer birth interval [71, 87–93]. For neonatal and infant mortality, using data collected between 1990 and 1997 from 17 developing countries, the risk of dying decreased with increasing birth interval up to 3 years, after which the slope plateaued, unlike with child mortality, for which the lower risk persisted even for an interval of 4 years or more [92]. Adjusted analysis, again using DHS data, indicated neonatal mortality to be reduced by 40% for preceding birth interval of 3 years or more compared with an interval of less than 2 years [94].

Several biologic and sociobehavioral pathways exist to explain the association of increased mortality with short birth interval. One such posited mechanism is related to the maternal depletion syndrome, although evidence for this may be limited. A second mechanism may be related to increased transmission of infectious disease, although total number of children may be a stronger predictor for this [87]. A third pathway through which birth interval may have an impact on mortality could be related to competition for scarce resources; the risk of mortality associated with a short interval was lower if the previous sibling had died [91, 95–96]. Alternately, a short subsequent interval may also increase the risk of mortality of an index child, again due to resources being diverted to a younger sibling [87, 88, 97–100].

### 4.3.5  Maternal Nutrition and Infant Mortality

Prepregnancy weight, height, and weight gain during pregnancy are associated with fetal growth and preterm and birth weight. These outcomes and their influence on perinatal and infant mortality were examined in Chapter 3. As mentioned in Chapter 3,

Table 4.3

Risk of 6-month infant mortality by low birth weight and its causes

| | Mortality | | | |
|---|---|---|---|---|
| *Causes* | *n* | *%* | *n* | *%* |
| Preterm only | 222 | 17.3 | 24 | 10.8 |
| Small for gestational age only | 895 | 69.8 | 40 | 4.5 |
| Both preterm and small for gestational age | 165 | 12.9 | 25 | 15.2 |

*Preterm* gestational age <37 weeks, *small for gestational age* birth weight below tenth centile of US national reference for fetal growth [105]

antenatal food supplementation has been found to improve birth weight and fetal growth in malnourished settings. A study in the Gambia clearly demonstrated that maternal supplementation during pregnancy with a daily high-calorie and protein food supplement would lead to a reduced incidence of low birth weight and perinatal mortality [101]. An antenatal supplementation trial conducted in rural Nepal demonstrated that folic acid with or without iron or zinc significantly reduced the risk of infant mortality among preterm infants [102]. Reduction in maternal anemia and low birth weight incidence may explain in part the beneficial impact on infant mortality. On the other hand, antenatal vitamin A supplementation has not been found to have an impact on either fetal loss or infant mortality [103], although among vitamin A-deficient night-blind women, infant mortality was significantly higher, and providing weekly vitamin A during pregnancy reduced infant mortality up to 3 months [104].

In the same study in Nepal, low birth weight only due to preterm occurred in just 17% of births, as compared with low birth weight due to an infant small for gestational age (70% of births) (P. Christian, unpublished data; Table 4.3). However, the 6-month IMR was double in the group whose low birth weight was due to preterm birth and threefold when both preterm and small-for-gestational-age infants were present, suggesting that the risk of mortality associated with preterm birth may be higher than that associated with fetal growth retardation despite the higher rates of small-for-gestational age infants in many developing countries. The mortality rate among full-term infants born greater than 2.5 kg was 2.7%.

In Nepal, where the hookworm is highly endemic, geohelminth infestation may be strongly associated with the etiology of maternal anemia during pregnancy [106]. In such a setting, deworming twice during pregnancy in the second and third trimesters was associated with a significant reduction in severe anemia during pregnancy and improved birth weight and infant survival [107], suggesting that in endemic areas where prevalence of anemia is high, antenatal anthelmintic treatment along with antenatal iron-folate supplementation should be routinely provided as per the international guidelines [108].

### 4.3.6 Breast-feeding

Breast-feeding has long been known to provide protection against infections and infectious mortality. The current World Health Organization (WHO)/UNICEF recommendation is to breast-feed exclusively for the first 6 months of life and beyond 6 months to continue breast-feeding while providing safe complementary foods into the first 2 years of life or more. The antimicrobial, anti-inflammatory, and immunomodulatory properties of breast milk [109, 110] combined with its nutritional composition that is best suited to an infant's needs during the early period of postnatal growth and development of the immature gut and the immune system make breast milk the ideal source of nutrition for an infant. These properties of human milk afford a survival benefit to the infant.

A three-country (Brazil, Pakistan, Philippines) pooled analysis provided an estimate of the magnitude of survival benefit afforded by breast-feeding by age in the first 12 months of life [111]. Breast-feeding was associated with improved survival for both boys (odds ratio [OR] = 3.5, 95% confidence interval [CI] 2.4–5.0) and girls (OR = 4.1, 95% CI 2.8–6.1) in the first 6 months of life, with the protective effect declining in the second 6-month period in both boys (OR = 1.8, 95% CI 1.1–3.0) and girls (OR = 2.9, 95% CI 1.6–5.2). In the first 6 months, protection against diarrheal disease mortality was higher (combined sex OR = 6.1, 95% CI 4.1–9.0) compared with that against acute lower respiratory infection (OR = 2.4, 95% CI 1.6–3.5). This difference between infectious causes of mortality disappeared in the second 6 months of life. Using secondary data from a multicenter randomized trial on immunization-linked vitamin A supplementation in Ghana, India, and Peru, non-breast-fed and partially breast-fed infants had a 10-fold and 2.5-fold increased risk, respectively, of dying compared to predominantly breast-fed infants [112]. Breast-feeding may also be protective for neonatal sepsis, hypothermia, and hypoglycemia [113, 114]. Reasons for terminating breast-feeding may also influence subsequent risk of mortality in children. In Guinea-Bissau, compared with weaning among healthy mothers and children, illness in either the child or mother or the onset of a new pregnancy as a reason for termination of breast-feeding was associated with a three or four times higher risk of infant/child mortality [115].

Even in countries with high HIV-1 prevalence, exclusive breast-feeding for the first 6 months of life is recommended in the absence of affordable, feasible, acceptable, sustainable, and safe replacement feeding [116]. Following 6 months, weaning to replacement feeding with complete cessation of breast-feeding is recommended, although the conditions under which replacement feeding is to be done remain the same. Simulation models predicting HIV-free survival of infants of HIV-1-positive mothers showed that breast-feeding is safer than replacement feeding between 7 days and 4 months of age. For the interval between 4 and 6 months, replacement feeding is similar to breast-feeding, and after 6 months replacement feeding is substantially safer than breast-feeding for infant HIV-free survival [117].

Using current data on risks of postnatal HIV transmission from mixed and exclusive breast-feeding, another simulation aims to inform policies regarding infant feeding practices among HIV-1-infected women [118]. This simulation demonstrated that, in low infant mortality settings (IMR <25/1,000), replacement feeding resulted in the highest HIV-free survival rates in the first 2 years of life. Conversely, in settings with higher IMR (25–100/1,000), exclusive breast-feeding up to 6 months and early breast-feeding cessation at 6 months produced the best survival, both relative to "no intervention," by which "usual" infant feeding involving early, predominant, and mixed breast-feeding continued for up to 2 years is practiced. In countries with IMR above 100/1,000, replacement feeding produced the best HIV-free survival. Such countries include Zambia, Tanzania, Ethiopia, Malawi, Rwanda, Cote de'Ivoire, Mali, Democratic Republic of the Congo, Angola, and Mozambique.

## 4.4   DIRECT AND UNDERLYING CAUSES OF INFANT MORTALITY

Despite the lack of adequate vital registration and autopsy data among infants, several estimates based on models using nationally representative surveys and special studies using parental verbal autopsies are available to establish causes of infant deaths. The current WHO estimates of major causes of death in children under 5 years [2] can be intrapolated for causes of deaths among infants. Worldwide, 73% of deaths in children in this age category can be attributed to the following causes: pneumonia (19%), diarrhea (17%), malaria (8%), neonatal causes (37%), AIDS/HIV (3%), measles (4%), injuries (3%), and others (10%). Causes of neonatal mortality are discussed in the next section. Another estimate based on a 42-country prediction model showed slightly different estimates, attributing 52.6% of deaths to neonatal causes, 14.1% to diarrhea, 8.2% to respiratory infections, 0.3% to AIDS, and 24.7% to other causes [1, 119].

The proportions of deaths caused by malaria and HIV/AIDS are much higher in Africa, although these proportions vary by existence of either or both these infections. MTCT is one of the primary causes of infection in the fetus, newborn, and breast-feeding infant. Infants in many African countries where malaria (predominantly caused by *Plasmodium falciparum*) is endemic are at a high risk of infection, severe anemia, and mortality [27, 120–124]. An analysis for the year 2000 from studies in 18 countries in middle and southern Africa estimated that, of 100 million children under 5 years old living in areas where malaria transmission occurs, about 804,000 died from the direct effects of malaria, suggesting that the mortality burden associated with this infection is high [125]. Malarial infection through maternal transmission at birth or in utero may also increase the risk of neonatal death. In Tanzania, cord parasitemia was associated with an almost ninefold risk of neonatal death [121].

Maternal malarial infection is associated with low birth weight and increased risk of infant mortality. Assuming that 25% of pregnant women in malaria-endemic areas in Africa have placental malaria, it is estimated that 5.7% of infant deaths could result from an indirect cause of malaria in pregnancy [126]. Mortality in infants in Burkina Faso has been shown to peak after the rainy season, primarily due to increase in malaria infections during this time period [27]. In Tanzania, a treated bed net project that involved both the public and private sectors led to a successful implementation of increased usage from 10% to 50% and a record 27% reduction in mortality in children 1 month to 4 years of age over the course of 3 years [127]. In Kenya, in a randomized community-based trial, adherence and usage of treated bed nets increased significantly in intervention versus control villages, and infant mortality was reduced by 22% [128].

Among 48 demographic surveillance studies, *P. falciparum* malaria was associated with a twofold increase in the risk of all-cause mortality in those under 5 years old, suggesting that malaria may explain a higher burden of childhood mortality in Africa [120]. While this pattern of mortality cause structure in sub-Saharan Africa has an impact on the proportion of causes related to neonatal deaths and therefore infant deaths, it does not have an impact on the contribution of diarrheal deaths or those due to pneumonia in older children [1].

When considering causes of infant mortality, both neonatal and postneonatal, one needs to consider (1) overlap or multiplicity of causes and (2) the role of undernutrition as an underlying cause for much of the infant mortality in low-income countries. For example, comorbidity of pneumonia and diarrhea is high, suggesting shared risk factors and exacerbation of risk due to coexistence of multiple morbidities (Fig. 4.4) [1, 129]. Often, measles is

**Fig. 4.4.** Overlap between deaths attributed to diarrhea and pneumonia [1].

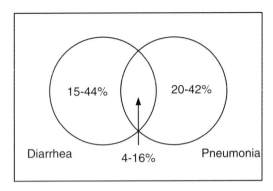

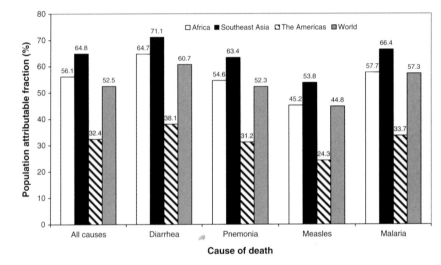

**Fig. 4.5.** Population attributable fraction for undernutrition of child deaths by cause in three high mortality WHO regions and the world. (Adapted from Ref. 133.)

also complicated by pneumonia and diarrhea [1]. Even with causes of neonatal mortality, a considerable overlap among sepsis, preterm delivery, and birth asphyxia has been observed using a neonatal verbal autopsy method in a rural setting in Nepal [130].

The work by Pellitier has long established the risk of child mortality attributable to undernutrition, especially mild-to-moderate [131, 132]. As underlying factors, both underweight (<1 standard deviation below reference weight/age using international reference population) and micronutrient deficiencies significantly reduce the risk of death due to diarrhea, pneumonia, malaria, and measles [133, 134]. Using longitudinal data from ten cohort studies and prevalence of weight for age by categories from 310 national nutrition surveys, 52.5% [95% CI 44.8–60.7%) of all deaths in young children (age range 0 to 72 months) were attributable to undernutrition (Fig. 4.5). The cause-specific population attributable fraction was 44.8% for measles, 57.3% for malaria, 52.3% for pneumonia, and 60.7% for diarrhea, although this may vary by region and proportion of deaths due to these causes. Reductions in rates of malnutrition (low weight for age) using longitudinal data from 59 countries between 1966 and 1996 have been significantly associated with improvements in child survival after controlling for socioeconomic and policy changes [135]. The authors estimated that reducing low weight for age by 5%

could reduce child (1–4.9 years old) mortality by approximately 30% and mortality for those under 5 years old by about 13%. The lower reduction in the mortality rate for those younger than 5 years, primarily driven by a lack of impact on infant mortality, may be because low weight for age in the postnatal period is not as critical a factor in affecting infant mortality, most of which occurs in the neonatal period. Including low birth weight in the model would enhance the role of undernutrition in affecting infant mortality.

The contribution of low birth weight and intrauterine growth retardation to infant mortality was discussed previously. Among other nutritional factors, underlying micronutrient deficiencies may also increase the risk of mortality. It is estimated that the risk of dying from diarrhea, measles, and malaria is increased by 20–24% among vitamin A-deficient children [136] and from diarrhea, pneumonia, and malaria by 13–21% among zinc-deficient children [137]. Currently, 647,000 deaths of those under 5 years are caused by vitamin A deficiency worldwide and are thus avertable with supplementation and fortification programs [136]. It has been shown that daily iron supplementation to children 2 weeks to 36 months of age is unlikely to affect infant/child mortality in South Asia [138] and may exacerbate severe malarial morbidity and mortality in a malarious region in Africa [139]. Daily zinc supplementation, on the other hand, may decrease mortality. Trials are currently under way in both settings to examine the magnitude of impact.

## 4.5   CONTRIBUTIONS OF NEONATAL MORTALITY TO INFANT MORTALITY: CAUSES AND RISK FACTORS

Neonatal mortality accounts for 38% of all deaths in children younger than 5 years and 60% of infant deaths. Furthermore, mortality is highest in the first 24 hours after birth, when 25–45% of all neonatal deaths will occur. Three quarters of neonatal deaths occur in the first week of birth. Unlike declines in child mortality observed in the past, the rates of neonatal mortality in the developing world have been slow to decline, resulting in disproportionately higher neonatal relative to postneonatal mortality (Figs. 4.6 and 4.7).

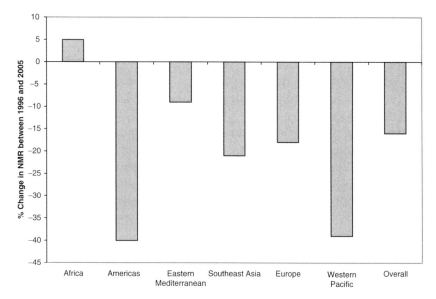

**Fig. 4.6.** Estimated percentage change in neonatal mortality (NMR) rate by World Health Organization (WHO) regions. (Adapted from [8].)

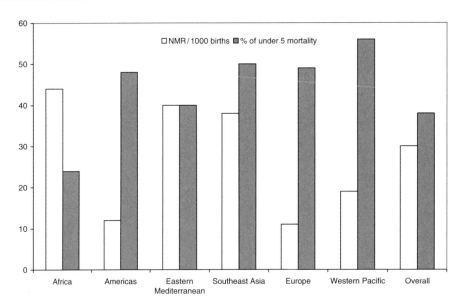

**Fig. 4.7.** Regional variations in neonatal mortality rate (NMR) and as proportion of deaths in children less than 5 years. (Adapted from [8].)

The main reason for this is related to the focus on pneumonia, diarrhea, and vaccine-preventable infectious diseases, which are important causes of postneonatal but not neonatal mortality [8]. Thus, many countries in the developing world are becoming more comparable with the developed world, where neonatal deaths contribute a large proportion of infant/child mortality. While 63% of deaths in children below 5 years occur in the neonatal period in high-income countries, that figure is 38% in low- and middle-income countries [8]. Following the child survival series in the *Lancet*, a series on neonatal survival reported epidemiologic data on newborn deaths in developing countries and evidence-based interventions to reduce them [8–11].

Less than 10% of neonatal deaths occur in countries where adequate vital registration exists. Thus, a majority of the data on neonatal mortality rates and numbers are derived from household surveys using the DHS. Globally, it is estimated that about 4 million newborns die in the first 28 days of life (neonatal period), with 99% of the deaths occurring in developing countries [8].

Causes of neonatal mortality are even more difficult to ascertain in the absence of hospital deaths and vital registration. Data collected using verbal autopsies tend to be inaccurate, although attempts have been made to better define and validate algorithms using symptoms [140–143]. Causes of death for neonates are also likely to be multiple and overlapping [130, 144, 145]. Based on statistical modeling, the major direct causes are preterm birth (27%); sepsis, including pneumonia (26%); asphyxia (23%); tetanus (7%); and congenital malformations (7%) [8]. The remaining 7% and 3% are due to other causes and diarrhea, respectively.

Maternal intrapartum complications and prenatal health contribute enormously to neonatal survival. Complications during labor, including obstructed labor and malpresentation, carry high risks [8, 146–149]. Perinatal conditions, at 6.2%, are the second leading cause of the global disability-adjusted life years (DALYs), after lower respiratory infections [150]. Maternal death will dramatically increase the risk of not only neonatal but also postneonatal mortality [71]. In Nepal, the odds of dying in the first 6 months of life in the event of a maternal death were more than 50-fold (95% CI 20.3–131.8) [51]. It has been shown that even among infants who survive despite a maternal death, fewer than 10% live beyond their first birthday [151]. Even maternal nutritional status may play a role; with every centimeter increase in maternal mid-upper arm circumference, the adjusted risk of mortality in the first week of life was lower by 12% (95% CI 5–19%) [51].

Skilled attendance at birth and delivery in a health facility are critical for alleviating risks associated with labor and delivery. Globally, only 56% of deliveries occur with a skilled attendant, although variability between countries and between regions in a country is high [152]. Interestingly, middle-income countries may face a different challenge, as demonstrated by a case study of three birth cohorts (1982, 1993, 2004) in Brazil [153], which showed a trend of increased preterm deliveries and a reduction in mean birth weight. This trend was attributed to the unregulated private and public care sector practices and increases in labor induction and cesarean section and inaccurate ultrasound estimations of gestational age. However, despite increases in preterm births, neonatal mortality rates have stayed constant perhaps due to improved newborn care. Countries such as Brazil are likely to face different challenges in attempting to achieve the MDGs.

## 4.6   INTERVENTIONS FOR REDUCING INFANT AND NEONATAL MORTALITY

To reduce infant mortality, the period of intervention begins in pregnancy, continues to the time of labor and delivery and into the first 28 days of life, and extends to the end of the first year of life. Public health interventions such as immunizations; integrated management of childhood infections, especially focusing on the infant; exclusive breastfeeding; prevention of MTCT; use of treated bed nets; and provision of safe drinking water are among the interventions reviewed in the child survival series [4]. This review identified low coverage of known effective interventions throughout the developing world as one of the largest constraints to successful infant and child mortality reductions (Fig. 4.8). The availability of interventions such as nevirapine and replacement feeding, insecticide-treated bed nets, preventive intermittent treatment for malaria, and others is even lower, with only 1–5% having access [4].

Also identified is the need to differentiate between interventions that are effective versus delivery strategies with design implementation and sustainability that are generally poor. The challenge for improving child survival in the future may lie in ways to effectively scale up programs and cater them to local needs and situations. Research priorities should be focused in this area of public health services [5]. In the past, research on quantifying health problems and identifying strategies to improve child health has been valuable in making progress toward reduction in child mortality [155].

A growing concern is that of a global problem of antimicrobial resistance, which is particularly cogent to the developing world [156, 157]. Antibiotic treatment of sepsis, pneumonia, and dysentery is an important intervention that is estimated to prevent

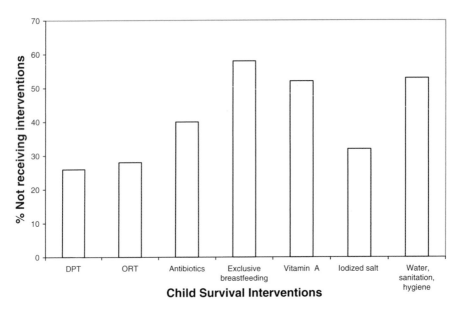

**Fig. 4.8.** Percentage of the world's children under 2 years of age not receiving known effective interventions for saving lives [154]. *DPT* diphtheria-pertussis-tetanus, *ORT* oral rehydration therapy.

approximately 1.5 million deaths of children under 5 years old through universal coverage [4].

The IMR will decline when the proportionately higher rates of neonatal deaths decline. Any strategy for reducing neonatal mortality will need to take antenatal as well as intrapartum risks into consideration and target both the neonate and the mother at the time of labor and delivery. A comprehensive discussion of the evidence for efficacious interventions is beyond the purview of this chapter, and the reader is referred to the child and neonatal survival series for a detailed description [9, 10]. Interventions known to be effective are tetanus toxoid vaccination, resuscitation, prevention and management of hypothermia, breast-feeding, and community-based management of pneumonia, among others [9]. Recent research has revealed innovative interventions that may be promising for future applications to programs. Dosing of a newborn with vitamin A at 50,000 IU within hours after birth has been shown to result in a 25% reduction in infant mortality [158] based on a randomized community-based trial in rural India that replicated the findings of a clinic-based small study in Indonesia, which showed a 64% reduction in infant mortality [159].

However, further research is still needed to adopt this as a policy in South and Southeast Asian countries. In Africa, among HIV-1-infected infants who seroconvert after 6 weeks of age, vitamin A given at birth may in fact cause an increase in mortality [160, 161], although it may also increase survival among infants who are infected in the intrapartum period [160].

Three recent community-based interventions are of note for their effect on neonatal mortality in rural Nepal, where antenatal care is low, a majority (>90%) of deliveries occur at home, and newborn care is home based. The first trial showed that newborn skin wiping with chlorhexadine solution reduced neonatal mortality by 28% among low birth weight infants [162]. Previously, relative to nonintervention time periods, both vaginal cleansing prior to delivery among women and full-body cleansing among newborns with 0.25% chlorhexadine were shown to reduce neonatal mortality by 22% in Malawi [163] and Egypt [164]. In the same population in Nepal, a nested, randomized trial of topical application of chlorhexadine to the umbilical cord on days 1–4, 6, 8, and 10 compared with dry cord care or cord care with soap and water significantly reduced the risk of omphalitis (by 25%) and neonatal mortality (by 24%) [165]. A third trial conducted in Nepal used a participatory intervention with women's groups in which a facilitator supported the group meetings to identify perinatal problems and strategies for addressing them [166]. Birth outcomes were monitored in a large cohort of 28,931 women. Relative to the control clusters, neonatal mortality was found to be significantly lower (by 30%) in the intervention clusters [166], demonstrating that a low-cost, local, and potentially sustainable intervention could have a huge impact on the risk of early infant deaths. Practices that were improved due to the intervention included antenatal care, institutional deliveries, trained birth attendance, and hygiene. Another such approach using traditional birth attendants who provided antenatal care and safe delivery kits led to a 30% reduction in perinatal mortality in Pakistan [167]. These trials provide encouraging results for simple community-based newborn interventions that can be effective on a large scale. In Gadchiroli, India, home-based neonatal care and identification of high-risk neonates has been successfully implemented over the past decade [168–172].

Thus, in resource-poor settings such home-based delivery models may be more feasible and affordable than regionalized care as practiced in the developing world involving primary, secondary, and tertiary care [173]. Results from several other such effectiveness studies are being awaited to inform the formulation of a newborn care package for addressing the high rates of neonatal mortality—the highest contributor to infant mortality—in the developing world. Cost-effectiveness analyses for sub-Saharan Africa and Southeast Asia suggested that the most effective mix of interventions were community-based newborn care package followed by antenatal care [174–176]. Packages were more effective than individual interventions due to synergies on costs, especially related to common delivery modes.

## 4.7    FUTURE ACTIONS

Current evidence exists to show that most infant and child deaths are preventable with low-cost, simple interventions that are somehow failing to reach those most in need. The two *Lancet* series, termed the Lancet's campaign on child survival [177], draw urgent attention to and provide a much-needed push for revitalizing efforts to reduce child and newborn deaths and thereby achieve MDG-4 by 2015 [178]. A wide group of institutions, agencies, scientists, policymakers, and programmers have begun meeting once every 2 years for a "Countdown 2015" to take stock of the progress being made in preventing child deaths [178]. Partnerships for the "continuum of care approach" involving the mother, the newborn, and the child have been formed, including the Healthy Newborn Partnership, Partnership for Safe Motherhood and Newborn Health, and the Child Survival Partnership created by several countries, agencies, and international organizations [179]. And yet, the UN 2005 Human Development Report (www.undp.org) has found indicators of development, public health, and education to be either slowing or stagnating, and there is concern that the MDGs will be missed by a large margin by most countries [180, 181].

Another barrier is related to the tracking of mortality in low-income countries that relies on extrapolations of trends and data from household surveys to monitor change. There is a need for coordination and consistent application of an agreed-on methodology for monitoring mortality trends [182]. The Child Mortality Coordination Group is such a group that is poised to provide technical and other assistance to countries in an effort to help strengthen their ability to collect and examine data [182]. However, urgent measures are simultaneously needed to initiate vital registration and certification systems for accurate assessment of trends and leading causes of infant and child mortality [183].

## REFERENCES

1. Black RE, Morris SS, Bryce J. Where and why are 10 million children dying every year? Child survival I. Lancet 2003;361:2226–2234.
2. Bryce J, Boschi-Pinto C, Shibuya K, Black RE, WHO Child Health Epidemiology Reference Group. WHO estimates of the causes of death in children. Lancet 2005;365:1147–1152.
3. United Nations International Children's Emergency Fund. The state of the world's children 2005. New York: United Nations Children's Fund, 2005.
4. Jones G, Steketee RW, Black RE, Bhutta ZA, Morris SS, Bellagio Child Survival Study Group. How many child deaths can we prevent this year? Child survival II. Lancet 2003;362:65–71.
5. Bryce J, el Arifeen S, Pariyo G, Lanata CF, Gwatkin D, Habicht J-P, Multi-Country Evaluation of IMCI Study Group. Reducing child mortality: can public health deliver? Child survival III. Lancet 2003;362:159–164.
6. Victora CG, Wagstaff A, Schellenberg JA, Gwatkin D, Claeson M, Habicht J-P. Applying an equity lens to child health and mortality: more of the same is not enough. Child survival IV. Lancet 2003;362: 233–241.
7. Bellagio Study Group on Child Survival. Knowledge into action for child survival. Child survival V. Lancet 2003;362:323–327.
8. Lawn JE, Cousens S, Zupan J, Lancet Survival Steering Team. Four million neonatal deaths: When? Where? Why? Neonatal survival 1. Lancet 2005;365:891–900.
9. Darmstadt GL, Bhutta ZA, Cousens S, Adam T, Walker N, de Bernis L, Lancet Neonatal Survival Steering Team. Evidence-based, cost-effective interventions: how many newborn babies can we save? Neonatal survival 2. Lancet 2005;365:977–988.
10. Knippenberg R, Lawn JE, Darmstadt GL, Begkoyian G, Fogstad H, Walelign N, Paul VK, Lancet Neonatal Survival Steering Team. Systematic scaling up of neonatal care in countries. Neonatal survival 3. Lancet 2005;365:1087–1098.
11. Martines J, Paul VK, Bhutta ZA, Koblinsky M, Soucat A, Walker N, Bahl R, Fogstad H, Costello A, Lancet Neonatal Survival Steering Team. Neonatal survival 4. Lancet 2005;365:1189–1197.
12. Mason E. Child survival: time to match commitments with action (comment). Lancet 2005;365:1286–1287.
13. Bryce J, Black RE, Walker N, Bhutta ZA, Lawn JE, Steketee RW. Can the world afford to save the lives of 6 million children each year? Lancet 2005; 365:2193–2200.
14. Costello A, Osrin D. The case for a new global fund for maternal, neonatal, and child survival. Lancet 2005;366:603–605.
15. Cutler D, Miller G. The role of public health improvements in health advances: the twentieth century United States. Demography 2005;42:1–22.
16. Condran GA, Crimmins-Gardner E. Public health measures and mortality in US cities in the late nineteenth century. Human Ecol 1978;6:27–54.

17. Ahmed OB, Lopez AD, Inoue M. The decline in child mortality: a reappraisal. Bull World Health Organ 2000;78:1175–1191.
18. World Health Organization. World health report 2002. Reducing risks, promoting healthy life. Geneva: World Health Organization, 2002. No. WHA 540.1.
19. Sachs JD, chair. Macroeconomics and health: investing in health for human development. Geneva: World Health Organization, 2001.
20. Claeson M, Waldman RJ. The evolution of child health programmes in developing countries: from targeting diseases to targeting people. Bull World Health Organ 2000;78:1234–1245.
21. United Nations International Children's Emergency Fund. Progress since the world summit for children: a statistical review. New York: United Nations International Children's Emergency Fund, 2001. Available at: http://www.unicef.org/pubsgen/wethechildren-stats/sgreport_adapted_stats_eng.pdf.
22. Rutstein SO. Factors associated with trends in infant mortality and child mortality in developing countries during the 1990s. Bull World Health Organ 2000;78:1256–1270.
23. Adetunji J. Trends in under-5 mortality rates and the HIV/AIDS epidemic. Bull World Health Organ 2000;78:1200–1206.
24. Newell M-L, Coovadia H, Cortina-Borja M, Rollins N, Gaillard P, Dabis F, Ghent International AIDS Society Working Group. Mortality of infected and uninfected infants born to HIV-infected mothers in Africa: a pooled analysis. Lancet 2004;364:1236–1243.
25. Korenromp EL, Williams BG, Gouws E, Dye C, Snow RW. Measurement of trends in childhood malaria mortality in Africa: an assessment of progress toward targets based on verbal autopsy. Lancet Infect Dis 2003;3:349–358.
26. Korenromp EL, Arnold F, Williams BG, Nahlen BL, Snow RW. Monitoring trends in under-5 mortality rates through national birth history surveys. Int J Epidemiol 2004;33:1293–1301.
27. Kynast-Wolf G, Hammer GP, Muller O, Kouyate B, Becher H. Season of death and birth predict patterns of mortality in Burkina Faso. Int J Epidemiol Advance Access August 2, 2005.
28. Rayco-Solon P, Moore SE, Fulford AJ, Prentice AM. Fifty-year mortality trends in three rural African villages. Trop Med Int Health 2004;9:1151–1160.
29. Vaahtera M, Kulmala T, Maleta K, Cullinan T, Salin ML, Ashorn P. Epidemiology and predictors of infant morbidity in rural Malawi. Paediatr Perinat Epidemiol 2000;14:363–371.
30. Borus PK, Cumberland P, Sonoiya S, Kombich J, Tukei PM, Cutts FT. Measles trends and vaccine effectiveness in Nairobi, Kenya. East Afr Med J 2003;80:361–364.
31. Becker S, Weng S. Seasonal patterns of deaths in Matlab, Bangladesh. Int J Epidemiol 1998;27: 814–823.
32. Bouvier P, Breslow N, Doumbo O, Robert CF, Picquet M, Mauris A, Dolo A, Dembele HK, Delley V, Rougemont A. Seasonality, malaria, and impact of prophylaxis in a West African village. II. Effect on birthweight. Am J Trop Med Hyg 1997;56:384–389.
33. Popkin BM, Guilkey DK, Schwartz JB, Flieger W. Survival in the perinatal period: a prospective analysis. J Biosoc Sci 1993;25:359–370.
34. Eregie CO, Ofovwe G. Observations from a cluster survey on seasonality in neonatal tetanus. East Afr Med J 1992;69:619–621.
35. Gonzalez Perez G, Galvez AM, Herrera Leon LL. Seasonal variations in infant mortality in Cuba. An Esp Pediatr 1988;28:521–525.
36. Victora CG, Vaughan JP, Barros FC. The seasonality of infant deaths due to diarrheal and respiratory diseases in southern Brazil, 1974–1978. Bull Pan Am Health Organ 1985;19:29–39.
37. Mosley WH, Chen LC. An analytical framework for the study of child survival in developing countries. 1984. Bull World Health Organ 2003;81:140–145.
38. Hill K. Frameworks for studying the determinants of child survival. Bull World Health Organ 2003;81:138–139.
39. United Nations International Children's Emergency Fund. The state of the world's children 1998. New York: Oxford University Press, 1998:24.
40. Shandra JM, Nobles J, London B, Williamson JB. Dependency, democracy, and infant mortality: a quantitative, cross-national analysis of less developed countries. Soc Sci Med 2004;59:321–333.
41. Philip E. Why infant mortality is low in Kerala. Indian J Pediatr 1985;52:439–443.

42. Bryant JH. Health for all: the dream and the reality. World Health Forum 1988;9:291–302; discussion 303–314.
43. Franke RW, Chasin BH. Kerala State, India: radical reform as development. Int J Health Serv 1992;22:139–156.
44. Save the Children. State of the world's mothers 2004. Westport, CT: Save the Children, 2004.
45. Bellew R, Raney L. Educating girls. Finance Dev 1992;29:54–56.
46. Caldwell J. The theory of fertility decline. New York: Academic, 1982.
47. Cebu Study Team. Underlying and proximate determinants of child health: The Cebu Longitudinal Health and Nutrition Study. Am J Epidemiol 1991;133:185–201.
48. Katz J, West KP Jr, Pradhan EK, LeClerq SC, Shakya TR, Khatry SK, Shrestha SR. Impact of providing a small income on women's nutritional status and household food expenditures in rural Nepal. Food Nutr Bull 2001;22:13–18.
49. Katz J, West KP Jr, Pradhan EK, LeClerq SC, Khatry SK, Shrestha SR. The impact of a small steady stream of income for women on family health and economic well-being. Global Public Health 2007;2:35–52.
50. Wimberley D. Investment dependence and alternative explanations of third world mortality: a cross-national study. Am Sociol Rev 1990;55:830–854.
51. Katz J, West KP Jr, Khatry SK, Christian P, LeClerq SC, Pradhan EK, Shrestha SR. Risk factors for early infant mortality in Sarlahi district, Nepal. Bull World Health Organ 2003;81:717–725.
52. Fauveau V, Koenig MA, Wojtyniak B. Excess female deaths among rural Bangladeshi children: an examination of cause-specific mortality and morbidity. Int J Epidemiol 1991;20:729–735.
53. Nielsen F, Alderson A. Income inequality, development, and dualism: results from an unbalanced cross-national panel. Am Sociol Rev 1995;60:674–701.
54. Fuse K, Crenshaw EM. Gender imbalance in infant mortality: a cross-national study of social structure and female infanticide. Soc Sci Med 2006;62:360–374.
55. Johnson NE, Sufian AJM. Effect of son mortality on contraceptive practice in Bangladesh. J Biosoc Sci 1992;24:9–16.
56. Jha P, Kumar R, Vasa P, Dhingra N, Thiruchelvam D, Moineddin R. Low male-to-female sex ratio of children born in India: national survey of 1.1 million households. Lancet 2006;367:211–218.
57. Amin R. Infant and child mortality in Bangladesh. J Biosoc Sci 1988;20:59–65.
58. Ahmed MF. Infant mortality in Bangladesh: a review of recent evidence. J Biosoc Sci 1991;23:327–336.
59. Curtis SL, Steele K. Variations in familial neonatal mortality risks in four countries. J Biosoc Sci 1996;28:141–159.
60. Desai S, Alva S. Maternal education and child health: is there a strong causal relationship? Demography 1998;35:71–81.
61. Asling-Monemi K, Pena R, Ellsberg MC, Persson LA. Violence against women increases the risk of infant and child mortality: a case-referent study in Nicaragua. Bull World Health Organ 2003;81:17–18.
62. Bhargava A, Chowdhury S, Singh KK. Healthcare infrastructure, contraceptive use and infant mortality in Uttar Pradesh, India. Econ Hum Biol 2005;3:388–404.
63. Cleland J, Bicego G, Fegan G. Socioeconomic inequalities in childhood mortality: the 1970s to the 1980s. Health Trans Rev 1992;2:1–18.
64. Arntzen A, Samuelsen SO, Bakketeig LS, Stoltenberg C. Socioeconomic status and risk of infant death. A population-based study of trends in Norway, 1967–1998. Int J Epidemiol 2004;33:279–288.
65. Brockerhoff M. Rural-to-urban migration and child survival in Senegal. Demography 1990;27:601–616.
66. Davanzo J, Butz WP, Habicht JP. How biological and behavioural influences on mortality in Malaysia vary during the first year of life. Pop Stud 1983;37:381–402.
67. Brockerhoff M, Derose LF. Child survival in East Africa: the impact of preventive health care. World Dev 1996;24:1841–1857.
68. Merrick TW. The effect of piped water on early childhood mortality in urban Brazil, 1970 to 1976. Demography 1985;22:1–24.
69. Davanzo J, Habicht JP. Infant mortality decline in Malaysia, 1946–1975: the roles of changes in variables and changes in the structure of the relationships. Demography 1986;23:143–160.
70. Paul BK. Health service resources as determinants of infant death in rural Bangladesh: an empirical study. Soc Sci Med 1991;32:43–49.

71. Becher H, Muller O, Jahn A, Gbangou A, Kynast-Wolf G, Kouyate B. Risk factors of infant and child mortality in rural Burkina Faso. Bull World Health Organ 2004;82:265–273.

72. James C, Morris SS, Keith R, Taylor A. Impact on child mortality of removing user fees: simulation model. BMJ 2005;331;747–749.

73. Bicego G, Ahmad OB. Infant and child mortality. Demographic and health surveys, comparative studies No. 20. Calverton, MD: Macro International, 1996.

74. Geronimus AT, Korenman S. The socioeconomic costs of teenage childbearing: evidence and interpretation. Demography 1993;30:281–290.

75. Manda SOM. Unobserved family and community effects on infant mortality in Malawi. Genus 1998;54:143–164.

76. Markovitz BP, Cook R, Flick LH, Leet TL. Socioeconomic factors and adolescent pregnancy outcomes: distinctions between neonatal and post-neonatal deaths? BMC Public Health 2005;5:79–85.

77. Mavalankar DV, Trivedi CR, Gray RH. Levels and risk factors for perinatal mortality in Ahmedabad, India. Bull World Health Organ 1991;69:435–442.

78. Van den Broeck J, Eeckels R, Massa G. Maternal determinants of child survival in a rural African community. Int J Epidemiol 1996;25:998–1004.

79. Hull TH, Gubhaju B. Multivariate analysis of infant and child mortality in Java and Bali. J Biosoc Sci 1986;18:109–118.

80. Leach A, McArdle TF, Banya WAS, Krubally O, Greenwood AM, Rands C, et al. Neonatal mortality in a rural area of the Gambia. Ann Trop Paediatr 1999;19:33–43.

81. Barros FC, Victoria CG, Vaughan JP, Estanislau HJ. Perinatal mortality in southern Brazil: a population-based study of 7,392 births. Bull World Health Organ 1987;65:95–104.

82. Greenwood AM, Greenwood BM, Bradley AK, Williams K, Shenton FC, Tulloch S, et al. A prospective survey of the outcome of pregnancy in a rural area of the Gambia. Bull World Health Organ 1987;65:635–643.

83. Kusin JA, Kardjati S, de With C. Infant mortality in Madura, Indonesia. Implications for action. J Trop Pediatr 1989;35:129–132.

84. Razzaque A, Ahmed K, Wai L. Twinning rates in a rural area of Bangladesh. Hum Biol 1990;62:505–514.

85. Chowdhury MK, Khan NU, Wai L, Bairagi R. Sex differences and sustained excess in mortality among discordant twins in Matlab, Bangladesh: 1977–1985. Int J Epidemiol 1990;19:387–390.

86. Katz J, West KP, Khatry SK, LeClerq SC, Christian P, Pradhan EK, Shrestha SR. Twinning rates and survival of twins in Nepal. Int J Epidemiol 2001;30:802–807.

87. Cleland J, Sathar ZA. The effect of birth spacing on childhood mortality in Pakistan. Pop Stud 1984;38:401–418.

88. Koenig MA, Phillips JF, Campbell OM, D'Souza S. Birth intervals and childhood mortality in rural Bangladesh. Demography 1990;27:251–265.

89. Miller JE, Trussell J, Pebley AR, Vaughan B. Birth spacing and child mortality in Bangladesh and the Philippines. Demography 1992;29:305–318.

90. Madise NJ, Diamond I. Determinants of infant mortality in Malawi: an analysis to control for death clustering within families. J Biosoc Sci 1995;27:95–106.

91. Whitworth A, Stephenson R. Birth spacing, sibling rivalry and child mortality in India. Soc Sci Med 2002;55:2107–2119.

92. Rutstein SO. Effects of preceding birth intervals on neonatal, infant and under-5 years mortality and nutritional status in developing countries: evidence from the demographic and health surveys. Int J Gynecol Obstet 2005;89:S7–S24.

93. Madise NJ. Infant mortality in Zambia: socioeconomic and demographic correlates. Soc Biol 2003;50:148–166.

94. Setty-Venugopal V, Upadhyay UD. Birth spacing: three to five saves lives. Baltimore, MD: Johns Hopkins University, Population Information Program, 2002.

95. De Sweemer C. The influence of child spacing on child survival. Pop Stud 1984;38:47–72.

96. Swenson I. Relationships between pregnancy spacing, sex of infants, maternal age, and birth order, and neonatal and post-neonatal mortality in Bangladesh. Soc Biol 1981;28:299–307.

97. Hobcraft JN, McDonald JW, Rutstein SO. Demographic determinants of infant and early child mortality: a comparative analysis. Pop Stud 1985;39:363–385.

98. Palloni A, Millman S. Effects of inter-birth intervals and breastfeeding on infant and early childhood mortality. Pop Stud 1986;40:215–236.

99. Pebley AR, Stupp PW. Reproductive patterns and child mortality in Guatemala. Demography 1987;24:43–60.

100. Retherford RD, Choe MK, Thapa S, Gubhaju BB. To what extent does breastfeeding explain birth-interval effects on early childhood mortality? Demography 1989;26:439–450.

101. Ceesay SM, Prentice AM, Cole TJ, Foord F, Weaver LT, Poskitt EM, Whitehead RG. Effects on birth weight and perinatal mortality of maternal dietary supplements in rural Gambia: 5 year randomised controlled trial. BMJ 1997;315:786–790.

102. Christian P. Micronutrients and reproductive health issues: an international perspective. J Nutr 2003;133:1969S–1973S.

103. Katz J, West KP Jr, Khatry SK, Pradhan EK, LeClerq SC, Christian P, Wu LSF, Adhikari RK, Shrestha SR, Sommer A. Maternal low-dose vitamin A or beta-carotene supplementation has no effect on fetal loss and early infant mortality: a randomized cluster trial in Nepal. Am J Clin Nutr 2000;71:1507–1576.

104. Christian P, West KP Jr, Khatry SK, LeClerq SC, Kimbrough-Pradhan E, Katz J, Shrestha SR. Maternal night blindness increases risk of mortality in the first 6 months of life among infants in Nepal. J Nutr 2001;131:1510–1512.

105. Alexander GR, Himes JH, Kaufman RB, Mor J, Kogan M. A United States national reference for fetal growth. Obstet Gynecol 1996;87:163–168.

106. Dreyfuss ML, Stoltzfus RJ, Shrestha JB, Pradhan EK, LeClerq SC, Khatry SK, Shrestha SR, Katz J, Albonico M, West KP Jr. Hookworms, malaria and vitamin A deficiency contribute to anemia and iron deficiency among pregnant women in the plains of Nepal. J Nutr 2000;130:2527–2536.

107. Christian P, Khatry SK, West KP Jr. Antenatal anthelmintic treatment, birthweight, and infant survival in rural Nepal. Lancet 2004;364:981–983.

108. Stoltzfus RJ, Dreyfuss ML. Guidelines for the use of iron supplements to prevent and treat iron deficiency anemia. International Nutritional Anemia Consultative Group, World Health Organization, United Nations Children's Fund. Washington, DC: ILSI, 1998.

109. Goldman AS, Chheda S, Garofalo R. Evolution of immunologic functions of the mammary gland and the postnatal development of immunity. Pediatr Res 1998;43:155–162.

110. Labbok MH, Clark D, Goldman AS. Breastfeeding: maintaining an irreplaceable immunological resource. Nat Rev Immunol 2004;4:565–572.

111. WHO Collaborative Study Team on the Role of Breastfeeding on the Prevention of Infant Mortality. Effect of breastfeeding on infant and child mortality due to infectious diseases in less developed countries: a pooled analysis. Lancet 2000;355:451–455.

112. Bahl R, Frost C, Kirkwood BR, Edmond K, Martines J, Bhandari N, Arthur P. Infant feeding patterns and risks of death and hospitalization in the first half of infancy: multicenter cohort study. Bull World Health Organ 2005;83:418–426.

113. Huffman SL, Zehner ER, Victora C. Can improvements in breast-feeding practices reduce neonatal mortality in developing countries? Midwifery 2001;17:80–92.

114. Ashraf RN, Jalil F, Zaman S, Karlberg J, Khan SR, Lindblad BS, Hanson LA. Breast feeding and protection against neonatal sepsis in a high risk population. Arch Dis Child 1991;66:488–490.

115. Jakobsen MS, Sodemann M, Molbak K, Alvarenga IJ, Nielsen J, Aaby P. Termination of breastfeeding after 12 months of age due to a new pregnancy and other causes is associated with increased mortality in Guinea-Bissau. Int J Epidemiol 2003;32:92–96.

116. World Health Organization. New data on the prevention of mother-to-child transmission of HIV and their policy implications: conclusions and recommendations. Geneva, October 11–13, 2000, approved January 15, 2001 [cited January 19, 2001]. Available at: http://www.who.int/child-adolescent-health/publications/NUTRITION/New_data.htm, 2000.

117. Ross JS, Labbok MH. Modeling the effects of different infant feeding strategies on infant survival and mother-to-child transmission of HIV. Am J Public Health 2004;94:1174–1180.

118. Piwoz EG, Ross JS. Use of population-specific infant mortality rates to inform policy decisions regarding HIV and infant feeding. J Nutr 2005;135:1113–1119.
119. Morris SS, Black RE, Tomaskovic L. Predicting the distribution of under-five deaths by cause in countries without adequate vital registration systems. Int J Epidemiol 2003;32:1041–1051.
120. Snow RW, Korenromp EL, Gouws E. Pediatric mortality in Africa: *Plasmodium falciparum* malaria as a cause or risk? Am J Trop Med Hyg 2004;71:16–24.
121. Villamor E, Msamanga G, Aboud S, Urassa W, Hunter DJ, Fawzi WW. Short report: adverse perinatal outcomes of HIV-1-infected women in relation to malaria parasitemia in maternal and umbilical cord blood. Am J Trop Med Hyg 2005;73:694–697.
122. Verhoeff FH, Cessie SL, Kalanda BF, Kazembe PN, Broadhead RL, Brabin BJ. Post-neonatal infant mortality in Malawi: the importance of maternal health. Ann Trop Paed 2004;24:161–169.
123. Merchant T, Schellenberg JA, Nathan R, Abdulla S, Mukasa O, Mshinda H, Lengeler C. Anaemia in pregnancy and infant mortality in Tanzania. Trop Med Int Health 2004;9:262–266.
124. Gemperli A, Vounatsou P, Kleinschmidt I, Bagayoko M, Lengeler C, Smith T. Spatial patterns of infant mortality in Mali: the effect of malaria endemicity. Am J Epidemiol 2004;159:64–72.
125. Rowe AK, Rowe SY, Snow RW, Korenromp EL, Armstrong Schellenberg JR, Stein C, Nahlen BL, Bryce J, Black RE, Steketee RW. The burden of malaria mortality among African children in the year 2000. Int J Epidemiol 2006 Advance Access February 28, 2006.
126. Guyatt HL, Snow RW. Malaria in pregnancy as an indirect cause of infant mortality in sub-Saharan Africa. Trans R Soc Trop Med Hyg 2001;95:569–576.
127. Armstrong Schellenberg JRM, Abdulla S, Natha R, et al. Effect of large-scale social marketing of insecticide-treated nets on child survival in rural Tanzania. Lancet 2001;357:1241–1247.
128. Lindblade KA, Eisele TP, Gimnig JE, Alaii JA, Odhiambo F, ter Kuile FO, Hawley WA, Wannemuehler KA, Phillips-Howard PA, Rosen DH, Nahlen BL, Terlouw DJ, Adazu K, Vulule JM, Slutsker L. sustainability of reductions in malaria transmission and infant mortality in western Kenya with use of insecticide-treated bednets. 4 to 6 years of follow-up. JAMA 2004;291:2571–2580.
129. Fenn B, Morris SS, Black RE. Comorbidity in childhood in northern Ghana: magnitude, associated factors, and impact on mortality. Int J Epidemiol 2005;34:368–375.
130. Freeman JV, Christian P, Khatry SK, Adhikari RK, LeClerq SC, Katz J, Darmstadt GL. Evaluation of neonatal verbal autopsy using physician review versus algorithm-based cause-of-death assignment in rural Nepal. Paediatr Perinat Epidemiol 2005;19:323–331.
131. Pelletier DL. The potentiating effects of malnutrition on child mortality: epidemiologic evidence and policy implications. Nutr Rev 1994;52:409–415.
132. Pelletier DL, Frongillo EA Jr, Schroeder DG, Habicht JP. The effects of malnutrition on child mortality in developing countries. Bull World Health Organ 1995;73:443–448.
133. Caulfield LE, de Onis M, Blossner M, Black RE. Undernutrition as an underlying cause of child deaths associated with diarrhea, pneumonia, malaria, and measles. Am J Clin Nutr 2004;80:193–198.
134. Caulfield LE, Richard SA, Black RE. Undernutrition as an underlying cause of malaria morbidity and mortality in children less than 5 years old. Am J Trop Med Hyg 2004;71:55–63.
135. Pelletier DL, Frongillo EA. Changes in child survival are strongly associated with changes in malnutrition in developing countries. J Nutr 2003;133:107–119.
136. Rice AL, West KP Jr, Black RE. Vitamin A deficiency. In: Comparative quantification of health risks. Global and regional burden of disease attributable to selected major risk factors, vol. 1. Ezzati M, Lopez AD, Rodgers A, Murray CJL, eds. Geneva: World Health Organization, 2004;4:211–256.
137. Caulfield L, Black RE. Zinc deficiency. In: Comparative quantification of health risks. Global and regional burden of disease attributable to selected major risk factors, vol. 1. Ezzati M, Lopez AD, Rodgers A, Murray CJL, eds. Geneva: World Health Organization, 2004;5:257–279.
138. Tielsch JM, Khatry SK, Stoltzfus RJ, Katz J, LeClerq SC, Adhikari R, Mullany LC, Shrestha S, Black RE. Effect of routine prophylactic supplementation with iron and folic acid on preschool child mortality in southern Nepal: community-based, cluster-randomised, placebo-controlled trial. Lancet 2006;367:144–152.
139. Sazawal S, Black RE, Ramsan M, Chwaya HM, Stoltzfus RJ, Dutta A, Dhingra U, Kabole I, Deb S, Othman MK, Kabole FM. Effects of routine prophylactic supplementation with iron and folic acid on

admission to hospital and mortality in preschool children in a high malaria transmission setting: community-based, randomised, placebo-controlled trial. Lancet 2006;367:133–143.

140. Datta N, Mand M, Kumar V. Validation of causes of infant death in the community by verbal autopsy. Indian J Pediatr 1988;55:599–604.

141. Kalter HD, Gray RH, Black RE, Gultiano SA. Validation of postmortem interviews to ascertain selected causes of death in children. Int J Epidemiol 1990;19:380–386.

142. Mirza NM, Macharia WM, Wafula EM, Agwanda RO, Onyango FE. Verbal autopsy: a tool for determining cause of death in a community. E Afr Med J 1990;67:693–698.

143. Snow B, Marsh K. How useful are verbal autopsies to estimate childhood causes of death? Health Policy Plan 1992;7:22–29.

144. Marsh DR, Sadruddin S, Fikree FF, Krishnan C, Darmstadt GL. Validation of verbal autopsy to determine the cause of 137 neonatal deaths in Karachi, Pakistan. Paed Perinat Epidemiol 2003;17:132–142.

145. Shrivastava SP, Kumar A, Ojha AK. Verbal autopsy determined causes of neonatal deaths. Indian Pediatr 2001;38:1022–1025.

146. Weiner R, Ronsmans C, Dorman E, Jilo H, Muhoro A, Shulman C. Labour complications remain the most important risk factors for perinatal mortality in rural Kenya. Bull World Health Organ 2003;81:561–566.

147. Kulmala T, Vaahtera M, Rannikko J, et al. The relationship between antenatal risk characteristics, place of delivery and adverse delivery outcome in rural Malawi. Acta Obstet Gynecol Scand 2000;79:984–990.

148. Chalumeau M, Salanave B, Bouvier-Colle MH, De Bernis L, Prual A, Breart G. Risk factors for perinatal mortality in West Africa: a population-based study of 20326 pregnancies. Acta Paediatr 2000;89:1115–1121.

149. Child Health Research Project. Reducing perinatal and neonatal mortality. Volume 3, No. 1. Report of a meeting May 10–12, 1999. Baltimore, MD: Johns Hopkins University, 1999.

150. World Health Organization. The world health report 2001. Geneva: World Health Organization, 2001.

151. Koblinsky MA, Tinker A, Daly P. Programming for safe motherhood: a guide to action. Health Policy Plan 1994;9:252–266.

152. United Nations International Children's Emergency Fund. State of the world's children report 2001. New York: United Nations International Children's Emergency Fund, 2000.

153. Barros FC, Victora CG, Barros AJD, Santos IS, Albernaz E, Matijasevich A, Domingues MR, Sclowitz IKT, Hallal PC, Silveira MF, Vaughan JP. The challenge of reducing neonatal mortality in middle-income countries: findings from three Brazilian birth cohorts in 1982, 1993, and 2004. Lancet 2005;365: 847–854.

154. Lancet. The world's forgotten children (comment). Lancet 2003;361:1.

155. Working Group on Women and Child Health. Improving child health: the role of research. BMJ 2002;324:1444–1447.

156. Okeke IN, Laxminarayan R, Bhutta ZA, Duse AG, Jenkins P, O'Brien TF, Pablos-Mendez A, Klugman KP. Antimicrobial resistance in developing countries. Part I: recent trends and current status. Lancet Infect Dis 2005;5:481–493.

157. Okeke IN, Klugman KP, Bhutta ZA, Duse AG, Jenkins P, O'Brien TF, Pablos-Mendez A, Laxminarayan R. Antimicrobial resistance in developing countries. Part II: strategies for containment. Lancet Infect Dis 2005;5:568–580.

158. Rahmathullah L, Tielsch JM, Thulasiraj RD, Katz J, Coles C, Devi S, John R, Prakash K, Sadanand AV, Edwin N, Kamaraj C. Impact of supplementing newborn infants with vitamin A on early infant mortality: community based randomised trial in southern India. BMJ 2003;327:254–259.

159. Humphrey JH, Agoestina T, Wu L, Usman A, Nurachim M, Subardja D, Hidayat S, Tielsch J, West KP Jr, Sommer A. Impact of neonatal vitamin A supplementation on infant morbidity and mortality. J Pediatr 1996;128:489–496.

160. Humphrey JH, Iliff PJ, Marinda ET, Mutasa K, Moulton LH, Chidawanyika H, Ward BJ, Nathoo KJ, Malaba LC, Zijenah LS, Zvandasara P, Ntozini R, Mzengeza F, Mahomva AI, Ruff AJ, Mbizvo MT, Zunguza CD, ZVITAMBO Study Group. Effects of a single large dose of vitamin A, given during

the postpartum period to HIV-positive women and their infants, on child HIV infection, HIV-free survival, and mortality. J Infect Dis 2006;193:860–871.

161. Fawzi, WW, Msamanga GI, Hunter D, et al. Randomized trial of vitamin supplements in relation to transmission of HIV-1 through breastfeeding and early child mortality. AIDS 2002;16:1935–1944.

162. Tielsch JM, Darmstadt GL, Mullany LC, Khatry SK, Katz J, LeClerq SC, Shrestha S, Adhikari R. Impact of newborn skin-cleansing with chlorhexadine on neonatal mortality in southern Nepal: a community-based, cluster-randomized trial. Pediatrics 2007;76:725–731.

163. Taha TE, Biggar RJ, Broadhead RL, et al. Effect of cleaning the birth canal with antiseptic solution on maternal and newborn morbidity and mortality in Malawi. BMJ 1997;315:216–220.

164. Bakr AF, Karkour T. Effect of predelivery vaginal antisepsis on maternal and neonatal morbidity and mortality in Egypt. J Womens Health 2005;14:496–501.

165. Mullany LC, Darmstadt GL, Khatry SK, Katz J, LeClerq SC, Shrestha S, Adhikari R, Tielsch JM. Topical applications of chlorhexidine to the umbilical cord prevent omphalitis and neonatal mortality in southern Nepal: a community-based, cluster-randomized trial. Lancet 2006; 367:910–918.

166. Manandhar DS, Osrin D, Shrestha BP, Mesko N, Morrison J, Tumbahangphe KM, Tamang S, Thapa S, Shrestha D, Thapa B, Shrestha JR, Wade A, Borghi J, Standing H, Manandhar M, de L Costello AM, MIRA Makwanpur Trial Team. Effect of a participatory intervention with women's groups on birth outcomes in Nepal: cluster-randomised controlled trial. Lancet 2004;364:970–979.

167. Jokhio AH, Winter HR, Cheng KK. An intervention involving traditional birth attendants and perinatal and maternal mortality in Pakistan. N Engl J Med 2005;352:2091–2099.

168. Bang AT, Bang RA, Stoll BJ, Baitule SB, Reddy HM, Deshmukh MD. Is home-based diagnosis and treatment of neonatal sepsis feasible and effective? Seven years of intervention in the Gadchiroli field trial (1996 to 2003). J Perinatol 2005;25S:S62–S71.

169. Reddy MH, Bang AT. How to identify neonates at risk of death in rural India: clinical criteria for the risk approach. J Perinatol 2005;25S:S44–S50.

170. Bang AT, Reddy HM, Bang RA, Deshmukh MD. Why do neonates die in rural Gadchiroli, India? (Part II): estimating population attributable risks and contribution of multiple morbidities for identifying a strategy to prevent deaths. J Perinatol 2005;25S:S35–S43.

171. Bang AT, Bang RA. Background of the field trial of home-based neonatal care in Gadchiroli, India. J Perinatol 2005;25S:S3–S10.

172. Bang AT, Bang RA, Reddy HM. Home-based neonatal care: summary and applications of the field trial in rural Gadchiroli, India (1993 to 2003). J Perinatol 2005;25S:S108–S122.

173. Paul VK, Singh M. Regionalized perinatal care in developing countries. Semin Neonatal 2004; 9:117–124.

174. Adam T, Lim SS, Mehta S, Bhutta ZA, Fogstad H, Mathai M, Zupan J, Darmstadt GL. Cost effectiveness analysis of strategies for maternal and neonatal health in developing countries. BMJ 2005;331:1107–1110.

175. Barnett S, Nair N, Lewycka S, Costello A. Community interventions for maternal and perinatal health (commentary). Int J Obstet Gynaecol 2005;112:1170–1173.

176. Borghi J, Thapa B, Osrin D, Jan S, Morrison J, Tamang S, Shrestha BP, Wade A, Manandhar DS, de L Costello AM. Economic assessment of a women's group intervention to improve birth outcomes in rural Nepal. Lancet 2005;366:1882–1884.

177. Horton R. Newborn survival: putting children at the centre (comment). Lancet 2005;365:821–822.

178. Bryce J, Victora CG. Child survival: countdown to 2015 (comment). Lancet 2005;365:2153–2154.

179. Tinker A, ten Hoppe-Bender P, Azfar S, Bustreo F, Bell R. A continuum of care to save newborn lives (comment). Lancet 2005;365:822–825.

180. Dyer O. Goals to reduce poverty and infant mortality will be missed. News BMJ 2005;331:593.

181. Lancet Infectious Diseases. Poor shooting at the millennium development goals (editorial). Lancet Infect Dis 2005;5:529.

182. Child Mortality Coordination Group. Tracking progress towards the Millenium Development Goals: reaching consensus on child mortality levels and trends. Bull World Health Organ 2006; 84:225–232.

183. Lopez AD. Commentary: estimating the causes of child deaths. Int J Epidemiol 2003;32:1052–1053.

# 5    Child Growth and Development

*Mercedes de Onis*

## 5.1    INTRODUCTION

The quality of life of infants and young children, as opposed to mere survival, is becoming increasingly important. Most developing countries have experienced dramatic decreases in their infant and under-5 mortality rates over the last three decades. As greater numbers of children survive, it becomes critical to pay closer attention to children's ability to develop their full physical and mental potentials. This will in turn have important consequences in adult life.

Child growth is internationally recognized as the best global indicator of physical well-being in children because poor feeding practices—in both quantity and quality—and infections, or more often a combination of the two, are major factors that affect physical growth and mental development in children [1]. Poor child growth is the consequence of a range of factors that are closely linked to the overall standard of living and whether a population can meet its basic needs, such as access to food, housing, and health care. Child growth assessment thus not only serves as a means for evaluating the health and nutritional status of children but also provides an excellent measurement of the inequalities in health faced by populations. Based on this principle, internationally set health goals for this century will be assessed on the basis of improvements in the rates of underweight among children younger than 5 years [2].

There is strong evidence that poor physical growth is usually associated with deficient or delayed mental development [3], and a number of studies have demonstrated a relationship between growth status and school performance and intellectual achievement [4, 5]. The precise mechanism linking impaired growth and poor mental development is not known. The association cannot be regarded as a simple causal relationship because of the complex environmental factors that affect both growth and development; many socioeconomic disadvantages that coexist with stunting or underweight may also detrimentally affect mental development. It is possible that more than one mechanism act together. For example, nutritionally deprived children are often described as lethargic, possibly because they reduce their activity as a protective measure to conserve energy [6]. This reduced activity limits the child's ability for exploration and interaction and thus may have negative consequences for children's motor and cognitive development. Children who do not practice their existing skills may be less likely to acquire new skills. At the same time, the apathy these children exhibit could lead adults to treat them

From: *Nutrition and Health: Nutrition and Health in Developing Countries, Second Edition*
Edited by: R. D. Semba & M. W. Bloem © Humana Press, Totowa, NJ

differently from nonstunted children. Undernutrition could also have a direct effect on children's central nervous system. These complex relationships make it difficult to disentangle the exact mechanisms of the association between deficits in growth and poor mental development.

Impaired growth is ultimately a response to limited nutrient availability or utilization at the cellular level. Although in the past most of the attention has been directed toward the negative consequences associated with inadequate protein-energy intake, there is increasing recognition of the important role that micronutrient deficiency plays in children's growth and development. At severe levels of protein-energy deficiency, linear growth probably stops, and body reserves are used as energy and protein sources to maintain vital functions. At less-severe stages, however, it may be possible to cope by simply slowing the rate of linear growth and other compensatory mechanisms, such as reduced activity. The negative consequences of micronutrient deficiencies range from altered immunity and increased risk of infectious diseases and death to reduced growth and mental development [7].

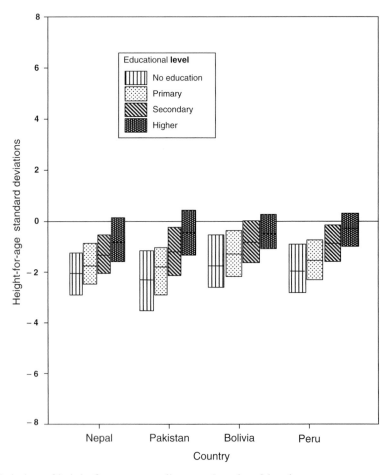

**Fig. 5.1.** Variation of height for age according to educational level.

Nutritional deficiencies in turn are deeply rooted in poverty and deprivation. Poverty breeds undernutrition, which in turn generates poverty in a vicious cycle that perpetuates across generations. The intrinsic links between poverty and nutrition have been reviewed in detail elsewhere [8]. Based on national-level data, Fig. 5.1 shows the effect of socioeconomic status on stunting (i.e., low height-for-age) for four countries in Asia and Latin America. These associations are consistent across those countries with similar dose-response relationship.

Regardless of the origin, the consequences of impaired growth and development in children can be long lasting and compromise academic performance and the ability to contribute to society. Most growth retardation occurs very early in life; the two periods of highest vulnerability are during intrauterine development and during the transition from reliance on breast milk to addition of other foods to the diet, generally beginning in the second 6 months of life [9]. In fact, almost all of the growth retardation documented in studies carried out in developing countries has its origin in the first 2 or 3 years of life [10]. Once present, growth retardation usually remains for life as growth deficits are generally not recuperated [11].

This chapter reviews concepts and indicators for measuring impaired fetal and child growth; describes the magnitude and geographical distribution of growth retardation in developing countries; discusses the links between fetal and child growth retardation; outlines the main health and social consequences of impaired growth in terms of morbidity, mortality, child development, and adult-life consequences; and reviews interventions aimed at promoting healthy growth and development.

## 5.2 MEASURING IMPAIRED GROWTH: CONCEPTS AND INDICATORS

Assessing childhood growth remains a mainstay of pediatric care in all settings, that is, in the most advanced health care centers and those faced with severe resource constraints. It is the most widespread approach for assessing body size, weight, composition, and proportions. It can be done inexpensively and noninvasively and is of inherent interest to caretakers responsible for children's welfare. Growth assessment's principal utility to health care stems from its screening value, such as assessing general well-being; identifying growth faltering and excessive growth; managing infant feeding; evaluating maternal lactation performance, the suitability of weaning practices, and related infant behaviours and the follow-up of children with medical conditions known to affect growth adversely (e.g., renal and cardiac patients). It is also useful for population health purposes, such as the assessment of community levels of over- and undernutrition, the prediction and ongoing assessments of feeding emergencies, and assessments of economic resource distribution.

### 5.2.1 Fetal Growth

Growth failure is a cumulative process that can begin in utero. Various criteria have been used to classify an infant as having experienced normal, subnormal, or supranormal growth in utero. An expert committee from the World Health Organization (WHO) recommended the tenth percentile of a birth-weight-for-gestational-age, sex-specific, single/twins risk curve for the classification of small for gestational age [1]. Strictly speaking, small-for-gestational-age infants are not synonymous to intrauterine growth restriction (IUGR); some small-for-gestational-age infants may merely represent the lower tail of the normal fetal growth distribution. In individual cases, however, it is usually very difficult to determine whether an observed birth weight that is low for gestational age is the result of true in utero growth restriction or represents a "normally small" infant. Classification of IUGR is therefore based on the established cutoff for small for gestational age. The higher the prevalence of infants small for gestational age in a given population, the greater the likelihood that small for gestational age is a result of IUGR [1].

Historically, because valid assessment of gestational age is often not available in developing countries, the incidence of low birth weight (LBW) has been used as a proxy to quantify the magnitude of IUGR in these settings. This approach, however, underestimates considerably the true magnitude of IUGR as it does not take into account those infants whose weight at birth falls below the tenth percentile but who weigh more than 2500 g; many of these infants are likely also to have IUGR [12]. It is thus important to improve the availability and quality of gestational age estimates on a population-wide basis in developing countries. This includes, if feasible, recording early in pregnancy the mother's recall of the date her last normal menstrual period began and the training of birth attendants in the physical assessment of the newborn. In developed countries, early ultrasound examination has improved the validity and reliability of gestational age assessment, although evidence from randomized trials did not demonstrate improvement in maternal or fetal/infant outcomes with routine early ultrasound [13].

The issue of which reference curve to use in assessing growth at birth has been a cause of debate. Based on the observations that children of well-off populations in developing countries experience similar growth patterns as those of healthy, well-nourished children in developed countries and that children of the same genetic background show differing growth performance depending on the environment in which they grow up, there is prevailing international consensus that children of all races have the same growth potential, and that country- or race-specific growth references are not advised [1]. Growth curves should certainly not be adjusted for factors that may be a cause of growth retardation. For example, making adjustments for the height of stunted parents in deprived populations could reinforce the wrong impression that children from these populations are born small for genetic reasons, and that not much can be done about this. On this basis, a group of international experts recommended that an international fetal growth reference curve should be developed based on pooled data from countries in different geographical regions where fetal growth is believed to be optimal [13].

There remain outstanding research questions in the classification and definition of IUGR. Although the use of a single, sex-specific international reference is justifiable, research is needed to assess whether infants of different genetic backgrounds born at a particular weight for gestational age are at substantially different risks for mortality and morbidity. Similarly, it would be important to determine whether infants who are born small because their mothers are primiparous or living at high altitude are at the same risk for adverse outcomes as those of equivalent size who are small because, for instance, their mothers are stunted, have preeclampsia, or are smokers. In addition, research is needed to base the criteria for defining IUGR on evidence of increased risk for important health outcomes, such as perinatal mortality. Because proportionality at birth may be related to adverse health outcomes [13, 14], an attempt should also be made to develop reference data and indicators for the classification of newborns as "wasted" and "stunted" and to quantifying the morbidity and mortality risks associated with these two types of infants.

### 5.2.2   Child Growth Indicators and Their Interpretation

In children, the three most commonly used indicators to assess growth status are weight-for-age, length/height-for-age, and weight-for-length/height. Weight-for-age is the most commonly applied and, for more than half of the world's countries, the sole anthropometric indicator used [15]. Although it is the easiest indicator to use when children's ages are known, weight-for-age lacks the biological specificity necessary to separate weight- from length/height-related deficits or excesses in growth. Conversely, length/height-for-age and weight-for-length/height permit the distinction of stunted, wasted, and overweight children and allow the appropriate targeting of interventions [16, 17]. The routine collection of length/height measurements (recumbent length up to 2 years of age and standing height for older children) is important because this enables the assessment of not only weight-for-height, but also body mass index (i.e., ratio of weight in kilograms to the square of height in meters), a valuable indicator proposed for monitoring the increasing public health problems of overweight and obesity in childhood [18].

The interpretation of the commonly used anthropometric indicators is as follows:

*Low weight-for-age*: Weight-for-age reflects body mass relative to chronological age. It is influenced by both the child's height (height-for-age) and weight (weight-for-height). Its composite nature makes interpretation complex. For example, weight-for-age fails to distinguish between short children of adequate body weight and tall, thin children. However, in the absence of significant wasting in a community, similar information is provided by weight-for-age and height-for-age in that both reflect an individual's or population's long-term health and nutritional experiences. Short-term changes, especially reductions in weight-for-age, reveal changes in weight-for-height. In general terms, the worldwide variation of low weight-for-age and its age distribution are similar to those of low height-for-age [19].

*Low height-for-age*: Stunted growth reflects a process of failure to reach linear growth potential as a result of suboptimal health or nutritional conditions. On a population basis, high levels of stunting are associated with poor socioeconomic conditions (Fig. 5.1) and increased risk of frequent and early exposure to adverse conditions such as illness or inappropriate feeding practices. Similarly, a decrease in the national stunting rate is usually indicative of improvements in overall socioeconomic conditions of a country [20]. The worldwide variation of the prevalence of low height-for-age is considerable, ranging from 5% to 65% among the less-developed countries [21]. In many such settings, prevalence starts to rise at about 3 months of age; the process of stunting slows at around 3 years of age, after which mean heights run parallel to the current international reference [10]. Therefore, the age modifies the interpretation of findings: For children in the age group below 2–3 years, low height-for-age probably reflects a continuing process of "failing to grow" or "stunting"; for older children, it reflects a state of "having failed to grow" or "being stunted." From the point of view of interventions, it is important to differentiate between these two groups.

*Low weight-for-height*: Wasting or thinness indicates in most cases a recent and severe process of weight loss, which is often associated with acute starvation or severe disease. However, wasting also may be the result of chronic unfavorable conditions. Provided there is no severe food shortage, the prevalence of wasting is usually below 5%, even in poor countries [19]. The Indian subcontinent, where a higher prevalence of wasting is found, is an important exception. A prevalence between 10% and 14% is regarded as serious and above or equal to 15% as critical [1]. Typically, the prevalence of low weight-for-height reaches a peak in the second year of life [19]. Lack of evidence of wasting in a population does not imply the absence of current nutritional problems: Stunting and other deficits may be present [22]. Given these characteristics wasting or thinness demands a careful assessment whenever it is encountered.

*High weight-for-height*: *Overweight* is the preferred term for describing high weight-for-height [1]. Even though there is a strong correlation between high weight-for-height and obesity as measured by adiposity, greater lean body mass can also contribute to high weight-for-height. On an individual basis, therefore, "fatness" or "obesity" should not be used to describe high weight-for-height. However, on a population-wide basis, high weight-for-height can be considered as an adequate indicator of obesity because the majority of individuals with high weight-for-height are obese. Strictly speaking, the term *obesity* should be used only in the context of adiposity measurements, for example, skinfold thickness.

Other available anthropometric indicators that are used to describe growth status during childhood include mid-upper arm circumference (MUAC), body mass index (BMI), skinfolds, and head circumference; however, none of these has achieved such widespread use as the height- and weight-based indicators mentioned due, in part, to the lack of widely acceptable pediatric reference data for their interpretation. For some of these measurements, technical difficulties result in high intra- and interindividual variation and require skilled individuals to perform the measurements accurately and precisely. For skinfolds, the cost of equipment also has precluded their wide application in children. MUAC-for-age has been proposed as an alternative indicator for use where the collection of height and weight measurements is difficult (e.g., refugee crises); however, its proper application requires the use of age-specific reference data for its accurate interpretation [1]. Its use also requires the ascertainment of age, an important drawback under difficult field conditions.

### 5.2.3 The International Reference Population

The designation of a child as having impaired growth implies some means of comparison with a "reference" child of the same age and sex. Thus, in practical terms, anthropometric values need to be compared across individuals or populations in relation to an acceptable set of reference values. This need has made the choice of a growth reference population an important issue that has received considerable attention in the last decades.

The international reference growth curves, the so-called National Center for Health Statistics (NCHS)/WHO international reference population, were formulated in the 1970s by combining growth data from two distinct data sets. All samples consisted of healthy, well-nourished US children as the curves were originally planned to serve as a reference for the United States. A detailed account of the historical background of the NCHS/WHO growth charts can be found elsewhere [23].

WHO adopted the reference curves of the NCHS for international use in the late 1970s based on the then-growing evidence that the growth patterns of well-fed, healthy preschool children from diverse ethnic backgrounds are very similar [23]. The adoption by WHO of the NCHS-based growth curves resulted in their wide international dissemination. Throughout the 1980s, several microcomputer-based software versions of the NCHS/WHO international growth reference were developed and supported by the Centers for Disease Control and Prevention (CDC) and WHO. These software-based references have contributed to the wide acceptance of the concept of the international growth reference because they simplified the handling of anthropometric data from surveys, surveillance, and clinical studies.

Although the NCHS/WHO international growth curves have served many useful purposes throughout these years, because of a number of serious drawbacks, the suitability of these curves for international purposes was challenged in the mid-1990s [1, 24]. Work conducted by WHO demonstrated that the NCHS/WHO international reference is sufficiently flawed that it interferes with the sound health and nutritional management of infants and young children. These flaws arise from both technical and biological considerations. In particular, the current international reference may lead to the early introduction of complementary foods in exclusively breast-fed infants, which often has adverse consequences for the health and nutritional well-being of infants [25, 26]. As a result, WHO began planning in 1994 for new references that reflect how children *should* grow in all countries rather than merely describing how they grew at a particular time and place [27, 28].

The WHO Multicentre Growth Reference Study (MGRS) (1997–2003) collected primary growth data and related information from 8,440 affluent children from widely differing ethnic backgrounds and cultural settings (Brazil, Ghana, India, Norway, Oman, and United States) [29]. The MGRS combined a longitudinal study from birth to 24 months with a cross-sectional study of children aged 18 to 71 months. In the longitudinal study, mothers and newborns were screened and enrolled at birth and visited at home a total of 21 times on weeks 1, 2, 4, and 6; monthly from 2 to 12 months; and bimonthly in the second year. Data were collected on anthropometry; motor development; feeding practices; child morbidity; perinatal factors; and socioeconomic, demographic, and environmental characteristics [29]. The new WHO growth curves based on these data represent the best description of physiological growth and establish the breast-fed infant as the biological norm for growth and development.

## 5.2.4  Issues in the Interpretation of Growth Data

One essential consideration is the appropriate use of the reference data. The way in which a reference is interpreted and the clinical and public health decisions that will be based on it are as important as the choice of the reference. The reference should be used as a general guide for screening and monitoring and not as a fixed standard that can be applied in a rigid fashion to individuals from different ethnic, socioeconomic, and nutritional and health backgrounds. For clinical or individual-based application, reference values should be used as a screening tool to detect individuals at greater risk of health or nutritional disorders, and they should not be viewed as a self-sufficient diagnostic tool.

For population-based application, the reference values should be used for comparison and monitoring purposes. In a given population, a high prevalence of anthropometric deficit will be indicative of significant health and nutritional problems. However, it is not only those individuals below the cutoff point who are at risk; the entire population is at risk, and the cutoff point should be used only to facilitate the application of the indicator [30].

There are three different systems by which a child or a group of children can be compared to the reference population: Z-scores (standard deviation [SD] scores), percentiles, and percent of median. For population-based assessment (including surveys and nutritional surveillance), the Z-score is widely recognized as the best system for analysis and presentation of anthropometric data because of its advantages compared to the other methods [1]. At the individual level, however, although there is substantial recognition that the Z-score is the most appropriate descriptor of malnutrition, health and nutrition centers (e.g., supplementary feeding programmes in refugee camps) have been in practice reluctant to adopt its use for individual assessment. A detailed description of the three systems, including a discussion of their strengths and weaknesses, can be found elsewhere [31].

In clinical applications, children are commonly classified using a cutoff value, often ≤ 2 and ≥ 2 Z-scores. The rationale for this is the statistical definition of the central 95% of a distribution as the "normal" range, which is not necessarily based on the optimal point for predicting functional outcomes. A better approach to classifying individual children would be to base the cutoffs on the relationship between growth deficits and health outcomes, such as mortality, morbidity, and child development [30]. The difficulty of this approach is that these relationships differ according to the prevalence of health and nutritional disorders, and thus it would be more advisable to develop practical methods for identifying local cutoffs that take account of local circumstances.

For population-based applications, a major advantage of the Z-score system is that a group of Z-scores can be subjected to summary statistics such as the mean and SD. The mean Z-score, although less commonly used, has the advantage of describing the nutritional status of the entire population directly without resorting to a subset of individuals below a set cutoff. A mean Z-score significantly lower than zero (the expected value for the reference distribution) usually means that the entire distribution has shifted downward, suggesting that most, if not all, individuals have been affected. Using the mean Z-score as an index of severity for health and nutrition problems results in increased awareness that, if a condition is severe, an intervention is required for the entire community, not just those who are classified as "malnourished" by the cutoff criteria [30, 32]. In addition, the observed SD value of the Z-score distribution is very useful for assessing data quality [1].

Last, experience with population surveillance has contributed to emphasizing the usefulness of identifying prevalence ranges to assess the severity of a situation as the basis for making public health decisions. For example, when 10% of a population is below the −2 SD cutoff for weight-for-height, is that too much, too little, or average? The intention of the so-called trigger levels is to assist in answering this question by giving some kind of guideline for the purpose of establishing levels of public health importance of a situation. Such classifications are very helpful for summarizing prevalence data and can be used for targeting purposes when establishing intervention priorities. It is

Table 5.1
Classification for assessing severity of growth deficits by prevalence ranges among children under 5 years of age

| Indicator | Severity of growth deficits by prevalence ranges (%) | | | |
|---|---|---|---|---|
| | Low | Medium | High | Very high |
| Stunting | <20 | 20–29 | 30–39 | ≥40 |
| Underweight | <10 | 10–19 | 20–29 | ≥30 |
| Wasting | <5 | 5–9 | 10–14 | ≥15 |

Source: Adapted with permission from [1].

important to note that the trigger levels vary according to the different anthropometric indicators. The prevalence ranges shown in Table 5.1 are those currently recommended [1] to classify levels of stunting, underweight, and wasting.

## 5.3. PREVALENCE OF GROWTH RETARDATION IN DEVELOPING COUNTRIES

An analysis using data from the WHO Global Database on Low Birth Weight quantified the magnitude of IUGR in different countries and regions of the world [12]. As summarized in Table 5.2, it is estimated that about 13.7 million babies in developing countries are already malnourished at birth, representing 11% (ranging from 1.9% to 20.9%) of all newborns in these countries. This rate is considerably higher than that estimated for developed countries (approximately 2%). Overall, the incidence of IUGR-LBW is about six times higher in developing than in developed countries [33]. The estimates of IUGR-LBW, however, greatly underestimate the magnitude of fetal growth retardation; the actual incidence of IUGR could be considerably higher. For example, if the rates of infants below the tenth percentile of the birth-weight-for-gestational-age reference curve are considered, 23.8% or approximately 30 million newborns per year would be affected (Table 5.2). There are nevertheless some healthy infants with birth weights below the tenth percentile, who represent the lower tail of a fetal growth distribution. However, in most developing countries a large proportion of newborns suffers from some degree of IUGR, as illustrated by the overall downward shift of the birth weight distribution. Unfortunately, a methodology to disentangle these two groups is not available. The risk of being born malnourished is highest in Asia, followed by Africa. Taking into consideration the number of total live births in each geographical region, nearly 75% of all affected newborns are born in Asia (mainly South-central Asia), 20% in Africa, and about 5% in Latin America [12].

Although there are constraints to deriving these estimates, mainly related to the qualitative and quantitative limitations of the available data, they still represent a valid approximation for descriptive and epidemiological purposes. These estimates confirm that IUGR is a major public health problem worldwide. In many countries, the high rates of impaired fetal growth exceed the recommended levels for triggering public health action [12]. A prevalence of IUGR in excess of 20% has been recommended as the cutoff point; in the absence of information on gestational age, a prevalence above 15% of LBW may be used as a proxy cutoff [1]. Population-wide interventions aimed at preventing fetal growth retardation are urgently needed in these high-prevalence countries.

Table 5.2
Summary estimates of impaired fetal growth in developing countries

| Indicator | Source | Rate (%) | Total number newborns affected per year[a] (in millions) |
|---|---|---|---|
| IUGR-LBW (<2,500 g; ≥ 37- week gestation) | Live births weighted average using LBW rates from WHO databank and regression model WHO databank and regression model | 11.0 (1.9–20.9)[b] | 13.699 |
| LBW (<2,500 g; all gestational ages) | Live births weighted average using LBW rates from WHO databank | 16.4 (5.8–28.3) | 20.423 |
| IUGR (<tenth percentile; all gestational ages) | From WHO Collaborative Study on Maternal Anthropometry and Pregnancy Outcomes | 23.8 (9.4–54.2) | 29.639 |

Source: Adapted with permission from [12].
IUGR intrauterine growth restriction, LBW low birth weight, WHO World Health Organization
[a] Total live births are based on the United Nations World Population Prospects.
[b] Range.

The WHO Global Database on Child Growth and Malnutrition [19] compiles data on height-for-age, weight-for-age, and weight-for-height of preschool children worldwide to monitor global progress in combating childhood malnutrition. The rigorous methodology and large coverage of the Global Database permits an accurate description of the magnitude and geographical distribution of child growth retardation in developing countries. At present, the Global Database covers over 95% of the total population of those under 5 years old (about 510 million children) living in developing countries or 84% of this age group worldwide. Based on this vast amount of data, Fig. 5.2 displays the geographical distribution of countries according to their prevalence of underweight [34]. Prevalences have been grouped according to the recommended trigger levels of public health importance (Table 5.1). The disaggregation by sex shows no consistent differences between male and female; however, prevalence rates are consistently higher in rural than in urban areas and can vary considerably by age and region within countries. Detailed information on national surveys concerning data disaggregated by age, sex, urban/rural residence, and region can be found in the Web site of the Global Database (www.who.int/nutgrowthdb).

Tables 5.3 and 5.4 present regional and global trends (1990–2005) for the prevalence and number of stunted and underweight children under 5 years old, respectively [35]. There was global progress in the reduction of child malnutrition during the 1990s, with stunting and underweight prevalence declining from 34% to 27% and 27% to 22%, respectively (Tables 5.3 and 5.4). The largest decline was achieved in eastern Asia, where stunting and underweight levels decreased by one half between 1990 and 2000.

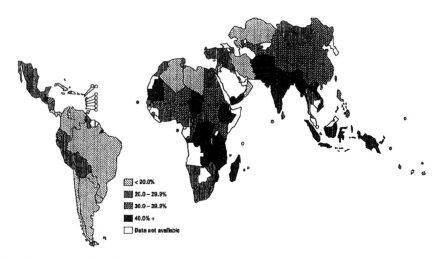

**Fig. 5.2.** 1 Percent with weight 2 standard deviations below the mean weight-for-age reference population.

Southeastern Asia also experienced substantial improvements, with stunting rates declining from 42% to 32% and underweight from 35% to 27%. South-central Asia continued to suffer from staggeringly high levels of child malnutrition, but rates were showing significant declines in stunting, from 51% to 40% and underweight from 50% to 41% during this period. Substantial improvements were also made in Latin America and the Caribbean, where a relative decrease of 25% in stunting (from 18% to 14%) and one third in underweight (from 9% to 6 %) occurred over the last 10 years of the time period. In Africa, however, there was little or no change in the last decade, and 35% and 24% of all those under 5 remained stunted and underweight, respectively. The actual number of malnourished children in Africa increased between 1990 and 2000, from 40 million to 45 million stunted and 25 million to 31 million underweight. The lack of progress observed in Africa was likely to be partly due to the effect of the HIV/AIDS epidemic. The disease has both direct and indirect effects: Infected children are more likely to be underweight, but also AIDS orphans or children of parents affected by AIDS are at increased risk of becoming malnourished. In sub-Saharan Africa, an estimated 333,000 children below 5 years of age died in 1999 with HIV infection [36], and 11 million were estimated to be orphaned because of AIDS [37]. The predictions of stunting and underweight made for 2005 might have been underestimates if the HIV/AIDS epidemic worsened in Africa or other regions.

An analysis forecasted trends of underweight to identify geographical regions unlikely to achieve the Millennium Development Goal of a 50% decrease in the 1990 prevalence by 2015 [34]. The authors concluded that an overall improvement in the global situation is anticipated; however, neither the world as a whole nor the developing regions are expected to achieve the goal. This is largely due to the deteriorating situation in Africa, where all subregions except northern Africa are expected to fail to meet the goal (Fig. 5.3).

The overall reduction in the prevalence of underweight is consistent with the increasing rates in childhood overweight observed in many developing countries. A global analysis in 1995 showed a rising trend in childhood overweight in 16 of 38 developing countries with more than one national survey [38]. Figure 5.4 presents trends in selected

Table 5.3

Estimated prevalence and numbers of stunted preschool children 1990–2005 with 95% confidence intervals by United Nations (UN) regions and subregions

| UN regions and subregions | Stunting (%) | | | | Numbers of stunted (in millions) | | | |
|---|---|---|---|---|---|---|---|---|
| | 1990 | 1995 | 2000 | 2005 | 1990 | 1995 | 2000 | 2005 |
| Africa | 36.9 | 36.1 | 35.2 | 34.5 | 39.6 | 41.9 | 45.1 | 48.5 |
| | 33.3–40.5 | 33.0–39.1 | 32.5–38.0 | 31.7–37.4 | 35.7–43.5 | 38.4–45.5 | 41.6–48.7 | 44.5–52.6 |
| Eastern | 44.4 | 44.4 | 44.4 | 44.4 | 15.8 | 17.3 | 19.4 | 21.6 |
| | 36.6–52.4 | 37.3–51.8 | 37.6–51.4 | 37.6–51.4 | 13.0–18.7 | 14.5–20.2 | 16.5–22.5 | 18.3–25.0 |
| Middle | 42.2 | 40.0 | 37.8 | 35.8 | 5.6 | 6.3 | 6.8 | 7.4 |
| | 34.2–50.5 | 34.0–46.2 | 33.7–42.1 | 33.0–38.6 | 4.5–6.7 | 5.4–7.3 | 6.0–7.6 | 6.9–8.0 |
| Northern | 27.4 | 24.4 | 21.7 | 19.1 | 5.8 | 5.1 | 4.6 | 4.2 |
| | 21.1–34.7 | 18.7–31.2 | 16.1–28.6 | 13.5–26.5 | 4.5–7.4 | 3.9–6.5 | 3.4–6.1 | 2.9–5.8 |
| Southern | 25.4 | 25.0 | 24.6 | 24.3 | 1.5 | 1.4 | 1.5 | 1.4 |
| | 23.7–27.1 | 22.6–27.6 | 21.5–28.1 | 20.4–28.6 | 1.4–1.6 | 1.3–1.6 | 1.3–1.7 | 1.2–1.7 |
| Western | 34.7 | 33.8 | 32.9 | 32.0 | 10.9 | 11.8 | 12.7 | 13.9 |
| | 28.7–41.2 | 29.9–37.9 | 30.2–35.7 | 28.4–35.7 | 9.0–13.0 | 10.4–13.2 | 11.7–13.8 | 12.4–15.5 |
| Asia | 41.1 | 35.4 | 30.1 | 25.7 | 154.6 | 130.8 | 109.4 | 92.4 |
| | 38.6–43.6 | 32.6–38.2 | 27.1–33.1 | 22.5–28.9 | 145.1–164.1 | 120.5–141.0 | 98.6–120.2 | 80.9–103.8 |
| Eastern | 30.0 | 21.5 | 14.8 | 10.0 | 37.5 | 23.5 | 15.2 | 9.5 |
| | 28.7–31.3 | 20.4–22.6 | 13.9–15.8 | 9.3–10.7 | 35.9–39.1 | 22.3–24.7 | 14.3–16.1 | 8.8–10.2 |
| South-central | 50.8 | 45.2 | 39.7 | 34.5 | 88.0 | 81.0 | 71.5 | 63.5 |
| | 46.1–55.4 | 40.2–50.3 | 34.4–45.3 | 29.0–40.5 | 79.9–96.0 | 72.0–90.2 | 62.0–81.6 | 53.3–74.4 |
| Southeastern | 41.8 | 36.8 | 32.1 | 27.7 | 23.9 | 21.3 | 18.1 | 15.3 |
| | 33.6–50.4 | 29.3–44.9 | 25.2–39.7 | 21.3–35.1 | 19.2–28.8 | 17.0–26.0 | 14.3–22.5 | 11.8–19.4 |
| Western | 25.0 | 21.7 | 18.7 | 16.1 | 5.2 | 5.0 | 4.5 | 4.1 |
| | 20.2–30.4 | 15.1–30.1 | 10.9–30.1 | 7.8–30.3 | 4.2–6.3 | 3.5–6.9 | 2.7–7.3 | 2.0–7.8 |
| Latin America and Caribbean | 18.3 | 15.9 | 13.7 | 11.8 | 10.0 | 8.8 | 7.6 | 6.5 |
| | 13.6–23.0 | 11.3–20.5 | 9.1–18.4 | 7.0–16.5 | 7.4–12.6 | 6.2–11.3 | 5.0–10.2 | 3.9–9.2 |

| Region | | | | | | | |
|---|---|---|---|---|---|---|---|
| Caribbean | 12.4 (6.8–21.5) | 9.6 (5.1–17.3) | 7.4 (3.8–14.1) | 5.7 (2.7–11.5) | 0.5 (0.3–0.9) | 0.4 (0.2–0.7) | 0.3 (0.1–0.5) | 0.2 (0.1–0.4) |
| Central America | 25.9 (16.3–38.4) | 23.0 (14.4–34.8) | 20.4 (12.5–31.5) | 18.0 (10.8–28.4) | 4.0 (2.5–5.9) | 3.7 (2.3–5.6) | 3.3 (2.0–5.1) | 2.9 (1.8–4.6) |
| South America | 15.7 (10.8–22.2) | 13.3 (8.6–20.0) | 11.3 (6.5–18.9) | 9.6 (4.9–18.2) | 5.5 (3.8–7.8) | 4.7 (3.0–7.1) | 4.0 (2.3–6.7) | 3.4 (1.7–6.5) |
| Oceania | n/a | n/a | 29.3 (7.9–66.7) | n/a | n/a | n/a | 0.32 (0.09–0.72) | n/a |
| All developing countries | 37.9 (35.9–39.8) | 33.5 (31.4–35.6) | 29.6 (27.5–31.7) | 26.5 (24.2–28.7) | 204.3 (193.7–214.9) | 181.5 (170.4–192.7) | 162.1 (150.4–173.8) | 147.5 (135.0–159.9) |
| Developed countries | 2.8 (0.8–9.1) | 2.8 (0.8–8.9) | 2.7 (0.8–8.7) | 2.6 (0.8–8.4) | 2.2 (0.7–7.1) | 2.0 (0.6–6.4) | 1.8 (0.5–5.7) | 1.6 (0.5–5.2) |
| Global | 33.5 (29.5–44.9) | 29.9 (23.0–40.0) | 26.7 (17.4–35.5) | 24.1 (12.9–31.4) | 206.5 (195.7–217.2) | 183.5 (172.2–194.8) | 163.9 (152.1–175.7) | 149.1 (136.6–161.6) |

*Source*: Adapted with permission from [35].
*n/a* not available due to insufficient data

Table 5.4

Estimated prevalence and numbers of underweight preschool children 1990–2005 with 95% confidence intervals by United Nation (UN) regions and subregions

| UN regions and subregions | Underweight (%) | | | | Numbers of underweight (in millions) | | | |
|---|---|---|---|---|---|---|---|---|
| | 1990 | 1995 | 2000 | 2005 | 1990 | 1995 | 2000 | 2005 |
| Africa | 23.6 | 23.9 | 24.2 | 24.5 | 25.3 | 27.8 | 30.9 | 34.5 |
| | 21.0–26.2 | 21.5–26.3 | 21.9–26.4 | 22.1–26.8 | 22.6–28.1 | 25.0–30.6 | 28.0–33.8 | 31.1–37.8 |
| Eastern | 26.7 | 27.9 | 29.2 | 30.6 | 9.5 | 10.9 | 12.8 | 14.8 |
| | 22.0–32.0 | 23.3–33.0 | 24.6–34.3 | 25.7–35.8 | 7.8–11.4 | 9.1–12.9 | 10.8–15.0 | 12.5–17.4 |
| Middle | 27.8 | 26.9 | 26.1 | 25.3 | 3.7 | 4.2 | 4.7 | 5.3 |
| | 19.8–37.5 | 21.0–33.8 | 21.8–30.8 | 21.6–29.3 | 2.6–5.0 | 3.3–5.3 | 3.9–5.5 | 4.5–6.1 |
| Northern | 12.3 | 10.9 | 9.7 | 8.6 | 2.6 | 2.3 | 2.1 | 1.9 |
| | 7.4–19.6 | 5.9–19.4 | 4.6–19.4 | 3.6–19.5 | 1.6–4.1 | 1.2–4.1 | 1.0–4.2 | 0.8–4.3 |
| Southern | 14.0 | 13.9 | 13.7 | 13.6 | 0.8 | 0.8 | 0.8 | 0.8 |
| | 9.9–19.5 | 9.8–19.2 | 9.7–19.0 | 9.6–18.8 | 0.6–1.1 | 0.6–1.1 | 0.6–1.2 | 0.6–1.1 |
| Western | 27.8 | 27.5 | 27.1 | 26.8 | 8.8 | 9.6 | 10.5 | 11.7 |
| | 23.6–32.4 | 24.2–31.0 | 24.2–30.3 | 23.6–30.3 | 7.4–10.2 | 8.4–10.8 | 9.4–11.7 | 10.3–13.2 |
| Asia | 35.1 | 31.5 | 27.9 | 24.8 | 131.9 | 116.3 | 101.2 | 89.2 |
| | 31.7–38.5 | 27.8–35.1 | 24.0–31.7 | 20.8–28.8 | 119.2–144.7 | 102.7–129.8 | 87.3–115.0 | 74.9–103.5 |
| Eastern | 18.5 | 13.2 | 9.3 | 6.5 | 23.1 | 14.5 | 9.5 | 6.1 |
| | 17.6–19.4 | 12.5–13.9 | 8.8–9.9 | 6.1–6.9 | 22.0–24.2 | 13.7–15.3 | 9.0–10.1 | 5.7–6.5 |
| South-central | 49.6 | 45.2 | 40.8 | 36.5 | 86.0 | 80.9 | 73.4 | 67.1 |
| | 42.4–56.8 | 37.9–52.6 | 33.5–48.5 | 29.3–44.4 | 73.5–98.5 | 67.9–94.3 | 60.3–87.3 | 53.9–81.5 |
| Southeastern | 35.2 | 31.2 | 27.4 | 23.9 | 20.2 | 18.1 | 15.5 | 13.2 |
| | 30.8–40.0 | 27.1–35.6 | 23.4–31.8 | 19.9–28.5 | 17.6–22.9 | 15.7–20.7 | 13.2–18.0 | 11.0–15.7 |
| Western | 12.9 | 12.1 | 11.3 | 10.6 | 2.7 | 2.8 | 2.8 | 2.7 |
| | 9.9–16.7 | 7.3–19.4 | 5.0–23.7 | 3.3–28.9 | 2.1–3.5 | 1.7–4.5 | 1.2–5.8 | 0.9–7.5 |
| Latin America and Caribbean | 8.7 | 7.3 | 6.1 | 5.0 | 4.8 | 4.0 | 3.4 | 2.8 |
| | 6.1–11.3 | 5.0–9.6 | 4.0–8.1 | 3.2–6.8 | 3.4–6.2 | 2.8–5.3 | 2.2–4.5 | 1.8–3.8 |

| | | | | | | | | |
|---|---|---|---|---|---|---|---|---|
| Caribbean | 10.0 | 7.8 | 6.1 | 4.7 | 0.4 | 0.3 | 0.2 | 0.2 |
| | 5.9–16.4 | 4.5–13.3 | 3.3–10.8 | 2.5–8.7 | 0.2–0.7 | 0.2–0.5 | 0.1–0.4 | 0.1–0.3 |
| Central America | 12.4 | 10.7 | 9.2 | 7.9 | 1.9 | 1.7 | 1.5 | 1.3 |
| | 7.5–19.9 | 6.3–17.6 | 5.2–15.7 | 4.3–14.0 | 1.2–3.1 | 1.0–2.8 | 0.9–2.6 | 0.7–2.3 |
| South America | 7.0 | 5.7 | 4.6 | 3.7 | 2.5 | 2.0 | 1.6 | 1.3 |
| | 4.5–10.8 | 3.6–8.9 | 2.9–7.4 | 2.3–6.1 | 1.6–3.8 | 1.3–3.1 | 1.0–2.6 | 0.8–2.2 |
| Oceania | n/a | n/a | n/a | n/a | n/a | n/a | n/a | n/a |
| All developing countries | 30.1 | 27.3 | 24.8 | 22.7 | 162.2 | 148.2 | 135.5 | 126.5 |
| | 27.6–32.5 | 24.8–29.9 | 22.2–27.3 | 20.1–25.4 | 149.1–175.3 | 134.4–162.0 | 121.3–149.7 | 111.8–141.2 |
| Developed countries | 1.6 | 1.4 | 1.3 | 1.1 | 1.2 | 1.0 | 0.8 | 0.7 |
| | 0.8–3.0 | 0.6–3.2 | 0.5–3.5 | 0.3–3.7 | 0.6–2.4 | 0.4–2.3 | 0.3–2.3 | |
| Global | 26.5 | 24.3 | 22.2 | 20.6 | 163.4 | 149.2 | 136.4 | 127.2 |
| | 24.3–28.6 | 22.1–26.6 | 19.9–24.5 | 18.2–22.9 | 150.3–176.6 | 135.3–163.1 | 122.2–150.6 | 112.5–141.9 |

*Source*: Adapted with permission from [35].

n/a not available due to insufficient data

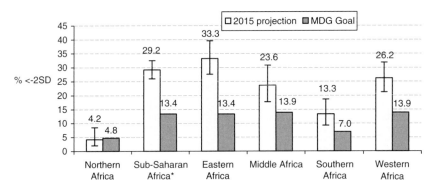

**Fig. 5.3.** Projections of underweight with 95% confidence intervals in African subregions in 2015 compared to Millennium Development Goal (MDG).

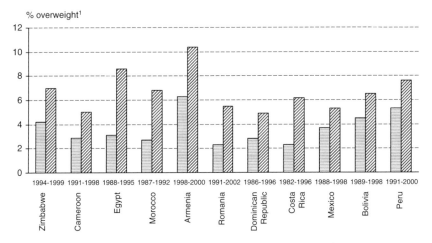

**Fig. 5.4.** Trends of child overweight in selected developing countries.[1]*Overweight* is defined as weight for height above two standard deviations of the National Center for Health Statistics/World Health Organization reference median value. (Adapted with permission from [39].)

developing countries based on national surveys included in the WHO Global Database on Child Growth and Malnutrition [39]. The comparison of both ends of the weight-for-height distribution suggest a population-wide shift, with overweight replacing wasting as countries undergo the nutrition transition [38]. Because of this transition, indicators of malnutrition based on weight will be more complex to interpret, and stunting will increasingly provide a more accurate indication of undernutrition than will underweight.

## 5.4 HEALTH AND SOCIAL CONSEQUENCES OF IMPAIRED GROWTH

The health and social consequences of the current high prevalences of fetal and child growth retardation in developing countries are severe. Fetuses suffering from growth retardation have higher perinatal morbidity and mortality [14, 40, 41], are at an increased risk of sudden infant death syndrome [42], and have higher infant mortality and childhood morbidity [43]. During childhood, they are more likely to have poor cognitive development [44, 45] and neurologic impairment [46–48]; in adulthood, they are at increased risk of cardiovascular disease [49], high blood pressure [50], obstructive lung disease [51], diabetes [52], high cholesterol concentrations [53], and renal damage [54]. Newborns with IUGR have lower levels of insulin-like growth factor 1 and higher growth hormone levels [55], indicating an endocrine process that could be related to these long-term impairments.

The major outcomes of poor growth during childhood can be classified in terms of mortality, morbidity (incidence and severity), and psychological and intellectual development. There are also important consequences in adult life in terms of body size, work and reproductive performances, and risk of chronic diseases.

A number of studies have demonstrated the association between increasing severity of anthropometric deficits and mortality [30]. It is now recognized that growth retardation has a far more powerful impact on child mortality than has been traditionally recognized, which in turn has important implications for policy and programs addressing child survival [56]. An analysis documented that the risk of mortality because of low weight-for-age was elevated for each cause of death and for all-cause mortality [57]. Overall, 52.5% of all deaths in young children were attributable to undernutrition, varying from 44.8% for deaths because of measles to 60.7% for deaths due to diarrhea [57]. The majority of deaths were caused by the potentiating effect of mild-to-moderate low weight-for-age as opposed to severe low weight-for-age. Thus, strategies that focus only on severely malnourished children will be insufficient to improve child survival in a meaningful way. The most significant impact can be expected when all grades of severity are targeted. Similarly, children suffering from impaired growth tend to have more severe diarrhoeal episodes and are more susceptible to several infectious diseases frequently seen in developing countries, such as malaria or meningitis [58, 59] (Fig. 5.5). The risk of pneumonia is also increased in these children [60].

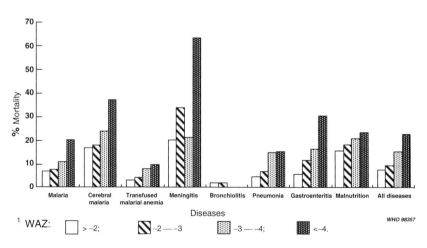

**Fig. 5.5.** Mortality of malaria, cerebral malaria, transfused malaria anemia, meningitis, bronchiolitis, pneumonia, gastroenteritis, malnutrition, and all diseases combined by weight for age (WAZ) expressed as z-score on admission.[1] (Adapted with permission from [59].)

There is strong evidence that poor growth is associated with impaired development [3, 5], and a number of studies have demonstrated a relationship between growth status and school performance and intellectual achievement [4]. Child stunting leads to significant reduction in adult size [4]; one of the main consequences of small adult size resulting from stunting during childhood is reduced work capacity [61], which in turn has an impact on economic productivity. For women, maternal size is associated with specific reproductive outcomes. Data from the Guatemalan Longitudinal Study [4] showed how the percentage of women with short stature varies strikingly according to the degree of stunting at 3 years of age. As shown in Fig. 5.6, 65% of the girls severely stunted at age of 3 had short stature when they became adults. Short women are at a greater risk for obstetric complications because of smaller pelvic size [1]. There is also a strong association between maternal height and birth weight [62]. This results in an intergenerational effect since LBW babies are themselves likely to have anthropometric deficits at later ages [63, 64]. These LBW babies, born to stunted mothers, contribute to closing the intergenerational cycle by which low maternal size and anemia predispose to LBW babies, which in turn predisposes to growth failure of children, leading back to small adults (Fig. 5.7). Also, the occurrence of early pregnancy will contribute both in terms of LBW and inducing premature cessation of growth in the mother. The implications of this vicious cycle are enormous for the human and socioeconomic development of the affected populations.

In summary, the magnitude of the problem and the severity of the health and social consequences associated with impaired growth cannot be overemphasized. Child growth is a major determinant of human development. There is thus an urgent need to develop or identify effective community-based interventions for improving child growth and development. Population-wide interventions aimed at preventing IUGR are also urgently

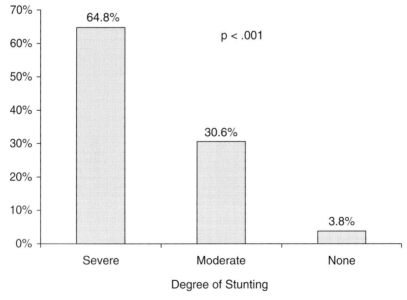

**Fig. 5.6.** Prevalence of short stature (<149 cm) in Guatemalan women (≥18 years) by degree of stunting at 3 years of age. (Adapted with permission from [4].)

Intergenerational cycle of growth failure

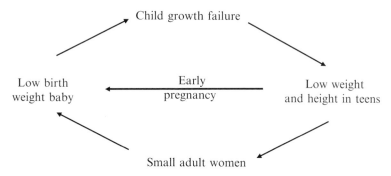

**Fig. 5.7.** Intergenerational cycle of growth failure.

required given the strong association between pre- and postnatal growth and the magnitude of fetal growth retardation in developing countries.

## 5.5 INTERVENTIONS AIMED AT PROMOTING HEALTHY GROWTH AND DEVELOPMENT

A comprehensive review of the evidence from 126 randomized controlled trials (RCTs) evaluating 36 prenatal interventions aimed at preventing or treating impaired fetal growth was carried out by Gülmezoglu et al. [65]. The same authors provided an in-depth analysis of nutritional interventions evaluated in RCTs [66]. RCTs are widely recognized as the most objective and rigorous available method to evaluate the effectiveness of health care interventions. Systematic reviews of RCTs provide an excellent tool for summarizing the results of interventions. By following a rigorous methodology, they reduce bias, improve reliability and accuracy of conclusions, and can establish if trial results are consistent and generalizable across populations, settings, and treatment variations. The strategies evaluated by Gülmezoglu et al. [65] included care and advice during pregnancy (e.g., social support for women at risk, strategies to stop smoking, nutritional advice); nutrition supplementation (e.g., protein-energy, vitamin and minerals, antianemic supplements, fish oil supplementation); and prevention/treatment of hypertensive disorders, fetal compromise, and infections.

Based on this review, only 2 of 24 nonnutritional interventions (i.e., strategies to reduce maternal smoking and antimalarial chemoprophylaxis in primigravidae) provided evidence they were beneficial (Table 5.5). Strategies to reduce smoking during pregnancy were associated with increased birth weight and lower rate of term LBW (typical odds ratio 0.80; 95% confidence interval [CI] 0.65–0.98). These effects have been greater in more compliant groups, and those groups who were more successful in stopping smoking showed the highest mean birth weight gains. The systematic review of the use of antimalarial drug chemoprophylaxis showed that malaria chemoprophylaxis was associated with higher maternal hemoglobin levels and birth weights. These effects were more prominent in primigravidae, who are known to be more susceptible.

Only 1 of the 12 nutritional interventions (i.e., balanced protein-energy supplementation) showed a reduction in the incidence of IUGR [65, 66]. Supplementation was

Table 5.5

Forms of care likely to be beneficial and forms of care of unknown effectiveness that merit further research for the prevention or treatment of impaired fetal growth

| Intervention | IFG outcome | Effect[a] | Comments |
|---|---|---|---|
| Forms of care likely to be beneficial | | | |
| Smoking cessation | Term LBW | 0.80 (0.65–0.98) | Effect stronger in more compliant women; intervention in agreement with overall health advise |
| Antimalarials—primigravidae | MBW | 112 g (41–183 g)[b] | Four trials of small sample size |
| Balanced protein-energy supplementation | SGA | 0.76 (0.58–1.01) | Borderline significance but does not include the new positive Gambia trial; lack of effective method to select women who will benefit the most |
| Forms of care of unknown effectiveness that merit further research | | | |
| Routine zinc | Term LBW | 0.77 (0.54–1.11) | Only the most recent trial showed positive effect |
| Routine folate | Term LBW | 0.60 (0.37–0.97) | Populations poorly defined and limitations in randomization procedures |
| Routine magnesium | Term LBW | 0.59 (0.37–0.93) | Trials have high numbers of exclusions and limitations in the randomization procedures |
| Abdominal decompression (for suspected IFG) | Term LBW | 0.21 (0.13–0.34) | Possibility of selection, observer, and analysis bias in the two RCTs; safety unknown; the large effect observed makes further exploration of this technique worthwhile |

*Source*: Adapted with permission from [65].

[a]Typical odds ratios (ORs) and 95 % confidence intervals (an OR < 1 indicates that the intervention resulted in favourable outcomes).

[b]Weighted mean difference between intervention and control groups.

*IFG* impaired fetal growth, *LBW* low birth weight, *MBW* mean birth weight, *RCT* randomized controlled trial, *SGA* small for gestational age

associated with increases in maternal weight gain and mean birth weight and a decrease of borderline statistical significance in the number of IUGR babies (Table 5.5). A community-based trial in rural Gambia, not included in the calculations of the typical odds ratio in Table 5.4, showed that supplementation significantly increased birth weight by 136 g [67]. The odds ratio for LBW babies in supplemented women was 0.61 (95% CI 0.47–0.79), supporting the results of the systematic review [66].

Overall, it is surprising how limited data are supporting the effectiveness of nutritional interventions during pregnancy, some of which are of widespread use even in women without nutritional deficiencies. However, it is obvious that women manifesting nutritional deficits can only benefit from reversing such a situation. On this basis, efforts to improve women's nutrition should be a priority, especially in developing countries, although the expected effect of maternal nutrition supplementation on birth weight may be modest (about 100 g). Similarly, the average effect associated with some interventions suggests a potential effect of considerable magnitude (Table 5.5). Zinc, folate, and magnesium supplementation should be rigorously evaluated. Trials to evaluate these and other promising interventions should target populations at risk for IUGR, should be based on sound epidemiological or basic science background information, and should follow rigorous methods, including adequate sample sizes to detect any impact on substantial outcomes [65, 66]. In countries where multiple pathologies coexist, it may be difficult to achieve beneficial results by testing a single intervention. Malaria and other parasites, malnutrition, and anemia coexist in many developing countries, and the presence of such a combination of conditions is probably worse than each one of them alone. Appropriate combinations of interventions (e.g., a combination of antianemic [iron-folate] and antimicrobial/antiparasite agents tested in population-based trials) should be rigorously evaluated since it is very unlikely that the intergenerational and intragenerational effect of deprivation and poverty on maternal and fetal health can be overcome by a single intervention or treatment. Simple solutions will not resolve the problem of fetal malnutrition and its associated outcomes [68].

The World Health Organization recently conducted a comprehensive review evaluating the effectiveness of interventions aimed at improving physical growth or psychological development during childhood [69]. The review concluded the following:

Nutrition interventions significantly improve physical growth in poor and malnourished populations. Balanced protein-energy supplementation during pregnancy improve birth weight and reduce the incidence of IUGR. Food supplementation for infants and young children has documented impacts on physical growth. Other types of effective nutrition interventions include caregiver education about feeding practices for young children, breast-feeding promotion, and zinc supplementation in zinc-deficient areas. Programmes that include education, food supplementation, or micronutrient supplementation can result in reductions in the prevalence of moderate and severe growth retardation.

Nutrition interventions significantly improve psychological development in disadvantaged populations. Increased intake of nutrients and energy during the first 2 years of life, and prenatally through supplements to mothers, have significant positive impacts on cognitive and motor development. For example, interventions to prevent iodine deficiency have dramatic effects on cognitive development as well as preventing the physical stunting that accompanies iodine deficiency.

Psychosocial interventions significantly improve psychological development. For example, children attending preschool center-based programmes gain an average of about 8 IQ points by the time they are ready to start school. They are also less likely to repeat primary school grades or be placed in special education classes.

Combined interventions to improve both physical growth and psychological development have even greater impact in disadvantaged populations at risk of malnutrition. The combination of supplementation and stimulation interventions appears to have a greater effect on cognitive development than either alone. These combined nutrition and psychological interventions had significant impacts on both growth and development in every study that tested this relationship.

There are a number of conditions under which the impact on growth and development is most likely to be seen. Interventions during the earliest periods of life (i.e., prenatally and during infancy and early childhood) are likely to have the greatest impact. The children at higher risk are generally the ones who show the greatest response to growth and development interventions. Growth and development programmes that utilize several types of interventions and more than one delivery channel are more efficacious than those that are more restricted in scope. Types of interventions include nutrition education on diet and feeding practices, providing supplementary food or micronutrient supplements, and demonstrating cognitive stimulation activities or other activities to improve parenting skills. Types of delivery channels are home visits, group counselling, child care centers, and mass media. Program efficacy and effectiveness appear to be greater when parents are more involved.

When discussing combined interventions, a number of challenges arise. Many potential models for combined interventions to promote physical growth and psychological development of infants and young children have not yet been implemented. Others have been implemented but not systematically evaluated, which is essential. There is a need to develop and evaluate a model of combined interventions that could reach a large proportion of children who are at risk of growth and development faltering. An example could be a culturally adaptable counselling package that combines nutrition counselling on complementary feeding (with food supplementation if necessary) with counselling on psychosocial care (e.g., warmth, attentive listening, proactive stimulation, and support for exploration and autonomy). There is also an urgent need to evaluate the effectiveness of different content, programme venues, and delivery channels.

Poor growth is part of a vicious cycle that includes poverty and disease. These three factors are interlinked in such a way that each contributes to the presence and permanence of the others. Given the complexity of the underlying causes of the problem, new efforts must also be made to understand the specific economic, behavioural, dietary, and other factors affecting child growth and development. A good technical package has proved to be insufficient by itself; a distinguishing feature of successful programmes has been community involvement in identifying the problems and mobilizing action to resolve them. Future interventions should thus be strongly community based. Special effort should be made to improve the situation of women as primary child caregivers, with particular attention to their health and nutrition throughout the life cycle. Similarly, a focus on complementary feeding combined with continued attention to the protection and promotion of breast-feeding remain key for tackling the problem.

## 5.6  CONCLUSIONS

The future of human societies relies on the ability of children to achieve their optimal physical growth and mental development. Never before has there been so much knowledge to assist families and societies in their desire to raise children to reach their full potential. A fundamental need is to focus the attention of policymakers on nutritional status as one of the main indicators of development and as a precondition for the socioeconomic advancement of societies in any significant long-term sense. A good start in life will pay off, in terms of both human capital and economic development.

# REFERENCES

1. World Health Organization. Physical status: the use and interpretation of anthropometry. Geneva: World Health Organization, 1995. Technical Report Series No. 854.
2. United Nations. Millennium development goals. Available at: http://www.un.org/millenniumgoals.
3. Pollitt E, Gorman KS, Engle PL, Martorell R, Rivera J. Early supplementary feeding and cognition. Monogr Soc Res Child Dev 1993;58:1–99.
4. Martorell R, Rivera J, Kaplowitz H, Pollitt E. Long-term consequences of growth retardation during early childhood. In: Human growth: basic and clinical aspects. Hernandez M, Argente J, eds. Amsterdam: Elsevier Science, 1992;143–149.
5. Pan American Health Organization. Nutrition, health and child development. Washington: Pan American Health Organization, 1998. Scientific Publication No. 566.
6. Spurr GB. Physical activity and energy expenditure in undernutrition. Prog Food Nutr 1990;14: 139–192.
7. Black RE, ed. Zinc for child health. Am J Clin Nutr 1998;68(suppl):414S–516S.
8. Administrative Committee on Coordination, Subcommittee on Nutrition (ACC-SCN). Nutrition and poverty. Geneva: ACC-SCN, 1997. Nutrition Policy Paper No. 16.
9. Brown KH, Begin F. Malnutrition among weanlings of developing countries: still a problem begging for solutions. J Pediatr Gastroenterol Nutr 1993;17:132–138.
10. Shrimpton R, Victora CG, de Onis M, Lima RC, Blössner M, Clugston G. Worldwide timing of growth faltering: implications for nutritional interventions. Pediatrics 2001;107:E75.
11. Martorell R, Kettel Khan L, Schroeder DG. Reversibility of stunting: epidemiological findings in children from developing countries. Eur J Clin Nutr 1994;48(suppl 1):S45–S57.
12. de Onis M, Blössner M, Villar J. Levels and patterns of intrauterine growth retardation in developing countries. Eur J Clin Nutr 1998;52:S1, S5–S15.
13. Bakketeig LS, Butte N, de Onis M, Kramer M, O'Donnell A, Prada JA, Hoffman HJ. Report of the IDECG Working Group on definitions, classifications, causes, mechanisms and prevention of IUGR. Eur J Clin Nutr 1998;52:S1, S94–S96.
14. Villar J, de Onis M, Kestler E, Bolaños F, Cerezo R, Berendes H. The differential neonatal morbidity of the intrauterine growth retardation syndrome. Am J Obstet Gynecol 1990;163:151–157.
15. de Onis M, Wijnhoven TMA, Onyango AW. Worldwide practices in child growth monitoring. J Pediatr 2004;144:461–465.
16. Uauy R, Kain J. The epidemiological transition: need to incorporate obesity prevention into nutrition programmes. Public Health Nutr 2002;5:223–229.
17. World Health Organization. Management of severe malnutrition: a manual for physicians and other senior health workers. Geneva: World Health Organization, 1999.
18. American Academy of Pediatrics Policy Statement. Prevention of pediatric overweight and obesity. Pediatrics 2003;112:424–430.
19. de Onis M, Blössner M. The World Health Organization global database on child growth and malnutrition: methodology and applications. Int J Epidemiol 2003;32:518–526.
20. Frongillo EA Jr, de Onis M, Hanson KMP. Socioeconomic and demographic factors are associated with worldwide patterns of stunting and wasting of children. J Nutr 1997;127:2302–2309.
21. de Onis M, Frongillo EA, Blössner M. Is malnutrition declining? An analysis of changes in levels of child malnutrition since 1980. Bull World Health Organ 2000;78:1222–1233.
22. Victora CG. The association between wasting and stunting: an international perspective. J Nutr 1992;122:1105–1110.
23. de Onis M, Yip R. The WHO growth chart: historical considerations and current scientific issues. Bibl Nutr Dieta 1996;53:74–89.
24. de Onis M, Habicht JP. Anthropometric reference data for international use: recommendations from a World Health Organization Expert Committee. Am J Clin Nutr 1996;64:650–658.
25. WHO Working Group on Infant Growth. An evaluation of infant growth: the use and interpretation of anthropometry in infants. Bull World Health Organ 1995;73:165–174.
26. WHO Working Group on Infant Growth. An evaluation of infant growth. Geneva: World Health Organization, 1994. Document WHO/NUT/94.8.

27. de Onis M, Garza C, Habicht JP. Time for a new growth reference. Pediatrics 1997;100(5). Available at: http://www.pediatrics.org/cgi/content/full/100/5/e8.

28. Garza C, de Onis M, for the WHO Multicentre Growth Reference Study Group. Rationale for developing a new international growth reference. Food Nutr Bull 2004;25:S5–S14.

29. de Onis M, Garza C, Victora CG, Onyango AW, Frongillo EA, Martines J, for the WHO Multicentre Growth Reference Study Group. The WHO Multicentre Growth Reference Study: planning, study design, and methodology. Food Nutr Bull 2004;25:S15–S26.

30. de Onis M. Measuring nutritional status in relation to mortality. Bull World Health Organ 2000;78:1271–1274.

31. Gorstein J, Sullivan K, Yip R, de Onis M, Trowbridge F, Fajans P, et al. Issues in the assessment of nutritional status using anthropometry. Bull World Health Organ 1994;72:273–283.

32. Yip R, Scalon K. The burden of malnutrition: a population perspective. J Nutr 1994;124:2043S–2046S.

33. Villar J, Ezcurra EJ, Gurtner de la Fuente V, Campodonico L. Pre-term delivery syndrome: the unmet need. In: New perspectives for the effective treatment of pre-term labor: an international consensus. Research and Clinical Forums 1994;16:9–38.

34. de Onis M, Blössner M, Borghi E, Frongillo EA, Morris R. Estimates of global prevalence of childhood underweight in 1990 and 2015. JAMA 2004;291:2600–2606.

35. de Onis M, Blössner M, Borghi E, Morris R, Frongillo EA. Methodology for estimating regional and global trends of child malnutrition. Int J Epidemiol 2004;33:1260–1270.

36. Walker N, Schwartländer B, Bryce J. Meeting international goals in child survival and HIV/AIDS. Lancet 2002;360:284–288.

37. United Nations International Children's Emergency Fund. The state of the world's children 2004. New York: United Nations International Children's Emergency Fund, 2004.

38. de Onis M, Blössner M. Prevalence and trends of overweight among preschool children in developing countries. Am J Clin Nutr 2000;72:1032–1039.

39. de Onis M. The use of anthropometry in the prevention of childhood overweight and obesity. Int J Obes Relat Metab Disord 2004;28:S81–S85.

40. Williams RL, Creasy RK, Cunningham GC, Hawes WE, Norris FD, Tashiro M. Fetal growth and perinatal viability in California. Obstet Gynecol 1982;59:624–32.

41. Balcazar H, Haas JD. Retarded fetal growth patterns and early neonatal mortality in a Mexico city population. Bull Pan Am Health Organ 1991;25:55–63.

42. Øyen N, Skjaerven R, Little R, Wilcot A. Fetal growth retardation in sudden infant death syndrome (SIDS) babies and their siblings. Am J Epidemiol 1995;142:84–90.

43. Ashworth A. Effects of intrauterine growth retardation on mortality and morbidity in infants and young children. Eur J Clin Nutr 1998;52:S1, S34–S42.

44. Paz I, Gale R, Laor A, Danon YL, Stevenson DK, Seidman DS. The cognitive outcome of full term small for gestational age infants at late adolescence. Obstet Gynecol 1995;85:452–456.

45. Low J, Handley-Derry M, Burke S, et al. Association of intrauterine fetal growth retardation and learning deficits at age 9 to 11 years. Am J Obstet Gynecol 1992;167:1499–1505.

46. Parkinson CE, Wallis S, Harvey DR. School achievement and behaviour of children who are small-for-dates at birth. Dev Med Child Neurol 1981;23:41–50.

47. Taylor DJ, Howie PW. Fetal growth achievement and neurodevelopmental disability. Br J Obstet Gynaecol 1989;96:789–794.

48. Villar J, Smeriglio V, Martorell R, Brown CH, Klein RE. Heterogenous growth and mental development of intrauterine growth-retarded infants during the first three years of life. Pediatrics 1984;74:783–791.

49. Osmond C, Barker DJ, Winter PD, Fall CH, Simmonds SJ. Early growth and death from cardiovascular disease in women. BMJ 1993;307:1519–1524.

50. Williams S, George I, Silva P. Intrauterine growth retardation and blood pressure at age seven and eighteen. J Clin Epidemiol 1992;45:1257–1263.

51. Barker DJP. The intrauterine origins of cardiovascular and obstructive lung disease in adult life: The Mark Daniels lecture 1990. J Royal Coll Phys London 1991;25:129–133.

52. Hales CN, Barker DJ, Clark PM, et al. Fetal and infant growth and impaired glucose tolerance at age 64. BMJ 1991;303:1019–1022.

53. Barker DJ, Martyn CN, Osmond C, Hales CN, Fall CH. Growth in utero and serum cholesterol concentrations in adult life. BMJ 1993;307:1524–1527.

54. Hinchliffe SA, Lynch MR, Sargent PH, Howard CV, Van Velzen D. The effect of intrauterine growth retardation on the development of renal nephrons. Br J Obstet Gynaecol 1992;99:296–301.

55. Nieto-Diaz A, Villar J, Matorras-Weinig R. Intrauterine growth retardation at term: association between anthropometric and endocrine parameters. Acta Obstet Gynecol Scand 1996;75:127–131.

56. Pelletier D, Frongillo EA, Habicht JP. Epidemiologic evidence for a potentiating effect of malnutrition on child mortality. Am J Public Health 1993;83:1130–1133.

57. Caulfield LE, de Onis M, Blössner M, Black RE. Undernutrition as an underlying cause of child deaths associated with diarrhea, pneumonia, malaria, and measles. Am J Clin Nutr 2004;80:193–198.

58. Tomkins A, Watson F. Malnutrition and infection: a review. Geneva: Administrative Committee on Coordination/Subcommittee on Nutrition, 1989. ACC/SCN State-of-the-Art Series, Nutrition Policy Discussion Paper No. 5.

59. Man WDC, Weber M, Palmer A, Schneider G, Wadda R, Jaffar S, Mulholland EK, Greenwood BM. Nutritional status of children admitted to hospital with different diseases and its relationship to outcome in the Gambia, West Africa. Trop Med Int Health 1998;3:1–9.

60. Victora CG, Fuchs SC, Flores A, Fonseca W, Kirkwood BR. Risk factors for pneumonia in a Brazilian metropolitan area. Pediatrics 1994;93(6 pt 1):977–985.

61. Spurr GB, Barac-Nieto M, Maksud MG: Productivity and maximal oxygen consumption in sugar cane cutters. Am J Clin Nutr 1977;30:316–321.

62. Kramer MS. Determinants of low birth weight: methodological assessment and meta-analysis. Bull World Health Organ 1987;65:663–737.

63. Klebanoff MA, Yip R. Influence of maternal birth weight on rate of fetal growth and duration of gestation. J Pediatr 1987;111:287–292.

64. Binkin NJ, Yip R, Fleshood L, Trowbridge FL. Birthweight and childhood growth. Pediatrics 1988;82:828–834.

65. Gülmezoglu M, de Onis M, Villar J. Effectiveness of interventions to prevent or treat impaired fetal growth. Obstet Gynecol Surv 1997;52:139–149.

66. de Onis M, Villar J, Gülmezoglu M. Nutritional interventions to prevent intrauterine growth retardation: evidence from randomized controlled trials. Eur J Clin Nutr 1998;52:S1, S83–S93.

67. Ceesay SM, Prentice AM, Cole TJ, Ford F, Weaver LT, Poskitt EME, Whitehead RG. Effects on birth weight and perinatal mortality of maternal dietary supplements in rural Gambia: 5 year randomised controlled trial. BMJ 1997;315:786–790.

68. Ferro-Luzzi A, Ashworth A, Martorell R, Scrimshaw N. Report of the IDECG Working Group on effects of IUGR on infants, children and adolescents: immunocompetence, mortality, morbidity, body size, body composition, and physical performance. Eur J Clin Nutr 1998;52:S1, S97–S99.

69. World Health Organization. A critical link: interventions for physical growth and psychological development. Geneva: Division of Child Health and Development, World Health Organization, 1999. Document WHO/CHS/CAH/99.3.

# 6 Diarrheal Diseases

## Claudio F. Lanata and Robert E. Black

## 6.1 INTRODUCTION

Diarrheal diseases are a leading cause of childhood morbidity and mortality in developing countries. An important contributing factor to these deaths is malnutrition. Diarrhea is a condition characterized by stools of decreased consistency and increased number and is usually caused by infection of the gastrointestinal tract by pathogenic viruses, bacteria, or parasites. There has been great variability in the literature regarding the definition of diarrhea as stool consistency and number can be influenced by age and type of diet. For most epidemiological studies, *diarrhea* is defined as a condition in which three or more liquid stools are passed within any 24-hour period [1, 2]. This definition may be less satisfactory for breastfeeding infants under 2 months of age, who often pass frequent, loose, "pasty" stools that are not considered to be diarrhea.

An episode of diarrhea is usually considered to be terminated when an individual has at least 2 days free of diarrhea as defined here. *Dysentery* is defined as diarrheal disease in which blood is present in liquid stools. *Persistent diarrhea* is defined as an episode of diarrhea that lasts for at least 14 days. In this chapter, we review the current knowledge of this important subject, reviewing the epidemiology, the pathogenesis, the interactions between nutritional and diarrheal diseases, the dietary management of these conditions, and the nutritional interventions that may prevent diarrheal diseases.

## 6.2 PUBLIC HEALTH IMPORTANCE

The World Health Organization (WHO) estimated that diarrheal diseases caused 1.8 million deaths annually in 2000–2003, an important decline from the 4.6 million deaths estimated for the year 1980 [3, 4]. Most of these deaths occurred within the first 2 years of life. Repeated attacks of diarrhea in children can lead to undernutrition, poor growth, decreased immunocompetence, and death. Attacks of diarrhea in undernourished children tend to be more severe and of longer duration, suggesting a vicious cycle of diarrhea and undernutrition.

From: *Nutrition and Health: Nutrition and Health in Developing Countries, Second Edition*
Edited by: R. D. Semba & M. W. Bloem © Humana Press, Totowa, NJ

## 6.3  HISTORICAL BACKGROUND

Diarrheal diseases are most commonly associated with poverty, poor sanitation and hygiene, inadequate water supplies, and limited education. In the 19th and early 20th centuries, diarrheal diseases contributed substantially to the high infant and young child mortality rates in Europe and the United States [5, 6]. Summer epidemics of diarrhea were commonly observed among infants and young children in large cities such as Paris and London during the mid- and late 19th century [7]. The conditions and problems with diarrheal disease in the United States and Europe up to the early 20th century were similar to those encountered in many developing countries today [8, 9]. With improvements in sanitation, hygiene, child feeding practices, and water supplies, the problems of diarrheal disease were greatly diminished in industrialized countries.

With its dramatic clinical course, epidemic nature, and high mortality, cholera has been probably the most widely studied of the diarrheal diseases through history [10, 11]. Cholera was endemic in South Asia and the East Indies in the 19th century and underwent several pandemics in the 19th century and into the 20th century, following trade routes and human migration [12]. Cholera and public health are discussed in Chapter 1.

The relationship between nutritional status and diarrheal diseases has been recognized since the early 1960s, after an increased prevalence of diarrhea was observed in malnourished children [13]. Since then, several carefully conducted epidemiological and clinical studies have documented clearly the relationship between nutrition and diarrheal diseases [14]. A significant development in the treatment of diarrheal diseases has been the increased use of oral rehydration therapy (ORT) using a single fluid such as glucose, sodium chloride, trisodium citrate dihydrate, and potassium chloride, collectively known as oral rehydration salts (ORS), mixed in water to form ORS solution. Oral rehydration was recognized as effective in the treatment of cholera in adults [15] and children [16] and was shown to be effective in treating diarrhea caused by other pathogens [17, 18].

## 6.4  EPIDEMIOLOGY

The epidemiology of diarrheal diseases in developing countries is complex and has been reviewed in detail elsewhere [19].

### 6.4.1  Geographical Distribution

Diarrheal diseases occur worldwide but are more common in developing countries, where conditions of poverty, poor hygiene and sanitation, lack of access to clean water, and limited education are found. Diarrheal diseases are also more common in urban slums, where crowding and inadequate housing may be common. The prevalence of diarrheal diseases may be more common in warmer climates, which facilitate the growth of pathogens in contaminated foods. Diarrheal deaths are concentrated in areas of high population density, extreme poverty, and poor access to health facilities, as shown with deaths due to rotavirus that occur primarily in sub-Saharan Africa and Southeast Asia (Fig. 6.1) [20].

### 6.4.2  Risk Factors

Whether an individual develops diarrheal disease is a consequence of exposure to pathogenic organisms and the susceptibility of the host to infection (age, nutritional status, immunity). Nearly all diarrheal diseases are transmitted by direct contact with

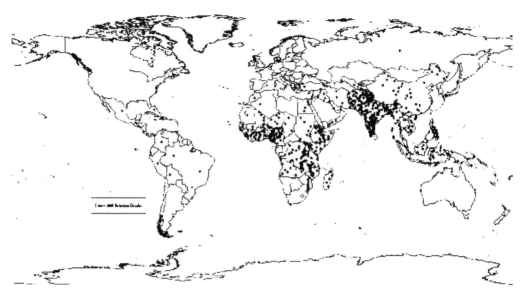

**Fig. 6.1.** Geographical distribution of deaths due to diarrheal disease.

Table 6.1
**Risk Factors for Diarrheal Diseases**

Limited access to clean water
Poor sanitation
Lack of latrine
Low socioeconomic status
Low maternal age
Low maternal education
Contaminated baby bottles
Contaminated weaning foods
Early introduction to solid foods
Fecal contamination of hands
Child defecation in common areas
Improper food preparation
Improper food storage
Contaminated eating utensils
Uncovered water reservoirs
Houseflies
Micronutrient deficiencies
Immunosuppression
Postmeasles attack

feces or by contact with water, food, utensils, fingers, flies, or soil that has been contaminated with feces. Many different risk factors have been identified for diarrheal disease (Table 6.1). Low socioeconomic status (SES) [21–24], crowding [22, 25, 26], less access to clean water and sanitation [25, 27, 28], low maternal age [29], and low maternal education [30] have been described as risk factors for diarrhea.

The lack of breast-feeding or not doing it exclusively during the first 6 months of life has been clearly demonstrated as a risk factor for the development of diarrhea and its duration. In a large longitudinal study done in the Philippines, children under 2 years of age who did not breast-feed had an increased risk (eight- to tenfold increased mortality rate) of both diarrheal morbidity and mortality, mostly during the first 6 months of life [31]. Poor feeding patterns seem to be related to the development of diarrheal diseases. In a case-control study in Brazil, children completely weaned had a fourteenfold increased risk of mortality owing to diarrheal diseases and fourfold increased risk of mortality owing to respiratory infections as compared with breast-fed children, controlling for confounding variables [32]. Several mechanisms in addition to the nutritional ones, including transfer of immunity by breast milk and avoidance of pathogens from contaminated weaning foods, may be involved [33–35]. Baby bottles are also known to be a risk factor for the development of acute otitis, diarrhea, and pneumonia [36]. Early introduction of solid foods are also a risk factor for the development of acute diarrhea [34, 37], likely through ingestion of enteropathogens with the foods.

Fecal contamination of mother's hands may occur at the time of defecation or when cleaning their children's feces [38]. An association between hand contamination with fecal coliform bacteria and the incidence of diarrhea has been observed in Bangladesh, with stronger association found in communities with unimproved water and sanitation [39]. Bacterial contamination of food has been documented extensively in developing countries [40]. The level of bacterial contamination is influenced by temperature of food preparation, the storage time between preparation and eating, and the use of refrigeration. Uncooked fruits and vegetables may be contaminated with fecal coliform bacteria, viruses, and other pathogens before reaching the home [41]. Irrigation with sewage-contaminated water may increase contamination of fruits and vegetables with fecal bacteria. Baby bottles, baby bottle nipples, cups and spoons, and food containers have frequently been found to be contaminated with fecal bacteria and diarrheal pathogens [42–44]. Waterborne transmission has been well documented for most enteropathogens, especially *Vibrio cholerae*, *Salmonella typhi*, and *Giardia lamblia*, and the use of contaminated unboiled drinking water has been associated with diarrhea [45, 46]. Contaminated water vessels and uncovered water reservoirs are associated with increased risk of diarrheal disease [24]. Houseflies have been implicated by some studies as a mode of transmission for diarrheal disease since fly control interventions have proven to be effective in reducing diarrheal incidence in developing countries [47]. Exposure of children to animal feces, such as chicken feces, has been implicated in transmission of *Campylobacter jejuni* diarrhea [48].

Host risk factors for diarrheal diseases include undernutrition, as reflected by low anthropometric status using a variety of indicators [26, 49, 50]; micronutrient deficiencies (such as that of vitamin A and zinc); a previous episode of diarrhea [51]; and hypochlorhydria [52]. Decreased immunity is also a risk factor for diarrheal disease. Malnutrition, micronutrient deficiencies, and immune status are discussed in Section 6.5.6.

### 6.4.3  Incidence

Diarrheal incidence has varied across studies, and this may be because of methodological differences, including the definition of diarrhea and the surveillance frequency and techniques used, or may be caused by actual differences in the study populations.

Despite these important differences, the median incidence of diarrhea reported from the review of published community-based studies worldwide since the 1980s has not changed. Snyder and Merson [3] estimated a median rate of 2.2 episodes per child under 5 years of age per year, reviewing studies published up to 1980, which used different diarrhea definitions and recall periods. This may explain why in the review of studies published between 1980 and 1990, selecting studies that used a standardized diarrhea definition and shorter recall periods, Bern et al. [53] estimated a median diarrhea incidence rate of 2.6 episodes per year per child younger than 5 years, and from the review of studies published between 1990 and 2000, Kosek et al. [54] estimated a rate of 3.2 episodes per year per child younger than 5 years. Work done by the Child Epidemiology Reference Group (CHERG) of WHO [55], reviewing community-based studies done since 1980 as well as national survey data from several countries in the world in different time periods, confirmed that diarrhea incidence has not been reduced since 1980, in contrast with the sharp decline of diarrhea mortality seen in the same period. These findings suggest that improvements in water and sanitation that have taken place since 1980 have not been enough to reduce diarrhea transmission. Other effective interventions, as reviewed in Section 6.8, need to be implemented worldwide to reduce the burden of diarrhea. The median incidence of diarrhea from studies published between 1990 and 2003 [55] by age is shown in Fig. 6.2. A high incidence of diarrhea is found in the first 2 years of life, with a peak incidence usually between 6 and 11 months of age.

### 6.4.4 Seasonality

In many developing countries, the incidence of diarrhea may have a peak during hot or wet months [21, 56]. Rotavirus infection may have little seasonality in tropical areas but often peaks in cool or dry season in temperate regions [57].

### 6.4.5 Duration

In most settings, diarrheal episodes are self-limited and resolve within 1 week, and a small fraction will take up to 2 weeks to resolve. Persistent diarrhea (greater than 14 days duration) rarely constitutes more than one fifth of all episodes in community-based

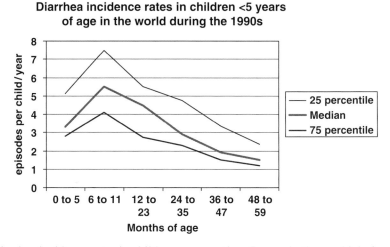

**Fig. 6.2.** Diarrhea incidence rates in children younger than 5 years in the world during the 1990s.

studies; the incidence of persistent diarrhea in children under 5 years of age has ranged up to 60 episodes per 100 child-years in different studies, and the incidence of persistent diarrhea also declines with age.

## 6.5  CLINICAL FEATURES/PATHOPHYSIOLOGY

Diarrheal disease may be accompanied by other associated problems, including dehydration, fever, electrolyte disturbances, anorexia, convulsions, measles, micronutrient deficiencies, and severe protein-energy malnutrition (PEM). Information on the clinical case management of diarrheal disease can be found elsewhere [58].

### 6.5.1  Major Pathogens Involved in Diarrheal Diseases in Children

The major pathogens involved in diarrheal diseases have been studied in both community-based and hospital-based studies. In a recent review of studies published since 1990 done by CHERG, enterotoxigenic *Escherichia coli* was found to be the leading enteropathogen, constituting about 14% of all episodes of diarrhea in community-based studies [59]. *Giardia lamblia*, enteropathogenic *E. coli* (EPEC), and rotavirus were identified as the next most common pathogens, with prevalence between 8 and 10%. Other common enteropathogens included *Campylobacter*, *Shigella*, *Cryptosporidium parvum*, and *Entamoeba histolytica*. Community-based studies best represent the overall occurrence of diarrhea illness regardless of severity of disease or care-seeking behavior. In clinic- or hospital-based studies, rotavirus has been the leading enteropathogen found, with prevalence between 18% and 25%, followed by bacterial pathogens such as enterotoxigenic *E. coli*, EPEC, *Campylobacter*, and *Shigella*. *Vibrio cholerae* may be frequent in some settings. In general, community-based studies have usually identified enteropathogens in about half the episodes of diarrhea studies, and facility-based studies have identified enteropathogens in 60–70%.

### 6.5.2  Pathophysiology

Acute diarrheal disease has been separated into two groups according to the pathogenesis and site of disease in the intestinal tract [60]. Enterotoxic and viral diarrheas are characterized by impaired absorption in the upper small intestine and a noninflammatory, often watery diarrhea. Enterotoxigenic *E. coli* has colonization factors, which allow the bacteria to adhere to the small bowel, and enterotoxins, which cause secretion of fluid and electrolytes into the intestinal lumen. *Vibrio cholerae* produces an enterotoxin that also causes loss of fluid and electrolytes in the intestinal lumen. Rotavirus can cause patchy mucosal changes in the small intestine, blunting of villi, reduced activity of lactase and other disaccharidases, and reduced absorption of carbohydrates. Invasive bacterial diarrheas such as *Shigella*, *Salmonella*, *Yersinia enterocolitica*, *C. jejuni*, and enteroinvasive *E. coli* can invade intestinal epithelial cells and cause an inflammatory diarrhea [61]. Invasive enteropathogens may also produce enterotoxins.

### 6.5.3  Effects of Malnutrition on Mortality

Early studies documented the increased risk of death owing to diarrheal diseases in malnourished children [62]. Malnourished children who were discharged from a hospital after treatment for diarrheal illnesses had 14 times greater risk of dying compared with better-nourished controls [63]. In a community-based study in rural India, severely malnourished children had a 24-fold higher diarrheal case fatality rate compared to normally nourished children [64]. In a case-control study in Mexico, diarrhea cases with previous history of malnutrition had a 7.5-fold greater chance of dying compared with those with severe diarrhea cases who survived [65].

The risk of dying from diarrheal diseases is proportional to the degree of malnutrition. In a review of six prospective studies, a consistent increase in mortality was observed with poorer nutritional status, as indicated by weight for age, with a synergistic effect of malnutrition and morbidity [66]. In a large prospective study done in the Philippines, the risk of mortality increased 1.6 times for each one-unit decrease in weight-for-age Z-score [67]. This study also documented a similar risk of increased mortality from diarrhea and acute respiratory illnesses, with mortality for diarrhea and lower respiratory illness increasing 1.7 times for each one-unit decrease in weight-for-age Z-score. The mortality associated with both acute lower respiratory diseases and diarrhea combined was doubled for each one-unit decrease in weight-for-age Z-score [67]. In a combined analysis of data from ten longitudinal, community-based studies, Caulfield et al. found that the relative risk of death from diarrhea was increased for children who were less than −1Z weight-for-age, and the risk increased progressively with each Z-score below the median [68]. Overall, 60.7% of diarrhea deaths could be attributed to underweight.

The mortality from diarrhea in malnourished children seems to be high in persistent diarrhea as compared with acute episodes. Persistent diarrhea per se is associated with greater mortality than acute diarrhea [64], but if persistent episodes (diarrheal episodes of 14 days or longer duration) were associated with severe malnutrition, the risk of death increased 68-fold in Bangladesh [69]. In conclusion, childhood malnutrition is consistently associated with an increased risk of death, both for diarrheal (persistent diarrhea in particular) and respiratory illnesses.

### 6.5.4 Effects of Malnutrition on Morbidity

Early studies documented a relationship between malnutrition and the prevalence of diarrheal diseases [13, 70–72]. This relationship is stronger for an increased duration of diarrheal illnesses in undernourished children, especially those episodes owing to *Shigella* sp. and enterotoxigenic *E. coli*, than for an increased incidence [73, 74]. The duration of diarrheal episodes owing to these organisms or episodes generally increased threefold or more for less-well-nourished children. Undernutrition is also a risk factor for persistent diarrhea [75, 76]. Poorer nutritional status has been documented as associated with an increased rate of stool output in children [77], leading to an increased risk of dehydration [78]. These mechanisms probably explain the increased risk for hospitalization and length of hospital stay owing to diarrheal disease in the presence of malnutrition [79–81].

Studies also showed an increased risk for diarrhea incidence. Prior malnutrition has been associated with a 1.5- to 2.0-fold increased risk of developing a diarrheal episode in several geographical areas [82–87]. This increased risk of diarrhea may explain why some studies have found that prior episodes of diarrhea were a strong predictor for diarrhea in a subsequent period in undernourished children [88–90]. Some organisms may be particularly selected as a cause of infection in malnourished children, like *C. parvum* infections [91].

### 6.5.5    Effects on Growth of Children

Several studies have clearly documented a negative effect of diarrhea on the weight and height gain of children during or after an episode of acute diarrhea [70, 71, 92–97]. The effect seems to be more consistent in reducing weight gain than in reducing height or length gain. The growth faltering observed has varied from 10–20% in countries with lower prevalence of malnutrition in the Americas [70, 72] to 70–80% in countries with high prevalence of malnutrition in Africa [71, 94, 98], suggesting that the negative effect of diarrheal diseases is greater in children with poorer nutritional status, most likely owing to their poorer diets. This negative effect can be reversed by 14–30 days after the episode if the child returns to his or her normal diet and remains healthy [92, 99]. As expected, the magnitude of the weight deficit is inversely related to the duration of the diarrheal episode [100]. Although the distribution of durations of diarrheal episodes is continuous and skewed toward the longer duration, episodes that last more than 14 days are a subgroup associated with higher risk of dying [69]. Persistent diarrheal episodes, which account for about 3–20% of all diarrheal episodes [100], occur in children who also have higher burden of diarrhea in general, and both the persistent episodes and the high prevalence adversely affect growth [100–102].

Both symptomatic and asymptomatic infections can cause an adverse effect on growth. A community-based study has indicated that both symptomatic and asymptomatic infections with *C. parvum* in Peruvian children were associated with a reduction of weight gain, controlling for other variables [103]. Even though the effect size was less in asymptomatic infections, because of its higher prevalence, asymptomatic infections played a greater role on the overall impact of *C. parvum* infection on growth than symptomatic infections. *Cryptosporidium parvum*-infected children, especially those infected when they were under 6 months of age or when they were stunted at the time of infection, did not have catch-up growth, showing significant differences in height even 1 year after the infection, compared with noninfected children, suggesting a long-lasting, adverse effect on linear growth [104].

The effect of diarrhea on growth could be owing to a reduced appetite, altered feeding practices, decreased nutrient absorption, or increased metabolic needs. Studies have described a modifying effect of diet on the relationship between diarrhea and growth. Diarrhea has a lesser effect on growth of breast-fed infants [105], among those whose usual dietary intake is greater or of better quality [106], or among children who receive food supplements [107, 108]. Thus, an adequate diet can protect from the nutritional impact of diarrhea. Also, children with an adequate diet will grow faster after an illness, experiencing what has been called catch-up growth, especially if they do not have recurrent infections [82, 109, 110].

### 6.5.6    Effect on Dietary Intake

Several clinical and community-based studies have found that diarrheal diseases are associated with some reduction in the dietary intake during illness [111–117]. Initial studies provided conflicting results because they did not distinguish between breast milk and other liquids and solids. Carefully conducted studies in children who were not breast-feeding any longer have indicated that common illnesses, including diarrhea, have reduced energy consumption by 15–20% [113, 114]. This reduction is of a lesser magnitude in infants who receive more than 50% of their energy intake from breast milk, for whom the reduction in dietary intake during illness only occurs from non-breast milk sources [116]. The reduction of energy intake during diarrhea seems greater in hospitalized children than at the community level [111, 112], possibly owing to the greater severity of illness or to a difference in the acceptability of hospital versus home diets. It was postulated that the characteristics of the diet may influence the dietary intake during illness, although a study done in Peru did not show that dietary viscosity influenced the energy consumption of a potato-based diet [118].

### 6.5.7   Effects on Nutrient Absorption and Intestinal Function

Diarrheal illnesses can reduce intestinal absorption as a result of several mechanisms: direct enterocyte and crypt cell destruction by the enteropathogen (or its toxins) or by the immune response of the individual; increased intestinal motility with a reduction of transit time; and reduced bile acids by increased fecal losses or bacterial hydrolysis [119]. Owing to these mechanisms, malabsorption or abnormal digestion of protein, fat, and especially carbohydrates occurs [120, 121], potentially increasing the intraintestinal fluid volume and fecal losses by its osmotic effect and worsening the diarrheal episode, especially with rotavirus diarrhea [122]. Diarrhea can also increase the intestinal permeability to test sugars, an effect that lasts after the end of the diarrheal episode and was associated with reduced growth in a West African study [123]. This increased permeability may also increase the risk of sensitization to dietary proteins and the development of food allergies [124]. Finally, diarrhea also increases the fecal excretion of selected micronutrients, like zinc and copper [125] and some vitamins [126].

### 6.5.8   Relationship with Nutrition and Immunity

#### 6.5.8.1   UNDERNUTRITION

Severe malnutrition is associated with a depressed immune response, which is one of the mechanisms that may explain the increased incidence and severity of infections in undernourished children. As initially documented in a study done in Peru, delayed cutaneous hypersensitivity to several antigens, as an indicator of cell-mediated immunity, has proven to be a very good predictor of the incidence of diarrhea, controlling for anthropometric status [127]. Studies done in Bangladesh [128] and Kenya [129] confirmed these findings; anergic children had 20–50% increased incidence of diarrheal diseases, independent of their nutritional status. Cell-mediated immune status was also an important predictor of persistent diarrhea [130] as anergic children experienced twice the incidence of persistent diarrhea in the period after their assessment. This increased risk can vary over time as children have been observed to change their delayed cutaneous hypersensitivity status when reevaluated 6–12 months later (C. F. Lanata, unpublished observations).

#### 6.5.8.2   VITAMIN A

Diarrheal disease has been associated with increased risk of developing vitamin A deficiency [131], and in turn, vitamin A deficiency has been associated with increased risk of developing diarrheal disease in preschool children [132]. Several studies have shown that children with diarrhea (especially more severe diarrhea and persistent diarrhea) have a strong association with xerophthalmia or low vitamin A status assessed by several indicators, including serum retinol levels [133]. The observation that serum retinol levels were lower in children with acute diarrhea seems to be explained partly by an increased urinary loss of vitamin A during acute diarrhea, especially those episodes associated with rotavirus or fever [134]. This urinary loss of retinol, which seems to be transient [135], occurs because of impaired tubular reabsorption of low molecular weight proteins, including the binding protein transporting retinol, as documented in children with shigellosis [136]. The relationship between vitamin A deficiency and diarrheal disease is also discussed elsewhere in this book (see Chapter 13).

### 6.5.8.3 ZINC

In contrast to vitamin A supplementation, the studies done with zinc supplementation have shown more consistent results in the prevention of diarrheal and respiratory diseases. It is now clear that zinc has an important role not only in growth, but also in the immune capacity of children to fight against diarrheal and respiratory diseases [137, 138]. Zinc deficiency is associated with skin and mucosal damage; reduced number of circulating lymphoid cells; poor function of B and T lymphocytes, neutrophils, monocytes, and macrophages; cytokine depression or suppression; and therefore poor immune function [138]. Because zinc-containing foods with the highest bioavailability are animal proteins—a dietary source underrepresented in the diet of children living in most developing countries—zinc deficiency may be one of the most important nutritional disorders in developing countries [137]. The potential role of zinc in prevention of diarrhea is discussed further in Section 6.7.3.

### 6.5.8.4 OTHER MICRONUTRIENTS

Other micronutrients may also play a role in the development of infectious diseases. Copper deficiency in children, a rare condition, is also associated with persistent diarrhea that disappears after supplementation [139, 140]. Selenium, another essential trace element, may have a more important role. Among several functions, it is needed in erythrocytes and granulocytes to metabolize $H_2O_2$, and together with vitamin E has antioxidant effects in tissues. Therefore, it may have antiproliferative and cancer-protecting effects [141]. Selenium requirements are greater in infants and young children and its concentration in human milk is affected by maternal intake [141]. In studies with pigs, selenium-deficient diets have been observed to cause a marked suppression of lymphocyte response to mitogens as well as an increased burst respiratory response of stimulated granulocytes [142]. In an experimental swine dysentery model, selenium supplementation was associated with improved clinical response as well as with greater weight gain in the recovery period [143]. Studies are needed to evaluate the role of selenium in diarrhea in infants.

## 6.6 DIAGNOSIS

Diarrhea, as mentioned, is defined as a condition in which three or more liquid stools are passed within a 24-hour period [1, 2]. On an individual level, the clinical concept of diarrhea can range from a subtle variation from normal to a rapidly fatal disease. Nausea, vomiting, fever, abdominal cramps, dehydration, and convulsions may also be present but are not necessary for the diagnosis of diarrhea. The clinical assessment of the patient and case management of diarrhea are beyond the scope of this chapter and can be found in a WHO treatment manual [58].

## 6.7 TREATMENT

### *6.7.1 Oral Rehydration Therapy*

Oral rehydration therapy (ORT) is the treatment of choice for patients with some dehydration. The purpose of ORT is to treat the deficits in water and electrolytes that occur with acute watery diarrhea. Approximately 95% of children who visit a health care facility for acute watery diarrhea can be successfully treated with ORT. A new low-osmolality oral rehydration solution has been shown to be associated with less vomiting, reduced stool output, and reduced need for intravenous solutions [144] and has replaced the old WHO/UNICEF (United Nations International Children's Emergency Fund) formulation.

### *6.7.2 Nutritional Management*

One of the strategies that has been considered to reduce the negative impact of diarrheal diseases on the nutritional status of children has been the dietary management of children during illness or immediately after recovering. For years, physicians have feared that food could be incompletely digested as a consequence of the malabsorption observed in diarrheal diseases, thereby increasing the stool output owing to osmotic effects, with an increase in the risk of dehydration and other diarrheal complications. This has caused many clinicians to be cautious with the introduction of foods during acute diarrheal diseases. Studies in several developing countries have provided evidence of the importance of an adequate dietary intake during and after diarrhea. These studies have included the timing of when to introduce feeding and the amount of food that could be given and the diet characteristics, including micronutrient contents, in both acute and persistent diarrhea.

#### 6.7.2.1 TIMING OF FEEDING

In a clinical trial conducted in Peru, children with acute diarrhea were randomized into four groups, with the objective of evaluating the consequences of introduction of a full-strength diet early in the course of an acute diarrheal episode on the clinical course of illness and the nutritional status of these children [145]. One group received a full-strength, lactose-free diet immediately after rehydration. A second group received a half-strength, lactose-free diet for 2 days prior to the introduction of the full-strength formulation. A third group received no diet and were kept on oral rehydration solutions for 2 days, followed by a half-strength diet for 2 days, and then the full-strength diet introduced 2 days later. The fourth group was similar to the third group but received only intravenous fluids for the first 2 days before the half- and full-strength diets were introduced.

The groups were comparable in their clinical and biological characteristics. The introduction of a full-strength diet after rehydration was not associated with any change in the stool output of these children. In contrast, children who received the full-strength diet gained weight continuously from the start of the study, whereas those who received the half-strength formula for 2 days gained weight only when they were given the full-strength formula, requiring 8 days to become similar in weight to the children receiving the full-strength formula earlier. Children who received no diet for the first 2 days lost weight during that period. They only gained weight once they were given the full-strength formula; however, even after 2 weeks of observation, they were still significantly less well nourished than the children given full-strength diets earlier. Similar findings were also observed in children under 1 year of age in Romania [146] and in a multicenter study conducted in several hospitals in Europe [147].

These studies have prompted WHO and pediatric societies to recommend continuing feedings with their usual diet in children with diarrhea as well as rapid reintroduction of usual feedings immediately after rehydrating a child with more severe diarrhea in a hospital setting [148].

### 6.7.2.2 LACTOSE

One of the major concerns related to the dietary management of children with diarrhea has been the lactose content of the diet. Because lactose malabsorption frequently occurs with diarrhea, there is a possibility that partially absorbed lactose will pass into the colon and increase the fluid volume in the lumen by osmotic pressure, leading to an increased stool output and dehydration. This was felt to be a strong reason to restrict lactose in the diet of children with diarrhea. Despite the fact that human milk contains more lactose than cow's milk, it is much better absorbed and tolerated. In a randomized trial during which continued or interrupted breast-feeding were compared in children with diarrhea, children who continued breast-feeding had a lower stool output than those who received only oral rehydration solution for the first 24 hours of hospitalization [149]. Breast milk may also have a direct effect on diarrhea by providing specific secretory immunoglobulin A (IgA) against viral or bacterial pathogens, as well as by the presence of lactadherin, a mucin-associated glycoprotein, which binds specifically to rotavirus, inhibiting its replication [150]. The evidence is strong that breast milk should be continued in children with diarrhea.

Several clinical trials have focused on the safety of providing nonhuman milk to children with diarrhea, with conflicting results. In a meta-analysis of 13 clinical trials, children who were fed undiluted lactose-containing diets had a 22% rate of treatment failure compared with 12% treatment failure in children who were given lactose-free diets [151]. The meta-analysis suggested that this effect was mainly seen among children who were moderately to severely dehydrated on admission. No significant differences on treatment failure existed between children who had mild-to-no dehydration. Based on this analysis, WHO recommends continuing with nondiluted, lactose-containing, nonhuman milk in children with diarrhea. Moderate or severe dehydration is infrequent, and these children require treatment in health facilities. Thus, they should be fed under close medical supervision. Some of these children who may not tolerate undiluted nonhuman milk may be infected with EPEC, as indicated by a study done in Brazil, where an increased stool output associated with a lactose-containing formula was mainly observed in children with EPEC infections [152]. A better alternative than providing water-diluted, nonhuman milk to those children with more severe diarrhea seems to be the mixture of milk with other foods, like potato, rice, or noodles.

### 6.7.2.3 MIXED DIETS

In a clinical trial in Peruvian children with acute diarrhea, a blend of toasted wheat and pea flour and a mixture of potato and milk were compared with a commercially available lactose-free, soy protein formula [153]. No difference in stool output or treatment failure occurred during the first 48 hours of admission. Even more, when the median durations of excretion of liquid stools were compared, the common food group had less than half the duration of the formula group (60 vs. 144 hours, respectively). Similar studies comparing bean- [154], chicken- [155], maize- [156], and rice- [157] based diets have confirmed these findings. Children with diarrhea who were fed with locally available mixtures of foods, even including nonhuman milk, had no adverse effects and had a reduction in the duration of diarrhea. In a prospective, community-based study in Peruvian children, the consumption of cereals during diarrhea was associated with shortening the duration of the episode by 1 day [158]. Maulen-Radovan [157] demonstrated that treatment failures due to recurring dehydration were significantly less in children fed a mixture of rice or chicken and other common foods than with a soy protein infant formula. In a study done in malnourished children recovering from a diarrheal episode owing to shigellosis in Bangladesh, providing a high-protein diet, as compared with a standard diet, during a 3-week period was associated with a significant gain in height when assessed 6 months later [159]. When a milk-cereal formula was offered for 10 days to these malnourished children with shigellosis, giving a higher-density diet (with the same proportion of protein) was associated with a significant weight gain, even 1 month after discharge from the hospital with no subsequent dietary intervention at home [160].

These studies highlight the importance of a good-quality diet, in terms of both energy density and protein content, to be offered to children with diarrhea and in the convalescent period, even when these diets may not be available thereafter. One way of achieving this is to increase the energy density of staple foods by fermentation or germination. Amylase-rich flour from germinated wheat can instantly liquefy a thick porridge, making it more acceptable to sick children and increase its energy density [161]. Amylase-treated porridge obtained from germinated wheat has been shown to increase the energy intake of children with diarrhea [162, 163]. It may be particularly important to provide a good-quality diet with adequate protein during shigellosis because this illness results in substantial loss of protein in the stool [164].

### 6.7.2.4 FIBER

Because of the consistent observations of reduced duration of diarrhea among children fed mixed diets, several investigators have studied the role of dietary fiber in the duration of diarrhea because most of these staple foods have a high fiber content. Dietary fiber—noncellulose polysaccharides that form the indigestible portion of the plant cell wall—together with lignins are not absorbed by the human intestinal tract. In the colon, they are partially digested by fecal bacteria, increasing the total fecal bacterial mass. Dietary fiber also has hydrophilic sites that bind to water. These two effects may explain the changes in stool consistency observed with the ingestion of high-fiber diets. Not all types of dietary fiber may have an effect on diarrheal duration, as demonstrated in a human volunteer study in which only psyllium increased fecal consistency and stool viscosity, and wheat bran or calcium polycarbophil did not [165]. This effect depends on the ratio between the concentration of water-binding insoluble solids in the distal colon, like psyllium, and the amount of fecal water reaching the colon [166]. The presence of fiber in the diet diminishes the intestinal transit time, even in the presence of a high flow rate of enteral feedings in experimental dog models, by intensifying inhibitory feedback from the distal gut to the upper intestine [167] through a cholecystokinin-mediated mechanism. Some dietary soluble fiber, like partially hydrolyzed guar gum (Sunfiber), not only reduces the duration of liquid stools during diarrhea but also increases flatulence as a result of fermentation of the soluble fiber in the colon. Concomitant production of short-chain fatty acids increases the intestinal absorption of water and sodium, as reviewed in Section 6.7.2.8 [168].

The consumption of dietary fiber in children with diarrhea has therefore been associated with a reduction of the duration of diarrhea as documented in studies done in the United States [169] and Belgium [170]. In a clinical trial done in Peruvian children with acute diarrhea, a group given a soy protein infant formula was compared with a group that received the same formula with soy polysaccharide fiber [171]. As expected, the group that received the fiber supplement had a substantial reduction in the median duration of diarrhea. This apparent reduction, however, was mainly owing to the characteristics of the stool because stool wet or dry weight was similar between the groups. Also, there were no differences in the absorption of macronutrients from the diet or changes in the anthropometric status of the study children. This osmotic "cosmetic" effect on diarrheal stools in children may be important, even if not translated into a nutritional benefit, because it diminishes liquid stools, which are always a concern to mothers. If some dietary fibers have the added effect of an increased water absorption in the distal gut by an increased production of short-chain fatty acids, this may be an important contribution to the management of children with diarrhea. Even if dietary fibers by themselves do not have a strong justification as supplements, the use during diarrhea of mixtures of locally available staple foods with high dietary fiber content in children with diarrhea is still recommended in light of these studies.

### 6.7.2.5 PROBIOTICS

Other dietary components that have been considered to play a role in the management of diarrhea are *probiotics*—viable bacteria in the food. Although they are not really food or nutrients to humans, when added to foods they can benefit humans by their action on some food components or by inhibiting the growth or function of pathogenic bacteria. Several such organisms have been studied as potential agents in the treatment or prevention of diarrhea. Organisms that are capable of fermenting lactose, like in yogurts, may diminish the lactose content of the diet, therefore increasing the digestibility of milk products in children with diarrhea. Because of this effect, yogurt may be better tolerated than nonhuman milk in children with diarrhea [172]. However, when nonhuman milk is given as part of a mixed diet in children with diarrhea, no benefits on the severity, duration, and treatment failure of diarrhea were seen when milk was substituted with yogurt, even in malnourished children [173].

Specific probiotic agents have also been evaluated individually. *Lactobacillus casei* GG, an acid- and bile-resistant strain that colonizes the intestinal mucosa, has been found to reduce the duration and severity of rotavirus diarrhea [174] and other diarrhea [175, 176]. When given combined with ORS in children hospitalized with acute diarrhea, it reduced diarrhea duration and shortened hospital stay in a multicenter European trial [177]. In rotavirus diarrhea, the supplementation with *Lactobacillus* GG not only decreased the diarrheal duration, but also reduced the excretion of rotavirus in the stools [178]. Furthermore, in a community-based study done in Peruvian children, *Lactobacillus* GG or placebo were given 6 days/week for 15 months to a large group of children in periurban Lima [179]. *Lactobacillus* GG supplementation was associated with a significant reduction in the incidence of acute diarrhea (13% reduction), especially in children who were not breast-feeding (20% reduction in non-breast-fed vs. none in breast-fed). Thus, supplementation with this organism not only reduces the duration and severity of an acute diarrheal episode, but also can prevent its development. *Lactobacillus* GG colonizes the gastrointestinal tract between 1 and 3 days in the majority of individuals, and some may be excreted for up to 1 week [180], indicating that it needs to be taken at least three times per week to be beneficial. This strain has also been found important in stimulating intestinal immunity, increasing IgA-secreting cells in the gut and the release of interferon into the lumen, explaining how it may work [180].

Other single organisms have also been tested. *Lactobacillus reuterii*, an organism of human origin that is a natural colonizer of the gastrointestinal tract, had similar effects in children hospitalized with rotavirus diarrhea in Finland [181], showing a dose response: 48% of children who received a dose of $10^{10}$ colony-forming units (cfu) of the organisms had watery diarrhea by the second day of treatment compared with 70% of those who received a lower dose ($10^7$ cfu) and 80% of those who received placebo [182]. Other bacteria, like *Bifidobacterium bifidum* and *Streptococcus thermophilus*, have been found to prevent the development of acute diarrhea and rotavirus shedding in infants admitted to a chronic medical care hospital [183]. The administration of *Enterococcus* SF 68 strain during diarrhea in adults was also associated with a significant reduction of the duration and severity of diarrhea [184]. The fermentation of mixed diets with *Lactobacillus acidophilus* has been shown to prevent the development of diarrhea with enterotoxigenic *E. coli* in mice [185]. In contrast, when adult volunteers were given a combination of *L. acidophilus* and *Lactobacillus bulgaricus* and then challenged with *E. coli* strains that produced heat-stable or heat-labile enterotoxins or both, there were no differences in the attack rate, incubation period, duration, and severity of diarrhea compared with volunteers who were given placebo [186]. *Saccharomyces boulardii* was able to prevent the development of diarrhea in critically ill tube-fed adults hospitalized in intensive care units [187] and the stool frequency and duration of diarrhea in hospitalized children, shortening their hospital stay [188].

From all these studies, it could be concluded that probiotics are promising agents in the management and prevention of diarrhea and deserve further evaluation in children in developing countries with different field conditions and etiologic agents. Each of the most promising organisms should be tested to confirm their potential use in the treatment and prevention of diarrhea [180, 188–191]. If efficacy is further demonstrated, studies of cost-effectiveness of these interventions will be needed to determine whether these approaches are useful.

### 6.7.2.6 PREBIOTICS

Because probiotics are beneficial to the host only when they are present in the gut, therefore requiring frequent oral administration to have a permanent effect, other mechanisms to manipulate the composition of the gut flora potentially to increase the growth of bacterial groups like bifidobacteria or lactobacillus have been tried. *Prebiotics*, nondigestible food ingredients in humans, are capable of selectively stimulating the growth or activity of one or a limited group of bacterial species in the gut. This could prevent a negative health impact caused by another type of bacteria [192, 193]. Nondigestible oligosaccharides, in particular fructooligosaccharides, naturally exist in a variety of plants and are used as a natural endulcorant. They have been shown to stimulate the growth of bifidobacteria in the gut, enabling them to become the predominant species in human feces [194, 195]. In a study done in Chilean children, the administration of a milk formula supplemented with prebiotics after a week of amoxicillin treatment increased the concentration of difidobacteria and *Lactobacillus* population in the gut as compared with a placebo control [196]. However, in a community-based trial, cereal supplemented with oligofructose, with or without zinc, failed to reduce diarrhea prevalence and the need to use health care in a Peruvian breast-fed population [197].

### 6.7.2.7  EPIDERMAL GROWTH FACTOR

Oral administration of the epidermal growth factor, which is present in human milk, has stimulated the recovery of the small intestinal morphology and function after rotavirus infection in pigs [198], improved weight gain, reduced small and large intestinal colonization with EPEC, improved the intestinal function in rabbits [199], and reduced colitis in mouse [200]. Intravenous administration of epidermal growth factor increased the number of microvilli in two Korean children with microvillus inclusion disease, a rare disorder with chronic diarrhea [201]. Further human studies are needed to confirm these preliminary findings.

### 6.7.2.8  SHORT-CHAIN FATTY ACIDS

In the large bowel, unabsorbed carbohydrates are fermented by the colonic flora to short-chain fatty acids, also producing gas. Animal studies have documented that the production of short-chain fatty acids in the large bowel function as a compensatory response to diarrhea because they are associated with an increase in the capacity to absorb fluids from the large bowel [202]. In small infants, owing to an immature fecal flora, short-chain fatty acids are not produced, and unabsorbed carbohydrates are not fermented, passing through the colon unchanged, contributing to diarrheal losses by their osmotic effects.

Whether unabsorbed carbohydrates cause diarrhea probably depends on the balance between the osmotic force of the carbohydrate and the colonic capacity to digest it by bacterial fermentation. Danish adult volunteers were given two nonabsorbable carbohydrates, one of which (lactulose) produced a high-osmolar product in the gut after colonic fermentation compared with the other (fructo-oligosaccharide, Idolax) [203]. Increasing doses of lactulose induced a higher fecal volume, indicating that the osmotic effect is the main mechanism of carbohydrate-induced diarrhea.

Short-chain fatty acids may also have a direct pharmacologic effect. The consumption of short-chain fatty acids by patients with diarrhea has resulted in a net absorption of sodium and water from the large bowel lumen, improving the function of the colonic mucosa, as documented in a study in Indian adults [204].

The mechanisms of the effect of short-chain fatty acids are not clearly understood. One short-chain fatty acid, butyrate, has been studied in some depth. It is absorbed from the colon via passive diffusion of the lipid-soluble form and by active mechanisms linked to various ion-exchange transporters, which may be affected by neuroendocrine factors [205]. Butyrate has been shown to regulate colonic motility, increase colonic blood flow, and may enhance colonic healing, as seen after colonic anastomosis [205]. In a rat model, short-chain fatty acids, butyrate in particular, increased NaCl absorption from the colon, in a mechanism mediated by cyclic adenosine monophosphate (cAMP) [206], and reduced water and Na secretion induced by cholera toxin in the colon [207]. In the rabbit, short-chain fatty acids reduced mucosal congestion, cellular infiltration, necrotic changes, and blood and mucus in the lumen induced by *Shigella flexneri* 2a [208]. The only use in humans has been butyrate given to a child with congenital chloride diarrhea over a 12-month period, with normalization of stool patterns and serum electrolytes, with no side effects [209]. Further studies in controlled, randomized, double-blind clinical trials are needed with short-chain fatty acids or with diets that manipulate their colonic production in children with diarrhea.

### 6.7.2.9 GLUTAMINE

Glutamine, a nonessential amino acid, is absorbed in the intestinal tract coupled with sodium. It is an important nitrogen-carrying amino acid and is one of the principal metabolic substrates for enterocytes. Because of these effects, it has been suggested that its addition to oral rehydration solutions may improve fluid and electrolyte absorption and may stimulate a more rapid healing process in the intestine, lessening the duration or severity of diarrhea.

Glutamine-based oral rehydration solution was associated with an increased water and electrolyte absorption compared with standard WHO oral rehydration solution or with Ringer's solution, used as a control in a perfused rabbit ileal loop model of secretory diarrhea induced by cholera toxin [210]. Morphological changes in the colon were also stimulated with the use of glutamine-based oral rehydration solution in calves with diarrhea induced by enterotoxigenic *E. coli* [211]. Diarrhea-induced changes in villus length and width, crypt depth and width, and villus surface area were prevented with the glutamine-based solution compared with WHO oral rehydration solution. In another animal model, however, this solution did not have any beneficial effect on diarrhea.

Several improved oral rehydration solutions, including glutamine-based solution, were tested in a model of piglet rotavirus enteritis [212]. None of the solutions tested had any significant effect in shortening the clinical illness or in stimulating the recovery of the mucosa. A randomized, double-blind, controlled trial of glutamine-based oral rehydration solution in infants showed that it had no additional therapeutic advantages compared to the standard WHO oral rehydration solution in noncholera diarrhea [213]. Amino acid-containing oral rehydration solutions are not recommended by WHO [214]. Glutamine supplements, however, were found effective in reducing diarrhea duration in children [215], deserving further clinical evaluation.

### 6.7.2.10 NUCLEOTIDES

Because some types of diarrhea (e.g., rotavirus) create extensive damage to the intestinal mucosa, there is a need to produce new villous cells in the recovery process. The intestinal mucosa has a limited capacity to synthesize nucleotides needed in the growth of tissue and obtains most of them either from the blood or the intestinal lumen (from the diet or sloughed mucosal cells) [216, 217]. The addition of nucleotides to the diet therefore could increase the recovery from diarrhea [218]. Dietary nucleotides influence lymphocyte maturation, activation, and proliferation; they contribute to the immunoglobin response in infancy [219]. In weanling rats after lactose-induced prolonged diarrhea, the use of a diet supplemented with nucleotides was associated with intestinal histologic and ultrastructural morphology closer to the normal tissue than in rats given a standard semipurified diet [220]. There is a need to further evaluate benefits of nucleotide supplementation during acute or persistent diarrhea in children from developing countries.

### 6.7.2.11  LECTINS

Lectins are molecules that bind specifically to sugar moieties (e.g., glycoproteins or glycolipids) present in the surface of several mucosal cells as well as other organisms like bacteria or parasites. Several staple foods contain relatively high concentrations of lectins, like beans, wheat, and lentils, many of which are poorly absorbed in the gastrointestinal tract and resistant to heat and digestive enzymes [221]. Dietary lectins have been hypothesized to facilitate the binding of bacteria to the intestinal mucosa as well as to be cytotoxic to damaged mucosal cells, promoting the development of diarrhea or its prolongation [222–225]. In rat studies, red kidney beans given to weanling rats caused diarrhea, increased fecal energy loss, and the translocation of indigenous intestinal bacteria (*Citrobacter* sp. and *E. coli*) to the mesenteric lymph nodes [226]. In Bangladesh, the consumption of lentils was associated with a 14% increase in the prevalence of diarrhea [100], although this was not observed in Peruvian children [158].

In contrast, other types of dietary lectins may be protective. In plants, lectins have antimicrobial activity and are thought to play a role in plant defense against bacteria [227]. Some of these plant lectins can have antibacterial activity to human pathogens like *E. coli* [228] and may play a role in some human infections [229]. Some types of feedings have the capacity to induce endogenous synthesis of lectins, which has been found to reduce the incidence of diarrhea and promote better weight gain in piglets [230]. Several surface carbohydrates of *G. lamblia* [231] and *C. parvum* [232] are specifically agglutinated by lectins from seaweed, wheat germ, and other plant lectins. Antigenic constituents of sporulated *C. parvum* oocyst antigens that reacted with antisera from orally infected mice were specifically bound to plant lectins, including wheat germ agglutinin [233]. In the mouse model of giardiasis, the administration of wheat germ agglutinin inhibited the growth of *G. lamblia* trophozoites in vitro as well as the development of *Giardia muris* infections in the adult mouse [234]. It can be concluded that dietary lectins may increase the risk of developing bacterial diarrhea as well as inhibit the development of protozoal infections in humans. Further randomized, placebo-controlled, double-blind clinical trials with dietary lectins are warranted, particularly in the treatment or prevention of *G. lamblia* and *C. parvum* infections.

## 6.7.3  *Micronutrient Supplementation*

Specific micronutrients like zinc and vitamin A have been evaluated as therapeutic agents in acute diarrheal diseases.

### 6.7.3.1  ZINC

In an initial study done in a small group of Indian children with acute diarrhea, a small reduction (9%) of diarrhea was reported after zinc supplementation, especially in those children who had a low zinc concentration in the rectal mucosal biopsy specimens [235]. In a controlled community-based study also done in India, children were randomized to receive a multivitamin preparation with or without 20 mg of elemental zinc provided as zinc gluconate during an acute diarrheal episode [236]. Zinc-supplemented children had a 23% faster recovery from the episode as well as a 39% reduction of the probability of the episode lasting more than 7 days if zinc supplementation was started within 3 days of the onset of the episode. Zinc supplementation was also associated with a reduction in the severity of diarrhea, as indicated by a reduced mean number of watery stools per day. Another study done in Bangladesh [237] showed similar findings.

In a pooled analysis of three of these trials, zinc supplements during an acute diarrheal episode were associated with a 15% faster recovery and a 20% reduction of the probability of an episode lasting more than 7 days [238]. No difference in the effect was seen by age, gender, and nutritional status of study children in the pooled analysis.

In total, there have been 14 published trials of zinc for the treatment of acute diarrhea. All but one of these reported that children had shorter episodes, passed fewer stools per day, and were less likely to progress to have diarrhea for more than 7 days; most of these effects were statistically significant [239]. Zinc supplementation during acute diarrhea improves intestinal permeability, as indicated by the urinary lactulose:manitol excretion ratio, suggesting increased healing of small bowel mucosal damage [240].

Zinc supplementation also has a therapeutic effect in persistent diarrhea. In a study done in Bangladesh, zinc supplementation in children with persistent diarrhea was associated with a 33% reduction of diarrheal duration, an effect that was greater among malnourished children and in boys [241]. Supplemented children also were able to maintain body weight during hospitalization as well as their serum zinc concentration compared with unsupplemented control children who lost weight and had a reduction on their serum zinc level. A study done in Peru had similar results but did not reach statistical significance [242]. In a pooled analysis of four clinical trials done in children with persistent diarrhea in Bangladesh, Peru, and Pakistan, zinc supplementation was associated with a 29% faster recovery and 49% lower rate of treatment failure or death than control children [238].

Zinc supplementation is an important therapeutic tool in children with acute and persistent diarrhea in developing countries. WHO and UNICEF in 2004 issued a joint recommendation that zinc be used in the therapy of all cases of diarrhea in children [243].

### 6.7.3.2 Vitamin A

Since vitamin A supplementation had a significant impact in reducing diarrhea-related mortality in children, several investigators have evaluated the effects of vitamin A supplementation in the treatment of diarrhea cases. Clinical trials have failed to demonstrate any benefit of vitamin A on the duration or severity of diarrhea if given as a treatment [244] unless the cases had clinical signs of vitamin A deficiency or malnutrition [245, 246].

In a large, double-blind controlled trial in 900 Indian children with acute diarrhea, vitamin A supplementation had no beneficial effects in all study children but was associated with a reduction in diarrhea duration, mean number of stools or proportion of watery stools, and diarrheal episodes that became persistent in the subgroup of children who were not breast-fed [247]. In contrast, another double-blind controlled trial in 684 Bangladeshi children failed to demonstrate any beneficial effect of vitamin A supplementation during acute diarrhea of any type [248], although another trial done in Bangladesh suggested that the clinical course of acute shigellosis may be benefited by vitamin A supplementation [249]. Vitamin A supplements also failed to improve stool output, weight loss, and recovery of persistent diarrhea in Bangladeshi children [250] or to improve severe diarrhea in South African children [251], Australian indigenous population [252], and Turkish children [253]. The current recommendation is not to give vitamin A supplementation as a treatment of diarrhea.

### 6.7.4  Dietary Management of Persistent Diarrhea

In children with persistent diarrhea, many of whom may also be malnourished, the presence of lactose or carbohydrate malabsorption has been recognized as a reason for treatment failures [254]. Inexpensive and widely available mixed diets have been effective in the management of these children. A chicken-based diet was similar to more expensive elemental or soy-based diets in malnourished children with persistent diarrhea in Mexico [255]. In Croatia, a chicken-based diet not only was as good as a semielemental diet but also was associated with a reduction of diarrheal duration [256]. In children with persistent diarrhea in India, cow's milk mixed with cereals was compared with a milk-free diet [257]. Both diets had similar results in terms of diarrhea recovery and nutritional benefits, indicating that milk mixed with other foods could be used in these children.

To standardize the dietary management of children with persistent diarrhea, WHO supported a multicenter study done in Bangladesh, India, Mexico, Pakistan, Peru, and Vietnam. All children were offered an initial diet with cereals, vegetable oil, animal milk, or yogurt, with vitamins and minerals added. If the patient did not improve on that initial diet, a lactose-free diet was then given to these children. Of the children, 65% were successfully managed only with the initial diet, whereas 80% were successfully managed with the combination of both diets [258]. As shown in other studies, treatment failures were mostly associated with the presence of associated illnesses that required specific antibiotics. This study proved that children with persistent diarrhea in developing countries can be managed with simple, cheap, and available foods.

## 6.8  PREVENTION

### 6.8.1  Breast-Feeding

Promotion of breast-feeding is considered a high priority in the prevention of diarrheal diseases. Non-breast-fed children also have up to a twofold increase in diarrheal duration and up to a sixfold increased risk of persistent diarrhea compared with partially or fully breast-fed children [149, 259, 260]. Breast-fed children have a reduced mortality risk [261]. Non-breast-fed or partially breast-fed children have up to a 25-fold increased risk of death [31, 262, 263]. Breast-feeding promotion has been estimated to reduce diarrhea prevalence by 40% in infants aged 0–2 months, 30% in those aged 3–5 months, and 10% in those aged 6–11 months [261]. Intervention studies to promote the introduction of exclusive breast-feeding in infants under 6 months of age are encouraging [264]. A randomized, controlled trial of home-based peer counseling to promote exclusive breast-feeding reported an increase in the rate of exclusive breast-feeding at 3 months postpartum after six visits (67% exclusive breast-feeding) or three visits (50% exclusive breast-feeding) counseling frequencies, compared with no counseling (12% exclusive breast-feeding) [265]. Duration of breast-feeding was longer in the intervention groups and diarrhea was less frequent in the intervention groups (12%) compared with the control group (26%).

Breast-feeding promotion through a regular health care program in Pakistan demonstrated a reduction in the time to initiate breast-feeding after birth, an increased rate of exclusive breast-feeding at 1 month of age, with significant reduction of diarrheal rates [266]. In a cluster randomized community-based trial of an educational campaign through existing primary health care services, the prevalence of exclusive breast-feeding at 6 months of age increased, reducing diarrheal morbidity in India [267]. In Manila, breast-feeding counseling in low birth weight (LBW) infants increased exclusive breast-feeding at six months of age and showed an impact on diarrhea morbidity [268]. These results documented the importance of breast-feeding promotion to improve infant health.

### 6.8.2    Improved Weaning Practices

Several epidemiological studies have clearly documented that diarrhea increases at the time of introduction of weaning foods. Diarrheal rates are greater in infants not receiving breast milk compared with those receiving exclusive or partial breast-feeding [261]. In infants under 6 months of age, the simple addition of water or infusions to breast milk are associated with a two- or threefold increase in diarrhea rates [33, 36]. Bacterial contamination of weaning foods in developing countries has been documented [269–271]. Food has been incriminated as a source of outbreaks of diarrheal diseases in developed countries [272] and as a source of traveler's diarrhea [273, 274], documenting its important role in the transmission of diarrhea. All major bacterial enteropathogens have been isolated from weaning food samples, in concentrations from $10^3$ to $10^8$ bacteria per gram or milliliter [270, 271]. Food seems to be more frequently contaminated and to have higher bacterial counts than drinking water in developing countries, presumably owing to multiplication of the bacteria in the food [275]. The promotion of an adequate weaning food under hygienic conditions would have the dual advantage of improving nutrient content and decreasing microbial contamination, which should be effective in reducing diarrheal diseases [276–278]. Randomized, controlled trials of improved weaning food practices to prevent diarrheal diseases are needed in developing countries.

### 6.8.3    Use of Safe Water

Contaminated water plays an important role in the transmission of some pathogens that cause diarrhea. In many developing countries, a large proportion of the population does not have access to safe water [279]. In spite of available potable water, further contamination with enteropathogens may occur in the home as a result of contaminated vessels and utensils. Point-of-use disinfectant by chemicals or solar light have been shown to reduce diarrheal rates in children, as do simple water-filtering systems that can be used at home [280, 281]. Provision of safe water must be accompanied by health education aimed at better hygiene and weaning practices.

### 6.8.4    Hand Washing

Hygiene education and hand washing may help to reduce the incidence of diarrheal diseases. The risk of diarrhea with lack of hand washing has been described in mothers after defecating or cleaning a child. The level of hand contamination with fecal coliforms is greater in communities with unimproved water and sanitation facilities, suggesting that the impact of hand washing may be greater in such communities [282]. Not only bacteria but also viruses can adhere to hands, as documented with rotavirus in

Bangladesh [283]. Hand washing with soap is effective in eliminating fecal contamination [284–286], even for viruses [287]. Hand washing does not necessarily need to be done with soap since using ash, mud, or other agents may also facilitate the removal of bacteria, being more effective than using water alone [288]. Hand washing interventions were found in a meta-analysis to reduce diarrheal incidence by 44% [289]. There is a need to develop and implement large intervention programs to increase the frequency of appropriate hand washing practices by children and mothers in developing countries.

### 6.8.5   *Latrines and Proper Disposal of Human Waste*

Because the fecal-oral route is the main route of transmission for diarrheal pathogens, the safe disposal of human feces would be expected to reduce transmission of most pathogens. In a meta-analysis of sanitation interventions, diarrhea rates were reduced by 32% [289]. Sanitation schemes such as latrines generally require proper education and active involvement of the community to be effective. It also should be recognized that, in many communities, young children may be allowed to defecate freely even though sanitation facilities such as latrines are available [290, 291]. The use of potties was identified as an important intervention to avoid fecal contamination of a household's soil by toddlers and should be further evaluated [292].

### 6.8.6   *Measles Immunization*

Major complications of measles infection include diarrheal disease, immune suppression, and a period of increased susceptibility to infectious diseases following an attack (see Chapter 8). Widespread measles immunization coverage would be expected to have an impact on diarrhea.

### 6.8.7   *Nutritional Interventions*

Improving the nutritional status of children should be effective in preventing diarrheal morbidity and mortality. Only recently has there been a comparative risk assessment of different risk factors that affect mortality and burden of diseases in the world. From the analysis of 26 selected risk factors in an extensive review of the literature, childhood and maternal underweight explained 9.5% of all disability-adjusted life years (DALYs) lost by children and adults worldwide, ranked fourth as a cause of death and first as a cause of DALYs [293]. However, randomized, controlled interventions that were able to document an improvement in the nutritional status of children (e.g., through food supplements) have not studied its effects in preventing diarrheal diseases. Preliminary results in nonrandomized studies, like the observed reduction in the incidence of diarrheal diseases following nutritional improvement through home garden production and nutrition education in Vietnamese children [294], need to be confirmed.

#### 6.8.7.1   ZINC

Low serum zinc levels have been found to be significant predictors of the incidence of diarrhea in general and severe diarrhea in particular, as well as an increased risk for the development of acute lower-respiratory infections, especially in boys [295]. In a community-based, double-blind, randomized trial done in India, zinc supplementation given daily for 6 months was associated with a significant reduction in diarrhea incidence (17–26% reduction) and prevalence (35% reduction), which was mainly seen in children older than 12 months, in boys, and in children with low serum zinc levels [296]. A similar effect was also observed in the prevention of persistent diarrhea and dysentery in this study. Zinc supplementation was associated with a 21% reduction of persistent diarrhea and 14% reduction of dysentery, which were not statistically significant overall [297]. Again, the effect was more apparent in boys, in children with low serum zinc levels prior to supplementation, and in children older than 11 months. A similar study done in Guatemala also found a 22% reduction in the incidence of acute and persistent diarrhea, mainly among poorly nourished boys [298].

Similar studies done in Mexico, Peru, and Vietnam were combined with the results observed in India and Guatemala in a pooled analysis. Zinc supplementation resulted in statistically significant reductions of 18% in the incidence and 25% in the prevalence of diarrhea and 41% in the incidence of pneumonia [299]. A trend was found for the prevention of persistent diarrhea and dysentery, without reaching statistical significance.

Overall, there have been 22 trials assessing the effect of daily zinc supplementation and 3 trials of weekly supplementation [239]. Of the 25 trials, 20 reported a benefit of the zinc supplements on diarrhea incidence, prevalence, or severity; 3 trials, 2 with weekly supplementation, reported no benefits.

Low serum zinc levels in mothers either early or late in gestation have been associated with LBW: the lower the serum zinc level in the mother, the lower the birth weight [300]. Zinc supplementation given daily during an 8-week period to LBW full-term infants in Brazil was associated with a 28% reduction in the prevalence of diarrhea and 33% reduction in the prevalence of cough [301]. In another study done in India, zinc supplementation given between 30 days and 9 months of life to a large group of infants who were small for their gestational age found that supplemented children had significantly lower mortality [302]. In a large, double-blind, placebo-controlled trial in Pemba, Zanzibar, evaluating a total of over 42,000 children aged 1–36 months, 10 mg of zinc supplements given daily for a mean of about 16 months was associated with a non-significant reduction in mortality of 7% [303].

### 6.8.7.2 VITAMIN A

An association between xerophthalmia and childhood mortality was noted in Indonesia [304], leading to several controlled intervention trials of vitamin A supplementation in developing countries endemic for vitamin A deficiency. There was an overall 23% reduction in mortality in children 6–59 months of age, as indicated in a meta-analysis of these studies [305]. In those trials in which cause-specific mortality data were obtained, vitamin A supplementation was associated with a 35–50% reduction in diarrhea-associated mortality [306–309]. When this association was evaluated in prospective, community-based trials of vitamin A supplementation, there were conflicting results. In a large study done in Ghana, in an area with high prevalence of xerophthalmia, it was demonstrated that vitamin A supplementation reduced the severity of diarrheal diseases rather than its incidence or prevalence [309, 310]. Supplemented children had a lower incidence of diarrheal episodes with a high number of liquid stools per day or with dehydration, which resulted in significant reductions in clinic visits (17% reduction) and hospitalizations (38% reduction) for diarrhea cases. In an additional trial done in nonxerophthalmic children in northeastern Brazil, vitamin A supplementation was associated with a reduced probability of having diarrheal episodes, especially those with high number of liquid stools per day [311]. No impact was observed on dysenteric diarrheal episodes.

On examining all of the studies of vitamin A supplementation, it was concluded, however, that there was little or no overall effect on diarrhea rates [305]. The most likely conclusion is that vitamin A supplementation reduces the severity of diarrheal episodes and complications but does not reduce the incidence of all diarrhea. One possible mechanism for this observation is that supplemented children are able to mount an acute-phase response after a diarrheal episode compared with those who received placebo [312]. A meta-analysis confirmed previous findings and suggested that high-dose vitamin A supplementation is only recommended for children living in areas with vitamin A deficiency [313].

### 6.8.7.3 NUCLEOTIDES

A strategy that has been considered for the prevention of diarrheal diseases is the provision of a dietary supplement with nucleotides. This hypothesis was tested in a large multicenter study done in infants from Spain. A formula with nucleotide supplementation was given for the first 6 months of life and compared with unsupplemented formula [314]. There was a 36% reduction on the incidence of diarrhea, as noted by participating mothers and by cases detected in 340 pediatric clinics. The duration and severity of diarrhea were also less in the supplemented infants compared with control infants. No impact on anthropometric indicators was found in these infants living in a developed country.

In a controlled, community-based study in Chilean children who received an infant formula with or without supplemental nucleotides [315], children who received the supplemented formula had a significant reduction in the incidence and prevalence of diarrhea, although no difference existed in the causes of diarrheal episodes or in their clinical characteristics. In a trial in Taiwanese newborns supplemented with nucleotide-containing infant formula for 12 months, significant protection against diarrhea was documented [316]. These findings were confirmed in a large multicenter study of Italian children [317]. These studies need to be replicated in developing countries with poor socioeconomic conditions. Other ways of providing dietary nucleotides, such as by consumption of staple foods that contain animal proteins with adequate amounts of nucleotides, need further evaluation.

### 6.8.8 Vaccines

Rotavirus may be responsible for 5% of all diarrheal episodes and for 20% of diarrheal deaths in children under 5 years of age [318]. A live rotavirus vaccine prepared from a rhesus rotavirus, to which specific antigens from human rotavirus were added by molecular techniques (rhesus-human, reassortant, tetravalent rotavirus vaccine), was effective in developed countries and was introduced into the United States in 1998 [319]. The efficacy of this vaccine in developing countries was not initially considered optimal owing to its lower level of protection as seen in field trials done in Peru [320] and Brazil [321]. However, a reanalysis of these two trials has suggested that the vaccine had similar vaccine efficacy against moderate and severe rotavirus diarrhea as in trials conducted in Venezuela and the United States [322]. Because of an association of intussusception with this rotavirus vaccine [323], the vaccine was put on hold [324] and withdrawn from the US market by the manufacturer.

This prompted the developed of alternative vaccines. Three oral doses of a bovine-based human reassortant rotavirus vaccine have been proved safe and effective in protecting mostly US and Finish children in a large vaccine trial [325]. This vaccine has been introduced into the United States and some Latin American markets. An attenuated human rotavirus vaccine has also been developed and proved safe and effective in a large vaccine trial done in several Latin American countries [326]. This vaccine has been introduced in the markets of several Latin American countries, with Brazil the first to use it in their public system. Other vaccines against cholera and typhoid fever are available in the market but seldom used in developing countries. New vaccines against shigellosis and enterotoxigenic *E. coli* are expected to become available in the near future.

### 6.8.9   Other Potential Interventions

As reviewed in this chapter, other potential interventions that could have a preventive effect on diarrheal diseases have been identified. The prevention of diarrheal diseases by the administration of probiotics, particularly *Lactobacillus* GG, needs to be further documented, as well as the potential benefit of the utilization of food-related products like epidermal growth factor or short-chain fatty acids.

### 6.9   FUTURE DIRECTIONS

As highlighted in this chapter, there has been considerable progress in documenting the importance of nutrition and its relationship with diarrheal diseases in children in developing countries. However, there are several research activities that should be conducted to develop a package of effective interventions that could be implemented in an inexpensive way in developing countries. Many gaps of information still exist in some critical areas, as indicated in this review, which are summarized only briefly next:

- The effect of diarrhea on growth and nutrition has been well documented. There is a further need to evaluate the nutritional cost of asymptomatic infections in children, as documented with *C. parvum* in Peru. This may cause an important burden owing to the high prevalence of asymptomatic infections.
- In the area of dietary management of diarrheal diseases, significant progress has occurred, with the identification of a variety of potential elements that may be effective in the management or treatment of these diseases. The use of probiotics, particularly *Lactobacillus* GG, in the treatment and prevention of diarrheal diseases is very promising. Studies are needed to evaluate further other strains that may have similar potential, as are effectiveness studies of these approaches in a public health context.
- Further studies are needed to elucidate the mechanisms of action of short-chain fatty acids in the gut. The direct effect of administering short-chain fatty acids to children with diarrhea, as antidiarrheal agents promoting water and electrolyte absorption as documented with butyrate, needs further evaluation. Similar studies are also needed with other agents that may be beneficial to children with diarrhea, like epidermal growth factor and nucleotides.
- The use of lectins to prevent the development of diarrhea associated with *G. lamblia* and *C. parvum* needs to be evaluated in controlled clinical trials.
- Effectiveness studies are needed to guide how to implement the recommendation that zinc be used for diarrhea treatment along with ORT.

- Further investigation is needed into the means of increasing the dietary intake of readily absorbed zinc in children, such as food fortification, taking into consideration the consumption of staple foods available for fortification in developing countries.
- Vitamin A supplementation deserves further evaluation as treatment for shigellosis.
- In the area of nutrition, there is overwhelming evidence indicating the importance of better nutritional status in the prevention of diarrheal diseases and their complications. However, few studies have documented an impact on improving the nutritional status of children in developing countries and the benefits of these changes on the rates of diarrheal diseases. Further controlled trials evaluating the impact of intervention programs promoting exclusive breast-feeding on diarrheal diseases, as well as an improved quality of weaning foods, are urgently needed.
- An area of investigation that deserves particular attention is food hygiene because it may be one of the most important, and yet neglected, mechanisms of transmission of enteropathogens in developing countries.

## 6.10   CONCLUSIONS

It can be concluded from this review that nutrition and diarrheal diseases are closely related. These infectious diseases have an important impact on the nutritional status of affected children, especially in developing countries where the consumption of a weaning diet of very low quality inhibits an adequate catch-up growth after recovery from these illnesses. Poorly nourished children, on the other hand, are at a greater risk of developing these illnesses as well as getting more severe episodes, including persistent diarrhea, with a significant increase in their risk of dying. Considerable knowledge exists today of adequate dietary management of diarrheal diseases, which should inhibit their negative effects on nutrition. However, in many developing countries, the unavailability of an adequate weaning food not only prevents adequate dietary management during illnesses but also, more importantly, has a pronounced and permanent effect on the nutritional status of these children.

Considerable progress has been made in identifying potential effective dietary interventions in the treatment and, in some cases, prevention of diarrheal diseases. The use of probiotics, epidermal growth factor, short-chain fatty acids, nucleotides, lectins, and micronutrients, particularly zinc, have opened whole new avenues for research in nutrition and disease control. It is likely that in the future, when studies will have clearly identified the cost-effectiveness of these potential interventions, public health officers in developing countries may consider not only ways to improve the diet of their population but also the interventions that will reduce morbidity and mortality. These advances may go beyond the immediate benefit of reducing the burden of illness and improve the quality of life (e.g., through enhanced cognitive development) as well.

## REFERENCES

1. Baqui AH, Black RE, Yunus MD, Hoque ARA, Chowdhury HR, Sack RB. Methodological issues in diarrhoeal diseases epidemiology: definition of diarrhoeal episodes. Int J Epidemiol 1991;20:1057–1063.
2. Morris SS, Cousens SN, Lanata CF, Kirkwood BR. Diarrhoea—defining the episode. Int J Epidemiol 1994;23:617–623.

3. Snyder JD, Merson MH. The magnitude of the global problem of acute diarrhoeal disease: a review of the active surveillance data. Bull World Health Organ 1982;60:605–613.

4. Bryce J, Boschi-Pinto C, Shibuya K, Black RE, WHO Child Health Epidemiology Reference Group. New WHO estimates of the causes of child deaths. *Lancet* 2005;365:1147–1152.

5. Woods R, Woodward J, eds. Urban disease and mortality in nineteenth century England. New York: St. Martin's Press, 1984.

6. Meckel RA. Save the babies: American public health reform and the prevention of infant mortality, 1850–1929. Baltimore, MD: Johns Hopkins University Press, 1990.

7. Newman G. Infant mortality: a social problem. London: Methuen, 1906.

8. Stuart HC. Mortality among infants and children and progress in reduction in rates from certain causes. J Pediatr 1938;15:266–276.

9. Newsholme A. Fifty years in public health: a personal narrative with comments. London: Allen and Unwin, 1935.

10. Creighton C. A history of epidemics in Britain. Cambridge, UK: Cambridge University Press, 1894.

11. Scott HH. A history of tropical medicine. London: Arnold, 1939.

12. Ackerknecht EH. History and geography of the most important diseases. New York: Hafner, 1965.

13. Gordon JE, Guzman MA, Ascoli W, et al. Acute diarrheal disease in less developed countries. I. An epidemiological basis for control. Bull World Health Organ 1964;31:1–7.

14. Chen LC, Scrimshaw NS, eds. Diarrhea and malnutrition: interactions, mechanisms, and interventions. New York: Plenum, 1983.

15. Nalin DR, Cash RA, Islam R, Molla M, Phillips RA. Oral maintenance therapy for cholera in adults. Lancet 1968;2:370–373.

16. Nalin DR, Cash RA. Oral or nasogastric maintenance therapy in pediatric cholera patients. J Pediatr 1971;78:355–358.

17. Sack DA, Chowdhury AMAK, Eusof A, Ali MA, Merson MH, Islam S, et al. Oral hydration in rotavirus diarrhoea: a double blind comparison of sucrose with glucose electrolyte solution. Lancet 1978;2:280–283.

18. Nalin DR, Levine MM, Mata L, De Cespedes C, Vargas W, Lizano C, et al. Oral rehydration and maintenance of children with rotavirus and bacterial diarrhoeas. Bull World Health Organ 1979;57:453–459.

19. Black RE, Lanata CF. Epidemiology of diarrheal diseases in developing countries. In: Infections of the gastrointestinal tract, 2nd ed. Blaser MJ, Smith PD, Ravdin JI, Greenberg HB, Guerrant RL, eds. Philadelphia: Lippincott, Williams and Wilkins, 2002:11–29.

20. Parashar UD, Gibson CJ, Bresee JS, Glass RI. Rotavirus and severe childhood diarrhea. Emerg Infect Dis 2006;12:304–306.

21. Guerrant RL, Kirchhoff LV, Shields DS, et al. Prospective study of diarrheal illnesses in northeastern Brazil: patterns of disease, nutritional impact, etiologies, and risk factors. J Infect Dis 1983;148:986–997.

22. Becker S, Black RE, Brown KH, Nahar S. Relations between socio-economic status and morbidity, food intake and growth in young children in two villages in Bangladesh. Ecol Food Nutr 1986;18:251–264.

23. Stanton BF, Clemens JD. Socioeconomic variables and rates of diarrhoeal disease in urban Bangladesh. Trans R Soc Trop Med Hyg 1987;81:278–282.

24. Yeager BAC, Lanata CF, Lazo F, Verastegui H, Black RE. Transmission factors and socioeconomic status as determinants of diarrhoeal incidence in Lima, Peru. J Diarrhoeal Dis Res 1991;9:186–193.

25. Rahaman M, Rahaman MM, Wojtyniak B, Aziz KMS. Impact of environmental sanitation and crowding on infant mortality in rural Bangladesh. Lancet 1985;2:28–31.

26. Sepulveda J, Willett W, Muñoz A. Malnutrition and diarrhea. A longitudinal study among urban Mexican children. Am J Epidemiol 1988;127:365–376.

27. Henry ES. Environmental sanitation, infection and nutritional status of infants in rural St. Lucia, West Indies. Trans R Soc Trop Med Hyg 1981;75:507–513.

28. Tomkins AM, Drasar BS, Bradley AK, Williamson WA. Water supply and nutritional status in rural northern Nigeria. Trans R Soc Trop Med Hyg 1978;72:239–243.

29. Esrey SA, Collett J, Miliotis MD, Koornhof HJ, Makhales P. The risk of infection from *Giardia lamblia* due to drinking water supply, use of water, and latrines among preschool children in rural Lesotho. Int J Epidemiol 1989;18:248–253.

30. Betrand WE, Walmus BF. Maternal knowledge, attitudes and practice as predictors of diarrhoeal disease in young children. Int J Epidemiol 1983;12:205–210.

31. Yoon PW, Black RE, Moulton LH, Becker S. Effect of not breastfeeding on the risk of diarrheal and respiratory mortality in children under 2 years of age in Metro Cebu, the Philippines. Am J Epidemiol 1996;143:1142–1148.

32. Victora CG, Smith PG, Vaughan JP, Nobre LC, Lombardi C, Teixeira AM, et al. Evidence for protection by breast-feeding against infant deaths from infectious diseases in Brazil. Lancet 1987;2:319–322.

33. Chandra RK. Prospective studies of the effect of breast feeding on incidence of infection and allergy. Acta Paediatr Scand 1979;68:691–694.

34. Brown KH, Black RE, Lopez de Romaña G, Creed de Kanashiro H. Infant feeding practices and their relationship with diarrheal and other diseases. Pediatrics 1989;83:31–40.

35. Lopez-Alarcon M, Villalpando S, Fajardo A. Breast-feeding lowers the frequency and duration of acute respiratory infection and diarrhea in infants under 6 months of age. J Nutr 1997;127:436–443.

36. Deb SK. Acute respiratory disease survey in Tripura in case of children below 5 years of age. J Indian Med Assoc 1998;96:111–116.

37. Popkin BM, Adair L, Akin JS, Black R, Briscoe J, Flieger W. Breast-feeding and diarrheal morbidity. Pediatrics 1990;86:874–882.

38. Han AM, Nwe OO, Aye T, Hlaing T. Personal toilet after defaecation and the degree of hand contamination according to different methods used. J Trop Med Hyg 1986;89:237–241.

39. Henry FJ, Rahim Z. Transmission of diarrhoea in two crowded areas with different sanitary facilities in Dhaka, Bangladesh. J Trop Med Hyg 1990;93:121–126.

40. Lanata CF. Studies of food hygiene and diarrhoeal disease. Int J Environ Health Res 2003;13:S175–S183.

41. Goldreich EE, Bordner RH. Fecal contamination of fruits and vegetables during cultivation and processing for the market. A review. J Milk Food Technol 1971;34:184–195.

42. Barrell RAE, Rowland MGM. Commercial milk products and indigenous weaning foods in a rural West African environment: a bacteriological perspective. J Hyg (Camb) 1980;84:191–202.

43. Phillips I, Lwanga SK, Lore W, Wasswa D. Methods and hygiene of infant feeding in an urban area of Uganda. J Trop Pediatr 1969;15:167–171.

44. Cherian A, Lawande RV. Recovery of potential pathogens from feeding bottle contents and teats in Zaria, Nigeria. Trans R Soc Trop Med Hyg 1985;79:840–842.

45. Huttly SRA, Blum D, Kirkwood BR, Emeh RN, Feachem RG. The epidemiology of acute diarrhoea in a rural community in Imo State, Nigeria. Trans R Soc Trop Med Hyg 1987;81:865–870.

46. Knight SM, Toodayan W, Caique WJC, Kyi W, Barnes A, Desmarchelier P. Risk factors for the transmission of diarrhoea in children: a case-control study in rural Malaysia. Int J Epidemiol 1992;21:812–818.

47. Chavasse DC, Shier RP, Murphy OA, Huttly SR, Cousens SN, Akhtar T. Impact of fly control on childhood diarrhea in Pakistan: community-randomized trial. Lancet 1999;353:22–25.

48. Grados O, Bravo N, Black RE, Butzler JP. Case-control study to identify risk factors for pediatric *Campylobacter* diarrhea in Lima, Peru. Bull World Health Organ 1988;66:369–374.

49. Schorling JB, McAuliffe JF, de Souza MA, Guerrant RL. Malnutrition is associated with increased diarrhoea incidence and duration among children in an urban Brazilian slum. Int J Epidemiol 1990;19:728–735.

50. Palmer DL, Koster FT, Alam AKMJ, Islam MR. Nutritional status: a determinant of severity of diarrhea in patients with cholera. J Infect Dis 1976;134:8–14.

51. El Samani EFZ, Willett WC, Ware JH. Association of malnutrition and diarrhoea in children aged under 5 years. A prospective follow-up study in a rural Sudanese community. Am J Epidemiol 1988;128:93–105.

52. Nalin DR, Levine RJ, Levine MM, Hoover D, Bergquist E, McLaughlin J, et al. Cholera, non-vibrio cholera, and stomach acid. Lancet 1978;2:856–859.

53. Bern C, Martines J, de Zoysa I, Glass RI. The magnitude of the global problem of diarrhoeal diseases: a ten-year update. Bull World Health Organ 1992;70:705–714.

54. Kosek M, Bern C, Guerrant RL. The global burden of diarrhoeal disease, as estimated from studies published between 1992 and 2000. Bull World Health Organ 2003;81(3):197–204.

55. Lanata CF, Mendoza W, Verastegui H, Black RE, WHO Child Epidemiology Reference Group. Trends on diarrhoea morbidity in children under 5 years of age since the 1980s: the need for effective preven-

tive interventions. Final report to WHO, May 2005. Available from the authors and at http://www.who. int/child_adolescent_health/data/cherg/en/index.html

56. Black RE, Merson MH, Rahman, ASMM, Yunus M, Alim AR, Huq I, et al. A 2 year study of bacterial, viral, and parasitic agents associated with diarrhea in rural Bangladesh. J Infect Dis 1980;142:660–664.

57. Cook SM, Glass RI, LeBaron CW, Ho MS. Global seasonality of rotavirus infections. Bull World Health Organ 1990;68:171–177.

58. World Health Organization. A manual for the treatment of diarrhoea for use by physicians and other senior health workers. Programme for the Control of Diarrhoeal Diseases. Geneva: World Health Organization, 1990. WHO/CDD/SER/80.2 Rev.2.

59. Lanata CF, Mendoza W, Black RE, WHO Child Epidemiology Reference Group. Improving diarrhea estimates. Final report to WHO, October 2003. Available from the authors.

60. Guerrant RL. Pathophysiology of the enterotoxic and viral diarrheas. In: Diarrhea and malnutrition: interactions, mechanisms, and interventions. Chen LC, Scrimshaw NS, eds. New York: Plenum, 1983:23–43.

61. Keusch GT. The epidemiology and pathophysiology of invasive bacterial diarrheas with a note on biological considerations in control strategies. In: Diarrhea and malnutrition: interactions, mechanisms, and interventions. Chen LC, Scrimshaw NS, eds. New York: Plenum, 1983:45–72.

62. Ryder RW, Reeves WC, Sack RB. Risk factors for fatal childhood diarrhea: a case-control study from two remote Panamanian islands. Am J Epidemiol 1985;121:605–610.

63. Roy SK, Chowdhury AK, Rahaman MM. Excess mortality among children discharged from hospital after treatment for diarrhoea in rural Bangladesh. BMJ 1983;287:1097–1099.

64. Bhandari N, Bhan MK, Sazawal S. Mortality associated with acute watery diarrhea, dysentery and persistent diarrhea in rural north India. Acta Paediatr Suppl 1992;381:3–6.

65. Tome P, Reyes H, Rodriguez L, Guiscafre H, Gutierrez G. Death caused by acute diarrhea in children: a study of prognostic factors. Salud Publica Mex 1996;38:227–235.

66. Pelletier DL, Frongillo EA Jr, Habicht J.P. Epidemiologic evidence for a potentiating effect of malnutrition on child mortality. Am J Public Health 1993;83:1130–1133.

67. Yoon PW, Black RE, Moulton LH, Becker S. The effect of malnutrition on the risk of diarrheal and respiratory mortality in children < 2 years of age in Cebu, Philippines. Am J Clin Nutr 1997;65:1070–1077.

68. Caulfield LE, de Onis M, Blossner M, Black RE Undernutrition as an underlying cause of child deaths associated with diarrhea, pneumonia, malaria and measles. Am J Clin Nutr 2004;80:193–198.

69. Fauveau V, Henry FJ, Briend A, Yunus M, Chakraborty J. Persistent diarrhea as a cause of childhood mortality in rural Bangladesh. Acta Paediatr Suppl 1992;381:12–14.

70. Martorell R, Habicht JP, Yarbrough C, Lechtig A, Klein RE, Western KA. Acute morbidity and physical growth in rural Guatemalan children. Am J Dis Child 1975;129:1296–1301.

71. Rowland MGM., Cole TJ, Whitehead RG. A quantitative study into the role of infection in determining nutritional status in Gambian village children. Br J Nutr 1977;37:441–450.

72. Condon-Paoloni D, Cravioto J, Johnston FE, De Licardie ER, Scholl TO. Morbidity and growth of infants and young children in a rural Mexican village. Am J Public Health 1977;67:651–656.

73. Black RE, Brown KH, Becker S. Malnutrition is a determining factor in diarrheal duration, but not incidence, among young children in a longitudinal study in rural Bangladesh. Am J Clin Nutr 1984;39:87–94.

74. Chen LC, Huq E, Huffman SL. A prospective study of the risk of diarrheal diseases according to the nutritional status of children. Am J Epidemiol 1981;114:284–292.

75. Deivanayagam N, Mala N, Ashok TP, Ratnam SR, Sankaranarayanan VS. Risk factors for persistent diarrhea among children under 2 years of age. Case control study. Indian Pediatr 1993;30:177–185.

76. Bhandari N, Bhan MK, Sazawal S, Clemens JD, Bhatnagar S, Khoshoo V. Association of antecedent malnutrition with persistent diarrhoea: a case-control study. BMJ 1989;298:1284–1287.

77. Black RE, Merson MH, Eusof A, Huq I, Pollard R. Nutritional status, body size and severity of diarrhoea associated with rotavirus or enterotoxigenic *Escherichia coli*. J Trop Med Hyg 1984;87:83–89.

78. Mathur R, Reddy V, Naidu AN, Ravikumar, Krishnamachari KA. Nutritional status and diarrhoeal morbidity: a longitudinal study in rural Indian preschool children. Hum Nutr Clin Nutr 1985;39:447–454.

79. Atalah E, Bustos P, Gomez E. Infantile malnutrition: social cost or respiratory and digestive pathology. Arch Latinoam Nutr 1983;33:395–408.

80. Victora CG, Barros FC, Kirkwood BR, Vaughan JP. Pneumonia, diarrhea, and growth in the first 4 years of life: a longitudinal study of 5,914 urban Brazilian children. Am J Clin Nutr 1990;52:391–396.

81. Man WD, Weber M, Palmer A, Schneider G, Wadda R, Jaffar S, et al. Nutritional status of children admitted to hospital with different diseases and its relationship to outcome in the Gambia, West Africa. Trop Med Int Health 1998;3:678–686.

82. Guerrant RL, Schorling JB, McAuliffe JF, de Souza MA. Diarrhea as a cause and an effect of malnutrition: diarrhea prevents catch-up growth and malnutrition increases diarrhea frequency and duration. Am J Trop Med Hyg 1992;47:28–35.

83. Biritwum RB, Isomura S, Assoku A, Torigoe S. Growth and diarrhoeal disease surveillance in a rural Ghanaian pre-school child population. Trans R Soc Trop Med Hyg 1986;80:208–213.

84. El Samani FZ, Willett WC, Ware JH. Predictors of simple diarrhoea in children under 5 years—a study of a Sudanese rural community. Soc Sci Med 1989;29:1065–1070.

85. Schorling JB, McAuliffe JF, de Souza MA, Guerrant RL. Malnutrition is associated with increased diarrhoea incidence and duration among children in an urban Brazilian slum. Int J Epidemiol 1990;19:728–735.

86. Lindtjorn B, Alemu T, Bjorvatn B. Nutritional status and risk of infection among Ethiopian children. J Trop Pediatr 1993;39:76–82.

87. Anand K, Sundaram KR, Lobo J, Kapoor SK. Are diarrheal incidence and malnutrition related in under five children? A longitudinal study in an area of poor sanitary conditions. Indian Pediatr 1994;31:943–948.

88. Sepulveda J, Willett W, Muñoz A. Malnutrition and diarrhea. A longitudinal study among urban Mexican children. Am J Epidemiol 1988;127:365–376.

89. El Samani EF, Willett WC, Ware JH. Association of malnutrition and diarrhea in children aged under 5 years. A prospective follow-up study in a rural Sudanese community. Am J Epidemiol 1988;128:93–105.

90. Chowdhury MK, Gupta VM, Bairagi R, Bhattacharya BN. Does malnutrition predispose to diarrhoea during childhood? Evidence from a longitudinal study in Matlab, Bangladesh. Eur J Clin Nutr 1990;44:515–525.

91. Sarabia-Arce S, Salazar-Lindo E, Gilman RH, Naranjo J, Miranda E. Case-control study of *Cryptosporidium parvum* infection in Peruvian children hospitalized for diarrhea: possible association with malnutrition and nosocomial infection. Pediatr Infect Dis J 1990;9:627–631.

92. Black RE, Brown KH, Becker S. Effects of diarrhea associated with specific enteropathogens on the growth of children in rural Bangladesh. Pediatrics 1984;73:799–805.

93. Bairagi R, Chowdhury MK, Kim YJ, Curlin GT, Gray RH. The association between malnutrition and diarrhoea in rural Bangladesh. Int J Epidemiol 1987;16:477–481.

94. Rowland MGM., Rowland SGJ., Cole TJ. Impact of infection on the growth of children from 0 to 2 years in an urban West African community. Am J Clin Nutr 1988;47:134–138.

95. Adair L, Popkin BM, Van Derslice J, Akin J, Guilkey D, Black R, et al. Growth dynamics during the first 2 years of life: a prospective study in the Philippines. Eur J Clin Nutr 1993;47:42–51.

96. Bittencourt SA, Leal MC, Rivera J. Diarrhea and growth among children under 18 months of age in Rio de Janeiro. Bull Pan Am Health Organ 1993;27:135–144.

97. Bhandari N, Sazawal S, Clemens JD, Kashyap DK, Dhingra U, Bhan MK. Association between diarrheal duration and nutrition decline: implications for an empirically validated definition of persistent diarrhea. Indian J Pediatr 1994;61:559–566.

98. Zumrawi FY, Dimond H, Waterlow JC. Effects of infection on growth in Sudanese children. Hum Nutr Clin Nutr 1987;41:453–461.

99. Moy RJ, de C Marshall TF, Choto RG, McNeish AS, Booth IW. Diarrhoea and growth faltering in rural Zimbabwe. Eur J Clin Nutr 1994;48:810–821.

100. Black RE. Persistent diarrhea in children of developing countries. Pediatr Infect Dis J 1993;12:751–761.

101. McAuliffe JF, Shields DS, de Sousa MA, Sakell J, Schorling J, Guerrant RL. Prolonged and recurring diarrhea in the northeast of Brazil: examination of cases from a community-based study. J Pediatr Gastroenterol Nutr 1986;5:902–906.

102. Baqui AH, Black RE, Sack RB, Yunus MD, Siddique AK, Chowdhury HR. Epidemiological and clinical characteristics of acute and persistent diarrhoea in rural Bangladeshi children. Acta Paediatr Suppl 1992;381:15–21.

103. Checkley W, Gilman RH, Epstein LD, Suarez M, Diaz JF, Cabrera L, et al. Asymptomatic and symptomatic cryptosporidiosis: their acute effect on weight gain in Peruvian children. Am J Epidemiol 1997;145:156–163.

104. Checkley W, Epstein LD, Gilman RH, Black RE, Cabrera L, Sterling CR. Effects of *Cryptosporidium parvum* infection in Peruvian children: growth faltering and subsequent catch-up growth. Am J Epidemiol 1998;148:497–506.

105. Brown KH, Peerson JM, Kanashiro H, Lopez de Romaña G, Black RE. The relationship between diarrheal prevalence and growth of poor infants varies with their age and usual energy intake. FASEB J 1991;5:A1079.

106. Marquis GS, Habicht JP, Lanata CF, Black RE, Rasmussen KM. Breast milk or animal-product foods improve linear growth of Peruvian toddlers consuming marginal diets. Am J Clin Nutr 1997;66:1102–1109.

107. Lutter CK, Mora JO, Habicht JP, Rasmussen KM, Robson DS, Sellers SG, Super CM, Herrera MG. Nutritional supplementation: effects on child stunting because of diarrhea. Am J Clin Nutr 1989;50:1–8.

108. Rivera J, Martorell R, Lutter CK. Interaction of dietary intake and diarrheal disease in child growth. Arch Latinoam Nutr 1989;39:292–307.

109. Black RE, Brown KH, Becker S. Influence of acute diarrhea on the growth parameters of children. In: Acute diarrhea: its nutritional consequences in children. Bellanti JA, ed. New York: Nestlé, Vevey/Raven, 1983:75–84.

110. Schorling JB, Guerrant RL. Diarrhoea and catch-up growth. Lancet 1990;335:599–600.

111. Hoyle B, Yunus M, Chen LC. Breast-feeding and food intake among children with acute diarrheal disease. Am J Clin Nutr 1980;33:2365–2371.

112. Molla AM, Molla A, Sarker SA, Rahaman MM. Food intake during and after recovery from diarrhea in children, In: Diarrhea and malnutrition: interactions, mechanisms, and interventions. Chen LC, Scrimshaw NS, eds. New York: Plenum, 1983:113–123.

113. Mata LJ, Kromal RA, Urrutia JJ, Garcia B. Effect of infection on food intake and the nutritional state: perspectives as viewed from the village. Am J Clin Nutr 1977;30:1215–1227.

114. Martorell R, Yarbrough C, Yarbrough S, Klein RE. The impact of ordinary illnesses on the dietary intake of malnourished children. Am J Clin Nutr 1980;33:345–350.

115. Brown KH, Black RE, Robertson AD, Becker S. Effects of season and illness on the dietary intake of weanlings during longitudinal studies in rural Bangladesh. Am J Clin Nutr 1985;41:343–355.

116. Brown KH, Stallings RY, Creed de Kanashiro CH, Lopez de Romana G, Black RE. Effects of common illnesses on infants energy intakes from breast milk and other foods during longitudinal community-based studies in Huascar (Lima), Peru. Am J Clin Nutr 1990;52:1005–1013.

117. Dickin KL, Brown KH, Fagbule D, Adedoyin M, Gittelsohn J, Esrey SA, Oni GA. Effect of diarrhea on dietary intake by infants and young children in rural villages of Kwara State, Nigeria. Eur J Clin Nutr 1990;44:307–317.

118. Marquis GS, Lopez T, Peerson JM, Brown KH. Effect of dietary viscosity on energy intake by breast-fed and non-breast-fed children during and after acute diarrhea. Am J Clin Nutr 1993;57:218–223.

119. O'Loughlin EV, Scott RB, Gall DG. Pathophysiology of infectious diarrhea: changes in intestinal structure and function. J Pediatr Gastroenterol Nutr 1991;12:5–20.

120. Jonas A, Avigad S, Diver-Haber A, Katznelson D. Disturbed fat absorption following infectious gastroenteritis in children. J Pediatr 1979;95:366–372.

121. Rosenberg IH, Solomons NW, Schneider RE. Malabsorption associated with diarrhea and intestinal infections. Am J Clin Nutr 1977;30:1248–1253.

122. Sack D, Rhoads M, Molla A, Molla AM, Wahed M. Carbohydrate malabsorption in infants with rotavirus diarrhea. Am J Clin Nutr 1982;36:1112–1118.

123. Lunn PG, Northrup-Clewes CA, Downes RM. Intestinal permeability, mucosal injury, and growth faltering in Gambian infants. Lancet 1991;338:907–910.

124. Isolauri E, Untunen M, Wiren S, Vuorinen P, Koivula T. Intestinal permeability changes in acute gastroenteritis: effects of clinical factors and nutritional management. J Pediatr Gastroenterol Nutr 1989;8:466–473.

125. Castillo-Duran C, Vial P, Uauy R. Trace mineral balance during acute diarrhea in infants. J Pediatr 1988;113:452–457.

126. Paerregaard A, Hjelt K, Krasilnikoff PA. Vitamin $B_{12}$ and folic acid absorption and hematological status in children with postenteritis enteropathy. J Pediatr Gastroenterol Nutr 1990;11:351–355.

127. Black RE, Lanata CF, Lazo F. Delayed cutaneous hypersensitivity: epidemiologic factors affecting and usefulness in predicting diarrheal incidence in young Peruvian children. Pediatr Infect Dis J 1989;8:210–215.

128. Baqui AH, Black RE, Sack RB, Chowdhury HR, Yunus M, Siddique AK. Malnutrition, cell-mediated immune deficiency, and diarrhea: a community-based longitudinal study in rural Bangladeshi children. Am J Epidemiol 1993;137:355–365.

129. Shell-Duncan B, Wood JW. The evaluation of delayed-type hypersensitivity responsiveness and nutritional status as predictors of gastro-intestinal and acute respiratory infection: a prospective field study among traditional nomadic Kenyan children. J Trop Pediatr 1997;43:25–32.

130. Baqui AH, Sack RB, Black RE, Chowdhury HR, Yunus M, Siddique AK. Cell-mediated immune deficiency and malnutrition are independent risk factors for persistent diarrhea in Bangladeshi children. Am J Clin Nutr 1993;58:543–548.

131. Sommer A, Tarwotjo I, Katz J. Increased risk of xerophthalmia following diarrhea and respiratory disease. Am J Clin Nutr 1987;45:977–980.

132. Sommer A, Katz J, Tarwotjo I. Increased risk of respiratory disease and diarrhea in children with preexisting mild vitamin A deficiency. Am J Clin Nutr 1984;40:1090–1095.

133. Salazar-Lindo E, Salazar M, Alvarez JO. Association of diarrhea and low serum retinol in Peruvian children. Am J Clin Nutr 1993;58:110–113.

134. Alvarez JO, Salazar-Lindo E, Kohatsu J, Miranda P, Stephensen CB. Urinary excretion of retinol in children with acute diarrhea. Am J Clin Nutr 1995;61:1273–1276.

135. Mitra AK, Alvarez JO, Wahed MA, Fuchs GJ, Stephensen CB. Predictors of serum retinol in children with shigellosis. Am J Clin Nutr 1998;68:1088–1094.

136. Mitra AK, Alvarez JO, Guay-Woodford L, Fuchs GJ, Wahed MA, Stephenson CB. Urinaryretinol excretion and kidney function in children with shigellosis. Am J Clin Nutr 1998;68:1095–1103.

137. Penny ME, Lanata CF. Zinc in the management of diarrhea in young children. N Engl J Med 1995;333:73–874.

138. Shankar AH, Prasad AS. Zinc and immune function: the biological basis of altered resistance to infection. Am J Clin Nutr 1998;68(suppl):447S–463S.

139. Cordano A, Baertl JM, Graham GG. Copper deficiency in infancy. Pediatrics 1964;34:324–326.

140. Cordano A. Clinical manifestations of nutritional copper deficiency in infants and children. Am J Clin Nutr. 1998;67(5 suppl):1012S–1016S.

141. Bedwal RS, Nair N, Sharma MP, Mathur RS. Selenium B: its biological perspectives. Med Hypotheses 1993;41:150–159.

142. Lessard M, Yang WC, Elliott GS, Rebar AH, Van Vleet JF, Deslauriers N, et al. Cellular immune responses in pigs fed a vitamin E- and selenium-deficient diet. J Anim Sci 1991;69:1575–1582.

143. Teige J, Tollersrud S, Lund A, Larsen HJ. Swine dysentery: the influence of dietary vitamin E and selenium on the clinical and pathological effects of *Treponema hyodysenteriae* infection in pigs. Res Vet Sci 1982;32:95–100.

144. CHOICE Study Group. Multicenter, randomized, double-blind clinical trial to evaluate the efficacy and safety of a reduced osmolarity oral rehydration salts solution in children with acute watery diarrhea. Pediatrics 2001;107:613–618.

145. Brown KH, Gastañaduy AS, Saavedra JM, Lembcke J, Rivas D, Robertson AD, et al. Effect of continued oral feeding on clinical and nutritional outcomes of acute diarrhea in children. J Pediatr 1988;112:191–200.

146. Nanulescu M, Condor M, Popa M, Muresan M, Panta P, Ionac S, et al. Early re-feeding in the management of acute diarrhoea in infants of 0–1 year of age. Acta Paediatr 1995;84:1002–1006.

147. Sandhu BK, Isolauri E, Walker-Smith JA, Banchini G, van Caillie-Bertrand M, Dias JA, et al. Early feeding in childhood gastroenteritis. J Pediatr Gastroenterol Nutr 1997;24:522–527.

148. Walker-Smith JA, Sandhu BK, Isolauri E, Banchini G, van Caillie-Bertrand M, Dias JA, et al. Guidelines prepared by the ESPGAN Working Group on acute diarrhoea. Recommendations for feeding in childhood gastroenteritis. European Society of Pediatric Gastroenterology and Nutrition. J Pediatr Gastroenterol Nutr 1997;24:619–620.

149. Khin-Maung-U, Nyunt-Nyunt-Wai, Myo-Khin, Mu-Mu-Khin, Tin-U, Thane-Toe. Effect on clinical outcome of breast feeding during acute diarrhoea. BMJ 1985;290:587–589.

150. Newburg DS, Peterson JA, Ruiz-Palacios GM, Matson DO, Morrow AL, Shults J, et al. Role of human-milk lactadherin in protection against symptomatic rotavirus infection. Lancet 1998;351:1160–1164.

151. Brown KH, Peerson JM, Fontaine O. Use of nonhuman milks in the dietary management of young children with acute diarrhea: a meta-analysis of clinical trials. Pediatrics 1994;93:17–27.

152. Palma D, Oliva CA, Taddei JA, Fagundes-Neto U. Acute diarrhea: stool water loss in hospitalized infants and its correlation with etiologic agents and lactose content in the diet. Arq Gastroenterol 1997;34:186–195.

153. Alarcon P, Montoya R, Perez F, Dongo JW, Peerson JM, Brown KH. Clinical trial of home available, mixed diets versus a lactose-free, soy-protein formula for the dietary management of acute childhood diarrhea. J Pediatr Gastroenterol Nutr 1991;12:224–232.

154. Alarcon P, Montoya R, Rivera J, Perez F, Peerson JM, Brown KH. Effect of inclusion of beans in a mixed diet for the treatment of Peruvian children with acute watery diarrhea. Pediatrics 1992;90:58–65.

155. Romer H, Guerra M, Piña JM, Urrestarazu MI, Garcia D, Blanco ME. Realimentation of dehydrated children with acute diarrhea: comparison of cows milk to a chicken-based formula. J Pediatr Gastroenterol Nutr 1991;13:46–51.

156. Grange AO, Santosham M, Ayodele B, Lesi FE, Stallings RY, Brown KH. Evaluation of a maize-cowpea-palm oil diet for the dietary management of Nigerian children with acute, watery diarrhea. Acta Paediatr 1994;83:825–832.

157. Maulen-Radovan I, Brown KH, Acosta MA, Fernandez-Varela H. Comparison of a rice-based, mixed diet versus a lactose-free, soy-protein isolate formula for young children with acute diarrhea. J Pediatr 1994;125:699–706.

158. Lanata CF, Black RE, Creed-Kanashiro H, Lazo F, Gallardo ML, Verastegui H, Brown KH. Feeding during acute diarrhea as a risk factor for persistent diarrhea. Acta Paediatr 1992;381(suppl):98–103.

159. Kabir I, Rahman MM, Haider R, Mazumder RN, Khaled MA, Mahalanabis D. Increased height gain of children fed a high-protein diet during convalescence from shigellosis: a 6-month follow-up study. J Nutr 1998;128:1688–1691.

160. Mazumder RN, Hoque SS, Ashraf H, Kabir I, Wahed MA. Early feeding of an energy dense diet during acute shigellosis enhances growth in malnourished children. J Nutr 1997;127:51–54.

161. Rahman MM, Mitra AK, Mahalanabis D, Wahed MA, Khatun M, Majid N. Absorption of nutrients from an energy-dense diet liquefied with amylase from germinated wheat in infants with acute diarrhea. J Pediatr Gastroenterol Nutr 1997;24:119–123.

162. Rahman MM, Mahalanabis D, Ali M, Mazumder RN, Wahed MA, Fuchs GJ. Absorption of macronutrients and nitrogen balance in children with dysentery fed an amylase-treated energy-dense porridge. Acta Paediatr 1997;86:1312–1316.

163. Darling JC, Kitundu JA, Kingamkono RR, Msengi AE, Mduma B, Sullivan KR, Tomkins AM. Improved energy intakes using amylase-digested weaning foods in Tanzanian children with acute diarrhea. J Pediatr Gastroenterol Nutr 1995;21:73–81.

164. Black RE, Levine MM. Intestinal protein loss in shigellosis. Nutr Res 1991;11:1215–1220.

165. Eherer AJ, Santa Ana CA, Porter J, Fordtran JS. Effect of psyllium, calcium polycarbophil, and wheat bran on secretory diarrhea induced by phenolphthalein. Gastroenterology 1993;104:1007–1012.

166. Wenzl HH, Fine KD, Schiller LR, Fordtran JS. Determinants of decreased fecal consistency in patients with diarrhea. Gastroenterology 1995;108:1729–1738.

167. Lin HC, Zhao XT, Chu AW, Lin YP, Wang L. Fiber-supplemented enteral formula slows intestinal transit by intensifying inhibitory feedback from the distal gut. Am J Clin Nutr 1997;65:1840–1844.

168. Homann HH, Kemen M, Fuessenich C, Senkal M, Zumtobel V. Reduction in diarrhea incidence by soluble fiber in patients receiving total or supplemental enteral nutrition. J Parenter Enteral Nutr 1994;18:486–490.

169. Vanderhoof JA, Murray ND, Paule CL, Ostrom KM. Use of soy fiber in acute diarrhea in infants and toddlers. Clin Pediatr (Phila) 1997;36:135–139.

170. Loeb H, Vandenplas Y, Wursch P, Guesry P. Tannin-rich carob pod for the treatment of acute-onset diarrhea. J Pediatr Gastroenterol Nutr 1989;8:480–485.

171. Brown KH, Perez F, Peerson JM, Fadel J, Brunsgaard G, Ostrom KM, MacLean WC Jr. Effect of dietary fiber (soy polysaccharide) on the severity, duration, and nutritional outcome of acute, watery diarrhea in children. Pediatrics 1993;92:241–247.

172. Boudraa G, Touhami M, Pochart P, Soltana R, Mary JY, Desjeux JF. Effect of feeding yogurt versus milk in children with persistent diarrhea. J Ped Gastroenterol Nutr 1990;11:509–512.

173. Bhatnagar S, Singh KD, Sazawal S, Saxena SK, Bhan MK. Efficacy of milk versus yogurt offered as part of a mixed diet in acute noncholera diarrhea among malnourished children. J Pediatr 1998; 132:999–1003.

174. Isolauri E, Juntunen M, Rautanen T, Sillanaukee P, Koivula T. A human lactobacillus strain (*Lactobacillus casei* sp. strain GG) promotes recovery from acute diarrhea in children. Pediatrics 1991;88:90–97.

175. Raza S, Graham SM, Allen SJ, Sultana S, Cuevas L, Hart CA. *Lactobacillus* GG promotes recovery from acute nonbloody diarrhea in Pakistan. Pediatr Infect Dis J 1995;14:107–111.

176. Pant AR, Graham SM, Allen SJ, Harikul S, Sabchareon A, Cuevas L, Hart CA. *Lactobacillus* GG and acute diarrhoea in young children in the tropics. J Trop Pediatr 1996;42:162–165.

177. Guandalini S, Pensabene L, Zikri MA, Dias JA, Casali LG, Hoekstra H et al. *Lactobacillus* GG administered in oral rehydration solution to children with acute diarrhea: a multicenter European trial. J Pediatr Gastroenterol Nutr 2000;30:54–60.

178. Guarino A, Canani RB, Spagnuolo MI, Albano F, Di Benedetto L. Oral bacterial therapy reduces the duration of symptoms and of viral excretion in children with mild diarrhea. J Pediatr Gastroenterol Nutr 1997;25:516–519.

179. Oberhelman RA, Gilman RH, Sheen P, Taylor DN, Black RE, Cabrera L, et al. A placebo-controlled trial of *Lactobacillus* GG to prevent diarrhea in undernourished Peruvian children. J Pediatr 1999;134: 15–20.

180. Gorbach SL. Probiotics and gastrointestinal health. Am J Gastroenterol 2000;95(1 suppl):S2–S4.

181. Shornikova AV, Casas IA, Isolauri E, Mykkanen H, Vesikari T. *Lactobacillus reuteri* as a therapeutic agent in acute diarrhea in young children. J Pediatr Gastroenterol Nutr 1997;24:399–404.

182. Shornikova AV, Casas IA, Mykkanen H, Salo E, Vesikari T. Bacteriotherapy with *Lactobacillus reuteri* in rotavirus gastroenteritis. Pediatr Infect Dis J 1997;16:1103–1107.

183. Saavedra JM, Bauman NA, Oung I, Perman JA, Yolken RH. Feeding of *Bifidobacterium bifidum* and *Streptococcus thermophilus* to infants in hospital for prevention of diarrhoea and shedding of rotavirus. Lancet 1994;344:1046–1049.

184. Buydens P, Debeuckelaere S. Efficacy of SF 68 in the treatment of acute diarrhea. A placebo-controlled trial. Scand J Gastroenterol 1996;31:887–891.

185. Rani B, Khetarpaul N. Probiotic fermented food mixtures: possible applications in clinical anti-diarrhoea usage. Nutr Health 1998;12:97–105.

186. Clements ML, Levine MM, Black RE, Robins-Browne RM, Cisneros LA, Drusano GL, Lanata CF, Saah AJ. *Lactobacillus* prophylaxis for diarrhea due to enterotoxigenic *Escherichia coli*. Antimicrob Agents Chemother 1981;20:104–108.

187. Bleichner G, Blehaut H, Mentec H, Moyse D. *Saccharomyces boulardii* prevents diarrhea in critically ill tube-fed patients. A multicenter, randomized, double-blind placebo-controlled trial. Intensive Care Med 1997;23:517–523.

188. Kurugol Z, Koturoglu G. Effects of Saccharomyces boulardii in children with acute diarrhea. Acta Paediatr 2005;94:44–7.

189. Saavedra JM. Microbes to fight microbes: a not so novel approach to controlling diarrheal disease. J Pediatr Gastroenterol Nutr 1995;21:125–129.

190. Elmer GW, Surawicz CM, McFarland LV. Biotherapeutic agents. A neglected modality for the treatment and prevention of selected intestinal and vaginal infections. JAMA 1996;275:870–876.

191. Szajewska H, Mrukowicz JZ. Probiotics in the treatment and prevention of acute infectious diarrhea in infants and children: a systematic review of published randomized, double-blind, placebo-controlled trials. J Pediatr Gastroenterol Nutr 2001;33(Suppl 2):S17–S25.

192. Gibson GR, Roberfroid MB. Dietary modulation of the human colonic microbiota: introducing the concept of prebiotics. J Nutr 1995;125:1401–1412.

193. Gibson GR. Dietary modulation of the human gut microflora using prebiotics. Br J Nutr 1998;80: S209–S112.

194. Bouhnik Y, Vahedi K, Achour L, Attar A, Salfati J, Pochart P, et al. Short-chain fructo-oligosaccharide administration dose-dependently increases fecal bifidobacteria in healthy humans. J Nutr 1999;129:113–116.

195. Fishbein L, Kaplan M, Gough M. Fructooligosaccharides: a review. Vet Hum Toxicol 1988;30: 104–107.

196. Brunser O, Gotteland M, Cruchet S, Figueroa G, Garrido D, Steenhout P. Effect of a milk formula with prebiotics on the intestinal microbiota of infants after an antibiotic treatment. Pediatr Res 2006;59:451–456.

197. Duggan C, Penny ME, Hibberd P, Gil A, Huapaya A, Cooper A, et al. Oligofructose-supplemented infant cereal: two randomized, blinded, community-based trials in Peruvian infants. Am J Clin Nutr 2003;77:937–942.

198. Zijlstra RT, Odle J, Hall WF, Petschow BW, Gelberg HB, Litov RE. Effect of orally administered epidermal growth factor on intestinal recovery of neonatal pigs infected with rotavirus. J Pediatr Gastroenterol Nutr 1994;19:382–390.

199. Buret A, Olson ME, Gall DG, Hardin JA. Effects of orally administered epidermal growth factor on enteropathogenic *Escherichia coli* infections in rabbits. Infect Immun 1998;66:4917–4923.

200. McCole DF, Rogler G, Varki N, Barrett KE. Epidermal growth factor partially restores colonic ion transport responses in mouse models of chronic colitis. Gastroenterology 2005;129:591–608.

201. Beck NS, Chang YS, Kang IS, Park WS, Lee HJ, Suh YL. Microvillus inclusion disease in two Korean infants. J Korean Med Sci 1997;12:452–456.

202. Lifschitz CH. Role of colonic scavengers of unabsorbed carbohydrates in infants and children. J Am Coll Nutr 1996;15(5 suppl):30S–34S.

203. Clausen MR, Jorgensen J, Mortensen PB. Comparison of diarrhea induced by ingestion of fructooligosaccharide Idolax and disaccharide lactulose: role of osmolarity versus fermentation of malabsorbed carbohydrate. Dig Dis Sci 1998;43:2696–2707.

204. Ramakrishna BS, Mathan VI. Colonic dysfunction in acute diarrhoea: the role of luminal short chain fatty acids. Gut 1993;34:1215–1218.

205. Velazquez OC, Lederer HM, Rombeau JL. Butyrate and the colonocyte. Production, absorption, metabolism, and therapeutic implications. Adv Exp Med Biol 1997;427:123–134.

206. Krishnan S, Ramakrishna BS, Binder HJ. Stimulation of sodium chloride absorption from secreting rat colon by short-chain fatty acids. Dig Dis Sci 1999;44:1924–1930.

207. Rabbani GH, Albert MJ, Rahman H, Chowdhury AK. Short-chain fatty acids inhibit fluid and electrolyte loss induced by cholera toxin in proximal colon of rabbit in vivo. Dig Dis Sci 1999;44:1547–1553.

208. Rabbani GH, Albert MJ, Hamidur Rahman AS, Moyenul IM, Nasirul Islam KM, Alam K. Short-chain fatty acids improve clinical, pathologic, and microbiologic features of experimental shigellosis. J Infect Dis 1999;179:390–397.

209. Canani RB, Terrin G, Cirillo P, Castaldo G, Salvatore F, Cardillo G, et al. Butyrate as an effective treatment of congenital chloride diarrhea. Gastroenterology 2004;127:630–634.

210. Silva AC, Santos-Neto MS, Soares AM, Fonteles MC, Guerrant RL, Lima AA. Efficacy of a glutamine-based oral rehydration solution on the electrolyte and water absorption in a rabbit model of secretory diarrhea induced by cholera toxin. J Pediatr Gastroenterol Nutr 1998;26:513–519.

211. Brooks HW, Hall GA, Wagstaff AJ, Michell AR. Detrimental effects on villus form during conventional oral rehydration therapy for diarrhoea in calves; alleviation by a nutrient oral rehydration solution containing glutamine. Vet J 1998;155:263–274.

212. Rhoads JM, Gomez GG, Chen W, Goforth R, Argenzio RA, Neylan MJ. Can a super oral rehydration solution stimulate intestinal repair in acute viral enteritis? J Diarrhoeal Dis Res 1996;14:175–181.

213. Ribeiro H Jr, Ribeiro T, Mattos A, Palmeira C, Fernandez D, Sant Ana I, et al. Treatment of acute diarrhea with oral rehydration solutions containing glutamine. J Am Coll Nutr 1994;13:251–255.

214. Bhan MK, Mahalanabis D, Fontaine O, Pierce NF. Clinical trials of improved oral rehydration salt formulations: a review. Bull World Health Organ 1994;72:945–955.

215. Yalcin SS, Yurdakok K, Tezcan I, Oner L. Effect of glutamine supplementation on diarrhea, interleukin-8 and secretory immunoglobulin A in children with acute diarrhea. J Pediatr Gastroenterol Nutr 2004;38:494–501.

216. Uauy R, Quan R, Gil A Role of nucleotides in intestinal development and repair: implications for infant nutrition. J Nutr 1994;124(8suppl):1436S–1441S.

217. Uauy R. Nonimmune system responses to dietary nucleotides. J Nutr 1994;124(1 suppl):157S–159S.

218. Leleiko NS, Walsh MJ. Dietary purine nucleotides and the gastrointestinal tract. Nutrition 1995;11:725–730.

219. Gil A. Modulation of the immune response mediated by dietary nucleotides. Eur J Clin Nutr 2002;56(suppl 3):S1–S4.

220. Bueno J, Torres M, Almendros A, Carmona R, Nunez MC, Rios A, Gil A. Effect of dietary nucleotides on small intestinal repair after diarrhoea. Histological and ultrastructural changes. Gut 1994;35:926–933.

221. Nachbar MS, Oppenheim JD. Lectins in the United States diet: a survey of lectins in commonly consumed foods and a review of the literature. Am J Clin Nutr 1980;33:2338–2345.

222. Banwell JG, Abramowsky CR, Weber F, Howard R, Boldt DH. Phytohemagglutinin-induced diarrheal disease. Dig Dis Sci 1984;29:921–929.

223. Pistole TG. Interaction of bacteria and fungi with lectins and lectin-like substances. Annu Rev Microbiol 1981;35:85–112.

224. Weiser MM. Dietary lectins and the possible mechanisms whereby they induce intestinal injury. In: Chronic diarrhea in children. Lebenthal E, ed. New York: Raven, 1984:279–287.

225. Thorne GM. Gastrointestinal infections-dietary interactions. J Am Coll Nutr 1986;5:487–499.

226. Shoda R, Mahalanabis D, Wahed MA, Albert MJ. Bacterial translocation in the rat model of lectin induced diarrhoea. Gut 1995;36:379–381.

227. Fritig B, Heitz T, Legrand M. Antimicrobial proteins in induced plant defense. Curr Opin Immunol 1998;10:16–22.

228. Ofek I, Goldhar J, Sharon N. Anti-*Escherichia coli* adhesin activity of cranberry and blueberry juices. Adv Exp Med Biol 1996;408:179–183.

229. Sharon N. Carbohydrate-lectin interactions in infectious disease. Adv Exp Med Biol 1996;408:1–8.

230. Goransson L, Martinsson K, Lange S, Lonnroth I. Feed-induced lectins in piglets. Feed-induced lectins and their effect on post-weaning diarrhoea, daily weight gain and mortality. Zentralbl Veterinarmed [B] 1993;40:478–484.

231. Hill DR, Hewlett EL, Pearson RD. Lectin binding by *Giardia lamblia*. Infect Immun 1981;34:733–738.

232. Llovo J, Lopez A, Fabregas J, Munoz A. Interaction of lectins with *Cryptosporidium parvum*. J Infect Dis 1993;167:1477–1480.

233. Luft BJ, Payne D, Woodmansee D, Kim CW. Characterization of the *Cryptosporidium* antigens from sporulated oocysts of *Cryptosporidium parvum*. Infect Immun 1987;55:2436–2441.

234. Ortega-Barria E, Ward HD, Keusch GT, Pereira ME. Growth inhibition of the intestinal parasite *Giardia lamblia* by a dietary lectin is associated with arrest of the cell cycle. J Clin Invest 1994;94:2283–2288.

235. Sachdev HPS, Mittal NK, Mittal SK, Yadav HS. A controlled trial on utility of oral zinc supplementation in acute dehydrating diarrhea in infants. J Pediatr Gastroenterol Nutr 1988;7:877–881.

236. Sazawal S, Black RE, Bhan MK, Bhandari N, Sinha A, Jalla S. Zinc supplementation in young children with acute diarrhea in India. N Engl J Med 1995;333:839–844.

237. Roy SK, Tomkins AM, Akramuzzaman SM, Behrens RH, Haider R, Mahalanabis D, Fuchs G. Randomized controlled trial of zinc supplementation in malnourished Bangladeshi children with acute diarrhoea. Arch Dis Child 1997;77:196–200.

238. Black RE for Zinc Investigators Collaborative Group. Zinc supplementation effects on diarrhea and pneumonia: a pooled analysis of randomized controlled trials. FASEB J 1999;A659.7.

239. Fischer Walker CL, Black RE. Functional indicators for assessing zinc deficiency. Food Nutr Bull 2007;28(3 suppl):S454–S479.

240. Alam AN, Sarker SA, Wahed MA, Khatun M, Rahaman MM. Enteric protein loss and intestinal permeability changes in children during acute shigellosis and after recovery: effect of zinc supplementation. Gut 1994;35:1707–1711.

241. Roy SK, Tomkins AM, Mahalanabis D, Akramuzzaman SM, Haider R, Behrens RH, Fuchs G. Impact of zinc supplementation on persistent diarrhoea in malnourished Bangladeshi children. Acta Paediatr 1998;87:1235–1239.

242. Penny ME, Peerson JM, Marin RM, Duran A, Lanata CF, Lonnerdal B, Black RE, Brown KH. Randomized, community-based trial of the effect of zinc supplementation, with and without other micronutrients, on the duration of persistent childhood diarrhea in Lima, Peru. J Pediatr 1999;135:208–217.

243. Fontaine O. Zinc and treatment of diarrhoea. Med Trop (Mars) 2006;66:306–309.

244. Henning B, Stewart K, Zaman K, Alam AN, Brown KH, Black RE. Lack of therapeutic efficacy of vitamin A for non-cholera, watery diarrhoea in Bangladeshi children. Eur J Clin Nutr 1992;46:437–443.

245. Dewan V, Patwari AK, Jain M, Dewan N. A randomized controlled trial of vitamin A supplementation in acute diarrhea. Indian Pediatr 1995;32:21–25.

246. Donnen P, Dramaix M, Brasseur D, Bitwe R, Vertongen F, Hennart P. Randomized placebo-controlled clinical trial of the effect of a single high dose or daily low dose of vitamin A on the morbidity of hospitalized, malnourished children. Am J Clin Nutr 1998;68:1254–1260.

247. Bhandari N, Bahl R, Sazawal S, Bhan MK. Breast-feeding status alters the effect of vitamin A treatment during acute diarrhea in children. J Nutr 1997;127:59–63.

248. Faruque AS, Mahalanabis D, Haque SS, Fuchs GJ, Habte D. Double-blind, randomized, controlled trial of zinc or vitamin A supplementation in young children with acute diarrhea. Acta Paediatr 1999;88:154–160.

249. Hossain S, Biswas R, Kabir I, Sarker S, Dibley M, Fuchs G, Mahalanabis D. Single dose vitamin A treatment in acute shigellosis in Bangladeshi children: randomized double blind controlled trial. BMJ 1998;316:422–426.

250. Khatun UH, Malek MA, Black RE, Sarkar NR, Wahed MA, Fuchs G et al. A randomized controlled trial of zinc, vitamin A or both in undernourished children with persistent diarrhea in Bangladesh. Acta Paediatr 2001;90:376–380.

251. Rollins NC, Filteau SM, Elson I, Tomkins AM. Vitamin A supplementation of South African children with severe diarrhea: optimum timing for improving biochemical and clinical recovery and subsequent vitamin A status. Pediatr Infect Dis J 2000;19:284–289.

252. Valery PC, Torzillo PJ, Boyce NC, White AV, Stewart PA, Wheaton GR, et al. Zinc and vitamin A supplementation in Australian indigenous children with acute diarrhea: a randomized controlled trial. Med J Aust 2005;182:530–535.

253. Yurdakok K, Ozmert E, Yalcin SS, Latell Y. Vitamin A supplementation in acute diarrhea. J Pediatr Gastroenterol Nutr 2000;31:234–237.

254. Bhatnagar S, Bhan MK, Singh KD, Shrivastav R. Prognostic factors in hospitalized children with persistent diarrhea: implications for diet therapy. J Pediatr Gastroenterol Nutr 1996;23:151–158.

255. Nurko S, Garcia-Aranda JA, Fishbein E, Perez-Zuniga MI. Successful use of a chicken-based diet for the treatment of severely malnourished children with persistent diarrhea: a prospective, randomized study. J Pediatr 1997;131:405–412.

256. Kolacek S, Grguric J, Percl M, Booth IW. Home-made modular diet versus semi-elemental formula in the treatment of chronic diarrhoea in infancy: a prospective randomized trial. Eur J Pediatr 1996;155:997–1001.

257. Bhatnagar S, Bhan MK, Singh KD, Saxena SK, Shariff M. Efficacy of milk-based diets in persistent diarrhea: a randomized, controlled trial. Pediatrics 1996;98:1122–1126.

258. International Working Group on Persistent Diarrhoea. Evaluation of an algorithm for the treatment of persistent diarrhoea: a multicenter study. Bull World Health Organ 1996;74:479–489.

259. Munir M. Infantile diarrhoea: breast and bottle feeding compared with special reference to their clinical role. Paediatr Indonesia 1985;25:100–106.

260. de Zoysa I, Rea M, Martines J. Why promote breastfeeding in diarrhoeal disease control programmes? Health Policy Plan 1991;6:371–379.

261. Feachem RG, Koblinsky MA. Interventions for the control of diarrhoeal disease among young children: promotion of breast-feeding. Bull World Health Organ 1984;62:271–291.

262. Victora CG, Smith PG, Vaughan JP, Nobre LC, Lombardi C, Teixeira AM, et al. Infant feeding and deaths due to diarrhea. A case-control study. Am J Epidemiol 1989;129:1032–1041.

263. Victora CG, Huttly RS, Fuchs SC, Nobre LC, Barros FC. Deaths due to dysentery, acute and persistent diarrhoea among Brazilian infants. Acta Paediatr 1992;381(suppl):7–11.

264. Davies-Adetugbo AA, Adetugbo K, Orewole Y, Fabiayi AK. Breast-feeding promotion in a diarrhoea programme in rural communities. J Diarrhoeal Dis Res 1997;15:161–166.

265. Morrow AL, Guerrero ML, Shults J, Calva JJ, Lutter C, Bravo J, et al. Efficacy of home-based peer counselling to promote exclusive breastfeeding: a randomised controlled trial. Lancet 1999;353:1226–1231.

266. Saleemi MA, Zaman S, Akhtar HZ, Jalil F, Ashraf RN, Hanson LA, et al. Feeding patterns, diarrhoeal illness and linear growth in 0–24 month old children. J Trop Pediatr 2004;50:164–169.

267. Bhandari N, Bahl R, Mazumdal S, Martines J, Black RE, Bhan MK. Effect of community-based promotion of exclusive breastfeeding on diarrhoeal illness and growth: a cluster randomized controlled trial. Lancet 2003;361:1418–1423.

268. Agrasada BV, Gustafsson J, Kylberg E, Ewald U. Postnatal peer counselling on exclusive breastfeeding of low-birthweight infants: a randomized, controlled trial. Acta Paediatr 2005;94:1109–1115.

269. Black RE, Lopez de Romana G, Brown KH, Bravo N, Bazalar OG, Kanashiro HC. Incidence and etiology of infantile diarrhea and major routes of transmission in Huascar, Peru. Am J Epidemiol 1989;129:785–799.

270. Barrell RAE, Rowland MGM. Infant foods as a potential source of diarrhoeal illness in rural West Africa. Trans R Soc Trop Med Hyg 1979;73:85–90.

271. Black RE, Brown KH, Becker S, Abdul Alim ARM, Merson MH. Contamination of weaning foods and transmission of enterotoxigenic *Escherichia coli* diarrhoea in children in rural Bangladesh. Trans R Soc Trop Med Hyg 1982;76:259–264.

272. Roberts D. Sources of infection: food. Lancet 1990;336:859–861.

273. Merson MH, Morris GK, Sack DA, Wells JG, Feeley JC, Sack RB, et al. Travelers diarrhea in Mexico: a prospective study of physicians and family members attending a congress. N Engl J Med 1976;294:1299–1305.

274. Tjoa WS, DuPont HL, Sullivan P, Pickering LK, Holguin AH, Olarte J, Evans DG, Evans DJ Jr. Location of food consumption and travelers diarrhea. Am J Epidemiol 1977;106:61–66.

275. Lanata CF. Studies of food hygiene and diarrhoeal disease. Int J Environ Health Res 2003;13:S175–S183.

276. World Health Organization (WHO). Research on improving infant feeding practices to prevent diarrhoea or reduce its severity: memorandum from a JHU/WHO meeting. Bull World Health Organ 1989;67:27–33.

277. Ashworth A, Feachem RG. Interventions for the control of diarrhoeal diseases among young children: weaning education. Bull World Health Organ 1985;63:1115–1117.

278. Esrey SA, Feachem RG. Interventions for the control of diarrhoeal diseases among young children: promotion of food hygiene. Geneva: World Health Organization, 1989. Document WHO/CDD/89.39.

279. United Nations International Children's Emergency Fund (UNICEF). The state of the world's children 1998. New York: Oxford University Press, 1998.

280. Addiss DG, Pond RS, Remshak M, Juranek DD, Stokes S, Davis JP. Reduction of risk of watery diarrhea with point-of-use water filters during massive outbreak of waterborne *Cryptosporidium* infection in Milwaukee, Wisconsin, 1993. Am J Trop Med Hyg 1996;54:549–553.

281. Rainey RC, Harding AK. Acceptability of solar disinfection of drinking water treatment in Kathmandu Valley, Nepal. Int J Environ Health Res 2005;15:361–372.

282. Henry FJ, Rahim Z. Transmission of diarrhoea in two crowded areas with different sanitary facilities in Dhaka, Bangladesh. J Trop Med Hyg 1990;93:121–126.

283. Samadi AR, Huq MI, Ahmed QS. Detection of rotavirus in hand-washings of attendants of children with diarrhoea. BMJ 1983;286:188.

284. Black RE, Dykes AC, Anderson KE, Wells JG, Sinclair SP, Gary GW Jr, Hatch MH, Gangarosa EJ. Handwashing to prevent diarrhea in day-care centers. Am J Epidemiol 1981;113:445–451.

285. Han AM, Nwe OO K, Aye T, Hling T. Personal toilet after defaecation and the degree of hand contamination according to different methods used. J Trop Med Hyg 1986;89:237–41.

286. Sprunt K, Redman W, Leidy G. Antibacterial effectiveness of routine hand washing. Pediatrics 1973;52:264–271.

287. Eggers HJ. Handwashing and horizontal spread of viruses. Lancet 1989;1:1452.

288. Hoque BA, Bruend A. A comparison of local handwashing agents in Bangladesh. J Trop Ped Hyg 1991;94:61–64.

289. Fewtrell L, Kauffmann RB, Kay D, Enanoria W, Haller L, Colford JH. Water, santitation, and hygiene interventions to reduce diarrhoea in less developed countries: a systematic review and meta-analysis. Lancet Infect Dis 2005;5:42–52.

290. Lanata CF, Huttly SRA, Yeager BAC. Diarrhoea: whose feces matter? Reflections from studies in a Peruvian shanty town. Pediatr Infect Dis J 1998;17:7–9.

291. Yeager BA, Huttly SR, Bartollini R, Rojas M, Lanata CF. Defecation practices of young children in a Peruvian shanty town. Soc Sci Med 1999;49:531–541.

292. Yeager BAC, Huttly SRA, Diaz J, Bartolini R, Marin M, Lanata CF. An intervention for the promotion of hygienic feces disposal behaviors in a shanty town of Lima, Peru. Health Educ Res 2002;17:761–773.

293. Ezzati M, Lopez AD, Rodgers A, Hoorn SV, Murria CJL, Comparative Risk Assessment Collaborating Group. Selected major risk factors and global and regional burden of disease. Lancet 2002;360:1347–1360.

294. English RM, Badcock JC, Giay T, Ngu T, Waters AM, Bennett SA. Effect of nutrition improvement project on morbidity from infectious diseases in preschool children in Vietnam: comparison with control commune. BMJ 1997;315:1122–1125.

295. Bahl R, Bhandari N, Hambidge KM, Bhan MK. Plasma zinc as a predictor of diarrheal and respiratory morbidity in children in an urban slum setting. Am J Clin Nutr 1998;68(2 suppl):414S–417S.

296. Sazawal S, Black RE, Bhan MK, Jalla S, Sinha A, Bhandari N. Efficacy of zinc supplementation in reducing the incidence and prevalence of acute diarrhea B a community-based, double-blind, controlled trial. Am J Clin Nutr 1997;66:413–418.

297. Sazawal S, Black RE, Bhan MK, Jalla S, Bhandari N, Sinha A, Majumdar S. Zinc supplementation reduces the incidence of persistent diarrhea and dysentery among low socioeconomic children in India. J Nutr 1996;126:443–450.

298. Ruel MT, Rivera JA, Santizo MC, Lönnerdal B, Brown KH. Impact of zinc supplementation on morbidity from diarrhea and respiratory infections among rural Guatemalan children. Pediatrics 1997;99:808–813.

299. Zinc Investigators Collaborative Group. Prevention of diarrhea and acute lower respiratory infection by zinc supplementation in developing country children: pooled analysis of randomized controlled trials. J Pediatr 1999;135:689–697.

300. Neggers YH, Cutter GR, Alvarez JO, Goldenberg RL, Acton R, Go RC., Roseman JM. The relationship between maternal serum zinc levels during pregnancy and birthweight. Early Hum Dev 1991;25:75–85.

301. Lira PI, Ashworth A, Morris SS. Effect of zinc supplementation on the morbidity, immune function, and growth of low-birth-weight, full term infants in northeast Brazil. Am J Clin Nutr 1998;68 (2 suppl):418S–424S.

302. Sazawal S, Black RE, Menon VP, Dhingra U, Dhingra P, Mazumder S, et al. Effect of zinc and mineral supplementation in small for gestational age infants on growth and mortality. FASEB J 1999;A309.7.

303. Sazawal S, Black RE, Ramsan M, Chwaya HM, Dutta A, Dhingra U, Stoltzfus RJ, Othman MK, Kabole M. Effects of zinc supplementation on mortality in children 1–48 months: A community-based randomised placebo-controlled trial. Lancet 2007;269: 927–934.

304. Sommer A, Tarwotjo I, Hussaini G, Susanto D. Increased mortality in children with mild vitamin A deficiency. Lancet 1983;2:585–588.

305. Beaton GH, Martorell R, L'Abbe KA, Edmonston B, McCabe G, Ross AC, Harvey B, eds. Effectiveness of vitamin A supplementation in the control of young child morbidity and mortality in developing countries. Final report to CIDA. Toronto: University of Toronto, 1992.

306. Rahmathullah L, Underwood BA, Thulasiraj RD, Milton RC, Ramaswamy K, Rahmathullah R, Babu G. Reduced mortality among children in Southern India receiving a small weekly dose of vitamin A. N Engl J Med 1990;323:929–935.

307. West KP Jr, Pokhrel RP, Katz J, LeClerq SC, Khatry SK, Shrestha SR, et al. Efficacy of vitamin A in reducing preschool child mortality in Nepal. Lancet 1991;338:67–71.

308. Daulaire NMP, Starbuck ES, Houston RM, Church MS, Stukel TA, Pandey MR. Childhood mortality after a high dose of vitamin A in a high risk population. BMJ 1992;304:207–210.

309. Ghana VAST Study Team. Vitamin A supplementation in northern Ghana: effects on clinic attendances, hospital admissions, and child mortality. Lancet 1993;342:7–12.

310. Arthur P, Kirkwood B, Ross D, Morris S, Gyapong J, Tomkins A, Addy H. Impact of vitamin A supplementation on childhood morbidity in northern Ghana. Lancet 1992;339:361–362.

311. Barreto ML, Santos LMP, Assis AMO, Araujo MPN, Farenzena GJ, Santos PAB, Fiaccone RL. Effect of vitamin A supplementation on diarrhoea and acute lower respiratory-tract infections in young children in Brazil. Lancet 1994;344:228–231.

312. Filteau SM, Morris SS, Raynes JG, Arthur P, Ross DA, Kirkwood BR, et al. Vitamin A supplementation, morbidity, and serum acute-phase proteins in young Ghanaian children. Am J Clin Nutr 1995;62:434–438.

313. Grotto I, Mimouni M, Gdalevich M, Mimouni D, Vitamin A supplementation and childhood morbidity from diarrhea and respiratory infections: a meta-analysis. J Pediatr 2003;142: 297–304.

314. Lama More RA, Gil-Alberdi Gonzalez B. Effect of nucleotides as dietary supplement on diarrhea in healthy infants. An Esp Pediatr 1998;48:371–375.

315. Brunser O, Espinoza J, Araya M, Cruchet S, Gil A. Effect of dietary nucleotide supplementation on diarrhoeal disease in infants. Acta Paediatr 1994;83:188–191.

316. Yau KI, Huang CB, Chen W, Chen SJ, Chou YH, Huang FY et al. Effect of nucleotides on diarrhea and immune responses in healthy term infants in Taiwan. J Pediatr Gastroenterol Nutr 2003;36:37–43.

317. Merolla R. Evaluation of the effects of a nucleotide-enriched formula on the incidence of diarrhea. Italian multicenter national study. Minerva Pediatr 2000;52:699–711.

318. De Zoysa I, Feachem RG. Interventions for the control of diarrhoeal diseases among young children: rotavirus and cholera immunization. Bull World Health Organ 1985;63:569–583.

319. Committee on Infectious Diseases, American Academy of Pediatrics. Prevention of rotavirus disease: guidelines for use of rotavirus vaccine. Pediatrics 1998;102:1483–1491.

320. Lanata CF, Midthum K, Black RE, Butron B, Huapaya A, Penny ME, et al. Safety, immunogenicity and protective efficacy of one or three doses of the rhesus tetravalent rotavirus vaccine in infants from Lima, Peru. J Infect Dis 1996;174:268–275.

321. Linhares AC, Gabbay YB, Mascarenhas JPD, et al. Immunogenicity, safety and efficacy of rhesus-human reassortant rotavirus vaccine in Belem, Brazil. Bull World Health Organ 1996;74:491–500.

322. Linhares AC, Lanata CF, Hausdorff WP, Gabbay YB, Black RE. Reappraisal of the Peruvian and Brazilian lower titer tetravalent rhesus-human reassortant rotavirus vaccine efficacy trials: analysis by severity of diarrhea. Ped Infect Dis J 1999;18:1001–1006.

323. Centers for Disease Control and Prevention. Intussusception among recipients of rotavirus vaccine. United States, 1998–1999. MMWR Morb Mortal Wkly Rep 1999;48:577–581.

324. Suzuki H, Katsushima N, Konno T. Rotavirus vaccine put on hold. Lancet 1999;354:1390.

325. Vesikari T, Mason DO, Dennehy P, Van Dame P, Santosham M, Rodriguez Z, et al. Safety and efficacy of a pentavalent human-bovine (WC3) reassortant rotavirus vaccine. N Engl J Med 2006;354:23–33.

326. Ruiz-Palacios GM, Perez-Schael I, Velazquez FR, Abate H, Breuer T, Costa-Clemens SA, et al. Safety and efficacy of an attenuated vaccine against severe rotavirus gastroenteritis. N Engl J Med 2006;354:11–22.

# 7 Acute Lower Respiratory Infections

## Claudio F. Lanata and Robert E. Black

### 7.1 INTRODUCTION

Acute respiratory infections are the leading cause of morbidity and mortality among infants and children in developing countries. It is estimated that pneumonia causes up to 2 million deaths per year in children under 5 years of age, and neonatal pneumonia or sepsis causes an additional 1 million deaths per year [1]; an important contributing factor to these deaths is malnutrition [2]. Acute respiratory infections include both acute upper-respiratory infections and acute lower-respiratory infections. Acute lower-respiratory infections consist primarily of pneumonia, but also include croup, tracheobronchitis, and bronchiolitis. The specific aims of this chapter are to present current knowledge regarding the epidemiology, pathophysiology, diagnosis, and treatment of acute lower-respiratory infections and the potential role of nutrition in treatment and prevention.

### 7.2 PUBLIC HEALTH IMPORTANCE

The recently published report of the Disease Control Priorities Project (DCPP) has estimated that lower-respiratory infections in general caused 3.7 million deaths in the world in 2001, representing 6.7% of all causes of deaths in all ages and 5.6% of all disability-adjusted life years (DALYs) lost in the world [3]. The number of deaths caused by lower-respiratory infections in children under 5 years of age was estimated to be 1.9 million in the year 2001, representing 18.3% of all child deaths, higher than for diarrheal diseases, which explained only 15.1% of all child deaths [4] (Fig. 7.1).

### 7.3 HISTORICAL BACKGROUND

Among the acute respiratory infections, influenza epidemics are well described in historical accounts from at least the 12th century [5]. Epidemics have been especially well documented in Great Britain [6]. Influenza is known to have occurred in many pandemics, with involvement of all areas of the globe and a characteristic geographical spread along the routes of human travel. The great influenza pandemic in 1918–1919 is considered to have accounted for the most deaths from an epidemic disease since the Black Death of the 14th century, killing an estimated 21 million people worldwide [7, 8]. The threat of the avian influenza virus H5N1 to mutate and be able to spread among humans has alerted the world of the current risk of a similar deadly pandemic [9, 10].

From: *Nutrition and Health: Nutrition and Health in Developing Countries, Second Edition*
Edited by: R. D. Semba & M. W. Bloem © Humana Press, Totowa, NJ

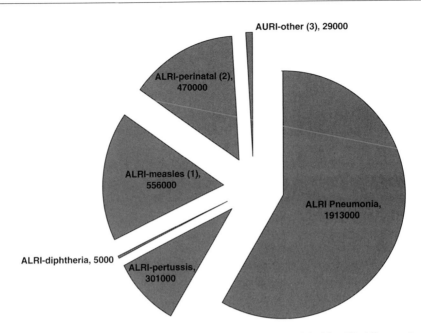

**Fig. 7.1.** Causes of acute lower-respiratory infection (ALRI) worldwide. (1) All measles-related deaths are assumed as due to ALRI. (2) All perinatal deaths not related to low birth weight or to birth asphyxia and birth trauma have been classified as ALRI. (3) All deaths due to acute upper respiratory infections (AURI) not due to otitis mostly represent croup. (Adapted with permission from [4].)

A common cause of pneumonia, pneumococcus (*Diplococcus* [*Streptococcus*] *pneumoniae*), was identified in 1881, and subsequent animal studies showed that it was involved in the causation of pneumonia [11]. By the turn of the century in the United States, it was estimated that mortality from pneumonia affected 1 of 500 individuals [12]. Antipneumoccocal sera were developed for the treatment of pneumonia; however, typing of the many pneumococcal strains was needed to ensure that the proper pneumococcal antisera were used. Sulfa antibiotics, which emerged in the late 1930s, were later shown to be more effective than serum therapy in the treatment of pneumococcal pneumonia [11]. Identification of many viral pathogens involved in acute respiratory infections, including respiratory syncytial virus (RSV), parainfluenza virus, and rhinoviruses, occurred in the 1950s [11].

## 7.4   EPIDEMIOLOGY

Several risk factors have been identified for acute lower-respiratory infections. These are reviewed briefly in this chapter (Table 7.1).

### 7.4.1   *Risk Factors*

#### 7.4.1.1   LOW BIRTH WEIGHT

Low birth weight (LBW) (<2,500 g) is associated with increased morbidity and mortality from acute lower-respiratory infections. Case-control studies from Brazil [13, 14], Sri Lanka [15], Chile [16], and the Bedouins in Israel [17] have documented that LBW

Table 7.1
**Risk factors for acute lower-respiratory infection**

Low birth weight
Lack of breast-feeding
Malnutrition
Vitamin A deficiency
Selenium deficiency
Zinc deficiency
Vitamin D or calcium deficiency
Immunosuppression
Attendance at day care centers
Crowding
Exposure to cooking fire
Parental smoking
Outdoor contaminants
Low socioeconomic status, poor housing
Household dampness
Respiratory disease in the household
Prior respiratory infections
Young age
Males
Season
Lack of immunization
Human immunodeficiency virus (HIV/AIDS)
Sickle-cell disease

was associated with an increased risk of acute lower-respiratory infection. LBW infants appeared to have a 50% greater risk of pneumonia compared with infants with birth weight of 2,500 g or more [11]. These findings have been confirmed by longitudinal studies done in Pelotas, Brazil [18], and in China [19], where LBW children had higher hospital admissions for respiratory disease. LBW has also been associated with repeated episodes of wheezing disorders during the first year of life [20]. In a prospective study of premature infants with birth weight less than 1,500 g in Rio de Janeiro, Brazil, respiratory morbidity was associated with previous mechanical ventilation, prolonged oxygen use (more than 28 days), and pneumonia in the neonatal period [21].

Epidemiologic studies have also shown an association between LBW and increased mortality from acute lower-respiratory infections in Brazil [22, 23], India [24], and the Philippines [25]. Infants born at term weighing 2,000–2,499 g at birth had neonatal mortality ten times greater than that of infants weighing 3,000–3,499 g [26]. This increased risk of mortality owing to respiratory diseases seems to be greater among LBW infants who were stunted at birth [26].

The incidence of LBW is greater in developing countries than in developed countries for several reasons [26]; one is poor maternal weight gain during pregnancy. Maternal weight gain of less than 10 kg was associated with a 40% increased risk of hospitalization owing to pneumonia in Brazil [27]. This increased risk of morbidity and mortality among LBW infants may be owing to impaired immunity or lung function [28]. The incidence of LBW, especially those infants small for gestational age born at term, continues to be an important public health problem in developing countries because of poor diet, infections, adolescent pregnancies, and other reasons.

### 7.4.1.2 LACK OF BREAST-FEEDING

Lack of breast-feeding has been identified as a major risk factor for morbidity and mortality in children with acute lower-respiratory infections. Children in China who were not breast-fed were twice as likely to be hospitalized as breast-fed children [19]. Lack of breast-feeding was found to be a risk factor for acute lower-respiratory infection, including radiologically confirmed pneumonia, in case-control studies in Argentina [29] and Porto Alegre, Brazil [13]. Non-breast-fed children were 17 times more likely to be hospitalized for pneumonia than breast-fed children in Pelotas, Brazil; this risk increased to 61 times in infants under 3 months of age [30]. In a birth cohort study in poor rural areas of Malawi, early introduction of complementary feeding was associated with increased risk of respiratory infections, particularly among illiterate women [31]. Similar findings have been reported in cohort studies done in Iran [32] and Nigeria [33]. Studies in developed countries also indicated that exclusive breast-feeding during the first months of life protects against asthma at 6 years of age [34], an effect that may also exist in developing countries.

Epidemiologic studies have also documented the relationship between lack of breast-feeding and the risk of death in children with acute lower-respiratory infections. A case-control study in Pelotas, Brazil, showed that risk of death from respiratory infections was higher in infants who were not breast-fed [35]. In a large prospective birth cohort study in slum areas of Dhaka, Bangladesh, partial or no breast-feeding in the first months of life was associated with a 2.4-fold increased risk of death due to acute respiratory infections [36]. In a secondary analysis of a multicenter study done in Ghana, India, and Peru, non-breast-fed infants had a high risk (hazard ratio of 32.7) of death due to acute lower-respiratory infections [37] Breast-feeding may be protective against acute respiratory infections because of transfer of immunity by breast milk, the presence of antibacterial and antiviral substances in breast milk, and avoidance of pathogens from contaminated weaning foods [38–40]. Baby bottles are also known to be a risk factor for the development of acute otitis, diarrhea, and pneumonia [41].

### 7.4.1.3 MALNUTRITION

The relationship between malnutrition and the incidence of respiratory diseases has only been evaluated critically since the 1990s [42]. A study done in the Philippines found an increased risk of acute respiratory infections in children with a Z-score less than −3 in weight-for-age compared with the National Center for Health Statistics median reference population [43]. This study found that undernourished children had a relative risk of 1.2 for an increased incidence of any acute respiratory illness and 1.9 for acute lower-respiratory infections [43]. These initial findings were confirmed by subsequent studies done in Bangladesh [44] and India [41].

These studies used a symptom-based definition of acute lower-respiratory infections without clinical or radiographic confirmation of pneumonia. In addition, an association between undernutrition and an increased risk of developing pneumonia seems to exist, as indicated by hospital-based studies done in the Gambia [45], Brazil [18], and Chile [46], where undernutrition was identified as a risk factor for hospitalizations owing to pneumonia. In a case-control study done in the Gambia, the development of pneumococcal infections was associated with a history of poor weight gain prior to illness compared with community controls [47]. Malnutrition seems to increase the severity of acute lower-respiratory infection, increasing its probability of having bacteremia (in many cases with multiple microbial organisms), pleural effusion, and other complications [48]. In a review of ten cohort studies done in Africa and Southeast Asia, the relative risk of mortality due to pneumonia varied from 2.01 in children with −1 to −2 standard deviation (SD) weight-for-age to 8.09 in children with less than 3 SDs [2]. That review concluded that 52.3% of all pneumonia deaths in the world were attributable to undernutrition. In conclusion, poor nutritional status in children seems to be associated with a modest increased risk for developing any acute respiratory disease and a moderate risk for developing acute lower-respiratory infection or pneumonia, increasing its severity and therefore explaining an important proportion of deaths due to pneumonia worldwide.

### 7.4.1.4 MICRONUTRIENT STATUS

Micronutrient status has been implicated as a risk factor in acute respiratory infections. Respiratory disease has been associated with increased risk of developing vitamin A deficiency [49], and in turn, vitamin A deficiency has been associated with increased risk of developing respiratory disease in preschool children [50, 51]. However, when respiratory diseases were assessed in carefully controlled prospective trials of vitamin A supplementation, no major reduction occurred in the mortality or morbidity associated with respiratory diseases, as indicated in an initial meta-analysis of available studies [52]. These findings were ratified by two meta-analyses [53, 54]. The initial association between low serum retinol levels and pneumonia may be explained by vitamin A that is lost in the urine during these infections [55], probably by mechanisms similar to those documented for diarrheal diseases [56].

Children with low plasma zinc concentrations in an urban slum setting had a mean prevalence rate of acute lower-respiratory infections that was 3.5-fold higher than children with normal plasma zinc concentrations [57]. In a randomized, double-blind, placebo-controlled trial in Bangladeshi children 2–23 months of age hospitalized with severe pneumonia, 20 mg of elemental zinc per day was associated with increased recovery and shorter hospital stay and duration of antibiotic treatment [58]. This study did not publish treatment effects by gender, although most children (65%) were male. In another double-blind, placebo-controlled trial in Indian children 2–24 months of age, 10 mg of zinc as acetate was associated with reduction of severe illness and fever, but in boys, not in girls [59]. Finally, in another Indian study, using a similar study design in hospitalized children 2–23 months of age, 10 mg of zinc sulfate did not have a beneficial effect on the treatment of severe pneumonia [60]. It is not clear if these differences could be due to lower zinc doses in the Indian studies, compared to the study in Bangladesh, or to other biological differences. In a controlled, double-blind study in Indian children 9 months to 15 years of age hospitalized with pneumonia associated with acute measles, 20 mg of zinc acetate did not showed any clinical benefit [61].

Further studies are needed to clarify the role of zinc supplements in the treatment of severe pneumonia in children. It is important to mention that in the Bangladeshi study, zinc supplementation did not show any benefit for children with wheezing disorders, only those with severe pneumonia [59]. It is now clear that zinc is important not only in growth but also in the immune function of children, which is affected in zinc-deficient children suffering diarrheal and respiratory diseases [62]. Most children in developing countries consume very little animal proteins—the dietary source of zinc with the highest bioavailability—explaining why zinc deficiency may be one of the most important nutritional disorders in children from developing countries [63].

Selenium deficiency may be a risk factor for the development of respiratory infections, particularly pneumonia, among critically ill patients and malnourished children. Premature infants may be particularly at risk. It is known that selenium serum concentration drops in premature infants after birth, especially in those who develop respiratory distress syndrome [64]. In a prospective study in LBW infants, low plasma selenium levels were associated with chronic lung disease and bronchopulmonary dysplasia, as well as with the total days of oxygen requirement. For each drop of 0.1 µmol/L of selenium in plasma, there was a 58% increase in days of oxygen dependency, controlling for gestational age and age when infants were fully fed orally [65]. Premature infants, especially those treated with oxygen, may warrant selenium supplementation. Supplementation with one dose of 1 mg sodium selenite to routine treatment of children hospitalized with pneumonia or wheezing disorders associated with RSV [66] or *Mycoplasma pneumonia* [67] has been found to have a beneficial clinical effect in China. Food additives containing selenium have also been reported to have a beneficial effect in children with pneumonia in Russia [68, 69]. Further clinical trials with selenium supplementation in children with pneumonia are warranted.

Other micronutrients may also play a role in susceptibility of children to pneumonia and other acute respiratory infections. In a case-control study done in Ethiopia, children with clinical or radiological evidence of rickets had a probability of pneumonia 13 times higher than did children without rickets, suggesting that vitamin D or calcium deficiency may also be important as a risk factor for pneumonia [70]. A review of the literature concluded that nutritional rickets was a risk factor for pneumonia in Ethiopian children [71]. In a case-control study done in Indian children, a low serum level of vitamin D was associated with severe acute lower-respiratory infections, adjusting for other risk factors [72]. Poor dietary calcium intake may potentiate the deficiency of vitamin D [73]. Clinical trials with vitamin D with or without calcium supplements should be done in areas where vitamin D deficiency is endemic.

### 7.4.1.5 Decreased Immunity

Some indicators of decreased immunity have been associated with the risk of acute respiratory diseases. Depressed cell-mediated immunity has been demonstrated to be an important predictor of both acute upper- (20% increased risk) [74] and lower- (80% increased risk) [44] respiratory infections in Bangladeshi children, controlling for nutritional status. A study done in Kenya found a similar association with acute respiratory infections (34% increased risk) [75]. This impaired immune capacity of children in developing countries seems to be related to micronutrient deficiencies (zinc in particular) and malnutrition.

### 7.4.1.6 Environmental and Socioeconomic Factors

Several environmental and socioeconomic factors have been associated with respiratory infections in children. Attendance at day care centers has been identified as a strong risk factor for acute upper- and lower-respiratory tract infections in children in several studies, both in developed [76, 77] and developing countries [13, 14, 78]. Children in day care centers have between 5 and 12 times greater risk of pneumonia than those cared for at home. This increased risk is not only for bacterial pneumonia, but also for other causes of pneumonia like *M. pneumoniae* [79] and RSV [80]. The very low rate of invasive pneumococcal disease observed in Switzerland between 1985 and 1994 has been attributed to the lower rate of day care attendance of Swiss children compared to other European countries [81]. Day care centers increase the contact between young children and facilitate the transmission of infections through respiratory droplets.

Similar to attendance at day care centers, crowding (number of persons in the household, number of persons sharing the bedroom, number of siblings under 5 years of age, greater parity) also favors the transmission of respiratory infections, as documented in case-control [13–15, 80, 82, 83] and longitudinal [84, 85] studies. Even at the turn of the twentieth century, household crowding was associated with an increased risk of death owing to measles-associated pneumonia [84]. Increased contact with other children or adults, whether at home or at institutions, is a strong risk factor for pneumonia and other respiratory diseases.

Another mechanism by which crowding may affect the risk of respiratory diseases is the exposure to smoking and other indoor air pollutants. Exposure to smoke during cooking and parental smoking was associated with deaths owing to acute lower-respiratory infections in a case-control study in the Gambia [86]. Maternal smoking (greater than or equal to five cigarettes/day) was associated with upper- and lower-respiratory diseases in a longitudinal study in Chile [82]. In a large prospective study of 1,459 children less than 2 years of age in periurban Lima, Peru, even the exposure of a child to a very low level of household members who smoke (mean consumption 11 cigarettes/week, only 6% of mothers reported smoking) was consistently associated with an increased risk of cough and respiratory illnesses [87]. Environmental exposure to tobacco smoke has been associated clearly with an increased risk of pneumonia, bronchitis, bronchiolitis, chronic middle ear effusion, and increased frequency and severity of attacks among asthmatics [88, 89]. Maternal smoking during pregnancy increases the risk of sudden infant death syndrome (SIDS) [90]. The Comparative Risk Assessment Collaborating Group has estimated that smoking may explain 2% of the DALYs lost to lower-respiratory infections in the world [91]. Developing countries are rapidly increasing their rate of maternal and household smoking, the reduction of which should be considered a public health priority. Breast-feeding protects children from this increased risk of lower-respiratory diseases associated with exposure to environmental tobacco smoke [90, 92], which is another reason for breast-feeding promotion.

Many households in developing countries utilize biomass fuels (wood, manure, carbon, agricultural waste, etc.), mostly because more efficient fossil fuels or electricity are either not available or not affordable [93]. These fuels are usually burned in inefficient stoves or openly within the family room without the use of a chimney, especially in rural areas in the highlands. Children exposed to these sources of indoor air pollution have increased risk of respiratory illnesses. In Nepal, the risk of severe respiratory diseases increased with the number of hours each infant spent near a stove [94, 95]. In the Gambia, carriage of a child on the mother's back while cooking was associated with acute lower-respiratory infections [96], as was the use of wood-burning stoves by Native Americans [97].

An increased incidence of acute lower-respiratory infection was reported associated with the use of kerosene stoves in India [98], but not in Peru [87].

Among different combustion products, a high concentration of suspended particulates with 0.1- to 10-μ diameter (PM10) has been linked to an increased risk of pneumonia. This effect seems to be mediated through an inhibition of the inflammatory response of alveolar macrophages by PM10 exposure, as documented with RSV infections [99]. Not only may indoor sources of air contaminants be important, but also environmental air pollution may play a role as a risk factor for pneumonia, especially among atopic individuals [100]. It has been estimated that indoor smoke from solid fuels explains 36% of DALYs lost to lower-respiratory infections in the world [91], while urban ambient air pollution may explain about 1% of mortality due to acute respiratory infections in children less than 5 years of age in the world [101].

Because of all these reasons, the incidence of acute lower-respiratory diseases has been reported to be higher in crowded urban areas of low socioeconomic status, where most of these factors are combined [41]. Lower social class [41, 82, 102], race [102], parental education [13, 27, 41, 82], and poor housing [29, 83] are variables associated with lower-respiratory infections through crowding, indoor air pollution, and environmental exposure to tobacco, as well as other nutritional factors. The presence of a pet animal at home [15] as well as household dampness [87, 103] are particular risk factors for wheezing disorders and childhood asthma, most likely by favoring the growth of molds [104] and the presence of other household allergens.

### 7.4.1.7 PRIOR INFECTIONS

Several studies have reported an increased risk of pneumonia or acute lower-respiratory infections in children who have had a prior episode of pneumonia or wheezing [13–15, 29]. Viral infections, particularly with RSV or influenza virus, also predispose to invasive pneumococcal disease for a period of 4 weeks [105]. In a case-control study in Brazil, wheezing disorders were associated with a sevenfold increased risk of pneumonia in children, controlling for other factors [106]. On the other hand, prior acute lower-respiratory infections (croup, bronchitis, bronchiolitis, or pneumonia) were also a risk factor for wheezing in infancy [20]. But, prior infection does not always seem to be a risk factor. Infections in early life seem to be related to the chances of developing asthma and allergic disorders later in life. An initial report from Japan documented that children 12 years old who had a positive tuberculin response predicted a lower incidence of asthma, lower serum immunoglobulin E (IgE) levels, and the predominance of a cytokine profile not associated with atopy [107]. This report was used to postulate that the reduction of early childhood infections, such as tuberculosis, owing to development and better living standards may be one reason for the increase in asthma and atopy observed in developed societies in the last 20 years [108].

The hygiene hypothesis suggested that an early life exposure to a contaminated environment primes the immune system in the direction of a Th1 (T helper type 1) profile, associated with a nonallergic phenotype; living in a cleaner environment would prime the immune system toward a Th2 (T helper type 2) profile, an allergic phenotype [109]. Some studies in developing countries have found supporting evidence for this hypothesis, with higher prevalence of atopic diseases and history of asthma in children in urban areas in Turkey [110] and Chinese [111] children; in contrast, the history of acute gastroenteritis, fever, and antibiotic use during infancy was associated with later development of asthma in Korean children [112]. Some have postulated that rather than environmental exposure to pathogens, persistent infections with certain microorganisms, like *Chlamydia pneumoniae*, may explain later development of asthma [113]. Others have suggested that lifestyle changes related to obesity may be the link with asthma and developed areas [114]. Systematic reviews of the literature also provided conflicting results regarding the hygiene hypothesis [115, 116], indicating that the association of an increased prevalence of asthma, eczema, and atopy in developed countries may be multifactorial, relating to the host, nutritional status, and environment, among other factors yet to be explained.

### 7.4.1.8 OTHER FACTORS

Other factors have been associated with pneumonia or acute lower-respiratory infections, like young age, male sex, young maternal age, and so forth. Infants and children under 2 years of age have the highest incidence of infections, particularly with RSV [80]. Mortality owing to lower-respiratory diseases is concentrated among infants under 6 months of age [1]. Males have a higher incidence of wheezing disorders or RSV infections in infancy than females [15, 80, 87, 117]. Those of young maternal age [13] and adolescent mothers [27] have been reported to have an increased risk of pneumonia in their children. Lack of immunization has also been associated with increased risk of respiratory morbidity [14, 41] and mortality [86].

The increased incidence of HIV infections in the heterosexual population is changing the epidemiology of respiratory infections in children from developed and developing countries. As the prevalence of HIV increases in women, the number of newborns infected with HIV through vertical transmission will also increase [118]. As documented in Haiti, a large proportion of HIV-infected newborns (60% in this study) will die before reaching 6 months of life, whether meningitis, sepsis, or pneumonia is the immediate cause of death [119]. Other conditions prevalent in developing countries, like sickle-cell disease, are also associated with an increased risk of invasive pneumococcal and *Haemophilus influenzae* infections [120]. Finally, lack of maternal antibodies is a risk factor for the development of infections in early infancy, as documented for RSV [80]. This association may offer the opportunity to protect newborns through maternal immunization, as discussed in Section 7.7.1.

## 7.4.2 Incidence

Before reviewing the information available on incidence of acute lower-respiratory infections in children, it is important to discuss briefly the definitions of pneumonia or acute lower-respiratory infection used in these studies because they have profound influence on the rates reported, as reviewed elsewhere [121]. Studies done in developed countries generally report cases diagnosed by physicians on clinical grounds, sometimes complemented by chest X-rays. In contrast, studies conducted in developing countries usually are based on diagnosis from respiratory signs and symptoms reported by the mother or identified by field-workers. Even though the presence of cough, rapid respiratory rates, and other respiratory signs are highly suggestive of pneumonia, as promoted by the World Health Organization (WHO) case-management guidelines, it is difficult to distinguish very clearly between pneumonia and other types of acute lower-respiratory infections, especially in community-based prospective studies [122, 123].

The methodology used in these studies is also critical. High variability exists on the normal respiratory-rate-by-age, which at some ages is very similar (within 1 SD) of the cutoff value used by WHO to consider that a child has tachypnea [124]. The technique used to measure the respiratory rate is also important [125]. Physical signs on chest examination have important variations when repeat observations are done with one or multiple observers [126]. Even chest X-rays may be negative in the presence of pneumonia proven by postmortem examination in children [127]. To complicate the issue further, rates will change if cases are identified at health facilities when mothers decide to bring their children for care (passive surveillance) as compared with frequent home visits by trained field-workers to identify respiratory infections (active surveillance). Because of these variables, studies using passive surveillance and chest X-ray to diagnose pneumonia report the lowest rates, and studies using active surveillance and symptom-based diagnosis of acute lower-respiratory infections report the highest rates. Because of these reasons, the comparison of acute lower-respiratory infection or pneumonia rates across studies and countries may not be valid and should be taken with caution if the methods used are not similar.

The incidence of acute respiratory infections (mostly upper) in developing countries has been reported as between four and seven episodes per child per year, being similar in America [128], Africa [129], and Asia [130]. The incidence of pneumonia, as diagnosed by physicians with or without radiology, has been reported as 53 episodes per 100 child-years in children under 3 years of age in Guatemala [128]; 30 episodes per 100 child-years in infants and children under 2 years of age in Peru [122, 131]; and 16.5 episodes per 100 child-years in children under 5 years of age in the Gambia [132]. In a systematic review of 28 high-quality community-based studies published since 1961, the median incidence rate of clinical pneumonia in children less than 5 years of age was 0.29 episodes per child-year, giving an estimated number of 150.7 million cases per year, with 7–13% of these children hospitalized in developing countries in the world [133]. The incidence in developed countries was estimated as 0.026 episodes per child-year, suggesting that 95% of all cases of pneumonia occur in developing countries. The age-specific incidence rates for acute respiratory infections are generally highest in infants at 6–11 months of age.

### 7.4.3 Seasonality

Seasonal distribution for incidence rates of acute respiratory infections and acute lower-respiratory infections has been examined in several initial studies [134]. Patterns of acute respiratory infections appear to vary by location. The highest incidence of acute respiratory infections in Colombia and Thailand was observed from September through December. In Guatemala, the highest rates were noted from January through July. Two peaks were observed in the Philippines, one in January and one in October. Seasonality was also observed for acute lower-respiratory infections in different location, but the patterns did not necessarily coincide with that for acute respiratory infections overall [134]. This variation is most likely owing to the mixture of pneumonia and wheezing disorders that are combined by the methodology used in these initial studies. Wheezing disorders or infections by RSV are more seasonal than pneumococcal or *H. influenzae* infections in tropical developing countries, being more common in winter or cold months [82]. Mortality owing to acute lower-respiratory infections, more so in neonates, is also higher in winter months [135].

These observations have led people to believe that exposure to cold weather or high humidity is associated with an increased risk of developing acute lower-respiratory infections or pneumonia. Volunteer studies with rhinoviruses after exposure to cold and to high humidity failed to demonstrate an increased risk of infection com-pared to a warm and dry environment [136]. Epidemiological studies done in England have also failed to demonstrate an association between indoor temperature and humidity and respiratory infections [137]. Most likely, cold weather induces individuals to reduce ventilation indoors, and the crowding that results from remaining indoors increases the risk of respiratory infections rather than the cold directly affecting the health. There is a need to better document this lack of association to clarify this issue.

### 7.4.4 Duration

Most episodes of acute respiratory infections and acute lower-respiratory infections last less than 2 weeks [134]. In a prospective home surveillance study done in Peru of respiratory signs and symptoms by frequent (twice weekly) home visits by trained field-workers, it was shown that cough and phlegm started developing 10–12 days prior to the diagnosis of pneumonia by a physician or a positive chest X-ray. It was also found that patients took 10–12 days to recover after diagnosis [122]. Rapid breathing, fever, loss of appetite, and ill appearance, as reported by the mother, appeared between 5 and 8 days prior to diagnosis and lasted 5–8 days after the diagnosis (except fever that disappeared in 24 hours after starting antibiotics) [122]. Thus, the duration of symptoms is related to their severity as well as to early treatment with antibiotics. Based on this study, it could be said that most respiratory signs and symptoms associated with pneumonia in the community usually would last no more than 15 days if diagnosed early and treated appropriately.

### 7.4.5 Case Fatality Ratios

Case fatality ratios for acute lower-respiratory infections in different hospital-based studies have ranged from 0.8% [138] to about 20% [139–142] in developing countries. Higher case fatality has been associated with age under 1 year [143–146], malnutrition [143–145, 147], increased respiratory rate (>70/min) [147], cyanosis and low oxygen saturation [143, 144, 146, 147], rickets [72, 144], loose stools [145], and late hospital admission [148]. Females have been reported to have an increased case fatality [134, 143]. In malnourished children, pneumonia is a predictor of mortality [149]. Gambian children who were hospitalized with severe pneumonia and survived were followed up after discharge from the hospital [150]. It was found that children who were malnour-ished while in the hospital had a threefold greater risk of death after being sent home than children without malnutrition, indicating the importance of nutritional recovery in the hospital before a patient is sent home [150].

Owing to the increase in the prevalence of penicillin-resistant strains of S. pneumoniae, concerns of greater case fatality rates in infections with resistant strains have emerged [151]. However, in several studies [152–154] the mortality associated with resistant strains did not increase even when penicillin or related drugs were used owing to the high concentration these antibiotics achieved in the lung tissue, several levels above the minimal inhibitory concentration of the strains [155]. On the contrary, resistant strains have higher mortality rates in meningitis owing to the lower antibiotic concentration in the cerebrospinal fluid [154, 155]. As expected, appropriate case management can reduce a high level of case fatality, as documented in Zambia when the WHO protocol for case management of pneumonia was introduced in a rural hospital [140].

## 7.5   CLINICAL FEATURES/PATHOPHYSIOLOGY

### 7.5.1   *Clinical Presentation*

Acute upper-respiratory infections are usually defined based on signs of at least one of the following: runny nose, sore throat, cough, or earache or ear discharge, without any findings of acute lower-respiratory infections [134]. Acute lower-respiratory infections are defined based on the presence of cough and at least one of the following signs: increased respiratory rate (>60 respirations per minute in infants under 2 months of age, >50 respirations per minute in infants 2–11 months old, and >40 respirations per minute in children 12 months and older); rales or crepitations; wheezing; stridor; or chest indrawing [134, 156–159]. The presence of cough and an increased respiratory rate or chest indrawing is about 70% sensitive and specific to identify pneumonia, especially in cases seen in an emergency room of a health facility [156–158]. In areas that do not have malaria, the presence of fever may increase the specificity without much drop in the sensitivity [123, 160], increasing its positive predictive value. The presence of chest indrawing, nasal flaring, and cyanosis are signs of more severe disease [122, 161, 162].

Severe and complicated pneumonia was associated with low weight, anemia, and a white blood cell (WBC) count below 15,000/mm$^3$ at the time of admission in Israeli children [162]. The presence of nasal mucus, of any color or consistency, was not associated with pneumonia in a longitudinal study in Peru [122], against the popular belief that purulent nasal discharge is associated with pneumonia. Bacteremic pneumococcal pneumonia is usually associated with high fever, increased WBC counts, and ill appearance [163]; in 80% of cases, they had a lobar pneumonia. However, in a prospective study done in Brazil, respiratory signs and symptoms did not distinguish bacterial from viral pneumonia [164]. Also, the majority of clinically diagnosed cases of pneumonia in outpatient settings in developing countries do not have an abnormal chest X-ray, even though they do respond to antibiotic treatment, indicating the importance of clinical judgment over X-ray or laboratory parameters [165].

In the laboratory, apart from a positive chest X-ray, children with pneumonia have an increased WBC count during the first 2 days of their clinical course, declining thereafter, reaching the lowest levels by day 4 [166]. The erythrocyte sedimentation rate follows an opposite course, being normal or mildly elevated during the start of the clinical course and increasing steadily thereafter [166]. Studies have documented the importance of hypoxemia in children with acute lower-respiratory infections, ranging from 6% to 9% in outpatient cases to 47% in children hospitalized with pneumonia, more so (72%) in children with a positive chest X-ray [167]. Hypoxemia is more frequent in children living in high altitude areas [167] and is frequently underrecognized in neonates [168].

### 7.5.2   *Major Pathogens Involved in Acute Lower Respiratory Diseases in Children*

Respiratory syncytial virus is the leading viral pathogen involved in acute lower-respiratory infections in children, isolated in 5–37% of patients [134, 138, 169–171].

Of children infected with RSV, 30% have pneumonia; bronchiolitis is the most common clinical presentation [172]. The association of RSV with asthma and reversible reactive airway disease in early childhood has been clearly recognized [173]. Epithelial cells are initially involved in an inflammatory response, in which cytokines and chemokines released from inflammatory cells trigger further inflammatory responses, which are more common in susceptible children with a family history of asthma or atopy [173, 174]. Recent studies have suggested that RSV may enhance the development of an allergic inflammatory response in susceptible hosts when exposed to allergens after being infected with RSV [175]. Other important viral causes of acute lower-respiratory infections are adenovirus, parainfluenza virus, and influenza virus [176, 177].

In 2001, a new, previously unidentified virus causing acute respiratory tract infections was reported from the Netherlands and was called human metapneumovirus (hMPV) [178], from the paramyxovirus group [180]. Since its initial report, it has been associated with respiratory illnesses in Europe, North and South America, Asia, Australia, and South Africa [178]. It is isolated in between 1% and 25% of cases with upper and lower respiratory tract infections, having similar epidemiological characteristics as RSV and influenza virus [174, 178, 179].

In November 2002, a severe acute respiratory syndrome (SARS) was reported from southern China, a disease later discovered to be caused by a coronavirus, probably from an animal source [180]. In February 2003, the virus was brought to Hong Kong, and from there, it spread rapidly to more than 30 countries in several continents, causing more than 8,000 cases and 916 deaths (11% case fatality) before the epidemic ended in June 2003 [180–182]. Because of its long incubation period (mean 6.4 days, range 2–11 days), it allowed asymptomatic air travelers to spread the disease globally. In children, SARS caused milder disease, with nonspecific chest X-ray changes [183].

Several zoonotic paramyxoviruses have also caused outbreaks of severe respiratory diseases in humans. The first was caused by what is now called Hendra virus, a lethal zoonotic agent able to cause the disease in horses and humans, initially described in Australia in 1984, 1999, and 2004, with a high case fatality rate [184–186]. The second and most frequent one is called the Nipah virus, initially described as causing an outbreak of severe febrile encephalitis with respiratory symptoms in Malaysia and Singapore in 1999 and later in Bangladesh, where it caused several outbreaks between 2001 and 2005 [185–188]. Its reservoir is large fruit bats (also called flying foxes), and virus can infect humans from bats, pigs, or infected humans [188]. Since its reemergence in 2003 in several Southeast Asian countries, a highly pathogenic avian influenza A virus (H5N1) has caused severe disease in humans exposed to sick or dead chickens or wild birds [9, 10]. There have been more than 200 human cases reported, including children, with a high case fatality rate (about 50%), but human-to-human transmission has not been documented yet. A fear exists that a mutation of the A/H5N1 influenza virus could allow it to spread within humans, causing another severe pandemic influenza in the world [10].

Identification of the bacterial causes of pneumonia is limited by the low rate of isolation of bacteria in blood cultures and the impracticality and risk involved with needle aspiration of the lung for culture. Cultures taken from the trachea or throat are invalid because they are usually contaminated by bacteria that grow in those settings, not necessarily representing the cause of the pneumonia. In cultured specimens taken from sterile sites (blood or lung tissue) in children with acute lower-respiratory infections, the most commonly identified bacterial pathogen has generally been *S. pneumoniae*, followed by *H. influenzae* [134, 138, 170, 171, 189]. Other important pathogens include *Bordetella pertussis* and *M. pneumoniae*. Pneumonia in cases with pertussis has been reported in 9.4% of cases, with the severity of the disease greater among infants less than 6 months old [190]. Pertussis in the very young infant or in individuals previously immunized can also occur. In very young infants, the disease is atypical and severe, requiring hospitalization [191]. In previously immunized individuals, pertussis is mild, prolonged (>4 weeks of symptoms), and atypical [192]. Despite the worldwide use of pertussis immunization, the incidence of pertussis has not been reduced as expected [193]. Pertussis still occurs, causing severe morbidity and mortality in unimmunized or partially immunized children, usually infected from adults or adolescents who have waning vaccine-induced immunity [194]. In some endemic areas, *Chlamydia trachomatis* should also be considered in cases with pneumonia, especially if the individual has concurrent conjunctivitis [195]. As with *M. pneumoniae*, *C. pneumoniae* is also a cause of pneumonia epidemics in schoolchildren and adults [196]. Mixed infections with different pathogens may occur.

Empyema can occur in *S. pneumoniae* pneumonia. However, *Staphylococcus aureus* is a common cause of empyema in developing countries, requiring thoracentesis and prolonged antibiotic therapy [197, 198]. Another complication of pneumococcal pneumonia is necrotizing pneumonia, usually associated with lung abscesses and cavitation, with better clinical course in children than in adults [199]. Croup in children is associated with older children (mean age 21 months), usually associated more with viral organisms than bacteria [200].

An important subgroup of children that has been recently studied in developing countries is infants under 3 months of age. In two studies done in Ethiopia [201] and Papua New Guinea [202], *Streptococcus pyogenes* and *S. pneumoniae* were the most common isolates, followed by *S. aureus*. RSV was the most common viral agent. Organisms frequently isolated in young infants in developed countries, like *Salmonella* group B and *Streptococcus agalactiae*, were rarely isolated. However, in a similar study done in the Philippines [203], *Salmonella* spp., *Enterobacter* spp., and gram-negative organisms were more common than *S. pneumoniae*, indicating that the pattern observed in developed countries may also be present in some developing countries. Further studies on the etiology of severe infectious diseases in infants under 3 months of age are needed. Because of the newly recognized need to protect against *S. pneumoniae* infection in young infants, WHO is now evaluating the use of maternal immunization to protect neonates [204, 205].

*Klebsiella pneumoniae* [206], blastomycosis [207], *Legionella* pneumonia [208], and melioidosis [209] are some of the opportunistic infections that may occur in premature babies and persons who are immunocompromised, have congenital diseases, or are given steroids. In some isolated rural areas with low immunization coverage, measles epidemics that are associated with up to 32% of pneumonia cases still occur [210].

### 7.5.3   *Pathophysiology*

The pathophysiology of acute lower-respiratory infections may vary depending on the pathogen involved. In general, the immune defenses in the lung are provided by a cough reflex, action of cilia in the tracheobronchial tree, mucus secretion by goblet cells, and phagocytic activity by alveolar macrophages. Pneumonia occurs when pathogenic organisms overwhelm these host defenses and infection occurs in the lower-respiratory tract. In the affected portion of the lung, polymorphonuclear leukocytes, erythrocytes, and proteinaceous secretions are present, and consolidation occurs, which may appear as a homogeneous density on chest radiograph. In general, consolidation occurs less among young infants. The affected individual may develop fever, tachycardia, and cyanosis, and sputum production may be present. Phagocytosis, antibody responses, and other immune mechanisms usually allow recovery from pneumonia within several days to a couple of weeks.

A series of elegant experimental studies have clarified the physiologic changes occurring in the lung with lobar pneumonia. Studies in dogs with pneumonia induced by inoculation with *S. pneumoniae* [211] or *Pseudomonas aeruginosa* [212] revealed that the exudate produced in the site of infection reduces the gas exchanged by filling the alveoli, preventing them from inflation. This causes a reduction in the total lung capacity as well as in the functional residual capacity, proportional to the magnitude of the lung involved. The lung reacts with hypoxia-induced pulmonary vasoconstriction in the affected area, initially thought to be an attempt to divert blood to ventilated lung tissues to maintain a high oxygen tension in the blood [213]. This, however, is not effective, and blood goes through the pneumonic, unventilated tissue, creating an arterial-venous shunt, which explains the hypoxia seen in severe pneumonia [214]. This pulmonary vasoconstriction induces pulmonary hypertension, which in severe pneumonia causes right ventricular cardiac failure, a condition that is associated with increased mortality and that does not respond to digoxin therapy [215]. Very few children with right ventricular failure will manifest the typical clinical signs of hepatomegaly, tachycardia, raised jugular venous pressure, or peripheral edema. They usually only have dilation of the right ventricle on ultrasound examination of the heart [215].

Oxygen administration reduces the vasoconstriction and increases the blood's oxygen tension through the preserved lung tissue, but the shunt remains unchanged because the pneumonic lung is not ventilated [216]. Intrapulmonary blood shunt is not the only reason for hypoxia because the pneumonic tissue increases its consumption of oxygen, and at the same time, fever and infection also increase the oxygen requirements in the rest of the body [217]. The involvement of lung tissue by pneumonia also causes a reduction of lung compliance and an increase in the work of breathing. In the dog model, administration of intravenous fluids that could increase the plasma volume and the pulmonary capillary wedge pressure is associated with large increases in lobar wet weights of the affected pneumonic lung, probably owing in part to transudation of plasma and crystalloid into alveolar spaces [218]. The magnitude of the intrapulmonary shunt may be increased by endogenous vasodilator mediators, exogenous systemically administered vasodilator drugs, positioning the patient with the affected lung down, and increasing the positive airway pressure by mechanical ventilation [219]. Factors that reduce shunt include effective hypoxic pulmonary vasoconstriction, inhaled locally acting vasodilators that act primarily on the ventilated lung, and positioning the patient with the affected lung up [219]. The blood's oxygen saturation is improved if the patient is in prone position rather than in supine position [220]. The administration of aerosolized vasodilators may be beneficial to patients by improving their ventilation in the ventilated lung, thereby improving the blood's oxygen tension [221].

The lung compliance of the remaining ventilated lung seems also to be reduced, possibly by a reduction in surfactant activity, further increasing the work of breathing [219]. Pulmonary surfactant is a complex material composed of lipids and proteins; it is found in the fluid lining of the alveolar surface of the lungs. Surfactant prevents alveolar collapse at low lung volume and preserves bronchiolar patency during normal and forced respiration [222]. It is also involved in the protection of the lung from injuries and infections caused by inhaled particles or microorganisms [222]. Pulmonary surfactant is absent in prematurity and is one of the reasons for respiratory distress syndrome and hyaline membrane disease in premature newborns [222]. But, surfactant abnormalities are also present in various degrees in asthma, bronchiolitis, pneumonia, cystic fibrosis, and HIV infections [222]. Natural and synthetic surfactants are now available for the prevention and treatment of respiratory distress syndrome in infants [223].

The recovery process in pneumonia is produced by clearing of fluids and other materials from the air space, improving ventilation, and in part by a reduction of perfusion of poorly ventilated areas of the lung [224]. The reduction of blood flow through the consolidated lung reduces the shunt and improves arterial oxygen concentration [219]. However, the lung is not always able to recover completely. Long-term consequences after childhood pneumonia have been reported in pulmonary function tests among adults, including a reduction of lung volume [225].

There have been discussions whether the abnormal pulmonary function seen with some acute lower-respiratory infections, like wheezing disorders, is a consequence of or a risk factor for the initial attack. In an elegant prospective study done in Taiwan, respiratory function was assessed by a single-occlusion technique and rapid thoracic compression technique in a group of infants at a mean of 2 months who were then followed for 2 years [226]. Infants who developed a subsequent attack of wheezing had low values of total respiratory compliance corrected for body weight compared with those infants who did not develop a wheezing attack. This study indicated that differences in lung function in early life, for reasons yet to be understood, predispose infants to acute lower-respiratory infection with wheezing disorders in their first 2 years of life.

### 7.5.4  *Impact of Acute Respiratory Infections on Nutrition and Growth*

Few studies have focused on the impact of respiratory diseases on nutrition and growth. Compared with tuberculosis, which has a prolonged course of illness with a pronounced impact on nutrition [227, 228], or diarrheal diseases, the role of acute respiratory diseases on the nutritional status of children has been not well documented. In a prospective study of a small cohort of Gambian children, acute lower-respiratory infections diagnosed by a pediatrician were associated with a loss of 14.7 g of weight per day of illness, greater than the reduction observed with diarrheal diseases [229]. Because of their higher prevalence, however, diarrheal diseases explained one half of weight loss, and acute lower-respiratory infections only accounted for 25% of observed weight deficit. One study in the Philippines documented the impact of febrile respiratory illness on weight gain [230]. In Papua New Guinea, weight gain was reduced during episodes of acute lower-respiratory infections in young children [231]. A large longitudinal study in Brazil suggested that hospitalization for pneumonia and subsequent height-for-age are significantly associated [18], and acute respiratory infections had a negative impact on weight gain in Guatemala [232].

Acute respiratory illnesses have been associated with a 10–20% reduction in food intake [233]. This could be caused by a reduction in the child's appetite—as has been well documented in a study in Peru [234]—the same mechanism that is postulated for the reduction of weight after a diarrheal episode or a febrile illness [235]. As with these other illnesses, catabolism may also play a role. Based on these studies, we can conclude that acute lower-respiratory illnesses, especially those associated with fever, have a negative impact on the nutritional status of children if the child's appetite is reduced, and there is a subsequent reduction of dietary intake. Further studies are needed to quantify the magnitude of this negative relationship between acute lower-respiratory infection and growth.

## 7.6  TREATMENT

### 7.6.1  Case Management of Pneumonia

A case management approach for pneumonia in children has been developed by WHO and is based on the assumptions that the main causes of fatal pneumonia are *S. pneumoniae* and *H. influenzae* [236], and that antibiotic treatment of pneumonia can reduce case fatality rates [237]. An algorithm based on clinical signs was developed to facilitate the recognition and management of acute respiratory infections by non-specialist doctors working in small hospitals with limited facilities [238, 239]. Several intervention studies using a case-management strategy for pneumonia were conducted in several developing countries. A meta-analysis of intervention trials on case management of pneumonia in nine community settings showed that the case-management strategy has a substantial effect on neonate, infant, and under 5 mortality rates, at least in settings where infant mortality rates are 49/1,000 live births or greater [240, 241]. Despite differences in study populations (location, immunization coverage, diarrhea management, prevalence of malnutrition, health services availability, maternal literacy, and infant mortality rates) and antibiotic (penicillin, ampicillin, cotrimoxazole) treatment in the different intervention trials, there was a consistent impact of case management on pneumonia mortality in neonates, infants, and children 1–4 years old. Case management of pneumonia was associated with a summary estimate from the pooled studies of 42% reduction (95% confidence interval [CI] 22–57%) of neonatal pneumonia mortality, of a 36% reduction (95% CI 20–48%) of infant pneumonia mortality, and of a 36% reduction (95% CI 20–49%) of pneumonia mortality among children 0–4 years old [241]. Reductions of total mortality by 27% (95% CI 18–35%) in neonates, 20% (95% CI 11–28%) in infants, and 24% (95% CI 14–33%) in children 0–4 years of age were also observed [241].

### 7.6.2  Nutritional Interventions for Treatment of Acute Respiratory Infections

#### 7.6.2.1  ZINC

As described in Section 7.4.1.4, zinc supplementation given to children hospitalized with severe pneumonia was found effective in reducing pneumonia severity and shortening hospital stay in Bangladeshi [58] and Indian children [59], findings that were not confirmed in another Indian study [60]. No effect on wheezing disorders was observed in these trials [59]. Zinc gluconate glycine lozenges have been suggested as a therapy for the common cold [242–244]. Initial meta-analyses of randomized, controlled clinical trials have suggested that zinc lozenges may be effective in the reduction of cold symptoms in adults and children, but the studies had many problems, including zinc dose; inadequate placebo control, and various formulations of the lozenge, which may include citric acid, sorbitol, mannitol, or tartaric acid, which may bind free zinc ion in the mouth, reducing its therapeutic effect [242, 243]. Initial zinc lozenges were associated with adverse effects in general, with bad taste and nausea as prominent symptoms [245]. Recent done trials, however, have documented that zinc lozenges were associated with reduction of duration and severity of cold symptoms [246, 247], especially when administered within 24 hours of the onset of common cold symptoms [248]. The use of zinc nasal sprays, gels, or lozenges given intranasally have caused important side effects and are not recommended [249, 250].

### 7.6.2.2   VITAMIN A

Recent meta-analysis of trials evaluating the clinical effect of vitamin A supplementation in nonmeasles childhood pneumonia indicated that there was no effect [53, 54]. One study even showed vitamin A supplementation associated with more severe disease compared with placebo recipients [251]. These studies indicated that vitamin A supplementation has no role in the therapy of pneumonia.

### 7.6.2.3   SELENIUM

Selenium may play a potentially important role in acute lower-respiratory infections, and this relationship has only been partly explored. In humans, it was recognized early that patients on total parenteral nutrition who developed selenium deficiency had a marked reduction in erythrocyte and granulocyte glutathione peroxidase activity, which inhibits the cell's capacity to metabolize $H_2O_2$, abnormalities that returned to normal after selenium supplementation [252]. In critically ill patients admitted to intensive care units, the frequency of ventilator-associated pneumonia, organ system failure, and mortality (especially in those who developed a systemic inflammatory response syndrome), were three times higher in patients with low plasma selenium concentration on admission [253]. This fall in plasma concentration of selenium seems to occur mostly in patients with septicemia or pneumonia compared with those who develop viral infections [254, 255]. In a double-blind, controlled trial in Chinese children, selenium supplementation in children hospitalized with pneumonia or bronchiolitis associated with RSV resulted in a faster recovery rate of specific respiratory signs or symptoms [66]. Selenium supplements have also improved clinical signs of children with *M. pneumoniae* [67], and food additives containing selenium have improved symptoms in children admitted with pneumonia in Russian hospitals [68, 69]. Further trials are needed to document the value of selenium in the management of acute lower-respiratory infections in children.

## 7.7   PREVENTION

Potential interventions for the reduction of morbidity and mortality of pneumonia in children under 5 years old include immunization, improving nutrition, reducing environmental pollution, reducing transmission of pathogens, and improvement of child care practices [28].

### 7.7.1 Immunization

Measles and pertussis are still causing an important proportion of acute respiratory infection-related deaths in the world's children under 5 years old [1]. Increasing immunization coverage with measles vaccine and with diphtheria-pertussis-tetanus vaccine would be expected to lower the deaths from these two vaccine-preventable causes of acute respiratory infections [256]. The seven-valent conjugated pneumococcal vaccine has been safe and effective against pneumonia and invasive pneumococcal disease in children in the United States and was introduced for universal immunization in children in 2000 [257]. The effect of this vaccine introduction was greater in adults not vaccinated but protected by herd immunity by their children's immunization [257]. A protective effect was also observed for antibiotic-resistant invasive pneumococcal infections in children and adults in the United States [258]. This vaccine also reduces the prevalence of nasopharyngeal carriage of vaccine-type *S. pneumoniae* serotypes, which are replaced by nonvaccine types [259]. Recent reports from the United States indicate that these replacing serotypes are causing a greater proportion of invasive disease than before, which is a concern over the long-term benefits of this vaccine [257, 258]. The effect of this vaccine on the prevention of acute otitis media is questionable [260], although it may reduce tympanostomy tube placement in children [261]. A nine-valent conjugate pneumococcal vaccine was tested in a large group of infants in the Gambia, where it was documented not only to be 37% effective against radiological pneumonia, 77% effective against invasive pneumococcal disease caused by vaccine-related serotypes, and 15% against all-cause hospital admissions, but also was 16% effective in reducing mortality [262]. This nine-valent vaccine was also effective in South African infants, mostly among those who were not infected with HIV [263]. The seven-valent vaccine is now licensed for commercial use in several developing countries, but due to its high price, its use in public immunization programs will not happen soon. Other pneumococcal vaccines are under the horizon that may allow their introduction in developing countries.

*Haemophilus influenzae* type b (Hib) vaccine has been effective in reducing childhood pneumonia and meningitis in some industrialized countries, and a trial in the Gambia showed that a conjugate Hib vaccine was 95% protective against all invasive Hib disease and 100% protective against Hib pneumonia [264]. Although Hib causes only a small proportion of pneumonia, the vaccine was able to be 21% protective against any type of radiologically defined pneumonia in young children, indicating its potential to control diseases in children and infants from developing countries. This newly available vaccine has been rapidly introduced to developed countries, followed a few years later to most countries in Latin America. With the support of the Global Alliance for Vaccines and Immunisation (GAVI), the Hib vaccine is being introduced in poor countries [265].

Another vaccine that was introduced in developed countries that may be widely used in developing countries is an inactivated, trivalent influenza vaccine. In 2002, it was recommended to be used in US children 6–23 months of age [266], and several Latin American countries have also introduced it in young children. A new, cold-adapted, live influenza vaccine has proved not only immunogenic in young infants but also more effective in preventing influenza illness than the inactivated influenza vaccine [267]. However, the use of the cold-adapted trivalent intranasal influenza virus vaccine in children and adolescents has been associated with an increased risk of asthma or reactive airway disease in children younger than 36 months [268]. This risk may be related to the intra-nasal route of administration since the use of a live attenuated trivalent influenza vaccine in children and adolescents has not been observed to increase the risk of asthma [272], including when it was tested in children and adolescents with asthma [270]. Finally, the use of the BCG vaccine in infants has been cost-effective in preventing severe childhood tuberculosis and should continue to be used [271].

The protection of the fetus by transplacental transfer of maternal antibodies has allowed the protection of infants against tetanus by maternal immunization. Similar approaches are also being considered to protect neonates against pneumococcal diseases, pertussis, group B streptococcal infections, and Hib infections [204, 272]. Other vaccines against human parainfluenza virus type 3 and RSV are also under development and may become available in the near future.

### 7.7.3  *Nutrition*

#### 7.7.3.1  BREAST-FEEDING

Promotion of breast-feeding has been found to protect against acute respiratory infections in infants from developing countries [36]. It has been estimated that breast-feeding would significantly reduce the mortality due to diarrhea and acute lower-respiratory diseases in the world [256]. An estimated 1.45 million lives and 117 million DALYs are lost due to suboptimal breast-feeding in developing countries [273].

#### 7.7.3.2  PREVENTION OF LBW

The prevention of LBW may hypothetically decrease pneumonia mortality in developing countries, depending on the prevalence of LBW and the magnitude of the reduction in LBW [28]. There is a need to identify effective ways to reduce the prevalence of LBW in developing countries. Zinc supplementation has shown some promising results.

#### 7.7.3.3  REDUCTION OF MALNUTRITION

The reduction in malnutrition among infants and young children has been estimated to prevent 40% of pneumonia deaths in the world [28, 91]. The improvement of the weaning diet of children 6–24 months of age is a public health priority [2]. A pivotal study demonstrated that an intervention in well-baby clinics of the Ministry of Health in Trujillo, Peru, has been effective in improving nutrition in children [274], a study that needs to be replicated in other parts of the world. Food supplementation has been considered as an alternative approach by many developing countries, whereas food fortification is used in very few countries in the developing world.

#### 7.7.3.4  ZINC SUPPLEMENTATION

Daily zinc supplementation of 10 mg to infants and 20 mg to older children younger than 3 years has been proven to reduce the incidence of pneumonia by 26% in Indian children [275]. A single 70-mg dose given weekly to Bangladeshi children 60 days to 12 months of age at enrollment and followed for 12 months reduced the incidence of pneumonia by 17% and prevented pneumonia-related deaths [276]. Zinc fortification followed by zinc supplementation has been cost-effective in developing countries [277]. Zinc deficiency has been estimated to explain 1.9% of the global burden of disease worldwide and 16% of the lower-respiratory infections [91]. Eliminating zinc deficiency is now considered a priority for developing countries [256]. Effective and sustainable ways to increase the dietary intake of bioavailable zinc in developing countries are needed.

### 7.7.3.5 VITAMIN A SUPPLEMENTATION

As reviewed in Section 7.4.1.4, vitamin A supplementation appears to have little impact on acute respiratory diseases in preschool children. When respiratory diseases were assessed in carefully controlled prospective trials of vitamin A supplementation, no major reduction occurred in the mortality or morbidity associated with respiratory diseases, as indicated in a meta-analysis of all available studies [52]. Vitamin A does not have any role in the prevention of respiratory diseases in children.

### 7.7.3.6 SELENIUM SUPPLEMENTATION

Selenium supplementation may have possible benefit in reducing the morbidity and mortality of acute respiratory diseases in humans. Dietary supplementation with selenium for dairy cattle has become a standard practice and has been associated with a reduction of calf losses owing to respiratory diseases [275]. In patients with major burns, supplementation with selenium combined with copper and zinc was associated with fewer bronchopneumonia infections and with a shorter hospital stay in a double-blind, placebo-controlled trial [276]. Selenium has also been incriminated in the pathogenesis of asthma. It has been postulated that the combination of dietary, environmental, and genetic factors that decrease the cellular reducing capacity will increase tissue vulnerability to oxidant stress. This will result in inflammation and tissue damage in the respiratory system and later in immune damage, leading to an increased risk to develop asthma [277]. Severely malnourished children often have very low plasma selenium concentrations and low erythrocyte and plasma glutathione peroxidase activity, which may predispose them to the development of serious infections [278]. Controlled, randomized, double-blind trials are needed with selenium supplementation for treatment or prevention of respiratory illnesses in children; toxicity should be also closely monitored [279].

## 7.7.4 Other Measures

Reducing indoor and outdoor air pollution, elimination of environmental tobacco smoke, and reduction of crowding are potential interventions that may prevent childhood pneumonia in developing countries [280]. Modifications of child care practices, including improvement of care-seeking, better maternal education, and increased child spacing, is also a potential area that may have an impact on reducing pneumonia in children. All these potential interventions require evaluation in controlled studies in developing countries before they can be considered.

## 7.8 FUTURE DIRECTIONS

As reviewed in this chapter, a series of studies is needed to be able to answer many of the questions raised. The most important ones are listed next.

## 7.8.1 Risk Factors for Pneumonia and Acute Lower-Respiratory Infection

- The impact of acute lower-respiratory infections on subsequent nutritional status and growth needs further elucidation in developing countries.

- There is a need to perform properly conducted studies to prove or disprove the relationship between cold or high-humidity exposure and pneumonia and other acute lower-respiratory infection.
- Further studies are needed to clarify if abnormal lung function precedes or is a consequence of pneumonia or acute lower-respiratory infection or both.
- There is a need to understand better the pathophysiology of intrauterine growth and how LBW could be avoided.
- The relationship between maternal immune status and the protection of neonates by transplacental immune mechanisms needs further study.
- Only zinc and vitamin A have been evaluated in relation to pneumonia and acute lower-respiratory infection. Other micronutrients, like selenium, vitamin D, and calcium, deserve further studies. There is a need to study further the relationship between indoor air pollutants and acute lower-respiratory infection, identifying the combustion products that are more closely related to these diseases, and describing their pathophysiology.

### 7.8.2   Clinical Aspects

- There is a need to standardize the methodology and definitions of pneumonia and acute lower-respiratory infection for the conduct of longitudinal prospective studies of acute lower-respiratory infection epidemiology.
- There is a need to improve the diagnostic capabilities of bacterial pathogens as causes of pneumonia and invasive diseases in infants and children to facilitate the clinical management of patients and the conduct of epidemiological studies.
- The results of the WHO-sponsored studies on the etiology of severe infections of infants under 3 months of age have indicated the need to reevaluate the clinical management of these cases in developing countries.
- The increased prevalence of antibiotic-resistant bacteria strains is worrisome. There is a need to monitor this trend and at the same time try to diminish the inappropriate use of antibiotics. Alternative methods for the treatment of these infections may be needed in the near future.

### 7.8.3   Prevention

- There is a need to replicate effective interventions that have improved weaning food practices and improved the nutritional status of children in developing countries from Africa and Southeast Asia and to study their impact on the incidence and severity of pneumonia and other acute lower-respiratory infections.
- The protective efficacy of breast-feeding promotion on pneumonia and other acute lower-respiratory infections needs further evaluation and documentation.
- Although zinc supplementation has been proven to reduce the incidence of pneumonia and acute lower-respiratory infection, there is a need to document its impact on mortality, which should facilitate the development of a sustainable approach to improve the zinc status of children in developing countries.
- Prospective studies as well as double-blind, placebo-controlled clinical trials with selenium as a treatment or prevention of respiratory diseases in children, particularly in premature or LBW infants, are needed.
- Maternal immunization seems to be a promising intervention for the control of infections in the neonatal period. Proposed vaccine candidates should be evaluated in properly designed studies.
- The search for effective and affordable vaccines against the most prevalent childhood illnesses for children in the developing world should continue.

- Ways to reduce the risk of transmission of respiratory pathogens in crowded areas and in day care centers are urgently needed. Effective interventions should be developed and tested in developing countries.
- The exposure of children in developing countries to indoor air pollutants, including environmental tobacco smoke, needs further evaluation. Appropriate interventions (such as improving stoves) should be developed and tested for their efficacy in preventing pneumonia and other acute lower-respiratory infection.

## 7.9   CONCLUSIONS

Acute lower-respiratory diseases are some of the most important diseases of infants and young children in developing countries and are closely associated with high morbidity and mortality. A series of factors that increase the risk of developing pneumonia and other types of acute lower-respiratory infections have been identified, whereas others require further studies. Although a considerable number of studies have been conducted to measure the incidence and clinical characteristics of these illnesses, there is still a need to standardize the methodology to be used in the field. Physician-based diagnostic methodologies seem to be preferable to symptom-based definitions of pneumonia, which are not capable of adequately separating pneumonia from wheezing disorders and other acute lower-respiratory infections; this explains the great variability of the rates reported in studies using that methodology. Recently conducted studies on the etiology of severe infections in infants less than 3 months of age have identified the increased rate of pneumococcal diseases even from the neonatal period. Maternal immunization may be an important public health tool to reduce severe infections during the neonatal and early postneonatal periods of infants.

Despite the considerable knowledge on risk factors for pneumonia and other acute lower-respiratory infection, there are relatively few proven interventions to prevent them. The most promising ones are vaccines. The new pneumococcal conjugate vaccines, combined with the Hib vaccine, may be important interventions to control severe invasive diseases caused by these bacteria.

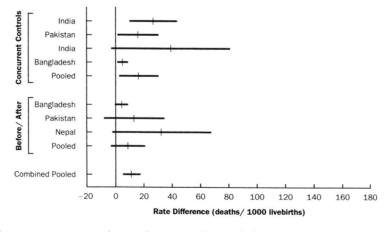

**Fig. 7.2.** Case management and acute lower-respiratory infection mortality in infants. (Adapted with permission from [240].)

While new vaccines are developed, tested, and implemented, other interventions are also needed that will focus on nutrition and the control of micronutrient deficiencies. Further studies are needed to identify sustainable interventions to improve the general nutritional status of children in developing countries as well as their families. The deficiencies of zinc, selenium, calcium, and vitamin D in children are also important and should be controlled. These studies also need to document their impact on pneumonia and other acute lower-respiratory infections in the affected population.

## REFERENCES

1. Bryce J, Boschi-Pinto C, Shibuya K, Black RE, WHO Child Health Epidemiology Reference Group. WHO estimates of the causes of death in children. Lancet 2005;365:1147–1152.
2. Caulfield LE, de Onis M, Blössner M, Black RE. Undernutrition as an underlying cause of child deaths associated with diarrhea, pneumonia, malaria, and measles. Am J Clin Nutr 2004;80:193–198.
3. Lopez AD, Mathers CD, Ezzati M, Jamison DT, Murray CJL. Measuring the global burden of disease and risk factors, 1990–2001. In: Global burden of disease and risk factors. Lopez AD, Mathers CD, Ezzati M, Jamison DT, Murray CJL, eds. Washington, DC: Oxford University Press, 2006:1–13.
4. Lopez AD, Begg S, Bos E. Demographic and epidemiological characteristics of major regions, 1990–2001. In: Global burden of disease and risk factors. Lopez AD, Mathers CD, Ezzati M, Jamison DT, Murray CJL, eds. Washington, DC: Oxford University Press, 2006:17–44.
5. Hirsch A. Handbook of geographical and historical pathology, vol. 1. Acute infective diseases. London: New Sydenham Society, 1883.
6. Thompson T. Annals of influenza or epidemic catarrhal fever in Great Britain from 1510 to 1837. London: Sydenham Society, 1852.
7. Jordan EO. Epidemic influenza: a survey. Chicago: American Medical Association, 1927.
8. Beveridge WIB. Influenza: The last great plague. New York: Prodist, 1977.
9. de Jong MD, Hien TT. Avian influenza A (H5N1). J Clin Virol 2006;35:2–13.
10. Wong SS, Yuen KY. Avian influenza virus infections in humans. Chest 2006;129:156–168.
11. Dowling HF. Fighting infection: conquests of the twentieth century. Cambridge: Harvard University Press, 1977.
12. US Bureau of the Census. Historical statistics of the United States, colonial times to 1957. Washington, DC: US Government Printing Office, 1960.
13. Victora CG, Fuchs SC, Flores JAC, Fonseca W, Kirkwood B. Risk factors for pneumonia among children in a Brazilian metropolitan area. Pediatrics 1994;93:977–985.
14. Fonseca W, Kirkwood BR, Victora CG, Fuchs SR, Flores JA, Misago C. Risk factors for childhood pneumonia among the urban poor in Fortaleza, Brazil: a case-control study. Bull World Health Organ 1996;74:199–208.
15. Dharmage SC, Rajapaksa LC, Fernando DN. Risk factors of acute lower respiratory tract infections in children under 5 years of age. Southeast Asian J Trop Med Public Health 1996;27:107–110.
16. Vejar L, Casteran JC, Navarrete P, Sanchez S, LeCerf P, Castillo C. Risk factors for home deaths due to pneumonia among low socioeconomic level Chilean children, Santiago de Chile (1994). Rev Med Chil 2000;128:627–632.
17. Coles CL, Fraser D, Givon-Lavi N, Greenberg D, Gorodischer R, Bar-Ziv J, Dagan R. Nutritional status and diarrheal illness as independent risk factors for alveolar pneumonia. Am J Epidemiol 2005;162:999–1007.
18. Victora CG, Barros FC, Kirkwood BR, Vaughan JP. Pneumonia, diarrhoea and growth in the first 4 years of life. A longitudinal study of 5,914 Brazilian children. Am J Clin Nutr 1990;52:391–396.
19. Chen Y, Shunzhang Y, Li W. Artificial feeding and hospitalization in the first 18 months of life. Pediatrics 1988;81:58–62.
20. Gold DR, Burge HA, Carey V, Milton DK, Platts-Mills T, Weiss ST. Predictors of repeated wheeze in the first year of life: the relative roles of cockroach, birth weight, acute lower respiratory illness, and maternal smoking. Am J Respir Crit Care Med 1999;160:227–236.

21. de Mello RR, Dutra MV, Ramos JR, Daltro P, Boechat M, Lopes JM. Neonatal risk factors for respiratory morbidity during the first year of life among premature infants. Sao Paulo Med J 2006;124:77–84.

22. Victora CG, Barros FC, Vaughan JP, Teixeira AMB. Birthweight and infant mortality: a longitudinal study of 5,914 Brazilian children. Int J Epidemiol 1987;16:239–245.

23. Victora CG, Smith PG, Vaughan JP, Nobre LC, Lombardi C, Teixeira AM, et al. Influence of birth weight on mortality from infectious diseases: a case-control study. Pediatrics 1988;81:807–811.

24. Datta N. Acute respiratory infection in low birth weight infants. Indian J Pediatr 1987;54:171–176.

25. Yoon PW, Black RE, Moulton LH, Becker S. Effect of not breastfeeding on the risk of diarrheal and respiratory mortality in children under 2 years of age in Metro Cebu, the Philippines. Am J Epidemiol 1996;143:1142–1148.

26. Ashworth A. Effects of intrauterine growth retardation on mortality and morbidity in infants and young children. Eur J Nutr 1998;52(suppl 1):S34–S41.

27. Cesar JA, Victora CG, Santos IS, Barros FC, Albernaz EP, Oliveira LM, et al. Hospitalization due to pneumonia: the influence of socioeconomic and pregnancy factors in a cohort of children in Southern Brazil. Rev Saude Publica 1997;31:53–61.

28. Victora GG, Kirkwood BR, Ashworth A, Black RE, Rogers S, Sazawal S, et al. Potential interventions for the prevention of childhood pneumonia in developing countries: improving nutrition. Am J Clin Nutr 1999;70:309–320.

29. Cerqueiro MC, Murtagh P, Halac A, Avila M, Weissenbacher M. Epidemiologic risk factors for children with acute lower-respiratory infection in Buenos Aires, Argentina: a matched case-control study. Rev Infect Dis 1990;12:S1021–S1028.

30. Cesar JA, Victora CG, Barros FC, Santos IS, Flores JA. Impact of breast feeding on admission for pneumonia during postneonatal period in Brazil: nested case-control study. BMJ 1999;318:1316–1312.

31. Kalanda BF, Verhoeff FH, Brabin BJ. Breast and complementary feeding practices in relation to morbidity and growth in Malawian infants. Eur J Clin Nutr 2006;60:401–407.

32. Khadivzadeh T, Parsai S. Effect of exclusive breastfeeding and complementary feeding on infant growth and morbidity. East Mediterr Health J 2004;10:289–294.

33. Onayadee AA, Abiona TC, Abayomi IO, Makanjuola RO. The first 6 month growth and illness of exclusively and non-exclusively breast-fed infants in Nigeria. East Afr Med J 2004;81:146–153

34. Oddy WH, Sherriff JL, de Klerk NH, Kendall GE, Sly PD, Beilin LJ, Blake KB, Landau LI, Stanley FJ. The relation of breastfeeding and body mass index to asthma and atopy in children: a prospective cohort study to age 6 years. Am J Public Health 2004;94:1531–1537.

35. Victora CG, Smith PG, Vaughan JP, Nobre LC, Lombardi C, Teixeira AMB, et al. Evidence for a protection by breast-feeding against infant deaths from infectious diseases in Brazil. Lancet 1987;2:319–322.

36. Arifeen S, Black RE, Antelman G, Baqui A, Caulfield L, Becker S. Exclusive breastfeeding reduces acute respiratory infection and diarrhea deaths among infants in Dhaka slums. Pediatrics 2001;108:E67. Available at: http://www.pediatrics.org/cgi/content/full/108/4/e67.

37. Bahl R, Frost C, Kirkwood BR, Edmond K, Martines J, Bhandari N, Arthur P. Infant feeding patterns and risks of death and hospitalization in the first half of infancy: multicentre cohort study. Bull World Health Organ 2005;83:418–426.

38. Chandra RK. Prospective studies of the effect of breast feeding on incidence of infection and allergy. Acta Paediatr Scand 1979;68:691–694.

39. Brown KH, Black RE, Lopez de Romaña G, Creed de Kanashiro H. Infant feeding practices and their relationship with diarrheal and other diseases. Pediatrics 1989;83:31–40.

40. Lopez-Alarcon M, Villalpando S, Fajardo A. Breast-feeding lowers the frequency and duration of acute respiratory infection and diarrhea in infants under six months of age. J Nutr 1997;127:436–443.

41. Deb SK. Acute respiratory disease survey in Tripura in case of children below 5 years of age. J Indian Med Assoc 1998;96:111–116.

42. Bale JR. Creation of a research program to determine the etiology and epidemiology of acute respiratory tract infection among children in developing countries. Rev Infect Dis 1990;12(suppl 8): S861–S866.

43. Tupasi TE, Lucero MG, Magdangal DM, Mangubat NV, Sunico ME, Torres CU, et al. Etiology of acute lower respiratory tract infection in children from Alabang, Metro Manila. Rev Infect Dis 1990;12:S929–S939.

44. Zaman K, Baqui AH, Yunus M, Sack RB, Bateman OM, Chowdhury HR, Black RE. Association between nutritional status, cell-mediated immune status and acute lower-respiratory infections in Bangladeshi children. Eur J Clin Nutr 1996;50:309–314.

45. Man WD, Weber M, Palmer A, Schneider G, Wadda R, Jaffar S, et al. Nutritional status of children admitted to hospital with different diseases and its relationship to outcome in the Gambia, West Africa. Trop Med Int Health 1998;3:678–686.

46. Atalah E, Bustos P, Gomez E. Infantile malnutrition: social cost or respiratory and digestive pathology. Arch Latinoam Nutr 1983;33:395–408.

47. O'Dempsey TJ, McArdle TF, Morris J, Lloyd-Evans N, Baldeh I, Laurence BE, et al. A study of risk factors for pneumococcal disease among children in a rural area of west Africa. Int J Epidemiol 1996;25:885–893.

48. Johnson WB, Aderele WI, Gbadero DA. Host factors and acute lower-respiratory infections in pre-school children. J Trop Pediatr. 1992;38:132–136.

49. Sommer A, Tarwotjo I, Katz J. Increased risk of xerophthalmia following diarrhea and respiratory disease. Am J Clin Nutr 1987;45:977–980.

50. Sommer A, Katz J, Tarwotjo I. Increased risk of respiratory disease and diarrhea in children with pre-existing mild vitamin A deficiency. Am J Clin Nutr 1984;40:1090–1095.

51. Bloem MW, Wedel M, Egger RJ, Speek AJ, Schrijver J, Saowakontha S, Schreurs WH. Mild vitamin A deficiency and risk of respiratory tract diseases and diarrhea in preschool and school children in northeastern Thailand. Am J Epidemiol 1990;131:332–339.

52. Vitamin A and Pneumonia Working Group. Potential interventions for the prevention of childhood pneumonia in developing countries: a meta-analysis of data from field trials to assess the impact of vitamin A supplementation on pneumonia morbidity and mortality. Bull World Health Organ 1995;73:609–619.

53. Grotto I, Mimouni M, Gdalevich M, Mimouni D. Vitamin A supplementation and childhood morbidity from diarrhea and respiratory infections: a meta-analysis. J Pediatr 2003;142:297–304.

54. Brown N, Roberts C. Vitamin A for acute respiratory infection in developing countries: a meta-analysis. Acta Paediatr 2004;93:1437–1442.

55. Lawrie NR, Moore T, Rajagopal KR. The excretion of vitamin A in urine. Biochem J 1941;35:825–836.

56. Alvarez JO, Salazar-Lindo E, Kohatsu J, Miranda P, Stephensen CB. Urinary excretion of retinol in children with acute diarrhea. Am J Clin Nutr 1995;61:1273–1276.

57. Bahl R, Bhandari N, Hambidge KM, Bhan MK. Plasma zinc as a predictor of diarrheal and respiratory morbidity in children in an urban slum setting. Am J Clin Nutr 1998;68(suppl 2):414S–417S.

58. Brooks WA, Yunus M, Santosham M, Wahed MA, Nahar K, Yeasmin S, Black RE. Zinc for severe pneumonia in very young children: double-blind placebo-controlled trial. Lancet 2004;363:1683–1688.

59. Mahalanabis D, Lahiri M, Paul D, Gupta S, Gupta A, Wahed MA, Khaled MA. Randomized, double-blind, placebo-controlled clinical trial of the efficacy of treatment with zinc or vitamin A in infants and young children with severe acute lower respiratory infection. Am J Clin Nutr 2004;79:430–436.

60. Bose A, Coles CL, Gunavathi, John H, Moses P, Raghupathy P, Kirubakaran C, Black RE, Brooks WA, Santosham M. Efficacy of zinc in the treatment of severe pneumonia in hospitalized children < 2 years old. Am J Clin Nutr 2006;83:1089–1096.

61. Mahalanabis D, Chowdhury A, Jana S, Bhattacharya MK, Chakrabarti MK, Wahed MA, Khaled MA. Zinc supplementation as adjunct therapy in children with measles accompanied by pneumonia: a double-blind, randomized controlled trial. Am J Clin Nutr 2002;76:604–607.

62. Shankar AH, Prasad AS. Zinc and immune function: the biological basis of altered resistance to infection. Am J Clin Nutr 1998;68(suppl):447S–463S.

63. Penny ME, Lanata CF. Zinc in the management of diarrhea in young children. N Engl J Med 1995;333:873–874.

64. Amin S, Chen SY, Collipp PJ, Castro-Magana M, Maddaiah VT, Klein SW. Selenium in premature infants. Nutr Metab 1980;24:331–340.

65. Darlow BA, Inder TE, Graham PJ, Sluis KB, Malpas TJ, Taylor BJ, Winterbourn CC. The relationship of selenium status to respiratory outcome in the very low birth weight infant. Pediatrics 1995;96:314–319.

66. Liu X, Yin S, Li G. Effects of selenium supplement on acute lower respiratory tract infection caused by respiratory syncytial virus. Zhonghua Yu Fang Yi Xue Za Zhi 1997;31:358–361.

67. Hu S, Liu X, Yin SA, Xu A. Effect of selenium on children suffered from Mycoplasma pneumonia. Wei Sheng Yan Jiu 1998;27:344–347.

68. Uglitskikh AK, Tsokova NB, Bmoshinskii IV, Mazo VK, Kon'IIa, Ostreikov IF. Experience with a selenium-containing biological active supplement used in children with pneumonias in an intensive care unit. Anesteziol Reanimatol 2006;1:45–48.

69. Bakulin IG, Novozhenov VG, Orlov AM, Gmoshinskii IV, Mazo VK. Correction of selenium deficiency in patients with pneumonia. Vopr Pitan 2004;73:12–14.

70. Muhe L, Lulseged S, Mason KE, Simoes EA. Case-control study of the role of nutritional rickets in the risk of developing pneumonia in Ethiopian children. Lancet 1997;349: 1801–1804.

71. Wondale Y, Shiferaw F, Lulseged S. A systematic review of nutritional rickets in Ethiopia: status and prospects. Ethiop Med J 2005;43:203–210.

72. Wayse V, Yousafzai A, Mogale K, Filteau S. Association of subclinical vitamin D deficiency with severe acute lower respiratory infection in Indian children under 5 years. Eur J Clin Nutr 2004;58:563–567.

73. Pettifor JM. Nutritional rickets: deficiency of vitamin D, calcium, or both? Am J Clin Nutr 2004;80(6 suppl):1725S–1729S.

74. Zaman K, Baqui AH, Yunus M, Sack RB, Chowdhury HR, Black RE. Malnutrition, cell-mediated immune deficiency and acute upper-respiratory infections in rural Bangladeshi children. Acta Paediatr 1997;86:923–927.

75. Shell-Duncan B, Wood JW. The evaluation of delayed-type hypersensitivity responsiveness and nutritional status as predictors of gastro-intestinal and acute respiratory infection: a prospective field study among traditional nomadic Kenyan children. J Trop Pediatr 1997;43:25–32.

76. Louhiala PJ, Jakkola N, Ruotsalainen R, Jaakkola JJ. Form of day care and respiratory infections among Finnish children. Am J Public Health 1995;85:1109–1112.

77. Celedon JC, Litonjua AA, Weiss ST, Gold DR. Day care attendance in the first year of life and illnesses of the upper and lower respiratory tract in children with a familial history of atopy. Pediatrics 1999;104:495–500.

78. Flores Hernandez S, Reyes Morales H, Perez Cuevas R, Guiscafre Gallardo H. The day care center as a risk factor for acute respiratory infections. Arch Med Res 1999;30:216–223.

79. Lind K, Bentzon MW. Ten and a half years seroepidemiology of *Mycoplasma pneumoniae* infection in Denmark. Epidemiol Infect 1991;107:189–199.

80. Holberg CJ, Wright AL, Martinez FD, Ray CG, Taussig LM, Lebowitz MD. Risk factors for respiratory syncytial virus-associated lower respiratory illnesses in the first year of life. Am J Epidemiol 1991;133:1135–1151.

81. Venetz I, Schopfer K, Muhlemann K. Paediatric, invasive pneumococcal disease in Switzerland, 1985–1994. Swiss Pneumococcal Study Group. Int J Epidemiol 1998;27:1101–1104.

82. Lopez Bravo IM, Sepulveda H, Valdes I. Acute respiratory illnesses in the first 18 months of life. Rev Panam Salud Publica 1997;1:9–17.

83. Cardoso MR, Cousen SN, de Goes Siqueira LF, Alves FM, D'Angelo LA. Crowding: risk factor or protective factor for lower respiratory disease in young children? BMC Public Health 2004;4:19.

84. Burstrom B, Diderichsen F, Smedman L. Child mortality in Stockholm during 1885–1910: the impact of household size and number of children in the family on the risk of death from measles. Am J Epidemiol 1999;149:1134–1141.

85. Hasan K, Jolly P, Marquis G, Roy E, Podder G, Alam K, Huq F, Sack R. Viral etiology of pneumonia in a cohort of newborns till 24 months of age in rural Mirzapur, Bangladesh. Scand J Infect Dis 2006;38:690–695.

86. De Francisco A, Morris J, Hall AJ, Armstrong Schellenberg JRM, Greenwood BM. Risk factors for mortality from acute lower respiratory tract infections in young Gambian children. Int J Epidemiol 1993;22:1174–1182.

87. Fitzgerald ME. Environmental risk factors for respiratory symptoms and disease in children birth to 30 months of age in Lima, Peru. PhD thesis. Baltimore, MD: Johns Hopkins University, 1994.

88. Jinot J, Bayard S. Respiratory health effects of exposure to environmental tobacco smoke. Rev Environ Health 1996;11:89–100.

89. Wald NJ, Hackshaw AK. Cigarette smoking: an epidemiological overview. Br Med Bull 1996;52:3–11.

90. Dybing E, Sanner T. Passive smoking, sudden infant death syndrome (SIDS) and childhood infections. Hum Exp Toxicol 1999;18:202–205.

91. Ezzati M, Vander Hoorn S, Dodgers A, Lopez AD, Mathers CD, Murray CJL, Comparative Risk Assessment Collaborating Group. Estimates of global and regional potential health gains from reducing multiple major risk factors. Lancet 2003;362:271–280.

92. Nafstad P, Jaakkola JJ, Hagen JA, Botten G, Kongerud J. Breastfeeding, maternal smoking and lower respiratory tract infections. Eur Respir J 1996;9:2623–2629.

93. Smith KR. Biofuels, air pollution, and health. A global review. New York: Plenum, 1987.

94. Pandey MR, Boleij JSM, Smith KR, Wafula EM. Indoor air pollution in developing countries and ARI in children. Lancet 1989a;1:427–429.

95. Chen BH, Hong CJ, Pandey MR, Smith KR. Indoor air pollution in developing countries. World Health Stat Q 1990;43:127–138.

96. Armstrong JR, Campbell H. Indoor air pollution exposure and lower respiratory infections in young Gambian children. Int J Epidemiol 1991;20:424–429.

97. Morris K, Morgenlander M, Coulehan JL, Gahagen S, Arena VC. Wood-burning stoves and lower respiratory tract infection in American Indian children. Am J Dis Child 1990;144:105–108.

98. Sharma S, Sethi GR, Rohtagi A, Chaudhary A, Shankar R, Bapna JS, et al. Indoor air quality and acute lower-respiratory infection in Indian urban slums. Environ Health Perspect 1998;106:291–297.

99. Becker S, Soukup JM. Exposure to urban air particulates alters the macrophage-mediated inflammatory response to respiratory viral infection. J Toxicol Environ Health 1999;57:445–457.

100. Corbo GM, Forastiere F, Dell'Orco V, Pistelli R, Agabiti N, De Stefanis B, et al. Effects of environment on atopic status and respiratory disorders in children. J Allergy Clin Immunol 1993;92:616–623.

101. Cohen AJ, Ross Anderson H, Ostro B, Pandey KD, Krzyzanowski M, Kunzli N, Gutschmidt K, Pope A, Romieu I, Samet JM, Smith K. The global burden of disease due to outdoor air pollution. J Toxicol Environ Health A 2005;68:1301–1307.

102. Levy A, Fraser D, Vardi H, Dagan R. Hospitalizations for infectious diseases in Jewish and Bedouin children in southern Israel. Eur J Epidemiol 1998;14:179–186.

103. Yang CY, Lin MC, Hwang KC. Childhood asthma and the indoor environment in a subtropical area. Chest 1998;114:393–397.

104. Etzel R, Rylander R. Indoor mold and children's health. Environ Health Perspect 1999;107 (suppl 3):463.

105. Kim PE, Musher DM, Glezen WP, Rodriguez-Barradas MC, Nahm WK, Wright CE. Association of invasive pneumococcal disease with season, atmospheric conditions, air pollution, and the isolation of respiratory viruses. Clin Infect Dis 1996;22:100–106.

106. Pereira JC, Escuder MM. Susceptibility of asthmatic children to respiratory infection. Rev Saude Publica 1997;31:441–447.

107. Shirakawa T, Enomoto T, Shumazu S, Hopkin JM. The inverse association between tuberculin responses and atopic disorders. Science 1997;275:77–79.

108. Cookson WOCM, Moffatt MF. Asthma: an epidemic in the absence of infection? Science 1997;275:41–42.

109. Renz H, Blumer N, Virna S, Sel S, Garn H. The immunological basis of the hygiene hypothesis. Chem Immunol Allergy 2006;91:30–48.

110. Zeyrek CD, Zeyrek F, Sevinc E, Demir E. Prevalence of asthma and allergic diseases in Sanliurfa, Turkey, and the relation to environmental and socioeconomic factors: is the hygiene hypothesis enough? J Investig Allergol Clin Immunol 2006;16:290–295.

111. Norback D, Zhao ZH, Wang ZH, Wieslander G, Mi YH, Zhang Z. Asthma, eczema, and reports on pollen and cat allergy among pupils in Shanxi province, China. Int Arch Occup Environ Health 2006.

112. Ahn KM, Lee MS, Hong SJ, Lim DH, Ahn YM, Lee HR, Lee MI, Lee MH, Shin YK, Kim KE. Fever, use of antibiotics, and acute gastroenteritis during infancy as risk factors for the development of asthma in Korean school-age children. J Asthma 2005;42:745–750.

113. Von HL. Role of persistent infection in the control and severity of asthma: focus on *Chlamydia pneumoniae*. Eur Respir J 2002;19:546–556.

114. Platts-Mills TA, Erwin E, Heymann P, Woodfolk J. Is the hygiene hypothesis still a viable explanation for the increased prevalence of asthma? Allergy 2005;60(suppl 79):25–31.

115. Ramsey CD, Celedon JC. The hygiene hypothesis and asthma. Curr Opin Pulm Med 2005;11:14–20.

116. Flohr C, Pascoe D, Williams HC. Atopic dermatitis and the "hygiene hypothesis": too clean to be true? Br J Dermatol 2005;152:202–216.

117. Bisgaard H, Dalgaard P, Nyboe J. Risk factors for wheezing during infancy. A study of 5,953 infants. Acta Paediatr Scand 1987;76:719–726.

118. Newell ML. Current issues in the prevention of mother-to-child transmission of HIV-1 infection. Trans R Soc Trop Med Hyg 2006;100:1–5.

119. Jean SS, Pape JW, Verdier RI, Reed GW, Hutto C, Johnson WD Jr., Wright PF. The natural history of human immunodeficiency virus 1 infection in Haitian infants. Pediatr Infect Dis J 1999;18:58–63.

120. Greenwood B. The epidemiology of pneumococcal infection in children in the developing world. Philos Trans R Soc Lond B Biol Sci 1999;354: 777–785.

121. Lanata CF, Rudan I, Boschi-Pinto C, Tomaskovic L, Cherian T, Weber M, Campbell H. Methodological and quality issues in epidemiological studies of acute lower respiratory infections in children in developing countries. Int J Epidemiol 2004;33:1362–1372.

122. Lanata CF. Incidence and evolution of pneumonia in children at the community level. In: Respiratory infections in children. Benguigui Y, Lopez Antuñano FJ, Schmunis G, Yunes J, eds. Washington, DC: Pan American Health Organization, 1999, 59–83.

123. Lanata CF, Quintanilla N, Verastegui H. Validity of a respiratory questionnaire to identify pneumonia in children in Lima, Peru. Int J Epidemiol 1994;23:827–834.

124. Berman S, Simoes EAF, Lanata C. Respiratory rate and pneumonia in infancy. Arch Dis Child 1991;66:81–84.

125. Simoes EAF, Roark R, Berman S, Esler LI, Murphy J. Respiratory rate: Measurement of variability over time and accuracy at different counting periods. Arch Dis Child 1991;66:1199–1203.

126. Spiteri MA, Cook DG, Clarke SW. Reliability of eliciting physical signs in examination of the chest. Lancet 1988;1:873–875.

127. Doherty JF, Dijkhuizen M, Wieringa FT, Moule N, Golden MHN. WHO guidelines on detecting pneumonia in children. Lancet 1991;338:1454.

128. Mata LJ. The children of Santa Maria Cauque: a prospective field study of health and growth. Cambridge, MA: MIT Press, 1978.

129. Wafula EM, Onyango FE, Mirza WM, Macharia WM, Wamola I, Ndinya-Achola JO, et al. Epidemiology of acute respiratory tract infections among young children in Kenya. Rev Infect Dis 1990;12(suppl 8):S1035–S1038.

130. Kielmann AA, Taylor CE, DeSweemer C, Uberoi IS, Takulia HS, Masih N, Vohra S. The Narangwal experiment on interactions of nutrition and infection: II. Morbidity and mortality effects. Indian J Med Res 1978;68(suppl):21–41.

131. Lopez de Romaña G, Brown KH, Black RE, Creed-Kanashiro H. Longitudinal studies of infectious diseases and physical growth of infants in Huascar, an underprivileged peri-urban community in Lima, Peru. Am J Epidemiol 1989;129:769–784.

132. Campbell H, Byass P, Lamont AC, Forgie IM, O'Neaill KP, Lloyd Evans N, Greenwood BM. Assessment of clinical criteria for identification of severe acute lower respiratory tract infections in children. Lancet 1989;1:297–299.

133. Rudan I, Tomaskovic L, Boschi-Pinto C, Campbell H;WHO Child Health Epidemiology Reference Group. Global estimate of the incidence of clinical pneumonia among children under 5 years of age. Bull World Health Organ 2004;82:895–903.

134. Selwyn BJ, Coordinated Date Group of BOSTID Researchers. The epidemiology of acute respiratory tract infection in young children: comparison of findings from several developing countries. Rev Infect Dis 1990;12(suppl 8):S870–S888.

135. Apostolidou I, Katsouyanni K, Touloumi G, Kalpoyannis N, Constantopoulos A, Trichopoulos D. Seasonal variation of neonatal and infant deaths by cause in Greece. Scand J Soc Med 1994;22: 74–80.

136. Douglas RG, Lindgram KM, Cough RB. Exposure to cold environment and rhynovirus cold: failure to demonstrate and effect. N Engl J Med 1968;279:742–747.

137. Ross A, Collins M, Sanders C. Upper respiratory tract infection in children, domestic temperatures, and humidity. J Epidemiol Community Health 1990;44:142–146.

138. Nacul LC, Kirkwood BR, Carneiro AC, Pannuti CS, Magalhaes M, Arthur P. Aetiology and clinical presentation of pneumonia in hospitalized and outpatient children in northeast Brazil and risk factors for severity. J Health Popul Nutr 2005;23:6–15.

139. Tall FR, Valian A, Curtis V, Traore A, Nacro B, Cousens S, et al. Acute respiratory infections in pediatric hospital at Bobo-Dioulasso. Arch Pediatr 1994;1:249–254.

140. Smyth A, Ridwan R, Cairns J. Impact of a case management protocol for childhood pneumonia in a rural Zambian hospital. Ann Trop Paediatr 1998;18:155–160.

141. Campbell JD, Sow SO, Levine MM, Kotloff KL. The causes of hospital admission and death among children in Bamako, Mali. J Trop Pediatr 2004;50:158–163.

142. Magree HC, Russell FM, Sa'aga R, Greenwood P, Tikoduadua L, Pryor J, Waqatakirewa L, Carapetis JR, Mulholland EK. Chext X-ray-confirmed pneumonia in children in Fiji. Bull World Health Organ 2005;83:427–433.

143. Spooner V, Baarker J, Tulloch S, Lehmann D, Marshall TF, Kajoi M, Alpers MP. Clinical signs and risk factors associated with pneumonia in children admitted to Goroka Hospital, Papua New Guinea. J Trop Pediatr 1989;35:295–300.

144. Smyth A, Carty H, Hart CA. Clinical predictors of hypoxaemia in children with pneumonia. Ann Trop Paediatr 1998;18:31–40.

145. Banajeh SM, al-Sunbali NN, al-Sanahani SH. Clinical characteristics and outcome of children aged under 5 years hospitalized with severe pneumonia in Yemen. Ann Trop Paediatr 1997;17:321–326.

146. Djelantik IG, Gessner BD, Sutanto A, Steinhoff M, Linehan M, Moulton LH, Arjoso S. Case fatality proportions and predictive factors for mortality among children hospitalized with severe pneumonia in a rural developing country setting. J Trop Pediatr 2003;49:327–332.

147. Sehgal V, Sethi GR, Sachdev HP, Satyanarayana L. Predictors of mortality in subjects hospitalized with acute lower respiratory tract infections. Indian Pediatr 1997;34:213–219.

148. Banajeh SM. Outcome for children under 5 years hospitalized with severe acute lower respiratory tract infections in Yemen: a 5 year experience. J Trop Pediatr 1998;44:343–346.

149. Gernaat HB, Dechering WH, Voorhoeve HW. Mortality in severe protein-energy malnutrition at Nchelenge, Zambia. J Trop Pediatr 1998;44:211–217.

150. West TE, Goetbhebuer T, Milligan P, Mulhollnd EK, Weber MW. Long-term morbidity and mortality following hypoxaemic lower respiratory tract infection in Gambian children. Bull World Health Organ 1999;77:144–148.

151. Ball P. Therapy for pneumococcal infection at the millennium: doubts and certainties. Am J Med 1999;107:77S–85S.

152. O'Dempsey TJ, McArdle TF, Lloyd-Evans N, Baldeh I, Lawrence BE, Secka O, Greenwood B. Pneumococcal disease among children in a rural area of west Africa. Pediatr Infect Dis J 1996;15:431–437.

153. Tan TQ, Mason EO Jr, Barson WJ, Wald ER, Schutze GE, Bradley JS, et al. Clinical characteristics and outcome of children with pneumonia attributable to penicillin-susceptible and penicillin-nonsusceptible *Streptococcus pneumoniae*. Pediatrics 1998;102:1369–1375.

154. Rios AM, de la Hoz F, Leal AL, Castillo O, Castaneda E. The impact of antimicrobial resistance and *Streptococcal pneumoniae* serotype distribution on the mortality of children under 5 years of age with invasive disease. Rev Panam Salud Public 1999;5:69–76.

155. Pallares R. Treatment of pneumococcal pneumonia. Semin Respir Infect 1999;14:276–284.

156. Harari M, Shann F, Spooner V, Meisner S, Carney M, de Campo J. Clinical signs of pneumonia in children. Lancet 1991;338:928–930.

157. Reed SC, Vreuls R, Metsing M, Mohobane PH, Patrick E, Moteetee M. Clinical signs of pneumonia in children attending a hospital outpatient department in Lesotho. Bull World Health Organ 1994;72:113–118.

158. Singhi S, Dhawan A, Kataria S, Walia BN. Validity of clinical signs for the identification of pneumonia in children. Ann Trop Paediatr 1994;14:53–58.

159. Shamo'on H, Hawamdeh A, Haddadin R, Jmeian S. Detection of pneumonia among children under 6 years by clinical evaluation. East Mediterr Health J 2004;10:482–487.

160. Taylor JA, Del Beccaro M, Done S, Winters W. Establishing clinically relevant standards for tachypnea in febrile children younger than 2 years. Arch Pediatr Adolesc Med 1995;149:283–287.

161. Basnet S, Adhikari RK, Gurung CK. Hypoxemia in children with pneumonia and its clinical predictors. Indian J Pediatr 2006;73:777–781.

162. Wexler ID, Knoll S, Picard E, Villa Y, Shoseyov D, Engelhard D, Kerem E. Clinical characteristics and outcome of complicated pneumococcal pneumonia in a pediatric population. Pediatr Pulmonol 2006;41:726–734.

163. Toikka P, Virkki R, Mertsola J, Ashorn P, Eskola J, Ruuskanen O. Bacteremic pneumococcal pneumonia in children. Clin Infect Dis 1999;29:568–572.

164. March M de F, Sant'Anna CC. Signs and symptoms indicative of community-acquired pneumonia in infants under 6 months. Braz J Infect Dis 2005;9:150–155.

165. Hazir T, Nisar YB, Qazi SA, Khan SF, Raza M, Zameer S, Masood SA. Chest radiography in children aged 2–59 months diagnosed with non-severe pneumonia as defined by World Health Organization: descriptive multicentre study in Pakistan. BMJ 2006;333:629.

166. Triga MG, Syrogiannopoulos GA, Thoma KD, Fezoulidis IB, Pastromas VG, Beratis NG. Correlation of leucocyte count and erythrocyte sedimentation rate with the day of illness in presumed bacterial pneumonia of childhood. J Infect 1998;36:63–66.

167. Lozano JM. Epidemiology of hypoxaemia in children with acute lower respiratory infections. Int J Tuberc Lung Dis 2001;5:496–504.

168. Duke T, Blaschke AJ, Sialis S, Bonkowsky JL. Hypoxaemia in acute respiratory and non-respiratory illnesses in neonates and children in a developing country. Arch Dis Child 2002;86:108–112.

169. Weissenbacher M, Carballal G, Avila M, Salomón H, Harisiadi J, Catalano M, et al. Etiologic and clinical evaluation of acute lower respiratory tract infections in young Argentinian children: an overview. Rev Infect Dis 1990;12:S889–S898.

170. Rahman M, Huq F, Sack DA, Butler T, Azad AK, Alam A, Nahar N, Islam M. acute lower-respiratory infections in hospitalized patients with diarrhea in Dhaka, Bangladesh. Rev Infect Dis 1990;12: S899–S906.

171. Forgie IM, O'Neill KP, Lloyd-Evans N, Leinonen M, Campbell H, Whittle HC, Greenwood BM. Etiology of acute lower-respiratory infections in Gambian children: I. Acute lower respiratory tract infections in infants presenting at the hospital. Pediatr Infect Dis J 1991;10:33–41.

172. Uduman SA, Ijaz MK, Kochiyil J, Mathew T, Hossam MK. Respiratory syncytial virus infection among hospitalized young children with acute lower respiratory illnesses in Al Ain, UAE. J Commun Dis 1996;28:245–252.

173. Ogra PL. Respiratory syncytial virus: the virus, the disease and the immune response. Paediatr Respir Rev 2004;5(suppl A):S119–S126.

174. Welliver RC. Respiratory syncytial virus and other respiratory viruses. Pediatr Infect Dis J 2003; 22(suppl 2):S6–S10.

175. Piedimonte G. Contribution of neuroimmune mechanisms to airway inflammation and remodeling during and after respiratory syncytial virus infection. Pediatr Infect Dis J 2003;22(suppl 2):S66–S74.

176. Ahn KM, Chung SH, Chung EH, Koh YJ, Nam SY, Kim JH, et al. Clinical characteristics of acute viral lower respiratory tract infections in hospitalized children in Seoul, 1996–1998. J Korean Med Sci 1999;14:405–411.

177. Videla C, Carballal G, Misirlian A, Aguila M. acute lower-respiratory infections due to respiratory syncytial virus and adenovirus among hospitalized children from Argentina. Clin Diagn Virol 1998;10:17–23.

178. Principi N, Bosis S, Esposito S. Human metapneumovirus in paediatric patients. Clin Microbiol Infect 2006;12:301–308.

179. Williams JV. The clinical presentation and outcomes of children infected with newly identified respiratory tract viruses. Infect Dis Clin North Am 2005;19:569–584.

180. Chan-Yeung M, Xu RH. SARS: epidemiology. Respirology 2003;8(suppl):S9–S14.

181. Chan-Yeung M, Ooi GC, Hui DS, Ho PL, Tsang KW. Severe acute respiratory syndrome. Int J Tuberc Lung Dis 2003;7:1117–1130.

182. Lam WK, Zhong NS, Tan WC. Overview on SARS in Asia and the world. Respirology 2003;8(suppl):S2–S5.

183. Emmanuel JV, Pua U, Wansaicheong GK, Goh JP, Tsou IY. Radiographic features of SARS in pae-diatric patients: a review of cases in Singapore. Ann Acad Med Singapore 2006;35:340–344.

184. Westbury HA. Hendra virus disease in horses. Rev Sci Tech 2000;19:151–159.

185. Mackenzie JS, Field HE. Emerging encephalitogenic viruses: lyssaviruses and henipaviruses trans-mitted by frugivorous bats. Arch Virol Suppl 2004;18:97–111.

186. Eaton BT, Broder CC, Wang LF. Hendra and Nipah viruses: pathogenesis and therapeutics. Curr Mol Med 2005;5:805–816.

187. Bellini WJ, Harcourt BH, Bowden N, Rota PA. Nipah virus: an emergent paramyxovirus causing severe encephalitis in humans. J Neurovirol 2005;11:481–487.

188. Epstein JH, Field HE, Luby S, Pulliam JR, Daszak P. Nipah virus: impact, origins, and causes of emergence. Curr Infect Dis Resp 2006;8:59–65.

189. Forgie IM, O'Neill KP, Lloyd-Evans N, Leinonen M, Campbell H, Whittle HC, Greenwood BM. Etiology of acute lower respiratory tract infections in Gambian children: II. Acute lower respira-tory tract infection in children ages one to nine years presenting at the hospital. Pediatr Infect Dis J 1991;10:42–47.

190. Halperin SA, Wang EE, Law B, Mills E, Morris R, Dery P, et al. Epidemiological features of pertussis in hospitalized patients in Canada, 1991–1997: report of the Immunization Monitoring Program—Active (IMPACT). Clin Infect Dis 1999;28:1238–1243.

191. Vegelin AL, van Vught AJ, Wolfs TF, Kimpen JL, Geelen SP. Pertussis in young infants. Ned Tijd-schr Geneeskd 1998;142:2657–2660.

192. Yaari E, Yafe-Zimerman Y, Schwartz SB, Slater PE, Shvarzmann P, Andoren N, et al. Clinical manifestations of *Bordetella pertussis* infection in immunized children and young adults. Chest 1999;115:1254–1258.

193. Greenberg DP, von Konig CH, Heininger U. Health burden of pertussis in infants and children. Pedi-atr Infect Dis J 2005;24(suppl 5):S39–S43.

194. Forsyth K, Tan T, von Konig CH, Caro JJ, Plotkin S. Potential strategies to reduce the burden of pertussis. Pediatr Infect Dis J 2005;24(suppl 5):S69–S74.

195. Lehmann D, Sanders RC, Marjen B, Rongap A, Tschappeler H, Lamont AC, et al. High rates of *Chla-mydia trachomatis* infections in young Papua New Guinean infants. Pediatr Infect Dis J 1999;18(10 suppl):S62–S69.

196. Hagiwara K, Ouchi K, Tashiro N, Azuma M, Kobayashi K. An epidemic of pertussis-like illness caused by *Chlamydia pneumoniae*. Pediatr Infect Dis J 1999;18:271–275.

197. Sarihan H, Cay A, Aynaci M, Akyazici R, Baki A. Empyema in children. J Cardiovasc Surg (Torino) 1998;39:113–116.

198. Goel A, Bamford L, Hanslo D, Hussey G. Primary staphylococcal pneumonia in young children: a review of 100 cases. J Trop Pediatr 1999;45:233–236.

199. Kerem E, Bar Ziv, Rudenski B, Katz S, Kleid D, Braanski D. Bacteremic necrotizing pneumococcal pneumonia in children. Am J Respir Crit Care Med 1994;149:242–244.

200. Leung AK, Kellner JD, Johnson DW. Viral croup: a current perspective. J Pediatr Health Care 2004;18:297–301.

201. Muhe L, Tilahun M, Lulseged S, Kebede S, Enaro D, Ringertz S, et al. Etiology of pneumonia, sepsis and meningitis in infants younger than three months of age in Ethiopia. Pediatr Infect Dis J 1999;18(10 suppl):S56–S61.

202. Lehmann D, Michael A, Omena M, Clegg A, Lupiwa T, Sanders RC, et al. Bacterial and viral etiol-ogy of severe infection in children less than 3 months old in the highlands of Papua New Guinea. Pediatr Infect Dis J 1999;18(10 suppl):S42–S49.

203. Gatchalian SR, Quiambao BP, Morelos AM, Abraham L, Gepanayao CP, Sombrero LT, et al. Bac-terial and viral etiology of serious infections in very young Filipino infants. Pediatr Infect Dis J 1999;18(10 suppl):S50–S55.

204. World Health Organization. Report on the meeting on maternal and neonatal pneumococcal immuni-zation. Geneva: World Health Organization, 1998. WHO/VRD/GEN/98.01.

205. Obaro SK, Deubzer HE, Newman VO, Adegbola RA, Greenwood BM, Henderson DC. Serotype-specific pneumococcal antibodies in breast milk of Gambian women immunized with a pneumococcal polysaccharide vaccine during pregnancy. Pediatr Infect Dis J 2004;23:1023–1029.

206. Bonadio WA. *Klebsiella pneumoniae* bacteremia in children. Fifty-seven cases in 10 years. Am J Dis Child 1989;143:1061–1063.

207. Varkey B. Blastomycosis in children. Semin Respir Infect 1997;12:235–242.

208. Levy I, Rubin LG. Legionella pneumonia in neonates: a literature review. J Perinatol 1998;18:287–290.

209. Thummakul T, Wilde H, Tantawichien T. Melioidosis, an environmental and occupational hazard in Thailand. Mil Med 1999;164:658–662.

210. Sniadack DH, Moscoso B, Aguilar R, Heath J, Bellini W, Chiu MC. Measles epidemiology and outbreak response immunization in a rural community in Peru. Bull World Health Organ 1999;77:545–552.

211. Mink SN, Light RB, Wood LD. Effect of pneumococcal lobar pneumonia on canine lung mechanics. J Appl Physiol 1981;50:283–291.

212. Hanly P, Light RB. Lung mechanics, gas exchange, pulmonary perfusion, and hemodynamics in canine model of acute *Pseudomonas* pneumonia. Lung 1987;165:305–322.

213. Hiser W, Pennan RW, Reeves JT. Preservation of hypoxic pulmonary pressor response in canine pneumococcal pneumonia. Am Rev Respir Dis 1975;112:817–822.

214. Light RB, Mink SN, Wood LD. Pathophysiology of gas exchange and pulmonary perfusion in pneumococcal lobar pneumonia in dogs. J Appl Physiol 1981;50:524–530.

215. Shann F, MacGregor D, Richens J, Coakley J. Cardiac failure in children with pneumonia in Papua New Guinea. Pediatr Infect Dis J 1998;17:1141–1143.

216. Gea J, Roca J, Torres A, Agusti AG, Wagner PD, Rodriguez-Roisin R. Mechanisms of abnormal gas exchange in patients with pneumonia. Anesthesiology 1991;75:782–789.

217. Light RB. Intrapulmonary oxygen consumption in experimental pneumococcal pneumonia. J Appl Physiol 1988;64:2490–2495.

218. Cooligan T, Light RB, Wood LD, Mink SN. Plasma volume expansion in canine pneumococcal pneumonia: its effects on respiratory gas exchange and pneumonia size. Am Rev Respir Dis 1982;126:86–91.

219. Light RB. Pulmonary pathophysiology of pneumococcal pneumonia. Semin Respir Infect 1999;14:218–226.

220. Chaisupamongkollarp T, Preuthipan, Vaicheeta S, Chantarojanasiri T, Kongvivekkajornkij W, Suwanjutha S. Prone position in spontaneously breathing infants with pneumonia. Acta Paediatr 1999;88:1033–1034.

221. Rodriguez-Roisin R, Roca J. Update '96 on pulmonary gas exchange pathophysiology in pneumonia. Semin Respir Infect 1996;11:3–12.

222. Griese M. Pulmonary surfactant in health and human lung diseases: state of the art. Eur Respir J 1999;13:1455–1476.

223. Ghodrat M. Lung surfactants. Am J Health Syst Pharm 2006;63:1504–1521.

224. Light RB, Mink SN, Cooligan RG, Wood LD. The physiology of recovery in experimental pneumococcal pneumonia. Clin Invest Med 1983;6:147–151.

225. Johnston ID. Effect of pneumonia in childhood on adult lung function. J Pediatr 1999;135:33–37.

226. Yau KI, Fang LJ, Shieh KH. Factors predisposing infants to lower respiratory infection with wheezing in the first 2 years of life. Ann Allergy Asthma Immunol 1999;82:165–170.

227. Hussey G, Chisholm T, Kibel M. Miliary tuberculosis in children: a review of 94 cases. Pediatr Infect Dis J 1991;10:832–836.

228. Nelson LJ, Wells CD. Global epidemiology of childhood tuberculosis. Int J Tuberc Lung Dis 2004;8:636–647

229. Rowland MGM., Rowland SGJ., Cole TJ. Impact of infection on the growth of children from 0 to 2 years in an urban West African community. Am J Clin Nutr 1988;47:134–138.

230. Adair L, Popkin BM, Van Derslice J, Akin J, Guilkey D, Black R, et al. Growth dynamics during the first 2 years of life: a prospective study in the Philippines. Eur J Clin Nutr 1993;47:42–51.

231. Smith TA, Lehman D, Coakley C, Spooner V, Alpers MP. Relationships between growth and acute lower-respiratory infections in children <5 y in a highland population of Papua New Guinea. Am J Clin Nutr 1991;53:963–970.

232. Cruz JR, Pareja G, de Fernandez A, Peralta F, Caceres P, Cano F. Epidemiology of acute respiratory tract infections among Guatemalan ambulatory preschool children. Rev Infect Dis 1990;12(suppl 8): S1029–S1034.

233. Pereira SM, Begum A. The influence of illnesses on the food intake of young children. Int J Epidemiol 1987;16:445–450.

234. Brown KH, Peerson JM, Lopez de Romaña G, Creed de Kanashiro H, Black RE. Validity and epidemiology of reported poor appetite among Peruvian infants from a low-income, periurban community. Am J Clin Nutr 1995;61:26–32.

235. Stephensen CB. Burden of infection on growth failure. J Nutr 1999;129(2S suppl):534S–538.

236. Shann F. Etiology of severe pneumonia in children in developing countries. Pediatr Infect Dis J 1986;5:247–252.

237. McCord C, Keilmann AA. A successful programme for medical auxiliaries in treating childhood diarrhea and pneumonia. Trop Doct 1978;8:220–225.

238. Shann F, Hart K, Thomas D. Acute lower respiratory tract infection in children: possible criteria for selection of patients for antibiotic therapy and hospital admissions. Bull World Health Organ 1984;62:749–753.

239. World Health Organization. Respiratory infections in children: management in small hospitals. A manual for doctors. Geneva: World Health Organization, 1988.

240. Sazawal S, Black RE. Meta-analysis of intervention trials on case-management of pneumonia in community settings. Lancet 1992;340:528–533.

241. Sazawal S, Black RE. Pneumonia case management trials group. Effect of pneumonia case management on mortality in neonates, infants, and preschool children: a meta-analysis of community-based trials. Lancet Infect Dis 2003;3:547–556.

242. Marshall S. Zinc gluconate and the common cold. Review of randomized controlled trials. Can Fam Physician 1998;44:1037–1042.

243. Jackson JL, Peterson C, Lesho E. A meta-analysis of zinc salts lozenges and the common cold. Arch Intern Med 1997;157:2373–2376.

244. Jackson JL, Lesho E, Peterson C. Zinc and the common cold: a meta-analysis revisited. J Nutr 2000;130(5S suppl):1512S–1515S.

245. Macknin ML, Piedmonte M, Calendine C, Janosky J, Wald E. Zinc gluconate lozenges for treating the common cold in children: a randomized controlled trial. JAMA 1998;279:1962–1967.

246. Prasad AS, Fitzgerald JT, Bao B, Beck FW, Chandrasekar PH. Duration of symptoms and plasma cytokine levels in patients with the common cold treatment with zinc acetate. A randomized, double-blind, placebo-controlled trial. Ann Intern Med 2000;133:245–252.

247. McElroy BH, Miller SP. An open-label, single-center, phase IV clinical study of the effectiveness of zinc gluconate lozenges (Cold-Eeze) in reducing the duration and symptoms of the common cold in school-age subjects. Am J Ther 2003;10:324–329.

248. Hulisz D. Efficacy of zinc against common cold viruses: an overview. J Am Pharm Assoc (Wash DC) 2004;44:594–603.

249. Eby GA. Zinc lozenges: cold cure or candy? Solution chemistry determinations. Biosci Rep 2004;24:23–39.

250. Eby GA, Halcomb WW. Ineffectiveness of zinc gluconate nasal spray and zinc orotate lozenges in common-cold treatment: a double-blind, placebo-controlled clinical trial. Altern Ther Health Med 2006;12:34–38.

251. Stephensen CB, Franchi LM, Hernandez H, Campos M, Gilman RH, Alvarez JO. Adverse effects of high-dose vitamin A supplements in children hospitalized with pneumonia. Pediatrics 1998;101:3.

252. Baker SS, Lerman RH, Krey SH, Crocker KA, Hirsh EF, Cohen H. Selenium deficiency with total parenteral nutrition: reversal of biochemical and functional abnormalities by selenium supplementation: a case report. Am J Clin Nutr 1983;38:769–774.

253. Forceville X, Vitoux D, Gauzit R, Combes A, Lahilaire P, Chappuis P. Selenium, systemic immune response syndrome, sepsis, and outcome in critically ill patients. Crit Care Med 1998;26:1536–1544.

254. Srinivas U, Braconier JH, Jeppsson B, Abdulla M, Akesson B, Ockerman PA. Trace element alterations in infectious diseases. Scand J Clin Lab Invest 1988;48:495–500.

255. Chen JR, Anderson JM. Legionnaires disease: concentrations of selenium and other elements. Science 1979;206:1426–1427.

256. Jones G, Steketee RW, Black RE, Bhutta ZA, Morris SS, Bellagio Child Survival Study Group. How many child deaths can we prevent this year? Lancet 2003;362:65–71.

257. Centers for Disease Control and Prevention. Direct and indirect effects of routine vaccination of children with seven-valent pneumococcal conjugate vaccine on incidence of invasive pneumococcal disease—United States, 1998–2003. MMWR Morb Mortal Wkly Rep 2005;54:893–897.

258. Kyaw MH, Lynfield R, Schaffner W, Craig AS, Hadler J, Reingold A, et al. Effect of introduction of the pneumococcal conjugated vaccine on drug-resistant *Streptococcus pneumoniae*. N Engl J Med 2006:354:1455–1463.

259. Millar EV, O'Brien KL, Watt JP, Bronsdon MA, Dallas J, Whitney CG, Reid R, Santosham M. Effect of community-wide conjugate pneumococcal vaccine use in infancy on nasopharyngeal carriage through 3 years of age: a cross-sectional study in a high-risk population. Clin Infect Dis 2006;43:8–15.

260. Straetemans M, Sanders EA, Veenhoven RH, Schilder AG, Damoiseaux RA, Zielhuis GA. Pneumococcal vaccines for preventing otitis media. Cochrane Database Syst Rev 2004;(1):CD001480.

261. Palmu AA, Verho J, Jokinen J, Karma P, Kilpi TM. The seven-valent pneumococcal conjugate vaccine reduces tympanostomy tube placement in children. Pediatr Infect Dis J 2004;23:732–738.

262. Cutts FT, Zaman SM, Enwere G, Jaffar S, Levine OS, Okoko JB, et al. Efficacy of nine-valent pneumococcal conjugate vaccine against pneumonia and invasive pneumococcal disease in the Gambia: randomized, double-blind, placebo-controlled trial. Lancet 2005;365:1139–1146.

263. Madhi SA, Kuwanda L, Cutland C, Klugman KP. The impact of a nine-valent pneumococcal conjugated vaccine on the public health burden of pneumonia in HIV-infected and -uninfected children. Clin Infect Dis 2005;40:1511–1518.

264. Mulholland K, Hilton S, Adegbola R, Usen S, Opraugo A, Omosigho C, et al. Randomised trial of *Haemophilus influenzae* type-b tetanus protein conjugate vaccine for prevention of pneumonia and meningitis in Gambian infants. Lancet 1997;349:1191–1197.

265. Wardlaw T, Salama P, Johansoon EW, Mason E. Pneumonia: the leading killer of children. Lancet 2006;368:1048–1050.

266. McMahon AW, Iskander J, Haber P, Chang S, Woo EJ, Braun MM, Ball R. Adverse events after inactivated influenza vaccination among children less than 2 years of age: analysis of reports from the vaccine adverse event reporting system, 1990–2003. Pediatrics 2005;115:453–460.

267. Ashkenazi S, Vertruyen A, Aristegui J, Esposito S, McKeith DD, Klemola T, et al. Superior relative efficacy of live attenuated influenza vaccine compared with inactivated influenza vaccine in young children with recurrent respiratory tract infections. Pediatr Infect Dis J 2006;25:870–879.

268. Bergen R, Black S, Shinefield H, Lewis E, Ray P, Hansen J, Walker R, Hessel C, Cordova J, Mendelman PM. Safety of cold-adapted live attenuated influenza vaccine in a large cohort of children and adolescents. Pediatr Infect Dis J 2004;23:138–144.

269. Piedra PA, Gaglani MJ, Riggs M, Herschler G, Fewlass C, Watts M, Kozinetz C, Hessel C, Glezen WP. Live attenuated influenza vaccine, trivalent, is safe in healthy children 18 months to 4 years, 5 to 9 years, and 10 to 18 years of age in a community-based, nonrandomized, open-label trial. Pediatrics 2005;116:397–407.

270. Fleming DM, Crovari P, Wahn U, Klemola T, Schlesinger Y, Langussis A, et al. Comparison of the efficacy and safety of live attenuated cold-adapted influenza vaccine, trivalent, with trivalent inactivated influenza virus vaccine in children and adolescents with asthma. Pediatr Infect Dis J 2006;25:860–869.

271. Trunz BB, Fine P, Dye C. Effect of BCG vaccination on childhood tuberculosis meningitis and military tuberculosis worldwide: a meta-analysis and assessment of cost-effectiveness. Lancet 2006;367:1173–1180.

272. Greenwood B. Maternal immunization in developing countries. Vaccine 2003;21:3436–3441.

273. Lauer JA, Betran AP, Barros AJ, de Onis M. Deaths and years of life lost due to suboptimal breast-feeding among children in the developing world: a global ecological risk assessment. Public Health Nutr 2006;9:673–685.

274. Penny ME, Creed-Kanashiro HM, Robert RC, Narro MR, Caulfield LE, Black RE. Effectiveness of an educational intervention delivered through the health services to improve nutrition in young children: a cluster-randomised controlled trial. Lancet 2005;365:1863–1872.

275. Gerloff BJ. Effect of selenium supplementation on dairy cattle. J Anim Sci 1992;70:3934–3940.

276. Berger MM, Spertini F, Shenkin A, Wardle C, Wiesner L, Schindler C, Chiolero RL. Trace element supplementation modulates pulmonary infection rates after major burns: a double-blind, placebo-controlled trial. Am J Clin Nutr 1998;68:365–371.

277. Greene LS. Asthma and oxidant stress: nutritional, environmental, and genetic risk factors. J Am Coll Nutr 1995;14:317–324.

278. Thomas AG, Miller V, Shenkin A, Fell GS, Taylor F. Selenium and glutathione peroxidase status in paediatric health and gastrointestinal disease. J Pediatr Gastroenterol Nutr 1994;19:213–219.

279. Pentel P, Fletcher D, Jentzen J. Fatal acute selenium toxicity. J Forensic Sci 1985;30:556–562.

280. Kirkwood BR, Gove S, Rogers S, Lob-Levyt J, Arthur P, Campbell H. Potential interventions for the prevention of childhood pneumonia in developing countries: a systematic review. Bull World Health Organ 1995;73:793–798.

# 8    Measles

*Gregory Hussey*

## 8.1    INTRODUCTION

Despite the availability of a cheap and effective vaccine, measles remains a problem in developing countries. It is a leading childhood killer, accounting for at least a third of all vaccine-preventable diseases. This chapter discusses important epidemiological, clinical, and management issues that are relevant in developing countries. The association between measles and nutrition, particularly vitamin A, is stressed. The need to reduce the disease burden through effective case management and immunization is highlighted.

## 8.2    DEFINITION

Measles is an acute infectious disease caused by an RNA paramyxovirus. The disease is characterized by a generalized maculopapular erythematous rash, high fever and coryza, conjunctivitis, cough, or stomatitis. Measles virus is related to other morbilli-viruses, such as rinderpest virus, peste des petits ruminants virus, and canine distemper virus. Experimental animal models involving some of these other morbilliviruses have been used to gain insight into measles infection in humans.

## 8.3    PUBLIC HEALTH IMPORTANCE

Measles is a major cause of childhood morbidity and mortality. The World Health Organization (WHO) has estimated that over 5 million measles cases and approximately 500,000 deaths occur annually in developing countries, mainly in sub-Saharan Africa (SSA) and Southeast Asia (SEA) [1]. Most deaths occur in infancy [2] and are a consequence of complications such as pneumonia, diarrhea, and malnutrition. In addition, countless thousands are disabled as a consequence of chronic lung disease, malnutrition, blindness, deafness, and recurrent infections [3]. WHO and the United Nations International Children's Emergency Fund (UNICEF) have identified 45 priority countries in SSA and SEA with high measles burden for implementation of comprehensive strategies for accelerated and sustained measles mortality reduction; the goal is a 90% reduction in measles mortality by 2010 compared to the 2000 level [1].

From: *Nutrition and Health: Nutrition and Health in Developing Countries, Second Edition*
Edited by: R. D. Semba & M. W. Bloem © Humana Press, Totowa, NJ

## 8.4   HISTORICAL BACKGROUND

Measles as a clinical entity has been known for centuries. A distinction between measles and smallpox was made as early as the 10th century by Rhazes [4]. In 1676, a detailed clinical description of measles was made by Thomas Sydenham [5]. During the 18th century, measles epidemics occurred in England in about once every 3 years [6] and in Germany about every 4 or 5 years [7]. In contrast, with the more isolated island population of Japan, measles epidemics occurred less frequently, at intervals of about 20–30 years during the Tokugawa period (1600–1868) [8]. One of the first detailed epidemiological descriptions of measles was by Peter Panum in 1846. In his study of the epidemic on the Faroe Islands, he defined the incubation period, mode of transmission (i.e., person-to-person via droplet infection), and showed that infection resulted in lifelong immunity [9]. Buccal spots, an early diagnostic sign in measles, were described by Henry Koplik, an American physician, in 1896 [10].

David Morley's studies in Nigeria in the 1950s and 1960s highlighted the importance of measles as a significant cause of childhood morbidity and mortality in developing countries [11]. In particular, he emphasized the important interaction between measles and malnutrition [12]. Until recently, the nutritional status of the child was generally believed to be one of the major determinants of disease severity in measles. However, Peter Aaby, in a number of studies in West Africa in the 1980s, showed that overcrowding and viral dose were probably the most significant predictors of mortality [13]. There is no specific treatment for measles. However, high-dose vitamin A therapy reduces the rate of complications and mortality [14, 15]. WHO recommends vitamin A as part of the standard case management for measles [16].

The measles virus was isolated in 1954 by Enders and Peebles and a serological test was developed [17]. Work on a vaccine against measles subsequently commenced, and in 1963 the first vaccine was licensed in the United States [18]. Despite the availability of a safe and effective vaccine, measles remained a significant problem in developing countries. One of the reasons for this was the inability to immunize young infants successfully because of passively derived maternal antibodies [19]. To overcome this problem, the high-dose Edmonston-Zagreb vaccine was recommended for use in developing countries for infants between 4 and 6 months of age [20]. However, it was found subsequently to be associated with increased child mortality in the months following immunization [21, 22]. The hypothesis was that the excess mortality was a consequence of immune suppression following exposure to the high viral titer [23]. This vaccine is no longer recommended for use in infants [24].

## 8.5   EPIDEMIOLOGY

Measles is a highly communicable disease and spreads from person to person via droplet infection. The probability of an exposed susceptible person contracting the disease on exposure is very high. The infectious period is from the onset of the illness until 4–5 days after the appearance of the rash. Humans are the only natural host.

Measles is currently endemic in a number of SEA and SSA countries, and cases occur predominantly in children aged less than 5 years. The improvement of measles vaccine coverage in some countries has led to a changing epidemiology, with outbreaks affecting predominantly older children and adolescents [25]. In developed countries, measles is rare and is usually a disease of older children and young adults who have not been immunized or in whom primary immunization has failed [26].

Areas where measles transmission is likely to occur include areas with high population density, poor socioeconomic status (SES), very low immunization coverage, and high numbers of measles cases or deaths from measles [27]. Overcrowded living conditions have been identified as an important determinant of intensity of exposure and subsequent disease outcome [13]. Secondary cases (children who contract measles from another case in a household or health center) have a higher case fatality rate than primary cases. This is probably because of increased exposure to a higher viral dose [28].

Other children at particular risk for developing severe disease include children less than 1 year old, those who are vitamin A deficient, the severely malnourished, the immunocompromised (including HIV-infected children), children who live in zones of armed conflict or in refugee camps, and children who are migrants [27, 29].

The widespread use of measles immunization since the 1960s has raised a potentially important issue regarding the timing of measles immunization. The level of protective antibodies against measles is lower in individuals who were immunized in childhood compared with individuals who originally had a wild-type measles infection. The level of protective antibodies becomes especially important during pregnancy as the level of passively transferred maternal antibodies against measles in infants is related to maternal levels of antibodies. Infants who have lower levels of maternal antibodies have a shorter period of protection against wild-type measles infection.

## 8.6   PATHOPHYSIOLOGY

The clinical expression of infection and consequently the complications of measles are governed by the extent of the virus-induced epithelial damage, by the degree of immune suppression [30], and by the patient's vitamin A status [31]. The pathologic effects of measles virus infection and vitamin A deficiency are remarkably similar in that both are responsible for epithelial damage and immune suppression. The epithelia of the respiratory and gastrointestinal tracts and the conjunctiva are particularly vulnerable. The reason for the dramatic decline in serum vitamin A levels during acute measles and other infections is not known. Contributing factors include reduced intake as a consequence of infection-induced anorexia; increased catabolism, utilization, and urinary excretion; and problems with retinol-binding protein homeostasis [32, 33].

The clinical significance of measles virus immunosuppression has been documented by findings indicating that lymphopenia owing to lower T- and B-cell levels, impaired antibody response, and reduced C3 levels were significant predictors of the clinical severity of measles [34]. In addition, persistent immune suppression may account for the increased morbidity and mortality associated with measles in the ensuing months after the acute infection [35].

The importance of vitamin A as a predictor of disease severity has been documented in a number of studies. In Zaire, children with measles, especially those under 2 years of age, who had a vitamin A level below 5 μg/dL had a three times greater risk of dying compared to children with higher levels [36]. In the United States, where clinical vitamin A deficiency does not occur, low serum vitamin A levels have been associated with an increased risk of hospitalization and severe disease [37, 38].

## 8.7   INTERACTION WITH NUTRITION

### 8.7.1   Effect of Measles on Nutrition

An acute attack of measles can have a significant adverse effect on the nutritional status of children [12, 39]. The mechanisms include infection-induced anorexia, refusal to take food because of the associated stomatitis or mouth ulceration, catabolic effects of infection, associated diarrhea and vomiting, and protein-losing enteropathy [40–43]. Energy balance studies in children with measles indicated significant increased fecal and urine losses and reduced intake [41].

Acute diarrhea is a common problem in children with measles and contributes to negative nitrogen balance and increased mortality [44–46]. Prolonged or persistent diarrhea has a major impact on nutritional status and may follow the acute episode in about 30% of cases [47]. Diarrhea in measles is a consequence of a number of interrelated factors [48]. The measles virus causes epithelial damage, which is compounded by the hyporetinemia that invariably occurs in the acute phase. In addition, both measles and vitamin A deficiency reduce immune competence, resulting in increased susceptibility to gastrointestinal pathogens. The net effect of the gastrointestinal damage is diarrheal disease and protein-losing enteropathy [40]. Measles is thus a common precipitating cause of kwashiorkor [11, 39].

Severe stomatitis and mouth ulcers, which are frequently caused by herpes simplex or *Candida* infections, are common complications of measles [49]. Superadded secondary bacterial infections may develop, especially if oral hygiene is poor. This may cause difficulty with feeding, result in dehydration, and aggravate malnutrition.

### 8.7.2   Effect of Malnutrition on Measles

Malnutrition is generally thought to be an important determinant of disease severity. A number of hospital-based studies have indicated that malnourished children with measles have a higher morbidity and mortality rate [50–53]. This, however, does not necessarily imply a causal relationship. Measles is an acute catabolic event associated with reduced intake, increased gastrointestinal losses, and rapid weight loss. Lower weight therefore may be a reflection of more severe disease. Malnourished children with measles have also been shown to have prolonged excretion of virus, impaired immunity, and increased susceptibility to secondary infection compared to well-nourished children [53]. An analysis of data from six countries suggested that 45% of deaths as a result of measles are attributable to undernutrition [28].

These assumptions have been challenged by findings in several community studies that have reported no relation between nutritional status and risk of severe or fatal measles. It has been argued that overcrowding and intensive exposure (i.e., virus dose) are more important determinants of disease severity and mortality [13, 28, 29].

## 8.8   CLINICAL FEATURES

The incubation period for measles is 8–12 days. The illness starts with a prodrome characterized by fever, cough, and coryza and lasts for 2–3 days. Koplik spots are visible on the buccal mucosa during this period. The maculopapular erythematous rash

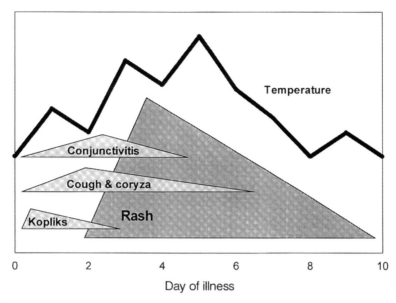

**Fig. 8.1.** Clinical course of measles.

then appears, starting on the neck, then spreading to the face and the rest of the body. The child has a high fever; is irritable; is photophobic; and usually has conjunctivitis, cough, and stomatitis (see Fig. 8.1). The illness lasts for about 4–5 days. The rash then fades or discolors. Desquamation occurs frequently and may persist for weeks.

Significant complications occur in 15–25% of all cases and include pneumonia, diarrhea, malnutrition, otitis media, severe mouth ulcers, and severe conjunctivitis [3]. The case fatality rate of children hospitalized with measles varies between 5% and 15%. Measles is a significant risk factor for the development of keratomalacia in developing countries and, if not recognized and treated early, will result in blindness [54]. Uncommon complications include encephalitis, myocarditis, nephritis, and pneumothorax [55, 56]. Subacute sclerosing panencephalitis is an extremely uncommon long-term complication of measles [57].

A number of studies have indicated that children who had measles have significantly increased morbidity and mortality in the ensuing months when compared with community controls [35, 58]. This is characterized by failure to thrive, recurrent infections, persistent pneumonia, and diarrhea. If present, vitamin A deficiency will aggravate these problems. Measles can be severe, atypical, and prolonged in immunocompromised HIV-infected children [59, 60].

## 8.9  DIAGNOSIS

The diagnosis of measles is usually based on the prodrome, Koplik's spots, and characteristic rash, and the diagnosis is seldom difficult. If necessary, serological diagnosis may be required. The diagnosis can also be confirmed by finding typical multinucleate giant cells in a buccal smear. The rash of measles can be confused with rubella, infectious mononucleosis, scarlet fever, Rocky Mountain spotted fever, and enteroviral infections.

## 8.10 TREATMENT

Although there is no specific therapy for measles, the adverse consequences can be reduced by treatment with vitamin A [14, 15, 61–65], providing good supportive medical care, and through the treatment of complications [66]. The basic principles of management are shown in Table 8.1. Children with specific complications of measles such as pneumonia, diarrhea, and malnutrition must be treated in accordance with current WHO recommendations for the specific problem [66].

Antibiotics should only be given if there is a specific indication, such as pneumonia, otitis media, or dysentery. There is little evidence that prophylactic antibiotics are of benefit in children with measles [67]. They may be useful in children who are at an additional risk for secondary bacterial infections, such as those with severe malnutrition, AIDS, and xerophthalmia. The indiscriminate use of antibiotics may result in unnecessary complications, such as antibiotic-associated diarrhea, severe drug reactions, and the emergence of drug-resistant organisms.

### 8.10.1 Nutritional Support

Because measles virus infection is a major catabolic event and associated with significant weight loss, careful attention must be paid to the nutritional needs of these children [68]. Mothers must be encouraged to feed the child even if diarrhea is present. Breast feeding must be maintained. In the children who are not breast fed, the energy content of the food must be increased by adding a teaspoon of vegetable oil and a teaspoon of sugar to the milk or cereal. The child must be given more fluids than usual to prevent dehydration. If dehydration is present, additional fluids must be provided in the form of oral or intravenous rehydration solution. Where available, additional vitamins and minerals such as multivitamin syrup must be provided. If a hospitalized child refuses to take food, then a nasogastric tube must be inserted, and liquid food and fluids given through the tube.

In many cultures, there is the mistaken custom to stop feeding or to reduce feeding of children with measles. Mothers and caregivers must be informed of the importance of maintaining adequate feeding during the acute and convalescent stage. Because failure

**Table 8.1**
Basic principles of measles case management

| |
|---|
| Treat the whole child. |
| Anticipate complications in high-risk groups. |
| Admit severely ill children to hospital. |
| Treat fever with paracetamol if the temperature is above 39°C. |
| Give vitamin A according to WHO recommendations. |
| Encourage breast feeding. |
| Provide nutritional support to all children. |
| Act promptly to treat eye lesions. |
| Use antibiotics only when there are clear indications. |
| Give oral rehydration solution for diarrhea. |

to thrive and recurrent infections are common in the months following measles [35, 58], it is therefore essential that children are closely monitored, and regular clinic attendance is recommended for at least 6 months following recovery from acute measles.

### 8.10.2 Vitamin A Therapy

Seven published clinical trials (six inpatient and one outpatient studies), have evaluated the effect of vitamin A supplementation on morbidity and mortality [14, 15, 61–65]. The studies differed in terms of their designs and the dose of vitamin A given. In Cape Town, South Africa [15], Tanzania [14], and India [64], the children received 200,000 IU on two successive days; in Kenya [63], a single dose, which varied with age, was given; in Zambia [65], they received a single dose of 200,000 IU; in Durban, South Africa [52], they received 100,000 IU (<1 year of age) or 200,000 IU (>1 year) on days 1, 2, and 8; and in England [61], they received approximately 20,000 IU daily in the form of cod-liver oil for 1–3 weeks (estimated dose of 140,000–400,000 IU altogether). All the studies were done on inpatients except for the Zambian study, which was done on outpatients.

In the UK trial, the case fatality rate in the treated group was 3.7% compared to 8.7% in the untreated group [61]. The relative risk (RR) of dying from measles following supplementation with vitamin A was 0.46 (95% confidence interval [CI] 0.26–0.81; $p = .018$) compared to those not supplemented. The effect was most noticeable with respect to deaths caused by pneumonia. In the Tanzanian clinical trial, 6 (7%) of the 88 vitamin A-supplemented children who were admitted to a rural hospital died, whereas there were 12/92 (13%) deaths in the control group. Although there were twice as many deaths in the placebo group, the difference was not significant (RR 0.52, 95% CI 0.21–1.33; $p = .25$). There was, however, a significant difference in mortality in children less than 2 years old (RR 0.15; $p = .03$) and for the cases complicated by croup [14]. In the Cape Town study done on children with severe measles who were admitted to an urban regional hospital, vitamin A therapy had a significant effect on mortality, with 10/97 (10%) deaths occurring in the placebo group and only 2/92 (2%) deaths in the vitamin A-treated group (RR 0.21, 95% CI 0.05–0.94; $p = .046$) [15]. The Durban study consisted of a small sample size (n = 60) and only one death was reported in the placebo group [62].

A meta-analysis of the four studies in the United Kingdom, South Africa, and Tanzania showed that vitamin A therapy reduced mortality by an impressive 67% ($p = .004$) [69]. In the Kenyan study, the overall case fatality was 2.7% and did not differ among treated (n = 146) and untreated (n = 148) children [63]. The study from India, which evaluated the impact of vitamin A therapy in children with postmeasles complications (the average time of hospitalization following onset of rash was about 8 days), reported a case fatality rate of 16% in the vitamin A-treated group compared to 32% in the group who did not receive vitamin A ($p < .02$) [64]. Mortality rates in these trials are summarized in Fig. 8.2.

A Cochrane systematic review of the literature indicated that two doses of vitamin A of 200,000 IU on successive days was significantly associated with a 82% reduction of mortality in children younger than 2 years, a 67% reduction in pneumonia-specific mortality, and a 47% reduction in croup incidence, but no significant reduction in the incidence of pneumonia and diarrhea [70].

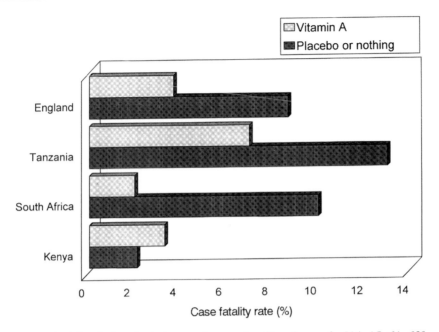

**Fig. 8.2.** Clinical trials of vitamin A therapy in measles. Based on refs. [14, 15, 61, 63]

Three African trials [15, 62, 63] specifically studied the impact of vitamin A on morbidity. In Cape Town, the treated children had a significantly shorter hospital stay and recovered more rapidly from pneumonia and diarrhea, and fewer children developed croup, persistent pneumonia, or persistent diarrhea [15]. In Durban, the vitamin A-treated children also recovered more rapidly overall and specifically from pneumonia. In addition, the integrated morbidity scores (determined by clinical findings and chest radiograph) at 1, 6, and 26 weeks following infection were reduced by 82%, 61%, and 85%, respectively, in the supplemented group [62]. In Kenya, children given vitamin A had a significantly lower risk of developing otitis media and recovered more rapidly from diarrhea [63].

Furthermore, three large-scale community intervention trials, one in South India [71] and two in Nepal [72, 73], evaluated the effect of prophylactic vitamin A supplements on childhood mortality and included in their analysis the effect on measles-related mortality. A meta-analysis of these studies showed a 36% reduction in mortality (RR 0.74, 95% CI 0.53–1.04; $p = .08$) [74]. These findings are consistent with those from the hospital-based studies.

The beneficial effects of vitamin A therapy reported in the aforementioned clinical trials have been confirmed in an evaluation of a vitamin A supplementation program implemented as part of the routine case management of all children hospitalized with measles in Cape Town [75]. The morbidity (hospital stay and intensive-care admissions) and mortality in children hospitalized during 1989 and 1990, after the implementation of the program, were significantly less than that in the children admitted during 1985 and 1986, the period prior to the implementation of vitamin A therapy. The significance of these findings is that vitamin A therapy provided protection against the complications of measles infection in everyday hospital practice.

Table 8.2
Vitamin A dosage

| Age | Immediately on diagnosis | Next day |
|---|---|---|
| Infants <6 mo | 50,000 IU | 50,000 IU |
| Infants <6–11 mo | 100,000 IU | 100,000 IU |
| Infants ≥ 12 mo | 200,000 IU | 200,000 IU |

All the clinical trials of vitamin A therapy in acute measles have been done in a hospital setting. One study from Zambia evaluated the effect of vitamin A therapy in an outpatient setting [65]. In a blinded, placebo-controlled trial, children were given a single high dose of vitamin A in oil. At baseline, 63% and 68% of treated and placebo treated children had pneumonia. After 4 weeks, pneumonia was absent in the treated group, but occurred in 12% of controls.

### 8.10.3   Vitamin A Dosage

The dosage schedule of vitamin A for children with measles is shown in Table 8.2. Note that if the child has any eye signs of vitamin A deficiency, then a third dose must be given at least 2 weeks after the second dose.

## 8.11   PREVENTION

### 8.11.1   Measles Vaccine

Most of the current live attenuated vaccines (including Schwarz, Moraten, Edmonston Zagreb, and AIK-C) in use throughout the world were derived from the original virus isolated and cultured by Enders and Peebles in 1954 [17]. Measles vaccine is safe and very effective. The vaccine may cause a minor febrile or measles-like illness 7–10 days after injection. When administered to children over the age of 12 months, as is the case in most developed countries, seroconversion is over 95% [76]. Under the age of 12 months, seroconversion is lower because of the interference of maternally derived antibodies [19]. However, because of the high probability of exposure to measles before the age of 1 year in many developing countries, and because disease is usually more severe in infants, WHO has advocated vaccination at 9 months of age [77]. If possible, a second measles vaccine dose should be given some time after the first birthday [1]. In developed countries, it is recommended that a child receive at least two measles vaccines after the age of 1 year [78]. In these countries, the measles vaccine is frequently administered together with mumps and rubella vaccine. Measles vaccine is recommended for children with HIV infection [60, 79]. Some authorities advise against its use in severely immunocompromised HIV-infected children [78].

By 1985, virtually all countries had incorporated measles vaccine into their national expanded program on immunization (EPI). Since then, the global coverage of children less than 1 year of age with one dose of measles vaccine has increased significantly, and it is now estimated to be about 80% [1]. The worldwide use of measles vaccine has also resulted in a dramatic decline in reported measles cases (Fig. 8.3). In many countries

Measles global annual reported incidence and MCV coverage, 1980-2004

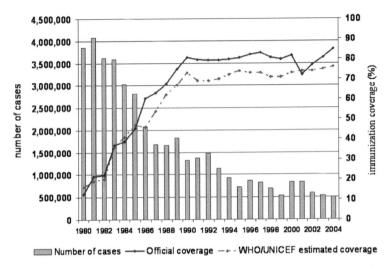

**Fig. 8.3.** Measles global annual reported incidence and MCV coverage, 1980–2004. (From http://www.who.int/immunization_monitoring/diseases/measles/en/index.html.)

(even some developing countries), measles is now under control; that is, the measles morbidity and mortality rate has been reduced to a small fraction of preimmunization levels, and in many instances the diseases has been virtually eliminated.

### 8.11.2   Improving Vitamin A Status of Children

Population-based studies indicated that vitamin A reduces childhood morbidity and mortality [69, 74]. The strategies of WHO and UNICEF for control and eventual elimination of vitamin A deficiency include the provision of vitamin A to children through a combination of strategies such as breast-feeding, vitamin A supplementation, food fortification, and dietary diversification [80].

WHO has also published guidelines for the simultaneous administration of vitamin A and measles vaccine as part of the routine EPI schedule [81]. The EPI is being viewed as the gateway to elimination of vitamin A deficiency. The program provides a greater number of opportunities for delivery of vitamin A to mothers and children than any other health program, reaching about 80% of the world's children in their first year of life as well as their mothers. Vitamin A can safely be administered at 9 months of age or older without having any effect on the production of antibodies to concurrently administered measles vaccine [82, 83].

### 8.12   RESEARCH NEEDS

One of the major impediments to measles control and elimination is the high rate of transmission among young children and infants coupled with the reduced efficacy of the vaccine in children less than 1 year old. WHO is exploring alternative strategies for immunization as well as evaluating new vaccines [84, 85]. In the context of the measles eradication strategy, simple diagnostic tests that can be utilized under field conditions are being assessed, as is the development and strengthening of measles surveillance systems. In addition, alternative routes of immunization, including the mucosal route, are being explored [86]. One of the biggest challenges facing developing countries is to develop strategies to reach the "hard-to-reach children," that is, children living in remote and often inaccessible geographical areas as well as the poor living in the large periurban slums.

## 8.13   CONCLUSIONS

Measles has long been a leading childhood killer, but major progress has been made in the last two decades in preventing measles through immunization and improving survival of affected children through effective case management. Global deaths due to measles have declined by almost 50%, from close to 1 million in 1999 to less than 500,000 in 2004 [1]. Although there is no specific therapy for measles, disease severity and mortality can be reduced by vitamin A therapy and the provision of good supportive care. Particular attention should be paid to the nutritional requirements of affected children.

Measles is a preventable disease. The goal should be to work toward the elimination and ultimately the eradication of measles by ensuring universal immunization, a goal that is attainable. However, it requires an injection of significant resources, particularly in developing countries where there is a poor primary health care infrastructure and where measles is endemic.

## REFERENCES

1. World Health Organization. Progress in reducing measles deaths: 1999–2004. Wkly Epidemiol Rec 2006;81:89–96
2. World Health Organization. Division of Diarrhoeal and Acute Respiratory Disease Control. Integrated management of the sick child. Bull World Health Org 1995;73:735–740.
3. Hussey GD, Clements CJ. Clinical problems in measles. Ann Trop Paediatr 1996;16:307–317.
4. Rhazes [Abu Bakr Muhammad ibn Zakariya al-Razi]. A treatise on the smallpox and measles. Translated from the Arabic by William Alexander Greenhil. London: Sydenham Society, 1848.
5. Sydenham T. Observationes medicae circa morborum acutorum historiam et curationem. Londini: Kettilby, 1676.
6. Creighton C. A history of epidemics in Britain. Cambridge, UK: Cambridge University Press, 1894.
7. Hirsch A. Handbook of geographical and historical pathology. London: New Sydenham Society, 1883.
8. Jannetta AB. Epidemics and mortality in early modern Japan. Princeton, NJ: Princeton University Press, 1987.
9. Panum PL. Observations made during the epidemic of measles in the Faroe Islands in the year 1846. Med Classics 1929;3:829–886.
10. Koplik H. The diagnosis of the invasion of measles from a study of the exanthema as it appears on the buccal mucous membrane. Arch Pediatr 1896;13:918–922.
11. Morley D, Woodland M, Martin WJ. Measles in Nigerian children: a study of the disease in West Africa, and its manifestations in England and other countries during different epochs. J Hyg Camb 1963;61:115–134.
12. Morley D. Severe measles in the tropics-1. BMJ 1969;1:297–300, 363–365.
13. Aaby P. Malnutrition and overcrowding/intensive exposure in severe measles infection: review of community studies. Rev Infect Dis 1988;10:478–491.
14. Barclay AJG, Foster A, Sommer A. Vitamin A supplements and mortality related to measles: a randomised clinical trial. BMJ 1987;294:294–296.
15. Hussey GD, Klein M. A randomised controlled trial of vitamin A in children with severe measles. N Engl J Med 1990;323:160–164.

16. World Health Organization. Global programme for vaccines and immunization. Treating measles in children. Geneva: World Health Organization, 1997. WHO/EPI/TRAM/97.02.

17. Enders JF, Peebles TC. Propagation in tissue cultures of cytopathogenic agents from patients with measles. Proc Soc Exp Biol Med 1954;86:277–286.

18. Katz SL, Kempe CH, Black FL, et al. Studies on an attenuated measles-virus vaccine. VII. General summary and evaluation of the results of vaccination. N Engl J Med 1960;273:180–184.

19. Sato H, Albrecht P, Reynolds DW, et al. Transfer of measles, mumps, and rubella antibodies from mother to infant. Its effect on measles, mumps and rubella immunization. Am J Dis Child 1979;133: 1240–1243.

20. Job JS, Halsey NA, Boulos R, et al. Successful immunization of infants at 6 months of age with high dose Edmonston-Zagreb measles vaccine. Pediatr Infect Dis J 1991;10:303–311.

21. Garenne M, Leroy O, Beau JP, et al. Child mortality after high-titre measles vaccines: prospective study in Senegal. Lancet 1991;338:903–907.

22. Aaby P, Samb B, Simondon F, et al. Divergent mortality for male and female recipients of low-titer and high-titer measles vaccine in rural Senegal. Am J Epidemiol 1993;138:746–755.

23. Hussey GD, Goddard EA, Hughes J, et al. The effect of Edmoonston-Zagreb and Schwarz measles vaccines on immune response in infants. J Infect Dis 1996;173:1320–1326.

24. World Health Organization. Expanded programme on immunication: global advisory group. Wkly Epidemiol Rec 1993;68:11–16.

25. Coetzee N. Hussey GD, Visser G, Barron P, Keen A. The 1992 measles epidemic in Cape Town: a changing epidemiological pattern. S Afr Med J 1994;84:145–149.

26. Clements CJ, Strassburg M, Cutts FT, Torel C. The epidemiology of measles. World Health Stat Q 1992;45:285–291.

27. World Health Organization. Measles control in the 1990's: Plan of action for global measles control. Geneva: World Health Organization, 1992. WHO/EPI/GEN/92.3.

28. Aaby P, Coovadia H. Severe measles: a reappraisal of the role of nutrition, overcrowding and virus dose. Med Hypotheses 1985;18:93–112.

29. Caulfield LE, de Onis M, Blossner M, Black RE. Undernutrition as an underlying cause of child deaths associated with diarrhoea, pneumonia, malaria and measles. Am J Clin Nutr 2004;80:193–198.

30. Anonymous. Immunology of measles. Lancet 1989;2:780–781.

31. Hussey GD, Klein M. Measles induced vitamin A deficiency. Ann NY Acad Sci 1992;669:188–196.

32. Tomkins A, Hussey GD. Vitamin A, immunity and infection. Nutr Res Rev 1989;2:17–28.

33. Stephensen CB, Alvarez JO, Kohatsu J, Hardmeier R, Kennedy JI, Gammon RD. Vitamin A is excreted in the urine during acute infection. Am J Clin Nutr 1994;60:388–392.

34. Coovadia HM, Wesley A, Brain P. Immunological events in acute measles influencing outcome. Arch Dis Child 1978;53:861–867.

35. Hull HF, Williams PJ, Oldfield F. Measles mortality and vaccine efficacy in rural West Africa. Lancet 1983;1:972–975.

36. Markowitz LE, Nzilambi N, Diskell WJ, et al. Vitamin A levels and mortality among hospitalized measles patients. J Trop Paediatr 1989;35:109–112.

37. Butler JC, Havens PL, Sowell AL, et al. Measles severity and serum retinol (vitamin A) concentration among children in the United States. Pediatrics 1993;91:1176–1181.

38. Frieden TF, Sowell AL, Henning KJ, Huff DL, Gunn RA. Vitamin A levels and severity of measles: New York City. Am J Dis Child 1992;146:182–186.

39. Reddy V. Interaction between nutrition and measles. Indian J Pediatr 1987;54:53–57.

40. Dossetor JFB, Whittle HC. Protein-losing enteropathy and malabsorption in acute measles enteritis. BMJ 1975;2:592–593.

41. Duggan MB, Milner RDG. Energy cost of measles infection. Arch Dis Child 1986;61:436–439.

42. Axton JHM. Measles and the state of nutrition. S Afr Med J 1979;55:125–126.

43. Bhaskaram P, Reddy V, Ray S, Bhatnagar RC. Effect of measles on the nutritional status of preschool children. J Trop Med Hyg 1984;87:21–25.

44. Coomey JOO, Richardson JE. Measles in Ghana. Ann Trop Paediatr 1984;4:189–194.

45. Varavithya W, Charuvantji A, Tarounotai T, et al. Diarrhoea in measles. J Med Assoc Thai 1985;68: 298–301.

46. Greenberg BL, Sack RB, Salazar-Lindo E, et al. Measles-associated diarrhea in hospitalized children in Lima, Peru: pathogenic agents and impact on growth. J Infect Dis 1991;163:495–502.

47. Koster FT, Curlin GC, Aziz KMA, Haque A. Synergistic impact of measles and diarrhoea on nutrition and mortality in Bangladesh. Bull World Health Org 1981;59:901–908.

48. Hussey GD, Klein M. Measles. Child Hosp Q 2:301–305.

49. Orren A, Kipps A, Moodie JW, et al. Increased susceptibility to herpes simplex virus infections in children with acute measles. Infect Immunol 1981;31:1–6.

50. Burgess W, Mduma B, Josephson GV. Measles in Mbeya, Tanzania, 1981–1983. J Trop Pediatr 1986;32:148–153.

51. Samsi TK, Ruspandji T, Susanto I, Gunawan K. Risk factors for severe measles. Southeast Asian J Trop Med Public Health 1992;23:497–503.

52. Alwar AJE. The effect of protein energy malnutrition on morbidity and mortality due to measles at Kenyatta National Hospital, Nairobi, Kenya. East Afr Med J 1992;69:415–418.

53. Dossetor J, Whittle HC, Greenwood BM. Persistent measles infection in malnourished children. BMJ 1977;1:1633–1635.

54. Foster A, Sommer A. Corneal ulceration, measles, and childhood blindness in Tanzania. Br J Ophthal 1987;71:331–343.

55. Tidstrom B. Complications in measles with special reference to encephalitis. Acta Med Scand 1968;184:411–415.

56. Miller DL. Frequency of complications of measles. BMJ 1964;2:75–78.

57. Zilber N, Rannon L, Alter M, Kahana E. Measles, measles vaccination, and risk of subacute sclerosing panencephalitis (SSPE). Neurology 1983;33:1558–1564.

58. Burstrom B, Aaby P, Mutie DM, Kimani G, Bjerregaard P. Severe measles outbreak in Western Kenya. East Afr Med J 1992;69:419–423.

59. Markowitz LE, Chandler FW, Roldan EO, et al. Fatal measles pneumonia without a rash: in a child with AIDS. J Infect Dis 1988;158:480–483.

60. Palumbo P, Hoyt L, Demasio K, Oleske J, Connor E. Population-based study of measles and measles immunization in human immunodeficiency virus-infected children. Pediatr Infect Dis J 1992;11:1008–1114.

61. Ellison JB. Intensive vitamin therapy in measles. BMJ 1932;2:708–711.

62. Coutsoudis A, Broughton M, Coovadia HM. Vitamin A supplementation reduces measles morbidity in young African children: a randomised, placebo-controlled, double-blind trial. Am J Clin Nutr 1991;54:890–895.

63. Ogaro FO, Orinda VA Onyango F, Black RE. Effect of vitamin A on diarrhoeal and respiratory complications of measles. Trop Geogr Med 1993;45:283–286.

64. Madhulika, Kabra SK, Talati A. Vitamin A supplementation in post-measles complications. J Trop Pediatr 1994;40:305–307.

65. Rosales FJ, Kjolhede C, Goodman L. Efficacy of a single oral dose of 200,000 IU of oil-soluble vitamin A in measles-associated morbidity. Am J Epidemiol 1996;143:413–422.

66. World Health Organization. Case management of measles: a policy document. Geneva: World Health Organization, 1996.

67. Shann F. Meta-analysis of trials of prophylactic antibiotics for children with measles: inadequate evidence. BMJ 1997;314:334–336.

68. Hussey GD. Managing measles. Integrated management reduces disease severity. BMJ 1997;314:316–317.

69. Glasziou PP, Mackerras DEM. Vitamin A supplementation in infectious diseases: a meta-analysis. BMJ 1993;306:366–370.

70. Huiming Y, Chaomin W, Meng M. Vitamin A for treating measles in children. Cochrane Database Syst Rev 2005(4):CD001479.

71. Rahmathullah L, Underwood B, Thulasiraj RD, et al. Reduced mortality among children in Southern India receiving a small weekly dose of vitamin A. N Engl J Med 1990;323:929–935.

72. West KP Jr., Pokhrel RP, Katz J, et al. Efficacy of vitamin A in reducing pre-school child mortality in Nepal. Lancet 1991;338:67–71.

73. Daulaire NM, Starbuck ES, Houston RM, Church MS, Stukel TA, Pandey MR. Childhood mortality after a high dose of vitamin A in a high risk population. BMJ 1992;304:207–210.

74. Beaton GH, Martorell R, Aronson KJ, et al. Effectiveness of vitamin A supplementation in the control of young child morbidity and mortality in developing countries. Geneva: Administrative Committee on Coordination/Subcommittee on Nutrition (ACC/SCN), 1993. Discussion paper no. 13.

75. Hussey GD, Klein M. Routine high dose vitamin A therapy for children hospitalized with measles. J Trop Paediatr 1993;39:342–345.

76. Preblud SR, Katz SL. Measles vaccine. In: Vaccines. Plotkin SA, Mortimer EA, eds. Philadelphia: Saunders, 1988:182–211.

77. World Health Organization: Global programme for vaccines and immunization. Immunization policy. Geneva: World Health Organization, 1995. WHO/EPI/GEN/95.03 REV.1.

78. Watson JC, Hadler SC, Dykewicz CA, Reef S, Phillips L. Measles, mumps, and rubella-vaccine use and strategies for elimination of measles, rubella, and congenital rubella syndrome and control of mumps: recommendations of the Advisory Committee on Immunization Practices (ACIP). MMWR Morb Mortal Wkly Rep 1998;47(RR-8):1–57.

79. Arpadi SM, Markowitz LE, Baughman AL, et al. Measles antibody in vaccinated human immunodeficiency virus type 1-infected children. Pediatrics 1996;97:653–657.

80. World Summit for Children—Mid-decade goal: VAD. Geneva: UNICEF-WHO Joint Committee on Health Policy Special Session, January 27–28, 1994. JCHPSS/94/2.8.

81. World Health Organization. Using immunization contacts as the gateway to eliminating vitamin A deficiency. Geneva: World Health Organization, 1994. WHO/EPI/GEN/94.9.

82. Semba RD, Akib A, Beeler J, et al. Effect of vitamin A supplementation on measles vaccination in nine-month-old infants. Public Health 1997;111:245–247.

83. Benn CS, Aaby P, Bale C, et al. Randomised trial of effect of vitamin A supplementation on antibody response to measles vaccine in Guinea-Bissau, West Africa. Lancet 1997;350:101–105.

84. Song MK, Vindurampulle CJ, Capozzo AV, et al. Characterisation of immune responses induced by intramuscualar vaccination with DNA vaccines encoding measles virus haemagglutinin and/or fusion proteins. J Virol 2005;79:9854–9861.

85. Chien-Hsiung P, Valsamakis A, Colella T, et al. Modulation of disease, T cell responses, and measles clearance in monkeys vaccinated with H-encoding alphavirus replicon particles. Proc Natl Acad Sci U S A 2005;102:11581–11588.

86. Dilraj A, Cutts FT, de Castro JF et al. Responses to different measles vaccine strains given by aerosol and subcutaneous routes to schoolchildren: a randomized trial. Lancet 2000;355:798–803.

# 9

## Malaria and Nutrition

*Anuraj H. Shankar*

### 9.1 INTRODUCTION

Malaria is the most significant parasitic disease of human beings and remains a major cause of morbidity, anemia, and mortality worldwide. Malaria currently accounts for approximately 200 million morbid episodes and 2–3 million deaths each year, estimates that have been increasing over the last three decades [1]. The disease is caused by protozoan organisms of the genus *Plasmodium*, which invade and replicate within red blood cells (RBCs), a process resulting in the manifestations of disease, including cyclical fevers, anemia, convulsions, and death. The parasite is transmitted from person to person by biting anopheline mosquitoes. There are four malaria species that infect humans: *Plasmodium falciparum*, *Plasmodium vivax*, *Plasmodium malariae*, and *Plasmodium ovale*. They are distributed in varying degrees throughout the tropical world and in some more temperate areas, wherever ecological and sociological conditions favor sufficient interactions between humans, mosquitoes, and parasites to maintain transmission. It is, however, important to acknowledge that the majority of acute morbidity and mortality is caused by *P. falciparum*, and that nearly 90% of all cases and fatalities occur in sub-Saharan Africa. Although all persons are at risk for malaria, in many settings the burden of disease is carried primarily by children below the age of 5 and by pregnant women.

Malaria is a treatable infection, and a variety of antimalarial drugs are available. However, drug resistance has become a major problem, and new effective compounds are needed. Prevention of malaria has focused on reduction of man–mosquito contact by application of insecticides, use of bed nets, and environmental management to reduce mosquito-breeding areas. The development of a malaria vaccine is currently a major focus of research. Clearly, additional low-cost and effective means to assist in the prevention and treatment of malaria are needed.

It has long been acknowledged that populations residing in malarious areas generally live under conditions leading to poor nutritional status. The groups at highest risk for the adverse effects of malaria, children and pregnant women, are also most affected by poor nutrition. Although it has been suspected that nutrition might influence susceptibility to infection by the malaria parasite or modify the course of disease, there have been comparatively few efforts to examine such interactions. Among the studies that have been done, early ones suggested that poor nutritional status was actually protective.

From: *Nutrition and Health: Nutrition and Health in Developing Countries, Second Edition*
Edited by: R. D. Semba & M. W. Bloem © Humana Press, Totowa, NJ

However, modern and more recent works indicated that macronutrient and certain forms of micronutrient malnutrition exacerbate malaria morbidity and mortality [2]. Indeed, several field trials of nutritional supplementation have begun to clarify which nutrients can significantly reduce the burden of malarial disease and which might be exacerbative. What is clear is that nutrition strongly influences the disease burden of malaria, and that malaria itself has a profound effect on host nutritional status. This chapter describes the history and current state of knowledge of malaria and nutrition and develops a rational paradigm for the development of targeted, nutrient-based interventions as adjuncts to current methods of malaria treatment and prevention.

## 9.2   HISTORICAL BACKGROUND

### 9.2.1   Historical Overview of Malaria

Human beings have long been afflicted with malaria. Medical writings dating from 2700 BC in China and India described what is most likely malaria, and the disease is described in writings of Homer [3]. Indeed, the Greeks had known the relation of fever to swamps and low-lying water since the 6th century BC, and Roman efforts to drain large areas of swampland were partially motivated by the desire to reduce malaria.

Effective treatment for malaria was not recognized in the West until the early 1600s, after Jesuit priests in Peru observed Amerindians treating cyclical fevers with a tea made from the bark of the cinchona tree. By 1820, the active ingredient from the bark, quinine, had been isolated, and its use for cyclic fevers became widespread. The malaria parasite itself was discovered in the blood of humans by Laveran in 1880. In 1898, Ross, working in India, and Grassi and colleagues, working in Italy, independently described the life cycle of malaria in birds and humans, respectively. Recognition of the role of mosquitoes in transmission led to efforts to reduce mosquito breeding through drainage and environmental control and reduction in human–mosquito contact through clothing, repellents, and bed nets.

### 9.2.2   Attempts to Eradicate Malaria

As mentioned, malaria control had initially been limited to reduction of mosquito-breeding habitat, use of bed nets, and treatment of cases with quinine. However, two developments changed the strategies used to combat malaria. First, in the 1930s chloroquine was developed as a derivative of quinine that was cheaper, was more effective, and had fewer side effects. Second, in 1940, DDT was synthesized and realized to be the most potent insecticide available to humans, remaining active for several months after application. In 1955, the World Health Organization (WHO), in response to the optimism engendered by the potential of these discoveries, formulated a plan for world-wide malaria eradication. By the late 1950s, one of the most ambitious health campaigns in history had been launched [4].

Early efforts were enormously successful in some countries such as the United States, Italy, Malta, and Sri Lanka but met with limited success in others. Unfortunately, implementation was minimal in Africa, where disease burden was greatest. By the late 1960s, it was clear that eradication operations were untenable in many countries, and further compounding problems was the emergence of anopheline resistance to insecticides and parasite resistance to antimalarials [5, 6]. A rapid resurgence of malaria and widespread emergence of chloroquine-resistant malaria followed the subsequent decline of the eradication effort.

### 9.2.3   Modern Approaches to Malaria Control

By the mid-1970s, the focus of combating malaria had shifted to control rather than eradication. There was also a gradual resurgence in malaria research that was fueled by developments in molecular biology and immunology. Despite major advances in understanding the biology of the parasite, diagnostic techniques, vector control methods, and antimalarial drugs, malaria has steadily increased over the last three decades. The current WHO Global Malaria Control strategy is focused on four goals: (1) provide early diagnosis and prompt treatment; (2) plan and implement selective and sustainable preventive measures, including vector control; (3) provide early detection to contain or prevent epidemics; and (4) strengthen local capacities in basic/applied research to permit the regular assessment of a country's malaria situation, in particular the ecological, social, and economic determinants of the disease.

The WHO Roll Back Malaria 'program initiated in 2000, and the ongoing funding from the Global Fund for HIV, Tuberculosis, and Malaria, exemplifies the renewed interest in controlling malaria and—determined not to repeat past mistakes—has genuinely prioritized on malaria in Africa. The WHO goals mentioned are being pursued through a variety of means, including provision of malaria treatment kits to village-based health workers or pharmacists and focused training and capacity building through networking. The most significant developments, however, have been the resurrection and improvement of an older technology, the bed net, and a focused effort on malaria vaccine development.

#### 9.2.3.1   INSECTICIDE-TREATED BED NETS

The use of curtains or fabric to shield sleeping persons from mosquitoes has been practiced since ancient times. Indeed, the use of mosquito nets was strongly advocated after Ross and Grassi had discovered that mosquitoes did indeed transmit malaria. Although useful if maintained and used properly, bed nets are easily rendered ineffective if holes develop in the netting or if improperly hung. In 1950. researchers observed that if bed nets were dipped in residual insecticides, mosquitoes flying against or landing on the net were exposed to lethal doses and died within minutes. Improved development has led to renewed interest in bed nets, specifically insecticide-treated nets (ITNs). Several trials [7–9] demonstrated that ITNs were very effective in reducing morbidity and mortality. Meta-analysis of these trials indicated overall reductions in malaria morbidity by 48% and mortality by 20–40% [10].

#### 9.2.3.2   VACCINE DEVELOPMENT

Rationale for the belief that a malaria vaccine could be developed was based on the clear epidemiological evidence that humans develop protective immunity against malaria when repeatedly exposed to the infection. In addition, the maturation of molecular biology and modern immunology provided novel tools and hope that malaria vaccines were feasible.

Initial studies focused heavily on the sporozoite, the stage inoculated to humans by the mosquito. Emphasis on the sporozoite as an immunological target for protection was motivated by observations made in the 1950s that humans could be protected against a challenge infection after exposure to the bite of irradiated malaria-infected mosquitoes [11, 12]. By the early 1980s, researchers at New York University had cloned the circumsporozoite protein (CSP), the predominant protein on the surface of the sporozoite and the first gene to be cloned from a human parasite. Following demonstration that rodents could be immunized with recombinant CSP, there was considerable optimism that a vaccine would soon be available. Unfortunately, phase II trials in humans, including experimental challenge infections [13], failed to demonstrate adequate protection. However, research continued, and initial results with newer vaccine formulations based on the CSP, such as RTS,S/AS02A, have been promising [14, 15] and are reviewed elsewhere [16].

By the late 1980s, the attention of malaria vaccine development had begun to shift to the blood stage of the parasite, with the rationale that the erythrocytic phase was responsible for clinical disease and mortality. Further impetus for this approach came from experiments in 1963 [17], demonstrating that infusion of antibody from resistant adults into children suffering acute clinical malaria resulted in rapid clearance of parasitemia. By the late 1980s, Pattaroyo and colleagues in Colombia developed a synthetic vaccine known as SPf66, which was based on several different blood stage antigens shown to be protective against experimental *P. falciparum* infection of monkeys [18]. SPf66 became the first vaccine to be tested in large-scale field trials. Although initial results of 30–70% efficacy in South America [19] and Tanzania [20] were promising, additional field trials in the Gambia [21], Thailand [22], and Tanzania [23] failed to demonstrate efficacy. Nevertheless, SPf66 demonstrated that a vaccine could be developed that could elicit partial protection in some settings. As such, development of blood stage vaccines has continued. and several candidates are undergoing field testing in Africa and Papua New Guinea [24] and are reviewed elsewhere [25].

There are currently at least 23 vaccine candidates in various stages of development. These include, but are not limited to, CSP, merozoite surface protein 1 (MSP-1), erythrocyte-binding antigen 175 (EBA 175), apical-merozoite antigen 1 (APA-1), gametocyte antigens (Pfs25), and pre-erythrocyte liver-stage antigen 3 (LSA-3). As insights are gained through ongoing immunological and field studies, it is anticipated that a vaccine with at least partial efficacy will be available within a decade.

## 9.3  EPIDEMIOLOGY

The starting point for understanding malaria as a disease, and the rationale behind control programs, must be an in-depth understanding of the intricate and often village-specific aspects of ecology, biology, and epidemiology of malaria. Such knowledge is also the basis for understanding nutritional modulation of malaria morbidity and mortality.

### 9.3.1  *Geographic Distribution and Disease Burden*

The relative importance of malaria varies greatly in different geographical areas of the world. As mentioned, nearly 90% of life-threatening *P. falciparum*-related disease continues to be in Africa, with the remaining 10% occurring primarily in Southeast Asia and India, followed by South America [1, 3, 26].

Both incidence and seriousness of disease define its public health significance. *Plasmodium falciparum* causes a variety of pathophysiological and potentially lethal conditions such as cerebral malaria and severe malaria anemia. Additional complications include splenomegaly and renal and pulmonary pathology. In much of tropical Africa, malaria is the leading disease burden on the population. In Ghana, for example, *P. falciparum* has long accounted for nearly 10% of all healthy life-years lost [27, 28], making it the greatest single health threat to the population. In many cases, malaria is a contributing factor to death even though the final cause may be attributed to another disease, such as diarrhea or pneumonia. Community-based intervention studies [29, 30] indicated that malaria may account for nearly half the under-5 mortality. When malaria is controlled, reductions in nonmalaria mortality also decrease. A report of the global burden of disease indicated that malaria was responsible for 18% of all childhood deaths, and 94% of all such deaths in Africa [31].

*Plasmodium vivax*, although not as overtly pathogenic as *P. falciparum*, continues to be a major cause of morbidity in parts of China, India, Southeast Asia, Polynesia, and South America. It is a significant cause of morbidity and anemia, and these effects may indirectly contribute to all-cause mortality. Likewise, *P. malariae* is not as pathogenic as *P. falciparum*, although an unusual and highly lethal nephrosis can occur. *Plasmodium ovale* is a relatively uncommon infection, and its contribution to overall malaria morbidity is not substantial.

In addition to the proximate effects of morbidity and death, malaria results in chronic effects of persistent anemia, long-term disability, poor educational and work performance, and the cost of coping with illness and death within the family and community. In many cases, severe anemia from malaria requires blood transfusion, and this in turn has been closely associated with transmission of HIV and with hepatitis B virus. Last, malaria during pregnancy, particularly with the first pregnancy, places the woman at special risk for severe anemia and death from malaria [32]. In addition, prenatal malaria can result in intrauterine growth retardation, low birth weight (LBW), premature delivery, fetal death, and miscarriage.

### 9.3.2 Life Cycle of the Malaria Parasite

The complex life cycle of *Plasmodium* spp. is given in Fig. 9.1. The parasite undergoes two developmental stages in the human host, resulting in asexual reproduction, and three in the mosquito, resulting from sexual reproduction. The parasite is transmitted to humans as a sporozoite in the saliva of an infected female anopheline mosquito taking a blood meal. Sporozoites enter the venous circulation through the capillary beds and invade liver cells within minutes. Over the next 5–15 days, the sporozoite replicates to produce about 40,000 daughter parasites, called *merozoites*. In the case of *P. vivax* and *P. ovale*, dormant forms known as *hypnozoites* sometimes develop in the liver cells, remaining viable for up to 50 years [33]. When released from liver cells, merozoites invade erythrocytes. These intraerythrocytic merozoites differentiate into trophozoites, which consume the intracellular hemoglobin and give rise to 6–24 daughter merozoites. The red cell eventually ruptures, releasing these merozoites to invade new erythrocytes and perpetuate the cycle.

Each erythrocytic cycle requires 48 hours for *P. falciparum*, *P. vivax*, and *P. ovale* but 72 hours for *P. malariae* [34, 35]. The different species of parasites also have different preferences for certain erythrocytes. *Plasmodium vivax* and *P. ovale* prefer younger nucleated red cells known as reticulocytes, whereas *P. malariae* prefers older red cells.

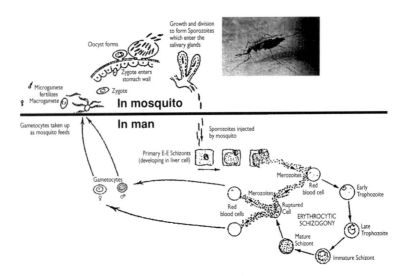

**Fig. 9.1.** Life cycle of Plasmodium.

*Plasmodium falciparum* has a marginal preference for younger cells but will readily infect all erythrocytes [34, 35]. In addition, *P. falciparum*-infected erythrocytes develop knob-like structures on their surface, which, along with several protein structures, lead to adherence of infected erythrocytes to the postcapillary venous endothelium [6, 36]. This results in sequestration of infected erythrocytes in the capillary beds, thereby preventing circulation of infected erythrocytes to the spleen, which is a major site of parasite removal. Moreover, rupture of infected erythrocytes occurs in an environment of tightly packed cells that facilitates reinvasion by daughter merozoites. For these reasons, as well as others, *P. falciparum* achieves the highest levels of erythrocytic infection and results in the greatest degree of pathology.

Within the erythrocyte, some merozoites differentiate into sexual forms known as *macrogametocytes* (female) and *microgametocytes* (male). When taken up in a blood meal, gametocytes emerge in the mosquito gut and begin sexual reproduction, leading to sporogonic development. The male and female gametes fuse, providing for genetic recombination, to form a zygote that transforms to the ookinete, which penetrates the gut wall and attaches to the epithelium. Over the next 7–12 days, the oocyst enlarges, forming about 10,000 sporozoites, and ruptures into the coelomic cavity. The sporozoites then migrate to the salivary glands and are ready be transmitted to the human host, thus completing the cycle.

The actual time required for replication in the mosquito depends on the species of parasite, mosquito, and particularly on the ambient temperature. Under optimal conditions at 30°C, *P. falciparum* requires 9 days, but at 20°C it takes 23 days [6]. With an average life span for most anophelines less than 3 weeks, ambient temperature is critical to transmission.

Once infected, the mosquito transmits sporozoites with each blood meal [6]. Fifty to sixty species of the genus *Anopheles* are known to be capable of transmitting malaria to humans. There is great variation in different species in their host feeding preferences and ability to support malaria replication. *Anopheles gambiae* is the most important vector in Africa and among the most efficient for malaria.

### 9.3.3 Classification Schemes of Malaria Endemnicity

The frequency of inoculation of the sporozoite into the human host is, of course, a primary determinant of infection. This is measured by determining the biting rate of anopheline mosquitoes and the proportion of mosquitoes that are infected with the parasite. The entomological inoculation rate (EIR) is the product of these numbers and represents the frequency at which the typical person is directly exposed to infection. The EIR ranges from a few bites a year to over 300 in high-transmission areas.

Malaria endemnicity has been classified into four broad categories based on percentages of children, ages 1–10, with enlarged spleens and the prevalence of circulating malaria parasites [37, 38]: (1) *Holoendemic* areas refer to areas with constantly high EIR and with prevalence and spleen rates exceeding 75%. Immunity typically develops rapidly such that by age 10, acute malaria morbidity and mortality is low. (2) *Hyperendemic* areas include regions with regular, often seasonal transmission, with spleen and parasite rates from 50% to 75%. Immunity is less developed, and adults also experience significant illness. (3) *Mesoendemic* areas have malaria transmission fairly regularly but at much lower levels, and spleen and parasite rates range from 10% to 50%. Such areas are prone to occasional epidemics involving those with little immunity, which may result in fairly high mortality. (4) *Hypoendemic* areas have limited malaria transmission. The population will have little or no immunity, and severe malaria epidemics involving all age groups can develop.

### 9.3.4 Clinical Disease

Disease processes in malaria result from the erythrocytic cycle of invasion and hemolysis. Along with the liberation of the merozoites, hemolysis releases several pyrogenic compounds from infected red cells; these stimulate the clinical paroxysms of fever and chills. In some patients, the erythrocytic cycle becomes synchronized so that virtually all merozoites are released every 48 or 72 hours. This accounts for the periodicity of these symptoms and is the basis for the older classification of malaria into tertian (every third day) and quartan (every fourth day) disease. However, clinical manifestations of infection, particularly in children, can range from the totally asymptomatic to severe disease and rapid death. Children may present with symptoms that include listlessness, pyrexia, abdominal cramping, difficulty breathing, mental disorientation, or convulsions.

The distinction between infection and disease is particularly important in malaria. Infection with the malaria parasite does not necessarily result in disease. In highly endemic areas, childhood prevalence rates exceed 50%, but few will have acute symptoms. Typically, in hyperendemic areas the prevalence and density of infection with *P. falciparum* peak in early childhood and decline thereafter, with density receding prior to prevalence. The density of infection at which symptoms appear is also greater in early life and becomes lower with age [39]. This indicates that separate immunological effectors modulate infection, parasite density, and febrile responses to the parasites.

It is also of interest that, even in areas of perennial transmission, the incidence of malarial disease is substantially greater with seasonal increases in transmission, suggesting that recent inoculation more frequently leads to disease [40]. Indeed, it appears that many individuals who become symptomatic have encountered a new parasite variant [41].

In the case of *P. vivax* and *P. ovale*, reactivation of dormant hypnozoites can result in long-term relapses. Although *P. falciparum* and *P. malariae* do not produce hypnozoites, untreated or inadequately treated infections may result in persistent low-grade parasitemia, leading to recrudescent disease [42].

### 9.3.5   Epidemiology of Severe Malaria

As the intensity of transmission increases, the proportion of severe malaria cases and mortality is concentrated in lower age groups. In high-transmission areas, severe malaria and death are generally restricted to those below 5 years of age, and most clinical disease occurs below 15 years of age [43, 44]. Severe malaria can include a variety of life-threatening manifestations but usually refers to either severe anemia or conditions with cerebral or neurological involvement [29, 43, 45, 46]. These are distinct clinical sequelae with different epidemiological patterns that are altered by transmission intensity.

In high-transmission areas (e.g., EIR > 100/year), severe anemia predominates in the youngest children from 6 to 24 months of age, whereas cerebral malaria is more common in older children from 36 to 48 months of age. In lower transmission areas (e.g., EIR < 10), severe disease is predominantly cerebral malaria in older children. Interestingly, despite the different manifestations, the number of children experiencing severe disease is similar [44, 47, 48].

These age-specific effects may be related to a combination of increased exposure as well as age-dependent maturation of the immune system [49]. In addition, constancy of transmission appears to influence severe disease. Areas of intense perennial transmission tend toward severe anemia, with cerebral malaria more frequent in areas of seasonal transmission [50]. There is also space-time clustering of severe malaria [51, 52], suggesting that severe malaria occurs in localized microepidemics.

### 9.3.6   Diagnosis and Drug Treatment of Malaria

#### 9.3.6.1   DIAGNOSIS

Diagnosis of malaria infection is generally made by microscopic detection of the parasite in a Geimsa-stained finger-prick blood sample smeared on a glass slide. A thick smear is usually viewed to detect and enumerate parasites, and a thin smear is used for speciation. The ability to detect low-grade infections depends on the number of fields examined and the experience of the technician viewing the slide. Although technologically simple, microscope-based diagnosis requires a trained technician to obtain reliable results.

Additional, although often more expensive, techniques have been developed that allow detection of the parasite by unskilled personnel [53]. Several of these tests, such as the ParaSight-F test, detect circulating malaria antigen in the blood and are available as a dipstick [54]. Others, such as the QBC column, concentrate parasites into a thin band in a centrifuged capillary tube, which is then viewed under a microscope.

#### 9.3.6.2   DRUG TREATMENTS

In non-Western countries, the history of herbal drug use goes back hundreds of years before any effective drugs were available in Europe. In China, derivatives of the plant

Qing-hao-su have been in use for centuries, and pre-Columbian Peruvian healers used tea made from the bark of the cinchona tree. The active ingredient of the cinchona bark, quinine, was extracted in 1820 in Europe. Since then, several drugs have been developed and are in use throughout the world. While a brief synopsis of several drugs is provided here, refer to an informative review for extensive coverage of this topic [55].

Chloroquine, a quinine derivative, was invented in the late 1930s and is active against asexual stages of all human malaria except drug-resistant strains of *P. falciparum*. It is well tolerated, even when taken chronically for long periods, and is safe for young children and pregnant women. It has a prolonged half-life of 33 days, which facilitates its use as a prophylactic drug. The most important side effect is pruritis reported almost uniquely but frequently by black Africans. Owing to its low toxicity and cost and high effectiveness, chloroquine remains the first-line drug of choice in many areas. Additional drugs described next offer various advantages and disadvantages over chloroquine.

Quinine continues to be an important therapeutic agent, especially for drug-resistant *P. falciparum* malaria. However, it has a relatively short shelf life and has more adverse reactions than chloroquine.

Artesunate and related compounds, derived from Qing-hao-su, have demonstrated a high degree of effectiveness with relatively low rates of adverse reactions. The mechanism of action involves rapid oxidative damage of the parasite and is distinct from the mechanism of action of quinine and related compounds. A rapidly absorbed suppository formulation of artesunate for young children is also available. Though relatively new, resistance to this drug has been observed in some patients.

Pyrimethamine and proguanil are effective drugs, but resistance generally occurs relatively quickly.

Sulfadoxine-pyrimethamine (SP), originally developed for efficacy against chloroquine-resistant *P. falciparum*, is widely used in areas of drug resistance and is a folate antagonist. However, prophylactic use has been associated with severe and often fatal adverse reactions. Increasing reports of SP-resistant *P. falciparum* are further limiting usefulness [26].

Mefloquine, another quinine derivative, is widely used for prophylaxis in areas with chloroquine resistance. It is more expensive and has more adverse reactions than chloroquine.

Primaquine is unique in that it has activity against all forms of the malaria parasite occurring in humans. Because of its effect on sporozoites and the hepatic forms, it can be used to prevent the establishment of infection in the liver. However, primaquine also causes hemolysis in those with glucose-6-phosphate dehydrogenase (G6PD) deficiency, a common trait in Africans.

Note that recent developments in chemotherapeutic agents for malaria involve multiple-drug therapy. It is believed that this provides optimal therapy because drugs can be combined that affect different aspects of parasite metabolism. Moreover, this limits emergence of drug-resistant parasites. Various combinations currently in use include artesunate–mefloquine and artesunate–sulfadoxine–pyrimethamine.

### 9.3.7   Host–Parasite Interactions and Immunity

Malaria is a very intense stimulator of the human immune system. Many biological defense systems are activated in response to malaria infections, including the reticuloendothelial system, with great enhancement of phagocytic activities in the spleen, lymph nodes, and liver to remove altered RBCs and other debris, an intense activation of humoral defenses. Indeed, humans can develop several grams per liter of immunoglobulin directed against malaria and a great range of cellular immune and cytokine cascade defenses. Some of these responses are protective, and others may contribute to the pathology.

Despite this intense immune activation, or perhaps because of it, humans do not develop complete immunity. Over a period of years of exposure to the parasite, antidisease immunity may develop in persons living in endemic areas. This is characterized as asymptomatic infections with relatively low levels of circulating parasites. It is currently thought that antibody, and possibly cell-mediated, responses are responsible for this. Individuals may also develop anti-infection immunity that results in decreased presence of new infections. In this case, cell-mediated immunity against the stages that infect liver cells is thought to be the primary effector. It is noteworthy that the exposure-induced immunity is species, and often strain, specific and fades within months if exposure to the parasite is interrupted. While immunity is poorly understood, as mentioned above antibodies to certain parasite proteins have been associated with protection against blood-stage parasites. Moreover, antibody against toxic factors produced by the parasite, such as the glycosylphosphatidyl inositol moiety, have been associated with protection from clinical illness.

As mentioned, *P. falciparum*-infected red cells undergo complex changes, including the expression of protein knobs on the red cell surface [6, 36]. These proteins are highly variable in their antigenic expression and are the products of highly variable "var" genes. Up to 150 different var genes have been identified, which occupy up to 5% of the malaria genome [6]. This commitment to antigenic diversity of the knobs reflects the key role they play in the survival of *P. falciparum*. The var gene proteins also confer adherence to noninfected red cells, a phenomenon known as *rosetting*. These processes facilitate sequestration of the parasite in the microvasculature and may facilitate maturation by keeping parasites in their preferred less-oxygenated blood.

Proteins expressed on vascular endothelium serve as receptors for attachment of infected erythrocytes. Immune mediators such as tumor necrosis factor-$\alpha$ (TNF-$\alpha$) released during infection may activate some of these. Much work has gone into efforts to relate specific phenotypic parasitic characteristics—such as the capacity to stimulate the release of cytokines including TNF-$\alpha$, the production of nitric oxide, and the cytoadherence and rosetting phenotypes (and their underlying genotypes)—to the diversity of clinical events provoked by *P. falciparum* that lead to severe disease [56–59]. Although the rosetting phenotype has been reported as associated with cerebral malaria, no clear association so far has been found between any particular cytoadherance phenotype and cerebral malaria or other forms of severe malaria [44, 60]. There is also evidence that parasites stimulate TNF-$\alpha$, but thus far no pattern has been consistently discerned. What is clear is that great antigenic diversity exists within any given *P. falciparum* population within humans or within vectors [61–63].

These factors underscore the discussed challenges with development of a vaccine against malaria. The relative importance of antibody- and cell-mediated immunity is unclear, but both seem to be involved. Moreover, as mentioned, malaria can vary some of its surface antigens, and different strains of the protozoa have different antigens.

It is anticipated that an effective vaccine against malaria would need to induce both humoral and cellular immunity, possibly against multiple stages of the parasite.

### 9.3.8 Modulating Factors of Malaria Morbidity and Mortality

The formation of small towns arising in concert with agricultural development in much of Africa, Asia, and South America has facilitated malaria transmission by concentrating populations in relatively confined areas near water supplies. The development of small dams and irrigation schemes has also added to anopheline breeding. In addition, the agricultural use of pesticides has been a factor in the development and spread of insecticide-resistant vectors.

From the biomedical perspective, the heavy morbidity and mortality caused by malaria has led to the selection of multiple genetic traits that confer some degree of protection. Most of these involve the red cell and include structural variants in hemoglobin. Variants in the β-globin chain of hemoglobin include hemoglobin S (sickle-cell trait), and hemoglobins C and E. Altered α- and β-chain production results in α- and β-thalassemias. Others traits include erythrocyte enzyme deficiency of G6PD, red cell cytoskeletal abnormalities such as ovalocytosis, and loss of red cell membrane proteins such as Duffy blood group factor [64–66]. In some cases, selection for polymorphisms of immunological effectors, such as TNF-α, has occurred [63]. Most of these genetic polymorphisms are somewhat deleterious to overall health but provide survival advantage in malarious areas.

## 9.4   EFFECTS OF NUTRITION ON MALARIA

### 9.4.1 Early Perceptions of the Impact of Nutrition on Malaria

Prior to 1950, it was widely accepted that malnutrition led to greater susceptibility to malaria. The Indian Famine Commission in 1898 reported that malaria was more frequent and fatal in those suffering from poor diets [67]. Likewise, historical accounts from the late 19th and early 20th centuries indicated that famines and poor economic conditions in north India and Sri Lanka tended to precipitate malaria epidemics, and that the poorer classes experienced greater mortality [68, 69]. Several reports from 1920 to 1940 in Corsica [70], Algeria [70], Vietnam [71], Turkey [72], and Ghana [73] stated that malaria was more frequent and severe among groups and individuals who were undernourished. In 1954, Garnham, a prominent malariologist of his time, stated that in Africa the clinical effects and mortality of malaria were more severe when superimposed on malnourished children [74]. Still, there were reports to the contrary. In 1897, an Italian industrialist unsuccessfully attempted to exploit the fertile but malaria-infested Pontine marshes near Rome by protecting farmers with generous provisions of food and quinine [75]. Some claimed there was no association between nutritional status and malaria morbidity [76], whereas others recounted that increases in food consumption following famines actually exacerbated malaria [77].

Unfortunately, most of these reports were based on qualitative clinical and epidemiological observations or even anecdotal information. Little, if any, quantitative data or methodological information was published to substantiate the conclusions. By the early 1950s, however, clinicians and malariologists began making attempts to quantify more carefully the interactions between nutrition and malaria. Three studies from Ghana and Nigeria published between 1954 and 1971 [78–80] were particularly influential and strongly promoted the notion that malnutrition was in fact protective for malaria. This idea was reinforced by a series of studies by Murray et al. [81–84] from 1975 to 1980 on refeeding and malaria in famine victims from Niger and Sudan. Animal studies appeared to support these reported malaria-suppressive effects of a poor diet, leading to the perception that malnourished children were less susceptible to malaria infection, morbidity, and mortality [85–88]. The following section of the chapter critically assesses these studies, reviews more recent data from humans, and reexamines data from the animal studies.

### 9.4.2 Malnutrition and Malaria: Synergism or Antagonism?

#### 9.4.2.1 MALNOURISHED INDIVIDUALS AND MALARIA MORBIDITY AND MORTALITY

Several studies have examined the association between malnutrition, usually protein-energy malnutrition (PEM), and malaria morbidity and mortality. These are presented in Tables 9.1 and 9.2. Some studies were based on clinic outpatients, whereas others were hospital admissions or community-based cross-sectional studies. Most were case-control studies, but some were longitudinal surveillance of cohorts. Studies with results consistent with the idea that malnutrition exacerbates malaria are labeled as synergistic, whereas those indicating malnutrition protects against malaria are referred to as antagonistic.

##### 9.4.2.1.1 Clinic-Based Studies.
Among the first studies of nutrition and malaria was a large-scale clinic-based study in Uganda [89, 90] (Table 9.1), which concluded that no association existed between nutritional status and malaria mortality. This study was less than ideal as nutritional status was based on qualitative and subjective indicators such as thin or pale hair or being "very" thin, and malaria diagnosis was based only on spleen enlargement, whereas m[ortality risk was estimated by presence or absence of sibling mortality. Another smaller clinic-based study in India reported progressively increasing parasite density with improved nutritional status [91], suggesting that malnutrition was protective. However, two additional studies, one in Brazil [92] and one done on Soviet army personnel [93], reported greater frequency or more severe malaria in those who were malnourished.

##### 9.4.2.1.2 Early Hospital-Based Studies of Severe Malaria.
As mentioned, early hospital-based studies strongly influenced current perceptions of malaria and malnutrition. First, in 1954, an autopsy report by Edington [78] indicated that four Ghanaian children who died from cerebral malaria were all well nourished. Other accounts from South Africa in 1960 [94] reported that malaria was rarely seen in malnourished children. This was followed by another qualitative report from Edington (1967) [95] in Nigeria stating that children dying of cerebral malaria were usually well nourished, and that cerebral malaria was rare in children suffering from kwashiorkor. Case-control studies from Nigeria by Hendrickse in 1967 [79] and 1971 [80] concluded that children suffering from malaria were less likely to be malnourished or have convulsions. Hendrickse also reaffirmed the apparent protection owing to kwashiorkor [79]. A subsequent autopsy report from Nigeria of 25 malnourished children indicated that only 2 had died of malaria [96].

**Table 9.1**

Interaction between malnutrition and *Plasmodium falciparum* (*Pf*): clinic and hospital-based studies

| Reference | Country | Study type | Number of subjects | Age group | Index of nutritional status[a] | Malaria-related outcome | Description of observations | Interaction |
|---|---|---|---|---|---|---|---|---|
| Gongora and colleagues 1959, 1960 [90] | Uganda | Clinic malaria outpatients | 22,000 | <6 yr | Malnutrition | Splenomegaly with sibling mortality | Higher reported sibling mortality in patients with spleen enlargement or malnutrition but no stronger association if both were present | Neutral |
| Ahmad et al. 1985 [91] | India | Clinic malaria outpatients | 75 | Birth–12 yr | Weight for age (Indian standard) | Parasite density | Patients with progressively greater malnutrition had lower *Pf* parasitemia[b] | Antagonistic |
| Pereira et al. 1995 [92] | Brazil | Clinic outpatients: *Pf* patients vs. healthy controls | 120 | 17–72 yr | Weight for height (Quetelet index) | Clinical malaria | *Pf* cases weighed 13% less than healthy controls | Synergistic |
| Liashenko 1997 [93] | Afghanistan, Vietnam, Cambodia | Clinical malaria outpatients: underweight vs. normal weight | 1,342 | Soviet army males ~20–28 yr | Underweight (18% below normal weight) | Clinical malaria immune response | Malnourished. *Pf* patients had lower antibody response to infection, which was associated with greater acute morbidity | Synergistic |
| Hendrickse 1967 [79] | Nigeria | Hospital admissions | 333 | Children | Malnutrition | Parasite density, mortality | Heavy infections more frequently seen in well-nourished children; among malnourished children the cause of death was rarely malaria | Antagonistic |

(continued)

241

Table 9.1 (continued)

Interaction between malnutrition and *Plasmodium falciparum (Pf)*: clinic and hospital-based studies

| Reference | Country | Study type | Number of subjects | Age group | Index of nutritional status[a] | Malaria-related outcome | Description of observations | Interaction |
|---|---|---|---|---|---|---|---|---|
| Hendrickse et al. 1971 [80] | Nigeria | Hospital admissions: *Pf* patients vs. febrile cases | 295 | Birth–10 yr | Malnutrition | Clinical malaria | Malaria patients were 0.82 times as likely to be malnourished, malnutrition in patients approximately six times more frequent than population; malnourished children 0.64 times as likely to have convulsions | Antagonistic and synergistic |
| Razanamparany et al. 1995 [99]; Randriamiharisoa et al. 1993 [100] | Madagascar | Hospital admissions: all *Pf* admissions | 1,549 | Birth–14 yr | Malnutrition (standardized but not described) | Malaria mortality | Malnourished malaria patients 2.5[b] times more likely to die; 73% of all malaria cases were malnourished | Synergistic |
| Olumese et al. 1997 [101] | Nigeria | Hospital admissions: cerebral malaria vs. other causes | 376 | 1–5 yr | Wellcome classification | Malaria mortality | Cerebral malaria patients were 0.40[b] times as likely to be malnourished, but malnourished cerebral malaria patients were 3.5[b] times more likely to die or suffer neurological deficits | Synergistic |

| Source | Country | Sample | N | Age | Measure | Outcome | Results | Interaction |
|---|---|---|---|---|---|---|---|---|
| Renaudin 1997 [113] | Chad | Hospital admissions: all Pf | 1,050 | 1 mo–5 yr | Weight for height (NCHS standard), $\leq 2$ SD | Malaria mortality | Malaria patients were 0.57[b] times as likely to be malnourished, malnourished malaria patients were 1.5[b] times more likely to die | Synergistic |
| Faye et al. 1998 [102] | Senegal | Hospital admissions: Pf death vs. Pf survivors | 104 | <5 | Weight for age (NCHS standard), $\leq 2$ SD | Malaria mortality | Underweight patients 2.8 times more likely to die[b] | Synergistic |
| Man et al. 1998 [104] | The Gambia | Hospital admissions: all Pf | 13,579 | Birth–5 yr | Weight for age (NCHS standard), $\leq 2$ SD | Malaria mortality | Malnourished by WAZ score $\leq 2$: malaria patients were 0.67 times as likely to be malnourished but weighed about 0.35 kg less than control children; overall, children with malaria were 1.30 times more likely to die | Synergistic |
| Nacher et al. 2003 [108] | Thailand | Hospital admissions: Pf cerebral malaria vs. Pf hyperparasitemia | 98 | | | | Cerebral malaria patients were 0.11 times as likely to be malnourished as those with hyperparasitemia[b] | Antagonistic |
| Ong'echa et al. 2006 [106] | Kenya | Hospital admissions | | | | | Wasting was associated with increased risk of malarial anemia[b] | Synergistic |

SD standard deviation

[a]Low height-for-age refers to stunting, low weight-for-age to underweight, and low height-for-age to wasting. In most cases, percentiles were determined by comparison with Harvard or National Center for Health Statistics (NCHS) standards for anthropometry. Malnutrition classification is based on subjective indicators rather than on some standard measure.

[b]Refers to statistically significant finding $p < .05$.

**Table 9.1 (continued)**

Interaction between malnutrition and *Plasmodium falciparum* (*Pf*): cross-sectional and longitudinal studies

| Reference | Country | Study type | Number of subjects | Age group | Index of nutritional status[a] | Malaria-related outcome | Description of observations | Interaction |
|---|---|---|---|---|---|---|---|---|
| Burgess et al. 1975 [109] | Malawi | Cross-sectional survey | 445 | Birth–5 yr | Weight-for-height (Harvard standard), < 80th percentile | Infection rate | Underweight children had greater prevalence of malaria[b] (data not in format that allowed risk estimate) | Synergistic |
| Wenlock 1979 [110] | Zambia | Cross-sectional survey | 6,938 | All ages | Weight-for-age (Harvard standard), < 80th percentile | Infection rate | Underweight children 1.27 times more likely to be infected[b] | Synergistic |
| Sharp and Harvey 1980 [111] | Papua New Guinea | Cross-sectional survey | 166 | Birth–5 yr | Height-for-age (Harvard standard), < 90th percentile | Spleen enlargement | Stunted children 1.9 times more likely to have an enlarged spleen[b] | Synergistic |
| Carswell et al. 1981 [117] | Tanzania | Cross-sectional survey | 244 | School-age children | Weight-for-age, weight-for-height, < 90th percentile | Immune response to parasite | No association between underweight children and antibody levels to malaria antigens | Neutral |
| Mongour et al. 1982 [118] | Burkina Faso | Cross-sectional survey | 165 | 6mo–3 yr | Weight-for-age (Harvard standard), < 70th percentile | Infection rate | Underweight children 0.90 times as likely to be infected | Neutral |
| El Samani et al. 1987 [112] | Sudan | Cross-sectional survey | 445 | Birth–5 yr | Weight-for-age (NCHS standard), < 90th percentile | Signs of malaria illness | Stunted children 1.4 times more likely to have recent malaria illness (not slide confirmed malaria)[b] | Synergistic |

244

| Author | Country | Study design | N | Age | Measure | Outcome | Finding | Synergistic or antagonistic |
|---|---|---|---|---|---|---|---|---|
| Dominiguez-Vasquez and Alzate Sanchez 1990 [116] | Colombia | Cross-sectional survey | 124 | Birth–6yr | Height-for-age, weight-for-height (Waterlow) | Immune response | Underweight children had decreased antibody responses to malaria antigens | Synergistic |
| Ranaudin and Lombart 1994 [113] | Chad | Cross-sectional survey | 144 | Birth–1yr | Weight-for-age (NCHS standard), <90th percentile | Infection rate | Malnourished children 1.54 times more likely to be infected[b] | Synergistic |
| Tshikuka et al. 1997 [114] | Zaire | Cross-sectional survey | 558 | 4mo–10yr | Height-for-age, weight-for-height (NCHS standard), ≤2 SD | Infection rate | Malnourished children 1.23 times more likely to be infected[b] | Synergistic |
| Mamiro et al. 2005 [120] | Tanzania | Cross-sectional survey | 309 | 6mo | | | Stunting associated with malaria infection[b] | Synergistic |
| Friedman et al. 2005 [121] | Kenya | Cross-sectional survey | | Birth–3yr | | | Stunted children 1.98 or 1.77 times more likely to be infected or have clinical malaria, respectively[b] | Synergistic |

(continued)

Table 9.1 (continued)
Interaction between malnutrition and *Plasmodium falciparum* (*Pf*): cross-sectional and longitudinal studies

| Reference | Country | Study type | Number of subjects | Age group | Index of nutritional status[a] | Malaria-related outcome | Description of observations | Interaction |
|---|---|---|---|---|---|---|---|---|
| Ehrhardt et al. 2006 [119] | Ghana | Cross-sectional survey | ~4000 | | | | Malnourished children 1.67 times more likely to have clinical malaria[b] | Synergistic |
| Sturchler et al. 1987 [239] | Tanzania | Longitudinal surveillance (multiple cross-sectional surveys of same cohort) | 170 | 1 mo–15 yr | Low growth | Infection rate | Children with low growth tended to be more frequently infected[b] | Synergistic |
| Snow et al. 1991 [126] | The Gambia | Longitudinal surveillance | 138 | 1–4 yr | Weight-for-age, height-for-age, weight-for-height (NCHS standard), ≦ 2 SD | Clinical malaria, parasite density | No impact of nutritional status on clinical malaria; nonsignificant tendency for higher parasite density in well-nourished children | Neutral |

246

| Reference | Country | Study design | No. | Age | Nutritional indicator | Malaria outcome | Findings | Conclusion |
|---|---|---|---|---|---|---|---|---|
| Williams et al. 1997 [123] | Vanuatu | Longitudinal surveillance of malaria attacks for 1 yr | 1511 | Birth–10 yr | | | Underweight children likely to have an attack of *P. vivax*[b] and a tendency toward more attacks by *Pf* | Synergistic |
| Genton et al. 1998 [121] | Papua New Guinea | Longitudinal surveillance of malaria attacks for 1 yr | 136 | 10 mo–5 yr | Height-for-age, weight-for-height (NCHS standard), ≦2 SD | Clinical malaria | Stunted children had lower risk for malaria attacks[b]; antimalaria cell-mediated immunity higher in stunted children,[b] but antibody responses to malaria lower in underweight children[b] | Antagonistic with some synergistic |
| Tonglet et al. 1999 [118] | Congo | Longitudinal surveillance (3-month staggered cohorts for 1 yr) | 842 | Birth–2 yr | Weight-for-age, height-for-age, arm circumference (NCHS standard), ≦2 SD | Clinical malaria (not slide confirmed) | Malnourished children tended to have more malaria attacks if <9 months old | Synergistic |
| Deen et al. 2002 [119] | The Gambia | Longitudinal surveillance | 487 | Birth–5 yr | | | Stunted children 1.35 times more likely to have malaria episode[b] | Synergistic |

(continued)

Table 9.1 (continued)

Interaction between malnutrition and *Plasmodium falciparum* (*Pf*): cross-sectional and longitudinal studies

| Reference | Country | Study type | Number of subjects | Age group | Index of nutritional status[a] | Malaria-related outcome | Description of observations | Interaction |
|---|---|---|---|---|---|---|---|---|
| Caulfield et al. 2004 [123] | Vanuatu [117], The Gambia [120], Ghana [125], Senegal [126], Guinea Bissau [127] | Meta-analysis of cross-sectional and longitudinal studies | Cross-sectional: |1828 Longitudinal: ~45,000 | Cross sectional: ? Longitudinal: Birth–1 yr or to 5 yr | | | Cross sectional: underweight children 1.31 times more likely to have clinical malaria (non-significant)<br><br>Longitudinal: underweight children more than 4 to 9 times more likely to die from malaria[b] | Synergistic<br><br>Synergistic |

*SD* standard deviation

[a]Low height-for-age refers to stunting, low weight-for-age to underweight, and low height-for-ageto wasting. In most cases, percentiles were determined by comparison with Harvard or National Center for Health Statistics (NCHS) standards for anthropometry. Malnutrition classification based on subjective indicators rather than on some standard measure.

[b]Refers to statistically significant finding $p < .05$.

**9.4.2.1.3 Critical Analysis of the Early Hospital-Based Studies.** Although these reports appeared convincing of a protective effect of malnutrition on malaria, several characteristics of the studies weaken such conclusions. Most important, the study populations were comprised of clinic cases or malnourished children, and comparisons were made between those with or without malaria. In the absence of healthy community controls, one can only conclude that malaria is less exacerbated by malnutrition than other conditions. The overall prevalence of malnutrition among malaria cases in these studies was remarkably high, suggesting possible synergy with malnutrition. A more informative analysis would have included the relationship between the degree of malnutrition among malaria cases and the risk of malaria mortality. Unfortunately, such analyses were not done, partly because relatively nonstandardized qualitative descriptors rather than quantitative assessments were used to categorize malnutrition. In some studies, incomplete analyses of the existing data were made. For example, Hendrickse reported decreased risk of convulsions in malnourished malaria patients, but the same decline in convulsion risk was also observed for malnourished nonmalaria patients [97]. Additional caveats reside in the lack of information on socioeconomic status (SES) or residence of the cases. Well-nourished cases may tend to come from the urban areas and have less acquired immunity, whereas malnourished cases could come from outlying higher-transmission areas, leading to greater immunity. Indeed, Edington reported that the children suffering from cerebral malaria tended to have less hookworm [95], an observation possibly related to SES. Last, the conclusions based on patients suffering from kwashiorkor may not be generalizable to overall malnutrition because aflatoxins, a causative agent of kwashiorkor, are toxic to malaria parasites in vitro and in vivo [97, 98].

**9.4.2.1.4 Modern Hospital-Based Studies of Severe Malaria.** In the last 15 years, additional studies have been completed on the relationship between malnutrition and malaria. These have tended to be larger studies that more carefully documented nutritional status by reference standards using height, weight, and age and have evaluated malnutrition as a risk factor for malaria mortality among hospital admissions. Studies (Table 9.1) conducted in Madagascar [99, 100], Nigeria [101], Senegal [102], Chad [103], the Gambia [104], and Ghana [105] indicated that malnourished patients are 1.3–3.5 times more likely to die or suffer permanent neurological sequelae compared to normally nourished malaria patients. In addition, the study from the Gambia indicated that malaria patients typically weighed 350 g less than healthy control children [104]. A recent study from Kenya among hospital admissions for severe malaria anemia indicated that wasting was strongly associated with this outcome [106].

It is also important to note that, in many of these studies, as seen by Hendrickse, malnourished hospital patients were less likely to be suffering from malaria as compared to other conditions. This is consistent with the notion that malaria may be exacerbated by malnutrition to a lesser degree than other diseases. Indeed, additional analyses in the Gambia study [104] confirmed the greater impact of malnutrition on risk of death from diarrhea and pneumonia.

In contrast to these reports, a study of 60 hospital patients in India indicated that parasitemia tended to increase with improving nutritional status; however, no data on clinical outcomes were presented [107]. A more recent hospital-based case-control study from Thailand indicated that adult patients suffering from cerebral malaria were more likely to be well nourished than those admitted for nonsevere malaria [108]. Unfortunately, because the controls were not systematically selected from the same geographical area as the cases, differences in parasite strains or other factors could not be excluded as contributors to this finding. Alternatively, one interpretation may be that the relationship between malnutrition and malaria is modulated by the local epidemiology of malaria and perhaps malnutrition. As such, malnutrition could possibly be protective in some areas and conditions and exacerbative in others. However, considering the available data in toto, it would appear that malnutrition considerably increases the risk of severe malaria morbidity and death.

It should also be appreciated that certain age-dependent relationships may underlie some inconsistencies linking malnutrition and malaria in humans. Severe clinical malaria is more frequent in young children (i.e., < 3 years) and tends toward severe malaria anemia. In contrast, for older children (i.e., > 3 years), cerebral malaria is more frequently encountered. Likewise, various indicators of nutritional status have age-dependent distributions. Wasting (low weight-for-height) is seen more frequently in young children than in older children, for whom stunting (low height-for-age) is generally more prevalent. Thus, if such age-based differences were not taken into account, a clinic or hospital-based study of severe malaria cases could erroneously conclude that wasting was protective for cerebral malaria.

Additional study of the epidemiology of hospital-based severe malaria would be useful to examine confounding factors such as age, SES, immunity and disease ecology.

**9.4.2.1.5   Cross-Sectional Studies of Malariometric Indicators.** Several cross-sectional surveys (Table 9.2) also favor a synergistic relationship between malnutrition and malaria. Studies carried out in Malawi [109], Zambia [110], Papua New Guinea [111], Sudan [112], Chad [113], Zaire [114], and Tanzania [115] indicated greater risk for infection [109, 110, 113, 114], malaria illness [112, 115], or spleen enlargement [111] among malnourished children. A study in Colombia indicated that malnourished children had lower antimalaria antibody levels [116]. This could be interpreted as a synergistic effect if malnutrition suppresses antibody response to malaria or possibly as antagonistic if malnutrition protects against infection, thereby precluding formation of parasite-specific antibody. In Tanzania, there was no effect of nutritional status on antiparasite antibody levels [117], and a study in Burkina Faso [118] found no association between malaria infection and nutritional status.

Several additional reports indicated significant associations between malnutrition and malaria. A survey of more than 4,000 children in northern Ghana indicated that malnutrition was associated with clinical malaria (odds ratio [OR] 1.67; 95% confidence interval [CI] 1.10–2.50) [119]. Similarly, a survey in Tanzania, where more than 50% of the infants are infected with *P. falciparum,* indicated that stunting was associated with malaria [120], and in Kenya stunted preschool children were about 1.5–2.5 times more likely to be infected and to have high-density parasitemia, clinical malaria, or severe malarial anemia [121].

**9.4.2.1.6   Longitudinal Cohort Studies and Effects of Nutrition on Drug-Resistant Malaria.** Last, longitudinal cohort studies in Tanzania [122], Vanuatu [123], and Congo [124] indicated that malnutrition predisposes children to malaria illness. Another longitudinal study from the Gambia also indicated that stunted, but not underweight or wasted, preschool children were at increased risk for malaria episodes [125]. In contrast, an earlier report from the Gambia [126] indicated little effect of malnutrition on malaria attacks. Another report from Papua New Guinea suggested that stunted children may be more resistant to malaria attacks [127], although this protection was not seen in underweight children. In this study, it is of interest that the stunted children also exhibited increased immune responses to malaria antigens, suggesting increased exposure, whereas the wasted children had suppressed responses. One additional semi-ilongitudinal study (multiple cross-sectional cohort surveys) in Zaire [128] reported no association between nutritional status and malaria mortality. It should, however, be noted that no causes of death were actually established, and the authors assumed that deaths were due to malaria. Another longitudinal follow-up study of daily active case detection from Burkina Faso found no association between malnutrition and clinical malaria [129]. The highly sensitive surveillance methodology used in this study would be biased toward detecting differences in the onset of a malaria episode and not necessarily the subsequent severity. Still, it may be of interest that the cross-sectional study from Burkina Faso mentioned also found no association between malaria and malnutrition.

An interesting study was published that estimated the proportion of global malaria morbidity and mortality due to malnutrition [130]. For malaria morbidity, the authors pooled longitudinal follow-up data from two [123, 126] field studies and interpreted the effects in the context of the global prevalence of underweight children. A similar process was performed for malaria deaths as determined by verbal autopsy from three studies [131–133]. The authors estimated that 8.2% of global malaria morbidity and 57% of malaria mortality were due to children being underweight. Despite the caveats of limited data, fusing morbidity data for *P. falciparum* and *P. vivax*, and reliance on verbal autopsies, the results provide a general estimate of the overall impact of malnutrition on malaria.

Additional evidence of an exacerbative role of malnutrition on malaria can be seen in several longitudinal drug resistance studies. Malnourished Rwandan refugees had slower parasite clearance, higher parasite titers at presentation, and more severe drug resistance [134]. Likewise, in the Solomon Islands, malnourished children were 3.6 times more likely to have drug-resistant malaria [135, 136]. More recent work in Malawi showed that severely malnourished children were three times more likely to experience treatment failures than those better nourished [137].

### 9.4.2.2 STUDIES IN FAMINE RELIEF

The Murray family examined the presence of malaria in famine victims during nutritional rehabilitation in a series of studies. During the Sahelian famine in Niger, victims were admitted to a hospital for refeeding, and it was observed that *P. falciparum* malaria developed in many of these individuals within a few days [82], often resulting in cerebral pathology. Because there was no transmission of malaria at the hospital, it was believed that feeding had provided essential nutrients for sequestered parasites, leading to recrudescent infection [81, 82]. In another study, famine victims were given either grain or milk for rehabilitation, and it was observed that those given grain were more likely to experience recrudescent cerebral malaria [83]. These studies suggested that quality as well as quantity of the diet is an important determinant of malaria morbidity. The previously mentioned 1945 report of the Bengal Famine Commission also stated that refeeding tended to precipitate malaria disease in those carrying low-grade infections [77]. The Murrays concluded that the interaction between poor diet and malaria is part of an ecological balance between humans and malaria, which was interpreted as a beneficial aspect of malnutrition.

### 9.4.2.3 STUDIES IN ANIMALS

A variety of animal experiments have also contributed to the idea that PEM reduces malaria morbidity. Early work showed that monkeys maintained on a low-protein diet did indeed have lower parasitemia [138–141]. However, the animals either were unable to clear the infection, resulting in multiple recrudescences [139], or parasitemia appeared earlier and lasted longer [141]. Immune responses were also suppressed [141]. However, for monkeys suffering from cerebral malaria, protein-deprived animals had fewer parasitized erythrocytes in the cerebral capillaries and did not develop the disrupted endothelium seen in normally fed monkeys. Still, cerebral and pulmonary edema was present in all animals irrespective of dietary regimen [142].

The primate experiments were complemented by a variety of informative data from studies of rodent malaria. A comprehensive series of investigations by Ramakrishnan et al. in the early 1950s indicated that malaria parasitemia was less severe in protein-deprived rats, and that survival was enhanced [143–147]. He also showed that methionine and para-amino benzoic acid (PABA) promoted infection in starving rats [143]. Importantly, it was also clear that protein-deprived animals were unable to clear the infection [147], and that protein restriction in young rats exacerbated malaria parasitemia and mortality [144]. Moreover, parasite densities were higher and more lethal during relapses in protein-deprived animals [147]. Last, starved animals experienced strong relapse infections when food was given [144].

Additional studies by Edirisinghe et al. [87, 148–151] documented that acute and chronic protein deprivation depressed peak parasitemia more than 75% and prevented death. However, as shown in previous work, the animals were unable to clear the infection [150], and antibodies preventing parasite growth did not adequately develop. Elegant work by Fern et al. [151] then demonstrated that readdition of threonine to a low-protein diet restored susceptibility, and that this effect was enhanced by valine, isoleucine, and methionine. However, phenylalanine, tyrosine, lysine, histidine, and tryptophan did not appear to have this promoting effect.

Subsequent studies in rats and mice confirmed that low-protein diets suppressed parasitemia [152–156] and inhibited cell-mediated immunity [152, 153], and that effects were reversible by addition of PABA [153]. Effects on mortality were, however, less consistent. In some cases, low-protein diets suppressed parasitemia, but mortality was higher, albeit delayed [157]. Addition of threonine and methionine to the low-protein diet decreased mortality [157], although methionine and threonine alone had no effect when added to the deficient diet. Others observed no effect on mortality in moderately malnourished mice, but increased death was seen in severely malnourished animals [158]. Protein-deficient diets were, however, consistently protective for rodent cerebral malaria [155, 156, 159].

### 9.4.2.4 SYNTHESIS OF DATA CONCERNING EFFECTS OF PROTEIN-ENERGY MALNUTRITION ON MALARIA

The considerable body of data from humans and animals, though complex, provides ample evidence to draw some conclusions regarding the interaction between malnutrition and malaria. Although it has been frequently mentioned that malnutrition is protective for malaria [85–88], modern and recent studies along with careful reexamination of the older human studies and data from animals indicate that malnutrition does indeed exacerbate malaria and considerably increases the likelihood of mortality.

The human hospital-based studies suggesting a protective effect of malnutrition are inconclusive owing to the many methodological and design issues mentioned. Similarly, the animal-based data, often cited as supportive evidence that malnutrition is protective, are not so clear when carefully examined. Closer inspection reveals that although parasitemia tends to be lower in poorly fed animals, they are unable to clear the infection, and immune responses to the parasite are suppressed. This leads to more chronic infections and more severe relapses. Also, the observation that malnutrition is particularly deleterious for malaria in younger animals is important. In cerebral malaria, poor diets appear protective for animals, but human data indicate that malnourished children are more likely to die from cerebral malaria. This discrepancy may be rooted in differences in the etiology of cerebral pathology in animals and humans.

The famine or starvation situation is, however, a special case, and it is consistently observed in humans and animals that refeeding an infected starved host reactivates low-grade infections. The implication is that antimalarial measures should be included during nutritional rehabilitation of famine victims.

### 9.4.3  Impact of Malaria on Growth

Although malnutrition appears to exacerbate malaria, it is also true that malaria itself results in growth failure and is a contributing factor to malnutrition. Several reports from Africa have noted a transient weight loss in young African children following a malaria attack [160–162]. In the Gambia, two longitudinal cohort studies indicated that *P. falciparum* malaria was significantly related to lower weight gain and growth faltering, particularly in children below 36 months of age [163, 164]. Other studies have attempted to compare weights in different communities with different levels of malaria. In El Salvador, no differences in weight or height were observed in areas with low or high transmission of *P. vivax* [165]. In contrast, researchers in Papua New Guinea found significantly greater malnourished individuals in villages with high *P. falciparum* transmission intensity compared to control villages with lower transmission [111], and longitudinal follow-up of preschool children in Kenya indicated that *P. falciparum* infection increased the risk of being underweight or stunted, particularly in children up to 2 years of age [166]. An interesting recent longitudinal study of male adolescents and adults in Kenya indicated that malaria infection and related production of TNF-$\alpha$, a proinflammatory cytokine, were associated with reduced weight gain [167].

Additional studies of chemoprophylaxis provided more definitive evidence for the effects of malaria on growth. A 1-year placebo-controlled trial of pyrimethamine prophylaxis in 176 Ghanaian 7-year old children resulted in a nonsignificant 78 g excess weight gain in those taking pyrimethanine [168]. In a small 2-year study in the Gambia [169] of 52 children randomized to chloroquine prophylaxis or placebo at birth, unprotected children weighed significantly less between 6 and 24 months. Another 2-year study in Nigeria that followed 198 children given chloroquine prophylaxis or a placebo shortly after birth found that protected children tended to have greater height, weight, mid-upper arm circumference (MUAC), and mean serum albumin levels, although the differences were relatively small [170]. Interestingly only 1 child given chloroquine died from malnutrition, compared to 6 such deaths in the control group.

Moderate effects on nutritional status were also observed following other malaria interventions. The Garki Project (1980) examined the effects of prolonged and large-scale insecticide spraying and chemoprophylaxis on nutritional parameters in a northern Nigerian community and observed small but significant changes in weight gain and MUAC [171]. However, similar interventions in Tanzania found no effect in 2- to 18-month-old children after malaria control [172] Snow et al. in Kenya followed 1,500 children 1–11 months of age, half of whom slept under insecticide-treated bed nets [173]. The number of children classified as malnourished was 25% less in those using ITNs, and MUACs were also increased. A similar study of bed nets and treatment on demand in Tanzania found that protected children gained more weight, with the strongest effects seen in those less than 18 months of age [174]. Likewise, bed nets were associated with a 1.2% increase in percent lean body mass in Kenyan children less than 13 years of age [175]. A study from Vietnam in which multiple annual anthropometric surveys were performed along with integrated malaria control measures over a 4- to 5-year period revealed an annual increase of height-for-age Z-score of 0.11–0.14 extending into preadolescent age [176].

### 9.4.4 Influence of Specific Nutrients on Malaria Morbidity

#### 9.4.4.1 IRON

Iron deficiency affects nearly 2 billion people worldwide, resulting in over 500 million cases of anemia [177]. Additional sequelae include poor neurological development, lower work capacity, LBW, and increased maternal and infant mortality [178, 179]. The burden of both iron deficiency and malaria falls primarily on preschool children and pregnant women [180, 181], and iron supplementation of these groups is the primary means of prevention and treatment of anemia. Multiple studies have attempted to evaluate the benefit of iron supplementation in malaria endemic areas [84, 182–202]. Some of these studies reported that iron supplementation increased the risk of developing or reactivating malarial illness [84, 182, 185], whereas others reported no significant adverse effects [190, 193, 203]. To resolve this issue, a systematic review and meta-analysis of controlled trials of iron supplementation was completed [204]. A search produced 13 trials [84, 182–193], totaling 5,230 subjects, from which data were pooled to obtain composite effects of iron supplements on malaria attack rates, parasite prevalence, parasite density, prevalence of enlarged spleens, hemoglobin levels, and anemia.

Iron supplementation resulted in a nonsignificant 9% (relative risk [RR] 1.09, 95% CI 0.92–1.30, n = 8) increase in the risk of a malaria attack. End-of-trial cross-sectional data indicated a 17% (RR 1.17, 95% CI 1.08–1.25, n = 13) greater risk of infection in those given iron. Qualitative assessment of parasite density suggested a tendency toward higher levels in those receiving iron. However, hemoglobin levels improved by 1.2 g/dL (95% CI 1.2–1.3, n = 11) following iron supplementation, and the risk of anemia was reduced by 50% (RR 0.50, 95% CI 0.45–0.54, n = 4). Thus, there were substantial benefits as well.

Although the meta-analysis indicated exacerbative effects of iron on malaria and reductions in anemia, it was unable to address the issue of severe malaria. However, a large-scale trial in Tanzanian preschool children indicated that daily oral iron supplementation at current WHO recommended doses resulted in an 11% (1–23%,

$p = .03$) increased risk of all-cause hospitalization and a nonsignificant 15% (−7 to 41, $p = .19$) increase in all-cause mortality [205]. These effects were not observed in a similar trial in Nepal, where malaria transmission is relatively low [206], suggesting a substantial role for *P. falciparum* in the excess morbidity and mortality. It should be noted that the children received folic acid along with the iron, and this may also have influenced the results. However, these data are consistent with other recent studies indicating adverse effects of iron supplementation on *P. vivax* [207, 208] and a report from Kenya indicating that iron-deficient children were less likely to experience *P. falciparum* morbidity [209].

The mechanisms for this effect on malaria remain unknown. However, recent discoveries indicated immunomodulatory effects of non-transferrin-bound iron (NTBI) [210]. Specifically, NTBI increased the expression of adhesion molecules, intracellular adhesion molecule 1 (ICAM-1), vascular cell adhesion molecule 1 (VCAM-1), and E-selectin, thereby indicating a role in adhesion-mediated processes that have been implicated in the pathology of *P. falciparum* malaria. In addition, it has been demonstrated that anemic erythrocytes containing elevated zinc protoporphyrin IX can inhibit parasite replication [211]. Iron supplementation may therefore lead to conditions that are more favorable for parasite growth. Additional pathways may involve the recently discovered iron-regulatory peptide known as hepcidin [212].

As a body of evidence, current data indicate that routine supplementation with iron in preschool children in areas with malaria can result in an increased risk of severe illness and death. As such, current guidelines for universal supplementation with iron may need to be revisited. If iron supplementation is considered, co-implementation with antimalaria activities would be strongly warranted. The role of iron-fortified foods or food additives for improving iron status should also be evaluated for potential adverse effects on malaria.

### 9.4.4.2 ZINC

Zinc is essential for normal immune function [213] and has been shown to reduce the incidence of diarrhea and pneumonia [214]. Indeed, zinc is essential for a variety of lymphocyte functions implicated in resistance to malaria, including production of immunoglobulin G (IgG), interferon-$\gamma$ (IFN-$\gamma$), and TNF-$\alpha$ and microbicidal activity of macrophages [213, 215].

Cross-sectional studies among school-aged children in Papua New Guinea [216] and pregnant women in Malawi [217] have reported inverse associations between measures of zinc status and *P. falciparum* parasitemia. In addition, a placebo-controlled trial of zinc supplementation in preschool children in the Gambia documented a 30% reduction in health center attendance owing to *P. falciparum* [218], although this was not statistically significant. Last, mildly zinc-deficient mice experienced mortality from a normally nonlethal strain of *P. yoelii* [219], and zinc supplements decreased markers of oxidative stress during infection with *P. berghei* [220].

A placebo-controlled trial of zinc supplementation of preschool children in Papua New Guinea provided additional evidence for the role of zinc in malaria. The study indicated that zinc supplementation reduced by 38% (95% CI 3–60, $p = .037$) the frequency of health center attendance owing to *P. falciparum* malaria. Moreover, a 69% (95% CI 25–87, $p = .009$) reduction was observed for malaria episodes accompanied by high levels of parasitemia (i.e., $\geq 100{,}000$ parasites/$\mu$L), suggesting that zinc may preferentially protect against more severe malaria episodes [221]. A subsequent trial of daily zinc supplementation of preschool children in Burkina Faso indicated no protective effect on *P. falciparum* [222]. However, the active daily case detection and rapid treatment, coupled with high levels of asymptomatic parasitemia, may have masked an effect of zinc on malaria attacks, particularly more severe ones. As such, these results are difficult to compare with those from the clinic-based surveillance in the trials from Papua New Guinea and the Gambia. A subsequent randomized controlled trial in the Peruvian Amazon of daily zinc and iron supplementation indicated that zinc, both alone and with iron, decreased *P. vivax* attacks more than 50% among children younger than 5 years [208]. Most recently, a large-scale trial in Tanzania evaluated the impact of daily zinc supplementation on mortality in preschool children. The study indicated a tendency for zinc supplements to reduce malaria mortality [223].

Given the initial reports of the effects of routine zinc supplementation on malaria, a multicenter trial was carried out to examine if zinc would reduce malaria morbidity if given as an adjunct to treatment. The results of this clinic-based study indicated that although a 4-day course of zinc improved plasma zinc status, there was no impact on parasitological or clinical outcomes for uncomplicated *P. falciparum* [224]. It may be that the mechanism by which zinc affects malaria requires more than several days of supplementation to have an impact. If so, one would not expect to observe an impact on treatment of malaria.

While additional information is needed to document the geographic regions and conditions of malaria transmission in which zinc might be effective, evidence is growing for a protective role of zinc on malaria. As such, it has been estimated based on existing data that zinc deficiency contributes about 20% to the global burden of malaria morbidity and mortality [130]. This provides considerable motivation for continued assessment of the impact of zinc on malaria and to explore the potential of improving zinc status as part of the integrated efforts to reduce the global burden of malaria.

### 9.4.4.3 VITAMIN A

Vitamin A is essential for normal immune function [225], and several studies suggested it could play a role in potentiating resistance to malaria. Early work in vitamin A-deficient ducks indicated that vitamin A deficiency exacerbated malaria, but it had little effect on malaria in chicks [226]. Further studies in vitamin A-deficient rats and mice showed an increased susceptibility to malaria that was readily reversed by supplementation [227, 228]. In addition, a genetic locus, which includes cellular retinol-binding protein 1, has been shown to modulate malaria mortality and parasitemia in mice [229]. Subsequent in vitro studies showed that addition of free retinol to *P. falciparum* cultures reduced parasite replication in two studies [230, 231], although this was not seen in another [232].

In humans, cross-sectional studies in preschool children and in adults have reported inverse associations between plasma vitamin A levels and *P. falciparum* parasitemia [233–238]. However, this observation could be due to the acute-phase response following infection, which tends to lower plasma vitamin A levels. One study observed that low baseline vitamin A status was associated with increased risk of parasitemia, but confounding by age could not be excluded [239]. Subsequently, a substudy of a vitamin A trial in preschool children in Ghana reported no statistically significant effects of vitamin A on *P. falciparum* morbidity or mortality [240]. However, longitudinal surveillance of slide-confirmed malaria morbidity was not conducted [241]. Another trial of vitamin A supplementation in children reported no effect on malaria parasitemia [242]. In contrast, additional evidence for a role of vitamin A in malaria infection includes selective depletion of plasma-borne provitamin A carotenoids during acute malaria attacks [233, 243] and some indication of modest protection against malaria morbidity from consumption of carotenoid-rich red palm oil [244].

The most definitive study to date of the effects of vitamin A on malaria was completed in Papua New Guinea [245]. The study, a double-blind, placebo-controlled trial, indicated that vitamin A supplementation reduced the frequency of *P. falciparum* episodes by 30% (95% CI 14–43, $p = .0013$) among preschool children. At the end of the study, geometric mean parasite density was 36% lower in the vitamin A than the placebo group, and the proportion of children with spleen enlargement was reduced by 11%, although neither difference was significant. However, it was clear that children aged 12–36 months benefited most, having 35% (95% CI 14–50, $p = .0023$) fewer malaria attacks, 26% fewer enlarged spleens, and a 68% reduction in parasite density.

These data have subsequently been affirmed by reports indicating that vitamin A supplements could offset the adverse effect of malaria on childhood growth [242], and that vitamin A supplements may protect pregnant women against malaria [246]. There is also preliminary evidence that vitamin A may reduce the severity of malaria when given as an adjunct to treatment [247]. While the mechanism underlying the effects of vitamin A on malaria are not fully characterized, one study indicated that vitamin A may help upregulate CD36 expression and facilitate phagocytosis of parasitized erythrocytes as well as limit pathological processes related to cerebral malaria [248].

Overall, the evidence indicates that vitamin A is important in resistance to malaria in humans, and quantitative estimates of disease burden indicated that vitamin A deficiency may account for about 20% of global malaria morbidity and mortality [130]. As for zinc, this provides impetus to improve vitamin A status as part of overall efforts to reduce the disease burden of malaria.

#### 9.4.4.4 B VITAMINS

##### 9.4.4.4.1 Folate.
Folate is a crucial nutrient for cellular growth, including cell-mediated immunity, and DNA and protein synthesis. It is crucial for erythrocyte production. As such, folate supplements are often given in conjunction with iron to treat or prevent anemia. For this reason, and for its role in preventing neural tube defects, folate supplementation along with iron is part of routine prenatal care in most countries. Given that folate metabolism of the parasite is also a target for several antimalarial drugs, such as SP, the interactions between host folate status and malaria are of interest. Indeed, the observation that some parasite strains can access exogenous folate, thereby bypassing drug-impaired folate synthesis, places greater importance on host folate status [249].

Initial studies indicated that folate deficiency enhanced susceptibility to avian malaria [250]. In contrast, primate malaria species were unable to survive in severely folate-deficient rhesus monkeys [251]. This protective effect of folate deficiency differs from observations in humans; low infection rates have been reported in pregnant women consuming a diet high in folates [252]. In addition, greater infection rates have been reported in those suffering from megaloblastic anemia [253], a sign of folate deficiency. However, these findings may be influenced by the observation that malaria itself may induce folate deficiency [253–255], and that folate utilization is dysregulated in infected erythrocytes [256].

A trial of prophylactic folate supplementation in preschool children in the Gambia [257] showed no adverse effects for malaria. A trial of folate supplements in pregnant women [258] showed no adverse effect on parasitemia, even though reticulocyte counts did increase. Two separate trials reported that development of *P. falciparum* in vivo was not affected by folate supplements given with pyrimethamine [258, 259]. In one case, the folate dose given was sufficient to reverse the side effects of high-dose pyrimethamine [260]. These studies led to the notion that folate supplementation affected neither malaria disease outcome nor the effect of drug treatment with pyrimethamine. Indeed, the routine use of folate supplements in malarious areas has been advocated [253, 261].

However, in the mid-1990s a randomized controlled trial from Africa indicated greater treatment failure for SP when folate supplements were given [262]. This finding, particularly the delayed clearance of parasitemia, was confirmed in two trials in Kenya and Zambia [263, 264] in which folic acid was given along with SP. However, it has also been demonstrated that intermittent prophylactic therapy with SP for pregnant women was not adversely affected by consumption of folic acid supplements [265].

As a whole, these data indicate that routine use of folic acid supplements in malarious areas may be contraindicated if SP is the primary treatment regimen, and that therapeutic supplementation with folic acid to treat malaria-related anemia may best be delayed until parasite clearance is achieved. Formal review of the existing evidence and subsequent recommendations are warranted.

**9.4.4.4.2   Riboflavin.** Riboflavin status also influences malaria morbidity. The relationship appears to be one of antagonism such that deficiency confers a degree of protection. Reports from Papua New Guinea [266, 267] indicated that riboflavin-deficient infants were less likely to be infected. Similar observations were made in India [268, 269] and the Gambia [270]. In India, clinical malaria was also less severe in riboflavin-deficient individuals [271]. However, a more recent study in Gabon using high-performance liquid chromatography to assess riboflavin status, rather than the traditional erythrocyte glutathione reductase assay, did not find an association between riboflavin status and parasitemia [272]. A study in which both methods are used would be useful, as would assessment of the effects of riboflavin on malaria in the context of a randomized trial.

Because riboflavin is an essential factor for the enzyme glutathione peroxidase, an antioxidative enzyme, it has been proposed that deficiency promotes an oxidative environment that leads to destruction of the parasite. Indeed, lipid peroxidation was increased in riboflavin-deficient children with malaria infection [273], and reduced glutathione peroxidase activity was observed in red cells from riboflavin-deficient infected individuals [274]. Consistent with this notion is the observation that reduced glutathione activity persists in some populations residing in malarious areas despite adequate riboflavin intake [275], suggesting that isoforms with reduced activity confer resistance to malaria.

There is evidence for other mechanisms as well. *Plasmodium falciparum*-infected erythrocytes have an increased requirement for riboflavin [276]. Moreover, riboflavin analogs inhibit the growth of parasites in vitro [277, 278] and in vivo in experimental murine malaria [278]. In some cases, these activities also correlated with reduced activity of glutathione reductase [277]. Riboflavin-deficient rats are also more resistant to malaria [279]. However, riboflavin-deficient chicks are more susceptible [280]. Interestingly, additional work in rats suggested that the protective effect may be mediated by mechanisms that do not involve increased susceptibility of erythrocytes to oxidative damage, hemolysis, or erythropoiesis [281].

Although human and animal data suggest riboflavin deficiency is protective, in vitro studies suggested that high doses of riboflavin suppress parasite growth by preventing the oxidation of hemoglobin needed by the parasite [282]. Thus, high-dose riboflavin therapy could possibly be of benefit. Interestingly, the protective or exacerbative effects of riboflavin are based on different sites of action for the same antioxidant properties. This again emphasizes the complex pathways through which nutrients may influence malaria parasites and host morbidity.

**9.4.4.4.3   Thiamine.** Reports from Thailand indicated that poor thiamine status is associated with greater risk of severe malaria and simple clinical malaria [283]. This is consistent with early experiments in which thiamine-deficient ducks were more susceptible to avian malaria [284]. There are also reports that acute cerebral ataxia following malaria can be treated with thiamine [285].

It is also of interest that the malaria parasite has been shown to synthesize thiamine [286] from proximal precursors. The significance of this vis-à-vis host thiamine status remains to be studied. In addition, it has been demonstrated that another B vitamin, pyridoxine [287], can be synthesized by *P. falciparum*. These pathways present potential new targets for the development of novel chemotherapeutics against malaria.

### 9.4.4.5   VITAMIN E AND OTHER ANTIOXIDANTS

Several reports indicated that deficiencies of vitamin E and other antioxidants tend to protect against malaria infection [288]. As discussed, the absence of antioxidants makes the parasite more vulnerable to damage by oxygen radical produced by the immune system. In humans, it was initially proposed that the exacerbative effects on cerebral malaria following refeeding of famine victims [83] with grain was caused by the vitamin E content of the grain that would be absent in the diet of those who received milk [289, 290].

The exacerbative effect of vitamin E on malaria was first described by Godfrey in 1957, who demonstrated that the antimalaria effects of cod-liver oil in mice were reversible by giving vitamin E [291]. Multiple studies in rodent systems confirmed the protective effects of vitamin E deficiency [292–296] and the ability of vitamin E to abrogate the protective effects of prooxidant compounds, such as peroxidizable fatty acids, on malaria [293–296]. Interesting, however, was the observation that vitamin E deficiency was also protective against murine cerebral malaria [297], in which oxidative damage plays a significant role. Studies of avian malaria in the duck also observed a protective effect of vitamin E deficiency [298].

With regard to selenium, there are no human studies addressing the role of selenium in malaria. A few animal studies have been published and indicated that selenium has little role in modulating rodent malaria [299, 300]. However, selenium-deficient ducks were more susceptible to avian malaria [298].

Vitamin C also has been studied in animals, but little has been done in humans. Experiments in monkeys indicated that vitamin C deficiency exacerbated malaria [301]. In mice, however, results have been mixed. Godfrey [291] indicated that large doses of vitamin C, as with vitamin E, could abrogate the protective effect of cod-liver oil. This was not the case, however, when lower doses were used in conjunction with vitamin E-deficient mice [288], and vitamin C supplements did not modify the course of parasitemia in normal mice.

These data indicated that, although antioxidant vitamins may have an exacerbative role under some conditions, it is difficult to predict the effect of a nutrient on malaria based on its antioxidant properties alone. For example, a study from Uganda indicated that the antioxidant lycopene was associated with more rapid parasite clearance following treatment [302]. In general, data are lacking for the effects of antioxidant nutrients on malaria morbidity, pathology, and mortality in humans. Additional studies in this area are clearly warranted.

## 9.5   CONCLUSIONS AND RECOMMENDATIONS

Malaria remains a very significant public health problem throughout the tropical world. The future success of malaria control lies in the ability to implement multiple, effective interventions that are technologically and economically sustainable. The current focus on early detection and treatment, insecticide-treated bed nets, and vector control through environmental management provides useful tools. There is also reason for optimism that a malaria vaccine with at least partial efficacy will be available for endemic areas within the coming decade.

This chapter elucidated the strong role that nutrition plays in modulating malaria morbidity and mortality and the potential that nutrient-based interventions might have in combating malaria. Indeed, given the clearly deleterious effects of poor nutritional status on malaria mortality, general improvements in dietary intake through improved childhood nutrition and economic development are likely to have a very large impact on reducing the disease burden of malaria. The observation that selective nutrient supplementation with vitamin A or zinc can substantially lower malaria attack rates suggests that targeted nutrient-based interventions can serve as useful adjuncts to malaria-control programs. At US $0.12 for a 1-year supply [303], vitamin A supplementation would rank among the more cost-effective interventions for malaria [304]. Moreover, both vitamin A and zinc supplementation have been demonstrated in several settings to reduce substantially morbidity from other infectious diseases [305–307].

The effects of other nutrients also require examination, as indicated by reported predisposition to severe and uncomplicated malaria owing to thiamine deficiency, carotenoids, unsaturated fatty acids, as well as others. In general, low cost, high safety, and potential efficacy of targeted nutritional supplementation or fortification suggest that a rational approach to development of such interventions might prove useful for prevention or as adjunctive therapy for *P. falciparum* malaria. Other benefits may also be gained. For example, nutrient supplementation may mitigate the delay in acquired immunity associated with bed nets [308] and chemoprophylaxis [180].

Although there is reason for concern over an exacerbative effect of some nutrients on malaria morbidity, such as iron and possibly folate and certain antioxidants, this should also be considered a challenge to scientists and public health professionals to discover and invent novel approaches to obtain the benefits of key nutrients while mitigating any adverse effects. Integrated approaches to malaria control and nutritional improvement should be adopted.

In addition, more detailed investigations should be undertaken to clarify the effects of specific micronutrients, as well as macronutrients, on malaria morbidity, pathology, immunity, and mortality. Although these should focus primarily on *P. falciparum* in Africa, other geographic areas and species should not be neglected. For example, it is likely that investigations of the role of nutrition in *P. vivax* malaria in Asia and Latin America will also prove informative. Specifically, there is a need for well-designed longitudinal and clinic-based studies to determine the mechanistic basis of how nutrients influence malaria. Additional public health issues include examination of different nutritional requirements for adults and children with respect to malaria and the specific physiology of malnutrition and malaria in severely malnourished individuals such as those encountered under famine conditions. It would also be useful to understand how malaria affects dietary intake, dietary patterns, and food beliefs surrounding malaria illness.

Last, nutritional modulation of malaria morbidity and mortality highlights the complex nature of resistance to malaria. It is clear that different nutrients, such as vitamin A, zinc, and iron, selectively modify different aspects of malaria immunity and pathology. Study of these effects and their underlying mechanisms may yield important insight to host–parasite interactions, possibly leading to new therapies or vaccines.

## REFERENCES

1. Guinovart C, Navia MM, Tanner M, Alonso PL. Malaria: burden of disease. Curr Mol Med. 2006 Feb;6(2):137–140.
2. Shankar AH, 2000. Nutritional modulation of malaria morbidity and mortality. J Infect Dis 182(suppl 1): S37–S53
3. Bruce-Chwatt LJ. History of malaria from prehistory to eradication. In: Malaria: principles and practice of malariology. Wernsdorfer WH, McGregor IA, eds. Edinburgh: Churchill Livingstone, 1988:1–69.
4. World Health Organization Expert Committee on Malaria. WHO Technical Report Series No. 357. Geneva: World Health Organization, 1967.
5. World Health Organization. Re-examination of the global strategy of malaria eradication. A report by the director general to the 22nd World Health Assembly. Geneva: World Health Organization, 1969.
6. Krishna S. Science, medicine, and the future. Malaria. BMJ 1997;315:730–732.
7. Binka FN, Kubaje A, Adjuik M, Williams LA, Lengeler C, Maude GH, et al. Impact of permethrin impregnated bednets on child mortality in Kassena-Nankana district, Ghana: a randomized controlled trial. Trop Med Int Health 1996;1:147–154.
8. Nevill CG, Some ES, Mung'ala VO, Mutemi W, New L, Marsh K, Lengeler C, Snow RW. Insecticide-treated bednets reduce mortality and severe morbidity from malaria among children on the Kenyan coast. Trop Med Int Health 1996;1:139–146.
9. D'Alessandro U, Olaleye B, Langerock P, Bennett S, Cham K, Cham B, Greenwood BM. The Gambian National Impregnated Bednet Programme: evaluation of effectiveness by means of case-control studies. Trans R Soc Trop Med Hyg 1997;91:638–642.
10. Lengeler C. Insecticide treated bednets and curtains for malaria control. Cochrane Review. In: The Cochrane Library, Issue 4. Oxford: Update Software, 1998.
11. Clyde DF, Most H, McCarthy VC, Vanderberg JP. Immunization of man against sporozoite-induced falciparum malaria. Am J Med Sci 1973;266:169–177.
12. Clyde DF. Immunization of man against falciparum and vivax malaria by use of attenuated sporozoites. Am J Trop Med Hyg 1975;24:397–401.

13. Hoffman SL, Sherwood JA, Hollingdale MR, et al. Safety and efficacy of a recombinant DNA *Plasmodium falciparum* sporozoite vaccine. Lancet 1987;1:1277–1281.

14. Stoute JA, Slaoui M, Heppner DG, Momin P, Kester KE, Desmons P, Wellde BT, Garcon N, Krzych U, Marchand M. A preliminary evaluation of a recombinant circumsporozoite protein vaccine against *Plasmodium falciparum* malaria. N Engl J Med 1996;336:86–91.

15. Alonso PL, Sacarlal J, Aponte JJ, Leach A, Macete E, Milman J, Mandomando I, Spiessens B, Guinovart C, Espasa M, Bassat Q, Aide P, Ofori-Anyinam O, Navia MM, Corachan S, Ceuppens M, Dubois MC, Demoitie MA, Dubovsky F, Menendez C, Tornieporth N, Ballou WR, Thompson R, Cohen J. Efficacy of the RTS,S/AS02A vaccine against *Plasmodium falciparum* infection and disease in young African children: randomised controlled trial. Lancet. 2004 Oct 16–22;364(9443):1411–1420.

16. Graves P, Gelband H. Vaccines for preventing malaria (pre-erythrocytic). Cochrane Database Syst Rev 2006 Oct 18;(4):CD006198.

17. McGregor IA, Carrington SP, Cohen S. Falciparum malaria with West African human gammaglobulin. Trans R Soc Trop Med Hyg 1963;57:170–175.

18. Patarroyo ME, Romero P, Torres ML, Clavijo P, Moreno A, Martinez A, et al. Induction of protective immunity against experimental infection with malaria using synthetic peptides. Nature 1987;328:629–632

19. Patarroyo ME, Amador R, Clavijo P, Moreno A, Guzman F, Romero P, et al. A synthetic vaccine protects humans against challenge with asexual blood stages of *Plasmodium falciparum* malaria. Nature 1988;332:158–61.

20. Alonso PL, Smith T, Schellenberg DM, et al. Randomised trial of efficacy of SPf66 vaccine against *Plasmodium falciparum* malaria in children in southern Tanzania. Lancet 1994;344:1175–1181.

21. D'Alessandro U, Leach A, Drakeley CJ, Bennett S, Olaleye BO, Fegan GW, et al. Efficacy trial of malaria vaccine Spf66 in Gambian infants. Lancet 1995;346:462–467.

22. Nosten F, Luxemburger C, Kyle DE et al. Randomized double blind placebo controlled trial of SPf66 malaria vaccine in children in northwestern Thailand. Shoklo SPf66 Malaria Vaccine Trial Group. Lancet 1996;348:701.

23. Acosta CJ, Galindo CM, Schellenberg DM, et al. Evaluation of the SPf66 vaccine for malaria control when delivered through the EPI scheme in Tanzania. Trop Med Int Health 1999;4:368–376.

24. Moorthy VS, Good MF, Hill AV. Malaria vaccine developments. Lancet 2004 Jan 10;363(9403):150–156.

25. Graves P, Gelband H. Vaccines for preventing malaria (blood-stage). Cochrane Database Syst Rev 2006 Oct 18;(4):CD006199.

26. Krogstad DJ. Malaria as a re-emerging disease. Epidemiol Rev 1996;18:77–79.

27. Ghatoura GBS. A quantitative method of assessing the health impact of different diseases in less developed countries. Int J Epidemiol 1981;73–80.

28. Hyder AA, Rotllant G, Morrow RH. Measuring the burden of disease: healthy life-years. Am J Public Health 1998;88:196–202.

29. Greenwood BM. Why do some African children develop severe malaria. Parasitol Today 1991;277–281.

30. Alonso PL, Lindsay SW, Armstrong JR, Conteh M, Hill AG, David PH, et al. The effect of insecticide-treated bed nets on mortality of Gambian children. Lancet 1991;337:1499–1502.

31. Bryce J, Boschi-Pinto C, Shibuya K, Black RE; WHO Child Health Epidemiology. WHO estimates of the causes of death in children. Lancet 2005 Mar 26–Apr 1;365(9465):1147–1152.

32. Brabin, B. The risks and severity of malaria in pregnant women. Geneva: World Health Organization, 1991. TDR/Applied Field Research in Malaria Reports, No. 1.

33. Krotoski WA, Collins WE, Bray RS, Garnham PC, Cogswell FB, Gwadz RW, et al. Demonstration of hypnozoites in sporozoite-transmitted *Plasmodium vivax* infection. Am J Trop Med Hyg 1982;31:1291–1293.

34. Russell PF. Practical malariology. Oxford: Oxford University Press, 1963.

35. Garnham PC. Malaria parasites and other hemosporidia. Oxford: Blackwell Scientific, 1966.

36. Su XZ, Heatwole VM, Wertheimer SP, Guinet F, Herrfeldt JA, Peterson DS, et al. The large diverse gene family var encodes proteins involved in cytoadherence and antigenic variation of *Plasmodium falciparum*-infected erythrocytes. Cell 1995;82:89–100.

37. Metselaar D. Two malaria surveys in the central mountains of the Netherlands and New Guinea. Am J Trop Med Hyg 1959;8:364–367.

38. Molineaux L. The epidemiology of human malaria as an explanation of its distribution including some implications for its control. Edinburgh: Churchill Livingstone, 1988:913–998.

39. Smith T, Genton B, Bawa K, Gibson N, Taime J, Narara A, et al. Relationships between *Plasmodium falciparum* infection and morbidity in an highly endemic area. Parasitology 1994;109:539–549.

40. Greenwood BM, Bradley AK, Greenwood AM, Byass P, Jammeh K, Marsh K, et al. Mortality and morbidity from malaria among children in a rural area of the Gambia, West Africa. Trans R Soc Trop Med Hyg 1987;81:478–486.

41. Lines J, Armstrong JRM. For a few parasites more: inoculum size, vector control and strain-specific immunity to malaria. Parasitol Today 1992;8:381–383.

42. Prevention of Malaria. Infect Dis Clin North Am Health Iss Int Travelers 1992:313–331.

43. Marsh K. Malaria: a neglected disease? Parasitology 1992;104:S53–S66.

44. Molineaux L. *Plasmodium falciparum* malaria: some epidemiological implications of parasite and host diversity. Ann Trop Med Parasitol 1996;90:379–393.

45. Molyneux ME, Taylor TE, Wirima JJ, Borgstein A. Clinical features and prognostic indicators in paediatric cerebral malaria: a study of 131 comatose Malawian children. Q J Med 1989;71:441–459.

46. Warrell DA. Severe and complicated malaria. R Soc Trop Med Hyg 1990;1–65.

47. Snow RW, Bastos de Azevedo I, Lowe BS, Kabiru EW, Nevill CG, et al. Severe childhood malaria in two areas of markedly different falciparum transmission in East Africa. Acta Trop 1994;57:289–300.

48. Snow RW. Will reducing *Plasmodium falciparum* transmission alter malaria mortality among African children? Parasitol Today 1995;188–190.

49. Marsh K, English M, Crawley J, Peshu N. The pathogenesis of severe malaria in African children. Ann Trop Med Parasitol 1996;90:396–402.

50. Slutsker L, Taylor TE, Wirima JJ, Steketee RW. In-hospital morbidity and mortality due to malaria-associated severe anaemia in two areas of Malawi with different patterns of malaria infection. Trans R Soc Trop Med Hyg 1994;88:548–551.

51. Snow RW, Schellenberg JR, Peshu N, Forster D, Newton CR, Winstanley PA, et al. Periodicity and space-time clustering of severe childhood malaria on the coast of Kenya. Trans R Soc Trop Med Hyg 1993;87:386–390.

52. Armstrong Schellenberg JRM. An analysis of the geographic distribution of severe malaria in children in the Kilifi District, Kenya. Int J Epidemiol 1998;323–329.

53. Oaks SC. Malaria: obstacles and opportunities. In: Institute of Medicine. Committee for the Study on Malaria Prevention and Control. Washington, DC: National Academy Press, 1991.

54. Shiff CJ, Premji Z, Minjas JN. The rapid manual ParaSight-F test. A new diagnostic tool for *Plasmodium falciparum* infection. Trans R Soc Trop Med Hyg 1993;87:646–648.

55. Baird JK. Effectiveness of antimalarial drugs. N Engl J Med 2005 Apr 14;352(15):1565–1577.

56. Allan RJ, Beattie P, Bate C, Van Hensbroek MB, Morris-Jones S, Greenwood BM, Kwiatkowski D. Strain variation in tumor necrosis factor induction by parasites from children with acute falciparum malaria. Infect Immun 1995;63:1173–1175.

57. Clark IA. The cytokine theory of human cerebral malaria. Parasitol Today 1994.

58. Clark IA, Rockett KA. Nitric oxide and parasitic disease. Adv Parasitol 1996;37:1–56.

59. Gupta S, Hill AV, Kwiatkowski D, Greenwood AM, Greenwood BM, Day KP. Parasite virulence and disease patterns in *Plasmodium falciparum* malaria. Proc Natl Acad Sci U S A 1994;91:3715–3719.

60. Treutiger CJ, Hedlund I, Helmby H, Carlson J, Jepson A, Twumasi P, et al. Rosette formation in *Plasmodium falciparum* isolates and anti-rosette activity of sera from Gambians with cerebral or uncomplicated malaria. Am J Trop Med Hyg 1992;46:503–510.

61. Babikker HA, Ranford-Cartwright LC, Currie D, Charlwood JD, et al. Random mating in natural population of the malaria parasite *Plasmodium falciparum*. Parasitology 1994;109:413–421.

62. Kwiatowski D, Nowak N. Periodic and chaotic host–parasite interactions. Proc Nat Acad Sci U S A 1991;88:5111–5113.

63. McGuire W, Hill AV, Allsopp CE, Greenwood BM, Kwiatkowski D. Variation in the TNF-alpha promotor region associated with susceptibility to cerebral malaria. Nature 1994;371:508–510.

64. Fleming AF, Storey J, Molineaux L, Iroko EA, Attai ED. Abnormal haemoglobins in the Sudan savanna of Nigeria. I. Prevalence of haemoglobins and relationship between sickle cell trait, malaria and survival. Ann Trop Med Parasitol 1979;73:161–172.

65. Weatherall DJ. Common genetic disorders of the red cell and the "malaria hypothesis." Ann Trop Med Parasitol 1987;81:539–548.

66. Miller LH. Impact of malaria on genetic polymorphism and genetic diseases in Africans and African Americans. Proc Natl Acad Sci U S A 1994;91:2415–2419.

67. Report of the Indian famine commission. Calcutta: Government of India, 1898.

68. Gill CA. The genesis of epidemics and the natural history of disease: an introduction to the science of epidemiology. London: Bailliere, Tindall, and Cox, 1928.

69. Christophers SR. Scientific memoirs by officers of the medical and sanitary departments of the government of India, 1911.

70. Roubaud E. Le bien-être dans le paludisme et les maladies a Trypanosomes. Bull Soc Pathol Exotique 1921;662–665.

71. Farinaud EM. Le paludisme à Poulo-Condore. Ann Inst Pasteur 1939;540–570.

72. Eckstein A. Malaria in childhood. Acta Med Orient 1943;2:123–132.

73. Williams CD. Clinical malaria in children. Lancet 1940;1:441–443.

74. Garnham PCC. Malaria in the African child. East Afr Med J 1954;31:155–159.

75. Hackett LW. Malaria in Europe; an ecological study. London: Oxford University Press, 1937.

76. James SP. Epidemiological results of a laboratory study of malaria in England. Trans R Soc Trop Med Hyg 1926;20:143–157.

77. Famine inquiry commission report on Bengal. New Delhi: Government of India, 1945:118.

78. Edington GM. Cerebral malaria in the Gold Coast African: four autopsy reports. Ann Trop Med Parasitol 1954;48:300–306.

79. Hendrickse RG. Interactions of nutrition and infection: experiene in Nigeria. In: Nutrition and infection. Wolstenhome GEW, O'Connor M, eds. Boston: Little, Brown, 1967:98–111.

80. Hendrickse RG, Hasan AH, Olumide LO, Akinkunmi A. Malaria in early childhood: an investigation of five hundred seriously ill children in whom a "clinical" diagnosis of malaria was made on admission to the children's emergency room at University College Hospital, Ibadan. Ann Trop Med Parasitol 1971;65:1–20.

81. Murray MJ, Murray NJ, Murray AB, Murray MB. Refeeding-malaria and hyperferraemia. Lancet 1975;1:653–654.

82. Murray MJ, Murray AB, Murray MB, Murray CJ. Somali food shelters in the Ogaden famine and their impact on health. Lancet 1976;1:1283–1285.

83. Murray MJ, Murray AB, Murray NJ, Murray MB. Diet and cerebral malaria: the effect of famine and refeeding. Am J Clin Nutr 1978;31:57–61.

84. Murray MJ, Murray AB, Murray MB, Murray CJ. The adverse effect of iron repletion on the course of certain infections. Br Med J 1978;2:1113–1115.

85. McGregor IA. Malaria: nutritional implications. Rev Infect Dis 1982;4:798–804.

86. McGregor IA. Malaria and nutrition. In: Malaria: principles and practice of malariology. Wernsdorfer WH, McGregor IA, eds. London: Churchill Livingstone, 1988:753–767.

87. Edirisinghe JS. Infections in the malnourished: with special reference to malaria and malnutrition in the tropics. Ann Trop Paediatr 1986;6:233–237.

88. Latham MC. Needed research on the interactions of certain parasitic diseases and nutrition in humans. Rev Infect Dis 1982;4:896–900.

89. Gongora J, McFie J. Malnutrition, malaria and mortality. Trans R Soc Trop Med Hyg 1959;53:238–247.

90. Gongora J. Malnutrition, malaria and mortality. Trans R Soc Trop Med Hyg 1960;54:471–473.

91. Ahmad SH, Moonis R, Shahab T, Khan HM, Jilani T. Effect of nutritional status on total parasite count in malaria. Indian J Pediatr 1985;52:285–288.

92. Periera PCM, Meira DA, Curi PR, deSouza N, Burini RC. The malarial impact on the nutritional status of Amazonian adult subjects. Rev Inst Med Trop Sao Paulo 1995;37:19–24.

93. Liashenko I. Primary tropical malaria in underweight patients. Voenno-Meditsinskii Zhurnal 1997;318:46–51.
94. Walt F. Anaemia and kwashiorkor. J Trop Pediatr 1960;6:3–9.
95. Edington GM. Pathology of malaria in West Africa. BMJ 1967;1:715–718.
96. Purtilo DT, Conner DH. Fatal infections in protein-calorie malnourished children with hymolymphatic atrophy. Arch Dis Child 1975;50:149–152.
97. Hendrickse RG. Of sick turkeys, kwashiorkor, malaria, perinatal mortality, heroin addicts and food poisoning: research on the influence of aflatoxins on child health in the tropics. Ann Trop Med Parasitol 1997;91:787–793.
98. Hendrickse RG, Lamplugh SM, Maegraith BG. Influence of aflatoxin on nutrition and malaria in mice. Trans R Soc Trop Med Hyg 1986;80:846–847.
99. Razanamparany MS, Randriamiharisoa FA, Razanamparany NJD, Ramialimanana V. L'epidémie de paludisme a Antananarivo de 1983 a 1994 vue a travers le service de pediatrie de l'hôpital général de Befelatanana. Cahiers Sante 1995;5:382–385.
100. Randriamiharisoa FA, Razanamparany NJD, Ramialimanana V, Razanamparany MS. Epidemiological data on children hospitalized with malaria from 1983 to 1992. Arch Inst Pasteur Madagascar 1993;60:38–42.
101. Olumese PE, Sodeinde O, Ademowo OG, Walker O. Protein energy malnutrition and cerebral malaria in Nigerian children. J Trop Pediatr 1997;43:217–219.
102. Faye O, Correa J, Camara B, et al. Malaria lethality in Dakar pediatric environment study of risk factors [in French]. Med Trop (Mars) 1998;58:361–364.
103. Renaudin P. Evaluation of the nutritional status of children less than 5 years of age in Moundou, Chad: correlations with morbidity and hospital mortality. Med Trop 1997;57:49–54.
104. Man WD, Weber M, Palmer A, et al. Nutritional status of children admitted to hospital with different diseases and its relationship to outcome in the Gambia, West Africa. Trop Med Int Health 1998;3: 678–686.
105. Mockenhaupt FP, Ehrhardt S, Burkhardt J, et al. Manifestation and outcome of severe malaria in children in northern Ghana. Am J Trop Med Hyg 2004;71:167–172.
106. Ong'echa JM, Keller CC, Were T, Ouma C, Otieno RO, Landis-Lewis Z, Ochiel D, Slingluff JL, Mogere S, Ogonji GA, Orago AS, Vulule JM, Kaplan SS, Day RD, Perkins DJ. Parasitemia, anemia, and malarial anemia in infants and young children in a rural holoendemic *Plasmodium falciparum* transmission area. Am J Trop Med Hyg. 2006 Mar;74(3):376–385.
107. Goyal SC. Protein energy malnutrition and cerebral malaria. J Trop Pediatr 1991;37:143–144.
108. Nacher M, Singhasivanon P, Treeprasertsuk S, Vannaphan S, Traore B, Looareesuwan S, Gay F. Intestinal helminths and malnutrition are independently associated with protection from cerebral malaria in Thailand. Ann Trop Med Parasitol. 2002 Jan;96(1):5–13.
109. Burgess HJL, Burgess AP, Driessen F. The nutritional status of children aged 0–5 years in Nkhotakota, Malawi. Trop Geog Med 1975;27:375–382.
110. Wenlock RW. The epidemiology of tropical parasitic diseases in rural Zambia and the consequences for public health. J Trop Med Hyg 1979;82:90–98.
111. Sharp PT, Harvey P. Malaria and growth stunting in young children of the highlands of Papua New Guinea. Papua New Guinea Med J 1980;23:132–140.
112. El Samani FZ, Willett WC, Ware JH. Nutritional and socio-demographic risk indicators of malaria in children under five: a cross-sectional study in a Sudanese rural community. J Trop Med Hyg 1987;90:69–78.
113. Renaudin P, Lombart JP. Anemia in infants less than 1 year old in Moundou, Chad: prevalence and etiology. Med Trop 1994;54:337–342.
114. Tshikuka J, Gray-Donald K, Scott M, Olela KN. Relationship of childhood protein-energy malnutrition and parasite infections in an urban African setting. Trop Med Int Health 1997;2: 374–382.
115. Mbago MCY, Namtua PP. Some determinants of nutritional status of 1 to 4-year-old children in low income urban areas in Tanzania. J Trop Pediatr 1991;38: 299–306.

116. Dominguez-Vazquez A, Alzate-Sanchez A. Nutritional status in children under 6 years of age and its relation to malaria and intestinal parasitism. Salud Publica de Mexico 1990;32:52–63.

117. Carswell F, Hughes AO, Palmer RI, Higginson J, Harland PS, Meakins RH. Nutritional status, globulin titers, and parasitic infections of two populations of Tanzanian school children. Am J Clin Nutr 1981;34:1292–1299.

118. Monjour L, Palminteri R, Froment A, Renault T, Alfred C, Gentilini M. Is cell-mediated immune response related to nutritional state, but unaffected by concomitant malarial infection? Ann Trop Med Parasitol 1982;76:575–577.

119. Ehrhardt S, Burchard GD, Mantel C, Cramer JP, Kaiser S, Kubo M, Otchwemah RN, Bienzle U, Mockenhaupt FP. Malaria, anemia, and malnutrition in African children—defining intervention priorities. J Infect Dis 2006 Jul 1;194(1):108–114.

120. Mamiro PS, Kolsteren P, Roberfroid D, Tatala S, Opsomer AS, Van Camp JH. Feeding practices and factors contributing to wasting, stunting, and iron-deficiency anaemia among 3–23-month old children in Kilosa district, rural Tanzania. J Health Popul Nutr 2005 Sep;23(3):222–230.

121. Friedman JF, Kwena AM, Mirel LB, Kariuki SK, Terlouw DJ, Phillips-Howard PA, Hawley WA, Nahlen BL, Shi YP, ter Kuile FO. Malaria and nutritional status among pre-school children: results from cross-sectional surveys in western Kenya. Am J Trop Med Hyg 2005 Oct; 73(4):698–704.

122. Tanner M, Burnier E, Mayombana C, et al. Longitudinal study on the health status of children in a rural Tanzanian community: parasitoses and nutrition following control measures against intestinal parasites. Acta Trop 1987;44:137–174.

123. Williams TN, Maitland K, Phelps L, et al. *Plasmodium vivax:* a cause of malnutrition in young children. Q J Med 1997;90:751–757.

124. Tonglet R, Mahangaiko Lembo E, Zihindula PM, Wodon A, Dramaix M, Hennart P. How useful are anthropometric, clinical, and dietary measurements of nutritional status as predictors of morbidity of young children in central Africa? Trop Med Int Health 1999;4:120–130.

125. Deen JL, Walraven GE, von Seidlein L. Increased risk for malaria in chronically malnourished children under 5 years of age in rural Gambia. J Trop Pediatr. 2002 Apr;48(2):78–83.

126. Snow RW, Byass P, Shenton FC, Greenwood BM. The relationship between anthropometric measurements and measurements of iron status and susceptibility to malaria in Gambian children. Trans R Soc Trop Med Hyg 1991;85:584–589.

127. Genton B, Al-Yaman F, Ginny M, Taraika J, Alpers MP. Relation of anthropometry to malaria morbidity and immunity in Papua New Guinean children. Am J Clin Nutr 1998;68:734–741.

128. van den Broeck J, Eeckels R, Vuylsteke J. Influence of nutritional status on child mortality in rural Zaire. Lancet 1993;341:1491–1495.

129. Muller O, Garenne M, Kouyate B, Becher H. The association between protein-energy malnutrition, malaria morbidity and all-cause mortality in West African children. Trop Med Int Health 2003; 8:507–511.

130. Caulfield LE, Richard SA, Black RE. Undernutrition as an underlying cause of malaria morbidity and mortality in children less than 5 years old. Am J Trop Med Hyg 2004 Aug;71(2 suppl):55–63.

131. Randomised trial to assess benefits and safety of vitamin A supplementation linked to immunisation in early infancy. WHO/CHD Immunisation-Linked Vitamin A Supplementation Study Group. Lancet 1998;352:1257–1263.

132. Andersen M, 1997. Anthropometric measurements in health programmes: epidemiological and statistical aspects. PhD dissertation. University of Copenhagen, Copenhagen, Denmark.

133. Garenne M, Garenne M, Maire B, Fontaine O, Dieng K, Briend A, 2000. Risks of dying associated with different nutritional status in pre-school aged children. Final report. Dakar: ORSTOM, September 1987:246. Reprinted by CEPED, Paris.

134. Wolday D, Kibreab T, Bukenya D, Hodes R. Sensitivity of *Plasmodium falciparum* in vivo to chloroquine and pyrimethamine-sulfadoxine in Rwandan patients in a refugee camp in Zaire. Trans R Soc Trop Med Hyg 1995;89:654–656.

135. Hess FI, Iannuzzi A, Leafasia J, et al. Risk factors of chloroquine resistance in *Plasmodium falciparum* malaria. Acta Trop 1996;61:293–306.

136. Hess FI, Nukuro E, Judson L, Rodgers J, Nothdurft HD, Rieckmann KH. Anti-malarial drug resistance, malnutrition and socio-economic status. Trop Med Int Health 1997;2:721–728.

137. Hamel MJ, Holtz T, Mkandala C, Kaimila N, Chizani N, Bloland P, Kublin J, Kazembe P, Steketee R. Efficacy of trimethoprim-sulfamethoxazole compared with sulfadoxine-pyrimethamine plus erythromycin for the treatment of uncomplicated malaria in children with integrated management of childhood illness dual classifications of malaria and pneumonia. Am J Trop Med Hyg 2005 Sep;73(3):609–615.

138. Geiman QM, McKee RW. Malarial parasites and their mode of life. Sci Month 1948;67:217.

139. Ray AP. Haematological studies on Simian malaria. II. Blood picture in monkeys during acute and chronic stages of *P. knowlesi* infection. Indian J Malariol 1957;4:360.

140. Tatke M, Bazaz-Malik G. Brain histomorphology in protein deprived rhesus monkeys with fatal malarial infection. Indian J Med Res 1989;89:404–410.

141. Bazaz-Malik G, Tatke M. Response to *Plasmodium cynomolgi* infection in a protein deficient host. Indian J Med Res 1982;76:527–533.

142. Tatke M, Malik GB. Pulmonary pathology in severe malaria infection in health and protein deprivation. J Trop Med Hyg 1990;93:377–382.

143. Ramakrishnan SP, Prakash S, Krishnaswami SP, Singh LC. Studies on *P. berghei* Vincki and Lips: effect of glucose, biotin PABA and mathionine on the course of blood induced infection in starving albino rats. Indian J Malariol 1953;7:225.

144. Ramakrishnan SP. Studies on *Plasmodium berghei* N. Sp. Vincke and Lips, 1948. VIII. The course of blood-induced infection in starved albino rats. Indian J Malariol 1953;7:53–60.

145. Ramakrishnan SP. Studies on *Plasmodium berghei* Vincke and Lips, 1948. XVI. Effect of ketogenic diet on the course of blood-induced infection in rats. Indian J Malariol 1954;8:85–88.

146. Ramakrishnan SP. Studies on *Plasmodium berghei* Vincke and Lips, 1948. XVIII. Effect of diet different in quality but adequate in quantity on the course of blood-induced infection in rats. Indian J Malariol 1954;8:97–105.

147. Ramakrishnan SP. Studies on *Plasmodium berghei*, Vincke and Lips, 1948. XVII. Effect of different quantities of the same diet on the course of blood-induced infection in rats. Indian J Malariol 1954;8:89–96.

148. Edirisinghe JS, Fern EB, Targett GAT. The influence of dietary protein on the development of malaria. Ann Trop Paediatr 1981;1:87–91.

149. Edirisinghe JS, Fern EB, Targett GAT. Dietary suppression of rodent malaria. Trans R Soc Trop Med Hyg 1981;75:591–593.

150. Edirisinghe JS, Fern EB, Targett GAT. Resistance to superinfection with *Plasmodium berghei* in rats fed a protein-free diet. Trans R Soc Trop Med Hyg 1982;76:382–386.

151. Fern EB, Edirisinghe JS, Targett GA. Increased severity of malaria infection in rats fed supplementary amino acids. Trans R Soc Trop Med Hyg 1984;78:839–841.

152. Bhatia A, Aggarwal A, Sehgal S, Chakravarti RN, Vinayak VK. Interactions of protein calorie malnutrition, malaria infection and immune responses. Aust J Exp Biol Med Sci 1983;61:589–597.

153. Bhatia A, Vinayak VK. Dietary modulation of malaria infection in rats. Indian J Malariol 1991;28: 237–242.

154. Ibekwe CAC, Ugwunna SC. The effects of host diet on *Plasmodium yoelii nigeriensis*. J Parasitol 1990;76:903–912.

155. Bakker NPM, Eling WMC, De Groot AMT, Sinkeldam EJ, Luyken R. Attenuation of malaria infection, paralysis and lesions in the central nervous system by low protein diets in rats. Acta Trop 1992;50:285–293.

156. van Doorne CW, Eling WMC, Luyken R. Rodent malaria in rats exacerbated by milk protein, attenuated by low-protein vegetable diet. Trop Med Int Health 1998;3:596–600.

157. Keshavarz-Valian H, Alger NE, Boissonneault GA. Effects of p-aminobenzoic acid, methionine, threonine and protein levels on susceptibility of mice to *Plasmodium berghei*. J Nutr 1985;115: 1613–1620.

158. Fagbenro-Beyioku AF, Oyerinde JPO. Effect of host-diet inadequacy on the course of infection of *Plasmodium yoelii nigeriensis*. West Afr J Med 1990;9:124–128.

159. Hunt NH, Manduci N, Thumwood CM. Amelioration of murine cerebral malaria by dietary restriction. Parasitology 1993;107:471–476.

160. Garnham PCC. Malarial immunity in Africans: effects in infancy and early childhood. Am J Trop Med Hyg 1949;43:47–61.

161. Bruce-Chwatt LJ. Malaria in African infants and effect on growth and development in children in southern Nigeria. Ann Trop Med Parasitol 1952;46:173–200.

162. Frood JDL, Whitehead RG, Coward WA. Relationship between pattern of infection and development of hypoalbuminaemia and hypo-β-lipoproteinaemia in rural Ugandan children. Lancet 1971;2: 1047–1049.

163. Rowland MGM, Cole TJ, Whitehead RG. A quantitative study into the role of infection in determining nutritional status in Gambian village children. Br J Nutr 1977;37:441–450.

164. Marsden PD. The Sukuta Project: a longitudinal study of health in Gambian children from birth to 18 months of age. Trans R Soc Trop Med Hyg 1964;58:455–489.

165. Faich GA, Mason J. The prevalence and relationships of malaria, anemia, and malnutrition in a coastal area of El Salvador. Am J Trop Med Hyg 1975;24:161–167.

166. Nyakeriga AM, Troye-Blomberg M, Chemtai AK, Marsh K, Williams TN. Malaria and nutritional status in children living on the coast of Kenya. Am J Clin Nutr 2004 Dec;80(6):1604–1610.

167. Friedman JF, Kurtis JD, Mtalib R, Opollo M, Lanar DE, Duffy PE. Malaria is related to decreased nutritional status among male adolescents and adults in the setting of intense perennial transmission. J Infect Dis 2003 Aug 1;188(3):449–457. Epub July 15, 2003.

168. Colbourne MJ. The effect of malaria suppression in a group of Accra school children. Trans R Soc Trop Med Hyg 1955;49:356–369.

169. McGregor IA, Gilles HM, Walters JH, Davies AH, Pearson FA. Effects of heavy and repeated malarial infections on Gamiban infants and children. BMJ 1956;686–692.

170. Bradley-Moore AM, Greenwood BM, Bradley AK, Kirkwood BR, Gilles HM. Malaria chemoprophylaxis with chloroquine in young Nigerian children III. Its effect on nutrition. Ann Trop Med Parasitol 1985;79:575–584.

171. Molineaux L, Gramiccia G. The Garki Project. Geneva: World Health Organization, 1980.

172. Draper KC, Draper CC. Observations on the growth of African infants with special reference to the effects of malaria control. J Trop Med Hyg 1960;63:165–171.

173. Snow RW, Molyneux CS, Njeru EK, et al. The effects of malaria control on nutritional status in infancy. Acta Trop 1997;65:1–10.

174. Shiff C, Checkley W, Winch P, Premji Z, Minjas J, Lubega P. Changes in weight gain and anaemia attributable to malaria in Tanzanian children living under holoendemic conditions. Trans R Soc Trop Med Hyg 1996;90:262–265.

175. Friedman JF, Phillips-Howard PA, Hawley WA, Terlouw DJ, Kolczak MS, Barber M, Okello N, Vulule JM, Duggan C, Nahlen BL, ter Kuile FO. Impact of permethrin-treated bed nets on growth, nutritional status, and body composition of primary school children in western Kenya. Am J Trop Med Hyg. 2003 Apr;68(4 suppl):78–85.

176. Hung LQ, de Vries PJ, Giao PT, Binh TQ, Nam NV, Chong MT, Kager PA. Nutritional status following malaria control in a Vietnamese ethnic minority commune. Eur J Clin Nutr. 2005 Aug;59(8): 891–899.

177. DeMaeyer E, et al. Preventing and controlling iron deficiency anaemia through primary health care: a guide for health administrators and programme managers. Geneva: World Health Organization, 1989.

178. Walter T. Early and long-term effect of iron deficiency anemia on child development. In: Nutritional anemias. Fomon SJ, Zlotkin S, eds. New York: Raven, 1992.

179. Fairbanks VF. Iron in medicine and nutrition. In: Modern nutrition in health and disease. Shils ME, Olson JA, Shike M, eds. Philadelphia: Lea and Febiger, 1994.

180. Gibson RS. Principles of nutritional assessment. New York: Oxford University Press, 1990.

181. Wyler DJ. Malaria: overview and update. Clin Infect Dis 1993;16:449–458.

182. Oppenheimer SJ, Gibson FD, Macfarlane SB, et al. Iron supplementation increases prevalence and effects of malaria: report on clinical studies in Papua New Guinea. Trans R Soc Trop Med Hyg 1986;80:603–612.

183. Menendez C, Kahigwa E, Hirt R, et al. Randomized placebo-controlled trial of iron supplementation and malaria chemoprophylaxis for prevention of severe anaemia and malaria in Tanzanian infants. Lancet 1997;350:844–850.

184. Chippaux JP, Schneider D, Aplogan A, Dyck JL, Berger J. Effets de la supplementation en fer sur l'infection palustre. Bull Soc Pathol Exot 1991;84:54–62.

185. Smith AW, Hendrickse RG, Harrison C, Hayes RJ, Greenwood BM. The effects on malaria of treatment of iron-deficiency anaemia with oral iron in Gambian children. Ann Trop Paediatr 1989;9: 17–23.

186. Mebrahtu T, Stoltzfus RJ, Chwaya HM, Jape JK, Savioli L, Montresor A, Albonico M, Tielsch JM. Low-dose daily iron supplementation for 12 months does not increase the prevalence of malarial infection or density of parasites in young Zanzibari children. J Nutr. 2004 Nov;134(11):3037–3041.

187. Lawless JW, Latham MC, Stephenson LS, Kinoti SN, Pertet AM. Iron supplementation improves appetite and growth in anemic Kenyan primary school children. J Nutr 1994;124:645–654.

188. Adam, Z. Iron supplementation and malaria: a randomized, placebo-controlled field trial in rural Ethiopia. Study in children study. London: University of London, 1996.

189. Gebreselassie, H. Iron supplementation and malaria infection: results of a randomized controlled field trial.Montreal: McGill University, 1996.

190. Harvey PWJ, Heywood PF, Nesheim MC, et al. The effect of iron therapy on malarial infection in Papua New Guinean school children. Am J Trop Med Hyg 1989;40:12–18.

191. Adam, Z. Iron supplementation and malaria: a randomized, placebo-controlled field trial in rural Ethiopia. Study in adult women. London: University of London, 1996.

192. Fleming AF, Ghatoura GBS, Harrison KA, Briggs ND, Dunn DT. The prevention of anaemia in pregnancy in primigravidae in the guinea savanna of Nigeria. Ann Trop Med Parasitol 1986;80:211–233.

193. Menendez C, Todd J, Alonso PL, et al. The effects of iron supplementation during pregnancy, given by traditional birth attendants, on the prevalence of anaemia and malaria. Trans R Soc Trop Med Hyg 1994;88:590–593.

194. Bates CJ, Powers HJ, Lamb WH, Gelman W, Webb E. Effect of supplementary vitamins and iron on malaria indices in rural Gambian children. Trans R Soc Trop Med Hyg 1987;81:286–291.

195. Ekvall H, Premji Z, Bjorkman A. Micronutrient and iron supplementation and effective antimalarial treatment synergistically improve childhood anemia. Trop Med Int Health 2000;5:696–705.

196. van den Hombergh J, Dalderop E, Smit Y. Does iron therapy benefit children with severe malaria-associated anaemia? A clinical trial with 12 weeks supplementation of oral iron in young children from the Turiani Division, Tanzania. J Trop Pediatr 1996;42:220–227.

197. Nwanyanwu OC, Ziba C, Kazembe PN, Gamadzi G, Gondwe J, Redd SC. The effect of oral iron therapy during treatment for *Plasmodium falciparum* malaria with sulphadoxine-pyrimethamine on Malawian children under 5 years of age. Ann Trop Med Parasitol 1996;90:589–595.

198. Boele van Hensbroek M, Morris-Jones S, Meisner S, et al. Iron, but not folic acid, combined with effective antimalarial therapy promotes haematological recovery in African children after acute falciparum malaria. Trans R Soc Trop Med Hyg 1995;89:672–676.

199. Gordeuk V, Thuma P, Brittenham G, et al. Effect of iron chelation therapy on recovery from deep coma in children with cerebral malaria. N Engl J Med 1992;327:1473–1477.

200. Oppenheimer SJ, Macfarlane SBJ, Moody JB, Harrison C. Total dose iron infusion, malaria and pregnancy in Papua New Guinea. Trans R Soc Trop Med Hyg 1986;80:818–822.

201. Masawe AEJ, Muindi JM, Swai GB. Infections in iron deficiency and other types of anaemia in the tropics. Lancet 1974;2:314–317.

202. Oppenheimer SJ. Iron and its relation to immunity and infectious disease. J Nutr 2001 Feb;131 (2S-2):616S–633S; discussion 633S–635S

203. Harvey PWJ, Bell RG, Nesheim MC. Iron deficiency protects inbred mice against infection with *Plasmodium chabaudi*. Infect Immun 1985;50:932–934.

204. International Nutritional Anemia Consultative Group. Safety of iron supplementation programs in malaria-endemic regions. Washington, DC: International Life Science Institute, 2000.

205. Sazawal S, Black RE, Ramsan M, Chwaya HM, Stoltzfus RJ, Dutta A, Dhingra U, Kabole I, Deb S, Othman MK, Kabole FM. Effects of routine prophylactic supplementation with iron and folic acid on admission to hospital and mortality in preschool children in a high malaria transmission setting: community-based, randomised, placebo-controlled trial. Lancet 2006 Jan 14;367(9505):133–143.

206. Tielsch JM, Khatry SK, Stoltzfus RJ, Katz J, LeClerq SC, Adhikari R, Mullany LC, Shresta S, Black RE. Effect of routine prophylactic supplementation with iron and folic acid on preschool child mortality in southern Nepal: community-based, cluster-randomised, placebo-controlled trial. Lancet 2006 Jan 14;367(9505):144–152.

207. Nacher M, McGready R, Stepniewska K, Cho T, Looareesuwan S, White NJ, Nosten F. Haematinic treatment of anaemia increases the risk of *Plasmodium vivax* malaria in pregnancy. Trans R Soc Trop Med Hyg 2003 May–Jun;97(3):273–276.

208. Richard SA, Zavaleta N, Caulfield LE, Black RE, Witzig RS, Shankar AH. Zinc and iron supplementation and malaria, diarrhea, and respiratory infections in children in the Peruvian Amazon. Am J Trop Med Hyg. 2006 Jul;75(1):126–132.

209. Nyakeriga AM, Troye-Blomberg M, Dorfman JR, Alexander ND, Back R, Kortok M, Chemtai AK, Marsh K, Williams TN. Iron deficiency and malaria among children living on the coast of Kenya. J Infect Dis 2004 Aug 1;190(3):439–447. Epub July 2, 2004.

210. Kartikasari AE, Georgiou NA, Visseren FL, van Kats-Renaud H, Sweder van Asbeck B, Marx JJ. Endothelial activation and induction of monocyte adhesion by nontransferrin-bound iron present in human sera. FASEB J. 2006 Feb;20(2):353–345. Epub December 20, 2005.

211. Iyer JK, Shi L, Shankar AH, Sullivan DJ Jr. Zinc protoporphyrin IX binds heme crystals to inhibit the process of crystallization in *Plasmodium falciparum*. Mol Med. 2003 May–Aug;9(5–8): 175–182.

212. Vyoral D, Petrak J. Hepcidin: a direct link between iron metabolism and immunity. Int J Biochem Cell Biol. 2005 Sep;37(9):1768–1773.

213. Shankar AH, Prasad AS. Zinc and immune function: the biological basis of altered resistance to infection. Am J Clin Nutr 1998;68:447S–463S.

214. Fischer Walker C, Black RE. Zinc and the risk for infectious disease. Annu Rev Nutr 2004;24: 255–275.

215. Good MF, Kaslow DC, Miller LH. Pathways and strategies for developing a malaria blood-stage vaccine. Ann Rev Immunol 1998;16:57–87.

216. Gibson RS, Heywood A, Yaman C, Sohlstrom A, Thompson LU, Heywood P. Growth in children from the Wosera subdistrict, Papua New Guinea, in relation to energy and protein intakes and zinc status. Am J Clin Nutr 1991;53:782–789.

217. Gibson RS, Huddle JM. Suboptimal zinc status in pregnant Malawian women: its association with low intakes of poorly available zinc, frequent reproductive cycling, and malaria. Am J Clin Nutr 1998;67:702–709.

218. Bates CJ, Evans PH, Dardenne M, et al. A trial of zinc supplementation in young rural Gambian children. Br J Nutr 1993;69:243–255.

219. Shankar AH, Kumar N, Scott AL. Zinc-deficiency exacerbates experimental malaria infection in mice. FASEB J 1995;9:A4269.

220. Arif AJ, Mathur PD, Chandra S, Singh C, Sen AB. Effect of zinc diet on xanthine oxidase activity of liver of mice infected with *Plasmodium berghei*. Indian J Malariol 1987;24:59–63.

221. Shankar AH, Genton B, Baisor M, Paino J, Tamja S, Adiguma T, Wu L, Rare L, Bannon D, Tielsch JM, West KP Jr, Alpers MP. The influence of zinc supplementation on morbidity due to *Plasmodium falciparum*: a randomized trial in preschool children in Papua New Guinea. Am J Trop Med Hyg. 2000 Jun;62:663–669.

222. Muller O, Becher H, van Zweeden AB, Ye Y, Diallo DA, Konate AT, Gbangou A, Kouyate B, Garenne M. Effect of zinc supplementation on malaria and other causes of morbidity in west African children: randomised double blind placebo controlled trial. BMJ 2001 Jun 30;322(7302):1567.

223. Sazawal S, Black RE, Ramsan M, Chwaya HM, Dutta A, Dhingra U, Stoltzfus RJ, Othman MK, Kabole FM. Effect of zinc supplementation on mortality in children aged 1–48 months: randomised placebo-controlled trial. Lancet 2007 Mar 17;369(9565):927–934.

224. Zinc Against Plasmodium Study Group. Effect of zinc on the treatment of *Plasmodium falciparum* malaria in children: a randomized controlled trial. Am J Clin Nutr 2002 Oct;76(4):805–812.

225. Semba RD. The role of vitamin A and related retinoids in immune function. Nutr Rev 1998;56: S38–S48.

226. Roos A, Hegsted DM, Stare FJ. Nutritional studies with the duck. IV. The effect of vitamin deficiencies on the course of *P. lophurae* infection in the duck and the chick. J Nutr 1946;32: 473–484.

227. Krishnan S, Krishnan AD, Mustafa AS, Talwar GP, Ramalingaswami V. Effect of vitamin A and undernutrition on the susceptibility of rodents to a malarial parasite *Plasmodium berghei*. J Nutr 1976;106:784–791.

228. Stoltzfus RJ, Jalal F, Harvey PWJ, Nesheim MC. Interactions between vitamin A deficiency and *Plasmodium berghei* infection in the rat. J Nutr 1989;119:2030–2037.

229. Foote SJ, Burt RA, Baldwin TM, et al. Mouse loci for malaria-induced mortality and the control of parasitaemia. Nature Genet 1997;17:380–381.

230. Davis TME, Skinner-Adam TS, Beilby J. In vitro growth inhibition of *Plasmodium falciparum* by retinol at concentrations present in normal human serum. Acta Trop 1998;69:111–119.

231. Hamzah J, Skinner-Adams TS, Davis TM. In vitro antimalarial activity of retinoids and the influence of selective retinoic acid receptor antagonists. Acta Trop 2003 Aug;87(3):345–353.

232. Samba DC, Basco LK, Bleiberg-Daniel F, Lemmonier D, Le Bras J. Absence of effect of retinol on the in vitro development of *Plasmodium falciparum*. Int J Vit Nutr Res 1992;62:99–100.

233. Thurnham DI, Singkamani R. The acute phase response and vitamin A status in malaria. Trans R Soc Trop Med Hyg 1991;85:194–199.

234. Galan P, Samba C, Luzeau R, Amedee-Manesme O. Vitamin A deficiency in pre-school age Congolese children during malarial attacks. Part 2: impact of parasitic disease on vitamin A status. Int J Vit Nutr Res 1990;60:224–228.

235. Samba D, Luzeau R, Mourey MS, Amedee-Manesme O. Consequences de l'acces palustre sur les reserves vitaminiques A. Gastroenterol Clin Biol 1989;13:A288.

236. Tabone MD, Muanza K, Lyagoubi M, et al. The role of interleukin-6 in vitamin A deficiency during *Plasmodium falciparum* malaria and possible consequences for vitamin A supplementation. Immunology 1992;75:553–554.

237. Filteau SM, Morris SS, Abbott RA, et al. Influence of morbidity on serum retinol of children in a community-based study in northern Ghana. Am J Clin Nutr 1993;58:192–197.

238. Friis H, Mwaniki D, Omondi B, et al. Serum retinol concentrations and *Schistosoma mansoni*, intestinal helminths, and malarial parasitemia: a cross-sectional study in Kenyan preschool and primary school children. Am J Clin Nutr 1997;66:665–671.

239. Sturchler D, Tanner M, Hanck A, et al. A longitudinal study on relations of retinol with parasitic infections and the immune response in children of Kikwawila village, Tanzania. Acta Trop 1987;44: 213–227.

240. Binka FN, Ross DA, Morris SS, et al. Vitamin A supplementation and childhood malaria in northern Ghana. Am J Clin Nutr 1995;61:853–859.

241. Shankar AH. Vitamin A and malaria. Am J Clin Nutr 1995;62:842–843.

242. Villamor E, Mbise R, Spiegelman D, Hertzmark E, Fataki M, Peterson KE, Ndossi G, Fawzi WW. Vitamin A supplements ameliorate the adverse effect of HIV-1, malaria, and diarrheal infections on child growth. Pediatrics. 2002 Jan;109(1):E6.

243. Nussenblatt V, Mukasa G, Metzger A, Ndeezi G, Eisinger W, Semba RD. Relationship between carotenoids and anaemia during acute uncomplicated *Plasmodium falciparum* malaria in children. J Health Popul Nutr. 2002 Sep;20(3):205–214.

244. Cooper KA, Adelekan DA, Esimai AO, Northrop-Clewes CA, Thurnham DI. Lack of influence of red palm oil on severity of malaria infection in pre-school Nigerian children. Trans R Soc Trop Med Hyg. 2002 Mar–Apr;96(2):216–223.

245. Shankar AH, Genton B, Semba RD, et al. Effect of vitamin A supplementation on morbidity due to *Plasmodium falciparum* in young children in Papua New Guinea: a randomised trial. Lancet 1999;354:203–209.

246. Cox SE, Staalsoe T, Arthur P, Bulmer JN, Tagbor H, Hviid L, Frost C, Riley EM, Kirkwood BR. Maternal vitamin A supplementation and immunity to malaria in pregnancy in Ghanaian primigravids. Trop Med Int Health. 2005 Dec;10(12):1286–1297.

247. Varandas L, Julien M, Gomes A, Rodrigues P, Van Lerberghe W, Malveiro F, Aguiar P, Kolsteren P, Van Der Stuyft P, Hilderbrand K, Labadarios D, Ferrinho P. A randomised, double-blind, placebo-controlled clinical trial of vitamin A in severe malaria in hospitalised Mozambican children. Ann Trop Paediatr 2001 Sep;21(3):211–222.

248. Serghides L, Kain KC. Mechanism of protection induced by vitamin A in falciparum malaria. Lancet 2002 Apr 20;359(9315):1404–1406.

249. Macreadie I, Ginsburg H, Sirawaraporn W, Tilley L, 2000. Antimalarial drug development and new targets. Parasitol Today 16: 438–444.

250. Seeler AO, Ott WH. Studies on nutrition and avian malaria. III. Deficiency of "folic acid" and other unidentified factors. J Infect Dis 1945;77:82–84.

251. Das KC, Virdi JS, Herbert V. Survival of the dietarily deprived: folate deficiency protects against malaria in primates. Blood 1992;80:281a.

252. Hamilton PJ, Gebbie DA, Wilks NE, Lothe F. The role of malaria, folic acid deficiency and haemoglobin AS in pregnancy at Mulago hospital. Trans R Soc Trop Med Hyg 1972;66:594–602.

253. Fleming AF, Werblinska B. Anaemia in childhood in the quinea savanna of Nigeria. Ann Trop Paediatr 1982;2:161–173.

254. Strickland GT, Kostinas JE. Folic acid deficiency complicating malaria. Am J Trop Med Hyg 1970;19:910–915.

255. Fleming AF, Hendrickse JP, Allan NC. The prevention of megaloblastic anaemia in pregnancy in Nigeria. J Obstet Gynaecol Br Commonw 1968;75:425–432.

256. Brabin BJ, van den Berg H, Nijmeyer F. Folacin, cobalamin, and hematological status during pregnancy in rural Kenya: the influence of parity, gestation, and *Plasmodium falciparum* malaria. Am J Clin Nutr 1986;43:803–815.

257. Fuller NJ, Bates CJ, Hayes RJ, et al. The effects of antimalarials and folate supplements on haematological indices and red cell folate levels in Gambian children. Ann Trop Paediatr 1988;8:61–67.

258. Gail K, Herms V. Influence of pteroylglutamic acid (folic acid) on parasite density (*Plasmodium falciparum*) in pregnant women in West Africa. Zeitschrift Tropenmed Parasitol 1969;20:440–450.

259. Hurley MGD. Administration of pyrimenthamine with folic and folinic acids in human malaria. Trans R Soc Trop Med Hyg 1959;53:410–411.

260. Tong MJ, Strickland GT, Votteri BA, Gunning J. Supplemental folates in the therapy of *Plasmodium falciparum* malaria. J Am Med Assoc 1970;214:2330–2333.

261. Topley E. Anaemia where malaria is endemic. Trop Doctor 1975;5:18–22.

262. van Hensbroek MB, Morris-Jones S, Meisner S, et al. Iron, but not folic acid, combined with effective antimalarial therapy promotes haematological recovery in African children after acute falciparum malaria. Trans R Soc Trop Med Hyg 1995;89:672–676.

263. Carter JY, Loolpapit MP, Lema OE, Tome JL, Nagelkerke NJ, Watkins WM. Reduction of the efficacy of antifolate antimalarial therapy by folic acid supplementation. Am J Trop Med Hyg. 2005 Jul;73(1):166–170.

264. Mulenga M, Malunga P, Bennett S, Thuma P, Shulman C, Fielding K, Greenwood B. Folic acid treatment of Zambian children with moderate to severe malaria anemia. Am J Trop Med Hyg. 2006 Jun;74(6):986–990.

265. Mbaye A, Richardson K, Balajo B, Dunyo S, Shulman C, Milligan P, Greenwood B, Walraven G. Lack of inhibition of the anti-malarial action of sulfadoxine-pyrimethamine by folic acid supplementation when used for intermittent preventive treatment in Gambian primigravidae. Am J Trop Med Hyg 2006 Jun;74(6):960–964.

266. Oppenheimer SJ, Bull R, Thurnham DI. Riboflavin deficiency in Madang infants. Papua New Guinea Med J 1983;26:17–20.

267. Thurnham DI, Oppenheimer SJ, Bull R. Riboflavin status and malaria in infants in Papua New Guinea. Trans R Soc Trop Med Hyg 1983;77:423–424.

268. Dutta P, Pinto J, Rivlin R. Antimalarial effects of riboflavin deficiency. Lancet 1985;2:1040–1043.

269. Thurnham DI. Antimalarial effects of riboflavin deficiency. Lancet 1985;2:1310–1311.

270. Bates CJ, Powers HJ, Lamb WH, Anderson BB, Perry GM, Vullo C. Antimalarial effects of riboflavin deficiency. Lancet 1986;1:329–330.

271. Das BS, Das DB, Satpathy RN, Patnaik JK, Bose TK. Riboflavin deficiency and severity of malaria. Eur J Clin Nutr 1988;42:277–283.

272. Traunmuller F, Ramharter M, Lagler H, Thalhammer F, Kremsner PG, Graninger W, Winkler S. Normal riboflavin status in malaria patients in Gabon. Am J Trop Med Hyg. 2003 Feb;68(2):182–185.

273. Das BS, Thurnham DI, Patnaik JK, Das DB, Satpathy R, Bose TK. Increased plasma lipid peroxidation in riboflavin-deficient, malaria-infected children. Am J Clin Nutr 1990;51:859–863.

274. Barraviera B, Machado PE, Meira DA. Glutathione reductase activity and its relation with riboflavin levels measured by methemoglobin reduction by cystamine in patients with malaria (preliminary report). Rev Instit Med Trop Sao Paulo 1988;30:107–108.

275. Anderson BB, Giuberti M, Perry GM, Salsini G, Casadio I, Vullo C. Low red blood cell glutathione reductase and pyridoxine phosphate oxidase activities not related to dietary riboflavin: selection by malaria? Am J Clin Nutr 1993;57:666–672.

276. Dutta P. Enhanced uptake and metabolism of riboflavin in erythrocytes infected with *Plasmodium falciparum*. J Protozool 1991;38:479–483.

277. Cowden WB, Clark IA. Antimalarial activity of synthetic riboflavin antagonists. Trans R Soc Trop Med Hyg 1987;81:533.

278. Cowden WB, Butcher GA, Hunt NH, Clark IA, Yoneda F. Antimalarial activity of a riboflavin analog against *Plasmodium vinckei* in vivo and *Plasmodium falciparum* in vitro. Am J Trop Med Hyg 1987;37:495–500.

279. Kaikai P, Thurnham DI. The influence of riboflavin deficiency on *Plasmodium berghei* infection in rats. Trans R Soc Trop Med Hyg 1983;77:680–686.

280. Seeler AO, Ott WH. Effect of riboflavin deficiency on the course of *Plasmodium Lophurae* infection in chicks. J Infect Dis 1944;75:175–178.

281. Dutta P, Gee M, Rivlin RS, Pinto J. Riboflavin deficiency and glutathione metabolism in rats: possible mechanisms underlying altered responses to hemolytic stimuli. J Nutr 1988;118:1149–1157.

282. Akompong T, Ghori N, Haldar K. In vitro activity of riboflavin against the human malaria parasite *Plasmodium falciparum*. Antimicrob Agents Chemother 2000;44:88–96.

283. Krishna S, Taylor AM, Supanaranond W, et al. Thiamine deficiency and malaria in adults from southeast Asia. Lancet 1999;353:546–549.

284. Ramo Rao R, Sirsi N. Avian malaria and B complex vitamins. I. Thiamine. J Indian Instit Sci 1956;38:108.

285. Adamolekun B, Eniola A. Thiamine-responsive acute cerebellar ataxia following febrile illness. Cent Afr J Med 1993;39:40–41.

286. Wrenger C, Eschbach ML, Muller IB, Laun NP, Begley TP, Walter RD. Vitamin B1 de novo synthesis in the human malaria parasite *Plasmodium falciparum* depends on external provision of 4-amino-5-hydroxymethyl-2-methylpyrimidine. Biol Chem. 2006 Jan;387(1):41–51.

287. Wrenger C, Eschbach ML, Muller IB, Warnecke D, Walter RD. Analysis of the vitamin B6 biosynthesis pathway in the human malaria parasite *Plasmodium falciparum*. J Biol Chem. 2005 Feb 18;280(7):5242–5248. Epub December 7, 2004.

288. Levander OA, Ager AL Jr. Malarial parasites and antioxidant nutrients. Parasitology 1993;107:S95–S106.

289. Kretschmar W. The importance of p-aminobenzoic acid to the course and immunity of malaria in animals (*Plasmodium berghei*) and in man (*Plasmodium falciparum*). 2. Studies on naturally fed small children. Z Trop Parasitol 1966;17:369–374.

290. Eaton JW, Eckman JR, Berger E, Jacob HS. Suppression of malaria infection by oxidant-sensitive host erythrocytes. Nature 1976;264:758–760.

291. Godfrey DG. Antiparasitic action of dietary cod liver oil upon *Plasmodium berghei* and its reversal by vitamin E. Exp Parasitol 1957;6:555–565.

292. Eckman JR, Eaton JW, Berger E, Jacob HS. Role of vitamin E in regulating malaria expression. Trans Assoc Am Physicians 1976;89:105–115.

293. Levander OA, Ager AL Jr, Morris VC, May RG. Menhaden-fish oil in a vitamin E-deficient diet: protection against chloroquine-resistant malaria in mice. Am J Clin Nutr 1989;50:1237–1239.

294. Levander OA, Ager AL Jr, Morris VC, May RG. *Plasmodium yoelii*: comparative antimalarial activities of dietary fish oils and fish oil concentrates in vitamin E-deficient mice. Exp Parasitol 1990;70:323–329.

295. Levander OA, Ager AL Jr, Morris VC, May RG. Protective effect of ground flaxseed or ethyl linolenate in a vitamin E-deficient diet against murine malaria. Nutr Res 1991;11:941–948.

296. Taylor DW, Levander OA, Krishna VR, Evans CB, Morris VC, Barta JR. Vitamin E-deficient diets enriched with fish oil suppress lethal *Plasmodium yoelii* infections in athymic and scid/bg mice. Infect Immun 1997;65:197–202.

297. Levander OA, Fontela R, Morris VC, Ager AL Jr. Protection against murine cerebral malaria by dietary-induced oxidative stress. J Parasitol 1995;81:99–103.

298. Yarrington JT, Whitehair CK, Corwin RM. Vitamin E-selenium deficiency and its influence on avian malarial infection in the duck. J Nutr 1973;103:231–241.

299. Levander OA. Selenium and sulfur in antioxidant protective systems: relationships with vitamin E and malaria. Proc Soc Exp Biol Med 1992;200:255–259.

300. Levander OA, Ager AL Jr, Morris VC, May RG. Qinghaosu, dietary vitamin E, selenium, and cod-liver oil: effect on the susceptibility of mice to the malarial parasite *Plasmodium yoelii*. Am J Clin Nutr 1989;50:346–352.

301. McKee RW, Geiman QM. Studies on malarial parasites. V. Effects of ascorbic acid on malaria (*Plasmodium knowlesi*) in monkeys. Proc Soc Exp Biol Med 1946;63:313–315.

302. Metzger A, Mukasa G, Shankar AH, Ndeezi G, Melikian G, Semba RD. Antioxidant status and acute malaria in children in Kampala, Uganda. Am J Trop Med Hyg 2001 Aug;65(2):115–119.

303. West KP Jr. Vitamin A deficiency: its epidemiology and relation to child mortality and morbidity. In: Vitamin A in health and disease. Blomhoff R, ed. New York: Dekker, 1994:585–614.

304. Graves PM. Comparison of the cost-effectiveness of vaccines and insecticide impregnation of mosquito nets for the prevention of malaria. Ann Trop Med Parasitol 1998;92:399–410.

305. Black RE. Therapeutic and preventive effects of zinc on serious childhood infectious diseases in developing countries. Am J Clin Nutr 1998;68:476S–479S.

306. Sazawal S, Black R, Jalla S, Bhan MK, Bhandari N, Sinha A. Zinc supplementation in young children with acute diarrhea in India. N Engl J Med 1995;333:839–844.

307. Sazawal S, Black R, Jalla S, Mazumdar S, Sinha A, Bhan MK. Zinc supplementation reduces the incidence of acute lower respiratory infections in infants and preschool children: a double-blind controlled trial. Pediatrics 1998;102:1–5.

308. Snow RW, Omumbo JA, Lowe B, et al. Relation between severe malaria morbidity in children and level of *Plasmodium falciparum* transmission in Africa. Lancet 1997;349:1650–1654.

# 10 Tuberculosis

## Monique van Lettow and Christopher Whalen

## 10.1 INTRODUCTION

### 10.1.1 Definitions

Tuberculosis is an infection caused by *Mycobacterium tuberculosis* or related organisms such as *Mycobacterium bovis*. *Mycobacterium tuberculosis*, a slowly growing, acid-fast-staining bacillus, is the most common cause of tuberculosis in humans and is the focus of this chapter. Tuberculosis is most commonly transmitted from person to person via the aerial route, and most individuals who are infected do not develop clinical disease. About 5% of those infected may develop clinical manifestations such as pulmonary or miliary disease, and disease may occur at the time of primary infection or may occur years later. Malnutrition and other immunosuppressive disorders such as human immunodeficiency virus (HIV) infection increase the risk of developing clinical disease (Fig. 10.1). In the absence of effective chemotherapy, tuberculosis is characterized by wasting and high mortality. The association of poor nutrition with tuberculosis is evident in older terms for tuberculosis, such as the Greek term *phthisis* or "to waste away" and "consumption."

### 10.1.2 Public Health Importance

Worldwide, tuberculosis is the second most common cause of death from infectious disease, after HIV/AIDS, accounting for 2 million deaths annually. About one third of the world's population, or 1.8 billion individuals, are infected with *M. tuberculosis*, representing an enormous pool of individuals at risk for development of future disease [1]. In sub-Saharan Africa, the Indian subcontinent, and Southeast Asia, half or more of adults have latent tuberculosis infection. Each year, between 7 and 8 million people throughout the world develop active tuberculosis, and the vast majority of cases occur in sub-Saharan Africa and Asia. Tuberculosis is responsible for about one quarter of all preventable deaths in developing countries, and many of these deaths are associated with underlying HIV infection.

The current global situation of tuberculosis is complicated by three factors: the evolving pandemic of human immunodeficiency virus type 1 (HIV), the emergence of multidrug-resistant tuberculosis, and the increased mobility of populations. The epidemics of tuberculosis and HIV overlap in many regions of the world, especially in sub-Saharan

From: *Nutrition and Health: Nutrition and Health in Developing Countries, Second Edition*
Edited by: R. D. Semba & M. W. Bloem © Humana Press, Totowa, NJ

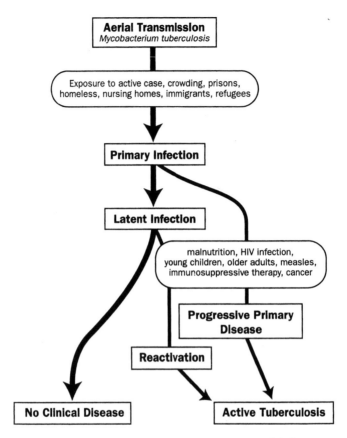

**ɤ. 10.1.** General model for tuberculosis infection and common risk factors.

Africa, and the potential of the disease to spread is enormous, especially in Asia, where the HIV epidemic is growing rapidly [2]. Multidrug-resistant tuberculosis represents a major threat to the global control of tuberculosis, and a global survey indicated that drug-resistant strains are being transmitted in every continent [3]. On both local and global levels, the mixing of potential or infectious cases of tuberculosis within populations of susceptible individuals has increased because of greater mobility in a modern world [4, 5]. War, political strife, famine, poverty, and refugee crises render the control of tuberculosis even more intractable.

## 10.2   HISTORICAL BACKGROUND

### 10.2.1   Antiquity

Tuberculosis has been described from the mummified remains of a priest who lived 3,000 years ago in the 21st dynasty of ancient Egypt [6, 7], and the disease has also been found in mummified remains of a child from pre-Columbian Peru [8]. A clinical description consistent with pulmonary tuberculosis appears in *Epidemics III* of the Hippocratic corpus from the fifth century BC [9]. The terms *phthisis*, *tabes*, and *marasmus* were used to describe diseases characterized by emaciation, including tuberculosis, and in Greek derivation these terms are close in signifying wasting away, weakness, and decay. Tuberculosis is mentioned by many medical writers from antiquity. Aretaeus the Cappadocian (81–?138 AD) provided a detailed description of advanced tuberculosis, and he recommended a generous diet of fresh eggs and milk as treatment [10]. In classical Rome, Galen (130–200 AD) considered milk a treatment for tuberculosis, suggesting that patients take milk directly from an ass [11].

### 10.2.2 Early Ideas About Tuberculosis

During the Middle Ages, scrofula (tuberculosis of the lymph glands of the neck) became known as "the King's Evil" because kings were thought to have the power to cure the condition by touching afflicted individuals [12, 13]. Scrofula and pulmonary tuberculosis were generally considered separate illnesses. Different forms of consumption were described by Richard Morton (1635–1698) in *Phthisiologia: or a Treatise of Consumptions,* and pulmonary consumption was considered a distinct entity, characterized by wasting, fever, and a dry, nonproductive cough that later became purulent. *Exulceration* was a process of coughing up material that resulted in cavities in the lung [14]. In the 18th century, the nosology, or classification of disease, emerged as an important approach, and it was largely influenced by the Linnaean system for the taxonomy of plants. Thus, diseases could be classified according to their symptoms. William Cullen (1710–1790), a physician in Scotland, devised a well-known classification of diseases in which *phthisis* was defined as a hectic fever accompanied by the expectoration of purulent matter from the lungs [15]. Wasting was not part of Cullen's definition of phthisis. Phthisis could arise from "acrimony" in the blood, which could produce tubercles and then ulceration. Symptoms followed. An interpretation of clinical observations of tuberculosis by Morton and Cullen has been presented in detail elsewhere [16].

The Paris medical school was preeminent in Europe during the early half of the 19th century, when medical knowledge became based on an integration of direct clinical observation of large numbers of patients with detailed postmortem examinations of those who died [17, 18]. Instead of viewing phthisis as a rather sudden presentation of illness, Gaspard-Laurent Bayle (1774–1816) considered phthisis to be a process in which different stages exist, which led to destruction of the lungs [19]. The invention of the stethoscope by René-Théophile-Hyacinthe Laennec (1781–1826) allowed inference about abnormalities inside the chest and correlation with other clinical findings. In *Traité de l'auscultation médiate* of 1819, Laennec used the term phthisis to refer to destructive diseases of the lung that were associated with the tubercle [20].

A dominant idea in cell theory toward the mid-19th century was that cells, with nucleus and outer membrane, could grow out of blastema, or morbid secretions [21]. Thus, blastema gave rise to tubercle formation. Advances in microscopy and more precise observations led Rudolf Virchow (1821–1902), a German pathologist, to refute the blastema theory and to conclude that exudation did not give rise to new cells, but that cells arose out of preexisting cells or *omnis cellula e cellula* (each cell from a cell). Virchow considered that caseation, or formation of cheese-like masses (i.e. the tubercle) was the result of cellular transformation, and that it was not specific for phthisis alone, occurring in cancer and suppuration as well. In Virchow's view, scrofula resulted from a weakness of the mother tissue plus a constitutional predisposition plus a location where cells went to pieces more easily.

### 10.2.3   Tuberculosis as an Infectious Disease

The idea that tuberculosis could be caused by a specific infectious agent was pursued by Jean-Antoine Villemin (1827–1892). Other diseases, such as syphilis, smallpox, and glanders, appeared to be caused by specific infectious agents. Villemin demonstrated that caseous material and tubercles from a human could cause tuberculosis in rabbits. He performed other experiments showing that sputum and bronchial secretions were also infectious in nature [22], and he concluded that tuberculosis was a transmissible disease. Robert Koch (1843–1910), a German physician, conducted microscopic studies that led to the description of the tubercle bacillus [23]. Koch devised a new staining technique that allowed the detection of rod-shaped bacteria in affected tissues, and he was able to grow the bacteria in artificial culture media. The pure culture, when injected into an animal host, resulted in tuberculosis. Koch later described a phenomenon in which an extract of tuberculosis injected in the skin could differentiate between a previously infected and uninfected animal, leading eventually to the development of the tuberculin skin test [24]. Koch's reputation suffered greatly when he claimed that tuberculin, an extract of tubercle bacilli, could cure tuberculosis.

Therapies for the treatment of tuberculosis in the 18th century included fresh air, which was thought to aid the healing and closing of cavities and ulcers in the lungs [25]. Moving to warmer climates and long sea voyages were sought by some afflicted with tuberculosis [26]. In Europe, the Swiss Alps became a popular destination for those seeking a cure in the latter half of the 19th century. The sanitorium became a prominent approach to tuberculosis treatment, and this institutionalized care, usually in sunny, rural locations, included fresh air, rest, regulated exercise, and supervised diet [26, 27]. Sunlight exposure, sea bathing, and radiation with ultraviolet light were also advocated for treatment of tuberculosis [28]. Collapse therapy of the lung (artificial pneumothorax) was used to treat pulmonary tuberculosis [29].

### 10.2.4   Cod-Liver Oil Therapy

The use of cod-liver oil deserves special mention in regard to nutrition and tuberculosis. In the 18th and 19th centuries in European cities, tuberculosis was widespread and the cause of 25% of all adult deaths [30]. During the early 19th century, the survival in adults with pulmonary tuberculosis was 2 years from the time of diagnosis, and no therapy was effective [31]. The therapy for tuberculosis was considered to have changed dramatically with the introduction of cod-liver oil [32]. Cod-liver oil is a rich source of vitamins A and D and was long known as having medicinal properties in fishing villages along the North Sea and in Norway. The use of cod-liver oil as a treatment for tuberculosis spread to Germany [33] and France [34]. After the introduction of cod-liver oil at Brompton Hospital, the main hospital for tuberculosis in London, using historical controls, the survival rate increased fourfold from an average 2 years to 8 years after diagnosis [31]. Cod-liver oil consumption at Brompton Hospital alone reached 1,500 gallons per year [35], and in addition to a decrease in mortality, weight gain was typically observed among those treated with cod-liver oil [36].

From 1820 until 1920, there are numerous reports of clinical improvement in pulmonary and lymphatic tuberculosis with cod-liver oil therapy [37]. In an early trial of cod-liver oil for adults with pulmonary tuberculosis complicated by intestinal involvement, 28 cases received symptomatic treatment only, and 50 cases were treated with cod-liver oil. Adults treated with cod-liver oil had a steady gain in weight, while adults in the control group had a continual loss of weight in 50 weeks of follow-up, with 10% mortality reported in the cod-liver oil treatment group versus 71% mortality in those receiving symptomatic treatment [38]. During the tuberculosis sanitarium movement in the United States in the early part of this century, cod-liver oil was often used as treatment. Cod-liver oil therapy for tuberculosis was largely superseded by antibiotic treatment in the 1940s, and in general, scientific interest in nutritional status and tuberculosis waned. Dietetic management of tuberculosis continued to include an "eggs-and-milk" approach in the 1940s and 1950s [39] and later an emphasis on high protein intake [40]. Because of the later emphasis on tuberculosis chemotherapy, most reports on the relationship between nutritional status and tuberculosis largely antedate 1950.

### 10.2.5   BCG Vaccine and Tuberculosis Chemotherapy

At the Pasteur Institute, efforts were made by Léon Charles Albert Calmette (1863–1933) and Camille Guérin (1872–1961) to develop a vaccine against tuberculosis. An attenuated strain of bovine tubercle bacilli, *Bacilli Calmette-Guérin*, was found to have a protective effect in calves, and later this vaccine, known as BCG, was tried in infants [41]. BCG vaccine was eventually accepted by many countries around the world and was recommended by the World Health Organization as part of tuberculosis control [42]; however, the vaccine was not adopted in the United States, despite evidence for efficacy of the vaccine [43, 44] in preventing disseminated forms of tuberculosis, because of the low and declining prevalence of disease in the country and the strategic choice to treat latent tuberculosis infection. The United States remains one of the few countries where BCG vaccination is not used in tuberculosis control.

Streptomycin was isolated in the laboratory of Selman Waksman (1888–1973), a Russian soil microbiologist who had migrated to the United States. A preliminary trial suggested that it could be effective against tuberculosis [45], and a large controlled clinical trial was conducted by the British Medical Research Council, which provided definitive evidence that streptomycin was an effective treatment for pulmonary tuberculosis [46]. A similar effort to evaluate streptomycin through a clinical trial at the Veterans Administration in the United States failed to provide persuasive therapeutic evidence because investigators abandoned the use of an untreated control group for comparison, delaying recommendations for more widespread use of the drug [47]. In the 1950s, isonicotinic acid hydrazide, or isoniazid, emerged as a new treatment for tuberculosis [48], and soon multiple therapy was initiated to treat tuberculosis and reduce the chance of drug resistance.

### 10.2.6   The Decline of Tuberculosis in Industrialized Countries

In the latter half of the 19th century and through the first half of the 20th century, mortality rates from pulmonary tuberculosis were steadily declining in England and Wales (Fig. 10.2). Thomas McKeown (1912–1988) hypothesized that the decline in tuberculosis mortality was largely the result of improvements in standards of living and nutrition

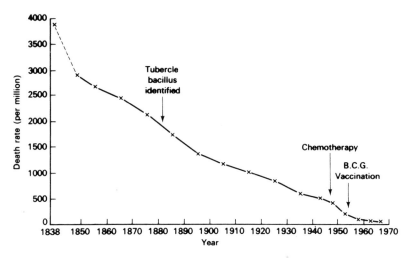

**Fig. 10.2.** Case fatality rates for tuberculosis. (Based on [49].)

rather than advances in medicine, such as antibiotics [49, 50]. Others have argued that government sanitary reforms and isolation of individuals with tuberculosis accounted for the decline in the disease. Tuberculosis often affects populations for whom poverty, inadequate housing, crowding, alcoholism, poor diet, and bad hygiene are present, and the decline of tuberculosis probably occurred because of a combination of factors, many of which are difficult to disentangle from historical epidemiology [51].

For further reading, general histories of tuberculosis can be found in older, standard texts, most of which have a medical orientation and celebrate individuals related to medicine and scientific progress through great discoveries [52–55], and in other texts that are more accessible to the general reader [56, 57]. The social history of tuberculosis in the United States [58, 59], France [51], Great Britain [27], and Japan [60] are discussed in other texts.

## 10.3   EPIDEMIOLOGY

### 10.3.1   Geographic Distribution

Tuberculosis is distributed throughout the world, but the main burden of tuberculosis infection and disease is found in developing countries. During the 1990s, Africa and Asia had the highest prevalence of both tuberculosis infection and active tuberculosis. The prevalence of tuberculosis ranges from 26% in the Americas to 44% in the Western Pacific. The annual risk of infection, a marker of *M. tuberculosis* transmission [61], is estimated at 1–2% per year [62]. Similarly for active tuberculosis, the annual global incidence increased from 62 cases/100,000 population in the 1980s to 75 cases/100,000 population in the 1990s [63]. The greatest increase in incidence occurred in Asia, where the annual incidence changed from 115 cases/100,000 population to 148 cases/100,000 population between 1985 and 1995, an increase of 25%. Africa had the second highest increase in tuberculosis incidence in this period, rising 19%, with an average incidence of 80 cases/100,000 population. In 2000, there were an estimated 8–9 million new cases of tuberculosis. Sub-Saharan Africa had the highest absolute incidence rate (290 per 100,000 population), but the most populous countries of Asia had the largest numbers of cases: India, China, Indonesia, Bangladesh, and Pakistan together accounted for more than half the global burden. Asia and Africa now account for 80% of the tuberculosis cases worldwide [1].

The global tuberculosis caseload appears to be growing slowly. Although case numbers have declined in western and central Europe, North and South America, and the Middle East, they have increased in countries of the former Soviet Union, in parts of Asia, and in sub-Saharan Africa. Economic decline and general failure of health services have increased tuberculosis rates in the former Soviet Union. The increase in tuberculosis incidence in Africa is strongly associated with the prevalence of HIV infection [1].

### 10.3.2  High-Risk Groups and Risk Factors

In considering the epidemiology of tuberculosis, it is useful to separate the risk of acquiring infection from the risk of developing active disease. The risks for infection relate to the probability of contact with an infected case, whereas the risk for developing disease once infected relate to the success of the host immune response in containing the infection. Groups at high risk for infection include close contacts of infectious cases [64], individuals living in congregate settings such as prisons [65], homeless [66], those in nursing homes [67], recent immigrants from countries where the prevalence of tuberculosis is high, and medically underserved or marginalized populations. In addition, individuals with a recent tuberculin skin test conversion from negative to positive are at risk for early progression of disease.

Once infected, an individual has about a 10% lifetime risk of developing active tuberculosis. Some recently infected individuals fail to contain the initial infection and progress to develop active tuberculosis, a situation known as *progressive primary disease*. Other individuals successfully contain the initial infection, become latently infected for a prolonged period of time, and then develop active disease years to decades after the infection [68, 69]. Common conditions associated with the risk of developing active tuberculosis are diseases associated with immunosuppression such as HIV infection, measles, and malnutrition. Other conditions associated with the reactivation of tuberculosis include fibrotic lung lesions consistent with previous untreated pulmonary tuberculosis, lymphoma, prolonged immunosuppressive therapy (e.g., corticosteroids), head and neck cancers, insulin-dependent diabetes mellitus, and end-stage renal disease. Host nutritional status may influence the risk of an infected individual developing active tuberculosis, as discussed in a section on nutrition.

### 10.3.3  Incidence and Prevalence of Tuberculosis in Vulnerable Populations

#### 10.3.3.1  HIV INFECTION

HIV infection confers the greatest known risk for the development of both progressive primary disease and reactivation tuberculosis. Among patients with advanced HIV disease, recent infection progresses to disease within 6 months in 30–40% of patients [69]. Among individuals with a reactive tuberculin skin test, defined as 5 mm or greater induration, the risk of disease depends on the population involved. In cohort studies of injection drug users, the risk is high, about 7% to 12% per year [70]. In Africa, the risk ranges from 3 to 8 cases per 100 person-years of observation [71, 72]. The risk of tuberculosis among tuberculin-negative persons is lower. Among HIV-infected individuals with cutaneous anergy to tuberculin and other skin test antigens (e.g., candida, mumps, tetanus), there appears to be an increased risk for developing active tuberculosis [73]. In sub-Saharan Africa, the seroprevalence rates of HIV infection in adults with tuberculosis range from 20% to over 75% [2, 74], and even higher seroprevalence rates of HIV occur among children [75, 76]. In 2000, an estimated 11% of new adult tuberculosis cases were infected with HIV, with wide variations among regions: 38% in sub-Saharan Africa, 14% in more developed countries, and 1% in the western Pacific Region. About two million people died of tuberculosis in 2000, with 13% also infected with HIV [1].

### 10.3.3.2 CHILDREN

Children younger than 5 years of age are particularly susceptible to tuberculosis, especially disseminated forms of disease such as tuberculous meningitis and miliary disease. In most instances, children are exposed to an infectious parent or relative through household contact. This exposure leads to an initial tuberculosis infection in about one half of contacts. The attack rate for active tuberculosis in children who are contacts is high, estimated to be 25% within 5 years of the exposure [77] or 400 cases/100,000 population for children less than 5 [68]. The risk for developing tuberculosis declines to minimal levels among adolescents until puberty, when the risk again increases.

### 10.3.3.3 OLDER ADULTS

Older adults represent another group at risk for the development of tuberculosis. Active tuberculosis in this population most likely represents reactivation of remote tuberculous infections. In the United States in 2004, the average rates of tuberculosis were about 60% higher in older adults compared to the national average (7.8 vs. 4.9 cases/100,000 population, respectively). Moreover, even today in the United States, tuberculosis among persons older than 65 years accounts for 20% of the total cases of tuberculosis. Older age has also been associated with increased mortality. Tuberculosis in the elderly is an important problem because of the potential for transmission in nursing homes. Tuberculosis incidence rates are 39 cases/100,000 population in nursing homes versus 21 cases/100,00 population in the community. It is likely that nursing homes represent sites for ongoing transmission, not only to other residents of the home but also to health-care providers. Another high-risk situation for the transmission of tuberculosis occurs where older grandparents live together with young children under age 5 in extended family households.

### 10.3.3.4 OTHER POPULATIONS AT RISK

Other populations at high risk for tuberculosis include some minority groups, the homeless, foreign-born immigrants from countries where the prevalence of tuberculosis is high, and prisoners. At-risk minority populations comprise 70% of the tuberculosis cases in the United States. Compared to the rate in non-Hispanic whites, the incidence rates in Asians is ten times greater, in non-Hispanic blacks eight times greater, and in Hispanics and Native Americans five times greater [78]. The homeless are a difficult group to track and make accurate estimates of incidence; however, the prevalence of tuberculosis in these individuals is high. In a study from New York City, 43% of men in a homeless shelter over a 5-year period had latent tuberculosis infection, and 6% had active tuberculosis [79]. Prisoners have an incidence rate for tuberculosis that is ten times the general population, with rates that range from 90 cases/100,000 inmates to 184 cases/100,000 inmates [80]. Foreign-born individuals residing in the United States comprise a disproportionate number of tuberculosis cases in the United States and accounted for 60% of the excess tuberculosis cases observed between 1985 and 1995 [81]. Similar trends in tuberculosis incidence have been observed in other industrialized countries with high levels of immigration from developing countries. The incidence rates among foreign-born in the United States depend on the country of origin and range from 12 cases to 177 cases/100,000 population [82], with countries of origin with the highest rates from Asia, Haiti, and sub-Saharan Africa.

### 10.3.4  Drug-Resistant Tuberculosis

Within months of the first use of streptomycin for the treatment of tuberculosis, drug-resistant strains of *M. tuberculosis* emerged. The development of drug resistance to a single drug was a harbinger of events to come as new antituberculous drugs were introduced into practice. The use of multiple drugs in the treatment regimen for tuberculosis prevented the emergence of drug-resistant strains [83] and has become the standard practice in treated active disease. Despite the standard multidrug treatment regimens, multidrug-resistant strains of *M. tuberculosis* have emerged, best documented in well-studied outbreaks of tuberculosis in the United States during the early 1990s.

The emergence of drug resistance is directly related to previous treatment for tuberculosis, whether through improper regimens, inadequate treatment, or incomplete adherence [84]. A nationwide survey in the United States indicated that resistance to one or more antituberculous drugs was present in 14% of cases, and resistance to both isoniazid and rifampin, the two most potent antituberculous drugs currently available, was present in 3.5% of specimens tested [85]. The problem of drug-resistant tuberculosis is global as a survey conducted by the World Health Organization of 35 countries throughout the world indicated that all countries reported cases of resistant tuberculosis [3]. Approximately 10% of strains tested were resistant to one or more antituberculous medications. The treatment and management of drug-resistant tuberculosis is one of the greatest challenges of the future facing tuberculosis control programs.

## 10.4  CLINICAL FEATURES/PATHOPHYSIOLOGY

### 10.4.1  Clinical Features of Tuberculosis

Tuberculosis is a disease produced by chronic infection with *M. tuberculosis*. The spectrum of disease ranges from asymptomatic latent tuberculosis infection to disseminated disease. The most common form of tuberculosis is latent infection. The standard way to make the diagnosis of latent tuberculosis infection is through tuberculin skin testing, although new methods to detect latent tuberculosis infection are now being tested.

Active tuberculosis, the form of disease that disrupts normal host physiology to produce symptoms, is generally classified as pulmonary or extrapulmonary. Pulmonary disease is the most common form of active tuberculosis, accounting for about 80% of cases. Cough is the most common symptom associated with pulmonary tuberculosis, occurring in over 95% of cases. The cough is usually chronic, lasting more than 1 month, and it is most often productive of sputum. Occasionally, hemoptysis (coughing up blood), dyspnea (shortness of breath), and chest pain develop. Other constitutional symptoms include fevers, night sweats, and weight loss. The physical examination for tuberculosis is nonspecific, but common findings include inanition and abnormal breath sounds in the affected parts of the lung. The chest radiograph is often used to confirm the presence and assess the extent of disease. Infiltrates are nearly universal, and cavitary lesions, usually in the upper lung segments, are often found, particularly in reactivation of latent infection.

Extrapulmonary disease accounts for about 20% of active tuberculosis cases. Although almost any site can be affected by tuberculosis, the most common extrapulmonary sites are the lymph nodes (most often the cervical lymph nodes), pleura, kidneys, meninges, and bone or joints. The diagnosis of tuberculosis at these sites requires a high level of clinical suspicion and proper diagnostic specimens taken for acid fast staining, mycobacterial culture, and histopathology. Even as the incidence of pulmonary tuberculosis was declining in the United States, the rate of extrapulmonary disease remained constant. With the HIV epidemic, the proportion of extrapulmonary tuberculosis increased as HIV-infected individuals are more susceptible to extrapulmonary disease.

### 10.4.2  Pathophysiology

*Mycobacterium tuberculosis* is transmitted through the airborne route from infectious cases to susceptible contacts. An infected individual will cough and produce an aerosol of tiny droplet particles, which contain live *M. tuberculosis*. When these particles are inhaled by a susceptible contact, they impact deep in the lung parenchyma in the alveoli. The initial interaction between the host immune system and *M. tuberculosis* occurs in the alveoli, where pulmonary macrophages engulf, process, and present mycobacterial antigens in conjunction with major histocompatibility complex (MHC) class II molecules. When the complex of mycobacterial antigen and MHC molecule is recognized by antigen-specific CD4 lymphocytes, the CD4 lymphocytes release interferon-γ (INF-γ) and interleukin 2 (IL-2). The INF-γ serves to activate macrophages and enhance their ability to contain mycobacteria. This response is regulated, in part, by IL-12, which induces differentiation of T helper type 1 (Th1) cells and augments the release of INF-γ from the T lymphocytes [86]. The activated macrophages release a number of cytokines, including tumor necrosis factor-α (TNF-α) [87], IL-1 [88], and IL-6 [89], that are responsible for the recruitment of cells to the site of infection, formation of granuloma, and development of the delayed-type hypersensitivity response. This process is downregulated by effects of monocyte-derived transforming growth factor-β (TGF-β) and IL-10 on CD4 lymphocytes [90, 91]. Within this network of cytokines, TNF-α appears to play a more central role in the pathogenesis of tuberculosis. TNF-α is essential for granuloma formation [92] and activates macrophage clearance of the organism. Further, proteins and polysaccharides of *M. tuberculosis* stimulate mononuclear phagocytes to express TNF-α as well as other cytokines [93]. Overexpression of TNF-α also appears to be responsible for many of the systemic signs and morbidity of tuberculosis, such as fever, night sweats, and cachexia.

## 10.4.3   Role of Nutrition

### 10.4.3.1   PROTEIN AND ENERGY STATUS

Malnutrition is well known among adults with tuberculosis. In adults with pulmonary tuberculosis in Malawi, weight, mid-upper arm circumference, and serum albumin were lower than controls on admission to the hospital, and these nutritional indices improved during treatment with effective chemotherapy, irrespective of clinical, nutritional, and radiographic features of tuberculosis on admission [94, 95]. A study of nutritional status in 148 adults with smear-positive pulmonary tuberculosis in Tanzania showed that 77% of males and 58% of females had a body mass index below 18.5 on admission [96]. In general, adults gained weight during 6 months of treatment with chemotherapy, but weight was lost after treatment had finished. The length of stay in the hospital was the primary determinant of weight gain in patients on chemotherapy, suggesting that nutritional intake in the hospital was better than could be achieved at home. Progressive nutritional recovery generally occurs during tuberculosis chemotherapy; however, serum albumin levels and mean arm muscle circumference have been reported as subnormal after 12 months, suggesting that body protein reserves may not be fully recovered during treatment [97].

Measurements of [$^{13}$C]leucine flux suggested that there is altered amino acid metabolism in adults with tuberculosis, and this abnormality, or "anabolic block" may contribute to wasting in tuberculosis despite nutritional support [98]. In adults with pulmonary tuberculosis who developed respiratory failure, serum albumin and hemoglobin were strong predictors of survival [99]. Body composition studies have shown that there are no large differences between HIV-positive and HIV-negative adults with tuberculosis; however, body cell mass, among other indicators of nutritional status, significantly decrease with increasing HIV disease [74, 100–103].

Less is known about nutritional status in children with tuberculosis. Children with severe protein energy malnutrition are at a higher risk of developing tuberculosis [104]. A study of children with pneumonia in the Gambia suggests that *M. tuberculosis* is not an uncommon cause of pneumonia, especially among children who are malnourished [105]. In Bulawayo, Zimbabwe, an autopsy series of 184 children aged under 5 who died at home showed that tuberculosis was present in 4%, and all of the children who died with tuberculosis had marasmus [106].

Experimental animal studies showed that protein calorie malnutrition has a marked effect on resistance to tuberculosis. Malnourished mice infected with *M. tuberculosis* had a fatal course of infection, and immunological abnormalities included tissue-specific decreases in expression of interferon-γ, TNF-α, and nitric oxide synthetase [107]. Restoration of a full protein diet could reverse the fatal course of tuberculosis in malnourished mice. Skin sensitivity to purified protein derivative (PPD) and lymphocyte proliferation were not affected by protein and calorie restriction in cattle infected with *M. bovis*, but alterations in the number of circulating CD2$^+$, CD8$^+$, and γδ T cells was noted in the malnourished cattle [108]. In a guinea pig model, animals on a protein-restricted diet were vaccinated with *M. bovis* BCG vaccine and then infected via the respiratory route with virulent *M. tuberculosis*. Protein deficiency was associated with loss of tuberculin skin sensitivity, reduced lymphocyte proliferation responses to mycobacterial antigens, decreased IL-2 production, and reduced CD2$^+$ lymphocytes in the thymus and peripheral blood [109, 110].

#### 10.4.3.2  VITAMIN A

Clinic-based studies using different indicators of vitamin A status suggested that vitamin A deficiency is not uncommon among adults and children with tuberculosis. Low circulating vitamin A levels [111–114], depleted hepatic stores of vitamin A [115, 116], and night blindness [117, 118] have been described in adults with tuberculosis. In a large study of children from Cebu island in the Philippines, xerophthalmia was associated with tuberculosis [119]. Factors that may contribute to the development of vitamin A deficiency during tuberculosis include decreased dietary intake of vitamin A, impaired absorption of vitamin A [120], increased utilization of vitamin A during infection, and abnormal losses of vitamin A in the urine.

In a cross-sectional study in Rwanda, 29% of adults with tuberculosis and HIV coinfection had serum vitamin A concentrations indicative of deficiency (<1.05 μmol/L) [121]. In a longitudinal study of 519 adults coinfected with tuberculosis and HIV in Kampala, Uganda, 36% had serum vitamin A concentrations consistent with deficiency (<1.05 μmol/L) at the time of presentation [122]. During follow-up (median) of 17 months, 30% of subjects with serum vitamin A below 1.05 μmol/L and 17% of subjects with serum vitamin A above 1.05 μmol/L died ($p < .01$). In multivariate analyses that adjusted for CD4+ lymphocyte count, age, sex, body mass index, and diarrheal morbidity, vitamin A deficiency was associated with increased risk of death (relative risk = 1.78, 95% confidence interval [CI] 1.2–2.6). In a cross-sectional study involving 801 adults with pulmonary tuberculosis in Zomba, Malawi, plasma retinol concentrations below 0.70 μmol/L and above 1.05 μmol/L occurred in 61% and 84%, respectively [102]. This study showed that wasting and higher HIV load were risk factors associated with vitamin A deficiency.

Animal studies suggested that vitamin A deficiency decreases resistance to experimental infection with *M. tuberculosis*. Early studies demonstrated that cod-liver oil had some impact on experimental tuberculosis in animals, such as dissemination of disease [123–125]. Among animals inoculated with virulent tubercle bacilli, mortality was higher among vitamin A-deficient rats than rats on a normal diet [126]; more severe infection and extensive lesions have been noted in such animals on histopathology compared with control rats [127]. In addition, rats given adequate vitamin A but restricted in protein or calories were not more susceptible to experimental tuberculosis infection, suggesting that increased susceptibility to tuberculosis was attributable to lack of vitamin A rather than protein-energy malnutrition. An accelerated course of tuberculosis has been reported in vitamin A-deficient rats [128]. Vitamin A-deficient mice have a more severe infection with *M. bovis* compared with mice supplemented with dietary β-carotene [129]. Chicks on a high vitamin A diet had 26% increased survival compared with chicks on a normal diet following experimental infection with *M. tuberculosis* [130]. In pigs experimentally infected with tuberculosis, those receiving cod-liver oil had greater weight gain and more limited tuberculous histopathology compared with pigs not receiving cod-liver oil [131].

In vitro studies with cell lines and animal studies suggest that vitamin A and its active metabolites may influence immunological responses to tuberculosis. Dietary vitamin A enhances T-cell proliferation responses and antibody responses to *M. tuberculosis* antigen in the chick model [132]. All-*trans* retinoic acid inhibits the multiplication of virulent *M. tuberculosis* in cultured human macrophages [133]. Defective production of IL-2 has been implicated in anergy to PPD and disseminated tuberculosis [86]. Vitamin A has been shown to enhance IL-2 production by activated T cells [134, 135], and vitamin A-supplemented mice challenged with *M. bovis* and treated with IL-2 have stronger delayed type hypersensitivity (DTH) responses and proliferation responses to PPD compared with control mice without supplementary vitamin A [136].

### 10.4.3.3 VITAMIN D

It has been postulated that vitamin D deficiency is associated with tuberculosis [137]. Unlike other respiratory diseases, the seasonality of tuberculosis in the United Kingdom shows a peak incidence in the summer, a time that follows low sunlight exposure and the low winter levels of vitamin D [138]. Hypovitaminosis D might increase the risk of tuberculosis because of the effects of vitamin D on immune function [139], and in vitro studies suggested that vitamin D status may influence resistance to tuberculosis. Cultured human monocytes and macrophages were protected against virulent tubercle bacilli by $1,25(OH_2)$-vitamin $D_3$, an active metabolite of vitamin D [140–143]. $1,25(OH_2)$-Vitamin $D_3$ may enhance the effects of pyrazinamide against tuberculosis [144]. Studies in vitamin D-deficient guinea pigs suggested that dietary vitamin D levels influence immunity to virulent *M. tuberculosis* [145].

Abnormalities in calcium homeostasis have been reported in patients with tuberculosis, and the relationship of these abnormalities to vitamin D status is unclear. In untreated pulmonary tuberculosis, calcium levels have been reported to be decreased [146], increased [147, 148], or normal [149] compared with healthy controls, and vitamin D levels are reported to be normal [150, 151] during tuberculosis. It has been suggested that plentiful sunlight may cause high levels of vitamin D and calcium in patients in Africa [152]. Isoniazid and rifampicin treatment for tuberculosis has been reported to depress [153] or have no effect [154] on vitamin D levels. Similarly, chemotherapy for tuberculosis has been reported to increase [155], decrease [156], or have no effect [157] on calcium levels.

### 10.4.3.4 B COMPLEX VITAMINS

There are limited data regarding the status of B complex vitamins in individuals with tuberculosis. Low serum folate levels are common in adults with tuberculosis both before and during tuberculosis chemotherapy [114, 158, 159]. In a study of adults with tuberculosis in Nigeria, serum vitamin $B_{12}$ levels were not significantly different from asymptomatic controls [160], and normal serum vitamin $B_{12}$ levels were also described in Finland among adults with tuberculosis [158].

### 10.4.3.5 VITAMIN C

A longitudinal study of 1,100 men was conducted in a low-income area of Philadelphia in the 1940s to determine whether nutritional deficiencies increased the risk of developing tuberculosis [161]. At baseline, vitamins A and C, hemoglobin, albumin, calcium, and phosphorus were measured, and all subjects had chest roentgenographic examination to exclude those with evidence of tuberculosis. The subjects were followed for 7 years, and 28 men subsequently developed tuberculosis. Low plasma levels of both vitamins A and C at baseline significantly increased risk of developing tuberculosis. There is some evidence from animal models that vitamin deficiency may influence susceptibility to intestinal tuberculosis [162], and the evidence for vitamin A has been discussed previously.

### 10.4.3.5  OTHER NUTRITIONAL PROBLEMS

Epidemiologic studies of tuberculosis among Asian immigrants in south London associated a vegetarian diet with tuberculosis [163, 164]. A case-control study was conducted among Asian immigrants to London from the Indian subcontinent and East Africa, and the single most important risk factor identified was vegetarianism, with the highest risk of tuberculosis among lactovegetarians (avoidance of meat or fish) [164]. In most of the cases, tuberculosis developed more than 5 years after arrival in the United Kingdom, suggesting that tuberculosis in these immigrant Asians was due to reactivation secondary to decreased immunity associated with micronutrient malnutrition. The vegetarian Asian diet is known to increase the risk of deficiencies of iron, vitamin $B_{12}$, and vitamin D [165] and probably zinc as well.

The effect of zinc deficiency on immunity to tuberculosis has been studied in a guinea pig model, and these studies showed that zinc-deficient animals had reduced tuberculin sensitivity and fewer circulating T lymphocytes but no apparent altered resistance to virulent *M. tuberculosis* [154]. Deficiencies of dietary protein or zinc interfere with immunological responses of guinea pigs to *M. bovis* BCG vaccination [166]. Anemia is common during tuberculosis [167], and it is probable that the anemia of chronic inflammation accounts for a large proportion of anemia [168, 169]. In Indonesia, patients with tuberculosis had significantly lower plasma zinc concentrations [170]. A case-control study from Miami showed that 12 people with tuberculosis were more likely to have low plasma selenium concentrations than 32 healthy controls [171]. In Malawi, among 801 adults with pulmonary tuberculosis, zinc and selenium deficiency occurred in 85% and 87%, respectively [102]. Another study from Malawi suggested that there is an association between selenium deficiency and anemia in adults with pulmonary tuberculosis [172]. Sammon speculated that, in countries where maize is the predominant staple food, the pattern of disease is largely determined by a change in immune profile caused by metabolites of dietary linoleic acid [173]. High intake of linoleic acid in a diet deficient in polyunsaturated fatty acids and riboflavin may result in high tissue production of Th1-like lymphocytes, which are primarily involved in mediation of cellular immunity. Such dietary immune modulation may affect resistance to tuberculosis in certain geographic areas [173].

### 10.4.4  Strength of Evidence Regarding Role of Nutrition

Although the association between malnutrition and tuberculosis is well known, there have been few controlled clinical trials conducted to investigate whether improved nutrition will reduce the risk of developing active disease or will improve the clinical outcome of tuberculosis. These issues have tremendous public health importance, but there are significant challenges in attempts to answer such questions. The incidence rates of active tuberculosis are low enough to require extremely large sample sizes (i.e., thousands of subjects) to determine with adequate statistical power whether a nutritional intervention would have an impact on the incidence of tuberculosis. The measurement of outcomes following clinical disease (i.e., sputum-positive disease, radiographic evidence) and relapse of disease are difficult to measure in nutritional studies of patients with tuberculosis.

Smaller intervention trials have been conducted that provided insight into the relationship between nutrition and tuberculosis, but none of these studies were definitive. One study conducted in Madras, India, was particularly influential in shaping health care programs as it showed that tuberculosis chemotherapy could be conducted on an outpatient basis rather than in a sanitorium [174]; 163three patients with tuberculosis were treated either in a sanitorium with a well-balanced diet or at home on a markedly poorer diet. Weight gain was greater in the patients treated in the sanitorium compared with patients treated at home. A higher proportion of sanitorium patients attained negative sputum cultures before the home patients, but the overall response to treatment was considered to be similar in both groups.

In Harlem, New York City, a trial was conducted in the 1940s to determine whether a vitamin-and-mineral supplement could reduce the incidence of tuberculosis in families who had an active case of tuberculosis. One hundred and ninety four families received either a vitamin-and-mineral supplement or no supplement. The attack rate of tuberculosis was 0.16/100 person-years in families who took the vitamins and minerals and 0.91/100 person-years among families in the control group [175].

The impact of vitamin A supplementation has been examined in small trials, but these studies have been limited by small sample size and insufficient statistical power to examine major outcomes. In a 1950s study, 78 adults with moderately advanced tuberculosis were divided into three treatment groups: control, different forms of synthetic vitamin A, and cod-liver oil therapy. Cod-liver oil had a significant impact on clinical outcome, with the most clinical failures noted in the control group [176]. In the synthetic vitamin A group, some patients were given intramuscular injections of vitamin A palmitate, in which vitamin A is absorbed irregularly. A controlled clinical trial involving 85 children with pulmonary tuberculosis in Cape Town suggested that two consecutive doses of vitamin A, 200,000 IU, at the commencement of tuberculosis chemotherapy had no apparent impact on serum vitamin A levels, hemoglobin, roentgenographic findings, or weight Z-scores at 6 weeks and 3 months later [177].

In a more recent placebo-controlled trial from Indonesia [178], daily supplements of vitamin A and zinc given to adults with pulmonary tuberculosis led to significant improvements in the lesion area observed on chest radiographs after 2 months of tuberculosis chemotherapy; this was not the case at the 6-month follow-up. The supplements resulted in earlier clearance of tubercle bacilli from sputum. However, no effects of the supplements were observed on the number of cavities, the surface area of cavities, hemoglobin concentrations, or different anthropometric indicators of nutritional status. In another trial among 110 new cases of active tuberculosis, subjects received tuberculosis chemotherapy alone or in addition to injectable thiamin, vitamin $B_6$, or vitamin C or an oral multivitamin supplement. All groups receiving any vitamin supplementation had significantly better lymphocyte proliferation responses (in response to phytohemagglutinin or PPD) than the arm of the study receiving no vitamin supplementation [179].

Another trial showed that vitamins C and E were effective in improving immune responses to tuberculosis when given as adjuncts to multidrug tuberculosis therapy [180]. A study assessed the effects of early nutritional intervention on lean mass and physical function in patients with tuberculosis and wasting. In this study, patients who started antituberculous therapy were randomly assigned to receive either standard nutritional counseling or nutritional counseling to increase their intake through diet and high-energy supplements. After 6 weeks, patients in the nutritional supplement group (n = 19) had a significantly greater increase in body weight, total lean mass, and grip strength than did the control subjects (n = 17) [181].

Two randomized, placebo-controlled clinical trials of multimicronutrient supplementation for adults with HIV infection and pulmonary tuberculosis were completed and yielded conflicting results. In a study involving 213 HIV-infected adults with pulmonary tuberculosis in Tanzania, daily supplementation with a multivitamin plus zinc for 8 months reduced mortality by 71% [182]. In contrast, a larger study with longer follow-up in Malawi did not corroborate these findings. The Malawi trial involved 821 HIV-infected adults with pulmonary tuberculosis and showed that daily supplementation with a multivitamin and mineral supplement for 24 months had no significant impact on mortality [183].

## 10.5   DIAGNOSIS

### 10.5.1   Clinical Diagnosis of Latent Tuberculosis Infection

The natural history of tuberculosis follows a two-stage process [184]. In the first stage, an asymptomatic, latent infection is established after exposure to and infection with *M. tuberculosis*. This stage of infection produces no symptoms and may persist for decades without ever progressing to active disease. Until recently, the only way to make the diagnosis of latent tuberculosis infection was with the use of the tuberculin skin test. Although the skin tests are performed today using a number of different techniques (e.g., Mantoux test and Heaf test) and antigens (e.g., Purified Protein Derivative and RT-23), all methods inject tuberculin antigens into the epidermis and examine the skin for signs of reaction after 2 to 3 days. Because there is no gold standard for detection of latent tuberculosis infection, a variety of criteria are used to classify people as being infected with *M. tuberculosis* or not, depending on the size of the reaction [185, 186]. In the clinical setting or in contact investigations, these criteria are interpreted as a positive or negative tuberculin skin test and are used as the basis for treatment of latent tuberculosis infection.

An individual with latent tuberculosis infection will generally have a positive tuberculin skin test, but false-positive and false-negative tuberculin skin tests can occur. False-positive skin tests may occur because of previous BCG vaccination or through infection with environmental mycobacteria. False-negative tests may occur in the setting of immunosuppression, such as with advanced HIV infection. Immune-based assays have been developed to measure INF-$\gamma$ responses to antigens of *M. tuberculosis* using either whole-blood cytokine assays or ELISpot assays [187]. These immune-based tests appear to be as sensitive as the tuberculin skin test but may be more specific when antigens found only in *M. tuberculosis* are used [187, 188].

### 10.5.2   Clinical and Laboratory Diagnosis of Active Tuberculosis

The diagnosis of tuberculosis is based on the clinical syndrome and the identification of *M. tuberculosis* in appropriate specimens taken from the patient. The identification of *M. tuberculosis* relies on four complementary methods: staining techniques, mycobacterial culture, histopathology, and molecular methods.

### 10.5.2.1 STAINING TECHNIQUES

Staining techniques are the most widely used methods for the identification and diagnosis of *M. tuberculosis* infection. Two staining methods are currently in widespread use: the Ziehl-Neelsen procedure and the auramine-rhodamine method. Both techniques depend on the ability of the mycobacterium to retain the dye even after treatment with an acid solution, hence the term acid fast [189]. Diagnostic specimens treated with theses stains are viewed with the light microscope for the presence of organisms and graded according to standard definitions [190]. The auramine-rhodamine method requires a fluorescence microscope. The sensitivity of staining techniques is about 50–75%, yet the specificity is uniformly high, about 95–99%. The advantage to this technique is that it is inexpensive, readily available, and easily performed. The disadvantage is that the stains do not identify the species of mycobacteria.

### 10.5.2.2 MYCOBACTERIAL CULTURE

Mycobacterial culture represents the gold standard for the diagnosis of tuberculosis and should supplement the staining methods when possible. Culture increases the sensitivity above the staining techniques and allows the identification of species involved. Sensitivity and specificity of culture have been reported at 82% and 98%, respectively [191]. Two general methods are used to culture *M. tuberculosis*. One method uses a solid medium, such as Middlebrook or Lowenstein-Jensen media, to grow the organism, but visible growth may take 3 to 8 weeks. The other method uses a liquid medium, or broth, combined with a radiometric marker of bacterial growth. This approach leads to more rapid identification of *M. tuberculosis*, usually within 2 weeks. Modern nucleic acid probes may also be used to verify the diagnosis of *M. tuberculosis* instead of other *Mycobacteria*.

### 10.5.2.3 MOLECULAR METHODS

Diagnostic tests have been developed in which polymerase chain reaction (PCR) is used to amplify the DNA of *M. tuberculosis* in sputum and other fluids. Theoretically, PCR can detect even one strand of DNA. The sensitivity of this technique has been reported at 90% or greater [192], but the use of these techniques in sputum smear-negative tuberculosis remains to be established.

### 10.5.2.4 HISTOPATHOLOGY

In the setting of extrapulmonary tuberculosis, the diagnosis may be suggested by the characteristic caseating granuloma seen in biopsied tissue. Fluorochrome staining with the auramine-rhodamine stain is useful in identifying acid-fast organisms within the granuloma and raises suspicion of active tuberculosis.

### 10.5.2.5 SPECIMEN COLLECTION AND LABORATORY SAFETY

Specimens for diagnostic testing are collected from involved sites. Expectorated sputum is used in the case of pulmonary tuberculosis. When cavitary lesions are present on the chest radiograph, the yield of acid-fast staining is high. When cavitary lesions are not present, sputum induction using nebulized saline often increases the yield. Diagnostic specimens may include urine, cerebrospinal fluid, pleural fluid, synovial fluid, or gastric lavage fluids. Biopsies are often taken of involved sites, including lymph nodes, pleura, synovium, bone, or other affected organs to increase the yield of diagnosis.

In some cases, surgical procedures or bronchoscopy are required to obtain the appropriate specimens for diagnosis. Because *M. tuberculosis* is a contagious microorganism, special precautions are needed to ensure the safety of medical and laboratory personnel during the collection and processing of samples. Biosafety guidelines are published for the handling of mycobacterial specimens [193].

### 10.5.3   Differential Diagnosis

The differential diagnosis for tuberculosis is extensive and includes other infectious etiologies, malignancy, development abnormalities, and inflammatory conditions. Other infectious diseases to be considered in the differential diagnosis of tuberculosis include necrotizing pneumonias caused by staphylococci or gram-negative bacteria and chronic lung abscess caused by anaerobic organisms. Fungal diseases such as histoplasmosis, blastomycosis, coccidiodomycosis, and aspergillosis can imitate tuberculosis. Lymphoma, bronochogenic carcinoma, and metastatic disease can produce a clinical picture that resembles tuberculosis. Rheumatoid nodules, sarcoidosis, Wegener's granulomatosis, and lymphocytic granulomatosis are also included in the differential diagnosis.

## 10.6   TREATMENT AND PREVENTION

### 10.6.1   General Considerations

The control of tuberculosis in a community is founded on four general interventions: (1) passive case detection and appropriate treatment of infectious cases, (2) treatment of tuberculosis infection, (3) BCG vaccination, and (4) environmental measures to interrupt transmission. A summary of each control strategy is given.

In the natural history of tuberculosis, there are two points that can be targeted for treatment: active tuberculosis and latent infection. The goal of treating active tuberculosis is twofold: to cure the patient of the disease and to reduce the risk of further transmission of infection to contacts in the community. Thus, treatment of active disease provides individual benefit to the patient and accrues public health benefit by curtailing the transmission of infection. The goal of treating latent tuberculosis infection is to reduce the pool of people in a population who are latently infected with *M. tuberculosis*. Treatment of latent tuberculosis infection has been referred to as "preventive therapy" or "chemoprophylaxis" for tuberculosis. These terms are ambiguous regarding the primary prevention of tuberculosis infection or prevention of disease in infected persons. Most experts agree today that the intervention is best referred to as the treatment of latent tuberculosis infection.

### 10.6.2   Treatment of Active Tuberculosis

#### 10.6.2.1   GENERAL TREATMENT REGIMENS

The recommendations for the treatment of active tuberculosis undergo periodic updating by the World Health Organization or the Centers for Disease Control and Prevention in the United States [194]. Although specific details about the timing of doses and duration of therapy may vary slightly, all treatment regimens contain an 8-week "intensive phase" that includes four different antituberculous medications, followed by an 18-week "continuation phase" with two antituberculosis medications. These regimens should be given using directly observed therapy (DOT) in all patients. The World

Health Organization places standard 6-month, supervised treatment at the center of their DOTS (DOT short-course) program, a tuberculosis treatment strategy rolled out beginning in 1993 [195, 196].

Three currently recommended regimens for the treatment of active pulmonary tuberculosis are shown in Table 10.1 [194]. In each regimen, daily isoniazid, rifampin, pyrazinamide, and ethambutol are used during the first 2 months of treatment, the intensive phase of therapy, followed by 4 months of isoniazid and rifampin. Ethambutol, or streptomycin, is usually included in the initial regimen until the results of the drug susceptibility testing are available or in areas where primary drug resistance to isoniazid is suspected to be high. If available, rifapentine may be substituted for rifampin in the continuation phase of therapy, thereby allowing weekly dosing. When rifampin is used, the regimens are best given daily, but intermittent dosing can be used if guided by expert advice. All drugs are given according to body weight. The principles of treating extrapulmonary tuberculosis are similar to pulmonary disease except that the continuation phase may need to be extended, especially for patients with tuberculous meningitis or in children with disseminated disease.

Treatment of active tuberculosis is always indicated as the risk of mortality is approximately 30% in untreated cases. Successful treatment of tuberculosis depends on regular dosing of multiple drugs to which the organism is susceptible for a sufficient length of time [197]. Because these drugs need to be given for 6 months, adherence with therapy is a major determinant of treatment outcome. Poor adherence has been associated with treatment failures, relapse cases, and the emergence of multiple-drug resistance. The problem of poor adherence becomes amplified when drug-resistant strains are transmitted to susceptible contacts.

To address the problem of nonadherence in tuberculosis treatment, DOT has been used [198, 199] and has been cost-effective [200]. In DOT, health care workers observe the ingestion of each dose of medication to ensure compliance. Intermittent regimens were developed to facilitate the use of DOT. When used, DOT can lead to treatment completion proportions as high as 90% when multiple enablers and enhancers are used in a patient-centered approach [201]. In areas where DOT has been used, incidence rates of tuberculosis have declined as well as the rates of multidrug-resistant tuberculosis [199] and relapse cases [202]. It should be noted that the only randomized clinical trial of DOT

Table 10.1
**Recommended regimens for the treatment of active tuberculosis**

| | |
|---|---|
| Option 1 | Daily isoniazid, rifampin, and pyrazinamide, ethambutol for 8 weeks, then isoniazid and rifampin daily or two to three times/week for 18 weeks |
| Option 2 | Daily isoniazid, rifampin, pyrazinamide, and ethambutol for 2 weeks, then same drugs for 6 weeks by DOT, then isoniazid and rifampin for 18 weeks by DOT |
| Option 3 | Daily isoniazid, rifampin, pyrazinamide, and ethambutol three times/week for 8 weeks, then isoniazid and rifampin three times per week for 18 weeks by DOT |

Directly observed therapy (DOT) is an integral part of the delivery of antituberculosis therapy.

[a]On all three options, consult a tuberculosis medical expert if the patient is symptomatic or smear or culture positive after 3 months.

failed to show a difference in completion rate when compared with self-administration therapy [203]. This study made the point that supportive patient–provider relations may accomplish the same goals as DOT.

Because of the success of DOT and the urgent need to control tuberculosis, the World Health Organization has developed an entire strategy around DOT, also known as DOTS. This strategy is a comprehensive program that promotes case detection, direct observation of each dose of treatment, counseling, monitoring for cure, and reporting to local and international authorities. In high-burden countries where DOTS has been implemented, the average treatment completion proportion was 82% in 1996, although only 12% of tuberculosis cases were treated by DOT.

### 10.6.2.2 SPECIAL CIRCUMSTANCES

HIV-infected persons with active pulmonary tuberculosis are generally treated with the standard short-course regimen. There are a number of caveats to this recommendation that must be considered before starting patients on antituberculosis therapy [194]. Intermittent dosing of antituberculosis treatment may not apply to patients with HIV-associated tuberculosis, especially with more advanced stages of HIV infection. The treatment of HIV-associated tuberculosis in patients receiving antiretroviral therapy is complex because of drug–drug interactions between rifamycins and antiretroviral medications. Although antiretroviral treatment should not be withheld from HIV-infected patients with active tuberculosis if indicated, the choice of treatment must be guided by availability of specific antituberculosis (e.g., rifabutin) and antiretroviral (e.g., efavirenz or abacavir) medications. As patients with HIV-associated tuberculosis have been treated with antiretroviral therapy, paradoxical reactions may be observed as a consequence of immune reconstitution. These paradoxical reactions may produce transient worsening of signs, symptoms, and radiographic findings after initiating antiretroviral therapy. In addition, since a study from Uganda showed evidence that cotrimoxazole had stabilizing effects on HIV disease progression and was associated with reduced mortality, daily cotrimoxazole prophylaxis has now been recommended as a basic component of tuberculosis and HIV care throughout Africa [204, 205].

In general, children with pulmonary disease and extrapulmonary disease in adults are all treated with the standard short-course regimen with good effect. Extrapulmonary disease in children is treated with 12 months of therapy. In pregnant women, the risk of active tuberculosis poses a greater threat to the mother and fetus than do the medications, so treatment is recommended. In pregnant women, isoniazid, rifampin, and ethambutol are recommended for treatment. Pyrazinamide is not currently recommended because possible teratogenic effects are unknown.

Treatment failure, relapse, and primary or secondary drug resistance pose special problems in the treatment and management of tuberculosis [194]. In these settings, one cannot assume that the organism is susceptible to the standard treatment regimens. Therefore, additional drugs to which the organism is susceptible must be added to the regimen. Until the drug susceptibility profile is known, it is recommended that at least two new drugs be added to the standard regimen. Once the drug susceptibility pattern is known, a tailored drug regimen can be chosen. Because of the complexity and potential toxicity of these drug regimens, treatment failures, relapses, and potential drug-resistant cases should be referred to experts in the field for management.

### 10.6.3    Treatment of Latent Tuberculosis Infection

Most individuals infected with *M. tuberculosis* manifest no signs or symptoms of disease. In fact, the only evidence of latent infection is a reactive tuberculin skin test. Yet, these latently infected individuals represent a large pool of people who are at risk for progression to active tuberculosis. Beginning in the 1970s, clinical trials were performed to determine whether treatment with isoniazid alone would reduce the risk of developing tuberculosis. The results of these trials in HIV-seronegative populations indicated that isoniazid given for between 6 and 12 months reduces the risk of tuberculosis by 75% [206]. The widespread use of isoniazid therapy for latent infection has been limited because of its toxicity profile and the adherence issues of long-term therapy, especially in individuals without symptoms of active disease.

Although the treatment of adults for latent tuberculosis infection is not uniformly recommended throughout the world, there are groups at high risk for progression to active tuberculosis who merit treatment of latent tuberculosis infection. These high-risk groups are children and HIV-infected persons. HIV infection confers the greatest known risk for the development of active tuberculosis. Children are at high risk because latent infection often indicates recent infection. During the 1990s a series of randomized clinical trials evaluated a number of approaches to the treatment of latent tuberculosis infection in HIV-infected persons [71, 72, 200–203, 207–210]. With the completion of these trials, there are new options for the treatment of latent infection. The choice of therapy will depend on the clinical and social circumstances.

Treatment of latent tuberculosis infection with isoniazid requires between 6 and 9 months of therapy. Although no clinical trial of 9 months of therapy has been performed, there is evidence from secondary analyses of several independent trials that 9 months of isoniazid provides better protection against tuberculosis than 6 months. These analyses form the basis for the preferred use of 9 months of therapy in most current recommendations. In some local settings, however, 6 months of therapy may be more cost-effective than 9 months and would be the preferred regimen.

In HIV-infected adults with reactive tuberculin skin tests, 2-month, rifampin-based regimens (rifampin and pyrazinamide) provide protection that is comparable to a 12-month course of isoniazid therapy in HIV-infected adults [211]. Despite initial enthusiasm for these short-term regimens, rifampin-pyrazinamide for 2 months is currently not recommended for treatment of latent tuberculosis infection because of the high risk for liver injury and death, especially in HIV-seronegative persons [212, 213].

### 10.6.4    BCG Vaccination

BCG is the mostly widely used vaccination throughout the world, yet it is one of the most controversial. The controversy stems from the variable protection it affords against active pulmonary disease. Since World War II, a vast literature has developed around the use of BCG vaccination, including clinical trials and observational studies. Meta-analysis of these studies led to some conclusions, although it did not resolve the controversies [43, 214]. There is general agreement that BCG vaccination provides uniform protection against the disseminated forms of tuberculosis often seen in children, such as meningeal and miliary tuberculosis. There is no question that BCG is effective in reducing not only the risk of tuberculosis in children but also mortality from tuberculosis. Regarding pulmonary disease, the protective efficacy varies from –10% to 80% [43]. Since pulmonary disease is responsible for the majority of *M. tuberculosis* transmission, an accurate assessment of protection against this form of disease is critical in basing public policy toward BCG vaccination on scientific grounds. The reasons for the variability in protection are unknown, although the type of BCG used, the population studies, the study design used, the geographic location, and genetic heterogeneity may all contribute to the variability [44]. In the end, one fact is clear: Despite its worldwide use, BCG vaccination has not prevented the worldwide resurgence of tuberculosis observed in the last decade of this century.

### 10.6.5   Environmental Measures

Outbreaks of tuberculosis in hospitals, nursing homes, and other health care facilities indicate that *M. tuberculosis* is readily transmitted in the health care setting. A number of environmental and personal measures can be taken to prevent the transmission of *M. tuberculosis* in these settings. In guidelines of the Centers for Disease Control and Prevention [215], the primary emphasis of tuberculosis infection control practice is based on three hierarchical levels of activity. First, administration measures must be in place to reduce the risk of exposure to an infectious case. This includes a strategy for the prompt diagnosis, isolation, and treatment of suspected cases of tuberculosis. Health care worker education, counseling, and screening form the cornerstone of tuberculosis surveillance and control in health care settings. Second, engineering controls should be in place to reduce the concentration of droplet nuclei in the air, thereby reducing the risk of transmission [216]. These measures include adequate ventilation, directional air flow, filtration of air, and the use of germicidal ultraviolet irradiation. Third, personal protective devices such as HEPA (high-efficiency particulate air) filter face masks may offer protection from exposure when worn properly by health care personnel.

### 10.7   SUMMARY AND CONCLUSIONS

Tuberculosis is a common infectious disease that accounts for major morbidity and mortality worldwide. One third of the world's population is infected with *M. tuberculosis*, and this represents a large proportion of the population who are at risk for development of future clinical disease. The evolving HIV/AIDS pandemic and the increased mobility of populations have contributed to a large resurgence of tuberculosis, especially in Africa and Asia. Populations at high risk for acquiring tuberculosis infection include close contacts of infected individuals, people in institutionalized settings (prisons, nursing homes, homeless shelters), and those living in poverty. Once infected, most people have latent disease, and in general, there is a 10% lifetime risk of developing clinical disease. The risk of developing clinical disease is higher in children, in individuals with immunosuppression (i.e., HIV infection, cancer, malnutrition), and in the elderly. Effective treatment regimens exist for both latent tuberculosis infection and active tuberculosis, but multidrug-resistant strains have emerged in different parts of the world.

### 10.8   RECOMMENDATIONS

Aggressive application of programs for the control and treatment of tuberculosis are urgently needed to contain the resurgence of tuberculosis in developing countries.

Implementation of DOT may reduce incidence rates of tuberculosis, rates of multidrug-resistant tuberculosis, and relapse rates. The association between malnutrition and tuberculosis is well known, but there are three major gaps in knowledge that are of public health importance:

- Although nutritional status seems to be related to the risk of developing active tuberculosis in individuals who have latent tuberculosis infection, it is unclear whether any type of nutritional intervention will help prevent infected individuals from developing active disease.
- Despite adequate chemotherapy for tuberculosis, morbidity and mortality can be high, especially among people who are coinfected with HIV. Whether adjunct nutritional support, in the form of micronutrient supplementation or other intervention, will improve clinical outcomes, such as morbidity, mortality, and relapse rates in those undergoing chemotherapy for tuberculosis, is not known.
- In individuals who have multidrug-resistant tuberculosis, host factors may play the most important role in resistance to M. tuberculosis. Whether nutritional interventions will help improve clinical outcomes for these individuals is unknown.

## REFERENCES

1. Frieden TR, Sterling TR, Munsiff SS, Watt CJ, Dye C. Tuberculosis. Lancet 2003;362:887–899.
2. De Cock KM, Soro B, Coulibaly IM, Lucas SB. Tuberculosis and HIV infection in sub-Saharan Africa. JAMA 1992;268:1581–1587.
3. Pablos-Mendez A, Raviglione M, Laszlo A, Binkin N, Rieder HL, Bustreo F, Cohn DL, Lambregts-van Weezenbeek CS, Kim SJ, Chaulet P, Nunn P. Global surveillance for antituberculous-drug resistance, 1994–1997. N Engl J Med 1998;338:1641–1649.
4. Small PM, Hopewell PC, Singh SP, Paz A, Parsonnet J, Ruston DC, Schecter GF, Daley CL, Schoolnik GK. The epidemiology of tuberculosis in San Francisco: a population-based study using conventional and molecular methods. N Engl J Med 1994;330:1703–1709.
5. Hermans PW, Messadi F, Guebrexabher H, van Soolingen D, de Haas PE, Heersma H, de Neeling H, Ayoub A, Portaels F, Frommel D, et al. Analysis of the population structure of Mycobacterium tuberculosis in Ethiopia, Tunisia, and the Netherlands: usefulness of DNA typing for global tuberculosis epidemiology. J Infect Dis 1995;171:1504–1513.
6. Smith GE, Ruffer MA. Pott'che Krankheit an einer ägyptischen Mumie. Giessen: Töpelmann, 1910.
7. Buikstra JE, Baker BJ, Cook DC. What diseases plagued the ancient Egyptians? A century of controversy considered. In: Biological anthropology and the study of ancient Egypt. Davies WV, Walker R, eds. London: British Museum, 1993.
8. Allison MJ, Mendoza D, Pezzia A. Documentation of a case of tuberculosis in pre-Columbian America. Am Rev Resp Dis 1973;107:985–891.
9. Chadwick J, Mann WN. The medical works of Hippocrates. Oxford: Blackwell Scientific, 1950.
10. Aretaeus the Cappadocian. The extant works of Aretaeus, the Cappadocian. Adams F, ed. and trans. London: Sydenham Society, 1856.
11. Galen. Librorum pars prima [-quinta] (5 volumes). Venetiis, in aedibus Aldi, et Andreae Asulani soceri, 1525.
12. Crawfurd R. The king's evil. Oxford: Clarendon Press, 1911.
13. Bloch M. The royal touch: sacred monarchy and scrofula in England and France. Montreal: McGill-Queen's University, 1973.
14. Morton R. Phthisiologia: or a treatise of consumptions, 2nd ed. London: Innys, 1720.
15. Cullen W. First lines of the practice of physic. Edinburgh: Elliot, and London: Cadell, 1786.
16. King LS. Medical thinking: a historical preface. Princeton, NJ: Princeton University Press, 1982.
17. Ackerknecht EH. Medicine at the Paris Hospital, 1794–1848. Baltimore, MD: Johns Hopkins, 1967.

18. Foucault M. The birth of the clinic: an archaeology of medical perception. New York: Pantheon, 1973.
19. Bayle GL. Recherches sur la phthisie pulmonaire. Paris: Gabon, 1810.
20. Laennec RTH. De l'auscultation médiate, ou traité de diagnostic des maladies des poumons et du coeur. Paris: Brosson and Claudé, 1819.
21. Schwann T. Microscopical researches into the accordance in the structure and growth of animals and plants. London: Sydenham Society, 1847.
22. Villemin JA. Etudes sur la tuberculose: preuves rationelles et expérimentales de sa spécifité et de son inoculabilité. Paris: Baillière, 1868.
23. Koch R. Die Aetiologie der Tuberkulose. Berlin klin Wschr 1882;19:221–230.
24. Koch R. Weitere Mittheilungen über ein Heilmittel gegen Tuberkulose. Dtsch med Wschr 1890; 16:1029–1032, 1891; 17:101–102, 1189–1192.
25. Bodington G. Essay on the treatment of and cure of pulmonary consumption. London: Longmans, 1840.
26. Rothman SM. Living in the shadow of death: tuberculosis and the social experience of illness in American history. Baltimore, MD: Johns Hopkins University Press, 1994.
27. Bryder L. Below the magic mountain: a social history of tuberculosis in 20th-century Britain. Oxford, UK: Clarendon Press, 1988.
28. Rollier A. Die Heliotherapie der Tuberkulose. Berlin: Springer, 1913.
29. Forlanini C. A contribuzione della terapia chirurgica della tisi; ablazione de polmone? pneumotorace artificiale? Gazz Osp Clin 1882;3:537, 585, 601, 609, 617, 625, 641, 657, 665, 689, 705.
30. Bates JH, Stead WW. The history of tuberculosis as a global epidemic. Med Clin North Am 1993;77:1205–1217.
31. Williams CJB, Williams CT. On the nature and treatment of pulmonary consumption. Lancet 1868;i:369–70, 403–404, 431–432, 552–554, 613–615, 711–713, 777–780; ii:3–4, 38–40, 107–109, 211–214.
32. Bennett JH. Treatise on the oleum jecoris aselli, or cod liver oil, as a therapeutic agent in certain forms of gout, rheumatism, and scrofula, with cases. London: Highley, 1841.
33. Schütte D. Beobachtungen über den Nutzen des Berger Leberthrans (Oleum jecoris aselli, von Gadus Asellus L.). Archiv f. med. Erfahrung 1824;79–92.
34. Taufflieb E. De l'huile de foie de morue et de son usage en médecine. Bull Trav Soc Med Prat Paris 1852;45–135.
35. Williams CJB, Williams CT. Pulmonary consumption, its etiology, pathology, and treatment. 2nd ed. London: Longmans, Green, 1889.
36. Bibliographical Record. The first annual report of the Hospital for Consumption and Diseases of the Chest, London, 1849. London J Med 1850;2:37–46.
37. Greenhow EH. On the employment of cod-liver oil in phthisis. With cases. Lancet 1854;ii:502–505, 542–545.
38. McConkey M. The treatment of intestinal tuberculosis with codliver oil and tomato juice. Am Rev Tuberc 1930;21:627–635.
39. Tui C, Kuo NH, Schmidt L. The protein status in pulmonary tuberculosis. Am J Clin Nutr 1954;2: 252–264.
40. Pottenger FM Jr, Pottenger FM. Adequate diet in tuberculosis. Am Rev Tuberc 1946;54:219.
41. Calmette LCA, Guérin C, Négre L, Boquet A. Sur la vaccination préventive des enfants nouveau-nés contre la tuberculose par le B. C. G. Ann Inst Pasteur 1927;41:201–232.
42. World Health Organization Expert Committee on Tuberculosis. Ninth Report. Geneva: World Health Organization, 1974. Technical Report Series No. 552.
43. Colditz GA, Brewer TF, Berkey CS, Wilson ME, et al. Efficacy of BCG vaccine in the prevention of tuberculosis. Meta-analysis of the published literature. JAMA 1994;271:698–702.
44. Comstock GW. Field trials of tuberculosis vaccines: how could we have done them better? Controlled Clin Trials 1994;15:247–276.
45. Hinshaw HC, Feldman WH. Streptomycin in the treatment of clinical tuberculosis: a preliminary report. Proc Mayo Clin 1945;20:313–318.
46. Medical Research Council. Streptomycin treatment of pulmonary tuberculosis. BMJ 1948;2:769–782.

47. Marks HM. The progress of experiment: science and therapeutic reform in the United States, 1900–1990. Cambridge, UK: Cambridge University Press, 1997.

48. Robitzek EH, Selikoff IJ, Orstein GG. Chemotherapy of human tuberculosis with hydrazine derivatives of isonicotinic acid. (Preliminary report of representative cases.) Q Bull Sea View Hosp 1952;13: 27–51.

49. McKeown T. The modern rise of population. New York: Academic, 1976.

50. McKeown T. The role of medicine: dream, mirage, or nemesis? Princeton, NJ: Princeton University Press, 1979.

51. Barnes DS. The making of a social disease: tuberculosis in nineteenth century France. Berkeley: University of California Press, 1995.

52. Flick LF. The development of our knowledge of tuberculosis. Philadelphia: privately printed, 1925.

53. Brown L. The story of clinical pulmonary tuberculosis. Baltimore, MD: Williams and Wilkins, 1941.

54. Waksman S. The conquest of tuberculosis. Berkeley: University of California Press, 1964.

55. Coury C. La tuberculose au cours des ages. Grandeur et déclin d'un maladie. Suresne: Lepetit, 1972.

56. Dubos R, Dubos J. The white plague: tuberculosis, man, and society. Boston: Little, Brown, 1952.

57. Daniel TM. Captain of death: the story of tuberculosis. Rochester: University of Rochester Press, 1997.

58. Bates B, Rothman S, Ellison D. Bargaining for life: a social history of tuberculosis, 1876–1938. Philadelphia: University of Pennsylvania Press, 1992.

59. Ott K. Fevered lives: tuberculosis in America culture since 1870. Cambridge: Harvard University Press, 1996.

60. Johnston W. The modern epidemic: a history of tuberculosis in Japan. Cambridge: Council on East Asian Studies, 1995.

61. Sudre P, ten Dam G. Tuberculosis: a global overview of the situation today. Bull World Health Organ 1992;70:149–159.

62. Styblo K. Overview and epidemiologic assessment of the current global tuberculosis situation with emphasis on control in developing countries. Rev Infect Dis 1989;11:S339–S345.

63. Raviglione MC, Snider DE, Kochi A. Global epidemiology of tuberculosis plus morbidity and mortality of a worldwide epidemic. JAMA 1995;273:220–226.

64. Loudon RG, Spohn SK. Cough frequency and infectivity in patients with pulmonary tuberculosis. Am Rev Resp Dis 1969;99:109–111.

65. Stead WW. Undetected tuberculosis in prison. JAMA 1978;240:2544–2547.

66. Nolan CM, Elarth AM, Barr H, Saeed AM, Risser DR. An outbreak of tuberculosis in a shelter for homeless men: a description of its evolution and control. Am Rev Resp Dis 1991;143:257–261.

67. Stead WW, Lofgren JP, Warren E, Thomas C. Tuberculosis as an endemic and nosocomial infection among the elderly in nursing homes. N Engl J Med 1985;312:1483–1487.

68. Comstock GW, Liveway VT, Woolpert SF. The prognosis of a positive tuberculin reaction in childhood and adolescence. Am J Epidemiol 1974;99:131–138.

69. Daley CL, Small PM, Schecter GF, Schoolnik GK, McAdam RA, Jacobs WR Jr, Hopewell PC. An outbreak of tuberculosis with accelerated progression among persons infected with the human immunodeficiency virus. N Engl J Med 1992;326:231–235.

70. Moreno S, Miralles P, Diaz MD, Baraia J, Padilla B, Berenguer J, Alberdi JC. Isoniazid preventive therapy in human immunodeficiency virus-infected persons. Long term effect on the development of tuberculosis and survival. Arch Intern Med 1997;157:1729–1734.

71. Whalen CC, Johnson JL, Okwera A, Hom DL, Huebner R, Mugyenyi P, Mugerwa RD, Ellner JJ. A trial of three regimens to prevent tuberculosis in Ugandan adults infected with the human immunodeficiency virus. N Engl J Med 1997;337:801–808.

72. Hawken MP, Meme HK, Elliott LC, Chakaya JM, Morris JS, Githui WA, Juma ES, Odhiambo JA, Thiong'o LN, Kimari JN, Ngugi EN, Bwayo JJ, Gilks CF, Plummer FA, Porter JD, Nunn PP, McAdam KP. Isoniazid preventive therapy for tuberculosis in HIV-1-infected adults: results of a randomised trial. AIDS 1997;11:875–882.

73. Moreno S, Baraia-Etxaburu J, Douza E. Risk for developing tuberculosis among anergic patients infected with HIV. Ann Intern Med 1993;119:194–198.

74. Lettow van M, Fawzi WW, Semba RD. Triple trouble: the role of malnutrition in tuberculosis and human immunodeficiency virus co-infection. Nutr Rev 2003;61:81–90.

75. Chintu C, Ganapati B, Luo C, Ravilgione M, Diwan V. Seroprevalence of human immunodeficiency virus type 1 infection in Zambian children with tuberculosis. Pediatr Infect Dis J 1993;12:499–504.

76. Sassan-Morokro M, De Cock KM, Ackah A, Vetter KM, Doorly R, Brattegaard K, Coulibaly D, Coulibaly IM, Gayle H. Tuberculosis and HIV infection in children in Abidjan, Cote d'Ivoire. Trans R Soc Trop Med Hyg 1994;88:178–181.

77. Kamat SR, Dawson JJY, Devadata S, Fox W, Janardhanam BJ, Radhakrishna S. A controlled trial of the influence of segregation of tuberculosis patients for 1-year on the attack rate of tuberculosis in a 5-year period in close family contacts in South India. Bull World Health Organ 1966;34:517–532.

78. Centers for Disease Control and Prevention. Prevention and control of tuberculosis in U.S. communities with at-risk minority populations. MMWR Morb Mortal Wkly Rep 1992;41:1–11.

79. McAdam JM, Brickner PW, Scharer LL, Crocco JA, Duff AE. The spectrum of tuberculosis in a New York City men's shelter clinic (1982–1988). Chest 1990;97:798–805.

80. Centers for Disease Control and Prevention. Prevention and control of tuberculosis in correctional facilities. MMWR Morb Mortal Wkly Rep 1996;45:1–23.

81. Cantwell MF, Snider DE Jr, Cauthen GM, Onorato IM. Epidemiology of tuberculosis in the United States, 1985 through 1992. JAMA 1994;272:535–539.

82. Zuber PL, McKenna MT, Binkin NJ, Onorato IM, Castro KG. Long-term risk of tuberculosis among foreign-born persons in the United States. JAMA 1994;278:304–307.

83. Cohn ML, Middlebrook G, Russel WF. Combined drug treatment of tuberculosis. I. Prevention of emergence of mutant populations of tubercle bacilli resistant to both streptomycin and isoniazid in vitro. J Clin Invest 1959;38:1349–1355.

84. Mahmoudi A, Iseman MD. Pitfalls in the care of patients with tuberculosis: common errors and their association with the acquisition of drug resistance. JAMA 1993;270:65–68.

85. Bloch AB, Cauthen G, Onorato IM, Dansbury KG, Kelly GD, Driver CR, Snider DE Jr. Nationwide survey of drug-resistant tuberculosis in the United States. JAMA 1994;271:665–671.

86. Toossi Z. Cytokine circuits in tuberculosis. Infect Agents Dis 1996;5:98–107.

87. Takashima T, Ueta C, Tsuyuguchi I, Kishimoto S. Production of tumor necrosis factor by monocytes from patients with pulmonary tuberculosis. Infect Immun 1990;58:3286–3292.

88. Wallis RS, Vjecha M, Amir-Tahmasseb M, Okwera A, Byekwaso F, Nyole S, Kabengera S, Mugerwa RD, Ellner JJ. Influence of tuberculosis on human immunodeficiency virus enhanced cytokine expression and elevated $\beta_2$-microglobulin in HIV-1-associated tuberculosis. J Infect Dis 1993;167:43–48.

89. Ogawa T, Uchida H, Kusumoto Y, Mori Y, Yamamura Y, Hamada S. Increase in tumor necrosis factor alpha and interleukin-1 secreting cells in peripheral blood mononuclear cells from subject infected with *Mycobacterium tuberculosis*. Infect Immun 1991;59:3021–3025.

90. Hirsch CS, Hussain R, Toossi Z, Dawood G, Shahid F, Ellner JJ. Cross-modulation by transforming growth factor beta in human tuberculosis: suppression of antigen-driven blastogenesis and interferon gamma production. Proc Natl Acad Sci U S A 1996;93:3193–3198.

91. Toossi Z, Gogate P, Shiratsuchi H, Young T, Ellner JJ. Enhanced production of transforming growth fatctor-β (TGF-β) by blood monocytes from patients with active tuberculosis and the presence of TGF-β in tuberculous granulomatous lungs lesions. J Immunol 1995;54:465–473.

92. Kindler V, Sappino AP, Grau GE, Piguet PF, Vassalli P. The inducing role of tumor necrosis factor in the development of bactericidal granulomas during BCG infection. Cell 1989;56:731–740.

93. Valone SE, Rich EA, Wallis RS, Ellner J. Expression of tumor necrosis factor αα in-vitro by human mononuclear phagocytes stimulated with whole *Mycobacterium bovis* BCG and mycobacterial antigens. Infect Immun 1988;56:3313–3315.

94. Nkhoma WA, Harries AD, Reeve PA, Nyangulu DS, Wirima JJ. Nutrition in pulmonary tuberculosis: a comparison of African patients from Malawi and Nigeria. East Afr Med J 1987;64:643–647.

95. Harries AD, Nkhoma WA, Thompson PJ, Nyangulu DS, Wirima JJ. Nutritional status in Malawian patients with pulmonary tuberculosis and response to chemotherapy. Eur J Clin Nutr 1988;42:445–450.

96. Kennedy N, Ramsay A, Uiso L, Gutmann J, Ngowi FI, Gillespie SH. Nutritional status and weight gain in patients with pulmonary tuberculosis in Tanzania. Trans R Soc Trop Med Hyg 1996;90:162–166.

97. Onwubalili JK. Malnutrition among tuberculous patients in Harrow, England. Eur J Clin Nutr 1988;42:363–366.

98. Macallan DC, McNurlan MA, Kurpad AV, de Souza G, Shetty PS, Calder AG, Griffin GE. Whole body protein metabolism in human pulmonary tuberculosis and undernutrition: evidence for anabolic block in tuberculosis. Clin Sci 1998;94:321–331.

99. Mehta JB, Fields CL, Byrd RP, Roy TM. Nutritional status and mortality in respiratory failure caused by tuberculosis. Tennessee Med October 1996:369–371.

100. Paton NI, Castello-Branco LR, Jenning G, et al. Impact of tuberculosis on the body composition of HIV-infected men in Brazil. J Acquired Immune Defic Syndr Hum Retrovirol 1999;20:265–271.

101. Shah S, Whalen C, Kotler DP, et al. Severity of human immunodeficiency virus infection is associated with decreased phase angle, fat mass and body cell mass in adults with pulmonary tuberculosis infection in Uganda. J Nutr 2001;131:2843–2847.

102. van Lettow M, Harries AD, Kumwenda JJ, Zijlstra EE, Clark TD, Taha TE, Semba RD. Micronutrient malnutrition and wasting in adults with pulmonary tuberculosis with and without HIV co-infection in Malawi. BMC Infect Dis 2004;4:61.

103. van Lettow M, van der Meer JJM, West C, van Crevel R, Semba RD. Interleukin-6 and HIV load, but not plasma leptin concentration, predict anorexia and wasting in adults with pulmonary tuberculosis in Malawi. J Clin Endocrinol Metab 2005;90:4771–4776.

104. Shimeles D, Lulseged S. Clinical profile and pattern of infection in Ethiopian children with severe protein-energy malnutrition. East Afr Med J 1994;71: 264–267.

105. Adegbola RA, Falade AG, Sam BE, Aidoo M, Baldeh I, Hazlett D, Whittle H, Greenwood BM, Mulholland EK. The etiology of pneumonia in malnourished and well-nourished Gambian children. Pediatr Infect Dis J 1994;13:975–982.

106. Ikeogu MO, Wolf B, Mathe S. Pulmonary manifestations in HIV seropositivity and malnutrition in Zimbabwe. Arch Dis Child 1997;76:124–128.

107. Chan J, Tian Y, Tanaka KE, Tsang MS, Yu K, Salgame P, Carroll D, Kress Y, Teitelbaum R, Bloom BR. Effects of protein calorie malnutrition on tuberculosis in mice. Proc Natl Acad Sci U S A 1996;93:14857–14861.

108. Doherty ML, Monaghan ML, Bassett HF, Quinn PJ, Davis WC. Effect of dietary restriction on cell-mediated immune responses in cattle infected with *Mycobacterium bovis*. Vet Immunol Immunopathol 1996;49:307–320.

109. Bartow RA, McMurray DN. Erythrocyte receptor (CD2)-bearing T lymphocytes are affected by diet in experimental pulmonary tuberculosis. Infect Immun 1990;58:1843–1847.

110. McMurray DN, Bartow RA. Immunosuppression and alteration of resistance to pulmonary tuberculosis in guinea pigs by protein undernutrition. J Nutr 1992;122:738–743.

111. Getz HR, Koerner TA. Vitamin A and ascorbic acid in pulmonary tuberculosis. Determination in plasma by the photoelectric colorimeter. Am J Med Sci 1941;202:831–847.

112. Getz HR, Westfall IS, Henderson HJ. Nutrition in tuberculosis as evaluated by blood analysis. Am Rev Tuberc 1944;50:96–111.

113. Prokopiev DI. Vitamin A content and carotene in blood plasma in pulmonary tuberculosis. Ter Arkh 1966;38:54–59.

114. Evans DIK, Attock B. Folate deficiency in pulmonary tuberculosis: relationship to treatment and to serum vitamin A and beta-carotene. Tubercle 1971;52:288–294.

115. Crimm PD, Short DM. Vitamin A content of the human liver in tuberculosis. Ann Intern Med 1939;13:61–63.

116. Moore T, Sharman IM. Vitamin A levels in health and disease. Br J Nutr 1951;5:119–129.

117. Getz HR, Hildebrand GB, Finn M. Vitamin A deficiency in normal and tuberculous persons as indicated by the biophotometer. J Am Med Assoc 1939;112:1308–1311.

118. Harris R, Harter JS. Night blindness and vitamin A deficiency in pulmonary tuberculosis. South Med J 1940;33:1064–1065.

119. Solon FS, Popkin BM, Fernandez TL, Latham MC. Vitamin A deficiency in the Philippines: a study of xerophthalmia in Cebu. Am J Clin Nutr 1978;31:360–368.

120. Breese BB, Watkins E, McCoord AB. The absorption of vitamin A in tuberculosis. J Am Med Assoc 1942;119:3–4.

121. Rwangabwoba JM, Fischman H, Semba RD. Serum vitamin A levels during tuberculosis and human immunodeficiency virus infection. Int J Tuberc Lung Dis 1998;2:771–773.

122. Langi P, Semba RD, Mugerwa RD, Whalen CC. Vitamin A deficiency and mortality among human immunodeficiency virus-infected adults in Uganda. Nutr Res 2003;23: 595–605.

123. Smith MI. Studies on nutrition in experimental tuberculosis. I. The effect of fat-soluble A vitamine on tuberculosis of the guinea pig, with especial reference to the value of codliver oil in experimental tuberculosis. Am Rev Tuberc 1923;7:33–48.

124. Steiner M, Greene MR, Kramer B. The effect of vitamin-A deficiency on experimental tuberculosis in the guinea pig and rabbit. Am Rev Tuberc 1937;36:222–238.

125. Otero PM, Koppisch E, Axtmayer JH. Influence of dietary factors upon the resistance of the white rat to experimental tuberculosis. I. Vitamin A deficiency. Puerto Rico J Publ Health Trop Med 1934;9:314–320.

126. Gloyne SR, Page DS. A preliminary note on the relationship between deficiency in vitamin A and tuberculosis. Tubercle 1921;3:577–579.

127. Sriramachari S, Gopalan C. Nutrition and tuberculosis: effect of some nutritional factors on resistance to tuberculosis. Indian J Med Res 1958;46:105–112.

128. Hagedorn K. Versuche an Ratten über den Einfluß des Vitaminmangels auf den Verlauf der Tuberkulose. Beitr Klin Tuberk spezif Tuberk Forsch 1928;70:389–407, 1929;72:1–31.

129. Finkelstein MH. Effect of carotene on course of B. tuberculosis infection of mice fed on a vitamin A deficient diet. Proc Soc Exp Biol Med 1932;29:969–971.

130. Solotorovsky M, Squibb RL, Wogan GN, Siegel H, Gala R. The effect of dietary fat and vitamin A on avian tuberculosis in chicks. Am Rev Resp Dis 1961;84:226–235.

131. Wells JW. A comparative study of the influence of cod-liver oil, and cod-liver oil emulsion upon the nutrition of normal and tuberculous pigs. Manchester, UK: Manchester University Press, 1907.

132. Sklan D, Melamed D, Friedman A. The effect of varying levels of dietary vitamin A on immune response in the chick. Poult Sci 1994;73:843–847.

133. Crowle AJ, Ross EJ. Inhibition by retinoic acid of multiplication of virulent tubercle bacilli in cultured human macrophages. Infect Immun 1989;57:840–844.

134. Malkovsky M, Medawar PB. Is immunological tolerance (non-responsiveness) a consequence of interleukin-2 deficit during the recognition of antigen? Immunol Today 1984;5:340.

135. Malkovsky M, Medawar PB, Thatcher DR, Toy J, Hunt R, Rayfield LS, Dore C. Acquired immunological tolerance of foreign cells is impaired by recombinant interleukin 2 or vitamin A acetate. Proc Natl Acad Sci U S A 1985;82:536–538.

136. Ferraro F, Mattei M, Colizzi V. Low doses of recombinant interleukin-2 enhanced delayed type hypersensitivity to PPD in mice infected with *Mycobacterium bovis*-BCG and fed a diet supplemented with vitamin A acetate. Z Erkrank Atm org 1988;171:45–49.

137. Davies PDO. A possible link between vitamin D deficiency and impaired host defence to *Mycobacterium tuberculosis*. Tuberculosis 1985;66:301–304.

138. Douglas AS, Strachan DP, Maxwell JD. Seasonality of tuberculosis: the reverse of other respiratory diseases in the UK. Thorax 1996;51:944–946.

139. Thomasset M. Vitamine D et systeme immunitaire. Pathol Biol (Paris) 1994;42:163–172.

140. Crowle AJ, Ross EJ, May MH. Inhibition by $1,25(OH)_2$-vitamin $D_3$ of the multiplication of virulent tubercle bacilli in cultured human macrophages. Infect Immun 1987;55:2945–2950.

141. Rook GA, Steele J, Fraher L, Barker S, Karmali R, O'Riordan J, Stanford J. Vitamin $D_3$, gamma interferon, and control of proliferation of *Mycobacterium tuberculosis* by human monocytes. Immunology 1986;57:159–163.

142. Rook GA, Taverne J, Steele J, Altes C, Stanford JL. Interferon gamma, cholecalciferol metabolites, and the regulation of anti-mycobacterial and immunopathological mechanisms in human and murine macrophages. Bull Int Union Tuberc Lung Dis 1987;62: 41.

143. Denis M. Killing of *Mycobacterium tuberculosis* within human monocytes: activation by cytokines and calcitriol. Clin Exp Immunol 1991;84:200–206.

144. Crowle AJ, Salfinger M, May MH. $1,25(OH_2)$-vitamin $D_3$ synergizes with pyrazinamide to kill tubercle bacilli in cultured human macrophages. Am Rev Respir Dis 1989;139:549–552.

145. McMurray DN, Bartow RA, Mintzer CL, Hernandez-Frontera E. Micronutrient status and immune function in tuberculosis. Ann N Y Acad Sci 1990;587:59–69.
146. Hafiez AA, Abdel-Hafez MA, Salem D, Abdou MA, Helaly AA, Aarag AH. Calcium homeostasis in untreated pulmonary tuberculosis. Kekkaku 1990;65:308–316.
147. Bradley GW, Sterling GM. Hypercalcaemia and hypokalaemia in tuberculosis. Thorax 1978;33:464–467.
148. Davies PD, Church HA, Brown RC, Woodhead JS. Raised serum calcium in tuberculosis patients in Africa. Eur J Respir Dis 1987;71:341–344.
149. Fuss M, Karmali R, Pepersack T, Bergans A, Dierckx P, Prigogine T, Bergmann P, Corvilain J. Are tuberculous patients at a great risk from hypercalcemia? Q J Med 1988;69:868–678.
150. Grange JM, Davies PD, Brown RC, Woodhead JS, Kardjito T. A study of vitamin D levels in Indonesian patients with untreated pulmonary tuberculosis. Tubercle 1985;66:187–191.
151. Chan TY, Poon P, Pang J, Swaminathan R, Chan CH, Nisar M, Williams CS, Davies PD. A study of calcium and vitamin D metabolism in Chinese patients with pulmonary tuberculosis. J Trop Med Hyg 1994;97:26–30.
152. Davies PD, Church HA, Brown RC, Woodhead JS. Raised serum calcium in tuberculosis patients in Africa. Eur J Respir Dis 1987;71:341–344.
153. Davies PD, Brown RC, Woodhead JS. Serum concentrations of vitamin D metabolites in untreated tuberculosis. Thorax 1985;40:187–190.
154. Williams SE, Wardman AG, Taylor GA, Peacock M, Cooke JN. Long term study of the effect of rifampicin and isoniazid on vitamin D metabolism. Tubercle 1985;66:49–54.
155. Kitrou MP, Phytou-Pallikari A, Tzannes Se, Virvidakis K, Mountokalakis TD. Serum calcium during chemotherapy for active pulmonary tuberculosis. Eur J Respir Dis 1983;64:347–354.
156. Brodie MJ, Boobis AR, Hillyard CJ, Abeyasekera G, MacIntyre I, Park BK. Effect of isoniazid on vitamin D metabolism and hepatic monooxygenase activity. Clin Pharmacol Ther 1981;30:363–367.
157. Perry W, Erooga MA, Brown J, Stamp TC. Calcium metabolism during rifampicin and isoniazid therapy for tuberculosis. J Roy Soc Med 1982;75:533–536.
158. Markkanen T, Levanto A. Sallinen V, Virtanen S. Folic acid and vitamin $B_{12}$ in tuberculosis. Scand J Haemat 1967;4:283–291.
159. Cameron SJ, Horne NW. The effect of tuberculosis and its treatment on erythropoiesis and folate activity. Tubercle 1971;52:37–48.
160. Knox-Macaulay HHM. Serum cobalamin concentration in tuberculosis. A study in the Guinea savanna of Nigeria. Trop Geog Med 1990;42:146–150.
161. Getz HR, Long ER, Henderson HJ. A study of the relation of nutrition to the development of tuberculosis. Influence of ascorbic acid and vitamin A. Am Rev Tuberc 1951;64:381–393.
162. McConkey M, Smith DT. The relation of vitamin C deficiency to intestinal tuberculosis in the guinea pig. J Exp Med 1933;58:503–512.
163. Finch PJ, Millard FJC, Maxwell JD. Risk of tuberculosis in immigrant Asians: culturally acquired immunodeficiency? Thorax 1991;46:1–5.
164. Strachan DP, Powell KJ, Thaker A, Millard FJC, Maxwell JD. Vegetarian diet as a risk factor for tuberculosis in immigrant south London Asians. Thorax 1995;50:175–180.
165. Chanarin I, Stephenson E. Vegetarian diet and cobalamin deficiency: their association with tuberculosis. J Clin Pathol 1988;41:759–762.
166. McMurray DN, Yetley EA. Response to *Mycobacterium bovis* BCG vaccination in protein- and zinc-deficient guinea pigs. Infect Immun 1983;39:755–761.
167. Corr WP Jr, Kyle RA, Bowie EJW. Hematologic changes in tuberculosis. Am J Med Sci 1964;248:709–714.
168. Baynes BD, Flax H, Bothwell TH, Bezwoda WR, MacPhail AP, Atkinson P, Lewis D. Haematological and iron-related measurements in active pulmonary tuberculosis. Scand J Haematol 1986;36:280–287.
169. Morris CDW, Bird AR, Nell H. The haematological and biochemical changes in severe pulmonary tuberculosis. Quart J Med 1989;272:1151–1159.
170. Karyadi E, Schultink W, Nelwan RHH, et al. Poor micronutrient status of active pulmonary tuberculosis patients in Indonesia. J Nutr 2000;130:2953–2958.

171. Shor-Posner G, Miguez MJ, Pineda LM, et al. Impact of selenium status on the pathogenesis of mycobacterial disease in HIV-1-infected drug users during the era of highly active antiretroviral therapy. J Acquir Immune Defic Syndr 2002;29:169–173.

172. van Lettow M, West C, van der Meer JJM, Wieringa F, Semba RD. Low plasma selenium concentrations, high plasma human immunodeficiency virus load and high interleukin-6 concentrations are risk factors associated with anemia in adults presenting with pulmonary tuberculosis in Zomba district, Malawi. Eur J Clin Nutr 2005;59:526–532.

173. Sammon AM. Dietary linoleic acid, immune inhibition and disease. Postgrad Med J 1999;75:129–132.

174. Ramakrishnan CV, Rajendran K, Jacob PG, Fox W, Radhakrishna S. The role of diet in the treatment of pulmonary tuberculosis. An evaluation in a controlled chemotherapy study in home and sanatorium patients in south India. Bull World Health Organ 1961;25:339–359.

175. Downes J. An experiment in the control of tuberculosis among Negroes. Milbank Mem Fund Q 1950;28:127–159.

176. Getz HR. A physiologic and clinical study of failures in vitamin A metabolism in tuberculous patients. Am Rev Tuberc Pulm Dis 1955;72:218–227.

177. Hanekom WA, Potgieter S, Hughes EJ, Malan H, Kessow G, Hussey GD. Vitamin A status and therapy in childhood pulmonary tuberculosis. J Pediatr 1997;131:925–927.

178. Karyadi E, West CE, Schultink W, et al. A double-blind, placebo-controlled study of vitamin A and zinc supplementation in persons with tuberculosis in Indonesia: effects on clinical response and nutritional status. Am J Clin Nutr 2002;75:720–727.

179. Volosevich GV. Functional activity of blood T-lymphocytes in patients with pulmonary tuberculosis treated with chemotherapeutic drugs and vitamins. Probl Tuberk 1982;3:47–50.

180. Safaryan MF, Karagezyan KG, Karapetyan ET, Avanesyan NA. Efficacy of antioxidative therapy in patients with pulmonary tuberculosis and correction of lipid peroxidation. Probl Tuberk 1990;5:40–44.

181. Paton NI, Chua YK, Earnest A, Chee CB. Randomized controlled trial of nutritional supplementation in patients with newly diagnosed tuberculosis and wasting. Am J Clin Nutr 2004;80:460–465.

182. Range N, Changalucha J, Krarup H, Magnussen P, Anderssen ÅB, Friis H. The effect of multivitamin/mineral supplementation on mortality during treatment of pulmonary tuberculosis: a randomized two-by-two factorial trial in Mwanza, Tanzania. Br J Nutr 2006;95:762–660.

183. Semba RD, Kumwenda J, Zijlstra E, Ricks MO, van Lettow M, Whalen C, et al. Micronutrient supplements and mortality of HIV-infected adults with pulmonary TB: a controlled clinical trial. Int J Tuberc Lung Dis 2007;11:854–859.

184. Comstock G. Epidemiology of tuberculosis. Am Rev Respir Dis 1982;125:8–15.

185. Centers for Disease Control and Prevention. Targeted tuberculin testing and treatment of latent tuberculosis infection. MMWR Morb Mortal Wkly Rep 2000;49(RR-6):1–5.

186. American Thoracic Society. Diagnostic standards and classification of tuberculosis. Am Rev Respir Dis 1990;142:725–735.

187. Whalen CC. New diagnostic tests for latent tuberculosis infection: measure for measure. JAMA 2005;293(22):2785–2787.

188. Pai M, Riley LW, Colford JM, Jr. Interferon-gamma assays in the immunodiagnosis of tuberculosis: a systematic review. Lancet Infect Dis 2004 December;4(12)761–776.

189. Kent PT, Kubica GP. Public health mycobacteriology: a guide for the level III laboratory. US Department of Public Health and Human Services, Public Health Service. Atlanta: Centers for Disease Control and Prevention, 1985.

190. International Union Against Tuberculosis and Lung Disease. Technical guide for sputum examination for tuberculosis by direct microscopy. Bull Int Union Tuberc Lung Dis 1986;61:1–16.

191. Levy H, Feldman C, Sacho H, van der Meulen H, Kallenbach J, Koornhof H. Reevaluation of sputum microscopy and culture in the diagnosis of pulmonary tuberculosis. Chest 1989;95:1193–1197.

192. Eisenach KD, Cave MD, Bates JH, Crawford JT. Polymerase chain reaction amplification of a repetitive DNA sequence specific for *Mycobacterium tuberculosis*. J Infect Dis 1990;161:977–981.

193. Anonymous. Biosafety in microbiology and biomedical laboratories. Washington, DC: US Government, 1993.

194. Centers for Disease Control and Prevention. Treatment of tuberculosis. American Thoracic Society, CDC, and Infectious Diseases Society of America. MMWR Morb Mortal Wkly Rep 2003;52(RR-11): 36–41.

195. Kochi A. The global tuberculosis situation and the new control strategy of the World Health Organization. Tuberc Lung Dis 1991;72:1–6.

196. World Health Organization. Framework for effective tuberculosis control. Geneva: World Health Organization, 1994. Report No. WHO/TB/94.179.

197. American Thoracic Society. Treatment of tuberculosis and tuberculosis infection in adults and children. Am J Resp Crit Care Med 1994;149:1359–1374.

198. McDonald RJ, Memon AM, Reichman LB. Successful supervised ambulatory management of tuberculosis treatment failure. Ann Intern Med 1982;96:297–302.

199. Chaulk CP, Moore-Rice K, Rizzo R, Chaisson RE. Eleven years of community-based directly observed therapy for tuberculosis. JAMA 1995;274:945–951.

200. Moore RD, Chaulk CP, Griffiths R, Cavalcante S, Chaisson RE. Cost-effectiveness of directly observed versus self-administered therapy for tuberculosis. Am J Resp Crit Care Med 1996;154: 1013–1019.

201. Caulk CP, Kazandjian VA. Directly observed therapy for treatment completion of pulmonary tuberculosis. Consensus statement of the Public Health Tuberculosis Guidelines Panel. JAMA 1998;279: 943–948.

202. Weis SE, Slocum PC, Blais FX, King B, Nunn M, Matney GB, Gomez E, Foresman BH. The effect of directly observed therapy on the rates of drug resistance and relapse in tuberculosis. N Engl J Med 1994;330:1179–1184.

203. Zwarenstein M, Schoeman JH, Vundule C, Lombard CJ, Tatley M. Randomised controlled trial of self-supervised and directly observed treatment for tuberculosis. Lancet 1998;352:1340–1343.

204. Mermin J, Lule J, Ekwaru JP, Malamba S, Downing R, Ransom R, Kaharuza F, Culver D, Kizito F, et al. Effect of co-trimoxazole prophylaxis on morbidity, mortality, CD4-cell count, and viral load in HIV infection in rural Uganda. Lancet 2004;364:1428–1434.

205. Zachariah R, Spielmann MP, Chinji C, Gomani P, Arendt V, Hargreaves NJ, Salaniponi FM, Harries AD. Voluntary counselling, HIV testing and adjunctive cotrimoxazole reduces mortality in tuberculosis patients in Thyolo, Malawi. AIDS 2003;2;17:1053–1061.

206. Ferebee SH. Controlled chemoprophylaxis trials in tuberculosis: a general review. Adv Tuberc Res 1970;17:28–106.

207. Pape JW, Jean SS, Ho JL, Hafner A, Johnson WD Jr. Effect of isoniazid prophylaxis on incidence of active tuberculosis and progression of HIV infection. Lancet 1993;342:268–272.

208. Gordin FM, Matts JP, Miller C, Brown LS, Hafner R, John SL, Klein M, Vaughn A, Besch CL, Perez G, Szabo S, El-Sadr W. A controlled trial of isoniazid in persons with anergy and human immunodeficiency virus infection who are at high risk for tuberculosis. N Engl J Med 1997;337: 315–320.

209. Chaisson RE, Gordin F, Matts J, Garcia L, Hafner R, Obrien R. A randomized trial of rifampin/ pyrazinamide for 2 months vs. INH for 12 months in HIV+ tuberculin+ adults. Twelfth World AIDS Conference, Geneva, June 28–July3, 1998, Conference Record, p. 287. Abstract 447/22126.

210. Halsey NA, Coberly JS, Desormeaux J, Losikoff P, Atkinson J, Moulton LH, Contave M, Johnson M, Davis H, Geiter L, Johnson E, Huebner R, Boulos R, Chaisson RE. Randomised trial of isoniazid versus rifampicin and pyrazinamide for prevention of tuberculosis in HIV-1 infection. Lancet 1998;351:786–792.

211. Gordin F, Chaisson RE, Matts JP, Miller C, de Lourdes GM, Hafner R, et al. Rifampin and pyrazinamide versus isoniazid for prevention of tuberculosis in HIV-infected persons: an international randomized trial. Terry Beirn Community Programs for Clinical Research on AIDS, the Adult AIDS Clinical Trials Group, the Pan American Health Organization, and the Centers for Disease Control and Prevention Study Group. JAMA 2000 March 15;283(11):1445–1450.

212. Centers for Disease Control and Prevention. Adverse event data and revised American Thoracic Society/CDC recommendations against the use of rifampin and pyrazinamide for treatment of latent tuberculosis infection—United States, 2003. MMWR Morb Mortal Wkly Rep 2003;52:735–739.

213. Gordin FM, Cohn DL, Matts JP, Chaisson RE, O'Brien RJ. Hepatotoxicity of rifampin and pyrazin-amide in the treatment of latent tuberculosis infection in HIV-infected persons: is it different than in HIV-uninfected persons? Clin Infect Dis 2004 August 15;39(4)561–565.

214. Rodrigues LA, Diwan VK, Wheeler JG. Protective effect of BCG against tuberculous meningitis and miliary tuberculosis: a meta-analysis. Int J Epidemiol 1993;22:1154–1158.

215. Centers for Disease Control and Prevention. Guidelines for the prevention of the transmission of *Mycobacterium tuberculosis* in health-care facilities. MMWR Morb Mortal Wkly Rep 1994;43: 1–111.

216. Segal-Maurer S, Kalkut GE. Environmental control of tuberculosis: continuing controversy. Clin Infect Dis 1994;19:299–308.

# 11 Human Immunodeficiency Virus Infection

*Eduardo Villamor, Karim Manji,*
*and Wafaie W. Fawzi*

## 11.1 INTRODUCTION

Human immunodeficiency virus (HIV) belongs to the lentivirus subfamily of retroviruses, which includes both HIV-1 and HIV-2 viruses. HIV infection causes a progressive decline in immunity that can lead to the acquired immunodeficiency syndrome (AIDS) and death.

HIV-1 infection is having a devastating impact in many developing countries. It is estimated that by the end of 2006, approximately 39.5 million people were living with HIV/AIDS, the highest number ever [1]. New infections totaled 4.3 million in 2006, and 2.9 million HIV-related deaths occurred in the same year; more than 20 million have died since the beginning of the epidemic in 1981. The most heavily affected geographical region is sub-Saharan Africa, which is home to about 63% (or approximately 24.7 million) of the world's total number of persons with HIV/AIDS. More than three quarters of women living with HIV/AIDS worldwide reside in sub-Saharan Africa; currently, 59% of all infected persons in this region are women. Mother-to-child transmission (MTCT) of HIV-1 occurs in 30–45% of cases, and sub-Saharan Africa accounts for approximately 90% of the children orphaned by AIDS. The epidemic is expanding rapidly in Asia, particularly in South/Southeast Asia, where there are about 7.8 million people with HIV/AIDS. Regional statistics and features of the HIV I AIDS epidemic are shown in Fig. 11.1.

The AIDS epidemic is having a major demographic effect in many countries where the prevalence of HIV is high. These effects include a dramatic reduction in life expectancy to less than 50 years, a decline in workforce groups like that of teachers, decreases of net family income, declines in child survival, and an increase in the number of orphans and vulnerable children. Three major challenges for developing countries are the prevention of heterosexual transmission of HIV, prevention of MTCT, and the use of highly active antiretroviral therapy (HAART) for eligible infected individuals.

This chapter focuses primarily on the problem of HIV-1 infection as it relates to developing countries and emphasizes the relationship between host nutritional status and the pathogenesis of HIV infection. In this chapter, HIV means HIV-1 infection and may be used interchangeably with AIDS.

From: *Nutrition and Health: Nutrition and Health in Developing Countries, Second Edition*
Edited by: R. D. Semba & M. W. Bloem © Humana Press, Totowa, NJ

ADULTS AND CHILDREN ESTIMATED TO BE LIVING
WITH HIV AS OF END 2004

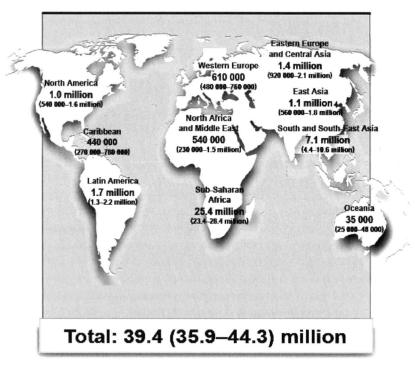

**Total: 39.4 (35.9–44.3) million**

**Fig. 11.1.** Global distribution of HIV/AIDS. Total: 39.5 million. (From [1]).

## 11.2   HISTORICAL BACKGROUND

In the early 1980s, a new acquired immunodeficiency syndrome was described among homosexual men [2–4], injection drug users [5], hemophiliacs [6], and infants [7]. Epidemiological observations suggested that there was an infectious agent transmitted from person to person by sexual intercourse, through blood transfusions, and from mother to infant [8]. A retrovirus was isolated from patients with AIDS [9–11], and antibodies to the retrovirus were described [12, 13]. AIDS research progressed rapidly from the initial observations in the 1980s to include more complete descriptions of the spectrum of disease, sequencing and cloning of HIV-1, and elucidation of the infectious cycle of HIV-1. In 1985, AIDS wasting syndrome, or "slim disease," was described in Uganda [14], and during the same year a diagnostic test was developed. The first world AIDS conference was held in Atlanta, Georgia. In 1987, zidovudine (ZDV) was found to decrease progression to AIDS [15], and the prophylactic use of oral trimethoprim-sulfamethoxazole was found to prevent *Pneumocystis* pneumonia [16]. In 1991, didanoside (ddI) was launched, followed by lamivudine (3TC) and stavudine (d4T) in 1994–1995. By 1996, triple-drug cocktails were available and included potent protease inhibitors. The use of these drugs reduced deaths due to AIDS by 80% in developed countries. Simultaneously, efforts to decrease MTCT were ongoing. A large trial known as the ACTG 076 used a regimen consisting of oral ZDV therapy to the mother during the second and third trimester, intravenous ZDV to the mother at delivery, ZDV to the infant for 6 weeks, and formula feeding from birth and was found to reduce MTCT of HIV by over half [17]. In 1999, the HIVNET 012 trial in Uganda showed that a single dose to the mother during labor and a single oral dose to the baby soon after delivery could achieve a similar reduction in intrapartum transmission of HIV-1 from mothers to children [18]. Most developing countries have started using this inexpensive, effective, and operationally efficient intervention in MTCT prevention programs.

In 2000, five major pharmaceutical companies agreed to slash the price of HIV/AIDS drugs in a breakthrough deal with the United Nations, and in 2002, the Global Fund to Fight AIDS, Tuberculosis, and Malaria was set up. On the World AIDS Day 2003, the World Health Organization (WHO) and UNAIDS launched a "3-by-5" initiative aimed at providing antiretroviral treatment to 3 million people living with AIDS by the year 2005. During the same year, enfuvirtide, the first fusion inhibitor, was launched. In 2004, the United Nations, the Global Fund, and the Clinton Foundation jointly signed an agreement to procure the distribution of inexpensive generic antiretroviral (ARV) medications in developing countries. By the end of the same year, a Global Coalition on Women and AIDS was launched to address issues of social injustice and violence against women. Also, an initiative from the US government called the President's Emergency Plan for AIDS Relief (PEPFAR) was announced as a commitment to provide $15 billion over 5 years to increase the availability of ARV in African countries. Scaling up treatment programs that provide life-prolonging ARV treatment remains a major public health challenge for the immediate future; in low- and middle-income countries, only about 20% of individuals with advanced AIDS have access to ARV treatment, and only about 9% of HIV-infected pregnant women receive ARV prophylaxis [19].

## 11.3   EPIDEMIOLOGY

### 11.3.1   Highest-Risk Groups

The two groups at highest risk of HIV infection in developing countries include sexually active adults and infants born to HIV-infected women, although reports on increased incidence from homosexual transmission and children subject to sexual abuse are emerging. Young women are at the highest risk particularly in sub-Saharan Africa, where 59% of all infected adults are women, and at least two thirds of all 15- to 24-year-olds living with HIV/AIDS are females. Women have little access to education, are more dependent on men economically, are not empowered to resist unprotected sex, and are more vulnerable to violence than men. Sex workers are high-risk groups found in both industrialized and developing countries, and HIV infection among injection drug users is increasingly reported from developing countries such as Thailand and Brazil and countries in Africa as well.

### 11.3.2   Prevalence and Incidence

The vast majority of individuals infected with HIV live in developing countries. Sub-Saharan Africa has been hardest hit by the AIDS epidemic, with an estimated 24.7 million, or about 63% of all individuals infected worldwide by 2006 and 75% of all women infected. The women-to-men ratio of infection in South Africa has been estimated at 20 to 10, while in Kenya and Mali, it is 45 to 10. The prevalence of HIV increased in every region in the world between 2004 and 2006. The greatest increases were observed in East Asia and in Eastern Europe and Central Asia, where the number of people living with HIV rose by 21% [19].

India has the largest number of people living with HIV outside South Africa, an estimated number of 5.1 million individuals. The HIV seroprevalence rates among pregnant women increased steadily in many urban centers in Africa from 1985 to 1997 [20]. Between 1997 and 2003, the prevalence among pregnant women remained stable at 5–10% in West and Central Africa, 10–15% in eastern Africa, and 15–40% in southern Africa [21]. This stabilization of rates may not necessarily indicate a decrease in the incidence of infection but a rise in mortality of untreated HIV-infected persons and migration.

The direct assessment of HIV incidence in population studies entails logistic and methodological challenges. Some of the figures available are derived from studies of groups that are likely to be at higher risk than the general population, for example, 2.5 per 100 person-years among military conscripts in Thailand [22], 3.4/100 person-years in women attending family-planning clinics in Tanzania [23], and 2.0/100 person-years in male factory workers from Zimbabwe [24]. A lower incidence of 0.7 per 100 person-years was found in rural Uganda between 1994 and 2000 [25]. The incidence among intravenous drug users in the United States varies between 0.15% and 2.85% per year [26]. The incidence of HIV infection in Eastern Europe and Central Asia increased by close to 70% in 2006 with respect to 2004; in Asia, the Middle East, and North Africa, it rose by 12–15% [19].

### 11.3.3  Risk Factors

#### 11.3.3.1  TRANSMISSION OF HIV

The three major modes of HIV transmission are through sexual contact, through MTCT, and through transmission by blood products. Factors that increase the risk of transmission of HIV through sexual contact include unprotected receptive anal intercourse [27], unprotected vaginal intercourse [28], and the presence of other concurrent sexually transmitted diseases (STDs) such as genital ulcers, chancroid, syphilis, gonorrhea, and genital herpes infection [29, 30]. Uncircumcised men [31] and women who use traditional vaginal desiccants [32] may be at higher risk for becoming infected with HIV during sexual intercourse. Sexual intercourse during menses may increase the risk of HIV transmission [33]. High plasma HIV load is associated with higher HIV load in seminal fluid in men [34] and higher vaginal shedding of HIV in women [35].

Risk factors for MTCT of HIV include preterm birth, birth order, premature rupture of membranes, low maternal CD4 lymphocyte counts, high maternal HIV load, and breast-feeding [36–42]. Maternal nutritional factors such as anemia [43] and wasting during pregnancy [44] have been associated with MTCT of HIV. Among HIV-infected breast-feeding women, high cell-free and cell-associated HIV loads in breast milk [45–47] and subclinical mastitis [48] are associated with higher MTCT of HIV. Natural history studies have shown that the rates of MTCT of HIV among women who do not breast-feed are about 15–25%, and that among women who breast-feed, the rates are about 25–45% [49]. In breast-feeding populations, about one third of the total MTCT is thought to occur through breast milk [40, 50–52]. Late postnatal transmission accounts for 42% of breast-feeding infection [53]. Efforts are being made in resource-limited settings to decrease MTCT using various regimens. With the use of short-course ARV therapy, transmission rates in developing countries can be reduced by 51% in non-breast-feeding populations and by almost 40% in breast-feeding populations [18, 54–56]. Long-course, triple-ARV therapy used in Europe, the United States, and Brazil has resulted in transmission rates around 1% [57]. Other interventions currently under investigation include the administration of ARV to the infant during breast-feeding and the administration of HAART to the mother during and after pregnancy.

Transmission by blood products usually occurs through the sharing of needles and syringes by individuals engaged in intravenous drug use. Nosocomial spread of HIV has been noted in outbreaks in Eastern Europe and attributed to contaminated needles and syringes. Screening of blood products has largely eliminated HIV transmission through blood transfusion, although sporadic reports suggest that transmission is still occurring through contaminated blood products when there are breakdowns in laboratory screening and in the health care system in general [58].

### 11.3.3.2 PROGRESSION OF THE DISEASE

The main indicators of disease progression during HIV infection are plasma HIV load [59] and circulating CD4 lymphocyte counts [60]. In many industrialized countries, it has become standard clinical practice to monitor these laboratory indicators. In the case of individuals on long-term ARV therapy, it has become imperative to measure plasma HIV load to monitor periodically for resistance of the virus to treatment. The measurement of either CD4 lymphocyte count or plasma HIV load requires relatively sophisticated and expensive laboratory instrumentation and facilities, trained personnel, and sustained support. Although access to these tests has slightly improved in less technologically developed settings during the past few years, monitoring of HIV disease progression usually depends on the monitoring of complications that accompany different stages of HIV disease, especially in periurban and rural settings.

## 11.4   CLINICAL FEATURES/PATHOPHYSIOLOGY

### *11.4.1   Clinical Features*

The clinical course of HIV infection may be highly variable. Primary HIV infection is generally followed by a period in which the individual is asymptomatic. Over months to years, there is usually a slow decline in CD4 lymphocyte count and an increase in HIV load, and certain illnesses such as bacterial pneumonia, *Herpes zoster,* and oral candidiasis may occur. With further decline of CD4 lymphocyte count, AIDS-defining illnesses, such as Kaposi's sarcoma, *Mycobacterium tuberculosis,* and esophageal candidiasis may occur. There are three staging classifications for HIV infection in use: the Centers for Disease Control and Prevention (CDC) classification, which is descriptive and intended for surveillance [61]; the Walter Reed classification, which relies on laboratory markers that are unavailable in many developing countries [62]; and a proposed WHO classification, which is intended to be universally applicable [63]. The WHO staging system for HIV infection and disease in adults and adolescents is shown in Table 11.1.

Table 11.1
**World Health Organization clinical staging of HIV/AIDS for adults and adolescents with confirmed HIV infection**

**Clinical stage 1**
Asymptomatic
Persistent generalized lymphadenopathy

**Clinical stage 2**
Moderate unexplained weight loss (<10% of presumed or measured body weight)
Recurrent upper-respiratory tract infections (sinusitis, tonsillitis, otitis media, and pharyngitis)
Herpes zoster
Angular cheilitis
Recurrent oral ulceration
Papular pruritic eruptions
Seborrheic dermatitis
Fungal nail infections

**Clinical stage 3**
Unexplained severe weight loss (>10% of presumed or measured body weight)
Unexplained chronic diarrhea for longer than 1 month
Unexplained persistent fever (above 37.6°C intermittent or constant, for longer than 1 month)
Persistent oral candidiasis
Oral hairy leukoplakia
Pulmonary tuberculosis (current)
Severe bacterial infections (such as pneumonia, empyema, pyomyositis, bone or joint infection, meningitis, or bacteremia)
Acute necrotizing ulcerative stomatitis, gingivitis, or periodontitis
Unexplained anemia (<8 g/dL), neutropenia (<0.5 × 10⁹/L), or chronic thrombocytopenia (<50 × 10⁹/L)

**Clinical stage 4**
HIV wasting syndrome
*Pneumocystis* pneumonia
Recurrent severe bacterial pneumonia
Chronic herpes simplex infection (orolabial, genital, or anorectal of more than 1-month duration or visceral at any site)
Esophageal candidiasis (or candidiasis of trachea, bronchi, or lungs)
Extrapulmonary tuberculosis
Kaposi's sarcoma
Cytomegalovirus infection (retinitis or infection of other organs)
Central nervous system toxoplasmosis
HIV encephalopathy
Extrapulmonary cryptococcosis, including meningitis
Disseminated nontuberculous mycobacterial infection
Progressive multifocal leukoencephalopathy
Chronic cryptosporidiosis (with diarrhea)
Chronic isosporiasis
Disseminated mycosis (coccidiomycosis or histoplasmosis)

(continued)

Table 11.1 (continued)
**World Health Organization clinical staging of HIV/AIDS for adults and adolescents with confirmed HIV infection**

Recurrent nontyphoidal *Salmonella* bacteremia
Lymphoma (cerebral or B-cell non-Hodgkin) or other solid HIV-associated tumors
Invasive cervical carcinoma
Atypical disseminated leishmaniasis
Symptomatic HIV-associated nephropathy or symptomatic HIV-associated cardiomyopathy

### 11.4.1.1 PRIMARY HIV INFECTION

Acute primary HIV infection is characterized by a high viremia and decrease in CD4 lymphocyte count within 2–6 weeks of initial infection. Within weeks, seroconversion to HIV occurs with the appearance of antibodies to HIV in the peripheral circulation. Symptoms of acute HIV infection include fever, joint pain, and night sweats, although some individuals may be asymptomatic [64]. High viremia during primary HIV infection is considered a predictor of long-term outcome after seroconversion [65]. During primary HIV infection, individuals may be highly infectious and are at higher risk of transmitting HIV to others during sexual intercourse [66].

### 11.4.1.2 ASYMPTOMATIC HIV INFECTION

After primary HIV infection, plasma HIV load usually drops to undetectable. During the asymptomatic phase of HIV infection, the CD4 lymphocyte count may slowly decline at a rate of 50–100 cells/μL per year [67], and there may be considerable variability in the rate of decline. HIV is not latent during this period but is actively replicating in lymphoid tissue. Other laboratory abnormalities, such as anemia and lymphopenia, may be detected. The infected individual may have lymphadenopathy but no other symptoms or signs. Asymptomatic HIV infection can last for many years.

### 11.4.1.3 SYMPTOMATIC HIV INFECTION

In early symptomatic HIV infection, fever, night sweats, fatigue, and headaches are common, and diarrhea and anorexia contribute to weight loss. Mucocutaneous disorders such as oral candidiasis, oral hairy leukoplakia, molluscum contagiosum, and seborrheic dermatitis are relatively common [68]. Varicella-zoster infection may be common in early symptomatic HIV infection. Late symptomatic HIV infection is usually associated with the appearance of one or more AIDS-defining illnesses. Oral candidiasis and lymphadenopathy were identified as the strongest predictors of HIV infection among adults in Tanzania [69].

### 11.4.1.4 ACQUIRED IMMUNE DEFICIENCY SYNDROME

According to WHO, AIDS in adults with confirmed HIV infection is defined as clinical diagnosis (presumptive or definitive) of any stage 4 condition or first-ever documented CD4 count less than 200 per mm³ or less than 15% [63]. The pattern of AIDS-associated illnesses appears to differ greatly between developed and developing countries. In Africa, for example, tuberculosis is a major AIDS-defining illness, and up to 75% of newly diagnosed tuberculosis patients are HIV infected. The presence of HIV in an individual increases the risk of developing tuberculosis tenfold. Cryptococcal meningitis is another major initial AIDS-defining illness in parts of Africa [70]. Prior to

HAART in North America and Europe, about one third of HIV-infected patients would develop cytomegalovirus (CMV) infection. Although CMV infection occurs in developing countries, it is not a leading AIDS-associated opportunistic infection, perhaps because of geographical differences in the epidemiology of CMV infection, differences in approaches to diagnosis, or different rates of survival among HIV-infected adults.

## 11.4.2  Pediatric HIV Infection

Nearly all cases of HIV infection in children are acquired through MTCT of HIV. The natural history of HIV infection in children is variable and tends to be more rapidly progressive when compared to adults. In the developed world, before the widespread use of ARV therapy, 30% of infected infants presented before 6 months of age, and 17–25% died within the first 18 months of life. By 6 years of age, up to 75% of children were alive, with 50% still alive by 9 years of age [71]. Survival of children with AIDS appears to be bimodal, with approximately 10–20% of infected children "rapid progressors," usually dying of AIDS before 4 years of age, whereas the remaining 80–90% of children have survival patterns more typical of adults with AIDS, with a mean survival of approximately 9–10 years [71]. Survival of children infected with HIV in Africa appears to be much shorter than that seen in Europe and the United States. In Uganda, median survival of HIV-infected children was 21 months, with 66.2% dying by 36 months of age [72]. In a cohort in Malawi, the mortality rates per 1,000 person-years of observation were 339, 46, and 36 in HIV-infected children, HIV-uninfected born to HIV-infected women, and HIV-uninfected born to HIV-negative women, respectively. Among HIV-infected children, the cumulative proportion surviving to age 24 months was 70%, and to 36 months the cumulative proportion surviving was 55% [73].

### 11.4.2.1  FACTORS AFFECTING DISEASE PROGRESSION IN CHILDREN

Progression of HIV infection in children may depend on the timing of transmission, the inoculum of virus, the phenotype of the virus, and the immune response. The timing of viral detection in the newborn period may serve as a prognostic indicator of subsequent clinical course. Several prospective cohorts have observed significant associations between early viral detection (in utero infection) and rapid disease progression in infancy. Kuhn et al. evaluated 432 infants born to mothers infected with HIV [74]. HIV was detected by polymerase chain reaction (PCR) or culture within the first 2 days of life in 28% of infants; the calculated relative risk for progression to AIDS or death was 2.6 (confidence interval [CI] 1.5–4.6). In children with virus detectable 48 hours after birth, 29% had died or developed AIDS by 1 year of age. A threefold increased risk for early disease progression among infants with early viral detection was reported by Mayaux et al. [75]. Currently, there is no demonstrable RNA threshold that can differentiate rapid from slow progressors in the first few months of life. Risk of disease progression has been related to high viral loads (>100,000 copies/mL), especially if CD4 counts are low [76].

Two related properties of HIV are syncytium induction and macrophage tropism. In adults and children, macrophage tropism has been associated with a nonprogressive clinical state. In contrast, the syncytium-inducing and CD4 lymphocyte-tropic phenotypes have been observed with the development of symptomatic progressive disease [77]. There is an association between the human leukocyte antigen (HLA) system and genetic susceptibility to HIV [78]. The discovery of the coreceptors CXCR4, CCR5,

CCR2, and CCR3 and the effects of their mutants have provided evidence of genetic variability in host susceptibility. Homozygosity to the CCR5 gene confers protection against nonsyncytium-inducing or macrophage-tropic HIV strains, and that heterozygosity is associated with slower disease progression in children and adults [79–81].

### 11.4.2.2 CLASSIFICATION OF HIV INFECTION IN CHILDREN

The World Health Organization has developed a classification system for HIV-infected children that is based on immunologic criteria such as CD4 lymphocyte counts and clinical criteria (Table 11.2).

Early clinical signs and symptoms that are suggestive of HIV infection in an infant include weight loss or failure to thrive, delayed milestones, persistent diarrhea, persistent

Table 11.2
**World Health Organization clinical staging of HIV/AIDS for children with confirmed HIV infection**

**Clinical stage 1**
Asymptomatic
Persistent generalized lymphadenopathy

**Clinical stage 2**
Unexplained persistent hepatosplenomegaly
Papular pruritic eruptions
Fungal nail infection
Angular cheilitis
Lineal gingival erythema
Extensive wart virus infection
Extensive molluscum contagiosum
Recurrent oral ulcerations
Unexplained persistent parotid enlargement
Herpes zoster
Recurrent or chronic upper-respiratory tract infections (otitis media, otorrhea, sinusitis, or tonsillitis)

**Clinical stage 3**
Unexplained moderate malnutrition or wasting not adequately responding to standard therapy
Unexplained persistent diarrhea (14 days or more)
Unexplained persistent fever (above 37.5°C intermittent or constant for longer than 1 month)
Persistent oral candidiasis (after first 6–8 weeks of life)
Oral hairy leukoplakia
Acute necrotizing ulcerative gingivitis or periodontitis
Lymph node tuberculosis
Pulmonary tuberculosis
Severe recurrent bacterial pneumonia
Symptomatic lymphoid interstitial pneumonitis
Chronic HIV-associated lung disease, including brochiectasis
Unexplained anemia (<8 g/dL), neutropenia (<0.5 × 10⁹/L), or chronic thrombocytopenia (<50 × 10⁹/L)

(continued)

Table 11.2 (continued)
World Health Organization clinical staging of HIV/AIDS for children with confirmed HIV infection

**Clinical stage 4**

Unexplained severe wasting, stunting, or severe malnutrition not responding to standard therapy

Pneumocystis pneumonia

Recurrent severe bacterial infections (such as empyema, pyomyositis, bone or joint infection, or meningitis but excluding pneumonia)

Chronic herpes simplex infection (orolabial or cutaneous of more than 1-month duration or visceral at any site)

Esophageal candidiasis (or candidiasis of trachea, bronchi, or lungs)

Extrapulmonary tuberculosis

Kaposi's sarcoma

Cytomegalovirus infection: retinitis or cytomegalovirus infection affecting another organ, with onset at age older than 1 month

Central nervous system toxoplasmosis (after 1 month of life)

Extrapulmonary cryptococcosis (including meningitis)

HIV encephalopathy

Disseminated endemic mycosis (coccidiomycosis or histoplasmosis)

Disseminated nontuberculous mycobacterial infection

Chronic cryptosporidiosis (with diarrhea)

Chronic isosporiasis

Cerebral or B-cell non-Hodgkin lymphoma

Progressive multifocal leukoencephalopathy

Symptomatic HIV-associated nephropathy or HIV-associated cardiomyopathy

---

fever, and severe or repeated pneumonia. In a large cohort study in Zaire, the incidence rates of acute diarrhea were 170 per 100 child-years in HIV-infected infants compared with 100 episodes per 100 child-years in uninfected infants [82]. The incidence of recurrent diarrhea was about twice as high and incidence of persistent diarrhea was about four times higher in HIV-infected infants compared with uninfected infants. Infants with HIV infection were shown to have a twofold increased risk of death from diarrhea [82].

In children with confirmed HIV infection, AIDS is defined as clinical diagnosis (presumptive or definitive) of any stage 4 condition or CD4 count below 200 per $mm^3$ in children 5 years of age or older (<15% of total lymphocytes in children 36–59 months old, < 20% if 12–35 months old, and < 25% if < 12 months of age [63]).

### 11.4.3 Pathogenesis

The pathogenesis of HIV infection depends on both virologic and host factors. The main cellular targets for HIV are human cells that express the CD4 differentiation antigen on cell surface, such as $CD4^+$ T lymphocytes, $CD4^+$ monocytes and macrophages, and $CD4^+$ dendritic cells. The outer envelope of HIV is covered with a surface glycoprotein known as gp120, and this glycoprotein specifically binds to the CD4 molecule. Various coreceptors, such as CCR5 and CXCR4, appear to be necessary for binding and

HIV entry into the host cell [83]. After fusion of viral and target cell membranes, viral RNA and proteins are deposited in the cytoplasm of the host cell. Uncoating results in the deposition of a reverse transcription complex in the cytoplasm, and this high molecular weight complex then translocates into the host cell nucleus. Through reverse transcription, viral complementary DNA (cDNA) is synthesized, and this proviral DNA is integrated into host cell DNA. Transcription of proviral DNA produces proteins such as Tat, Rev, and Nef and important gene products such as gag, gag/pol, and other accessory gene products are expressed. Viral RNA is enclosed in an envelope glycoprotein, and further maturation steps occur before mature virions bud off from the host cell.

Lymphoid tissues serve as the primary site of viral replication and are the main reservoir for the virus. During acute HIV syndrome, the virus is disseminated widely in lymphoid tissues, plasma HIV load is high, and the infected individual responds with a specific immune response against HIV. After the appearance of an immune response, within 6 months to 1 year, the plasma HIV load decreases and then stabilizes to what has been termed a *set point*". This set point is of considerable importance as it appears to correlate directly with the rate of HIV disease progression [65]. The initial immune response to the virus during acute HIV syndrome may thus be a major determinant of the set point. The immune response to HIV consists of nonspecific immune responses, HIV-specific antibody responses, and an HIV-specific cytotoxic T-lymphocyte response by CD8+ lymphocytes. Among these immune responses, the cytotoxic T-lymphocyte response may be the most important [84].

A period of clinical latency may last for years, during which immune activation and viral replication occur without any obvious signs or symptoms of HIV infection. During this period, CD4 lymphocyte counts in peripheral blood may slowly decline until eventually the immune compromise results in the appearance of clinical disease. The loss of CD4 lymphocytes is the main immunologic abnormality of HIV infection. The rate of progression from primary HIV infection to AIDS may be 2–3 years in some individuals, who have been termed *rapid progressors*, or may be 20 years or more in other individuals, who have been termed *long-term survivors* [85]. The possible reasons for the large differences in AIDS-free survival include host immune responses, host genetic factors, and viral strain and phenotype. Individuals with a mutant allele for the coreceptor CCR5 have significantly slower HIV disease progression [86].

## 11.4.4 Role of Nutrition

There is a bidirectional relationship between HIV infection and the nutritional status. On the one hand, malnutrition affects HIV transmission and disease progression. On the other, HIV infection can lead to undernutrition, including micronutrient deficiencies and body mass depletion through decreased food intake, malabsorption, and increased utilization and excretion of nutrients [87]. This vicious cycle contributes to further deterioration of the health of patients and ultimately leads to mortality.

### 11.4.4.1 THE ROLE OF NUTRITIONAL FACTORS IN HIV PROGRESSION AND TRANSMISSION

**11.4.4.1.1 Vitamins and Disease Progression.** The relations between vitamins and HIV disease progression and transmission have been examined in observational and, more recently, intervention studies. In some observational studies, the status of vitamins was assessed through the measurement of serum concentrations, whereas others examined the dietary intake of nutrients from foods and supplements. Lower plasma concentrations of vitamin A [88] were related to increased mortality, while decreased levels of vitamins E [89] and $B_{12}$ [90] were associated with progression to AIDS. These biochemical markers may be limited in their correlation with the true underlying micronutrient status. Low vitamin A, for example, is associated with the acute-phase response to infection [91] and may be a marker of HIV disease stage rather than a reflection of limited liver stores of the nutrient.

Reverse causality may provide another explanation for the association between low plasma concentrations and health outcomes: HIV infection could adversely affect absorption and metabolism of nutrients, leading to biochemical deficiency. Several observational studies that examined the associations between intakes of individual vitamins or use of multivitamin supplements and risk of HIV disease progression suggested the potential for beneficial effects. Daily use of multivitamin supplements in a group of HIV-infected men in the United States was related to decreased progression to AIDS and higher CD4 counts [92]; in another study, individuals with average vitamin A intakes between 9,000 and 20,000 IU had lower risk of disease progression and death than those above or below the range [93, 94]. Higher intakes of niacin, vitamins $B_1$, $B_2$, $B_6$, and C were associated with slower progression to AIDS and with 40–60% reductions in the risk of death after 8 years of follow-up [88, 89]. Noticeably, the risk reductions were apparent at levels of intake that were several times the recommended dietary allowance (RDA) and could only be reached through the intake of supplements. This could suggest that supplementation at high doses may enhance the immune function even among individuals who are not nutritionally deficient, or that HIV-infected persons develop very profound micronutrient deficiencies that may only be corrected through large supplemental doses. The latter was supported by a study in South Africa among subjects likely to suffer from undernutrition in which daily intake of B-complex vitamin supplements was associated with significantly lower risk of disease progression [95].

A number of intervention studies have examined the effect of vitamin supplements on HIV disease progression. High doses of β-carotene (180 mg/day) resulted in higher $CD4^+$ cell counts in one study [96] but had no effect on $CD4^+$ cell counts or viral load in another [97]. Daily multimicronutrient supplements during 2 weeks had no effects on persistent diarrhea, CD4 cell counts, or clinical markers of disease severity in Zambian individuals [98]. In a trial of vitamins E and C, supplementation for 3 months suggested a beneficial effect on viral load, but the study was too small for this effect to become statistically significant [99]. The efficacy and safety of daily multivitamin supplementation on clinical outcomes was examined in two randomized, double-blind, placebo-controlled trials from Thailand and Tanzania. In Thailand, supplements that included 21 nutrients were associated with reduction in mortality among HIV-infected men and women; the results were statistically significant among individuals with very low baseline $CD4^+$ cell counts. No significant effects were noted on $CD4^+$ cell counts or viral load [100].

Further evidence in support of the benefits of vitamin supplementation to HIV-infected subjects comes from a large, double-blind, placebo-controlled randomized trial conducted in Tanzania among 1,078 HIV-infected women who were not on ARV therapy. In this study, daily supplements of multivitamins B, C, and E resulted in large and statistically significant reductions in the risk of progression to WHO stage 4 or AIDS-related death, decreased symptoms and signs of HIV disease [101], and wasting [102]. Multivitamins also resulted in significantly higher CD4$^+$ and CD8$^+$ cell counts and significantly lower viral load. These findings are probably generalizable to HIV-infected women in early stages of disease in developing countries, as supported by a smaller trial of the same nutrients plus selenium, which found a significant increase in CD4 cell counts among nonpregnant, HIV-infected women from Kenya [103]. The mechanisms through which multivitamins B, C, and E delay progression to AIDS are not completely known. They are likely to be mediated through improvements in specific aspects of the immunity function. For example, vitamin E supplementation can improve the cutaneous delayed-type hypersensitivity (DTH) response, an indicator of T-cell-dependent macrophage activation [104–106]; lymphocyte proliferation, interleukin (IL) 2 production [104], and antibody concentrations [105]. Vitamin C supplements have been related to increased lymphocyte proliferation in the elderly [107].

A potential role for vitamin D in HIV disease progression has been suggested in observational studies. HIV infection was inversely related to serum concentrations of vitamin D in some settings [108–110], and in a small longitudinal study of HIV-infected persons, low vitamin D concentrations at baseline appeared to be related to greater risk of mortality [110]. This association could be mediated through increased severity of mycobacterial opportunistic infections against which vitamin D could normally be protective. Additional epidemiological evidence is warranted on this promising field of research.

**11.4.4.1.2 Vitamins, Pregnancy Outcomes, and Child Health.** Some observational studies suggested that low serum vitamin A concentrations among HIV-infected pregnant women were associated with a higher risk of morbidity and mortality among children [111] and with vertical transmission of HIV [112, 113]. These results motivated the implementation of randomized, placebo-controlled intervention studies, which constitute the best design to assess the relations between nutrients and health outcomes. Results from three such trials have been reported to date.

In Malawi, HIV-infected pregnant women were randomized to either 10,000 IU vitamin A or placebo during the prenatal period. No effect was noted on transmission of the virus at 6 weeks or by 12 months or on the risk of prematurity, but an improvement in birth weight was reported [114]. In South Africa, supplements of preformed vitamin A and β-carotene during the prenatal period resulted in a reduction in prematurity but had no significant effect on birth weight or the risk of HIV infection in infants by 3 months of age [115]. While both trials from Malawi and South Africa provided vitamin A or placebo regimens during the antenatal period only, pregnant women in Tanzania were randomized to daily vitamin A (preformed vitamin A and β-carotene) or multivitamins (vitamin B complex, C, and E) using a two-by-two factorial design, and these supplements were provided daily during the antenatal period and beyond. Multivitamin supplements (including vitamin B complex, C, and E), but not vitamin A/β-carotene alone, resulted in approximately 40% reductions in the risks of fetal loss, low birth weight, and severe prematurity [116] and a significant increase in weight gain during pregnancy [117]. Daily supplements of multivitamins had no effect on the risk of overall vertical transmission of HIV in utero or during the intrapartum and early breast-feeding periods (up to 6 w eeks of age) [118]; however, children born to women on multivitamins who were in relatively poorer nutritional or immunological conditions at baseline experienced large and significant reductions in the risks of these endpoints. Maternal multivitamin supplementation resulted in significant benefits to child health outcomes, including lower child mortality among HIV-negative children [119], an overall significant reduction in the risk of diarrhea, and a large increase in CD4 cell counts [120], and significant improvement in attained weight by 24 months of age [121]. Contrary to the original hypothesis, vitamin A/β-carotene resulted in a significant increase of 38% in the risk of vertical transmission of the virus [119]. Vitamin A/β-carotene supplementation also resulted in a significant increase in lower genital viral shedding [122]. In a trial conducted in Kenya, daily administration of 10,000 IU vitamin A alone (i.e., without β-carotene) to HIV-infected, nonpregnant women had no effect on CD4 cell counts and plasma or genital viral load after 6 weeks [123].

The efficacy of a single large dose of vitamin A given to women in the early postpartum period (200,000 IU) or to neonates (50,000 IU) was examined in Zimbabwe. Supplementing HIV-infected mothers or their infants resulted in significantly increased risk of infant HIV infection or death, although providing the supplement to both mother and infant had no effect compared to placebo [124].

The mechanisms by which vitamin A/β-carotene could increase HIV shedding and transmission of HIV are not clear. It has been hypothesized that by increasing the multiplication and differentiation of lymphoid and myeloid cells, preformed vitamin A leads to increased density of CCR5 receptors that are expressed on these cells and are necessary for attachment and subsequent replication of the virus [125]. It is also possible that the adverse effect noted in the Tanzania study is due to the β-carotene component of the vitamin A intervention. Although high doses of β-carotene provided for short periods of time to HIV-infected individuals were apparently safe [96, 97], there is no study of the safety of prolonged supplementation.

Four placebo-controlled trials have examined the efficacy of direct vitamin A supplementation of children with HIV infection. In South Africa, vitamin A supplements provided to HIV-infected children resulted in an approximately 50% reduction in diarrheal morbidity [126]. Compared with placebo, vitamin A supplements given every 4 months to Tanzanian children resulted in significant reductions in mortality and morbidity and improvements in growth; these effects were larger among HIV-infected children than HIV-negative ones [127–129]. In another trial from South Africa among HIV-infected children, vitamin A administered before influenza vaccination was associated with a dampening in the increase in human immunodeficiency viral load associated with the vaccination [130]. In a trial from Uganda, vitamin A supplementation to HIV-infected children resulted in a 46% reduction in mortality and decreased the point prevalence of persistent cough and chronic diarrhea [131]. The benefits of vitamin A in children could be mediated by the many roles that vitamin A plays as an immunomodulatory agent [132]. Vitamin A is fundamental for the growth and function of T and B cells, antibody responses, and maintenance of mucosal epithelia, including that of the respiratory, gastrointestinal, and genitourinary tracts.

The evidence reviewed suggests that supplementation of vitamins B complex, C, and E at multiples of the RDA should be considered among HIV-infected, pregnant, or lactating women. Daily supplementation with vitamin A and β-carotene to HIV-infected women is not advised with current evidence. While there is no strong evidence in support of providing vitamin A supplements to HIV-infected adults, vitamin A is an essential nutrient, and HIV-infected individuals should ensure RDA dietary intake. Among children, periodic vitamin A supplementation after 6 months of age still constitutes a powerful public health tool to decrease mortality and morbidity from some infections, independent of the child's HIV status.

**11.4.4.1.3   Vitamins and Horizontal Transmission of HIV.** There is scarce evidence regarding the potential role of vitamin status on heterosexual transmission of HIV, and it is limited to vitamin A and β-carotene. Higher serum retinol concentrations have been related to increased risk of seroconversion in small case-control studies conducted in Kenya [125] and India [133]; in the latter study, an inverse association between β-carotene concentrations and horizontal transmission was reported. Differences in the distribution of serum retinol between cases and controls were not apparent in studies from Rwanda [134] and Tanzania [135]. In a randomized clinical trial of postpartum women from Zimbabwe, supplementation with 400,000 IU vitamin A had no effect on the incidence of HIV infection, although low serum retinol concentrations were significant risk factors for seroconversion [136].

**11.4.4.1.4   Minerals.** Most of the research on the roles of minerals in the context of HIV infection has focused on selenium and zinc. Selenium is a critical part of the antioxidant enzyme glutathione peroxidase. In adults infected with HIV, low plasma selenium concentrations have been associated with large increases in the risks of death [137, 138], disease progression [138], and the occurrence of opportunistic events such as mycobacterial disease [139]. In pregnant women, low selenium concentrations have been related to fetal death and increased risk of intrapartum HIV transmission [140]. Among HIV-infected children, low plasma selenium has also been related to a higher risk of mortality [141, 142].

Several small intervention studies of HIV-infected individuals provided evidence suggestive of beneficial effects of selenium supplementation. For example, supplementation with 100 µg of selenium daily for 1 year resulted in higher glutathione peroxidase activity and glutathione levels among HIV-infected persons [143]. A small crossover trial showed a significant increase in percentage of CD4$^+$ cells and CD4/CD8 ratio while the glutathione activity remained unchanged [144], and in a randomized trial in the United States, 200 µg of selenium per day resulted in a significant decrease in total hospital admission rates and hospitalizations due to infections [145]. In another randomized trial of 174 HIV-infected adults, 200 µg selenium daily for 9 months appeared to decrease viral load [146]. Overall, the available body of evidence implicates selenium deficiency as an independent predictor for accelerated progression of HIV disease. Additional randomized controlled trials are needed to elucidate the impact of selenium supplementation on clinical outcomes among HIV-infected adults and children.

Observational studies that examined the relationships between zinc status and HIV-related outcomes have provided conflicting results. Higher levels of zinc intake were associated with significantly faster disease progression and higher mortality among asymptomatic HIV-infected men in a prospective cohort study of asymptomatic HIV-infected men in the United States [93, 94]. In contrast, plasma zinc concentrations were inversely associated with mortality in another study [147]. As for vitamin A, plasma zinc concentrations may be low as a result of the infection state and do not necessarily reflect poor nutritional status among individuals.

The effects of zinc supplementation on pregnancy outcomes and hematologic and T-cell counts were examined in a randomized clinical trial among HIV-infected pregnant women in Tanzania [148]. Daily supplementation with 25 mg zinc during pregnancy had no effect on adverse pregnancy outcomes, including low birth weight, prematurity less than 37 weeks, small for gestational age, or fetal loss. While both zinc and placebo groups experienced an increase in hemoglobin levels between baseline and 6 weeks postpartum, the rise in hemoglobin was significantly lower in the zinc group compared with the placebo group. The effect on hematologic status may have been due to the adverse effect of zinc on iron absorption, as previously observed in other studies [149]. Zinc supplements had no effect on CD4 cell counts, maternal viral load, or MTCT up to 6 weeks postpartum [150].

A small randomized clinical trial of 96 South African children 6–60 months old with symptomatic HIV infection suggested that daily supplementation with 10 mg oral zinc for 6 months was associated with fewer episodes of watery diarrhea and had no effect on viral load or CD4 cell counts [151]. By contrast, zinc supplementation had no effect on persistent diarrhea in a short-term randomized trial of Peruvian HIV-infected adults who were zinc deficient [152]. Larger and longer-term studies are warranted to examine the effect of zinc on HIV disease progression and associated mortality in both children and adults.

Anemia is a recognized risk factor for HIV disease progression [153–155]. Current WHO recommendations include daily iron-folate supplements (400 μg folate and 60 mg iron) during 6 months of pregnancy to prevent anemia and twice-daily supplements to treat severe anemia. Although there are concerns about potential adverse effects of iron supplementation in the context of HIV infection [156, 157], more data are needed before this recommendation is changed. Analysis from a historical cohort showed that 60 mg iron supplementation was not associated with changes in viral load [158], but the effects of larger doses remain unknown as well as the impact on clinical outcomes.

As the availability of ARV therapy increases in developing countries, it is important to ascertain whether the benefits shown by supplementation with some micronutrients in ARV-naïve patients are also apparent in those receiving HAART [159]. One trial of multiple vitamins and minerals showed no significant effects on mortality [160]. Two trials with antioxidants suggested an increase in oxidative defenses [161–163], and one of them showed a decrease in oxidative stress [163]. No effects on viral load have been demonstrated [161, 164], although increased CD4 cell counts were reported in two intervention studies [145, 164]. Three trials failed to show an impact of micronutrients on adverse effects related to HAART [160, 164, 165]. Stronger evidence is needed before recommending routine micronutrient supplementation to HIV-infected patients receiving HAART.

**11.4.4.1.5  Breast-feeding.** Breast-feeding is the gold standard of infant nutrition in developing countries. Among HIV-infected women from regions where ARV therapy is not readily available, there is a dilemma between the risk of MTCT through breast milk and the health and survival benefits of breast-feeding. Breast-feeding accounts for more than one third of MTCT in sub-Saharan Africa, where this practice is almost universal [53], and few interventions are known that could diminish this risk. Inactivation of HIV through expression and heat treatment of breast milk, although potentially efficacious [166], is impractical in many settings due to stigmatization and socioeconomic factors. Total avoidance of breast-feeding is also not a realistic option given the high cost of formula, the lack of adequate hygienic conditions in most countries affected by the epidemic, and the greater morbidity that not-breast-fed infants experience [167]. Current evidence indicates that exclusive breast-feeding is associated with the lowest risk of MTCT when compared to predominant or mixed breast-feeding [168, 169]. A short course of nevirapine (NVP) administered to the mother during labor and to the infant in the immediate postpartum period has the potential of reducing transmission throughout the first 18 months of age [170], and in infants receiving ZDV prophylaxis, breast-feeding is associated with lower mortality than formula feeding [171]. Ongoing studies are evaluating the efficacy of ARV regimens to breast-feeding infants or mothers in preventing HIV infection.

The impact of breast-feeding to the mothers has been a matter of debate. In a study from Kenya, it was hypothesized that breast-feeding may result in higher mortality among women [172], possibly through depletion of maternal nutritional status. However, these findings were not confirmed by studies in South Africa [173], Tanzania [174], or Malawi [175].

In settings where replacement feeding is not acceptable, feasible, affordable, sustainable, and safe (AFASS), WHO [176] currently recommends exclusive breast-feeding for the first 6 months of life. If at 6 months replacement feeding is still not AFASS, WHO recommends continuation of breast-feeding with additional complementary foods and periodic assessment of the mother and baby. All breast-feeding is to stop when once a nutritionally adequate and safe diet can be provided without breast milk.

**11.4.4.1.6 Protein-Energy Malnutrition.** The question of how protein-energy malnutrition affects HIV disease progression and transmission poses a methodological challenge given that HIV infection itself induces wasting and undernutrition through various mechanisms. Wasting, an involuntary loss of fat and lean body mass, is a strong predictor of adverse outcomes among HIV-infected subjects independent of other markers of disease progression, which suggests that malnutrition per se could be causally related to worsened prognosis. Several studies conducted mostly in developed settings [177–183] have found that the proportion of body weight loss in HIV-positive adults is positive and linearly associated with the risks of progression to AIDS and death and the occurrence of opportunistic episodes, both infectious and oncological. The effect of wasting on mortality appears to be particularly strong when the loss of body mass occurs at the expense of metabolically active tissue as measured through lean mass [177, 184] and through decreases in indicators of the integrity of membranes [184, 185]; this effect is present even in patients who receive ARV treatment.

In developing countries, the burden of wasting is likely to be aggravated by high rates of underlying undernutrition, specific nutrient deficiencies, and increased prevalence of infections such as malaria, tuberculosis, and intestinal parasitoses. A few studies have examined the impact of wasting and protein-energy malnutrition on HIV-related outcomes in these settings. In the Gambia, body mass index (BMI) at the time of HIV infection diagnosis was a strong and independent predictor of mortality among adults [186]. Wasting measured as maternal weight loss during pregnancy was strongly associated with the risk of perinatal HIV transmission in a study in Tanzania, independent of CD4 cell counts and viral load [44]. Wasting also appeared to augment viral shedding in genital secretions and was significantly related to increased rates of fetal loss, low birth weight, and preterm delivery [187]. In children, protein-energy malnutrition also appears to have a significant impact on HIV progression. Infant wasting and growth failure have been reported as frequent risk factors for mortality in studies of HIV-positive children from Malawi, Uganda, and Rwanda [73, 188, 189]. In a study of HIV-infected and uninfected preschool children in Tanzania, wasting was a strong predictor of mortality only among those who were HIV infected [190]. The effect of improving protein and energy intake on HIV-related outcomes in developing countries is largely unknown at this point.

### 11.4.4.2 THE IMPACT OF HIV INFECTION ON NUTRITIONAL STATUS

**11.4.4.2.1 Child Growth.** The adverse effect of HIV infection on child growth starts in utero. Children born to HIV-infected mothers are at higher risk of intrauterine growth retardation (IUGR) than those with HIV-negative mothers according to studies conducted in both in and developing countries. The risk of low birth weight (<2,500 g) is estimated to be twice as high for HIV-infected compared to uninfected women according to a meta-analysis of 17 studies [191]. In addition to maternal disease stage and nutritional factors, fetal infection with HIV could be one important cause of IUGR, as suggested by a study in Rwanda in which birth weight, head circumference, ponderal index, and weight-to-head circumference ratio were significantly lower among the babies who were HIV positive at birth compared to those who remained uninfected [192].

HIV infection also contributes to extrauterine growth impairments. Early reports on growth alterations came from studies of prepubertal boys with hemophilia, in which asymptomatic carriers of HIV were found to be one quartile shorter in height-for-age than uninfected hemophiliacs [193]. As recently reviewed [194], in the majority of longitudinal studies conducted in Africa HIV infection was related to large and significant linear and ponderal growth delays in children below 2 years of age. In these settings, growth retardation appeared early in life, between birth and 3 months, and affected accrual of both length-for-age and weight-for-age. There were no differences in growth between children born to HIV-negative mothers and those born to HIV-positive mothers who did not become infected themselves (seroreverters).

Numerous causes of growth retardation in children infected with HIV have been identified in studies conducted in developed countries [195–198]. These include decreased protein and energy intake, increased utilization of nutrients and losses secondary to malabsorption, advanced stage of HIV disease as indicated by high viral load and low CD4 cell counts, exposure to ARV treatment, alterations in the growth hormone axis, and psychosocial factors. Much less evidence is available on the mechanisms through which HIV infection causes growth retardation among African preschool children. Some studies suggested that the micronutrient status plays an important role. Low serum vitamin A and carotenoid concentrations have been related to decreased weight and height velocities in Ugandan children [199], and vitamin A supplementation in Tanzanian HIV-infected infants resulted in rapid catch-up linear growth [129]. Other possible causes of growth retardation among HIV-positive children include secondary infections. Diarrhea and respiratory infections are likely to have a more severe impact on the growth pattern of HIV-infected children than among uninfected children. Evidence to support this hypothesis, however, is lacking.

**11.4.4.2.2 Wasting Syndrome.** Wasting consists of a progressive involuntary loss of lean and fat body mass that often accompanies HIV infection. Clinically, HIV-related wasting in adults is defined in terms of the proportion of body weight unintentionally lost over time as follows: 10% over 12 months, 7.5% over 6 months, or 5% over 3 months

[200, 201]. Alternatively, a measurement of BMI below $20 \, \text{kg/m}^2$ is also suggestive of wasting, as well as a decrease in the proportion of body cell mass (BCM, an indicator of lean body mass) below 35% in men and 23% in women. The validity of these definitions in settings with a high underlying prevalence of protein-energy malnutrition is unknown.

In a study in the Gambia, the sensitivity and specificity of BMI below 18 was comparable to that of CD4 cell counts below $200/\text{mm}^3$ in predicting short-term mortality among HIV-infected adults [186]. In children below 13 years, the US CDC [202] defined *wasting* as (1) persistent weight loss of more than 10% of baseline; (2) downward crossing of at least two percentile lines on the weight-for-age chart in a child aged 1 year or older; or (3) less than the fifth percentile on the weight-for-height chart on two consecutive measurements at least 30 days apart plus chronic diarrhea or documented fever for at least 30 days, whether intermittent or constant. These definitions are yet to be validated against adverse outcomes and efficacy of available interventions in developing countries.

Although the key characteristic of wasting is an alteration in the metabolism of protein and energy, there are multiple causes of weight loss in persons with HIV, for which the independent contribution to wasting may be difficult to set apart. The basic metabolic disturbances that lead to wasting appear to represent an adaptive response to a generalized inflammatory state and are mediated by increased secretion of proinflammatory cytokines, including tumor necrosis factor-$\alpha$ (TNF-$\alpha$), interferon-$\gamma$ (INF-$\gamma$), and interleukins (ILs) 1 and 6 [203, 204]. Both TNF-$\alpha$ and INF-$\gamma$ inhibit myosin expression in muscle cells [205], and the former induces anorexia [206]. Other factors that lead to a negative energy balance and protein catabolism include (1) decreased intake of nutrients due to poor appetite and malabsorption from opportunistic gastrointestinal infections [207]; (2) increased resting energy expenditure [208, 209]; and (3) impaired protein anabolism through hypogonadism [210] or by a direct effect of HIV infection even when dietary intake is adequate [211]. In developing countries, additional factors are likely to contribute to the pathophysiology of wasting in HIV-infected people. These include highly prevalent infections like malaria, intestinal parasitoses [212], and tuberculosis [213]; specific micronutrient deficiencies; and low dietary intake of proteins with high biological value due to poverty [214]. This last aspect may have particularly important implications in the design of strategies to prevent and treat wasting since essential amino acids appear to be limiting factors for protein anabolism among HIV-infected persons [215], and consumption of animal products by asymptomatic HIV-infected subjects is related to improved iron, albumin, and lipid profiles [216].

Research is urgently needed on therapeutic approaches against wasting that could be practicable in resource-limited settings. A role of micronutrients has been suggested in some clinical trials; in Tanzania, supplementation with vitamins B, C, and E prevented weight loss during pregnancy [117] and diminished the risk of reaching a mid-upper arm circumference less than 22 cm [102]. Among infants, vitamin A supplementation improved linear growth [129]. The effect of increasing protein and caloric intake in developing countries is unknown. Other specific interventions that have proven efficacious in studies conducted in industrialized countries include treatment with growth hormone, testosterone, and anabolic steroids [217].

**11.4.4.2.3 Micronutrient Status.** HIV infection could impair micronutrient status through malabsorption, decreased dietary intake secondary to anorexia, increased utilization from oxidative stress, and greater renal losses in the case of nephropathy. Malabsorption particularly affects vitamin $B_{12}$ [218, 219] and the fat-soluble vitamins A and E through impaired absorption of fat. Elevated urinary losses of vitamins A and E could also contribute to deficiency of these nutrients [220, 221]. The prevalence of micronutrient deficiencies during HIV infection seems to vary widely, depending on the study population and stage of disease. Low serum concentrations of vitamins A [112, 222–224], E [225–228], C [225, 226, 229, 230], $B_6$ [226], $B_{12}$ [218, 231, 232], D [110], niacin [225, 229], folate [233, 234], and provitamin A carotenoids [223–225, 229, 235] have been found in various studies from different settings. Injection drug users from large inner cities, pregnant women, and children seem to be at the highest risk.

Hematopoietic abnormalities are common during HIV infection. Malabsorption of iron, HIV infection itself, CMV, and *Mycobacterium avium intracellulare* have been implicated as factors contributing to abnormal hematopoiesis [236]. Bone marrow biopsies and serum studies showed that over one -third of symptomatic HIV-infected children had iron deficiency [236]. Iron deficiency in HIV-infected children is associated with intestinal iron malabsorption and anemia [237]. During HIV infection, serum copper levels consistent with deficiency were not found in heterosexual adults [229], but were noted in 3–11% of homosexual men and injection drug users [225, 226]. Higher serum copper levels were found in HIV-infected homosexual men, and these high levels may reflect an increase in serum caeruloplasmin levels during the acute-phase response [147]. Serum magnesium levels consistent with deficiency have been described in about 20–50% of HIV-infected adults [225, 226], but the significance of magnesium deficiency during HIV infection is unknown. Low serum concentrations of zinc [226, 238] and selenium [239–241] are also common in HIV-infected adults.

A limitation of the use of biomarkers in assessing the impact of HIV infection on micronutrient status is that serum concentrations may change as a result of the acute-phase response and may not represent the underlying nutritional status. The possibility of reverse causality also needs to be considered in the interpretation of these studies since micronutrient deficiencies could be predictors of HIV disease progression and transmission. The effect of micronutrient supplementation in the context of HIV infection was reviewed separately here.

## 11.5  DIAGNOSIS

The laboratory diagnosis of HIV infection in adults and children over the age of 15 months is usually made on the basis of two positive tests for antibody to HIV using two different enzyme-linked immunosorbent assays (ELISAs) on a single serum or plasma sample. If the results of the two different HIV ELISAs are not concordant, a Western blot may be used to confirm the diagnosis. In individuals who have recently been exposed to HIV, there is a serological window between exposure to the virus and the development of antibodies, and seroconversion usually occurs within 6 months of exposure [242]. There is a variety of HIV "rapid tests" that are commercially available, and some of these tests do not require refrigeration or laboratory instrumentation. Infants born to HIV-infected mothers represent a special case for diagnosis of HIV infection because passively acquired maternal antibodies to HIV can yield positive HIV antibody testing even though the infant may not be HIV infected. In many developing countries, passively acquired maternal antibodies usually have disappeared by the time the infant is 15 months of age. Qualitative HIV DNA PCR [243] or quantitative HIV RNA PCR have the highest sensitivity and specificity for diagnosis of HIV infection in infants.

## 11.6    TREATMENT

The approaches to management of patients with HIV infection vary widely in developing countries and are often dependent on local conditions and socioeconomic factors. Much of the disparity in care is owing to the problem that many drugs, especially ARV medications, are expensive. Many countries in Africa that have been hit hard by the AIDS epidemic are still dealing with basic issues of clean water, sanitation, hygiene, nutrition, and primary care, and in this setting of limited health care resources, expensive AIDS care must compete with other priorities in health care.

The World Health Organization periodically updates its guidelines for treatment of HIV-infected persons. These guidelines, available at http://www.who.int/hiv/pub/guidelines/en/, provide detailed recommendations for initiation of treatment in adults/adolescents and infants/children and schemes for first- and second-line ARV regimens. In adults and adolescents, the decision to treat depends on the clinical stage of disease and the CD4 cell count or the total lymphocyte count if the latter is unavailable. Four first-line ARV regimens are recommended for adults and adolescents. These regimens consist of a thymidine analog nucleoside reverse transcriptase inhibitor (NRTI) (i.e., d4T or ZDV); a thiacytidine NRTI (i.e., 3TC), and a nonnucleoside reverse transcriptase inhibitor (NNRTI) (i.e., NVP or efavirenz [EFV]). In children, the decision to initiate ARVs depends on the availability of CD4 cell counts, age, availability of definitive virological diagnosis, and clinical stage of disease. The recommended first line of treatment involves a combination of d4T or ZDV, 3TC, and NVP or EFV if older than 3 years or weight is above 10 kg. Further specific details on medical treatment of HIV/AIDS that are beyond the scope of this book are presented in detail in the WHO guidelines documents. These include the algorithms to decide initiation of treatment, dosages and adverse effects, monitoring of treatment failures, second lines of treatment, and prevention of opportunistic infections

## 11.7    PREVENTION

Strategies to reduce the sexual transmission of HIV include the use of latex condoms [244–247], treatment of STDs [247–249], and HIV counseling, testing, and education. Recent clinical trials found that male circumcision could significantly reduce the risk of acquiring HIV [250–252]. As for the prevention of MTCT, the most effective therapeutic method includes a combination of ARV drugs, formula feeding, and cesarean section, which can reduce MTCT of HIV to about 1% [253]. Prenatal and intrapartum transmission can be reduced by the administration of a short course of ZDV during pregnancy [54] or NVP to the mother during labor plus a single dose to the infant in the immediate postpartum [18]. In support of current WHO recommendations for selecting one of these two interventions, they have been recently reported to have comparable efficacy in reducing MTCT up to 6 weeks postpartum in breast-feeding populations [254]. Nevertheless, a combination of ZDV plus 3TC has greater efficacy than any regimen consisting of a single drug [254, 255]. It appears that the peripartum NVP regimen

[170], but not the ZDV plus 3TC [255], could have the potential to decrease late breast-feeding transmission. Still, any short-course regimens to prevent early MTCT need to be accompanied by other interventions that minimize the risk of transmission through breast-feeding. Since cesarean sections and total avoidance of breast-feeding may not be practicable in many resource-limited settings, a combination of short-course peripartum regimens with early cessation of breast-feeding has become a major strategy in prevention of MTCT. The administration of ARV therapy to breast-feeding women also has some potential to decrease the risk of MTCT [55, 56, 256]; ongoing clinical trials are examining the efficacy of prophylactic ARV therapy administered to the breast-feeding child or the mother.

## 11.8   SUMMARY AND CONCLUSIONS

HIV/AIDS is the single leading infectious cause of death in developing countries. Over 70% of infected individuals live in developing countries. The HIV/AIDS pandemic continues to spread with major demographic impact in sub-Saharan Africa and South and Southeast Asia. Two major challenges to controlling the epidemic are the prevention of sexual transmission of HIV through counseling, testing, education, and condom use and the prevention of MTCT through short-course ARV regimens and other low-cost interventions. The pathogenesis of HIV infection may depend on both virologic factors (viral strain and phenotype) and host factors (genetic and nutritional).

There is a bidirectional relation between HIV infection and the nutritional status. On the one hand, nutritional deficiencies may play a role in the pathogenesis of HIV infection because of the role of some micronutrients as antioxidants and in immune function. On the other hand, HIV infection affects the nutritional status through anorexia, diarrhea, malabsorption, and altered storage and metabolism. Multivitamin supplementation is a low-cost intervention that has been effective in delaying disease progression and decreasing mortality from AIDS. Important areas of future research include the role of macronutrients and elements such as iodine, selenium, and zinc on HIV progression and transmission.

In many developing countries, the primary health care infrastructure needs to be strengthened to include better access to HIV testing, counseling, and AIDS education, and measures must be taken so that such infrastructure can be sustained. These measurements include adequate clinic and hospital facilities to deal with the epidemic, improved infrastructure to deal with the orphan crisis, adoption of pediatric guidelines on the use of prophylaxis for opportunistic infections, the establishment of voluntary counseling and testing depots based outside the hospital setting, adequate access to STD treatment and condoms/barrier methods, drug security and distribution infrastructure, and access to lower-cost ARV therapy to prevent vertical transmission of HIV-1. Upscaling of life-saving ARV treatment is a critical aspect in decreasing the burden of HIV infection in developing countries. Current multipartner initiatives need to be strengthened and promoted, and additional resources need to be urgently devoted to increasing ARV availability and distribution.

The relationship in developing countries between HIV and other common infectious diseases, including malaria, filariasis, schistomiasis, and intestinal parasitoses, needs further elucidation.

# REFERENCES

1. UNAIDS. AIDS epidemic update: 2006. Geneva: World Health Organization, 2006.
2. Gottlieb MS, Schroff R, Schanker HM, et al. *Pneumocystis carinii* pneumonia and mucosal candidiasis in previously healthy homosexual men: evidence of a new acquired cellular immunodeficiency. N Engl J Med 1981;305:1425–1431.
3. Masur H, Michelis MA, Greene JB, et al. An outbreak of community-acquired Pneumocystis carinii pneumonia: initial manifestation of cellular immune dysfunction. N Engl J Med 1981;305:1431–1438.
4. Siegal FP, Lopez C, Hammer GS, et al. Severe acquired immunodeficiency in male homosexuals, manifested by chronic perianal ulcerative herpes simplex lesions. N Engl J Med 1981;305:1439–1444.
5. Centers for Disease Control and Prevention. Update on acquired immune deficiency syndrome (AIDS)–United States. MMWR Morb Mortal Wkly Rep 1982;31:507–508, 513–514.
6. Centers for Disease Control and Prevention. *Pneumocystis carinii* pneumonia among persons with hemophilia A. MMWR Morb Mortal Wkly Rep 1982;31:365–367.
7. Centers for Disease Control and Prevention. Unexplained immunodeficiency and opportunistic infections in infants—New York, New Jersey, California. MMWR Morb Mortal Wkly Rep 1982;31:665–667.
8. Centers for Disease Control and Prevention. Acquired immune deficiency syndrome (AIDS): precautions for clinical and laboratory staffs. MMWR Morb Mortal Wkly Rep 1982;31:577–580.
9. Barre-Sinoussi F, Chermann JC, Rey F, et al. Isolation of a T-lymphotropic retrovirus from a patient at risk for acquired immune deficiency syndrome (AIDS). Science 1983;220:868–871.
10. Gallo RC, Salahuddin SZ, Popovic M, et al. Frequent detection and isolation of cytopathic retroviruses (HTLV-III) from patients with AIDS and at risk for AIDS. Science 1984;224:500–503.
11. Popovic M, Sarngadharan MG, Read E, Gallo RC. Detection, isolation, and continuous production of cytopathic retroviruses (HTLV-III) from patients with AIDS and pre-AIDS. Science 1984;224:497–500.
12. Brun-Vezinet F, Rouzioux C, Barre-Sinoussi F, et al. Detection of IgG antibodies to lymphadenopathy-associated virus in patients with AIDS or lymphadenopathy syndrome. Lancet 1984;1:1253–1256.
13. Sarngadharan MG, Popovic M, Bruch L, Schupbach J, Gallo RC. Antibodies reactive with human T-lymphotropic retroviruses (HTLV-III) in the serum of patients with AIDS. Science 1984;224:506–508.
14. Serwadda D, Mugerwa RD, Sewankambo NK, et al. Slim disease: a new disease in Uganda and its association with HTLV-III infection. Lancet 1985;2:849–852.
15. Fischl MA, Richman DD, Grieco MH, et al. The efficacy of azidothymidine (AZT) in the treatment of patients with AIDS and AIDS-related complex. A double-blind, placebo-controlled trial. N Engl J Med 1987;317:185–191.
16. Fischl MA, Dickinson GM, La Voie L. Safety and efficacy of sulfamethoxazole and trimethoprim chemoprophylaxis for *Pneumocystis carinii* pneumonia in AIDS. JAMA 1988;259:1185–1189.
17. Connor EM, Sperling RS, Gelber R, et al. Reduction of maternal-infant transmission of human immunodeficiency virus type 1 with zidovudine treatment. Pediatric AIDS Clinical Trials Group Protocol 076 Study Group. N Engl J Med 1994;331:1173–1180.
18. Guay LA, Musoke P, Fleming T, et al. Intrapartum and neonatal single-dose nevirapine compared with zidovudine for prevention of mother-to-child transmission of HIV-1 in Kampala, Uganda: HIVNET 012 randomised trial. Lancet 1999;354:795–802.
19. UNAIDS. Report on the global AIDS epidemic. 2006. Available at: http://www.unaids.org/en/HIV_data/2006GlobalReport/default.asp.
20. UNAIDS. AIDS epidemic update: 1998. Geneva: World Health Organization, 1998.
21. UNAIDS. AIDS epidemic update: 2004. Geneva: World Health Organization, 2004.
22. Celentano DD, Nelson KE, Lyles CM, et al. Decreasing incidence of HIV and sexually transmitted diseases in young Thai men: evidence for success of the HIV/AIDS control and prevention program. Aids 1998;12:F29–F36.
23. Kapiga SH, Lyamuya EF, Lwihula GK, Hunter DJ. The incidence of HIV infection among women using family planning methods in Dar es Salaam, Tanzania. Aids 1998;12:75–84.
24. Gregson S, Machekano R, Donnelly CA, Mbizvo MT, Anderson RM, Katzenstein DA. Estimating HIV incidence from age-specific prevalence data: comparison with concurrent cohort estimates in a study of male factory workers, Harare, Zimbabwe. Aids 1998;12:2049–2058.

25. Quigley MA, Kamali A, Kinsman J, et al. The impact of attending a behavioural intervention on HIV incidence in Masaka, Uganda. AIDS 2004;18:2055–2063.

26. Kral AH, Page-Shafer K, Edlin BR, et al. Persistent HIV incidence among injection drug users in San Francisco during the 1990s: results of five studies. J Acquir Immune Defic Syndr 2004;37:1667–1669.

27. Detels R, English P, Visscher BR, et al. Seroconversion, sexual activity, and condom use among 2,915 HIV seronegative men followed for up to 2 years. J Acquir Immune Defic Syndr 1989;2:77–83.

28. Holmberg SD, Horsburgh CR Jr, Ward JW, Jaffe HW. Biologic factors in the sexual transmission of human immunodeficiency virus. J Infect Dis 1989;160:116–125.

29. Plummer FA, Simonsen JN, Cameron DW, et al. Cofactors in male-female sexual transmission of human immunodeficiency virus type 1. J Infect Dis 1991;163:233–239.

30. Cameron DW, Simonsen JN, D'Costa LJ, et al. Female to male transmission of human immunodeficiency virus type 1: risk factors for seroconversion in men. Lancet 1989;2:403–407.

31. Bongaarts J, Reining P, Way P, Conant F. The relationship between male circumcision and HIV infection in African populations. Aids 1989;3:373–377.

32. Dallabetta GA, Miotti PG, Chiphangwi JD, Liomba G, Canner JK, Saah AJ. Traditional vaginal agents: use and association with HIV infection in Malawian women. Aids 1995;9:293–297.

33. European Study Group on Heterosexual Transmission of HIV. Comparison of female to male and male to female transmission of HIV in 563 stable couples. BMJ 1992;304:809–813.

34. Dulioust E, Tachet A, De Almeida M, et al. Detection of HIV-1 in seminal plasma and seminal cells of HIV-1 seropositive men. J Reprod Immunol 1998;41:27–40.

35. Mostad SB, Jackson S, Overbaugh J, et al. Cervical and vaginal shedding of human immunodeficiency virus type 1-infected cells throughout the menstrual cycle. J Infect Dis 1998;178:983–991.

36. Italian Multicentre Study. Epidemiology, clinical features, and prognostic factors of paediatric HIV infection. Lancet 1988;2:1043–1046.

37. Goedert JJ, Mendez H, Drummond JE, et al. Mother-to-infant transmission of human immunodeficiency virus type 1: association with prematurity or low anti-gp120. Lancet 1989;2:1351–1354.

38. Ryder RW, Nsa W, Hassig SE, et al. Perinatal transmission of the human immunodeficiency virus type 1 to infants of seropositive women in Zaire. N Engl J Med 1989;320:1637–1642.

39. European Collaborative Study. Risk factors for mother-to-child transmission of HIV-1. Lancet 1992;339:1007–1012.

40. Dunn DT, Newell ML, Ades AE, Peckham CS. Risk of human immunodeficiency virus type 1 transmission through breastfeeding. Lancet 1992;340:585–588.

41. Landesman SH, Kalish LA, Burns DN, et al. Obstetrical factors and the transmission of human immunodeficiency virus type 1 from mother to child. The Women and Infants Transmission Study. N Engl J Med 1996;334:1617–1623.

42. Newell ML. Mechanisms and timing of mother-to-child transmission of HIV-1. AIDS 1998;12:831–837.

43. St Louis ME, Kamenga M, Brown C, et al. Risk for perinatal HIV-1 transmission according to maternal immunologic, virologic, and placental factors. JAMA 1993;269:2853–2859.

44. Villamor E, Saathoff E, Msamanga G, O'Brien ME, Manji K, Fawzi WW. Wasting during pregnancy increases the risk of mother-to-child HIV-1 transmission. J Acquir Immune Defic Syndr 2005;38:622–626.

45. Li HC, Biggar RJ, Miley WJ, et al. Provirus load in breast milk and risk of mother-to-child transmission of human T lymphotropic virus type I. J Infect Dis 2004;190:1275–1278.

46. Rousseau CM, Nduati RW, Richardson BA, et al. Longitudinal analysis of human immunodeficiency virus type 1 RNA in breast milk and of its relationship to infant infection and maternal disease. J Infect Dis 2003;187:741–747.

47. Koulinska IN, Villamor E, Chaplin B, et al. Transmission of cell-free and cell-associated HIV-1 through breast-feeding. J Acquir Immune Defic Syndr 2006;41:93–99.

48. Semba RD, Kumwenda N, Hoover DR, et al. Human immunodeficiency virus load in breast milk, mastitis, and mother-to-child transmission of human immunodeficiency virus type 1. J Infect Dis 1999;180:93–98.

49. The Working Group on Mother-To-Child Transmission of HIV. Rates of mother-to-child transmission of HIV-1 in Africa, America, and Europe: results from 13 perinatal studies. J Acquir Immune Defic Syndr Hum Retrovirol 1995;8:506–510.

50. Leroy V, Newell ML, Dabis F, et al. International multicentre pooled analysis of late postnatal mother-to-child transmission of HIV-1 infection. Ghent International Working Group on Mother-to-Child Transmission of HIV. Lancet 1998;352:597–600.

51. Miotti PG, Taha TE, Kumwenda NI, et al. HIV transmission through breastfeeding: a study in Malawi. JAMA 1999;282:744–749.

52. Fawzi W, Msamanga G, Spiegelman D, et al. Transmission of HIV-1 through breastfeeding among women in Dar es Salaam, Tanzania. J Acquir Immune Defic Syndr 2002;31:331–338.

53. Coutsoudis A, Dabis F, Fawzi W, et al. Late postnatal transmission of HIV-1 in breast-fed children: an individual patient data meta-analysis. J Infect Dis 2004;189:2154–2166.

54. Shaffer N, Chuachoowong R, Mock PA, et al. Short-course zidovudine for perinatal HIV-1 transmission in Bangkok, Thailand: a randomised controlled trial. Bangkok Collaborative Perinatal HIV Transmission Study Group. Lancet 1999;353:773–780.

55. Wiktor SZ, Ekpini E, Karon JM, et al. Short-course oral zidovudine for prevention of mother-to-child transmission of HIV-1 in Abidjan, Cote d'Ivoire: a randomised trial. Lancet 1999;353:781–785.

56. Dabis F, Msellati P, Meda N, et al. Six-month efficacy, tolerance, and acceptability of a short regimen of oral zidovudine to reduce vertical transmission of HIV in breastfed children in Cote d'Ivoire and Burkina Faso: a double-blind placebo-controlled multicentre trial. DITRAME Study Group. Diminution de la Transmission Mere-Enfant. Lancet 1999;353:786–792.

57. Chersich MF, Gray GE. Progress and emerging challenges in preventing mother-to-child transmission. Curr Infect Dis Rep 2005;7:393–400.

58. Lackritz EM. Prevention of HIV transmission by blood transfusion in the developing world: achievements and continuing challenges. Aids 1998;12(suppl A):S81–S86.

59. Mellors JW, Rinaldo CR Jr, Gupta P, White RM, Todd JA, Kingsley LA. Prognosis in HIV-1 infection predicted by the quantity of virus in plasma. Science 1996;272:1167–1170.

60. Stein DS, Korvick JA, Vermund SH. CD4+ lymphocyte cell enumeration for prediction of clinical course of human immunodeficiency virus disease: a review. J Infect Dis 1992;165:352–363.

61. Centers for Disease Control and Prevention. 1993 revised classification system for HIV infection and expanded surveillance case definition for AIDS among adolescents and adults. MMWR Recomm Rep 1992;41:1–19.

62. Redfield RR, Wright DC, Tramont EC. The Walter Reed staging classification for HTLV-III/LAV infection. N Engl J Med 1986;314:131–132.

63. World Health Organization. WHO case definitions of HIV for surveillance and revised clinical staging and immunological classification of HIV-related disease in adults and children. 2006. Available at: http://www.who.int/entity/hiv/pub/guidelines/HIVstaging150307.pdf.

64. Bollinger RC, Brookmeyer RS, Mehendale SM, et al. Risk factors and clinical presentation of acute primary HIV infection in India. JAMA 1997;278:2085–2089.

65. Mellors JW, Kingsley LA, Rinaldo CR Jr, et al. Quantitation of HIV-1 RNA in plasma predicts outcome after seroconversion. Ann Intern Med 1995;122:573–579.

66. Koopman JS, Jacquez JA, Welch GW, et al. The role of early HIV infection in the spread of HIV through populations. J Acquir Immune Defic Syndr Hum Retrovirol 1997;14:249–258.

67. Pantaleo G, Graziosi C, Fauci AS. New concepts in the immunopathogenesis of human immunodeficiency virus infection. N Engl J Med 1993;328:327–335.

68. Tschachler E, Bergstresser PR, Stingl G. HIV-related skin diseases. Lancet 1996;348:659–663.

69. Miller WC, Thielman NM, Swai N, et al. Diagnosis and screening of HIV/AIDS using clinical criteria in Tanzanian adults. J Acquir Immune Defic Syndr Hum Retrovirol 1995;9:408–414.

70. Moosa MY, Coovadia YM. Cryptococcal meningitis in Durban, South Africa: a comparison of clinical features, laboratory findings, and outcome for human immunodeficiency virus (HIV)-positive and HIV-negative patients. Clin Infect Dis 1997;24:131–134.

71. Rogers MF, Caldwell MB, Gwinn ML, Simonds RJ. Epidemiology of pediatric human immunodeficiency virus infection in the United States. Acta Paediatr Suppl 1994;400:5–7.

72. Marum L, Bagenda D, Guay LA, et al. Three-year mortality in a cohort of HIV-1-infected and -uninfected Ugandan children. Eleventh International Conference on AIDS and STDs; Vancouver; July 1996. Abstract WeB312.

73. Taha TE, Kumwenda NI, Broadhead RL, et al. Mortality after the first year of life among human immunodeficiency virus type 1-infected and uninfected children. Pediatr Infect Dis J 1999;18:689–694.

74. Kuhn L, Steketee RW, Weedon J, et al. Distinct risk factors for intrauterine and intrapartum human immunodeficiency virus transmission and consequences for disease progression in infected children. Perinatal AIDS Collaborative Transmission Study. J Infect Dis 1999;179:52–58.

75. Mayaux MJ, Burgard M, Teglas JP, et al. Neonatal characteristics in rapidly progressive perinatally acquired HIV-1 disease. The French Pediatric HIV Infection Study Group. JAMA 1996;275:606–610.

76. Mofenson LM, Korelitz J, Meyer WA 3rd, et al. The relationship between serum human immunodeficiency virus type 1 (HIV-1) RNA level, CD4 lymphocyte percent, and long-term mortality risk in HIV-1-infected children. National Institute of Child Health and Human Development Intravenous Immunoglobulin Clinical Trial Study Group. J Infect Dis 1997;175:1029–1038.

77. De Rossi A, Ometto L, Masiero S, Zanchetta M, Chieco-Bianchi L. Viral phenotype in mother-to-child HIV-1 transmission and disease progression of vertically acquired HIV-1 infection. Acta Paediatr Suppl 1997;421:22–28.

78. Kiepiela P, Leslie AJ, Honeyborne I, et al. Dominant influence of HLA-B in mediating the potential co-evolution of HIV and HLA. Nature 2004;432:769–774.

79. Mummidi S, Ahuja SS, Gonzalez E, et al. Genealogy of the CCR5 locus and chemokine system gene variants associated with altered rates of HIV-1 disease progression. Nat Med 1998;4:786–793.

80. Vallat AV, De Girolami U, He J, et al. Localization of HIV-1 co-receptors CCR5 and CXCR4 in the brain of children with AIDS. Am J Pathol 1998;152:167–178.

81. Misrahi M, Teglas JP, N'Go N, et al. CCR5 chemokine receptor variant in HIV-1 mother-to-child transmission and disease progression in children. French Pediatric HIV Infection Study Group. JAMA 1998;279:277–280.

82. Thea DM, St Louis ME, Atido U, et al. A prospective study of diarrhea and HIV-1 infection among 429 Zairian infants. N Engl J Med 1993;329:1696–1702.

83. Berger EA. HIV entry and tropism: the chemokine receptor connection. AIDS 1997;11(suppl A): S3–S16.

84. Borrow P, Lewicki H, Hahn BH, Shaw GM, Oldstone MB. Virus-specific CD8+ cytotoxic T-lymphocyte activity associated with control of viremia in primary human immunodeficiency virus type 1 infection. J Virol 1994;68:6103–6110.

85. Munoz A, Kirby AJ, He YD, et al. Long-term survivors with HIV-1 infection: incubation period and longitudinal patterns of CD4+ lymphocytes. J Acquir Immune Defic Syndr Hum Retrovirol 1995;8:496–505.

86. Dean M, Carrington M, Winkler C, et al. Genetic restriction of HIV-1 infection and progression to AIDS by a deletion allele of the CKR5 structural gene. Hemophilia Growth and Development Study, Multicenter AIDS Cohort Study, Multicenter Hemophilia Cohort Study, San Francisco City Cohort, ALIVE Study. Science 1996;273:1856–1862.

87. Keusch GT, Farthing MJ. Nutritional aspects of AIDS. Annu Rev Nutr 1990;10:475–501.

88. Semba RD, Caiaffa WT, Graham NM, Cohn S, Vlahov D. Vitamin A deficiency and wasting as predictors of mortality in human immunodeficiency virus-infected injection drug users. J Infect Dis 1995;171:1196–1202.

89. Tang AM, Graham NM, Semba RD, Saah AJ. Association between serum vitamin A and E levels and HIV-1 disease progression. Aids 1997;11:613–620.

90. Tang AM, Graham NM, Chandra RK, Saah AJ. Low serum vitamin B-12 concentrations are associated with faster human immunodeficiency virus type 1 (HIV-1) disease progression. J Nutr 1997;127:345–351.

91. Baeten JM, Richardson BA, Bankson DD, et al. Use of serum retinol-binding protein for prediction of vitamin A deficiency: effects of HIV-1 infection, protein malnutrition, and the acute phase response. Am J Clin Nutr 2004;79:218–225.

92. Abrams B, Duncan D, Hertz-Picciotto I. A prospective study of dietary intake and acquired immune deficiency syndrome in HIV-seropositive homosexual men. J Acquir Immune Defic Syndr 1993;6:949–958.

93. Tang AM, Graham NMH, Kirby AJ, McCall AD, Willett WC, Saah AJ. Dietary micronutrient intake and risk progression to acquired immunodeficiency syndrome (AIDS) in human immunodeficiency virus type 1 (HIV-1)-infected homosexual men. Am J Epidemiol 1993;138:1–15.

94. Tang AM, Graham NMH, Saah AJ. Effects of micronutrient intake on survival in human immunodeficiency virus type 1 infection. Am J Epidemiol 1996;143:1244–1256.

95. Kanter AS, Spencer DC, Steinberg MH, Soltysik R, Yarnold PR, Graham NM. Supplemental vitamin B and progression to AIDS and death in black South African patients infected with HIV. J Acquir Immune Defic Syndr 1999;21:252–253.

96. Coodley GO, Nelson HD, Loveless MO, Folk C. Beta-carotene in HIV infection. J Acquir Immune Defic Syndr 1993;6:272–276.

97. Nimmagadda AP, Burri BJ, Neidlinger T, O'Brien WA, Goetz MB. Effect of oral beta-carotene supplementation on plasma human immunodeficiency virus (HIV) RNA levels and CD4$^+$ cell counts in HIV-infected patients. Clin Infect Dis 1998;27:1311–1313.

98. Kelly P, Musonda R, Kafwembe E, Kaetano L, Keane E, Farthing M. Micronutrient supplementation in the AIDS diarrhoea-wasting syndrome in Zambia: a randomized controlled trial. AIDS 1999;13:495–500.

99. Allard JP, Aghdassi E, Chau J, et al. Effects of vitamin E and C supplementation on oxidative stress and viral load in HIV-infected subjects. AIDS 1998;12:1653–1659.

100. Jiamton S, Pepin J, Suttent R, et al. A randomized trial of the impact of multiple micronutrient supplementation on mortality among HIV-infected individuals living in Bangkok. AIDS 2003;17:2461–2469.

101. Fawzi WW, Msamanga GI, Spiegelman D, et al. A randomized trial of multivitamin supplements and HIV disease progression and mortality. N Engl J Med 2004;351:23–32.

102. Villamor E, Saathoff E, Manji K, Msamanga G, Hunter DJ, Fawzi WW. Vitamin supplements, socioeconomic status, and morbidity events as predictors of wasting in HIV-infected women from Tanzania. Am J Clin Nutr 2005;82:857–865.

103. McClelland RS, Baeten JM, Overbaugh J, et al. Micronutrient supplementation increases genital tract shedding of HIV-1 in women: results of a randomized trial. J Acquir Immune Defic Syndr 2004;37:1657–1663.

104. Meydani SN, Barklund PM, Liu S, et al. Vitamin E supplementation enhances cell-mediated immunity in healthy elderly subjects. Am J Clin Nutr 1990;52:557–563.

105. Meydani S, Meydani M, Blumberg J, et al. Vitamin E supplementation and in vivo immune response in healthy elderly: a randomized controlled trial. JAMA 1997;277:1380–1386.

106. Pallast EG, Schouten EG, de Waart FG, et al. Effect of 50- and 100-mg vitamin E supplements on cellular immune function in noninstitutionalized elderly persons. Am J Clin Nutr 1999;69:1273–1281.

107. Kennes B, Dumont I, Brohee D, Hubert C, Neve P. Effect of vitamin C supplements on cell-mediated immunity in old people. Gerontology 1983;29:305–310.

108. Teichmann J, Stephan E, Discher T, et al. Changes in calciotropic hormones and biochemical markers of bone metabolism in patients with human immunodeficiency virus infection. Metabolism 2000;49:1134–1139.

109. Teichmann J, Stephan E, Lange U, et al. Osteopenia in HIV-infected women prior to highly active antiretroviral therapy. J Infect 2003;46:221–227.

110. Haug C, Muller F, Aukrust P, Froland SS. Subnormal serum concentration of 1,25-vitamin D in human immunodeficiency virus infection: correlation with degree of immune deficiency and survival. J Infect Dis 1994;169:889–893.

111. Semba RD, Miotti PG, Chiphangwi JD, et al. Infant mortality and maternal vitamin A deficiency during human immunodeficiency virus infection. Clin Infect Dis 1995;21:966–972.

112. Semba RD, Miotti PG, Chiphangwi JD, et al. Maternal vitamin A deficiency and mother-to-child transmission of HIV-1. Lancet 1994;343:1593–1597.

113. Graham NM, Munoz A, Bacellar H, Kingsley LA, Visscher BR, Phair JP. Clinical factors associated with weight loss related to infection with human immunodeficiency virus type 1 in the Multicenter AIDS Cohort Study. Am J Epidemiol 1993;137:439–446.

114. Kumwenda N, Miotti PG, Taha TE, et al. Antenatal vitamin A supplementation increases birth weight and decreases anemia among infants born to human immunodeficiency virus-infected women in Malawi. Clin Infect Dis 2002;35:618–624.

115. Coutsoudis A, Pillay K, Spooner E, Kuhn L, Coovadia HM. Randomized trial testing the effect of vitamin A supplementation on pregnancy outcomes and early mother-to-child HIV-1 transmission in Durban, South Africa. South African Vitamin A Study Group. Aids 1999;13:1517–1524.

116. Fawzi WW, Msamanga GI, Spiegelman D, et al. Randomised trial of effects of vitamin supplements on pregnancy outcomes and T cell counts in HIV-1-infected women in Tanzania. Lancet 1998;351:1477–1482.
117. Villamor E, Msamanga G, Spiegelman D, et al. Effect of multivitamin and vitamin A supplements on weight gain during pregnancy among HIV-1-infected women. Am J Clin Nutr 2002;76:1082–1090.
118. Fawzi WW, Msamanga G, Hunter D, et al. Randomized trial of vitamin supplements in relation to vertical transmission of HIV-1 in Tanzania. J Acquir Immune Defic Syndr 2000;23:246–254.
119. Fawzi WW, Msamanga GI, Hunter D, et al. Randomized trial of vitamin supplements in relation to transmission of HIV-1 through breastfeeding and early child mortality. Aids 2002;16:1935–1944.
120. Fawzi WW, Msamanga GI, Wei R, et al. Effect of providing vitamin supplements to human immunodeficiency virus-infected, lactating mothers on the child's morbidity and CD4+ cell counts. Clin Infect Dis 2003;36:1053–1062.
121. Villamor E, Saathoff E, Bosch RJ, et al. Vitamin supplementation of HIV-infected women improves postnatal child growth. Am J Clin Nutr 2005;81:880–888.
122. Fawzi W, Msamanga G, Antelman G, et al. Effect of prenatal vitamin supplementation on lower-genital levels of HIV type 1 and interleukin type 1 beta at 36 weeks of gestation. Clin Infect Dis 2004;38:716–722.
123. Baeten JM, McClelland RS, Overbaugh J, et al. Vitamin A supplementation and human immunodeficiency virus type 1 shedding in women: results of a randomized clinical trial. J Infect Dis 2002;185:1187–1191.
124. Humphrey JH, Iliff PJ, Marinda ET, et al. Effects of a single large dose of vitamin A, given during the postpartum period to HIV-positive women and their infants, on child HIV infection, HIV-free survival, and mortality. J Infect Dis 2006;193:860–871.
125. MacDonald KS, Malonza I, Chen DK, et al. Vitamin A and risk of HIV-1 seroconversion among Kenyan men with genital ulcers. Aids 2001;15:635–639.
126. Coutsoudis A, Bobat RA, Coovadia HM, Kuhn L, Tsai WY, Stein ZA. The effects of vitamin A supplementation on the morbidity of children born to HIV-infected women. Am J Public Health 1995;85:1076–1081.
127. Fawzi WW, Mbise RL, Hertzmark E, et al. A randomized trial of vitamin A supplements in relation to mortality among human immunodeficiency virus-infected and uninfected children in Tanzania. Pediatr Infect Dis J 1999;18:127–133.
128. Fawzi WW, Mbise R, Spiegelman D, Fataki M, Hertzmark E, Ndossi G. Vitamin A supplements and diarrheal and respiratory tract infections among children in Dar es Salaam, Tanzania. J Pediatr 2000;137:660–667.
129. Villamor E, Mbise R, Spiegelman D, et al. Vitamin A supplements ameliorate the adverse effect of HIV-1, malaria, and diarrheal infections on child growth. Pediatrics 2002;109:E6.
130. Hanekom WA, Yogev R, Heald LM, Edwards KM, Hussey GD, Chadwick EG. Effect of vitamin A therapy on serologic responses and viral load changes after influenza vaccination in children infected with the human immunodeficiency virus. J Pediatr 2000;136:550–552.
131. Semba RD, Ndugwa C, Perry RT, et al. Effect of periodic vitamin A supplementation on mortality and morbidity of human immunodeficiency virus-infected children in Uganda: A controlled clinical trial. Nutrition 2005;21:25–31.
132. Villamor E, Fawzi WW. Effects of vitamin a supplementation on immune responses and correlation with clinical outcomes. Clin Microbiol Rev 2005;18:446–464.
133. Mehendale SM, Shepherd ME, Brookmeyer RS, et al. Low carotenoid concentration and the risk of HIV seroconversion in Pune, India. J Acquir Immune Defic Syndr 2001;26:352–359.
134. Moore PS, Allen S, Sowell AL, et al. Role of nutritional status and weight loss in HIV seroconversion among Rwandan women. J Acquir Immune Defic Syndr 1993;6:611–616.
135. Villamor E, Kapiga SH, Fawzi WW. Vitamin A serostatus and heterosexual transmission of HIV: case-control study in Tanzania and review of the evidence. Int J Vitam Nutr Res 2006;76:81–85.
136. Humphrey JH, Hargrove JW, Malaba LC, et al. HIV incidence among post-partum women in Zimbabwe: risk factors and the effect of vitamin A supplementation. AIDS 2006;20:1437–1446.
137. Baum MK, Shor-Posner G, Lai S, et al. High risk of HIV-related mortality is associated with selenium deficiency. J Acquir Immune Defic Syndr Hum Retrovirol 1997;15:370–374.

138. Kupka R, Msamanga GI, Spiegelman D, et al. Selenium status is associated with accelerated HIV disease progression among HIV-1-infected pregnant women in Tanzania. J Nutr 2004;134:2556–2560.

139. Shor-Posner G, Miguez MJ, Pineda LM, et al. Impact of selenium status on the pathogenesis of mycobacterial disease in HIV-1-infected drug users during the era of highly active antiretroviral therapy. J Acquir Immune Defic Syndr 2002;29:169–173.

140. Kupka R, Garland M, Msamanga G, Spiegelman D, Hunter D, Fawzi W. Selenium status, pregnancy outcomes, and mother-to-child transmission of HIV-1. J Acquir Immune Defic Syndr 2005;39:203–210.

141. Campa A, Shor-Posner G, Indacochea F, et al. Mortality risk in selenium-deficient HIV-positive children. J Acquir Immune Defic Syndr Hum Retrovirol 1999;20:508–513.

142. Kupka R, Msamanga GI, Spiegelman D, Rifai N, Hunter DJ, Fawzi WW. Selenium levels in relation to morbidity and mortality among children born to HIV-infected mothers. Eur J Clin Nutr 2005;59:1250–1258.

143. Delmas-Beauvieux MC, Peuchant E, Couchouron A, et al. The enzymatic antioxidant system in blood and glutathione status in human immunodeficiency virus (HIV)-infected patients: effects of supplementation with selenium or beta-carotene. Am J Clin Nutr 1996;64:101–107.

144. Look MP, Rockstroh JK, Rao GS, et al. Sodium selenite and N-acetylcysteine in antiretroviral-naive HIV-1-infected patients: a randomized, controlled pilot study. Eur J Clin Invest 1998;28:389–397.

145. Burbano X, Miguez-Burbano MJ, McCollister K, et al. Impact of a selenium chemoprevention clinical trial on hospital admissions of HIV-infected participants. HIV Clin Trials 2002;3:483–491.

146. Hurwitz BE, Klaus JR, Llabre MM, et al. Suppression of human immunodeficiency virus type 1 viral load with selenium supplementation: a randomized controlled trial. Arch Intern Med 2007;167:148–154.

147. Graham NM, Sorensen D, Odaka N, et al. Relationship of serum copper and zinc levels to HIV-1 seropositivity and progression to AIDS. J Acquir Immune Defic Syndr 1991;4:976–980.

148. Fawzi WW, Villamor E, Msamanga GI, et al. A trial of zinc supplements in relation to pregnancy outcomes, hematologic indicators, and T-cell counts among HIV-1 infected women in Tanzania. Am J Clin Nutr 2005;81:161–167.

149. Lind T, Lonnerdal B, Stenlund H, et al. A community-based randomized controlled trial of iron and zinc supplementation in Indonesian infants: interactions between iron and zinc. Am J Clin Nutr 2003;77:883–890.

150. Villamor E, Aboud S, Koulinska IN, et al. Zinc supplementation to HIV-1-infected pregnant women: effects on maternal anthropometry, viral load, and early mother-to-child transmission. Eur J Clin Nutr 2006;60:862–869.

151. Bobat R, Coovadia H, Stephen C, et al. Safety and efficacy of zinc supplementation for children with HIV-1 infection in South Africa: a randomised double-blind placebo-controlled trial. Lancet 2005;366:1862–1867.

152. Carcamo C, Hooton T, Weiss NS, et al. Randomized controlled trial of zinc supplementation for persistent diarrhea in adults with HIV-1 infection. J Acquir Immune Defic Syndr 2006;43:197–201.

153. O'Brien M E, Kupka R, Msamanga GI, Saathoff E, Hunter DJ, Fawzi WW. Anemia is an independent predictor of mortality and immunologic progression of disease among women with HIV in Tanzania. J Acquir Immune Defic Syndr 2005;40:219–225.

154. Belperio PS, Rhew DC. Prevalence and outcomes of anemia in individuals with human immunodeficiency virus: a systematic review of the literature. Am J Med 2004;116(suppl 7A):27S–43S.

155. Semba RD, Martin BK, Kempen JH, Thorne JE, Wu AW. The impact of anemia on energy and physical functioning in individuals with AIDS. Arch Intern Med 2005;165:2229–2236.

156. Clark TD, Semba RD. Iron supplementation during human immunodeficiency virus infection: a double-edged sword? Med Hypotheses 2001;57:476–479.

157. Traore HN, Meyer D. The effect of iron overload on in vitro HIV-1 infection. J Clin Virol 2004;31(suppl 1):92–98.

158. Olsen A, Mwaniki D, Krarup H, Friis H. Low-dose iron supplementation does not increase HIV-1 load. J Acquir Immune Defic Syndr 2004;36:637–638.

159. Drain PK, Kupka R, Mugusi F, Fawzi WW. Micronutrients in HIV-positive persons receiving highly active antiretroviral therapy. Am J Clin Nutr 2007;85:333–345.

160. Austin J, Singhal N, Voigt R, et al. A community randomized controlled clinical trial of mixed carotenoids and micronutrient supplementation of patients with acquired immunodeficiency syndrome. Eur J Clin Nutr 2006;60:1266–1276.

161. Spada C, Treitinger A, Reis M, et al. An evaluation of antiretroviral therapy associated with alpha-tocopherol supplementation in HIV-infected patients. Clin Chem Lab Med 2002;40:456–459.

162. de Souza Junior O, Treitinger A, Baggio GL, et al. alpha-Tocopherol as an antiretroviral therapy supplement for HIV-1-infected patients for increased lymphocyte viability. Clin Chem Lab Med 2005;43:376–382.

163. Jaruga P, Jaruga B, Gackowski D, et al. Supplementation with antioxidant vitamins prevents oxidative modification of DNA in lymphocytes of HIV-infected patients. Free Radic Biol Med 2002;32:414–420.

164. Kaiser JD, Campa AM, Ondercin JP, Leoung GS, Pless RF, Baum MK. Micronutrient supplementation increases CD4 count in HIV-infected individuals on highly active antiretroviral therapy: a prospective, double-blinded, placebo-controlled trial. J Acquir Immune Defic Syndr 2006;42:523–528.

165. Jensen-Fangel S, Justesen US, Black FT, Pedersen C, Obel N. The use of calcium carbonate in nelfinavir-associated diarrhoea in HIV-1-infected patients. HIV Med 2003;4:48–52.

166. Jeffery BS, Webber L, Mokhondo KR, Erasmus D. Determination of the effectiveness of inactivation of human immunodeficiency virus by Pretoria pasteurization. J Trop Pediatr 2001;47:345–349.

167. Coutsoudis A, Pillay K, Spooner E, Coovadia HM, Pembrey L, Newell ML. Morbidity in children born to women infected with human immunodeficiency virus in South Africa: does mode of feeding matter? Acta Paediatr 2003;92:890–895.

168. Iliff PJ, Piwoz EG, Tavengwa NV, et al. Early exclusive breastfeeding reduces the risk of postnatal HIV-1 transmission and increases HIV-free survival. AIDS 2005;19:699–708.

169. Coovadia HM, Rollins NC, Bland RM, et al. Mother-to-child transmission of HIV-1 infection during exclusive breastfeeding in the first 6 months of life: an intervention cohort study. Lancet 2007;369:1107–1116.

170. Jackson JB, Musoke P, Fleming T, et al. Intrapartum and neonatal single-dose nevirapine compared with zidovudine for prevention of mother-to-child transmission of HIV-1 in Kampala, Uganda: 18-month follow-up of the HIVNET 012 randomised trial. Lancet 2003;362:859–868.

171. Thior I, Lockman S, Smeaton LM, et al. Breastfeeding plus infant zidovudine prophylaxis for 6 months vs formula feeding plus infant zidovudine for 1 month to reduce mother-to-child HIV transmission in Botswana: a randomized trial: the Mashi Study. JAMA 2006;296:794–805.

172. Nduati R, Richardson BA, John G, et al. Effect of breastfeeding on mortality among HIV-1 infected women: a randomised trial. Lancet 2001;357:1651–1655.

173. Coutsoudis A, Coovadia H, Pillay K, Kuhn L. Are HIV-infected women who breastfeed at increased risk of mortality? AIDS 2001;15:653–655.

174. Sedgh G, Spiegelman D, Larsen U, Msamanga G, Fawzi WW. Breastfeeding and maternal HIV-1 disease progression and mortality. AIDS 2004;18:1043–1049.

175. Taha TE, Kumwenda NI, Hoover DR, et al. The impact of breastfeeding on the health of HIV-positive mothers and their children in sub-Saharan Africa. Bull World Health Organ 2006;84:546–554.

176. World Health Organization. WHO HIV and infant feeding technical consultation. Consensus statement. 2006. Available at: http://www.who.int/child-adolescent-health/New_Publications/NUTRITION/consensus_statement.pdf.

177. Kotler DP, Tierney AR, Wang J, Pierson RNJ. Magnitude of body-cell-mass depletion and the timing of death from wasting in AIDS. Am J Clin Nutr 1989;50:444–447.

178. Suttmann U, Ockenga J, Selberg O, Hoogestraat L, Deicher H, Muller MJ. Incidence and prognostic value of malnutrition and wasting in human immunodeficiency virus-infected outpatients. J Acquir Immune Defic Syndr Hum Retrovirol 1995;8:239–246.

179. Wheeler DA, Gibert CL, Launer CA, et al. Weight loss as a predictor of survival and disease progression in HIV infection. Terry Beirn Community Programs for Clinical Research on AIDS. J Acquir Immune Defic Syndr Hum Retrovirol 1998;18:80–85.

180. Maas JJ, Dukers N, Krol A, et al. Body mass index course in asymptomatic HIV-infected homosexual men and the predictive value of a decrease of body mass index for progression to AIDS. J Acquir Immune Defic Syndr Hum Retrovirol 1998;19:254–259.

181. Shor-Posner G, Campa A, Zhang G, et al. When obesity is desirable: a longitudinal study of the Miami HIV-1-infected drug abusers (MIDAS) cohort. J Acquir Immune Defic Syndr 2000;23:81–88.

182. Malvy E, Thiebaut R, Marimoutou C, Dabis F. Weight loss and body mass index as predictors of HIV disease progression to AIDS in adults. Aquitaine cohort, France, 1985–1997. J Am Coll Nutr 2001;20:609–615.

183. Jones CY, Hogan JW, Snyder B, et al. Overweight and human immunodeficiency virus (HIV) progression in women: associations HIV disease progression and changes in body mass index in women in the HIV epidemiology research study cohort. Clin Infect Dis 2003;37(suppl 2):S69–S80.

184. Ott M, Fischer H, Polat H, et al. Bioelectrical impedance analysis as a predictor of survival in patients with human immunodeficiency virus infection. J Acquir Immune Defic Syndr Hum Retrovirol 1995;9:20–25.

185. Schwenk A, Beisenherz A, Romer K, Kremer G, Salzberger B, Elia M. Phase angle from bioelectrical impedance analysis remains an independent predictive marker in HIV-infected patients in the era of highly active antiretroviral treatment. Am J Clin Nutr 2000;72:496–501.

186. Van Der Sande MA, Van Der Loeff MF, Aveika AA, et al. Body mass index at time of HIV diagnosis: a strong and independent predictor of survival. J Acquir Immune Defic Syndr 2004;37:1288–1294.

187. Villamor E, Dreyfuss ML, Baylin A, Msamanga G, Fawzi WW. Weight loss during pregnancy is associated with adverse pregnancy outcomes among HIV-1 infected women. J Nutr 2004;134:1424–1431.

188. Berhane R, Bagenda D, Marum L, et al. Growth failure as a prognostic indicator of mortality in pediatric HIV infection. Pediatrics 1997;100:e7.

189. Lepage P, Msellati P, Hitimana DG, et al. Growth of human immunodeficiency type 1-infected and uninfected children: a prospective cohort study in Kigali, Rwanda, 1988 to 1993. Pediatr Infect Dis J 1996;15:479–485.

190. Villamor E, Misegades L, Fataki MR, Mbise RL, Fawzi WW. Child mortality in relation to HIV infection, nutritional status, and socio-economic background. Int J Epidemiol 2005;34:61–68.

191. Brocklehurst P, French R. The association between maternal HIV infection and perinatal outcome: a systematic review of the literature and meta-analysis. Br J Obstet Gynaecol 1998;105:836–848.

192. Bulterys M, Chao A, Munyemana S, et al. Maternal human immunodeficiency virus 1 infection and intrauterine growth: a prospective cohort study in Butare, Rwanda. Pediatr Infect Dis J 1994;13:94–100.

193. Jason J, Gomperts E, Lawrence DN, et al. HIV and hemophilic children's growth. J Acquir Immune Defic Syndr 1989;2:277–282.

194. Villamor E, Fataki MR, Bosch RJ, Mbise RL, Fawzi WW. Human immunodeficiency virus infection, diarrheal disease and sociodemographic predictors of child growth. Acta Paediatr 2004;93:372–379.

195. Miller TL, Easley KA, Zhang W, et al. Maternal and infant factors associated with failure to thrive in children with vertically transmitted human immunodeficiency virus-1 infection: the prospective, P2C2 human immunodeficiency virus multicenter study. Pediatrics 2001;108:1287–1296.

196. Lindsey JC, Hughes MD, McKinney RE, et al. Treatment-mediated changes in human immunodeficiency virus (HIV) type 1 RNA and CD4 cell counts as predictors of weight growth failure, cognitive decline, and survival in HIV-infected children. J Infect Dis 2000;182:1385–1393.

197. Arpadi SM, Cuff PA, Kotler DP, et al. Growth velocity, fat-free mass and energy intake are inversely related to viral load in HIV-infected children. J Nutr 2000;130:2498–502.

198. McKinney RE Jr, Johnson GM, Stanley K, et al. A randomized study of combined zidovudine-lamivudine versus didanosine monotherapy in children with symptomatic therapy-naive HIV-1 infection. The Pediatric AIDS Clinical Trials Group Protocol 300 Study Team. J Pediatr 1998;133:500–508.

199. Melikian G, Mmiro F, Ndugwa C, et al. Relation of vitamin A and carotenoid status to growth failure and mortality among Ugandan infants with human immunodeficiency virus. Nutrition 2001;17:567–572.

200. Polsky B, Kotler D, Steinhart C. HIV-associated wasting in the HAART era: guidelines for assessment, diagnosis, and treatment. AIDS Patient Care STDS 2001;15:411–423.

201. Wanke C, Kotler D. The approach to diagnosis and treatment of HIV wasting. J Acquir Immune Defic Syndr 2004;37:S284–S288.

202. Center for Disease Control and Prevention. 1994 revised classification system for human immunodeficiency virus infection in children less than 13 years of age. MMWR Morb Mortal Wkly Rep 1994;43:1–19.

203. Godfried MH, van der Poll T, Jansen J, et al. Soluble receptors for tumour necrosis factor: a putative marker of disease progression in HIV infection. AIDS 1993;7:33–36.

204. Rimaniol AC, Zylberberg H, Zavala F, Viard JP. Inflammatory cytokines and inhibitors in HIV infection: correlation between interleukin-1 receptor antagonist and weight loss. AIDS 1996;10:1349–1356.

205. Acharyya S, Ladner KJ, Nelsen LL, et al. Cancer cachexia is regulated by selective targeting of skeletal muscle gene products. J Clin Invest 2004;114:370–378.

206. Tracey KJ, Beutler B, Lowry SF, et al. Shock and tissue injury induced by recombinant human cachectin. Science 1986;234:470–474.

207. Kotler DP. Human immunodeficiency virus-related wasting: malabsorption syndromes. Semin Oncol 1998;25:70–75.

208. Melchior JC, Salmon D, Rigaud D, et al. Resting energy expenditure is increased in stable, malnourished HIV-infected patients. Am J Clin Nutr 1991;53:437–441.

209. Grunfeld C, Pang M, Shimizu L, Shigenaga JK, Jensen P, Feingold KR. Resting energy expenditure, caloric intake, and short-term weight change in human immunodeficiency virus infection and the acquired immunodeficiency syndrome. Am J Clin Nutr 1992;55:455–460.

210. Bhasin S, Storer TW, Berman N, et al. Testosterone replacement increases fat-free mass and muscle size in hypogonadal men. J Clin Endocrinol Metab 1997;82:407–413.

211. Paton NI, Ng YM, Chee CB, Persaud C, Jackson AA. Effects of tuberculosis and HIV infection on whole-body protein metabolism during feeding, measured by the [15N]glycine method. Am J Clin Nutr 2003;78:319–325.

212. Villamor E, Msamanga G, Spiegelman D, Peterson KE, Antelman G, Fawzi WW. Pattern and predictors of weight gain during pregnancy among HIV-1 infected women from Tanzania. J Acquir Immune Defic Syndr 2003;32:560–569.

213. van Lettow M, Fawzi WW, Semba RD. Triple trouble: the role of malnutrition in tuberculosis and human immunodeficiency virus co-infection. Nutr Rev 2003;61:81–90.

214. Villamor E, Saathoff E, Mugusi F, Bosch RJ, Urassa W, Fawzi WW. Wasting and body composition of adults with pulmonary tuberculosis in relation to HIV-1 coinfection, socioeconomic status, and severity of tuberculosis. Eur J Clin Nutr 2005;60:163–171.

215. Laurichesse H, Tauveron I, Gourdon F, et al. Threonine and methionine are limiting amino acids for protein synthesis in patients with AIDS. J Nutr 1998;128:1342–1348.

216. Vorster HH, Kruger A, Margetts BM, et al. The nutritional status of asymptomatic HIV-infected Africans: directions for dietary intervention? Public Health Nutr 2004;7:1055–1064.

217. Moyle GJ, Schoelles K, Fahrbach K, et al. Efficacy of selected treatments of HIV wasting. J Acquir Immune Defic Syndr 2004;37:S262–S276.

218. Harriman GR, Smith PD, Horne MK, et al. Vitamin B12 malabsorption in patients with acquired immunodeficiency syndrome. Arch Intern Med 1989;149:2039–2041.

219. Ehrenpreis ED, Carlson SJ, Boorstein HL, Craig RM. Malabsorption and deficiency of vitamin B12 in HIV-infected patients with chronic diarrhea. Dig Dis Sci 1994;39:2159–2162.

220. Jolly PE, Moon TD, Mitra AK, del Rosario GR, Blount S, Clemons TE. Vitamin A depletion in hospital and clinic patients with acquired immunodeficiency syndrome—a preliminary report. Nutr Res 1997;17:1427–1441.

221. Jordao Junior AA, Silveira S, Figueiredo JF, Vannucchi H. Urinary excretion and plasma vitamin E levels in patients with AIDS. Nutrition 1998;14:423–426.

222. Semba RD. Vitamin A and human immunodeficiency virus infection. Proc Nutr Soc 1997;56:459–469.

223. Phuapradit W, Chaturachinda K, Taneepanichskul S, Sirivarasry J, Khupulsup K, Lerdvuthisopon N. Serum vitamin A and beta-carotene levels in pregnant women infected with human immunodeficiency virus-1. Obstet Gynecol 1996;87:564–567.

224. Friis H, Gomo E, Koestel P, et al. HIV and other predictors of serum beta-carotene and retinol in pregnancy: a cross-sectional study in Zimbabwe. Am J Clin Nutr 2001;73:1058–1065.

225. Bogden JD, Baker H, Frank O, et al. Micronutrient status and human immunodeficiency virus (HIV) infection. Ann N Y Acad Sci 1990;587:189–195.

226. Beach RS, Mantero-Atienza E, Shor-Posner G, et al. Specific nutrient abnormalities in asymptomatic HIV-1 infection. AIDS 1992;6:701–708.

227. Baum MK, Shor-Posner G, Lu Y, et al. Micronutrients and HIV-1 disease progression. AIDS 1995;9:1051–1056.

228. Mastroiacovo P, Ajassa C, Berardelli G, et al. Antioxidant vitamins and immunodeficiency. Int J Vit Nutr Res 1996;66:141–145.

229. Skurnick JH, Bogden JD, Baker H, et al. Micronutrient profiles in HIV-1-infected heterosexual adults. J Acquir Immune Defic Syndr Hum Retrovirol 1996;12:75–83.

230. Coodley G, Girard DE. Vitamins and minerals in HIV infection. J Gen Intern Med 1991;6:472–479.

231. Burkes RL, Cohen H, Krailo M, Sinow RM, Carmel R. Low serum cobalamin levels occur frequently in the acquired immune deficiency syndrome and related disorders. Eur J Haematol 1987;38:141–147.

232. Paltiel O, Falutz J, Veilleux M, Rosenblatt DS, Gordon K. Clinical correlates of subnormal vitamin B12 levels in patients infected with the human immunodeficiency virus. Am J Hematol 1995;49:318–322.

233. Friis H, Gomo E, Koestel P, et al. HIV and other predictors of serum folate, serum ferritin, and hemo-globin in pregnancy: a cross-sectional study in Zimbabwe. Am J Clin Nutr 2001;73:1066–1073.

234. Boudes P, Zittoun J, Sobel A. Folate, vitamin B$_{12}$, and HIV infection. Lancet 1990;335:1401–1402.

235. Ullrich R, Schneider T, Heise W, et al. Serum carotene deficiency in HIV-infected patients. Berlin Diarrhoea/Wasting Syndrome Study Group. AIDS 1994;8:661–665.

236. Mueller BU, Tannenbaum S, Pizzo PA. Bone marrow aspirates and biopsies in children with human immunodeficiency virus infection. J Pediatr Hematol Oncol 1996;18:266–271.

237. Castaldo A, Tarallo L, Palomba E, et al. Iron deficiency and intestinal malabsorption in HIV disease. J Pediatr Gastroenterol Nutr 1996;22:359–363.

238. Koch J, Neal EA, Schlott MJ, et al. Zinc levels and infections in hospitalized patients with AIDS. Nutrition 1996;12:515–518.

239. Dworkin BM, Rosenthal WS, Wormser GP, Weiss L. Selenium deficiency in the acquired immunode-ficiency syndrome. JPEN J Parenter Enteral Nutr 1986;10:405–407.

240. Mantero-Atienza E, Beach RS, Gavancho MC, Morgan R, Shor-Posner G, Fordyce-Baum MK. Sele-nium status of HIV-1 infected individuals. JPEN J Parenter Enteral Nutr 1991;15:693–694.

241. Cirelli A, Ciardi M, de Simone C, et al. Serum selenium concentration and disease progress in patients with HIV infection. Clin Biochem 1991;24:211–214.

242. Horsburgh CR Jr, Ou CY, Jason J, et al. Duration of human immunodeficiency virus infection before detection of antibody. Lancet 1989;2:637–640.

243. Biggar RJ, Miley W, Miotti P, et al. Blood collection on filter paper: a practical approach to sample collection for studies of perinatal HIV transmission. J Acquir Immune Defic Syndr Hum Retrovirol 1997;14:368–373.

244. Saracco A, Musicco M, Nicolosi A, et al. Man-to-woman sexual transmission of HIV: longitudinal study of 343 steady partners of infected men. J Acquir Immune Defic Syndr 1993;6:497–502.

245. Hanenberg RS, Rojanapithayakorn W, Kunasol P, Sokal DC. Impact of Thailand's HIV-control pro-gramme as indicated by the decline of sexually transmitted diseases. Lancet 1994;344:243–245.

246. de Vincenzi I. A longitudinal study of human immunodeficiency virus transmission by heterosexual part-ners. European Study Group on Heterosexual Transmission of HIV. N Engl J Med 1994;331:341–346.

247. Laga M, Alary M, Nzila N, et al. Condom promotion, sexually transmitted diseases treatment, and declining incidence of HIV-1 infection in female Zairian sex workers. Lancet 1994;344:246–248.

248. Ghys PD, Fransen K, Diallo MO, et al. The associations between cervicovaginal HIV shedding, sexu-ally transmitted diseases and immunosuppression in female sex workers in Abidjan, Cote d'Ivoire. AIDS 1997;11:F85–F93.

249. Grosskurth H, Mosha F, Todd J, et al. Impact of improved treatment of sexually transmitted diseases on HIV infection in rural Tanzania: randomised controlled trial. Lancet 1995;346:530–536.

250. Auvert B, Taljaard D, Lagarde E, Sobngwi-Tambekou J, Sitta R, Puren A. Randomized, controlled intervention trial of male circumcision for reduction of HIV infection risk: the ANRS 1265 trial. PLoS Med 2005;2:e298.

251. Gray RH, Kigozi G, Serwadda D, et al. Male circumcision for HIV prevention in men in Rakai, Uganda: a randomised trial. Lancet 2007;369:657–666.

252. Bailey RC, Moses S, Parker CB, et al. Male circumcision for HIV prevention in young men in Kisumu, Kenya: a randomised controlled trial. Lancet 2007;369:643–656.

253. Mandelbrot L, Le Chenadec J, Berrebi A, et al. Perinatal HIV-1 transmission: interaction between zid-ovudine prophylaxis and mode of delivery in the French Perinatal Cohort. JAMA 1998;280:55–60.

254. Leroy V, Sakarovitch C, Cortina-Borja M, et al. Is there a difference in the efficacy of peripartum antiret-roviral regimens in reducing mother-to-child transmission of HIV in Africa? Aids 2005;19:1865–1875.

255. Petra Study Team. Efficacy of three short-course regimens of zidovudine and lamivudine in prevent-ing early and late transmission of HIV-1 from mother to child in Tanzania, South Africa, and Uganda (Petra study): a randomised, double-blind, placebo-controlled trial. Lancet 2002;359:1178–1186.

256. Shapiro RL, Holland DT, Capparelli E, et al. Antiretroviral concentrations in breast-feeding infants of women in Botswana receiving antiretroviral treatment. J Infect Dis 2005;192:720–7.

# 12 Malnutrition

## Dirk G. Schroeder

## 12.1 INTRODUCTION

Malnutrition is widespread among disadvantaged populations living in developing countries. The consequences of malnutrition are severe and long lasting. Children who are malnourished have longer and more severe illnesses [1, 2] and have a higher risk of dying [3, 4] compared to better-nourished children. Malnourished children also have delayed motor development [5] and lower cognitive function and school performance [6]. In adulthood, individuals who were malnourished as children have impaired work capacity [7] and worse reproductive performance [8]. Finally, malnutrition can have negative effects not only on those afflicted but also on their offspring [9].

The causes of malnutrition are numerous. These causes are intertwined with each other and are hierarchically related. The most immediate (or proximate) determinants of malnutrition are poor diet and illness [10]. Poor diet and illness are themselves caused by a set of underlying factors that include family access to food and maternal care-taking practices. Finally, these underlying factors are influenced by the basic socioeconomic and political conditions within which poor families are attempting to raise well-nourished children. An accurate understanding of the relationships among these various causes of malnutrition and the relative contribution of each is essential for the design of efficient and effective programs to reduce malnutrition and its consequences. Because the resources directed at improving nutritional status are relatively scarce, it is critical that these resources are directed at interventions that will have the largest "bang for the buck" and will lead to lasting improvements.

The primary objectives and content of this chapter are as follows: In the first sections, key terms are defined, and the global prevalence of malnutrition is described. Next, a conceptual framework and the epidemiological evidence of the primary determinants and consequences of malnutrition are presented. Programmatic implications of these findings are then examined. The chapter concludes by identifying key gaps in knowledge that would benefit from additional research, focusing on those most likely to increase the effectiveness of interventions and programs aimed at ameliorating malnutrition.

### 12.1.1 Definitions and Historical Overview

*Malnutrition* is a common and widely used term to refer to suboptimal nutritional health. In international health (and in this chapter), malnutrition generally refers to undernutrition (e.g., poor growth) rather than overnutrition (e.g., obesity).

From: *Nutrition and Health: Nutrition and Health in Developing Countries, Second Edition*
Edited by: R. D. Semba & M. W. Bloem © Humana Press, Totowa, NJ

A wide range of terms has been used to refer to the clinical and functional manifestations of undernutrition. A familiarity with the historical evolution of these terms is instructive because, as would be expected, the introduction and use of these terms closely reflected the evolving scientific understanding of the causes of, and solutions to, malnutrition. Table 12.1 summarizes the introduction of key terms since 1900. More detailed accounts of the history of international nutrition may be found elsewhere [11].

In the early decades of the 19th century, health workers in Latin America identified a clinical syndrome that they referred to as *Distrofia pluricarencial*, meaning "multiple deficiency state" (Table 12.1). The clinical signs of this syndrome were likely similar to those identified in West African infants by Cicely Williams in the mid-1930s, who adopted for the syndrome the local name of *kwashiorkor*. The causes of kwashiorkor were unknown at the time, but Williams suggested that "some amino acid or protein deficiency cannot be excluded" [12].

Between the mid-1930s and late-1950s, the international nutrition community focused almost exclusively on kwashiorkor with the belief that it was "the most serious and

Table 12.1
Origin and introduction of some terms describing nutritional deficiency among children in developing countries

| Year(S) | Term | Notes |
|---|---|---|
| 1990– 1930 | Distrofia Pluricarencial | Term used by early Latin American workers meaning "multiple deficiency state." |
| 1935 | Kwashiorkor | From the Ga language of West Africa. Translation is "the disease of the deposed child." |
| 1955 | Protein deficiency | Term reflected current thinking on primary cause of Kwashiorkor. |
| 1959–1960 | Protein-calorie malnutrition (PCM) | PCM first introduced late 1950s. |
|  | Protein-energy malnutrition (PEM) | Evolved into protien-energy malnutrition (PEM). Used to cover whole range of malnutrition other than states caused primarily by specific nutrients (e.g., Vitatmin C deficiency, pellagra). PEM still widely used. |
| 1980s–90s | Energy-nutrient malnutrition (ENM) | In recognition that other nutients besides protein (e.g., zinc, Vitamin A) significantly contribute to malnutrition and growth faltering. Not widely used. |
| 1990s | Micronutrient malnutrition | Used to refer to key micronutrient deficiencies: vitamin A, iodine, and iron |
| Late 1990s | Malnutrition | Term used widely by international organizations (e.g., UNICEF) to refer to ENM and growth-faltering. |

widespread nutritional disorder known to medical and nutritional sciences" [13]. This perspective, along with the belief that kwashiorkor was caused by a protein deficiency, led to the suggestion that improving protein intakes *alone* would solve the problem of malnutrition in poor countries. From a programmatic standpoint, activities during the 1950s and 1960s thus focused on increasing protein intakes through such means as improving the protein quality of grains [14]. Collectively, these efforts were commonly referred to as the "Green Revolution." At about the same time, a great deal of effort was invested in the development of protein-rich, vegetable-based food mixtures, such as *Incaparina* [15], still in use throughout Central America.

As early as the 1950s, however, the focus on protein as the exclusive cause of malnutrition and poor growth began to be questioned. Data began emerging that suggested that severely malnourished children could gain weight well on high-energy/low-protein diets [16, 17]. Also, surveys from areas other than Africa indicated the existence of forms of malnutrition besides kwashiorkor, including marasmus and nonspecific stunting, both of which were thought to be primarily caused by deficiencies in energy rather than protein. In recognition of these early findings, Jelliffe [18] introduced the term *protein-calorie malnutrition* (PCM). This evolved into protein-energy malnutrition (PEM), a term still widely used today.

Research during the 1960s further shifted the focus from protein to energy. Dietary studies suggested that protein intakes and the protein/energy ratio from traditional foods were generally near requirements, but that total energy intakes fell far short of requirements [19]. By not meeting energy needs, protein, however ample in the diet, would tend to be metabolized for its energy, causing signs of protein deficiency to appear. Conversely, it was believed that providing energy, even "empty calories," would "spare" protein and improve nutritional status. Finally, scientists began to question whether kwashiorkor itself was caused by protein deficiency, a controversy that remains to the present.

Together, these findings led some international nutritionists to conclude in the mid-1970s that the "protein gap is a myth and that what really exists, even for vulnerable groups, is a food gap and an energy gap" [19]. The focus on protein by the international scientific community and the resources spent to close this gap were termed a "fiasco" [20]. Such authors argued that if most traditional diets were consumed at levels sufficient to satisfy energy needs, protein needs would also be met. Programmatic efforts during the late 1970s and early 1980s thus emphasized simple recommendations to increase energy intake, such as "add 2 tablespoons of oil to the child's diet" [21, 22].

In the mid-1980s, however, the focus shifted yet again. Scientific evidence began accumulating that the continued high rates of growth stunting around the globe could not be overcome simply by providing more energy from more of the same foods. Rather, certain micronutrients were identified as playing a key role in linear growth and infection. Specifically, vitamin A and iron, and more recently, zinc, have been suggested as key growth-limiting nutrients [23]. Traditional diets given to young children are generally low in these key micronutrients and of poor dietary quality. It is also now recognized that multiple nutrient deficiencies frequently coexist, and that the type of food (e.g., animal vs. vegetable) affects utilization; this has initiated discussions of the importance of "dietary quality" [24]. A review of the current scientific evidence for the role of specific nutrients and dietary quality for growth is presented separately in this chapter.

In sum, the scientific understanding of the primary causes of undernutrition and poor growth came "full circle" during the 20th century. As was recognized by workers in Latin America nearly a century ago, the clinical, somatic, and functional consequences of inadequate nutrition are most commonly caused by multiple nutrient deficiencies, usually in combination with high rates of disease. Only in very rare cases is the poor growth seen among children in the developing world due to inadequacies of a single nutrient. The term *malnutrition* is thus used throughout this chapter as it is currently employed by the international health and nutrition community in general: to refer to the syndrome of inadequate intakes of protein, energy, and micronutrients, combined with frequent infections, which result in poor growth and body size. Because poor growth is such an important result and indicator of undernutrition, a brief overview of the issues related to measuring and evaluating growth in an international context is presented next.

## 12.2   MEASURING PHYSICAL STATUS AND GROWTH

### 12.2.1   *Anthropometric Indices of Nutritional Health*

*Anthropometry* is the external measuring of the human body. The tools used for anthropometry (i.e., scales, tapes) can be simple and portable and are therefore widely used in developing countries for determining body growth, proportions, size, and composition [25, 26]. In children, weight and height (or length) are the most commonly measured, although mid-upper arm circumference (MUAC) is also used. Supine length rather than height is commonly measured in children under 2 years old, but there is wide variation among programs in this regard. Young (2- to 3-year-old) children measured standing are approximately 0.5–1 cm shorter than if measured lying down [27]. For simplicity, the term *height* is used throughout this chapter to refer to both supine length and standing height.

Individual measures such as weight and height are uninformative on their own. When combined with age (i.e., weight-for-age, height-for-age) or each other (i.e., weight-for-height) and compared to reference values, however, they create useful indices that describe the physical status of individuals and populations. Deficits in height-for-age, weight-for-height, and weight-for-age usually reflect distinct processes or outcomes of growth impairment and have been described using a range of terms, some of which are more accurate than others [28].

Low height-for-age in younger children (under 2 to 3 years of age) in poor countries reflects an ongoing process of "failing to grow" or "stunting," whereas in older children, it reflects the state of "having failed to grow" or "being stunted" [29]. The term *chronic malnutrition* is frequently used in association with low height-for-age, but this term can be misleading and should be discouraged [28]. Low weight-for-height measures "thinness" and is best described as "wasting." One of the advantages of weight-for-height is that it does not require age, which is often unknown or inaccurately reported in developing countries. The terms *acute malnutrition*, *current malnutrition*, and *severe malnutrition* are commonly used but are less appropriate descriptors than wasting [28].

Weight-for-age is a measure of body mass relative to chronological age. Because body mass is determined by both height and weight, it is often difficult to determine whether a child who is low weight-for-age is stunted, wasted, or both. After 3 years of age, low weight-for-age is primarily caused by stunting in most developing countries, although in famine situations or in certain key countries, such as India, low weight-for-age among older children may in fact represent wasting. The terms *lightness* and *underweight* are the preferred terms for low weight-for-age [28].

The development economist Peter Svedberg has proposed an alternative to conventional anthropometric indices that consists of an aggregate indicator of undernutrition termed the composite index of anthropometric failure (CIAF) [30]. The CIAF consists of six subgroups that are combinations of stunting, wasting, underweight, or normal. The CIAF has been applied to anthropometric data to provide a single aggregated figure of the number of undernourished children [31], but the validity of the classification has been criticized [32].

The MUAC has been promoted as an alternative measure of wasting because of the high portability of the equipment (i.e., a measuring tape) and the belief that MUAC is independent of age [33]. The belief that MUAC is age and sex independent has led to the promotion of fixed cutoff points (usually 12.5 or 13.0 cm). Research, however, suggested that MUAC does in fact increase over the first 5 years of life [34]. The World Health Organization (WHO) has therefore concluded that MUAC-for-age or MUAC-for-height, rather than a fixed cutoff, should be promoted [35]. MUAC-for-age reference data have been published [36]. Importantly, the use of MUAC without age if rapid identification is essential (i.e., in famine situations if ages are unknown) is acceptable in that this will tend to overidentify younger children, who are most at risk for morbidity and mortality [34] (see also Chapter 24, on emergencies).

Under research conditions, in which small changes in growth are measured over short time periods, alternate and more accurate anthropometric methods than just weight and height may be necessary. For example, kneemometers to measure knee-heel length are increasingly used [37].

### 12.2.2  Growth References

In privileged populations, differences in growth and attained height within an ethnic group are primarily owing to differences in genetic potential [38], whereas in disadvantaged societies, environmental factors account for much of the variation among individuals. At a population level, the large variation in child growth seen worldwide among social classes and among countries is fundamentally owing to environmental factors, such as poor diets and high burdens of infection, rather than genetic makeup [39]. Children of varying ethnic origins born into environments in which diets are adequate and the burden of morbidity is low will attain similar preadolescent heights [40]. This, along with the desire to be able to compare the nutritional status of populations across all parts of the world, has led to the promotion and widespread use of a single international growth reference [39].

The recommended international growth reference as of the writing of this chapter is referred to as the National Center for Health Statistics/World Health Organization (NCHS/WHO) growth reference. The data for this reference come from US children and were collected before 1975 [41, 42]. These NCHS/WHO curves are the basis for the majority of growth monitoring "road to health" cards used throughout much of the developing world. In the nearly 30 years since its adoption, the NCHS/WHO reference has been criticized on a number of points. One set of criticisms has focused on the technical flaws in the curves [43], a discussion of which is outside the scope of this chapter and may be found elsewhere [43, 44]. Other areas of continued debate are whether breast- and bottle-fed children grow similarly in relation to the reference [45] and the appropriateness of a single international reference for use in all ethnic groups [46].

East and Southeast Asian populations have been identified as most likely to be genetically shorter than other ethnic groups [47, 48]. Studies from Thailand [49], Indonesia [50], and the United States [51], however, provided evidence that Asian children can grow as tall as other children of similar socioeconomic strata. For example, Droomers et al. [50] reported that the mean height-for-age Z-score of preschool age (2–5 years) Indonesian children from high socioeconomic strata living in Jakarta, Indonesia, was $0.24 \pm 0.94\,Z$, above the NCHS reference median.

In sum, differences in the genetic potential of child growth among ethnic groups, even among East and Southeast Asian children, are likely to be very small. Differences in adult height owing to ethnicity are likely less than 2 cm on average compared to deficits of 10 cm or more at age 5 years owing to the poor diets and infection found in poor countries. The use of a single international reference is thus still recommended [28]. However, a WHO expert panel concluded that the NCHS/WHO reference is not the best choice for this single reference, and that a new reference should be developed [52].

The WHO Multicentre Growth Reference Study (MGRS) is a community-based, multicountry project to develop new growth references for infants and young children (see also Chapter 5, Child Growth and Development) [53]. It was thought that a new international growth reference should describe how children should grow rather than how they grow, and that the reference should reflect the similarity in child growth among diverse ethnic groups. New WHO child growth standards were derived from an international sample of healthy breast-fed infants from Brazil, Ghana, India, Norway, Oman, and the United States and young children who were raised in environments that do not constrain growth [54].

### 12.2.3   Expression of Anthropometry

Anthropometric data may be expressed as centiles (percentiles), percent of median, and standard deviation (SD) (or Z) scores relative to the reference [55]. A centile score reflects a child's size (e.g., weight) relative to the entire distribution of reference values at a certain age. A value falling below the third centile is commonly used as an indicator of growth retardation. Percent of median is the child's achieved size relative to the reference median value with cutoffs of less than 80% of median commonly used as indicating growth retardation. Finally, Z-scores indicate the number of SDs the child's value is from the reference mean. Two SD below the mean ($\leq 2\,Z$) is often used as an indicator of growth retardation.

Centiles are more commonly used in industrialized countries, whereas in developing countries, percent of median is more common, in part because so many children in developing countries fall below the third percentile cutoff. Z-scores are recommended for research purposes because they are easier to interpret across various anthropometric variables and ages [28, 56]. In summary, anthropometry along with a single international reference make up the best and most common method of assessing nutritional status in developing countries.

### 12.2.4   Severe Malnutrition

*Severe malnutrition* is defined by a weight-for-height Z-score of −3 or less (severe wasting) or the presence of nutritional edema [57]. The prevalence of severe malnutrition is about 2% in least-developed countries and about 1% in developing countries, which together account for about 10 million severely malnourished children at one time [57]. Severe malnutrition is associated with 1–2 million preventable child deaths each year [58]. Severe malnutrition is a life-threatening condition that requires urgent treatment, and the Standing Committee on Nutrition has recently reviewed the methods of diagnosing severe malnutrition and its treatment [59]. For community-based screening for severe malnutrition, a MUAC below 110 mm or the presence of bipedal edema was found to be the best indicator [60]. The approach to treatment of severe malnutrition has been transformed with the advent of new therapeutic diets, as discussed in Section 12.5.2.

## 12.3  PATTERNS AND TIMING OF GROWTH RETARDATION

### 12.3.1  *Prevalence and Patterns of Global Anthropometric Status*

At the close of the 20th century, approximately half a billion children under age 5 were living in developing countries. Of these, about 37% were stunted, 11% were wasted, and 30% were underweight [10]. Although mortality rates have declined substantially over the last three decades, rates of malnutrition have declined more modestly during this time [61]. Between 1980 and 1995, under-5 mortality rates in the developing world declined from 133 per 1,000 to 80 per 1,000, while percent underweight went from 38% to 31% [62, 63]. And, owing to increases in global population, the total number of undernourished children has remained essentially stable, at about 170 million, during this period.

There are regional differences in the patterns of malnutrition. Over three quarters of children with wasting are in India, Pakistan, and Bangladesh [64]. Weight deficits, particularly in relation to height, tend to be highest in Asia and lowest in Latin America. Regions with high rates of stunting do not necessarily have a lot of wasting, however. Victora [65], in an analysis that used country as the unit of analysis, found that the correlation between wasting and stunting within countries was highest in Asia and the eastern Mediterranean (Pearson's correlation coefficient of approximately 0.7), nonexistent in Africa, and actually inverse in Latin America (correlation of −0.3). This last finding is caused by the apparently contradictory existence of very high rates of stunting in Latin America, but almost no wasting. Based on this ecological analysis, Victora suggested that the determinants for stunting are different from those for wasting. Empirical evidence confirming this hypothesis and the importance of national-level factors were published by Frongillo and colleagues [66], although additional research in this area is critically needed.

In sum, malnutrition and poor growth among children are enormous problems throughout the developing world. The timing at which this growth faltering occurs in a child's life and the potential for recovering these deficits (i.e., catch-up growth) are examined next.

### 12.3.2  *Timing of Growth Faltering and Potential for Catch-Up Growth*

The process of growth retardation frequently begins even before birth (i.e., in utero) in poor societies [67]. Ultrasound studies conducted among pregnant women in Guatemala showed that maternal weight gain from the first to the second trimester of pregnancy was associated with fetal growth and infant length at birth [68]. Placental volume and growth also are related to fetal size [69]. Good research on intrauterine growth is rare; however, this can be inferred from the high prevalence of low birth weight (LBW) in developing countries:

17% in developing countries compared to 6% in industrialized countries [70]. Even fewer studies have examined the prevalence of intrauterine stunting (IUS) at birth in developing countries or whether IUS predicts stunting later in life. In rural Malawi, Neufeld and colleagues [71] found that 48% of full-term infants were below the tenth percentile of the reference length-for-gestational age. In Guatemala, at 15 days of age, full-term infants were on average about −1.0Z below the NCHS/WHO reference length-for-age Z-score, representing an absolute difference of around 2–3 cm [68], with 13% of the sample more than 2 SD below the reference median [72]. The magnitude of these length deficits is similar to those found in Pakistan [73]. Shortness at birth is a strong predictor of subsequent growth during childhood. Some research showed that IUS is the best predictor of stunting at 3 years of age compared to measures of growth retardation based on birth weight, intrauterine growth retardation (IUGR), or LBW [74].

Growth in weight between birth and approximately 3 months of age in developing countries is generally similar or even a little better than reference values from developed countries [75]. Linear growth during the first 3 months of life generally tracks reference values; in other words, no additional faltering occurs on top of the deficits seen at birth [76], although fattening during this early period has been documented in Guatemala [77]. These good growth rates during the first 3 months of life have been attributed to the high rates of breast-feeding initiation during the early postnatal period. By about 3 months of age, however, linear growth in many developing country communities begins to falter, and by 9 to 12 months of age, stunting in these populations is often severe, with length-for-age Z-scores of close to −2 not uncommon [76, 78, 79]. Figure 12.1 presents data from Guatemala of typical growth patterns of poor developing country children.

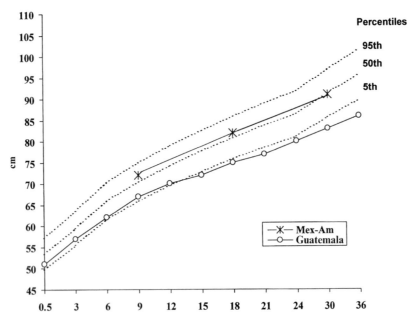

**Fig. 12.1.** Linear growth among children in Guatemala and in US Mexican-Americans, to 36 months of age, ref. [77].

It is important to reiterate that the exact timing at which severe growth faltering is initiated during infancy depends on the specific conditions to which the infant is exposed and will thus vary both within and across populations. An important task for programmers is to determine the age at which faltering occurs in the local situation. Accurate knowledge of the age at which growth begins to falter will provide important clues to the determinants of the faltering and thus allow the design of effective interventions to prevent it.

Some of the difficulty in determining the timing of growth faltering of infants in developing countries is because the current NCHS/WHO growth reference is based on formula- rather than breast-fed children [46]. Research has shown that growth differs between these two feeding modes, even among otherwise healthy children [80] and infants born small for gestational age in industrialized conditions [81]. The use of a fully breast-fed reference leads to different conclusions concerning the age at which children in developing countries begin faltering in weight, although the effect is less for length [80]. The new international growth reference includes predominantly breast-fed children [54], as mentioned.

At about 3 years of age, growth faltering relative to reference values plateaus, and between about 3 years and adolescence, linear growth velocity of developing country children generally parallels reference centile lines [72], although continued decline through school age (7- to 14-year-olds) has been documented in Zanzibar [82]. Growth during adolescence in developing countries is poorly documented. Maturation is often delayed, and the growth period may be prolonged in poor societies by 2 or more years, such that a small portion of the early growth deficit in height may be made up [83].

In general, however, once individuals are growth stunted, these deficits are rarely recovered (i.e., through catch-up growth) [83]. The exception is for very young children who are born into poor environments but then are exposed to radically improved dietary and environmental conditions through, for example, adoption. The biological mechanisms promoting catch-up growth, when it occurs, are complex and still relatively poorly understood [84]. For example, with adoption, maturity may be "overly accelerated," and short stature may result.

In summary, more than a third of all children under 5 in developing countries experience malnutrition to a significant enough degree to become permanently growth retarded. This growth retardation, particularly linear growth retardation, generally begins very early in the child's life and, once it has occurred, is rarely reversible. Put another way, this means that most of the absolute height deficits seen in adults in developing countries are already present by about 3 years of age.

But, you may ask, what is so bad about a person being smaller? Some have argued that individuals can be "small but healthy," and that there are, in fact, global advantages to populations being smaller in that smaller people eat less food [85]. This view has been criticized by other authors, who point out that focusing on growth is important not so much because it is essential that each individual achieve maximal adult height, but because poor growth is an excellent indicator that the body is compromised and performing suboptimally on a wide range of other functions (e.g., immune function) [86, 87].

In the next sections, the current epidemiologic evidence of the substantial consequences and complex causes of poor malnutrition and growth are reviewed in detail.

## 12.4    EPIDEMIOLOGIC EVIDENCE

### *12.4.1    Conceptual Diagram*

A modified version of the United Nations International Children's Emergency Fund (UNICEF) conceptual framework [10, 88] of child health and survival is used to guide the next sections of this chapter (Fig. 12.2). The strength of this framework is that it recognizes and integrates the biomedical consequences as well as the underlying socioeconomic determinants, and consequences, of malnutrition. Landmark articles of such integrated models include those by Mosley and Chen [89] and Bongaarts [90].

In the next sections of this chapter, the contribution of malnutrition (poor growth) to higher mortality (arrow 1 in Fig. 12.2), more infection (arrow 2), and other functional impairments (arrow 3) are reviewed first. Next, the key proximate determinants of malnutrition, namely infection (arrow 4) and inadequate diet (arrow 5) are reviewed. An examination of the bidirectional relationship between dietary intakes and infection (arrows 7 and 8) and the impact of infectious disease on mortality (arrow 9) are outside the scope of this chapter. The underlying determinants of dietary intake and disease, namely insufficient access to food (arrow 10), inadequate child care practices (arrow 11), poor water and sanitation and inadequate health services (arrow 12) are then presented, primarily in relation to programmatic efforts to alleviate malnutrition. A discussion of the basic causes of malnutrition (e.g., the agricultural and economic environment) is outside the scope of this chapter but may be found elsewhere [91].

### *12.4.2    Consequences of Malnutrition*

#### 12.4.2.1    MORTALITY

Approximately 12 million children under 5 years of age die each year in developing countries [10]. Until recently, the "causes" of these deaths were overwhelmingly attributed to diseases such as diarrhea, pneumonia, and vaccine-preventable diseases. Figure 12.3 is

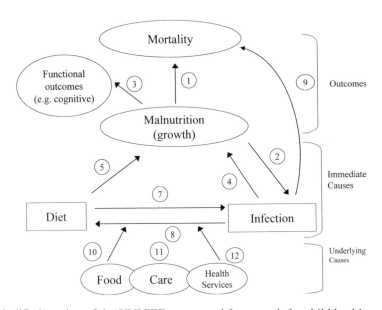

**Fig. 12.2.** Modified version of the UNICEF conceptual framework for child health and survival.

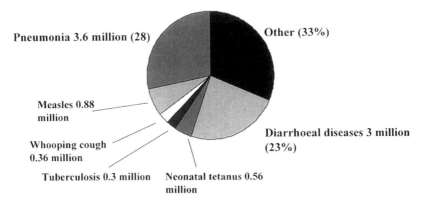

**Fig. 12.3.** Main causes of child death.

reproduced from a 1993 UNICEF document that classified the causes of child deaths and is representative of the historical lack of importance given to malnutrition; in this case, it is only briefly mentioned in the footnote.

This focus on disease as the "main" cause of death among children essentially ignored the long-recognized synergistic relation between malnutrition and infection on mortality. As Scrimshaw et al. [92] noted in 1968, "The simultaneous presence of malnutrition and infection results in an interaction that is more serious for the host than would be expected from the combined effect of the two working independently." Thus, most children in the developing world die not from an infectious disease or frank starvation alone, but from the simultaneous presence of malnutrition and infection that together greatly increase the child's risk of death.

Despite the broad theoretical acceptance of this dual causality, attempts to improve child survival in developing countries have focused disproportionately on preventing or managing infectious diseases rather than eliminating or addressing malnutrition [93]. In 1990, UNICEF spent just 13% of expenditures on direct nutrition activities [94]. The reasons for this emphasis on infectious disease included the apparently higher feasibility of addressing disease compared with malnutrition [95] and the belief that if infections could be reduced, improvements in nutritional status [96] and survival [97] would certainly follow.

By the 1990s, child mortality rates in the developing world had dropped dramatically, from 216 per 1,000 in 1960 to 97 per 1,000 in 1996 [10]. During the same period, epidemiologic information was accumulating that strongly suggested that the majority of deaths that were still not being prevented were caused by the potentiating effects of malnutrition.

In the early 1990s, a series of articles were published that reviewed all previous prospective studies that had examined the relation between anthropometric status and risk for mortality [3, 4, 98, 99]. In the review by Pelletier [3], 28 community-based, prospective studies in 12 Asian and sub-Saharan African countries were examined. Mortality rates from the 8 most comparable studies that reported nutritional status as weight-for-age are presented in Fig. 12.4 and were used to estimate overall relative risks by weight-for-age nutritional status category.

Deaths per 1000 per Year

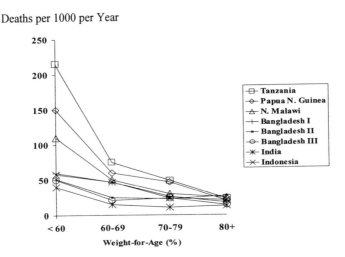

**Fig. 12.4.** Mortality rates by weight-for-age in eight community-based studies.

A key finding from these analyses was that, in the vast majority of studies, the risk of mortality was increased not only with severe malnutrition, but also with mild and moderate malnutrition, a finding that contradicted an early, landmark article on this topic [100]. Summary estimates based on these studies found that the risk of death was 8.4, 4.6, and 2.5 times greater for a child whose weight-for-age was below 60%, 60–69%, and 70–79% of the reference median [3], respectively, compared to a child whose weight-for-age was above 80% of the reference median. Thus, decrements in nutritional status were found to increase risk of death in an exponential, rather than linear, fashion. Calculated another way, the risk of mortality increased at a compounded rate of 5.9% ($\pm 0.8\%$ standard error) for each decrease of 0.1 Z-score units below $-1.0$ [99].

In subsequent articles by Pelletier and coauthors [101, 102], these summary relative risk estimates were used in conjunction with prevalence rates of the various levels of malnutrition to calculate population-attributable risks (PARs). In this case, PAR is an estimate of the percentage of child deaths attributable to malnutrition's potentiating impact on infectious disease. As noted by Yip and Scanlon [103], PAR is the "bottom line" when expressing the cost of malnutrition on mortality.

The PAR estimates were calculated for 53 developing countries with nationally representative data on children's weight-for-age [103]. Results indicated that 56% of child deaths (aged 6–59 months) were attributable to malnutrition's potentiating effect, and that 83% of these were attributable to mild-to-moderate rather than severe malnutrition. These two findings, that over half of all child deaths are owing, in part, to malnutrition and that mild-to-moderate malnutrition accounts for the vast majority of these malnutrition-related deaths, have led many international organizations to reconceptualize their global strategies to child survival. A concrete example of the impact of this work is represented in more recent presentations of the causes of global child mortality in which the role of malnutrition is literally placed "front and center" (Fig. 12.5).

In an analysis of ten cohort studies, Caulfield and colleagues calculated the proportion of deaths attributable to undernutrition for cause-specific and all-cause mortality

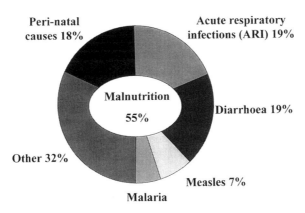

**Fig. 12.5.** Malnutrition and child mortality. Adapted with permission from ref. [99].

[104]. Overall, 52.5% of all deaths in young children were attributable to undernutrition, with a range from 44.8% of deaths because of measles to 60.7% of deaths due to diarrhea [104].

#### 12.4.2.2 INFECTION AND DISEASE

One of the reasons that there is such a strong association between malnutrition and child mortality is that a malnourished child tends to suffer more days of infectious disease. The total number of days of disease a child experiences is a combination of the number of episodes (i.e., incidence) and the duration of each episode. Early studies of these relationships suggested that malnutrition results in longer durations of disease but not more episodes. An early article by Black et al. [1], for example, found that malnutrition was associated with longer diarrheal durations, but not incidence, among young Bangladeshi children. Figure 12.6, adapted from this article, shows the clear relationship between anthropometric status at the start of an episode and the average duration of diarrheal episodes associated with enterotoxigenic *Escherichia coli*.

Subsequent studies have confirmed this strong relationship between initial nutritional status and duration or severity of an infectious disease episode [105], and some studies found an association with an increased number (incidence) of episodes as well [106, 107]. In a study from Brazil, for example, Guerrant and colleagues [105] found that children with weight-for-age 3 SD or more below the median (i.e., $\leq -3\,Z$) had 37% more episodes, 73% longer durations, and 100% more days of diarrhea than their better-nourished counterparts. However, it should be noted that the relationship between nutritional status and diarrhea incidence is highly subject to confounding by socioeconomic and environmental context; not all analyses have adequately controlled for these factors.

Mechanisms by which malnutrition increases the incidence and prevalence of infectious disease are numerous and complex. Some of the factors include impaired host defenses, including protective mucus, gastric acidity, and humoral and cellular immunity. In-depth reviews of these factors are available elsewhere [108].

It should be noted that malnutrition is not associated with more disease in all cases. For example, Aaby et al. argued that malnutrition has little to do with measles incidence [109]; however, more importantly, there is strong evidence that the severity of measles infection is related to malnutrition (see Chapter 8, Measles). Also, a study by Genton and colleagues

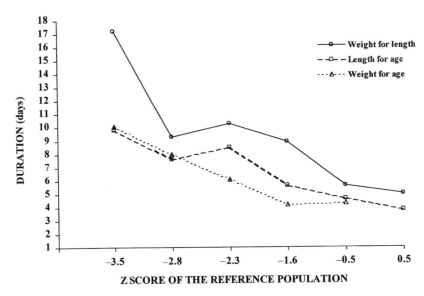

**Fig. 12.6.** Relationship between anthropometric status and duration of diarrheal episodes. Adapted with permission from ref. [1].

[110] found that stunting among Papua New Guinean children was actually protective against malaria. These instances, however, are the exceptions (see Chapter 9, Malaria). Overall, the evidence that malnutrition increases the burden of illness is consistent and strong [111].

### 12.4.2.3  FUNCTIONAL OUTCOMES

Malnutrition impairs functional performance. These impairments may be physical, such as reduced physical activity and work capacity, as well as cognitive and behavioral. A challenge in understanding these myriad effects of malnutrition is that many of these functional outcomes (e.g., physical activity and social interaction) are highly related [112]. The impact of malnutrition on cognitive and behavioral development is briefly summarized next. The impact of malnutrition on other functional outcomes, such as work capacity and reproductive health, can be found elsewhere [113].

A number of reviews of the impact of malnutrition on mental development are available [114, 115]. The chapter by Martorell [115] thoroughly reviewed the published literature and came to nine key generalizations regarding the impact of undernutrition during pregnancy or early childhood on cognitive and behavioral development. These generalizations are summarized in Table 12.2.

Two points should be highlighted from this list. First, the theories by which malnutrition leads to developmental delays have changed radically over the past 40 years or so. In the mid-1960s, many scientists believed the impact of malnutrition on cognitive deficits was caused exclusively by physical damage to the brain during critical periods [116]. It is now recognized that malnutrition hinders cognitive abilities through a variety of interrelated routes, as presented in Fig. 12.7 (adapted from [117]). As seen in this figure, a poorly nourished child may be less physically active and therefore less likely to interact with his or her environment, which may or may not lead to impaired learning.

Table 12.2

Nine generalizations about the impact of undernutrition during pregnancy or early childhood on cognitive and behavioral development

| Area | Findings |
| --- | --- |
| Effects are severe and varied | Poor nutrition during intrauterine life and early years leads to profound and varied effects that include:<br><br>Delayed physical growth and motor development; Impaired cognitive development and lower IQs; More behavioral problems and deficient social skills; and Decreased attention, impaired learning, and lower educational achievement. |
| Not only the severely malnourished are affected | Mild-to-moderate malnutrition as well as severe malnutrition can have significant negative effects |
| Mechanisms | Both organic-based mechanisms (e.g., damage to the brain) as well as such mechanisms as reduced exploration and interest in stimuli, separately or in combination, likely play a role. |
| Who is affected? | The poorest segments of society are most likely to be malnourished and the negative effects of malnutrition on cognitive development are likely to be greatest among these populations. |
| Which nutrients? | It is difficult to identify one or two key nutrient deficiencies that are most associated with impaired development because nutritional deficiencies tend to cluster. The safest course is to make sure children meet all of their requirements for all nutrients from breast and complementary foods. |
| Which ages? | There is strong evidence that the earlier the nutritional intervention in the life of the child, the greater the benefit in preventing impaired physical and cognitive development. |
| Effects are largely irreversible | Although there is scientific evidence that improvements in cognition can be achieved through intensive educational and dietary therapy, few children in developing countries have the benefit of such therapy. Thus, in poor countries, once cognition is impaired, it is largely permanent. |
| Effects are long lasting | Nutritional supplementation trials have found that improved nutrition during preschool age persists as long as adolescence and adulthood. |
| Stimulation | Combining stimulation programs with nutritional programs results in greater cognitive development than either alone. |

Source: Adapted with permission from [102].

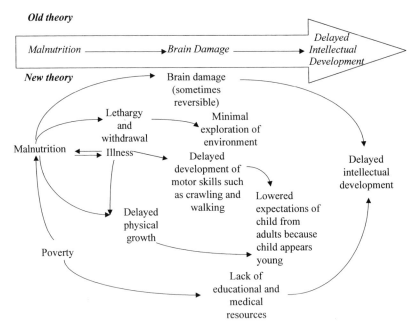

**Fig. 12.7.** Malnutrition and delayed intellectual development. Adapted with permission from ref. [117].

The second point to be highlighted relates to the timing of the insult. In general, the earlier the malnutrition in the life of the child, the more severe, longer-lasting, and less amenable to reversal are the negative consequences. Also, like the effects on mortality reviewed here, even mild and moderate forms of malnutrition can have measurable effects on cognition and behavior. Finally, there are not one or two single nutrients that can be held most responsible for the relationship between malnutrition and cognitive deficits. This finding parallels the evidence for the impact of specific nutrients on physical growth, as discussed in a separate section.

### 12.4.2.4 SUMMARY

In summary, the consequences of malnutrition are varied, severe, and long lasting, particularly if the malnutrition occurs early in the child's life. It is not only children with severe malnutrition who suffer additional negative consequences; rather, there is now ample evidence that mild and moderate forms of malnutrition have significant, measurable consequences. And, at a population level, because most children who are malnourished have mild or moderate rather than severe forms of malnutrition, the overwhelming proportion of the impairments owing to malnutrition is due to these milder or moderate forms.

Thus, it is clear that malnutrition should be prevented. But how? In the next sections, the literature on the main causes of malnutrition is summarized. An accurate understanding of these causes is essential for designing effective programs.

### 12.4.3 Causes of Malnutrition and Poor Growth

The most immediate (or proximate) causes of malnutrition are illness (infection) and poor diet. The evidence that these conditions negatively impact growth, particularly linear growth, is summarized next. The focus on linear growth is in recognition of the fact that relative weight (i.e., weight-for-height) may be lost and more easily recovered, whereas linear growth deficits are generally permanent.

### 12.4.3.1 INFECTION

It is indisputable that infectious diseases have an important and significant impact on the growth of individual children. Diarrheal disease and lower-respiratory infections have been particularly implicated in this regard. One of the first studies that documented this in a developing country was directed by Leonardo Mata in the community of Santa María Cauqué, Guatemala, between 1962 and 1967 [118]. During this study, Mata followed 45 children from birth and daily gathered information on growth, illnesses, and stool samples, among other information. Mata then plotted weight gains of these children against growth references and superimposed the illnesses and durations of illnesses that they experienced. An example of these plots is presented in Fig. 12.8, often referred to as a "Matagram."

The biological mechanisms that underlie the impact of infectious disease on growth are well documented and include decreased dietary intakes owing to catabolism, malabsorption, and anorexia [119], among others.

Although the impact of infection on growth of individual children is clear, the impact of infectious disease on growth at the population level is more controversial. The central question is: How much of the average growth deficits seen among developing country children is caused by infectious disease versus, for example, poor diet? Early community-based studies suggested that infections were the primary causes of poor childhood growth at the population level [120, 121]. For example, Rowland and colleagues [122] analyzed data on 126 Gambian infants who were followed from birth until 2 years of age and calculated that lower respiratory-tract infections (LRTIs) reduced weight gain by 14.7 g/day of infection and diarrheal diseases reduced weight gain by 3.7 g/day during the first 2 years of life. Because

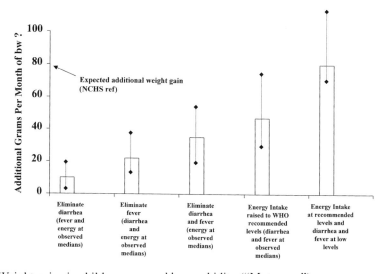

**Fig. 12.8.** Weight gains in children, grouped by morbidity ("Matagram").

children were sick with diarrhea most often, the overall impact of the diseases on weight gain at the community level was greatest for diarrheal diseases. The authors estimated that diarrheal diseases were responsible for approximately one half and LRTI for one -quarter of the approximate 1.2 kg shortfall in weight below the NCHS reference at age 1 year. Notably, infectious diseases were not found to have any impact on length gain. Also, negative effects of diarrhea were much reduced in breast-fed children, a phenomenon that subsequently was confirmed by Lutter and colleagues [123].

In the late 1980s, however, the widely accepted notion that diarrhea and other infectious diseases were the primary causes of poor childhood growth began to be questioned. In a novel analysis of a community-based study of Bangladeshi children (6–35 months), Briend and colleagues [124] compared weight and length gains in which diarrhea had occurred at the beginning to those that occurred at the end of 3-month intervals. Based on 1,772 such 3-month intervals, the authors found that although weight gain and linear growth were lower in intervals with diarrhea than in intervals without diarrhea, comparison of weight and height gains in intervals during which diarrhea occurred at the beginning or at the end showed that after nonbloody diarrheas children catch up, and that deficits in weight gain and linear growth were no longer apparent a few weeks later. The authors thus concluded that the effect of diarrhea on growth is transient, and that efforts to control diarrhea are unlikely to improve children's nutritional status in the long term.

This and similar analyses prompted a series of review articles that asked whether the elimination of diarrheal disease would significantly reduce malnutrition [111, 125]. Black [125], for example, noted that the magnitude of impact of diarrheal diseases on growth was very dependent on a number of other factors, including feeding practices during and after the illness. A summary table of the aforementioned studies, along with others that have been published since these reviews quantified the impact of diarrheal disease on length gain deficits, is presented in Table 12.3. As seen, diarrheal disease likely accounts for only approximately 10–15% of the overall total length deficits seen in developing countries.

In summary, although it is indisputable that infectious disease has detrimental effects on the growth of individual children, infectious disease does not appear to be the primary cause of growth retardation at the population level. Of the approximately

Table 12.3
Impact of diarrhea on linear growth

| Author, Year | Reference | Country | Age (months) | % Total length deficits |
|---|---|---|---|---|
| Schorling and Guerrant (1990) | 107 | Brazil | | 21 |
| Black et al. (1984) | 1 | Bangladesh | 2–48 | 20 |
| Briend (1989) | 124 | Bangladesh | 6–35 | 20 |
| Martorell et al. (1975) | 120 | Guatemala | 0–84 | 10 |
| Rowland (1988) | 122 | Gambia | 0–24 | NS[a] |

[a]NS, nonsignificant.

10 cm that children are linearly growth retarded by 5 years of age, it appears that this shortfall could only be reduced by 2 to 3 cm by programmatic efforts focused exclusively on bring infectious disease rates in developing countries down to those seen in industrialized countries. Black [125] and others have thus concluded that, although reduction of infectious diseases is desirable for many reasons, the relative feasibility of eliminating or significantly reducing infectious diseases to improve nutritional status should be balanced against the cost, feasibility, and effectiveness of more direct nutrition interventions.

So, what accounts for the remaining 7- to 8-cm shortfall in heights seen among children in developing countries? Some of this deficit is owing to intergenerational effects in which shorter mothers give birth to shorter newborns [9]. The balance of the deficit, however, is mostly because of the young child's diet and, perhaps more importantly, the combined impact of simultaneous exposure to poor diet and high rates of infection. In addition, among poor families, parental tobacco use, especially smoking by the father, may divert precious household income from food to tobacco, increasing the risk of stunting of children in these households (see Chapter 23, Impact of Parental Tobacco Use on Child Malnutrition and Survival).

### 12.4.3.2 DIET

Dietary intakes unquestionably affect nutritional status and growth. Dietary intakes of infants and young children in developing countries come from a combination of breast milk and complementary (or transitional) foods. As presented in the historical overview, the scientific understanding regarding which nutrients are most responsible for the widespread growth faltering seen in developing countries, however, has evolved significantly over the past half-century. In this section, the most up-to-date evidence for the impact of individual nutrients is briefly summarized; more detailed reviews are available elsewhere [23, 126].

*Breast-Feeding.* The epidemiologic evidence for the advantages of exclusive breast-feeding early in life and the continuation of breast-feeding during the first 2 years of life is extensive and convincing. The literature on benefits of breast-feeding has been reviewed and summarized elsewhere, so it is not addressed here. Particularly important, however, is the evidence that exclusive breast-feeding early in life protects against infections (arrow 7 in Fig. 12.2), even in industrialized countries [127–129]. And, when a child does become ill, the breast-feeding child suffers less in terms of reduced intakes and growth faltering than the non-breast-fed child [119].

*Nutritional Determinants of Growth.* The literature on the nutritional determinants of growth has been reviewed by me as well as others [23, 126, 130]. In these reviews, the evidence for the relation between specific nutrient deficiencies, alone and in combination, and growth was reviewed; some of the key findings of these articles are summarized in Table 12.4.

One of the key limitations of attempting to draw conclusions about the role of specific nutrients and growth is that many of the published studies did not adequately take into account the fact that the nutrients of interest were also being provided along with other nutrients. For example, many of the studies that concluded that calcium intake increases growth were based on an observed association between cow's milk intake and growth,

Table 12.4

**Evidence for the nutritional determinants of childhood growth in developing countries**

| Nutrient | Availability of good-quality studies | Likelihood that provision of nutrient/food will improve growth | Notes (key references) |
|---|---|---|---|
| *Macronutrients* | | | |
| Energy alone | Low | Low-moderate | Few studies have isolated the effect of energy. |
| Protein alone | High | Low | |
| *Individual vitamins and minerals* | | | |
| Vitamin A | High | Low-moderate | Improved growth with vitamin A apparently limited to the severely vitamin A deficient. |
| Vitamin $B_6$ | Low | Low-moderate | Lactating infants of supplemented mothers grew better. |
| Vitamin $B_{12}$ | Low | ? | Very few studies. Difficult to separate Vitamin $B_{12}$ from other components of animal products. |
| Calcium | Moderate | Low | Most positive studies based on studies with cow's milk. Supplementation trials generally found no impact. |
| Copper | Low | Moderate | Most studies have been too short to measure impact on linear growth. |
| Folic acid | Low | ? | Very few studies. |
| Iodine | Moderate | Low | Widespread programs to increase fortification with iodine provides opportunity to test impact on growth. |
| Iron | High | ? | Effects likely depend on degree of iron depletion, baseline nutritional status, and underlying causes of iron deficiency. |
| Zinc | High | Moderate-high | Meta-analysis found significant impact of zinc supplementation on both weight and length [133]. |
| *Other* | | | |
| Multiple micro-nutrients | Low | Moderate | Programmers are considering widespread supplementation with multiple micronutrients, despite lack of good studies. |
| Animal products | Low | Moderate | Correlational results studies consistently positive, but open to confounding (e.g., SES). Randomized trials needed. |
| Dietary quality | Low-moderate | Moderate | Definitions highly variable. Need more consistent definition. |

*SES* socioeconomic status.

without adequately considering the other nutrients that are also present in cow's milk (e.g., zinc, protein) [131]. Randomized, supplementation trials with calcium, on the other hand, generally failed to find an impact on growth [132].

Of the individual nutrients examined in these reviews, the evidence for an impact of zinc on growth appeared to be the most consistently positive. In a meta-analysis of randomized zinc trials, the overall effects of sizes were significant but small (at about 0.22 SD units and 0.26 SD for height and weight, respectively), but effects were about twice as large in children who were stunted ($\leq 2$ height-for-age Z-score (HAZ) on entry. The authors of a meta-analysis of randomized trials that examined the impact of studies of zinc on child growth thus concluded that, "There is now sufficient information to indicate that, in those settings with high rates of stunting and/or low plasma zinc concentrations, programs to enhance zinc status should be considered to improved children's growth" [133] (see Chapter 15, Zinc Deficiency).

The more mixed results seen in the studies that attempted to isolate the impact of a single nutrient on growth are likely owing, as least in part, to the fact that malnourished children are typically deficient in a number of nutrients simultaneously. If one nutrient is increased through supplementation, the nutrient that is the next most deficient then becomes limiting [134]. Thus, there is currently great interest in determining whether provision of multiple micronutrients will improve growth [131, 132]. To date, there have been just four well-designed studies examining the impact of multiple-micronutrient supplements on growth [135–138], and only one of these has found a significant impact on growth [see Chapter 18]. As suggested by Ramakrishnan and Huffman in Chapter 18, the extent of deficiencies and age of the children are likely important factors in whether the supplements have positive and sustainable effects on growth.

The International Research on Infant Supplementation (IRIS) studies, conducted among 1,134 infants in Indonesia, Peru, South Africa, and Vietnam, showed that daily multiple-micronutrient supplementation was associated with greater weight gain and less anemia than a daily iron supplement or weekly multiple-micronutrient supplement [139, 140]. Meta-analyses showed that supplementation with multiple micronutrients improves child growth, whereas supplementation with iron or vitamin A alone did not improve child growth [141].

In spite of the current lack of scientific evidence of the benefits and risks of supplementation with multiple micronutrients, there is serious discussion among the large, multinational organizations (e.g., UNICEF) about going ahead with large-scale supplementation with multiple micronutrients [142]. Many in the scientific community believe that such large-scale efforts may be premature.

An alternative, or perhaps complementary, strategy for improving diets of developing country children is to focus not on specific nutrients, but on specific types of foods (e.g., animal products or even the whole diet), a concept often referred to as *dietary quality.*

A high-quality diet is defined as one that has the proper concentrations, balance, and bioavailability of both the macro- and micronutrients needed for growth and health [24]. Some of the best reports on the importance of dietary quality come from the nutrition Collaboration Research Support Program (CRSP) studies in Mexico, which showed that while intake of individual nutrients failed to predict size, dietary patterns, such as consumption of more animal products and fruit, were associated with larger size, whereas high tortilla consumption was associated with small body size. This finding was in spite of the fact that the high tortilla consumption pattern was associated with higher total intake of such individual nutrients as iron, thiamine, zinc, energy, calcium, and niacin among preschoolers. This apparent contradiction between high absolute nutrient intake from tortillas, but worse growth, was attributed to the low bioavailability of nutrients from tortillas owing to the high fiber and phytate content [143].

Inclusion of animal products may be a key strategy for improving dietary quality. Observational studies in developing countries consistently find a strong positive correlation between animal product intake and height [144]. This correlation is often attributed to the extra protein found in animal products [145–148], but nutritional aspects of animal products other than protein may in fact be responsible [148, 149]. Animal products are an excellent source of a number of micronutrients and minerals, including iron, zinc, calcium, vitamin A, and phosphorus; vitamin $B_{12}$, of course, is only found in animal products. Alternately, it has been suggested that sulfur, primarily found in amino acids such as methionine and cysteine [150, 151], or the higher dietary fat content of animal foods [152] are responsible for the associations. Regardless of the reasons for the effect, it is generally agreed that increased consumption of animal products would likely have a significant impact on increased growth among children in developing countries [126]. Remarkably few well-designed, randomized studies of the use of animal products, however, have been conducted. This is an important area of research for the future.

*Impact of State-of-the Art Dietary Interventions on Growth and Mortality.* To what degree can improving dietary intake among children alone reduce global malnutrition and improve survival? There are strikingly few good studies that can be used to answer this question. Caulfield and colleagues [153] summarized programmatic efforts to improve dietary intake and growth of 6- to 12-month-old infants in five efficacy trials and 16 programs conducted in 14 different countries. Improvements in dietary intake (ranging from 65 to 302 kcal/day) were found in almost all of these trials and programs. Caulfield et al. calculated that such improvements in intake were associated with improvements in growth range of 0.10–0.50 SD units. The authors also estimated that improvements of this magnitude would translate into reductions in malnutrition ($\leq 2$ SD weight-for-age) at 12 months of 1–19%, and that these reductions in malnutrition could in turn reduce deaths owing to malnutrition by 2–13%, depending on the initial prevalence of malnutrition in the target community.

*Summary.* In summary, poor dietary intakes, both by pregnant women and by young children, are responsible for a significant portion of the growth stunting that occurs in developing countries. As seen from this review, however, lack of no single nutrient can be highlighted as primarily responsible. This is in contrast to our earlier understanding of the causes of poor growth, which focused, for example, on protein as the main cause of malnutrition. Rather, diets served to young children by poor mothers in developing countries do not allow optimal nutrition and growth for a number of reasons; such diets are often inadequate in a variety of nutrients, especially certain micronutrients; contain high amounts of inhibitors, such as phytates, that reduce the absorption of the nutrients that are consumed; and are low in promoters of absorption, such as vitamin C and fat.

### 12.4.3.3 RELATIVE AND COMBINED EFFECTS OF INFECTION AND POOR DIET ON CHILD GROWTH

The previous two sections summarized the strong epidemiologic evidence that high burdens of infection and poor diet are each important, independent determinants of the widespread growth retardation seen in developing countries. Most of the studies cited examined the impact of either infection or diet on growth. A key question for programmers, however, is which approaches will have the greatest impact on improving growth—reducing infection, improving diets, or both? These questions go to the heart of the design of international nutrition policies and distribution of resources.

Strikingly few published studies have examined the effects of the simultaneous improvements in diet and health on growth. A notable exception is a study by Becker and colleagues [154] that used random-effect regression methods to model monthly weight changes in 70 children aged 5 to 18 months from two Bangladeshi villages. Estimates indicated that increasing energy intakes to the recommended WHO level would have a significantly greater effect on weight gain than would the elimination of diarrhea and fever (Fig. 12.9). With energy at recommended intake and diarrhea and fever prevalence as found in US children, weight gain was predicted to be near that of the international reference population. The authors concluded, therefore, that interventions aimed at improving dietary intake may be as important as infection control programs for improving growth of children in poor developing nations. Additional research on the magnitude of the improvements in child growth if diets are improved and infections are reduced is urgently needed.

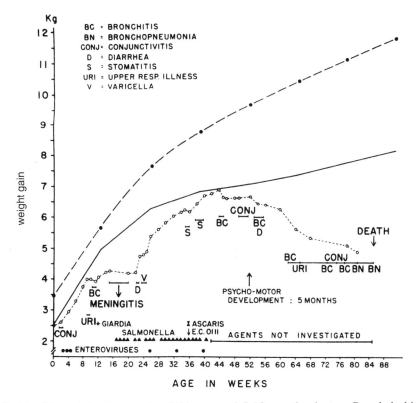

**Fig. 12.9.** Monthly weight changes in children, aged 5-18 months, in two Bangladeshi villages. Adapted with permission from ref. [154].

### *12.4.4   The Underlying Determinants: Food, Care, and Heath*

The UNICEF conceptual framework identifies three primary underlying causes of poor diet and excess disease: insufficient food; inadequate maternal and child care and poor environment; and inadequate health services. Historically, nutritionists have focused primarily on increasing food availability, while the medical community has emphasized the availability of health services. The recognition of the importance of "care" in this equation, however, is new. As noted by WHO:

> *The placement of child care as one of the three critical determinants of adequate nutrition, along with access to food and health services, represents an important breakthrough in the understanding of good nutrition as more than just a problem of food security and health.* [126]

Reviews of the scientific data on the importance of food security, maternal feeding behaviors, and the health care sector are outside the scope of this chapter. Monographs on these topics provide additional detail [126, 155].

#### 12.4.4.1   Programmatic Implications

The relatively slow decline in the rates of malnutrition and consistently massive number of malnourished suggests that past approaches to improve child nutritional status over the past three decades could have been more effective. In part, this may be because of the emphasis on elimination of infectious disease as a primary means to reduce malnutrition. It is now much more widely recognized that improving dietary intakes of the pregnant women and children under 5 years old is essential if there is to be significant and sustained reductions in childhood malnutrition. As indicated, improvements in diets will contribute not only to better nutrition but also to reductions in illness burden prevalence and mortality.

The next question is, How can the aim of improving dietary intakes and quality for women and young children be achieved in a timely, effective, and cost-effective manner?

## 12.5   NUTRITION-ORIENTED INTERVENTIONS AND PROGRAMS: NECESSARY ELEMENTS AND OPTIMAL DESIGNS

Nutrition programs are perceived by many to be extremely complex or ineffective. Reviews of past nutrition program experiences indicated that this perception is at least partially accurate because such programs have often been too rigid in their design (i.e., not adapted to local needs and conditions) and inadequately targeted (e.g., at older children), among other flaws [156].

During the 1980s and 1990s, however, a great deal of effort was invested in addressing these design flaws and developing improved and novel approaches. Furthermore, it was found that programs that are effective at reducing undernutrition have a number of common features [115, 153, 157]. These features can be grouped as follows: who should receive the most attention, when should the target individuals receive this attention, what should the content of the nutrition interventions be, and how should these interventions be delivered, as summarized in Table 12.5.

Programs that are likely to have the most significant impact on reducing global malnutrition are those targeted at the populations for which inadequate nutrition has its largest effects, namely, pregnant women and children under 3 years of age. It is in these

Table 12.5
Characteristic of programs that will effectively promote child growth

| | |
|---|---|
| Who and when | Women, especially when pregnant |
| | Young children, less than 2–3 yr of age |
| What | Adequate dietary intakes during pregnancy |
| | Exclusive breast feeding to around 6 mo |
| | Partial breast feeding through the second year of life |
| | High-quality, locally available complementary foods of high nutrient densities fed with adequate frequency and encouragement |
| | Supplementary feeding when necessary |
| | Micronutrients, through foods, supplements and /or fortification for both pregnant women and young children |
| How | Built around gaining weight (during pregnancy) and promoting healthy growth of young children |
| | Behaviour change through communication and dialogue |
| | Participant involvement in process and design of interventions |
| | Integrated with health services when appropriate well-maintained and adequately staffed Strong local and political commitment |
| Other | Combine with psychosocial stimulation |

populations and during these ages that nutritional interventions have the greatest potential for benefit. In children, a clear relationship between earlier supplementation and greater improvements in growth per unit of supplement has been documented [158].

Effective programs will promote adequate diets for pregnant women. For the newborn, promotion of exclusive breast-feeding for newborns through 6 months of age and partial breast-feeding through 2 years is recommended. Once the child reaches about 6 months of age, programs should emphasize the promotion of complementary foods that are of high quality, particularly in respect to micronutrient density. Ample amounts of these foods should be served by caretakers frequently enough and with a gentle persistence, such that young children consume adequate quantities of the foods, especially during illness.

A key conceptual shift is that, in the end, the ultimate objective of nutrition programs is to change behavior. Whether the intervention involves development of a new food, fortification of an existing product, or simply educating mothers to feed the foods they already feed more frequently, success can only be achieved if caretakers change their current practices. Another paradigm shift is that nutritional problems and the solutions to these problems are very context specific. There is not and will unlikely ever be a single "magic bullet" that significantly and sustainably improves child growth across a wide variety of settings. Rather, the components of a nutrition-oriented program must be tailored to the particular problems, cultural conditions, and resource constraints of the local context.

It should be noted that this is in stark contrast to the promotion of universal recommendations for child feeding that many international organizations still promote. For example, standardized recommendations such as "add 2 tablespoons of oil to children's foods" have been widely promoted in the past though such media as UNICEF's Facts for Life [159]. Such recommendations may be appropriate for certain communities or mothers, but in areas where energy and energy density is not the problem, the addition of oil to foods may even be harmful in that it actually decreases the micronutrient densities of the food mixtures.

In sum, state-of-the-art approaches to improving young child feeding recognize that it is essential that behavior change strategies are based on the local needs and conditions of the population, and that they take advantage of the knowledge and resources of which caretakers can feasibly avail themselves. In addition, these strategies need to be based on well-grounded behavior change theory, be flexible enough to take into account changing individual participant situations and needs (e.g., seasonality), and have long-term community and national support.

### 12.5.1 Manuals and Guides to Assist with Designing Programs

A number of manuals are available that guide the user in how to develop strategies for improving maternal and young child diets. One of the most comprehensive is *Designing by Dialogue*, produced by the Academy for Educational Development in Washington, DC [160]. This manual provides a step-by-step approach to developing a behavior change strategy that avoids unidirectional proselytizing (i.e., "education") and builds on bidirectional conversation with local caretakers and populations.

Another manual, produced by Save the Children, utilizes the concept of "positive deviance" to identify behaviors that are being used by poor mothers to raise well-nourished children [161]. This approach thus employs a technique that has been identified as a common element of successful programs in the past, that is, building on what mothers already "do right" [153]. Another key aspect of the positive deviance approach is that it emphasizes the importance of community involvement in identifying the positive deviant families and the behaviors. The positive deviance approach has been applied in Vietnam, Haiti, and Pakistan [162]. It has been hypothesized that much of the success with the positive deviant approach is owing to this community involvement, which causes families and the community to become more empowered to solve not only the nutritional problems of their children, but also other health and well-being problems [163]. Another manual, published by Helen Keller International, focuses on increasing the consumption of micronutrient-rich foods [164]. Finally, an integrated strategy for improving child feeding was developed UNICEF and WHO [165].

### 12.5.2 Treatment of Severe Malnutrition

The development of ready-to-use therapeutic food (RUTF) spread has greatly advanced the treatment of severe malnutrition. RUTF spread is an energy-dense food that is made of powdered ingredients that are embedded in a lipid-rich paste [166]. Milk powder, powdered vitamins and minerals, sugar, vegetable oil, and peanut butter are mixed together and have an energy density of about 23 kJ/g (5.5 kcal/g) [166]. Because the water content of the mixture is low, the RUTF resists microbial contamination and can be stored at ambient tropical conditions for 3–4 months. RUTF, as the name implies, does not require any cooking, and a severely malnourished child needs to consume a few spoonfuls of RUTF several times a day to have a sufficient nutrient intake for recovery [166]. RUTF can be produced locally with a standard planetary bakery mixer, and the main precaution in quality control is the procurement of properly stored peanuts that do not have aflatoxin contamination. Community-based approaches to the treatment of severe malnutrition include day care nutrition centers, residential nutrition centers, primary health clinics, and domiciliary care, and the provision of high energy, high protein, and micronutrients was deemed essential for the success of these approaches [167].

The limitations of the traditional approach to treatment of severe malnutrition in inpatient facilities became apparent with large-scale humanitarian crises, such as the famine in south Sudan in 1998, and community-based therapeutic care was designed to address these limitations [168]. Acutely malnourished children are identified through screening of the affected population or self-referral, and three types of treatment are provided, depending on the child's condition: (1) for moderate acute malnutrition, supplementary feeding program with dry take-home rations and simple medicines; (2) for severe acute malnutrition with no medical complications, provision of RUTF and routine medicines to be taken at home, with weekly check-ups and resupply of RUTF; (3) for acute malnutrition with medical complications, treatment at an inpatient stabilization center until well enough to proceed with outpatient care. The first pilot community-based therapeutic care program was implemented during the 2000 famine in Ethiopia and was followed by larger programs in Darfur, Sudan, in 2001 [168]. A field manual for community-based therapeutic care was prepared by Valid International in 2006 [168].

## 12.6   RESEARCH NEEDS AND PRIORITIES

Gaps in our understanding of the causes and consequences of malnutrition have been noted throughout this review. Research into a number of these areas would significantly improve the design and therefore effectiveness of a program aimed at preventing malnutrition in developing countries.

There is ample information on the patterns of growth failure in developing countries. There is still a great deal yet unknown about the causes of growth failure. In particular, there is poor understanding of why malnutrition rates and the patterns of stunting and wasting vary so widely across different regions. For example, it has been hypothesized that the significantly greater rates of malnutrition seen in Southeast Asia compared to Africa may be owing, in part, to women's perceived self-efficacy and how their role in the family and society affect women's control over, and abilities related to, child care [169]. Future research should consider both underlying and proximate determinants of malnutrition (Fig. 12.2) and distinguish between stunting and wasting-type growth failure.

There are numerous additional examples of needed research with each domain that has been examined in this chapter. This review found that there is renewed recognition that malnutrition is a key determinant of child mortality, and that adequate young child feeding is an essential element of preventing malnutrition. It was also noted, however, that the manner in which programmers can best improve young child feeding in an efficient, cost-effective, and sustainable manner is still evolving. Specific examples of research gaps in the area of complementary feeding are therefore listed in Table 12.6.

Research needs more directly related to breast-feeding promotion are available elsewhere. A similarly detailed listing of research topics related to promotion of improved dietary practices of pregnant women should be drawn up.

In addition to the more biological and epidemiological type of research listed in Table 12.6, more rigorous evaluations of the efficiency, effectiveness, and costs of programmatic efforts are also desperately needed. There are literally thousands of organizations, both governmental and nongovernmental, that are working throughout the developing world to improve child health and nutrition. Extremely few of the lessons learned through these attempts, however, are documented and made available to the larger international

Table 12.6
Research recommendations related to complementary feeding

| Area | Examples of specific research gaps |
|------|-----------------------------------|
| Relationship between breast feeding and complementary feeding | Which factors (e.g., maternal nutritional status) affect the appropriate timing of the introduction of complementary foods? |
| | How do various presentations of complementary foods (e.g., liquid vs. solid) and methods of serving these foods (e.g., cup vs. spoon) affect breast milk intakes? |
| Factors affecting intake of complementary foods and total intakes | What is the relationship between energy density, feeding frequency, total daily energy intake, and energy intake from breast milk and complementary foods? |
| | What are the causes of poor appetite among children? |
| | What are the effects of aggressively feeding children with poor appetites? |
| Macronutrient content of complementary foods | More information is needed on essential fatty acid requirements of young children. |
| | What is the ability of low-protein staple foods (e.g., cassava) to meet protein requirements, and what can be done to improve protein content of these foods? |
| Micronutrient content of complementary foods | Additional information on the absorption and utilization of micronutrients, especially problem nutrients (iron, zinc, calcium, and vitamin A) from complementary foods is needed. |
| | Approaches to improve overall micronutrient content and bioavailability of local diets are needed. |
| Organoleptic characteristics of complementary foods | Additional information on the viscosity of traditional complementary foods and the impact of varying viscosity on intakes is needed |
| | The influence of other organoleptic characteristics of complementary foods, i.e., flavor, aroma, color, texture, in developing country settings is almost totally undocumented. |
| Feeding behaviors | Additional research on caregiver techniques (e.g., passive/active) and how these affect child intakes. |
| | What is the effect of feeding mode (cup, self-feeding, etc.) on intakes? |
| Food processing | More information is needed on the effects of different food-processing techniques on nutritional value of foods, acceptability, toxicology, etc. |
| | Additional strategies for reducing viscosity of foods should be explored. |
| Planning and evaluating programmatic interventions | How can current information on nutritional needs of children be adapted to local circumstances? |
| | Additional evaluations that assess the efficacy, effectiveness, efficiency, and costs of different approaches are needed. |

*Source*: Adapted from [126].

health community. Designers and financial backers of these programs are encouraged to invest the relatively small additional resources that are required to rigorously evaluate and document their efforts. Key issues regarding the design and interpretation of such program-based evaluations were described by Habicht and colleagues [170]. Wider application and publication of the lessons learned through such evaluations will allow other programmers to use their own resources more effectively.

## 12.7 SUMMARY AND CONCLUSIONS

In summary, this review has provided an overview of malnutrition in the developing world. The evolution of the various terms that have been used in relation to undernutrition and the perceived causes of this malady over the past century have been described. An in-depth review of the current scientific knowledge of the causes and determinants of malnutrition was then presented.

Through this review, the substantial effects that malnutrition, even in its mild or moderate forms, have on child mortality and impaired cognitive and behavior outcomes were noted. In terms of the causes of malnutrition, there has been a shift away from a belief that preventing infectious disease would necessarily lead to significantly lower rates of malnutrition. Rather, it is now very widely recognized that inadequate young child feeding, regarding both breast-feeding and complementary feeding, is perhaps the key determinant of poor child growth in developing countries. It is also increasingly recognized that many of the previous efforts to address malnutrition were poorly designed. Over the past decade or so, more effective interventions that are targeted at the pregnant mother and the very young child and are flexible and situation specific, among other attributes, have been developed.

Over the next decade, it is critical that these new approaches are adequately supported, rigorously evaluated, and further refined so that the scourge of malnutrition can become a historical footnote. The widespread application of these approaches within the context of integrated efforts to improve the socioeconomic and societal status of poor women and families could significantly improve the growth and nutritional status of young children throughout the developing world. The economic and social benefits to the global society of significantly reducing malnutrition are immense. The ethical reasons for doing so are unquestionable.

## REFERENCES

1. Black RE, Brown KH, Becker S. Malnutrition is a determining factor in diarrheal duration, but not incidence, among young children in a longitudinal study in rural Bangladesh. Am J Clin Nutr 1984;39:87–94.
2. Sepulveda J, Willett W, Munoz A. Malnutrition and diarrhea: a longitudinal study among urban Mexican children. Am J Epidemiol 1988;127:365–376.
3. Pelletier DL. The relationship between child anthropometry and mortality in developing countries: implications for policy, programs and future research. J Nutr 1994;124:2047S–2081S.
4. Schroeder DG, Brown KH. Nutritional status as a predictor of child survival: summarizing the association and quantifying its global impact. Bull World Health Organ 1994;72:569–579.
5. Pollitt E, Husaini MA, Harahap H, Halati S, Nugraheni A, Sherlock A. Stunting and delayed motor development in rural West Java. Am J Hum Biol 1994;6:627–635.
6. Pollitt E. Malnutrition and infection in the classroom. Paris: UNESCO, United Nations, 1990.
7. Haas JD, Martinez EJ, Murdoch E, Conlisk E, Rivera JA, Martorell R. Nutritional supplementation during the preschool years influences body size and composition of Guatemalan adolescents. J Nutr 1995;125:1078S–1089S.

8. Martorell R, Ramakrishnan U, Schroeder DG, Ruel M. Reproductive performance and nutrition during childhood. Nutr Rev 1996;54:S15–S21.

9. Ramakrishnan U, Martorell R, Schroeder DG, Flores R. Role of intergenerational effects on linear growth. J Nutr 1999;129:544S–549S.

10. The state of the world's children. Geneva: United Nations International Children's Emergency Fund, Oxford University Press, 1998.

11. Waterlow JC. Protein-energy malnutrition. London: Edward Arnold, 1992.

12. Williams CD. A nutritional disease of childhood associated with a maize diet. Arch Dis Child 1933;8:423.

13. Brock JF, Autret M. Kwashiorkor in Africa. Monograph Series, No. 8. Geneva: World Health Organization, 1952.

14. Autret M. In: Meeting protein needs of infants and children. Washington, DC: National Academy of Sciences, National Research Council, 1961:12(84):537. Publication 843.

15. Wise RP. The case of incaparina in Guatemala. Food Nutr Bull 1980;2:3–8.

16. Ashworth A, Waterlow JC. Calorie and protein intakes and growth. Lancet 1969;1:776–777.

17. Gopalan C, Swamminathan MC, Kumari VKK, Rao DH, Vijayaraghavan K. Effect of calorie supplementation on growth of undernourished children. Am J Clin Nutr 1973;26:563–566.

18. Jelliffe DB. Protein-calorie malnutrition in tropical pre-school children. J Pediatr 1959;54:227–256.

19. Waterlow JC, Payne PR. The protein gap. Nature 1975;258:113–117.

20. McLaren DS. The great protein fiasco. Lancet 1974;(ii):93–96.

21. King M. Medical Care in developing countries: a primer on the medicine of poverty and a symposium from Makerere, Nairobi. London: Oxford University Press, 1966.

22. Jelliffe DB, Jelliffe EFP. Multimixes as weaning food. J Trop Pediatr 1967;13:46–50.

23. Allen LH. Nutritional influences on linear growth: a general review. Eur J Clin Nutr 1994;48:S75–S89.

24. Brown KH. The importance of dietary quality versus quantity for weanlings in less developed countries: a framework for discussion. Food Nutr Bull 1991;13:86–94.

25. deOnis M, Habicht J-P. Anthropometric reference data for international use: recommendations from a World Health Organization Expert Committee. Am J Clin Nutr 1996;64:650–658.

26. Zemel BS, Riley EM, Stallings VA. Evaluation of methodology for nutritional assessment in children: anthropometry, body composition, and energy expenditure. Annu Rev Nutr 1997;17:211–235.

27. Roche AF, Davila GH. Differences between recumbent length and stature within individuals. Growth 1974;38:313–320.

28. World Health Organization. Physical status: the use and interpretation of anthropometry. Geneva: World Health Organization, 1995. Report of a WHO Expert Committee, World Health Organization Technical Report Series, No. 854.

29. Beaton GH, Kelly A, Kevany J, Martorell R, Mason J. Appropriate uses of anthropometric indices in children: a report based on an ACC/SCN workshop, New York, United Nations Administrative Committee on Coordination/Subcommittee on Nutrition. ACC/SCN State-of-the-Art Series. Geneva: ACC/SCN, 1990. Nutrition Policy Discussion Paper No. 7.

30. Svedberg P. Poverty and undernutrition: theory, measurement and policy. New Delhi: Oxford India Paperbacks, 2000.

31. Nandy S, Irving M, Gordon D, Subramanian SV, Smith GD. Poverty, child undernutrition and morbidity: new evidence from India. Bull World Health Organ 2005;83:210–216.

32. Bhattacharyya AK. Composite index of anthropometric failure (CIAF) classification: is it more useful? Bull World Health Organ 2006;84:335.

33. Shakir A, Morley D. Measuring malnutrition. Lancet 1974;58–759.

34. Hall G, Chowdhury S, Bloem M. Use of mid-upper-arm circumference Z-scores in nutritional assessment (letter). Lancet 1993;341:1481.

35. Mei Z, Grummer-Strawn LM, de Onis M, Yip R. The development of a MUAC-for-height reference, including a comparison to other nutritional status screening indicators. Bull World Health Organ 1997;74:333–341.

36. deOnis M, Yip R, Mei Z. Mid-upper-arm circumference-for-age reference data: recommendations from a WHO Expert Committee. Bull World Health Organ 1997;75:11–18.

37. Skinner AM, Cieslak Z, MacWilliam L, Solimano A, Kinson HF. The measurement of knee-heel length in newborn infants using a simple vernier calipers. Acta Pediatr 1997;86:512–517.
38. Bouchard C. Genetic aspects of anthropometric dimensions relevant to assessment of nutritional status. In: Anthropometric assessment of nutritional status. Himes JR, ed. New York: Wiley-Liss, 1991:213–232.
39. Habicht JP, Martorell R, Yarbrough C, Malina RM, Klein RE. Height and weight standards for preschool children. How relevant are ethnic differences in growth potential? Lancet 1974;611–615.
40. Martorell R. Child growth retardation: a discussion of its causes and of its relationship to health. In: Nutritional adaptation in man. Blaxter KL, Waterlow JC, eds. London: Libbey, 1985:13–29.
41. Waterlow JC, Buzina R, Keller W, Lane JM, Nichaman MZ, Tanner JM. The presentation and use of height and weight data for comparing nutritional status of groups of children under the age of 10 years. Bull World Health Organ 1977;55:489–498.
42. Hamill PV, Drizd TA, Johnson CL, Reed RB, Roche AF, Moore WM. Physical growth: National Center for Health Statistics percentiles. Am J Clin Nutr 1979;32:607–629.
43. Dibley MJ, Staehling N, Nieburg P, Trowbridge FL. Interpretation of Z-score anthropometric indicators derived from the international growth reference. Am J Clin Nutr 1987;46:749–762.
44. deOnis M, Yip R. The WHO growth chart: historical considerations and current scientific issues. Bibl Nutr Dieta 1996;53:74–89.
45. Victora CG, Morris SS, Barros FC, deOnis M, Yip R. The NCHS reference and the growth of breast- and bottle-fed infants. J Nutr 1998;128:1134–1138.
46. Macfarlane SB. A universal growth reference or fool's gold? Eur J Clin Nutr 1995;49:745–753.
47. Davis DP. The importance of genetic influences in early childhood with particular reference to children of Asiatic origin. In: Linear growth retardation in less developed countries. Nestle Nutrition Workshop Series, vol. 14. Waterlow JC, ed. New York: Raven, 1988:75–90.
48. Eveleth PB, Tanner JM. Worldwide variation in human growth. Cambridge, UK: Cambridge University Press, 1990.
49. Chusilp K, Somnasang P, Kirdpon W, Wongkham S, Sribonlue P, Mahaverawat U, et al. Observations on the development of stunting in children of the Khon Kaen region of Thailand. Eur J Clin Nutr 1992;46:475–487.
50. Droomers M, Gross R, Schultink W, Sastroamidjojo S. High socio-economic class preschool children from Jakarta, Indonesia are taller and heavier than NCHS reference population. Eur J Clin Nutr 1995;49:740–744.
51. Yip R, Scanlon K, Trowbridge F. Improving growth status of Asian refugee children in the United States. JAMA 1992;267:937–940.
52. deOnis M, Garza C, Habicht JP. Time for a new growth reference. Pediatrics 1997;100:E8.
53. de Onis M, Garza C, Victora CG, Onyango AW, Frongillo EA, Martines J. The WHO Multicentre Growth Reference Study: planning, study design, and methodology. Food Nutr Bull 2004;25:S15–S26.
54. WHO Multicentre Growth Reference Study Group. WHO child growth standards based on length/ height, weight, and age. Acta Paediatr Suppl 2006;450:76–85.
55. Cole TJ. The use and construction of anthropometric growth reference standards. Nutr Res Rev 1993;6:19–50.
56. Gorstein J, Sullivan K, Yip R, de Onis M, Trowbridge F, Fajans P, Clugston G. Issues in the assessment of nutritional status using anthropometry. Bull World Health Organ 1994;72:273–283.
57. Briend A, Prudhon C, Prinzo ZW, Daelmans BMEG, Mason JB. Putting the management of severe malnutrition back on the international health agenda. Food Nutr Bull 2006;27:(suppl 3):S3–S5.
58. Collins S, Dent N, Binns P, Bahwere P, Sadler K, Hallam A. Management of severe acute malnutrition in children. Lancet 2006;368:1992–2000.
59. Prudhon C, Briend A, Prinzo ZW, Daelmans BMEG, Mason JB, eds. WHO, UNICEF, and SCN informal consultation on community-based management of severe malnutrition in children. SCN Nutrition Policy Paper No. 21. Food Nutr Bull 2007;27:S3–S108.
60. Myatt M, Khara T, Collins S. A review of methods to detect cases of severely malnourished children in the community for their admission into community-based therapeutic care programs. Food Nutr Bull 2006;27(suppl 3):S7–S23.

61. Administrative Committee on Coordination/Subcommittee on Nutrition (ACC/SCN). Second report on the world nutrition situation, vol. 1: global and regional results. Geneva: World Health Organization, 1992.

62. de Onis M, Blossner M. WHO global database on child growth and malnutrition. Geneva: World Health Organization, 1997.

63. World development report: knowledge for development. New York: World Bank/Oxford University Press, 1998.

64. Gross R, Webb P. Wasting time for wasted children: severe child undernutrition must be resolved in non-emergency settings. Lancet 2006;367:1209–1211.

65. Victora CG. The association between wasting and stunting: an international perspective. J Nutr 1992;122:1105–1110.

66. Frongillo EA Jr, deOnis M, Hanson KM. Socioeconomic and demographic factors are associated with worldwide patterns of stunting and wasting of children. J Nutr 1997;127:2302–2309.

67. Falkner F, Holzgreve W, Schloo RH. Prenatal influences on postnatal growth: overview and pointers for needed research. Eur J Clin Nutr 1994;48:S15–S24.

68. Neufeld LM, Haas JD, Grajeda R, Martorell R. Changes in maternal weight form the first to the second trimester of pregnancy are associated with fetal growth and infant length at birth. Am J Clin Nutr 2004;79:646–652.

69. Thame M, Osmond C, Bennett F, Wilks R, Forrester T. Fetal growth is directly related to maternal anthropometry and placental volume. Eur J Clin Nutr 2004;58:894–900.

70. United Nations International Children's Emergency Fund. The state of the world's children. Oxford, UK: Oxford University Press, 1996.

71. Neufeld LM, Pelletier DL, Haas JD. The timing hypothesis and body proportionality of the intra-uterine growth retarded infant. Am J Hum Biol 1999;11:638–646.

72. Martorell R, Schroeder DG, Rivera JA, Kaplowitz HJ. Patterns of linear growth in rural Guatemalan adolescents and children. J Nutr 1995;125:1060S–1067S.

73. Ruel MT, Neufeld L, Habicht J-P, Martorell R. Stunting at birth: a simple indicator that predicts both risk and benefit among stunted populations. FASEB J 1996;10:A289.

74. Karlberg J, Engstrom I, Karlberg P, Fryer JG. Analysis of linear growth using a mathematical model. I. From birth to 3 years. Acta Paediatr Scand 1987;76:478–488.

75. Neumann CG, Harrison GG. Onset and evolution of stunting in infants and children. Examples from the Human Nutrition Collaborative Research Support Program. Kenya and Egypt studies. Eur J Clin Nutr 1994;48:S90–S102.

76. Huttly SRA, Victora CG, Barros FC, Teixeira AMB, Vaughan JP. The timing of nutritional status determination: implications for interventions and growth monitoring. Eur J Clin Nutr 1991;45:85–96.

77. Rivera J, Ruel MT. Growth retardation starts in the first 3 months of life among rural Guatemalan children. Eur J Clin Nutr 1997;51:92–96.

78. Espo M, Kulmala T, Maleta K, Cullinan T, Salin ML, Ashorn P. Determinants of linear growth and predictors of severe stunting during infancy in rural Malawi. Acta Paediatr 2002;91:1364–1370.

79. Waterlow JC. Observations on the natural history of stunting. In: Linear growth retardation in less developed countries. Waterlow JC, ed. Vevey: Raven Press, New York: Nestle Nutrition, 1988.

80. Dewey KG, Peerson JM, Brown KH, Krebs NF, Michaelsen KF, Persson LA, et al. Growth of breast-fed infants deviates from current reference data: a pooled analysis of US, Canadian, and European Data Sets. Pediatrics 1995;96:495–503.

81. Lucas A, Fewtrell MS, Davies PS, Bishop NJ, Clough H, Cole TJ. Breast-feeding and catch-up growth in infants born small for gestational age. Acta Paediatr 1997;86(6)/:564–569.

82. Stoltzfus RJ, Albobnico M, Tielsch JM, Chwaya HM, Savioli L. Linear growth retardation in Zanzibari school children. J Nutr 1997;127:1099–1105.

83. Martorell R, Kettel Khan L, Schroeder DG. Reversibility of stunting: epidemiological findings in children from developing countries. Eur J Clin Nutr 1994;48:S45–S57.

84. Boersma B, Witt JM. Catch-up growth. Endocr Rev 1997;18(5):646–661.

85. Seckler D. Small but healthy: a basic hypothesis in the theory, measurement, and policy of malnutrition. In: Newer concepts in nutrition and their implications for policy. Sukhatme PV, ed. Pune, India: Maharashtra Association for the Cultivation of Science Research Institute, 1982.

86. Martorell R. Body size, adaptation and function. Hum Organ 1989;48:15–20.
87. Martorell R. Promoting health growth: rationale and benefits. In: Child growth and nutrition in developing countries. Pelletier D, Alderman H, eds. Ithaca, NY: Cornell University Press, 1995:15–31.
88. United Nations International Children's Emergency Fund. Strategy for improved nutrition of children and women in developing countries. New York: United Nations International Children's Emergency Fund, 1990. UNICEF Policy Review 1990–1 (E/ICEF/1990/L.6).
89. Mosley WH, Chen LC. An analytical framework for the study of child survival in developing countries. Pop Dev Rev 1984;10:25–45.
90. Bongaarts J. Does malnutrition affect fecundity? A summary of evidence. Science 1980;208:564–569.
91. Mebrahtu S, Pelletier D, Pinstrup-Andersen P. Agriculture and nutrition. In: Child growth and nutrition in developing countries. Pelletier D, Alderman H, eds. Ithaca, NY: Cornell University Press, 1995:220–242.
92. Scrimshaw NS, Taylor DI, Gordon JE. Interactions of nutrition and infection. Geneva: World Health Organization, 1968.
93. World Health Organization/United Nations International Children's Emergency Fund. The management of diarrhoea and use of oral rehydration therapy. Geneva: World Health Organization, 1985.
94. Parker D, Jesperson E. Mobilizing resources for children in the 1990's. UNICEF Staff Working Papers. New York: United Nations International Children's Emergency Fund, 1994.
95. Walsh JA, Warren KS. Selective primary health care: an interim strategy for disease control in developing countries. N Engl J Med 1979;301:967–974.
96. Mata LJ, Kromal RA, Urrutia JJ, Garcia B. Effect of infection on food intake and the nutritional state: perspectives as viewed from the village. Am J Clin Nutr 1977;30:1215–1227.
97. Grant JP. The state of the world's children. Oxford, UK: Oxford University Press, 1984.
98. Pelletier DL. The relationship between child anthropometry and mortality in developing countries: implications for policy, programs and future research. Monograph No. 12. Ithaca, NY: Cornell Food and Nutrition Policy Program, Cornell University, 1991.
99. Pelletier DG, Frongillo EA, Habicht J-P. Epidemiologic evidence for a potentiating effect of malnutrition on child mortality. Am J Public Health 1993;83:1130–1133.
100. Chen LC, Chowdhury, AKA, Huffman SL. Anthropometric assessment of energy: protein malnutrition and subsequent risk of mortality among preschool aged children. Am J Clin Nutr 1980;33:1836–1845.
101. Pelletier DL, Frongillo EA, Schroeder DG, Habicht J-P. A Methodology for estimating the contribution of malnutrition to child mortality in developing countries. J Nutr 1994;124:2106S–2122S.
102. Pelletier DL, Frongillo EA, Schroeder DG, Habicht J-P. The effects of malnutrition on child mortality in developing countries. Bull World Health Organ 1995;7(4):443–448.
103. Yip R, Scanlon K. The burden of malnutrition: a population perspective. J Nutr 1994;124(suppl 10):2043S–2046S.
104. Caulfield LE, de Onis M, Blossner M, Black RE. Undernutrition as an underlying cause of child deaths associated with diarrhea, pneumonia, malaria, and measles. Am J Clin Nutr 2004;80:193–198.
105. Guerrant RL, Schorling JB, McAuliffe JF, Auxiliadora de Souza M. Diarrhea as a cause and an effect of malnutrition: diarrhea prevents catch-up growth and malnutrition increases diarrhea frequency and duration. Am J Trop Hyg 1992;47:28–35.
106. El Samani EFZ, Willett WC, Ware JH. Association of malnutrition and diarrhea in children aged under 5 years. A prospective follow-up study in a rural Sudanese community. Am J Epidemiol 1988;128:93–105.
107. Schorling JB, McAuliffe JF, Auxiliadora de Souza M, Guerrant RL. Malnutrition is associated with increased diarrhoea incidence and duration among children in an urban Brazilian slum. Int J Epidemiol 1990;19:728–735.
108. Calder PC, Field CJ, Gill HS, eds. Nutrition and immune function. Oxon, UK: CABI, 2002.
109. Aaby P, Bukh J, Kronborg D, Lisse IM, Clotide de Silva M. Delayed excess mortality after exposure to measles during the first 6 months of life. Am J Epidemiol 1990;132:211–219.

110. Genton B, Al-Yaman F, Ginny M, Taraika J, Alpers MP. Relation of anthropometry to malaria morbidity and immunity in Papua New Guinean children. Am J Clin Nutr 1998;68:734–741.

111. Briend A. Is diarrhoea a major cause of malnutrition among the under-fives in developing countries? A review of available evidence. Eur J Clin Nutr 1990;44:611–628.

112. Pollitt E, Gorman K. Long-term developmental implications of motor maturation and physical activity in infancy in a nutritionally at risk population, Cambridge, MA. In: Activity, energy expenditure and energy requirements of infants and children. Schürch B, Scrimshaw NS, eds. International Dietary Energy Consultative Group Workshop, November 14–17, 1989.

113. Haddad LJ, Bouis HE. The impact of nutritional status on agricultural productivity: wage evidence from the Philippines. Oxford Bull Econ Stat 1990;53(1):45–68.

114. Grantham-McGregor SM. A review of the studies of the effect of severe malnutrition on mental development. J Nutr 1995;125:2233S–2238S.

115. Martorell R. Undernutrition during pregnancy and early childhood: consequences for cognitive and behavioral development. In: Early child development: investing in our children's future. Young ME, ed. Amsterdam: Elsevier, 1997:39–83.

116. Levitsy DA, Strupp BJ. Malnutrition and the brain: changing concepts, changing concerns. J Nutr 1995;125:2212S–2220S.

117. Brown JL, Pollitt E. Malnutrition, poverty and intellectual development. Sci Am 1996;274:38–43.

118. Mata L. The children of Santa Maria Cauqué. Cambridge, MA: Massachusetts Institute of Technology, 1978.

119. Brown KH, Black RE, Lopez de Romana G, Creed de Kanashiro H. Infant-feeding practices and their relationship with diarrheal and other diseases in Huascar (Lima), Peru. Pediatrics 1989;83:678.

120. Martorell R, Habicht J-P, Yarbrough C, Lechtig A, Klein RE, Western KA. Acute morbidity and physical growth in rural Guatemalan children. Am J Dis Child 1975;129:1296–1301.

121. Rowland MGM, Cole TJ, Whitehead RG. A quantitative study into the role of infection in determining nutritional status in Gambian village children. Br J Nutr 1977;37:441–450.

122. Rowland MG, Rowland SG, Cole TJ. Impact of infection on the growth of children from 0 to 2 years in an urban West African community. Am J Clin Nutr 1988;47:134–138.

123. Lutter CK, Mora JO, Habicht JP, Rasmussen KM, Robson DS, Sellers SG, et al. Nutritional supplementation: effects on child stunting because of diarrhea. Am J Clin Nutr 1989;50:1–8.

124. Briend A, Hasan KH, Aziz KMA, Hoque BA. Are diarrhoea control programmes likely to reduce childhood malnutrition? Observations from rural Bangladesh. Lancet 1989;2:319–322.

125. Black RE. Would control of childhood infectious diseases reduce malnutrition? Acta Paediatr Scand (suppl) 1991;374:133–140.

126. Brown KH, Dewey K, Allen L. Complementary feeding of young children in developing countries: a review of current scientific knowledge. Geneva: World Health Organization, 1998.

127. Scariati PD, Grummer-Strawn LM, Fein SB. A longitudinal analysis of infant morbidity and the extent of breastfeeding in the United States. Pediatrics 1997;99:E5.

128. Feachem RG, Koblinsky MA. Interventions for the control of diarrhoeal diseases among young children: promotion of breast-feeding. Bull World Health Organ 1984;62:271–291.

129. de Zoysa I, Rea M, Martines J. Why promote breast-feeding in diarrhoeal disease control programmes? Health Policy Plan 1991;6:371–379.

130. Waterlow JC, Schürch B. Summary of causes and mechanisms of linear growth retardation (stunting). Eur J Clin Nutr 1994;48:S210.

131. Takahashi E. Secular trend in milk consumption and growth in Japan. Hum Biol 56:427–437.

132. Lee WTK, Leung SSF, Xu YC, Zeng WP, Lau J, Oppenheimer SJ, Cheng JCY. Double-blind, controlled calcium supplementation and bone mineral accretion in children accustomed to a low-calcium diet. Am J Clin Nutr 1994;60:744–750.

133. Brown KH, Peerson JM, Allen LH. Effect of zinc supplementation on children's growth: a meta-analysis of intervention trials. Bibl Nutr Dieta 1998;54:76–83.

134. Allen LH. The nutrition CRSP: what is marginal malnutrition, and does it affect human function? Nutr Rev 1993;51:255–267.

135. Gershoff SN, McGandy RB, Nondasuta A, Tantiwongse P. Nutrition studies in Thailand: effects of calories, nutrient supplements, and health interventions on growth of preschool Thai village children. Am J Clin Nutr 1988;48:1214–1218.

136. Liu D-S, Bates CJ, Yin T-A, Wang X-B, Lu C-Q. Nutritional efficacy of a fortified weaning risk in a rural area near Beijing. Am J Clin Nutr 1993;57:506–511.

137. Rivera JA, González-Cossío T, Flores M, Romero M, Rivera M, Téllez-Rojo MM, et al. Multiple micronutrient supplementation increases the growth of Mexican infants. Am J Clin Nutr 2001;74:657–663.

138. Thu BD, Schultink W, Dillon D, Gross R, Leswara ND, Khoi HH. Effect of daily and weekly micronutrient supplementation on micronutrient deficiencies and growth in young Vietnamese children. Am J Clin Nutr 1999;69:80–86.

139. Smuts CM, Lombard CJ, Benade AJ, Dhansay MA, Berger J, Hop le T, et al. Efficacy of a foodlet-based multiple micronutrient supplement for preventing growth faltering, anemia, and micronutrient deficiency of infants: the four country IRIS trial pooled data analysis. J Nutr 2005;135:631S–638S.

140. Allen L, Shrimpton R. The International Research on Infant Supplementation Study: implications for programs and further research. J Nutr 2005;135:666S–669S.

141. Ramakrishnan U, Aburto N, McCabe G, Martorell R. Multimicronutrient interventions but not vitamin A or iron interventions alone improve child growth: results of three meta-analyses. J Nutr 2004;134:2592–2602.

142. Huffman SL, Baker J, Shumann MA, Zehner ER. The case for promoting multiple vitamin/mineral supplements for women of reproductive age in developing countries. Washington, DC: USAID/LINKAGES, 1998.

143. Allen KG, Backsstrand J, Stanek EJ, Pelto GH, Chavez A, Molina E, et al. The interactive effects of dietary quality on the growth and attained size of young Mexican children. Am J Clin Nutr 1992;56:353–364.

144. Torres A, Orav J, Willett W, Chen L. Association between protein intake and 1-y weight and height gains in Bangladeshi children aged 3–11 years. Am J Clin Nutr 1994;60:448–454.

145. Chernichovsky D, Coate D. The choice of diet for young children and its relation to children's growth. J Hum Res 1980;15:255–263.

146. Smith T, Earland J, Bhatia K, Heywood P, Singleton N. Linear growth of children in Papua New Guinea in relation to dietary, environmental and genetic factors. Ecol Food Nutr 1993;31:1–25.

147. Sigman M, Neumann CG, Baksh M, Bwibo NO, McDonald MA. Relation between nutrition and development in Kenyan toddlers. J Pediatr 1989;115:357–364.

148. Beaton GH, Calloway DH, Murphy SP. Estimated protein intakes of toddlers: predicted prevalence of inadequate intakes in village populations in Egypt, Kenya, and Mexico. Am J Clin Nutr 1992;55:902–911.

149. Allen LH, Backstrand JR, Pelto GH, Mata MP, Chavez A. The interactive effects of dietary quality on the growth and attained size of young Mexican children. Am J Clin Nutr 1992;56:353–364.

150. Golden MHN. Nutritional deficiency as a cause of growth failure. In: Human growth: basic and clinical aspects. Hernández M, Argente J, eds. Proceedings of the Sixth International Congress of Auxology, Madrid, Spain, September 15–19, 1991. Amsterdam: Excerpta Medica, 1992:175–182.

151. Golden MHN. Is complete catch-up possible for stunted malnourished children? Eur J Clin Nutr 1994;48:S58–S71.

152. Kaplan RM, Toshima MT. Does a reduced fat diet cause retardation in child growth? Prev Med 1992;21:33–52.

153. Caulfield LE, Huffman SL, Piwoz EG. Interventions to improve the complementary food intakes of 6–12 month old infants in developing countries: impact on growth, prevalence of malnutrition and potential contribution to child survival. Food Nutr Bull 1999;20:183–200.

154. Becker S, Black RE, Brown KH. Relative effects of diarrhea, fever, and dietary energy intake on weight gain in rural Bangladeshi children. Am J Clin Nutr 1991;53:1499–1503.

155. Engle P, Lhotska L. The role of care in programmatic actions for nutrition: designing programmes involving care. Food Nutr Bull 1999;20:121–135.

156. Beaton GH, Ghassemi H. Supplementary feeding programs for young children in developing countries. Am J Clin Nutr 1982;35:864–916.

157. Pinstrup-Andersen P, Pelletier D, Alderman H. Enhancing child growth and nutrition: lessons for action. In: Child growth and nutrition in developing countries: priorities for action. Pinstrup-Andersen P, Pelletier D, Alderman H, eds. Ithaca, NY: Cornell University Press, 1995:335–348.

158. Schroeder DG, Martorell R, Rivera J, Ruel M, Habicht J-P. Age differences in the impact of nutritional supplementation on growth. J Nutr 1995;125:1051S–1059S.

159. United Nations International Children's Emergency Fund. Facts for life. Geneva: United Nations International Children's Emergency Fund, 1991.

160. Dicken K, Griffiths M, Piwoz E. Designing by dialogue. Washington, DC: Academy for Educational Development, 1997.

161. Sternin M, Sternin J, Marsh. Designing a community-based nutrition program using the hearth model and the positive deviance approach: a field guide. Westport, CT: Save the Children, 1998.

162. Marsh DR, Schroeder DG. The positive deviance approach to improve health outcomes: experience and evidence from the field: preface. Food Nutr Bull 2002;23(suppl 4):3–6.

163. Fetterman DM, Kaftarian SJ, Wandersman A, eds. Empowerment evaluation: knowledge and tools for self-assessment and accountability. London: Sage, 1996.

164. Helen Keller International. Changing behaviors: guidelines on using research to increase consumption of micronutrients. Washington, DC: Helen Keller International, 1998.

165. United Nations International Children's Emergency Fund/World Health Organization. Global strategy for infant and young child feeding. Geneva: World Health Organization, 2003.

166. Manary MJ. Local production and provision of ready-to-use therapeutic food (RUTF) spread for the treatment of severe childhood malnutrition. Food Nutr Bull 2006;27(suppl 3):S83–S89.

167. Ashworth A. Efficacy and effectiveness of community-based treatment of severe malnutrition. Food Nutr Bull 2006;27(suppl 3):S24–S48.

168. Valid International. Community-based therapeutic care (CTC): a field manual. Oxford, UK: Valid International, 2006.

169. Gillespie S. Nutrition and poverty: overview. ACC/SCN Symposium Report, Nutrition Policy Paper 16. Geneva: World Health Organization, 1997.

170. Habicht JP, Victora CG, Vaughan JP. Program evaluations. Int J Epidemiol 1999;28:10–18.

# 13  Vitamin A Deficiency

## Keith P. West Jr. and Ian Darnton-Hill

## 13.1  INTRODUCTION

Vitamin A deficiency affects an estimated 125–130 million preschool-aged children and 7 million pregnant women in low-income countries [1]. Prevalent cases of preschool xerophthalmia are believed to number about 5 million, of which 10% can be considered potentially blinding, continuing to make this ocular condition the leading cause of preventable pediatric blindness in the developing world [2]. While there has been substantial progress toward its global control into the new millennium [3, 4], vitamin A deficiency remains an underlying cause of at least 650,000 early childhood deaths due to diarrhea, measles, malaria, and other infections each year [5]. It is an increasingly recognized problem among women of reproductive age in many developing countries [1, 6–10], appearing to reflect a chronicity of dietary deficiency that may extend from early childhood into adolescence [11] and adulthood. As has been observed at younger ages, maternal vitamin A deficiency may increase risks of maternal morbidity [12] and mortality [13, 14] in chronically undernourished and underserved populations.

This chapter provides a brief orientation to the vitamin itself, including its chemical structure, dietary sources, absorption, metabolism, and functions followed by discussions of the ocular, health, and survival consequences of vitamin A deficiency, its epidemiology in childhood and during the reproductive years, its clinicopathologic features, diagnosis, treatment, and approaches to prevention through dietary improvement, supplementation, and fortification.

## 13.2  THE NUTRIENT: VITAMIN A

Vitamin A is essential in regulating numerous key biologic processes in the body, including those involved in morphogenesis, growth, maturation, vision, reproduction, immunity, and more broadly, cellular differentiation and proliferation throughout life. Neither humans nor animals can synthesize or survive without vitamin A. Thus, it must be provided from the diet in sufficient amounts to meet all physiologic needs. Excellent, comprehensive reviews exist on the structure, absorption, metabolism, and functions of vitamin A [15, 16].

From: *Nutrition and Health: Nutrition and Health in Developing Countries, Second Edition*
Edited by: R. D. Semba & M. W. Bloem © Humana Press, Totowa, NJ

### 13.2.1  Structure and Nomenclature

The term vitamin A generically refers to compounds with biologic activity of all-*trans* retinol (R-OH) that, as depicted in Fig. 13.1, also include retinaldehyde (retinal) (R-CHO), various retinyl esters (the dominant form in food) (R-OO), and retinoic acids (R-OOH), among other vitamin A-active metabolic intermediates [15, 16]. Geometric isomers, in *trans* (straight-chained) and *cis* (bent-chained) configuration, are known to occur with retinal (e.g., in the visual cycle) and retinoic acid (e.g., that interact with nuclear receptors to activate gene transcription). Naturally occurring vitamin A compounds are considered a subset of a much larger family of "retinoids" that share a common, monocyclic, double-bonded chemical structure with various functional terminal groups. The vast majority of retinoids, however, are synthetic, investigative compounds that are not found in the diet and do not possess vitamin A activity [16, 17].

Lipid-soluble, yellow and orange pigments known as carotenoids, found mostly in plants, provide the precursor form of vitamin A to all mammalian diets. There are about 600 known carotenoids in nature, most of which have the general chemical structure $C_{40}H_{56}O_n$, where $n$, the number of oxygen molecules, can vary from 0 to 6.

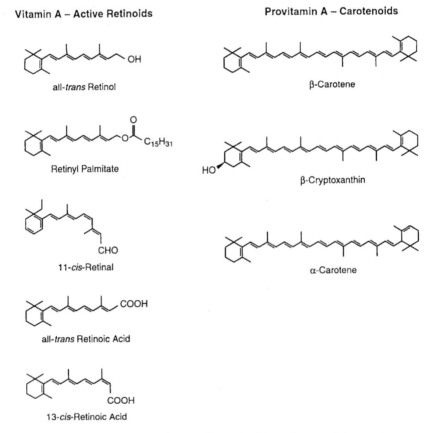

**Fig. 13.1.** Chemical structure of vitamin A-active retinoids and some of the most common provitamin A carotenoids. Ring and side-chain structures to which end groups are attached are referred in the text as R. (Adapted from [16] and [19]).

The colors of carotenoids derive from their extensive double-bond structures that absorb light. Carotenoids lacking oxygen in their chemical makeup are termed *hydrocarbon carotenoids* or *carotenes* (e.g., β-carotene, α-carotene, and lycopene), while those containing oxygen within their polar functional group are known as *xanthophylls* (e.g., β-cryptoxanthin). Among the many carotenoids, about 50 have been shown to possess biological activity of vitamin A, although far fewer are considered of nutritional importance in the human diet [16, 18, 19]. β-Carotene is the most ubiquitous carotenoid in foods and most efficient in its bioconversion to vitamin A, with a structure that, when centrally cleaved by enzyme action in the intestine, yields two identical molecules of retinal that can be reduced to retinol [20]. Asymmetric (or excentric) cleavage of β-carotene may also occur, generating molecules of different chain length called β-apocarotenals, the longer of which can still be shortened to form a molecule of either retinal or retinoic acid (Fig. 13.1) [16, 20]. Chemical structures of all-*trans* β-carotene, α-carotene, and β-cryptoxanthin, comprising the most abundant provitamin A carotenoids, are depicted in Fig. 13.1.

### 13.2.2  *Absorption and Transport*

As fat-soluble compounds, vitamin A and its precursor carotenoids are digested and absorbed by mechanisms common to lipids and thus require the presence of dietary fat. Approximately 5–10 g of fat in a meal appears to be sufficient to ensure absorption [16]. Preformed vitamin A esters are hydrolyzed to retinol by pancreatic and brush border enzymes, mixed with micelles, and absorbed by diffusion, although protein carriers may also facilitate uptake [21]. Within the enterocyte, most retinol from preformed and provitamin A sources is reesterified, incorporated into chylomicrons with other lipophilic molecules (including β-carotene), and secreted through intestinal lymph into portal circulation. A small proportion of unesterified retinol is also released into general circulation so that it can nourish tissues directly [16, 21]. Prior to reaching the liver, chylomicrons are reduced in size to remnants that, because of their lipophilic nature, retain most of the vitamin A. On reaching the liver, deposited retinyl esters are hydrolyzed to retinol and transferred to stellate cells to be stored as esters. Of the stored vitamin A in the body, 50–80% resides in the liver, from where it is released into circulation in association with retinol-binding protein (RBP) and transthyretin, a protein complex that transports the vitamin to tissue sites, where it is delivered to cells via RBP receptors located on the cell surface [16]. Within the cell, binding proteins escort retinoids to their cytoplasmic and nuclear sites of action.

### 13.2.3  *Metabolism and Functions*

Among numerous cellular mechanisms influenced by vitamin A, at least two reveal its essentiality and underscore its public health importance: one is the optical sensing mechanism in the visual cycle, the description of which earned George Wald the Nobel Prize in 1964 [22], and the other is in regulating gene transcription, which affects cellular differentiation and function.

#### 13.2.3.1  VISUAL CYCLE

Participation of vitamin A in the visual cycle enables vision under conditions of dim light. Inadequate vitamin A nutriture can sufficiently deprive rod cells to impair night vision and lead to "night blindness" (XN), a well-known disorder and clinical indicator of vitamin A deficiency [2]. In the cascade of events that enable low-light vision, vitamin A, in its aldehyde form (11-*cis* retinal), acts as a light-absorbing component (chromophore) of the visual pigment rhodopsin (known as visual purple), a protein that resides at the outer segments of rod photoreceptor cells in the retina [23, 24].

The initial step in vision occurs when light strikes photoreceptors and causes 11-*cis* retinal to isomerize to its all-*trans* form. The reaction induces a change in the conformation of rhodopsin that activates another protein, transducin, which initiates a change in cell membrane potential and a cascade of neurochemical reactions that transmit signals along the optic nerve to the brain, creating a visual image [24–26]. As all-*trans* retinal dissociates from rhodopsin, the visual pigment becomes colorless, at which point it is said to be "bleached." The open protein remains deactivated until it reattaches another molecule of 11-*cis* retinal to form rhodopsin and regain its photoreactive potential [24, 25].

The 11-*cis* retinal required to react with opsin comes from retinol that is either delivered to the retinal pigment epithelium (RPE) of the eye via choroidal circulation or has been recycled via the visual (or retinoid) cycle [24], depicted in Fig. 13.2. In this cycle, the all-*trans* retinal released from rhodopsin after bleaching is reduced to all-*trans* retinol and escorted by an interphotoreceptor retinoid-binding protein (IRBP) from the rod through an interstitial matrix to the RPE, where it is esterified, hydrolyzed, isomerized, and finally oxidized to 11-*cis* retinal. A parallel, light-induced pathway also exists in the RPE that forms 11-*cis* from all-*trans* retinal [24, 25]. The retinoid cycle is completed when the 11-*cis* isomer of retinal is escorted by the IRBP back from the pigment epithelium to the rod outer segment, where it attaches to opsin to form rhodopsin.

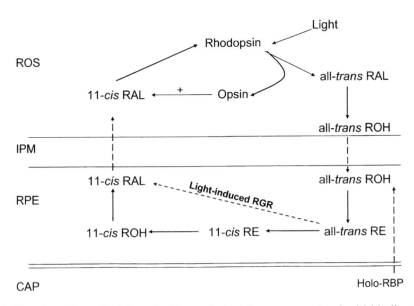

**Fig. 13.2.** The visual (or retinoid) cycle. Heavy dashed lines represent retinoid-binding transport of vitamin A. The lighter dashed line represents a light-induced conversion pathway to 11-*cis* retinal in the RPE. *CAP* choriocapillaris, *IPM* interphotoreceptor matrix, *RAL* retinal (retinaldehyde), *RE* retinyl ester, *RBP* retinol-binding protein, *RGR* retinal G-protein-linked receptor, *ROH* retinol, *ROS* rod photoreceptor outer segment; *RPE* retinal pigment epithelium.

### 13.2.3.2 GENE REGULATION

A second major function of vitamin A involves its ability to regulate gene transcription, representing the pathways by which vitamin A is likely to mediate most, although not all, of its effects on morphogenesis; organogenesis (e.g., lung, heart, vasculature, central nervous system, kidney, and limbs); immune function; tissue epithelialization (including the corneal and conjunctival surfaces of the eye); hematopoiesis; and bone growth and development [16, 27]. In the nucleus of the cell, all-*trans* and 9-*cis* retinoic acids complex with, and activate, retinoic acid (RAR) and retinoid X (RXR) receptors that bind to short sequences of deoxyribonucleic acid (DNA) known as retinoic acid response elements (RAREs) located within or near target genes. These interactions signal the process of gene transcription by ribonucleic acid (RNA) (Fig. 13.3), a process that leads to translation and synthesis of regulatory proteins that regulate cell differentiation, signaling, and apoptosis [16, 29, 30]. Over 500 genes are thought to respond to retinoic acid, either via the direct, activated RARE pathway or other, indirect, transcriptional mechanisms [16, 30]. Depletion in vitamin A nutriture alters molecular dynamics, which can lead to pathological changes in cell phenotype; these changes are most observable in rapidly dividing, bipotential cells, such as those that line the epithelial linings of the body. During vitamin A depletion, columnar and mucus-secreting goblet cells of the respiratory tract undergo reversible squamous metaplasia and keratinization [31, 32]. When these changes occur on the ocular surface, xerosis (drying) of the conjunctiva or cornea ensues, a histopathological feature of xerophthalmia [33].

### 13.2.4 Dietary Sources and Intake Recommendations

Dietary vitamin A is consumed in the human diet as preformed retinyl esters, from animal sources or fortified food items, or as provitamin A carotenoids obtained primarily from plant sources.

Preformed vitamin A activity can be estimated from food composition tables, in which 1 µg of retinol is the standard, defined as 1 µg of retinol activity equivalent (RAE)

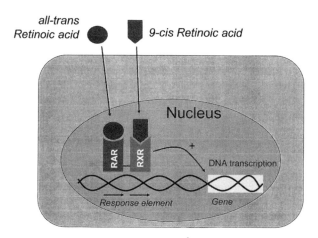

**Fig. 13.3.** Vitamin A mechanisms in gene regulation. Retinoic acids activate retinoic acid (RAR) or retinoid X (RXR) receptors that induce response elements on a DNA strand to signal gene transcription by messenger RNA. (Adapted from [28]).

[15, 34]. If the retinol content is reported as an ester, the molecular weight is factored in; for example, 1.83 µg of retinyl palmitate (the most common vitamin A ester in food) is equal to 1 µg RAE. It is generally held that 70–90% of preformed vitamin A from esters in the diet is absorbed and utilized [16]. Animal sources of preformed vitamin A include liver, fish liver oils, butter, cheese, milk fat, other dairy products and egg yolk [35]. Animal liver typically provides 5,000 to 12,000 µg RAE, cod liver oil about 4,200 µg RAE, whole cow or goat milk 30–60 µg RAE, and cheeses 100–200 µg RAE per 100 g edible portion [36]. Fortified foods provide another major dietary source of preformed vitamin A; these foods include ready-to-eat cereals, snack foods, beverages, margarine, and processed dairy products [37]. In developing countries, vitamin A-fortified foods remain limited in availability but may include sugar, cereal flours, edible oils [37, 38], margarine [39], and noodles [40]. Approximately 25% to 75% of the total vitamin A intake is preformed in developed countries, with North America at the upper end of this range [41, 42]. In many developing countries, preformed vitamin A intake typically lies at the lower end or below this range [15].

Breast milk provides in many poor settings the sole reliable source of vitamin A for the first 6 months of life or longer. Over 90% of its vitamin A content derives from highly bioavailable esters. Among healthy women, mature breast milk contains 600–700 µg of vitamin A per liter [36, 43], which, at an intake of about 725 mL per day, provides a breast-fed infant with 435–500 µg dietary vitamin A [43], an amount considered adequate during infancy [34]. In undernourished settings, breast milk can contain half this concentration [43, 44] but still provides clinically protective amounts to infants and toddlers [45, 46].

Provitamin A carotenoids represent the major source of dietary vitamin A in the developing world, among which β-carotene is the most ubiquitous and bioavailable [16, 19, 20]. Food sources of provitamin A carotenoids include dark green leafy vegetables, egg yolk, and deeply colored yellow and orange vegetables and fruits. Common items include carrot, ripe mango and papaya, yellow sweet potato, pumpkin, winter squash, apricot, and a number of indigenous fruits and plants [47, 48], in which β-carotene content typically ranges from about 3 to 18 mg per 100 g edible portion [18, 36, 47]. However, absorption and bioconversion of dietary β-carotene and other provitamin A carotenoids into retinol (i.e., bioefficacy) are part of a complex process that is influenced by numerous factors captured by the mnemonic SLAMENGHI [49–51], a term that reflects the effects of *s*pecies of carotenoid and its molecular *l*inkage; the *a*mount of carotenoid consumed in a meal; the source food *m*atrix (a dominant influence); *e*ffectors that may enhance or impair digestion, absorption, and bioconversion; the *n*utritional status, *g*enetic makeup, and *h*ealth status of the host; and nutrient *i*nteractions. Table 13.1 provides examples of these influences, several of which (i.e., food matrix and effectors) can be modified by food choices and the ways food is processed. For example, yellow fruit, cooked yams, added dietary fat, reduced fiber in meals, and various processes of cooking, mincing, or pureeing (e.g., of carrots and spinach) are all factors that favor bioavailability [55–61].

Historically, the molar retinol equivalency of dietary β-carotene and other provitamin A carotenoids has been assumed to be 6:1 and 12:1, respectively [15, 64]. For decades, these conversion factors guided vitamin A-carotenoid research and inferences [16] as well as food composition database estimates of vitamin A in meals and food supplies [36]. In 2001, based on evidence that had accumulated on the intakes of β-carotene

Table 13.1

SLAMENGHI mnemonic on factors that affect carotenoid bioavailability and bioconversion to vitamin A (modified from [49–51])

| | Factors | Examples |
|---|---|---|
| S | Species of carotenoid | All-trans β-carotene may be better absorbed than 9-*cis* β-carotene [50, 52] |
| L | Molecular linkage | Carotenoids in esters may be absorbed differently than in free form [50] |
| A | Amount of carotenoid eaten | Proportion absorbed may decrease with amount eaten at a meal [53]; Amount absorbed is proportionate to area under the concentration vs time curve [54] |
| M | Matrix in which carotenoid sits | β-carotene is better absorbed from soft yellow fruit than dark green leaves [55]; cooking, mincing or pureeing improves bioavailability [56–58] |
| E | Effectors of absorption & bioconversion | Fibre, pectin, cellulose, chlorophyll, type of fat & other carotenoid in food affect β-carotene bioavailability [52, 59]; 5-10 g of fat in meals improve β-carotene bioavailability [60–62] |
| N | Nutrient status of host | Low vitamin A status enhances enzyme cleavage & bioavailability of β-carotene (63); low protein & zinc status may reduce β-carotene bioavailability [52] |
| G | Genetic make-up of host | May partly explain differences in β-carotene response to dietary interventions (ie, carotenoid "responders" vs "non-responders") [52], or gender differences in serum β-carotene responses [51] |
| H | Health status of host | Carotenoid absorption may be reduced in intestinal and malabsorptive diseases [51, 52] |
| I | Interactions (biological) with other nutrients | Supplementation with one carotenoid may increase or decrease plasma concentrations of other carotenoids [51] |

required to prevent and cure night blindness [65], these ratios were doubled to 12:1 and 24:1, respectively, by the Institute of Medicine in the United States [34, 64].

While representing a major revision, carotenoid bioconversion to vitamin A may be even less efficient than indicated in these new ratios in undernourished populations [66], where retinol equivalencies for consuming β-carotene from mixtures of vegetables and fruit may be as high as about 21:1 [49, 67, 68]. Still, halving the retinol activity equivalency of provitamin A carotenoids in food had two immediate effects: It halved the bioavailable vitamin A content of the world's human food supply from carotenoid-rich foods and in doing so revealed a previous 55% overestimate of the vitamin A content in the global food supply (Fig. 13.4) [69], amplifying concern for populations that are largely dependent on vegetables and fruits to meet dietary vitamin A requirements [49].

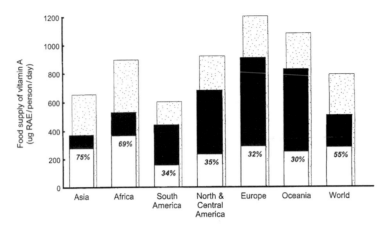

**Fig. 13.4.** Vitamin A activity in the regional and world food supplies as provitamin A carotenoids with their percent of total (based on a 12:1 β-carotene:retinol conversion ratio, white segments) and as preformed retinyl esters (black segments). Stippled bar represents the previous estimate of total vitamin A using a 6:1 conversion ratio, reflecting a 55% overestimate globally. (Based in part on [69]).

Table 13.2

Dietary reference intakes [34, 64] (DRI), recommended nutrient intakes [35] (RNI) and dietary requirements for vitamin A for children and adults by age and gender

| Age Group | Gender | DRI (34-IOM, 2001) Ug RAE per day | RNI (FAO, 2002) ug RE per day | Amount of β-Carotene-rich Food (gm) Required to Meet RDA | |
|---|---|---|---|---|---|
| | | | | Conversion Ratio | |
| | | RDA | RNI | 12:1 | 21:1 |
| Children | | | | | |
| 1-3 yr | M & F | 300 | 400 | 90 | 160 |
| 4-6 yr | M & F | 400 | 450 | 120 | 210 |
| 7-8 yr | M & F | 400 | 500 | 120 | 210 |
| 9 yr | M & F | 600 | 500 | 180 | 315 |
| Adolescents | | | | | |
| 10-13 yr | M/F | 600/600 | 400/600 | 180 | 315 |
| 14-18 yr | M/F | 900/700 | 400/600 | 240 | 420 |
| Adults | | | | | |
| 19-65 yr | M/F | 900/700 | 600/500 | 240 | 420 |
| Pregnancy | | ~760 | 850 | 320 | 320 |

Food items include an illustrative mixture of dark green leaves (spinach, kangkong or swamp cabbage, mustard greens) and one fruit (ie, mango), providing a mean beta-carotene content of 3 mg per 100 g [71], equal to 250 ug retinol activity equivalents (RAE) at a 12:1 beta-carotene:retinol equivalency ratio [34, 64] or 143 μg RAE at a conversion ratio of 21:1 [49]. Amounts required to meet the RDA assumes that 25% of the allowance is already being met by dietary sources of preformed vitamin A. An average RDA of 800 ug RAE represents the dietary target for ages 14-18 and 19-65 yr.

For example, in South Asia where historic per capita preformed vitamin A content of food has been less than 100 µg per day, the new 12:1 bioconversion ratio leads to a 42% reduction (or a 72% overestimate) in the calculated vitamin A content of food in the region (Fig. 13.4).

Second, the change made clear the virtual impossibility for most poor, young children to meet their vitamin A requirements through vegetable and fruit intake alone [7]. The problem is illustrated in Table 13.2, in which gram amounts of a provitamin A-containing food basket needed to meet the recommended dietary allowances (RDAs) [34, 64] are given by age, according to a 12:1 bioconversion ratio (for β-carotene), in a typical poor setting where, say, 25% of the RDA is eaten as preformed vitamin A. In this setting, a 4- to 6-year-old child needs to consume 120 g of vegetables and fruit daily to meet his or her RDA, depending on the ratio adopted, or at least a 40-g serving of such foods three times a day. The required intake is 75% more than this gram weight if a 21:1 ratio were accepted as the bioconversion ratio [49, 68].

Where less preformed vitamin A is typically consumed, the required intakes of vegetables and fruits increase further. The recommended nutrient intakes (RNIs) of the Food and Agricultural Organization (FAO) [35] are also listed, which, when used as the referent, produce similar estimates of intake to meet the vitamin A requirements from vegetables and fruits. The recent equivalency changes have also brought insight to decades of seemingly paradoxical epidemiologic data reporting the coexistence of xerophthalmia amid ample supplies of dark green leaves and other vegetable sources of vitamin A [72].

## 13.3 PUBLIC HEALTH SIGNIFICANCE OF VITAMIN A DEFICIENCY

Public health consequences that can be attributed to vitamin A deficiency are defined as *vitamin A deficiency disorders* or VADDs [73], which include the specific ocular manifestations of xerophthalmia and its blinding sequelae as well as nonspecific consequences such as anemia, immune dysfunction, increased susceptibility to infection, poorer growth, and mortality (Fig. 13.5). VADDs may also eventually come to include consequences in adult life that, in the future, might be causally linked to early-life exposure to vitamin A deficiency but for which human evidence is currently lacking [74–77]. At present, VADDs are known to occur in children and women of reproductive age.

### 13.3.1 Prevalence

The extent of vitamin A deficiency can be assessed by biochemical measures such as plasma or serum retinol or retinol-binding concentrations [78]. These indicators reflect status but are not disorders per se. On the other hand, the clinical stages of xerophthalmia (Greek *xeros* "drying"; *ophthalmia* "of the eye") [33] as well as their early, antecedent stages of squamous metaplasia that can be detected by impression cytology or impaired dark adaptation that precedes outright night blindness [79], serve both as physiologic indicators of deficiency and health consequences, or disorders, of vitamin A deficiency.

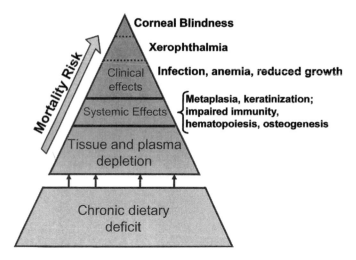

**Fig. 13.5.** Vitamin A deficiency disorders (VADDs). (Adapted from [1].).

#### 13.3.1.1 PRESCHOOL-AGED CHILDREN

A recent global analysis of data from low-income countries reported that about 25%, or 127 million, preschool-aged children are estimated to be vitamin A deficient (Table 13.3) [1]. The estimate is based on proportions of surveyed children with a serum retinol concentration below the conventional cutoff of 0.70 μmol/L [80]. A prevalence of deficiency of more than 15% among preschool children 6 to 71 months of age is considered to represent a public health problem [73, 80] (Table 13.4). Nearly 4.5 million preschoolers residing in the developing world, or nearly 1%, are thought to have xerophthalmia [1]. Highest-risk populations are in periequatorial regions of the world, especially in South and Southeast Asia, where about 45% of all cases reside, and in sub-Saharan Africa, which accounts for approximately 25% and 35% of the burdens of biochemical deficiency and xeropthhalmia, respectively [1].

The combined prevalence of xerophthalmia and serum retinol concentration below 0.70 μmol/L is depicted in Fig. 13.6. The lower threshold of 0.5% for xerophthalmia represents the World Health Organization (WHO) cutoff for Bitot's spots (X1B), while the 1.5% cutoff represents the sum of both thresholds for Bitot's spots (0.5%) and night blindness (1.0%) [73]. The resultant geographic pattern roughly parallels broad ecological indices of poverty and undernutrition. Findings of more recent surveys in China [81], India [82, 83], Nepal [7], Nigeria [84], Brazil [85], Venezuela [86], Cambodia [87], and the Western Pacific [88] generally uphold the conservative estimates in Table 13.3. Some studies have identified vitamin A deficiency at levels of public health concern in populations not previously considered deficient, such as in Turkey [89, 90] and among seminomadic Bedouin populations in Israel [91], where 15–20% of preschoolers have serum retinol concentrations below 0.70 μmol/L. Other studies have shown conditions to worsen amid conflict, such as in Afghanistan, where at least 7% of young children in Kabul City alone have xerophthalmia [92].

Table 13.3

Global prevalence of preschool child and maternal gestational vitamin A deficiency and xerophthalmia with numbers of cases, by region and selected countries [1][1]

| Region/Country | Under Five Years of Age | | | | | Pregnant Women | | | | |
| --- | --- | --- | --- | --- | --- | --- | --- | --- | --- | --- |
| | Population | Serum Retinol <0.70 µmol/L | | Xerophthalmia | | Live Births Per Year[2] | Serum Retinol <1.05 µmol/L | | Night Blindness | |
| | (000) | % | No. (000) | % | No. (000) | (000) | % | No. (000) | % | No. (000) |
| Africa | 103,934 | 32 | 33,406 | 1.5 | 1,593 | 24,425 | 22 | 5,383 | 4.4 | 1,075 |
| Ethiopia | 11,032 | 61 | 6,752 | 4.8 | 530 | 2,699 | 20 | 551 | 16.0 | 431 |
| Kenya | 4,462 | 41 | 1,812 | 2.0 | 89 | 992 | 23 | 231 | 2.2 | 21 |
| Nigeria | 17,880 | 28 | 5,024 | 1.0 | 179 | 4,176 | 10 | 426 | 2.4 | 100 |
| Senegal | 1,596 | 35 | 551 | 0.4 | 6 | 364 | 31 | 111 | 2.2 | 9 |
| South Africa | 4,909 | 33 | 1,635 | 1.6 | 79 | 1,055 | 24 | 258 | 2.2 | 23 |
| Other Countries | 64,055 | 28 | 17,632 | 1.1 | 710 | 15,139 | 25 | 3,806 | 3.3 | 492 |
| Eastern Mediterranean | 59,818 | 21 | 12,664 | 0.9 | 510 | 12,003 | 18 | 2,094 | 3.2 | 384 |
| Egypt | 8,081 | 12 | 962 | 0.3 | 26 | 1,720 | 20 | 351 | 9.4 | 162 |
| Morocco | 3,215 | 26 | 820 | 0.2 | 15 | 703 | 46 | 325 | 2.2 | 15 |
| Pakistan | 23,793 | 24 | 5,710 | 0.2 | 57 | 5,349 | 13 | 687 | 2.2 | 116 |
| Sudan | 4,162 | 24 | 991 | 1.7 | 72 | 944 | 6 | 60 | 2.2 | 20 |
| Other Countries | 20,597 | 20 | 4,181 | 1.7 | 340 | 3,287 | 20 | 671 | 2.2 | 71 |
| South/Southeast Asia | 169,009 | 33 | 55,812 | 1.2 | 2,026 | 36,214 | 24 | 8,797 | 10.9 | 3931 |
| Bangladesh | 15,120 | .31 | 4,649 | 0.6 | 94 | 3,504 | 22 | 788 | 12.8 | 449 |
| India | 114,976 | 31 | 35,355 | 1.6 | 1,790 | 24,489 | 23 | 5,583 | 12.1 | 2,963 |

(continued)

Table 13.3 (continued)

Global prevalence of preschool child and maternal gestational vitamin A deficiency and xerophthalmia with numbers of cases, by region and selected countries [1][1]

| Region/Country | Under Five Years of Age | | | | | Pregnant Women | | | | |
| | Population | Serum Retinol <0.70 µmol/L | | Xerophthalmia | | Live Births Per Year[2] | Serum Retinol <1.05 µmol/L | | Night Blindness | |
| | (000) | % | No. (000) | % | No. (000) | (000) | % | No. (000) | % | No. (000) |
|---|---|---|---|---|---|---|---|---|---|---|
| Sri Lanka | 1,597 | 35 | 564 | 1.6 | 26 | 328 | 27 | 89 | 3.7 | 12 |
| Other Countries | 11,825 | 12 | 1,375 | 0.2 | 20 | 2,497 | 14 | 336 | 3.1 | 78 |
| Western Pacific | 122,006 | 14 | 17,128 | 0.2 | 220 | 24,806 | 11 | 2,702 | 1.9 | 467 |
| China | 97,793 | 12 | 11,442 | 0.2 | 170 | 19,821 | 4 | 793 | 1.0 | 198 |
| Philippines | 9,800 | 38 | 3,724 | 0.1 | 7 | 2,064 | 44 | 916 | 8.6 | 178 |
| Viet Nam | 8,454 | 12 | 998 | 0.2 | 17 | 1,654 | 44 | 719 | 0.7 | 11 |
| Other Countries | 5,959 | 16 | 964 | 0.4 | 26 | 1,267 | 22 | 273 | 6.3 | 79 |
| Region of the Americas | 47,575 | 17 | 8,218 | 0.2 | 75 | 9,967 | 8 | 799 | 3.8 | 376 |
| Brazil | 15,993 | 14 | 2,187 | 0.1 | 20 | 3,344 | 5 | 167 | 3.7 | 125 |
| Guatemala | 1,816 | 13 | 244 | 0 | 0 | 399 | 11 | 45 | 1.9 | 7 |
| Peru | 2,898 | 13 | 377 | 0 | 0 | 610 | 9 | 55 | 7.6 | 46 |
| Other Countries | 26,868 | 20 | 5,410 | 0.2 | 55 | 5,614 | 10 | 533 | 3.5 | 197 |
| European Region[3] | 152 | 30 | 45 | 0 | 0 | ND | ND | ND | ND | ND |
| TOTAL | 502,494 | 25 | 127,273 | 0.9 | 4,424 | 129,304 | 18 | 19,776 | 5.8 | 6,233 |

[1] Combined and modified from Tables 1 and 2 in West, 2002 [1]. Numbers rounded from original report. Individual country survey references available in original report.

[2] Number of live births is used as a proxy for number of pregnancies.

[3] Based solely on one survey in Macedonia as reported by the Micronutrient Deficiency Information System of the World Health Organization (see reference 1).

ND=not determined.

Table 13.4

IVACG/WHO xerophthalmia classification and minimum indicator prevalence criteria for vitamin A deficiency to be a public health problem (73)

| Definition (Code) | Minimum Prevalence |
|---|---|
| Children 2-5 years of age | |
| Night blindness (XN) | 1.0% |
| Conjunctival xerosis (XIA) | – |
| Bitot's spots (X1B) | 0.5% |
| Cornea xerosis (X2) | |
| Corneal ulceration/ Keratomalacia (X3) | 0.01% |
| Xerophthalmic corneal scar (XS) | 0.05% |
| Serum retinol <0.70 μmol/L | 15.0% |
| Women of Childbearing Age | |
| Night blindness (XN) during most recent pregnancy | 5.0% |

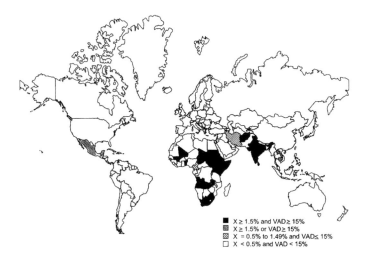

X ≥ 1.5% and VAD≥ 15%
X ≥ 1.5% or VAD≥ 15%
X = 0.5% to 1.49% and VAD≤ 15%
X < 0.5% and VAD < 15%

**Fig. 13.6.** Global distribution of preschool child vitamin A deficiency defined by joint prevalence distributions of deficient serum retinol concentration (<0.70 μmol/L) or abnormal conjunctival impression cytology (both defining vitamin A deficiency, labeled VAD), or xerophthalmia (labeled X) [1].

### 13.3.1.2 NEWBORNS AND NEONATES

Early infancy is a precarious period as limited materno-fetal transfer of retinol endows infants with only a 2-week to 2-month hepatic supply of vitamin A and low circulating retinol concentrations [93–95]. Whereas body vitamin A stores rise toward normal during infancy in well-nourished societies [95, 96], the status of infants reared under vitamin A-deprived and infection-exposed conditions tends to remain depressed [95,

97], which may increase risks of morbidity and mortality in the first 6 to 12 months of life, as discussed in Section 13.3.3. Prematurity exacerbates the vitamin A-depleted state at birth [98]. However, poor access to newborns and their high mortality in the developing countries coupled with difficulties in drawing blood and uncertainty about the plasma retinol cutoff have left the extent and severity of neonatal vitamin A deficiency unknown at this time.

### 13.3.1.3 SCHOOL-AGED CHILDREN

In undernourished populations, vitamin A deficiency may extend into the periadolescent years, as appears to be the case in Southeastern Asia, where limited data suggest that 23% of children 5 to 15 years of age, or about 83 million children, may have serum retinol concentrations below 0.70 μmol/L and nearly 3% to have nonblinding, mild xerophthalmia (night blindness or Bitot's spots) [99]. While risk factors and health consequences of deficiency at this age are unknown, poor adolescent vitamin A nutriture may predispose girls to chronic vitamin A deficiency in adult life that could exacerbate deficiency during pregnancy and lactation [12].

### 13.3.1.4 WOMEN OF REPRODUCTIVE AGE

Vitamin A deficiency afflicts women of child-bearing ages in undernourished societies, especially in the latter half of pregnancy when nutritional demands are high, circulating vitamin A is relatively low and risk of developing night blindness greatest [12]. Population data on serum retinol distributions during and following pregnancy, however, remain sparse. The current best estimate is that between about 10% and 45% of pregnant women in low-income countries have marginal-to-deficient serum retinol concentrations (<1.05 μmol/L), with the average prevalence 18%, or about 20 million affected gravida in a given year [1] (Table 13.3). On the other hand, because a history of night blindness can be reliably ascertained [100], a number of surveys have elicited a history of maternal night blindness, yielding an overall prevalence estimate of about 6%, with estimates generally ranging from 10% to 20% where malnutrition and childhood vitamin A deficiency are known to exist [1]. A provisional cutoff of more than 5% has been set for classifying night blindness during pregnancy as a public health problem (Table 13.4) [73, 100].

### 13.3.2 *Effects on Child Morbidity and Mortality*

Vitamin A deficiency has long been known as the "anti-infective" vitamin [101, 102]. Decades of animal experiments showed that progressive vitamin A depletion leads to poor growth, weight loss, infection, and death, usually before eye signs develop [103]. The regulatory roles of vitamin A in maintaining epithelial cell differentiation and function and immune competence [104, 105] provide biologic plausibility to its importance in decreasing severity and mortality from infectious diseases [2].

A modern era of epidemiologic investigation into the role of vitamin A deficiency in child mortality was launched with community-based studies of Sommer and colleagues in the late 1970s, which found Indonesian children with mild xerophthalmia, but no other obvious nutritional stress, to be two to three times more likely to develop diarrhea or respiratory infection [106] and more likely, in a dose-responsive fashion, to die [107] than children without eye signs (Fig. 13.7). Additional longitudinal studies in India [108]

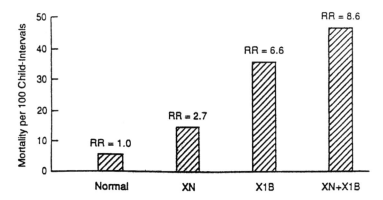

**Fig. 13.7.** Mortality rates of Indonesian preschool children without xerophthalmia (normal) and by severity of "mild" xerophthalmia [XN < X1B < (XN + X1B)]. *RR* relative risk, X1*B* Bitot's spots, XN night blindness (Adapted from [107].).

and Thailand [109] have generally corroborated increased risks of incident morbidity among children with mild xerophthalmia or hyporetinolemia, respectively.

Between 1986 and 1992, six of eight population-based intervention trials that enrolled more than 165,000 children in Southeast Asia [110, 111], South Asia [112–115], and Africa [116, 117] found that vitamin A supplementation, achieved by periodic high-potency dosing (e.g., 200,000 IU if > 12 months of age, half-dose below 12 months), weekly low-potency dosing (15,000 IU), or food fortification, could reduce child mortality by 6% to 54% (Fig. 13.8). Meta-analyses of findings from these trials have shown that, in areas of endemic vitamin A deficiency, all-cause preschool child mortality can be reduced, on average, by 23% to 34% by vitamin A interventions [118–121], with the effect size depending on the studies included and analytic approaches taken. Subsequent program effectiveness analyses, based on non-experimental designs, continue to support a favorable impact of vitamin A on child survival. In the Yemen, admissions and case fatality for severe, dehydrating diarrhea among preschoolers presenting to four major hospitals in Sana'a were reduced by 25% and about 50%, respectively, after the first year of semiannual vitamin A supplementation [122]. In Nepal, the 2001 Demographic and Health Survey, conducted after several years of national supplementation activities, estimated vitamin A receipt to be consistent with an approximately 50% decline in 1- to 4-year-old child mortality [123]. With greater emphasis given to vitamin A supplementation in recent years, it appears that global progress has been made to reduce child deaths from vitamin A deficiency, with estimates having fallen from 1.3 to 2.5 million preventable deaths [124] to about 650,000 deaths [125] annually from 1992 to 2003.

The remarkably consistent effect on mortality can be partly explained by an ability of vitamin A to lower case fatality from measles by about 50%, as observed in field trials and hospital-based treatment trials [2, 126–129] (Fig. 13.9). Vitamin A can be expected to lower risk of fatality from severe diarrhea and dysentery by about 40% [112, 114, 115, 130] and possibly *Plasmodium falciparum* malaria as well, based on findings from a trial in Papua New Guinea [131]. A recent WHO-sponsored analysis to calculate global and regional burdens of disease estimated about 50% reductions in case fatality from

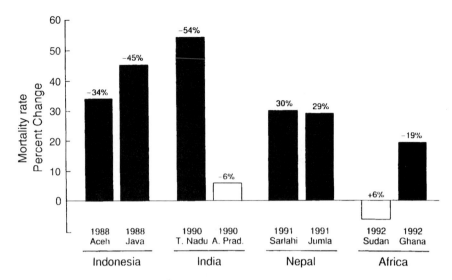

**Fig. 13.8.** Percent changes in mortality rates of children between about 6 or 12 months to less than 84 months of age receiving vitamin A compared to children receiving control supplements while participating in community intervention trials in Southeast Asia (Aceh [110] and Java [111], Indonesia); South Asia (Tamil Nadu [112] and Andhra Pradesh [113], India); Sarlahi [114] and Jumla [115], Nepal; and Africa (Ghana [116] and Sudan [117]). Total number of enrolled children more than 165,000 [2]. Black bars = Statistically significant difference from control group; White bars = Difference not significant

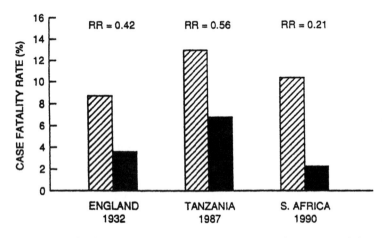

**Fig. 13.9.** Fatality rates of children hospitalized with severe measles who participated in clinical vitamin A trials in England [126], Tanzania [127], and South Africa [128]. Risk of mortality among vitamin A recipients was less than 50% that of controls in each study. *RR* relative risk (From [125]).

diarrhea and measles among vitamin A recipients [125]. Similarly, high-potency vitamin A supplementation of HIV-infected children in several African trials has reduced adverse outcomes by 50% or more, including all-cause and diarrhea-associated mortality [132, 133], diarrhea incidence or duration [133, 134], and stunting [135] over 18- to 24-month periods of follow-up. Notwithstanding these protective effects against several potentially fatal infectious diseases, vitamin A supplementation has had little influence on risk of mortality from acute lower-respiratory infections, unrelated to measles, for reasons that remain poorly understood [136].

### 13.3.3  Effects on Infant Morbidity and Mortality

Vitamin A may favor infant survival in undernourished populations, depending on the age dosed, "route" of supplementation, nutritional status, and dominant disease patterns. In both Nepal [137] and Tanzania [138], reaching the fetus and infant via routine maternal supplementation with vitamin A or β-carotene during pregnancy and lactation had no overall effect on infant mortality, except for a subset of infants born to night-blind women in Nepal who were more likely to survive following maternal vitamin A supplementation [139]. Direct dosing trials in South Asia and Africa, where infants were periodically given oral vitamin A (ranging from 25,000 to 100,00 IU per dose) from about 1 to 5 months of age, also failed to benefit infant survival [140, 141]. On the other hand, in recent years three randomized, double-blind, placebo-controlled trials in Southern Asia (Indonesia, India, and Bangladesh) reported reductions of 64% [142], 23% [143], and 15% (R. Klemm et al., unpublished data, 2007) in mortality during the first year of life following oral supplementation with about 50,000 IU of vitamin A (one fourth the standard vitamin A prophylactic dosage) in oil shortly after birth. Survival curves for the first two newborn vitamin A trials are depicted in Fig. 13.10. While causal

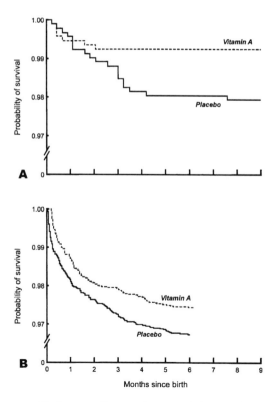

**Fig. 13.10.** Survival curves of infants orally supplemented shortly after birth with either vitamin A (~50,000 IU) or placebo in **A** Indonesia [142] and **B** southern India [143].

paths uniquely responsive to early neonatal (vs. later) high-potency vitamin A receipt remain poorly understood, diseases in early infancy that could plausibly respond include respiratory infections (e.g., from *Streptococcus pneumoniae*) [144], diarrhea, sepsis, and necrotizing enterocolitis [95].

Only one newborn vitamin A trial to date has been conducted outside Asia, in an urban population in Zimbabwe, where mothers were otherwise normal in their vitamin A status (i.e., <1% with a serum retinol concentration below 0.70 μmol/L). In this setting, a 50,000 IU oral dose of vitamin A given to either HIV-positive [145] or HIV-negative [146] infants at birth failed to confer a survival benefit during infancy. Maternal receipt of 400,000 IU of vitamin A immediately after birth also failed to improve infant survival in this population [145, 146]. Additional trials are needed in Africa, especially, to assess effects of newborn vitamin A on infant survival in malnourished, malaria-endemic areas.

### 13.3.4   Effects on Maternal Morbidity and Mortality

In chronically undernourished populations, vitamin A deficiency can pose a health risk to women during pregnancy and lactation. In rural South Asia [147–150] and sub-Saharan Africa [1] and in poor, urban areas of Latin America [1, 151], 10–20% of women have reported night blindness in pregnancy. Maternal night blindness is likely due to maternal vitamin A deficiency as it often develops late in pregnancy [12], when serum retinol is low [152], and then typically resolves within days after childbirth. The condition is associated with a poor diet, anemia, wasting undernutrition, and increased occurrence of diarrhea and other morbid symptoms [12, 149, 150, 153].

In Nepal, women who developed night blindness during pregnancy were at about a four-fold higher risk of dying during pregnancy through the first 2 years after parturition (3,600 per 100,000 person-years) than mothers who reported not having the condition (Fig. 13.11). Most often, causes of death among women who were night blind were associated with infection [14]. Under such high-risk conditions, such as in southern Nepal where maternal

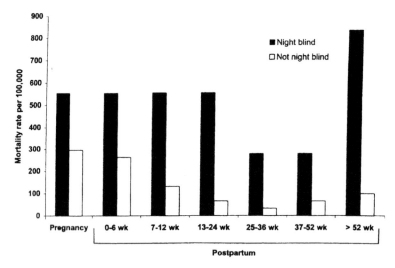

**Fig. 13.11.** Mortality rates per 100,000 person-years for up to 2 years postparturition among Nepalese mothers who prospectively reported being or not being night blind during pregnancy [14].

mortality rates exceed 600 per 100,000, once-weekly supplementation with either vitamin A or β-carotene at dosages that approximated an RDA (7000 μg RAE or 42 mg, respectively), reduced all-cause pregnancy-related mortality by 40% and 49%, respectively [13]. Given the plethora of physiologic effects of vitamin A, it is plausible that several potentially fatal causal paths could have responded to improved vitamin A (or β-carotene) nutriture, such as puerperal sepsis, other infections, anemia-involved causes, hypertensive diseases, and hemorrhage [154]. Notably, the value of late-gestational vitamin A therapy for prophylaxis against puerperal sepsis was recognized in humans and animals as early as the 1930s [155]. Higher maternal serum retinol concentration and vitamin A supplement receipt were associated with improved proinflammatory cytokine responses to infection among Ghanaian gravida [156]. However, it is likely that thresholds, or plateaus, in response to vitamin A may exist. For example, in a trial recently completed in Bangladesh, weekly antenatal vitamin A or β-carotene, at recommended levels, failed to improve maternal or infant survival in a population in whom vitamin A status was marginal to normal and maternal mortality far lower than in Nepal (K. West et al., unpublished data, 2007).

In HIV-positive populations, vitamin A deficiency is clearly associated with adverse pregnancy health. A strong dose–risk gradient has been demonstrated between maternal serum retinol concentration and risk of vertical transmission of HIV [157]. Cervico-vaginal shedding of HIV DNA [158], genital tract infections [159], and more variably, clinical mastitis [160, 161] have also been associated with poor maternal vitamin A status. The strength and consistency of the evidence of association suggests that vitamin A interventions could improve maternal health and infant survival and reduce HIV transmission [162]. However, vitamin A and related interventions in HIV settings have had mixed results.

In Tanzania, daily vitamin A (5,000 IU) plus high-dose β-carotene (30 mg) supplementation of HIV-infected pregnant women beginning in the third trimester failed to reduce risks of low birth weight or perinatal mortality [163] and may have increased lower genital tract shedding [164] and transmission of HIV from mother to infant [165]. However, when the same vitamin A plus β-carotene supplement was tested among South African HIV-infected pregnant women, no differences in fetal loss, infant mortality, or HIV transmission were noted relative to controls [166]. Mothers receiving vitamin A and β-carotene were less likely to deliver preterm (11% vs. 17% in controls, $p = .03$) [167], and their infants were better able to maintain normal gut permeability compared to controls [168]. In Malawi, antenatal receipt of 10,000 IU of vitamin A from 18–28 weeks gestation onward improved birth weight by 90 g, reduced low birth weight (<2.5 kg) by 33%, and nearly halved the rate of anemia in infants at 6 weeks of age but had no impact on vertical HIV transmission [169]. In Zimbabwe, a single, 400,000 IU dose of vitamin A given to vitamin A-sufficient, HIV-negative mothers shortly after delivery had no effect on infant mortality HIV [145]. The supplement also did not affect the survival or overall risk of HIV transmission among infants born to vitamin A-supplemented HIV-positive mothers [146]. These mixed effects do not clearly support an anti-HIV role for maternal vitamin A use, with or without β-carotene, in sub-Saharan Africa at this time.

## 13.4    HISTORICAL BACKGROUND

Several excellent treatises offer rich, historical accounts of the diverse paths to the discovery of vitamin A and its functions by scientific pioneers, especially in the modern era of the 19th and 20th centuries [170–173]. Vitamin A deficiency, manifest as xerophthalmia, has plagued humankind for at least 3,500 years. Night blindness and its treatment with foods now known to be rich in preformed vitamin A esters such as roasted ox, ass, or beef liver was reported from ancient Assyria, Egypt, and Greece [170] (Table 13.5). Medical treatises from Europe, China, the Middle East, and Southeast Asia throughout the first and second millennia documented the occurrence of night blindness and therapeutic value of animal liver. Clinical descriptions of corneal xerophthalmia first appeared in England in the 18th century, followed by additional reports in the 19th and early 20th centuries of its occurrence, in association with infection and poor growth, and its cure with animal and fish liver and oil products [170]. Characterization of conjunctival xerosis with superficial accumulation of keratinized cells and bacilli, named a Bitot's spot, was described as early as 1860 by von Huebbenet and then by its namesake, Bitot, in France in 1863.

In the 1870s, the foundation for understanding the visual cycle was laid by Franz Boll and Willy Kuhne in Germany. Working with frog eyes, they observed that light bleached the purple pigment (they termed *visual purple*) in retinal rod cells, and that its regeneration required interaction with the RPE [173]. Recognition of the existence of indispensable, accessory nutritional factors emerged in the late 19th century. In Japan, in 1904, Mori drew attention to the inadequacy of rice- and barley-based diets of children with *Hikan* (a disease that included keratomalacia) and the condition's rapid clinical response to cod liver oil [174]. Interestingly, the therapeutic or preventive value of dark green leaves (rich dietary β-carotene source) against xerophthalmia was not reported in the early literature. Indeed, Westhoff, working in Indonesia in 1911, drew attention to more frequent occurrence of xerophthalmia in areas where green leafy vegetables were often consumed [175].

The dawning of modern, experimental animal nutrition in the early 20th century led to the discovery of "vitamines" [172]. McCollum and Davis [176] and, at nearly the same time, Osborne and Mendel [177] showed that the addition of an ether-soluble extract from butter, egg yolk, or milk to the diets of young rats could promote growth, reduce morbidity, and enhance survival. McCollum called the extract "fat-soluble A," which was shortly thereafter renamed "Vitamine A."

The clinical relevance of the animal findings became quickly apparent. Bloch, a Danish pediatrician during World War I, observed how orphans subsisting on a fat-free milk, oatmeal, and barley soup diet were at greater risk of keratomalacia, infection, and poor growth, similar to McCollum's vitamin A-deficient animals, compared to children whose diet included a modest amount of whole milk [178]. He surmised vitamin A deficiency to be the underlying cause of "dystrophia alipogenetica." With Wolbach and Howe's classic description in 1923 of metaplasia and keratinization of epithelial linings in vitamin A-depleted animals [179], loss of the "barrier function" of epithelial linings became a plausible explanation for their decreased resistance to infection.

Animal experiments in the 1920s led Green and Melanby to coin vitamin A as an "anti-infective" factor [172, 180], while seminal clinical studies in humans through the 1940s continued to relate vitamin A deficiency or xerophthalmia to infectious disease risk [181, 182]. The 1930s found George Wald piecing together the many components of the visual cycle that earned him a Nobel Prize in 1966 [183]. During this time, observations emerged of an inverse relationship between febrile illness and plasma vitamin A concentration [184] and urinary excretion of vitamin A during disease [185], both now

**Table 13.5**
Historical benchmarks the discovery of vitamin A, its deficiency and prevention

| | | |
|---|---|---|
| *Antiquity* | | *Night blindness recognized in Egypt, Greece, Asyria* |
| 460–325 BC | | Ancient egyptians and greeks cured night blindness with roasted oken liver [170] |
| 19th C | | Magendie reports corneal xerophthalmia in dogs following dietary manipulation von Hubbenet and Bitot describe conjunctival xerosis with "Bitot's Spots" [195] Boll discovers in frogs that light bleaches the retina; Kuhne refines observations and discovers "visual purple" [173] |
| | | Budd, in England, describes corneal xerophthalmia in East Indians and Livingston notes [xerophthalmic] corneal lesions in Africans subsisting on manioc diet [170] |
| | | Guggenheim reports night blindness with keratomalacia in Russian children during Great Lenten Fast [170] Lunnin points to other indispensable survival factors in whole milk [than those known at the time] [172] |
| 20th C | 1904 | Mori reports "Hikan" in Japanese children which responds to cod liver oil and liver [174] |
| | 1912 | Hopkins postulates "accessory factors" necessary for life; Funk names these factors "vitamines" [172] |
| | 1913 | McCollum and Davis [176], and Osborne and Mendell [177] discover "fat soluble A" |
| | 1919 | Bloch finds xerophthalmia in Danish orphans subsisting on milk-fat free, oatmeal diet [178] |
| | 1928 | Green and Melanby coin term "anti-infective" for vitamin A [180] |
| | 1931 | Green and Pindar show cod liver oil reduces puerperal fever [155] |
| | 1932 | Ellison reports that vitamin A reduces measles fatality [189] |
| | 1935 | Wald describes "the visual cycle" [183] |
| | 1948 | Ramalingaswami relates "nutritional diarrhea" to vitamin A deficiency [182] |
| | 1960 | Gopalan draws global attention to endemic vitamin A deficiency in India [190] |
| | 1966 | McLaren publishes detailed photo accounts of xerophthalmia [191] |
| | 1964 | Wald wins the Nobel Prize for describing the visual cycle [173] |
| | | Oomen, McLaren and Escapini publish "Epidemiology and Public Health Aspects of Hypovitaminosis A" [192] |
| | 1974 | The International Vitamin A Consultative Group is established [194] |

(continued)

Table 13.5 (continued)
Historical benchmarks the discovery of vitamin A, its deficiency and prevention

| Antiquity | Night blindness recognized in Egypt, Greece, Asyria |
|---|---|
| 1983–84 | Sommer and colleagues in Indonesia report mild xerophthalmia is associated with increased risk of incident child morbidity [106] and mortality [107] |
| 1986 | Sommer and colleagues report that vitamin A can reduce child mortality in Indonesia [110] |
| 1989 | UNICEF World Summit for Children considers vitamin A essential for child survival [197] |
| 1992 | At the International Conference on Nutrition in Rome, countries commit to preventing vitamin A deficiency [198] |
| 1995 | Bioavailability of provitamin A carotenoids in vegetables challenged by Clive West and coworkers in Indonesia [66–68, 70] |
| 1998 | Christian and colleagues in Nepal reveal maternal night blindness as indicator of maternal vitamin A deficiency, poor health and survival [12,14] |
| 1999 | West and coworkers in Nepal report vitamin A or B-carotene supplementation can lower maternal mortality [13] |
| 2001 | Institute of Medicine in the United States revises the β-carotene:retinol conversion ratio from 6:1 to 12:1, and the ratio for other provitamin A carotenoids from 12:1 to 24:1 [64] |
| 2002 | Annecy Accords define "vitamin A deficiency disorders", add maternal night blindness as an indicator of deficiency, recognize inability of young children to eat adequate amounts of vitamin A from vegetables alone [73]. |
| 2003 | Ramathullah et al report from India a 23% reduction in infant mortality by giving newborns a single ~50,000 IU oral dose of vitamin A [143], affirming earlier work by Humphrey et al. in Indonesia [142]. |

understood to be part of the acute-phase response to inflammation [186–188]. Successful therapeutic applications of vitamin A were also reported in those years, for example, in reducing childhood fatality from measles [189], puerperal fever in mothers [155], and other infectious conditions [172].

Epidemiologic studies since the 1950s have guided our understanding of the public health consequences of vitamin A deficiency and benefits of its prevention in human populations. Clinical investigations by Gopalan et al. in India [190] and McLaren et al. in Jordan [191] provided photographic and clinical detail of conjunctival and corneal xerophthalmia and its interactions between vitamin A and protein-energy deficiencies. In 1964, Oomen, McLaren, and Escapini's 46-country FAO/WHO "survey" of national health and nutrition institutions from extant reports on xerophthalmia revealed the global extent of this problem throughout the developing world [192]. While the lack of population-based data and biases inherent in this type of data were appreciated, the report mobilized further surveys, research, and commitment to prevent vitamin A deficiency and served as the forerunner of the current WHO micronutrient deficiency information system [193]. By 1974 the International Vitamin A Consultative Group (IVACG) was formed, which provided essential global scientific and policy leadership in vitamin A deficiency prevention for over a quarter of a century [194].

The modern era of understanding the public health consequences of childhood vitamin A deficiency and the impact of its prevention was ushered in with a national survey, longitudinal study, and a series of hospital-based clinical studies of xerophthalmia by Sommer and colleagues in Indonesia in the late 1970s [195]. Most notable from this work were reports that children with nonblinding, mild xerophthalmia (night blindness and Bitot's spots) were at higher risks of death (Fig. 13.7) [107], diarrhea, and respiratory infections [106] than children without these eye signs, and that an estimated 5 million potentially blinding cases of corneal xerophthalmia occurred each year [196]. The dose-response nature of mortality risk with mild eye signs suggested a causal association, prompting intervention trials that came to reveal that vitamin A could reduce child mortality (Fig. 13.8).

## 13.5 EPIDEMIOLOGY

Our understanding of the epidemiology of vitamin A deficiency derives largely from studies of the mild and more frequent stages of xerophthalmia (night blindness [XN] and Bitot's spots [X1B]) and evidence of association with low serum retinol concentrations. The distribution of deficiency by location, person, and time can identify risk factors that may be proximal and causal (e.g., diet, care, and morbidity), that may be less proximal but having causal influence (e.g., socioeconomic status [SES], seasonal food availability), or that reflect indirect association. Knowledge of risk factors can influence the design and targeting of interventions and provide the "context" within which vitamin A deficiency exists.

### 13.5.1  Location

Vitamin A deficiency is a public health problem in approximately 78 developing countries [193] largely spanning periequatorial regions of the world (Fig. 13.6) [1], where vast numbers of rural and urban poor are exposed to inadequate dietary vitamin A and frequent infections. The extent and severity of deficiency appears most widespread across large areas of South and Southeast Asia and Sahelian and sub-Saharan Africa, where, on an ecological level, food supplies lack preformed vitamin A [69] (Fig. 13.4).

Vitamin A deficiency tends to cluster within countries, providing insight into causation and groups for targeting. Where national surveys or surveillance data exist [199–201], it is clear that regions with a high prevalence of xerophthalmia share common dietary and other ecologic exposures (e.g., poverty, high levels of infectious diseases, poor development and health infrastructures, and strong seasonal fluctuation in food availability). Clustering of risk appears to intensify within smaller, disadvantaged groupings. Population-based surveys in Africa (Malawi and Zambia), South Asia (Bangladesh and Nepal), and Southeast Asia (Indonesia) revealed a consistent 1.5- to 2.0-fold risk of xerophthalmia among children in villages where other children have the condition [202, 203]. More striking is a 7- to 13-fold higher risk of having, or developing, xerophthalmia among children whose siblings have the condition compared to children whose siblings are nonxerophthalmic [202] (Table 13.6). A similar parent–child intensity of clustering has been observed in Cambodia, where young children were four or five times more likely to have xerophthalmia when the mother was night blind, who in turn was nine times more likely to be night blind if one of her children had xerophthalmia [87]. This high level of shared risk of vitamin A deficiency is likely due to common exposures to a chronic poor diet [204, 205] and inadequate care, malnutrition, and disease that characterize mothers [206] and children

Table 13.6

Crude and age-adjusted village and household pairwise odds ratios for risk of xerophthalmia among preschool children[1] [202]

| Odds Ratio | Malawi | | Zambia | | Indonesia | | Nepal | |
|---|---|---|---|---|---|---|---|---|
| | n | OR[2] | n | OR | n | OR | n | OR |
| Unadjusted estimates | | | | | | | | |
| Village | 50 | 1.2 | 110 | 1.7 | 460 | 1.7 | 40 | 2.2 |
| | | (1.0–1.4)[3] | | (0.9–3.1) | | (1.4–2.2) | | (1.5–3.2) |
| Household | 2899 | 4.4 | 2449 | 7.4 | 16337 | 9.7 | 2909 | 7.7 |
| | | (2.2–8.8) | | (3.0–17.9) | | (6.6–14.2) | | (4.5–13.2) |
| Age-adjusted estimates | | | | | | | | |
| Village | | 1.2 | | 1.7 | | 1.8 | | 2.3 |
| | | (1.0–1.5) | | (0.9–3.2) | | (1.4–2.2) | | (1.6–3.4) |
| Household | | 7.3 | | 7.9 | | 10.5 | | 13.2 |
| | | (3.2–16.7) | | (3.5–17.8) | | (7.0–15.7) | | (6.0–29.0) |

[1] Numbers of children <6 years of age in each country: Malawi (n = 5441); Zambia (n = 4316); Indonesia (n = 28,586); and Nepal (n = 4764).

[2] Pairwise odds ratio based on alternating logistic regression.

[3] 95% confidence intervals in parentheses.

in high-risk families. For example, in Cambodia xerophthalmia was more likely found among children or mothers in homes where diarrhea was common [87]. Children in Nepalese households with a sibling history of xerophthalmia faced a twofold higher risk of early childhood death [207] than children in nonxerophthalmic households. Thus, xerophthalmia in early childhood or a positive history of maternal night blindness are not only indications for treatment [33, 73] but also serve to emphasize a need for preventive services within households and the communities of cases.

### 13.5.2  Persons at Risk

#### 13.5.2.1  AGE

Xerophthalmia (vitamin A deficiency) follows rather consistent patterns with respect to age, gender, and socioeconomic factors. Based on hospital admissions data from Indonesia [195] and Nepal [208], the incidence of corneal xerophthalmia, which rarely affects more than 0.1% of a population even in high-risk areas [195], appears to peak at 2 to 3 years of age (Fig. 13.12). Acute onset of corneal disease may follow any combination of recent weaning from the breast with sole dependence on a poor household diet, an episode of severe measles, persistent diarrhea, other severe febrile illness, or wasting malnutrition, coupled with poor child care [2, 195]. Although the incidence of corneal disease declines beyond age 3, the prevalence of healed, corneal scarring (XS), which represents permanent, potentially blinding sequelae, continues to rise among survivors [2, 195].

The prevalence of mild xerophthalmia (XN and X1B) typically, although not always [209], rises with age through the fifth year of life and often beyond, irrespective of area of the world or age-specific rates of deficiency [200, 210–218] (Fig. 13.13). This pattern may reflect a rise seen over time as children in high-risk populations continue to be exposed to a poor diet, lacking breast milk [219–221] and sufficient vegetables, fruits, and animal products with adequate vitamin A content [222–225]. A similar, although

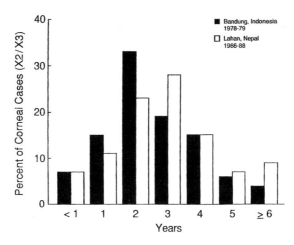

**Fig. 13.12.** Percent distribution of consecutive cases of corneal xerosis (X2) and ulceration/ keratomalacia (X3) by age admitted to eye hospitals in Indonesia (n = 162) [195] and Nepal (n = 295) [208].

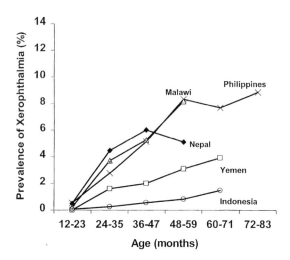

**Fig. 13.13.** Prevalence of xerophthalmia by age from population-based eye surveys in five countries: Philippines [211], Malawi [213], Nepal [215], Yemen [212], and Indonesia [216].

less well documented, rise in subclinical vitamin A deficiency (based on serum retinol) may occur with age during the preschool years [226, 227] in undernourished populations that is not evident in well-nourished settings [228], which may give rise to a high prevalence of marginal-to-deficient vitamin A status in school-aged years [99, 229]. It is plausible that chronic deficiency could persist into the reproductive years of women [1, 230–233], thereby raising the risk of night blindness during pregnancy [12, 14].

### 13.5.2.2 GENDER

Boys tend to show a higher prevalence of mild xerophthalmia than girls throughout the preschool and early school-aged years [2, 234–236]. Animal experiments also often revealed increased vulnerability of male versus female risks to vitamin A depletion with respect to growth, vitamin A status, and survival [237], suggesting there may be, in part, a genetic basis to this risk difference. The gender bias is less apparent for subclinical (biochemical) deficiency [226] and has not been observed in severe, corneal xerophthalmia [195]. Variation in feeding by gender may, however, be a more dominant cause of this risk difference in humans [210, 237, 238].

### 13.5.2.3 SOCIOECONOMIC STATUS

In general, socioeconomic status (ses) covaries inversely with the risk of vitamin A deficiency, presumably by influencing both availability and accessibility to an adequate diet and appropriate hygiene and care that can lead to less illness among poorer children. Low household SES is typically associated with xerophthalmia in young children, reflected by less parental education [195, 199, 207, 223, 227, 236–241] and landholding [195, 199, 207, 236, 242], poorer housing quality [195, 207, 223] and hygiene [195, 207, 240], fewer small assets [207, 236, 237, 239] and draft animals [204, 236, 239] owned, and a more frequent history of child mortality in the family [195, 207, 223]. Not surprisingly, women with night blindness also come from socioeconomically disadvantaged families, exhibiting a poor diet, less asset ownership, and increased risks of anemia and infection [12, 206]. Typically, odds ratios (ORs) for xerophthalmia lie between 1.5 and 2.5 when comparing risks among families with lower versus higher SES. Socioeconomic influence on variation in serum retinol has been less consistently observed [214, 226, 243], perhaps related to homeostatic mechanisms that maintain serum retinol across a wide range of status, making this association more difficult to detect when serum retinol is expressed on a continuous scale. At the community level, high-risk villages, marked by the presence of more than 1 child with xerophthalmia, tend to be poorer than those where no children have xerophthalmia [223]. Differentials in SES are not reliable for prediction of risk of vitamin A deficiency but do provide the context in which vitamin A deficiency occurs and, in part, a basis for understanding how vitamin A deficiency clusters within households and communities.

### 13.5.3  Periodicity

Periodicity in risk of vitamin A deficiency is captured mostly by the influence of season and long-term trends on incidence or prevalence. Spring peaks in xerophthalmia were widely noted in early 20th century China, Europe, and Japan, variably coinciding with the spring growth spurt, changes in diet, and the diarrhea season [2]. Drought increases risk of xerophthalmia [244, 245]. In rural South Asia, the incidence of xerophthalmia follows a predictable seasonality, waxing during the hot, dry season (March–June) and waning during the monsoon period (July–August) to a low level that is sustained beyond the major rice harvest months of November and December [246].

This annual cycle has been best depicted by Sinha and Bang, who clinically examined 300 preschool children in the Village of Ichag, West Bengal, each month for over 2 years (Fig. 13.14) [247]. The seasonal peak of night blindness and Bitot's spots was preceded by a period of high growth that followed the major harvest, which presumably drew down vitamin A reserves, and coincided with a period of low intake of fruits and vegetables and high incidence of diarrhea and measles [246, 248]. Appearance of the mango season coupled with slowed growth may partly explain the decrease in xerophthalmia late in the monsoon period. Seasonal patterns provide insight into the timing and nature of interventions, which should aim to mute the seasonal peak (e.g., distributing high-potency vitamin A prior to the highest-risk season) and, if feasible, address dietary

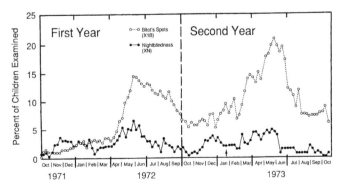

**Fig. 13.14.** Seasonality of prevalence of mild xerophthalmia in Ichag Village, West Bengal, India, over a 2-year period. Data to right of arrow represent control group only among children who participated in a placebo-controlled vitamin A trial [247].

and morbidity-related causes (e.g., promoting gardens or vegetable marketing, ensuring high measles vaccine coverage) wherever feasible [33, 248, 249, 250].

Risk of vitamin A deficiency can also shift over long periods of time that likely reflect gradual improvements in economic development, food security, and health services [251]. Although time trend data are absent, the past century witnessed the virtual disappearance of xerophthalmia from industrialized Western Europe, North America, and Japan. More recently, in Indonesia, the risk of potentially blinding vitamin A deficiency markedly decreased from the late 1970s to the early 1990s, reflected by a 75% reduction in the national prevalence of xerophthalmia [216] and a well-documented decline in xeroph-thalmia admissions to the Cicendo Eye Hospital in Bandung (Fig. 13.15) [252]. Such progress, however, can be reversed in the presence of political and economic turmoil, as when xerophthalmia began to reappear in Indonesia following its economic collapse in the late 1990s [253].

### 13.5.4  Proximal Causes

Vitamin A deficiency, as a public health problem, results from a chronic dietary insuf-ficiency of vitamin A, either preformed or from precursor carotenoids. It often occurs in association with protein-energy malnutrition, other micronutrient deficiencies, and as part of a "vicious cycle" with infection, in which one exacerbates and increases suscep-tibility to the other.

#### 13.5.4.1  BREAST-FEEDING

In affluent populations, newborns are normally born with low liver stores of vitamin A that increase rapidly thereafter throughout the preschool years (reviewed in [95]), presumably reflecting dietary sufficiency from breast milk and complementary foods

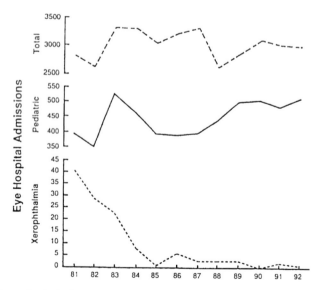

**Fig. 13.15.** Number of admissions at the Cicendo Eye Hospital, Bandung, Indonesia, between 1981 and 1992 [252]. The decline in xerophthalmia admissions likely reflected a true decrease (bottom line), given rising pediatric admissions (middle line) and stable total admissions (top line) over the same time period.

that promote storage of vitamin A in relation to normal requirements for growth and other needs. In malnourished societies, liver vitamin A stores may fail to accumulate beyond early infancy [71, 95]. This may be due in part to a combination of low breast milk vitamin A concentration, which can often be half that of breast milk from well-nourished populations of women [43, 44], and stress from chronic infection [104].

Still, breast milk provides a critical dietary source of vitamin A [254] that may protect children from xerophthalmia. In many populations, breast-feeding through the third year of life is associated with age-adjusted odds ratios of 0.1 to 0.5, representing 50% to 90% reductions in the probability of having xerophthalmia compared to children who have ceased breast-feeding [195, 219, 221, 255–258]. In Malawi, accelerated weaning, involving both premature introduction of complementary foods (at 3 versus 4 months of age) and early cessation of breast-feeding was associated with increased risk of preschool xerophthalmia [220]. A dose-response association was observed in Nepal: Children who were breast-fed up to ten or more times per day were 68% and 88%, respectively, less likely to have xerophthalmia than children of the same age who had ceased breast-feeding [207] (Fig. 13.16A). Infectious illnesses, such as protracted diarrhea, measles, or severe respiratory infection may weaken the protection that is apparent with breast-feeding [219], possibly due to increased demands and urinary losses of vitamin A that accompany infections [259].

### 13.5.4.2 COMPLEMENTARY FEEDING

The mix of complementary foods offered to weanlings can modify or even eliminate the excess risk of xerophthalmia associated with the loss of breast milk from the diet. In Indonesia, where no association existed between breast-feeding and xerophthalmia in the preschool years (Fig. 13.16B), children not routinely given milk, egg, yellow fruits and vegetables, dark green leaves, or meat/fish in the first 12 months of weaning were about three times more likely to be xerophthalmic than matched-control children given these foods [223]. Similarly, in Nepal, protective odds ratios against xerophthalmia in the preschool years ranged from 0.09 to 0.41 for regular (> three times per week) consumption of meat, fish, egg, and mango in the first 2 years of life [207]. Feeding histories of younger siblings in the first 2 years of life were similar to the cases and controls in the study (Table 13.7) [204], reflecting a chronically poor diet in high-risk households.

Numerous epidemiologic studies provided the basis for a progression of complementary feeding that appears to guard children from xerophthalmia through the preschool years. Intake of sweet, yellow fruit (mango and papaya) is strongly protective in the second and third years of life, denoted by a solid line in Fig. 13.17. As the influence of breast feeding weakens, stippled line dark green leafy vegetables appear strongly protective from the third year onward. Finally, after infancy, routine consumption of animal foods with preformed vitamin A (egg, dairy products, fish, and liver) appears to be highly protective [2, 195, 223, 255, 257, 258, 260–263].

How and with whom children eat their meals may affect their risk of vitamin A deficiency. Detailed ethnographic studies in Nepal have shown that rural children are twice as likely to consume vegetables, fruits, pulses, meat or fish, and dairy products when they share a plate with another relative during meals than when left to eat alone. Among plate sharers, however, chronically vitamin A-deficient children (i.e., those with a known history of xerophthalmia) were nearly twice as likely to share a plate at mealtime with an adult male (OR 1.7 95% confidence interval [CI] 1.0–2.8) than lower-risk

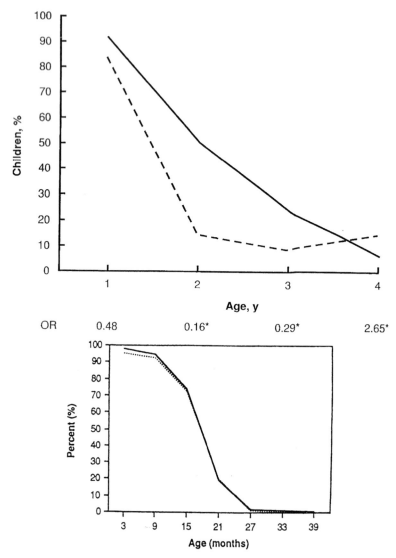

**Fig. 13.16. A** Percent of rural Nepalese children breast-feeding by age among cases of xerophthalmia (dashed line) and age- and sex-matched nonxerophthalmic controls (solid line). *OR* odds ratio for breast-feeding among cases relative to controls *A 95% confidence interval excluding 1.0 [207] **B** Percent of rural Indonesian children breast-feeding by age among cases of xerophthalmia (dotted line) and their age- and sex[-matched nonxerophthalmic controls (solid line) [223].

children residing in nonxerophthalmic households [264]. Sharing a plate at mealtime with a female of any age, on the other hand, was "protective" against xerophthalmia (OR 0.6, 95% CI 0.4–0.9), possibly reflecting female behavior that is more nurturing toward younger children.

### 13.5.4.3 INFECTIOUS DISEASE MORBIDITY

Vitamin A deficiency and infection interact within a vicious cycle [103] in which one exacerbates and increases susceptibility to the other. The bidirectional relationship

Table 13.7

Correlations in sibling feeding patterns and reported frequencies of intake
of foods (n = 67 focus child and younger sibling pairs1) [204]

| | Correlation Between Siblings | |
|---|---|---|
| Specific Food Items | Spearman's Rank Correlation | P value |
| Preformed vitamin A sources | | |
|    Meat | 0.38 | <0.002 |
|    Fish | 0.39 | <0.002 |
|    Traditional tonic | 0.38 | <0.002 |
|    Animal milk | 0.66 | <0.001 |
|    Other breast milk | 0.50 | <0.001 |
|    Eggs | 0.53 | <0.001 |
| Carotenoid sources | | |
| Mango | 0.54 | <0.001 |
| Dark green leaves | 0.33 | <0.007 |
| Papaya | 0.14 | 0.27 |

[1] Only younger siblings who were >24 months at time of interview used in analysis.

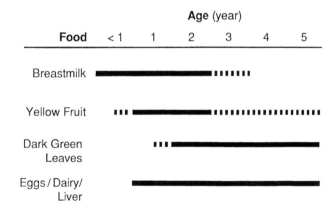

**Fig. 13.17.** Composite depiction of age-specific protection against xerophthalmia conferred by food sources of vitamin A based on epidemiologic studies in Southern Asia and Africa. Solid bar denotes strong, consistent evidence of protection; dash indicates weaker epidemiologic evidence [26].

complicates frequent cross-sectional evidence of depressed plasma retinol levels with diarrhea, acute respiratory infections, measles, malaria, HIV/AIDS, and other infectious illnesses that can be attributed in part to an acute-phase response [265–267]. However, prospective studies showed that infection can induce vitamin A deficiency through a variety of ways, depending on the cause, duration, and severity of infection and vitamin A status of the host at onset. Serum retinol may be depressed because of decreased dietary intake or malabsorption due to diarrhea or intestinal pathogens [268–270], impaired release or accelerated depletion of hepatic retinol reserves [271], increased retinol utilization by target tissues, or increased urinary losses [259, 272–274]. Hyporetinolemia may adversely affect immune competence, which could exacerbate or predispose children to infection [104].

Urinary retinol loss, reflecting losses in body stores, can vary greatly by type and severity of infection. In a Bangladesh study, 6%, 19%, 17%, and 65% of children hospitalized with dysentery, watery diarrhea, pneumonia, or sepsis, respectively, excreted more than 0.70 μmol (20 μg) of retinol in urine per day, corresponding to 10% of a preschool child's estimated metabolic requirement. Total urinary excretion of retinol per episode of sepsis was 6.0 μmol, amounting to about 20% of an average young child's (3-month) liver reserve of 35 μmol or 75% of a marginally vitamin A-nourished child's much lower liver reserve (e.g., 8 μmol) [259]. This suggests that severe infection acutely decompensates vitamin A nutriture, which could precipitate xerophthalmia. Indeed, in a prospective study in Indonesia, preschoolers with either diarrhea or acute respiratory disease were twice as likely to have developed xerophthalmia in a subsequent 3-month period than healthier children [275]. Severe diarrhea, dysentery, measles, and other severe febrile illnesses are frequently reported to precede corneal xerophthalmia [2].

## 13.6  CLINICOPATHOLOGICAL FEATURES

### 13.6.1  Xerophthalmia

Conjunctival and corneal xerosis, corneal ulceration and necrosis, and retinal dysfunction causing poor dark adaptation and night blindness are the ocular consequences of vitamin A deficiency. Active "xerophthalmia" includes all of these clinical stages, plus less-studied and understood lesions in the retinal pigment epithelium, described as the "xerophthalmic fundus" [195, 276]. These fundal changes are not considered further here. Healed corneal scars resulting from corneal xerophthalmia are not considered "active" but represent the potentially blinding sequelae of xerophthalmia [33, 195].

#### 13.6.1.1  NIGHT BLINDNESS (XN)

Night blindness is the earliest, specific clinical manifestation of vitamin A deficiency and is usually the most prevalent stage of xerophthalmia. Its occurrence reflects a failure in rod photoreceptor cells in the retina to maintain peripheral vision under dim light that can be detected by dark adaptometry. Impaired dark adaptation occurs in the presence of depressed serum retinol concentrations [277, 278] and is responsive to vitamin A supplementation [279]. Typically, a history of night blindness can be elicited using a local term for the condition, often translated as "chicken eyes" (domestic fowl lack rods and thus night vision) or "twilight" or "evening" blindness [2, 33, 195]. A history of night blindness is associated with low-to-deficient serum retinol concentrations in preschool-aged children [2, 195, 241, 280, 281] and pregnant women [12] compared to individuals without the condition. Night blindness during pregnancy can be reliably elicited by history, which can serve as an indicator of individual and community risk of vitamin A deficiency [100].

#### 13.6.1.2  CONJUNCTIVAL XEROSIS WITH BITOT'S SPOTS (X1B)

Vitamin A deficiency leads to a keratinizing metaplasia of mucosal surfaces of the body, including the bulbar conjunctiva. In chronic deficiency, xerosis of the conjunctiva appears as a dry, nonwettable, rough or granular surface, best seen on oblique illumination from a hand light [2, 33, 195, 276]. On the ocular surface, the tear film breaks up, revealing a xerotic surface that has been likened to "sandbanks at the receding tide" [282]. Histologically, the lesions represent a transformation of normal, surface, columnar epithelium, with abundant mucus-secreting goblet cells, to a stratified, squamous epithelium that lacks goblet cells [33, 276]. In advanced xerosis, gray-yellow patches of keratinized cells and saprophytic bacilli, called Bitot's spots, may aggregate on the surface, temporal to the limbus and, in more severe cases, on nasal surfaces as well (Fig. 13.18). The lesions may be bubbly, foamy, or cheese-like in appearance [276].

### 13.6.1.3  CORNEAL XEROSIS (X2), ULCERATION, AND NECROSIS (X3)

Corneal xerophthalmia represents acute decompensation of the cornea, which is a sight-threatening medical emergency [2, 33, 195, 276] that is also associated with high case fatality [195]. Mild xerosis ("drying") presents as superficial punctate erosions that lend a hazy, nonwettable, and irregular appearance to the cornea on hand-light examination. Usually both eyes are involved. With increased severity, the cornea becomes edematous and takes on a dry, granular appearance, described like the "peel of an orange" [195]. Vitamin A therapy successfully treats corneal xerosis, although in advanced disease, thick plaques of cornified epithelium form that may slough off. Ulceration can be round or oval in appearance, shallow or deep to the stroma, usually sharply demarcated, and often peripheral to the visual axis. Usually, only one ulcer forms in the affected eye. Vitamin A treatment will heal the tissue, leaving an opaque stromal scar or leukoma. Ulcers that perforate the entire cornea (through Descemet's membrane) and are plugged with iris will, on healing, form an adherent leukoma. These are often at the periphery of the cornea and leave central vision of a healed eye intact [33, 276]. Keratomalacia ("corneal melting or softening") refers to necrosis of the cornea, forming initially opaque localized lesions that can expand rapidly to cover and blind the cornea (Fig. 13.19). Therapy with

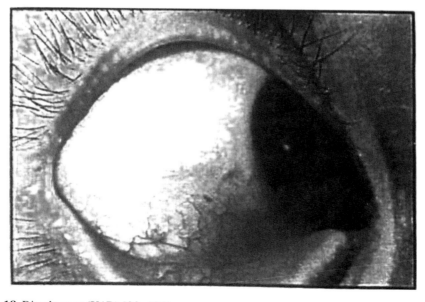

**Fig. 13.18.** Bitot's spot (X1B) [33, 195].

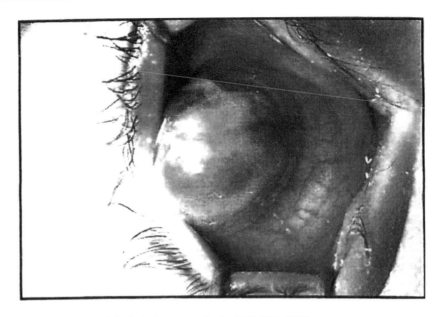

**Fig. 13.19.** Corneal xerophthalmia/keratomalacia (X3) [33, 195].

vitamin A leaves a densely scarred cornea, often with resultant phthisis (shrunken globe) or staphyloma (protuding cornea) [276].

### 13.6.2   Infection

Vitamin A deficiency predisposes individuals to severe infection [106] and a higher risk of mortality in children (Figs. 13.7 and 13.8) and women, at least during nutritionally stressing periods of pregnancy and lactation [13, 14]. Multiple roles of vitamin A in maintaining epithelial barrier function and regulating cellular and antibody-mediated immunity [104, 105] provide biologic plausibility for vitamin A deficiency as a cause of morbidity.

### 13.6.3   Poor Growth

Experimental vitamin A depletion in animals causes a deceleration in weight gain to a "plateau," as hepatic retinol reserves become exhausted, and eventual weight loss [176, 177, 237]. This dynamic is difficult to observe in children. Corneal xerophthalmia is associated with severe linear growth stunting and acute wasting malnutrition, likely due to a combination of protein-energy malnutrition, infection, and multiple micronutrient deficiencies [2, 195]. Mild xerophthalmia (XN or X1B) is associated with moderate stunting and mild wasting in children [2, 195, 223, 263] and wasting in pregnant women [12]. Spontaneous recovery from xerophthalmia, likely due to dietary improvement, has been associated with gain in weight but less noticeable catch-up in linear growth over a 6-month period [283].

In general, vitamin A supplementation cannot be expected to measurably improve weight or height gain in a population [284–289], although it may lead to measurable increases in lean body mass, reflected by incremental upper arm muscle area [287, 290], and there may be growth responses in subsets of a population [290] or on a seasonal basis [287, 291]. In some settings, vitamin A may result in accelerated linear growth [111, 292–294], particularly among children who are moderately to severely vitamin A deficient and for whom the deficiency may be growth limiting [287, 293, 294]. Repeated bouts of infection may blunt the growth response [295], an effect that may also explain seasonal growth responses to vitamin A [296]. Moderately ill (e.g., children recovering from severe measles), wasted, or clinically vitamin A-deficient children may show marked ponderal and apparent lean body gains following vitamin A supplementation [287, 297, 298].

## 13.7   TREATMENT

Children with any stage of xerophthalmia should be treated with vitamin A according to WHO treatment guidelines, that is, with high potency vitamin A at presentation, the next day, and 1 to 4 weeks later (Table 13.8). Supportive nutritional and antibiotic therapy should be considered, as indicated by the patient's condition, along with dietary counseling.

Night blindness responds within 24–48 hours of high-potency vitamin A treatment, leading to a return to normal scotopic (nighttime) vision [33, 280]. The efficacy of the treatment guidelines for night blind women is presumed. In Nepal, long-term, weekly supplementation with about 23,000 IU only prevented about two thirds of maternal night blindness cases [149], suggesting that a higher, more frequent, or sustained dosage may be needed in some undernourished settings to resolve this symptom.

Bitot's spots (X1B) in preschool children generally respond to high-potency vitamin A within 2–5 days, becoming smaller in size and disappearing within 2 weeks. A small percentage of lesions may persist as smaller aggregates on the conjunctival surface for months [33, 195]. In older children, X1B may be more refractory to vitamin A. Although

Table 13.8
**Vitamin A treatment and prevention schedules [299]**

| Age | Treatment at Diagnosis[1] | Prevention Dosage | Frequency |
|-----|---------------------------|-------------------|-----------|
| <6 months | 50,000 IU | 50,000 IU | With each vaccine visit at 10, 14 & 16 weeks of age; with polio vaccine |
| 6-11 months | 100,000 IU | 100,000 IU | Every 4-6 months |
| >1 year | 200,000 IU | 200,000 IU | Every 4-6 months |
| Women | 200,000 IU[2] | 400,000 IU | <6 weeks after delivery |

*Source:* 299

[1] Treat all cases of xerophthalmia with the same age-specific dosage on days 1, 2 and 14; treat measles cases on days 1 and 2; treat cases of severe malnutrition (ie, kwashiorkor or weight for height $< - 3$ Z-scores below the international referent median) on day 1.

[2] For women of reproductive age (13–49 yr) with active corneal lesions give 200,000 IU on days 1, 2 and 14; treat women with milder eye signs (night blindness or Bitot's spots) with 10,000 IU per day or 25,000 IU per week for >3 months.

similar in clinical appearance, factors associated with responsive and nonresponsive X1B differ: The latter are more frequent with age, associated with localized versus more generalized metaplasia and goblet cell loss, less often associated with night blindness, and observed at higher serum retinol concentrations than responsive X1B [300–302].

Corneal xerophthalmia can rapidly lead to blindness without immediate vitamin A treatment. Corneal xerosis quickly responds to vitamin A, usually within 2 to 5 days of therapy, with the cornea returning to normal without permanent sequelae within 1 to 2 weeks [33, 195]. Shallow, small corneal ulcers, which usually form peripheral to the visual axis, heal with minimal structural damage or risk of visual loss. Ulcers will form an opaque stromal scar or leukoma. Corneal necrosis (keratomalacia) must be treated immediately with standard vitamin A therapy coupled with topical antibiotics and other nutritional measures [33, 195]. Healing may induce large lesions to slough, forming decemetoceles [276].

Children with severe measles should always receive vitamin A (Table 13.8) as they are very likely to be benefit from such therapy both in terms of saving sight and reducing case fatality [2].

## 13.8  PREVENTION

The main cause of vitamin A deficiency is an insufficient dietary intake of vitamin A, likely compounded by poor bioavailability of provitamin A carotenoids from vegetable-based diets [49, 50, 55, 66, 67] that dominate the developing world (Fig. 13.4). Other important contributing factors include the increased requirements for vitamin A at certain stages in the life cycle (i.e., growth, pregnancy, and lactation) and following episodes of infection (especially measles) [303]. Sociocultural factors such as intrahousehold distribution and gender preference and other economic constraints to achieving an adequate diet and health provide the context within which deficiency occurs and prevention must take place [304–306]. However, control of vitamin A deficiency cannot await correction of "root" causes of poverty that, in the long run, would be expected to relieve most poor populations of the burden of malnutrition, including vitamin A deficiency, as indeed happened in the industrialized world [238].

Effective prevention should increase vitamin A intake to adequate levels alongside efforts to reduce infectious diseases. Prevention, for purposes of implementation and estimating resource needs, can be categorized into three partly overlapping and complementary approaches [307]:

1. **Dietary diversification**: increasing vitamin A intake from available and accessible foods, achieved through nutrition education, social marketing, home or community garden programs, and other measures to improve food security
2. **Fortification**: taking advantage of existing consumption patterns of fortifiable foods to carry vitamin A into the diets of populations
3. **Supplementation**: encompassing community-based efforts to provide vitamin A supplements to high-risk groups, typically preschool-aged children on a periodic basis and mothers within 6–8 weeks after childbirth

There are four levels of activity required for any prevention program to be successful: (1) the family level, at which acceptance, compliance, contact, or behavior change must occur among targeted beneficiaries (e.g., home gardening, supplement receipt, breast-feeding, etc.); (2) the community and district level, at which planning, organization, logistics, and often political investment are required to launch and sustain programs; (3) the national level, at which policy, funding, and legislation are required to enact national programs; and (4) the global level, at which multilateral, international, and trade bodies interact to create favorable political and financial climates for policies and programs to be planned and funded. Enactment and long-term change are less likely to be sustained without the more distal, "higher" levels being addressed and becoming engaged [308].

### 13.8.1 Dietary Diversification

Improving dietary intake of high-risk groups requires an adequate, affordable, and diverse supply of food sources of vitamin A, which preferably includes preformed sources of vitamin A throughout the year, consumed in sufficient amounts, especially by those at highest risk: infants, young children, adolescent girls, and women of reproductive age. A first-line, dietary intervention to protect infants and young children from vitamin A deficiency is extended breast-feeding, which consistently exhibits a protective association against xerophthalmia even through the fourth year of life [2, 219, 220, 221, 255–257], although effectiveness data are lacking to show a change in vitamin A status from breast-feeding promotion. This was also the rationale for the IVACG recommendation to give postpartum women 400,000 IU of vitamin within 6 weeks of delivery [299], although WHO continues to recommend 200,000 IU. Although it has been possible to demonstrate increased retinol levels in the breast milk for 2 to 8 months after maternal postpartum vitamin A supplementation [97, 233, 309], the effects of this intervention have not been evaluated with respect to infant survival [310]. With weaning, routine provision of soft yellow fruits and vegetables, dark green leaves, eggs, and other food sources of vitamin A should be provided [2, 195, 223, 232, 255], which in controlled studies have been shown to raise low serum retinol concentrations in children [2].

Where food sources of vitamin A are inadequate, homestead gardening, which combines horticultural, credit, and nutrition education or social marketing services [311–314], has raised vitamin A intakes [249], improved household economic return, and therefore improved food security [315]. Further, food-based interventions that promote participation of women and rally community support through creative social marketing appear capable of changing behavior and enhancing vitamin A intake [248, 304, 316–319] and, in some instances, have been shown to improve vitamin A status [304, 320]. Given evidence of poorer bioavailability of green leaf and other vegetable-based provitamin A carotenoids than previously thought [49, 64], approaches that include the promotion of food sources of preformed vitamin A (animal and fortified foods), a wider variety of carotenoid-containing foods [249, 260, 321], and food preparation methods that enhance carotenoid absorption (Table 13.1) may offer new tactics for improving the effectiveness of local dietary interventions [2].

Innovative approaches are currently being developed or tested to reduce dependency on external funding in the future. These include the use of fortified rice premix [322], β-carotene-rich crops such as orange-fleshed sweet potatoes [323], and genetically modified foods such as "golden rice" [324] and increased use of animal-source foods through home gardening programs [325]. Still, firm evidence of the impact on vitamin A status, sustainability, and costs to different participants of food-based interventions is lacking. In one instance, homestead gardening was shown to significantly reduce the risk of night blindness in Bangaldeshi children who had not received a vitamin A capsule through the national program [326], and to empower women in ways that were likely to improve the health of their children [327].

### 13.8.2 Fortification

Fortification represents an increasingly important food-based approach to control vitamin A and other micronutrient deficiencies as fortifiable foods ("vehicles") gain entry into markets of the developing world and as fortification of food aid commodities becomes more common [328, 329]. Numerous foods have long been fortified in economies in which food production and marketing systems are highly industrialized, integrated, and readily reach the consumer [330, 331]. Fortification is likely to be most effective when one or more food vehicles are widely consumed by high-risk groups, and their intake is reasonably narrow across other segments of a population (to minimize risk of overconsumption), processing and distribution are centralized (in a limited number of facilities to maintain quality control), organoleptic change from addition of vitamin A is imperceptible over time under ambient conditions, and costs of fortification are both small relative to the product itself and absorbable by the consumer [2, 329, 330, 332, 333].

Fortification has been slow in effectively scaling up in developing countries compared with experiences in the industrialized world. This has been due largely to a lack of production and market potential for fortifiable foods in most food economies where vitamin A deficiency remains a public health problem [330]. Some notable successes exist, however, especially with respect to vitamin A fortification of sugar in Guatemala and other Central American countries. Over a period of two decades, effectiveness studies demonstrated improved vitamin A status, and vigorous and persistent efforts were made by government and the food industry to find sound solutions to recoup costs, develop enabling legislation, and successfully market vitamin A-fortified sugar in these countries [332, 334–336]. Vitamin A-fortified monosodium glutamate, widely consumed throughout Southeast Asia as a meal flavor enhancer, improved breast milk and serum retinol concentrations [292, 337, 338] as well as the growth and survival of preschool-aged children [111] in Indonesia and the Philippines. However, product discoloration, problems with stability and packaging under highly humid conditions, difficulties in product pricing, and loss of manufacturer confidence [2, 339, 340] led to failure in scaling up this potentially effective fortified product. Fortification of margarine that does not require refrigeration [341] and wheat flour [342], both consumed by the rural poor in the Philippines, has been shown to improve vitamin A status of children. These results, added to acceptable retention of vitamin A in such products under tropical, humid conditions [341–343], add to a growing variety of foods that can be fortified with vitamin A. Further, a staple such as wheat flour offers the opportunity for multinutrient fortification that could lead to the prevention of several micronutrient deficiencies [344].

Penetration of fortified foods into poor, geographically remote markets remains a major challenge [328, 333]. Cost analysis data are sparse but findings, for example, from Guatemala suggest that, where the critical targeting and central processing conditions are met, fortification can be two to four times more cost-effective in reaching beneficiaries with adequate amounts of vitamin A than vitamin A capsule distribution or dietary diversification efforts [345].

Encouraging findings on impact and cost, increasing numbers of food vehicles, and a greater global momentum bode well for expanding fortification to prevent micronutrient malnutrition [328, 346]. Additional vehicles for vitamin A fortification include fats and oils, tea, milk/milk powder, cereals, other flours, instant noodles, whole wheat, rice, salt, soybean oil, and infant formulas [2, 331, 346]. Naturally high sources of vitamin A can also be protected during processing or used to fortify other products. For example, in India, red palm oil is added to other edible oils, and Malaysia has done much work to retain the β-carotene content of palm oil during processing [347]. Fortification of cooking oils is moving beyond the pilot phase in several African countries [348]. Fortified rice premixes made from extruded rice flour and resembling natural milled grains have been developed and are awaiting expanded testing and use [322]. Innovation will be required to advance fortification as an effective and practical measure of control in the developing world.

### 13.8.3 Supplementation

Periodic high-dose vitamin A supplementation remains the most widely practiced, direct means by governments throughout the world to prevent deficiency [349–351]. Each year, UNICEF procures and distributes over 400 million vitamin A supplements to nearly 80 countries. This number excludes supplements distributed in several other countries of high vitamin A deficiency endemicity (i.e., China, India, Indonesia, and Viet Nam) (N. Dalmiya, UNICEF, personal communication, 1999). The rationale for supplementation with a high dose of vitamin A rests on the assumption that, as a fat-soluble nutrient, it is stored in the body, principally in the liver, and released in association with transport proteins to meet demands of body tissues as required. The same physical form of oral supplement (i.e., typically a gelatinous capsule or oily syrup delivered with a spoon) used for treatment is also used for prophylaxis, varying only in dosage (fraction or multiples of a standard dose) according to purpose and age of recipients [33]. This facilitates greatly the logistics of supplying supplements for programs. Thus, a theoretical 4- to 6-month supply (usually 100,000–200,000 IU or about 30–60 mg RAE) provided at one time can establish a nutritional reserve for use during periods of reduced dietary intake or increased need [352], as well as for routine twice-yearly supplementation. Increasingly, high-potency vitamin A supplements are being distributed through semiannual, highly organized, national Child Health Days or Weeks. This experience extends the momentum of several years of National Immunization Days (NIDs) for Polio Eradication, during which "piggybacked" vitamin A delivery achieved extremely high levels of coverage in some of the most poorly resourced countries in the world, including in West Africa [353].

The efficacy of high-dose vitamin A prophylaxis appears to be about 90% in preventing any stage of xerophthalmia for 6 months in children [2], despite a likely dosage absorption of only 30–50% under prevalent conditions of morbidity and malnutrition often found in developing countries [2, 349, 354, 355] and including intercurrent infection that can reduce the period of protection afforded against low serum retinol and liver store depletion [271]. Program effectiveness, however, is lower. Assuming sufficient, albeit nearly always incomplete, coverage (e.g., >85% of targeted children) and a degree of dosage inadequacy, community-based periodic vitamin A delivery can be expected to be about 75% effective in preventing children from developing xerophthalmia in high-risk populations [2, 197, 349, 350, 356]. Protection against hyporetinolemia (i.e., serum retinol < 20 μg/dL or < 0.70 μmol/L) may be less well sustained as serum retinol remains elevated for only up to about 2 months following high-potency vitamin A receipt

[2]. Similar levels of protection against maternal night blindness (67%) and postpartum serum hyporetinolemia (69%) 6 months following delivery have been reported with weekly low-dose vitamin A supplementation [149] and high-potency vitamin A receipt at delivery [230], respectively.

High-potency vitamin A is well tolerated by children, although up to about 10% of preschoolers may experience transient side effects (nausea, vomiting, headache, diarrhea, or fever have been reported) following receipt of 200,000 IU [357]; up to approximately 2% of young infants (<6 months) may show a bulging fontanel following a single dose of 50,000 IU or more [142, 358–360], although a larger proportion (4–8%) may experience such an effect following repeated dosing during the first 6 months of life [361].

A bulging fontanel following receipt of 50,000 IU has not been accompanied by an increase in intracranial pressure [362], has returned to normal usually within 48 hours [358–360, 362], and has not been associated with long-term developmental abnormalities [363]. Administration of 100,000 IU as a single dose to infants under 6 months of age may be excessive [140] and therefore should be reserved for treatment [33, 195].

High-potency vitamin A supplements can be delivered to high-risk populations in several ways. One approach is to restrict vitamin A use to health care settings for the treatment of xerophthalmia and case management of severe infections such as measles [126–128, 297, 303], malaria [131], severe malnutrition, diarrhea, and respiratory disease [299]. This approach incorporates both elements of what has been termed "therapeutic" or "targeted" [33, 349, 352]. Its advantage lies in its effort to reach the most vitamin A deficient, and thus the most responsive individuals, and being cost-efficient as few new resources are required beyond the supplements themselves, minimal health personnel training, and existing delivery capabilities [352]. However, coverage may be poor as it depends fully on access of vulnerable groups to health and other "carrier" services, and attributed costs may not be trivial if a supplement program requires additional assessment procedures or nutrition education services to be added [364]. In many of the most affected countries, health systems are typically poorly functioning and very underresourced.

Second, vitamin A may be delivered for primary prevention in an "opportunistic" way, that is, one that maximizes vitamin A receipt once, intermittently, or periodically through multiple, existing service programs (not initially motivated or designed for vitamin A distribution) that reach large proportions of target groups. Examples include the Expanded Programme for Immunization and NIDs [365] and routine growth monitoring clinics [349, 366]. Integrating vitamin A delivery with immunization services provides a timely opportunity to deliver 25,000 or 50,000 IU during each of three routine contacts in the first 6 months of life, 200,000 IU to the mothers at the first 6-week postpartum visit, 100,000 IU to infants in late infancy at the time of measles vaccination, and a 200,000 IU supplement to older children who may be accessible on the day of community contact [365]. The advantages of such program integration, however, remain theoretical as in practice few programs have carried out such a combined approach. While initial concerns about concurrent vitamin A dosing interfering with seroconversion to vaccine have been dispelled [367, 368], periodic vitamin A dosing of infants younger than 6 months of age has nonetheless not improved infant survival [140, 141], unlike what appears possible when dosing is done shortly after birth [142, 143] or 5 months of age [110–120]. Growth-monitoring clinics provide regular access to children for vitamin A receipt, although coverage is often low, especially among older preschool aged children [366, 369].

Universal coverage represents the third, broadest coverage approach to vitamin A prophylaxis. Supplement distribution may be combined with other national or regional community programs (such as a NID) or stand alone as a "vertical" activity, sweeping through communities in high-risk regions to dose children of the target age (6 months to 4 or 5 years) on a planned timetable, usually every 4 to 6 months [349, 352, 369]. Historically poor coverage rates, typically under 50% [199, 221, 349, 350], have been vastly improved to 80% or more in recent years through campaign approaches that focus all distribution activities on two set days, 6 months apart, each year [370].

Child Health Days or Child Health Weeks, designed initially as the alternate 6-month dosing opportunity during the NIDs years, are proving to be a viable universal approach for delivering vitamin A in a way that also integrates other semiannual child health care services [370]. Key to success appears to be a strong social marketing approach to secure active and sustained community involvement in distribution activities [371], although, as with many public programs, goals of sustainability are best met in times of political and economic stability [250]. Community and household factors associated with adequate coverage tend to vary by country setting [199, 221, 350, 353]. Cost data for universal vitamin A distribution are sparse [349, 371–373], making it difficult to estimate program efficiency. It has been estimated that universal vitamin A distribution costs roughly US $0.25 per delivered dose, of which the capsule (if from UNICEF) costs US $0.02 [349, 373], although costs of delivery may rise sharply in reaching remote populations [351, 374, 375]. As a basic rule, universal vitamin A coverage should be a programmed activity in malnourished refugee child populations, with a goal to dose new arrivals followed by periodic delivery [2, 352, 376].

The feasibility and degree to which each preventive strategy can be pursued simultaneously depends on the prevalence and severity of deficiency, resources including infrastructure, political commitment, financial capacity, and potential benefits and safety [369]. The need to change behavior of groups—families, communities, industry, government—remains an essential part of each strategy. Sustainability remains an important consideration, and experience in a resource-poor country such as Niger in West Africa suggests five important factors: (1) leadership and ownership by the Ministry of Public Health (or equivalent); (2) district-level planning and implementation; (3) effective training and flexible delivery mechanisms; (4) effective social information and communication and mobilization; and (5) responsiveness of responsible ministry and partners [371]. It will be important in the next few years to test the impact of the last decade's programs, although the methodological challenges such as partitioning effects and costs of other concurrent interventions, will continue to represent challenges to evaluation.

## 13.9 CONCLUSION

Vitamin and mineral deficiencies rarely occur alone, rarely have a single cause, and always occur in a wider ecological, social, and political environment. Poor-quality diets low in micronutrients are invariably a consequence of poverty, itself of a consequence of local, national, and global inequities. Increasingly, it is recognized that while scaling-up integrated vitamin A supplementation programs [351], nations need to be simultaneously looking to strengthen other approaches, such as fortification and improving diets, women's education, and development programs aimed at improving social inequities.

## REFERENCES

1. West KP Jr. Extent of vitamin A deficiency among preschool children and women of reproductive age. J Nutr 2002;132:2857S–2866S.
2. Sommer A, West KP Jr. Vitamin a deficiency: health, survival, and vision. New York: Oxford University Press, 1996.
3. Dalmiya N, Darnton-Hill I, Greig A, Palmer A, Wardlaw T. Vitamin A supplementation: progress for child survival. Working paper. New York: UNICEF, December 2006.
4. Bloem MW, Kiess L, Moench-Pfanner R. Process indicators for monitoring and evaluating vitamin A programs. J Nutr 2002;132:2934S–2939S.
5. Rice A, West KP Jr, Black RE. Vitamin A deficiency, in comparative quantification of health risks. In: Global and regional burden of disease attributable to selected major risk factors, vol. 1. EEsszti M, Lopez AD, Rodgers A, Murray CJL, eds. Geneva: World Health Organization, 2004:211–256.
6. Katz J, Khatry SK, West KP, Humphrey JH, LeClerq SC, Pradhan EK, et al. Night blindness is prevalent during pregnancy and lactation in rural Nepal. J Nutr 1995;125:2122–2127.
7. Gorstein J, Shrestha RK, Pandey S, Adhikari RK, Pradhan A. Current status of vitamin A deficiency and the national vitamin A control program in Nepal: results of the 1998 national micronutrient status survey. Asia Pac J Clin Nutr 2003;12:96–103.
8. Ahmed F, Azim A, Akhtaruzzaman A. Vitamin A deficiency in poor, urban, lactating women in Bangladesh: factors influencing vitamin A status. Public Health Nutr 2003;6:447–452.
9. Semba RD, de Pee S, Panagides D, Poly O, Bloem MW. Risk factors for nightblindness among women of childbearing age in Cambodia. Eur J Clin Nutr 2003;57:1627–1632.
10. Saunders C, do Carmo Leal M, Gomes, MM, Campos LF, dos Santos Silva BA, de Lima APPT, et al. Gestational nightblindness among women attending a public maternity hospital in Rio de Janeiro, Brazil. J Health Pop Nutr 2004;22:348–356.
11. Singh V, West KP Jr. Vitamin A deficiency and xerophthalmia among school-aged children in Southeastern Asia. Eur J Clin Nutr 2004;58:1342–1349.
12. Christian P, West KP Jr, Khatry SK, Katz J, Shrestha SR, Pradhan EK, et al. Night blindness of pregnancy in rural Nepal—nutritional and health risks. Int J Epidemiol 1998;27:231–237.
13. West KP Jr, Katz J, Khatry SK, LeClerq SC, Pradhan EK, Shrestha SR, et al. Double blind, cluster randomised trial of low dose supplementation with vitamin A or β-carotene on mortality related to pregnancy in Nepal. BMJ 1999;318:570–575.
14. Christian P, West KP Jr, Khatry SK, Kimbrough-Pradhan E, LeClerq SC, Katz J, et al. Night blindness during pregnancy and subsequent mortality among women in Nepal: effects of vitamin A and β-carotene supplementation. Am J Epidemiol 2000;152:542–547.
15. Solomons NW. Vitamin A. In: Present knowledge in nutrition, 9th ed., vol. 1. Bowman BA, Russell RM, eds. International Life Sciences Institute. Washington, DC: ILSI, 2006:157–183.
16. Blomhoff R, Blomhoff HK. Overview of retinoid metabolism and function. J Neurobiol 2006;66:606–630.
17. Dawson MI, Hobbs PD. The synthetic chemistry of retinoids. In: The retinoids: biology, chemistry, and medicine, 2nd ed. Sporn MB, Roberts AB, Goodman DS. New York: Raven Press, 1994:5–178.
18. Rodriguez-Amaya DB. A guide to carotenoid analysis in foods. OMNI Research, International Life Sciences Institute, Human Nutrition Research Institute. Washington, DC: ILSI, 1999:1–64.
19. Krinsky NI, Johnson EJ. Carotenoid actions and their relation to health and disease. Mol Aspects Med 2005;26:459–516.
20. Nagao A. Oxidative conversion of carotenoids to retinoids and other products. J Nutr 2004;134:237S–240S.
21. Harrison EH, Hussain MM. Mechanisms involved in the intestinal digestion and absorption of dietary vitamin A. J Nutr 2001;131:1405–1408.
22. Wald G. Molecular basis of visual excitation. Science 1968;162:230–239.

23. Hargrave PA. Rhodopsin structure, function and topography: the Friedenwald Lecture. Invest Ophthalmol Vis Sci 2001;42:3–9.

24. Lamb TD, Pugh EN Jr. Dark adaptation and the retinoid cycle of vision. Prog Retinal Eye Res 2004;23(3):307–380.

25. Pepperberg DR, Crouch RK. An illuminating new step in visual-pigment regeneration. Lancet 2001;358:298–299.

26. West KP Jr, McLaren DS. The epidemiology of vitamin A disorders. In: The epidemiology of eye disease, 2nd ed. Johnson G, Minassian DC, Weale RA, West SK, eds. London: Arnold, 2003:241–259.

27. Zile MH. Function of vitamin A in vertebrate embryonic development. J Nutr 2001;131:705–708.

28. West CE. Recent advances in vitamin A research: improving the vitamin status of populations. Twenty-first IVACG meeting, Marrakech, Morocco, February 3–5, 2003.

29. Omori M, Chytil F. Mechanism of vitamin A action. J Biol Chem 1982;257:14370–14374.

30. Balmer JE, Blomhoff R. Gene expression regulation by retinoic acid. J Lipid Res 2002;43:1773–1808.

31. McDowell EM, Keenan KP, Huang M. Effects of vitamin A-deprivation on hamster tracheal epithelium. Virchows Arch [Cell Pathol] 1984;45:197–219.

32. McDowell EM, Keenan KP, Huang M. Restoration of mucociliary tracheal epithelium following deprivation of vitamin A. Virchows Arch [Cell Pathol] 1984;45:221–240.

33. Sommer A. Vitamin A deficiency and its consequences: a field guide to their detection and control. 3rd ed. Geneva: World Health Organization, 1995.

34. Otten JJ, Hellwig JP, Meyers LD, eds. Dietary reference intakes: the essential guide to nutrient requirements. Institute of Medicine of the National Academy of Sciences. Washington, DC: National Academies, 2006:170–181.

35. Human vitamin and mineral requirements. A report of a joint FAO/WHO expert consultation, Bangkok, Thailand. Rome: World Health Organization and Food and Agricultural Organization of the United Nations, 2002:87–108.

36. Hands ES. Nutrients in food. Baltimore, MD: Lippincott, Williams and Wilkins, 2000.

37. Dary O, Mora JO. Food fortification to reduce vitamin A deficiency: International Vitamin A Consultative Group recommendations. J Nutr 2002;132:2927S–2933S.

38. Solon FS, Klemm RD, Sanchez L, Darnton-Hill I, Craft NE, Christian P, et al. Efficacy of a vitamin A-fortified wheat-flour bun on the vitamin A status of Filipino schoolchildren. Am J Clin Nutr. 2000;72:738–744.

39. Solon FS, Solon MS, Mehansho H, West KP Jr, Sarol J, Perfecto C, et al. Evaluation of the effect of vitamin A-fortified margarine on the vitamin A status of preschool Filipino children. Eur J Clin Nutr 1996;50:720–723.

40. Melse-Boostra A, de Pee S, Martini E, Halati S, Sari M, Kosen S, et al. The potential of various foods to serve as a carrier for micronutrient fortification, data from remote areas in Indonesia. Eur J Clin Nutr 2000;54:822–827.

41. US Department of Agriculture, Agricultural Research Service, 2004. What we eat in America, NHANES 2001–2002. Food Surveys Research Group. Available at: http://www.barc.usda.gov/bhnrc/foods.

42. Cotton PA, Subar AF, Friday JE, Cook A. Dietary sources of nutrients among US adults, 1994 to 1996. J Am Diet Assoc 2004;104:921–930.

43. Haskell MJ, Brown KH. Maternal vitamin A nutriture and the vitamin A content of human milk. J Mammary Gland Biol Neoplasia 1999;4:243–257.

44. Wallingford JC, Underwood BA. Vitamin A deficiency in pregnancy, lactation and the nursing child. In: Vitamin A deficiency and its control. Bauernfiend JC, ed. Orlando, FL: Academic, 1986:101–152.

45. West KP Jr, Chirambo MC, Katz J, Sommer A, the Malawi Survey Group. Breastfeeding, weaning patterns and the risk of xerophthalmia in southern Malawi. Am J Clin Nutr 1986;44:690–697.

46. Khatry SK, West KP Jr, Katz J, LeClerq SC, Pradhan EK, Shu-Fune L, et al. Epidemiology of xerophthalmia in Nepal. Arch Ophthalmol 1995;113:425–429.

47. Rodriguez-Amaya, DB. Carotenoids and food preparation: the retention of provitamin A carotenoids in prepared, processed and stored foods. Washington, DC: OMNI Project/John Snow, 1997:1–88.

48. Engleberger L, Darnton-Hill I, Coyne T, Fitzgerald MH, Marks GC. Carotenoid-rich bananas: a potential food source for alleviating vitamin A deficiency. Food Nutr Bull 2003;24:303–318.

49. West CE, Eilander A, van Lieshout M. Consequences of revised estimates of carotenoid bioefficacy for dietary control of vitamin A deficiency in developing countries. J Nutr 2002;132:2920S–2926S.

50. West CE, Castenmiller JJJM. Quantification of the "SLAMENGHI" factors for carotenoid bioavailability and bioconversation. Int J Vit Nutr 1998;68:371–377.

51. Castenmiller JJM, West CE. Bioavailability and bioconversion of carotenoids. Annu Rev Nutr 1998;18:19–38.

52. De Pee S, West CE. Dietary carotenoids and their role in combating vitamin A deficiency: a review of the literature. Eur J Clin Nutr 1996;50:S38–S53.

53. Food and Agriculture Organization of the United Nations. Requirements of vitamin A, iron, folate and vitamin $B_{12}$. Report of a Joint FAO/WHO Expert Consultation. Rome: Food and Agriculture Organization, 1988.

54. Parker RS, Swanson JE, You C-S, Edwards AJ, Huang T. Bioavailability of carotenoids in human subjects. Proc Nutr Soc 1999;58:1–8.

55. de Pee S, West CE, Permaesih D, Martuti S, Muhilal, Hautvast JGAJ. Orange fruit is more effective than are dark-green, leafy vegetables in increasing serum concentrations of retinol and β-carotene in schoolchildren in Indonesia. Am J Clin Nutr 1998;68:1058–1067.

56. Rock CL, Lovalvo JL, Emenhiser C, Ruffin MT, Flatt SW, Schwartz SJ. Bioavailability of β-carotene is lower in raw than in processed carrots and spinach in women. J Nutr 1998;128:913–916.

57. Castenmiller JJM, West CE, Linssen JPH, van het Hof KH, Voragen AGJ. The food matrix of spinach is a limiting factor in determining the bioavailability of β-carotene and to a lesser extent of lutein in humans. J Nutr 1999;129:349–355.

58. Ncube TN, Greiner T, Malaba LC, Gebre-Medhin M. Supplementing lactating women with pureed papaya and grated carrots improved vitamin A status in a placebo-controlled trial. J Nutr 2001;131:1497–1502.

59. Reidl J, Linseisen J, Hoffman J, Wolfram G. Some dietary fibers reduce the absorption of carotenoids in women. J Nutr 1999;129:2170–2176.

60. Takyi EEK. Children's consumption of dark green, leafy vegetables with added fat enhances serum retinol. J Nutr 1999;129:1549–1554.

61. Drammeh BS, Marquis GS, Funkhouser E, Bates C, Eto I, Stephensen CB. A randomized, 4-month mango and fat supplementation trial improved vitamin A status among young Gambian children. J Nutr 2002;132:3693–3699.

62. Ribaya-Mercado JD. Influence of dietary fat on β-carotene absorption and bioconversion into vitamin A. Nutr Rev 2002;60:104–110.

63. Van Vliet T, van Vlissingen MF, van Schaik F, van den Berg H. β-Carotene absorption and cleavage in rats is affected by the vitamin A concentration of the diet. J Nutr 1996;126:499–508.

64. Dietary reference intakes for vitamin A, vitamin K, arsenic, boron, chromium, copper, iodine, iron, manganese, molybdenum, nickel, silicon, vanadium, and zinc. Institute of Medicine. Washington, DC: National Academy, 2001:82–161.

65. Russell RM, Ross AC, Trumbo PR, West KP. Retinol equivalency ratio of β-carotene (Letter). J Nutr 2003;133:2915–2916.

66. de Pee S, West CE, Muhilal, Karyadi D, Hautvast JGAJ. Lack of improvement in vitamin A status with increased consumption of dark green leafy vegetables. Lancet 1995;346:75–81.

67. de Pee S, Bloem MW, Gorstein J, Sari M, Satoto, Yip R, et al. Reappraisal of the role of vegetables in the vitamin A status of mothers in Central Java, Indonesia. Am J Clin Nutr 1998;68:1068–1074.

68. van Lieshout M, de Pee S. Vitamin A equivalency estimates: understanding apparent differences. Am J Clin Nutr 2005;81:943–944.

69. FAO/WHO Expert Consultation. Requirements of vitamin A, iron, folate and vitamin $B_{12}$. FAO Food Nutrition Ser 1988;23:16–32.

70. West CE Meeting requirements for vitamin A. Nutr Rev 2000;58:341–345.

71. Miller M, Humphrey J, Johnson E, Marinda E, Brookmeyer R, Katz J. Why do children become vitamin A deficient? J Nutr 2002;132:2867S–2880S.

72. Olson JA. Needs and sources of carotenoids and vitamin A. Nutr Rev 1994;52:67–73.

73. Sommer A, Davidson FR. Assessment and control of vitamin A deficiency. J Nutr 2002;132:2845S–2850S.

74. Zile MH. Function of vitamin A in vertebrate embryonic development. J Nutr 2001;131:705–708.
75. Matthews KA, Rhoten WB, Driscoll HK, Chertow BS. Vitamin A deficiency impairs fetal islet development and causes subsequent glucose intolerance in adult rats. J Nutr 2004;134:1958–1963.
76. Chailley-Heu B, Chelly N, Lelievre-Pegorier M, Barlier-Mur A-M, Merlet-Benichou M, Bourbon J. Mild vitamin A deficiency delays fetal lung maturation in the rat. Am J Respir Cell Mol Biol 1999;21:89–96.
77. Lelievre-Pegorier M, Vilar J, Ferrier M-L, Moreau E, Freund N, Gilbert T, et al. Mild vitamin A deficiency leads to inborn nephron deficit in the rat. Kidney Int 1998;54:1455–1462.
78. de Pee S, Dary O. Biochemical indicators of vitamin A deficiency: serum retinol and serum retinol binding protein. J Nutr 2002;132:2895S–2901S.
79. Congdon NG, West KP Jr. Physiologic indicators of vitamin A status. J Nutr 2002;132:2889S–2894S.
80. de Pee S, Dary O. Biochemical indicators of vitamin A deficiency: serum retinol and serum retinol binding protein. J Nutr 2002;132:2895S–2901S.
81. Mi J, Lin LM, Ma GF, Gu X, Liu M, Cheng H, Hou DQ, Tan ZW, Lie CY. Prevalence of vitamin A deficiency in children under 6 years of age in Tibet, China. Zhonghua Yu Fang Yi Xue Za Zhi 2006;37:419–422.
82. Toteja GS, Singh P, Dhillon BS, Saxena BN. Vitamin A deficiency disorders in 16 districts of India. Indian J Pediatr 2002;69:603–605.
83. Feldon F, Bahl S, Bhatnagar P, Wenger J. Severe vitamin A deficiency in India during pulse polio immunization (correspondence). Indian J Med Res 2005;122:265–267.
84. Maziya-Dixon BB, Akinyele IO, Sanusi RA, Oguntona TE, Nokoe SK, Harris EW. Vitamin A deficiency is prevalent in children less than 5 years of age in Nigeria. J Nutr 2006;136:2255–2261.
85. Martins MC, Santos LMP, Assis AMO. Prevalence of hypovitaminosis A among preschool children from northeastern Brazil, 1998. Rev Saude Pub 2004;38:537–542.
86. Castejon HV, Ortega P, Amaya D, Gomez G, Leal J, Castejon OJ. Co-existence of anemia, vitamin A deficiency and growth retardation among children 24–84 months old in Maracaibo, Venezuela. Nutr Neurosci 2004;7:113–119.
87. Semba RD, de Pee S, Panagides D, Poly O, Bloem MW. Risk factors for xerophthalmia among mothers and their children and for mother–child pairs with xerophthalmia in Cambodia. Arch Ophthalmol 2004;122:517–523.
88. Palafox NA, Gamble MV, Dancheck B, Ricks MO, Briand K, Semba RD. Vitamin A deficiency, iron deficiency, and anemia among preschool children in the Republic of the Marshall Islands. Nutrition 2003;19:405–408.
89. Kurugol Z, Egemen A, Keskinoglu P, Darcan S, Aksit S. Vitamin A deficiency in healthy children aged 6–59 months in Izmir Province of Turkey. Paediat Perinat Epidemiol 2000;14:64–69.
90. Inandi T, Ertekin V, Guraksin A, Keles S, Yildirim AK. Vitamin A deficiency in healthy children aged 6–71 months in eastern Turkey. Ann Trop Paediatr 2004;24:107–108.
91. Coles CL, Levy A, Gorodischer R, Dagan R, Deckelbaum RJ, Blaner WS, Fraser D. Subclinical vitamin A deficiency in Israeli-Bedouin toddlers. Eur J Clin Nutr 2004;58:796–802.
92. Mihora LD, Jatla KK, Little T, Campbell M, Rahim A, Enzenauer RW. Vitamin A deficiency in Afghanistan. Eye Contact Lens 2004;30:159–162.
93. Olson JA, Gunning DB, Tilton RA. Liver concentrations of vitamin A and carotenoids, as a function of age and other parameters, of American children who died of various causes. Am J Clin Nutr 1984;39:903–910.
94. Gebre-Medhin M, Vahlquist A. Vitamin A nutrition in the human foetus. Int J Vitam Nutr Res 1983;53:13–18.
95. West KP Jr. Public health impact of preventing vitamin A deficiency in the first 6 months of life. In: Micronutrient deficiencies in the first 6 months of life. Nestle Nutrition Workshop Series Pediatric Program. Basel: Karger AG, 2002;52:103–127.
96. Lindblad BS, Patel M, Hamadeh M, Helmy N, Ahmad I, Dawodu A, et al. Age and sex are important factors in determining normal retinol levels. J Trop Pediatr 1998;44:96–99.
97. Humphrey JH, Rice AL. Vitamin A requirements of young infants: re-examining its need and importance. Lancet 2000;356:422–424.
98. Mactier H, Weaver T. Vitamin A and preterm infants: what we know, what we don't now, and what we need to know. Arch Dis Child Fetal Neonatal Ed 2005;90:103–108.

99. Singh V, West KP Jr. Vitamin A deficiency and xerophthalmia among school-aged children in Southeastern Asia. Eur J Clin Nutr 2004;58:1342–1349.

100. Christian P. Recommendations for indicators: night blindness during pregnancy—a simple tool to assess vitamin A deficiency in a population. J Nutr 2002;132:2884S–2888S.

101. Mellanby E, Green HN. Vitamin A as an anti-infective agent. BMJ 1929;i:984–986.

102. Semba RD. Vitamin A as "anti-infective" therapy, 1920–1940. J Nutr 1999;129:783–791.

103. Scrimshaw NS, Taylor CE, Gordon JE. Interactions of nutrition and infection. WHO Monograph Series. Geneva: World Health Organization, 1968.

104. Semba RD. Vitamin A, immunity, and infection. Clin Infect Dis 1994;19:489–499.

105. Stephenson CB. Vitamin A, infection and immune function. Ann Rev Nutr 2001;21:167–192.

106. Sommer A, Katz J, Tarwotjo I. Increased risk of respiratory disease and diarrhea in children with preexisting mild vitamin A deficiency. Am J Clin Nutr 1984;40:1090–1095.

107. Sommer A, Hussaini G, Tarwotjo I, Susanto D. Increased mortality in children with mild vitamin A deficiency. Lancet 1983;2:585–588.

108. Milton RC, Reddy V, Naidu AN. Mild vitamin A deficiency and childhood morbidity—an Indian experience. Am J Clin Nutr 1987;46:827–829.

109. Bloem MW, Wedel M, Egger RJ, Speek AJ, Schrijver J, Saowakontha S, et al. Mild vitamin A deficiency and risk of respiratory tract diseases and diarrhea in preschool and school children in northeastern Thailand. Am J Epidemiol 1990;131:332–339.

110. Sommer A, Tarwotjo I, Djunaedi E, West KP Jr, Loedin AA, Tilden R, et al. Impact of vitamin A supplementation on childhood mortality: A randomized controlled community trial. Lancet 1986;1:1169–1173.

111. Muhilal, Permaesih D, Idjradinata YR, Muherdiyantiningsih, Karyadi D. Vitamin A-fortified monosodium glutamate and health, growth, and survival of children: a controlled field trial. Am J Clin Nutr 1988;48:1271–1276.

112. Rahmathullah L, Underwood BA, Thulasiraj RD, Milton RC, Ramaswamy K, Rahmathullah R, et al. Reduced mortality among children in southern India receiving a small weekly dose of vitamin A. N Engl J Med 1990;323:929–935.

113. Vijayaraghavan K, Radhaiah G, Prakasam BS, Sarma KVR, Reddy V. Effect of massive dose vitamin A on morbidity and mortality in Indian children. Lancet 1990;336:1342–1345.

114. West KP Jr, Pokhrel RP, Katz J, LeClerq SC, Khatry SK, Shrestha SR, et al. Efficacy of vitamin A in reducing preschool child mortality in Nepal. Lancet 1991;338:67–71.

115. Daulaire NMP, Starbuck ES, Houston RM, Church MS, Stukel TA, Pandey MR. Childhood mortality after a high dose of vitamin A in a high risk population. BMJ 1992;304:207–210.

116. Ghana VAST Study Team. Vitamin A supplementation in northern Ghana: effects on clinic attendances, hospital admissions, and child mortality. Lancet 1993;342:7–12.

117. Herrera MG, Nestel P, el Amin A, Fawzi, WW, Mohamed KA, Weld L. Vitamin A supplementation and child survival. Lancet 1992;340(8814):267–71.

118. Tonascia JA. Meta-analysis of published community trials: impact of vitamin A on mortality. In: Bellagio meeting on vitamin A deficiency and childhood mortality. Proceedings of Public Health Significance of Vitamin A Deficiency and Its Control. New York: Helen Keller International, 1993:49–51.

119. Beaton GH, Martorell R, Aronson KJ, Edmonston B, McCabe G, Ross AC, et al. Effectiveness of vitamin A supplementation in the control of young child morbidity and mortality in developing countries. Geneva: Administrative Committee on Coordination–Sub-Committee on Nutrition (ACC/SCN), 1993. ACC/SCN State of the Art Series Nutrition Policy Discussion Paper No. 13.

120. Fawzi WW, Chameres TC, Herrera MG, Mosteller F. Vitamin A supplementation and child mortality. JAMA 1993;269:898–903.

121. Glasziou PP, Mackerras DEM. Vitamin A supplementation in infectious diseases: a meta-analysis. BMJ 1993;306:366–370.

122. Banajeh SM. Is 12-monthly vitamin A supplementation of preschool children effective? An observational study of mortality rates for severe dehydrating diarrhea in Yemen. S Afr J Clin Nutr 2003;16:137–142.

123. Thapa S, Choe MK, Retherford RD. Effects of vitamin A supplementation on child mortality: evidence from Nepal's 2001 Demographic and Health Survey. Trop Med Int Health 2005;10:782–789.

124. Humphrey JH, West KP Jr, Sommer A. Vitamin A deficiency and attributable mortality among under-5-year-olds. Bull World Health Organ 1992;70:225–232.

125. Rice AL, West KP Jr, Black RE. Vitamin A deficiency. In: Comparative quantification of health risks. Global and regional burden of disease attributable to selected major risk factors, vol. 1. Ezzati M, Lopez AD, Rodgers A, Murray CJL, eds. Geneva: World Health Organization, 2004;4:211–256.

126. Ellison JB. Intensive vitamin therapy in measles. BMJ 1932;2:708–711.

127. Barclay AJG, Foster A, Sommer A. Vitamin A supplements and mortality related to measles: a randomised clinical trial. BMJ 1987;294:294–296.

128. Hussey GD, Klein M. A randomized, controlled trial of vitamin A in children with severe measles. N Engl J Med 1990;323:160–164.

129. West KP Jr. Vitamin A deficiency: its epidemiology and relation to child mortality and morbidity. In: Vitamin A in health and disease. Blomhoff R, ed. New York: Dekker, 1994.

130. Arthur P, Kirkwood B, Ross D, et al. Impact of vitamin A supplementation on childhood morbidity in northern Ghana. Lancet 1992;339:361–362.

131. Shankar AH, Genton B, Semba RD, Baisor M, Paino J, Tamja S, et al. Effect of vitamin A supplementation on morbidity due to *Plasmodium falciparum* in young children in Papua New Guinea: a randomised trial. Lancet 1999;354:203–209.

132. Fawzi WW, Mbise RL, Hertzmark E, Fataki MR, Herrera MG, Ndossi G, et al. A randomized trial of vitamin A supplements in relation to mortality among human immunodeficiency virus-infected and uninfected children in Tanzania. Pediatr Infect Dis J 1999;18:127–133.

133. Semba RD, Ndugwa C, Perry RT, Clark TD, Jackson JB, Melikian G, et al. Effect of periodic vitamin A supplementation on mortality and morbidity of human immunodeficiency virus-infected children in Uganda: a controlled clinical trial. Nutrition 2005;21:25–31.

134. Coutsoudis A, Bobat RA, Coovadia HM, Kuhn L, Tsai WY, Stein ZA. The effects of vitamin A supplementation on the morbidity of children born to HIV-infected women. Am J Public Health 1995;85:1076–1081.

135. Villamor E, Mbise R, Spiegelman D, Hertzmark E, Fataki M, Peterson KE, et al. Vitamin A supplements ameliorate the adverse effect of HIV-1, malaria, and diarrheal infections on child growth. Pediatrics 2002;109:E6.

136. Vitamin A and Pneumonia Working Group. Potential interventions for the prevention of childhood pneumonia in developing countries: a meta-analysis of data from field trials to assess the impact of vitamin A supplementation on pneumonia morbidity and mortality. Bull World Health Organ 1995;73:609–619.

137. Katz J, West KP Jr, Khatry SK, Pradhan EK, LeClerq SC, Christian P, et al. Maternal low-dose vitamin A or β-carotene supplementation has no effect on fetal loss and early infant mortality: a cluster randomized trial in Nepal. Am J Clin Nutr 2000;71:1570–1576.

138. Fawzi WW, Msamanga GI, Hunter D, Renjifo B, Antelman G, Bang H, et al. Randomized trial of vitamin A supplements in relation to transmission of HIV-1 through breastfeeding and early child mortality. AIDS 2002;16:1935–1944.

139. Christian P, West KP Jr, Khatry SK, LeClerq SC, Kimbrough-Pradhan E Katz J, et al. Maternal night blindness increases risk of infant mortality in the first 6 months of life in Nepal. J Nutr 2001;131:1510–1512.

140. West KP Jr, Katz J, Shrestha SR, Le Clerq SC, Khatry SK, Pradhan EK, et al. Mortality of infants <6 months of age supplemented with vitamin A: a randomized double-masked trial in Nepal. Am J Clin Nutr 1995;62:143–148.

141. WHO/CHD Immunisation-Linked Vitamin A Supplementation Study Group. Randomized trial to assess benefits and safety of vitamin A supplementation linked to immunisation in early infancy. Lancet 1998;352:1257–1263.

142. Humphrey JH, Agoestina T, Wu L, Usman A, Nurachim M, Subardja D, et al. Impact of neonatal vitamin A supplementation on infant morbidity and mortality. J Pediatr 1996;128:489–496.

143. Rahmathullah L, Tielsch JM, Thulasiraj RD, Katz J, Coles C, Devi S, et al. Impact of supplementing newborn infants with vitamin A on early infant mortality: community based randomised trial in southern India. BMJ 2003;327:254–259.

144. Coles CL, Rahmathullah L, Kanungo R, Thulasiraj RD, Katz J, Santhosham M, et al. Vitamin A supplementation at birth delays pneumococcal colonization in South Indian infants. J Nutr 2001;131:255–261.

145. Malaba LC, Iliff PJ, Nathoo KJ, Marinda E, Moulton LH, Zijenah LS, et al. Effect of postpartum maternal or neonatal vitamin A supplementation on infant mortality among infants born to HIV-negative mothers in Zimbabwe. Am J Clin Nutr 2005;81:454–456.

146. Humphrey JH, Iliff PJ, Marinda ET, Mutasa K, Moulton LH, Chidawanyika H, et al. Effects of a single large dose of vitamin A, given during the postpartum period to HIV-positive women and their infants, on child HIV infection, HIV-free survival, and mortality. J Infect Dis 2006;193:860–871.

147. Katz J, Khatry SK, West KP Jr, Humphrey JH, LeClerq SC, Pradhan EK, et al. Night blindness is prevalent during pregnancy and lactation in rural Nepal. J Nutr 1995;125:2122–2127.

148. United Nations International Children's Emergency Fund. Progotir Pathey on the road to progress. Achieving the goals for children in Bangladesh. Bangladesh: Bangladesh Bureau of Statistics, Ministry of Planning, Government of the People's Republic of Bangladesh, United Nations Children's Fund, 1998.

149. Christian P, West KP Jr, Khatry SK, Katz J, LeClerq S, Pradhan EK, et al. Vitamin A or β-carotene supplementation reduces but does not eliminate maternal night blindness in Nepal. J Nutr 1998;128:1458–1463.

150. Semba RD, de Pee S, Panagides D, Poly O, Bloem MW. Risk factors for night blindness among women of childbearing age in Cambodia. Eur J Clin Nutr 2003;57:1627–1632.

151. Saunders C, Mamalho RA, Thiapo de Lima APP, Gomes MM, Campos LF, Silva BAS, et al. Association between gestational night blindness and serum retinol in mother/newborn pairs in the city of Rio de Janeiro, Brazil. Nutrition 2005;21:456–461.

152. Sivakumar B, Panth M, Shatrugna V, Raman L. Vitamin A requirements assessed by plasma response to supplementation during pregnancy. Int J Vit Nutr Res 1997;67:232–236.

153. Christian P, Schulze K, Stoltzfus RJ, West KP Jr. Hyporetinemia, illness symptoms, and acute phase protein response in pregnant women with and without night blindness. Am J Clin Nutr 1998;67:1237–1243.

154. Faisel H, Pittrof R. Vitamin A and causes of maternal mortality: association and biological plausibility. Public Health Nutr 2000;3:321–327.

155. Green HN, Pindar D, Davis G, Mellanby E. Diet as a prophylactic agent against puerperal sepsis. BMJ 1931;ii:595–598.

156. Cox SE, Arthur P, Kirkwood BR, Yeboah-Antwi, Riley EM. Vitamin A supplementation increases ratios of proinflammatory to anti-inflammatory cytokine responses in pregnancy and lactation. Clin Exp Immunol 2006;144:392–400.

157. Semba RD, Miotti PG, Chiphangwi JD, Saah AJ, Canner JK, Dallabetta GA, et al. Maternal vitamin A deficiency and mother-to-child transmission of HIV-1. Lancet 1994;343:1593–1597.

158. Mostad SB, Overbaugh J, DeVange DM, Welch MJ, Chohan B, Mandaliya K, et al. Hormonal contraception, vitamin A deficiency, and other risk factors for shedding of HIV-1 infected cells from the cervix and vagina. Lancet 1997;350:922–927.

159. Belec L, Mbopi-Keou F-X, Roubache J-F, Mayaud P, Paul J-L, Gresenguet G. Vitamin A deficiency and genital tract infections in women living in Central Africa. J Acquir Immune Defic Syndr 20062:29:203–206.

160. Semba RD, Kumwenda N, Taha TE, Hoover DR, Quinn TC, Lan Y, et al. Mastitis and immunological factors in breast milk of human immuno-deficiency virus-infected women. J Hum Lactation 1999;15:301–306.

161. Nussenblatt V, Lema V, Kumwenda N, Broadhead R, Neville MC, Taha TE, et al. Epidemiology and microbiology of subclinical mastitis among HIV-infected women in Malawi. Int J STD AIDS 2005;16:227–232.

162. Dorosko SM. Vitamin A, mastitis, and mother-to-child transmission of HIV-1 through breast-feeding: current information and gaps in knowledge. Nutr Rev 2005;63:332–346.

163. Fawzi WW, Msamanga GI, Spiegelman D, Urassa EJN, McGrath N, Mwakagile D, et al. Randomised trial of effects of vitamin supplements on pregnancy outcomes and T cell counts in HIV-1-infected women in Tanzania. Lancet 1998;351:1477–1482.

164. Fawzi WW, Msamanga GI, Antelman G, Xu C, Hertzmark E, Spiegelman D, et al. Effect of prenatal vitamin supplementation on lower genital levels of HIV type 1 and interleukin type 1 beta at 36 weeks of gestation. Clin Infect Dis 2004;38:716–722.

165. Fawzi WW, Msamanga GI, Hunter D, Renjifo B, Antelman G, Bang H, et al. Randomized trial of vitamin supplements in relation to transmission of HIV-1 through breastfeeding and early child mortality. AIDS 2002;16:1935–1944.

166. Kennedy CM, Coustoudis A, Kuhn L, Pillay K, Mburu A, Stein Z, et al. Randomized controlled trial assessing the effect of vitamin A supplementation on maternal morbidity during pregnancy and postpartum among HIV-infected women. J Acquir Immune Defic Syndr 2000;24:37–44.

167. Cousoudis A, Pillay L, Spooner E, Kuhn L. Coovadia HM. Randomized trial testing the effect of vitamin A supplementation on pregnancy outcomes and early mother-to-child HIV-1 transmission in Durban, South Africa. South African Vitamin A Study Group. AIDS 1999;13:1517–1524.

168. Filteau SM, Rollins NC, Coutsoudis A, Sullivan KR, Willumsen JF, Tomkins AM. The effect of antenatal vitamin A and β-carotene supplementation on gut integrity of infants of HIV-infected South African women. J Pediatr Gastroenterol Nutr 2001;32:464–470.

169. Kumwenda N, Miotti PG, Taha TE, Broadhead R, Biggar RJ, Jackson JB, et al. Antenatal vitamin A supplementation increases birth weight and decreases anemia among infants born to human immunodeficiency virus-infected women in Malawi. Clin Infect Dis 2002;35:618–624.

170. Wolf G. A history of vitamin A and retinoids. FASEB J 1996;10:1102–1107.

171. Wolf G. Early research into the vitamins: the work of Wilhelm Stepp. J Nutr 1997;127:1255–1259.

172. Semba RD Vitamin A as "anti-infective" therapy. J Nutr 1999;129:783–791.

173. Wolf G. The discovery of the visual function of vitamin A. J Nutr 2001;131:1647–50.

174. Mori M. Uber den sog Hikan (Xerosis conjunctivae infantum ev Keratomalacie). Jahrb Kinderheilk 1904;59:175–194.

175. Westhoff CHA. Eenige opmerkingen omtrent oogziekten op Java. Feestbundel Geneesk Tijdschr Ned Indie 1911;141.

176. McCollum EV, Davis M. The necessity of certain lipins in the diet during growth. J Biol Chem 1913;15:167–175.

177. Osborne TB, Mendel LB. The influence of butter-fat on growth. J Biol Chem 1913;16:423–437.

178. Bloch CE. Clinical investigation of xerophthalmia and dystrophy in infants and young children (xerophthalmia et dystropia alipogenetica). J Hygiene 1921;19:283–304.

179. Wolbach SB, Howe PR. Tissue changes following deprivation of fat-soluble A vitamin. J Exp Med 1925;42:753–777.

180. Green HN, Mellanby E. Vitamin A as an anti-infective agent. BMJ 1928;20:691–696.

181. Blackfan KD, Wolbach SB. Vitamin A deficiency in infants. A clinical and pathological study. J Pediatr 1933;3:679–706.

182. Ramalingaswami V. Nutritional diarrhoea due to vitamin A deficiency. Indian J Med Sci 1948;2:665–674.

183. Wald G. Carotenoids and the visual cycle. J Gen Physiol 1935;19:351–357.

184. Clausen SW, McCoord AB. The carotenoids and vitamin A of the blood. J Pediatr 1938;13:635–650.

185. Laurie NR, Moore T, Rajagopal KR. The excretion of vitamin A in urine. Biochemical J 1941;35:825–836.

186. Thurnham DI, Mburu ASW, Mwaniki DL, Ed Wagt A. Micronutrients in childhood and the influence of subclinical inflammation. Proc Nutr Soc 2005;64:502–509.

187. Filteau SM, Morris SS, Abbott RA, Tomkins AM, Kirkwood BR, Arthur P, et al. Influence of morbidity on serum retinol of children in a community-based study in northern Ghana. Am J Clin Nutr 1993;58:192–197.

188. Mitra AK, Alvarez J, Stephensen CB. Increased urinary retinol loss in children with severe infections. Lancet 1998;351:1033–1034.

189. Ellison JB. Intensive vitamin A therapy in measles. BMJ 1932;2:708–711.

190. Gopalan C, Venkatachalam PS, Bhavani B. Studies of vitamin A deficiency in children. Am J Clin Nutr 1960;8:833–840.

191. McLaren DS, Oomen HAPC, Escapini H. Ocular manifestations of vitamin A deficiency in man. Bull World Health Organ 1966;34:357–361.

192. Oomen HAPC, McLaren DS, Escapini H. Epidemiology and public health aspects of hypovitaminosis A. A global survey of xerophthalmia. Trop Geogr Med 1964;4:271–315.

193. Micronutrient Deficiency Information System. Global prevalence of vitamin A deficiency. Geneva: World Health Organization, WHO/NUT/95.3, 1995. MDIS Working Paper No. 2.

194. Reddy V. History of the International Vitamin A Consultative Group 1975–2000. J Nutr 2002;132:2852S–2856S.

195. Sommer A. Nutritional blindness: xerophthalmia and keratomalacia. Oxford, UK: Oxford University Press, 1981.

196. Sommer A, Tarwotjo I, Hussaini G. Incidence, prevalence and scale of blinding malnutrition. Lancet 1981;1:1407–1408.

197. World. The World Summit for Children. New York: United Nations International Children's Emergency Fund, 1990.

198. World declaration and global plan of action, International Conference on Nutrition. Rome: Food and Agriculture Organization/World Health Organization, 1992.

199. Cohen N, Rahman H, Mitra M, Sprague J, Islam S, Leemhuis de Regt E, et al. Impact of massive doses of vitamin A on nutritional blindness in Bangladesh. Am J Clin Nutr 1987;45:970–976.

200. Cohen N, Rahman H, Sprague J, Jalil MA, Leemhuis de Regt E, Mitra M. Prevalence and determinants of nutritional blindness in Bangladeshi children. World Health Stat Q 1985;38:317–330.

201. Wolde-Gebriel Z, Demeke T, West CE. Xerophthalmia in Ethiopia: a nationwide ophthalmological, biochemical and anthropometric survey. Eur J Clin Nutr 1991;45:469–478.

202. Katz J, Zeger SL, Tielsch JM. Village and household clustering of xerophthalmia and trachoma. Int J Epidemiol 1988;17:865–869.

203. Katz J, Zeger SL, West KP Jr, Tielsch JM, Sommer A. Clustering of xerophthalmia within households and villages. Int J Epidemiol 1993;22:709–715.

204. Gittelsohn J, Shankar AV, West KP, Ram R, Dhungel C, Dahal B. Infant feeding practices reflect antecedent risk of xerophthalmia in Nepali children. Eur J Clin Nutr 1997;51:484–490.

205. Gittelsohn J, Shankar AV, West KP Jr, Faruque F, Gnywali T, Pradhan EK. Child feeding and care behaviors are associated with xerophthalmia in rural Nepalese households. Soc Sci Med 1998;47:477–486.

206. Semba RD, de Pee S, Panagides D, Poly O, Bloem MW. Risk factors for nightblindness among women of childbearing age in Cambodia. Eur J Clin Nutr 2003;57:1627–1632.

207. Khatry SK, West KP Jr, Katz J, LeClerq SC, Pradhan EK, Wu LS, et al. Epidemiology of xerophthalmia in Nepal: a pattern of household poverty, childhood illness and mortality. Arch Ophthalmol 1995;113:425–429.

208. Hennig A, Foster A, Shrestha SP, Pokhrel RP. Vitamin A deficiency and corneal ulceration in south-east Nepal: implications for preventing blindness in children. Bull World Health Organ 1991;69:235–239.

209. Bloem MW, Wedel M, Egger RJ, Speek AJ, Chusilp K, Saowakontha S, et al. A prevalence study of vitamin A deficiency and xerophthalmia in Northeastern Thailand. Am J Epidemiol 1989;129:1095–1103.

210. Solon FS, Popkin BM, Fernandez TL, Latham MC. Vitamin A deficiency in the Philippines: a study of xerophthalmia in Cebu. Am J Clin Nutr 1978;31:360–368.

211. Klemm RDW, Villate EE, Tuason CS, Bayugo G, Mendoza OM. A prevalence study of xerophthalmia in the Philippines: implications for supplementation strategies. SE Asian J Trop Med Public Health 1993;24:617–623.

212. Rosen DS, al Sharif Z, Bashir M, al Shabooti A, Pizzarello LD. Vitamin A deficiency and xerophthalmia in western Yemen. Eur J Clin Nutr 1996;50:54–57.

213. Tielsch JM, West KP Jr, Katz J, Chirambo MC, Schwab L, Johnson GJ, et al. Prevalence and severity of xerophthalmia in southern Malawi. Am J Epidemiol 1986;124:561–586.

214. Danks J, Kaufman D, Rait J. A clinical and cytological study of vitamin A deficiency in Kiribati. Aust N Z J Ophthalmol 1992;20:215–218.

215. Katz J, West KP Jr, Khatry SK, Thapa MD, LeClerq SC, Pradhan EK, et al. Impact of vitamin A supplementation on prevalence and incidence of xerophthalmia in Nepal. Invest Ophthalmol Vis Sci 1995;36:2577–2583.

216. Muhilal, Tarwotjo I, Kodyat B, Herman S, Permaesih D, Karyadi D, et al. Changing prevalence of xerophthalmia in Indonesia, 1977 to 1992. Eur J Clin Nutr 1994;48:708–714.

217. Santos LMP, Dricot JM, Asciutti LS, Dricot-D'Ans C. Xerophthalmia in the state of Paraiba, north-east of Brazil: clinical findings. Am J Clin Nutr 1983;38:139–144.

218. Fawzi WW, Herrera MG, Willett WC, el Amin A, Nestel P, Lipsitz S, et al. Vitamin A supplementation and dietary vitamin A in relation to the risk of xerophthalmia. Am J Clin Nutr 1993;58:385–391.

219. Mahalanabis D. Breast feeding and vitamin A deficiency among children attending a diarrhoea treatment centre in Bangladesh: a case-control study. BMJ 1991;303:493–496.

220. West KP, Jr., Chirambo M, Katz J, Sommer A, Malawi Survey Group. Breast-feeding, weaning patterns, and the risk of xerophthalmia in Southern Malawi. Am J Clin Nutr 1986;44:690–697.

221. Bloem MW, Hye A, Wijnroks M, Ralte A, West KP Jr, Sommer A. The role of universal distribution of vitamin A capsules in combatting vitamin A deficiency in Bangladesh. Am J Epidemiol 1998;142:843–855.

222. Tarwotjo I, Tilden RL, Pettiss ST, Sommer A, Soedibjo S, Hussaini G, et al. Interactions of community nutritional status and xerophthalmia in Indonesia. Am J Clin Nutr 1983;37:645–651.

223. Mele L, West KP Jr, Kusdiono, Pandji A, Nendrawati H, Tilden RL, et al. Nutritional and household risk factors for xerophthalmia in Aceh, Indonesia: a case-control study. Am J Clin Nutr 1991;53:1460–1465.

224. Khan NC, Khoi HH, Dung PK, Anh HM, Dung NC, West CE. Dietary patterns in relation to vitamin A deficiency in children in the Red River Region of Vietnam. Eur J Clin Nutr 1996;50:S78–S79.

225. Hussain A, Kvale G. Serum vitamin A in relation to socio-economic, demographic and dietary characteristics in Bangladeshi children. Acta Paediatr 1996;85:971–976.

226. Kjolhede CL, Stallings RY, Dibley MJ, Sadjimin T, Dawiesah S, Padmawati S. Serum retinol levels among preschool children in Central Java: Demographic and socioeconomic determinants. Int J Epidemiol 1995;24:399–403.

227. Rosen DS, Sloan NL, Delrosar A, Delapza TC. Risk factors for vitamin A deficiency in rural areas of the Philippines. J Trop Pediatr 1994;40:82–87.

228. Ballew C, Bowman BA, Sowell AL, Gillespie C. Serum retinol distributions in residents of the United States: third National Health and Nutrition Examination Survey, 1988–94. Am J Clin Nutr 2001;73:586–593.

229. Pant I, Gopaldas T. Effect of mega doses of vitamin A on the vitamin A status of underpriviledged school-age boys (7–15 years). Indian J Med Res 1987;86:196–206.

230. Stoltzfus RJ, Hakimi M, Miller KW, Rasmussen KM, Dawiesah S, Habicht JP, et al. High dose vitamin A supplementation of breast feeding Indonesian mothers: effects on the vitamin A status of mother and infant. J Nutr 1993;123:666–675.

231. Ahmed F, Hasan N, Kabir Y. Vitamin A deficiency among adolescent female garment factory workers in Bangladesh. Eur J Clin Nutr 1997;51:698–702.

232. Ahmed F. Vitamin A deficiency in Bangladesh: a review and recommendations for improvement. Public Health Nutr 1999;2:1–14.

233. Rice AL, Stoltzfus RJ, de Francisco A, Chakraborty J, Kjolhede CL, Wahed MA. Maternal vitamin A or β-carotene supplementation in lactating Bangladeshi women benefits mothers and infants but does not prevent subclinical deficiency. J Nutr 1999;129:356–365.

234. Cohen N, Jalil MA, Rahman H, Leemhuis de Regt E, Spragus J, Mitra M. Blinding malnutrition in rural Bangladesh. J Trop Pediatr 1986;32:73–78.

235. Djunaedi E, Sommer A, Pandji A, Kusdiono, Taylor HR, Aceh Study Group. Impact of vitamin A supplementation on xerophthalmia: a randomized controlled community trial. Arch Ophthalmol 1988;106:218–222.

236. Tielsch JM, Sommer A. The epidemiology of vitamin A deficiency and xerophthalmia. Annu Rev Nutr 1984;4:183–205.

237. West KP Jr. Dietary vitamin A deficiency: effects on growth, infection, and mortality. Food Nutr Bull 1991;13:119–131.

238. Darnton-Hill I. Vitamin A in the third world. Proc Nutr Soc Aust 1989;14:13–23.

239. Tielsch JM, West KP Jr, Katz J, Chirambo MC, Schwab L, Johnson GJ, et al. Prevalence and severity of xeropthalmia in southern Malawi. Am J Epidemiol 1986;124:561–568.

240. Nestel P, Herrera MG, El Amin A, Fawzi W, Mohammed KA, Weld L. Risk factors associated with xerophthalmia in northern Sudan. J Nutr 1993;123:2115–2121.

241. Hussain A, Kvale G, Ali K, Bhuyan AW. Determinants of night blindness in Bangladesh. Int J Epidemiol 1993;22:1119–1126.

242. Cohen N, Jalil MA, Rahman H, Matin MA, Sprague J, Islam J, et al. Landholding, wealth and risk of blinding malnutrition in rural Bangladeshi households. Soc Sci Med 1985;21:1269–1272.

243. Ahmed F, Mohiduzzaman M, Barua A, Shaheen N, Margetts BM, Jackson AA. Effect of family size and income on the biochemical indices of urban school children in Bangladesh. Eur J Clin Nutr 1992;46:465–473.

244. Oomen HAPC, ten Doesschate J. The periodicity of xerophthalmia in South and East Asia. Ecol Food Nutr 1973;2:207–217.

245. Desai NC, Desai S, Desai R. Xerophthalmia clinics in rural eye camps. Int Ophthalmol 1992;16:139–145.

246. Sinha DP, Bang FB. Seasonal variation in signs of vitamin-A deficiency in rural West Bengal children. Lancet 1973;2:228–231.

247. Sinha DP, Bang FB. The effect of massive doses of vitamin A on the signs of vitamin A deficiency in preschool children. Am J Clin Nutr 1976;29:110–115.

248. 1998 Nutrition Surveillance Project annual report. National and divisional trends among children and households in rural Bangladesh. New York: Helen Keller International and Institute of Public Health Nutrition, 1999.

249. Bloem MW, Huq N, Gorstein J, Burger S, Kahn T, Islam N, et al. Production of fruits and vegetables at the homestead is an important source of vitamin A among women in rural Bangladesh. Eur J Clin Nutr 1996;50S:62–67.

250. Bloem MW, de Pee S, Darnton-Hill I. New issues in developing effective approaches for the prevention and control of vitamin A deficiency. Food Nutr Bull 1998;19:137–148.

251. Bloem MW, Darnton-Hill I. Micronutrient deficiencies: first link in the chain of nutritional and health events in economic crises. In: Preventive nutrition. Vol. 2: primary and secondary prevention. Totowa, NJ: Humana Press, 2007: in press.

252. Semba RD, Susanto B, Muhilal, Natadisastra G. The decline of admissions for xerophthalmia at Cicendo Eye Hospital, Indonesia, 1981–1992. Int Ophthalmol 1995;19:39–42.

253. Soewarta K, Bloem MW. The role of high-dose vitamin A capsules in preventing a relapse of vitamin A deficiency due to Indonesia's current crisis. Indonesia Crisis Bull 1999;1:1–4.

254. Brown KH, Black RE, Becker S, Nahar S, Sawyer J. Consumption of foods and nutrients by weanlings in rural Bangladesh. Am J Clin Nutr 1982;36:878–889.

255. Tarwotjo I, Sommer A, Soegiharto T, Susanto D, Muhilal. Dietary practices and xerophthalmia among Indonesian children. Am J Clin Nutr 1982;35:574–581.

256. Cohen N, Measham C, Khanum S, Khatun M, Ahmed N. Xerophthalmia in urban Bangladesh. Implications for vitamin A deficiency preventive strategies. Acta Paediatr Scand 1983;72:531–536.

257. Stanton BF, Clemens JD, Wojtyniak B, Khair T. Risk factors for developing mild nutritional blindness in urban Bangladesh. Am J Dis Child 1986;140:584–588.

258. Schaumberg DA, O'Connor J, Semba RD. Risk factors for xerophthalmia in the Republic of Kiribati. Eur J Clin Nutr 1996;50:761–764.

259. Mitra AK, Alvarez JO, Stephensen CB. Increased urinary retinol loss in children with severe infections. Lancet 1998;351:1033–1034.

260. Shankar AV, West KP Jr, Gittelsohn J, Katz J, Pradhan R. Chronic low intakes of vitamin-A rich foods in households with xerophthalmic children: a case-control study in Nepal. Am J Clin Nutr 1996;64:242–248.

261. De Sole G, Belay Y, Zegeye B. Vitamin A deficiency in southern Ethiopia. Am J Clin Nutr 1987;45:780–784.

262. Cohen N, Rahman H, Sprague J, Jalil MA, Leemhuis de Regt E, Mitra M. Prevalence and determinants of nutritional blindness in Bangladeshi children. World Health Stat Q 1985;38:317–330.

263. Hussain A, Lindtjorn B, Kvale G. Protein energy malnutrition, vitamin A deficiency and night blindness in Bangladeshi children. Ann Trop Paed 1996;16:319–325.

264. Shankar AV, Gittelsohn J, West KP Jr, Stallings R, Gnywali T, Faruque F. Eating from a shared plate affects food consumption in vitamin A-deficient Nepali children. J Nutr 1998;128:1127–1133.

265. Thurnham DI, McCabe GP, Northup-Clewes CA, Nestel P. Effects of subclinical infection on plasma retinol concentrations and assessment of prevalence of vitamin A deficiency: meta-analysis. Lancet 2003;362:2052–2058.

266. Thurnham DI, Singkamani R. The acute phase response and vitamin A status in malaria. Trans R Soc Trop Med Hyg 1991;85:194–199.
267. Rwangabwoba J-M, Fischman H, Semba RD. Serum vitamin A levels during tuberculosis and human immunodeficiency virus infection. Int J Tuberculosis Lung Dis 1998;2:771–773.
268. Sivakumar B, Reddy V. Absorption of labelled vitamin A in children during infection. Br J Nutr 1972;27:299–304.
269. Reddy V, Sivakumar B. Studies on vitamin A absorption in children. Indian Pediatr 1972;9:307–310.
270. Salazar-Lindo E, Salazar M, Alvarez JO. Association of diarrhea and low serum retinol in Peruvian children. Am J Clin Nutr 1993;58:110–113.
271. Campos FACS, Flores H, Underwood BA. Effect of an infection on vitamin A status of children as measured by the relative dose response (RDR). Am J Clin Nutr 1987;46:91–94.
272. Stephensen CB, Alvarez JO, Kohatsu J, Hardmeier R, Kennedy JI Jr, Gammon RB Jr. Vitamin A is excreted in the urine during acute infection. Am J Clin Nutr 1994;60:388–392.
273. Alvarez JO, Salazar-Lindo E, Kohatsu J, Miranda P, Stephensen CB. Urinary excretion of retinol in children with acute diarrhea. Am J Clin Nutr 1995;61:1273–1276.
274. Semba RD, Muhilal, West KP Jr, Natadisastra G, Eisinger W, Lan Y, et al. Hyporetinolemia and acute phase proteins in children with and without xerophthalmia. Am J Clin Nutr 2000;72:146–153.
275. Sommer A, Tarwotjo I, Katz J. Increased risk of xerophthalmia following diarrhea and respiratory disease. Am J Clin Nutr 1987;45:977–980.
276. Wittpenn J, Sommer A. Clinical aspects of vitamin A deficiency. In: Vitamin A deficiency and its control. Bauernfeind JC, ed. Orlando, FL: Academic, 1986.
277. Wondmikun Y. Dark adaptation pattern of pregnant women as an indicator of functional disturbance at acceptable serum vitamin A levels. Eur J Clin Nutr 2002;56:462–466.
278. Taren DL, Duncan B, Shrestha K, Shrestha N, Genaro-Wolf D, Schleicher RL, et al. The night vision threshold test is a better predictor of low serum vitamin A concentration than self-reported night blindness in pregnant urban Nepalese women. J Nutr 2004;134:2573.
279. Congdon NG, Dreyfuss ML, Christian P, Navitsky RC, Sanchez AM, Wu LSF, et al. Responsiveness of dark-adaptation threshold to vitamin A and β-carotene supplementation in pregnant and lactating women in Nepal. Am J Clin Nutr 2000;72:1004–1009.
280. Sommer A, Hussaini G, Muhilal, Tarwotjo I, Susanto D, Saroso JS. History of nightblindness: a simple tool for xerophthalmia screening. Am J Clin Nutr 1980;33:887–891.
281. Hussain A, Kvale G, Odland M. Diagnosis of night blindness and serum vitamin A level: a population-based study. Bull World Health Organ 1995;73:469–476.
282. McLaren DS, Oomen HAPC, Escapini H. Ocular manifestations of vitamin-A deficiency in man. Bull World Health Organ 1966;34:257–361.
283. Tarwotjo I, Katz J, West KP Jr, Tielsch JM, Sommer A. Xerophthalmia and growth in preschool Indonesian children. Am J Clin Nutr 1992;55:1142–1146.
284. Rahmathullah L, Underwood BA, Thulasiraj RD, Milton RC. Diarrhea, respiratory infections, and growth are not affected by a weekly low-dose vitamin A supplement: a masked, controlled field trial in children in southern India. Am J Clin Nutr 1991;54:568–577.
285. Fawzi WW, Herrera G, Willett WC, Nestel P, El Amin A, Mohamed KA. The effect of vitamin A supplementation on the growth of preschool children in the Sudan. Am J Public Health 1997;87:1359–1362.
286. Kirkwood BR, Ross DA, Arthur P, Morris SS, Dollimore N, Binka F, et al. Effect of vitamin A supplementation on the growth of young children in northern Ghana. Am J Clin Nutr 1996;63:773–781.
287. West KP Jr, LeClerq SC, Shrestha SR, Wu LSF, Pradhan EK, Khatry SK, et al. Effects of vitamin A on growth of vitamin A-deficient children: field studies in Nepal. J Nutr 1997;127:1957–1965.
288. Lie C, Ying C, En-Lin W, Brun T, Geissler C. Impact of large-dose vitamin A supplementation on childhood diarrhoea, respiratory disease and growth. Eur J Clin Nutr 1993;47:88–96.
289. Ramakrishnan U, Latham MC, Abel R. Vitamin A supplementation does not improve growth of preschool children: a randomized, double-blind field trial in South India. J Nutr 1995;125:202–211.
290. West KP Jr, Djunaedi E, Pandji A, Kusdiono, Tarwotjo I, Sommer A, et al. Vitamin A supplementation and growth: a randomized community trial. Am J Clin Nutr 1988;48:1257–1264.
291. Bahl R, Bhandari N, Taneja S, Bhan MK. The impact of vitamin A supplementation on physical growth of children is dependent on season. Eur J Clin Nutr 1997;51:26–29.

292. Muhilal, Murdiana A, Azis I, Saidin S, Jahari AB, Karyadi D. Vitamin A-fortified monosodium glutamate and vitamin A status: a controlled field trial. Am J Clin Nutr 1988;48:1265–1270.

293. Donnen P, Brasseur D, Dramaix M, Vertongen F, Zihindula M, Muhamiriza M, et al. Vitamin A supplementation but not deworming improves growth of malnourished preschool children in Eastern Zaire. J Nutr 1998;128:1320–1327.

294. Hadi H, Stoltzfus RJ, Dibley MJ, Moulton LH, West KP Jr, Kjolhede CL, et al. Vitamin A supplementation selectively improves linear growth of Indonesian preschool children: a randomized controlled trial. Am J Clin Nutr 2000;71:507–513.

295. Hadi H, Stoltzfus RJ, Moulton LH, Dibley MJ, West KP Jr. Respiratory infections reduce the growth response to vitamin A supplementation in a randomized controlled trial. Int J Epidemiol 1999;28:874–881.

296. Hadi H, Dibley MJ, West KP Jr. Complex interactions with infection and diet may explain seasonal growth responses to vitamin A in preschool aged Indonesian children. Eur J Clin Nutr 2004;58:990–999.

297. Coutsoudis A, Broughton M, Coovadia HM. Vitamin A supplementation reduces measles morbidity in young African children: a randomized, placebo-controlled, double-blind trial. Am J Clin Nutr 1991;54:890–895.

298. Donnen P, Dramaix M, Brasseur D, Bitwe R, Vertongen F, Hennart P. Randomized placebo-controlled clinical trial of the effect of a single high dose or daily low doses of vitamin A on the morbidity of hospitalized, malnourished children. Am J Clin Nutr 1998;68:1254–1260.

299. Ross D. Recommendations for vitamin A supplementation. J Nutr 2002;131:2902S–2906S.

300. Sommer A, Emran N, Tjakrasudjatma S. Clinical characteristics of vitamin A responsive and nonresponsive Bitot's spots. Am J Ophthalmol 1980;90:160–171.

301. Semba RD, Wirasasmita S, Natadisastra G, Muhilal, Sommer A. Response of Bitot's spots in preschool children to vitamin A treatment. Am J Ophthalmol 1990;110:416–420.

302. Sovani I, Humphrey JH, Kuntinalibronto DR, Natadisastra G, Muhilal, Tielsch JM. Response of Bitot's spots to a single oral 100,000- or 200,000-IU dose of vitamin A. Am J Ophthalmol 1994;118:792–796.

303. West CE. Vitamin A and measles. Nutr Rev 2000;58:S46–S54.

304. de Pee S, Bloem MW, Satoto, Yip R, Sukaton A, Tjiong R, et al. Impact of a social marketing campaign promoting dark-green leafy vegetables and eggs in Central Java, Indonesia. Int J Vit Nutr Res 1998;68:389–398.

305. Darnton-Hill I, Webb P, Harvey PWJ, Hunt JM, Dalmiya N, Chopra M, et al. Micronutrient deficiencies and gender: social and economic costs. Am J Clin Nutr 2005;81(suppl):1198S–205S.

306. Webb P, Nishida C, Darnton-Hill I. Age and sex as factors in the distribution of global micronutrient deficiencies. Nutr Rev 2007;65:233–245.

307. Ramakrishnan U, Darnton-Hill I. Vitamin A deficiency disorders: assessment and control of VADD. J Nutr 2002;132(9S):2947S–2953S.

308. Chopra M, Darnton-Hill I. Responding to the crisis in sub-Saharan Africa: the role of nutrition. Public Health Nutr 2006;9:544–550.

309. Rice AL, Stoltzfus RJ, de Francisco A, Kjolhede C. Evaluation of serum retinol, the modified-relative-dose-response ratio, and breast-milk vitamin A as indicators of response to postpartum maternal vitamin A supplementation. Am J Clin Nutr 2000;71:799–806.

310. Sommer A 2005. Innocenti micronutrient research report No. 1, paper presented to the International Vitamin A Consultative Group Conference. Available at: http://ivacg.ilsi.org/file/Innocenti.pdf.

311. Talukder A, Bloem MW. Homegardening activities in Bangladesh. Dhaka, Bangladesh: Helen Keller International, 1992.

312. Talukder A, Khan TA, Baker SK, Zakaria AKM, Bloem MW, Kiess LK. Home gardening activities in Bangladesh. Mapping report and inventory. Dhaka, Bangladesh: Helen Keller International, 1997.

313. Talukder A, Islam N, Klemm R, Bloem M. Home gardening in South Asia. The complete handbook. Dhaka, Bangladesh: Helen Keller International, 1993.

314. Talukder A, Kiess L, Huq N, de Pee S, Darnton-Hill I, Bloem MW. Increasing the production and consumption of vitamin A-rich fruits and vegetables: lessons learned in taking the Bangladesh homestead gardening programme to a national scale. Food Nutr Bull 2000;21:165–172.

315. Marsh R. Building on traditional gardening to improve household food security. FAO Food Nutr Agric 1998;22:4–14.

316. Solon MA. Control of vitamin A deficiency by education and the public health approach. In: Vitamin A deficiency and its control. Bauernfeind JC, ed. Orlando, FL: Academic, 1986.

317. Hagenimana V, Oyunga MA, Low J, Njoroge SM, Gichuki ST, Kabira J. The effects of women farmers' adoption of orange-fleshed sweet potatoes: raising vitamin A Intake in Kenya. Washington, DC: International Center for Research on Women, 1999.

318. Ayalew W, Wolde Gebriel Z, Kassa H. Reducing vitamin A deficiency in Ethiopia: linkages with a women-focused dairy goat farming project. Washington, DC: International Center for Research on Women, 1999.

319. Smitasiri S, Attig GA, Dhanamitta S. Participatory action for nutrition education: social marketing vitamin A-rich foods in Thailand. Ecol Food Nutr 1992;28:199–210.

320. Johnson-Welch C. Focusing on women works: research on improving micronutrient status through food-based interventions. Washington, DC: International Center for Research on Women, 1999.

321. Devadas RP, Saroja S, Murthy NK. Availability of β-carotene from papaya fruit and amaranth in pre-school children. Indian J Nutr Dietet 1989;17:41–44.

322. Griener T, Kertson K. PATH's Ultra Rice© project. 2005. Available at: www.path.org.

323. van Jaarsveld PJ, Faber M, Tanumihardjo SA, Nestel P, Lombard CJ, Spinnler Benadé AJ. β-Carotene-rich orange-fleshed sweet potato improves the vitamin A status of primary school children assessed with the modified-relative-dose-response test. Am J Clin Nutr 2005;81:1080–1087.

324. Toenniessen GH. Crop genetic improvement for enhanced human nutrition. J Nutr 2002;132:2943S–2946S.

325. Helen Keller International. Integration of animal husbandry into home gardening programs to increase Vitamin A intake from foods: Bangladesh, Cambodia, and Nepal. Jakarta: Helen Keller International, Asia-Pacific Regional Office, special issue 2003. Available at: http://www.hki.org/research/homestead_food.html.

326. Kiess L, Bloem MW, de Pee S, Hye,A, Khan T, Talukder A, et al. Bangladesh: xerophthalmia free. The result of an effective vitamin A capsule program and homestead gardening (abstract). In: American Public Health Association 126th annual meeting report. Washington, DC: American Public Health Association, 1998:361.

327. Bushamuka VN, de Pee S, Talukder A, Kiess L, Panagides D, Taher A, et al. Impact of a homestead gardening program on household food security and empowerment of women in Bangladesh. Food Nutr Bull 2005;26:17–25.

328. Darnton-Hill I. Overview: rationale and elements of a successful food fortification program. Food Nutr Bull 1998;19:92–100.

329. US Department of Agriculture. Commodity specifications for various products procured for title II PL480 program. Kansas City, MO: USDA Kansas City Commodity Office, 1994.

330. Darnton-Hill I, Nalubola R. Food fortification as a public health strategy to meet micronutrient needs-successes and failures. Proc Nutr Soc 2002;61:231–41.

331. Bauernfeind JC, Arroyave G. Control of vitamin A deficiency by the nutrification of food approach. In: Vitamin A deficiency and its control. Bauernfeind JC, ed. Orlando, FL: Academic, 1986;12:359–388.

332. Dary O, Mora JO. Food fortification to reduce vitamin A deficiency: International Vitamin A Consultative Group recommendations. J Nutr 2002;132:2927S–2933S.

333. Darnton-Hill I, Bloem MW, de Benoist B, Brown L. Micronutrient restoration and fortification: communicating change, benefits and risk. Asia Pacific J Clin Nutr 2000;11(S6):S184–S196.

334. Arroyave G, Aguilar JR, Flores M, Guzman MA. Evaluation of sugar fortification with vitamin A at the national level. Washington, DC: Pan American Health Organization, 1979:1–82.

335. Arroyave G. Vitamin A deficiency control in Central America. In: Vitamin A deficiency and its control. Bauernfeind JC, ed. Orlando, FL: Academic, 1986;14:405–424.

336. Raphael A. Sugar fortification in Guatemala. Guatemala City: United Nations International Children's Emergency Fund, 1994–1995.

337. Solon FS, Fernandez TL, Latham MC, Popkin BM. An evaluation of strategies to control vitamin A deficiency in the Philippines. Am J Clin Nutr 1979;32:1445–1453.

338. Latham MC, Solon FS. Vitamin A deficiency control in the Philippines. In: Vitamin A deficiency and its control. Bauernfeind JC, ed. Orlando, FL: Academic, 1986;15:425–443.

339. Solon FS, Latham MC, Guirriec R, Florentino R, Williamson DF, Aguilar J. Fortification of MSG with vitamin A: the Philippines experience. Food Technol 1985;39:71–79.

340. Hall HS. Vitamin A fortification in a high stress environment. Unpublished report. Chicago: ACS National Meeting, 1993.

341. Solon FS, Solon MS, Mehansho H, West KP Jr, Sarol J, Perfecto C, et al. Evaluation of the effect of vitamin A-fortified margarine on the vitamin A status of preschool Filipino children. Eur J Clin Nutr 1996;50:720–723.

342. Solon FS, Klemm RDW, Sanchez L, Darnton-Hill I, Craft NE, Christian P, et al. Evaluation of the efficacy of vitamin A-fortified wheat-flour bun on the vitamin A status of Filipino school children. Am J Clin Nutr 2000;72:738–744.

343. Solon FS, Solon MA, Nano TA, Limson ERP, Mendoza O, Sanchez LE, et al. Wheat flour fortification with vitamin A. Final report. Manila: Nutrition Center of the Philippines, 1998.

344. Nalubola R, Nestel P, Dexter P, Alnwick D. Fortification of wheat flour with vitamin A. An update. Arlington, VA: OMNI Project/John Snow, 1998.

345. Phillips M, Sanghvi T, Suarez R, McKigney J, Fiedler J. The costs and effectiveness of three vitamin A interventions in Guatemala. Soc Sci Med 1996;42:1661–1668.

346. Lotfi M, Mannar MGV, Merx RJHM, Naber-van den Heuvel P. Micronutrient fortification of foods: current practices, research, and opportunities. Ottawa: Micronutrient Initiative/International Agricultural Centre, 1996.

347. Ong ASH. Nutritional aspects of palm oil: an introductory review. Asia Pacific J Clin Nutr 1994;3:201–206.

348. Fortifying Africa's future—Fortifier l'avenir de l'Afrique. Available at: www.fortaf.org/fortification_afc.htm. Accessed March 13, 2007.

349. West KP Jr, Sommer A. Delivery of oral doses of vitamin A to prevent vitamin A deficiency and nutritional blindness. Rome: United Nations Administrative Committee on Coordination, Subcommittee on Nutrition, 1993. State-of-the-Art Series, Nutrition Policy Discussion Paper No. 2 (second printing).

350. Darnton-Hill I, Sibanda F, Mitra M, Ali MM, Drexler AE, Rahman H, et al. Distribution of vitamin A capsules for the prevention and control of vitamin-A deficiency in Bangladesh. Food Nutr Bull 1988;10:60–70.

351. Dalmiya N, Palmer A, Darnton-Hill I. Sustaining vitamin A supplementation requires a new vision. Lancet 2006;368: DOI:10.1016/S0140-6736(06)69336-7.

352. World Health Organization. Vitamin A supplements dosage. Geneva: World Health Organization, 1997. Paper NUT/97.1.

353. Aguayo V, Baker SK, Crespin X, Hamani H, MamadoulTaïbou A. Maintaining high vitamin A supplementation coverage in children: lessons from Niger. Food Nutr Bull 2005;26:26–31.

354. Ahmed F, Darnton-Hill I. Vitamin A. In: Public health nutrition. The Nutrition Society textbook series. Gibney MJ, Margetts B, Kearney JM, Arab L, eds. Oxford, UK: Blackwell Sciences, 2004;192–215.

355. Vitamin A deficiency and xerophthalmia. Report of a joint WHO/USAID meeting. WHO technical report series. Geneva: World Health Organization, 1976;590:1–83.

356. Sinha DP, Bang FB. The effect of massive doses of vitamin A on the signs of vitamin A deficiency in preschool children. Am J Clin Nutr 1976;29:110–115.

357. Florentino RF, Tanchoco CC, Ramos AC, Mendoza TS, Natividad EP, Tangco JBM, et al. Tolerance of preschoolers to two dosage strengths of vitamin A preparation. Am J Clin Nutr 1990;52:694–700.

358. West KP Jr, Khatry SK, LeClerq SC, Adhikari R, See L, Katz J, et al. Tolerance of young infants to a single, large dose of vitamin A: a randomized community trial in Nepal. Bull World Health Organ 1992;70:733–739.

359. Stabell C, Bale C, da Silva AP, Olsen J, Aaby P. No evidence of fontanelle-bulging episodes after vitamin A supplementation of 6- and 9-month-old infants in Guinea Bissau. Eur J Clin Nutr 1995;49:73–74.

360. Iliff PJ, Humphrey JH, Mahomva AI, Zvandasara P, Bonduelle M, Malaba L, et al. Tolerance of large doses of vitamin A given to mothers and their babies shortly after delivery. Nutr Res 1999;19:1437–1446.

361. Baqui AH, de Francisco A, Arifeen SE, Siddique AK, Sack RB. Bulging fontanelle after supplementation with 25,000 IU of vitamin A in infancy using immunization contacts. Acta Paediatr 1995;84(8):863–866.

362. Agoestino T, Humphrey JH, Taylor GA, Usman A, Subardja D, Hidayat S, et al. Safety of one 52-µmol (50,000 IU) oral dose of vitamin A administered to neonates. Bull World Health Organ 1994;72:859–868.

363. Humphrey JH, Agoestina T, Juliana A, Septiana S, Widjaja H, Cerreto MC, WILLS, Ichord RN, Katz J, West KP Jr. Neonatal Vitamin A Supplementation: Effect on Development and Growth at 3 y of Age. AM J Chin Nutr 1998;68:109–17.

364. Fiedler JL. The Nepal National Vitamin A Program: prototype to emulate or donor enclave? Health Policy Plan 2000;15:145–56.

365. Global Programme for Vaccines and Immunization/Expanded Programme on Immunization. Integration of vitamin A supplementation with immunization: policy and programme implications. Report of a meeting, January 12–13, 1998. New York: United Nations International Children's Emergency Fund; Geneva: World Health Organization, 1998.

366. Berger RA, Courtright P, Barrows J. Vitamin A capsule supplementation in Malawi villages: missed opportunities and possible interventions. Am J Public Health 1995;85:718–719.

367. Semba RD, Muhilal, Mohgaddam NEG, Munasir Z, Akib A, Permaesih D, et al. Integration of vitamin A supplementation with the expanded program on immunization does not affect seroconversion to oral poliovirus vaccine in infants. J Nutr 1999;129:2203–2205.

368. Rahman MM, Mahalanabis D, Hossain S, Wahed MA, Alvarez JO, Siber GR, et al. Simultaneous vitamin A administration at routine immunization contact enhances antibody response to diphtheria vaccine in infants younger than six months. J Nutr 1999;129:2192–2195.

369. de Benoist B, Martines J, Goodman T (guest editors). Vitamin A supplementation and the control of vitamin A deficiency. Food Nutr Bull 2001;22:213–340.

370. Dalmiya N. Results from the Child Health Days assessments. Preliminary findings—Ethipia, Tanzania and Uganda. Presented at the Global Immunization meeting. United Nations, New York; February 13–15, 2007.

371. Aguayo VM, Baker SK. Vitamin A deficiency and child survival in sub-Saharan Africa: a reappraisal of challenges and opportunities. Food Nutr Bull 2005;26:348–55.

372. Arhin DC, Ross DA, Kufour F. Costs of vitamin A supplementation: the opportunity for integration with immunization in Ghana. Health Policy Plan 1993;8:339–348.

373. Loevinsohn BP, Sutter RW, Costales MO. Using cost-effectiveness analysis to evaluate targeting strategies: the case of vitamin A supplementation. Health Policy Plan 1997;12:29–37.

374. Tarwotjo I, West KP Jr, Mele L, Nur S, Nendrawati H, Kraushaar D, et al. Determinants of community-based coverage: periodic vitamin A supplementation. Am J Public Health 1989;79:847–849.

375. West KP Jr, Pokhrel RP, Khatry SK. Estimating the relative efficiency of a vitamin A intervention from population-based data. J Nep Med Assoc 1992;30:159–162.

376. Nieburg P, Waldman RJ, Leavell R, Sommer A, DeMaeyer EM. Vitamin A supplementation for refugees and famine victims. Bull World Health Organ 1988;66:689–697.

# 14 Nutritional Rickets and Vitamin D Deficiency

## John M. Pettifor

## 14.1 INTRODUCTION

Since the 1970s, nutritional rickets has received considerable attention from public health specialists in a number of developed countries as there appears to have been a resurgence in the prevalence of the disease over this period, having almost been eradicated by the middle of the last century in many of these countries. In many developing countries, attention has been focused on the disease, not only because of its effects on bone growth and mineral homeostasis but also because of its association with increased infant and childhood mortality, especially when accompanying lower-respiratory tract infections. Further, the long-term sequelae of the bony deformities, which are characteristic of the acute disease, may be associated with considerable morbidity during childbirth and have permanent effects on the joints of affected individuals.

As discussed in Section 14.5, it is now apparent that nutritional rickets is caused not only by vitamin D deficiency but also by low dietary calcium intake, and that it is likely that these two factors play synergistic roles in many patients who develop the disease.

## 14.2 DEFINITION

Rickets is a disease of growing bones that results from a failure of or delay in the calcification of newly formed cartilage at the growth plates of long bones, and the disease is associated with a failure of mineralization of newly formed osteoid (this feature is termed *osteomalacia*) at the trabecular bone surfaces and the endosteal and periosteal surfaces of cortical bone (Fig. 14.1). These osseous changes result in the long bones in particular no longer being able to maintain their normal shapes in response to physical forces, such as produced by weight bearing or muscle insertions. The results are the characteristic bony deformities, which are described in Section 14.6.

There are numerous causes of rickets; however, they can be divided broadly into three large categories: those associated with a primary inability to maintain serum calcium concentrations (calciopenic rickets), those associated with a primary inability to maintain normal serum phosphorus concentrations (phosphopenic rickets), and those associated

From: *Nutrition and Health: Nutrition and Health in Developing Countries, Second Edition*
Edited by: R. D. Semba & M. W. Bloem © Humana Press, Totowa, NJ

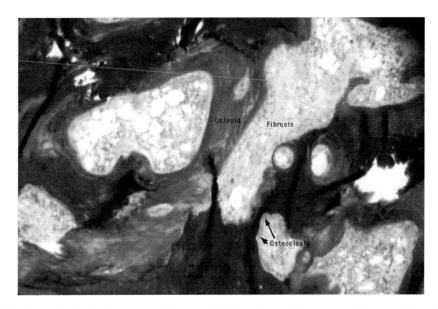

**Fig. 14.1.** The histological features of osteomalacia on bone biopsy. An Iliac crest bone biopsy showing excessive osteoid (light grey) lining the trabecular surfaces. Mineralized bone appears dark grey or black.

with a primary defect of mineralization. Nutritional rickets is a form of calciopenic rickets and is classically associated with vitamin D deficiency.

## 14.3   PUBLIC HEALTH IMPORTANCE

The global prevalence of rickets is not known as many of the community surveys that have been conducted rely on the finding of bony deformities that are not specific to rickets for the diagnosis of the disease. Furthermore, these deformities do not necessarily imply the presence of active rickets because deformities that develop during the active stage of the disease may persist for months or years after the disease has been treated. Despite the lack of accurate information, it is clear that rickets and vitamin D deficiency are common in many countries throughout the world, including Middle Eastern countries [1, 2] and a number of developing countries, such as Ethiopia [3], the Yemen [4], and areas of Asia, such as China [5] and Mongolia [6]. Furthermore, the disease is prevalent among immigrant and dark-skinned populations in a number of developed countries.

Besides the classical effects of active rickets on bone growth and development and on calcium homeostasis (Section 14.6), vitamin D deficiency may have adverse effects on a number of other systems. These include effects on the immune system [7]. A study from Ethiopia found that children admitted to hospital with pneumonia had a 13 times greater incidence of rickets than children without pneumonia, and the combination was associated with a 40% mortality rate [8]. In a study from Jordan, 11% of children under 2 years of age admitted for acute illnesses were found to have rickets, and 85% of those with rickets had lower-respiratory tract infections compared to only 30% of the children without rickets [9]. There are several possible mechanisms for rickety children to be predisposed to lower-respiratory tract infections; the first is that vitamin D, or more specifically 1,25-dihdroxyvitamin D, plays a role in the maturation and differentiation of immune cells; a second mechanism relates to the muscle weakness and hypotonia that is characteristic of severe vitamin D deficiency; and the third is the effect of rickets and osteomalacia on the rigidity and support provided by the ribs during respiration.

During pregnancy and early infancy, vitamin D deficiency is associated with poorer maternal weight gain, a higher incidence of neonatal hypocalcaemia, poor neonatal bone mineralization and fractures, and reduced longitudinal growth [10]. Further, there is evidence to suggest that there is an increased risk of type 1 diabetes mellitus in later life [11]. It has also been suggested that a number of neurological disorders are associated with vitamin D deficiency during pregnancy or early neonatal life; these include multiple sclerosis and bipolar disorder [12].

Epidemiological studies have provided interesting but as yet unproven data that suggest that low vitamin D status during adulthood may increase the risk of colon and prostate cancers, among a number of others [13]. The mechanisms through which vitamin D exerts its effects are varied, ranging from altering the calcium concentration in the colonic contents to providing substrate for the local formation of 1,25-dihydroxyvitamin D, which is important in regulating cellular division and differentiation.

## 14.4   HISTORICAL BACKGROUND

Although there are reported to be references to rickets in Greek and Roman writings nearly 2,000 years ago and a report has been published of skeletal evidence of rickets in an infant skeleton found in South Africa [14], which was radiocarbon dated to nearly 5000 BP, it has been only in the last 400 years that good descriptions of the disease have been recorded.

Nutritional rickets is a disease associated with urbanization and the industrial revolution. The first clear descriptions of the disease were published in the middle of the 17th century by Francis Glisson (1597–1677) and Daniel Whistler (1619–1684) [15], at which time it became known as the "English disease" because of the high prevalence of the condition among urban English children at that time. Francis Glisson provided a clear description of its peak prevalence in children between the ages of 6 and 30 months. At that time, the disease was more common among children of the affluent than the poor, reflecting the parental protection of affluent infants from sunlight [16]. However, with the development of inner-city slums with their narrow, sunless streets and atmospheric pollution, the disease became much more prevalent among the infants and young children of the poor and destitute. A number of hypotheses were proposed at that time regarding its aetiology, including digestive disturbances, poor and incorrect feeding, and the breathing of foul air.

A couple of centuries later, Trousseau, the famous French physician (1801–1867), noted that the disease was "unquestionably more common in damp cold countries than elsewhere," and that cod-liver oil and fish oils in general were effective in its management [17]; however, it was not until the beginning of the 20th century that his advice was generally accepted.

In the 18th, 19th, and early 20th centuries, a number of studies noted the almost-universal finding of the features of rickets in infants and young children living in the industrialised cities of northern Europe and northern North America [18, 19]. It was also noted that children living in rural and farming communities were generally spared [20].

A number of physicians had concluded in the late 1800s that sunlight was beneficial in both preventing and treating the disease [16, 21]; however, it was not until the early 20th century that the discovery of vitamin D by McCollum [22] and the role of ultra-violet (UV) light in the formation of vitamin D in the 1920s [23] provided a rational and acceptable approach to the prevention and management of vitamin D-deficiency rickets. Following the isolation of vitamin D, a number of countries introduced supplementation programmes and food fortification, especially infant milk formulas almost universally and cow's milk in the United States and Canada. These measures were associated with a rapid reduction in the prevalence of rickets in young children, and by the latter half of the 20th century, infantile rickets had become a relatively uncommon disease in many developed countries in the more northern latitudes. However, the relatively recent encour-agement of exclusive breast-feeding during the first months of life and the immigration of darker-skinned populations into many of these industrialised countries after World War II have seen a resurgence of the disease in certain communities in these countries [24–26]. Until recently, little attention has been paid to the prevalence of rickets in other countries, but it is clear that rickets has been and remains a problem in northern Asian countries, in the Middle East, and in a number of countries in Africa (see Section 14.5).

## 14.5   EPIDEMIOLOGY

Although humans can obtain their vitamin D supply through two routes (namely, through the diet or via skin synthesis under the influence of UV-B radiation), it is the epidermal synthesis that plays the major role in maintaining the vitamin D status of the majority of populations [27] (Fig. 14.2). Few unfortified foods, except for example oily fish and fish oils, contain adequate quantities of vitamin D to ensure vitamin D sufficiency [28].

Ultraviolet-B radiation between the wavelengths of 290 and 315 nm induces the pho-tolysis of 7-dehydrocholesterol in the skin to form previtamin $D_3$, which then undergoes thermal isomerisation over the next 24 to 36 hours to vitamin $D_3$ (cholecalciferol). Once formed in the deeper layers of the epidermis, vitamin $D_3$ is transported in the blood-stream attached to the vitamin D binding protein to the liver, where it is hydroxylated to 25-hydroxyvitamin $D_3$ [25(OH)$D_3$]. This last compound is the major circulating form of the vitamin, and measurement of its serum concentration provides a good index of the vitamin D status of an individual. Ingested and absorbed vitamin D (in the form of either vitamin $D_2$ or $D_3$) is also transported to the liver and hydroxylated to 25(OH)D (the absence of a subscript is used to denote that the vitamin D compound may be derived from either vitamin $D_2$ or $D_3$). Vitamin $D_2$ (ergocalciferol) is formed by the UV radiation of the plant sterol, ergosterol. Neither vitamin D nor its hydroxylated compound 25(OH)D is physiologically active at normal physiological concentrations; 25(OH)D must first be converted to 1,25-dihydroxyvitamin D [1,25-(OH)$_2$D] in the proximal tubules of the kidney before becoming a calciotropic hormone. 1,25-(OH)$_2$D acts largely though its intracellular vitamin D receptor to influence gene transcription and protein synthesis; its major target organs related to calcium and bone homeostasis are the gastrointestinal tract, where it enhances dietary calcium and to a lesser extent phosphorus absorption,

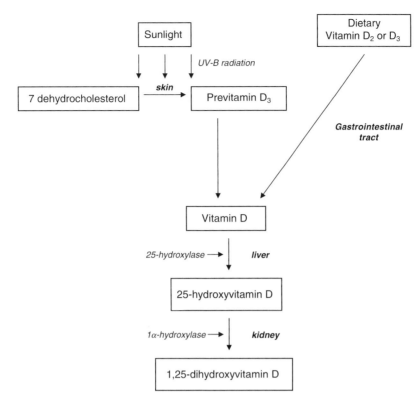

**Fig. 14.2.** Vitamin D metabolism.

and the bone itself, where it stimulates bone resorption and the release of calcium and phosphorus into the bloodstream. It has minor effects on the kidney, where it increases calcium reabsorption, and on the parathyroid gland, where it influences parathyroid hormone secretion (see [29] for a review of vitamin D physiology).

The amount of vitamin $D_3$ formed in the skin is dependent on a number of factors (Table 14.1) [30], the most important of these is the amount of solar UV-B radiation that is available at the skin surface. This is dependent to a large extent on the zenith angle of the sun, which in turn is dependent on the latitude of the country, the season of the year, and the time of day. Cities in countries at the extremes of northern and southern latitudes (such as Boston [42°N] or Calgary [52°N] in the north and Ushuaia [55°S] in the south) receive negligible amounts of UV-B radiation during the winter months [31, 32]. Even in Cape Town at 32°S the amount of vitamin D that can be formed during sunlight hours during the winter months is small (Fig. 14.3) [33]. A further factor that influences UV-B radiation is the extent of atmospheric pollution, such that in areas of high atmospheric pollution in an industrialised city, the UV radiation is reduced compared to that in less-polluted areas in the same city [34].

Personal factors also influence the formation of vitamin D in the skin. These include the amount of time spent out of doors, the extent of skin area exposed to sunlight, the time of day of the sunlight exposure, and the use of sunscreens, which can very effectively

Table 14.1
Factors influencing the formation of vitamin D in the skin

The amount of UV-B reaching the earth
   The zenith angle of the sun (the distance from the equator)
   The season of the year
   Time of day
   Atmospheric pollution
   Cloud cover
Human factors
   Amount of skin exposed (clothing coverage)
   Duration of exposure
   Use of sunscreens
   Degree of melanin pigmentation
   Amount of 7-dehydrocholesterol in the skin (aging)

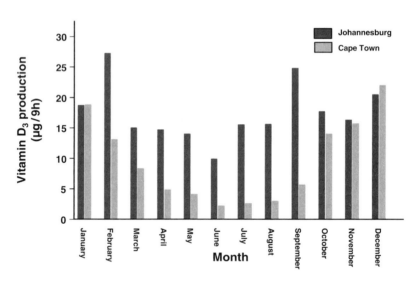

**Fig. 14.3.** The formation of vitamin D in cities at two different latitudes in South Africa. Johannesburg has a latitude of 26°S, while Cape Town has a latitude of 32°S. Vials containing 7-dehydrocholesterol were placed in the sun for 9 hours on 1 day a month throughout the year. The vitamin D formed in the vials was measured. Note the limited vitamin D formation that occurred during the winter months from April through September in Cape Town. (Reproduced with permission from [33].)

prevent UV penetration into the skin. Further, the degree of melanin pigmentation has a major effect on the amount of vitamin D formed in the skin. In numerous studies, in which serum concentrations of 25(OH)D were compared between black and white subjects, values in black and Asian subjects were significantly lower than those of their white peers living in the same community [10, 35, 36].

It is clear from the discussion that vitamin D-deficiency rickets is characteristically a disease of infants and young children as once children start to walk, they will tend to spend more time out of the house in the open air and thus be exposed to sunlight.

Furthermore, it is typically a disease of young children living in countries at high latitude. Breast-fed infants are further disadvantaged as breast milk normally contains very little vitamin D or its metabolites (estimated to be between 20 and 60 IU/L) [37, 38]. It is estimated that a lactating mother probably requires 4,000 IU/day of vitamin D (some ten times the currently recommended intake) to provide sufficient vitamin D in breast milk to maintain vitamin D sufficiency in the nursing baby who has limited access to sunlight [39]. Of all the vitamin D metabolites, 25(OH)D crosses the placenta most readily. The newborn infant has circulating levels of 25(OH)D that are approximately 60% of the mother's; thus, the infant is protected for several months from vitamin D deficiency without an additional source of vitamin D, provided the mother is vitamin D replete [40]. However, many studies have highlighted that many pregnant mothers have either vitamin D insufficiency or deficiency; this is particularly true of mothers with increased melanin pigmentation living in countries at high latitude (e.g., African Americans and the Asian communities in the United Kingdom and Europe) [41–44]. These low maternal levels predispose the young infant to earlier and more severe rickets.

Since 1980, rickets has been described from all the inhabited continents of the world. In the United States, African American infants are mainly at risk. The age group is typically less than 30 months, and the vast majority of affected infants are or have been breast-fed (96%) [24]. An interesting study by Carpenter and his group from the East Coast of the United States [45] suggested that low dietary calcium intake may also play a role in the pathogenesis of the disease as many of the infants who developed rickets had normal concentrations of 25(OH)D and had been weaned to diets low in calcium. In Canada, darker-skinned breast-fed infants are also at risk, and it is suggested that breast-fed infants living north of the 55th parallel should be supplemented with 800 IU/day vitamin D rather than the customary 400 IU/day [46].

In Europe, it is the Asian community (Pakistani and Indian immigrants) living in the United Kingdom that has been the most investigated as numerous reports have highlighted the high prevalence of vitamin D deficiency not only in infants but also in adolescents and pregnant mothers [26, 47–49]. Although vitamin D deficiency is central to the pathogenesis of the disease in this community, it is suggested that low dietary calcium intake associated with the high phytate content of the typical vegetarian diet increases vitamin D requirements through increased catabolism of 25(OH)D [50] (Fig. 14.4). Besides the increased melanin pigmentation, it appears that greater clothing coverage of the skin and less time spent out of doors might contribute to the greater prevalence of vitamin D deficiency in the Asian community compared to the indigenous population. In other northern European countries, reports of rickets as more prevalent in dark-skinned immigrants have also appeared [51–54].

Vitamin D deficiency and rickets are common in Middle Eastern countries, where social and religious customs, such as purdah and veiling, which prevent adequate skin exposure to UV-B radiation, are primarily responsible [55–57]. Vitamin D deficiency in young infants is also aggravated by a high prevalence of vitamin D deficiency in pregnant mothers [58]. Low calcium and high phytate intakes have been reported as responsible for osteomalacia among the Bedouins in Israel [59]. In the Yemen, some 50% of children admitted to the hospital for pneumonia had rickets [4], a finding similar to that noted in Ethiopia.

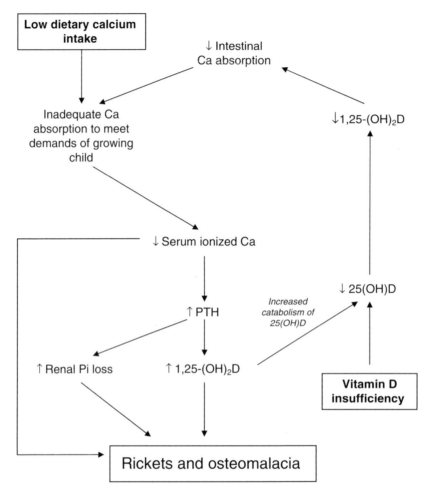

**Fig. 14.4.** The pathogenesis of rickets. The interrelationship between low dietary calcium intake and vitamin D insufficiency is shown.

As Africa straddles the Equator, it might be thought that rickets should be uncommon on that continent; yet, the disease has been reported from a number of African countries, including Algeria, Tunisia, Libya, Egypt, Sudan, Ethiopia, Nigeria, and South Africa. In the majority of these countries, the disease presents in infants and young children [53, 60–63] and is likely to be due to vitamin D deficiency caused by poverty and social and religious customs preventing sunlight exposure [54]. However, in Nigeria the mean age of presentation is older (46 months), and a number of researchers have noted that affected children have 25(OH)D concentrations above the accepted vitamin D-deficient range and elevated $1,25$-$(OH)_2D$ levels [65–66]. Furthermore, the bone disease responds to dietary calcium supplements alone [65, 67, 68]. Calcium intake in these children is typically low (~200 mg/day) as the diet is almost devoid of milk and dairy products, and the phytate content of the diet is high. However, in the Nigerian studies, no difference in calcium

intakes between control and affected children has been found [66]. Thus, although it appears that low dietary calcium intakes play a pivotal role in the pathogenesis of the disease in these children, other unknown factors may predispose susceptible children to the development of the disease.

In South Africa, vitamin D deficiency was frequently seen some 50 years ago in infants in the southernmost regions [63], but the prevalence has dropped markedly with the use of vitamin D supplements and the fortification of infant milk formulas with vitamin D. More recently, calcium-deficiency rickets in association with normal 25(OH)D and elevated 1,25-(OH)$_2$D concentrations has been described in children (aged between 4 and 16 years) living in rural parts of the country. As in the Nigerian children, the calcium intakes were estimated to be very low (150–250 mg/day); however, unlike the Nigerian situation, calcium intakes of control children were generally higher than those of affected children [69–72].

Rickets is well described in northern China [73, 74] (including Tibet, where the prevalence of clinical rickets was estimated at about 66% in one study [5]) and Mongolia [6]. Not only is the disease prevalent during infancy but also low vitamin D status and symptomatic hypocalcaemia are reported during the winter months in adolescents [75]. Excellent descriptions of the effects of osteomalacia on the skeleton and in particular on the pelvis of women in China were made by Maxwell over 70 years ago [76].

In India, the prevalence of rickets is more common in the Muslim than Hindu communities [77], and although vitamin D deficiency probably plays the dominant role in the pathogenesis of the disease, there is evidence emerging that low dietary calcium intake may be an important contributor in young children [78]. In urban communities, air pollution and overcrowding probably play a role in the pathogenesis of vitamin D deficiency [34]. Endemic fluorosis is well described in certain parts of India [79], and studies suggested that vitamin D deficiency and low dietary calcium intake might aggravate the clinical picture [80].

Dietary calcium-deficiency rickets has been described in the southeastern region of Bangladesh [81], where 0.9% of children between the ages of 1 and 15 years were found to have radiological disease [82].

Rickets and vitamin D deficiency in South America are uncommon because most countries are reasonably close to the equator. However, vitamin D deficiency is well described in the southernmost region of Argentina, especially during the winter months [83], and rickets is also described from this region and from urban areas around Buenos Aires, where it is associated with overcrowding and low socioeconomic status [84].

In Australia, a growing concern is apparent about the rising prevalence of rickets in the major cities, such as Sydney. Between 1993 and 2003, over 125 cases were diagnosed as having vitamin D-deficiency rickets in three large teaching hospitals. As in other developed countries, the disease is now occurring almost exclusively in children of immigrant families, especially from the Indian subcontinent, Africa, and the Middle East [25], although some 30 years ago a study from Melbourne suggested that it was immigrants from the Mediterranean region who were most at risk [85]. Studies also indicated that many of the pregnant women of immigrant families are vitamin D deficient, thus exposing their newborn infants to a greater risk of more severe and earlier rickets [86].

## 14.6 PATHOPHYSIOLOGY/CLINICAL FEATURES

Nutritional rickets is primarily a result of disturbed calcium homeostasis consequent to impaired dietary calcium absorption or inadequate dietary calcium intake to meet the demands of the growing skeleton. As discussed, the principle physiological role of vitamin D [or more specifically 1,25-(OH)$_2$D] is the control of intestinal calcium absorption; thus, a deficiency of vitamin D results in impaired absorption and hypocalcaemia. The latter stimulates secondary hyperparathyroidism, which results in a reduction in urinary calcium excretion and an increase in urinary phosphate loss. Further, increased parathyroid hormone secretion increases bone resorption and bone turnover, resulting in bone loss. The combination of hypocalcaemia and hypophosphataemia results in impaired mineralization at the growth plate and the development of the typical pathological features of rickets (see [87] for a more detailed discussion).

Clinically, the typical features of rickets are a result of the widening and splaying of the growth plates and resultant deformities of the metaphyses of the long bones. Thus, widening of the wrists, knees, and ankles; palpable and enlarged costochondral junctions (the rickety rosary); and deformities of the long bones as a result of weight bearing are the characteristic features [88]. The type of long-bone deformity is dependent on the age of the child; in young infants, deformities associated with fractures of the forearm are not uncommon and are associated with swaddling, while in the lower limb, anterior bowing of the distal third of the tibia may be found as a result of the infant lying with the legs crossed. In the child who has just started walking, bowlegs are a common feature, while in the older child, knock-knees or a windswept deformity are more common (Fig. 14.5). In the young infant, softening of the skull and a delay in mineralization result in craniotabes (ping-pong sign over the petrous temporal bone) and enlargement and delay in closure of the anterior fontanelle. In young children with severe rickets, softening of the ribs with narrowing of the lateral diameter of the chest produces the "violin case deformity," and the development of the Harrison's sulcus along the site of attachment of the diaphragm to the inner surface of the ribs may result in severe respiratory distress and recurrent lower-respiratory tract infections. Fractures of ribs and long bones are common manifestations of severe rickets.

Hypotonia and myopathy associated with vitamin D deficiency (possibly in association with bone pain) result in delayed motor milestones. In older children, this may present with difficulty in walking up stairs or rising from the sitting position [89].

Hypocalcaemia may manifest clinically without features of bony deformities, especially in the early stages of vitamin D deficiency in the young infant [90, 91]. In the neonate, hypocalcaemia with apnoeic attacks, convulsions, or tremor is more common in infants born to vitamin D-deficient mothers [92, 93]. Hypocalcaemic symptoms without bony deformities are also frequently noted in adolescent children [57].

## 14.7 DIAGNOSIS

The diagnosis of rickets is made clinically by the presence of the typical bony deformities [88]; however, these do not necessarily indicate active disease as they may persist for months or years following the correction of dietary calcium or vitamin D deficiencies. Craniotabes also may occur in young normal infants, especially in those born prematurely [94].

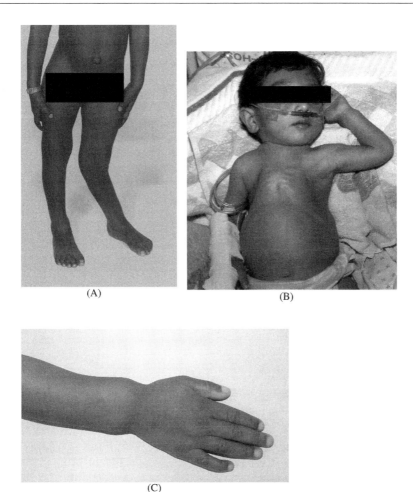

(A)

(B)

(C)

**Fig. 14.5.** Typical bony deformities associated with rickets. **A** Windswept deformities in a child with dietary calcium deficiency rickets. **B** Chest deformities in a child with severe rickets. The child presented with severe respiratory distress. **C** Enlarged wrist in a child with vitamin D deficiency.

Rickets is confirmed by radiological examination of the growth plates of rapidly growing regions of the skeleton. The wrists and knees are the typical sites examined radiographically. Early features of the disease are a loss of the provisional zone of calcification at the junction of the growth plate and metaphysis and progressive widening of the growth plate [95]. As the growth plates widen, physical forces disrupt the normal cartilage plates and undermineralized metaphyses causing cupping, fraying, and splaying of the metaphyses (Fig. 14.6). The epiphyses are typically underdeveloped, and the trabecular pattern of the metaphyses is coarse and sparse. The cortices of the diaphyses are thin, and periosteal new bone formation may be seen, especially during the early stages of healing. Fractures of the long bones and ribs are frequently noted in severe rickets.

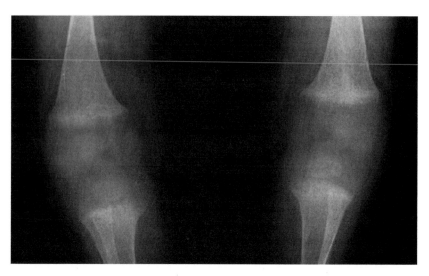

**Fig. 14.6.** Radiographic changes at the knees of an 18-month-old child with severe rickets. Note the loss of the provisional zone of calcification at the end of the metaphyses, the widening of the growth plates, and splaying, irregularity, and fuzziness of the metaphyses.

A grading system of the radiographic changes at the knees and wrists has been useful in assessing the severity of rickets and its response to treatment [96].

Biochemically, active rickets manifests classically with hypocalcaemia, hypophosphataemia, and elevated alkaline phosphatase and parathyroid hormone concentrations. In the early stages of vitamin D deficiency, hypocalcaemia may be the only biochemical finding, but as the disease progresses and hyperparathyroidism becomes manifest, hypocalcaemia may partially correct, and hypophosphataemia and elevated alkaline phosphatase levels become apparent. In the severe stages of the disease, calcium levels once again fall as the homeostatic mechanisms fail to maintain normocalcaemia.

Confirmation of vitamin D deficiency is dependent on the finding of low 25(OH)D concentrations. It is generally considered that values below 10–12 ng/mL (25–30 nmol/L) are indicative of vitamin D deficiency; however, children with vitamin D deficiency rickets typically have values below 5 ng/mL (12.5 nmol/L) [97]. The measurement of $1,25\text{-}(OH)_2D$ concentrations is not helpful in the diagnosis of vitamin D deficiency as levels have been found to be low, normal, or elevated [97–99].

Rickets due to dietary calcium deficiency presents with very similar biochemical findings to those of vitamin D deficiency. However, 25(OH)D levels are characteristically within the normal range, and $1,25\text{-}(OH)_2D$ concentrations are elevated [66, 67, 70].

## 14.8  TREATMENT

Vitamin D deficiency rickets responds rapidly to vitamin D supplements or adequate UV radiation. Thus, radiographic changes, hypocalcaemia and elevated alkaline phosphatase levels may normalise during the summer months in children living in countries at high latitude [100]. Vitamin D deficiency rickets is most frequently treated with

oral vitamin $D_2$ or $D_3$ at doses ranging from 5,000 to 15,000 IU/day for 4 to 8 weeks. Response to therapy may be assessed by an improvement in serum calcium or phosphorus values within 2 to 3 weeks, while radiographic signs of healing may be seen within a month [97]. Elevated alkaline phosphatase values may persist for several months after the commencement of therapy.

A single large dose (150,000 to 600,000 IU) of oral or parenterally administered vitamin D has been useful when patient compliance may be problematic. Healing occurs more rapidly than when smaller daily doses of vitamin D are administered, and no evidence of hypercalcaemia has been noted if doses between 150,000 and 300,000 IU are used [101].

In most developing countries and in certain situations in industrialised countries, vitamin D deficiency is frequently associated with low dietary calcium intake; thus, it is prudent to provide calcium supplements at the same time as correcting vitamin D deficiency as response to therapy is more rapid [68, 102]. A daily supplement of 50 mg/kg of elemental calcium for several months is recommended.

If dietary calcium deficiency is suspected to be the primary aetiological factor in the pathogenesis of the disease, as in Nigeria, in Bangladesh, or in older children in South Africa, children have been shown to respond rapidly to calcium supplements alone (1,000 mg/day) [68]; however, unless the measurement of 25(OH)D concentrations is readily available, it is appropriate to combine the calcium supplements with vitamin D therapy [78]. Vitamin D alone is less effective than either calcium alone or a combination of calcium and vitamin D in these situations [68].

## 14.9 PREVENTION

Since the discovery of vitamin D over 80 years ago, cheap and effective means of preventing vitamin D deficiency rickets have existed. Yet, despite this, rickets prevention has not been universally effective, as highlighted by the resurgence of rickets in certain communities in the United States and Europe and its still-common occurrence in many developing countries.

Several different approaches have been taken to address the high prevalence of rickets that existed in children living in temperate climates at the turn of the last century. In the United States and Canada, fortification of all dairy milk and infant milk formulas with vitamin D (400 IU/quart) has dramatically reduced the prevalence of the disease. However, the promotion of exclusive breast-feeding for the first 6 months of life, the greater use of sunscreens, and the advice to avoid direct sunlight in the early months of life have all increased the risk for developing rickets in young children. In the United Kingdom, vitamin D fortification of a number of foods, including milk, took place in the middle of the last century, but because of a suspected (but not proven) link to an apparent increase in distal renal tubular acidosis, this practice was discontinued, although margarines and a few cereals remain fortified.

Recommendations in North America are that all infants and children require a dietary intake of 200 IU/day vitamin D [103]; in the United Kingdom, recommendations of between 340 and 280 IU/day are provided for infants and children less than 3 years of age, respectively [104]. Despite these recommendations, children in some minority communities still remain at risk; thus, the American Academy of Pediatrics suggests that all breast-fed infants or those children not drinking at least 500 mL of cow's milk (infant formula or dairy milk) should receive a supplement of 200 IU/day [105]. Questions have been raised regarding whether 200 IU/day is sufficient as it is becoming more apparent that vitamin D has other actions than its recognised central role in calcium homeostasis [106], and it is unclear at what levels of 25(OH)D these other functions are optimised [107].

In the United Kingdom, vitamin D supplementation of all breast-fed at-risk infants is recommended. However, many paediatricians believe that vitamin D supplementation should be routine for all infants [108] and for all children who do not get sufficient sunlight exposure because of clothing or religious or social customs.

Certainly, more attention must be paid to pregnant women in many countries. There is indeed a greater awareness of the role that maternal vitamin D deficiency plays in exacerbating the development of vitamin D deficiency and rickets in infants, but it appears that health care professionals pay little attention to the recommendation that dark-skinned mothers should be supplemented during pregnancy [93].

Education programmes targeting at-risk communities have met with some success, but the messages need continual reinforcement and a champion within the health sector to ensure that health professionals comply with the recommendations.

The prevention of rickets in developing countries is even more problematic than in industrialised nations. The enormous burden of infectious diseases (including HIV), malnutrition, and poverty means that little attention is paid by health authorities to the problem of rickets, especially when health resources are severely curtailed. In these countries, rickets also is more likely to be due to a combination of vitamin D deficiency and low dietary calcium intake as once breast-feeding ceases the diets are typically devoid of dairy products.

Several studies have reported the effectiveness of intermittent large doses of vitamin D orally or parenterally. In areas where parental compliance or regular vitamin D supplies may be problematic, the use of 100,000 IU vitamin D every 3 months has been shown to maintain normal serum 25(OH) levels [109]. Doses higher than this have resulted in markedly elevated levels of 25(OH)D and occasional episodes of hypercalcaemia. Further studies are required to see if intermittent doses can be linked to the extended programme of immunization in countries where the prevalence of rickets in infants is high (e.g., China, Mongolia, Ethiopia, and countries in the Middle East).

Dairy products are expensive and often not accessible in many developing countries; thus, national or community programmes to increase calcium intake in children who have been weaned may be difficult as there are few cheap and acceptable alternative foods high in calcium. In countries or areas where dried fish is available, this can be ground with the fish bones and may provide an acceptable condiment to be added to porridge. Powder limestone, added to porridge, has also been shown to be an effective way of treating children with rickets (T. D. Thacher, P. R. Fischer, J. M. Pettifor, unpublished data). The addition of limestone to corn in the manufacture of tortillas markedly improves calcium intake in populations in Central America and is an accepted part of the diet. Similar food additions to staples should be experimented with in other developing countries where dietary calcium intake is low and is associated with rickets.

## 14.10   FUTURE DIRECTIONS

The control of rickets in developing countries is dependent on the control of poverty and overcrowding and the development of effective primary health care facilities and programmes. Further, dietary diversification is an important aspect of the improvement of calcium intake. In areas where social or religious customs militate against adequate sunlight exposure in young infants, attention must be paid to ensuring the adequate vitamin D status of pregnant women through the provision of vitamin D supplements during antenatal care. Health promotion and education programmes should highlight the ease of combating vitamin D deficiency and the prevention of long-term morbidity through ensuring adequate sunlight exposure or vitamin D supplementation.

International bodies must highlight the continuing morbidity and mortality associate with nutritional rickets in many developing countries and attention must be paid to placing programmes for the prevention of the disease on the world health agenda.

Although a lot is known about the pathogenesis and treatment of nutritional rickets, there are still a number of unanswered questions concerning the interrelationship between environmental and genetic factors that may predispose individual children to the development of rickets. For instance, in Nigeria, dietary calcium intake of children with and without rickets has been similar [66], yet the disease in affected children is cured by the provision of calcium supplements alone. This finding suggests that other genetic or environmental factors may play a role in the pathogenesis. Some 30 years ago, Greek researchers suggested that there was a genetic component to the predisposition for the development of vitamin D-deficiency rickets [110], and more recent work from the United States points to increased catabolism of vitamin D in Asian Indians compared to whites living in the same country [111], possibly indicating genetic differences and a predisposition to develop vitamin D deficiency.

## 14.11   CONCLUSIONS

Despite cheap and effective means of both treating and preventing nutritional rickets, the disease remains a major cause of infant and young child morbidity and mortality in a number of developing countries. Rickets continues as a public health problem in developing countries lying at high latitude in the temperate zones, while in the Middle East and some other countries, religious customs often prevent adequate sunlight exposure not only in young infants but also in adolescent children and pregnant women. In other tropical countries, increasing evidence is accumulating that indicates that low dietary calcium intake by itself or in synergy with relative vitamin D deficiency exacerbates and promotes the development of the disease.

Effective prevention programmes are not in place in most developing countries; thus, there needs to be a concerted effort from international agencies to ensure that rickets is placed on the health agenda of these countries. Treatment of most patients with rickets can be effectively managed using daily vitamin D supplements for several months; however, consideration should be given to the use of single large doses of vitamin D when compliance might be problematic. In all cases, attention should be paid to ensuring an adequate dietary calcium intake during treatment.

# REFERENCES

1. Lubani MM, Al-Shab TS, Al-Saleh QA et al. Vitamin-D-deficiency rickets in Kuwait: the prevalence of a preventable disease. Ann Trop Paediatr 1989;3:134–139.
2. Fida NM. Assessment of nutritional rickets in western Saudi Arabia. Saudi Med J 2003;24(4): 337–340.
3. Lulseged S, Fitwi G. Vitamin D deficiency rickets: socio-demographic and clinical risk factors in children seen at a referral hospital in Addis Ababa. East Afr Med J 1999;76(8):457–461.
4. Banajeh SM, al Sunbali NN, al Sanahani SH. Clinical characteristics and outcome of children aged under 5 years hospitalized with severe pneumonia in Yemen. Ann Trop Paediatr 1997;17(4):321–326.
5. Harris NS, Crawford PB, Yangzom Y, Pinzo L, Gyaltsen P, Hudes M. Nutritional and health status of Tibetan children living at high altitudes. N Engl J Med 2001;344(5):341–347.
6. Tserendolgor U, Mawson JT, MacDonald AC, Oyunbileg M. Prevalence of rickets in Mongolia. Asian Pacific J Clin Nutr 1998;7:325–328.
7. DeLuca HF, Cantorna MT. Vitamin D: its role and uses in immunology. FASEB J 2001;15(14): 2579–2585.
8. Muhe L, Luiseged S, Mason KE, Simoes EAF. Case-control study of the role of nutritional rickets in the risk of developing pneumonia in Ethiopian children. Lancet 1997;349:1801–1804.
9. Najada AS, Habashneh MS, Khader M. The frequency of nutritional rickets among hospitalized infants and its relation to respiratory diseases. J Trop Pediatr 2004;50(6):364–368.
10. Pawley N, Bishop NJ. Prenatal and infant predictors of bone health: the influence of vitamin D. Am J Clin Nutr 2004;80(6):1748S–1751S.
11. Harris SS. Vitamin D in type 1 diabetes prevention. J Nutr 2005;135(2):323–325.
12. Grant WB, Holick MF. Benefits and requirements of vitamin D for optimal health: a review. Altern Med Rev 2005;10(2):94–111.
13. Holick MF. Vitamin D: importance in the prevention of cancers, type 1 diabetes, heart disease, and osteoporosis. Am J Clin Nutr 2004;79(3):362–371.
14. Pfeiffer S, Crowder C. An ill child among mid-Holocene foragers of southern Africa. Am J Phys Anthropol 2004;123(1):23–29.
15. Dunn PM. Francis Glisson (1597–1677) and the "discovery" of rickets. Arch Dis Child Fetal Neonatal Ed 1998;78(2):F154–F155.
16. Gibbs D. Rickets and the crippled child: an historical perspective. J R Soc Med 1994;87:729–732.
17. Dunn PM. Professor Armand Trousseau (1801–67) and the treatment of rickets. Arch Dis Child Fetal Neonatal Ed 1999;80(2):F155–F157.
18. Chick DH. Study of rickets in Vienna 1919–1922. Med Hist 1976;20(1):41–51.
19. Larocque R. [Deaths at an early age in the city of Quebec, seventeenth–nineteenth centuries]. Can Bull Med Hist 1999;16(2):341–361.
20. Snow J. On the adulteration of bread as a cause of rickets. Int J Epidemiol 2003;32(3):336–337.
21. Holick MF. Photosynthesis, metabolism, and biologic actions of vitamin D. In: Nestle nutrition workshop series. Glorieux FH, ed. New York: Nestec, Vevey/Raven, 1991:1–20.
22. Rafter GW. Elmer McCollum and the disappearance of rickets. Perspect Biol Med 1987;30(4): 527–534.
23. Rajakumar K, Thomas SB. Reemerging nutritional rickets: a historical perspective. Arch Pediatr Adolesc Med 2005;159(4):335–341.
24. Weisberg P, Scanlon KS, Li R, Cogswell ME. Nutritional rickets among children in the United States: review of cases reported between 1986 and 2003. Am J Clin Nutr 2004;80(6):1697S–1705S.
25. Robinson PD, Hogler W, Craig ME, et al. The re-emerging burden of rickets: a decade of experience from Sydney. Arch Dis Child 2005;91(7):564–568.
26. Iqbal SJ, Kaddam I, Wassif W, Nichol F, Walls J. Continuing clinically severe vitamin D deficiency in Asians in the UK (Leicester). Postgrad Med J 1994;70:708–714.
27. Norman AW. Sunlight, season, skin pigmentation, vitamin D, and 25-hydroxyvitamin D: integral components of the vitamin D endocrine system. Am J Clin Nutr 1998;67:1108–1110.
28. Calvo MS, Whiting SJ, Barton CN. Vitamin D intake: a global perspective of current status. J Nutr 2005;135(2):310–316.

29. Jones G, Strugnell SA, DeLuca HF. Current understanding of the molecular actions of vitamin D. Physiol Rev 1998;78(4):1193–1231.

30. Holick MF. Environmental factors that influence the cutaneous production of vitamin D. Am J Clin Nutr 1995;61(3 suppl):638S–645S.

31. Webb AR, Kline L, Holick MF. Influence of season and latitude on the cutaneous synthesis of vitamin $D_3$: exposure to winter sunlight in Boston and Edmonton will not promote vitamin $D_3$ synthesis in human skin. J Clin Endocrinol Metab 1988;67:373–378.

32. Ladizesky M, Lu Z, Oliveri B et al. Solar ultraviolet B radiation and photoproduction of vitamin $D_3$ in central and southern areas of Argentina. J Bone Miner Res 1995;10(4):545–549.

33. Pettifor JM, Moodley GP, Hough FS et al. The effect of season and latitude on in vitro vitamin D formation by sunlight in South Africa. S Afr Med J 1996;86:1270–1272.

34. Agarwal KS, Mughal MZ, Upadhyay P, Berry JL, Mawer EB, Puliyel JM. The impact of atmospheric pollution on vitamin D status of infants and toddlers in Delhi, India. Arch Dis Child 2002;87(2): 111–113.

35. Looker AC, Dawson-Hughes B, Calvo MS, Gunter EW, Sahyoun NR. Serum 25-hydroxyvitamin D status of adolescents and adults in two seasonal subpopulations from NHANES III. Bone 2002;30(5): 771–777.

36. Harris SS, Dawson-Hughes B. Seasonal changes in plasma 25-hydroxyvitamin D concentrations of young American black and white women. Am J Clin Nutr 1998;67:1232–1236.

37. Specker BL, Tsang RC, Hollis BW. Effect of race and diet on human-milk vitamin D and 25-hydroxyvitamin D. Am J Dis Child 1985;139:1134–1137.

38. Hollis BW, Roos BA, Draper HH, Lambert PW. Vitamin D and its metabolites in human and bovine milk. J Nutr 1981;111:1240–1248.

39. Hollis BW, Wagner CL. Vitamin D requirements during lactation: high-dose maternal supplementation as therapy to prevent hypovitaminosis D for both the mother and the nursing infant. Am J Clin Nutr 2004;80(6):1752S–1758.

40. Hillman LS, Haddad JG. Human perinatal vitamin D metabolism 1: 25-hydroxyvitamin D in maternal and cord blood. J Pediatr 1974;84:742–749.

41. Nesby-O'Dell S, Scanlon KS, Cogswell ME, et al. Hypovitaminosis D prevalence and determinants among African American and white women of reproductive age: third National Health and Nutrition Examination Survey, 1988–1994. Am J Clin Nutr 2002;76(1):187–192.

42. Brunvand L, Haug E. Vitamin D deficiency amongst Pakistani women in Oslo. Acta Obstet Gynecol Scand 1993;72:264–268.

43. Grover SR, Morley R. Vitamin D deficiency in veiled or dark-skinned pregnant women. Med J Aust 2001;175(5):251–252.

44. Mukamel MN, Weisman Y, Somech R et al. Vitamin D deficiency and insufficiency in Orthodox and non-Orthodox Jewish mothers in Israel. Isr Med Assoc J 2001;3(6):419–421.

45. DeLucia MC, Mitnick ME, Carpenter TO. Nutritional rickets with normal circulating 25-hydroxyvitamin D: a call for reexamining the role of dietary calcium intake in North American infants. J Clin Endocrinol Metab 2003;88(8):3539–3545.

46. Ward LM. Vitamin D deficiency in the twentieth century: a persistent problem among Canadian infants and mothers. CMAJ 2005;172(6):769–770.

47. Dunnigan MG, Paton JPJ, Haase S, McNicol GW, Gardner MD, Smith CM. Late rickets and osteomalacia in the Pakistani community in Glasgow. Scot Med J 1962;7:159–167.

48. Datta S, Alfaham M, Davies DP et al. Vitamin D deficiency in pregnant women from a non-European ethnic minority population—an interventional study. Br J Obstet Gynaecol 2002;109(8): 905–908.

49. Dunnigan MG, McIntosh WB, Ford JA. Rickets in Asian immigrants. Lancet 1976;i:1346.

50. Clements MR. The problem of rickets in UK Asians. J Hum Nutr Diet 1989;2:105–116.

51. Meulmeester JF, van den Berg H, Wedel M, Boshuis PG, Hulshof KFAM, Luyken R. Vitamin D status, parathyroid hormone and sunlight in Turkish, Moroccan and Caucasian children in the Netherlands. Eur J Clin Nutr 1990;44:461–470.

52. Pedersen P, Michaelsen KF, Molgaard C. Children with nutritional rickets referred to hospitals in Copenhagen during a 10-year period. Acta Paediatr 2003;92(1):87–90.

53. Markestad T, Elzouki AY. Vitamin D-deficiency rickets in Northern Europe and Libya. In: Rickets. Glorieux FH, ed. New York: Nestec, Vevey/Raven, 1991:203–213.
54. Yeste D, Carrascosa A. [Nutritional rickets in childhood: analysis of 62 cases]. Med Clin (Barc) 2003;121(1):23–27.
55. Gannage-Yared MH, Chemali R, Yaacoub N, Halaby G. Hypovitaminosis D in a sunny country: relation to lifestyle and bone markers. J Bone Miner Res 2000;15(9):1856–1862.
56. Taha SA, Dost SM, Sedrani SH. 25-Hydroxyvitamin D and total calcium: extraordinarily low plasma concentrations in Saudi mothers and their neonates. Pediatr Res 1984;18(8):739–741.
57. Narchi H, El Jamil M, Kulaylat N. Symptomatic rickets in adolescence. Arch Dis Child 2001;84(6): 501–503.
58. Elidrissy ATH, Sedrani SH, Lawson DEM. Vitamin D deficiency in mothers of rachitic infants. Calcif Tissue Int 1984;36:266–268.
59. Shany S, Hirsh J, Berlyne GM. 25-Hydroxycholecalciferol levels in bedouins in the Negev. Am J Clin Nutr 1976;29:1104–1107.
60. Al Hag AI, Karrar ZA. Nutritional vitamin D deficiency rickets in Sudanese children. Ann Trop Paediatr 1995;15:69–76.
61. Lawson DEM, Cole TJ, Salem SI et al. Aetiology of rickets in Egyptian children. Hum Nutr Clin Nutr 1987;41C:199–208.
62. el Hag AI, Karrar ZA. Nutritional vitamin D deficiency rickets in Sudanese children. Ann Trop Paediatr 1995;15(1):69–76.
63. Dancaster CP, Jackson WPU. Studies in rickets in the Cape Peninsula II. Aetiology. S Afr Med J 1961;35:890–894.
64. Belachew T, Nida H, Getaneh T, Woldemariam D, Getinet W. Calcium deficiency and causation of rickets in Ethiopian children. East Afr Med J 2005;82(3):153–159.
65. Okonofua F, Gill DS, Alabi ZO, Thomas M, Bell JL, Dandona P. Rickets in Nigerian children: a consequence of calcium malnutrition. Metabolism 1991;40:209–213.
66. Thacher TD, Fischer PR, Pettifor JM, Lawson JO, Isichei C, Chan GM. Case-control study of factors associated with nutritional rickets in Nigerian children. J Pediatr 2000;137:367–373.
67. Oginni LM, Worsfold M, Oyelami OA, Sharp CA, Powell DE, Davie MW. Etiology of rickets in Nigerian children. J Pediatr 1996;128(5 pt 1):692–694.
68. Thacher TD, Fischer PR, Pettifor JM, et al. A comparison of calcium, vitamin D, or both for nutritional rickets in Nigerian children. N Engl J Med 1999;341(8):563–568.
69. Pettifor JM, Ross P, Wang J, Moodley G, Couper-Smith J. Rickets in children of rural origin in South Africa: is low dietary calcium a factor? J Pediatr 1978;92:320–324.
70. Pettifor JM, Ross FP, Travers R, Glorieux FH, DeLuca HF. Dietary calcium deficiency: a syndrome associated with bone deformities and elevated serum 1,25-dihydroxyvitamin D concentrations. Metab Bone Rel Res 1981;2:301–305.
71. Marie PJ, Pettifor JM, Ross FP, Glorieux FH. Histological osteomalacia due to dietary calcium deficiency in children. N Engl J Med 1982;307:584–588.
72. Eyberg C, Pettifor JM, Moodley G. Dietary calcium intake in rural black South African children. The relationship between calcium intake and calcium nutritional status. Hum Nutr Clin Nutr 1986;40C: 69–74.
73. Fraser DR. Vitamin D-deficiency in Asia. J Steroid Biochem Mol Biol 2004;89–90:491–495.
74. Strand MA, Peng G, Zhang P, Lee G. Preventing rickets in locally appropriate ways: a case report from north China. In Q Community Health Educ 2003;21(4):297–322.
75. Du X, Greenfield H, Fraser DR, Ge K, Trube A, Wang Y. Vitamin D deficiency and associated factors in adolescent girls in Beijing. Am J Clin Nutr 2001;74(4):494–500.
76. Maxwell JP. Further studies in adult rickets (osteomalacia) and foetal rickets. Proc R Soc Med 1934;28:265–300.
77. Bhattacharyya AK. Nutritional rickets in the tropics. In: Nutrtional triggers for health and in disease. Simopoulos AP, ed. Basel: Karger, 1992:140–197.
78. Balasubramanian K, Rajeswari J, Gulab, et al. Varying role of vitamin D deficiency in the etiology of rickets in young children vs. adolescents in northern India. J Trop Pediatr 2003;49(4):201–206.

79. Teotia SP, Teotia M. Endemic fluorosis in India: a challenging national health problem. J Assoc Physicians India 1984;32(4):347–352.

80. Khandare AL, Harikumar R, Sivakumar B. Severe bone deformities in young children from vitamin D deficiency and fluorosis in Bihar-India. Calcif Tissue Int 2005;76(6):412–418.

81. Fischer PR, Rahman A, Cimma JP et al. Nutritional rickets without vitamin D deficiency in Bangladesh. J Trop Pediatr 1999;45(5):291–293.

82. Kabir ML, Rahman M, Talukder K et al. Rickets among children of a coastal area of Bangladesh. Mymensingh Med J 2004;13(1):53–58.

83. Olivieri MB, Ladizesky M, Mautalen CA, Alonso A, Martinez L. Seasonal variations of 25 hydroxyvitamin D and parathyroid hormone in Ushuaia (Argentina), the southernmost city of the world. Bone Miner 1993;20:99–108.

84. Oliveri MB, Ladizesky M, Sotelo A, Griffo S, Ballesteros G, Mautalen CA. Nutritional rickets in Argentina. In: Rickets. Glorieux FH, ed. New York: Nestec, Vevey/Raven, 1991:233–245.

85. Mayne V, McCredie D. Rickets in Melbourne. Med J Aust 1972;2:873–875.

86. Nowson CA, Margerison C. Vitamin D intake and vitamin D status of Australians. Med J Aust 2002;177(3):149–152.

87. Pettifor JM. Nutritional rickets. In: Pediatric bone: biology and diseases. Glorieux FH, Pettifor JM, Juppner H, eds. San Diego, CA: Academic, 2003:541–565.

88. Thacher TD, Fischer PR, Pettifor JM. The usefulness of clinical features to identify active rickets. Ann Trop Paediatr 2002;22(3):229–237.

89. Glerup H, Mikkelsen K, Poulsen L et al. Hypovitaminosis D myopathy without biochemical signs of osteomalacic bone involvement. Calcif Tissue Int 2000;66(6):419–424.

90. Bonnici F. Functional hypoparathyroidism in infantile hypocalcaemic stage I vitamin D deficiency rickets. S Afr Med J 1978;54:611–612.

91. Fraser D, Kooh SW, Scriver CR. Hyperparathyroidism as the cause of hyperaminoaciduria and phosphaturia in human vitamin D deficiency. Pediatr Res 1967;1:425–435.

92. Zeghoud F, Vervel C, Guillozo H, Walrant-Debray O, Boutignon H, Garabedian M. Subclinical vitamin D deficiency in neonates: definition and response to vitamin D supplements. Am J Clin Nutr 1997;65:771–778.

93. Shenoy SD, Swift P, Cody D, Iqbal J. Maternal vitamin D deficiency, refractory neonatal hypocalcaemia, and nutritional rickets. Arch Dis Child 2005;90(4):437–438.

94. Pettifor JM, Pentopoulos M, Moodley GP, Isdale JM, Ross FP. Is craniotabes a pathognomonic sign of rickets in 3-month-old infants? S Afr Med J 1984;65:549–551.

95. Steinbach HL, Noetzli M. Roentgen appearance of the skeleton in osteomalacia and rickets. Am J Roentgen 1964;91:955–972.

96. Thacher TD, Fischer PR, Pettifor JM, Lawson JO, Manaster BJ, Reading JC. Radiographic scoring method for the assessment of the severity of nutritional rickets. J Trop Pediatr 2000;46:132–139.

97. Kruse K. Pathophysiology of calcium metabolism in children with vitamin D-deficiency rickets. J Pediatr 1995;126(5 pt 1):736–741.

98. Markestad T, Halvorsen S, Seeger Halvorsen K, Aksnes L, Aarskog D. Plasma concentrations of vitamin D metabolites before and during treatment of vitamin D deficiency rickets in children. Acta Paediatr Scand 1984;73:225–231.

99. Chesney RW, Zimmerman J, Hamstra A, DeLuca HF, Mazess RB. Vitamin D metabolite concentrations in vitamin D deficiency. Am J Dis Child 1981;135:1025–1028.

100. Gupta MM, Round JM, Stamp TCB. Spontaneous cure of vitamin-D deficiency in Asians during summer in Britain. Lancet 1974;i:586–588.

101. Cesur Y, Caksen H, Gundem A, Kirimi E, Odabas D. Comparison of low and high dose of vitamin D treatment in nutritional vitamin D deficiency rickets. J Pediatr Endocrinol Metab 2003;16(8): 1105–1109.

102. Kutluk G, Cetinkaya F, Basak M. Comparisons of oral calcium, high dose vitamin D and a combination of these in the treatment of nutritional rickets in children. J Trop Pediatr 2002;48(6):351–353.

103. Food and Nutrition Board. Sub-committee on the Tenth Edition of the RDAs. Recommended dietary allowances. Washington, DC: National Academy, 1989:1–184.

104. Department of Health. Nutrition and bone health: with particular reference to calcium and vitamin D. London: Her Majesty's Stationery Office, 1998.
105. Gartner LM, Greer FR. Prevention of rickets and vitamin D deficiency: new guidelines for vitamin D intake. Pediatrics 2003;111(4 pt 1):908–910.
106. Greer FR. Issues in establishing vitamin D recommendations for infants and children. Am J Clin Nutr 2004;80(6):1759S–1762S.
107. Whiting SJ, Calvo MS. Dietary recommendations to meet both endocrine and autocrine needs of Vitamin D. J Steroid Biochem Mol Biol 2005;97(1–2):7–12.
108. Wharton B, Bishop N. Rickets. Lancet 2003;362(9393):1389–1400.
109. Zeghoud F, Ben-Mekhbi H, Djeghri N, Garabedian M. Vitamin D prophylaxis during infancy: comparison of the long-term effects of three intermittent doses (15, 5, or 2.5 mg) on 25-hydroxyvitamin D concentrations. Am J Clin Nutr 1994;60:393–396.
110. Doxiadis S, Angelis C, Karatzas P, Vrettos C, Lapatsanis P. Genetic aspects of nutritional rickets. Arch Dis Child 1976;51:83–90.
111. Awumey EM, Mitra DA, Hollis BW, Kumar R, Bell NH. Vitamin D metabolism is altered in Asian Indians in the southern United States: a clinical research center study. J Clin Endocrinol Metab 1998;83(1):169–173.

# 15 Zinc Deficiency

## Roger Shrimpton and Anuraj H. Shankar

## 15.1   INTRODUCTION

Zinc deficiency has long been considered a common but overlooked problem in developing countries [1]. Unique chemical properties confer on zinc an important role in a wide variety of biological processes, including a fundamental role in gene expression, cell development, and replication. Although zinc occurs in the divalent state ($Zn^{2+}$), it does not exhibit redox chemistry in living organisms and so does not cause oxidative damage. It has a high affinity for electrons and typically binds to proteins, amino acids, peptides, and nucleotides, permitting both catalytic and structural functions. Intakes of zinc in populations are commonly lower than recommended levels, but adaptation mechanisms preclude the development of severe deficiency states. There is increasing evidence, however, that adaptation to low zinc intakes is not without consequence. A large and growing literature on zinc and immune function emphasizes the importance of mild zinc deficiency in reducing resistance to infection [2]. Increasing evidence has shown that zinc supplementation reduces the morbidity and mortality from common childhood infectious diseases, such as diarrhea, acute lower-respiratory tract infections, and malaria [3]. Momentum is now gathering to develop zinc intervention programs.

## 15.2   PUBLIC HEALTH SIGNIFICANCE

The extent of zinc deficiency worldwide is undetermined but probably affects between a quarter and a third of preschool children and their mothers. The lack of a simple quantitative biochemical or functional marker of zinc status has undermined efforts to quantify the global prevalence of zinc deficiency. Overall, approximately 20.5% of the world population is estimated to be at risk of inadequate zinc intake, varying across regions from 9% in the United States and Canada to 33.1% in Southeast Asia [4]. Zinc deficiency is considered to be among the ten largest contributing factors to the burden of disease in developing countries with high mortality [5]. Improving zinc status through supplementation or fortification is part of a group of interventions that, if successfully implemented, could together help reduce child deaths globally by 63% [6].

From: *Nutrition and Health: Nutrition and Health in Developing Countries, Second Edition*
Edited by: R. D. Semba & M. W. Bloem © Humana Press, Totowa, NJ

## 15.3   HISTORICAL BACKGROUND

Zinc was first recognized as an essential factor for the growth of *Aspergillus niger* in 1869 [7], and amounts common in foodstuffs were determined in the early part of the 19th century [8]. Early attempts to demonstrate the essentiality of zinc in animals were unsuccessful, largely because of problems of contamination. Reversible zinc deficiency was finally successfully produced in the rat for the first time in the early 1930s [9]. Studies of Chinese subjects with beriberi in the 1940s showed that the hair and toenails were very low in zinc, suggesting that zinc deficiency might be a concomitant of thiamin deficiency, stated to be widespread in the poor Chinese communities of Taiwan at that time [10, 11]. Balance studies in US schoolchildren in the 1940s led to the conclusion that zinc had a much higher requirement than was previously thought and was certainly not needed just as a "trace." An average intake of 16 mg, of which 5 mg was retained, put zinc on a similar footing to iron in quantitative terms [12].

Despite the variations in the concentrations of zinc in tissues, however, no characteristic manifestations of a suspected zinc deficiency were identified [13]. The universal distribution of zinc in nature, the extreme difficulty with which zinc deficiency had been produced in rats, and the small supplements that prevented symptoms convinced most authorities that zinc deficiency as a practical problem in animals or humans was improbable [14–16].

It came as a surprise, therefore, when parakeratosis, an endemic disease of swine, was shown to be due to inadequate dietary zinc [17], especially because the ration contained ten times the recognized requirement of the rat. The paradox was resolved when it was demonstrated that phytate, the phosphorus storage compound of plant seeds, reduced zinc availability in the soybean-based diet [18]. The original attempts to produce zinc deficiency in the rat had used synthetic diets based on casein or egg-white protein.

In 1961, Prasad and colleagues described a syndrome of iron-deficiency anemia, hepatosplenomegaly, hypogonadism, and dwarfism among young males in Iran who ate little animal protein, subsisted on unleavened wheat bread, and practiced geophagia [19]. After zinc supplementation, the subjects grew pubic hair, and their genitalia size increased [20]. Further studies showed that zinc supplementation was effective in increasing growth in these subjects [21]. Then, Moynahan in the United Kingdom in 1974 showed that the rare inherited disorder acrodermatitis enteropathica, lethally affecting young children after they were weaned from breast milk, was attributable to a defect in zinc absorption and was reversible by zinc supplementation [22].

The World Health Organization (WHO) first established provisional standards for recommended intakes of zinc in 1973 [23]. The Food and Nutrition Board of the National Research Council of the National Academy of Sciences established a recommended dietary allowance (RDA) for zinc in the United States for the first time in 1974 [24].

## 15.4   EPIDEMIOLOGY

The incidence and prevalence of zinc deficiency around the world have not been defined. Three factors appear to be contributing to this large gap in knowledge. First, since there is a lack of a sensitive, practical, and accepted indicator for zinc deficiency, population-based surveys have not been done. Second, marginal zinc deficiency is not

Table 15.1
**Risk factorss for zinc deficiency**

Insufficient dietary intake of zinc (low-protein diet)
High phytate and/or fiber cotent of food (vegetarian)
Diarrheal disease
Malabsorption syndromes
Parasitosis
Hot, humid climate
Lactation
Rapid multiplicative cell growth (pregnancy, infancy, adolescence)
Genetic disease (acrodermatitis enteropatthica, sickle cell anemia)

*Source*: Adapted with permission from [48].

characterized by a highly specific deficiency syndrome. Third, severe clinical deficiency in humans is not seen owing to either adaptation to low intakes or death. It is not surprising therefore that the importance of zinc nutrition for public health has only recently become more widely recognized.

The risk factors for zinc deficiency are multiple, as shown in Table 15.1. The risk of zinc deficiency is highest among infants, young children, pregnant women, and lactating women, for whom needs are comparatively higher owing to the extra demands of multiplicative cell growth. Zinc is commonly the most deficient nutrient in complementary food mixtures fed to infants during weaning in developing countries [25]. Women of childbearing age also have insufficient dietary zinc intake in many populations [26]. Eighty percent of women globally and 100% of women in developing countries have usual intakes of zinc considered inadequate to meet the normative needs of pregnancy [27].

Other risk factors for zinc deficiency include those that contribute to insufficient dietary intake, including poverty, food taboos, and special diets (including vegetarian diets that are high in phytate and fiber). Individuals with specific disease states may also be at higher risk, including those with malabsorption syndromes, diarrhea, and parasitic diseases. Individuals with genetic diseases such as acrodermatitis enteropathica, sickle-cell disease, and cystic fibrosis are also at special risk of deficiency.

## 15.5   METABOLISM OF ZINC

### 15.5.1   *Zinc Absorption*

Zinc apparently can be absorbed at all levels of the small intestine. Dietary zinc is digested free of its protein matrixes before becoming available for absorption. Pancreatic secretions that help digest food deliver an amount of zinc into the duodenum equivalent to that provided by most meals. The intestine must therefore recover appropriate amounts of zinc from both dietary and endogenous sources to maintain a favorable zinc balance. The total body zinc content of adults may be maintained with the absorption of about 5 mg/day of zinc. Zinc is absorbed both by passive diffusion and through a carrier-mediated process on the brush border of enterocytes [28, 29]. Zinc absorbed from the intestinal lumen is bound to many different molecules within the enterocytes, and metallothionein and cysteine-rich intestinal proteins play a role in transmucosal transport [30]. The absorption of zinc depends on both zinc status and the dietary intake of zinc [31]. During periods of high intake, zinc absorption decreases, and excretion of endogenous zinc into the gastrointestinal lumen is enhanced. In contrast, during periods of low intake, absorption of zinc is enhanced, and secretion of endogenous zinc into the gastrointestinal lumen is suppressed. During pregnancy and lactation, women increase their zinc absorption rates. Californian women consuming 50% of the recommended dietary intake increased absorption rates from 15% preconceptually to 25% during lactation [32]. Lactating women in the Amazon region, consuming a diet providing only 34% of the recommended intake, showed absorption rates of between 60% and 80% of dietary zinc [33].

### 15.5.2   Zinc Transport

Zinc released into the mesenteric capillaries and the portal circulation is bound initially to albumin, and two thirds of portal zinc is taken up by the liver [34]. Peripheral circulating zinc is firmly bound to $\alpha_2$-macroglobulin (30–40%), loosely bound to albumin (60–70%), and 7% chelated by amino acids [35, 36]. The latter fraction is involved in nutritionally relevant transport and distribution. There does not appear to be any homeostatic mechanisms for regulating circulating zinc levels and keeping them constant. Limited experimental studies in humans on low-zinc, high-energy diets showed that significant reductions in serum zinc levels take from 3–6 weeks [37, 38]. Consumption of a low-zinc, low-energy diet causes amino acids to be mobilized from muscle for gluconeogenesis in the liver, liberating zinc into circulation and maintaining serum zinc levels even in the face of depletion.

### 15.5.3   Zinc Storage

The total zinc content of the human body is estimated to be 60 mg in newborns [39] or 20 µg zinc/g, increasing to 30 µg zinc/g during growth and maturation; by adulthood, the total body zinc content is estimated to be about 1.5 g in women and 2.5 g in men. Zinc is found in all tissues and fluids in the body, but it is primarily an intracellular ion. There is no specific storage organ for zinc. It is estimated that 60% of total body zinc is in striated muscle, 20% in bone, 5% in blood and liver, and 3% in the skin and gastrointestinal tract. The highest concentrations of zinc are found in the choroid of the eye and prostatic fluids. Kinetic studies suggested that there are two major zinc pools in the body, one with a short half-life and another with a long half-life. The rapid turnover in zinc appears to occur in the liver, pancreas, kidney, and spleen. In lactating women consuming low-zinc diets in the Amazon region, the short-term pool size was reduced to about half of expected values. Although the total body zinc turnover rates seemed normal, plasma zinc turnover rates were double that expected [33].

### 15.5.4   Zinc Excretion

Zinc is excreted mostly in the feces. Fecal losses of zinc are a combination of unabsorbed dietary zinc and endogenous secretions of zinc from the pancreas, gallbladder, stomach, and duodenum. Zinc loss from enterocytes appears to be partly under homeostatic control. Urinary losses, although normally low, can be high in catabolic states.

During starvation, when amino acids are mobilized from muscle to the liver for glu-coneogenesis, much of the zinc liberated is lost through the urine [40]. Zinc loss also occurs through turnover of skin, hair, and nails and through sweat, menstrual blood loss, and semen. In tropical countries, sweat losses can be considerable. An ejaculation contains about 1 mg zinc because of the high zinc content of seminal fluid [41]. Lacta-tion is a form of zinc excretion in which about 2–3 mg of zinc is excreted per day in the first several weeks postpartum, decreasing to 1 mg/day by 2–3 months postpartum, and declining dramatically beyond this period [42].

## 15.6  BIOLOGICAL FUNCTIONS OF ZINC

Zinc is essential for many important biological functions, including immunity, growth, neurological transmission, and reproduction [43]. Zinc is the most abundant trace ele-ment inside most cells, with the exception of red blood cells with iron and bone cells with calcium. Zinc is not limited, as are calcium and iron, to a few functional roles.

### 15.6.1  Zinc Metalloenzymes

Zinc is needed for the function of about 300 zinc metalloenzymes [44], and among the classes of enzymes with zinc metalloenzymes are oxidoreductases, transferases, hydrolases, lyases, isomerases, and ligases. These zinc metalloenzymes are broadly involved in structural, regulatory, catalytic, and noncatalytic functions. Presumably, these enzymes are influenced by zinc status, but direct evidence of a link between zinc status and impaired function of a zinc-requiring enzyme in higher organisms is still quite limited. Evidence for the much-hypothesized effects of zinc deficiency on vitamin A metabolism, for example, was considered inconclusive in humans until recently [45]. Zinc supplementation has now been shown to improve conversion of β-carotene to reti-nol in pregnant women in Indonesia [46].

### 15.6.2  Zinc Fingers

The binding of regulatory proteins to specific recognition sequences of genes is important to gene expression and regulation. Zinc fingers are protein complexes that form a tetrahedral complex with zinc and provide structural stability for small polypep-tides [47]. The region of the protein containing the zinc-binding domains is essential for binding to DNA and plays a role in protein–protein interaction. Zinc-finger domains are found in regulatory proteins in the nucleus and the cytoplasm and among signal transduction factors. Zinc deficiency is postulated to be associated with increased risk of DNA damage, leading to cancer [48] and to birth defects [49].

### 15.6.3  Zinc and Biomembranes

Zinc is a common divalent ion within the cytoplasm of cells, and zinc may play an important role in the structure and function of biomembranes because of its ability to stabilize thiol groups and phospholipids and to quench free radicals [50].

### 15.6.4  Zinc and Immune Function

Given that cells produced by the immune system in response to infection have a large number of zinc-dependent enzymes, it is not surprising that zinc deficiency has profound effects on immune function [2]. Zinc may also have an important role in immunity because of its function as an antioxidant and its role in apoptosis. Zinc has a role in both nonspecific immunity and adaptive immunity mechanisms. Zinc deficiency is associated with impaired T- and B-lymphocyte function and the generation of antibody responses. Lymphocytes become less responsive to cytokine activation, and microbicidal ability of macrophages and neutrophils is suppressed [51] It has also been demonstrated that experimentally induced zinc deficiency in humans results in an imbalance between T helper type 1 (Th1) and 2 (Th2) cell subpopulations such that Th1 function is selectively suppressed [52]. Even subclinical zinc deficiency has a profound effect on immune status. T-cell and B-cell production is compromised in the thymus and bone marrow because of an increase in apoptosis in precursors of these cells [53]. Interestingly, production of cells of the neutrophil and macrophage lineages appears to be less affected, although function may be compromised, thereby preserving some level of innate immunity [54].

### 15.6.5   Other Functions of Zinc

Zinc has been implicated as playing a potential role in many other important biological functions, including synaptic transmission, the activity of growth hormone, the polymerization of tubulin, and signal transduction [43].

### 15.7   PATHOPHYSIOLOGY OF ZINC DEFICIENCY

Zinc deficiency may generally occur owing to one or more mechanisms, including inadequate intake of zinc; interference with absorption and bioavailability of dietary zinc; increased losses of zinc; impaired utilization of zinc; and increased requirement for zinc, as during pregnancy, lactation, and periods of rapid growth. Constitutive zinc metalloenzymes are part of the basic cellular structure and are relatively stable. Moreover, loss of 10–20% of a non-rate-limiting enzyme may not severely compromise metabolic function and cellular survival. If, however, a small pool of free zinc must provide ions for receptors and other transcription factors as needed for the immediate induction of fresh supplies of new enzymes, then even modest deficits of free zinc might seriously erode homeostatic adaptability and growth and development [55].

### 15.7.1   Dietary Sources and Intake of Zinc

The zinc content of foods is closely correlated with the protein content. The richest dietary sources of zinc are animal products such as shellfish, red meat, liver, and poultry. Dark meat has twice the zinc content of white meat. The plant protein sources such as beans, lentils, chickpeas, and peas are also relatively rich in zinc. In whole cereal grains, zinc is contained in the bran and germ portions, which are normally lost through milling. Consequently, white rice and white bread are relatively poor zinc sources. Dairy products contain only moderate amounts of zinc, and drinking water is a minor source of zinc in most populations.

The zinc content of some common foods is shown in Table 15.2, with foods classified according to their zinc energy densities [56]. Foods that will ensure that zinc needs are met if energy needs are met are classified as rich. Even in developed countries, zinc intakes are commonly suboptimal because of the excessive consumption of very poor

Table 15.2
Zinc content of some common foods

| Zinc category (mg/1,000 kcal) | Foods |
| --- | --- |
| Very poor (0–2) | Fats, oils, butter, cream cheese, sweets, chocolates, soft drinks, alcoholic drinks, preserves |
| Poor (1–5) | Fish, fruits, refined cereal products, pastries, biscuits, cakes, puddings, tubers, plantains, sausages, chips |
| Rich (4–12) | Whole grains, pork, poultry, milk, low-fat cheese, yogurt, eggs, nuts |
| Very rich (12–882) | Lamb, leaf and root vegetables, crustacea, beef, kidney, liver, heart, mollusks |

*Source:* Adapted with permission from [48].

zinc sources such as soft drinks, refined breads, cakes and sweets, and potato chips. In many populations in developing countries, the consumption of meat and animal products is low, such that suboptimal zinc intakes are also very common. Food taboos in Asia, especially, commonly contribute to preventing pregnant and lactating women and young children getting "hot" zinc- and protein-rich foods.

A comprehensive analysis and review of the complementary feeding of young children in developing countries concluded that meeting the micronutrient needs from complementary foods was the biggest challenge. Adequate amounts of iron and zinc can only be met if animal products are consumed in quantities unlikely to be feasible [57]. Of complementary foods fed during the second semester of life to infants in the Amazon, none met recommended zinc-to-energy levels, and 88% were below 70% of the recommended level [58]. It is also possible to estimate the percentage of individuals at the national level at risk of having inadequate zinc intakes based on the overall availability of food as estimated in food balance sheets compared with dietary requirements [4].

### 15.7.2 Absorption and Bioavailability of Zinc

There are several important factors in foods that can interfere with absorption of dietary zinc. Zinc in animal foods is generally more available than the zinc in vegetable foods. Animal and human studies have shown that the phytate (inositol hexaphosphate) content of plant foods can inhibit zinc absorption [18, 59], and the fiber, oxalate, tannin, and lignin content of plant foods can also reduce the absorption of zinc [60]. Whole grains, legumes, and leafy vegetables contain high amounts of these factors. Zinc forms insoluble complexes with phytate at alkaline pH [61] and at pH values usually found in foods. Soaking and fermentation of plant foods are among some strategies that can be used to reduce intake of phytic acid [62] as phytate is partially hydrolyzed to other analogous metabolites that have a lower capacity to bind zinc. The populations of the Middle East, where zinc deficiency was originally described, had high zinc intakes, but the zinc source was unleavened whole-wheat bread rich in phytate. The leavening of bread through the action of yeast reduces phytate content. Soy protein-based infant formulas may have a phytate content that reduces the absorption of zinc [63, 64]. Diarrheal diseases also interfere with the absorption of zinc and contribute to accelerated fecal losses of both dietary and endogenous zinc.

### 15.7.3  Zinc Dietary Requirements

The Food and Agriculture Organization (FAO) of the United Nations and WHO have reviewed their estimates of zinc requirements [65] and concluded that the estimates developed in the 1996 WHO/FAO/IAEA (International Atomic Energy Agency) report were still valid and useful for assessment of the adequacy of zinc intakes in population groups. Three general categories of diets have been proposed according to the availability of zinc (Table 15.3). Zinc requirements are higher during pregnancy and lactation and in infants and children during periods of rapid growth. During the third trimester of pregnancy, the physiological requirement for zinc is about twice as high as that in women who are not pregnant. Breast-fed infants are considered to absorb up to 80% of the zinc in breast milk. Diets with a high availability of zinc (50%) are characterized by a low cereal fiber content, low phytate content, and adequate protein content of meats and fish. Also included in this category are semisynthetic formula diets based on animal proteins. Diets with a moderate availability of zinc (30%) include mixed diets containing

Table 15.3
Recommended nutrient intakes (RNIs) for dietary zinc (mg/day) to meet the normative storage requirements for different population groups from diets differing in zinc bioavailability[a]

| Population group | Assumed body weight (kg) | High bioavailability | Moderate bioavailability | Low bioavailability |
|---|---|---|---|---|
| Infants and children | | | | |
| 0–6 months | 6 | 1.1[b] | 2.8[c] | 6.6[c] |
| 7–12 months | 9 | 0.8[b], 2.5[c] | 4.1 | 8.4 |
| 1–3 years | 12 | 2.4 | 4.1 | 8.3 |
| 4–6 years | 17 | 12.9 | 4.8 | 9.6 |
| 7–9 years | 25 | 3.3 | 5.6 | 11.2 |
| Adolescents | | | | |
| Females, 10–18 years | 47 | 4.3 | 7.2 | 14.4 |
| Males, 10–18 years | 49 | 5.1 | 8.6 | 17.1 |
| Adults | | | | |
| Females, 19–65 years | 55 | 3.0 | 4.9 | 9.8 |
| Males, 19–65 years | 65 | 4.2 | 7.0 | 14.0 |
| Females, 65+ years | 55 | 3.0 | 4.9 | 9.8 |
| Males, 65+ years | 65 | 4.2 | 7.0 | 14.0 |
| Pregnant women | | | | |
| First trimester | – | 3.4 | 5.5 | 11.0 |
| Second trimester | – | 4.2 | 7.0 | 14.0 |
| Third trimester | – | 6.0 | 10.0 | 20.0 |
| Lactating women | | | | |
| 0–3 months | – | 5.8 | 9.5 | |
| 3–6 months | – | 5.3 | 8.8 | |
| 6–12 months | – | 4.3 | 7.2 | |

[a]Based on World Health Organization/Food and Agricultural Organization estimates of zinc availability in three general types of diet [65].
[b]Infants fed exclusively human milk.
[c]Formula-fed infants.

animal or fish protein; lacto-ovo, ovovegetarian, or vegan diets that are not primarily based on unrefined cereals; and diets with a moderately high phytate/zinc molar ratio. Diets with a low availability of zinc (15%) include diets high in unrefined, unfermented, and ungerminated cereal grain, diets with a high phytate/zinc ratio, diets in which high-phytate soya protein constitutes the primarily source of protein, diets high in energy intake from high-phytate foods, and diets high in inorganic calcium salts.

## 15.8 CLINICAL MANIFESTATIONS OF ZINC DEFICIENCY

The clinical manifestations of zinc deficiency are generally nonspecific, vary widely, and depend on the severity of deficiency (Table 15.4). Severe zinc deficiency, noted in conditions such as acrodermatitis enteropathica and among patients fed total parenteral nutrition without zinc, is characterized by alopecia, diarrhea, skin lesions in the extremities and perioral area, and anorexia. Such patients, if not fed zinc, die from common infections such as diarrhea. Zinc deficiency is a nutritionally acquired immunodeficiency disorder and is associated with greater morbidity and mortality from infectious diseases [2]. In the original clinical observations in Iran, hypogonadism, delayed sexual maturation, and severe growth retardation were noted [19]. Marginal zinc deficiency may be associated with nonspecific clinical manifestations such as growth retardation, increased frequency of infections, failure to thrive, and impaired taste (hypogeusia). Zinc deficiency is common in the elderly, especially if hospitalized, and may be associated with poor wound healing.

Severe protein energy malnutrition has been associated with zinc deficiency. Zinc supplementation of such malnourished infants was shown to rapidly increase the size of the thymus, suggesting that zinc deficiency may play a part in the thymic atrophy and infections associated with malnutrition [66]. In the recovery of malnourished children, it has been shown that if the zinc-to-energy ratio of the diet was not sufficient, it could limit the rate of weight gain [67]. The weight gained could also be of different sorts of tissues. Rats on low zinc-to-energy diets deposit less lean tissue, and more adipose tissue is created.

Table 15.4
**Clinical manifestations of zinc deficiency**

Growth retardation
Hypogonadism
Delayed sexual maturation
Immunodeficiency
Increased infections
Delayed wound healing
Skin lesions
Alopecia
Hypospermia
Night blindness
Diarrhea
Behavioral disturbances
Anorexia
Hypogeusia

Zinc deficiency during pregnancy is associated with adverse maternal and fetal outcomes [26]. Severe maternal zinc deficiency has been associated with birth defects and
spontaneous abortion. Fetal growth retardation, low birth weight, preterm delivery, and
increased complications during delivery have been associated with marginal zinc deficiency [68]. Zinc deficiency impairs estrogen-dependent gene expression in the uterus
via the receptor for the hormone, which contains a zinc-finger protein. This lack of effect
of estrogen impairs the conversion of the uterus from its passive state to one capable
of concerted contractions with sufficient force to expel a fetus [69]. Maternal and early
infant zinc deficiencies may have an adverse influence on infant neurodevelopment,
including motor development, cognition, and activity [70].

## 15.9  ASSESSMENT OF ZINC STATUS

The diagnosis of zinc deficiency is hampered by the lack of a single, sensitive, and
specific low-cost indicator of zinc status. This has different implications for the determination of zinc status at the population level, in large epidemiological studies for public
health decision making, than at the individual level for clinical management of individual patients.

### 15.9.1  Plasma or Serum Zinc Concentrations

Plasma or serum zinc concentrations are the most widely used indicator for zinc status.
In general, during zinc deficiency, plasma or serum zinc concentrations will decrease.
The amount of zinc circulating in plasma is only less than 0.2% of the total body zinc
content, and most of the total body content of zinc is contained in muscle and liver.
Thus, small changes in the uptake or release of zinc in tissues can have a large effect
on plasma or serum zinc concentrations. There are several factors that may confound
the use of plasma or serum zinc concentrations, including infection [71], inflammation,
chronic disease, liver disease, pregnancy [72], and malnutrition [73].

Serum zinc concentrations have been determined in a large population of apparently
healthy individuals in the United States and age- and sex-related trends in zinc concentrations described [74]. The cutoff points most commonly used to assess the risk of zinc
deficiency using plasma and serum zinc concentrations is below 10.71 µmol/L (<70 µg/dL)
for morning fasting blood samples and less than 9.95 µmol/L (<65 µg/dL) for nonfasting
blood samples [75]. Further cutoffs have been proposed for assessing serum zinc concentrations in population studies, which consider age, sex, time of day, fasting state, and
pregnancy [76]. Although it is recognized that it is difficult to standardize the time of day
and fasting state during the collection of blood samples in surveys, it is recommended
that these characteristics of the sample be noted for better interpretation of results.

For the assessment of zinc status of children in developing countries, plasma or
serum zinc concentrations are the best indicators. Although zinc concentrations may
decrease during an acute-phase response, this does not appear to limit the use of plasma
zinc concentrations as an indicator of zinc status in community-based studies of children in developing countries. In cross-sectional, community-based studies conducted
among young children in Peru [77], Guatemala [78], and Zimbabwe [79], no significant
relations were found between the presence of infection and the plasma or serum zinc
concentrations.

Among hospitalized individuals or among adults, the effects of infection, inflammation, or other processes as mentioned may limit the usefulness of plasma zinc concentrations as an indicator of zinc status. The most reliable method for diagnosis of zinc deficiency may be the response of plasma or serum zinc concentrations to zinc supplementation [75].

Zinc plasma or serum concentrations can be measured by flame atomic absorption spectroscopy [80], and more recent methods include ashing small-volume samples in a graphite furnace followed by flameless atomic absorption spectroscopy. Several practical considerations must be made in collecting plasma or serum samples for the assessment of zinc concentrations. Ideally, the setting for the collection of blood samples should be standardized as much as possible in relation to meals, exercise, or other stress [75]. Plasma or serum should be separated as quickly as possible as zinc concentrations may change if the plasma or serum has not been separated from the blood within 1 hour [81]. In this regard, plasma may be preferable to serum in field studies. Hemolyzed samples should not be used as zinc concentrations are higher in erythrocytes than in plasma. Trace element-free syringes, pipette tips, and storage tubes are widely available from major laboratory supply houses and should be used for the collection of plasma or serum samples for zinc determinations as zinc contamination may occur with use of regular blood-drawing equipment and supplies [82].

### 15.9.2 Dietary Assessment

The assessment of dietary zinc intake in a population requires a complex approach: food intake distributions of a population, analysis of local staple foods, and a comparison of zinc intake from these foods with estimates of the requirements for adequate intake of zinc [83]. Dietary assessment can be based on the recall of an individual for food consumed or based on weighed food records compiled by research assistants. A 24-hour dietary recall has been developed for assessment of the adequacy of trace mineral intakes in illiterate populations [84]. In many developing countries, local food composition tables may be unavailable, and the investigator must develop such a table by collecting foods for analysis and measuring trace mineral content by atomic absorption spectroscopy [85]. Other dietary components may limit the dietary availability of zinc, including phytates, calcium, and dietary fiber, and these must be considered in the food analyses [83]. The observed or reported zinc intakes for a population can be used to derive a distribution of usual zinc intakes. The estimated bioavailability of zinc must be taken into account as estimates of zinc absorption can vary widely, depending on phytates and other factors in the food. For developing countries, the requirement estimates for zinc have been established by WHO based on the availability of zinc in the diet, as discussed in Section 15.7.3 (Table 15.3) [65].

### 15.9.3 Other Methods

Hair zinc concentrations have been used as an indicator of zinc status in children, but this method may be confounded by effects of malnutrition [86]. Erythrocyte zinc concentrations are insensitive indicators for zinc deficiency. Leukocytes contain high concentrations of zinc and have been examined as a possible indicator of zinc deficiency [87]; however, the laboratory technique is difficult and laborious, and contamination of leukocyte samples with erythrocytes and platelets is problematical. Diminished taste acuity (hypogeusia) is one feature of marginal zinc deficiency in children and has been used as a basis for a functional test of zinc status [88]. Stable isotope techniques may help provide further insight into zinc deficiency and the effects of zinc interventions [89]. At the population level, the use of a composite index for predicting the national risk of zinc deficiency has been proposed that uses a combination of stunting rates and adequacy of zinc in the national food supply [76].

## 15.10   ZINC SUPPLEMENTATION AS A PUBLIC HEALTH INTERVENTION

Zinc supplementation has been shown to have both preventive and therapeutic benefit in reducing the morbidity and mortality of a variety of childhood infectious diseases as well as a positive effect on child growth in certain situations. Efforts to build zinc interventions into diarrheal disease control programs have already begun.

### 15.10.1   Diarrheal Disease in Children

Strong evidence exists that zinc supplements improve the prognosis of children being treated for diarrheal disease. A pooled analysis of randomized controlled trials of therapeutic zinc in children with diarrhea showed that children with acute diarrhea given zinc supplements had a 15% lower probability of continuing diarrhea on a given day compared with those in the control group; children with persistent diarrhea had a 24% lower probability of continuing diarrhea. In addition, children with persistent diarrhea had a 42% lower rate of treatment failure or death if given zinc supplements [90]. A subsequent study in Bangladesh indicated that field implementation of diarrheal treatment that included daily zinc supplementation for 2 weeks reduced subsequent childhood mortality by 50% [91].

The most effective way to deliver zinc supplements as an adjunct to oral dehydration treatment in diarrheal disease control programs is still being explored. WHO and the United Nations International Children's Emergency Fund (UNICEF) currently recommend blister packs of ten dispersible tablets of 20 mg zinc for daily consumption as part of the treatment of diarrhea [92]. It may also be beneficial to add zinc to oral rehydration solution as zinc supplementation reduces the duration and severity of diarrheal episodes, and one of the shortcomings of oral rehydration therapy is that the frequency and volume of stools are not reduced. Studies of the efficacy of including zinc in oral rehydration solutions have not proven to be beneficial, however [93]. In addition, many countries promote the use of home-made fluids. The use of zinc as an adjunct therapy significantly improves the cost-effectiveness of standard management of diarrhea [94]. A five-country randomized controlled trial showed that zinc supplementation as an adjunct to oral rehydration therapy is well accepted, does not interfere with the oral rehydration, and reduces the use of other medications [95]. However, it is already proving difficult to achieve and maintain high coverage of oral rehydration therapy for diarrheal disease control [96]. The challenge of promoting zinc supplements as part of the treatment of diarrhea is therefore considerable, even if the rewards are likely to be great.

### 15.10.2   Respiratory Disease in Children

Regular zinc supplements have also been shown to prevent respiratory disease, especially in children with lower birth weights and those with stunted growth or zinc deficiency. The supplementation of low birth weight infants in Brazil from birth for 8 weeks reduced both diarrhea and coughs by a third in the first 6 months of life [97]. Zinc supplementation of babies with low birth weight in India reduced mortality during infancy by a third [98]. Pooled analysis of randomized controlled trials found that zinc supplements reduced diarrheal diseases by 18% and pneumonia by 41% in preschool children [99]. Community-based controlled trials in India [100] and Bangladesh [101] have shown that routine daily or weekly zinc supplementation reduces the incidence of pneumonia by 26% and 17%, respectively. The latter study also reported a reduction in mortality. Several studies are under way to examine the impact of zinc on childhood mortality. Thus, prophylactic zinc supplementation has the potential to greatly reduce the incidence and possibly the mortality of acute respiratory infections, which is remarkable considering the challenge that pneumonia presents from a child health perspective [102].

The use of zinc as an adjunct therapy for case management of pneumonia has also been evaluated. One trial in Bangladesh indicated that zinc reduced the duration of severe pneumonia by 30% [103] However, another carried out in India showed no additional benefit of zinc given as an adjunct to treatment [104] While there is some indication that adjunctive therapy may help, additional information is needed to confirm the effect and conditions of efficacy.

### 15.10.3   Malaria in Children

Zinc is essential for a variety of lymphocyte functions, many of which are implicated in resistance to malaria, including production of immunoglobulin G (IgG), interferon-$\gamma$, and tumor necrosis factor-$\alpha$ (TNF-$\alpha$) and microbicidal activity of macrophages [105]. A community-based, placebo-controlled trial in the Gambia showed that young children supplemented with zinc had 32% fewer clinic visits for malaria due to *Plasmodium falciparum*, although this was not statistically significant [106]. A placebo-controlled trial in Papua New Guinea showed that preschool children receiving 10 mg zinc/day had a significant 38% reduction in health center visits due to *P. falciparum* malaria [107]. Moreover, a 69% reduction was observed for malaria episodes accompanied by high levels of parasitemia (i.e., $> 100,000$ parasites/$\mu$L), suggesting that zinc may preferentially protect against more severe malaria episodes. A subsequent study in Burkina Faso did not observe a protective effect of daily zinc supplementation on *P. falciparum* attacks. However, the daily surveillance methodology that was used biased the study toward assessing impact on less-severe malaria attacks [108]. A five-country randomized controlled trial also found that zinc does not appear to provide a beneficial effect in the treatment of acute, uncomplicated *P. falciparum* malaria in preschool children [109]. Additional information is needed to document the geographic regions and conditions of malaria transmission in which zinc might be effective.

### 15.10.4   Growth and Development of Children

Zinc supplementation may also help prevent, or at least reduce, child growth failure, although the evidence is weaker than for prevention of disease and seems to depend on certain predisposing factors. A meta-analysis of randomized controlled trials of the effects of supplemental zinc on growth of prepubertal children found that height and weight growth were moderately improved, with the greatest responses shown by children who were initially underweight or stunted [110]. As has been noted previously, most zinc supplementation trials looking at growth outcomes have not focused on the age group of 6–12 months, when growth faltering is occurring [1]. Zinc supplementation trials in infants with birth weights above 2.5 kg have shown little effect on preventing growth faltering in the second half of infancy in Indonesia [111, 112]. In Ethiopia, zinc supplements increased length growth of stunted infants, but these infants were not selected on birth weight criteria [113]. Trials in infants from birth to 6 months in Bangladesh showed growth effects only in those with initial low zinc status [114]. Zinc supplementation of young children aged 6–36 months of age in Burkina Faso showed no effect on growth despite a high prevalence of undernutrition [115].

In India, zinc supplementation was noted to affect high-movement activities among infants and young children [116]. Zinc supplementation, 10 mg/day, was noted to affect the activity patterns of infants in rural Guatemala [117]. Zinc supplementation has been shown to benefit psychomotor development in undernourished children in Jamaica, and the benefits were enhanced if stimulation was also provided [118].

### 15.10.5   *Maternal Health*

Zinc supplementation during pregnancy may play a role in improving both maternal and child health [26]. Studies have been conducted to determine whether zinc supplementation will improve birth weight, and the results have been mixed, but many were conducted in well-nourished populations. A trial conducted among low-income women in Alabama showed that daily antenatal zinc supplementation, 25 mg/day, significantly increased birth weight [119], whereas in Lima, Peru, 15 mg/day zinc supplementation had no significant impact on birth weight or prematurity [120]. In Peru, however, they did find evidence of more advanced neurological development of the fetus, increased transfer of immunoglobulin, especially IgG, to the fetus, as well as reduced levels of acute respiratory infections (ARI) and diarrheal morbidity in the first year of life [121]. Furthermore, the length of the femur bone was greater at birth in the zinc-supplemented group [122]. In Bangladesh and the United States, zinc supplementation during pregnancy showed no beneficial effect on mental development and behavior of infants [123, 124]. Although there were no differences in growth or serum zinc concentrations in infants of mothers in Bangladesh who received zinc or placebo during pregnancy, low birth weight babies born to mothers in the zinc-supplemented group had reduced risks for acute diarrhea, dysentery, and impetigo at age 6 months compared with those born with low birth weight in the placebo group. These reductions were not seen in babies born with normal birth weight [125].

Postpartum zinc supplementation appears to have no effect on the breast milk zinc content [42], but it does have other effects. Although zinc supplementation of women during lactation in the Amazon did not influence milk zinc levels, milk retinol levels were double in the supplemented mothers as compared to the placebo control group at 4 months postpartum [126]. There were also growth and morbidity effects, with infants of zinc-supplemented mothers gaining half a kilogram more than controls by 5 months postpartum, with three times less diarrheal days compared to placebo controls [127]. There was also a relationship between maternal zinc status and the levels of secretory immunoglobulin A in breast milk [128].

Thus, there is increasing evidence that zinc supplementation during pregnancy and lactation improves fetal and infant growth and development, even though this may not be manifested as an improvement in birth weight. No trials so far have tried to evaluate the benefits of zinc supplementation for the health of the mother herself.

## 15.10.6  *Human Immunodeficiency Virus Infection*

Low serum or plasma zinc levels have been reported in 26% of asymptomatic homosexual men [129] and 29% of hospitalized patients with AIDS [130]. Low serum zinc levels were associated with reduced secretory function of the thymus [131] and HIV disease progression in homosexual men [132, 133]. Zinc levels can decrease during the acute-phase response, and it has been suggested that these low zinc levels may reflect HIV replication [132], and the possibility that zinc supplementation could enhance viral replication has been postulated. However, daily zinc supplementation, 200 mg/days for 30 days, reduced infectious disease morbidity in adults with AIDS in Italy [134], and in South Africa 10 mg/day zinc supplementation in preschool children with HIV-1 infection did not result in increased plasma viral load and reduced the diarrheal disease morbidity compared to placebo controls [135]. In Tanzania, the use of a multiple-micronutrient supplement, including zinc, during the treatment of pulmonary tuberculosis reduced mortality in those coinfected with HIV [136]. More research is needed to further explore the benefits of using zinc as an adjunct therapy in the treatment of HIV infections.

## 15.11  PREVENTION OF ZINC DEFICIENCY

Strategies to prevent zinc deficiency should consider the immediate, underlying, and basic causes of the deficiency. These should not be seen as either/or options but instead as a multiple-prong approach with shifting of priorities over time depending on resources available. The immediate causes operate at the level of the individual and include inadequate ingestion of zinc or excessive losses due to disease and can be fixed rapidly in the short term by measures such as supplementation and medication. Such measures should be a priority in the short term, although they may be difficult to maintain for long periods. Underlying causes operate at the level of the family and community and include household food security; availability of health, water, and sanitation services; and the caring practices that determine how mothers and their children are treated and looked after by their families and communities. These causes, few of which are specific for zinc deficiency, are more difficult to resolve and require a medium-term perspective, but if achieved are more likely to be sustainable. Basic causes operate at the societal level and include natural resources, national laws and policies, national infrastructure, mass media, education, culture, and religion, among others. Again, these are not necessarily specific for zinc; they take longer to implement, but once achieved they are very sustainable.

There are several shortcomings to using zinc supplements alone as a preventive intervention, and mounting evidence points toward multiple-micronutrient supplements as the best way to deliver preventive zinc interventions. Zinc supplementation is obviously an important option to use as a short-term solution in the treatment of infectious diseases, especially diarrhea [137]. But, for more prolonged use for preventive purposes, there are several problems that need to be resolved. First, it is thought that supplements must be given often (i.e., daily), and it is generally difficult to maintain high levels of compliance with these regimes. But, supplementation still has a preventive role for short periods in high-risk situations, such as pregnancy, lactation, and early childhood [138]. The other problem, however, is that zinc deficiency rarely occurs alone since people who are zinc deficient are most often also iron deficient and indeed have multiple micronutrient deficiencies. Giving zinc alone may either show no impact because it is not the first limiting nutrient or even exacerbate other deficiencies [139]. It also makes little logistical sense to try to deliver iron/folate tablets and zinc tablets as separate supplements for pregnant and lactating women, who commonly have these micronutrient deficiencies concurrently [140]. Combined iron and zinc supplements are not the ideal solution, however, as these two elements show interactions and combined are less effective than either alone in improving their respective status indicators [111, 141].

Fortunately, there is increasing evidence that multiple-micronutrient supplements that contain zinc and iron together with other micronutrients that are commonly limiting in complementary foods are more efficacious than iron or zinc alone for improving child growth and development as well as resolving the problems of zinc deficiency, iron deficiency, and anemia [142–144]. There is also evidence that the one RDA multiple-micronutrient supplement approach is not a large enough dose to reverse or prevent the anemia common during infancy in developing country settings, and that supplementation should start before 6 months of age, or during pregnancy, as well as be combined with infection and parasite control measures [145]. Trials in women during pregnancy are ongoing in eight countries comparing a multiple-micronutrient supplement containing zinc and another 12 nutrients with iron/folate supplements, looking at various birth outcomes [140]. In populations affected by emergency situations, WHO, the World Food Programme (WFP), and UNICEF recommend the use of such multiple-micronutrient supplements for pregnant and lactating women and children aged 6 to 59 months [146].

The underlying causes of zinc deficiency, which operate at the family and community levels, include hygiene and health services, dietary diversification and modification, as well as caring practices. The promotion of exclusive breast-feeding for the first 6 months is one important preventive measure that operates at the immediate and underlying levels. Other dietary approaches include increasing the intakes of foods that enhance zinc absorption, modifying foods through fermentation, soaking, or other measures to reduce phytic acid content [62]. These approaches are more complicated to organize, are best achieved through participatory community-based efforts, should not be developed just for improving zinc status, and are more sustainable over the medium term.

Basic-level determinants of zinc status can be tackled by increasing access and availability to zinc-rich foods. Increasing the intake of foods with a high content of zinc such as meat and animal products may be an economic challenge in many settings in developing countries. Promoting their preferential consumption by women and children instead of by men may be more feasible. A potential complementary strategy to reduce zinc deficiency at the basic cause level is that of breeding plants that are low in phytic acid and high in sulfur-containing amino acids, which promote zinc absorption [147], and or that have higher zinc content [148]. Initial trials of the efficacy of such approaches are not yet convincing, however [149]. Another option is food fortification with zinc [150], but again the problems of multiple-micronutrient deficiencies and interactions between fortificants need to be carefully considered. Most experience in food fortification comes from industrialized countries, where few governments mandate zinc fortification. Research into zinc fortification as part of a multiple-micronutrient approach is still incipient [137]. Further caution is necessary since the upper levels of recommended intake can easily be surpassed. In the United States, for example, the average intake of toddlers is already over the recommended levels due to the increasing trend for voluntary fortification of foods for children by the food industry [151].

## 15.12   CONCLUSIONS

Zinc is essential for many important biological processes, including gene expression, immune function, growth, and reproduction. Zinc deficiency is a major public health problem worldwide, with the most vulnerable groups infants and young children and pregnant and lactating women. Considerable capacity exists to adapt to inadequate zinc intake, such that overt clinical deficiency is rare. These adaptive mechanisms are not without consequence, however, and clinical trials have now shown that zinc supplementation in children reduces the morbidity and mortality due to diarrheal disease, respiratory disease, malaria, and possibly HIV/AIDS. Momentum is gathering to develop zinc intervention programs, especially in the treatment of the most common infectious diseases that cause the majority of child deaths. They are likely to have enormous impact if they can be established at scale in the countries with the highest levels of infant mortality.

Although it is less clear to what extent maternal zinc supplementation has a preventive benefit for maternal health, there is increasing evidence that it improves child health and development outcomes, and that zinc deficiency during early pregnancy has effects that are manifest throughout the course of life. Preventive zinc supplementation interventions during pregnancy, lactation, and infancy need to be further tested in large-scale programmatic settings, preferably as part of a multiple-micronutrient supplementation approach.

## 15.13   RECOMMENDATIONS

- The study of zinc deficiency in developing countries has been hampered by a lack of a good indicator of zinc status. Further investigation is needed to develop an inexpensive, sensitive, and specific indicator for zinc status in individuals.
- More national surveys of zinc intakes and serum zinc concentrations are needed to begin to better determine the extent of zinc deficiency in populations and to serve as baselines against which to judge the effectiveness of zinc intervention programs.
- The effectiveness of preventive zinc supplementation as part of a multiple-micronutrient approach for tackling anemia in pregnant and lactating women needs to be explored further, especially in populations in developing countries with the highest mortality.
- The potential mortality reduction effects of improving zinc nutrition in women and infants should be measured in populations likely to have extensive marginal deficiency.
- Dietary-based interventions to improve zinc nutriture need further evaluation, especially for complementary foods.
- The effect of zinc deficiency and supplementation on various aspects of immune function needs to be further investigated, especially during pregnancy, while looking at life course consequences.
- Further corroborative data are needed to demonstrate the efficacy of zinc supplementation in reducing the morbidity of *P. falciparum* malaria in developing countries.
- The potential use of zinc for fortification of foodstuffs needs to be tested at scale in developing country settings.
- The possibility of improving zinc nutriture through plant breeding also needs to be more fully explored.

# REFERENCES

1. Shrimpton R. Zinc deficiency: is it widespread but under-recognized? In: Subcommittee on Nutrition News, vol. 9. Geneva: United Nations Administrative Committee on Coordination, 1993:24–27.
2. Shankar AH, Prasad AS. Zinc and immune function: the biological basis of altered resistance to infection. Am J Clin Nutr 1998;68(suppl):447S–463S.
3. Black RE. Therapeutic and preventive effects of zinc on serious childhood infectious diseases in developing countries. Am J Clin Nutr 1998;68(suppl):476S–479S.
4. Wuehler SE, Peerson JM, Brown KH. Use of national food balance data to estimate the adequacy of zinc in national food supplies: methodology and regional estimates. Public Health Nutr 2005;8(7): 812–819.
5. World Health Organization. The world health report 2002: reducing risks, promoting healthy life. Geneva: World Health Organization, 2002.
6. Jones G, Steketee RW, Black RE, Bhutta ZA, Morris SS, Bellagio Child Survival Study Group. How many child deaths can we prevent this year? Lancet 2003;362:65–71.
7. Raulin J. Études cliniques sur la vegetation. Ann Sci Nat 11 Bot 1869:93. Ann Sci Nat (5th series) 1869;2:224.
8. Birkner V The zinc content of some foods. J Biol Chem 1919;38:191–203.
9. Todd WR, Elvehjem CA, Hart EB. Zinc in the nutrition of the rat. Am J Physiol 1934;107:146–156.
10. Eggleton WGE. Zinc content of epidermal structures in beri-beri. Biochem J 1939;33:403–406.
11. Eggleton WGE. Zinc and copper content of blood in beri-beri in conditions associated with protein deficiency and in diabetes mellitus. China J Physiol 1940;15:33–44.
12. Macy IG. Nutrition and chemical growth in childhood, vol. 1, evaluation. Springfield, IL: Thomas, 1942:198–202.
13. Youmans JB. Nutritional deficiencies: diagnosis and treatment. Philadelphia: Lippincott, 1943.
14. Hegsted, DM, McKibbin JM, Drinker CK. The biological, hygienic and medical properties of zinc and zinc compounds. US Public Health Rep Suppl 1945:179.
15. Darby WJ. Trace elements in human nutrition. In: Symposium on nutrition. Herriot RM, ed. Baltimore, MD: Johns Hopkins, 1953:229–261.
16. Monty KJ. Trace element deficiencies. In: Control of malnutrition in man. Subcommittee on Control of Nutritional Diseases of the Committee on Evaluation and Standards. Washington, DC: American Public Health Association, 1960:40.
17. Tucker HF, Salmon ND. Parakeratosis or zinc deficiency disease in pig. Proc Soc Exp Biol Med 1955;88:613–616.
18. O'Dell BL, Savage JE. Effect of phytic acid on zinc availability. Proc Soc Exp Biol Med 1960;103: 304–306.
19. Prasad AS, Halsted JA, Nadimi M. Syndrome of iron deficiency anemia, hepatosplenomegaly, hypogonadism, dwarfism, and geophagia. Am J Med 1961;31:532–546.
20. Prasad AS, Miale A, Farid Z, Schulert AR, Sandstead HH. Zinc metabolism in patients with the syndrome of iron deficiency anemia, hypogonadism, and dwarfism. J Lab Clin Med 1963;61:537–549.
21. Sandstead HH, Prasad AS, Schulert AR, Farid Z, Miale A Jr, Bassily S, Darby WJ. Human zinc deficiency, endocrine manifestations, and response to treatment. Am J Clin Nutr 1967;20:422–442.
22. Moynahan EJ. Acrodermatitis enteropathica: a lethal inherited human zinc-deficiency disorder. Lancet 1974;2:399–400.
23. World Health Organization. Trace elements in human nutrition. Geneva: World Health Organization, 1973. Technical Report Series 532:1–65.
24. Food and Nutrition Board. Recommended dietary allowances. Washington, DC: National Research Council, National Academy of Sciences, 1974:140.
25. Dewey KG, Brown KH. Update on technical issues concerning complementary feeding of young children in developing countries and implications for intervention programmes. Food Nutr Bull 2003;24(1):5.
26. Tamura T, Goldenberg RL. Zinc nutriture and pregnancy outcome. Nutr Res 1996;16:138–181.
27. Caulfield LE, Zavaletta N, Shankar AH, Merialdi M. Potential contribution of maternal zinc supplementation during pregnancy to maternal and child survival. Am J Clin Nutr 1998;68(suppl):499S–508S.

28. Steel L, Cousins RJ. Kinetics of zinc absorption by luminally and vascularly perfused rat intestine. Am J Physiol 1985;248:G46–G53.

29. Raffaniello RD, Wapnir RA. Zinc uptake by isolated rat enterocytes: effect of low molecular weight ligands. Proc Soc Exp Biol Med 1989;192:219–224.

30. Hempe JM, Cousins RJ. Cysteine-rich intestinal protein binds zinc during transmucosal zinc transport. Proc Natl Acad Sci U S A 1991;88:9671–9674.

31. Cousins RJ, Lee-Ambrose LM. Nuclear zinc uptake and interactions and metallothionein gene expression are influenced by dietary zinc in rats. J Nutr 1992;122:56–64.

32. Fung EB, Ritchie LD, Woodhouse LR, Roehl R, King J. Zinc absorption in women during pregnancy and lactation: a longitudinal study. Am J Clin Nutr 1997;66(1):80–88.

33. Jackson MJ, Giugliano R, Giugliano LG, Oliveira EF, Shrimpton R, Swainbank IG. Stable isotope metabolic studies of zinc nutrition in slum dwelling lactating in the Amazon valley. Br J Nutr 1988;59:193–203.

34. Cousins RJ. Regulation of zinc absorption: Role of intracellular ligands. Am J Clin Nutr 1979;32:339–345.

35. Prasad AS, Oberleas D. Binding of zinc to amino acids and serum proteins "in vitro." J Lab Clin Med 1970;76:416–425.

36. Giroux EL, Henkin RI. Competition for zinc among serum albumin and amino acids. Biochem Biophys Acta 1972;273:64–72.

37. Hess FM, King JC, Margen S. Zinc excretion in young women on low zinc intakes and oral contraceptive agents. J Nutr 1977;107:1610–1620.

38. Prasad AS, Rabbani P, Abbassi A, Bowersox E, Fox MRS. Experimental zinc deficiency in humans. Ann Int Med 1978;89:483–490.

39. Swanson CA, King JC. Zinc and pregnancy outcome. Am J Clin Nutr 1987;46:763–771.

40. Spencer H, Osis D, Kramer L, Norris C. Intake, excretion and retention of zinc in man. In: Trace elements in human health and disease, vol. 1. Prasad AS, ed. New York: Academic, 1976:345–361.

41. Baer MT, King JC. Tissue zinc levels and zinc excretion during experimental zinc depletion in young men. Am J Clin Nutr 1984;39:556–570.

42. Krebs NF, Reidinger CJ, Hartley S, Robertson AD, Hambidge KM. Zinc supplementation during lactation: effects on maternal status and milk concentrations. Am J Clin Nutr 1995;61:1030–1036.

43. Walsh CT, Sandstead HH, Prasad AS, Newberne PM, Fraker PJ. Zinc: health effects and research priorities for the 1990s. Environ Health Perspect 1994;102(suppl 2):5–46.

44. Vallee BL, Auld DS. Zinc coordination, function, and structure of zinc enzymes and other proteins. Biochemistry 1990;29:5647–5659.

45. Christian P, West KP Jr. Interactions between zinc and vitamin A: an update. Am J Clin Nutr 1998 Aug;68(2 suppl):435S–441S.

46. Dijkhuizen MA, Wieringa FT, West CE, Muhilal. Zinc plus β-carotene supplementation of pregnant women is superior to β-carotene supplementation alone in improving vitamin A status in both mothers and infants. Am J Clin Nutr 2004;80(5):1299–307.

47. Berg JM, Shi Y. The galvanization of biology: a growing appreciation for the roles of zinc. Science 1996;271:1081–1085.

48. Ho E. Zinc deficiency, DNA damage and cancer risk. J Nutr Biochem 2004 Oct;15(10):572–578.

49. Duffy JY, Overmann GJ, Keen CL, Clegg MS, Daston GP. Cardiac abnormalities induced by zinc deficiency are associated with alterations in the expression of genes regulated by the zinc-finger transcription factor GATA-4. Birth Defects Res B Dev Reprod Toxicol 2004;71(2):102–109.

50. Bettger WJ, O'Dell BL. Minireview: a critical physiological role of zinc in the structure and function of biomembranes. Life Sci 1981;28:1425–1438.

51. Fraker PJ, King LE, Laakko T, Vollmer TL. The dynamic link between the integrity of the immune system and zinc status. J Nutr 2000;130(5S suppl):1399S–1406S.

52. Prasad AS. Effects of zinc deficiency on Th1 and Th2 cytokine shifts. J Infect Dis 2000;182:S62–S68.

53. Fraker P, Telford W. Regulation of apoptotic events by zinc. In: Nutrition and gene expression. Berdanier C, ed. Boca Raton, FL: CRC, 1996:189–208.

54. Fraker PJ, King LE. Reprogramming of the immune system during zinc deficiency. Annu Rev Nutr 2004;24:277–298.

55. Bunce GE. Interactions between zinc, vitamins A and D and hormones in the regulation of growth. In: Nutrient regulation during pregnancy, lactation and infant growth. Allen L, King J, Lonnerdal B, eds. New York: Plenum, 1994:257–264.

56. Solomons NW, Shrimpton R. Zinc. In: Tropical and geographical medicine. Warren K, Mahmoud AF, eds. New York: McGraw-Hill, 1983:1059–1063.

57. World Health Organization. Complementary feeding of young children in developing countries: a review of current scientific knowledge. Geneva: World Health Organization, 1998.

58. Shrimpton R. Zinc intake from non-breast milk sources in the first year of life in a poor urban slum in Manaus, Amazonas Brazil. Proc Nutr Soc 1997;56:19A.

59. Turnlund JR, King JC, Keyes WR, Gong B, Michel MC. A stable isotope study of zinc absorption in young men: effects of phytate and α-cellulose. Am J Clin Nutr 1984;40:1071–1077.

60. Solomons NW, Jacob RA, Pineda O, Viteri FE. Studies on the bioavailability of zinc in man. II. Absorption of zinc from organic and inorganic sources. J Lab Clin Med 1979;94:335–343.

61. Mills CF. Dietary interactions involving trace elements. Ann Rev Nutr 1985;5:173–193.

62. Gibson RS, Yeudall F, Drost N, Mtitimuni B, Cullinan T. Dietary interventions to prevent zinc deficiency. Am J Clin Nutr 1998;68(suppl):484S–487S.

63. Lönnderdal B, Cederblad Å, Davidsson L, Sandström B. The effect of individual components of soy formula and cows' milk formula on zinc bioavailability. Am J Clin Nutr 1984;1064–1070.

64. Sandström B, Cederblad Å, Lönnderdal B. Zinc absorption from human milk, cow's milk, and infant formulas. Am J Dis Child 1983;137:726–729.

65. World Health Organization/Food and Agricultural Organization. Zinc. In: Vitamin and mineral requirements in human nutrition. 2nd ed. Geneva: World Health Organization, 2004:230–245.

66. Golden MH, Jackson AA, Golden BE. Effect of zinc on thymus of recently malnourished children. Lancet 1997;2(8047):1057–1059.

67. Golden BE, Golden MH. Plasma zinc, rate of weight gain, and the energy cost of tissue deposition in children recovering from sever malnutrition on a cow's milk or soya protein based diet. Am J Clin Nutr 1981;34:892–899.

68. Jameson S. Zinc status in pregnancy: the effect of zinc therapy on perinatal mortality, prematurity, and placental ablation. Ann NY Acad Sci 1993;678:178–192.

69. Bunce GE, Lytton F, Gunesekera B, Vessal M, Kim C. Molecular basis for abnormal parturition in zinc deficiency in rats. In: Nutrient regulation during pregnancy, lactation and infant growth. Allen L, King J, Lonnerdal B, eds. New York: Plenum, 1994:209–234.

70. Black MM. Zinc deficiency and child development. Am J Clin Nutr 1998;68:464S–469S.

71. Brown KH. Effect of infections on plasma zinc concentrations and implications for zinc status assessment in low-income countries. Am J Clin Nutr 1998;68(suppl):425S–429S.

72. Swanson CA, King JC. Reduced serum zinc concentration during pregnancy. Obstet Gynecol 1983;62:313–318.

73. Solomons NW. On the assessment of zinc and copper nutriture in man. Am J Clin Nutr 1979;32: 856–871.

74. Pilch SM, Senti FR. Analysis of zinc data from the second National Health and Nutrition Examination Survey (NHANES II). J Nutr 1985;115:1393–1397.

75. Gibson RS. Principles of nutritional assessment. New York: Oxford University Press, 1990.

76. Brown KH, Rivera JA, Bhutta Z, et al. International Zinc Consultative Group (IZiNCG) Technical document 1. Assessment of the risk of zinc deficiency in populations and options for its control. Food Nutr Bull 2004;25(1 suppl 2):S99–S203.

77. Brown KH, Lanata CF, Yuen ML, Peerson JM, Butron B, Lönnerdal B. Potential magnitude of the misclassification of a population's trace element status due to infection: example from a survey of young Peruvian children. Am J Clin Nutr 1993;58:549–554.

78. Ruz M, Solomons NW, Mejia LA, Chew F. Alterations of circulating micronutrients with overt and occult infections in anaemic Guatemalan preschool children. Intl J Food Sci Nutr 1995;46:257–265.

79. Friis H, Ndhlovu P, Kaondera K, Sandstrom B, Michaelsen KF, Vennervald BJ, Christensen NO. Serum concentration of micronutrients in relation to schistosomiasis and indicators of infection: a cross-sectional study among rural Zimbabwean school children. Eur J Clin Nutr 1996;50:386–391.

80. Smith JC Jr, Butrimovitz GP, Purdy WC. Direct measurement of zinc in plasma by atomic absorption spectroscopy. Clin Chem 1979;25:1487–1491.

81. English JL, Hambidge KM. Plasma and serum zinc concentrations: effect of time between collection and separation. Clin Chim Acta 1988;175:211–216.

82. Smith JC, Holbrook JT, Danford DE. Analysis and evaluation of zinc and copper in human plasma and serum. J Am Coll Nutr 1985;4:627–638.

83. Gibson RS, Ferguson EL. Assessment of dietary zinc in population. Am J Clin Nutr 1998;68(suppl): 430S–434S.

84. Ferguson EL, Gadowsky SL, Huddle JM, Cullinan TR, Gibson RS. An interactive 24-hour recall technique for assessing the adequacy of trace mineral intakes of rural Malawian women: its advantages and limitations. Eur J Clin Nutr 1995;49:565–578.

85. Ferguson EL, Gibson RS, Opare-Obisaw C, et al. The phytate, nonstarch polysaccharide, zinc, calcium, copper, and manganese contents of 78 locally grown and prepared African foods. J Food Comp Anal 1993;6:87–99.

86. Hambidge KM. Hair analyses: worthless for vitamins, limited for minerals. Am J Clin Nutr 1982;36: 943–949.

87. Jones RB, Keeling PW, Hilton PJ, Thompson RP. The relationship between leukocyte and muscle zinc in health and disease. Clin Sci 1981;60:237–239.

88. Hambidge KM, Hambidge C, Jacobs M, Baum JD. Low levels of zinc in hair, anorexia, poor growth, and hypogeusia in children. Pediatr Res 1972;6:868–874.

89. Hambidge KM, Krebs NF, Miller L. Evaluation of zinc metabolism with use of stable-isotope techniques: implications for the assessment of zinc status. Am J Clin Nutr 1998;68:410S–413S.

90. Zinc Investigators Collaborative Group. Therapeutic effects of oral zinc in acute and persistent diarrhea in children in developing countries: pooled analysis of randomised controlled trials. Am J Clin Nutr 2000;72:1516–22.

91. Baqui AH, Black RE, El Arifeen S, et al. Effect of zinc supplementation started during diarrhoea on morbidity and mortality in Bangladeshi children: community randomised trial. BMJ 2002;325: 1059–1065.

92. World Health Organization/United Nations International Children's Emergency Fund. Joint statement on the management of acute diarrhoea. Geneva: World Health Organization, 2004.

93. Bahl R, Bhandari N, Saksena M, Strand T, Kumar GT, Bhan MK, et al. Efficacy of zinc-fortified oral rehydration solution in 6–35 month old children with acute diarrhea. J Pediatr 2002;141:677–682.

94. Robberstad B, Strand T, Black RE, Somerfelt H. Cost effectiveness of zinc as an adjunct therapy for acute childhood diarrhoea in developing countries. Bull World Health Organ 2004;82:523–31.

95. Awasthi S;INCLEN Childnet Zinc Effectiveness for Diarrhea (IC-ZED) Group. Zinc supplementation in acute diarreia is acceptable, does not interfere with oral rehydration, and reduces the use of other medications: a randomized control trial in five countries. J Pediatr Gastroenterol Nutr 2006;42(3):300–305.

96. Bryce J, el Arifeen S, Parlyo G, Lanata CF, Gwatkin D, Habicht J-P, et al. Reducing child mortality: can public health deliver? Lancet 2003;362:159–64.

97. Lira PIC, Ashworth A, Morris SS. Effect of zinc supplementation on the morbidity, immune function, and growth of low-birth-weight, full-term infants in northeast Brazil. Am J Clin Nutr 1998;68(suppl):418S–424S.

98. Sazawal S, Black RE, Menon VP, Dinghra P, Caulfield LE, Dhingra U, et al. Zinc supplementation in infants born small for gestational age reduces mortality: a prospective, randomised controlled trial. Pediatrics 2001;108:1280–1286.

99. Zinc Investigators Collaborative Group. Prevention of diarrhea and pneumonia by zinc supplementation in children in developing countries: pooled analysis of randomised controlled trials. J Pediatr 1999;135:689–697.

100. Bhandari N, Bahl R, Taneja S, et al. Effect of routine zinc supplementation on pneumonia in children aged 6 months to 3 years: randomised controlled trial in an urban slum. BMJ 2002;324:1358–1362.

101. Brooks WA, Santosham M, Naheed A, et al. Effect of weekly zinc supplements on incidence of pneumonia and diarrhoea in children younger than 2 years in an urban, low-income population in Bangladesh: randomised controlled trial. Lancet 2005;366:999–1004.

102. Black RE, Morris SS, Bryce J. Where and why are 10 million children dying every year? Lancet 2003;361:226–234.

103. Brooks WA, Yunus M, Santosham M, et al. Zinc for severe pneumonia in very young children: double-blind placebo-controlled trial. Lancet 2004;363:1683–1688.

104. Mahalanabis D, Chowdhury A, Jana S, et al. Zinc supplementation as adjunct therapy in children with measles accompanied by pneumonia: a doubleblind, randomized controlled trial. Am J Clin Nutr 2002;76:604–607.

105. Good MF, Kaslow DC, Miller LH. Pathways and strategies for developing a malaria blood-stage vaccine. Annu Rev Immunol 1998;16:57–87.

106. Bates CJ, Evans PH, Dardenne M, et al. A trial of zinc supplementation in young rural Gambian children. Br J Nutr 1993;69:243–255.

107. Shankar AH, Genton B, Baisor M, et al. The influence of zinc supplementation on morbidity due to *Plasmodium falciparum*: a randomized trial in preschool children in Papua New Guinea. Am J Trop Med Hyg 2000;62:663–669.

108. Muller O, Becher H, van Zweeden AB, et al. Effect of zinc supplementation on malaria and other causes of morbidity in West African children: randomized double blind placebo controlled trial. BMJ 2001;322:1567–1572.

109. Zinc Against Plasmodium Study Group. Effect of zinc on the treatment of *Plasmodium falciparum* malaria in children: a randomized controlled trial. Am J Clin Nutr 2002;76(4):805–812.

110. Brown KH, Peerson JM, Rivera J, Allen LH. Effect of supplemental zinc on the growth and serum zinc concentrations of prepubertal children: a meta-analysis of randomized controlled trials. Am J Clin Nutr 2002 Jun;75(6):1062–1071.

111. Dijkhuizen MA, Wieringa FT, West CE, Martuti S, Muhilal. Effects of iron and zinc supplementation in Indonesian infants on micronutrient status and growth. J Nutr 2001;131:2860–2865.

112. Lind T, Lonnerdal B, Stenlund H, Gamayanti IL, Ismail D, Seswandhana R, Persson LA. A community-based randomized controlled trial of iron and zinc supplementation in Indonesian infants: effects on growth and development. Am J Clin Nutr 2004;80(3):729–736.

113. Umeta M, West CE, Haider J, Derenburg P, Hautvast JGAJ. Zinc supplementation and stunted infants in Ethiopia: a randomised controlled trial. Lancet 2000;355:2021–2026.

114. Osendarp SJ, Santosham M, Black RE, Wahed MA, van Raaij JM, Fuchs GJ. Effect of zinc supplementation between 1 and 6 months of life on growth and morbidity of Bangladeshi infants in urban slums. Am J Clin Nutr 2002;76(6):1401–1408.

115. Muller O, Garenne M, Reitmaier P, Van Zweeden AB, Kouyate B, Becher H. Effect of zinc supplementation on growth in West African children: a randomized double-blind placebo-controlled trial in rural Burkina Faso. Int J Epidemiol 2003 Dec;32(6):1098–1102.

116. Sazawal S, Bentley M, Black RE, Dhingra P, George S, Bhan MK. Effect of zinc supplementation among observed activity in preschool children in an urban slum population. Pediatrics 1996;98:1132–1137.

117. Bentley ME, Caulfield LE, Ram M, Santizo MC, Hurtado E, Rivera JA, Ruel MT, Brown KH. Zinc supplementation affects the activity patterns of rural Guatemalan infants. J Nutr 1997;127:1333–1338.

118. Meeks Gardner JM, Powell AC, Baker-Henningham H, Walker SP, Cole TJ, Grantham-McGregor SM. Zinc supplementation and psychosocial stimulation: effects on the development of undernourished Jamaican children. Am J Clin Nutr 2005;82:399–405.

119. Goldenberg RL, Tamura T, Neggers Y, Copper RL, Johnston KE, DuBard MB, Hauth JC. The effect of zinc supplementation on pregnancy outcome. JAMA 1995;274:463–468.

120. Caulfield LE, Zavaleta N, Figueroa A, Leon A. Maternal zinc supplementation does not affect size at birth or pregnancy duration in Peru. J Nutr 1999;129:1563–1568.

121. Merialdi M, Caulfield LE, Zavaleta N, Figueroa A, DiPietro JA. Adding zinc to prenatal iron and folate tablets improves fetal neurobehavioural development. Am J Obstet Gynecol 1999;180(2pt 1):483–490.

122. Merialdi M, Caulfield LE, Zavaleta N, Figueroa A, Costigan KA, Dominici F, Dipietro JA. Randomized controlled trial of prenatal zinc supplementation and fetal bone growth. Am J Clin Nutr. 2004;79(5):826–830.

123. Hamadani JD, Fuchs GJ, Osendarp SJ, Huda SN, Grantham-McGregor SM. Zinc supplementation during pregnancy and effects on mental development and behaviour of infants: a follow-up study. Lancet. 2002;360(9329):290–294.
124. Tamura T, Goldenberg RL, Ramey SL, Nelson KG, Chapman VR. Effect of zinc supplementation of pregnant women on the mental and psychomotor development of their children at 5 years of age. Am J Clin Nutr 2003;77(6):1512–1516.
125. Osendarp SJ, van Raaij JM, Darmstadt GL, Baqui AH, Hautvast JG, Fuchs GJ. Zinc supplementation during pregnancy and effects on growth and morbidity in low birthweight infants: a randomised placebo controlled trial. Lancet 2001;357(9262):1080–1085.
126. Shrimpton R, Franca TS, Rocha YS, Alencar FH. Zinc supplementation in urban Amazonian mothers: concentrations of zinc and retinol in maternal serum and milk. Proc Nutr Soc 1983;42:122A.
127. Shrimpton R, Allencar, FH, Vasconcellos JC, Rocha YR. Effects of maternal zinc supplementation on growth and diarrhoeal status of breastfed infants. Nutr Res 1985;suppl 1:338–342.
128. Shrimpton R, Lehti K. Influence of zinc supplementation on breastmilk SigA levels. In: Trace elements on man and animals TEMA 5. Mill CF, Bremner I, Chester JK, eds. Slough, UK: Commonwealth Agricultural Bureaus, 1985:90–93.
129. Beach RS, Mantero-Atienza E, Shor-Posner G, Javvier JJ, Szapocznik J, Morgan R, et al. Specific nutrient abnormalities in asymptomatic HIV-1 infection. AIDS 1992;6:701–708.
130. Koch J, Neal EA, Schlott MJ, Garcia-Shelton YL, Chan MF, Weaver KE, Cello JP. Zinc levels and infections in hospitalized patients with AIDS. Nutrition 1996;12:515–518.
131. Falutz J, Tsoukas C, Gold P. Zinc as a cofactor in human immunodeficiency virus-induced immunosuppression. JAMA 1988;259:2850–2851.
132. Graham NMH, Sorensen D, Odaka N, Brookmeyer R, Chan D, Willett WC, et al. Relationship of serum copper and zinc levels to HIV-1 seropositivity and progression to AIDS. J Acquir Immune Defic Syndr 1991;4:976–980.
133. Baum MK, Shor-Posner G, Lu Y, Rosner B, Sauberlich HE, Fletcher MA, et al. Micronutrients and HIV-1 disease progression. AIDS 1995;9:1051–1056.
134. Mocchegiani E, Veccia S, Ancarani F, Scalise G, Fabris N. Benefit of oral zinc supplementation as an adjunct to zidovudine (AZT) therapy against opportunistic infections in AIDS. Int J Immunopharm 1995;17:719–727.
135. Bobat R, Coovadia H, Stephen C, Naidoo KL, McKerrow N, Black RE, Moss WJ. Safety and efficacy of zinc supplementation for children with HIV-1 infection in South Africa: a randomised double-blind placebo-controlled trial. Lancet 2005;366(9500):1862–1867.
136. Range N, Changalucha J, Krarup H, Magnussen P, Andersen AB, Friis H. The effect of multi-vitamin/mineral supplementation on mortality during treatment of pulmonary tuberculosis: a randomised two-by-two factorial trial in Mwanza, Tanzania. Br J Nutr 2006;95(4):762–770.
137. Shrimpton R, Gross R, Darnton-Hill I, Young M. Zinc deficiency: what are the most appropriate interventions? BMJ 2005;330(7487):347–349.
138. Allen LH. Zinc and micronutrient supplements for children. Am J Clin Nutr 1998;68:495S–498S.
139. Solomons NW, Ruz M, Gibson RS. Single-nutrient interventions with zinc. Am J Clin Nutr 1999;70(1):111–113.
140. Shrimpton R, Shrimpton R, Schultink W. Can supplements help meet the micronutrient needs of the developing world? Proc Nutr Soc 2002;61(2):223–229.
141. Lind T, Lonnerdal B, Stenlund H, Ismail D, Seswandhana R, Eksrom E-C, Persson L-A. A community-based randomised controlled trial of iron and zinc supplementation in Indonesian infants: interactions between iron and zinc. Am J Clin Nutr 2003;77:883–890.
142. Smuts CM, Lombard CJ, Benade AJ, Dhansay MA, Berger J, Hop le T, Lopez de Romana G, Untoro J, Karyadi E, Erhardt J, Gross R, International Research on Infant Supplementation (IRIS) Study Group. Efficacy of a foodlet-based multiple micronutrient supplement for preventing growth faltering, anemia, and micronutrient deficiency of infants: the four country IRIS trial pooled data analysis. J Nutr 2005;135(3):631S–638S.
143. Sandstead HH, Penland JG, Alcock NW, Dayal HH, Chen XC, Li JS, Zhao F, Yang JJ. Effects of repletion with zinc and other micronutrients on neuropsychologic performance and growth of Chinese children. Am J Clin Nutr 1998 Aug;68(2 suppl):470S–475S.

144. Untoro J, Karyadi E, Wibowo L, Erhardt MW, Gross R. Multiple micronutrient supplements improve micronutrient status and anemia but not growth and morbidity of Indonesian infants: a randomized, double-blind, placebo-controlled trial. J Nutr 2005;135(3):639S–645S.

145. Allen L, Shrimpton R. The International Research on Infant Supplementation study: implications for programs and further research. J Nutr 2005;135(3):666S–669S.

146. World Health Organization/World Food Programme/United Nations International Children's Emergency Fund. Preventing and controlling micronutrient deficiencies in populations affected by an emergency. Geneva: World Health Organization, 2005.

147. Ruel MT, Bouis HE. Plant breeding: a long-term strategy for the control of zinc deficiency in vulnerable populations. Am J Clin Nutr 1998;68:488S–494S.

148. Nestel P, Bouis HE, Meenakshi JV, Pfeiffer W. Biofortification of staple food crops. J Nutr 2006;136(4):1064–1067.

149. Mazariegos M, Hambidge KM, Krebs NF, Westcott JE, Lei S, Grunwald GK, Campos R, Barahona B, Raboy V, Solomons NW. Zinc absorption in Guatemalan schoolchildren fed normal or low-phytate maize. Am J Clin Nutr 2006;83(1):59–64.

150. Rosado JL. Zinc and copper: proposed fortification levels and recommended zinc compounds. J Nutr 2003;133(9):2985S–2989S.

151. Arsenault JE, Brown KH. Zinc intake of US preschool children exceeds new dietary reference intakes. Am J Clin Nutr 2003;78(5):1011–1017.

# 16 Iron Deficiency and Anemia

## Usha Ramakrishnan and Richard D. Semba

## 16.1 INTRODUCTION

Iron deficiency is one of the most common nutrition disorders worldwide, affecting a large proportion of children and women in the developing world. In addition, iron deficiency is probably the only nutrient deficiency of significant prevalence in virtually all developed countries. Iron is element 26 in the periodic table and has an atomic weight of 55.85. In aqueous solution, iron exists in two oxidation states, either $Fe^{2+}$, the ferrous form, or $Fe^{3+}$, the ferric form. Iron changes between these forms, enabling it to serve as a catalyst in redox reactions by donating or accepting electrons. Iron-containing compounds play key roles in oxygen and energy metabolism. Iron is one of the most extensively investigated and understood nutrients. Although the burden and causes of iron deficiency are well established, the challenge remains for the adequate prevention and control of iron deficiency. This will require greater effort in embarking on public health measures that are feasible and cost-effective [1].

## 16.2 DEFINING ANEMIA AND IRON DEFICIENCY

Anemia is a commonly used indicator to screen for iron deficiency in clinical settings or to define the burden of iron deficiency in population-based surveys. Although anemia in itself is not specific for iron deficiency, especially in areas where other conditions such as malaria are common, there is a close association between anemia and iron deficiency. Iron deficiency, as defined by specific biochemical tests, is the most common cause of anemia in most parts of the world. Iron deficiency anemia represents the severe end of the spectrum of iron deficiency and requires the fulfillment of both the definition of anemia and iron deficiency [2]. Iron deficiency without anemia represents a moderate form of iron deficiency in which iron-dependent function is impaired, but anemia is not present. Depleted iron stores represent the mildest form of iron deficiency when there are no functional impairments or anemia. *Anemia* is defined as hemoglobin concentration below −2 standard deviations (SD) of the age- and sex-specific normal reference. The most commonly used cutoff for anemia is hemoglobin below 110 gm/L for children under 5 years old and pregnant women, below 120 gm/L for nonpregnant women, and below 130 gm/L for men.

From: *Nutrition and Health: Nutrition and Health in Developing Countries, Second Edition*
Edited by: R. D. Semba & M. W. Bloem © Humana Press, Totowa, NJ

## 16.3  HISTORICAL BACKGROUND

An early study on the composition of blood was conducted by Robert Boyle (1627–1691) in 1684. Various chemical analyses were conducted, and ashing of blood produced a brick-red substance [3]. Vincenzo Menghini (1704–1759), a chemist and physician in Italy, demonstrated in 1747 that particles of dried, powdered blood were attracted to a lodestone, suggesting the existence of iron in blood [4]. Based on experimental studies, Jean Baptiste Boussingault (1802–1887), a French agricultural chemist, determined that iron was an essential nutrient for animals [5]. Iron tablets were used in the 19th century for treatment of chlorosis, an early term for anemia in young women. Gustav von Bunge (1844–1920), a professor at the University of Dorpat in Estonia, showed that milk was a poor source of iron; thus, infants largely depended on prenatal iron reserves [6]. Helen Mackay (1891–1965) demonstrated that anemia could be alleviated in infants in East London by provision of iron-fortified milk [7].

The relationships among hookworm infection, iron deficiency, and poor growth and cognition in children were described in the 19th century and early part of the 20th century. *Ancyclostoma duodenale* was described in 1843 [8] and implicated as a cause of profound anemia [9]. In 1902, *Necator americanus* (*Uncinaria americana*) was described by the parasitologist Charles Wardell Stiles (1867–1941) [10]. Bailey K. Ashford (1873–1934) showed that the widespread tropical anemia in Puerto Rico was due to hookworm [11, 12]. Hookworm infection was found to be widespread in the American South [13]. The US Public Health Service began campaigns to treat hookworm with deworming and to prevent new hookworm infection with emphasis on sanitation [14].

In 1909, the Rockefeller Sanitary Commission for the Eradication of Hookworm Disease was established, and the commission had three goals: to determine the geographical distribution of the disease and degree of infection, to cure those who were infected, and to take measures to stop soil pollution to remove the source of infection [15]. In a survey of over a half a million rural schoolchildren in 11 states in the American South, nearly 40% were infected with hookworm [16]. From 1911 through 1914, the Rockefeller Sanitary Commission sponsored a dispensary campaign, examining and providing treatment for over a million persons [16].

In 1926, the physician Wilson G. Smillie (1886–1971) showed that deworming of heavily infected schoolchildren improved hemoglobin concentrations and increased growth [17, 18]. Hookworm infection was associated with poor mental development [19, 20]. Edward K. Strong (1884–1963) of the Rockefeller Sanitary Commission, demonstrated that infected children who were treated for hookworm had better performance on mental development tests than infected children who were not treated [21]. School-based deworming programs were undertaken in heavily affected areas of the South such as Covington County, Alabama [22]. The rural school was considered the unit of control, and installation of sanitary toilets was combined with mass treatment with anthelminthics [22].

## 16.4  EPIDEMIOLOGY

### 16.4.1  *Prevalence of Iron Deficiency and Anemia*

Using anemia as an indicator and data collected from multiple countries, the World Health Organization (WHO) estimated that about 4–5 billion people are iron deficient worldwide [23]. Although there is considerable variation by region, young children and

Table 16.1
Prevalence of anemia in developing and industrialized countries and in World Health Organization (WHO)-classified regions [23]

|  | Pregnant women (%) | Nonpregnant women (%) | School-aged children (%) |
|---|---|---|---|
| Industrialized countries | 18 | 12 | 9 |
| Developing countries | 56 | 44 | 53 |
| WHO regions |  |  |  |
| Africa | 51 |  | 52[a] |
| Americas | 35 |  | 23[a] |
| South-East Asia | 75 |  | 63[a] |
| Europe | 25 |  | 22[a] |
| Eastern Mediterranean | 55 |  | 45[a] |
| Western Pacific | 43 |  | 21[a] |

[a]Five- to 14-year-olds.

women of reproductive age are at greatest risk, followed by the elderly and men. Recent data from the nationally representative Demographic Health Surveys, which included the measurement of hemoglobin, showed that more than half of preschool-aged children (6–59 months) and women of reproductive age are anemic in many countries from South Asia and sub-Saharan Africa (Table 16.1). Although progress has been made in the reduction of anemia in parts of Central and South America, the rates continue to be high in countries such as Peru, Bolivia, and Haiti [23, 24]. In contrast, an estimated 7–12% of children and women are iron deficient in developed countries [25, 26].

Although not all anemias are caused by iron deficiency, in areas where the prevalence of anemia exceeds 30–40%, most anemia is caused in part or in total by iron deficiency. This assumption, however, may be a problem in certain parts of the world, such as sub-Saharan Africa, where conditions such as thalassemia and infections such as malaria are endemic. Similarly, other nutrient deficiencies, such as those of vitamin A, folic acid, vitamin $B_{12}$, and the like, may also contribute to the etiology of anemia. The complex etiology of anemia in certain settings may explain the limitation of using hemoglobin as an indicator of response for programs aiming to reduce the burden of iron deficiency. Nevertheless, because the presence of anemia reflects a more severe form of iron deficiency, it is safe to assume that the actual presence of iron deficiency is about two to three times that of the prevalence of iron deficiency anemia. For example, if a survey found that 30% of young children were anemic and further testing using an iron-specific test found that two of three children had clear evidence of iron deficiency, then 20% of the children would have iron deficiency anemia. The estimated prevalence of iron deficiency for this childhood population would be 40–60%.

### 16.4.2  Risk Factors for Iron Deficiency

The highest-risk groups for iron deficiency are preterm and low birth weight (LBW) infants, infants, and children during periods of rapid growth, children consuming milk who have a sensitivity to cow's milk, premenopausal women, pregnant women, and individuals with nematode infections in the gastrointestinal tract (Table 16.2). Low

Table 16.2
Some risk factors for iron deficiency
Pregnancy
Prematurity
Low birth weight
Rapid growth
Sensitivity to cow's milk
Low consumption of meat
High consumption of phytates
Menstruation
Nematode infection in gastrointestinal tract

consumption of iron-containing foods and consumption of foods that interfere with iron absorption, such as phytates, also increase the risk of iron deficiency. These individual risk factors are discussed throughout the following sections.

## 16.5  METABOLISM OF IRON

The average total body iron is about 3.8 g in men and 2.3 g in women. The iron-containing compounds in the body are grouped into functional iron, in which iron serves a metabolic or enzymatic function, and storage iron, in which iron is transported or stored. Most functional iron is in the form of heme proteins, that is, proteins that contain an iron-porphyrin prosthetic group. The basic structure of heme is a protoporphyrin-9 molecule with one iron atom. About two thirds of the iron in the body is functional iron, mostly in the form of hemoglobin within erythrocytes. Hemoglobin has a molecular weight of 68,000 and is composed of four heme units. Other functional iron includes myoglobin and iron-containing enzymes. In men, about one third of the total body iron is in the form of iron stores, whereas in women storage iron accounts for about one eighth of total body iron.

### 16.5.1  *Absorption of Iron*

Iron absorption is influenced by several factors, including dietary iron content, the bioavailability of dietary iron, the amount of storage iron in the body, and the rate of erythrocyte production. Dietary iron consists primarily of either nonheme iron and heme iron, and these are absorbed by different mechanisms [27]. Nonheme iron accounts for approximately 85% or more of the diet, and it consists primarily of iron salts found in plant and dairy products. The absorption of nonheme iron depends on how the entire meal affects iron solubility. Heme iron comes primarily from hemoglobin and myoglobin found in meat, poultry, and fish. Although heme iron comprises a smaller proportion of iron in the diet, the absorption of heme iron is two to three times greater than nonheme iron and is less affected by the overall composition of the diet. Women absorb approximately 13% of total dietary iron compared with men, who absorb about 6% of total dietary iron, and these differences may relate to the lower iron stores in women and the increased absorption of iron, which helps to compensate for menstrual losses of iron. The absorption of iron appears to be regulated by mucosal cells of the small intestine and is related to body iron stores. Thus, individuals with low hemoglobin absorb a greater fraction of nonheme iron from the diet.

Hepcidin, a recently discovered peptide hormone, is considered to be a major regulator of iron metabolism [28, 29]. Hepcidin is a cysteine-rich peptide found in human plasma and urine [30, 31] that is synthesized primarily in the liver [30–32]. The hepcidin gene encodes an 84-amino acid prepropeptide that is amino-terminally processed to the 25-amino acid peptide (hep25) [31]. The prepropeptide has no known biological activity. Hep25 forms a hairpin loop that is stabilized by four disulfide bridges, including an unusual vicinal disulfide bridge at the turn of the hairpin [33]. In addition to hep25, the dominant and active isoform of hepcidin found in plasma and urine, there are two other isoforms that contain 20 and 22 amino acids [31]. The 20-amino acid form is inactive [34], and the 22-amino acid form appears to be poorly active or inactive [35].

Evidence from animal studies indicated that hepcidin regulates iron metabolism by inhibiting duodenal iron absorption at the level of intestinal epithelium [36]. Hepcidin binds to the iron exporter ferroportin, inducing its internalization and degradation [34]. Ferroportin is the only mammalian iron exporter identified to date, and its function is necessary for maternofetal iron transfer and iron efflux from duodenal enterocytes, macrophages, and hepatocytes [37]. Ferroportin messenger RNA levels are also regulated by iron [38]. The synthesis of hepcidin is regulated by iron status, erythropoiesis, hypoxia, and inflammation [32, 39, 40] (Fig. 16.1). In humans, the relationships among hepcidin, hemoglobin, iron status, and inflammation have mostly been studied in patients with sepsis or hemochromatosis, and there is a paucity of data from community-dwelling or population-based studies. Hemojuvelin, a recently discovered protein, is expressed by liver, heart, skeletal muscle, and some other tissues and also appears to modulate hepcidin expression [28]. In normally healthy persons, hepcidin levels are thought to decrease during iron deficiency and increase in states of iron sufficiency [29].

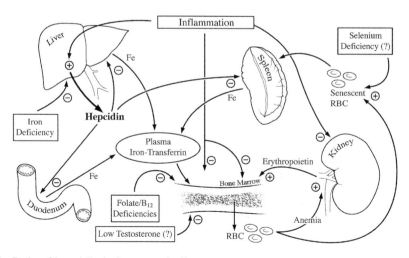

**Fig. 16.1.** Role of hepcidin in iron metabolism.

### 16.5.2   Transport of Iron

Heme iron and nonheme iron are transported from the intestine to the tissues by a plasma transport protein, transferrin. Transferrin delivers iron to tissues through surface receptors specific for transferrin, or transferrin receptor [41]. The receptors bind to the transferrin–iron complex at the cell surface and carry the complex into the cell, where iron is released. The iron supply of the body is reflected in the iron saturation of transferrin. A low transferrin saturation indicates undersupply of iron or deficiency, and a high transferrin saturation indicates oversupply of iron. Transferrin saturation can also be altered during inflammatory conditions such as a febrile response.

Transferrin receptors are found in high concentrations on tissues that have a high uptake of iron, including erythroid precursors, placenta, and liver. The expression of transferrin receptors on tissues is highly regulated in response to the availability of iron. In an iron-rich environment, the number of transferrin receptors decreases. In an iron-poor environment or when iron demand increases, the number of transferrin receptors increases. The concentration of circulating plasma or serum transferrin receptors is proportional to the expression of transferrin receptors on cell surfaces, and this is the basis for the use of circulating transferrin receptors as an indicator of iron status.

### 16.5.3   Storage of Iron

The major iron-storage compounds are ferritin and hemosiderin, which are found primarily in the liver, spleen, reticuloendothelial cells, and bone marrow. In the liver, iron is stored mainly in parenchymal cells or hepatocytes, and iron is also stored in reticuloendothelial cells or Kupffer cells. In the bone marrow and spleen, iron is stored mainly in reticuloendothelial cells. Stored iron is used primarily for the production of hemoglobin and for meeting other cellular needs for iron. Wide variations in the amount of storage iron can occur without any apparent effect on body functions. Storage iron is usually almost entirely depleted before the development of iron deficiency anemia. Full-term infants are born with a substantial store of iron, which usually can meet the infant's iron needs until 6 months of age [42]. Preterm and LBW infants generally have less storage iron than full-term infants, and as a consequence, these infants may deplete their iron stores as early as 2–3 months of age. Once infants have exhausted their body stores of iron, it is difficult to build up substantial iron stores because of the rapid growth and high iron requirement that occurs up to 24 months of age. After 24 months of age, the growth rate slows and iron stores usually begin to accumulate [43].

### 16.5.4   Iron Turnover and Loss

The production and destruction of erythrocytes accounts for most of the turnover of iron in the body. The average life span of erythrocytes is about 120 days, and in an adult, the daily iron turnover is about 20 mg. Most of the iron from degraded erythrocytes is recaptured for the synthesis of hemoglobin. Iron losses in the feces are about 0.6 mg/day from bile, desquamated mucosal cells, and minute amounts of blood [44]. Other routes of iron loss include desquamated skin and sweat (0.2–0.3 mg/day), urine (<0.1 mg/day). The average daily iron loss from adult men is 1.0 mg/day (range 0.5–2.0 mg/day). Premenopausal women need to replace the iron in menstrual blood loss, which accounts for 0.4–0.5 mg/day, combined with other iron losses for a total average iron loss of 1.3 mg/day [45].

### 16.5.5 Iron–Nutrient Interactions

Zinc and iron have significant interactions, as shown in a review of clinical trials involving supplementation with iron or zinc [46]. No significant differences in outcomes were noted when iron alone and iron and zinc were given to pregnant women, but when iron and zinc were given together to children, zinc appeared to reduce the benefit of iron supplementation [46]. Zinc supplementation has been shown to reduce the morbidity of diarrheal disease and pneumonia, but it is unclear whether concurrent supplementation with iron will reduce the effect of zinc.

Interactions have also been described between vitamin A and iron. Vitamin A supplementation has been shown to reduce anemia, and one of the biological mechanisms appears to be through increased mobilization of iron from the liver [47]. The increased availability of iron from the liver may potentially explain the reduction of serum erythropoietin and increased reticulocyte index described among severely anemic preschool children in Zanzibar who were supplemented with vitamin A [48]. More recently, there has also been interest in the bioavailability of iron in multivitamin-mineral supplements compared to just iron-folate or iron-only supplements. Studies showed that prenatal multivitamin-mineral supplements containing 60 mg of iron are as effective as standard iron-folate or iron-only supplements in improving hemoglobin and ferritin levels in pregnant women and women of reproductive age [49–51]. Findings from the recently completed UNIMAP trials, which used a prenatal multivitamin-mineral supplement with a lower dosage (i.e., 30 mg), will be very interesting [52].

## 16.6 ROLE OF IRON IN BIOLOGICAL FUNCTIONS

### 16.6.1 Hemoglobin

Hemoglobin plays an essential role in the transfer of oxygen from the lungs to tissues in erythrocytes. Hemoglobin combines with oxygen in the pulmonary circulation and becomes largely deoxygenated in the capillary circulation of tissues. In severe anemia, the hemoglobin content of erythrocytes is reduced, decreasing oxygen delivery to tissues and leading to chronic tissue hypoxia.

### 16.6.2 Myoglobin

Myoglobin is found in muscle, where it transports and stores oxygen needed for muscle contraction. The structure of myoglobin is a single heme group with a single globin chain. Myoglobin accounts for about 10% of the total body iron.

### 16.6.3 Cytochromes

Cytochromes contain heme and are essential to respiration and energy metabolism. Cytochromes a, b, and c are involved in oxidative phosphorylation and the production of cellular energy. Cytochromes serve as electron carriers in transforming adenosine disphosphate (ADP) to adenosine triphosphate (ATP), the primary energy storage compound. Cytochrome P450 is found in microsomal membranes of liver and intestinal mucosal cells.

### 16.6.4  Other Iron-Containing Enzymes

NADH (nicotinamide adenine dinucleotide phosphate) dehydrogenase and succinate dehydrogenase are two nonheme, iron-containing enzymes involved in energy metabolism. Hydrogen peroxidases also contain iron and protect against the accumulation of hydrogen peroxide. Catalase and peroxidase are two heme-containing enzymes that convert hydrogen peroxide to water and oxygen. Other iron-containing enzymes include aconitase, phosphoenolpyruvate carboxykinase, and ribonucleotide reductase.

### 16.6.5  Iron and Immune Function

Although animal studies suggested that some immune compartments may be affected adversely by iron deficiency, there still is no convincing evidence from human studies that iron deficiency has an adverse effect on immunity [53]. Some studies suggested that better iron status may benefit certain microorganisms during infection; however, the relationship between iron status and immunity is complex and has often been greatly oversimplified.

## 16.7  PATHOGENESIS OF IRON DEFICIENCY AND ANEMIA

### 16.7.1  Increased Requirement for Iron

In general, the etiology of iron deficiency can be viewed as a negative balance between iron intake and iron loss. Whenever there is rapid growth, as occurs during infancy, early childhood, adolescence, and pregnancy, iron requirement is much higher, and hence a positive iron balance is difficult to maintain. The blood volume expands in parallel with growth, with a corresponding increase in iron requirement [54]. Iron loss, related to monthly menstrual blood loss as well as iron transfer to the fetus during pregnancy, is a major factor in the increased risk of iron deficiency for women of childbearing age [55]. Table 16.3 compares the iron requirement of infants, women, and men. It is clear that infancy and pregnancy are times when requirement is high, increasing the risk for iron deficiency.

Table 16.3
**Iron requirements in infants, women, and men**

| Group | Age | Recommended intake (mg/day) |
|---|---|---|
| Infants | 0–3 months | – |
|  | 3–6 months | 6.6 |
|  | 6–12 months | 8.8 |
| Children | 1–10 years | 10 |
| Females |  |  |
|   Nonpregnant | 10–45 years | 15 |
|   Pregnant |  | 45 |
|   Postmenopausal |  | 10 |
| Males | 10–18 years | 12 |
|  | >18 years | 10 |

### 16.7.2   Poor Dietary Intake

Worldwide, the majority of iron deficiency is the direct result of low dietary iron content, especially of bioavailable iron. The dietary source of iron strongly influences the efficiency of the absorption. For infants, the iron content of milk consumed is a major determinant of iron status. The iron content of breast milk is low in comparison to that of cow's milk. However, 50% of the iron in breast milk can be absorbed, in contrast to less than 10% from cow's milk. The higher absorption efficiency of human breast milk does not entirely make up for the low iron content. After 6 months of age, breast-fed infants require an additional source of iron from the diet to meet their iron requirement. Unfortunately, in most settings, complementary food is low in iron content and availability. The amount of iron absorption from a variety of foods ranges from less than 1% to more than 20%. Foods of vegetable origin are at the lower end of the range, dairy products are in the middle, and meat is at the upper end. Meat is a good source of iron because most iron is in the form of heme iron, which has an absorption efficiency of 10–20%, which is two to three times greater than that for nonheme iron (2–7%). Nonheme iron found in plant foods and fortified food products is not only less well absorbed, the absorption is strongly influenced by the other foods ingested at the same meal. Ascorbic acid and meat protein are among the most potent enhancers of nonheme iron absorption. Tannin in tea and phytic acid in grain fibers are among the better known inhibitors of nonheme iron absorption.

### 16.7.3   Abnormal Iron Loss

The normal turnover of intestinal mucosa with some blood loss can be regarded as physiological blood, which is accounted for in the daily requirement. Normal menstrual blood loss is also an obligatory or physiological loss. The most common reason for abnormal blood loss in infants and younger children is the sensitivity of some children to the protein in cow's milk, resulting in increased gastrointestinal occult blood loss. In many tropical communities where hygienic conditions are inadequate, hookworm infection is a major cause of gastrointestinal blood loss for older children and adults. Hookworms cause bleeding in the upper intestine, and the severity of blood loss as measured by the hemoglobin content of feces is proportional to the intensity of the hookworm infestation. Studies showed that, in endemic areas, upward of 40% of the iron deficiency anemia and a majority of the severe anemia can be attributed to hookworm infections. There are two common forms of hookworm, *Necator americanus* and *Ancyclostoma duodenale*, and for the same worm load, *N. americanus* causes a greater level of bleeding. *Tricurius*, found in the colon, has also been shown to contribute to blood loss, but to a much lesser extent than hookworm.

## 16.8   FUNCTIONAL CONSEQUENCES OF IRON DEFICIENCY

Hemoglobin contains the majority of functional iron in the body; in addition, there are a number of other iron-dependent enzymes that can be adversely affected by iron deficiency [56]. The functional consequences of iron deficiency, which are of major public health importance, are briefly reviewed here.

### 16.8.1 Anemia and Mortality

Although mild anemia (10–20 gm/L below the cutoff) is not accompanied by health impairment, at a moderate level of anemia reduced oxygen-carrying capacity begins to interfere with aerobic function [57]. In areas where severe anemia (hemoglobin < 80 gm/L) is common, iron deficiency is usually one of multiple causes of anemia [58]. Very severe anemia (hemoglobin < 50 gm/L) is associated with increased childhood and maternal mortality and is often regarded as the underlying cause of death [59, 60]. Deaths associated with severe anemia generally occur in time of increased physiological stress, for example, during an acute febrile illness for a young child or during the peripartum period, when oxygen delivery and cardiovascular function are further compromised by worsening hemoglobin concentrations. In contrast to the known effects of severe anemia, the role of mild-to-moderate anemia and iron deficiency in reducing mortality remains controversial [61–63]. The causal association between iron deficiency and maternal mortality has been questioned, and a major limitation is the dearth of controlled trials, which are difficult to conduct in settings where there may be an impact since iron-folate supplementation is part of routine care [64, 65]. Evidence of increased risk of dying among young children in a controlled iron supplementation trial that was conducted in Zanzibar has renewed concerns about the safety of iron supplementation in malaria-endemic areas [66, 67].

### 16.8.2 Birth Outcomes

The impact of iron deficiency and anemia during pregnancy on birth outcomes such as LBW, prematurity, and infant iron status has been a topic of considerable interest for several decades. The U-shaped relationship between maternal hemoglobin and birth weight is well known, but the mechanisms explaining the increased risk of LBW at both ends of the distribution may be different. While low hemoglobin levels may be due to iron deficiency, high hemoglobin levels may be due to factors such as insufficient plasma volume expansion [68]. Similar to maternal mortality, there are few well-designed controlled trials of iron supplementation for pregnant women that have examined outcomes such as birth weight.

Although a meta-analysis [69] confirmed the conclusion of earlier reviews [64, 65] that there are insufficient data to conclude that iron supplementation during pregnancy improves birth size or the risk of premature delivery, a few controlled trials from the United States [70, 71] and Nepal [72] suggested that iron supplementation may reduce the risk of LBW. It should be noted that the trials conducted by Cogswell and colleagues [70] and Siega-Riz and colleagues [71] examined the effect of prenatal iron supplementation during early gestation among iron-replete women from low-income households in the United States and found that the reductions in the prevalence of LBW were primarily due to the effects on gestational age and not intrauterine growth retardation. In contrast, the study by Christian and colleagues [72] was a large, cluster-randomized trial that was conducted in a setting where the prevalence of LBW, anemia, and iron deficiency was high. No differences were seen in gestational age, but the prevalence of LBW was 34% among women who received iron-folate supplements compared to 43% among those who received placebo. It should be noted that this study also examined other nutrient combinations, and all participants received vitamin A. Clearly, more work is needed, and there may be benefits for both the mother and infant in terms of improved iron status and psychosocial benefits.

### 16.8.3   Child Behavior and Development

In recent years, the relationship between iron nutritional status and the cognitive development of younger children has been an area of active investigation. Consistently, children with iron deficiency anemia test less well in psychomotor development compared with iron-sufficient children [73]. When various developmental test scores are standardized, the magnitude of the deficient associated with iron deficiency is approximately 1 SD, a deficit greater than that observed for mild childhood lead poisoning. However, some deficit may be associated with iron deficiency without anemia [74, 75]. Although short-term iron treatment has been shown to reverse some aspects of the cognitive effect, the few long-term studies suggested that moderately severe iron deficiency in early childhood can lead to irreversible developmental disadvantage [76]. For this reason, control of childhood iron deficiency anemia should be based on primary prevention rather than relying on the detection of anemia in children after significant iron deficiency has occurred. It should be noted, however, that interventions aimed toward reducing iron deficiency are unlikely to improve physical growth [77]. Another area of interest is the evidence that demonstrated that iron-deficient women may be at increased risk of depression, which in turn would influence child growth and development [78]. Iron supplementation of women during the postpartum period has been shown to improve cognitive functioning [79].

### 16.8.4   Work Performance and Productivity

It is well established that significant anemia related to iron deficiency will reduce work performance. The classic study by Viteri and Torun demonstrated a linear dose-response relationship between hemoglobin concentration and Harvard step-test performance [80]. The adverse effect of iron deficiency on work or energy output appears to be mediated through a combination of decreased oxygen-carrying capacity from anemia and the effect of iron deficiency on muscle function. In animal studies, it has been shown that both aerobic and anaerobic functions are reduced [81].

In developing countries, where a large proportion of the economic output is based on physical labor, a major reduction in work capacity can be of great economic consequence. Iron supplementation studies among rubber tappers in Indonesia and tea pickers in Sri Lanka have clearly shown gain in productivity secondary to treatment of significant anemia [82, 83]. If the average reduction in productivity is 20% for an anemic individual, in a country where 50% of the women and 20% of the men are affected, the impact of iron deficiency anemia equals a total loss of 5–7% of the national economic output. Therefore, the economic consequence of iron deficiency for some poor countries may be substantial.

### 16.8.5   Heavy Metal Absorption

In developed countries such as the United States and in some situations in developing countries, an important consequence of iron deficiency is an increased risk of lead poisoning [84]. In the United States, young children who have iron deficiency have a three to four times higher prevalence of lead poisoning than children who are not iron deficient [85]. This association is partly socioeconomic: Poor children are more likely to have nutritional disorders and are also more likely to live in inadequate housing where risk to lead exposure is greater [85]. However, there is strong evidence of a direct association between iron deficiency and lead toxicity, related to the fact that iron-deficient individuals have increased efficiency of lead absorption [86]. This increased absorptive capacity is not specific for iron, and the absorption of other divalent metals, including toxic heavy metals such as lead and cadmium, is also increased [87]. The microcytic anemia thought in the past to be owing to lead poisoning is in fact iron deficiency anemia, which is frequently observed among children with lead poisoning [88]. Prevention of iron deficiency would reduce the number of children who are susceptible to lead poisoning through greater lead absorption, and one study suggested that iron treatment of children with lead poisoning may also help reduce their lead burden [89]. A controlled clinical trial conducted among lead-exposed Mexican schoolchildren showed that daily supplementation with iron or zinc reduced blood lead concentrations but had no impact of improving cognition [90]. The investigators concluded that iron or zinc supplementation could not be recommended as the sole treatment for improving cognition in lead-exposed children.

### 16.8.6    Iron and Infection

Iron is a pro-oxidant and in theory could potentially increase oxidative stress and exacerbate some types of infections. There are few solid data from observational studies that showed that iron deficiency increased the morbidity and mortality of infectious diseases [91], and it appears to be fairly clear that increased infectious disease morbidity is not part of the syndrome of iron deficiency. Oral iron supplementation has not been associated with a reduction in the morbidity of infectious diseases [91], and a systematic review of 28 controlled clinical trials showed that iron supplementation had no apparent effect on the incidence of infectious diseases, including malaria, except for a slightly increased risk of diarrhea [91]. However, a large, community-based controlled clinical trial conducted in a malaria holoendemic region in Zanzibar showed that routine supplementation with iron and folic acid increased hospitalizations and mortality [66]. Another large controlled clinical trial from lowland Nepal showed that iron and folic acid supplementation did not have an adverse impact on child morbidity or mortality [92]. In contrast to the trial in Zanzibar, the trial in Nepal was conducted in an area without significant malaria transmission [92]. Although current WHO recommendations for iron supplementation have not been changed, a joint statement by WHO and the United Nations International Children's Emergency Fund (UNICEF) recommended caution in areas where malarias transmission is intense and the possible need for targeting children who are iron deficient in these areas [67].

Although it has been speculated that iron supplementation may worsen HIV infection because of pro-oxidant effects and upregulation of HIV expression through NFκ-B (nuclear factor kappa B), there is currently little evidence from interventional studies that iron supplementation will worsen clinical outcomes in HIV infection [93]. A controlled clinical trial conducted among 458 female injection drug users with a high prevalence of iron deficiency showed that daily iron supplementation reduced anemia and improved iron status but had no adverse impact on hepatitis C viral load, plasma HIV load, liver enzymes, or CD4+ lymphocyte counts [94].

Table 16.4

Assessment of iron deficiency and iron deficiency anemia [95, 97]

| Indicator | Measure | Cutoffs | Indication | Commonly used methods | Special considerations in developing countries |
|---|---|---|---|---|---|
| Serum ferritin | Total body iron stores | <15 µg/L | Depleted iron stores | Venous or capillary blood, dried blood spots (DBS) ELISA | Infection and inflammation may cause inflated ferritin values. Use of DBS convenient for fieldwork |
| Serum transferrin concentration (TIBC) | Concentration of iron-transport protein | 360 µg/dL | Depleted iron stores | Venous blood | Influenced by infection and inflammation |
| | | | | Assay in which transferrin is saturated with excess iron; chromogenic methods | More complicated laboratory procedure that requires quality control sera |
| Serum transferrin saturation | Iron transport protein | <15% | Iron-deficient erythropoiesis | Venous blood | Influenced by infection and inflammation |
| | | | | Calculated from TIBC and serum iron values | Diurnal variation |
| Soluble serum transferrin receptor (STfR) | Expression of STfR, which binds ferritin for uptake in cells | High (10 mg/L) | Iron-deficient erythropoiesis | Venous blood Enzyme-linked immunosorbent assay (ELISA) | Possible to quantify STfR using a DBS. Not significantly influenced by infection and inflammation. Can be influenced by other nutritional deficiencies, such as $B_{12}$ and folate deficiencies, and specifically by acute malaria infection |
| Free erythrocyte protoporphyrin (FEP) | Serves as a precursor in heme biosynthesis | >70 mmol FEP/mol heme | Iron-deficient erythropoiesis | Whole blood (drop) Hemofluorometry | Influenced by infection and inflammation. Portable hemafluorometer available |

(continued)

Table 16.4 (continued)
Assessment of iron deficiency and iron deficiency anemia [95, 97]

| Indicator | Measure | Cutoffs | Indication | Commonly used methods | Special considerations in developing countries |
|---|---|---|---|---|---|
| Hemoglobin (SCN 2000) | Blood hemoglobin concentration | <11.0 g/dL | Anemia in pregnant women, children | Venous or capillary blood | Influenced by certain parasitic infections and other micronutrient deficiencies |
| | | | | Dried blood spot | It is necessary to make adjustments to cutoff values for persons living at high altitudes |
| | | <12.0 g/dL | Anemia in nonpregnant women > 15 years | HemoCue or cyanmethemoglobin method | Less-expensive, field-friendly equipment available |
| | | <13.0 g/dL | Anemia in men | | |
| Hematocrit | Packed red blood cell volume | <0.36 | Anemia in non-pregnant women > 15 years | Whole blood | Less expensive but methods can be difficult to standardize in a field setting |
| | | <0.33 | Anemia in pregnant women | Centrifugation method | |
| Erythrocyte | Color and shape of erythrocyte | Microcytic or hypochromic | Anemia | Whole blood Microscopy | |

*Source:* Adapted from refs. 95 and 97.

## 16.9   ASSESSMENT OF IRON NUTRITIONAL STATUS

### 16.9.1   Tests for Iron Deficiency

A number of hematologic and biochemical tests enable the characterization of iron status. Often, iron deficiency is defined by one or more abnormal iron biochemical tests: serum ferritin, transferrin saturation, transferrin receptor, and erythryocyte protoporphyrin (Table 16.4). *Iron deficiency anemia* is defined as meeting the criteria for both iron deficiency and anemia based on hemoglobin testing. Low serum ferritin per se is regarded as low or depleted iron stores. Even though all iron-related tests respond to changes in iron status, each test reflects different aspects of iron metabolism. For this reason, various tests are of different utility, and results may not always agree between tests.

Serum ferritin is a well-accepted marker of body iron stores and can be determined in venous or capillary bloods or dried blood spots using enzyme-linked immunosorbent assays (ELISAs) or two site immunoradiometric assays [95, 96]. Although still expensive for field-based settings, the ability to measure serum ferritin from blood spots is a major contribution. One of the problems with serum ferritin, however, is that infection and inflammation can falsely elevate the levels and are therefore a concern in areas where infections and parasitic diseases are common. The inclusion of a marker of infection such as C-reactive protein or a slightly higher cutoff value (<15 µg/L vs. 12 µg/L) has been recommended to address this concern [97].

Other markers of iron status are based on the transport form, namely, transferrin, which can be measured using chromogenic methods. More recently, the measurement of serum transferrin receptors from either venous blood or whole blood using ELISA techniques has been suggested as a better indicator of iron status. Elevated expression of serum transferrin receptors is indicative of iron-deficient erythropoiesis, which may be common in regions where iron deficiency is common but the prevalence of anemia is not that high. Similarly, elevated levels of free erythrocyte protoporphyrin (FEP) are indicative of impaired heme synthesis due to lack of iron and can be measured in whole blood using hematofluorometry. Although field-friendly equipment have been developed, problems remain in the use of these methods for large population-based surveys. It should be noted that a recent WHO and Centers for Disease Control and Prevention (CDC) Technical Consultation on the Assessment of Iron Status at the Population Level recommended the use of hemoglobin and serum ferritin as the most efficient combination for monitoring programs that aim to improve iron status [98].

### 16.9.2   The Meaning of Anemia

Anemia as measured by low hemoglobin concentration, or low hematocrit is by far the most commonly used indicator for detecting iron deficiency. Common causes of anemia other than iron deficiency include malaria; hereditary hemoglobinopathies or red cell production defects such as thalassemia minor; recent or current infections, including HIV infection; and any chronic conditions with an inflammatory response. On an individual basis, anemia cannot be used to detect those with milder forms of iron deficiency (iron deficiency without anemia). Because it is not generally feasible to perform iron biochemistry tests in many settings, hemoglobin response to iron treatment is a common approach in diagnosing iron deficiency. An increase in hemoglobin concentration of 10 g/L or more with a course of oral iron for those with anemia is indicative of iron deficiency. For population-based assessment or monitoring, prevalence of anemia is a useful indicator to define the severity of iron deficiency. One common reason for the misdiagnosis of anemia is inadequate laboratory procedures for hemoglobin determination related to capillary blood sampling or owing to inaccurate laboratory methods or procedures.

### 16.9.3   Field Testing for Hemoglobin

A portable photometer, the HemoCue system (Anglholm, Sweden) has been used in many different field surveys for the evaluation of anemia [99]. This system consists of a battery-operated photometer and a disposable cuvet, which is coated with the dried reagent (sodium azide) and serves as the blood collection device. This one-step blood collection, using a cuvet without a wet reagent, makes the system uniquely suited for rapid field surveys. Nonlaboratory personnel can be quickly and easily trained to operate the device, which is not dependent on electricity. In addition to these operational features, laboratory evaluation using standard methods found the HemoCue system to have satisfactory accuracy and precision [100]. Long-term field experience also demonstrated that the instrument is stable and durable. These features make the HemoCue system suitable for the inclusion of hemoglobin measurements in nutrition surveys.

### 16.9.4   Detection of Anemia by Clinical Examination

In resource-poor settings where it is not feasible to detect anemia by measurement of hemoglobin or hematocrit, clinical examination has been widely used to detect those with severe anemia. Clinical evidence regarding pallor of skin, conjunctiva, tongue, and palms is used to formulate an impression. In one study, the detection of severe anemia (hemoglobin <70 g/L), the sensitivity of clinical detection was reported to reach the range of 50–60% and 90% for specificity [101].

### 16.9.5   Use of Frequency Distributions of Hemoglobin
###              in Assessing Iron Status

When iron nutrition is included as a component of a nutrition survey, the traditional method of measurement is hemoglobin values among children, whereas a specific anemia survey usually examines a sample of children and women. The prevalence of anemia then serves as the index of severity of iron deficiency in the population. This approach is useful in areas where iron deficiency is the predominant cause of anemia, as is generally the case in developed countries. When poor iron intake is the main etiologic factor present in the population, children and women are disproportionately affected, and the hemoglobin concentration of adult men is virtually unaffected. If conditions other than poor dietary iron intake also present at a significant level, men can also have a high prevalence of anemia. For this reason, inclusion of a sample of men for anemia surveys can be useful in defining the nature of a high prevalence of anemia among children and women. If the prevalence of anemia for men is low, poor dietary iron intake is almost certain to be the cause of anemia in children and women. If men also have a high prevalence of anemia, factors other than poor dietary iron intake are usually present. This can include severe hookworm infection, causing iron deficiency owing to blood loss.

### 16.9.6    The Diagnosis of Multiple Conditions Contributing to Anemia

If other conditions are suspected to be contributing to anemia, proper evaluation of multiple factors using biochemical testing is often difficult. For example, both infections and vitamin A deficiency can cause depression of transferrin saturation and elevation of erythrocyte protoporphyrin measurements, which might lead to an incorrect interpretation that only iron deficiency is present [95]. Measurement of serum or plasma transferrin receptor has been considered helpful in distinguishing the anemia of chronic infection from iron deficiency anemia [102], but the sensitivity and specificity of serum or plasma transferrin receptor need further evaluation in different settings and among different risk groups.

Although the inclusion of indicators of iron status besides hemoglobin is desirable, areas with high rates of severe anemia are often found in developing countries where laboratory resources are limited. One method for the evaluation of different causes of anemia is the measurement of hemoglobin concentrations in the field before and after different interventions. For example, Suharno and colleagues [103] investigated anemia among pregnant women in rural Indonesia where vitamin A deficiency was also present. Treatment of anemia with a combination of iron and vitamin A resulted in a much better response of hemoglobin concentrations than either iron or vitamin A alone, demonstrating that virtually all the anemia in this population was attributed to vitamin A and iron deficiency.

## 16.10    CONTROL OF IRON DEFICIENCY

Despite the fact that the general strategy for improving iron nutrition is similar for infants and adult women (i.e., increasing dietary iron intake), the lack of overlap between infant and adult diet requires that separate approaches for intervention are considered. Combining strategies that address both diet quality and quantity with public health interventions such as improved hygiene and sanitation, routine deworming, and increased access to health service are often needed in many settings where the etiology of iron deficiency and anemia is complex.

### 16.10.1    Primary Health Care-Based Approaches

#### 16.10.1.1    IRON SUPPLEMENTATION

There are two general approaches to iron supplementation through the primary health care system. One approach is appropriate for areas where the prevalence of iron deficiency anemia is relatively low (i.e., less than 10–15%), and this approach involves screening for anemia and providing iron supplements only to those found to be anemic. The dosage of iron treatment is 3 mg/kg of elemental iron for children under 5 or 60 mg elemental iron daily for adults for 3 months. The second approach is to provide universal supplementation where the prevalence of iron deficiency anemia is high and where the majority of the population is affected by iron deficiency. For practical purposes, the former approach is suitable in developed areas, and the latter approach is suitable for most developing countries. In most developing countries, there is a general lack of adequate iron in the infant diet, and as a result, the prevalence of anemia exceeds 50% by 1 year of age, indicating that the majority of children are iron deficient. Currently, for such a purpose UNICEF recommends a daily dose of 12.5 mg of elemental iron for infants 6–12 months old. However, the findings of large trials from Zanzibar [66] and Nepal [92] have called for caution in the implementation of iron supplementation programs for children in regions where malaria is holoendemic [67].

It should be noted that very few developing countries have effective iron supplementation programs for young children and have been hampered by the lack of low-cost preparation or drops for distribution in developing countries and lack of experience for large-scale supplementation. Nevertheless, considerable progress has been made during the past decade in the development and testing of alternative approaches to deliver micronutrients such as iron along with other critical nutrients such as vitamin A, zinc, and so on to young children. These include microencapsulated sprinkles that can be added to complementary foods; low-cost, fortified, processed complementary foods; micronutrient foodlets or enriched spreads; and more that have been efficacious in improving iron status but are yet to be evaluated in large programmatic settings [104].

Routine iron supplementation is the current cornerstone of efforts to reduce iron-deficiency anemia during pregnancy. The current WHO recommendation is a 6-month regimen of a daily supplement containing 60 mg of elemental iron along with 400 µg of folic acid for all pregnant women. In settings where the prevalence of anemia is high (>40%), an additional 3 months of treatment during the postpartum period is recommended [105].

One major limitation of the iron supplementation strategy is the need to establish a system for supply and distribution of iron tablets through the primary health care system, and such supply and distribution is not always reliable in a resource-constrained setting. As with any system where there are multiple steps in getting supplies to a target population, it is not uncommon to have breakdowns in the supply chain.

Poor compliance is another common problem for any medication required over a long period of time by asymptomatic individuals. At higher doses of iron (>60 mg elemental iron), the gastrointestinal side effects are common and may contribute to a lack of compliance. To overcome these problems, proper education on the importance of the supplement and potential side effects need to be provided as part of the distribution program.

Although routine iron-folate supplementation is common practice in many countries, the prevalence of maternal anemia often remains high, suggesting that the effectiveness of such a program is not high. Efforts to improve the effectiveness of the program include ensuring the supply and distribution and communication to primary health care workers and women on the benefits of supplementation [106, 107]. One potential reason for lack of substantial anemia reduction could be the presence of other limiting factors, such as vitamin A deficiency or infections such as malaria or HIV infection. Thus far, the evidence indicates that greater effort is still needed to improve the effectiveness of such programs. One effort has been to test weekly instead of daily iron supplementation as an alternative to control maternal anemia. Although daily supplementation has been shown to be more effective, a study demonstrated that the benefit was dose dependent, that is, it depended on the total number of pills consumed rather than the frequency [108].

Another approach under investigation is whether to provide multivitamin-mineral supplements instead of iron-folate supplements during pregnancy. However, the findings to date are inconclusive (see Chapter 18). Timing of supplementation is another area of concern; many women in developing countries are already iron deficient when they become pregnant, which calls for earlier intervention [109]. Under supervised conditions, weekly iron administration has the potential to improve iron status of women of childbearing age and in turn prevent severe anemia during a subsequent pregnancy [110]. Weekly iron supplementation during the school age has been useful in correcting iron deficiency anemia.

#### 16.10.1.2 CONTROL OF INTESTINAL HELMINTH INFECTION

Studies from Zanzibar and Vietnam found that hookworm infestation can account for up to 40% of the iron deficiency anemia in highly endemic areas. In such settings, the potential impact of deworming can be justified as part of the anemia control program. Current evidence suggests that it is safe to deworm women after the first trimester of pregnancy, and the decision to deworm all children and women can be based on local prevalence because screening and treatment on the individual level may be less feasible.

### 16.10.2 Nutrition Education and Promotion

Among various micronutrients of interest, more is known about the bioavailability of iron in dietary sources than perhaps any other micronutrient. Factors that can either enhance or inhibit iron absorption have been well studied. To date, there is limited evidence from developing countries that suggests that dietary selection is an effective approach to improving iron status. This might be attributed to the fact that the main iron-rich foods are animal sources, which are relatively expensive. There is some encouraging evidence from developed countries that nutrition education can lead to improved feeding patterns and iron status among infants and younger children because iron-fortified foodstuffs such as infant cereal are commonly used. In most developing country settings, however, complementary foods are mainly local items with both low iron content and low iron bioavailability, which can also interfere with the absorption of iron in breast milk. Promotion of exclusive breast-feeding may help protect the higher absorption of iron from breast milk. Promoting the earlier introduction of meat-based complementary foods may be helpful. In the Middle East and northern Africa, tea is often introduced during infancy. Education efforts to delay the age at which tea is introduced and avoiding tea near mealtimes can be considered part of the education-based approach. The promotion of certain traditional food-processing techniques such as fermentation and germination, which can reduce phytate levels and thereby increase iron bioavailability, has also been successful in some settings [111].

### 16.10.3 Fortification

Iron fortification of commonly consumed foods (in settings where it is feasible) is likely the most cost-effective option. Ferrous sulfate, a highly soluble form of iron, is usually used to fortify infant formula and bread. In foods that are stored for a long period of time in air-permeable packages, ferrous sulfate and other highly soluble forms of iron may increase fat oxidation and rancidity; thus, less-soluble forms of iron such as ferric orthophosphate and ferric pyrophosphate are often used to fortify these types of foods.

One of the best examples of the effectiveness of fortification in the prevention of iron-deficiency anemia was seen in a project to fortify milk powder with iron and vitamin C for low-income families in Chile [112]. Another project demonstrated that iron status of school-aged children could be improved through provision of heme-iron-fortified cookies in schools [113]. Iron fortification of common food items such as wheat flour will affect the iron intake of all segments of the population except for infants. Women of childbearing age may potentially gain the most from this nontargeted approach. Experience to date indicates that it is highly feasible to fortify wheat flour with iron and other micronutrients. The additional cost of fortification is approx 0.5% of the overall cost of the processed flour. This is a small margin that can reasonably be passed on to the consumer without undue burden.

One argument against iron fortification is that it is only suitable for areas with a high consumption of wheat flour (>80–100 kg/person/year). In reality, even at lower consumption levels, iron fortification of flour can be of great value in improving iron status. For example, in a population with an average per capita consumption of 30 kg/year, if the flour is fortified at 60 parts per million, the total amount of extra iron consumed will be 1,800 mg/year or about 5 mg/day. This amount is about one third of the daily intake requirement of a nonpregnant woman or equivalent of a weekly intake of 30 mg as a supplement. At this level of consumption, iron deficiency anemia can be corrected over a year or can help build iron stores substantially. Based on the current experience, the fortification of wheat flour with iron should be considered in areas with at least a moderate consumption of wheat flour. Other food items that have been useful for iron fortification include curry powder, soy sauces, salt and fish sauce, and milk powder [114, 115].

Efforts have been made in examining the feasibility of biofortification as a potential means of improving iron status, especially in populations who consume staples such as wheat and maize, which have high levels of phytates that inhibit iron absorption [116]. Traditional plant-breeding techniques along with more modern techniques are being pursued to develop and promote varieties of staples that have high content of bioavailable iron by either increasing the actual iron content or reducing phytate levels. These approaches are promising and may be highly cost-effective, but still need to be evaluated [117].

## 16.10.4   Iron Overload

Concerns have been raised that iron fortification may potentially harm the few individuals who may be at risk for iron overload owing to various diseases that cause excess iron accumulation, such as hereditary hemochromatosis, a genetic condition in which iron absorption is enhanced. Hereditary hemochromatosis is an autosomal recessive disorder with a homozygote frequency of 100–500 per 100,000 in North America and Europe [118]. It is possible to screen for affected individuals and treat these individuals with prophylactic phlebotomy to prevent clinical disease [119]. In developing countries, incidence of hereditary hemochromatosis is lower because it is a genetic disorder that is generally associated with northern European ancestry. In Asia and Africa, rare and severe hereditary anemias such as thalassemia major are more common, and these affected individuals often become iron overloaded because of repeated transfusion. For the most part, these individuals have been identified, and specific measures can be taken to protect these individuals from iron overload.

Other concerns have been raised regarding the possible contribution of high iron levels to the development of chronic diseases. The evidence for this association is contradictory [120, 121], and it is possible that chronic disease may alter iron metabolism, giving rise to an apparent association that is not causal in nature. However, there is no advantage to higher iron stores as long as the body's iron requirement is met. The association between higher iron status and chronic diseases should be viewed as hypothetical, requiring more refined confirmatory studies. Because chronic diseases are the leading cause of mortality in many countries, these studies have generated a great deal of concern and have affected efforts to improve iron nutrition even in areas with severe iron deficiency.

## 16.11  CONCLUSIONS

Considerable progress has been made in our understanding of the causes and consequences of iron deficiency and anemia, but there is a lot of work to be done in moving toward the elimination of these conditions in many developing countries [122, 123]. Without doubt, the challenge of reducing iron deficiency and anemia worldwide depends on the development of sound approaches to intervention but also needs the commitment of the public, private, and civic sectors to work together. The most promising approach is dietary improvement by iron fortification of common staples, while for selected groups at risk such as infants, young children, and pregnant women, iron supplementation will also be needed. Unfortunately, increasing consumption of animal products is not always a practical solution because of economic barriers. The programmatic approaches to improving iron nutrition among adult women and among infants must be developed separately because there is little overlap between the diet consumed by the two groups. Prevention of iron deficiency anemia among younger children should be considered a high-priority issue because of the clear evidence that iron deficiency anemia impairs childhood development. Assessing iron status for monitoring program impact does not always require the full compendium of iron laboratory tests. The effective use of hemoglobin in combination with serum ferritin can be implemented easily even in settings with limited resources.

## 16.12  RECOMMENDATIONS

Although iron deficiency is perhaps the best characterized of all nutritional deficiency disorders, there are several areas that need to be characterized further through scientific investigation.

- Further studies are needed to characterize the effects of iron supplementation on immune responses to different infectious diseases.
- Large-scale community trials are needed to examine the efficacy of iron supplementation for the prevention of anemia in infancy and early childhood.
- Further investigation is needed to determine whether nutrition promotion and an education-based approach will improve iron status in various settings in developing countries.
- The association between chronic diseases and iron status needs further elucidation.
- The role of hepcidin, the recently described iron regulatory hormone, in the pathogenesis of iron deficiency and iron deficiency anemia needs further characterization in humans.
- The role of hemojuvelin, a recently described protein that modulates hepcidin expression, in the pathogenesis of iron deficiency and iron deficiency anemia needs further characterization in humans.
- Further research is needed to determine which indicators of anemia associated with iron deficiency will be most efficient for screening children who will benefit the most from iron supplements.

- Further research is urgently needed to develop effective strategies to control iron deficiency and anemia in regions where malaria transmission is intense and the prevalence of infection is high.
- More work is needed to examine the effects of joint iron and zinc supplementation on infectious disease morbidity, growth, and child development.

## REFERENCES

1. Yip R. The challenge of improving iron nutrition: limitations and potentials of major intervention approaches. Eur J Clin Nutr 1997;51(suppl 4):S16–S24.
2. Yip R, Dallman PR. Iron. In: Present knowledge in nutrition, 7th ed. Ziegler EE, Filer LJ Jr, eds. Washington, DC: International Life Sciences Institute, 1996.
3. Boyle R. Memoires for the natural history of humane blood. London: Smith, 1684.
4. Menghini V. De ferrearum particularum sede in sanguine. In: De Bononiensi scientiarum et artium instituto atgue academia commentarii, II, pt 2,1746, 244–266.
5. Boussingault JB. Compt Rendu 1867;64:1353.
6. Bunge G von. Z physiol Chem 1886;10:453.
7. Mackay HM. Anaemia in infancy: prevalence and prevention. Arch Dis Child 1928;3:117–146.
8. Dubini A. Nuovo verme intestinale umano (*Agchylostoma duodenale*), costituente un sesto genere dei Nematoidei proprii dell'uomo. Ann Univ Med (Milano) 1843;106:5–51.
9. Perroncito E. Osservazioni elmintologiche relative alla malattia sviluppatasi endemica negli operai del Gottardo. Atti della R. Accademia dei Lincei 1879–1880(3 ser);7:381–433.
10. Stiles CW. A new species of hookworm (*Uncinaria americana*) parasitic in man. Am Med 1902;3: 777–778.
11. Porto Rico Anemia Commission. Report of the Permanent Commission for the Suppression of Uncinariasis in Porto Rico, 1906–1907. San Juan, Puerto Rico: Bureau of Printing and Supplies, 1907.
12. Ashford BK, Gutiérrez Igaravidez P. Uncinariasis (hookworm disease) in Porto Rico: a medical and economic problem. San Juan, Porto Rico, August 5, 1910. U.S. 61st Congress, 3d Session, Senate Doc. 808. Washington, DC: Government Printing Office, 1911.
13. Stiles CW. Report upon the prevalence and geographic distribution of hookworm disease (*Uncinariasis or Anchylostomiasis*) in the United States. Washington, DC: Government Printing Office, 1903. Hygienic Laboratory Bulletin No. 10.
14. Stiles CW. Early history, in part esoteric, of the hookworm (uncinariasis) campaign in our southern United States. J Parasitol 1939;25:283–308.
15. Rockefeller Sanitary Commission for the Eradication of Hookworm Disease. Organization, activities, and results up to December 31, 1910. Washington, DC: Offices of the Commission, 1910.
16. Rockefeller Sanitary Commission for the Eradication of Hookworm Disease. Fifth annual report for the year 1914. Washington, DC: Offices of the Commission, 1915.
17. Smillie WG, Augustine DL. Hookworm infestation. The effect of varying intensities on the physical condition of school children. Am J Dis Child 1926;31:151–168.
18. Smillie WG, Augustine DL. The effect of varying intensities of hookworm infestation upon the development of school children. South Med J 1926;19:19–28.
19. Smillie WG, Spencer CR. Mental retardation in school children infested with hookworms. J Educ Psychol 1926;17:314–321.
20. Waite JH, Neilson IL. Effects of hookworm infection on mental development of North Queensland schoolchildren. J Am Med Assoc 1919;73:1877–1879.
21. Strong EK. Effects of hookworm disease on the mental and physical development of children. New York: Rockefeller Foundation, 1916. Rockefeller Foundation. International Health Commission Publication No. 3.
22. Smillie WG. Control of hookworm disease in south Alabama. South Med J 1924;17:494–499.
23. Standing Committee on Nutrition. The fifth report on the world nutrition situation: nutrition for improved development outcomes. Geneva: Standing Committee on Nutrition, United Nations System, 2004.
24. Ologoudou K. Trends in the prevalence and determinants of anemia in Latin America. Master's thesis. Atlanta: Program in Nutrition and Health Sciences, Emory University, 2006.

25. Looker AC, Dallman PR, Carroll MD, Gunter EW, Johnson CL. Prevalence of iron deficiency in the United States. JAMA 1997;277:973–976.

26. Hallberg L. Results of surveys to assess iron status in Europe. Nutr Rev 1995;53:314–322.

27. Björn-Rasmussen E, Hallberg L, Isaksson B, Arvidsson B. Food iron absorption in man: application of the two-pool extrinsic tag method to measure heme and non-heme iron absorption from the whole diet. J Clin Invest 1974;34:55–68.

28. Roy CN, Andrews NC. Anemia of inflammation: the hepcidin link. Curr Opin Hematol 2005;12:107–111.

29. Ganz T. Hepcidin—a regulator of intestinal iron absorption and iron recycling by macrophages. Best Pract Res Clin Haematol 2005;18:171–182.

30. Krause A, Neitz S, Hans-Jürgen M, Schulz A, Forssmann WG, Schulz-Knappe P, Adermann K. LEAP-1, a novel highly disulfide-bonded human peptide, exhibits antimicrobial activity. FEBS Lett 2000;480:147–150.

31. Park CH, Valore EV, Waring AJ, Ganz T. Hepcidin, a urinary antimicrobial peptide synthesized in the liver. J Biol Chem 2001;276:7806–7810.

32. Pigeon C, Ilyin G, Courselaud B, Leroyer P, Turlin B, Brissot P, Loréal O. A new mouse liver-specific gene, encoding a protein homologous to human antimicrobial peptide hepcidin, is overexpressed during iron overload. J Biol Chem 2001;276:7811–7819.

33. Hunter HN, Fulton DB, Ganz T, Vogel HJ. The solution structure of human hepcidin, a peptide hormone with antimicrobial activity that is involved in iron update and hereditary hemochromatosis. J Biol Chem 2002;277:37597–37603.

34. Nemeth E, Tuttle MS, Powelson J, Vaughn MB, Donovan A, Ward DM, Ganz T, Kaplan J. Hepcidin regulates cellular iron efflux by binding to ferroportin and inducing its internalization. Science 2004;306:2090–2093.

35. Nemeth E, Preza GC, Jung CL, Kaplan J, Waring AJ, Ganz T. The N-terminus of hepcidin is essential for its interaction with ferroportin: structure-function study. Blood September 1, 2005 (E-pub in advance of print).

36. Nicolas G, Bennoun M, Porteu A, Mativet S, Beaumont C, Grandchamp B, Sirito M, Sawadogo M, Kahn A, Vaulont S. Severe iron deficiency anemia in transgenic mice expressing liver hepcidin. Proc Natl Acad Sci USA 2002;99:4596–4601.

37. Donovan A, Lima CA, Pinkus JL, Pinkus GS, Zon LI, Robine S, Andrews NC. The iron exporter ferroportin/Slc40a1 is essential for iron homeostasis. Cell Metab 2005;1:191–200.

38. McKie AT, Marciani P, Rolfs A, Brennan K, Wehr K, Barrow D, Miret S, Bomford A, Peters TJ, Farzaneh F, Hediger MA. A novel duodenal iron-regulated transporter, IREG1, implicated in the basolateral transfer of iron to the circulation. Mol Cell 2000;5:299–309.

39. Nicolas G, Chauvet C, Viatte L, Danan JL, Bigard X, Devaux I, Beaumont C, Kahn A, Vaulont S. The gene encoding the iron regulatory peptide hepcidin is regulated by anemia, hypoxia, and inflammation. J Clin Invest 2002;110:1037–1044.

40. Weinstein DA, Roy CN, Fleming MD, Loda MF, Wolfsdorf JI, Andrews NC. Inappropriate expression of hepcidin is associated with iron refractory anemia: implications for the anemia of chronic disease. Blood 2002;100:3776–3781.

41. Huebers HA, Finch CA. The physiology of transferrin and transferrin receptors. Physiol Rev 1987;67:520–581.

42. Dallman PR, Siimes MA, Stekel A. Iron deficiency in infancy and childhood. Am J Clin Nutr 1980;33:86–118.

43. Yip R. Age related changes in iron metabolism. In: Iron metabolism in health and disease. Brock JH, Halliday JW, Pippard MJ, Powell LW, eds. London: Saunders, 1994:427–448.

44. Green R, Charlton RW, Seffel H, et al. Body iron excretion in man: a collaborative study. Am J Med 1968;45:336–353.

45. Hallberg L, Högdahl A, Nilsson L, Rybo G. Menstrual blood loss: a population study. Acta Obstet Gynecol Scand 1966;45:320–351.

46. Fischer Walker C, Kordas K, Stoltzfus RJ, Black RE. Interactive effects of iron and zinc on biochemical and functional outcomes in supplementation trials. Am J Clin Nutr 2005;82:5–12.

47. Semba RD, Bloem MW. The anemia of vitamin A deficiency: epidemiology and pathogenesis. Eur J Clin Nutr 2002;56:271–281.

48. Cusick SE, Tielsch JM, Ramsan M, Jape JK, Sazawal S, Black RE, et al. Short-term effects of vitamin A and antimalarial treatment on erythropoiesis in severe anemic Zanzibari preschool children. Am J Clin Nutr 2005;82:406–412.

49. Christian P, Shrestha SR, Leclerq SC, Khatry SK, Jiang T, Wagner T, et al. Supplementation with micronutrients in addition to iron and folic acid does not further improve hematologic status of pregnant women in rural Nepal. J Nutr 2003;133:3492–3498.

50. Ramakrishnan U, Neufield L, Gonzalez-Cossio T, Villalpando S, Garcia-Guerra A, et al. Multiple micronutrient supplements during pregnancy do not reduce or improve iron status compared to iron-only supplements in semirural Mexico. J Nutr 2004;134:898–903.

51. Moriarty-Craige SE, Ramakrishnan U, Neufeld L, Rivera J, Martorell R. Multivitamin-mineral supplementation is not as efficacious as iron supplementation in improving hemoglobin concentration in non-pregnant women living in Mexico. Am J Clin Nutr 2004;80:1308–1311.

52. United Nations International Children's Emergency Fund/World Health Organization/United Nations University Study Team. Multiple micronutrient supplementation during pregnancy (MMSDP): efficacy trials. London: Centre for International Child Health, Institute of Child Health, University College London, March 4–8, 2002.

53. Walter T, Olivares M, Pizarro F, Muñoz C. Iron, anemia, and infection. Nutr Rev 1997;55:111–124.

54. Dallman PR. Changing iron needs from birth through adolescence. In: Nutritional anemias. Fomon SJ, Zlotkin S, eds. New York: Raven, 1992:29–38.

55. Bothwell TH, Charlton RW, Cook JD, Finch CA. Iron metabolism in man. Oxford, UK: Blackwell Scientific, 1979.

56. Dallman PR. Tissue effects of iron deficiency. In: Iron in biochemistry and medicine. Jacobs A, Worwood M, eds. London: Academic, 1974.

57. Varat MA, Adolph RJ, Fowler NO. Cardiovascular effects of anemia. Am Heart J 1972;83:416–426.

58. Brooker S, Peshu N, Warn PA, Mosobo M, Guyatt HL, Marsh K, Snow RW. The epidemiology of hookworm infection and its contribution to anaemia among pre-school children on the Kenyan coast. Trans R Soc Trop Med Hyg 1999;93:240–246.

59. Allen LH. Pregnancy and iron deficiency: unresolved issues. Nutr Rev 1997;55:91–101.

60. Murphy JF, O'Riordan J, Newcombe RG, et al. Relation of haemoglobin levels in the first and second trimesters to outcome of pregnancy. Lancet 1986;1:992–994.

61. Rush D. Nutrition and maternal mortality in the developing world. Am J Clin Nutr 2000;72:212S–240S.

62. Brabin B, Hakimi M, Pelletier D. An analysis of anemia and pregnancy-related maternal mortality. J Nutr 2001;131:604S–614S; discussion 614S–615S.

63. Brabin BJ, Premji Z, Verhoeff F. An analysis of anemia and child mortality. J Nutr 2001;131:636S–645S.

64. Rasmussen K. Is there a causal relationship between iron deficiency or iron deficiency anemia and weight at birth, length of gestation and perinatal mortality? J Nutr 2001;131:590S–601S; discussion 601S–603S.

65. Ramakrishnan U. Functional consequences of nutritional anemia during pregnancy and early childhood. In: Nutritional anemias. Ramakrishnan U, ed. Boca Raton, FL: CRC, 2001:43–68.

66. Sazawal S, Black RE, Ramsan M, Chwaya HM, Stolzfus RJ, Dutta A, et al. Effects of routine prophylactic supplementation with iron and folic acid on admission to hospital and mortality in preschool children in a high malaria transmission setting: community-based, randomised, placebo-controlled trial. Lancet 2006;367:133–143.

67. World Health Organization/United Nations International Children's Emergency Fund Joint Statement. Iron supplementation of young children in regions where malaria transmission is intense and infectious diseases highly prevalent. Geneva: World Health Organization, 2006.

68. Yip R. Significance of an abnormally low or high hemoglobin concentration during pregnancy: special consideration of iron nutrition. Am J Clin Nutr 2000;72:272S–279S.

69. Pena-Rosas J, Viteri F. Effects of routine oral iron supplementation with or without folic acid for women during pregnancy. Cochrane Pregnancy and Childbirth Group. Cochrane Database Syst Rev 2006;3: CD004736.

70. Cogswell ME, Parvanta I, Ickes L, Yip R, Brittenham GM. Iron supplementation during pregnancy, anemia, and birth weight: a randomized controlled trial. Am J Clin Nutr 2003;78:773–781.

71. Siega-Riz AM, Hartzema AG, Turnbull C, Thorp J, McDonald T, Cogswell ME. The effects of prophylactic iron given in prenatal supplements on iron status and birth outcomes: a randomized controlled trial. Am J Obstet Gyn 2006;194:512–519.

72. Christian P, Khatry SK, Katz J, Pradhan EK, LeClerq SC, Shrestha SR, et al. Effects of alternative maternal micronutrient supplements on low birth weight in rural Nepal: double blind randomised community trial. BMJ 2003;326:571–576.

73. De Andraca I, Castillo M, Walter T. Psychomotor development and behavior in iron-deficiency anemic infants. Nutr Rev 1997;55:125–132.

74. Oski FA, Honig AS, Helu B, Howanitz P. Effect of iron therapy on behavior performance in nonanemic, iron-deficient infants. Pediatrics 1983;71:877–880.

75. Walter T, Kovalskys J, Stekel A. Effect of mild iron deficiency on infant mental development scores. J Pediatr 1983;102:519–522.

76. Lozoff B, Wachs TD. Functional correlates of nutritional anemias in infancy and early childhood—child development and behavior. In: Nutritional anemias. Ramakrishnan U, ed. Boca Raton, FL: CRC, 2001:69–88.

77. Ramakrishnan U, Aburto N, McCabe G, Martorell R. Multi-micronutrient supplements but not vitamin A or iron supplements alone improve child growth: results of three meta-analyses. J Nutr 2004;134:2592–2602.

78. Makrides M, Crowther CA, Gibson RA, Gibson RS, Skeaff CM. Efficacy and tolerability of low-dose iron supplements during pregnancy: a randomized controlled trial. Am J Clin Nutr 2003;78:145–153.

79. Beard JL, Hendricks MK, Perez EM, Murray-Kolb LE, Berg A, et al. Maternal iron deficiency anemia affects postpartum emotions and cognition. J Nutr 2005;135:267–272.

80. Viteri FE, Torun B. Anemia and physical work capacity. Clin Hematol 1974;3:609–626.

81. McLane JA, Fell RD, McKay RH, et al. Physiological and biochemical effects of iron deficiency on rat skeletal muscle function. Am J Physiol 1981;241:C47–C54.

82. Basta SS, Soekirman, Karyadi D, Schrimshaw NS. Iron deficiency anemia and the productivity of adult males in Indonesia. Am J Clin Nutr 1979;32:916–925.

83. Edgerton VR, Gardner GW, Ohira Y, Gunawardena KA, Senewiratne B. Iron-deficiency anaemia and its effect on worker productivity and activity patterns. BMJ 1979;2:1546–1549.

84. Kwong W, Friello P, Semba RD. The epidemiology and pathophysiology of iron deficiency and lead poisoning. Sci Total Environ 2004;330:21–27.

85. Yip R. Iron status of children with elevated blood lead concentrations. J Pediatr 1981;98:922–925.

86. Yip R. Multiple interactions between childhood iron deficiency and lead poisoning: evidence that childhood lead poisoning is an adverse consequence of iron deficiency. In: Recent knowledge on iron and folate deficiencies in the world, vol. 197. Hercberg S, Galan P, Dupin H, eds. Paris: INSERM, 1990:523–532.

87. Tandon SK, Khandelwal S, Jain VK, Mathur N. Influence of dietary iron deficiency on acute metal intoxication. Biometals 1993;6:133–138.

88. Clark M, Royal J, Seeler R. Interaction of iron deficiency and lead and the hematologic findings in children with severe lead poisoning. Pediatrics 1988;81:247–254.

89. Hammad TA, Sexton M, Langenberg P. Relationship between blood lead and dietary iron intake in preschool children. A cross-sectional study. Ann Epidemiol 1996;6:30–33.

90. Rico JA, Kordas K, López P, Rosado JL, Vargas GG, Ronquillo D, et al. Efficacy of iron and/or zinc supplementation on cognitive performance of lead-exposed Mexican schoolchildren: a randomized, placebo-controlled trial. Pediatrics 2006;117:e518–e527.

91. Gera T, Sachdev HPS. Effect of iron supplementation on incidence of infectious illness in children: systematic review. BMJ 2002;325:1142–1151.

92. Tielsch JM, Khatry SK, Stoltzfus RJ, Katz J, LeClerq SC, Adhikari R, et al. Effect of routein prophylactic supplementation with iron and folic acid on preschool child mortality in southern Nepal: community-based, cluster-randomised, placebo-controlled trial. Lancet 2006;367:144–152.

93. Clark TD, Semba RD. Iron supplementation during human immunodeficiency virus infection: a double-edged sword? Med Hypotheses 2001;57:476–479.

94. Semba RD, Ricketts EP, Mehta S, Netski D, Thomas D, Kirk G, Wu AW, Vlahov D. Effect of micronutrients and iron supplementation on hemoglobin, iron status, and plasma hepatitis C and HIV RNA in female injection drug users: a controlled clinical trial. J Acquir Immune Defic Syndr 2007;45:298–303.

95. Gibson R. Principles of nutritional assessment. 2nd ed. Oxford, UK: Oxford University Press, 2005.

96. Ahluwalia N, Lonnerdal B, Lorenz SG, Allen LH. Spot ferritin assay for serum samples dried on filter paper. Am J Clin Nutr 1998;67:88–92.

97. Lynch S, Green R. Assessment of nutritional anemias. In: Nutritional anemias. Ramakrishnan U, ed. Boca Raton, FL: CRC, 2001:23–42.

98. World Health Organization/Centers for Disease Control. Assesssing the iron status of populations. A joint report of a World Health Organization and Centers of Disease Control and Prevention Technical Consultation on Assessment of Iron Status of Populations. Geneva: World Health Organization, 2005.

99. Cohen AR, Seidl-Friedman J. HemoCue system for hemoglobin measurement. Evaluation in anemic and nonanemic children. Am J Clin Pathol 1988;90:302–305.

100. Hudson-Thomas M, Bingham KC, Simmons WK. An evaluation of the HemoCue for measuring haemoglobin in field studies in Jamaica. Bull World Health Organ 1994;72:423–426.

101. Gjorup T, Bugge PM, Hendriksen C, Jensen AM. A critical evaluation of the clinical diagnosis of anemia. Am J Epidemiol 1986;124:657–665.

102. Ahluwalia N. Diagnostic utility of serum transferrin receptor measurement in assessing iron status. Nutr Rev 1998;56:133–141.

103. Suharno D, West CE, Muhilal, Karyadi D, Hautvast JG. Supplementation with vitamin A and iron for nutritional anaemia in pregnant women in West Java, Indonesia. Lancet 1993;342:1325–1328.

104. Neufeld LM, Ramakrishnan U. Specific strategies to address micronutrient deficiencies in the young child: targeted fortification. In: Micronutrient deficiencies during the weaning period and the first years of life. Pettifor JM, Zlotkin S, eds. Nestlé Nutrition Workshops Series: Pediatric Program, Nestec. Basel, Switzerland: Karger, 2004;54:213–232.

105. World Health Organization. Iron deficiency anemia: assessment, prevention and control: a guide for programme managers. Geneva: United Nations International Children's Emergency Fund//United Nations University/World Health Organization, 2001.

106. Ekstrom EC. Supplementation for nutritional anemias. In: Nutritional anemias. Ramakrishnan U, ed. Boca Raton, FL: CRC, 2001:129–152.

107. Galloway R. Anemia prevention and control: what works. USAID, The World Bank, UNICEF, PAHO, FAO, The Micronutrient Initiative. Washington, DC: USAID, 2003.

108. Ekstrom EC, Hyder SMZ, Chowdhury AMR, Chowdhury SA, Lonnerdal B, et al. Efficacy and trial effectiveness of weekly and daily iron supplementation among pregnant women in rural Bangladesh: disentangling the issues. Am J Clin Nutr 2002;76:1392–1400.

109. Viteri FE, Berger J. Importance of pre-pregnancy and pregnancy iron status: can long-term weekly preventive iron and folic acid supplementation achieve desirable and safe status? Nutr Rev 2005;63: S65–S76.

110. Cavalli-Sforza T, Berger J, Smitasiri S, Viteri F. Weekly iron-folic acid supplementation of women of reproductive age: impact overview, lessons learned, expansion plans, and contributions toward achievement of the millennium development goals. Nutr Rev 2005;63:S152–S158.

111. Gibson RS, Hotz C. Dietary diversification/modification strategies to enhance micronutrient content and bioavailability of diets in developing countries. Br J Nutr 2001;85(suppl 2):S159–S166.

112. Heresi G, Pizarro F, Olivares M, Cayazzo M, Hertrampf E, Walter T, et al. Effect of supplementation with an iron-fortified milk on incidence of diarrhea and respiratory infection in urban-resident infants. Scand J Infect Dis 1995;27:385–389.

113. Walter T, Hertrampf E, Pizarro F, Olivares M, Llaguno S, Letelier A, Vega V, Stekel A. Effect of bovine-hemoglobin-fortified cookies on iron status of schoolchildren: a nationwide program in Chile. Am J Clin Nutr 1993;57:190–194.

114. Thuy PV, Berger J, Davidsson L. Regular consumption of NaFeEDTA-fortified fish sauce improves iron status and reduces the prevalence of anemia in anemic Vietnamese women. Am J Clin Nutr 2003;78:284–290.

115. Mannar V, Gallego EB. Iron fortification: country level experiences and lessons learned. J Nutr 2002;132:856S–858S.

116. Bouis HE. Micronutrient fortification of plants through plant breeding: can it improve nutrition in man at low cost? Proc Nutr Soc 2003;62:403–411.

117. Welch RM, Graham RD. Agriculture: the real nexus for enhancing bioavailable micronutrients in food crops. J Trace Elem Med Biol 2005;18:299–307.
118. Olynyk JK, Cullen DJ, Aquilia S, Rossi E, Summerville L, Powell LW. A population-based study of the clinical expression of the hemochromatosis gene. N Engl J Med 1999;341:718–724.
119. Felitti VJ, Beutler E. New developments in hereditary hemochromatosis. Am J Med Sci 1999;318:257–268.
120. Giles WH, Anda RF, Williamson DF, et al. Body iron stores and the risk of coronary heart disease. N Engl J Med 1994;331:1159–1160.
121. Sempos CT, Looker AC, Gillum RF, Makuc DM. Body iron stores and the risk of coronary heart disease. N Engl J Med 1994;330:1119–1124.
122. Mason J, Lotfi M, Dalmiya N, Sethuraman K, Deitchler M, Geibel S, et al. Progress in controlling micronutrient deficiencies. MI/Tulane University/UNICEF. The Micronutrient Initiative, 2001.
123. Galloway R, Dusch E, Elder L, Achadi E, Grajeda R, Hurtado E et al. Women's perceptions of iron deficiency and anemia prevention and control in eight developing countries. Soc Sci Med 2002;55:529–544.

# 17 Iodine Deficiency Disorders

## Richard D. Semba and François Delange*

## 17.1 INTRODUCTION

Iodine, a nonmetallic solid in the halogen family, is an essential constituent of the thyroid hormones thyroxine ($T_4$) and triiodothyronine ($T_3$). Thyroid hormones are involved in a wide range of biological functions and modulate gene expression through specific nuclear receptors. Iodine is present in small amounts in soil, water, plants, and animals, and insufficient dietary intake of iodine is generally related to lack of iodine in the environment.

The iodine deficiency disorders consist of a wide spectrum, including mental retardation, impaired physical development, increased perinatal and infant mortality, hypothyroidism, cretinism, and goiter. *Goiter* is defined as an enlargement of the thyroid gland, and *cretinism* is a term used for a severe form of iodine deficiency characterized by severe mental retardation. The effects of iodine deficiency are most pronounced during periods of rapid growth, that is, in the fetus, neonate, infant, and young children, and this may have a major effect on brain development. The ongoing global effort to eliminate iodine deficiency disorders through iodization of salt represents one of the largest public health efforts of the 20th century.

## 17.2 PUBLIC HEALTH SIGNIFICANCE

It was estimated that in 1990, there were 1,572 million people worldwide who consumed inadequate amounts of iodine and were at risk for iodine deficiency disorders [1–3]. Iodine deficiency is the leading cause of preventable mental retardation in the world [4]. The prevalence of iodine deficiency is related to the local availability of iodine in water and iodine in plants and foods, and the problem of iodine deficiency is global, with mountainous regions and large river deltas the most well-known areas for endemic iodine deficiency disorders.

## 17.3 HISTORICAL BACKGROUND

Descriptions of goiter and cretinism have been found in written records and iconography since antiquity, and seaweed or thyroid extracts were empirically known to be effective treatments for goiter [5]. Iodine was discovered by a saltpeter manufacturer

*deceased*

From: *Nutrition and Health: Nutrition and Health in Developing Countries, Second Edition*
Edited by: R. D. Semba & M. W. Bloem © Humana Press, Totowa, NJ

near Paris, Bernard Courtois (1777–1838) in 1811. Seaweed ash from Normandy was used in the production of saltpeter, and Courtois observed violet vapors and formation of black crystals when an extract of this burned seaweed was heated [5, 7]. This substance was named iodine by the French chemist Joseph Louis Gay-Lussac (1778–1850) after the Greek word for "violet." Further investigations by chemists showed that iodine was found in various seaweeds, algae, and marine sponges but was present only in trace quantities in other sources in nature. The qualitative estimation of iodine was facilitated by the discovery of the iodine–starch reaction, in which free iodine formed a blue color when combined with starch. A physician in Geneva, Jean-François Coindet (1774–1834), found that pure iodine was a remedy for goiter [8]. While working in Bogota, Colombia, Jean Baptiste Boussingault (1802–1887) noted that goiter was not endemic in communities that utilized iodine-containing salt from certain salinas, and before his return to France in 1831, he advised the Colombian government to provide for distribution of this naturally iodized salt for the health of the community [9].

During the mid-19th century, Gaspard Adolphe Chatin (1813–1901), a professor in the School of Pharmacy of Paris, conducted investigations of iodine in plants, water, and animals, and he concluded that lack of iodine in the drinking water could be the cause of goiter and cretinism [10]. Public health authorities in three departments (Bas-Rhin, Seine-Inférieure, Haute-Savoie) started prophylactic measures of giving schoolchildren daily iodine tablets, and a large reduction in goiter was noted [11]. The French program of iodine prophylaxis used high doses of 0.1 to 0.5 mg/kg for iodization of salt and daily iodine tablets containing 0.01 g potassium iodide. Although schoolchildren seemed to have tolerated the doses well, some adults with goiter may have experienced iodine-induced hyperthyroidism (Jod-Basedow reaction), and consequently the iodine prophylaxis program was abandoned [5]. The French Goitre Commission was also skeptical about Chatin's theory that iodine deficiency caused goiter and cretinism, noting that some of the 420,000 individuals with goiter in France lived in places where the air and soil contained iodine; instead, the Commission implicated toxins in the water and food as the cause of goiter [12].

By the late 19th century, the geographical distribution of endemic goiter and cretinism was recognized to extend around the world, with detailed accounts available from many countries in Europe [13]. In detailed studies in northwest India, Robert McCarrison (1878–1960) distinguished neurological, or "nervous" cretinism from hypothyroid or "myxoedematous" cretinism [14].

In the United States, large-scale trials of iodine for goiter prophylaxis were conducted by David Marine (1880–1976) and Oliver P. Kimball among schoolgirls in Akron, Ohio, between 1916 and 1920 [15–19]. Sodium iodide was found to be effective in preventing goiter and in treating existing goiter, and by 1924, iodized salt was introduced in Michigan for general prophylaxis [20]. Iodized salt for prophylaxis of goiter was implemented in various cantons in Switzerland in the early 1920s, an effort that had to overcome many difficulties, including disagreement among scientists and local opposition [5, 21]. With more widespread use of iodized salt, there was a decline in goiter and cretinism in parts of Europe.

Goiter and cretinism gained renewed attention in studies conducted in Papua New Guinea in the 1950s and 1960s. These studies showed that injections of iodized oil could prevent goiter and cretinism in isolated mountain villages [22, 23].

Although various international organizations called for the eradication of iodine deficiency from 1974 to 1983, little action took place during this decade [24]. The term

**Table 17.1**
**Spectrum of iodine deficiency disorders**

| | |
|---|---|
| Fetus | Abortions |
| | Stillbirths |
| | Congenital anomalies |
| | Increased perinatal mortality |
| | Increased infant mortality |
| | Neurological cretinism: mental deficiency, deaf mutism, spastic diplegia, squint |
| | Myxoedematous cretinism: dwarfism, mental deficiency |
| | Psychomotor defects |
| Neonate | Neonatal goiter |
| | Neonatal hypothyroidism |
| Child and adolescent | Goiter |
| | Juvenile hypothyroidism |
| | Retarded physical development |
| Adult | Goiter with its complications |
| | Hypothyroidism |
| | Impaired mental function |
| | Iodine-induced hyperthyroidism |

*Source:* After [25].

*iodine deficiency disorders* was introduced in 1983 to encompass the wide spectrum of the effect of iodine deficiency on health, including physical impairment and mental retardation (Table 17.1) [25]. A report by a special committee of the European Thyroid Association showed that iodine deficiency disorders were still a serious problem in many European countries in the 1980s, contrary to the general impression that the problem had largely been eradicated in Europe [26]. The International Council for Control of Iodine Deficiency Disorders (ICCIDD) was established in 1985 with the support of United Nations International Children's Emergency Fund (UNICEF) [24], and this expert council remains a driving force behind the global eradication of iodine deficiency disorders.

## 17.4   EPIDEMIOLOGY

### 17.4.1   Geographical Distribution

There is a natural cycle of iodine in nature between the ocean, the atmosphere, rainfall, and runoff of rainfall into streams and rivers (Fig. 17.1) [24]. The ocean contains most of the iodine on the earth's surface, with a concentration of iodide of 50–60 µg/L. Sunlight oxidizes iodide in seawater to elemental iodine, which is volatile and evaporates from the surface of the ocean. The concentration of iodine in the air is about 0.7 µg/m$^3$. Iodine in the atmosphere is returned to the surface of the earth by rain, which has iodine concentrations of 1.8 to 8.5 µg/L. Iodine is leached from the soil by rain, flooding, deforestation, and glaciation. Crops and animals raised on iodine-poor soils will have low iodine content. Thus, iodine deficiency disorders tend to occur most commonly in areas where the soil is poor in iodine, especially mountainous regions such

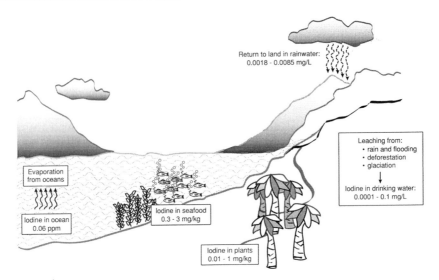

**Fig. 17.1.** Natural cycle of iodine.

as the Alps, Andes, and Himalayas, and large river floodplains and deltas, such as that of the Ganges and Irawaddy. The iodine content of the soil is usually reflected in the concentration of iodine in drinking water. For example, in India the iodine content of drinking water in iodine-deficient areas is 0.1–1.2 µg/L, and in the city of New Delhi, which is not iodine deficient, it is 9.0 µg/L [24].

### 17.4.2 Prevalence

The largest populations at risk of iodine deficiency disorders used to be in the eastern Mediterranean region, followed by Africa and Latin America (Table 17.2). It was estimated in 1990 that there were 655 million individuals in the world with goiter. In Asia, goiter prevalence was highest in China, Indonesia, and countries along the Himalayan mountains, such as India, Bhutan, Nepal, and Pakistan. Among countries with a high prevalence of goiter in Africa were Zaire, Tanzania, Sudan, and Cameroon. Goiter remained a major problem in countries along the Andean chain, such as Peru, Bolivia, Colombia, and Ecuador.

Long-term iodine prophylaxis has contributed to the decline of goiter in some parts of Europe [27], but even as late as the mid-1980s, goiter was a major problem in some European countries, such as Germany, Spain, Portugal, Italy, Turkey, and Greece, where national programs to iodize salt did not exist [28–31]. Even by 1992, iodine deficiency was considered to be under control in Europe only in several northern European countries and Switzerland [32]. The global prevalence of goiter and cretinism has markedly decreased in most regions and countries in the face of efforts to iodize salt worldwide, but because of a more accurate evaluation of the status of iodine nutrition in many parts of the world, the prevalence of iodine deficiency worldwide was still 38% in 1999 [33] and was 36.5% in school-aged children in 2003 [34].

Table 17.2

Total number of people and percent of regional population living in areas at risk of iodine deficiency disorder (IDD) or affected by IDD and cretinism in 1990

| WHO region | Total Population (millions) | At risk of IDD | | Affected by goiter | | Affected by cretinism | |
|---|---|---|---|---|---|---|---|
| | | Millions | % of region | Millions | % of region | Millions | % of region |
| Africa | 550 | 181 | 32.8 | 86 | 15.6 | 1.1 | 0.2 |
| Americas | 727 | 168 | 23.1 | 63 | 8.7 | 0.6 | 0.9 |
| Eastern Med | 406 | 173 | 42.6 | 93 | 22.9 | 0.9 | 2.3 |
| Europe | 847 | 141 | 16.7 | 97 | 11.4 | 0.9 | 1.1 |
| Southeast Asia | 1,355 | 486 | 35.9 | 176 | 13.0 | 3.2 | 1.3 |
| Western Pacific | 1,553 | 423 | 27.2 | 141 | 9.0 | 4.5 | 2.9 |
| Total | 5,438 | 1,572 | 28.9 | 655 | 12.0 | 11.2 | 2.0 |

*Source:* After [3].

## 17.4.3   Risk Factors

The most important risk factor for iodine deficiency disorders is residence in an area where soil and water are poor in iodine and where the primary sources of plant and animal foods are locally derived. Substances known as goitrogens are widely found in some vegetables and can interfere with the metabolism of iodine [35]. Cabbage, sweet potato, brussel sprouts, and turnips contain goitrogens. Cassava contains high concentrations of thiocyanates (SCNs) and has been implicated in the pathogenesis of goiter in Zaire [36]. Women of reproductive age, pregnant women, and young children are at the highest risk of iodine deficiency because of the impact of iodine deficiency on brain development. Among schoolchildren, girls appear to be at a higher risk of goiter than boys.

## 17.5   METABOLISM OF IODINE

### 17.5.1   Iodine Absorption and Transport

Dietary iodide (inorganic, bound form of iodine) is rapidly absorbed in the stomach and intestine. Iodate, the form of iodine used in iodized salt, is reduced in the blood and rapidly absorbed. The normal requirement for iodine is 100 to 150 μg per day [37]. Iodide circulates freely in the blood, not bound to proteins, and it is trapped by the thyroid and kidney. Iodine is excreted by the kidney, and the concentration of urinary iodine correlates well with the intake of iodine. Small amounts of iodine are excreted in saliva, sweat, and tears.

### 17.5.2   Iodine Storage

The human body contains about 15 to 20 mg of iodine, of which 70–80% is found in the thyroid gland. The thyroid traps iodine through an active transport mechanism known as the *iodine pump*, and iodine trapping is regulated by thyroid-stimulating hormone (TSH), or thyrotrophin, released from the pituitary gland. More trapping of iodine occurs if an individual has had long-standing iodine deficiency rather than in a situation of adequate iodine intake. The thyroid must trap about 60 µg of iodine per day to maintain an adequate supply of thyroxine [24]. The iodine content of the thyroid is generally related to iodine intake. If the iodine supply has been abundant, the thyroid may contain 10–20 mg of iodine, but in a situation of chronic iodine deficiency, the thyroid may contain as little as 200 µg of iodine.

### 17.5.3   Synthesis of Thyroid Hormones

The thyroid is a highly vascularized organ that contains many follicles. The follicles consist of thyroid cells surrounding colloid, and the main constituent of the colloid is thyroglobulin, a storage form of thyroid hormones. Iodine is an essential constituent of thyroid hormones 3,5,3',5'-tetraiodothyronine, thyroxine ($T_4$) and triiodothyronine ($T_3$). Thyroglobulin is synthesized from amino acids in thyroid cells and moves into the colloid. Iodide moves into the colloid of the thyroid by passive diffusion. In the colloid, iodide is oxidized by hydrogen peroxide from the thyroid peroxidase system, combines with tyrosine in thyroglobulin to form monoiodotyrosine (MIT) and diiodo-tyrosine (DIT). MIT and DIT continue oxidation and couple to form iodotyrosines. The iodinated thyroglobulin is absorbed back into the thyroid cell by pinocytosis and subsequently undergoes proteolysis, and $T_3$ and $T_4$ are released into the blood.

Iodine metabolism and the synthesis of thyroid hormones are regulated by complex interactions involving the brain, pituitary, thyroid, and iodine intake. Iodine uptake by the thyroid, synthesis of MIT and DIT, and secretion of $T_3$ and $T_4$ are regulated by TSH, which is secreted by the pituitary. Secretion of TSH in turn is regulated by the level of circulating $T_4$ and by thyrotrophin-releasing hormone (TRH) secreted by the hypothalamus. TRH release is influenced by neurotransmitters such as adrenalin, noradrenalin, serotonin, and dopamine. Further details of this complex regulation can be found elsewhere [38].

### 17.5.4   Transport and Turnover of Thyroid Hormones

In the blood, $T_3$ and $T_4$ are bound by different proteins produced in the liver, such as transthyretin, albumin, and thyroid-binding globulin (TBG). About three quarters of $T_4$ is normally bound to TBG. $T_4$ is found in much higher concentrations in the blood than $T_3$, and most of the $T_3$ in plasma is derived from peripheral tissues, where it is generated by monodeiodination of $T_4$. Other metabolic derivatives of thyroid hormones, such as $rT_3$ and 3,3'-diiodo-L-thyronine, are also found in the blood. Three deiodinases have been identified that catalyze monodeiodination of the outer ring [39]. Further deiodination of the inner ring deactivates $T_3$ and $T_4$. The three deiodinases contain selenocysteine; thus, selenium status may have an important influence on thyroid hormone metabolism, as discussed elsewhere in this chapter (see Section 17.8).

### 17.5.5   Thyroid Hormones and Gene Expression

Thyroid hormones are involved in the regulation of development and differentiation of nearly all organs and systems through their influence on gene expression. $T_3$ influences gene expression through thyroid hormone receptors (TRs), nuclear receptors that belong to a superfamily of DNA-binding proteins that includes receptors for retinoic acid (RAR; retinoic X receptor [RXR]), vitamin D (VDR), and steroids. Different isoforms of TRs

($TR\alpha_1$, $TR\alpha_2$, $TR\beta_1$, and $TR\beta_2$) have been described [40], and the expression of the TR isoform varies by organ type [41]. Specific sequences of DNA that bind TRs are known as thyroid hormone response elements (TREs) [42]. TRs bind $T_3$ and form heterodimers with retinoid X receptors (RXRs) in the form of RXR-TR [43]. The ligand for RXR is 9-*cis* retinoic acid. In addition, RXR can form heterodimers with the VDR [44]. $T_3$-responsive genes can be repressed by RXR-RXR homodimers [45]. A complex network of interaction exists among TRs, retinoid receptors, and other nuclear receptors. Thyroid hormone coactivators, corepressors, and cointegrators are involved in regulation of transcription by TR, and transcriptional activities are regulated by the relative presence or absence of $T_3$ [46, 47].

## 17.6 ROLE OF IODINE IN BIOLOGICAL FUNCTIONS

### 17.6.1 Metabolism

Thyroid hormones have major effects on the metabolism of proteins, carbohydrates, and lipids and are prime regulators of the basal metabolic rate. Thus, a wide variety of physiological activities, including heart rate, respiration, oxygen consumption, and nutrient metabolism are affected. Much of this regulation occurs through modulation of gene transcription by thyroid hormones. Thyroid hormones may also influence energy metabolism through direct and indirect regulation of mitochondrial activities [48].

### 17.6.2 Growth and Development

The synthesis of growth hormone is regulated in part by thyroid hormones [49], and physiological concentrations of circulating thyroid hormones appear to be necessary to maintain normal secretion of growth hormone by the pituitary [50]. Thyroid hormones play a role in normal bone cell growth and development [51], and in vitro studies suggested that thyroid hormones influence osteoblastic differentiation [52].

### 17.6.3 Brain Development

Thyroid hormones are involved in the early growth and differentiation of the brain and nervous system of the fetus [53–57]. The consequence of iodine deficiency during pregnancy is impaired synthesis of thyroid hormones by the mother and the fetus. An insufficient supply of thyroid hormones to the developing brain may result in mental retardation. Thyroid hormones appear to ensure the coordination of developmental events through regulation of oligodendroglial and neuronal differentiation and cell death [58]. $T_3$ has been shown to regulate several specific brain genes [58].

Brain growth is characterized by two periods of maximal growth velocity [59]. The first one occurs during the first and second trimesters between the third and the fifth months of gestation. This phase corresponds to neuronal multiplication, migration, and organization. The second phase takes place from the third trimester onward up to the second and third years postnatally. It corresponds to glial cell multiplication, migration, and myelization. The first phase occurs before fetal thyroid has reached its functional capacity. It is now largely agreed that during this phase, the supply of thyroid hormones to the growing fetus is almost exclusively of maternal origin, while during the second phase, the supply of thyroid hormones to the fetus is essentially of fetal origin [60].

As a matter of fact, an important recent issue on thyroid function and regulation in the fetus is the concept that thyroid hormones are transferred from mother to fetus both before and probably after the onset of fetal thyroid function, contrasting with the previous dogma that this transfer is minimal or does not exist [61]. In humans, $T_4$ can be found in the first trimester coelomic fluid from 6 weeks of gestational age, a long time before the onset of secretion of $T_4$ by the fetal thyroid, which occurs at the 24th week of gestation [62]. Nuclear $T_3$ receptors and the amount of $T_3$ bound to these receptors increase about six- to tenfold between 10 and 16 weeks, also before the secretion of hormones by the fetal thyroid [63]. The $T_4$ and $T_3$ found in early human fetuses up to midgestation are likely to be entirely or mostly of maternal origin. This transfer is decreasing but persists during later gestation as Vulsma et al. [64] suggested that up to 30% of serum $T_4$ in cord blood at birth could be of maternal origin, although a much lower percentage was reported by Delange et al. [65].

### 17.6.4   Iodine and Immune Function

There is some indirect evidence that iodine deficiency may contribute to abnormalities in immune function, but research in this area has largely been limited to animal studies of hypothyroidism and studies of the in vitro effects of thyroid hormones on immune effector cells. Thyroid hormones appear to be essential for normal lymphopoiesis and generation of antibody responses. Removal of the thyroid gland in rats resulted in the reduction of circulating peripheral blood lymphocytes, depression of antibody responses to experimental antigens, and reduced proliferative responses of spleen cells to mitogen, and abnormal immune responses could be restored by injections with thyroxine [66]. Antibody responses to sheep erythrocytes were depressed by a thyroid block in an avian model [67]. $T_3$-treated mice had higher antibody responses to sheep red blood cells [68]. Natural killer cell activity was enhanced by $T_4$ administration in mouse studies [69, 70]. Decreased proliferative responses of thymocytes to mitogen have been noted in chicks with hypothyroidism [71]. $T_3$ enhanced proliferation of murine lymphocytes to phytohemagglutinin in vitro [72] and enhanced differentiation of human B lymphocytes in vitro [73, 74]. In western India, the seroprevalence of toxoplasmosis was significantly higher among children with grade II goiter than children with no goiter or grade I goiter [75].

## 17.7   PATHOPHYSIOLOGY OF IODINE DEFICIENCY

### 17.7.1   Dietary Sources and Intake of Iodine

The richest dietary sources of iodine are seafood and seaweeds. Meat from animals that have grazed in areas with sufficient iodine in the soil can also constitute a significant source of iodine. Crops grown in iodine-sufficient soils may supply some dietary iodine. In most populations, iodized salt is the primary source of dietary iodine. Iodine in drinking water is usually only a small part of total iodine intake, providing less than 10% of daily iodine in the most iodine-rich areas. Some iodine is usually lost from foods during cooking; for example, during frying or boiling, as much as half the iodine content of fish may be lost.

### 17.7.2   Goitrogens

Environmental goitrogens are substances found in foods and water that interfere with the metabolism of iodine and in some circumstances will exacerbate iodine deficiency. These goitrogens include cyanogenic glycosides, thioglycosides, isothiocyanates, and

SCNs [76], and goitrogens can compete with iodine at the site of the iodine pump of the thyroid [24]. Several goiter endemias have been attributed to environmental goitrogens, for example, in Tasmania, eastern Nigeria, Colombia, and Greece [77]. It has been shown in Zaire that cassava plays a definite role in the development of endemic goiter. Cassava contains linamarin, a cyanogenic glucoside that is converted into SCN in the liver. Elevated serum levels of SCN were found in all age groups in the affected populations. SCN aggravates the effects of iodine deficiency by inhibiting the trapping of iodide by the thyroid gland [36, 78]. In general, iodized salt or other interventions with iodine can overcome the negative effects of environmental goitrogens

### 17.7.3   Iodine Dietary Requirements

Recommended intakes of iodine have been made by the World Health Organization (WHO), and recommendations are highest for pregnant and lactating women (Table 17.3) [79]. Very recently, the recommended iodine intake for pregnant and lactating women was increased to $250\,\mu g$/day [80].

## 17.8   CLINICAL MANIFESTATIONS OF IODINE DEFICIENCY DISORDERS

### 17.8.1   Goiter

Goiter, an enlargement of the thyroid gland, usually represents thyroid hyperplasia in response to insufficient iodine intake [81]. With iodine deficiency, $T_4$ concentrations in the blood fall, and the feedback of low $T_4$ on the pituitary leads to increased production of TSH. TSH stimulates hyperplasia of the thyroid with increased uptake of iodide, and the size of the thyroid increases, resulting in a goiter. By palpation on physical examination, *goiter* is defined as enlargement of the thyroid such that the lateral lobes are larger than the terminal phalanx of the thumb of the person who is being examined. The severity of goiter is usually proportional to the severity of iodine deficiency, and with persistent enlargement of the thyroid, nodules can form. Extremely large goiters may compress the trachea and interfere with respiration. In areas of goiter endemics, the daily iodine intake is usually well below $100\,\mu g$/day, and in the most severe goiter endemics, iodine intakes as low as $10\,\mu g$/day are known [82].

Endemic goiter has been occasionally associated with malnutrition [83, 84], although protein calorie malnutrition decreases the prevalence of goiter, to be expected on the basis of iodine intake [36]. Nutritional status and blood retinol concentrations were lower among individuals with goiter [85]. Impaired intestinal absorption of iodine has

Table 17.3
**Recommended daily intakes of iodine**

| Age/state | Micrograms/day |
| --- | --- |
| 0–59 months | 90 |
| 7–12 years | 120 |
| 12 years to adulthood | 150 |
| Pregnancy | 250 |
| Lactation | 250 |

*Source*: From refs. 79 and 80.

been described in children with malnutrition [86]. In Senegal, preschool children with acute malnutrition had lower serum $T_3$ concentrations than controls, and levels returned to normal after 2 weeks of refeeding [87]. Selenium deficiency has been implicated in the pathogenesis of goiter and cretinism, and this may be related to the selenocysteine involved in thyroid hormone metabolism [88–90]. Multiple micronutrient deficiencies have been associated with poor iodine status in children [91].

### 17.8.2 Cretinism

Endemic cretinism is usually found where the prevalence of endemic goiter is higher than 30% and the median urinary iodine concentration is less than 25 µg/g creatinine [92]. Endemic cretinism is characterized by mental retardation, which may be mild to severe, and a continuous spectrum of growth and neurological manifestations [93]. Two extreme types of cretinism have been described: neurological cretinism and myxoedematous, or hypothyroid, cretinism [24, 93]. In neurological cretinism, stature is usually normal, mental retardation is often severe, and deaf-mutism and cerebral diplegia are often present. In hypothyroid cretinism, severe growth retardation is present, mental retardation is less severe, and coarse, dry skin, and husky voice are present, but deaf-mutism and cerebral diplegia are absent. Intermediate forms between the two extreme types of cretinism are frequently reported [24, 93].

Neurological signs of endemic cretinism appear to be the result of hypothyroxinemia in the mother and fetus occurring during early pregnancy [56, 94]. Iodine treatment to the mother up to the end of the second trimester of pregnancy can prevent fetal brain damage due to iodine deficiency [95], but iodine treatment is probably most effective in preventing endemic cretinism when given prior to conception [96]. The hypothyroid signs in cretinism are due to thyroid failure acquired lately during pregnancy and early in the postnatal period, for example, under the influence of combined iodine and selenium deficiencies [88, 90, 93].

Sporadic cretinism, or sporadic congenital hypothyroidism, is not related to iodine deficiency and is used to describe a congenital defect in thyroid hormones or congenital absence or defect of a thyroid gland. Its incidence is 3 in 10,000 in industrialized countries that are receiving adequate iodine [97, 98].

### 17.8.3 Growth and Development

Maternal iodine deficiency during pregnancy causes retarded development of the fetus, and the more severe consequences include cretinism, as mentioned in the preceding section. Other, more insidious effects include impaired psychomotor and cognitive development [57, 99]. Children growing in iodine-deficient areas appear to have impaired psychomotor development and lower school performance. Impaired psychomotor development was found in apparently normal schoolchildren from an area of iodine deficiency in Iran [100]. Lower school performance and significant differences in IQ have been reported in various studies comparing children from iodine-deficient and iodine-sufficient areas [101]. In a case-control study of preschool children in northern Zaire, endemic goiter without cretinism was not associated with any major growth impairment, but no studies of thyroid status were performed in either cases or controls [102]. Thyroid function was evaluated in children with short stature in north India, and nearly half the children had abnormal thyroid function [103].

### 17.8.4    Reproductive Failure

Iodine deficiency in women is associated with infertility [104] and impaired fetal development [105]. Higher rates of spontaneous abortions and stillbirths have been reported from areas of iodine deficiency [24], and correction of hypothyroidism in pregnant women reduces these adverse outcomes [106]. Treatment with oral iodized oil during pregnancy significantly lowered the rates of abortions, stillbirths, and premature births in a mountainous area in Algeria [107]. Trends in salt iodization suggested that improvement of iodine status was associated with reductions in stillbirth and congenital anomalies [108].

### 17.8.5    Perinatal, Infant, and Child Mortality

High perinatal mortality has been associated with goiter during pregnancy [109]. Clinical trials conducted in different parts of the world suggested that iodine supplementation, in the form of iodized oil injections, oral iodized oil, or iodinated water supply, can reduce neonatal, infant, and child mortality (Table 17.4). Infant mortality was lower among infants born to women who were treated with intramuscular iodized oil around the 28th week of pregnancy compared with infants born to control women in Zaire [110]. In a controlled clinical trial in Papua New Guinea, cumulative long-term survival of children was significantly higher among those whose mothers received iodinated oil before conception (Fig. 17.2) [111]. The causes of death of children in this study were not known. In a rice-farming community in West Java, Indonesia, oral iodized oil, 100 mg, given directly to 6-week-old infants reduced mortality between 6 weeks and 6 months by about 50% compared with placebo (Fig. 17.3) [112]. Comparison of infant mortality rates between villages that received iodine in irrigation water versus control villages that did not in rural China suggested that iodinated water could reduce infant mortality by approximately half (Fig. 17.4) [113].

## 17.9    ASSESSMENT OF IODINE STATUS

Several indicators exist for the assessment of iodine status, both on the individual and population levels. WHO has developed criteria for iodine deficiency as a public health problem in populations [3] (Table 17.5).

Table 17.4
Controlled trials of iodine supplementation and perinatal, infant, and child mortality

| Location | Subjects | n | Treatment effect | Reference |
|---|---|---|---|---|
| Zaire | Pregnant women | 5,471 | One-third reduction in infant mortality | 109 |
| Papua New Guinea | Women, infants | 522 | 50% reduction in 15-year mortality | 111 |
| Indonesia | Infants, 6 weeks old | 617 | 50% reduction in mortality to 6 months | 112 |
| China | Villages, all population | 37,000 | 50% reduction in infant mortality | 113 |

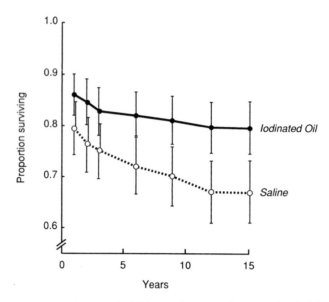

**Fig. 17.2.** Cumulative survival rates of children whose mothers received either iodinated oil or saline (bars indicate 95% confidence interval) [111].

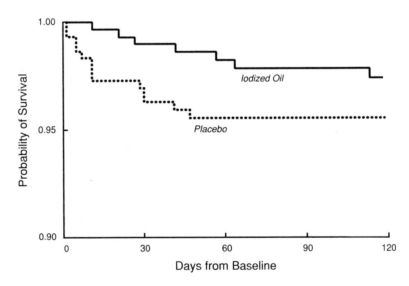

**Fig. 17.3.** Survival curves of infants receiving oral iodized oil or placebo in West Java, Indonesia [112].

### 17.9.1  Goiter Rate

The goiter rate is often used for the assessment of iodine status in a population, and the goiter rate includes both visible and palpable goiter. WHO has adopted a grading classification for goiter (Table 17.6) [3]. Determination of thyroid size by ultrasonography is more accurate than palpation, especially in areas where iodine deficiency is mildly

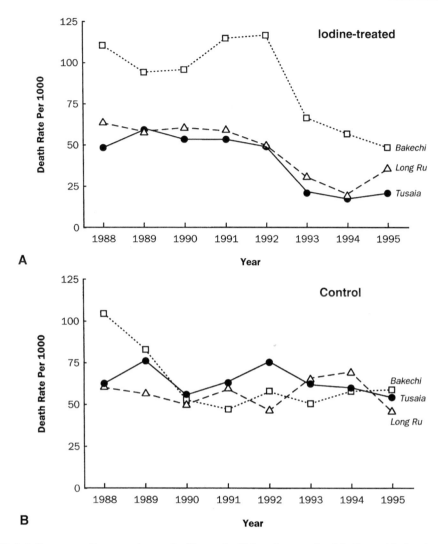

**Fig. 17.4.** Infant mortality rates in rural villages in China that received iodinated irrigation water (**A**) or were control villages (**B**). (Adapted with permission from [113].)

Table 17.5
**World Health Organization criteria for iodine deficiency as a public health problem in populations**

| Indicator | Population assessed | Mild | Moderate | Severe |
|---|---|---|---|---|
| Goiter by palpation (%) | School children | 5–19.9 | 20–30 | >30 |
| Thyroid volume by ultrasound (>97th percentile) (%) | School children | 5–19.9 | 20–30 | >30 |
| Median urinary iodine (μg/L) | School children | 50–99 | 20–49 | <20 |
| Thyroid-stimulating (>5 mU/L whole blood) hormone | Neonates | 3–19.9 | 20–40 | >40 |

Source: From [3].

**Table 17.6**
**Classification for goiter**

| | |
|---|---|
| Grade 0 | No palpable or visible goiter |
| Grade 1 | A mass in the neck that is consistent with an enlarged thyroid that is palpable but not visible when the neck is in the normal position; it moves upward in the neck as the subject swallows; nodular alterations can occur even when the thyroid is not enlarged |
| Grade 2 | A swelling in the neck that is visible when the neck is in a normal position and is consistent with an enlarged thyroid when the neck is palpated |

*Source:* From [3].

endemic and goiters in children are small. Health workers who are well trained in ultrasonography can conduct up to 200 examinations per day [114]. WHO and ICCIDD has recently recommended reference values for thyroid volume in school-aged children [114] based on variation in thyroid size varies by age, height, and weight [115] and data from a survey from 12 European countries [116]. These reference values were subsequently updated by a WHO working group [117].

### 17.9.2    *Urinary Iodine Concentrations*

Urinary iodine concentrations are a good indicator of iodine status in representative groups of subjects [3], and iodine can be easily measured in large numbers of samples [118]. Because urinary iodine concentrations tend to be skewed, the median value is usually used in describing urinary iodine concentrations in a population. Urinary iodine concentrations are classified as less than 20 µg/L (severe deficiency), 20–49 µg/L (moderate deficiency), 50–99 µg/L (mild deficiency), and 100–200 µg/L (adequate) [3]. A large study conducted among schoolchildren in Indonesia [119] and many others confirmed that urinary iodine concentrations are the best indicator for field studies for the assessment of iodine deficiency.

### 17.9.3    *Blood Thyroid-Stimulating Hormone*

Blood TSH can be used as an indirect indicator of iodine status [120] and has been used for screening of neonatal hypothyroidism. Heel-stick blood samples can be collected from neonates, spotted on filter paper, dried, and later eluted and measured using enzyme-linked immunosorbent assay [121]. A normal range of TSH is 0.17–2.90 µU/mL. The degree of iodine deficiency in a population can be evaluated on the basis of the frequency of neonatal blood TSH above the cutoff point of 3 µU/mL (Table 17.5).

### 17.10    PREVENTION OF IODINE DEFICIENCY DISORDERS

Iodized salt is currently the primary strategy for the prevention of iodine deficiency disorders worldwide, and oral iodized oil is being used in some areas to target specific communities at risk of iodine deficiency disorders. Intramuscular iodized oil injections were used in earlier investigations of iodine deficiency disorders. Iodination of the water supply has been a useful strategy in some communities but is limited to conditions where the whole population and the livestock have access to a single source of water.

### 17.10.1  Iodized Salt

Iodized salt is a term used to describe two different forms of iodine in salt: iodide, such as potassium iodide (KI), and potassium iodate (KIO$_3$) [24]. Potassium iodide was first used in salt iodization, but iodate is more stable under different climatic conditions and is now the recommended form for salt iodization. *Universal salt iodization* is defined as fortification of all salt for human and animal consumption [122, 123]. The goal of salt iodization is to provide about 150 μg of iodine per day in dietary salt, taking into account factors such as heat and humidity. Warm and humid conditions can influence the retention of iodate in salt. In typical circumstances, in which about 20% of the iodine is lost from salt from the production site to the household and another 20% is lost during cooking before consumption, and the average individual salt intake is 10 g/day, the iodine concentration in salt at the point of production should be within the range of 20–40 mg of iodine per kilogram of salt (20–40 ppm of iodine) [124]. This is estimated to provide 150 μg of iodine per person per day. In countries where iodized salt is used in processed foods, the iodine content in salt should be closer to the lower end of this range and vice versa [124]. The usual salt intakes can vary from country to country, but the usual consumption levels are 5–15 g/day for children and adults [3, 125].

Some studies suggested that the level of iodine in salt is often below the minimum required by local governments. A survey of iodine in salt samples across the country in Guatemala showed that more than 60% of samples were below the legally mandated level for iodized salt [126]. A national survey in Kenya in 1990 and 1991 showed that most samples of iodized salt did not reach the minimal iodine concentrations as required by government regulation [127]. Under the National Iodine Deficiency Disorder Control Programme in India, iodized salt containing at least 15 ppm iodine is supposed to be provided to beneficiaries; however, a survey of salt samples showed that nearly a fifth of samples did not contain adequate iodine [128]. On the other hand, it occurred occasionally that, on the contrary, the iodine content of salt largely exceeded the recommended level. This resulted in the occurrence of sporadic cases of iodine-induced hyperthyroidism (IIH) [129]. Therefore, adequate monitoring of the level of salt iodization and of the status of iodine nutrition of the populations has to be strictly organized [130].

In spite of these regrettable side effects, it is recognized that the benefits of correcting iodine deficiency by iodized salt by far outweigh the risks [131, 132]. Salt iodization appears as a particularly successful public health program as the access to iodized salt in households increased from 5–10% in 1990 to 68% in 1999 [33] and was accompanied by a spectacular decrease in the occurrence of brain damage and mental retardation due to iodine deficiency [34, 133].

### 17.10.2  Oral Iodized Oil

Oral iodized oil has been used to prevent iodine deficiency disorders in populations located where iodized salt is difficult to procure and where certain groups (i.e., pregnant women) are at high risk [134, 135]. In adults, a single dose of 460 mg of iodine is recommended [134], and a single annual dose of 240 mg of iodine seems to be adequate for children [135]. Lower doses of 47 mg and 118 mg of iodine in oral iodized oil were also found to be effective in reducing hypothyroidism in children in Zaire [136]. Among schoolchildren in western Sudan, oral iodized oil was as effective as an iodized oil injection in reducing goiter and preventing the recurrence of goiter [137], and in a clinical trial in eastern Zaire, oral iodized oil was also found to be an effective alternative to iodized oil injections [138, 139]. Oral iodized oil seemed to increase the mental performance of school-aged girls in a trial conducted in Bolivia [140].

For correction of iodine deficiency in children, single oral doses of 240 mg iodine in poppy seed oil appeared to be the optimal dose for 6-month coverage [141]. A trial conducted among schoolchildren in Malawi suggested that intestinal parasitic infections may interfere with the absorption of oral iodized oil [142]. Oral iodized oil is considered to be safe for pregnant women and can be given any time during pregnancy [143, 144].

Childhood immunization programs may provide infrastructure for the delivery of oral iodized oil to infants in areas where iodine deficiency disorders are a public health problem and iodized salt is not readily available [145]. There was initial concern that oral iodized oil might theoretically interfere with trivalent oral poliovirus vaccine when given together because the iodide could potentially inactivate the live poliovirus. In vitro studies suggested that there was no interference [146], and a clinical trial in Indonesia demonstrated that oral iodized oil given at 6 weeks of age did not interfere with seroconversion to trivalent oral poliovirus vaccine [147]. WHO recommends the following doses of oral iodized oil every 12–18 months in areas where iodine deficiency disorders are a serious problem: for children younger than 1 year, 0.5 mL (240 mg); for children older than 1 year and for women of childbearing age, 1.0 mL (480 mg) [148].

### 17.10.3   Iodized Oil Injections

Much knowledge about the use of iodized oil injections came from studies conducted in Papua New Guinea, Latin America, and Zaire from the late 1960s and 1970s [24, 149, 150]. In part because of concern over the AIDS pandemic and use of needles, oral iodized oil has largely replaced iodized oil injections.

### 17.10.4   Other Strategies

Monthly administration of 30 mg iodine in the form of a 10% potassium iodide oral solution was effective in the prophylaxis of iodine deficiency in schoolchildren in Zimbabwe [151]. Iodization of drinking water has been used as a strategy to reduce iodine deficiency disorders in developing countries such as Malaysia [152] and Mali [153]. Iodization of irrigation water improved iodine content of soil, crops, and animals in an area of rural China, and the annual costs of the project ranged from $0.05/person in the first year to $0.12/person in the second year [154]. In a study in western Sudan, iodine-saturated silicon matrices placed in wells and hand pumps significantly increased media urinary iodine concentrations and greatly reduced the prevalence of goiter [155].

Other strategies that have been proposed for prevention of iodine deficiency disorders include iodine fortification of flour [156], addition of iodine to fertilizers, and incorporation of iodine into school snacks and beverages. Increasing the dietary iodine consumption by chickens and livestock by the use of fish flour, seaweed, or iodine supplementation may be another strategy to increase the iodine content of meat, poultry, and dairy products. However, because of the difficulties in controlling the iodine intake by means of these different procedures, the current recommendation is to focus on the strategy of universal salt iodization with possible additional programs of iodine supplementation in pregnant and lactating women and young infants, that is, in the most susceptible age groups to the effects of iodine deficiency as long as the programs of salt iodization have not yet adequately covered the whole population [80].

## 17.11   CONCLUSIONS

Iodine deficiency is the leading cause of preventable mental retardation in the world and is a preventable cause of morbidity and mortality. Great progress has been made in providing access to iodized salt. As indicated by a WHO/UNICEF/ICCIDD report to the World Health Assembly in 1999 [33], of 5 billion people living in countries with iodine-deficiency disorders, 68% now have access to iodized salt. Of 130 countries affected by iodine deficiency disorders, 104 countries (81%) now have an intersectoral coordinating body, and 98 (75%) have legislation in place for iodized salt.

Major challenges remain in ensuring the sustainability of salt iodization through monitoring and enforcement. The goals for monitoring include salt iodine at a level of 90% effectively iodized and urine iodine in the normal range (median excretion of 100–300 µg/L). The lower level of 100 µg/L is necessary to ensure normal brain development in the fetus and young infant, and the upper level of 300 µg/L is to minimize the occurrence of iodine-induced hyperthyroidism. Further momentum on the governmental level and in the scientific and medical communities should help ensure the practical elimination of iodine deficiency disorders worldwide.

## REFERENCES

1. United Nations International Children's Emergency Fund. The state of the world's children 1995. New York: Oxford University Press, 1995.
2. Hetzel BS, Pandav CS. SOS for a billion: the conquest of iodine deficiency disorders. New York: Oxford University Press, 1994.
3. World Health Organization/United Nations International Children's Emergency Fund /International Council for Control of Iodine Deficiency Disorders. Indicators for assessing iodine deficiency disorders and their control through salt iodization. Geneva: World Health Organization, 1994.
4. Stanbury JB, ed. The damaged brain of iodine deficiency. New York: Cognizant Communication, 1994.
5. Merke F. History and iconography of endemic goitre and cretinism. Berne, Switzerland: Huber 1984.
6. Courtois MB. Découverte d'une substance nouvelle dans le Vareck. Ann Chim Paris 1813;88:304–310.
7. Clow A, Clow NL. The chemical industry: interaction with the industrial revolution. In A history of technology. Singer C, Holmyard EJ, Hall AR, Williams TI, eds. New York: Oxford University Press, 1958:230–257.
8. Coindet JF. Découverte d'un nouveau remède contre le goître. Bibl universelle 1820;14:190–198.
9. Boussingault JB. Memoire sur les salines iodiferes des Andes. Ann Chim Phys 1833;54:163.
10. Chatin A. Existence de l'iode dans l'air, les eaux, le sol et les produits alimentaires. Ann Soc Météorol France 1859;7:50–107.
11. Anonymous. Goitre in Savoy. Lancet 1869;2:518.
12. Baillarger JGF. Enquête sur le goître et le crétinisme. Recueil des Travaux du Comité Consultatif d'Hygiène Publique de France. Paris: Baillière, 1873.
13. Hirsch A. Handbook of geographical and historical pathology. Vol. 2. Chronic infective, toxic, parasitic, septic and constitutional diseases. London: New Sydenham Society, 1885.

14. McCarrison R. The thyroid gland in health and disease. New York: Wood, 1917.

15. Marine D, Kimball OP. The prevention of simple goiter in man. A survey of the incidence and types of thyroid enlargements in the schoolgirls of Akron (Ohio), from the 5th to the 12th grades, inclusive: the plan of prevention proposed. J Lab Clin Med 1917–1918;3:40–48.

16. Kimball OP, Marine D. The prevention of simple goiter in man. Second paper. Arch Intern Med 1918;22:41–44

17. Kimball OP, Rogoff JM, Marine D. The prevention of simple goiter in man. Third paper. J Am Med Assoc 1919;73:1873–1874.

18. Marine D, Kimball OP. Prevention of simple goiter in man. Fourth paper. Arch Intern Med 1920;25:661–672.

19. Kimball OP. The prevention of simple goiter in man. Am J Med Sci 1922;163:634–649.

20. Altland JK, Brush BE. Goiter prevention in Michigan: results of 30 years' voluntary use of iodized salt. J Mich State Med Soc 1952;51:985–989.

21. Bürgi H., Supersaxo Z. and Selz B. Iodine deficiency diseases in Switzerland 100 years after Theodor Kocher's survey: a historical review with some new goitre prevalence data. Acta Endocrinol (Kbh) 1990;123:577–590.

22. McCullagh SF. The Huon Peninsula endemic: I. The effectiveness of an intramuscular depot of iodized oil in the control of endemic goitre. Med J Aust 1963;1:769–777.

23. Hetzel BS, Pharoah POD, eds. Endemic cretinism. Papua New Guinea: Institute of Human Biology, 1971.

24. Hetzel BS. The story of iodine deficiency: an international challenge in nutrition. Oxford, UK: Oxford University Press, 1989.

25. Hetzel BS. Iodine deficiency disorders (IDD) and their eradication. Lancet 1983;2:1126–1129.

26. Subcommittee for the Study of Endemic Goitre and Iodine Deficiency of the European Thyroid Association. Goitre and iodine deficiency in Europe. Lancet 1985;1:1289–1293.

27. Lamberg BA, Haikonen M, Mäkelä M, Jukkara A, Axelson E, Welin MG. Further decrease in thyroid uptake and disappearance of endemic goitre in children after 30 years of iodine prophylaxis in the east of Finland. Acta Endocrinol (Copenh) 1981;98:205–209.

28. Scriba PC. Goiter and iodine deficiency in Europe: a review. In: Treatment of endemic and sporadic goiter. Reinwein D, Scriba PC, eds. Stuttgart: Schattauer, 1985:19.

29. Sanchez-Franco F, Ferreiro Alaez L, Cacicedo L, Carcia MD, Morreale de Escobar G, Escobar del Rey F. Alteraciones por deficiencia de yodo en las Hurdes. III. Cretinismo. Endocrinologia (Barcelona) 1987;34(suppl 2):88–93.

30. Vigneri R. Studies on the goiter endemia in Sicily. J Clin Endocrinol Metab 1988;11:831–843.

31. Gutekunst R, Scriba PC. Goiter and iodine deficiency in Europe. The European Thyroid Association report as updated in 1988. J Endocrinol Invest 1989;12:209–220.

32. Delange F, Dunn JT, Glinoer D, eds. Iodine deficiency in Europe: a continuing concern. New York: Plenum, 1993.

33. World Health Organization. Progress towards the elimination of iodine deficiency disorders (IDD). WHO/NHD/99.4. Geneva: World Health Organization/United Nations International Children's Emergency Fund/International Council for Control of Iodine Deficiency Disorders, 1999.

34. Andersson M, Takkouche B, Egli I, Allen H E, de Benoist B. Global iodine status and progress over the last decade towards the elimination of iodine deficiency. Bull World Health Organ 2005;83:518–525.

35. Gaitan E. Environmental goitrogenesis. Boca Raton, FL: CRC, 1989.

36. Delange F, Iteke FB, Ermans AM, eds. Nutritional factors involved in the goitrogenic action of cassave. Ottawa: International Developmental Research Centre, 1982.

37. World Health Organization Study–Group on Endemic Goitre. Final report. Bull World Health Organ 1953;9:293–309.

38. DeGroot LJ, Larsen PR, Henneman G. The thyroid and its diseases. 6th ed. New York: Churchill Livingstone, 1996.

39. Kohrle J. Local activation and inactivation of thyroid hormones: the deiodinase family. Mol Cell Endocrinol 1999;151:103–119.

40. White P, Dauncey MJ. Differential expression of thyroid hormone receptor isoforms is strikingly related to cardiac and skeletal muscle phenotype during postnatal development. J Mol Endocrinol 1999;23:241–254.

41. Shahrara S, Drvota V, Sylven C. Organ specific expression of thyroid hormone receptor mRNA and protein in different human tissues. Biol Pharm Bull 1999;22:1027–1033.

42. Umesono K, Murakami KK, Thompson CC, Evans RM. Direct repeats as selective response elements for the thyroid hormone, retinoic acid, and vitamin $D_3$ receptors. Cell 1991;65:1255–1266.

43. Zhang XK, Hoffmann B, Tran PBV, Graupner G, Pfahl M. Retinoid X receptor is an auxiliary protein for thyroid hormone and retinoic acid receptors. Nature (London) 1992;355:441–446.

44. Thompson PD, Hsieh JC, Whitfield GK, Haussler CA, Jurutka PW, Galligan MA, Tillman JB, Spindler SR, Haussler MR. Vitamin D receptor displays DNA binding and transactivation as a heterodimer with the retinoid X receptor, but not with the thyroid hormone receptor. J Cell Biochem 1999;75:462–480.

45. Lehmann JM, Zhang XK, Graupner G, Lee MO, Hermann T, Hoffmann B, Pfahl M. Formation of retinoid X receptor homodimers leads to repression of $T_3$ response: hormonal cross talk by ligand-induced squelching. Mol Cell Biol 1993;13:7698–7707.

46. Koenig RJ. Thyroid hormone receptor coactivators and corepressors. Thyroid 1998;8:703–713.

47. Lee H, Yen PM. Recent advances in understanding thyroid hormone receptor coregulators. J Biomed Sci 1999;6:71–78.

48. Goglia F, Moreno N, Lanni A. Action of thyroid hormones at the cellular level: the mitochondrial target. FEBS Lett 1999;452:115–120.

49. Spindler SR, Mellon SH, Baxter JD. Growth hormone gene transcription is regulated by thyroid and glucocorticoid hormones in cultured rat pituitary tumor cells. J Biol Chem 1982;257:11627–11632.

50. Giustina A, Wehrenberg WB. Influence of thyroid hormones on the regulation of growth hormone secretion. Eur J Endocrinol 1995;133:646–653.

51. Perry HM. Thyroid hormones and mineral metabolism. In: Bone and mineral research, vol. 6. Peck WA, ed. New York: Elsevier, 1989:113–137.

52. Klaushofer K, Varga F, Glantschnig H, Fratzl-Zelman N, Czerwenka E, Leis HJ, Koller K, Peterlik M. The regulatory role of thyroid hormones in bone cell growth and differentiation. J Nutr 1995;125(suppl 7):1996S–2003S.

53. Mussa GC, Zaffaroni M, Mussa F. Thyroid and growth: thyroid hormones and development of the nervous system. J Endocrinol Invest 1989;12(suppl 3):85–89.

54. Chan S, Kilby M D. Thyroid hormone and central nervous system development. J Endocrinol 2000;165:1–8.

55. Morreale de Escobar G, Obregon MJ, Escbar del Rey F. Role of thyroid hormone during early brain development. Eur J Endocrinol 2004;151:U25–U37.

56. Auso E, Lavado-Autric R, Cuevas E, Escobar del Rey F, Morreale de Escobar G, Berbel P. A moderate and transient deficiency of maternal thyroid function at the beginning of fetal neocorticogenesis alters neuronal migration. Endocrinology 2004;145:4037–4047.

57. Delange F. Iodine deficiency as a cause of brain damage. Postgrad Med J 2001;77:217–220.

58. Bernal J, Nunez J. Thyroid hormones and brain development. Eur J Endocrinol 1995;133:390–398.

59. Dobbing J and Sands J. Quantitative growth and development of human brain. Arch Dis Child 1973;48:757–767.

60. Morreale de Escobar G, Obregon MJ, Escobar del Rey F. Is neuropsychological development related to maternal hypothyroidism or to maternal hypothyroxinemia? J Clin Endocrinol Metab 2000;85:3975–3987.

61. Fisher DA, Dussault JH, Sack J Chopra IJ. Ontogenesis of hypothalamic-pituitary-thyroid function and metabolism in man, sheep and rat. Recent Prog Horm Res 1977;35:59–116.

62. Contempré B, Jauniaux E, Calvo R, Jurkovic D, Campbell S, Morreale de Escobar G. Detection of thyroid hormones in human embryonic cavities during the first trimester of gestation. J Clin Endocrinol Metab 1993;77:1719–1722.

63. Bernal J, Pekonen F. Ontogenesis of the nuclear 3,5,3'-triiodothyronine receptor in the human fetal brain. Endocrinology 1984;114:677–679.

64. Vulsma T, Gons MH, de Vijlder JJM. Maternal-fetal transfer of thyroxine in congenital hypothyroidism due to a total organification defect or thyroid agenesis. N Engl J Med 1989;321:13–16.

65. Delange F, Fisher DA, Glinoer D. Research in congenital hypothyroidism. New York: Plenum Press, 1989;1–367

66. Fabris N. Immunodepression in thyroid-deprived animals. Clin Exp Immunol 1973;15:601–611.

67. Keast D, Ayre DJ. Antibody regulation in birds by thyroid hormone. Dev Comp Immunol 1980;4:323–330.

68. Chen Y. Effect of thyroxine on the immune response of mice in vivo and in vitro. Immunol Commun 1980;9:269–276.

69. Sharma SD, Tsai V, Proffitt MR. Enhancement of mouse natural killer cell activity by thyroxine. Cell Immunol 1982;73:83–97.

70. Provinciali M, Muzzioli M, Fabris N. Thyroxine-dependent modulation of natural killer activity. J Exp Pathol 1987;3:617–622.

71. Yam D, Heller D, Snapir N. The effect of the thyroidal state on the immunological state of the chicken. Dev Comp Immunol 1981;5:483–490.

72. Keast D, Taylor K. The effect of tri-iodothyronine on the phytohaemagglutinin response to T lymphocytes. Clin Exp Immunol 1982;47:217–220.

73. Paavonen T. Enhancement of human B lymphocyte differentiation in vitro by thyroid hormone. Scand J Immunol 1982;15:211–215.

74. Paavonen T. Hormonal regulation of lymphocyte functions. Med Biol 1987;65:229–240.

75. Singh S, Singh N, Pandav R, Pandav CS, Karmarkar MG. *Toxoplasma gondii* infection and its association with iodine deficiency in a residential school in a tribal area of Maharashtra. Indian J Med Res 1994;99:27–31.

76. Van Etten CH. Goitrogens. In: Toxic constituents of plant foodstuffs. Liener IE, ed. New York: Academic, 1969:103–134.

77. Gaitan E. Goitrogens in the etiology of endemic goiter. In: Endemic goiter and endemic cretinism. Iodine nutrition in health and disease. Stanbury JB, Hetzel BS, eds. New York: Wiley, 1980.

78. Vanderpas J, Bourdoux P, Lagasse R, Rivera M, Dramaix M, Lody D, Nelson G, Delange F, Ermans AM, Thilly CH. Endemic infantile hypothyroidism in a severe endemic goitre area of central Africa. Clin Endocrinol 1984;20:327–340.

79. World Health Organization, United Nations International Children's Emergency Fund, International Council for Control of Iodine Deficiency Disorders. Assessment of the iodine deficiency disorders and monitoring their elimination. Geneva: World Health Organization, 2001. WHO/NHD/01.1:1–107.

80. de Benoist B, Delange F. Report of a WHO Technical Consultation on prevention and control of iodine deficiency in pregnancy, lactation, and in children less than 2 years of age. Public Health Nutr 2007;10(1A):1–167.

81. Stanbury JB, Brownell GL, Riggs DS, Perinetti H, Itoiz J, del Castillo EB. Endemic goiter. The adaptation of man to iodine deficiency. Cambridge: Harvard University Press, 1954.

82. Beckers C, Delange F. Iodine deficiency. In: Endemic goiter and endemic cretinism. Iodine nutrition in health and disease. Stanbury JB, Hetzel BS, eds. New York: Wiley, 1980:199–217.

83. Ingenbleek Y, Barclay D, Dirren H. Nutritional significance of alterations in serum amino acid patterns in goitrous patients. Am J Clin Nutr 1986;43:310–319.

84. Koutras DA, Christakis G, Trichopoulos D, et al. Endemic goiter in Greece: nutritional status, growth, and skeletal development of goitrous and nongoitrous populations. Am J Clin Nutr 1973;23:1360–1368.

85. Ingenbleek Y, Luypaert B, De Nayer P. Nutritional status and endemic goitre. Lancet 1980;1:388–391.

86. Ingenbleek Y, Beckers C. Evidence for intestinal malabsorption of iodine in protein-calorie malnutrition. Am J Clin Nutr 1973;26:1323–1330.

87. Ingenbleek Y, Beckers C. Triiodothyronine and thyroid-stimulating hormone in protein-calorie malnutrition in infants. Lancet 1975;2:845–848.

88. Vanderpas JB, Contempre B, Duale NL, Goossens W, Bebe N, Thorpe R, et al. Iodine and selenium deficiency associated with cretinism in northern Zaire. Am J Clin Nutr 1990;52:1087–1093.

89. Thilly CH, Vanderpas JB, Bebe N, Ntambue K, Contempre B, Swennen B, et al. Iodine deficiency, other trace elements, and goitrogenic factors in the etiopathogeny of iodine deficiency disorders (IDD). Biol Trace Elem Res 1992;32:229–243.

90. Dumont JE, Corvilain B, Contempre B. The biochemistry of endemic cretinism: roles of iodine and selenium deficiency and goitrogens. Mol Cell Endocrinol 1994;100:163–166.

91. Wolde-Gebriel Z, West CE, Gebru H, Tadesse AS, Fisseha T, Gabre P, et al. Interrelationship between vitamin A, iodine and iron status in schoolchildren in Shoa Region, Central Ethiopia. Br J Nutr 1993;70:593–607.

92. Hetzel BS. Towards a global strategy for the eradication of iodine deficiency disorders. International Symposium on Iodine Nutrition, Thyroxine and Brain Development (3A). New Delhi: All India Institute of Medical Sciences, 1985.

93. Delange FM. Endemic cretinism. In: The thyroid: a fundamental and clinical text. Braverman LE, Utiger RD, eds. Philadelphia: Lippincott, Williams and Wilkins, 2005:731–744.

94. Chaouki ML, Maoui R, Benmiloud M. Comparative study of neurological and myxoedematous cretinism associated with severe iodine deficiency. Clin Endocrinol 1988;28:399–408.

95. Yi CX, Min JX, Hong DZ, Rakeman MA, Li ZM, O'Donnell K, et al. Timing of vulnerability of the brain to iodine deficiency in endemic cretinism. N Engl J Med 1994;331:1739–1744.

96. Pharoah POD, Buttfield IN, Hetzel BS. Neurological damage to the fetus resulting from severe iodine deficiency during pregnancy. Lancet 1971;1:308–310.

97. Dussault J H, Walker P. Congenital hypothyroidism. New York: Dekker, 1983.

98. Delange F. Neonatal screening for congenital hypothyroidism: results and perspectives. Horm Res 1997;48:51–61.

99. Pharoah POD, Connolly KJ, Ekins RP, Harding AG. Maternal thyroid hormone levels in pregnancy and the subsequent cognitive and motor performance of the children. Clin Endocrinol 1984;21:265–270.

100. Azizi F, Sarshar A, Nafarabadi M, Ghazi A, Kimiagar M, Noohi S, et al. Impairment of neuromotor and cognitive development in iodine-deficient schoolchildren with normal physical growth. Acta Endocrinol 1993;129:501–504.

101. Bleichrodt N, Born M. A metaanalysis of research on iodine and its relationship to cognitive development. In: The damaged brain of iodine deficiency. Stanbury JB, ed. New York: Cognizant Communication, 1994:195–200.

102. Van den Broeck J, Eeckels R, Van Loon H, Van Miert M. Growth of children in a iodine-deficient area in northern Zaïre. Ann Human Biol 1993;20:183–189.

103. Virmani A, Menon PSN, Karmarkar MG, Kochupillai N, Seth V, Ghai OP, et al. Evaluation of thyroid function in children with undiagnosed short stature in north India. Ann Trop Paediatr 1987;7:205–209.

104. Longombe AO, Geelhoed GW. Iodine deficiency disorders and infertility in northeast Zaïre. Nutrition 1997;13:342–343.

105. Pharoah POD, Ellis SM, Williams ES. Maternal thyroid function, iodine deficiency and fetal development. Clin Endocrinol 1976;5:159–166.

106. McMichael AJ, Potter JD, Hetzel BS. Iodine deficiency, thyroid function, and reproductive failure. In: Endemic goiter and endemic cretinism. Stanbury JB, Hetzel BS, eds. New York: Wiley, 1980:445–460.

107. Chaouki ML, Benmiloud M. Prevention of iodine deficiency disorders by oral administration of lipiodol during pregnancy. Eur J Endocrinol 1994;130:547–551.

108. Potter JD, McMichael AJ, Hetzel BS. Iodization and thyroid status in relation to stillbirths and congenital anomalies. Int J Epidemiol 1979;8:137–144.

109. Thilly C, Lagasse R, Roger G, Bourdoux P, Ermans AM. Impaired fetal and postnatal development and high perinatal death-rate in a severe iodine deficient area. In: Thyroid research VIII. Proceedings of the Eighth International Thyroid Congress, Sydney, Australia, February 3–8, 1980. Stockigt JR, Nagataki S, eds. Oxford, UK: Pergamon, 1980:20–23.

110. Thilly CH. Goître et crétinisme endémiques, rôle étiologique de la consommation de manioc et stratégie d'éradication. Bull Acad Med Belg 1981;136:389–412.

111. Pharoah POD, Connolly KJ. A controlled trial of iodinated oil for the prevention of endemic cretinism: a long-term follow-up. Int J Epidemiol 1987;16:68–73.

112. Cobra C, Muhilal, Rusmil K, Rustama D, Djatnika, Suwardi SS, et al. Infant survival is improved by oral iodine supplementation. J Nutr 1997;127:574–578.

113. DeLong GR, Leslie PW, Wang SH, Jiang XM, Zhang ML, Rakeman M, et al. Effect on infant mortality of iodination of irrigation water in a severely iodine-deficient area of China. Lancet 1997;350:771–773.

114. World Health Organization and International Council for Control of Iodine Deficiency Disorders. Recommended normative values for thyroid volume in children aged 6–15 years. Bull World Health Organ 1997;75:95–97.

115. Vitti P, Martino E, Aghini-Lombardi F, Rago T, Antonangeli L, Maccherini D, et al. Thyroid volume measurement by ultrasound in children as a tool for the assessment of mild iodine deficiency. J Clin Endocrinol Metab 1994;79:600–603.

116. Delange F, Benker G, Caron Ph, Eber O, Ott W, Peter F, et al. Thyroid volume and urinary iodine in European schoolchildren: standardization of values for assessment of iodine deficiency. Eur J Endocrinol 1997;136:180–187.

117. Zimmermann M, Hess SY, Molinari L, de Benoist B, Delange F, Braverman LE, et al. New reference values for thyroid volume by ultrasound in iodine-sufficient schoolchildren : a World Health Organization/Nutrition for Health and Development Iodine Deficiency Study Group report. Am J Clin Nutr 2004;79:231–237.

118. Dunn JT, Crutchfield HE, Gutekunst R, Dunn AD, eds. Methods for measuring iodine in urine. Fonte, The Netherlands: International Council for Control of Iodine Deficiency Disorders/United Nations International Children's Emergency Fund/World Health Organization, 1993.

119. Pardede LVH, Hardjowasito W, Gross R, Dillon DHS, Totoprajogo OS, Yosoprawoto M, et al. Urinary iodine excretion is the most appropriate outcome indicator for iodine deficiency at field conditions at district level. J Nutr 1998;128:1122–1126.

120. Delange F. Screening for congenital hypothyroidism used as an indicator of IDD control. Thyroid 1998;8:1185–1192.

121. Burrow GN, Dussault JH, ed. Neonatal thyroid screening. New York: Raven, 1980.

122. World Health Organization. Iodine and health: eliminating iodine deficiency disorders safely through salt iodization. Geneva: World Health Organization, 1994.

123. Mannar MGV, Dunn JT. Salt iodization for the elimination of iodine deficiency. MI/ICCIDD/UNICEF/WHO. The Netherlands: International Council for Control of Iodine Deficiency Disorders, 1995.

124. World Health Organization/United Nations International Children's Emergency Fund/International Council for Control of Iodine Deficiency Disorders. Assessment of iodine deficiency disorders and monitoring their elimination. A guide for programme managers. 2nd ed. Geneva: World Health Organization, 2001.

125. World Health Organization. WHO recommended iodine levels in salt: guidelines for monitoring their adequacy and effectiveness. Geneva: World Health Organization, 1996. WHO/NUT/96.13.

126. Stewart C, Solomons N, Mendoza I. Salt iodine variation within an extended Guatemalan community. The failure of intuitive assumptions. Food Nutr Bull 1996;17:258–261.

127. Muture BN, Wainaina JN. Salt iodation in Kenya for national prophylaxis of iodine deficiency disorders. East Afr Med J 1994;71:611–613.

128. Kapil U, Bhasin S, Goindi G, Nayar D. Iodine content of salt in National Capital Territory of Delhi. Asia Pacific J Clin Nutr 1995;4:257–258.

129. Todd CH, Allain T, Gomo ZAR. Hasler JA, Ndiweni M Oken E. 1995. Increase in thyrotoxicosis associated with iodine supplements in Zimbabwe. Lancet 1995;346:1563–1564.

130. Delange F, de Benoist B, Alnwick D. Risks of iodine-induced hyperthyroidism following correction of iodine deficiency by iodized salt. Thyroid 1999;9:545–556.

131. Braverman LE. Adequate iodine intake-the good far outweighs the bad. Eur J Endocrinol 1998;139:14–15.

132. Delange F, Lecomte P. Iodine supplementation : benefits outweigh risks. Drug Safety 2000;22:89–95.

133. Delange F, de Benoist B, Pretell E Dunn J. Iodine deficiency in the world: where do we stand at the turn of the century? Thyroid 2001;11:437–447.

134. Dunn JT. Iodized oil in the treatment and prophylaxis of IDD. In: The prevention and control of iodine deficiency disorders. Hetzel BS, Dunn JT, Stanbury JB, eds. Amsterdam: Elsevier, 1987:127–134.

135. Ermans AM. Prevention of iodine deficiency disorders by oral iodized oil. Eur J Endocrinol 1994;130:545–546.

136. Tonglet R, Bourdoux P, Minga T, Ermans AM. Efficacy of low oral doses of iodized oil in the control of iodine deficiency in Zaire. N Engl J Med 1992;326:236–241.

137. Eltom M, Karlsson FA, Kamal AM, Boström H, Dahlberg PA. The effectiveness of oral iodized oil in the treatment and prophylaxis of endemic goiter. J Clin Endocrinol Metab 1985;61:1112–1117.

138. Phillips DIW, Lusty TD, Osmond C, Church D. Iodine supplementation: comparison of oral or intramuscular iodized oil with oral potassium iodide. A controlled trial in Zaire. Int J Epidemiol 1988;17:142–147.

139. Phillips DIW, Osmond C. Iodine supplementation with oral or intramuscular iodized oil. A 2-year follow-up of a comparative trial. Int J Epidemiol 1989;18:907–910.

140. Bautista A, Barker PA, Dunn JT, Sanchez M, Kaiser DL. The effects of oral iodized oil on intelligence, thyroid status, and somatic growth in school-age children from an area of endemic goiter. Am J Clin Nutr 1982;35:127–134.

141. Benmiloud M, Chaouki ML, Gutekunst R, Teichert HM, Wood WG, Dunn JT. Oral iodized oil for correcting iodine efficiency: optimal dosing and outcome indicator selection. J Clin Endocrinol Metab 1994;79:20–24.

142. Furnée CA, West CE, van der Haar F, Hautvast JGAJ. Effect of intestinal parasite treatment on the efficacy of oral iodized oil for correcting iodine deficiency in schoolchildren. Am J Clin Nutr 1997;66:1422–1427.

143. World Health Organization. Safe use of iodized oil to prevent iodine deficiency in pregnant women. Bull World Health Organ 1996;74:1–3.

144. Delange F. Administration of iodized oil during pregnancy: a summary of the published evidence. Bull World Health Organ 1996;74:101–108.

145. Expanded Programme on Immunization. Potential contribution of the Expanded Programme on Immunization to the control of vitamin A deficiency and iodine deficiency disorders. Geneva: World Health Organization, 1987. Document EPI/GAG/87/W.P.17.

146. Bruning JH, van Nimwegen FW, Oostvogel P, van Steenis G, Cohen N. Effects of iodized oil on trivalent oral polio vaccine in vitro. Int J Vit Nutr Res 1994;64:125–129.

147. Taffs RE, Enterline JC, Rusmil K, Muhilal, Suwardi SS, Rustama D, et al. Oral iodine supplementation does not reduce neutralizing-antibody responses to oral poliovirus vaccine. Bull World Health Organ 1999;77:484–491.

148. World Health Organization. Vitamin A and iodine supplementation. World Health Organ Wkly Epidemiol Rec 1990;65:61–68.

149. Dunn J T. Iodized oil in the treatment and prophylaxis of IDD. In: The prevention and control of iodine deficiency disorders. Hetzel BS, Dunn JT, Stanbury JB, eds. Amsterdam: Elsevier, 1987:127–134.

150. Wolff J. Physiology and pharmacology of iodized oil in goiter prophylaxis. Medicine 2001;80:20–36.

151. Todd CH, Dunn JT. Intermittent oral administration of potassium iodide solution for the correction of iodine deficiency. Am J Clin Nutr 1998;67:1279–1283.

152. Maberly GF, Eastman CJ, Corcoran JM. Effect of iodination of a village water-supply on goitre size and function. Lancet 1981;2:1270–1272.

153. Fisch A, Pichard E, Prazuck T, et al. A new approach to combating iodine deficiency in developing countries: the controlled release of iodine in water by a silicone elastomer. Am J Public Health 1993;83:540–545.

154. Cao XY, Jiang XM, Kareem A, Dou ZH, Rakeman MA, Zhang ML, et al. Iodination of irrigation water as a method of supplying iodine to a severely iodine-deficient population in Xinjiang, China. Lancet 1994;344:107–110.

155. Elnagar B, Eltom M, Karlsson FA, Bourdoux PP, Gebre-Medhin M. Control of iodine deficiency using iodination of water in a goitre endemic area. Int J Food Sci Nutr 1997;48:119–127.

156. Clements FW, Gibson HB, Howeler-Coy JF. Goitre prophylaxis by addition of potassium iodate to bread. Experience in Tasmania. Lancet 1970;1:489–492.

# 18 Multiple Micronutrient Malnutrition
## *What Can Be Done?*

## *Usha Ramakrishnan and Sandra L. Huffman*

## 18.1 INTRODUCTION

The basic cause of malnutrition (protein-energy malnutrition and micronutrient malnutrition) is poverty. Although lack of care, health, and environmental conditions are important components in the etiology of malnutrition, lack of access to food is still one of the major underlying causes of malnutrition. There is a strong correlation between gross national product and the level of malnutrition. However, the challenge facing nutritionists and other professionals in the field of health is to identify strategies to prevent malnutrition that are economically feasible.

While originally protein was considered the main factor in the etiology of malnutrition (see Chapter 12 on malnutrition), lack of energy was later understood to be more important as the underlying cause. Since the 1980s, much work has been carried out in the field of micronutrient deficiencies. The role of vitamin A deficiency in children had a major impact on the role and implications of micronutrient deficiencies. The poor strata in developing countries have a lack of purchasing power and spend a large percentage of their income on staple food. Animal products and fruits that are important sources of micronutrients are often more expensive and unaffordable; therefore, it can be expected that multiple-micronutrient deficiencies rather than singular deficiencies to be common in these settings [1–3]. The micronutrient deficiencies of concern are deficiencies of vitamin A, vitamin B complex, vitamin C, iron, iodine, and zinc. Although reduced energy intake remains a problem in many settings, suboptimal intakes of several micronutrients are more widespread and may be present even when energy needs are met.

Micronutrients can affect a variety of health and disease outcomes, for example, child growth and development, via (1) direct independent effects (e.g., zinc, folic acid [FA]) or (2) indirect effects through interactions with each other (e.g., vitamin A, zinc, and iron) and promoting appetite, which leads to increased food intake and therefore intake of other macro- and micronutrients.

From: *Nutrition and Health: Nutrition and Health in Developing Countries, Second Edition*
Edited by: R. D. Semba & M. W. Bloem © Humana Press, Totowa, NJ

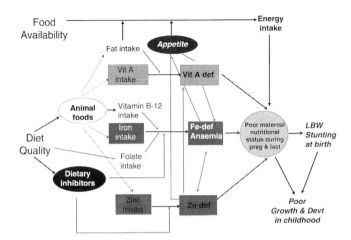

**Fig. 18.1.** Causes and consequences of multiple micronutrient malnutrition.

The conceptual framework that describes the mechanisms by which multiple-micronutrient malnutrition can affect health and disease outcomes is shown in Fig. 18.1. Poor dietary quality and inadequate intake are the underlying determinants of several micronutrient deficiencies. Diets are often low in several nutrients simultaneously due to low intake of animal products and fortified products. For many micronutrients, bioavailability is affected by the mix of foods eaten, presence of inhibitors, mode of preparation and drug–diet interactions [4, 5]. Exceptions would be trace elements such as iodine and selenium; the concentrations of these nutrients in foods depend on the soil or water content of the region where they are grown or harvested. Infections that cause diarrhea and parasitic infestations, which are common in these settings, can also contribute to multiple-micronutrient malnutrition by influencing nutrient absorption, utilization, and excretion [6, 7]. However, these infections are also exacerbated by micronutrient deficiencies.

At the physiological and metabolic level, there is considerable evidence of several micronutrient interactions that may have the potential to affect outcomes such as child growth and development. The interactions are more important when nutrient intakes are inadequate. There is some evidence that suggests that multiple-micronutrient deficiencies result in decreased appetite and anorexia, and these conditions disappear as soon as a dietary balance is restored [8, 9].

Micronutrients can also interact at the level of nutrient absorption. For example, vitamin C is a known enhancer of iron absorption, whereas zinc and calcium can interfere with the absorption and availability of iron [10]. The interrelationship between iron and zinc may also be bidirectional, although results are contradictory. In a recent review of supplementation trials, Walker et al. [11] concluded that while zinc supplementation alone does not affect iron status in children, zinc along with iron does not improve iron status to the same extent as when iron is given alone. Similarly, although iron does not affect zinc status, the findings are mixed for clinical outcomes such as morbidity, and more research is needed in helping guide policy about the most effective way to deliver more than one nutrient. A study among children in Peru improved iron absorption by giving ferrous sulfate and zinc sulfate supplements at least an hour apart [12]. Another study among women in Peru, however, found that prenatal iron supplements resulted in reduced zinc status [13]. In terms of nutrient utilization, studies have also shown that vitamin A affects both iron and zinc metabolism. For example, zinc is required for the synthesis of retinol-binding protein, which is required to transport vitamin A in the body. This interaction has been extensively studied in animal models and to a certain extent in young children [12, 14, 15]. Vitamin A deficiency also inhibits iron utilization and thereby accelerates the development of anemia. Some studies have shown that improving vitamin A status improves hematological indices in both children and pregnant women [16–18]. Alarcon et al.'s study in Peru found that inclusion of vitamin A with iron and zinc did not increase the impact on iron status [12]. Copper and zinc metabolisms are also interrelated.

The focus of this chapter is examination of the significance of multiple-micronutrient malnutrition by addressing the role of micronutrient interactions and the potential benefits of strategies to increase the intake of multiple micronutrients simultaneously. Specifically, the prevalence, functional consequences, and programmatic implications of multiple-micronutrient malnutrition are discussed. Details of the direct independent effects of various single micronutrients, which are described elsewhere, are not included.

## 18.2 PREVALENCE OF MULTIPLE-MICRONUTRIENT MALNUTRITION

Considerable data have accumulated on the prevalence of several micronutrient deficiencies, especially vitamin A, iron, zinc, folate, and so on, but much less is known about the prevalence of multiple-micronutrient deficiencies [19, 20]. Dietary surveys, including the Nutrition Collaborative Research Support Program (CRSP) in Mexico, Kenya, and Egypt have shown that multiple-micronutrient deficiencies, rather than single deficiencies, are common, and that low dietary intake and poor bioavailability of micronutrients account for the high prevalence of this complex of multiple deficiencies [5, 21, 22]. Women of reproductive age and children are at risk of suffering two or more micronutrient deficiencies, as described next. Other groups that may also be at risk include refugees and the elderly.

### 18.2.1 Women of Reproductive Age

Micronutrient malnutrition is common among women of reproductive age, particularly during pregnancy and lactation when demands are high. About 40% of women in the developing world are anemic, mostly caused by iron deficiency. Other reported deficiencies include iodine, zinc, vitamin A, and vitamin B complex, including thiamin, riboflavin, FA, $B_6$, and $B_{12}$ [20, 23]. Based on a review of studies conducted in Latin America, Mora and Mora [24] reported that riboflavin, thiamin, niacin, vitamins E and C, as well as folate and vitamin $B_{12}$ in pregnant women appear to affect important segments of the population, mostly rural low-income groups. Significant rates of $B_{12}$, $B_6$, riboflavin, and folate deficiency have also been reported among women in India [25].

Co-occurrence of micronutrient deficiencies has been observed among pregnant and postpartum women in Indonesia for zinc, vitamin A, and iron [20, 26]. For example, Dijkhuizen et al. [26] found that vitamin A deficiency was associated with an increased risk of anemia (odds ratio [OR] = 3.8, 95% confidence interval [CI] 1.4–10.0) and iron deficiency (OR = 4.8, 95% CI 2–11.6) among lactating women in Indonesia (the prevalence of anemia was 52%). In a Kenyan study, 6–8% of anemia in pregnancy was related to folate deficiency among the 48% of pregnant women found to be anemic [27]. A study of pregnant women in four rural and urban areas of China also found that those who had iron-deficiency anemia had higher rates of vitamin C, folate, and vitamin $B_{12}$ deficiencies when compared to those in the nonanemic subjects [28]. Multiple-micronutrient deficiencies have also been reported in studies of pregnant women in India [29], Mexico [30], and Nepal [31]. For example, in Nepal, 22% of pregnant women in their first trimester had two or more deficiencies, and 18% had five or more deficiencies. Over 60% were deficient in zinc, the most prevalent deficiency (see Fig. 18.2).

Deficiencies of folate, riboflavin, vitamin $B_6$, and vitamin $B_{12}$ can lead to elevated plasma homocysteine concentrations [32], which in turn has been associated with an elevated risk of adverse pregnancy outcomes including increased blood pressure, preeclampsia, stillbirths, risk of placental abruption, risk of prematurity, and low birth weight [33–35]. Homocysteinemia has been reported among pregnant women in developing countries [35–37]. In Bangladesh [36], 26% of pregnant women studied had high homocysteine levels (homocysteine > 10.4 μmol/L), and in Nepal, 68% had homocysteine levels above 7.5 μmol/L [37]. Urban Nepali pregnant women had a 65% prevalence of low plasma $B_{12}$, with deficiency associated with higher plasma homocysteine [35].

## 18.2.2   Children

Several studies have assessed micronutrient deficiencies in addition to those addressed in this volume (vitamin A, zinc, iron, and iodine), but less is known about the prevalence of multiple-micronutrient deficiencies. In Mexico, in a rural study among toddlers, deficiencies of iron, vitamin A, vitamin $B_{12}$, vitamin E, and riboflavin were found among significant proportions of children: about one third of children were deficient in serum $B_{12}$, riboflavin, and vitamin A; about two thirds had low hemoglobin; 70% had low plasma vitamin E. Since supplementation with iron improved serum ferritin but left many children with low hemoglobin and hematocrit, anemia was suggested to be caused by multiple deficiencies, not only iron [38]. Vitamin A deficiency has also been associated with a two- to threefold increased risk of anemia and zinc deficiency among Indonesian infants [26].

Lartey et al. [39] found a high prevalence of several micronutrient deficiencies among Ghanaian 6- and 12-month-old infants; respective deficiency values were as follows:

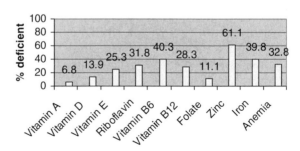

**Fig. 18.2.** Prevalence of multiple deficiencies among pregnant women (first trimester) in Nepal. (Adapted from [31].)

iron (hemoglobin < 100 g/L) 30% and 34%; plasma ferritin (<12 mg/L) 17% and 43%; plasma zinc (<10.7 mmol/L) 4% and 6%; vitamin A (<0.7 mmol/L) was 26% and 26%; and riboflavin (erythrocyte riboflavin < 200 μmol/L of packed red cells) was 14% and 10%. In a study of Bangladeshi infants 8–12 months of age [40], mean dietary intakes were particularly low for iron (8–9% of the recommended nutrient intake [RNI]), vitamin D (12–13% of the RNI), zinc (40–45% of the RNI), and vitamin $B_6$ (50% of the RNI). Ahmed et al. [41] also reported several nutrient deficiencies among anemic adolescent girls in Bangladesh. Almost 90% had riboflavin deficiency, whereas the prevalence of iron, FA, and vitamin A deficiency ranged from 25% to 40%). Albalak et al. [42] found that 21.6% of young children (12–36 months of age) in Honduras had both anemia (hemoglobin < 11 g/dL) and vitamin A deficiency (serum retinol < 30 μg/dl) using nationally representative data, but this proportion was not appreciably higher than what would have been expected based on the prevalence of the individual conditions. Clearly, more work is needed to document the epidemiology and prevalence of multiple micronutrient malnutrition in different settings.

## 18.3 CONSEQUENCES OF MULTIPLE-MICRONUTRIENT MALNUTRITION DURING THE LIFE CYCLE

Most of the research and programmatic efforts to eliminate micronutrient malnutrition to date have focused on single nutrients, especially vitamin A, iodine, iron, and zinc. This is a major concern in light of the limited resources that are available to many programs and countries worldwide and the need for more cost-effective and sustainable strategies. The rationale and scientific evidence supporting the role of multiple micronutrient malnutrition in determining important health outcomes over the life course, especially during vulnerable periods such as pregnancy, lactation, and childhood, are described in this section. The following sections examine the evidence, especially that based on controlled trials that have examined the effects of providing interventions such as multiple-micronutrient supplements or fortified foods on outcomes such as maternal and infant mortality; adverse pregnancy outcomes such as birth defects, prematurity, and low birth weight (LBW); early childhood growth and development; and health and nutritional status.

### 18.3.1 Pregnancy

Considerable research has been done to date supporting the role of micronutrients in determining maternal mortality and adverse pregnancy outcomes such as prematurity, intrauterine growth retardation, and birth defects [43]. In a review of micronutrients and pregnancy outcomes, Ramakrishnan et al. [43] concluded that while some nutrients have been studied extensively (e.g., calcium, zinc), most studies have used the *single-nutrient* approach (i.e. they examined the relationship between one specific nutrient and pregnancy outcomes), and that little is known about the significance of selected nutrient interactions and multiple-micronutrient malnutrition. Significant progress, however, has been made since then, and the evidence from prospective longitudinal studies and intervention trials on the role some of these interactions and multivitamin and mineral (MVM) supplements for improved pregnancy and other related reproductive health outcomes is reviewed in the following sections.

### 18.3.1.1  TWO-WAY MICRONUTRIENT INTERACTIONS IN PREGNANCY

**18.3.1.1.1  Iron and Zinc.** The provision of a daily supplement of zinc gluconate (30 mg Zn) along with routine iron supplementation during pregnancy has been shown to reduce the incidence of fetal distress, fetal demise (stillbirths and neonatal deaths), preterm deliveries, as well as infection rates when compared to iron supplementation alone in a randomized controlled trial of high-risk African American women [44]. Iron-deficient women who began zinc supplementation early in pregnancy also gave birth to longer infants compared to those who had adequate iron status and received zinc supplements later in pregnancy. Head and chest circumferences were also larger among infants born to the zinc-treated anemic women. However, two controlled trials in Peru [45] and Bangladesh [46] found that the provision of zinc supplements along with routine iron-folate supplements during pregnancy did not improve birth outcomes, including birth size, when compared to those who received a placebo. It should be noted that the study in Peru also found supplements containing zinc did improve zinc status in both mothers and neonates [47], with benefits for infant development [48]. However prenatal iron supplements reduced zinc absorption in pregnant women [13], but when zinc was included with iron in the supplement, this inhibitory effect was reduced. A review of several randomized control trials reported that neonatal immune status, early neonatal morbidity, and infant infections were improved in women consuming zinc in pregnancy [49].

**18.3.1.1.2  Iron and Vitamin A.** In a randomized, double-blind trial of pregnant women (n = 251) in Indonesia, the proportion of anemic women who became nonanemic (hemoglobin [Hb] < 110 g/L) following 16 weeks of supplementation was 97%, 68%, 35%, and 19% for those who received iron and vitamin A, iron only, vitamin A only, and placebo, respectively [17]. However, the effects on other outcomes such as birth weight are not known.

**18.3.1.1.3  Iron and Folate.** Folic acid and vitamin $B_{12}$ are provided with iron supplements as part of routine antenatal care to treat nutritional anemia in some parts of the world. The benefits of this combination in improving pregnancy outcomes, especially in reducing the prevalence of LBW, have been studied. Christian et al. [50] in Nepal found that FA in addition to iron and vitamin A was more beneficial than FA and vitamin A in reducing LBW. Achadi et al. [51], in a study in Indonesia, reported that the consumption of one or more iron-FA pills per week by pregnant women was associated with an increase in birth weight (172 g) and length (1 cm). A double-blind, randomized clinical trial conducted in nine hospitals in Mexico examined the impact of providing iron or iron plus FA on anemia. The results showed increased hemoglobin levels among women given both nutrients for 2 months in contrast to iron alone [52].

**18.3.1.1.4  Vitamin A and Zinc.** A supplement containing both vitamin A and zinc reduced night blindness to a greater extent that vitamin A alone in Nepal among pregnant women [53]. In Indonesia, Dijkhuizen et al. [54] found that zinc supplementation in addition to β-carotene during pregnancy improved the vitamin A status of mothers and infants postpartum more than β-carotene alone.

The following section examines the evidence from prospective and controlled trials that have evaluated the effects of prenatal MVM supplements in different settings.

### 18.3.1.2 PRENATAL MULTIVITAMIN-MINERAL SUPPLEMENTS

In one of the earliest prospective studies of drugs and pregnancy conducted in the 1960s in Sweden, Kullander and Kallen [55] found that the prevalence of LBW was significantly lower among women who reported the use of iron or MVM supplement during pregnancy. However, data on other potential confounding factors, such as the use of prenatal care, smoking, and other nutritional factors that may have been associated with supplement use were lacking. Scholl et al. [56], in a well-designed prospective follow-up study of low-income, urban women in the United States, reported that the risk of preterm delivery (<33 weeks) and LBW was reduced by at least half among women who used prenatal MVM supplements regularly compared to those who did not, after adjusting for several known confounders. The protective effect of the supplements was greater if started earlier (first vs. second trimester) and for very LBW. The plausibility of these findings was also strengthened by the fact that the blood levels of several micronutrients were similar for both users and nonusers at entry, and they increased significantly by 28 weeks of gestation among the users. Wu et al. [57], using data from the 1988 National Maternal and Infant Health Survey, found that regular MVM supplement use during pregnancy might reduce the risk of fetal death associated with maternal smoking, after adjusting for several confounders. Although supplement use was not associated with a reduced risk for fetal death in nonsmokers, these findings suggest potential benefits for "high-risk" individuals. In another retrospective case-control study, Shaw et al. [58] found that women who consumed multivitamin supplements containing FA during the periconceptual period (4 months) were 62% less likely (OR = 0.38, 95% CI 0.16–0.88) to deliver a preterm baby when compared to those who did not consume supplements. There were no differences in the prevalence of LBW. Vahratian et al. [59], found that while periconceptual and prenatal use of multivitamins was not related to preterm birth, preconceptual use may be associated with a reduced risk of preterm birth among women in North Carolina.

The majority of randomized clinical trials using MVM supplements that have been conducted in developed countries, originally, demonstrated that the periconceptual use of supplements containing FA reduced the risk of occurrence and recurrence of neural tube defects [60–62]. Periconceptual use of MVM supplements has also been shown to affect other reproductive health outcomes, for instance, more regular menstrual cycles, 5% increase in the rate of conception, and an increased risk of multiple births [63–66]. Reductions in the occurrence of other congenital abnormalities, such as cleft palate, congenital urinary tract anomalies [67], and cardiovascular malformations, have also been associated with MVM supplements [61, 68–71]. However, these events are less common and rare when compared to the prevalence of adverse pregnancy outcomes such as maternal mortality, prematurity, and LBW in developing countries.

Of the two large experimental trials that compared the efficacy of different combinations of MVM supplements on neural tube defects, only one permitted us to draw probabilistic causal associations between the use of MVM supplements and birth weight; it was the prospective, double-blind, randomized trial conducted in Hungary on a sample of 4,753 women who received different combinations of micronutrient supplements from preconception throughout pregnancy [61]. One group (group 1) was given all water-soluble vitamins; vitamins A, D, and E; and calcium, phosphorus, magnesium, iron, copper, manganese, and zinc. Group 2 was given only copper, manganese, zinc, and vitamin C. Group 1 had a significantly lower proportion of congenital abnormalities, but no differences were found in birth weight between the two groups. Although there was no evidence of micronutrient deficiency in this sample, the rates of ectopic pregnancies, miscarriages, and stillbirths as well as preterm births and LBW were significantly lower for both the supplemented groups when compared to the population figures [61]. Both groups also had greater mean birth weights than the general population.

In the trial that was conducted among women who were at risk of giving birth to infants with neural tube defects in the United Kingdom [62], significant reductions were found in the recurrence of neural tube defects (relative risk [RR] 0.28) for those who received MVM supplements containing FA when compared to those who received the placebo. There were no differences in the rates of miscarriages or stillbirths. Although the study design of this trial would have permitted comparisons in birth weight, these data were not reported. In a randomized controlled trial in France, Hininger et al. [72] found that prenatal MVM (excluding iron; see Tables 18.1 and 18.2) led to increased birth weights: mean birth weights were 3,049 + 460 g in the control group compared to 3,300 + 474 g ($p = .03$), and the number of infants weighing more than 2,700 g was 9 of 32 born to women in the control group compared to 2 of 31 women in the MVM group. Birth weight was also related to higher vitamin C blood levels.

Several randomized controlled intervention trials have evaluated the benefits of prenatal MVM supplements in developing countries where poor dietary intakes and multiple-micronutrient malnutrition are common. Most of these studies examined birth outcomes such as LBW and prematurity, while some of them also examined outcomes such as mortality and maternal nutritional status. Some addressed the effect of supplements in HIV-infected pregnant women. Key features of these studies (study setting, sample size, supplement composition, etc.) are summarized in Tables 18.1 and 18.2 [73–88]. Two of the trials [87, 88] were part of the World Health Organization/United Nations International Children's Emergency Fund/United Nations University (WHO/UNICEF/UNU) multicenter trials of prenatal MVM supplements using a standard MVM and designed to be pooled [89]. While WHO recommends iron and FA currently for pregnant women to prevent iron-deficiency anemia in pregnancy, it now recommends MVM for pregnant women in disaster settings [90] and for pregnant women who are HIV positive [91]. The multicenter trials were conducted to assess the impact of the WHO/UNICEF/UNU proposed supplement containing 15 nutrients (UNIMAPP, UN multiple micronutrient preparation) compared to iron and FA to determine whether the current WHO recommendation should be revised.

**18.3.1.2.1   Multiple Supplements in HIV-Infected Pregnant Women.** Since MVM supplements may have different effects among HIV-infected women compared to those who are not, this section summarizes impacts of multiple supplements on HIV-infected women. The earliest trial conducted of MVM supplementation in a developing country setting was the one from Tanzania [73], in which 1,078 HIV-infected pregnant women were randomized to any one of the following four treatments: (1) placebo; (2) megadose β-carotene plus preformed vitamin A only; (3) multivitamins excluding megadose β-carotene plus preformed vitamin A; (4) multivitamins including megadose β-carotene plus preformed vitamin A. Women were recruited between 12 and 29 weeks of gestation

**Table 18.1**

Description of randomized controlled trials of multiple-micronutrient supplementation in pregnant women

| Study site (reference) | Study period | Subjects | Experimental group | Control group | Weeks pregnant at recruitment |
|---|---|---|---|---|---|
| France [72] | 2001 | Pregnant women, 32–33 per group | MVM with 12 nutrients | Placebo | 12–16 |
| Tanzania [73–78] | April 1995 to July 1997 | 257–270 per group | 1. MVM with VA (+9 other nutrients) 2. MVM without VA (+9 other nutrients) 3. Vitamin A + FC + FA 120 mg Fe + 5 mg FA also given to all groups | Placebo | 12–27 |
| Zimbabwe [79] | 1996–1997 | Pregnant women (including 33% HIV infected), 832–837 per group | MVM with 13 nutrients | 120 mg Fe + 5 mg FA also given Placebo FeFA offered part of antenatal care | 25–32 |
| Sarlahi, Nepal [50, 80, 81] | December 1998 to April 2001 | Pregnant women, 772–876 per group | 1. Vitamin A + FA 2. MVM with Vitamin A + FA + Fe 3. MVM with Vitamin A + FA + Fe + Zn 4. MVM with 15 nutrients | 1000 µg RE VA | 9–17 |
| Mexico [82–85] | 1997–2000 | Pregnant women, 322–323 per group | MVM with 13 nutrients | 60 mg Fe | <13 |
| Tanzania [86] | August–October 1999 | Pregnant women, 127–132 per group | MVM fortified beverage with 11 nutrients (+768 kJ) | Placebo (+768 kJ) | 12–34 |
| Janakpur (Central) Nepal [87] | August 2002 to July 2004 | Pregnant women, 517–537 per group | MVM with 13 nutrients | 60 mg Fe + 400 µg FA | ≤20 |
| Guinea-Bissau [88] | January 2001 to October 2002 | Pregnant women, 519–542 per group | 1. MVM with 13 nutrients 2. Two MVM daily (except with 60 mg Fe) | 60 mg Fe + 400 µg FA | <37 |

*FA* folic acid, *MVM* multivitamin and minerals.

**Table 18.2**

Comparison of nutrient levels in multivitamin and mineral (MVM) supplements (>2 nutrients) used in randomized controlled trials in pregnant women

| | France [72] | Tanzania [73–78] | Zimbabwe [79] | Sarlahi, Nepal [50, 80, 81] | | | Mexico [82–85] | Tanzania [86] | Janakpur, Nepal [87], Guinea-Bissau [88] |
| --- | --- | --- | --- | --- | --- | --- | --- | --- | --- |
| | | | | MVM with vitamin A + FA + Fe | MVM with vitamin A + FA + Fe + Zn | MVM with 15 nutrients | | | |
| Vitamin A (µg RE) | 4.8 | 5,000 IU | 3,000 | 1,000 | 1,000 | 1,000 | 646 | 1,050 | 800 |
| β-Carotene (mg) | | 30 | 3.5 | | | | | | |
| Vitamin D (µg) | 10 | | 10 | | | 10 | 7.7 | | 5 |
| Vitamin E (mg) | | 30 | 10 | | | 10 | 5.7 | 21 | 10 |
| Vitamin K (µg) | | | | | | 65 | | | |
| Folic acid (µg) | 200 | 800 | | 400 | 400 | 400 | 215 | 280 | 400 |
| Thiamin (mg) | 1.4 | 20 | 1.5 | | | 1.6 | 0.9 | 1.2 | 1.4 |
| Riboflavin (mg) | 1.6 | 20 | 1.6 | | | 1.8 | 1.9 | | 1.4 |
| Niacin (mg) | 15 | 100 | 17 | | | 20 | 15.5 | 10 | 18 |
| Vitamin B$_{12}$ (µg) | 1 | 50 | 4.0 | | | 2.6 | 2.0 | 6 | 2.6 |
| Vitamin B$_6$ (mg) | | 25 | 2.2 | | | 2.2 | 1.9 | 1.4 | 1.9 |
| Vitamin C (mg) | 60 | 500 | 80 | | | 100 | 66.5 | 144 | 70 |
| Pantothenic acid (mg) | 6 | | | | | | | | |
| Iron (mg) | | | | 60 | 60 | 60 | 62.4 | 10.8 | 30 |
| Iodine (µg) | | | | | | | | 90 | 150 |
| Selenium (µg) | | | 65 | | | | | | 65 |
| Copper (mg) | | | 1.2 | | | 2 | | | 2 |
| Magnesium (mg) | 87.5 | | | | | 100 | 252 | | |
| Zinc (mg) | 10.5 | | 15 | | 30 | 30 | 12.9 | | 15 |
| Calcium (mg) | 100 | | | | | | | | |

*RE* retinol equivalent.

and followed until delivery; they were given supplements containing 2 to 38 times the recommended dietary allowance (RDA) of several vitamins and iron either with or without megadose β-carotene plus preformed vitamin A; the placebo group received only iron/FA. Multivitamin supplementation resulted in improved immune status (measured by increase in CD4, CD8, and CD3 and proportion of CD4 cells) and a significant reduction in the risk of fetal death, LBW (44%), severe preterm birth (39%), and small size for gestational age (43%); megadose β-carotene plus preformed vitamin A supplementation alone did not confer any benefits. The groups were similar at baseline, ruling out possible confounding. Increased weight gain during pregnancy was also seen among women who received the MVM supplements [74], and they were less likely to experience HIV-related morbidity [75]. There was a reduced the risk of hypertension during pregnancy by 38% (RR 0.62, 95% CI 0.40–0.94, $p = .03$) [76]. The authors hypothesized that the vitamin C or E reduced hypertension due to their antioxidative stress properties. Alternately, they suggested that B vitamins in the supplement reduced serum homocysteine and thereby improved endothelial function. Infants of supplemented women experienced improved immune and micronutrient status [77] and increased weight gain [78]. This study provided compelling evidence supporting the benefits of this low-cost supplementation to HIV-positive pregnant women in a developing country setting. Friis et al. [79] also found evidence of improved birth weight in the subsample of HIV-positive women who participated in the randomized controlled trial that was conducted in Zimbabwe. However, micronutrient supplements in Kenya resulted in higher levels of genital HIV-1 shedding compared with placebo, and this was greater among women who had been selenium deficient [92].

**18.3.1.2.2  Impacts on Birth Weight.** In the randomized clinical trial in Sarlahi, Nepal, significant increases in birth weight were noted for women consuming a MVM supplement with 15 nutrients and for those consuming a MVM supplement containing vitamin A plus iron and FA [80] compared to three other groups (see Table 18.1). These results included a reduction in the percent of infants with LBW (from 43% for vitamin A only to 35% for MVM with 15 nutrients and 34% for MVM with A, iron, FA) and an increase in mean birth weight of 64 g (95% CI 12–115 g) for the MVM group with 15 nutrients and 37 g (95% CI −16 to 90 g) for the MVM with A, iron, and FA compared to vitamin A alone. Since no placebo was used, we do not know the impact of vitamin A alone on birth weight. The authors reported that the proportion of women with heavier babies (>3.3 kg) was greater in the MVM group than in the other groups. The earlier trial of weekly vitamin A supplementation in Nepal that did have a placebo group did not report birth weight [93].

Osrin et al. [87] in Janakpur, Nepal, showed a reduction of LBW from 43% to 34% and an increase in mean birth weight of 77 g in the MVM group compared to the group with iron and FA. While they reported that when women were divided into groups by body mass index (BMI), a significant difference in birth weight was seen only among women with BMI > 18.5 kg/m², the trend was the same in thinner women; smaller sample sizes of thinner women may not have allowed sufficient size to detect significant changes in them. In Guinea-Bissau, birth weights of infants who received one daily MVM were 53 g (95% CI: −19 to 125 g) higher than controls, which was significant when other factors were adjusted [88]. Those consuming two daily MVM supplements had infants whose birth weights were 95 g (95% CI: 24–166 g) higher than controls, which was significant both adjusted and not adjusted. The proportion of LBW did not differ, however (13.6%, 12.0%, and 10.1%, respectively; $p > .05$). Among anemic women (Hb < 100 g/L at enrollment) in the MVM 2 group, the mean birth weight was 218 g (95% CI: 81–354 g) higher than the controls, and the proportion of LBW decreased from 18.6% to 7.4% ($p = .019$). In this study, birth weights measured within 3 days after delivery were available for 66% of the women in the study, with nearly all taken in the hospital (95%) in the first day. Women who delivered at home whose babies' birth weights were measured after the third day were thinner and had lower parity and lower education but were similar in terms of age and hemoglobin. This study eliminated birth weights after 3 days; thus, the results on birth weights are not representative of women most at risk.

In two studies with low baseline rates of LBW, there was no effect on birth weight associated with MVM supplementation. In the randomized clinical trial by Ramakrishnan et al. [82] in Mexican pregnant women, for whom the baseline percent LBW was less than 9%, birth weights were no different. In the randomized clinical trial in Harare, Zimbabwe, the LBW rate among HIV-negative women was 8.4%, and there was a 26 g *nonsignificant* higher birth weight in the MVM group and no difference in the proportion with LBW [79]. Lack of power due to limited sample size was not an issue in these two studies. It should be noted that although the findings from the randomized clinical trials suggest limited benefits of MVM supplements, Rao et al. [94] found that birth size was positively associated with intakes of green leafy vegetables (GLVs), which are high in FA, carotenoids, iron, and antioxidants, and fruit (high in vitamin C and antioxidants) at 28-week gestation and milk (high-quality protein, fat, calcium, riboflavin, vitamin A, and D) intake at 18 weeks. The odds ratio for delivering an infant at LBW was 0.43 (95% CI 20.12–0.99) in mothers who ate GLVs at least every other day compared with 1.0 in mothers who never ate them, with the unadjusted mean birth weights of 2,742 + 350 g (every other day) versus 2,571 + 351 g (never). Even once FA intake was controlled, GLVs continued to have an effect on birth weight, suggesting that nutrients other than FA contribute to the relationship. The effect on growth was mediated through increases in gestational age.

**18.3.1.2.3  Impact on Stillbirths.** Results of the studies concerning impacts on stillbirths are mixed. In Janakpur, Nepal, there was no significant difference in the rates of stillbirths. The rate of stillbirth was significantly less in the one MVM group 28/1,000 (n = 31) than in the control 56/1,000 (n = 15), $p < .05$ in Guinea-Bissau. However, the rate among women consuming two MVM supplements was not different from the control (44/1,000, n = 25). In Sarlahi, Nepal, the stillbirth rates were slightly higher (though not significantly) in the MVT group (51/1000) compared to 44/1,000 in the vitamin A-only group, 46/1,000 in the vitamin A and iron group; 36/1,000 in the vitamin A, iron, FA group; and 36/1,000 in the vitamin A, iron, FA, and zinc group. Interestingly, the percent of fetal loss that was due to stillbirths was highest in the MVM with 15 nutrients group (28.7%) compared to 23.8% in the vitamin A control group and to 17.0% in the group given MVM with A, iron, and FA. Since early fetal loss rates were similar in all five groups, there may have been a shift from early loss to stillbirths in the MVM group.

**18.3.1.2.4  Impacts on Neonatal Mortality.** Most neonatal deaths occur during the first 7 days of life (days 0–6). For example, the proportion of neonatal mortality occurring during the first 7 days among women receiving a MVM with over 10 nutrients ranged from 66% in Sarlahi, Nepal, to 76% in Janakpur, and to 96% in Guinea-Bissau.

Perinatal mortality includes both stillbirths and early neonatal deaths. Thus, reporting on both perinatal mortality and neonatal mortality can be misleading. This section therefore reports on results for neonatal mortality (deaths occurring during days 0–27 of life). The Guinea-Bissau, Mexican, or Zimbabwe study did not report differences in neonatal mortality by MVM group. However, the two studies in Nepal reported nonsignificant increases in neonatal mortality associated with MVM use in pregnancy. The Sarlahi study [81] compared neonatal deaths between women consuming vitamin A alone to several other combinations, and the authors found nonsignificantly different rates of neonatal mortality of 46/1,000 in those consuming the vitamin A control supplement compared to 36/1,000 for those receiving vitamin A and FA; 36/1,000 for those with vitamin A, iron, and FA; 38/1,000 for those receiving MVM with vitamin A, iron, and zinc; and 54/1,000 for those receiving a MVM supplement with 15 nutrients. Since there all groups supplements contained vitamin A, we do not know how the results compare with a placebo or iron and FA, although there was no impact of vitamin A on neonatal mortality in the earlier trial conducted in the same study setting [93]. The authors [81] also reported differences in asphyxia between supplement groups, with the MVM group showing a rate of 36% compared to 35% in the vitamin A only group; 25% in the MVM group with vitamin A, iron, and FA; 25% in the vitamin A and FA group; and 10% in the vitamin A, iron, FA, and zinc group. Another interesting finding of this study was that infant mortality through 3 months of age was reduced in the vitamin A and FA alone and vitamin A plus FA and iron groups, but only in premature infants. The small number of deaths, the lack of impact on fetal loss or neonatal mortality in premature infants, and the lack of similar findings in full-term infants suggest that these results may have been caused by chance rather than by differences in intake of the type of micronutrients. The Janakpur study also found a nonsignificant increase in neonatal deaths between 31/1,000 in the MVM group versus 20/1,000 in the iron and FA group. There were, however, no differences between supplement groups by causes of death in infants (infection, preterm birth, and birth asphyxia). Although these neonatal mortality differences in Nepal were not significant, the finding of higher levels of neonatal mortality led to the authors raising concerns about the findings [87, 95]. Others have questioned the validity of these findings [96, 97]. Since several efficacy studies have now been conducted in other developing countries (including Indonesia, Pakistan, Bangladesh, China, and Burkina Faso) that were designed to be pooled to address mortality concerns, the analyses of these WHO/UNICEF/UNU trials should be able to clarify how MVM supplementation affects pregnancy outcome [89].

**18.3.1.2.5 Impacts on Maternal Nutritional Status.** Most trials to date have shown that MVM supplements are *as effective as* iron and FA on prevention of iron-deficiency anemia and anemia in pregnancy. In Sarlahi, Nepal, the prevalence of iron deficiency (serum ferritin $< 12\,\mu g/L$) at 32-week gestation was 44% for the vitamin A-only controls, 51.5% for vitamin A plus FA, and 12.2–17.9% for the other three groups (see Table 18.2 for study groups) [50]. The proportion who were anemic (Hb $< 110\,g/L$) at 6 weeks postpartum was 39.8% for vitamin A only, 33.7% for FA and vitamin A, and 12.3–15.2% for the other three groups. In Janakpur, Nepal, rates of anemia dropped in both intervention and control groups from 37–39% to 25–29% [87], although lower levels of iron were used in the MVM supplement (30 mg) compared to the iron and FA supplement (60 mg). In Tanzania, the fortified beverage after 8 weeks use during pregnancy was associated with an improvement in serum ferritin, and the risk of becoming iron deficient decreased by 53% compared to the placebo [86]. In Mexico [83], there was no significant difference in hemoglobin or serum ferritin among women studied at 1 month postpartum, although there was a slight difference ($p < .01$) in hemoglobin at 32-week gestation in the MVM group (mean of 104.2 g/L (95% CI 102.5–106.0) versus in the control group receiving only iron (mean of 108.1 g/L, 95% CI 106.4–109.8) but not in serum ferritin when adjusted for initial serum ferritin. Although no differences were seen in weight gain during pregnancy, this trial showed that, compared to iron, MVM supplements may lead to greater postpartum weight retention among overweight women [84], which may be a concern in populations for whom overweight and obesity are increasing.

Only a few studies have as yet assessed impacts of MVM supplementation on the status of other nutrients. Improvements in retinol and vitamin E were seen in the women who received MVM supplementation in Janakpur, Nepal. In Tanzania, among HIV-positive women, the proportion of women deficient in vitamin A (<20 μg/dL) was 22% for those receiving supplements containing megadose β-carotene plus vitamin A compared to 50% in those who did not [73]. The consumption of the fortified beverage in Tanzania was not, however, related to improvement in retinol levels [85]. Similarly, no differences were seen in folate or zinc status in the Mexico study [85]. In the French study of healthy, well-nourished women, MVM supplementation led to improved blood levels of vitamins E and C, β-carotene, FA, and vitamins $B_2$ and $B_6$ but not to improved zinc plasma levels [72].

In summary, the evidence from research to date suggests that the benefits of provision of multiple-micronutrient supplements to pregnant women are difficult to assess and may be more important in specific subgroups, such as HIV-positive women. There appears to be a benefit on improving birth weights in some populations, and MVM supplements may be as effective as iron-FA supplements in reducing iron deficiency while enhancing maternal nutrient status, such as of B vitamins, vitamin E, and retinol. Little is known about the benefits to outcomes such as infant growth and morbidity, early childhood development, and women's health and nutrition.

### 18.3.2  Lactation

While considerable research has been done on the relationship among breast milk intake, its energy content, and child growth, little work has been done on the micronutrient content of breast milk in developing countries. The mother's nutritional status during pregnancy or lactation should, in theory, affect the growth of the newborn during the early postnatal period by determining the level of nutrient reserves in the newborn and the breast milk quantity and quality, including micronutrient concentrations. Allen [98], in a review on the importance of maternal micronutrient status during lactation, concluded that in general, milk composition is most affected by the woman's intake of water-soluble vitamins, less by the consumption of fat-soluble vitamins, and relatively unaffected by mineral intake or status. According to Allen, micronutrients can be classified into two priority categories for lactating women, as described next:

*Priority 1 micronutrients* are those for which deficiencies have been shown to result in lower concentrations in breast milk but are responsive to supplementation. They are vitamins A, $B_1$, $B_2$, $B_6$, and $B_{12}$ and perhaps iodine and selenium in deficient populations. For example, postpartum high-dose vitamin A supplementation or consumption of fortified foods by lactating women living in vitamin A-deficient populations has been shown to increase breast milk retinol concentrations [99, 100]. Studies in the Gambia have shown that riboflavin, vitamin A, and ascorbic acid concentrations in breast milk can also be improved by micronutrient supplementation of lactating women [101–103]. In a double-blind study of low-income, lactating women in the United States, breast milk levels of vitamin $B_6$, $B_{12}$, and folate increased in the micronutrient supplement group [104].

On the other hand, *priority 2 micronutrients* are those with levels in breast milk that appear to be relatively protected even during maternal deficiency and do not seem to respond to maternal supplementation. These include vitamin D, folate, iron, calcium, copper, and zinc. For example, although zinc may be an important limiting nutrient for child growth, the zinc content of breast milk does not appear to be affected by supplementation during lactation [105–107]. Similarly, iron supplementation during the last trimester of pregnancy did not alter the concentrations of iron, copper, selenium, and zinc in breast milk in a randomized clinical trial of pregnant women in Niger [107]. No studies to date have assessed the benefits of correcting multiple-micronutrient malnutrition on lactation performance. The study using prenatal MVM supplements in Mexico did, however, find that vitamin A levels were improved in breast milk [108] when compared to the control group, who received only iron. In Zimbabwe, MVM use between 22- and 35-week gestation through the first 3 months postpartum resulted in reduced mastitis in HIV-positive women but not HIV-negative women [109]. A study in Tanzania found that mastitis could be reduced by providing sunflower oil to the pregnant women in the last trimester. Vitamin E levels were also higher in their breast milk [110, 111].

## 18.3.3   Childhood

### 18.3.3.1   GROWTH

Recent estimates indicate that nearly half of the young children in South Asia, which represents a large segment of the world's population, are underweight (below −2 standard deviations [SD] of the international reference for weight-for-age), and 10–30% are underweight in Latin America and sub-Saharan Africa [112]. In these settings, severe growth retardation occurs during the prenatal and early postnatal periods, and although there may be potential for catching up during adolescence, currently available data indicate that this does not generally occur [113]. Therefore, identifying interventions aimed at preventing growth retardation during pregnancy and early childhood should be high priority and may help prevent adverse outcomes during early childhood and perhaps later in adolescence and during adulthood [114].

The role of nutrition in determining child growth has been an area of considerable research since the 1950s. Historically, the strong belief until the 1960s was that improving protein intakes *alone* would solve the problem of malnutrition in poor countries. The focus, however, moved from protein to energy during the late 1970s and early 1980s, when it was shown that (1) while protein intakes were satisfactory, it was total energy intakes that fell far short of requirements in these settings; and (2) severely malnourished children could gain weight well on high-energy/low-protein diets [115, 116]. Subsequently, in the late 1980s, certain micronutrients were identified as playing a key role in child growth. To date, considerable research has been done in identifying the role of selected single micronutrients in promoting child growth, notably vitamin A, iron, and zinc. A meta-analysis of over 20 intervention trials concluded that zinc supplementation can be expected to improve both height and weight in young children [117], whereas another meta-analyses of controlled trials concluded that neither vitamin A nor iron only improve child growth [118].

The recognition that multiple nutrient deficiencies frequently coexist and that the type of food (e.g., animal vs. vegetable) affects utilization initiated discussions of the importance of "dietary quality" for growth and efforts to evaluate MVM interventions such as MVM supplements, sprinkles, fortified complementary foods, and so on [119]. For example, some studies have shown the importance of animal foods, which are rich in several key micronutrients (vitamin A, $B_{12}$, iron, zinc) in promoting growth [120–123]. Several intervention trials using multiple-micronutrient supplements or fortified foods (Tables 18.3–18.6) have been conducted in various settings with varying degrees of impact on child growth [124–148]. A meta-analysis [118] concluded that MVM interventions improved both linear and ponderal growth (the effect sizes were 0.28, 95%CI 0.16–0.41 for height and 0.28, 95%CI –0.07 to 0.63 for weight), but these findings were based only on five studies that varied in terms of study setting, mode of intervention, and age range. Since this analysis, the multicountry International Research on Infant Supplementation (IRIS) trials that provided daily and weekly multiple-micronutrient supplements in four countries among children 6–12 months of age did not find impacts on growth [132–135]. In addition, studies in Peru [126], Bangladesh [127], China [137], Ghana [138], and South Africa [139, 140], all among young children under age 3, did not find impacts on growth. The studies from Mexico using both a MVM syrup [125, 129] and a fortified complementary food [141] all these studies found impacts on growth, as did the two studies in school-aged children in Botswana [145] and Tanzania [146] and [140] that used fortified beverages. In Vietnam, improvements in growth were only seen among children who were initially stunted [124]. A multicenter WHO/USAID study in India, Nepal, and Zanzibar is assessing the impact of iron, zinc, and FA dispersable tablets on child growth, but the results are not yet available. Impacts on growth are likely to be affected by maternal nutritional status and birth weight, underlying micronutrient deficiencies, food intake, and morbidity patterns, and thus the lack of consistency in findings is not surprising.

### 18.3.3.2  Micronutrient Status

In contrast to the findings on growth, clear benefits of MVM supplementation on children's micronutrient status have been found in trials of daily and weekly MVM supplements, including improvements in iron and retinol status. Improvements in hemoglobin levels were not always seen, however [131, 141]. Some studies have found improvements in zinc status [124, 126, 145, 148]. The IRIS trials also showed improvements in riboflavin status and reductions in homocysteine [148], whereas the study by Abrams et al. [145] found improvements in vitamin C in addition to the improvements just mentioned. As with MVM supplementation in women, multiple-micronutrient supplements in children led to improvements in micronutrient status in addition to improvements in hemoglobin.

### 18.3.3.3  Morbidity

Several micronutrients play essential roles in immune function, including vitamin A; thiamin; riboflavin; vitamins $B_6$, $B_{12}$, C, and E; FA; zinc; and iron [149]. Several intervention trials have also examined the benefits of providing nutrients such as vitamin A, iron,

**Table 18.3**
Characteristics of intervention studies of multiple micronutrients in children

| Author | Year | Country | Age | Duration (mo) | Number of participants | Type of supplement | Experimental group | Control group |
|---|---|---|---|---|---|---|---|---|
| **Infants and toddlers** | | | | | | | | |
| ***Syrup*** | | | | | | | | |
| Thu et al. [124] | 1999 | Vietnam | 6–24 mo | 3 | 54–55 | Syrup | 1. Daily MVM 2. Weekly MVM | Placebo |
| Rivera et al. [125] | 2001 | Mexico | 8–14 | 12 | 168–169 | Syrup | Daily fort with 30 mL (126 kJ, 30 kcal) | Unfort 126 kJ (30 kcal) |
| Penny et al. [126] | 2004 | Peru | 6–36 | 6 | 79–81 children with persistent diarrhea | Syrup | Daily 1. Zn + MVM 2. Zn | Placebo |
| Baquie, Black, et al. [127, 128] | 2003, 2004 | Bangladesh | 6 mo | 6 | 154–169 | Syrup | Daily 1. 20 mg Fe + 1 mg riboflavin 2. 20 mg Fe + 20 mg Zn+ 1 mg riboflavin 3. 20 mg Fe, Zn, riboflavin 4. MVM | 1 mg riboflavin |
| Ramakrishnan [129] | | Mexico | 3 mo | 18 | 650 | Syrup | Daily MVM | Iron + vitamin A |
| **Sprinkles and foodlets** | | | | | | | | |
| IRIS [132–135] | 2005 | Indonesia Peru | 6–12 mo | 6 | 60–69 63–74 | Foodlet | 1. Daily MVM 2. Weekly MVM + placebo | Placebo |

(continued)

**Table 18.3** (continued)
Characteristics of intervention studies of multiple micronutrients in children

| Author | Year | Country | Age | Duration (mo) | Number of participants | Type of supplement | Experimental group | Control group |
|---|---|---|---|---|---|---|---|---|
| | | South Africa | | | 46–50 | | 3. Daily iron | |
| | | Vietnam | | | 73–77 | | | |
| Martini et al., 2004, Vitalita [136] | 2005 | Indonesia | 6–30 | 6 | 266–551 | Sprinkles | Daily MVM | Placebo |
| **Fortified complementary foods** | | | | | | | | |
| Liu et al. [137] | 1993 | China | 6–13 mo | 3 | ~113 | Rusk | Daily fort rusk | Unfort rusk |
| Lartey et al. [138] | 1999 | Ghana | 6–12 mo | 6 | 26–29 | Porridge | Daily 1. Fort porridge 2. Porridge with fish powder 3. Fermented porridge with fish powder | Unfort porridge |
| Faber [139] | 2005 | South Africa | 6–12 mo | 6 | 144–145 | Porridge | Daily Fort porridge 40 g dry product containing 617 kJ per day (in sachets of 20 g each) | Unfort porridge |
| Oelofse [140] | 2003 | South Africa | 6 mo | 6 | 60 | Porridge | Daily Fort porridge 60 g dry product (1,304 kJ/d) | None |
| Rivera [141] | 2004 | Mexico | <12 mo | 24 | 650 | Porridge | Daily Fort papilla | None |

| Reference | Year | Country | Age | | Sample | Form | Intervention | Placebo |
|---|---|---|---|---|---|---|---|---|
| Lopriore et al. [142] | 2004 | Algeria | 3–6 yr | 4 | 125–135 children with HAZ ≤ 2 Algerian refugee camp | Peanut butter paste | Daily 1. Fort spread 2. Unfort spread 3. Fort spread + metronidazole 4. Unfort + metronidazole | Placebo spread |
| **Children and adolescents** | | | | | | | | |
| Friis et al. [143, 144] | 2003 | Kenya | 9–18 yr | 8 | 287–296 | Tablet | Five days per week 1. MVM 2. MVM + anthelminthics 3. Placebo + anthelminthics | Placebo |
| Abrams et al. [145] | 2003 | Botswana | 6–11 yr | 2 | 118–145 | Beverage | Daily Fort beverage 240 mL and provided 419 kJ (100 kcal) | Isocaloric placebo beverage |
| Ash et al. [146] | 2003 | Tanzania | 6–11 yr | 6 | 382–392 | Beverage | Daily Fort beverage (90 kcal) | Isocaloric placebo beverage |
| Ahmed et al. [41] | 2005 | Bangladesh | 14–18 | 3 | 89 | Tablet | Twice weekly MVM | Twice weekly Fe, FA |

*FA folic acid, fort fortified, MVM multivitamin and mineral, unfort unfortified HA-height for age Z score.*

**Table 18.4**

Comparison of nutrient levels in multivitamin and mineral (MVM) supplements used in randomized controlled trials in young children

| | Vietnam [124] daily/wkly | Mexico [125] | Peru [126] | Bangladesh [127, 128] | Mexico [129–131] 3–11 mo | Mexico [129–131] 12–24 mo | IRIS trials [132–135] daily/wkly | Vitalita, Indonesia [136] |
|---|---|---|---|---|---|---|---|---|
| Vitamin A (μg RE) | 333/1,700 | 450 | 450 | | 450 | 480 | 375/750 | 375 |
| β-Carotene (mg) | | | | | | | | |
| Vitamin D (μg) | | 10 | 6.4 | 20 | 400 | 400 | 5/10 | 50 |
| Vitamin E (mg) | | 6 | 8.5 | 8 | 4.0 | 6.0 | 6/12 | 6 |
| Vitamin K (μg) | | 15 | | | | | | |
| Folic acid (μg) | | 50 | 283 | 70 | 35.0 | 50.0 | | |
| Thiamin (mg) | | 0.7 | 1.75 | 0.8 | 0.40 | 0.70 | 0.5/1 | 0.5 |
| Riboflavin (mg) | | 1.2 | 1.45 | 1 | 0.75 | 1.20 | 0.5/1 | 0.5 |
| Niacin (mg) | | 9 | 11.5 | 12 | 6.0 | 9.0 | 6/12 | 6 |
| Vitamin $B_{12}$ (μg) | | 1.05 | 6.5 | 1.0 | 0.75 | 1.05 | 0.9/1.8 | 0.9 |
| Vitamin $B_6$ (mg) | | 1.0 | 1.55 | 1.2 | 0.60 | 0.10 | 0.5/1 | 0.5 |
| Vitamin C (mg) | 20/20 | 40 | 50 | 70 | 52.5 | 60.0 | 35 | 35 |
| Pantothenic acid (mg) | | 3 | | 6 | | | | |
| Iodine (μg) | | 70 | | 100 | | | 59/118 | 50 |
| Selenium (μg) | | 20 | 23 | 30 | | | | |
| Copper (mg) | | 1 | 0.65 | 1.2 | | | 0.6/1.2 | 0.6 |
| Magnesium (mg) | | | 50 | | 60.0 | 80.0 | | |
| Iron (mg) | 8/20* | 15* | 10* | 20* | 15.0 | 15.0 | 10/20 | 10 |
| Zinc (mg) | 5/17 zinc sulfate | 15 | 10(Zn gluconate) | 20(Zn acetate) | 7.5 | 15.0 | 10/20 | 5 |
| Manganese (mg) | | 1 | | | | | | |
| Biotin (μg) | | 15 | | 1.6 | | | | |

RE retinol equivalent *Fe sulfate.

**Table 18.5**
Comparison of nutrient levels of fortified complementary foods used in randomized control trials in young children

| | China [137] (per rusk) | Ghana [138] per 100 g dry wt | South Africa [139] per 40 g dry product | South Africa [140] per 60 g dry product | Mexico [141] per 44 g | Algeria [142] per 50 g |
|---|---|---|---|---|---|---|
| Vitamin A (µg RE) | | | | 1,200 | 400 | 1,000 |
| β-Carotene (mg) | | | 3 | | | |
| Vitamin D (µg) | 4 | | | 160 | | 25 |
| Vitamin E (mg) | | | 2.5 | 4 | 6 | 10 |
| Vitamin K (µg) | | | | | | |
| Folic acid (µg) | 25 | 307 | | 17.6 | 50 | 250 |
| Thiamin (mg) | 0.15 | 1.35 | | 0.64 | | 2 |
| Riboflavin (mg) | 0.2 | 0.98 | 0.4 | 0.24 | | 2 |
| Niacin (mg) | 2.5 | 14.9 | | 3.2 | | 25 |
| Vitamin B$_{12}$ (µg) | 0.3 | 3.5 | 0.25 | 0.6 | 0.7 | 2 |
| Vitamin B$_6$ (mg) | | 1.74 | 0.15 | 0.24 | | 2 |
| Vitamin C (mg) | | 39.1 | 56 | 40 | 40 | 53 |
| Pantothenic acid (mg) | | | | 0.6 | | 12.5 |
| Iodine (µg) | | | | 26 | | |
| Selenium (µg) | | | 10 | | | |
| Copper (mg) | | 1.3 | 0.11 | | | 1 |
| Magnesium (mg) | | 140 | | | | 78 |
| Iron (mg) | | | 11 (Fe fumarate) | 8 | 10 | 21 |
| Zinc (mg) | | | 3 (zinc sulfate) | 5.6 | 10 | 20.5 |
| Calcium (mg) | 300 | 895 | | 368 | | 500 |
| Manganese (mg) | | | | | | |
| Biotin (µg) | | | | 20 | | |

*RE* retinol equivalent.

**Table 18.6**
Comparison of nutrient levels of multivitamin and mineral (MVM) supplements used in randomized control trials in school-aged children

| | Kenya [144] | Botswana [145] | Tanzania [146] (24-g sachet) | Philippine [147] (25-g sachet) | Bangladesh [41] |
|---|---|---|---|---|---|
| Vitamin A (µg RE) | 1,000 | 2,400 | 1,750 IU | 700 IU | 800 |
| β-Carotene (mg) | | | | | |
| Vitamin D (µg) | | | | | 200 |
| Vitamin E (mg) | | 7.5 | 10.5 | 2.5 | 10 |
| Vitamin K (µg) | | | | | |
| Folic acid (µg) | 150 | 140 | 140 | 60 | 400 |
| Thiamin (mg) | 1.4 | | | | 1.4 |
| Riboflavin (mg) | 1.6 | 0.40 | 0.6 | 0.46 | 1.4 |
| Niacin (mg) | 16 | 2.7 | | 2.5 | 18 |
| Vitamin $B_{12}$ (µg) | 2 | 1.0 | 3 | 0.5 | 2.6 |
| Vitamin $B_6$ (mg) | 1.7 | 0.5 | 0.7 | 0.5 | 1.9 |
| Vitamin C (mg) | 50 | 60 | 72 | 75 | 70 |
| Pantothenic acid (mg) | | | | | |
| Iodine (µg) | 150 | 60 | 45 | 48 | 150 |
| Selenium (µg) | 40 | 120 | | | 65 |
| Copper (mg) | 2.0 | | | | 2 |
| Magnesium (mg) | | | | | |
| Iron (mg) | 18 | | 5.4 | 4.8 | 30 |
| Zinc (mg) | 20 | 3.75 (zinc gluconate) | 5.25 | 3.75 | 15 |

*RE* retinol equivalent.

and zinc, of which the greatest benefits were seen for zinc supplements, which have been shown to reduce the incidence of acute and persistent diarrhea as well as acute lower-respiratory infections [150], both of which are the leading cause of death in young children in developing countries. Interestingly, much less is known about the effects of MVM interventions in reducing morbidity during childhood (both early and the school years) despite the number of trials that examined growth as an outcome. MM supplementation was associated with a reduction in the prevalence of acute respiratory infection and fever in Peru [133], but no differences were seen in Indonesia [132] and South Africa [134]. The Vietnam study did not report on morbidity [135]. In Kenya, children who received MVM supplementation were reinfected with *Schistosoma mansoni* at only 69% of the intensity of those who received placebo [151].

### 18.3.3.4 MOTOR AND MENTAL DEVELOPMENT

Inadequate nutrition can also disrupt cognition and intellectual functioning. In a 1997 review of the published literature, Martorell [152] concluded that poor nutrition during early childhood, especially in developing country settings, can have varied effects on intellectual functioning. Our knowledge of the mechanisms by which malnutrition during these years disrupts these functional outcomes, however, is still evolving. Brown and Pollitt [153] proposed that malnutrition can hinder cognitive development through several interactive routes. For example, malnutrition could lead to delayed motor development and physical growth, lethargy, and withdrawal, which in turn may result in reduced exploration of the environment or reduced caregiver expectations and thereby delayed intellectual development and behavioral deficits, especially in suboptimal learning environments.

The association between generalized protein energy malnutrition and mental development has been examined in several observational and intervention trials carried out in many developing countries [154]. Pollitt and Oh, in a meta-analysis of nutrition intervention trials [155], concluded that there were beneficial effects of supplementation on the motor development of infants 8–19 months of age and on the motor and mental development of older children. However, these studies did not permit us to isolate the role of micronutrients versus energy or protein since the food supplements provided energy, protein, and other nutrients.

Most of our knowledge on the role of micronutrients for motor and mental development is limited to iodine and iron. Cretinism, an outcome of severe iodine deficiency, is typically characterized by serious and irreversible mental retardation that occurs during fetal life and postnatally [156]. Mental deficits have also been documented even among noncretinous populations residing in iodine-deficient areas. A meta-analysis of 18 studies concluded that a reduction of about 1 standard deviation in cognitive development could be attributed to iodine-deficiency disorders [157], but only a few of them were randomized controlled trials. Iron-deficiency anemia has also been associated with impaired performance on the mental and motor scores of the Bayley or similar scales used for infants and toddlers. Anemic infants treated with iron as early as 2–3 months of age and fully rehabilitated to normal hemoglobin levels have shown improvements later, but the findings are less consistent in the case of nonanemic iron-deficient children [158]. Iron supplementation of children over 2 years of age with iron-deficiency anemia can also improve some cognitive functions and school achievement [159].

Behavioral data from observational studies, especially the CRSP study from Egypt, suggest a role for several other micronutrients, namely, vitamins $B_6$ and $B_{12}$ and calcium in child development [160]. Poor vitamin $B_6$ status has been associated with reduced attention and child–caregiver interaction in Egyptian infants, which in turn may influence cognitive development [29, 161–162]. Neonates who were more responsive to adverse stimuli, more easily consoled, and less likely to show extreme distress were born to mothers with higher levels of vitamin $B_6$ in their breast milk [163]. Vitamin $B_{12}$ status has also been positively associated with the amount of symbolic play in infants [160].

Another nutrient of interest is zinc, which has been shown to play a role in brain function and development in animal models. Evidence of reduced activity and responsiveness in animals suggests that zinc may play a role in learning, attention, and memory [164]. Several studies have examined its role in young child development. Two randomized trials that examined the effects of zinc supplementation on cognitive development of preschool children in Canada [165] and school-aged children in Guatemala [166] failed to detect any differences. In another study in Guatemala, zinc-supplemented infants aged 6–9 months followed for 7 months were more frequently observed sitting up and playing compared to the nonsupplemented infants [167]. These infants were also somewhat less likely to be observed whining and crying compared to the placebo group. Sazawal et al. [168] reported a positive effect of zinc supplementation on the motor activity of children 12–24 months of age studied in a periurban community in north India. Ashworth et al. [169] reported that daily zinc supplementation (5 mg/day) during the first 8 weeks of life improved responsiveness in LBW infants in Brazil, but the study did not detect any significant differences in mental and psychomotor development at 6 and 12 months of age when compared to those who received a placebo.

Despite the evidence relating several micronutrients with child development, little is known about the impact of multiple-micronutrient deficiencies [170]. An observational study from Guatemala found that dietary quality based on the intake of animal foods was predictive of age at walking [171]. Preliminary findings from a study of school-aged children in Thailand indicated that a fortified seasoning powder containing one third of the Thai RDA for iron, iodine, zinc, and vitamin A per serving was associated with improved cognitive development [172]. Whaley et al. [173] also found that supplementation with animal products led to improvements in cognitive function in school-aged children in rural Kenya. Faber et al. [139] found significantly higher motor development scores in the group of children who received fortified porridge compared to those who received unfortified porridge. The trial from Mexico found evidence of selective benefits [130]. Specifically, among children whose mothers consumed iron only, those in the MVM group were less likely to show poorer motor development than children receiving iron plus vitamin A, with the largest benefit seen among the lowest tertile of socioeconomic status (SES). For children in the low-SES group, prenatal supplementation with MVM seemed most important for higher mental development at 24 months of age; whereas children in the middle- and high-SES groups benefited from receiving MVM during both the prenatal and postnatal periods, with the largest effects (~4.5 points) in the highest tertile of SES. Thus, it appears that improvements in multiple-micronutrient status have benefits for child development, although these are difficult to measure.

## 18.3.4  Adult Morbidity

Several studies have examined the role of micronutrients and HIV, including effects on immune response, progression to AIDS, and maternal–infant transmission of HIV [174]. HIV-infected individuals often have low serum concentrations of vitamins A, $B_6$, $B_{12}$, C, and E and folate, carotenoids, selenium, and magnesium [175], even in developed countries where intakes of these nutrients are relatively high. In developing countries where intakes are often inadequate, micronutrient status is even further compromised. A randomized clinical trial in Bangkok reported reductions in mortality among adult HIV-infected men who received MVM supplements, which is promising [176].

Few randomized trials have examined the role of multiple micronutrients on infection. The elderly represent a population known to show a decline in immune response, which has been hypothesized to be partially attributed to nutritional deficiencies found among the elderly due to their lower intake of food and gastric problems influencing absorption. Older adults are, in some ways, similar to populations in developing countries with low nutrient intake. Thus, several studies have tried to improve immune status through supplementation with micronutrients. Zinc, selenium, MVM supplements, and vitamin E supplements have all been associated with improved immune status among the elderly [149, 177–179].

Another factor affecting illnesses is related to oxidative stress. The immune response releases oxygen radicals that can be damaging to cell membranes. Nutrients that act as antioxidants (including iron, zinc, vitamin C, vitamin E, and selenium) can reduce the damage done to cells. Deficiencies in antioxidants and associated increases in oxidative stress injure T cells and therefore compromise cell-mediated immunity. Oxidative stress appears also to be related to cancer and to coronary heart disease (CHD), and several antioxidant nutrients (especially vitamin E and selenium) have been related to a reduced risk of these illnesses [175]. It has also been suggested that oxidative stress may increase HIV replication [180].

There is an emerging epidemic of cardiovascular disease in developing countries, in part due to increased life expectancy so that more people are now susceptible and because of increased levels of obesity, decreased exercise, adverse dietary changes, and increased smoking [181]. Low intake of several micronutrients (including FA and vitamins $B_6$, $B_{12}$, and E) have been implicated in an increased risk of cardiovascular disease. Both increased FA and vitamin $B_6$ intake have been shown in large-scale epidemiological studies to be associated with reduced risk of fatal CHD and nonfatal myocardial infarctions and with decreased risk of arteriosclerosis among women [182, 183].

A case-control study that was conducted in 19 centers in nine European countries assessed the relationship between homocysteine levels and cardiovascular risk [184]. Subjects in the top 20% of the control distribution had a twofold increase in the risk of vascular disease compared to the lower 80%, a risk similar to that of hypercholesterolemia or smoking. Plasma folate, $B_6$, and $B_{12}$ concentrations were inversely related to homocysteine levels, and users of vitamin preparations containing these nutrients had a .38 relative risk (95% CI 0.2–0.72) of cardiovascular disease compared to nonusers. A meta-analysis of 20 studies found an increased risk of coronary artery disease, with the odds ratio 1.6 for men and 1.5 for women, with a 5 μmol/L increase in total plasma or serum homocysteine [185]. A study found that inclusion of $B_{12}$ along with FA in a supplement was more effective in lowering homocysteine levels than FA alone [186].

Evidence is considerable that consumption of fruits and vegetables is associated with a decreased risk of cardiovascular disease, hypertension, and some cancers, presumably for their antioxidant effects [187]. Vitamin E has been suggested to offer a protective effect against atherosclerosis because of the recognition that oxidized low-density lipoproteins are involved in atherogenesis and because of studies showing the association of vitamin E supplementation with reduced risk of disease [188]. However, the association of other antioxidants such as vitamin C and β-carotene is less clear, leading to the interpretation that components of fruits and vegetables other than vitamins (such as phenolic compounds) may be have stronger antioxidant effects [187]. Increasing fruit and vegetable intake was shown to decrease significantly the risk for CHD, ischemic stroke, and lung cancer [189]. Lock et al. [189] estimated that 2.6 million deaths and 31% of cardiovascular disease may be attributed to inadequate consumption of fruits and vegetables.

## 18.4 PROGRAMMATIC IMPLICATIONS

Combining multiple micronutrients in a single delivery mechanism has been suggested as a cost-effective way to achieve multiple benefits. Approaches available to do so include improving dietary intake through increased consumption of nutrient-rich foods, fortified foods, and micronutrient supplements. Each has particular benefits and constraints.

### 18.4.1 *Improving Dietary Intake*

When feasible, improving the diet to include animal products, fruits, vegetables, and legumes will benefit nutrient status for several micronutrients simultaneously. Increasing consumption of animal flesh products results in improvements especially in iron and zinc status, as well as vitamins $B_6$, $B_{12}$, thiamin, and riboflavin. Increased consumption of organ meat also improves vitamins A, E, and D and folate intake.

Raising intakes of red and orange fruits and vegetables increases intake of provitamin A carotenoids. While improved intake of β-carotene from vegetables or fruits improves vitamin A status, it does not appear to do as well as preformed vitamin A or purified β-carotene, for example, in the form of red palm oil [190, 191]. Thus, animal products (fortified milk, eggs, liver) containing vitamin A are also needed. Increased consumption of dark GLVs can improve the status of FA, vitamin A, calcium, and vitamin C. Intake of legumes can enhance thiamin, riboflavin, and folate status. Increasing consumption of fruits and vegetables will also increase the intake of antioxidants other than vitamins, which appear to be important in preventing cardiovascular disease and some cancers.

Methods to improve dietary intakes center on (1) behavioral change (counseling / nutrition education) to increase micronutrient intake and to modify food preparation and processing practices to increase absorption of micronutrients by increasing intake of absorption enhancers and reducing phytate content of cereals and (2) promotion of small-livestock production and aquaculture to increase consumption of animal source foods (ASFs) and encouragement of home gardens [192].

#### 18.4.1.1 BEHAVIOR CHANGE PROGRAMS

Breast milk is an optimal animal food source. Numerous programs have documented improvements in breast-feeding practices with counseling and other behavior change interventions [193–195]. While the impact of improved breast-feeding practices on micronutrient status of infants is generally not evaluated, due to the high levels of multiple micronutrients (vitamin A, riboflavin, vitamin C, folate, $B_{12}$, etc.) in breast milk, even among malnourished women, and comparably lower levels in breast milk substitutes (such as diluted milk, teas), such programs are undoubtedly beneficial for childhood micronutrient status in developing countries.

In addition to breast milk, promoting increased intake of other animal food sources, fruits, and vegetables can lead to improved micronutrient intake. In Niger, mass media, including use of drama, radio skits, as well as counseling cards, led to increases in the proportion of mothers who fed their young children dark leafy greens. In the week prior to the survey, the proportion of children who had eaten dark GLVs increased from 57% to 94%. The proportion of mothers who had eaten liver in the week prior to the survey increased from 43% to 73% [196]. A social marketing campaign in Indonesia increased consumption of both eggs and dark GLVs among mothers and young children, which would benefit not only vitamin A intake but also vitamin D, riboflavin, and $B_{12}$ [197]. A study in Bangladesh measured the ability of mothers to feed dark GLVs to their young children to assess whether the children were able to consume sufficient (40 g) quantities to meet vitamin A requirements. Median intakes among 118 children were 41 g for children 6–11 months of age, 71 g for those aged 12–17 months, and 129 g for those aged 18–35 months [198].

Gibson et al. [199] tested the impact of (1) increasing consumption of whole dried fish with bones and orange-red fruits (papayas and mangoes); (2) encouraging inclusion of absorption enhancers of iron, zinc, provitamin A carotenoids, and vitamin A in household diets; and (3) germination, fermentation, and soaking to reduce the phytate content of maize in research among rural Malawi children 6–23 months of age. They found that intakes of energy, protein, calcium, riboflavin, available zinc, and available iron were higher in the intervention children than in controls, as was mid-upper arm circumference and arm muscle area. However, weight and height Z-score were not different between groups [199]. A study in Tanzania compared a complementary food processed to reduce phytates compared to an unprocessed food and found no difference in iron levels in children [200]. Had iron and other micronutrients been added to the food, these results would likely have been different.

Several programs have trained health workers to provide counseling on young child feeding that have led to benefits in micronutrient intake. Using a positive-deviance approach to counseling mothers of malnourished children in Vietnam, Save the Children found, in addition to benefits on child growth, a higher proportion of children in the intervention group were fed high-nutrient foods (peanuts, soybeans, meat, eggs, fish, shrimp) and were fed them more frequently than control children [201]. Government health workers in Haryana, India, were trained to provide counseling to mothers of young children [202]. Opportunities for counseling conducted by Anganwadi workers included monthly home visits for births until aged 12 months and weighing once every 3 months for children under 2 years of age. Counseling also took place during immunization clinics run by the auxiliary nurse midwives and sick child contacts with health care providers. In addition, messages on infant feeding were discussed at monthly meetings conducted by the auxiliary nurse midwives with community representatives, who held neighborhood meetings once a month with caretakers of children under 2 years old. This program led to improvements in diets of children at 9 months postpartum. The study observed a significant increase in the proportion of children fed milk (92% vs. 83%), legumes (18% vs. 7%), and vegetables (7% vs. 2%) in the intervention group compared to the control group, respectively. Many of these improvements were also found at 18 months. There was no difference in meat or egg consumption between groups (<1% ate these at 9 and 18 months).

A program to improve the quality and quantity of nutrition education offered by health workers in Peru found that a significantly higher proportion of children in the intervention group received chicken liver, fish, or egg than did controls at ages 6 and 8 months. Iron and zinc intake and adjusted mean increases in weight and length were all significantly greater in the intervention area than in the control area [203]. The Integrated Management of Childhood Illnesses (IMCI) program includes training on nutrition counseling for health providers, and nutrition counseling is expected to be done at encounters with young children. To evaluate the effectiveness of this approach, a study was conducted in 28 health centers in Pelotas, Brazil. The average age of children in the study was 6 months. Advice given to mothers was significantly greater for the intervention group compared to controls (including advice to give their children egg yolks, chicken/mince-meat, chicken liver, beans, and GLVs) [204].

### 18.4.1.2  PROMOTING ANIMAL PRODUCTION AND HOME GARDENING

Helen Keller International, in conjunction with numerous Bangladeshi nongovernmental organizations, promoted home gardens. The baseline study showed that women in families who had home gardens with more varieties of fruits and vegetables had higher intakes of vitamin A than those with fewer varieties. An evaluation of another program to increase production of carotene-rich foods in Bangladesh showed it had a measurable impact on the diets of children under 3 years of age [205]. While the focus was on pro-vitamin A-rich foods, increased consumption of vegetables was also likely to have improved intake for other nutrients.

Another study in Bangladesh assessed the impact of the Participatory Livestock Development Project, which encouraged production of poultry. Although monthly egg production increased in the intervention households, women and girls ate similar amounts of poultry and eggs in both groups. However, those in the intervention group ate higher quantities of small fish [206]. Thus, even though the eggs and chicken were sold, the increased incomes resulted in improved dietary intakes. Finally, the Food and Agricultural Research Management (FARM)-Africa evaluated the impact of a goat-raising project among 5,500 women in rural Ethiopia on milk consumption. They found that after 1 year of the project, the proportion of children who consumed milk 7 days a week increased dramatically [207].

### 18.4.2  Fortification

*Fortification* is the addition of nutrients at levels higher than those found in the original or comparable food. Requirements for both iron and zinc during pregnancy [208] generally cannot be met through dietary sources alone unless foods have been fortified. It is particularly difficult to promote complementary foods adequate in all nutrients without fortification [209, 210]. Fortification of staple foods with multiple micronutrients has become more common in developing countries, particularly in Latin America. Wheat flour is the most common vehicle for multiple-micronutrient fortification;

more recently, maize flour has been fortified with multiple micronutrients. Iron fortification of wheat is mandatory in most countries of Latin America, and it usually involves more than one nutrient [211]. While thiamin, riboflavin, and niacin previously were commonly added along with iron, currently FA is also being used in many countries. Fortification of staples with vitamin A, zinc, calcium, copper, or other minerals is as yet uncommon. Aside from mandatory fortification, voluntary fortification is also possible, with foods such as margarine, milk, and sugar commonly fortified with one or several nutrients.

In the mid 1990s, the United States passed regulations mandating fortification of flour with FA at a level of 140 μg FA to every 100 g of grain, which was projected to result in a mean additional intake of 100 μg FA per day [212]. However, to reduce neural tube defects substantially, an additional 200–400 μg of FA has been suggested to be needed. This is why the Centers for Disease Control in the United States recommends that women of reproductive age consume a supplement containing 400 μg of FA daily [213].

The results of mandated fortification with FA are impressive. Choumenkovitch et al. [214] compared data on FA intake among adults older than 19 years in the Framingham Offspring Cohort Study before and after the fortification program took place. The proportion of individuals with intakes less than the recommended 320 μg dietary folate equivalents/day decreased from 49% to 7%. The mean levels increased by 323 μg dietary folate equivalents/day among nonsupplement users. The higher level of intake observed over what was predicted may in part be explained by higher levels of FA found in some fortified foods over that stated on the labels. Red blood cell (RBC) folate increased among those exposed to fortification. In addition, mean total homocysteine concentration decreased from 10.1 to 9.4 μmol/L, as did the prevalence of high homocysteine concentrations (>13 μmol/L), which decreased from 18.7% to 9.8% [215]. Analyses of the National Health and Nutrition Examination Survey (NHANES) found that folate intake increased dramatically in the United States following fortification [216] for women of reproductive age (15–44 years) who did not use supplements. Fortification resulted in increases in mean serum folate from 10.7 nmol/L (prefortification) to 28.6 nmol/L (postfortification). In Canada, Ray et al. [217] also observed increases in red cell folate associated with the mandated fortification of foods. They reported that among 38,000 Ontarian women aged 18 to 42 years, mean RBC folate increased from prefortification levels of 527 nmol/L to 741 nmol/L after January 1, 1998.

The prevalence of neural tube defects decreased dramatically in both Canada and the United States after flour was fortified with FA [216–218]. Ray et al. [217] reported a 50% decline in open neural tube defects in Ontario, Canada, between 1994 and 2000, with a corresponding increase in serum folate levels. Persad et al. [218] found similar results in Nova Scotia. In the United States, the Centers for Disease Control and Prevention reported a decline of 26% in neural tube defects between 1995–1996 and 1999–2000 [219].

Several developing countries have also mandated folate fortification, especially in the Americas. Costa Rica has mandated fortification of milk (in 2001), wheat (in 1998), and corn flour (1999) [220]. Folate deficiency was reduced from 19% to 3% in urban areas and from 31% to 12% in rural areas among women 15–44 years of age between 1996 and 2001. The rate of neural tube defects also decreased accordingly, from 9.7 per 1,000 live births to 6.3. Flour is also fortified with iron. Similar success was also reported in Chile [221]. As countries expand fortification efforts, there are many logistical and quality control measures needed for fortificants to be added and sustained at appropriate levels. It will also be necessary to ensure that the target population consumes sufficient quantities of the fortified products. However, even in the United States, where fortification of foods has been a long-standing practice, because of the low intakes of certain foods and limited number of foods that are fortified, significant proportions of women consume less than adequate micronutrients.

Many countries have voluntary fortification of products, such as the fortification of margarine, noodles, and orange drink in the Philippines with vitamin A and the fortification of soy sauce in China with iron (sodium EDTA) and fish sauce in Vietnam. However, micronutrient deficiencies are still highly prevalent in many countries, and often most of the fortified products are mainly consumed by the middle class. Zinc is added to many breakfast cereals in the United States and is included in the standard formula for fortified blended foods used by the World Food Program. Premixes are usually used to add fortificants to foods. They include a blend of several micronutrients, a filler (cornstarch, wheat starch, or calcium sulfate), and a free-flowing agent (such as tricalcium phosphate). The bioavailability and stability of the nutrient and its organoleptic properties are especially important concerns for premixes. *CODEX Alimentarius* (p. 63) [222] specifies that "when a supplementary food for older infants and young children is supplemented with one or more nutrients, the total amount of the vitamins and minerals should be at least 2/3 the reference daily requirements per 100 g of the food on a dry matter basis." However, the *CODEX* also states that this table is "simply a guideline to emphasize the nutrients to be considered in the development of a supplementary food," and that "appropriate modifications might have to be made for adapting them (the guidelines) to specific conditions".

Encouraging the involvement of industry in promotion of fortified foods targeted to at-risk groups (such as fortified complementary foods for toddlers and fortified tonics for pregnant and breast-feeding women) is an important mechanism to improve multiple-micronutrient status in developing countries. Also, educating industry and governments on the benefits of multiple fortification of staples with additional nutrients (iron, zinc, FA, vitamin A) would help address deficiencies of these nutrients. Examples of such collaborations are discussed next.

In Mexico, a national program currently called Oportunidades (previously known as Progresa: Program for Education, Health, and Nutrition) was developed in 1997 to address malnutrition in low-income young children. It currently reaches 20% of Mexico's families. The program provides a fortified food to pregnant women and young children. The food (papilla) consists of dry whole milk, sugar, and maltodextrin and contains per 44-g ration the following: 5.8 g protein, 194 kcal energy, 6.6 g fats, and carbohydrates in addition to the nutrients shown in Table 18.5. Improvements in iron status were not as great as expected, which led to studies of bioavailability of iron in the food. These studies found that ferrous sulfate is more effective as a fortificant to milk-based products than reduced iron or ferrous fumarate [223].

Other countries, including Ecuador, Colombia, Guatemala, and Peru, have also distributed fortified complementary foods produced by local industries for young child feeding [224]. With increasingly urban populations buying increasing proportions of their food, such fortified foods could be a major means of improving young child nutritional status. Lutter and Dewey [225] suggested appropriate levels of over 15 micronutrients for a fortified complementary food. Other programs to increase micronutrient intakes of young children are now being tried on a large-scale basis. Micronutrient sprinkles have been developed using encapsulated forms of some of the nutrients, which allows multiple-nutrient combinations [210, 226]. They are less costly to produce and ship than a fortified complementary food and can be used to fortify foods fed to young children [224]. The impact of sprinkles containing iron and zinc was tested over a 2-month period in anemic toddlers in Ghana, and compliance was high (82% of children consumed it at least five times a week). Results of the study found that both iron and zinc combined and iron-containing sprinkles alone led to reductions in anemia, although iron alone was more effective [227]. More recently, MVM sprinkles have been effective in improving nutrient status.

Several countries have provided sprinkles for use in feeding young children (Guyana, Bolivia, Haiti, Mongolia, Ghana), and the sprinkles are being sold through a social marketing program by Population Services International in pilot programs in Haiti and Pakistan. In Mongolia, World Vision distributed sprinkles to over 10,000 children starting in 2001 as a way to reduce rickets and iron deficiency [228]. HKI is distributing multiple-micronutrient sprinkles or foodlets to tsunami victims aged 6 months to 12 years for a duration of 3 months [229]. A pilot program provided weekly MVM capsules (Nutrivit) to 20,000 women of child-bearing age and weekly foodlets to 8,000 children under age 5 years in low-income urban areas of Chiclayo Peru. This program was conducted by the Integrated Food Security Program in 2001 (A. Lechtig, personal communication) with supplements distributed by community volunteers.

Large-scale programs are planned through the public sector primary health care program implemented by Ministry of Health in Pakistan. BRAC, in Bangladesh, is planning to distribute sprinkles through their Female Community Health Worker program (popularly known as *Shastha Shebika*). In both countries, sprinkles would be produced locally through public–private partnerships via a technology transfer agreement. The cost per daily sachet of locally produced sprinkles is estimated to range from US $0.010 to US $0.015 compared to US $0.020 to US $0.025 if imported [230].

Another fortified product, which is a fat-based spread (like peanut butter), has been fortified with multiple micronutrients. Because it is fat-based and contains no water, the micronutrients in the spread do not react with each other, which results in a longer shelf life than that of a powder. Local production has been done in Malawi (Project Peanut Butter), Niger, and the Congo and is to start in Zimbabwe and in Mozambique at a cost of about US$.06 per 100 kcal [231]. The effect of such fat-based spreads is currently being tested at a community level among HIV-infected populations and as a means of feeding infants of HIV-infected mothers once the mothers stop breast-feeding (E. Piwoz, personal communication).

Comparison among sprinkles, foodlets, and fortified peanut paste has found that while all three improved micronutrient status compared to controls, the fortified peanut paste was the only one to improve growth (S. Adu-Afarwuah, personal communication). The fortified paste is preferable from a growth viewpoint, and future analyses of impacts on other nutrients may illustrate additional benefits for nutrient absorption as well. However, the cost of the fortified paste is about three times that for the sprinkles, which would likely affect coverage.

### 18.4.3  Multiple-Micronutrient Supplements

Though improving micronutrient intake through dietary approaches is the desirable method, supplements can play a particularly important role for selected nutrients. For example, dietary approaches have not been effective strategies in Asia, specifically the Indian subcontinent, while in fact vitamin A supplementation has been one of the few successful strategies in those countries. Supplements can be especially important during pregnancy, for adolescents and women of reproductive age, and for the elderly. For children under the age of 2 y, because of the need to have a liquid supplement, it is logistically difficult to provide sufficient quantities of supplements at low cost. Trials using MVM sprinkles or a foodlet containing micronutrients for addition to complementary foods are providing new alternatives to liquid supplements, as described in this chapter under fortification.

Only a few countries provide multiple-micronutrient supplements through the health system. In Cuba, a multiple supplement containing 35 mg of iron is provided to pregnant women. At prenatal care visits, pregnant women in Honduras and Thailand receive a multiple supplement. The only country to distribute multiple vitamins on a population basis is Cuba, in response to the neuropathy epidemic related to thiamin and other micronutrient deficiencies. National distribution of supplements to Cubans over 1 year of age began in 1993 [232]. Several effectiveness trials (in Bangladesh, India, Indonesia, Niger, the Philippines, Tanzania, and Viet Nam) have distributed MVM supplements to pregnant women through the public health sector and found that compliance with supplements has been high. Some programs are assessing the impact of providing supplements to women before marriage to improve nutritional status prior to pregnancy.

In 1992, the UK Department of Health began recommending that all women who plan to become pregnant should consume additional FA prior to conception and during the first 12 weeks of pregnancy by eating more folate-rich foods and taking a dietary supplement of 400 µg of FA. In a study of 411 women attending antenatal clinics between July and October 1993, only 14% of the pregnancies were unplanned. However, only 2% of the women had increased their intake of folate-rich foods, only 3% had taken folate-containing supplements prior to conception, and none had done both [233]. Only one third of the women had heard of the recommendation, and of those, only 37% received information before conception.

The Centers for Disease Control and Prevention also recommend that pregnant women should consume 30 mg/day of iron supplements starting at the first prenatal visit [234], and that women of reproductive age should take FA supplements. Other than these recommendations, there is no recognized policy in the United States concerning multiple-supplement use. Even so, 97% of pregnant women reported being advised to take supplements during pregnancy in the National Maternal and Infant Health Survey, conducted in 1988. This survey also found that 81% of women reported consuming supplements at least 3 days a week during the 3 months after they found out they were pregnant [235].

The National Health Interview Surveys collect information regarding supplement use in the past year by US adults. Data are available for 1987, 1992, and 2000. In the 1987 survey, 22% of adults reported that they had consumed A vitamin or mineral supplement on a daily basis. This rate was 23% in 1992 and increased to 30% in 2000 [236]. The 1989–1991 Continuing Survey of Food Intakes by Individuals found that

34% of white men and 43% of white women reported using supplements every day or "every so often" [237]. A 1997 national telephone survey found that 43% of women of reproductive age reported consuming a supplement containing FA, with 32% consuming it on a daily basis and 12% taking it less than daily [238]. Analyses of the NHANES [239] conducted between 1994 and 1998 found that 44% of women aged 20–39 y took vitamin and mineral supplements, mostly multiples. Radimer et al. [240] analyzed the NHANES 1999–2000 data and found that 52% of adults had taken supplements in the month before the survey, and 35% took multiples.

Thus, in the United States, a country where animal products provide 60% of food consumption and where there is widespread availability of fruits, vegetables, and fortified foods, supplements form an important component of nutrient intake for a large proportion of the population. While in the United States and other developed countries supplements are easily accessible, the availability of appropriate supplements is limited in most developing countries. High-quality multiple-micronutrient supplements are currently available from UNICEF, but the International Dispensary Association (IDA) and other nonprofit agencies procure them for sale to nonprofit organizations and developing country governments, and these may be inappropriate because of insufficient quantities of iron, zinc, copper, vitamin A, or FA. Assessments of supplements available for retail sale in several developing countries found limited availability, high cost, and inappropriate levels of nutrients in supplements, low levels of iron, and poor packaging [241, 242].

While multiple supplements are currently recommended for consumption on a daily basis, their use on a weekly basis, especially for women of reproductive age and adolescents, is a strategy that should be tested. Weekly or biweekly doses of iron, iodine, vitamin A, vitamin D, and riboflavin have been shown to be effective [243–245]. Theoretically, daily supplementation should not be necessary since requirements are based on *average* daily intakes, although a meta-analysis of daily versus weekly iron supplements concluded that iron should be provided daily during pregnancy [245].

Multivitamin and mineral supplements are widely prescribed by obstetricians and pediatricians in many developed countries. However, the effectiveness of these supplements in promoting better maternal and child health in well-nourished populations has been questioned. Although the presence of multiple-micronutrient deficiencies offers justification for the use of these supplements in developing areas, the cost of the supplements is an important limitation. Evidence of positive effects on maternal, fetal, and infant health would increase the rationale for multinutrient supplements to be used. Expanding the availability of supplements to consumers through private sector involvement, especially with social marketing of products to keep costs low, would help meet some of the current constraints to increased supplement use in developing countries.

Social marketing of multiple supplements has increased in the last several years. In 2002, Population Services International sold 16.3 million micronutrient supplements throughout the developing world, including multiple supplements for women of reproductive age in Bolivia, India, Pakistan, Paraguay, Togo, Venezuela, and Zambia and iron folate tablets in India [241]. An evaluation of a social marketing campaign targeting women of reproductive age in Santa Cruz, Bolivia, illustrated that such efforts are able to reach low-income women. In this program, conducted in 1998, ever-use of multivitamins rose 11% to 25% among all women, but the increase was greatest in those with lower SES (7% to 20%) compared to 17% to 33% in those with higher SES. Of all women, 11% had ever tried VitalDia (the marketed product), and 7% had consumed it in the last 3 months [246].

## 18.5  CONCLUSIONS

Results of interventions focused on improving multiple-micronutrient status are mixed. Multiples (usually containing zinc) have slightly less impact on iron status than iron alone, but they increase levels of other important nutrients beneficial for health (zinc, FA, vitamin A, etc.). Supplements in pregnant women may or may not benefit the birth weight of the child, depending on the health and nutritional status of the mother. However, improving a woman's micronutrient status is a benefit in and of itself. Clearly, increasing FA intake has benefits for both women's health (reduced homocysteine) and child health (reduced neural tube defects).

Optimally, improving dietary intake is a preferred way to increase multiple-micronutrient status. Increasing fruits and vegetable intake will lead to improvements simultaneously in numerous micronutrients, with additional benefits for other factors (e.g., other antioxidants, fiber) in these foods. Increasing ASFs may be beneficial especially in very poor countries as a means of increasing micronutrients, but the long-term impacts on health (due to relationships with obesity, diabetes, and cardiovascular disease) mean addressing trends in overconsumption as well [247].

Some have suggested that dietary approaches are the most sustainable or cost-effective strategies. However, data to support this are limited. Promotion of dietary changes often necessitates continued counseling and other behavior change efforts, which have their own costs. Each approach may be needed, depending on the context. An effort to increase egg consumption in Indonesia held great promise for improving the status of several micronutrients. However, the Asian economic crisis in the early 2000s led to reductions in the availability of chickens, and thus this approach became less viable.

Multiple fortification of staple foods with iron, FA, other B vitamins, and other nutrients when feasible (vitamin A, iodine) can have high impacts at low cost. A randomized controlled trial illustrated the different *biologic* effects that each of these approaches can have on improving folate status [248]. Women who received FA supplements had significantly greater intakes of FA than those who received fortified foods, foods high in folate, dietary advice on which foods to consume to improve folate status, or controls. Improvements in red cell folate were four to five times higher in those who received supplements or fortified foods than the dietary folate or dietary advice groups. However, these two groups still showed some improvement over controls in red cell folate.

Another analysis compared three approaches for increasing FA intake in relation to reducing cardiovascular disease. Boushey et al. [249] compared projected savings in lives with three strategies to increase folate intake: increases in fruits and vegetables, fortification of flour and cereal products, and use of supplements. If dietary interventions were able to increase the consumption of fruits and vegetables by two to three more times per day, resulting in 100 µg of additional folate per day, and if 40% of the population complied with this change, the number of prevented deaths annually would be 7,500 in men and 6,000 in women. Fortification of grain products with 350 µg/100 grams FA was estimated to reduce 30,000 deaths among men and 19,000 deaths among women annually. Use of supplements containing 400 µg by 50% of the population would result in 15,500 and 12,500 preventable deaths among men and women, respectively.

Such analyses are extremely useful in developing program options. All the issues associated with program interventions (education, social marketing, procurement, monitoring, distribution, compliance, etc.) and the costs to optimize the success of each strategy need to be considered in the selection of strategies to improve multiple-micronutrient intake.

Effectiveness trials are currently under way to assess the large-scale impact of providing multiple-micronutrient supplements to pregnant women, sprinkles and foodlets to young children, and fortified peanut spreads to HIV-infected populations in developing countries. These results along with continued monitoring of food consumption and fortification patterns will be helpful for educating policymakers about the best approaches to improve overall micronutrient status.

## REFERENCES

1. Rosado J, Bourges H, Saint-Martin B. Deficiencia de vitaminas y minerales en México. Una revisión crítica del estado de la información: I. Deficiencia de minerales. Salud Pub Mex 1995;37:130–139.
2. Rosado J, Bourges H, Saint-Martin B. Deficiencia de vitaminas y minerales en México. Una revisión crítica del estado de la información: II. Deficiencia de vitaminas. Salud Pub Mex 1995;37:452–461.
3. Rivera J, Long K, Gonzales-Cossio T, et al. Nutrición y Salud: Un menú para la familia. In: Cuadernos de salud. Problemas pretasicionales. Secretería de Salud, México, 1994.
4. Caballero B. Nutritional implications of dietary interactions: a review. Food Nutr Bull 1988;10(2):9–20.
5. Rosado JL, López P, Morales M, Munoz E, Allen LH. Bioavailability of energy, nitrogen, fat, zinc, iron and calcium from rural and urban Mexican diets. Br J Nutr 1992;68:45–58.
6. Hambidge KM. Zinc and diarrhea. Acta Paediatr 1992;81:82–86.
7. Jalal F, Nesheim MC, Agus Z, Sanjur D, Habicht JP. Serum retinol concentrations in children are affected by food sources of β-carotene, fat intake and anthelminthic drug treatment. Am J Clin Nutr 1998;68:623–629.
8. Wallwork JC, Fosmire GI, Sandstead H. Effect of zinc deficiency on appetite and plasma aminoacid concentrations in the rat. Br J Nutr 1981;43:127–136.
9. Golden BE, Golden HN. Relationship among dietary quality, children's appetites, growth stunting and efficiency of growth in poor populations. Food Nutr Bull 1991;13:105–109.
10. Skikne B, Baynes RD. Iron absorption. In: Iron metabolism in health and disease. Brock JH, Halliday JW, Pippard MJ, Powell LW, eds. London: Saunders, 1994:151–187.
11. Walker FC, Kordas K, Stoltzfus RJ, Black RE. Interactive effects of iron and zinc on biochemical and functional outcomes in supplementation trials. Am J Clin Nutr 2005;82:5–12.
12. Alarcon K, Kolsteren PW, Prada AM, Chian AM, Velarde RE, Pecho IL, et al. Effects of separate delivery of zinc or zinc and vitamin A on hemoglobin response, growth, and diarrhea in young Peruvian children receiving iron therapy for anemia. Am J Clin Nutr 2004;80:1276–1282.
13. O'Brien KO, Zavaleta N, Caulfield LE, Wen J, Abrams SA. Prenatal iron supplements impair zinc absorption in pregnant Peruvian women. J Nutr 2000;130:2251–2255.
14. Udomkesmalee E, Dhanamitta S, Sirisinha S, Charoenkiatkul S, Tuntipopipat S, Banjong O, et al. Effect of vitamin A and zinc supplementation on the nutriture of children in northeast Thailand. Am J Clin Nutr 1992;56:50–57.
15. Christian P, West KP Jr. Interactions between zinc and vitamin A: an update. Am J Clin Nutr 1998;68(suppl):435S–441S.
16. Mejia LA, Arroyave G. The effect of vitamin A fortification of sugar on iron metabolism in Central American children. Am J Clin Nutr 1982;36:87–93.
17. Suharno D, West CE, Muhilal, Karyadi D, Hautvast JG. Supplementation with vitamin A and iron for nutritional anaemia in pregnant women in West Java, Indonesia. Lancet 1993;342:1325–1328.

18. Shatrugna V, Raman L, Uma K, Sujatha T. Interaction between vitamin A and iron: effects of supplements in pregnancy. Int J Vitam Nutr Res 1997;67:145–148.

19. Ramakrishnan U. Prevalence of micronutrient malnutrition worldwide. Nutr Rev 2002;60(5): S46–S52.

20. UNICEF, Micronutrient Initiative. Vitamin and mineral deficiency: a Global Progress Report, 2004. Available at: http://www.micronutrient.org/reports/copy%20of%20report.asp.

21. Allen LH, Backstrand JR, Chávez A, Pelto GH. People cannot live by tortillas alone: the results of the Mexico Nutrition CRSP. Storrs, CT: Department of Nutritional Sciences, University of Connecticut, 1992.

22. Allen LH. The Nutrition CRSP: what is marginal malnutrition, and does it affect human function? Nutr Rev 1993;51(9):255–267.

23. Gitau R, Makasa M, Kasonka L, Sinkala M, Chintu C, Tomkins A, et al. Maternal micronutrient status and decreased growth of Zambian infants born during and after the maize price increases resulting from the southern African drought of 2001–2002. Public Health Nutr 2005;8(7):837–843.

24. Mora JO, Mora OL. Deficiencias de micronutrients en America Latina y el Caribe. Vitamins. Washington, DC: Pan American Health Organization, 1998.

25. Bamji MS, Lakshmi AV. Less recognized micronutrient deficiencies in India. NFI Bull 1998;19(2):5–8.

26. Dijkhuizen MA, Wieringa FT, West CE, Muherdiyantiningsih M. Concurrent micronutrient deficiencies in lactating mothers and their infants in Indonesia. Am J Clin Nutr 2001;73:786–791.

27. Calloway DH, Murphy SP, Beaton GH. Food intake and human function: a cross-project perspective. University of California, Berkeley, 1988.

28. Ma AG, Chen XC, Wang Y, Xu RX, Zheng MC, Li JS. The multiple vitamin status of Chinese pregnant women with anemia and nonanemia in the last trimester. J Nutr Sci Vitaminol (Tokyo) 2004;50(2):87–92.

29. Pathak P, Kapil U, Kapoor SK, Saxena R, Kumar A, Gupta N, et al. Prevalence of multiple micronutrient deficiencies amongst pregnant women in a rural area of Haryana. Indian J Pediatr 2004;71(11):1007–1014.

30. Neufeld LM, Ramakrishnan U, Gonzales-Cossio T, Rivera J, Martorell R. Prevalence of multiple micronutrient malnutrition during pregnancy in a semi-rural community in Mexico [abstract]. IUNS Congress, Vienna, Austria, August 27–September 1, 2001.

31. Jiang T, Christian P, Khatry SK, Wu L, West KP Jr. Micronutrient deficiencies in early pregnancy are common, concurrent, and vary by season among rural Nepali pregnant women. J Nutr 2005;135(5):1106–1112.

32. Ganji VK, Mohammmad R. Demographic, health, lifestyle, and blood vitamin determinants of serum total homocysteine concentrations in the third National Health and Nutrition Examination Survey, 1988–1994. Am J Clin Nutr 2003;77:826–833.

33. Vollset SE, Refsum H, Irgens, LM, Emblem BM, Tverdal A, Gjessing HK, et al. Plasma total homocysteine, pregnancy complications, and adverse pregnancy outcomes: the Hordaland Homocysteine Study. Am J Clin Nutr 2000;71:962–968.

34. Murphy MM, Scott JM, Arija V, Molloy AM, Fernandez-Ballart JD. Maternal homocysteine before conception and throughout pregnancy predicts fetal homocysteine and birth weight. Clin Chem 2004;50(8):1406–1412.

35. Bondevik G, Lie R, Ulstein,M, Kvåle G. Seasonal variation in risk of anemia among pregnant Nepali women. Int J Gynaecol Obstet 2000;69(3):215–222.

36. Gamble MV, Ahsan H, Liu X, Factor-Litvak P, Ilievski V, Slavkovich V, et al. Folate and cobalamin deficiencies and hyperhomocysteinemia in Bangladesh. Am J Clin Nutr 2005;81:1372–1377.

37. Bondevik GT, Schneede J, Refsum H, Lie RT, Ulstein M, Kvale G. Homocysteine and methylmalonic acid levels in pregnant Nepali women. Should cobalamin supplementation be considered? Eur J Clin Nutr 2001;55:856–864.

38. Allen LH, Rosado JL, Casterline JE, Lopez P, Munoz E, Garcia OP, et al. Lack of hemoglobin response to iron supplementation in anemic Mexican preschoolers with multiple micronutrient deficiencies. Am J Clin Nutr 2000;71:1485–1494.

39. Lartey A, Manu A, Brown KH, Dewey KG. Predictors of micronutrient status among 6- to 12-month-old breast-fed Ghanaian infants. J Nutr 2000;130(2):199–207.

40. Kimmons JE, Dewey KG, Haque E, Chakraborty J, Osendarp SJ, Brown KH. Low nutrient intakes among infants in rural Bangladesh are attributable to low intake and micronutrient density of complementary foods. J Nutr 2005;135(3):444–451.

41. Ahmed F, Khan MR, Akhtaruzzaman M, Karim R, Marks GC, Banu CP, et al. Efficacy of twice-weekly multiple micronutrient supplementation for improving the hemoglobin and micronutrient status of anemic adolescent schoolgirls in Bangladesh. Am J Clin Nutr 2005;82(4):829–835.

42. Albalak R, Ramakrishnan U, Stein AD, van der Haar F, Haber MJ, Schroeder DG, et al. Co-occurrence of nutrition problems in Honduran children. J Nutr 2000;130(9):2271–2273.

43. Ramakrishnan U, Majrekar, R, Gonzales-Cossio T, Rivera J, Martorell R. Micronutrients and pregnancy outcomes: a review of the literature. Nutr Res 1999;19:103–159.

44. Cherry FF, Sandstead HH, Wickeremasinghe AR. Adolescent pregnancy: zinc supplementation and iron effects. Ann N Y Acad Sci 1993;678:330–333.

45. Caulfield LE, Zavaleta N, Figueroa A, Leon Z. Maternal zinc supplementation does not affect size at birth or pregnancy duration in Peru. J Nutr 1999;129:1563–1568.

46. Osendarp SJM, van Raaij JMA, Arifeen SE, Wahed M, Caqui AH, Fuchs GJ. A randomized, placebo-controlled trial of the effect of zinc supplementation during pregnancy on pregnancy outcome in Bangladesh urban poor. Am J Clin Nutr 2000;71:114–119.

47. Caulfield LE, Zavaleta N, Figueroa A. Adding zinc to prenatal iron and folate supplements improves maternal and neonatal zinc status in a Peruvian population. Am J Clin Nutr 1999;69:1257–1263.

48. Merialdi M, Caulfield LE, Zavaleta N, Figueroa A, DiPietro JA. Adding zinc to prenatal iron and folate tablets improves neurobehavioral development. Am J Obstet Gynecol 1999;180:483–490.

49. Osendarp SJ, West CE, Black RE, Maternal Zinc Supplementation Study Group. The need for maternal zinc supplementation in developing countries: an unresolved issue. J Nutr 2003;133:817S–827S.

50. Christian P, Shrestha SR, Leclerq SC, Khatry SK, Jiang T, Wagner T, et al. Supplementation with micronutrients in addition to iron and folic acid does not further improve hematologic status of pregnant women in rural Nepal. J Nutr 2003;133:3492–3498.

51. Achadi EL, Hansell MJ, Sloan NL, Anderson MA. Women's nutritional status, iron consumption and weight gain during pregnancy in relation to neonatal weight and length in West Java, Indonesia. Int J Gynaecol Obstet 1995;48(suppl):S103–S119.

52. Juarez-Vazquez J, Bonizzoni E, Scotti A. Iron plus folate is more effective than iron alone in the treatment of iron deficiency anaemia in pregnancy: a randomised, double blind clinical trial. BJOG 2002;109(9):1009–1014.

53. Christian P, Khatry SK, Yamini S, Stallings R, LeClerq SC, Shrestha SR, et al. Zinc supplementation might potentiate the effect of vitamin A in restoring night vision in pregnant Nepalese. Am J Clin Nutr 2001;73(6):1045–1051.

54. Dijkhuizen MA, Wieringa FT, West CE, Muhilal. Zinc plus β-carotene supplementation of pregnant women is superior to β-carotene supplementation alone in improving vitamin A status in both mothers and infants. Am J Clin Nutr 2004;80(5):1299–1307.

55. Kullander S, Kallen B. A prospective study of drugs and pregnancy. Acta Obstet Gynecol Scand 1976;55:287–295.

56. Scholl TO, Hediger ML, Bendich A, Schall JI, Smith WK, Krueger PM. Use of multivitamin/mineral prenatal supplements: influence on the outcome of pregnancy. Am J Epidemiol 1997;146(2):134–141.

57. Wu T, Buck G, Mendola P. Maternal cigarette smoking, regular use of multivitamin/mineral supplements, and risk of fetal death: the 1988 National Maternal and Infant Health Survey. Am J Epidemiol 1998;148(2):215–221.

58. Shaw GM, Liberman RF, Todoroff K, Wasserman CR. Low birth weight, preterm delivery, and periconceptional vitamin use. J Pediatr 1997;130(6):1013–1014.

59. Vahratian A, Siega-Riz AM, Savitz DA, Thorp JM Jr. Multivitamin use and the risk of preterm birth. Am J Epidemiol 2004;160(9):886–889.

60. Smithells RW, Sheppard S, Schorah CJ, Seller MJ, Nevin NC, Harris R, et al. Possible prevention of neural tube defects by periconceptional vitamin supplementation. Lancet 1980;1:339–340.

61. Czeizel AE. Controlled studies of multivitamin supplementation on pregnancy outcomes. Ann N Y Acad Sci 1993;687:266–275.

62. MRC Vitamin Study Research Group. Prevention of neural tube defects: results of the medical research council vitamin study. Lancet 1991;338(8760):131–137.

63. Dudás I, Rockenbauer M, Czeizel AE. The effect of preconceptional multivitamin supplementation on the menstrual cycle. Arch Gynecol Obstet 1995;256:115–123.

64. Czeizel AE, Métneki J, István D. The effect of preconceptional multivitamin supplementation on fertility. Int J Vitam Nutr Res 1996;66:55–58.

65. Czeizel AE, Métneki J, Dudás I. Higher rate of multiple births after periconceptional vitamin supplementation. N Engl J Med 1994;23:1687–1689.

66. Werler MM, Cragan JD, Wasserman CR, Shaw GM, Erickson JD, Mitchell AA. Multivitamin supplementation and multiple births. Am J Med Genet 1997;71:93–96.

67. Li DK, Daling JR, Mueller BA, Hickok DE, Fantel AG, Weiss NS. Periconceptional multivitamin use in relation to the risk of congenital urinary tract anomalies. Epidemiology 1995;6:212–218.

68. Czeizel AE. Reduction of urinary tract and cardiovascular defects by periconceptional multivitamin supplementation. Am J Med Genet 1996;62:179–183.

69. Khoury MJ, Shaw GM, Moore CA, Lammer EJ, Mulinare J. Does periconceptional multivitamin use reduce the risk of neural tube defects associated with other birth defects? Data from two population-based studies. Am J Med Genet 1996;61:30–36.

70. Botto LD, Khoury MJ, Mulinare J, Erickson JD. Periconceptional multivitamin use and the occurrence of conotruncal heart defects: results from a population-based, case-control study. Pediatrics 1996;98(5):911–917.

71. Yang Q, Khoury MJ, Olney R, Mulinare J. Does periconceptional multivitamin use reduce the risk for limb deficiency in offspring? Epidemiology 1997;8(2):157–161.

72. Hininger I, Favier M, Arnaud J, Faure H, Thoulon JM, Hariveau E, et al. Effects of a combined micronutrient supplementation on maternal biological status and newborn anthropometrics measurements: a randomized double-blind, placebo-controlled trial in apparently healthy pregnant women. Eur J Clin Nutr 2004;58:52–59.

73. Fawzi WW, Msamanga GI, Spiegelman D, Urassa EJ, McGrath N, Mwakagile D, et al. Randomised trial of effects of vitamin supplements on pregnancy outcomes and T cell counts in HIV-1-infected women in Tanzania. Lancet 1998;351:1477–1482.

74. Villamor E, Msamanga G, Spiegelman D, Antelman G, Peterson KE, Hunter DJ, et al. Effect of multivitamin and vitamin A supplements on weight gain during pregnancy among HIV-1-infected women. Am J Clin Nutr 2002;76:1082–1090.

75. Fawzi WW, Msamanga GI, Spiegelman D, Wei R, Kapiga S, Villamor E, et al. A randomized trial of multivitamin supplements and HIV disease progression and mortality. N Engl J Med 2004;351:23–32.

76. Merchant AT, Msamanga G, Villamor E, Saathoff E, O'Brien M, Hertzmark E, et al. Multivitamin supplementation of HIV-positive women during pregnancy reduces hypertension. J Nutr 2005;135:1776–1781.

77. Baylin A, Villamor E, Rifai N, Msamanga G, Fawzi WW. Effect of vitamin supplementation to HIV-infected pregnant women on the micronutrient status of their infants. Eur J Clin Nutr 2005;59:960–968.

78. Villamor E, Saathoff E, Manji K, Msamanga G, Hunter DJ, Fawzi WW. Vitamin supplements, socioeconomic status, and morbidity events as predictors of wasting in HIV-infected women from Tanzania. Am J Clin Nutr 2005;82:857–865.

79. Friis H, Gomo E, Nyazema N, Ndhlovu P, Krarup H, Kaestel P, et al. Effect of multimicronutrient supplementation on gestational length and birth size: a randomized, placebo-controlled, double-blind effectiveness trial in Zimbabwe. Am J Clin Nutr 2004;80(1):178–184.

80. Christian P, Khatry SK, Katz J, Pradhan EK, LeClerq SC, Shrestha SR, et al. Effects of alternative maternal micronutrient supplements on low birth weight in rural Nepal: double blind randomised community trial. BMJ 2003;326:571–576.

81. Christian P, West KP, Khatry SK, Leclerq SC, Pradhan EK, Katz J, et al. Effects of maternal micronutrient supplementation on fetal loss and infant mortality: a cluster-randomized trial in Nepal. Am J Clin Nutr 2003;78:1194–1202.

82. Ramakrishnan U, Gonzalez-Cossio T, Neufeld LM, Rivera J, Martorell R. Multiple micronutrient supplementation during pregnancy does not lead to greater infant birth size than does iron-only supplementation: a randomized controlled trial in a semirural community in Mexico. Am J Clin Nutr 2003;77:720–725.

83. Ramakrishnan U, Neufield L, Gonzalez-Cossio T, Villalpando S, Garcia-Guerra A, Rivera J, et al. Multiple micronutrient supplements during pregnancy do not reduce or improve iron status compared to iron-only supplements in semirural Mexico. J Nutr 2004;134:898–903.

84. Ramakrishnan U, Gonzales-Cossio T, Neufeld LM, Rivera J, Martorell R. Effect of prenatal multiple micronutrient supplements on maternal weight and skinfold changes: a randomized double-blind clinical trial in Mexico. Food Nutr Bull 2005;26(3):273–280.

85. García-Guerra A, Neufeld LM, González-Cossío T, Villalpando S, Rivera J, Martorell Ret al. Zinc, vitamin A and folate status of women supplemented with micronutrients or iron only during pregnancy: results of a randomized controlled trial in semi-rural Mexico [abstract]. International Vitamin A Consultative Group Meeting, Lima, Peru, 2004.

86. Makola D, Ash DM, Tatala SR, Latham MC, Ndossi G, Mehansho H. A micronutrient-fortified beverage prevents iron deficiency, reduces anemia and improves the hemoglobin concentration of pregnant Tanzanian women. J Nutr 2003;133(5):1339–1346.

87. Osrin D, Vaidya A, Shrestha Y, Baniya RB, Manandhar DS, Adhikari RK, et al. Effects of antenatal multiple micronutrient supplementation on birthweight and gestational duration in Nepal: double-blind, randomised controlled trial. Lancet 2005;365:955–962.

88. Kæstel P, Michaelsen KF, Aaby P, Friis H. Effects of prenatal multimicronutrient supplements on birth weight and perinatal mortality: a randomised, controlled trial in Guinea-Bissau. Eur J Clin Nutr 2005;59:1081–1089.

89. United Nations International Children's Emergency Fund/World Health Organization/United Nations University Study Team. Multiple Micronutrient Supplementation During Pregnancy (MMSDP): efficacy trials. London: Centre for International Child Health, Institute of Child Health, University College London, March 4–8, 2002.

90. World Health Organization/United Nations International Children's Emergency Fund. Preventing and controlling micronutrients deficiencies in people affected by the Asian tsunami: multiple vitamin and mineral supplements for pregnant and lactating women and for children aged 6 to 59 months. Joint Statement by the WHO and UNICEF. Geneva: World Health Organization, 2005.

91. World Health Organization. Nutrient requirements for people living with HIV/AIDS. Report of a Technical Consultation. Geneva: World Health Organization, May 13–15, 2003.

92. McClelland RS, Baeten JM, Overbaugh J, Richardson BA, Mandaliya K, Emery S, et al. Micronutrient supplementation increases genital tract shedding of HIV-1 in women: results of a randomized trial. J Acquir Immune Defic Syndr 2004;37(5):1657–1663.

93. Katz J, West KP, Khatry SK, Pradhan EK, Le Clerq SC, Christian P, et al. Maternal low-dose vitamin A or β-carotene supplementation has no effect on fetal loss and early infant mortality: a randomized cluster trial in Nepal. Am J Clin Nutr 2000;71:1570–1576.

94. Rao S, Yajnik CS, Kanade A, Fall CH, Margetts BM, Jackson AA, et al. Intake of micronutrient-rich foods in rural Indian mothers Is associated with the size of their babies at birth: Pune Maternal Nutrition Study. J Nutr 2001;131:1217–1224.

95. Christian P, Osrin D, Manandhar DS, Khatry SK, de L Costello AM, West KP Jr. Antenatal micronutrient supplements in Nepal. Lancet 2005;366:711–712.

96. Huffman SL, Habicht JP, Scrimshaw N. Micronutrient supplementation in pregnancy. Lancet 2005;366:2001.

97. Shrimpton R, Dalmiya N, Darnton-Hill I, Gross R. Micronutrient supplementation in pregnancy. Lancet 2005;366:2001–2002.

98. Allen LH. Maternal micronutrients malnutrition: effects on breast milk and infant nutrition, and priorities for intervention. SCN News Mid-1994;11:21–24.

99. Stoltzfus RJ, Hakimi M, Miller KW, Rasmussen KM, Dawiesah S, Habicht JP, et al. High dose vitamin A supplementation of breast feeding Indonesian mothers: effects on the vitamin A status of mother and infant. J Nutr 1993;123:666–675.

100. Arroyave G, Beghin I, Flores M, Soto de Guido CS, Ticas JM. [Effects of the intake of sugar fortified with retinol by pregnant women and infant whose diet is usually low in vitamin A. Study of the mother and child.] Arch Latinoam Nutr 1974;24(4):485–512.

101. Villard L, Bates CJ. Effect of vitamin A supplementation on plasma and breast milk vitamin A levels in poorly nourished Gambian women. Hum Nutr Clin Nutr 1987;41(1):47–58.

102. Bates CJ, Prentice AM, Paul AA, Sutcliffe BA, Watkinson M, Whitehead RG. Riboflavin status in Gambian pregnant and lactating women and its implications for recommended dietary allowances. Am J Clin Nutr 1981;34:928–935.

103. Bates CJ, Prentice AM, Prentice A, Lamb WH, Whitehead RG. The effect of vitamin C supplementation on lactating women in Keneba, a West African rural community. Int J Vitam Nutr Res 1983:53(1):68–76.

104. Sneed SM, Zane C, Thomas MR. The effects of ascorbic acid, vitamin B-6, vitamin B-12 and folic acid supplementation on the breast milk and maternal status of low socioeconomic lactating women. Am J Clin Nutr 1981;34(7):1338–1346.

105. Krebs NF, Reidinger CJ, Hartley S, Robertson AD, Hambidge KM. Zinc supplementation during lactation: effects on maternal status and milk zinc concentrations. Am J Clin Nutr 1995;61(5):1030–1036.

106. Krebs NF. Zinc supplementation during lactation. Am J Clin Nutr 1998;68(2S):495S–498S.

107. Arnaud J, Prual A, Prezoisi P, Cherouvrier F, Favier A, Galan P, et al. Effect of iron supplementation during pregnancy on trace element (Cu, Se, Zn) concentrations in serum and breast milk from Nigerian women. Ann Nutr Metab 1993;37(5):262–271.

108. Hernandez-Cordero S, Rivera J, Villalpando S, Gonzalez-Cossio T, Neufeld LM, Ramakrishnan U, et al. Multiple micronutrient supplementation during pregnancy: effect on breast milk retinol concentration at one month postpartum [abstract]. Fifteenth International Vitamin A Consultative Group Meeting, Hanoi, Vietnam, 12–15 February, 2001. FASEB J 2001;15(4). Abstract 505.7.

109. Gomo E, Filteau SM, Tomkins AM, Ndhlovu P, Michaelsen KF, Friis H. Subclinical mastitis among HIV-infected and uninfected Zimbabwean women participating in a multimicronutrient supplementation trial. Trans R Soc Trop Med Hyg 2003;97(2):212–216.

110. Filteau SM, Lietz G, Mulokozi G, Bilotta S, Henry CJ, Tomkins AM. Milk cytokines and subclinical breast inflammation in Tanzanian women: effects of dietary red palm oil or sunflower oil supplementation. Immunology 1999;97(4):595–600.

111. Tomkins A. Nutrition and maternal morbidity and mortality. Br J Nutr 2001;85(suppl 2):S93–S99.

112. United Nations International Children's Emergency Fund statistics. Monitoring the situation of women and children 2005. Available at: http://www.childinfo.org/areas/malnutrition/.

113. Schroeder DG. Malnutrition. In: Nutrition and health in developing countries. Semba RD, Bloem MW, eds. Totowa, NJ: Humana Press, 2001:393–426.

114. De Onis M. Child growth and development. In: Nutrition and health in developing countries. Semba RD, Bloem MW, eds. Totowa, NJ: Humana Press, 2001:71–91.

115. Ashworth A, Waterlow JC. Calorie and protein intakes and growth. Lancet 1969;1:776–777.

116. Gopalan C, Swamminathan MC, Kumari VKK, Rao DH, Vijayaraghavan K. Effect of calorie supplementation on growth of undernourished children. Am J Clin Nutr 1973;26:563–566.

117. Brown KH, Peerson JM, Rivera J, Allen LH. Effect of supplemental zinc on the growth and serum zinc concentrations of prepubertal children: a meta-analysis of randomized controlled trials. Am J Clin Nutr 2002;75:1062–1071.

118. Ramakrishnan U, Aburto N, McCabe G, Stoltzfus R, Martorell R. Multi-micronutrient supplements but not vitamin A or iron supplements alone improve child growth: results of three meta-analyses. J Nutr 2004;134:2592–2602.

119. Neufeld LM, Ramakrishnan U. Specific strategies to address micronutrient deficiencies in the young child: targeted fortification. In: Micronutrient deficiencies during the weaning period and the first years of life. Nestlé Nutrition Workshops Series Vol. 54: pediatric program, Nestec Ltd. Pettifor JM, Zlotkin S, eds. Basel, Switzerland: Karger, 2004:213–232.

120. Allen LH, Backstrand JR, Stanek EJ, Pelto GH, Chavez A, Molina E, et al. The interactive effects of dietary quality on the growth and attained size of young Mexican children. Am J Clin Nutr 1992;56:353–364.

121. Guldan GS, Zhang MY, Zhang YP, Hong JR, Zhang HX, Fu SY, et al. Weaning practices and growth in rural Sichuan infants: a positive deviance study. J Trop Pediatr 1993;39:168–175

122. Hop LT. Programs to improve production and consumption of animal source foods and malnutrition in Vietnam. J Nutr 2003;133(11 suppl 2):4006S–4009S.

123. Neumann CG, Bwibo NO, Murphy SP, Sigman M, Whaley S, Allen LH, et al. Animal source foods improve dietary quality, micronutrient status, growth and cognitive function in Kenyan school children: background, study design and baseline findings. J Nutr 2003;133(11 suppl 2):3941S–3949S.

124. Thu BD, Schultink W, Dillon D, Gross R, Leswara ND, Khoi HH. Effect of daily and weekly micronutrient supplementation on micronutrient deficiencies and growth in young Vietnamese children. Am J Clin Nutr 1999;69:80–86.

125. Rivera JA, Gonzalez-Cossio T, Flores M, Romero M, Rivera M, Tellez-Rojo MM, et al. Multiple micronutrient supplementation increases the growth of Mexican infants. Am J Clin Nutr 2001;74: 657–663.

126. Penny ME, Marin RM, Duran A, Peerson JM, Lanata CF, Lonnerdal B, et al. Randomized controlled trial of the effect of daily supplementation with zinc or multiple micronutrients on the morbidity, growth, and micronutrient status of young Peruvian children. Am J Clin Nutr 2004;457–465.

127. Baqui AH, Zaman K, Persson LA, El Arifeen S, Yunus M, Begur N, et al. Simultaneous weekly supplementation of iron and zinc is associated with lower morbidity due to diarrhea and acute lower respiratory infection in Bangladeshi infants. J Nutr 2003;133(12):4150–4157.

128. Black MM, Baqui AH, Zaman K, Ake Persson L, El Arifeen S, Le K, et al. Iron and zinc supplementation promote motor development and exploratory behavior among Bangladeshi infants. Am J Clin Nutr 2004;80:903–910.

129. Ramakrishnan U, Neufeld LM, Gonzalez-Cossio T, DiGirolamo A, Rivera J, Martorell R. Effects of multiple micronutrient supplements on child growth: a randomized controlled trial in semi-rural Mexico [abstract]. FASEB J 2004. Abstract 1522.

130. DiGirolamo AM, Ramakrishnan U, Neufeld LM, Rivera J, Gonzalez-Cossio T, Martorell R. Effects of multiple micronutrient supplements on child development in semi-rural Mexico [abstract]. FASEB J 2004. Abstract 3113.

131. Neufeld LM, García A, García R, Villalpando S, Rivera J, Martorell R et al. Effects of multiple micronutrient supplements on iron status and anemia prevalence: a randomized controlled trial in semi-rural Mexico [abstract]. FASEB J 2004. Abstract 564.5.

132. Untoro J, Karyadi E, Wibowo L, Erhardt MW, Gross R. Multiple micronutrient supplements improve micronutrient status and anemia but not growth and morbidity of Indonesian infants: a randomized, double-blind, placebo-controlled trial. J Nutr 2005;135(3):639S–645S.

133. López de Romaña G, Cusirramos S, López de Romaña D. Efficacy of multiple micronutrient supplementation for improving anemia, micronutrient status, growth, and morbidity of Peruvian infants. J Nutr 2005;135(3):646S–652S.

134. Smuts CM, Dhansay MA, Faber M, van Stuijvenberg ME, Swanevelder S, Gross R, et al. Efficacy of multiple micronutrient supplementation for improving anemia, micronutrient status, and growth in South African infants. J Nutr 2005;135(3):653S–659S.

135. Hop LT, Berger J. Multiple micronutrient supplementation improves anemia, micronutrient nutrient status, and growth of Vietnamese infants: double-blind, randomized, placebo-controlled trial. J Nutr 2005;135(3):660S–665S.

136. Martini E, Foote D, de Pee S, et al. Efficacy of "sprinkles" home fortification to reduce anemia and micronutrient deficiencies in young children in Indonesia [abstract]. INACG, Lima, Peru, 2004.

137. Liu D-S, Bates CJ, Yin T-A, Wang XB, Lu CQ. Nutritional efficacy of a fortified weaning rusk in a rural area near Beijing. Am J Clin Nutr 1993;57:506–511.

138. Lartey A, Manu A, Brown KH, Peerson JM, Dewey KG. A randomized, community-based trial of the effects of improved, centrally processed complementary foods on growth and micronutrient status of Ghanaian infants from 6 to 12 months of age. Am J Clin Nutr 1999;70:391–404.

139. Faber M, Kvalsvig JD, Lombard CJ, Benade AJ. Effect of a fortified maize-meal porridge on anemia, micronutrient status, and motor development of infants. Am J Clin Nutr 2005;82:1032–1039.

140. Oelofse A, van Raaij JM, Benade AJ, Dhansay MA, Tolboom JJ, Hautvast JG. The effect of a micronutrient-fortified complementary food on micronutrient status, growth and development of 6- to 12-month-old disadvantaged urban South African infants. Int J Food Sci Nutr 2003;4(5):399–407.

141. Rivera JA, Sotres-Alvarez D, Habicht J-P, Shamah T, Villalpando S. Impact of the Mexican program for education, health, and nutrition (Progresa) on rates of growth and anemia in infants and young children: a randomized effectiveness study. JAMA 2004;291(21):2563–2570.

142. Lopriore C, Guidoum Y, Briend A, Branca F. Spread fortified with vitamins and minerals induces catch-up growth and eradicates severe anemia in stunted refugee children aged 3–6 years. Am J Clin Nutr 2004;80:973–981.

143. Friis H, Mwaniki D, Omondi B, Muniu E, Thiong'o F, Ouma J, et al. Effects on haemoglobin of multi-micronutrient supplementation and multi-helminth chemotherapy: a randomized, controlled trial in Kenyan school children. Eur J Clin Nutr 2003;57(4):573–579.

144. Mwaniki D, Omondi B, Muniu E, Thiong'o F, Ouma J, Magnussen P, et al. Effects on serum retinol of multi-micronutrient supplementation and multi-helminth chemotherapy: a randomised, controlled trial in Kenyan school children. Eur J Clin Nutr 2002;56(7):666–673.

145. Abrams SA, Mushi A, Hilmers DC, Griffin IJ, Davila P, Allen L. A multinutrient-fortified beverage enhances the nutritional status of children in Botswana. J Nutr 2003;133:1834–1840.

146. Ash DM, Tatala SR, Frongillo EA Jr, Ndossi GD, Latham MC. Randomized efficacy trial of a micronutrient-fortified beverage in primary school children in Tanzania. Am J Clin Nutr 2003;77:891–898.

147. Solon FS, Sarol JN Jr, Bernardo AB, Solon JA, Mehansho H, Sanchez-Fermin LE, et al. Effect of a multiple-micronutrient-fortified fruit powder beverage on the nutrition status, physical fitness, and cognitive performance of schoolchildren in the Philippines. Food Nutr Bull 2003;24(4 suppl):S129–S140.

148. Allen L, Shrimpton R. The International Research on Infant Supplementation study: implications for programs and further research. J Nutr 2005;135(3):666S–669S.

149. Ramakrishnan U, Webb A, Ologoudou K. Infections, immunity and vitamins. In: Handbook on nutrition and immunity. Gershwin D, Nestel P, eds. Totowa, NJ: Humana Press, 2004:93–115

150. Bhutta ZA, Black RE, Brown KH, Gardner JM, Gore S, Hidayat A, Khatun F, et al. Prevention of diarrhea and pneumonia by zinc supplementation in children in developing countries: pooled analysis of randomized controlled trials. Zinc Investigators' Collaborative Group. J Pediatr 1999;135:689–697.

151. Olsen A, Thiong'o FW, Ouma JH, Mwaniki D, Magnussen P, Michaelsen KF, et al. Effects of multimicronutrient supplementation on helminth reinfection: a randomized, controlled trial in Kenyan schoolchildren. Trans R Soc Trop Med Hyg 2003;97(1):109–114.

152. Martorell R. Undernutrition during pregnancy and early childhood: consequences for cognitive and behavioral development. In: Early child development: investing in our children's future. Young ME, ed. Dordrecht: Elsevier Science, 1997.

153. Brown JL, Pollitt E. Malnutrition, poverty and intellectual development. Sci Am 1996;274:38–43.

154. Grantham-McGregor SM, Walker SP, Chang S. Nutritional deficiencies and later behavioural development. Proc Nutr Soc 2000;59:47–54.

155. Pollitt E, Oh S-Y. Early supplementary feeding, child development, and health policy. Food Nutr Bull 1994;15(3):208–214.

156. Stanbury JB. Iodine and human development, Med Anthro 1992;13:413–423.

157. Bleichrodt N, Born MP. Meta-analysis of research on iodine, and its relationship to cognitive development. In: The damaged brain of iodine deficiency: neuromotor, cognitive, behavioral and educative aspects. Stanbury JB, ed. New York: Cognizant Communication, 1994.

158. Lozoff B, Wachs TD. Functional correlates of nutritional anemia in infancy and early childhood—child development and behavior. In: Nutritional anemias. Ramakrishnan U, ed. Boca Raton, FL: CRC Press, 2001:69–88.

159. Watkins WE, Pollitt E. Iron deficiency and cognition among school age children. In: Recent advances in research on the effects of health and nutrition on children's development and school achievement in the Third World. Grantham-McGregor SM, ed. Washington, DC: Pan American Health Organization, 1998.

160. Wachs TD, Moussa W, Bishry Z, Yunis F, Sobhy A, McCabe G, et al. Relations between nutrition and cognitive performance in Egyptian toddlers. Intelligence 1993;17:151–172.

161. McCullough A, Kirksey A, Wachs TD, McCabe GP, Bassily NS, Bishry Z, et al. Vitamin B-6 status of Egyptian mothers: relation to infant behavior and maternal-infant interactions. Am J Clin Nutr 1990;41:1067–1074.

162. Rahmanifar A, Kirksey A, Wachs TD, McCabe GP, Bishry Z, Galal OM, et al. Diet during lactation associated with infant behavior and caregiver–infant interaction in a semirural Egyptian village. J Nutr 1993;123:164–175.

163. Snyderman SE, Holt LE Jr, Carretero R, Jacobs K. Pyridoxine deficiency in the human infant. Am J Clin Nutr 1953;1:200–207.

164. Golub MS, Keen CL, Gershwin ME, Hendrickx AG. Developmental zinc deficiency and behavior. J Nutr 1995;125(8 suppl):2263S–2271S.

165. Smit Vanderkooy PD, Gibson RS. Food consumption patterns of Canadian preschool children in relation to zinc and growth status. Am J Clin Nutr 1987;45:609–616.

166. Cavan KR, Gibson RS, Graziso CF, Isalgue AM, Ruz M, Solomons NW. Growth and body composition of periurban Guatemalan children in relation to zinc status: a longitudinal zinc intervention trial. Am J Clin Nutr 1993;57:344–352.

167. Bentley ME, Caulfield LE, Ram M, Santizo MC, Hurtado E, Rivera JA, et al. Zinc supplementation affects the activity patterns of rural Guatemalan infants. J Nutr 1997;127:1333–1338.

168. Sazawal S, Bentley M, Black RE, Dhingra P, George S, Bhan MK. Effect of zinc supplementation on observed activity in low socioeconomic Indian preschool children. Pediatrics 1996;98:1132–1137.

169. Ashworth A, Morris SS, Lira PI, Grantham-McGregor SM. Zinc supplementation, mental development and behaviour in low birth weight term infants in northeast Brazil. Eur J Clin Nutr 1998;52(3):223–227.

170. Black MM. Micronutrient deficiencies and cognitive functioning. J Nutr 2003;133(11 suppl 2):3927S–3931S.

171. Kuklina EV, Ramakrishnan U, Stein AD, Barnhart HH, Martorell R. Growth and diet quality are associated with the attainment of walking in rural Guatemalan infants. J Nutr 2004;134:3296–3300.

172. Manger MS, Winichagoon P, Pongcharoen T, Gorwachirapan S, Boonpraderm A, McKenzie J, et al. Multiple micronutrients may lead to improved cognitive function in NE Thai schoolchildren. Asia Pac J Clin Nutr 2004;13(suppl):S46.

173. Whaley SE, Sigman M, Neumann C, Bwibo N, Guthrie D, Weiss RE, et al. The impact of dietary intervention on the cognitive development of Kenyan school children. J Nutr 2003;133:3965S–3971S.

174. Fawzi W. Micronutrients and human immunodeficiency virus type 1 disease progression among adults and children. Clin Infect Dis 2003;37(suppl 2):S112–S116.

175. Tang A, Graham NH, Saah A. Effects of micronutrient intake on survival in human immunodeficiency virus type 1 infection. Am J Epidemiol 1996;143(12):1244–1256.

176. Jiamton S, Pepin J, Suttent R, Filteau S, Mahakkanukrauh B, Hanshaoworakul W, et al. A randomized trial of the impact of multiple micronutrient supplementation on mortality among HIV-infected individuals living in Bangkok. AIDS 2003;17(17):2461–2469.

177. Fortes C, Forastiere F, Agabiti N, Fano V, Pacifici R, Virgili F, et al. The effect of zinc and vitamin A supplementation on immune response in an older population. J Am Geriatr Soc 1998;46(1):19–26.

178. Girodon F, Lombard M, Galan P, Brunet-Lecomte P, Monget AL, Arnaud J, et al. Effect of micronutrient supplementation on infection in institutionalized elderly subjects: a controlled trial. Ann Nutr Metab 1997;41:98–107.

179. Bogden JD, Louria DB. Micronutrients and immunity in older people. In: Preventive nutrition: the comprehensive guide of health professionals. 3rd ed. Bendich A, Deckelbaum RJ, eds. Totowa, NJ: Humana Press, 2005:551–572.

180. Patterson RE, White E, Kristal AR, Neuhouser ML, Potter JD. Vitamin supplements and cancer risk: the epidemiologic evidence. Cancer Causes Control 1997;8:786–802.

181. Hursten L. Global epidemic of cardiovascular disease predicted. Lancet 1998;352:1530.

182. Rimm EB, Willett AC, Hu FB, Sampson L, Colditz GA, Manson JE, et al. Folate and vitamin $B_6$ from diet and supplements in relation to risk of coronary heart disease among women. JAMA 1998;279(5):359–364.

183. Robinson K, Arheart K, Refsum H, Brattstrom L, Boers G, Ueland P, et al. Low circulating folate and vitamin $B_6$ concentrations: risk factors for stroke, peripheral vascular disease, and coronary artery disease. Circulation 1998;97(5):437–443.

184. The European Concerted Action Project. Plasma homocysteine as a risk factor for vascular disease. JAMA 1997;277(22):1775–1781.

185. Beresford SA, Boushey CJ. Homocysteine, folic acid, and cardiovascular risk. In: Preventive nutrition: the comprehensive guide for health professionals. Bendich A, Deckelbaum RJ, eds. Totowa, NJ: Humana Press, 1997.

186. Brouwer IA, van Dusseldorp M, Thomas CM, Duran M, Hautvast JG, Eskes TK, et al. Low-dose folic acid supplementation decreases plasma homocysteine concentrations: a randomized trial. Am J Clin Nutr 1999;69:99–104.

187. Cao G, Russell RM, Lischner N, Prior RL. Serum antioxidant capacity is increased by consumption of strawberries, spinach, red wine or vitamin C in elderly women. J Nutr 1998;128:2383–2390.

188. Chan AC. Vitamin E and atherosclerosis. J Nutr 1998;128:1593–1596.
189. Lock K, Pomerleau J, Causer L, Altmann DR, McKee M. The global burden of disease attributable to low consumption of fruit and vegetables: implications for the global strategy on diet. Bull World Health Organ 2005;83(2):100–108.
190. de Pee S, Bloem MW, Gorstein J, Sari M, Satoto, Yip R, et al. Reappraisal of the role of vegetables in the vitamin A status of mothers in Central Java, Indonesia. Am J Clin Nutr 1998;68:1068–1074.
191. de Pee S, West CE, Permaesih D, Martuti S, Muhilal, Hautvast JG. Orange fruit is more effective than dark-green leafy vegetables in increasing serum concentrations of retinol and beta-carotene in school children in Indonesia. Am J Clin Nutr 1998;68:1058–1067.
192. Gibson RS. Strategies for preventing micronutrient deficiencies in developing countries. Asia Pac J Clin Nutr 2004;13(suppl):S23.
193. World Health Organization. Community-based strategies for breastfeeding promotion and support in developing countries. Geneva: World Health Organization, 2003.
194. Haider R, Ashworth A, Kabir I, Huttly SR. Effect of community-based peer counsellors on exclusive breastfeeding practices in Dhaka, Bangladesh: a randomized controlled trial. Lancet 2000;356:1643–1647.
195. Morrow AL, Guerrero ML, Shults J, Calva JJ, Lutter C, Bravo J, et al. Efficacy of home-based peer counseling to promote exclusive breastfeeding: a randomised controlled trial. Lancet 1999;353:1226–1231.
196. Parlato M, Seidel R. Large-scale application of nutrition behavior change approaches: lessons from West Africa. Arlington, VA: Basics, 1998.
197. Bloem MW. The Central Java Project: maternal postpartum vitamin A supplementation, increased intake of vitamin-A rich foods and early childhood survival in central Java. Helen Keller International Special Report. Jakarta: Helen Keller International, 1997.
198. Rahman MM, Mahalanabis D, Islam MA. Can infants and young children eat enough green leafy vegetables from a single traditional meal to meet their daily vitamin A requirements? Eur J Clin Nutr 1993;47:68–72.
199. Gibson RS, Yeudall F, Drost N, Mtitimuni BM, Cullinan TR. Experiences of a community-based dietary intervention to enhance micronutrient adequacy of diets low in animal source foods and high in phytate: a case study in rural Malawian children. J Nutr 2003;133:3992S–3999S.
200. Mamiro PS, Kolsteren PW, van Camp JH, Roberfroid DA, Tatala S, Opsomer AS. Processed complementary food does not improve growth or hemoglobin status of rural Tanzanian infants from 6–12 months of age in Kilosa district, Tanzania. J Nutr 2004;134:1084–1090.
201. Mackintosh UA, Marsh DR, Schroeder DG. Sustained positive deviant child care practices and their effects on child growth in Viet Nam. Food Nutr Bull 2002;23(4 suppl):18–27.
202. Bhandari N, Mazumder S, Bahl R, Martines J, Black RE, Ghan MK, Infant Feeding Study Group. An educational intervention to promote appropriate complementary feeding practices and physical growth in infants and young children in rural Haryana, India. J Nutr 2004;134:2342–2348.
203. Penny ME, Creed-Kanashiro HM, Robert RC, Narro MR, Caulfield LE, Black RE. Effectiveness of an educational intervention delivered through the health services to improve nutrition in young children: a cluster-randomised controlled trial. Lancet 2005;365(9474):1863–1872.
204. Santos I, Cesar CG, Martines J, Concalves H, Gigante DP, Valle NJ, et al. Nutrition counseling increases weight gain among Brazilian children. J Nutr 2001;131:2866–2873.
205. Greiner T, Mitra SN. Evaluation of the impact of a food-based approach to solving vitamin A deficiency in Bangladesh. Food Nutr Bull 1995;16:193–205.
206. Nielsen H, Roos N, Thilsted SH. The impact of semi-scavenging poultry production on the consumption of animal source foods by women and girls in Bangladesh. J Nutr 2003;133:4027S–4030S.
207. Ayele Z, Peacock C. Improving access to and consumption of animal source foods in rural households: the experiences of a women-focused goat development program in the highlands of Ethiopia. J Nutr 2003;133:3981S–3986S.
208. Gibson RS. Zinc nutrition in developing countries. Nutr Res Rev 1994;7:151–173.
209. Brown KH, Dewey KG, Allen LH. Complementary feeding of young children in developing countries: a review of current scientific knowledge. Geneva: World Health Organization, 1998. WHO/NUT/98.1.

210. Brown KH, Dewey KG. Update on technical issues concerning complementary feeding of young children in developing countries and implications for intervention programs. Food Nutr Bull 2003;24(1):5–28.

211. Pan American Health Organization. Interagency Meeting: Iron Fortification in the Americas. May 17, 1998. Meeting report. Washington, DC: Pan American Health Organization, International Life Sciences Institute, Inter-American Development Bank, 1998.

212. Daly S, Mills JL, Molloy AM, Conley M, Lee YJ, Kirke PN, et al. Minimum effective dose of folic acid for food fortification to prevent neural-tube defects. Lancet 1997;350:1666–1669.

213. Oakley G, Erikson J, Adams MJ. Urgent need to increase folic acid consumption. JAMA 1998;274(21):1717–1718.

214. Choumenkovitch SF, Selhub J, Wilson PWF, Rader JI, Rosenberg IH, Jacques PF. Folic acid intake from fortification in United States exceeds predictions. J Nutr 2002;132:2792–2798.

215. Jacques PF, Selhub J, Bostom AG, et al. The effect of folic acid fortification on plasma folate and total homocysteine concentrations. N Engl J Med 2000;340:1449–1454.

216. Bailey LB. Folate and vitamin $B_{12}$ recommended intakes and status in the United States. Nutr Rev 2004;62(6 pt 2):S14–S20.

217. Ray JG, Meier C, Vermeulen MJ, Boss S, Wyatt PR, Cole DE. Association of neural tube defects and folic acid food fortification in Canada. Lancet 2002;360:2047–2048.

218. Persad VL, Van den Hof MC, Dube JM, Zimmer P. Incidence of open neural tube defects in Nova Scotia after folic acid fortification. CMAJ 2002;167:241–245.

219. Centers for Disease Control and Prevention. Spina bifida and anencephaly before and after folic acid mandate—United States, 1995–1996 and 1999–2000. MMWR Morb Mortal Wkly Rep 2004;53(17):362–365.

220. Chen LT, Rivera MA. The Costa Rican experience: reduction of neural tube defects following food fortification programs. Nutr Rev 2004;62(6 pt 2):S40–S43.

221. Hertrampf E, Cortés F, Erickson JD, Cayzzo M, Freire W, Bailey LB, et al. Consumption of folic acid-fortified bread improves folate status in women of reproductive age in Chile. J Nutr 2003;133:3166–3169.

222. Food and Agricultural Organization. CODEX alimentarius. Geneva: World Health Organization, 1997.

223. Perez-Exposito AB, Villalpando S, Rivera JA, Griffin IJ, Abrams SA. Ferrous sulfate is more bioavailable among preschoolers than other forms of iron in a milk-based weaning food distributed by PROGRESA, a national program in Mexico. J Nutr 2005;135(1):64–69.

224. Lutter CK. Macrolevel approaches to improve the availability of complementary foods. Food Nutr Bull 2003;24(1):83–103.

225. Lutter CK, Dewey K. Proposed nutrient composition for fortified complementary foods. J Nutr 2003;133:3011S–3020S

226. Zlotkin S, Arthur P, Antwi KY, Yeung G. Treatment of anemia with microencapsulated ferrous fumarate plus ascorbic acid supplied as sprinkles to complementary (weaning) foods. Am J Clin Nutr 2001;74:791–795.

227. Zlotkin S, Arthur P, Schauer C, Antwi KY, Yeung G, Piekarz A. Home-fortification with iron and zinc sprinkles or iron sprinkles alone successfully treats anemia in infants and young children. J Nutr 2003;133:1075–1080.

228. Mongolia evaluation of the distribution of micronutrient sprinkles in over 10,000 Mongolian infants using a non-governmental organization (NGO) model. Sprinkles Global Health Initiative. Available at: http://www.supplefer.com/mongolia.html.

229. Helen Keller International. Vitamins and minerals are crucial components of first line emergency response because they markedly reduce mortality and severity of disease. Tsunami Relief Bull January 2005, Issue 1.

230. Zlotkin SH, Schauer C, Christofides A, Sharieff W, Tondeur MC, Hyder SMZ. Micronutrient sprinkles to control childhood anaemia: a simple powdered sachet may be the key to addressing a global problem. PLOS Med [serial online] 2005 January;2(1):e1.

231. Nestel P, Briend A, de Benoist B, Decker E, Ferguson E, Fontaine O, et al. Complementary food supplements to achieve micronutrient adequacy for infants and young children. J Pediatr Gastroenterol Nutr 2003;36(3):316–328.

232. Macias-Matos C, Rodriguez-Ojea A, Chi N, Jiménez S, Zulueta D, Bates CJ. Biochemical evidence of thiamine depletion during Cuban neuropathy epidemic, 1992–1993. Am J Clin Nutr 1996;64:347–353.

233. Clark N, Fisk NM. Minimal compliance with the Department of Health recommendations for routine folate prophylaxis to prevent fetal neural tube defects. Br J Obstet Gynecol 1994;101:709–710.

234. Centers for Disease Control and Prevention. Recommendations to prevent and control iron deficiency in the United States. MMWR Recomm Rep 1998;47(RR-3):1–29.

235. Yu SM, Keppel KG, Singh GK, Kessel W. Preconceptional and prenatal vitamin-mineral supplement use in the 1988 National Maternal and Infant Health Survey. Am J Public Health 1996;86:240–242.

236. Subar A, Block G. Use of vitamin and mineral supplements: Demographics and amounts of nutrients consumed. Am J Epidemiol 1990;132(6):1091–1101.

237. Pelletier D, Kendall A. Supplement use may not be associated with better food intake in al. population groups. Fam Econ Nutr Rev 1997;10(4):32–44.

238. Centers for Disease Control and Prevention. Use of folic acid supplements among women of child-bearing age-United States. MMWR Morb Mortal Wkly Rep 1997;47:131–134.

239. Ervin RB, Wright JD, Reed-Gillette D. Prevalence of leading types of dietary supplements used in the Third National Health and Nutrition Examination Survey, 1988–94. Advance Data 2004;349:1–7.

240. Radimer K, Bindewald B, Hughes J, Ervin B, Swanson C, Picciano MF. Dietary supplement use by US adults: data from the National Health and Nutrition Examination Survey, 1999–2000. Am J Epidemiol 2004;160(4): 339–349.

241. Population Services International. Meeting a fundamental need social marketing of micronutrients prevents anemia, saves lives. Washington, DC. November 2003. Available at: http://www.psi.org/resources/pubs/micronutrients.pdf.

242. Huffman SL, Baker J, Shumann J, Zehner ER. The case for promoting multiple vitamin and mineral supplements for women of reproductive age in developing countries. Food Nutr Bull 1999;20(4): 379–394.

243. Beaton GH, McCabe GP. Efficacy of intermittent iron supplementation in the control of iron deficiency anemia in developing countries: an analysis of experience. Micronutrient Initiative, Toronto, Canada, April 1999.

244. Alnwick D. Weekly iodine supplements work. Am J Clin Nutr 1998;67(6):1103–1104.

245. Bates CJ, Flewitt A, Prentice AM, Lamb WH, Whitehead RG. Efficacy of a riboflavin supplement given at fortnightly intervals to pregnant and lactating women in rural Gambia. Hum Nutr Clin Nutr 1983;37:427–432.

246. Warnick E, Dearden KA, Slater S, Butron B, Lanata CF, Huffman SL. Social marketing improved the use of multivitamin and mineral supplements among resource-poor women in Bolivia. J Nutr Educ Behav 2004;36(6):290–297.

247. Popkin B, Du S. Dynamics of the nutrition transition toward the animal foods sector in China and its implications: a worried perspective. J Nutr 2003;133:3898S–3906S.

248. Cuskelly G, McNulty H, Scott J. Effect of increasing dietary folate on red-cell folate: Implications for prevention of neural tube defects. Lancet 1996;347:657–659.

249. Boushey CJ, Beresford SA, Omenn GS, Motulsky AG. A quantitative assessment of plasma homocysteine as a risk factor for vascular disease. Probable benefits of increasing folic acid intakes. JAMA 1995;274(13):1049–1057.

# 19 Nutrition in the Elderly in Developing Countries

*Noel W. Solomons and Odilia I. Bermúdez*

*Aging can be defined in practical terms as a series of time-related processes that ultimately bring life to a close.*

Busuttil, Dolle, Campisi, and Vijga [1]

## 19.1 THE BIOLOGY OF HUMAN AGING AND SURVIVAL: AN EVOLUTIONARY PERSPECTIVE

### 19.1.1 Overview

Through the millennia of human evolution, nutrient and physical activity requirements evolved to satisfy the hunter-gatherer lifestyle, survival to reproductive age occurred for a select few, and almost no one survived to advanced age. Yet, there is an underlying chronobiology of *Homo sapiens* that produces senescent changes from the cellular to the whole-body level and limits total life span to about 120 years. Today, more and more individuals are surviving into their eighth decade and beyond, including in developing countries, and median life span is extending throughout the world. Soon, more than three quarters of all persons over 60 years will live in developing or transitional nations. The challenge to medical care services and public health policy and programs in low-income societies is the lack of systematic information on gerontological diet and nutrition.

Persons advancing to older age in low-income tropical and semitropical settings can be seen as having a series of dual burdens. First, the poverty and environmental adversities of developing societies combine with the senescent change of aging. Second, they face the double burden of malnutrition, with deficiencies coexisting with overnutrition. Although recommended nutrient intakes have been developed for persons over 60 years of age, their applicability under the ecological conditions of developing societies is unknown. In many instances, the physical activity and food selection guidance for prevention of chronic diseases is already part of the traditional cultural patterns of developing societies. Finally, features of aging, ethnicity, and life in developing countries confound the conventional assumptions underlying the clinical, anthropometric, and laboratory assessment of nutritional status.

From: *Nutrition and Health: Nutrition and Health in Developing Countries, Second Edition*
Edited by: R. D. Semba & M. W. Bloem © Humana Press, Totowa, NJ

For every species, there is a maximal longevity span; that is, there is an age beyond which no member will survive. For humans, this span is judged to be about 120 years [2, 3]; beyond that age, the human organism cannot persist. In the wilds of Nature, the risks of infections, the vagaries of food supplies, and a food chain based on a hierarchy of predation ensures that most organisms born or hatched do not even survive to reproduce, and even fewer survive beyond the reproductive period. As such, for most species, the members do not come close to approaching the maximal biological life span.

### 19.1.2  Evolutionary Perspective on Aging

For over 90% of the up to 400,000 years of the evolution of the genus *Homo*, our ancestors were part of the community of animal and plant species in a natural wilderness. Humans were just one more wild species. Our way of life was that of migratory hunter-gatherer clans and tribes. Although a few individuals probably survived to advanced age throughout all epochs of prehistory, the majority of individuals succumbed early in life. As a contemporary anecdote, the multicenter, international survey research protocol *Food Habits in Later Life* called for the enrollment of a cohort of individuals aged 70 years or beyond [4]. When investigators tried to apply it among Aboriginal peoples in the north of Australia, however, the effort was quickly abandoned as the researchers found no potential subject older than 47 years. Such a truncated age pyramid was probably the order of the day among hunter-gatherer tribes and pastoralist nomadic groups throughout our history. With this evolutionary context, therefore, we might conclude that Nature never intended there to be aging societies or large numbers of older persons in the human populations.

### 19.1.3  The Evolutionary Paradoxes

Human evolution has been considered to be adaptive [5]. Darwinian theory, correctly interpreted, alludes to "survival of the fittest" in the sense of demographic dominations by the bearers of those genetic traits that provide reproductive superiority. That is, the bearers have a higher propensity to survival to adult life, better chances for procreation, and greater fecundity. The strength and agility that made for a better hunter could be generalized over generations as those men with better skills would both survive the rigors of the hunt and dominate the procreation within the tribe in polygamous societies.

Because the internal and external challenges to the aging organism occur *after* the peak reproductive years, anatomic and functional outcomes in human aging do not obey the conventional norms of natural selection. As a consequence, there is no way for a process of differential fecundity to select for traits that express themselves or become beneficial only *later* in life. In fact, in *Homo sapiens'* natural selection process, we may have accumulated genetic traits directed toward survival within a hunter-gatherer way of life; these traits could actually affect health detrimentally into the middle and later years of a much longer life span.

We also use the word *evolution* in the connotation of cultural adaptation [5]. Besides successful reproduction, adequate nutrition is the other fundamental pillar for the basic survival of a species. Until the advent of domestication of animals and the emergence of pastoralist lifestyles some 40,000 years ago [6], tribal hunter-gatherers dominated humanity. Paleonutritionists vary on the exact composition of "typical" Stone Age fare [7, 8], but successful hunting societies could have derived over 50% of their calories from the flesh and visceral organs of the available fauna. Animal protein, in the form of dairy foods and meat, has been the dietary fare of pastoralists throughout their history. With respect to aging, one could argue that the cultural (diet and lifestyle) attributes that made for success as a young and vigorous hunter or herder could sow the seeds of poorer health and function if one had the fortune to survive the peak reproductive years.

In summary, when the basic issues of survival confront the individuals of a society on a minute-to-minute and day-to-day basis, genetic biology and cultural adaptation must focus on getting enough individuals to survive to the age of reproduction to ensure the mere maintenance of the population. Making provision for long-term survival was among the lowest priorities of the evolutionary imperative for any species in the wild, including for us humans.

### 19.1.4   The Biology of Aging

When the conditions for surviving early and middle life are ensured, as with captive wild animals, domesticated pets and livestock, and humans, it becomes evident that underlying senescent processes are operating from conception and throughout life. Since the evolutionary purpose for individuals is reproduction for the maintenance of their species, more redundancy of capacity was focused onto procreative functions; this came about at the expense of capacity for infinite repair of the cells of the host. Molecular gerontology is currently revealing cellular senescence as the basis of the aging process for the whole organism. These changes involve altered remodeling of the chromatin in the nuclear apparatus (telomeres) [9], leakage of free radicals from the energy generation in increasingly porous mitochondria [10], or mutations in their single-stranded DNA [11] and alteration of apoptosis (programmed cell death) [12].

The late Dr. Nathan Shock, a pioneering gerontological physiologist working in Baltimore, Maryland, generalized to the aging process the differential—but inevitable—decline in physiological capacity of almost all human organ systems [13]. Shock and his group were working with white North American men in the middle of the 20th century; the degree to which the genetic constitution of other ethnic groups across the globe might vary in their projected rates of diminished physiological function is still a matter for prospective evaluation. Furthermore, with respect to the developing country perspective and its general social, lifestyle, and environmental features, we must take what is currently known about physiological senescence in two speculative directions. What would be the *theoretical* effects of lifestyle and environmental exposures for preservation or deterioration of organ system functions? What would the *projected* effect of physiological decline on day-to-day living demands for older individuals in low-income societies? The specific physiological and pathophysiological issues of the alimentary tract and its relation to diet and nutrition are discussed in a section of this chapter. For the general biological aging of humans, a brief profile of physiological senescence of the other systems is illustrative.

### 19.2   SENESCENCE OF TISSUE AND ORGAN FUNCTION WITH AGING

For the integumentary system (hair, skin, nails), which provides the external protective barrier, greater sun exposure might accelerate the loss of elasticity and the development of wrinkles. Darker skin pigmentation in certain African, Pacific Islander, and Amerindian populations, however, might counteract the aging of skin. To the extent that cuts and bruise injuries might be more common among elders in developing countries, delayed wound healing might present a greater risk to cutaneous infection.

The pulmonary-respiratory system function declines due to changes in chest wall compliance and diaphragmatic weakening. Obviously, lifelong indoor exposure to open hearth cooking fires damages the alveolar soft tissues of the lungs themselves. To the extent that relatively strenuous exertion may still be required of older men and women in preindustrialized settings, greater limitation on desired activities may be imposed by dwindling lung capacity. A similar restriction may be the consequence of cardiovascular and circulatory aging [14]. For the last systems, however, the fitness conditioning derived from strenuous daily demands may delay various aspects of physiological decline.

An intact musculoskeletal system to maintain agility of movement and weight-bearing capacity is as important for rigorous labor in later life as are the roles of breathing and circulation. With respected to joints, bones, and muscles, the lifestyle demands of typical low-income manual labor have differential effects. For cartilaginous tissue (joints), wear and tear of running, climbing, and lifting will accelerate their decline. For bones, the opposite is generally true, with weight bearing serving to strengthen the vertebral and long bones and retard demineralization [15]. Sarcopenia is an age-associated alteration in muscle structure and function with loss of muscle fibers and tensile strength and infiltration of muscle bundles with fat [16].

Physiological capacity of the hematological, renal, urogenital, and gonadal and reproductive systems declines with age. These systems are relatively less differentiated in their sensitive to the behavioral and environmental features superimposed on basic aging changes. The other endocrine responses (thyroidal, adrenal, somatotropic) dependent on the pituitary gland also decline in capacity with age. Decreased growth hormone secretion and tissue responsiveness of aging (somatopause) has implications for body composition and muscle strength [17]. In this same metabolic domain, aging is generally associated with a decline in lean body mass and an increase in adiposity, even without overall changes in body weight. Lower muscle mass affects the gait of older persons, making them more prone to fails and therefore to bone fractures [18].

The function of the immune system and its adequate regulation has important health implication for the aging individual. Given its dependency on continuously turning over immune cells, diet and nutrition play a determinant role in immune regulation. Host defenses against microbial pathogens may decline, exposing the older person to infections. The inflammatory response becomes dysregulated, and excess production of inflammatory cytokines, such as interleukin 6, advances with age. Tumor vigilance is an aspect of immune protection that takes on increasing importance with aging; the variation in its function represents one of the factors of differential risk of cancer among aging individuals. Autoimmune dysregulation increases with advancing age, increasing an individual's risk to diseases of autoimmunity.

The function of the nervous system declines with age in both the sensory and motor domains of peripheral nerves and at the central level with the special senses and mental cognition. The changes include altered pain sensation and loss of fine-motor functions. Sight, hearing, taste, smell, and touch all become less acute with age. Studies have shown that older individuals in all populations around the world suffer a loss of memory and cognitive functions.

### 19.2.1   Function of the Alimentary and Digestive Tract in Aging

Aging affects the structure and function of the digestive system from the oral cavity with loosening or loss of dentition and decreased saliva flow to slowing of propulsive (peristaltic) motility throughout the entire length of the tract. Fecal evacuations become less frequent and more difficult (constipation); the more fiber-rich traditional diets of rural cultures in developing societies would tend to counteract the constipating features of neural aging.

The secretion of bile and pancreatic juice, beginning with a ninefold secretory capacity in young adulthood, is rarely challenged by aging. Gastric *Helicobacter pylori* infection is more common under the poor sanitation conditions of developing countries [19]. The parietal cells lining the stomach of older persons, however, often suffer exhaustion. The nutritional consequences are reduced iron solubility and insufficient intrinsic factor for vitamin $B_{12}$ absorption. Assimilation of most other micronutrients, as well as of the macronutrients, is generally adequate to meet nutritional needs throughout the life span. The background sanitation in the developing world challenges inhabitants of all ages with the risks of intestinal helminthic and protozoal infestations and recurrent diarrheal episodes.

## 19.3   SUCCESSFUL AGING, NORMATIVE AGING, AND FRAIL AGING OF INDIVIDUALS WITHIN A POPULATION

One of the hallmark characteristics of an older population is the heterogeneity in functional status that one finds looking across individuals of the same age, that is, persons of a birth cohort during the same year 60, 70, or 80 years ago. This "splaying" of variation increases with advancing age [20]. One way to conceptualize this heterogeneity is as dissociation within individuals of *biological* aging and *chronological* aging [4]. The same cumulative numbers of years may have elapsed, but the advance in changes in the anatomic structure, metabolism, and physiological function (biological aging) is very nonuniform across a population, even of persons of the same ethnicity and culture living in the same habitat. The interplay of at least three factors contributes to this dissociation: genetic constitution, environmental exposure, and the burden of disease experience.

The eminent gerontologist Prof. John Rowe [21] advanced the term *successful aging* to characterize the process of growing older while retaining satisfactory health, function, and independence. This is contrasted to two other conditions: normative aging and frailty. *Normative aging* is the experience that covers most of the advanced years of most older persons in which multiple chronic diseases appear, and function is compromised to some degree. *Frailty* is at the other end of the spectrum; persons have severe decline in cognitive and physical function, losing independence in activities of daily living, often becoming wheelchair bound or bedridden, and requiring assistance and care [22].

## 19.4   DEMOGRAPHY OF AGING OF POPULATIONS IN DEVELOPING COUNTRIES

The aging of individuals within a population and the aging of a population are not exactly the same phenomenon. Both, however, are increasingly relevant to developing societies [23]. An individual's growing older is a product of surviving the hazards to health and physical safety in the society and environment. The aging of a *population* is seen in the distribution of a society among different age strata. The typical broad-based pyramidal form of the age pyramid of a young society transforms into a more columnar shape with extension of longer life and falling birth rates. Today, across the world, the most prominent feature of human demography is the aging of individuals and the aging of populations.

The fastest-growing subpopulation in the world, in terms of rate of increase, are persons surviving to 100 years of age. In developed countries, whereas once children had only a slight chance of ever knowing their grandfather, some 50% of those born today will come to know their great-grandparents [24]. Life expectancy still lags in developing countries, with a median life expectancy of 36 years in Botswana. A general tendency toward longer lives, however, can be seen throughout developing and transitional societies on all of the southern continents. By the year 2020, there will be 7.6 billion inhabitants on earth, with over 1 billion or 13.3% over the age of 60 years; this is up from 8.5% in 1990. Three quarters of these elderly will be living in developing countries. By region, 17% of East Asians, 12% of Latin Americans, and 10% of Southeast Asians will be over 60 years. China, with 231 million estimated for that year, and India with 145 million will be the two most populous nations in terms of elderly citizens [23].

## 19.5   THE BURDEN OF CHRONIC DISEASES IN THE AGING

It was conventional wisdom and epidemiological experience in low-income societies that acute infectious diseases, often life threatening, were common, but chronic, degenerative diseases were rare. The aforementioned extension of longevity in developing countries has been termed the *demographic transition* [25], which leads in turn to a change in disease patterns, the so-called *epidemiological transition* [26].

### 19.5.1   *Nontransmissible Disease Epidemiology in Developing Country Populations*

The epidemiology of nontransmissible or chronic diseases is not well documented in developing countries. This derives in part from the relatively recent emergence of the so-called double burden of diseases [27, 28]. The classical diseases of poverty, related to infections and nutritional deficiency, have not gone away—but have been joined by a growing incidence of degenerative illness. According to Yach et al. [29], chronic, nontransmissible illnesses are the most important cause of global mortality, with 29 million deaths annually caused by cardiovascular disease, cancer, chronic respiratory disease, and diabetes. Noting that the public health response by professionals, governments, and even agencies of the United Nation (UN) system remains inadequate, they pondered the reasons and found them in a set of entrenched beliefs and attitudes that do not assimilate and heed the aforementioned epidemiological reality. Yach and associates [29] asserted:

> *Reasons for this include that up-to-date evidence related to the nature of the burden of chronic diseases is not in the hands of decision makers and strong beliefs persist that chronic diseases afflict only the affluent and the elderly, that they arise solely from freely acquired risks, and that their control is ineffective and too expensive and should wait until infectious diseases are addressed.*

### 19.5.2   Relationship of Chronic Disease to Diet and Nutrition in Developing Countries

The last two decades have seen the emergence of interest in the nutritional science community with the relationships of diet and nutrition to the risk of chronic disease [30, 31]. To date, however, most nutritional epidemiology inquiry has been focused on dietary patterns in relation to the incidence of overweight, metabolic syndrome, cardiovascular disease, and neoplasms in affluent populations of developed, industrialized nations.

The question of policy and program relevance for developing countries of accumulated nutritional epidemiology understanding is important to older persons in low-income societies. Until recently, for instance, the patterns of cancers were sharply distinct between low-income countries in the tropics and high-income countries in temperate zones. Whereas sites in lung and large bowel and the family of hormonal cancers (breast, ovarian, prostatic) were predominant in industrialized populations, the oropharyngeal area, the upper digestive tract, and the liver were the most common sites across the developing world. Dietary factors, including nutrient deficiencies, food and beverage constituents, and temperature and charring of foods are clearly implicated in esophageal and gastric malignancy [32]. Overgrowth of staple grains and nuts with mycotoxins (aflatoxin, fumonisins) is a dietary risk factor for liver cancer [33]. Daily consumption of coffee has been identified as a protective dietary factor against hepatic carcinoma [34]. Many of the putative risk factors for cardiac and circulatory diseases relate to dietary practices, including sodium intake, hypertriglyceridemia, hypercholesterolemia, elevated homocysteinemia, systemic inflammation, and glycemic load.

Human dietary substances such as alcohol, red wine, chocolate, omega-3 fatty acids, and calcium can provide certain putative protective factors for these diseases [35–38]. Within the basic generalization of a traditional diet of low-income populations based on a major staple grain or tuber and low amounts in animal protein, few of the aforementioned or protective dietary components would be expected to be consumed widely. Protection, however, could come from the fiber and phytochemicals in these largely vegetarian fares plus the absence of the noxious components in animal sources.

The projection of epidemiological transition reviewed in the previous section portends a rising incidence of chronic diseases across the Third World. To the degree that endemic chronic illness can be prevented, it will improve quality of life of the populace and the budget perspectives of national health authorities. It is important to determine whether the same principles of protective diets and lifestyle are operative in populations emerging from economic underdevelopment as have been shown in societies of established affluence.

## 19.6   NUTRITIONAL REQUIREMENTS, NUTRIENT INTAKE RECOMMENDATIONS, AND GUIDELINES FOR HEALTHFUL EATING FOR THE ELDERLY

Since survival into later life has been infrequent until recent decades, there is also a paucity of information on nutritional requirements of the elderly. Until the mid-1990s, there was insufficiently detailed scientific evidence to differentiate nutrient recommendations for adults over 50 years into any more refined age groupings based on advancing age. This was true both for the US recommended dietary allowance (RDA) and the recommended nutrient intakes (RNI) of the UN system. Until 1997, a uniform requirement level was assigned for everyone over 51 years of age. It has only been recently that official bodies have ventured to specify age-specific recommendations for the oldest segments of populations; these recommendations were based on accumulation of new, age-specific experimental data. The dietary reference intakes (DRIs) for the United States and Canada [39–45] and for the 2004 (RNI), which come from the UN system [46], to apply across the developing world, new specificity is given to the elderly. The UN system defines 65 years as older, whereas the US-Canadian system uses two categories for older adults: 50–70 and above 70 years of age. A series of conceptual definitions govern the expression for normative intakes of macro- and micronutrients; these are provided in Table 19.1. The intake recommendations related to specific categories of risk for low or excessive intakes are provided in Tables 19.2 and 19.3 for older men and women, respectively. With

Table 19.1

**Definitions related to nutrient intake recommendations**

For the UN system (FAO/WHO/IAEA/UNU):

**Recommended nutrient intake (RNI):** The daily intake, set at the EAR plus 2 standard deviations (SD), which meets the nutrient requirements of almost all apparently healthy individuals in an age- and sex-specific population group.

For the dietary reference intakes (referent to the United States and Canada):

**Estimated average requirement (EAR):** The average daily nutrient intake level estimated to meet the requirement of half the healthy individuals in a particular life stage and gender group.

**Recommended dietary allowance (RDA):** The average daily nutrient intake level sufficient to meet the nutrient requirement of nearly all (97–98%) healthy individuals in a particular life stage and gender group.

**Adequate intake (AI):** A recommended average daily nutrient intake level based on observed or experimentally determined approximation or estimates of nutrient intake by a group (or groups) of apparently healthy people that are assumed to be adequate; –used when an recommended dietary allowances RDA cannot be determined.

**Tolerable upper intake level:** The highest average daily nutrient intake level likely to pose no risk of adverse health effects to almost all individuals in the general population; as intake increases above the tolerable upper intake level (UL), the potential risk of adverse effects increases.

**Acceptable range of macronutrient distribution (ARMD):** A range of intakes for a particular energy source that is associated with a reduced risk of chronic disease while providing adequate intakes of essential nutrients.

**Estimated energy requirement (EER):** The average dietary energy intake that is predicted to maintain energy balance in a healthy adult of a defined age, gender, weight, height, and level of physical activity consistent with good health.

*FAO* Food and Agricultural Organization, *UN* United Nations, *UNU* United Nations University, *WHO* World Health Organization, *IAEA* International Atomic Energy Agency.

Table 19.2
Nutrient intake recommendations for older men

| | WHO/FAO/IAEA | IoM for US/Canada | | | |
| | 65+ years | 51–70 years | | >70 years | |
| | RNI[a] | RDA/AI/AMDR[b] | UL[b] | RDA/AI/AMDR[b] | UL[b] |
|---|---|---|---|---|---|
| **Vitamins** | | | | | |
| Vitamin A (µg RAE) | 600 (µg RE) | 900 | 3,000 | 900 | 3,000 |
| Vitamin D (mg) | **15** | **10**[c] | 50 | **15**[c] | 50 |
| Vitamin E (mg α-tocopherol) | 10 (mg α-TE) | 15 | 1,000 | 15 | 1,000 |
| Vitamin K (µg) | 65 | 120[c] | ND | **120**[c] | ND |
| Vitamin C (mg) | 45 | 90 | 2000 | 90 | 2,000 |
| Thiamin (mg) | 1.2 | 1.2 | ND | 1.2 | ND |
| Riboflavin (mg) | 1.3 | 1.3 | ND | 1.3 | ND |
| Niacin (mg) | 16 | 16 | 35 | 16 | 35 |
| Vitamin B$_6$ (mg) | 1.7 | 1.7 | 100 | 1.7 | 100 |
| Biotin (mg) | – | 30[c] | ND | 30[c] | ND |
| Pantothenic acid (mg) | 5 | 5[c] | ND | 5[c] | ND |
| Folate (µg) | 400 | 400 | 1,000 | 400 | 1,000 |
| Vitamin B$_{12}$ (µg) | 2.4 | 2.4 | ND | 2.4 | ND |
| Choline (mg) | – | 550[c] | 3,500 | 550[c] | 3,500 |
| **Elements** | | | | | |
| Boron (mg) | – | ND | 20 | ND | 20 |
| Sodium (mg) | – | 1.3[c] | 2.3 | 1.2[c] | 2.3 |
| Potassium (mg) | – | 4.7[c] | – | 4.7[c] | – |
| Chloride (mg) | – | 2.0[c] | 3.6 | 1.8[c] | 3.6 |
| Calcium (mg) | **1,300** | **1,200**[c] | 2,500 | **1,200**[c] | 2,500 |
| Phosphorus (mg) | – | 700 | 4,000 | 700 | 3,000 |
| Magnesium (mg) | **230** | 420 | (350)[f] | 420 | (350)[f] |
| Iron (mg) | 14[d] | 8 | 45 | 8 | 45 |
| Zinc (mg) | 7.0[e] | 11 | 40 | 11 | 40 |

(continued)

Table 19.2 (continued)

Nutrient intake recommendations for older men

| | WHO/FAO/IAEA | IoM for US/Canada | | | |
| | 65+ years | 51–70 years | | >70 years | |
| | RNF[a] | RDA/AI/AMDR[b] | UL[b] | RDA/AI/AMDR[b] | UL[b] |
|---|---|---|---|---|---|
| Fluoride (mg) | – | 4[c] | 10 | 4[c] | 10 |
| Manganese (mg) | – | 2.3[c] | 11 | 2.3[c] | 11 |
| Chromium (µg) | – | **30**[c] | – | **30**[c] | – |
| Selenium (µg) | **34** | 55 | 400 | 55 | 400 |
| Molybdenum (µg) | – | 45 | 2,000 | 45 | 2,000 |
| **Macronutrients** | | | | | |
| Energy (EER[b] kcal) | – | **2,204** | – | **2,054** | – |
| Water (L) | – | **3.7**[c] | – | **2.1**[c] | – |
| Carbohydrate (AMDR) | – | 45–65% | – | 45–65% | – |
| Protein (AMDR) | – | 10–35% | – | 10–35% | – |
| Total fat (AMDR) | – | 20–35% | – | 20–35% | – |
| n-6 PUFA (AMDR) | – | 5–10% | – | 5–10% | – |
| n-3 PUFA (AMDR) | – | 0.6–1.2% | – | 0.6–1.2% | – |
| Dietary fiber (g) | – | **30**[c] | – | **30**[c] | – |

*Note:* The figures in **bold** denote recommendations specifically modified for aging.

*FAO* Food and Agricultural Organization, *IoM* Institute of Medicine, *ND* values not determined, *RAE* retinol activity equivalent, *WHO* World Health Organization, *RE* retinol equivalents, *TE* tocopherol equivalents, *PUFA* polyunsaturated fatty acids, *IAEA* International Atomic Energy Agency.

[a]Recommended nutrient intakes from the UN system (WHO/FAO/IAEA). Older adults: ≥65 years.

[b]Dietary reference intakes from US/Canada system. *AI* adequate intake, *AMDR* adequate macronutrient distribution range, *EER* estimated energy requirement, *RDA* recommended dietary allowance, *UL* tolerable upper intake level.

[c]Recommendation in the form of AIs.

[d]Based on 10% bioavailability of iron from the diet.

[e]Based on the assumption of moderate bioavailability of zinc.

[f]Based on supplemental intake only.

respect to nutrient recommendations for older persons, they remain unchanged from the levels recommended from age 19 onward, without any modifications for age. This is true for protein and water requirements. For one nutrient, iron, the recommendation declines in the later stages of the lifespan, and for another, vitamin D, it increases, according to the DRIs. The upper tolerable level for phosphorus is modified by age. The energy requirement, calculated as the estimated energy requirement (EER), is adjusted by age. There is no RDA for energy to prevent the expected weight gain that might occur with energy intakes above the EER [44]. The adequate intake (AI) for fiber is also adjusted for age.

The values in Table 19.2 and 19.3 should only be considered first approximations for the purposes of setting them for the elderly in developing countries. To advance to greater certainty and applicability, continuing research efforts are needed. With the exception of a few nutrients, notably riboflavin [47], the studies on requirements were conducted in subjects living in industrialized country settings. Moreover, we have the disclaimer in all systems of nutrient recommendations that they apply only to *healthy* individuals. One can reasonably argue that a diminishingly small number of individuals are totally "healthy" with increasing age. Thus, the recommendations in the tables would strictly apply to only a minority of elderly persons in any population.

Aside from the aging aspect, there is a dimension of the environmental features within human habitats of developing, tropical—often rural—societies. It has been argued that issues from humidity and high ambient temperatures to the intense concentrations of ecto- and endoparasites and microbes in the environment produce stress [48]. Nutrient requirements may not be a simple linear function of body mass but rather may have a relation with the underlying composition of tissues. Individuals with short stature, due to early chronic undernutrition, may present this type of metabolic variance. Similarly, the intensive daily physical efforts demanded by unmechanized agriculture may provoke increased requirements for certain nutrients.

The newer concepts embodied in the DRIs include a provision for setting a recommendation considering "health benefits" of a nutrient above and beyond the basic needs for the nutrients. The recent doubling of folate recommendations was motivated by the protective function this can have against neural tube defects in preconceptional women [41, 46]; it was later discovered, however, that a favorable effect on cardiovascular disease due to suppression of homocysteine levels occurs in fortified populations [49]. Generally, however, recommendation panels have been timid in invoking the health benefits criterion, citing the paucity of generalizable evidence and widespread confirmation for findings of demonstrated health benefits from suprarequirement intakes of nutrients.

Supplementation with amounts of nutrients not easily obtained with foods has demonstrated biological effects in older subjects. Doses of vitamin E in the range of 200–800 mg enhance in vitro indicators of immune function [50]. Zinc supplements of 100 mg daily for a month enhanced in vitro lymphocyte responses [51]. The oxocarotenes, zeaxanthin and lutein, found in certain corn and certain dark green vegetables, seem to play a protective role in the fovea of the ocular retina, and enhanced intakes are suggested to be preventive against macular degeneration associated with age [52].

Table 19.3
Nutrient intake recommendations for older women

| | WHO/FAO/IAEA | IoM for US/Canada | | | |
| | 65+ years | 51–70 years | | >70 years | |
| | RNI[a] | RDA/AI/AMDR[b] | UL[b] | RDA/AI/AMDR[b] | UL[b] |
|---|---|---|---|---|---|
| **Vitamins** | | | | | |
| Vitamin A (μg RAE) | 600 (μg RE) | 700 | 3,000 | 700 | 3,000 |
| Vitamin D (mg) | **15** | **10**[c] | 50 | **15**[c] | 50 |
| Vitamin E (mg α-tocopherol) | 7.5 (mg α-TE) | 15 | 1,000 | 15 | 1,000 |
| Vitamin K (μg) | 55 | 90[c] | ND | **90**[c] | ND |
| Vitamin C (mg) | 45 | 75 | 2,000 | 75 | 2,000 |
| Thiamin (mg) | 1.1 | 1.1 | ND | 1.1 | ND |
| Riboflavin (mg) | 1.1 | 1.1 | ND | 1.1 | ND |
| Niacin (mg) | 14 | 14 | 35 | 14 | 35 |
| Vitamin B$_6$ (mg) | 1.5 | 1.5 | 100 | 1.5 | 100 |
| Biotin (mg) | – | 30[c] | ND | 30[c] | ND |
| Pantothenic acid (mg) | 5 | 5[c] | ND | 5[c] | ND |
| Folate (μg) | 400 | 400 | 1,000 | 400 | 1,000 |
| Vitamin B$_{12}$ (μg) | 2.4 | 2.4 | ND | 2.4 | ND |
| Choline (mg) | – | 425[c] | 3,500 | 425[c] | 3,500 |
| **Elements** | | | | | |
| Boron (mg) | – | ND | 20 | ND | 20 |
| Sodium (mg) | – | 1.3[c] | 2.3 | 1.2[c] | 2.3 |
| Potassium (mg) | – | 4.7[c] | – | 4.7[c] | – |
| Chloride (mg) | – | 2.0[c] | 3.6 | 1.8[c] | 3.6 |
| Calcium (mg) | **1,300** | **1,200**[c] | 2,500 | **1,200**[c] | 2,500 |
| Phosphorus (mg) | – | 700 | 4,000 | 700 | 3,000 |
| Magnesium (mg) | **190** | 320 | (350)[f] | 320 | (350)[f] |
| Iron (mg) | 11[d] | 8 | 45 | 8 | 45 |
| Zinc (mg) | 4.9[e] | 8 | 40 | 8 | 40 |

| | | | | | |
|---|---|---|---|---|---|
| Iodine (µg) | 110 | 150 | 1,100 | 150 | 1,100 |
| Copper (µg) | — | 900 | 10,000 | 900 | 10,000 |
| Fluoride (mg) | — | 3[c] | 10 | 3[c] | 10 |
| Manganese (mg) | — | 1.8[c] | 11 | 1.8[c] | 11 |
| Chromium (µg) | — | **20[c]** | — | **20[c]** | — |
| Selenium (µg) | **26** | 55 | 400 | 55 | 400 |
| Molybdenum (µg) | — | 45 | 2,000 | 45 | 2,000 |
| **Macronutrients** | | | | | |
| Energy (EER[b] kcal) | — | **1,978** | — | **1,873** | — |
| Water (L) | — | 2.7[c] | — | 2.1[c] | — |
| Carbohydrate (AMDR) | — | 45–65% | — | 45–65% | — |
| Protein (AMDR) | — | 10–35% | — | 10–35% | — |
| Total fat (AMDR) | — | 20–35% | — | 20–35% | — |
| n-6 PUFA (AMDR) | — | 5–10% | — | 5–10% | — |
| n-3 PUFA (AMDR) | — | 0.6–1.2% | — | 0.6–1.2% | — |
| Dietary fiber (g) | — | 21[c] | — | 21[c] | — |

*Note*: The figures in **bold** denote recommendations specifically modified for aging.

*FAO* Food and Agricultural Organization, *IoM* Institute of Medicine, *ND* values not determined, *RAE* retinol activity equivalent, *WHO* World Health Organization, *RE* retinol equivalents, *TE* tocopherol equivalents, *PUFA* polyunsaturated fatty acids, *IAEA* International Atomic Energy Agency.

[a]Recommended nutrient intakes from the UN system (WHO/FAO/IAEA). Older adults: ≥ 65 years.

[b]Dietary reference intakes from US/Canada system. *AI* adequate intake, *AMDR* adequate macronutrient distribution range, *EER* estimated energy requirements, *RDA* recommended dietary allowance, *UL* tolerable upper intake level.

[c]Recommendation in the form of AIs.

[d]Based on 10% bioavailability of iron from the diet.

[e]Based on the assumption of moderate bioavailability of zinc.

[f]Based on supplemental intake only.

## 19.7  DIETARY INTAKE AND EATING BEHAVIOR BY ELDERLY IN DEVELOPING COUNTRIES

### 19.7.1  Assessing Dietary Intakes in Older Subjects: Caveats for Developing Countries

Among the consequences of the global demographic and epidemiological transitions, one could include the increasing numbers of older adults who require nutritional services adequate to their emotional, cultural, social, economic, and health needs for which appropriate assessment of their dietary intakes is needed. Dietary data, interpreted in the context of these various needs, would help to identify those dietary factors associated with declining health and the development of chronic conditions. Those linkages between diet and health or diet and disease are only perceived in events followed during periods of time as the effects of specific dietary practices might take months or even years to influence health.

Several techniques are usually applied for the assessment of dietary intakes and food patterns of older adults in developed countries, with the addition of sophisticated memory-enhancing tools that improve short-term memory among elders with compromised cognitive function or with declining physical health. To extract information about historical patterns, a widely used method consists of obtaining food consumption history with the application of food frequency questionnaires [53–55]. One of the most commonly used methodologies for dietary assessment is the 24-hour recall. The basic premise is the accurate recalling one could get as it only requests information from the previous 24 hours before the information is collected. In addition, the systematization of the five-step technique developed by the US Department of Agriculture expert group [56] has also improved greatly the application of this technique, particularly in the elderly. Diet history collected in food records (or food diaries) is another methodology used with older adults in developed countries. However, this methodology requires educated, highly motivated subjects, which could limit its application in some elderly groups.

There is a shortage of information about which instruments for dietary assessment are practical and reliable for extracting the information in older adults from *developing countries*. In addition, prior to the adoption of instruments developed in other latitudes, food lists (if food frequency questionnaires are used) and probing prompts (if 24-hour recalls are used) are needed as type of foods and eating patterns differ from country to country.

Among the elderly in developing countries, it is presumed that their ability of recalling food consumption and other related dietary facts could be modified not only by their cognitive status and declining health, but also by their education level and their lack of experience as informants. On the other hand, obtaining dietary information from older adults in developing countries could be facilitated by the monotonous diets that are traditionally associated with population groups from developing countries. Moreover, among those groups, there are usually a limited number of staple foods that are consumed frequently and with small variations in portion sizes. It has been observed that in countries like Guatemala, families are very consistent in the dimensions of their homemade tortillas, and people usually consume the same amount of them, making it relatively easy to collect information about amounts and frequencies of use of this food product. Rice is the main staple food for older Puerto Ricans living in the US mainland, independent of their length of residency [57], and it is also the main component in diets of older Panamanians [58].

To estimate nutrient and energy composition of foods consumed by older adults, reliable and accurate nutrient databases or food composition tables are needed. However, these reference instruments are scarce in developing countries, and in many cases, those that are available are outdated and limited in the number of nutrients for analysis and correlations with health outcomes. To correct for these limitations, the International Network of Food Data Systems (INFOODS) has been working worldwide to collect, systematize, and enhance international collaborations around food and nutrient databases [59].

Standards and reference patterns such as nutrient recommendations (discussed in the previous section) as well as dietary guidelines and graphic representations of food groups are used in the interpretation and application of dietary data. After the promulgation of the World Health Organization/Food and Agricultural Organization (WHO/FAO) guidelines for the development of food-based dietary guidelines [60], countries around the world have produced their own guidelines and used them to guide their efforts in policy making, program planning and evaluation. The FAO, through its Nutrition Information, Communication, and Education Department, makes efforts to divulge those dietary guidelines from its online site [61]. Despite all the efforts in improving tools for dietary assessment, few of them have been designed specifically for the elderly, particularly those in developing countries.

### 19.7.2   *Patterns of Dietary Consumption in Later Life*

Traditionally, elderly people had developed lifelong eating patterns partly modulated by sociodemographic and psychosocial determinants of their food-related behaviors as well as by the environmental circumstances associated with access and availability of their food supply [62]. The attachment of the elderly to their traditional eating practices represents a challenge for interventions to modify intake for the correction of nutritional imbalances and poor health. One could think that food intake of elders from developing countries, especially those residing in economically deprived areas, could be less than optimal because of food availability issues. All this is in addition to the increased requirements for several nutrients due to physiological changes associated with aging and to pathological effects of some chronic conditions at the same time that energy intakes are decreasing. However, there is evidence that, whereas for some elder groups their traditional diets are more health protective than more "modern" ones, for other groups their diet improves with the incorporation of new foods. Studies among elderly in Greece and in Australia revealed that those with traditional eating patterns had lower overall mortality and longer survival [63–65], and these patterns may be protective for obesity [66]. Among Mexican women in the United States, those of more recent arrival had higher protein, calcium, and vitamins A, C, and folate intakes and greater overall mean adequacy ratios (constructed with eight nutrients) than their counterparts in the country for more than a generation [67]. On the contrary, acculturation to the US culture seems to be positively associated with dietary quality [68] and diet diversity [69] among elderly Puerto Ricans in the United States. Moreover, older Puerto Ricans attached to their traditional food patterns with rice as their main source of energy have higher risk for obesity than those who had incorporated more variety into their eating patterns [70].

The evidence about changes in food accessibility and intake in several countries around the globe are suggestive of the risk for obesity and the malnutrition-related nontransmissible diseases. In Latin America, for example, it was observed that although nutrient availability differs in magnitude across countries, the overall patterns were remarkably consistent. Availability of total fat, animal products, and sugars were all increasing at the same time that rapid declines in the availability of cereals, fruit, and vegetables were occurring [71]. Mondini and Monteiro also observed drastic changes in dietary patterns of Brazilian populations, including declines in the relative consumption of cereals, beans, roots, and tubercles; increase in the relative consumption of eggs, milk, and dairy products; and replacement of lard, bacon, and butter by vegetable oils and margarine [72].

Although worldwide corrections of poor dietary habits and inadequate food intakes in the elderly are a challenge and could overwhelm governments of developing countries, the acceleration and magnitude of the changes already occurring in most of those countries are giving little option but to confront and look for viable solutions for the potential risks of having elderly populations with the triple burden of being old, poor, and malnourished.

## 19.8  NUTRITIONAL DEFICIENCY AND EXCESS AND ITS ASSESSMENT IN THE ELDERLY OF DEVELOPING COUNTRIES

The elderly of developing countries are most likely to suffer in their care and assessment by confusion of the blanket application of the norms and standards of the population at large to this more unique and heterogeneous population in later life. Nutritional status has three domains: The first is global, constitutional nutrition (formerly discussed in terms of "protein-energy" status), related to body composition; the second is status with respect to the body's reserves or availability of micronutrients (vitamins, minerals); and the third relates to hydration and fluid and electrolyte balance. The aging process itself conditions changes that make nutritional assessment more difficult.

### 19.8.1  Deficiency and Undernutrition States in Developing Country Elderly

The most commonly considered imbalance in nutritional status is undernutrition. Chronic energy deficiency is a concern in older persons in all societies. In developed countries, however, recent weight loss is often secondary, a consequence of a chronic degenerative disease. Although poverty creates the risk for primary dietary deficiencies, a differential diagnosis for underweight representing a secondary consequence of occult illness should be maintained in the elderly of low-income societies as well.

Primary vitamin and mineral deficiency can arise from consuming diets with low micronutrient density, with poor nutrients of poor bioavailability, or both. The primarily plant-based fare of traditional agrarian societies, combined with environmental stress that includes parasitoses and recurrent infections, is an established conditioning scenario for undernutrition with respect to a subset of vitamins and minerals. Among the vitamin deficiencies recorded as commonly endemic in low-income settings are those of vitamin A, riboflavin, and vitamin $B_{12}$. Folic acid deficiency occurs in certain populations largely dependent on boiled maize. Iodine deficiency is widespread across the globe due to environmental depletion of this element. Iron deficiency and its associated iron-deficiency anemia are reputed to be the most widespread deficiency disorders of humankind. A widespread vulnerability to subadequate zinc deficiency has been appreciated [73]. Selenium deficiency occurs when soils are particularly depleted of this mineral.

Specific micronutrient surveys focusing on elderly subpopulations in developing countries are scarce. In Guatemala, Boisvert et al. [47] found a majority of older persons screened had inadequate riboflavin status. It is widely regarded that gastric hyposecretion adversely influences vitamin $B_{12}$ status with increasing age. Vitamin D deficiency was previously considered to be of a lesser concern in tropical countries, which experience year-round direct penetration of the UV spectrum of sunlight. In fact, little survey experience on vitamin D status in developing country elderly is available. However, in the absence of general consumption of dairy items or marine fish, tropical populations are virtually totally dependent on solar-dependent vitamin D production. The dermal capacity decreases with aging, and outdoor activities may be curtailed with advancing age. In the context of degenerative diseases, greater amounts of vitamin D than have been considered normative may be protective against them [74]. Better across-the-board vitamin D nutriture may emerge as a public health necessity among elderly not only in non-tropical latitudes but also in the tropics as epidemiological and intervention trial data continue to emerge.

Since iron is of slow turnover, reserves of this element actually tend to build with the passage of time. With menopause, the monthly menstrual blood losses cease. For these reasons, the elderly should be considered the most resistant to iron-deficiency anemia in any society, and its occurrence raises the specter of some abnormal blood loss condition. Where hookworm or schistosomiasis is common, bleeding from parasitic lesions may produce anemia in any age group, including the elderly [75]. Gastric atrophy interferes with solubility for its intestinal absorption. However, iron deficiency or anemia in an older individual in a tropical country can have the same ominous clinical significance that it has in a developed country setting; that is, it signifies a malignancy at some level of the gastrointestinal tract.

As individuals age, several processes occur that make issues of hydration and water and electrolyte balance more precarious. With aging, there is a blunting in thirst sensation, renal function declines, and the vascular response to altered blood volume diminishes. Especially in hot humid climates, this would increase the susceptibility to hypovolemia and dehydration.

### 19.8.1.1 Diagnosing Undernutrition

The principles of any diagnosis are clinical history, physical examination, and laboratory testing. The human aging process itself confounds the assessment of nutritional status of the older individual both in the clinical setting and at the population level in epidemiological screening. Nutritional assessment as applied to the elderly must take into consideration physiological and social changes that occur with advancing age [76]. Cognitive decline distorts the accuracy of answers in clinical histories, and low levels of schooling and linguistic issues complicate the interview in developing societies. Keys to successful and reliable diagnostic evaluation for undernutrition of the elderly in general—and developing country elders in particular—are a knowledge of the most common deficiency states, as discussed above, and an understanding of the nuances, caveats and pitfalls of assessment techniques with advancing age.

Reflection of undernutrition (underweight) by anthropometric measurements, specifically the body mass index (BMI; kg/m$^2$), is confounded by short stature. The international standards define a BMI below 18.5 kg/m$^2$ as chronic energy deficiency, but up to 40% of free-living populations in South Asia can have values in that range. Adults lose stature due to settling and curvature of the spine with aging, and arm span [77] and knee height [78] have been proposed as surrogate measures. Short stature, however, is not an index of ongoing undernutrition in individuals beyond adolescence, such that "stunting" is not applicable in older adults. The laxness of the skin and redistribution of body fat confound the use of skinfold thickness for representative measurement of subcutaneous fat. Similarly, to the extent that skin turgor is to be used clinically to assess the hydration state, dermal changes with aging can confound assessment. Moisture of mucosal surfaces is a more reliable indicator of hydration of the elderly [76].

Aging has minimal effects on hematological parameters, such that universal standards for hemoglobin, hematocrit, and blood cell indices and counts are applicable in later life. Aging per se is associated with elevation of the binding protein of copper (ceruloplasmin) and a slight reduction in albumin concentration [15]. When urinary excretion of nutrient metabolites is employed in nutritional assessment, especially as ambient concentrations or timed excretion, the age-related changes in renal physiology must be considered to avoid diagnostic errors.

Some biochemical and laboratory measures of nutritional status are distorted by fundamental conditions prevailing in developing countries, such as inflammatory stimulation by microbes and parasites. This produces redistribution of circulating nutrients (e.g., iron, zinc, vitamin A, and copper) and distortion of nutrient indicators (e.g., plasma ferritin). Dehydration in hot climates would tend to produce hemoconcentration, decreasing the acuity of circulating biomarkers to detect deficiency states.

### 19.8.2  Excess and Overnutrition States in Developing Country Elderly

The popular image of developing countries is of populations living in rural poverty. It was also widely regarded that poverty was a restraint on obesity. Contemporary realities debunk both of these generalizations to the status of obsolete myths [79], showing that a lack of social power, choice, and a safe environment are more likely to produce weight excess, especially among poor in urban settings.

In real-world experience, the micronutrients most likely to produce adverse effects on the *high* side of exposure for older individuals are vitamin A, folic acid, iron, calcium, phosphorus, and sodium. Preformed vitamin A has interesting implications in later life as a postprandial load is cleared more slowly with advancing age [80], and bone demineralization has been related to vitamin A from animal sources [81]. As discussed, however, culinary customs and economic constraints generally act to produce lower intakes of this form of vitamin A as well as that of the other mentioned nutrients in diets of low-income societies.

The interaction of folic acid and vitamin B$_{12}$ has long been topical for the nutritional health of the elderly. In some developed countries, general folic acid fortification has raised some concerns about negative consequences in the face of vitamin B$_{12}$ scarcity [82]. Folic acid fortification lags behind in most developing countries, but when Chile instituted its national program, fortification levels were almost double those in most other nations with folic acid fortification mandates [83]. Hemochromatosis is rare among the ethnic groups native to developing countries; a poorly understood syndrome of iron accumulation found in southern Africa (Bantu siderosis) produces damaging iron overload when soluble forms of iron are available in the diet [84].

### 19.8.2.1 Diagnosing Overnutrition

Aging and Third World residence impose certain recognized challenges to diagnostic assessment of overnutrition. The BMI increases through the seventh decade and then decreases in survivors beyond this age. The value of the BMI for any given body weight is influenced by short stature, decreasing the value of the denominator term. Moreover, age-related height loss distorts the accurate assessment of an appropriate reference stature for an older individual [77]. Beyond mere body weight are changing proportions of lean and fat mass, with increased visceral deposition of lipids and fatty infiltration of skeletal muscles [18]. All of these aging features are reflected in the widely documented observation that individuals with identical BMIs can have vastly different percentage of body weights as fat or lean across ethnic groups [85, 86]. The "Indian paradox" derives from the development of cardiovascular and metabolic risk in South Asians at much lower BMIs [87], leading to a suggested adjustment for a lower cutoff for "overweight" for the populations of southern and southeastern Asia [27]. Finally, the health consequences of a given excessive body mass differ markedly across races [88].

Diagnosis of overload and toxicity states for micronutrients is difficult under any circumstances and in all age groups, requiring interpretive assessment of blood levels of nutrients and metabolites or tissue biopsy findings. No systematic understanding of how aging distorts these challenging diagnoses of vitamin and mineral excess has yet been developed.

## 19.9 CONCLUSIONS

The fact that the populations of developing countries are aging and more older persons are surviving is a virtual brave new world for public health for low-income societies. The consequences for diet and nutrition of the older members of developing societies have been little explored and are poorly understood. The nutrition transition is bringing forth a dual burden of malnutrition, with problems of under- and overweight. Epidemiological transition is emerging for the populations of developing countries with increasing prevalence of the components of the metabolic syndrome and malignant disease.

In the absence of a strong and prolific tradition of "tropical gerontology," the prudent course is to synthesize the substantial knowledge about the unique conditions and challenges in low-income societies and the accumulated understanding of aging biology and senescent changes from affluent societies and prepare an active agenda for inquiry. One would expect a series of interactions between the two domains in which the prevailing conditions of life in developing nations exacerbate processes of structural and functional senescence as well as those in which the traditional diet and rigorous physical activity will prove protective. This chapter bears testimony to the demographic transition and the prudence of recognizing that older individuals and chronic diseases are important emerging elements across the panorama of developing country health and nutrition.

# REFERENCES

1. Busuttil RA, Dolle M, Campisi J, Vijga J. Genomic instability, aging, and cellular senescence. Ann N Y Acad Sci 2004:1019;245–255.
2. Harper AE. Dietary goals—a skeptical view. Am J Clin Nutr 1978;31:310–321.
3. Kehayias JJ, Fiatarone MA, Zhuang H, Roubenoff R. Total body potassium and body fat: relevance to aging. Am J Clin Nutr 1997;66:904–910.
4. Wahlqvist ML, Davies L, Hsu-Hage BH-H, Kouris-Blazos A, Scrimshaw NS, Steen B, eds. Food habits in later life: a cross-cultural approach. Melbourne: United Nations University Press/Asia Pacific Journal of Clinical Nutrition, 1996.
5. Frisancho AR, ed. Human adaptation and accommodation. Ann Arbor: University of Michigan Press, 1996.
6. Simoons FD. Primary adult lactose intolerance and the milking habit: a problem in biological and cultural interrelations II. A culture history perspective. Am J Dig Dis 1970;23:963–980.
7. Eaton SB, Konner M. Paleolithic nutrition: a consideration of its nature and current implication. N Engl J Med 1985. 312:283–289.
8. Nestle M. Paleolithic diets: a skeptical view. Nutr Bull 2000;25:43–47.
9. Ahmed A, TT. Telomerase, telomerase inhibition, and cancer. J Anti Aging Med 2003;6:315–325.
10. Huang H, Manton KG The role of oxidative damage in mitochondria during aging: a review. Front Biosci 2004;9:100–117.
11. Khrapko K, Ebralidse K, Kraytsberg Y. Where and when do somatic mtDNA mutations occur? Ann N Y Acad Sci 2004;1019:240–244.
12. Fraker PJ, Lill Elghanian DA. The many roles of apoptosis in immunity as modified by aging and nutritional status. J Nutr Health Aging 2004;8:56–63.
13. Shock NR. Physiological aspects of aging. J Am Diet Assoc 1970;56:491–496.
14. Sussman MA, Anversa P. Myocardial aging and senescence: where have the stem cells gone? Annu Rev Physiol 2004;66:29–48.
15. Solomons NW. Older persons. Physiological changes. In: Encyclopedia of human nutrition. 2nd ed. Caballero B AL, Prentice AM, eds. London: Elsevier, 2004:431–436.
16. Mishra SK, Misra V. Muscle sarcopenia: an overview. Acta Myol 2003;22:43–47.
17. Lanfranco F, Gianotti L, Giordano R, Pellegrino M, Maccario M, Arvat E. Ageing, growth hormone and physical performance. J Endocrinol Invest 2003;26:861–872.
18. Kinney, JM. Nutritional frailty, sarcopenia and falls in the elderly. Curr Opin Clin Nutr Metab Care 2004;7(1):15–20.
19. Perez-Perez GI, Rothenbacher D, Brenner H. Epidemiology of *Helicobacter pylori* infection. Helicobacter 2004;9(suppl 1):1–6.
20. Henry CJK, Ritz P, Roth GS, Lane M, Solomons NW. Impact of human aging on energy and protein metabolism and requirements. Eur J Clin Nutr 2000;54(suppl 3):S157–S159.
21. Rowe JW, Kahn RL. Human aging: Usual and successful. Science 1987;237:143–149.
22. Lipsitz LA. Physiological complexity, aging and the path to frailty. Sci Aging Knowl Environ 2004;16:16.
23. Solomons NW. Demographic and nutritional trends among the elderly in developed and developing regions. Eur J Clin Nutr 2000;54(suppl 3):S1–S13.
24. Laslett P. Interpreting the demographic changes. Phil Trans R Soc London B Biol Sci 1997;352:1805–1809.
25. Manton KG. The dynamics of population aging: demography and policy analysis. Milbank Q 1991;69:309–338.
26. Manton KG. The global impact of noncommunicable diseases: estimates and projections. World Health Stat Q 1988;41:255–266.
27. World Health Organization. Diet, nutrition and the prevention of chronic diseases. Geneva: World Health Organization, 2001. WHO Technical Report Series 916.
28. Uauy R, Solomons N. Role of the international community in addressing the dual burden of malnutrition with a common agenda. SCN News 2006;32: 24–37.
29. Yach D, Hawkes C, Gould CL, Hofman KJ. The global burden of chronic diseases: overcoming impediments to prevention and control. JAMA 2004;291:2616–2622.

30. Willett W. Nutritional epidemiology. 2nd ed. New York: Oxford University Press, 1999.
31. Margetts BM, Nelson M, eds. Design concepts in nutritional epidemiology. Oxford, UK: Oxford University Press, 1991.
32. World Cancer Research Fund. Diet, nutrition and prevention of cancer: a global perspective. London: World Cancer Research Fund, 1997.
33. Riley RT, Morred WP, Bacon CW. Fungal toxins in foods. Recent concerns. Annu Rev Nutr 1993;13:167–189.
34. Kurozawa Y, Ogimoto I, Shibata A, Nose T, Yoshimura T, Suzuki H, Sakata R, Fujita Y, Ichikawa S, Iwai N, Tamakoshi A, JACC Study Group. Coffee and risk of death from hepatocellular carcinoma in a large cohort study in Japan. Br J Cancer 2005;93:607–610.
35. Hendriks HF, van Tol A. Alcohol. Handb Exp Pharmacol 2005;170:339–361.
36. Keen CL, Holt RR, Oteiza PI, Fraga CG, Schmitz HH. Cocoa antioxidants and cardiovascular health. Am J Clin Nutr 2005;81(1 suppl):298S–303S.
37. Siddiqui RA, Shaikh SR, Sech LA, Yount HR, Stillwell W, Zaloga GP. Omega 3-fatty acids: health benefits and cellular mechanisms of action. Mini Rev Med Chem 2004;4:859–871.
38. Peterlik M, Cross HS. Vitamin D and calcium deficits predispose for multiple chronic diseases. Eur J Clin Invest 2005;35:290–304.
39. Food and Nutrition Board and Standing Committee of the Scientific Evaluation of Dietary Reference Intakes. Dietary reference intakes for calcium, phosphorus, magnesium, vitamin D, and fluoride. Washington, DC: National Academy Press, 1999.
40. Food and Nutrition Board and Standing Committee of the Scientific Evaluation of Dietary Reference Intakes. Dietary reference intakes for vitamin C, vitamin E, selenium, and carotenoids. Washington, DC: Institute of Medicine, 2000.
41. Food and Nutrition Board Standing Committee of the Scientific Evaluation of Dietary Reference Intakes. Dietary reference intakes for thiamin, riboflavin, niacin, vitamin $B_6$, folate, vitamin $B_{12}$, pantothenic acid, biotin, choline. Washington, DC: Institute of Medicine, 2000.
42. Food and Nutrition Board Standing Committee of the Scientific Evaluation of Dietary Reference Intakes. Dietary reference intakes for vitamin A, vitamin K, arsenic, boron, chromium, copper, iodine, iron, manganese, molybdenum, nickel, silicon, vanadium, zinc. Washington, DC: Institute of Medicine, National Academy of Science, 2001.
43. Food and Nutrition Board Standing Committee of the Scientific Evaluation of Dietary Reference Intakes. Dietary reference intakes: applications in dietary assessment. A report of the Subcommittees on Interpretation Uses of Dietary Reference Intakes Upper Reference Levels of Nutrients, the Standing Committee on the Scientific Evaluation of Dietary Reference Intakes. Washington, DC: Institute of Medicine, National Academy of Science, 2001.
44. Food and Nutrition Board and Standing Committee of the Scientific Evaluation of Dietary Reference Intakes. Dietary reference intakes for energy, carbohydrates, fiber, fat, protein and amino acids (macronutrients). Washington, DC: Institute of Medicine, National Academy of Science, 2002:936.
45. Food and Nutrition Board and Standing Committee of the Scientific Evaluation of Dietary Reference Intakes. Dietary reference intakes for water, potassium, sodium, chloride, and sulfate. Washington, DC: Institute of Medicine, National Academy of Science, 2004.
46. World Health Organization and Food and Agricultural Organization. Human vitamin and mineral requirements. Geneva: World Health Organization, 2004.
47. Boisvert WA, Mendoza I, Castañeda C, Portocarrero L, Solomons NW, Gershoff SN, Russell RM. Riboflavin requirements of the healthy elderly and its relationship to macronutrient composition of the diet. J Nutr 1993;123:915–925.
48. Solomons NW, Kaufer-Horwitz M, Bermudez OI. Harmonization for mesoamerican nutrient-based recommendations: regional unification or national specification? Arch Latinoam Nutr 2004;54(4):363–373.
49. Malinow MR, Duell PB, Hess DL, Anderson PH, Kruger WD, Phillipson BE, Gluckman RA, Block PC, Upson BM. Reduction of plasma homocyst(e)ine levels by breakfast cereal fortified with folic acid in patients with coronary heart disease. N Engl J Med;1998:338:1009–1015.
50. Meydani SN, Han SN. Nutrient regulation of the immune response: the case of vitamin E. In: Present knowledge in nutrition, 8th ed. Bowman BA, Russell RM, eds. Washington, DC: ILSI Press, 2001:449–462.

51. Duchateau J, Delepesse G, Vrijens R, Collet H. Beneficial effect of oral zinc supplementation on the immune response of old people. Am J Med 1981;70:1001–1004.

52. Mozaffarieh M, Sacu S, Wedrich A. The role of the carotenoids, lutein and zeaxanthin, in protecting against age-related macular degeneration: a review based on controversial evidence. J Nutr 2003;2:20.

53. Block G, Hartman AM, Dresser CM, Carroll MD, Gannon J, Gardner L. A data-based approach to diet questionnaire design and testing. Am J Epidemiol 1986;124(3):453–469.

54. Tucker KL, Bianchi L, Maras J, Bermudez OI. Adaptation of a food frequency questionnaire to assess diets of Puerto Rican and non-Hispanic adults. Am J Epidemiol 1998;148:507–518.

55. Willett WC, Reynolds RD, Cottrell-Hoehner S, Sampson L, Browne ML. Validation of a semi-quantitative food frequency questionnaire: comparison with 1-year diet record. J Am Diet Assoc 1987;87:43–47.

56. Conway JM, Ingwersen LA, Vinyard BT, Moshfegh AJ. Effectiveness of the US Department of Agriculture five-step multiple-pass method in assessing food intake in obese and nonobese women. Am J Clin Nutr 2003;77:1171–1178.

57. Bermudez OI, Falcon LM, Tucker KL. Intake and food sources of macronutrients among older Hispanic adults: association with ethnicity, acculturation and length of residence in the United States. J Am Diet Assoc 2000;100:665–673.

58. Ministry of Health of Panama. Study about nutritional status and quality of life among older adults attending health centers in Panama City Metropolitan area. Valdes VE, Bermudez O, DeMas M, eds. Panama City, Panama: Ministry of Health, Social Security Institute, Pan American Health Organization, Institute of Nutrition for Central America and Panama and Tufts University, 2003.

59. Food and Agricultural Organization, Agriculture, Biosecurity, Nutrition and Consumer Protection Department. The international network of food data systems. 2006. Available at: http://www.fao.org/infoods/index_en.stm. Accessed May 18, 2006.

60. World Health Organization and Food and Agriculture Organization of the United Nations. Preparation and use of food-based dietary guidelines. Nicosia, Cyprus: World Health Organization and Food and Agriculture Organization.

61. Food and Agriculture Organization, Nutrition Information, Communication and Education Department. Food guidelines by country. 2005. Available at: http://www.fao.org/ag/agn/nutrition/education_guidelines_country_en.stm. Accessed December 18, 2005.

62. Bermudez OI, Tucker KL. Cultural aspects of food choices in various communities of elders. Generations 2004;28:22–27.

63. Trichopoulou A, Kouris-Blazos A, Wahlqvist ML, Gnardellis C, Lagiou P, Polychronopoulos E, Vassilakou T, Lipworth L, Trichopoulos D. Diet and overall survival in elderly people. BMJ 1995;311:1457–1460.

64. Trichopoulou A, Lagiou P, Trichopoulos D. Traditional Greek diet and coronary heart disease. J Cardiovasc Risk 1994;1:9–15.

65. Kouris-Blazos A, Gnardellis C, Wahlqvist ML, Trichopoulos D, Lukito W, Trichopoulou A. Are the advantages of the Mediterranean diet transferable to other populations? A cohort study in Melbourne, Australia. Br J Nutr 1999;82:57–61.

66. Wahlqvist ML, Kouris-Blazos A, Wattanapenpaiboon N. The significance of eating patterns: an elderly Greek case study. Appetite 1999;32:23–32.

67. Guendelman S, Abrams B. Dietary intake among Mexican-American women: generational differences and a comparison with white non-Hispanic women. Am J Public Health 1995;85:20–25.

68. Bermudez OI. Relationship of acculturation, health and socioeconomic factors to dietary status of Puerto Rican elderly. Amherst: University of Massachusetts, 1994.

69. Khan LK, Martorell R. Diet diversity in Mexican Americans, Cuban Americans and Puerto Ricans. Ecol Food Nutr 1997;36:401–415.

70. Lin H, Bermudez OI, Tucker KL. Dietary patterns of Hispanic elders are associated with acculturation and obesity. J Nutr 2003;133:3651–3657.

71. Bermudez OI, Tucker KL. Trends in dietary patterns of Latin American populations. Cad Saude Publica 2003;19(suppl 1):S87–S99.

72. Mondini L, Monteiro CA. Changes in the diet pattern of the Brazilian urban population (1962–1988) [in Portuguese]. Rev Saude Publica 1994;28:433–439.

73. Wuehler SE, Peerson JM, Brown KH. Use of national food balance data to estimate the adequacy of zinc in national food supplies: methodology and regional estimates. Public Health Nutr 2005;8:812–819.

74. Holick MF. Vitamin D: importance in the prevention of cancers, type 1 diabetes, heart disease, and osteoporosis. Am J Clin Nutr 2004;79:362–371.

75. Elias D, Wolff K, Klassen P, Bulux J, Solomons NW. Intestinal helminths and their on indicators of iron status in the elderly. J Nutr Health Aging 1997;1:167–173.

76. Solomons NW, Young VR. Metabolism. In: Manual of clinical nutrition, Paige DM, ed. Margate, NJ: Nutrition Publications, 1982:2.1–2.15.

77. Rabe B, Thamarin, Gross R, Solomons NW, Schultink W. Body mass index of the elderly derived from height and arm span. Asia Pac J Clin Nutr 1996;5:79–83.

78. Bermudez OI, Becker EK, and Tucker KL. Development of gender-specific equations for correction of stature of frail elderly Hispanics living in the northeastern United States. Am J Clin Nutr 1999;69: 992–998.

79. Monteiro CA, Benicio MH, Conde WL, Popkin BM. Shifting obesity trends in Brazil. Eur J Clin Nutr 2000;54: 342–346.

80. Solomons NW. Vitamin A and carotenoids. In: Present knowledge in nutrition. 8th ed. Bowman BA, et al., eds. Washington, DC: ILSI Press, 2001:127–145.

81. Crandall C. Vitamin A intake and osteoporosis: a clinical review. J Women's Health (Larchmt) 2004;13:939–953.

82. Flood VM, Webb KL, Smith W, Mitchell P, Bantick JM, Macintyre R, Sindhusake D, Rubin GL. Folate fortification: potential impact on folate intake in an older population. Eur J Clin Nutr 2001;55: 793–800.

83. Hertrampf E, Cortes F, Erickson JD, Cayazzo M, Freire W, Bailey LB, Howson C, Kauwell GP, Pfeiffer C. Consumption of folic acid-fortified bread improves folate status in women of reproductive age in Chile. J Nutr 2003;133:3166–3169.

84. Gordeuk V, Mukiibi J, Hasstedt SJ, Samowitz W, Edwards CQ, West G, Ndambire S, Emmanual J, Nkanza N, Chapanduka Z. Iron overload in Africa: interaction between a gene and dietary iron content. N Engl J Med 1992;326:95–100.

85. Deurenberg-Yap M, Chew SK, Deurenberg P. Elevated body fat percentage and cardiovascular risks at low body mass index levels among Singaporean Chinese, Malays and Indians. Obes Rev 2002;3:209–215.

86. Fernandez JR, Heo M, Heymsfield SB, Pierson RN Jr, Pi-Sunyer FX, Wang ZM, Wang J, Hayes M, Allison DB, Gallagher D. Is percentage body fat differentially related to body mass index in Hispanic Americans, African Americans, and European Americans? Am J Clin Nutr 2003;77:71–75.

87. Singh RB, Rastogi SS, Niaz MA, Postiglione A. Association of central obesity and insulin resistance with high prevalence of diabetes and cardiovascular disease in an elderly population with low fat intake and lower than normal prevalence of obesity: the Indian paradox. Coron Artery Dis 1998;9:559–565.

88. Stevens J, Juhaeri, Cai J, Jones DW. The effect of decision rules on the choice of a body mass index cutoff for obesity: examples from African American and white women. Am J Clin Nutr 2002;75:986–992.

# 20 The Nutrition Transition and Its Relationship to Demographic Change

## Barry M. Popkin

## 20.1 INTRODUCTION

Scientists have long recognized the importance of the demographic and epidemiological transitions in higher-income countries and have more recently understood that similar sets of broadly based changes are occurring in lower-income countries. What has not been recognized is that concurrent changes are occurring in nutrition with equally important resource allocation implications for many low-income countries. This chapter provides a heuristic framework that accommodates the dynamic nature of nutrition.

Human diet and nutritional status have undergone a sequence of major shifts among characteristic states, defined as broad patterns of food use and corresponding nutrition-related disease.[1] Over the last three centuries, the pace of dietary change appears to have accelerated to varying degrees in different regions of the world. The concept of the nutrition transition focuses on large shifts in diet, especially its structure and overall composition. These dietary changes are reflected in nutritional outcomes, such as changes in average stature and body composition. Further, dietary changes are paralleled by major changes in health status as well as by major demographic and socioeconomic changes.

This chapter uses data from nationwide surveys to present a brief case study of an issue of international importance that has emerged over the last two decades the coexistence of the problems of side-by-side under- and overnutrition. In many low-income countries,

---

[1] Two extant theories of change address key factors that affect and are affected by nutritional change. One relates to the demographic transition—the shift from a pattern of high fertility and high mortality to one of low fertility and low mortality (typical of modern industrialized nations). Even more directly relevant is the concept of the epidemiologic transition, first described by Omran [1]. The epidemiologic transition describes the shift from a pattern of high prevalence of infectious diseases and malnutrition, resulting from pestilence, famine, and poor environmental sanitation, to a pattern of high prevalence of chronic and degenerative diseases strongly associated with lifestyle. A fourth pattern of delayed degenerative diseases has been more recently formulated [2]. Accompanying this progression is a major shift in age-specific mortality patterns and life expectancy. The concepts of demographic and epidemiologic transition share a focus on the ways in which populations move from one pattern to the next. The framework developed here mirrors these concepts of demographic and disease change.

From: *Nutrition and Health: Nutrition and Health in Developing Countries, Second Edition*
Edited by: R. D. Semba & M. W. Bloem © Humana Press, Totowa, NJ

this rapid transition in diet is creating this situation. Thus, in some nations that are still developing, policies to address nutritional problems related to poverty and problems related to excess have begun to appear. Such a situation is rapidly developing in China, Indonesia, and a number of other Middle Eastern, African, and Asian countries, inter alia. In others in South America, obesity is the dominant concern now.

The rapid shift in the structure of diet in many low-income countries does not mean that the thesis posed by Behrman and others that income changes are not improving diet is invalid [3, 4]. Rather, it is important to note that these researchers, whose primary concern was poverty elimination, focused on improvements in caloric and protein intake and missed many of the more subtle and equally important changes in nutrition that occur with development.

This chapter reviews patterns of dietary change that have occurred in the period after World War II in East Asia and that are emerging in other low-income regions and the former Soviet Union to provide some context for a brief discussion of policy issues that either are already being faced by others or will soon become prominent.

## 20.2   BACKGROUND: PATTERNS OF THE NUTRITION TRANSITION

A summary of changes in nutrition and the major features of each pattern are presented in five broad patterns in Table 20.1. These patterns are not restricted to particular periods of human history. For convenience, the patterns are outlined in past tense as historical developments; however, "earlier" patterns are not restricted to the periods in which they first arose but continue to characterize certain geographic and socioeconomic subpopulations.

*Pattern 1: Collection of Food.* The diet at this time was high in carbohydrates and fiber and low in fat, especially saturated fat [5, 6]. In the wild animal meat consumed, the proportion of fat that was polyunsaturated was significantly higher than in modern domesticated animal meat [7]. These early humans were relatively tall but had short life expectancies (some speculate that the benefits of a good diet were offset by high levels of infectious disease; see [7]).

*Pattern 2: Famine.* In the famine pattern, the diet became much less varied and subject to larger variations and episodic periods of extreme hunger. These dietary changes are hypothesized to be associated with nutritional stress and a reduction in stature (estimated by some at about 4 inches; [8, 9]). During the later phases of this pattern, social stratification began to appear, and dietary variation according to gender and social status increased [10]. The pattern of famine (as with each of the patterns) was manifested heterogeneously over time and space. Some civilizations were more successful than others in alleviating famine and chronic hunger, at least for their more privileged citizens [11]. This pattern of famine accompanied the development of agriculture (the "first agricultural revolution"); however, the causal relationship between these developments is widely debated.

*Pattern 3: Receding Famine.* The consumption of fruits and vegetables and animal protein increased during the pattern of receding famine, and starchy staples became less important in the diet. Many earlier civilizations did make great progress in reduc-

**Table 20.1**
The nutrition transition

| Transition profile | Pattern 1: Collecting food | Pattern 2: Famine | Pattern 3: Receding famine | Pattern 4: Degenerative disease | Pattern 5: Behavioral change |
|---|---|---|---|---|---|
| **1. Nutrition profile** | | | | | |
| Diet | Plants, low-fat wild animals; varied diet | Cereals predominant; diet less varied | Fewer starchy staples; more fruits, vegetables, animal protein; low variety continues | More fat (especially from animal products), sugar, and processed foods; less fiber | Less fat and processing; increased carbohydrates, fruits, and vegetables |
| Nutritional status | Robust, lean, few nutritional deficiencies | Children, women suffer most from low fat intake; nutritional deficiency diseases emerge; stature declines | Continued maternal and child (MCH) nutrition problems; many deficiencies disappear; weaning diseases emerge; stature grows | Obesity: problems for elderly (bone health, etc.); many disabling conditions | Reduced body-fat levels and obesity; improved bone health |
| **2. Economy** | Hunter-gatherers | Agriculture, animal husbandry, home-making begin; shift to monocultures | Second agricultural revolution (crop rotation, fertilizer); Industrial Revolution; women join labor force | Fewer jobs with heavy physical activity; service sector and mechanization; household technology revolution | Service sector mechanization, industrial robotization dominate; leisure exercise grows to offset sedentary jobs |
| Household production | Primitive; onset of fire | Labor-intensive, primitive technology begins (clay cooking vessels) | Primitive water systems; clay stoves; cooking technology advances | Household technology mechanizes and proliferates | Food preparation cost falls significantly with technological change |
| Income and assets | Subsistence; primitive stone tools | Subsistence; few tools | Increasing income disparity; agricultural tools; industrialization rises | Rapid growth in income and income disparities; technology proliferation | Income growth slows; home and leisure technologies increase |

(continued)

**Table 20.1** (continued)
The nutrition transition

| Transition profile | Pattern 1: Collecting food | Pattern 2: Famine | Pattern 3: Receding famine | Pattern 4: Degenerative disease | Pattern 5: Behavioral change |
|---|---|---|---|---|---|
| **3. Demographic profile** | | | | | |
| Mortality/ fertility | Low fertility, high mortality, low life expectancy | Age of Malthus; high natural fertility, low life expectancy, high infant and maternal mortality | Slow mortality decline, later rapid; fertility static, then declines; small, cumulative population growth, later explosion | Life expectancy hits unique levels (60s–70s); huge fertility declines and fluctuations (e.g., postwar baby boom) | Life expectancy extends to 70s, 80s; disability-free period increases |
| Morbidity | Much infectious disease; no epidemics | Epidemics; endemic disease (plague, smallpox, polio, tuberculosis); deficiency disease begins; starving common | Tuberculosis, smallpox, infection, parasitic disease, polio, weaning disease (diarrhea, retarded growth) expand, later decline | Chronic disease related to diet, pollution (heart disease, cancer); infectious disease declines | Increased health promotion (preventive and therapeutic); rapid decline in coronary heart disease, slower change in age-specific cancer profile |
| Age structure | Young population | Young; very few elderly | Chiefly young; shift to older population begins | Rapid fertility decline; elderly proportion increases rapidly | Increasing proportion of elderly > 75 |
| Residency patterns | Rural, low density | Rural; a few small, crowded cities | Chiefly rural; move to cities increases; international migration begins; megacities develop | Urban population disperses; rural green space reduced | Lower-density cities rejuvenate; urbanization of rural areas encircling cities increases |
| **4. Food processing** | Nonexistent | Food storage begins | Storage process (drying, salting); canning and processing technologies; increased food refining and milling | Numerous food-transforming technologies | Technologies create foods and food constituent substitutes (e.g., macronutrient substitutes) |

*Source:* Reprinted with permission from [47].

ing chronic hunger and famines, but it is only in the last third of this millennium that these changes became widespread and led to marked shifts in diet. However, famines continued well into the 18th century in portions of Europe and still continue in some regions of the world. Spatially, famine has become limited mainly to sub-Saharan and southern Africa over the past decade.

*Pattern 4: Degenerative Disease.* A diet high in total fat, cholesterol, sugar, and other refined carbohydrates and low in polyunsaturated fatty acids and fiber, often accompanying an increasingly sedentary life, is characteristic of most high-income societies (and increasingly of portions of the population in lower-income societies), resulting in increased prevalence of obesity and contributing to the degenerative diseases of Omran's final epidemiologic stage [1].

*Pattern 5: Behavioral Change.* Consumption patterns resemble more the pattern of collecting food than that of the pattern of degenerative disease. Increased intake of fruits, vegetables, and carbohydrates and reduced intake of processed foods, meat, and dairy products are some aspects of this pattern. This "new" dietary pattern appears to be emerging as a result of changes in diet evidently associated with the desire to prevent or delay degenerative diseases and prolong health. Whether these changes, instituted in some countries by consumers and in others by a combination of government policy and consumer behavior, will constitute a large-scale transition in diet structure and body composition remains to be seen [12–14]. If they do occur, they may be very important in our goal of enhancing successful aging, which is the period between the age at which a person suffers permanent infirmity and the age at death [15, 16].

## 20.3  ECONOMIC CHANGE AND THE NUTRITION TRANSITION

A major change in economic structure associated with the nutrition transition is the shift from a preindustrial agrarian economy to industrialization. This transformation then accelerates; the service sector grows rapidly, industrial production is dominated by capital-intensive processes, and time-allocation patterns change dramatically. Associated socioeconomic changes especially important in the nutrition transition are changes in the role of women (especially with respect to patterns of time allocation), in income patterns, in household food preparation technology, in food production and processing technology, and in family and household composition [17]. Some of the effects of income changes are reviewed to put in context much of the recent debate on the question, "Does income matter?"

Only since the Industrial Revolution have widespread variations in income and large income discrepancies among segments of the population become important, and only with these developments has diet become consistently related to income. The patterns of receding famine and of degenerative disease are characterized by restructuring of the diet as income increases. The rapidity and the nature of this restructuring depends on many factors. With increasing income, the proportion of energy in the diet from various sources changes in the following ways:

Unseparated animal fat and animal protein increase.
Unseparated vegetable fat and vegetable protein decrease.
Carbohydrate decreases.
Sugar and separated edible fat increase [18, 19].

The well-known relationship based mainly on cross-country comparisons, but buttressed with a number of within-country time series studies, is summarized in Fig. 20.1 [20]. The responsiveness of dietary total energy, total and saturated fat, and other macro- and micronutrients to income change depends on the nature of the demand for particular foods as well as overall eating patterns. For example, in the Philippines, the coconut palm is a major source of cooking oil, and income increases are associated with increased away-from-home consumption of foods that are frequently fried; thus, saturated fat and total fat consumption are highly responsive to income increases, particularly income increases accruing to women [21]. Similarly, in China, pork consumption is highly responsive to increases in income, which thus results in large increases in the proportion of energy from fat [22, 23]. In contrast, where income increases are spent on more elaborate packaging and processing or higher quality of specific foods, rather than larger quantities of food or shifts in the types of foods, changes in income will have little effect on dietary structure.

Another apparent relationship between income and diet is that as income increases (beyond the point at which total food energy needs are met), people spend more per food item [24], partly to obtain higher quality. As many have shown, food demand is much more price- and income-elastic among the poor than among higher-income groups [25, 26]. Changes in diet with increased income also relate to the reduced time needed to consume higher-quality and higher-priced goods that have undergone more processing before purchase [27].

Much controversy surrounds study of the process by which increases in income lead to increased energy intake. Clearly, changes in income per capita at the national level will not necessarily translate into short-term improvements in diet. Variations in the distribution of income, how it is spent, and other factors mean that improved national income will not necessarily translate into improved purchasing power for the poor or, in turn, improved diets for the most needy households. Behrman and his colleagues argued that increased income does not affect quantity of diet [3, 4, 28]; their analyses focused primarily on short-term effects of income on energy and protein intake. Behrman

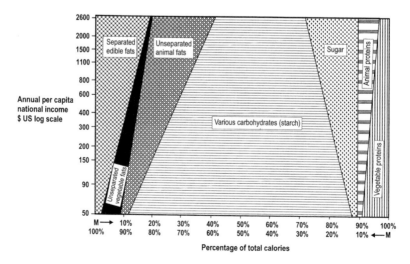

**Fig. 20.1.** Structure of the diet and income (country-level sources of energy, 1962).

et al. [4] summarized changes associated with income increases that improve the quality of the diet, although not necessarily by increasing its protein or energy content. These include a shift from broken and dirtier grains to whole and cleaned grains; increased processing of the product before it is purchased (a remarkable example is the effect of the introduction of portable rice-milling machinery in Indonesia); a shift from consumption of root crops to cereals as the staple; a switch from inferior to superior grains (e.g., corn to rice); and an increase in the variety of foods consumed.

For lower-income countries, a crucial dimension of the relationship between socioeconomic status and nutrition is the distribution of chronic disease risk factors by income group.[2] In particular, a World Bank study on adult health in Brazil [36] indicated that where income constraints among the poor are not too severe, many risk factors for cardiovascular disease will likely be greater among the poor than among the rich. Monteiro et al. [37, 38] used 1996 data from Brazil to show that there is an independent effect of economic variables on the risk of female obesity only in rural areas (the poorer the woman, the lower the risk of overweight). In the urban context, income does not matter, and either formal education or access to information is independently and inversely related to overweight [38].

## 20.4  DEMOGRAPHIC CHANGE AND THE NUTRITION TRANSITION

Urbanization is the major demographic force linked with the nutrition transition, but it is not the only important population factor in terms of effects on diet. Recent decades have seen remarkable shifts in fertility and mortality patterns and, with them, a shift toward an older age distribution in all regions of the world. In many lower-income countries, rapid fertility declines have led to larger increases in the proportion of persons aged over 65 than in higher-income countries [39]. The influence of such a shift in age distribution on diet is not clear. However, physical and psychological difficulties associated with aging are expected to have major effects on dietary patterns. In addition, significant cohort effects may change overall dietary patterns.

### 20.4.1  Key Dimensions of World Urbanization

Several major demographic shifts began after World War II; they continue unabated and have even accelerated in some regions. One is the vast increase in the proportion of persons who reside in urban areas. A second is urban agglomeration. A third is the shift of poverty toward the urban areas, particularly toward squatter and slum areas.

---

[2] Economists have given a great deal of attention to another dimension of economic change, namely, the transition from a subsistence to a cash economy. The most impressive body of knowledge on the dietary effects of commercialization comes from six large case studies conducted by the International Food Policy Research Institute (IFPRI) in the Philippines, Guatemala, the Gambia, Rwanda, Kenya, and Malawi. These studies indicated that commercialization substantially helped to alleviate hunger; however, increased income alone did not solve the problems of malnutrition [29–35]. In some cases (e.g., the Gambia), income increases were converted directly into food consumption; in others, particularly in environments where food markets were undeveloped, such as Rwanda, diet was still more influenced by the subsistence economy than by cash income.

### 20.4.2  Proportion Living in Cities

Urban growth was relatively modest before the Industrial Revolution. Rapid urban development first occurred in the higher-income countries; now, lower-income countries are undergoing even more rapid urbanization. In Table 20.2, United Nations population research is used to show that the higher-income world is comprised predominantly of urban residents today, while that is not the case for the less-developed and poorest least-developed countries. Nevertheless, by 2025 urban residency will be the common form of residence throughout all but the poorest African countries.

The rates of population growth are far greater in urban than rural areas because of the continuation of long-term patterns of in-migration. Table 20.3 shows that these patterns will accelerate in the next century.

**Table 20.2**
**Urban population 1970, 1994, and 2025**

| Region | Urban population (millions) | | | Urban share (percentage) | | |
|---|---|---|---|---|---|---|
| | 1970 | 1994 | 2025 | 1970 | 1994 | 2025 |
| World | 1,353 | 2,521 | 5,065 | 36.6 | 44.8 | 61.1 |
| Less-developed regions | 676 | 1,653 | 4,025 | 25.1 | 37.0 | 57.0 |
| Least-developed countries | 38 | 122 | 506 | 12.6 | 21.9 | 43.5 |
| More-developed regions | 677 | 868 | 1,040 | 67.5 | 74.7 | 84.0 |

*Source*: Adapted with permission from [37].

**Table 20.3**
**Average annual growth rate of urban and rural population, less-developed regions (percentage)**

| Region | 1965–1970 | 1990–1995 | 2020–2025 |
|---|---|---|---|
| Less-developed region | | | |
|   Urban | 3.58 | 3.51 | 2.33 |
|   Rural | 2.18 | 0.96 | −0.28 |
| Africa | | | |
|   Urban | 4.64 | 4.38 | 3.34 |
|   Rural | 1.98 | 2.03 | 0.72 |
| Asia | | | |
|   Urban | 3.28 | 3.68 | 2.31 |
|   Rural | 2.34 | 0.81 | −0.57 |
| Latin America | | | |
|   Urban | 3.97 | 2.60 | 1.26 |
|   Rural | 0.81 | −0.20 | −0.61 |
| Oceania | | | |
|   Urban | 7.26 | 3.13 | 3.32 |
|   Rural | 1.62 | 1.90 | 0.22 |

*Source*: From [62; urban figures from Table 16, p. 27; rural figures from Table 19, p. 29]. The United Nations is the author of the original data.

### 20.4.3  Concentrated Population Growth

Urban growth, particularly in lower-income countries, has been skewed toward a few larger cities, often called *urban conglomerates*. As is seen in Table 20.4, the most explosive growth of these megacities is in Asia.

### 20.4.4  Shift in the Proportion of Poor Living in Cities

Concomitant with increased concentration of the population in urban areas is a dramatic shift in the proportion of poor people living in cities. In absolute and relative terms, the majority of the poor of the lower-income world live in cities. At the same time, a disproportionate share of the higher income middle- and upper-income population also lives in urban areas.

One of the most influential changes has been in the spatial distribution of population. Rapid growth in urban populations profoundly affects diet [40]. Compared with rural diets, urban diets show trends toward increased consumption of grains that are felt to be more desirable or superior (e.g., rice or wheat rather than corn or millet) to more milled and polished grains (e.g., rice, wheat), food higher in fat, more animal products, more sugar, more food prepared away from the home, more processed foods, and reduced breast-feeding and earlier supplementation of infant diets.

Some of the key factors responsible for the urban dietary patterns are improved transportation and food distribution systems, greater penetration of commercial food sector marketing practices, increased heterogeneity of diet, changes toward occupational patterns less compatible with home food production and consumption, changes in household composition and structure, and differences in disease and health service availability patterns.

In one recent study, it was shown that the effect of urbanization on diet led to a significant increase in the consumption of edible oils and sweeteners, even in the very lowest-income countries [18]. They used national food balance data for most countries along with urbanization and income patterns. A cross-national regression model was used to examine the effect of rapid urbanization on the structure of diet shown in Fig. 20.1. At lower-income levels, according to the regression model, urbanization can more than double the amount of sweeteners in the diet and increases considerably the total fat consumed. The model confirms previous observations that people living in urban areas consume diets distinct from those of their rural counterparts. The potential impact of

**Table 20.4**
**Megacities (number), 1970–2015**

| Region | 1970 | 1994 | 2000 | 2015 |
|---|---|---|---|---|
| World | 11 | 22 | 25 | 33 |
| Less-developed region | 5 | 16 | 19 | 27 |
|   Africa | 0 | 2 | 2 | 3 |
|   Asia | 2 | 10 | 12 | 19 |
|   Latin America | 3 | 4 | 5 | 5 |
| More-developed regions | 6 | 6 | 6 | 6 |

*Megacities* cities with 8 million or more residents.
*Source*: From [62, Table 2, p. 6]. The United Nations is the author of the original data.

urbanization in flattening the income–sweetener relationship deserves further analysis; however, it is clear that the increased urbanization of lower-income nations is accelerating the shift to increased consumption of sweeteners and fats [18].

A separate study explored in further detail the sweetening of the world's diet [18]. In this study, increased consumption of caloric sweetener was one element in the world's dietary changes, represented by a 74 calorie/day increase between 1962 and 2000. Moreover, the level of change varied significantly by urbanization of the country.

An important dimension of urban growth is its associated pattern of migration. Migration from rural areas to cities (and to a lesser extent from small to larger cities) and international migration have affected diet profoundly. For example, populations of Samoans who moved to San Francisco, Polynesians and Maori who moved to New Zealand, Japanese who moved to the United States, and Yemenite Jews who moved to Israel all showed large changes in diet, followed by large increases in diet-related chronic diseases [41, 42]. Similarly, migration within countries is believed to affect the diets of the migrants and the diets of their communities of origin and destination; however, the causes and dimensions of such dietary changes are poorly understood. Lower-income countries, with much larger differences in dietary patterns between urban and rural populations, are experiencing the most rapid changes in population distribution now. Migrants to urban areas tend to adopt the urban dietary pattern, although the timing of such changes is unstudied (see [43] for a review of this subject).

There are clearly other crucial determinants of the nutrition transition. These include the shifting role and impact of the food industry, household technology, women's roles, and knowledge and attitudes related to food.

## 20.5    THE NATURE AND PACE OF THE NUTRITION TRANSITION

The interaction among these epidemiologic, socioeconomic, and demographic changes determines the nature and pace of nutritional change. This section outlines patterns of recent dietary change in several countries. We begin with countries in East Asia, which have undergone major economic change in the last 40 years.

### 20.5.1    Japanese and Korean Accelerated Model

Energy intake in Japan increased during the period after World War II slowly toward a peak around 1970 to 1975, whereas intake of animal products and fat increased continuously from 1946 to 1987. During this period, daily per capita consumption of animal products increased by 257 g, daily per capita total fat consumption increased 341%, and the proportion of energy from fat increased from 8.7% to 24.8% [44, 45]. Fat intake in Japan is still only about two thirds the US level, and the Japanese diet includes much more marine fish; average consumption of omega-3 fatty acids (thought to be protective against coronary heart disease) in Japan is more than twice that in the United States [46]. However, older Japanese consume much more marine fish and much less of the foods high in saturated fat than do younger Japanese, and overall consumption of marine fish is decreasing [47]. Thus, as the population ages, the younger cohort whose diet resembles the "Western diet" may begin to experience the associated health problems.

South Korea, another Asian country that has achieved remarkably rapid economic growth during the last three or four decades, appears to be experiencing a change in dietary structure similar to that of Japan. Trends in the South Korean diet for the last three decades include a marked decline in consumption of grains and a large increase in consumption of fish, meat, and milk [48, 49]. Increased consumption of animal products, particularly in the last decade, is reflected in an increasing proportion of energy from animal fat, which rose from about 2% in 1961 to 8% in 1988. By the late 1980s, total fat intake as a proportion of energy in Korea had reached only 15%; Japan reached this level in 1965, and the value increased to 25% of energy from fat by 1987 [45]. The South Korean diet might be expected to continue changing rapidly in a similar manner, resulting in a transition in disease patterns similar to that experienced by Japan. However, a unique combination of government education programs worked very well in South Korea to keep their vegetable intake level much higher and their edible oil intake much lower, resulting in a much lower than expected obesity level [48, 49].

### 20.5.2 Low-Income Countries with Rapid Income Increases: The Case of China

During the 1980–2006 period, real income in China more than doubled in urban areas and tripled in rural areas, and rapid income changes continue unabated. In China, energy availability increased dramatically from 1961 to 1988; since the 1980–1984 period, the main change has been in dietary structure, including increases in intake of total fat and animal fat. Total intake of animal source foods has also risen [50]. These effects are amplified in certain subpopulations; for children (aged 2 to 6) and adults (aged 20 to 45), increased income is associated with a marked increase in the proportion of energy from fat and from animal fat and in adult obesity [50]. Coronary heart disease and its precursors high serum cholesterol levels and hypertension have also increased in China, particularly in the subpopulations that have changed their diets most rapidly [51].

### 20.5.3 Degenerative Dietary and Epidemiologic Transition with Limited or No Economic Improvement

Prior to the current economic adjustment period, Eastern European countries and the former Soviet Union consumed a diet with over 25% of energy from animal fat and over 40% of energy from fat. This high-saturated fat diet is thought to be one of the causes of Russia's pattern of high obesity and corresponding high cardiovascular mortality rate—the highest in the world. In the past two decades in the Russia, consumption of cereals and starchy roots (mainly potatoes) declined greatly, and consumption of sugar and red meat increased (see Fig. 20.2). For added detail on the nutrition situation in Russia, see the work of Popkin et al. [52, 53].

This Russian diet was found among all social classes. In 1991, the poor in Russia (the bottom 12% of the income distribution, or about 18 million people) consumed about 2,121 kcal per capita daily, with about 28% of energy from meat and dairy sources (as shown in Table 20.5).

In the more recent reform period, price subsidies on meat and dairy products were removed, and there has been a marked shift in the proportion of energy from fat and a smaller shift in the proportion of energy from protein [54]. Fat as a percentage of energy decreased to 31.6%, and protein as a percentage of energy decreased from 14.3% to 12.5%. Overweight (determined by body mass index [BMI] $\geq$ 25) prevalence

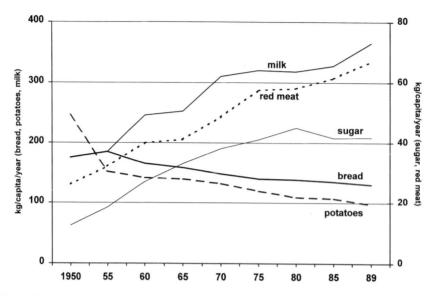

**Fig. 20.2.** Changes in food consumption: annual intake of selected foods, Soviet Union, 1950–1989.

**Table 20.5**
**Food consumption of the poor in the Russian Federation, 2nd quarter, 1991[a]**

|  | At-home consumption (kg/cap/yr) | Away from home (kg/cap/yr) | Calorie intake (per kcal/day) |
|---|---|---|---|
| 1. Bread products | 98.76 | 3.67 | 874 |
| 2. Potatoes | 107.40 | 3.89 | 179 |
| 3. Vegetables | 39.24 | 1.44 | 26 |
| 4. Melons | 0.36 | | |
| 5. Fruits, grapes | | | |
| 6. Sugar and confectioneries | 21.12 | 0.78 | 237 |
| 7. Meat and meat products | 38.16 | 1.40 | 229 |
| 8. Milk and milk products | 296.40 | 10.82 | 367 |
| 9. Eggs | 147.96 | 0.03 | 48 |
| 10. Fish and fish products | 7.44 | 0.28 | 16 |
| 11. Vegetable oil | 2.16 | 0.09 | 54 |
| 12. Margarine | 1.68 | 0.06 | 33 |
| Total | | | 2,112 |

Sample size of study (n = 60,000).
[a] Poor households have a monthly income below 150 rubles per capita or the poorest 12%.
*Source*: From [54].

remained relatively stable at about 50%, and obesity (BMI ≥ 30) prevalence increased from 13.3% to 16.0% of the adult population. Women consumed less energy than men and displayed higher prevalence of overweight and obesity in all time periods of the period 1992–2004. There was an income effect among men in all time periods, with higher-income men consuming more calories, fat, and protein than lower-income men; this effect was not apparent in women except in the proportion of fat and protein intake [55].

Russia is the exception that in many ways proves one component of the nutrition transition—the power of education. When Russia experienced the sudden removal of subsidies of meat and dairy products, the structure of diet shifted markedly, and people shifted toward a healthier diet lower in saturated fat. However, there was no education of the population on the adverse impact of higher intake of saturated fats on cardiovascular disease in Russia. Thus, as income improved, people went back quickly to their earlier dietary pattern.

### 20.5.4  Other Low-Income Countries

The changes in diet noted in China and Korea are also seen in many Central and South American countries, particularly in countries where income increases have been greatest, such as Chile, Brazil, Colombia, and Argentina and in Malaysia. For example, Malaysia has experienced more moderate and slower economic progress than China, but its income level is much higher, and it is at a higher current level of obesity [56, 57]. Its diet shifted markedly in the 1980s so that over 25% of the energy is now derived from fat. Brazil and Chile are two of the other countries that have moved far along in the transformations of their diets [58, 59].

In all other Latin American and Caribbean countries, all Asian countries, and most African and Middle Eastern countries, the urban populations have begun to consume this diet as well. Thus, diseases of affluence, often those associated with higher-fat and lower-fiber diets, have begun to appear in these populations. Moreover, with increased economic development, chronic disease risk factors are likely to increase disproportionately among the lower-income populations [36]. For example, elsewhere we present evidence for urban Brazil that showed a negative correlation between socioeconomic factors and obesity [37, 58].

## 20.6  CONCLUSION

An important aspect of the nutrition transition concept lies in its ability to help us understand the manner in which modern diets of large segments of the population of many developing countries seem to be converging on a pattern of high saturated fat, sugar, and refined foods and low fiber, while other segments of the population experience hunger and undernutrition. Often termed the *Western diet*, this dietary pattern is felt by many to be associated with high levels of chronic and degenerative diseases and with reduced disability-free time [60, 61]. Our purpose is not just to understand the dietary and health changes taking place, but also to begin to focus attention on defining the program and policy changes that could redirect the nutrition transition in many regions of the world.

# REFERENCES

1. Omran AR. The epidemiologic transition. A theory of the epidemiology of population change. Milbank Mem Fund Q 1971;49(4):509–538.

2. Olshansky SJ, Ault AB. The fourth stage of the epidemiologic transition: the age of delayed degenerative diseases. Milbank Q 1986;64(3):355–391.

3. Behrman J, Wolfe BL. More evidence on nutrition demand: income seems overrated and women's schooling underemphasized. J Dev Econ 1984;14:105–128.

4. Behrman J, Deolaikar AB, Wolfe BL. Nutrients: impacts and determinates. World Bank Econ Rev 1988;2:299–320.

5. Harris D. The prehistory of human subsistence: a speculative outline. In: Food, nutrition and evolution: food as an environmental factor in the genesis of human variability. Walcher DN, Kretchmer N, eds. New York: Masson, 1981.

6. Truswell AS. Diet and nutrition of hunter-gatherers. Health and diseases in tribal societies. Amsterdam: Elsevier, 1977.

7. Eaton SB, Shostak M, Konner M. The paleolithic prescription: a program of diet and exercise and a design for living. New York: Harper & Row, 1988.

8. Eaton SB, Konner M. Paleolithic nutrition: a consideration on its nature and current implications. N Engl J Med 1985;312:283–289.

9. Vargas LA. Old and new transitions and nutrition in Mexico. In: Disease in populations in transition: anthropological and epidemiological perspectives. Swedlund AC, Armelagos GJ, eds. New York: Bergin and Garvey, 1990.

10. Gordon KD. Evolutionary perspectives on human diet. In: Nutritional anthropology. Johnston FE, ed. New York: Liss, 1987.

11. Newman LF, Crossgrove W, Kates R, Matthews R, Millman S. Hunger in history: food shortage, poverty, and deprivation. Cambridge, MA: Blackwell, 1990.

12. Popkin BM, Zizza C, Siega-Riz AM. Who is leading the change? US dietary quality comparison between 1965 and 1996. Am J Prev Med 2003;25(1):1–8.

13. Popkin BM, Siega-Riz AM, Haines PS. A comparison of dietary trends among racial and socioeconomic groups in the United States. N Engl J Med 1996;335(10):716–720.

14. Popkin BM, Haines PS, Patterson RE. Dietary changes in older Americans, 1977–1987. Am J Clin Nutr 1992;55(4):823–830.

15. Crimmins EM, Saito Y, Ingegneri D. Changes in life expectancy and disability-free life expectancy in the United States. Pop Dev Rev 1989;15:235–267.

16. Manton KG, Soldo BJ. Dynamics of health changes in the oldest old: new perspectives and evidence. Milbank Mem Fund Q Health Soc 1985;63(2):206–285.

17. McGuire J, Popkin BM. Beating the zero sum game: women and nutrition in the Third World. Food Nutr Bull 1989;11:38–63.

18. Popkin BM, Nielsen SJ. The sweetening of the world's diet. Obes Res 2003;11(11):1325–1332.

19. Popkin B, Drewnowski A. Dietary fats and the nutrition transition: new trends in the global diet. Nutr Rev 1997;55:31–43.

20. Drewnowski A, Popkin BM. The nutrition transition: new trends in the global diet. Nutr Rev 1997;55(2):31–43.

21. Bisgrove EZ. Work and income as determinants of urban Filipino women's nutrient intake from commercially prepared at home prepared foods. Chapel Hill: University of North Carolina at Chapel Hill, 1991.

22. Chen C. Dietary guidelines for food and agricultural planning in China. In: Proceedings of the International Symposium on Food, Nutrition and Social Economic Development. Beijing: Chinese Academy of Preventive Medicine, 1991.

23. Popkin BM, Keyou G, Zhai F, Guo X, Ma H, Zohoori N. The nutrition transition in China: a cross-sectional analysis. Eur J Clin Nutr 1993;47(5):333–346.

24. Chaudri R, Timmer CP. The impact of changing affluence on diet and demand patterns for agricultural commodities. The World Bank, Washington, DC: 1986.

25. Alderman H. New research on poverty and malnutrition: what are the implications for research and policy? In: Including the poor: Proceedings of a symposium organized by the World Bank and the International Food Policy Research Institute. Lipton M, Van der Gaag J, eds. Washington, DC: World Bank Regional and Sectoral Studies, The World Bank, 1992.

26. Timmer CP, Falcon WP, Pearson SR. Food policy analysis. Baltimore, MD: Johns Hopkins University Press for the World Bank, 1984.

27. Mincer J. Market prices, opportunity costs, and income effects. In: Measurement in economics: studies in mathematical economics and econometrics in memory of Yehuda Grunfeld. Christ CF, Friedman M, Goodman LA, et al., eds. Stanford, CA: Stanford University Press, 1963.

28. Behrman J, Kenan WR. Nutrition and incomes: tightly wedded or loosely meshed? In: Pew/Cornell lecture series on food and nutrition policy. Ithaca, NY: Cornell Food and Nutrition Policy Program, Division of Nutritional Sciences, 1988.

29. Bouis HE. Effects of agricultural commercialization on land tenure, household resource allocation, and nutrition in the Philippines. Washington, DC: International Food Policy Research Institute in collaboration with the Research Institute for Mindanao Culture, 1990.

30. Kennedy ET, Cogill B. The effects of sugarcane production on food security, health, and nutrition in Kenya: A longitudinal analysis. Washington, DC: International Food Policy Research Institute, 1989.

31. Kennedy ET, Cogill B. Income and nutritional effects of the commercialization of agriculture in southwestern Kenya. Washington, DC: International Food Policy Research Institute, 1987.

32. von Braun J. The importance of non-agricultural income sources for the rural poor in Africa and implications for food and nutrition policy. In: Pew/Cornell lecture series on food and nutrition policy. Ithaca, NY: Cornell Food and Nutrition Policy Program, Division of Nutritional Sciences, 1989.

33. von Braun J, Hotchkiss D, Immink M. Nontraditional exports in Guatemala: effects on production, income, and nutrition. Washington D.C.: International Food Policy Research Institute in collaboration with the Institute of Nutrition of Central America and Panama, 1989.

34. von Braun J, Puetz D, Webb P. Irrigation technology and commercialization of rice in the Gambia: effects on income and nutrition. Washington, DC: International Food Policy Research Institute, 1989.

35. von Braun J, de Haen H, Blanken J. Commercialization of agriculture under population pressure: effects on production, consumption, and nutrition in Rwanda. Washington, DC: International Food Policy Research Institute, 1991.

36. Briscoe J. Brazil: the new challenge of adult health. Washington, DC: World Bank, 1990.

37. Monteiro CA, Conde WL, Popkin BM. Independent effects of income and education on the risk of obesity in the Brazilian adult population. J Nutr 2001;131(3):881S–886S.

38. Monteiro C, D'A Benicio MH, Mondini L, Popkin B. A shift in the obesity social paradigm is emerging: economic and cultural-educational predictors of adult obesity in Brazil. Int J Obesity 1998;22:10.

39. Jamison DT, Mosley WH, Measham AR, Bobadilla JL. Disease control priorities in developing countries. New York: Oxford University Press for the World Bank, 1993.

40. Mendez MA, Popkin B. Globalization, urbanization and nutritional change in the developing world. Electronic J Agr Dev Econ 2005;1:220–41.

41. Marmot M, Syme S, Kagan A, Hiroo K, Rhoads G. Epidemiologic studies of CHD and stroke in Japanese men living in Japan, Hawaii, and California: prevalence of coronary and hypertensive heart disease an associated risk factors. Am J Epidemiol 1975;102:514–522.

42. Prior L, Tasman-Jones C. New Zealand Maori and Pacific Polynesians. In: Western diseases: their emergence and prevention. Trowell HC, Burkitt DP, eds. Cambridge, MA: Harvard University Press, 1981.

43. Popkin B, Bisgrove EZ. Urbanization and nutrition in low-income countries. Food Nutr Bull 1988;10:3–23.

44. Yamaguchi K. Changes in nutritional and health status in Japan after the Second World War. In: Proceedings of international symposium on food, nutrition, and social economic development. Beijing: Chinese Academy of Preventive Medicine; 1991:394–401.

45. Popkin B. Nutritional patterns and transitions. Pop Dev Rev 1993;19(1):138–157.

46. Lands WE, Hamazaki T, Yamazaki K, et al. Changing dietary patterns. Am J Clin Nutr 1990;51(6): 991–993.

47. Fukuba H. Positive and negative effects of nutritional improvement in Japan. Tokyo: Japan Science Council, 1990.

48. Lee MJ, Popkin BM, Kim S. The unique aspects of the nutrition transition in South Korea: the retention of healthful elements in their traditional diet. Public Health Nutr 2002;5(1A):197–203.

49. Kim S, Moon S, Popkin BM. The nutrition transition in South Korea. Am J Clin Nutr 2000;71(1): 44–53.

50. Du S, Lu B, Zhai F, Popkin BM. A new stage of the nutrition transition in China. Public Health Nutr 2002;5(1A):169–174.

51. Popkin BM, Horton S, Kim S, Mahal A, Shuigao J. Trends in diet, nutritional status, and diet-related noncommunicable diseases in China and India: the economic costs of the nutrition transition. Nutr Rev 2001;59(12):379–390.

52. Popkin B, Kohlmeier L, Zohoori N, Baturin A, Martin D, Deev A. Nutritional risk factors in the former Soviet Union. In: Premature death in the new independent states. Bobadilla JL, Costello C, Mitchell F, eds. Washington, DC: National Academy Press, 1997:314–334.

53. Popkin B, Baturin A, Kohlmeier L, Zohoori N. Russia: monitoring nutritional change during the Reform Period. In: Implementing dietary guidelines for healthy eating. Wheelock V, ed. London: Chapman and Hall, 1997.

54. Zohoori N, Mroz TA, Popkin B, et al. Monitoring the economic transition in the Russian Federation and its implications for the demographic crisis—the Russian Longitudinal Monitoring Survey. World Development 1998;26:1977–1993.

55. Jahns L, Baturin A, Popkin BM. Obesity, diet, and poverty: trends in the Russian transition to market economy. Eur J Clin Nutr 2003;57(10):1295–1302.

56. Popkin BM. The nutrition transition and its health implications in lower-income countries. Public Health Nutr 1998;1(1):5–21.

57. Popkin BM, Doak CM. The obesity epidemic is a worldwide phenomenon. Nutr Rev 1998;56(4 pt 1):106–114.

58. Monteiro CA, Mondini L, de Souza AL, Popkin BM. The nutrition transition in Brazil. Eur J Clin Nutr 1995;49(2):105–113.

59. Levy-Costa RBS, Pontes NdS, Monteiro CA. Household food availability in Brazil: distribution and trends (1974–2003). Revista de Saúde Pública 2005;39:1–10.

60. National Research Council (US) Committee on Diet and Health. Diet and health: implications for reducing chronic disease risk. Washington, DC: National Academy, 1989.

61. United States Office of the Assistant Secretary for Health. Surgeon general's report on nutrition and health. Washington, DC: US Department of Health and Human Services, Public Health Service, 1988.

62. United Nations, Department for Economic and Social Information. World urbanization prospects: the 1994 revision. New York: United Nations, 1995. ST/ESA/SER.A/150.

# 21  The Rapid Emergence of Obesity in Developing Countries

## Colleen M. Doak and Barry M. Popkin

## 21.1  INTRODUCTION

The last century witnessed a remarkable change in patterns of disease. The control of infectious disease, together with changing life styles, led to longer life expectancies and the emergence of chronic disease as a primary cause of death. This change from infectious to chronic disease, first described by Omran [1], is known as the *epidemiologic transition*. However, as a result of the occurrence of HIV and related drug-resistant infections, some countries have witnessed a reversal in the expected trends [2]. In spite of HIV and related rises in the prevalences of infectious disease, obesity and chronic disease prevalences are still emerging at an accelerated rate in many developing countries [3–5]. In fact, prevalences of overweight/obesity exceed that of undernutrition in a majority of 37 developing countries studied in both urban and rural areas [6].

Overweight and obesity are emerging in developing countries as a result of rapidly changing lifestyle patterns, such as those of diet and physical activity, leading to an accelerated increase in overweight, obesity, and related chronic diseases. A transition in diet and physical activity patterns, leading to an energy-dense diet and a sedentary lifestyle, is known as the *nutrition transition* [7]. The nutrition transition as a global phenomenon has been documented to include the industrialized nations of Europe and North America as well as lower- and middle-income countries of Asia, Latin America, the Caribbean, Africa, and the Middle East.

Previously, we reported on data based on adults available from a number of countries in each region of the world [4, 8]. Elsewhere, we showed that there are equally important problems emerging among children and adolescents in lower-income countries. However, we focus our attention here on adults since there is insufficient data on adolescents to include them in this chapter [9]. Recent trends show the rising obesity prevalence has spread to more countries, and that the emergence of obesity has further accelerated.

In low-income countries experiencing the nutrition transition, obesity is usually observed first in urban areas and in the high-income elite. Urban lifestyles are associated with diet and activity patterns associated with the nutrition transition, contributing further to obesity [6, 10]. Although the urban elite are usually the first to experience

From: *Nutrition and Health: Nutrition and Health in Developing Countries, Second Edition*
Edited by: R. D. Semba & M. W. Bloem © Humana Press, Totowa, NJ

it, the obesity epidemic is also shifting to the middle and lower classes. Articles by Monteiro et al. [11, 12] showed that as gross national product (GNP) increases, the burden of obesity tends to shift toward lower socioeconomic groups.

The shift of the burden of obesity toward the poor is also accompanied by different risks by age and gender. Low-income women are at greater risk than low-income men at lower levels of economic development [12]. Other studies also showed high prevalences of overweight/obesity in women even in communities where there were also high prevalences of undernutrition for children [13]. Detailed analysis comparing the obesity trends in multiple countries showed a pattern in which adults experience higher absolute increases in the rates of obesity as compared to children [14]. Further evidence for differences in obesity risk are illustrated by studies showing overweight/obese adults clustering together with undernourished children [15, 16].

In the next section, we outline the methods used in this chapter. Large nationwide surveys were used for determining trends in obesity prevalence. Then, we focus briefly on some of the public health effects related to this epidemic.

## 21.2  METHODS

### 21.2.1  Survey Design and Sample

Data come from a large number of sources. Analyses conducted for this chapter that have not been published elsewhere are based on Chinese and Russian surveys. A thorough presentation is made of the China Health and Nutrition Survey (CHNS), an ongoing longitudinal survey covering eight provinces in China. A multistage, random, cluster-sampling procedure was used to draw the sample from each province. Additional detail on the research design of this survey is presented elsewhere [17]. Other data sets presented in detail are those of the Russian Longitudinal Monitoring Survey (RLMS), the first nationally representative sample of the Russian Federation. Additional details on the research design of this survey are found elsewhere [18, 19]. Data collection was identical with that for the China survey except that in China doctors and nutritionists collected all data, while in Russia trained nonmedical interview specialists collected the data.

In addition, we used data from published surveys conducted in all regions of the world. We focused mainly on large representative samples of adults. Our selection criteria for presenting data from other surveys was size, sampling design, and geographic area. If a study were representative of a region or country, it was always used. If it came from a country with few studies and did not fit our criteria of national representativeness, we used it if the sample size was large and seemed reasonably representative of the population sampled. Since there are few studies of trends in obesity, those that provided reasonably comparable measurement and sampling criteria were selected.

### 21.2.2  Measures

Body mass index (BMI) is the standard measure of overweight and obesity status used in large-scale surveys of nutritional status in adults. The World Health Organization BMI cutoffs for adults were used to delineate obesity: less than 18.5 for thinness (chronic energy deficiency), 18.5 to 24.99 for normal, 25.0 to 29.99 for overweight grade I, 30.0 to 39.99 for overweight grade II, and 40.0 and above for overweight grade III [20]. For this chapter, grades II and III were combined.

## 21.3   RESULTS

Elsewhere, we present some information on comparable trends in higher-income countries [8]. This chapter focuses on lower-income countries.

### 21.3.1   The Prevalence in Lower- and Middle-Income Countries

Before exploring trends in individual countries, we provide an overview of current knowledge on the prevalence of obesity. We have data from nationally representative surveys from a range of middle- and lower-income countries. We also have very large surveys from selected population groups in other countries. We report both sets of results in Table 21.1 for adults. We look at three measures of obesity and overweight, grade I (overweight), grades II and above (obesity), and grades I and above (overweight and obesity). Overall, the results showed that the highest levels of obesity (grade II and above) were in the Middle East, Western Pacific, and Latin America. In contrast, countries in sub-Saharan Africa and Asia have some of the lowest prevalences for overweight and obesity.

#### 21.3.1.1   LATIN AMERICA

The levels of overweight and obesity in Latin America are reasonably high (see Fig. 21.1). For example, more than 50% percent of the population is overweight (grade I) in Mexico. Table 21.1 shows that 59.6% of females were overweight based on the National Nutrition Surveys in 1999 [21]. Results further show an even higher prevalence of overweight for urban females in Mexico; 65% were overweight in 1999 [6]. Results from other parts of Latin America are similar. Figures are also high in other countries; over 30% are overweight in Peru. With the exception of Columbia in 1988–1989 and the 1989 data from Brazil, the prevalences for overweight and obesity are also high in other South American countries. Several of these South American examples come from urban-only samples. Other information is based on the Demographic Health Surveys and is only available for women [6]. In most countries, where we have gender-specific data, women have higher levels of overweight and obesity than do men. The exception is the later surveys from Brazil, where the prevalences are similar for men and women. There are few large-scale surveys in the Caribbean; however, based on other studies and the Cuban data presented here, Caribbean nations may also have high levels of obesity [22]. The Dominican Republic shows obesity prevalences that exceed those of Cuba, with over 40% overweight in women. However, the prevalences for Haiti are much lower.

#### 21.3.1.2   ASIA

Figure 21.1 shows grade I and grade II obesity. The countries are arranged in order of economic development, with the Kygyryz Republic having the lowest GNP and Malaysia having the highest GNP. Apart from a few exceptions, there was less grade II and above obesity in Asia versus other regions. Most countries had levels in the 5–15% range for grade I (Fig. 21.2). The documented exceptions are urban Thailand, Malaysia, and the Central Asian countries such as Kyrgyzstan that were members of the Soviet Union prior to 1992. Figure 21.2 shows a pattern of females with slightly higher prevalences of overweight and obesity (grades I and II). The high prevalence of obesity in Malaysia and urban Thailand may be related to a relatively higher level of economic development.

Table 21.1
Obesity patterns in adults in lower- and middle-income countries: studies with large sample size

| Country | Year | Sample (n) | Obesity criteria (BMI) | Age group | Percent obese | | |
|---|---|---|---|---|---|---|---|
| | | | | | Males | Females | Total |
| **Latin America** | | | | | | | |
| Bolivia [6] | 1998 | 845 (U) | ≥25 | 20–49 | | 57.9 | |
| | 1998 | 615 (R) | ≥25 | 20–49 | | 47.1 | |
| Brazil [24] | 1989 | 23,544 | >30 | 25–64 | 5.9 | 13.3 | 9.6 |
| Brazil [6] | 1996 | 2,421 (U) | ≥25 | 20–49 | | 42.8 | |
| | 1996 | 679 (R) | ≥25 | 20–49 | | 33.0 | |
| Brazil [25] | 1996/1997 | 5,137 for women | ≥25 | 20+ | | 39.0 | |
| Brazil [14] | 2003 | 59,204 | ≥25 | 18+ | 38.2 | 38.1 | 38.1 |
| Colombia [57] | 1988–1989 | 1,572 | 27.3 | 18–44 | – | 11.1 | – |
| Guatemala [6] | 1998 | 957 (U) | ≥25 | 20–49 | | 61.9 | |
| | 1998 | 1,521 (R) | ≥25 | 20–49 | | 42.6 | |
| Colombia [6] | 2000 | 2,410 (U) | ≥25 | 20–49 | | 48.8 | |
| | 2000 | 937 (R) | ≥25 | 20–49 | | 51.4 | |
| Mexico [21] | 1995 | 2,042 (U) | 25 | Adults | 50.0 | 58.0 | |
| | 1995 | 2,042 (U) | 30 | Adults | 11.0 | 23.0 | |
| Mexico [6] | 1999 | 10,395 (U) | ≥25 | 20–49 | | 65.4 | |
| | 1999 | 3,767 (R) | ≥25 | 20–49 | | 58.6 | |
| Mexico [21] | 1999 | 13,877 | ≥25 | 18–49 | | 59.6 | |
| Peru [58] | 1975/1976 | 3,145 | 25 | Adults | – | – | 33.8 |
| | 1975/1976 | 3,145 | >30 | Adults | – | – | 9.0 |
| Peru [6] | 2000 | 15,010 (U) | ≥25 | 20–49 | | 65.4 | |
| | 2000 | 6,160 (R) | ≥25 | 20–49 | | 58.6 | |
| **Caribbean** | | | | | | | |
| Cuba [59] | 1982 | 30,063 | 25 | 20–59 | 31.5 | 39.4 | 36.4 |
| | 1982 | 20,539 (U) | 25 | 20–59 | 36.0 | 41.8 | 39.7 |
| | 1982 | 9,513 (R) | 25 | 20–59 | 22.6 | 33.9 | 29.4 |

| Country | Year | n | BMI | Age | | | |
|---|---|---|---|---|---|---|---|
| Dominican Republic [6] | 1996 | 3,855 (U) | ≥25 | 20–49 | | 50.2 | |
| | 1996 | 2,352 (R) | ≥25 | 20–49 | | 40.2 | |
| Haiti [6] | 1994 | 686 (U) | ≥25 | 20–49 | | 20.4 | |
| | 1994 | 1,417 (R) | ≥25 | 20–49 | | 8.0 | |
| **Asia** | | | | | | | |
| China [30] | 1992 | 54,006 | >25 | >20 yr | 11.9 | 17.0 | 14.6 |
| China [14] | 1992 | 18,472 (U) | >25 | >20 yr | 20.8 | 25.1 | 23.1 |
| | 1992 | 35,534 (R) | >25 | >20 yr | 7.4 | 12.7 | 10.2 |
| China | 2000 | 4,722 | ≥25 | ≥18 | 22.1 | 24.6 | 23.4 |
| China | 2000 | 4,046 | ≥25 | 20–45 | 20.2 | 19.3 | |
| China [6] | 1997 | 895 (U) | ≥25 | 20–49 | | 20.5 | |
| | 1997 | 1,962 (R) | ≥25 | 20–49 | | 15.2 | |
| India [60] | 1989 | 1,784 (U) | 25 | 15–76 | 36.9 | 44.1 | 40.9 |
| India [58] | 1988/1990 | 21,361 | 25 | Adults | | – | 3.5 |
| | 1988/1990 | 21,361 | >30 | Adults | | – | 0.5 |
| India [61] | 1994 | 1,832 | >25 | 12–47 | | 6.6 | – |
| India [6] | 1993–1994 | 1,319 (U, slum) | >25 | 12–47 | | 11.6 | – |
| | 1999 | 2,024 (U) | ≥25 | 20–49 | | 26.4 | |
| | 1999 | 5,584 (R) | ≥25 | 20–49 | | 5.6 | |
| Indonesia [14] | 2000 | 22,725 | ≥25 | ≥18 | 11.4 | 22.1 | 17.0 |
| Kazakhstan [6] | 1999 | 1,091 (U) | ≥25 | 20–49 | | 36.3 | |
| | 1999 | 844 (R) | ≥25 | 20–49 | | 36.3 | |
| Kyrgyz Republic | 1993 | 4,053 | 30 | 18–59 | 4.2 | 10.7 | – |
| | 1993 | 4,053 | 25–<30 | 18–59 | 26.4 | 24.3 | – |
| Kyrgyz Republic [6] | 1997 | 1,100 (U) | ≥25 | 20–49 | | 34.7 | |
| | 1997 | 1,956 (R) | ≥25 | 20–49 | | 34.5 | |
| Malaysia [62] | 1990 | 4,747 | >25–30 | 18–64 | 24.0 | 18.1 | 21.4 |
| | 1990 | 4,747 | >30 | 18–64 | 4.7 | 7.9 | 6.1 |
| Philippines [63] | 1993 | 9,585 | >30 | 20 yr | 1.7 | 3.4 | – |
| | 1993 | 9,585 | 25–30 | 20 yr | 11.0 | 11.8 | – |

(continued)

**Table 21.1** (continued)
Obesity patterns in adults in lower- and middle-income countries: studies with large sample size

| Country | Year | Sample (n) | Obesity criteria (BMI) | Age group | Males | Females | Total |
|---|---|---|---|---|---|---|---|
| | | | | | | *Percent obese* | |
| Thailand [64] | 1985 | 3,495 (U) | 25 | 35–54 | 25.5 | 21.4 | 24.6 |
| | 1985 | 3,495 (U) | 30 | 35–54 | 2.2 | 3.0 | 2.4 |
| Uzbekistan | 1996 | 1,320 (U) | ≥25 | 20–49 | | 32.4 | |
| | 1996 | 2,118 (R) | ≥25 | 20–49 | | 26.1 | |
| **West Pacific** | | | | | | | |
| Fiji, Fijians [65] | 1993 | 1,190 | ≥27 | >18 | 26.6 | 47.4 | 37.8 |
| Fiji, Fijians [65] | 1993 | 1,226 | ≥25 | >18 | 18 | 33.9 | 25.9 |
| Micronesia [66] | 1987/1988 | 3,588 | >30 | 15–49 | | 31.9 | |
| | 1987/1988 | 3,588 | 25–<30 | 15–49 | | 33.2 | |
| Nauru [67] | 1994 | 1,344 | >30 | 25–69 | 80.2 | 78.6 | 79.4 |
| New Caledonia [68] | 1992–1994 | 6,503 (R) | 25 (F), 27 [69] | 30–59 | 44.6 | 71.4 | 59.0 |
| | 1992–1994 | 641 (U) | 25 (F) 27 [69] | 30–59 | 59.1 | 79.6 | 72.7 |
| American Samoa [48] | 1994 | 345 | ≥25 | 25–58 | 63.8 | 96.9 | 83.5 |
| | | | >30 | 25–58 | 45.9 | 87.8 | 70.8 |
| Western Samoa [48] | 1995 | 475 | ≥25 | 25–58 | 83.8 | 92.2 | 88.2 |
| | | | >30 | 25–58 | 37.1 | 66.2 | 52.2 |
| Tonga [70] | 1986 | 654 | >32 [69] >30 (F) | 20–49 | 10 | 39.1 | |
| | | | >26 [69] >24 (F) | 20–49 | 47.6 | 77.9 | |
| **Northern Africa/ Middle East** | | | | | | | |
| Bahrain [71] | 1991/1992 | 290 | >30 | >20 | 26.3 | 29.4 | 27.9 |
| Egypt [72] | 1983–1985 | 433 (R) | NCHS OB | 15–74 | 6.8 | 10.1 | 9.0 |
| Egypt [72] | 1983–1985 | 433 (R) | NCHS OVE | 15–74 | 12.9 | 25.1 | 21.0 |
| Egypt [6] | 1995 | 3,197 (U) | ≥25 | 20–49 | | 69.9 | |
| | 1995 | 4,220 (R) | ≥25 | 20–49 | | 46.6 | |
| Jordan [73] | 1994–1996 | 2,836 | >30 | > 25 yr | 32.7 | 59.8 | 49.7 |

| Country | Year | Sample size | BMI cutoff | Age (yr) | Men | Women | Both sexes |
|---|---|---|---|---|---|---|---|
| Jordan [6] | 1997 | 2,798 (U) | ≥25 | 20–49 | | 69.9 | |
| | 1997 | 775 (R) | ≥25 | 20–49 | | 46.6 | |
| Kuwait [74] | 1993–1994 | 3,435 | >30 | 18 | 32.3 | 40.6 | 36.4 |
| | 1993–1994 | 3,435 | >25–30 | 18 | 35.2 | 32.3 | 33.8 |
| Morocco [75] | 1984–1985 | 41,921 | >30 | Adults | — | — | 5.2 |
| | 1984–1985 | 41,921 | 25–29.99 | Adults | — | — | 18.7 |
| Morocco [6] | 1992 | 1,615 (U) | ≥25 | 20–49 | — | 50.3 | |
| | 1992 | 1,596 (R) | ≥25 | 20–49 | — | 27.9 | |
| Morocco [75] | 1984–1985 | 41,921 | >30 | Adults | — | — | 5.2 |
| | 1984–1985 | 41,921 | 25–29.99 | Adults | — | — | 18.7 |
| Saudi  Arabia [76] | 1996 | 13,177 | >30 | 15–95 | 16.0 | 24.0 | 19.8 |
| | 1996 | 13,177 | 25–30 | 15–95 | 29.0 | 27.0 | 28.0 |
| Senegal [6] | 1998 | 1,386 (U) | ≥25 | 20–49 | | 33.0 | |
| | 1998 | 1,779 (R) | ≥25 | 20–49 | | 11.0 | |
| Tunisia [58] | 1990 | 8,611 | >30 | Adults | 2.4 | 8.3 | 5.3 |
| | 1990 | 8,611 | 25 | Adults | 20.0 | 32.7 | 26.3 |
| Turkey [6] | 1998 | 1,087 (U) | ≥25 | 20–49 | | 63.2 | |
| | 1998 | 2,123 (R) | ≥25 | 20–49 | | 65.6 | |
| **Sub-Saharan Africa** | | | | | | | |
| Benin [6] | 1996 | 1,000 (U) | ≥25 | 20–49 | | 18.4 | |
| | 1996 | 1,603 (R) | ≥25 | 20–49 | | 10.5 | |
| Burkina Faso [6] | 1992 | 543 (U) | ≥25 | 20–49 | | 21.3 | |
| | 1992 | 3,079 (R) | ≥25 | 20–49 | | 5.4 | |
| Cameroon [6] | 1998 | 717 (U) | ≥25 | 20–49 | | 36.7 | |
| | 1998 | 886 (R) | ≥25 | 20–49 | | 19.5 | |
| Central African Republic [6] | 1994 | 926 (U) | ≥25 | 20–49 | | 12.3 | |
| | 1994 | 1,443 (R) | ≥25 | 20–49 | | 5.6 | |
| C'ote d'Ivoire [6] | 1994 | 1,256 (U) | ≥25 | 20–49 | | 30.7 | |
| | 1994 | 1,757 (R) | ≥25 | 20–49 | | 8.4 | |
| Congo [58] | 1986/1987 | 2,295 | 25 | >18 | — | 15.2 | — |

(continued)

**Table 21.1** (continued)
Obesity patterns in adults in lower- and middle-income countries: studies with large sample size

| Country | Year | Sample (n) | Obesity criteria (BMI) | Age group | Percent obese | | |
|---|---|---|---|---|---|---|---|
| | | | | | Males | Females | Total |
| Congo [77] | 1986/1987 | 2,295 | >30 | >18 | – | 3.4 | – |
| | 1991 | 3,004 (U) | >25 | 18 | – | – | 23.6 |
| | 1992 | 1,344(R) | >25 | 18 | – | – | 4.1 |
| Ghana [6] | 1998 | 773 (U) | ≥25 | 20–49 | | 32.2 | |
| | 1998 | 1,448 (R) | ≥25 | 20–49 | | 12.2 | |
| Kenya [6] | 1998 | 869 (U) | ≥25 | 20–49 | | 27.9 | |
| | 1998 | 2,499 (R) | ≥25 | 20–49 | | 15.3 | |
| Madagascar [6] | 1997 | 681 (U) | ≥25 | 20–49 | | 10.3 | |
| | 1997 | 1,898 (R) | ≥25 | 20–49 | | 3.6 | |
| Malawi [6] | 1992 | 361 (U) | ≥25 | 20–49 | | 27.0 | |
| | 1992 | 2,393 (R) | ≥25 | 20–49 | | 10.5 | |
| Mali [58] | 1991 | 4,868 | 25 | Adults | – | – | 7.2 |
| | 1991 | 4,868 | >30 | Adults | – | – | 0.8 |
| Mali [6] | 1996 | 1,353 (U) | ≥25 | 20–49 | | 21.6 | |
| | 1996 | 1,401 (R) | ≥25 | 20–49 | | 6.1 | |
| Namibia [6] | 1992 | 725 (U) | ≥25 | 20–49 | | 41.1 | |
| | 1992 | 1,810 (R) | ≥25 | 20–49 | | 15.2 | |
| Niger [6] | 1998 | 630 (U) | ≥25 | 20–49 | | 31.6 | |
| | 1998 | 2,834 (R) | ≥25 | 20–49 | | 4.5 | |
| Nigeria [6] | 1992 | 885 (U) | ≥25 | 20–49 | | 23.9 | |
| | 1992 | 1349 (R) | ≥25 | 20–49 | | 23.4 | |
| South Africa [78] | 1979 | 7,187 | >30 | 15–64 | 14.7 | 18.0 | 16.5 |
| | 1979 | 7,187 | 25–30 [69] 24–30 (F) | 15–64 | 41.9 | 38.8 | 40.3 |
| South Africa [79] | 1990 | 986 (BI) | 30 | 15–64 | 7.9 | 44.4 | 28.0 |
| South Africa [6] | 1998 | 2,293 (U) | ≥25 | 20–49 | | 61.0 | |
| | 1998 | 2,066 (R) | ≥25 | 20–49 | | 55.8 | |

| Country | Year | N | Cutoff | Age | | | |
|---|---|---|---|---|---|---|---|
| Tanzania [6] | 1996 | 1,064 (U) | ≥25 | 20–49 | | 28.5 | |
| | 1996 | 2,891 (R) | ≥25 | 20–49 | | 11.4 | |
| Mauritius [32] | 1992 | 5,111 | >30 | 25–74 | 5.3 | 15.1 | 10.6 |
| | 1992 | 5,111 | >25 | 25–74 | 35.7 | 47.7 | 42.2 |
| Uganda [6] | 1995 | 423 (U) | ≥25 | 20–49 | | 23.3 | |
| | 1995 | 2,961 (R) | ≥25 | 20–49 | | 9.4 | |
| Zambia [6] | 1996 | 1,600 (U) | ≥25 | 20–49 | | 25.9 | |
| | 1996 | 2,482 (R) | ≥25 | 20–49 | | 11.5 | |
| Zimbabwe [6] | 1994 | 619 (U) | ≥25 | 20–49 | | 36.8 | |
| | 1994 | 1,329 (R) | ≥25 | 20–49 | | 23.7 | |

*Bl* black, *NCHS* National Center for Health Statistics, *R* rural, *U* urban, *F* female, *NCHS OB* obesity based on NCHS criteria, *NCHS OVE* overweight based on NCHS criteria.

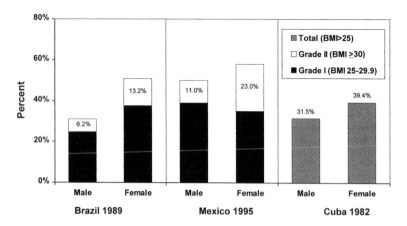

**Fig. 21.1.** Obesity patterns in Latin America.

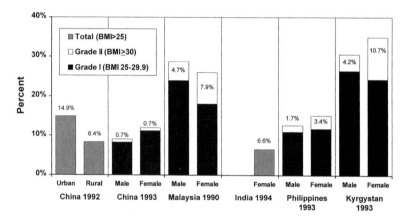

**Fig. 21.2.** Obesity patterns in Asia.

### 21.3.1.3  WESTERN PACIFIC

The island nations such as Samoa and Nauru, Fiji, and Melanesia have been the subject of many studies. The interest in this region is due to unusually high rates of obesity in the population as well as high rates of chronic disease. In some countries, over half the population had grade II or above obesity (Fig. 21.3). In most countries, obesity was much greater for females than it is for males.

### 21.3.1.4  MIDDLE EAST

The limited data for the oil-exporting countries such as Kuwait and Saudi Arabia indicate over a third of the adult population is overweight or obese (data not shown for overweight prevalence) (Fig. 21.4). In the North African countries, the situation reflects an emerging problem, with considerable grade I overweight and less grade II and above. Again, female obesity was higher in all countries where data were available for both genders.

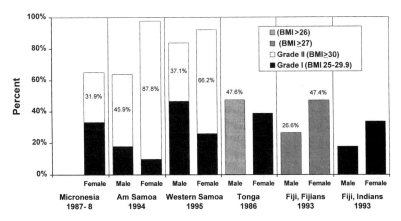

**Fig. 21.3.** Obesity patterns in Western and South Pacific.

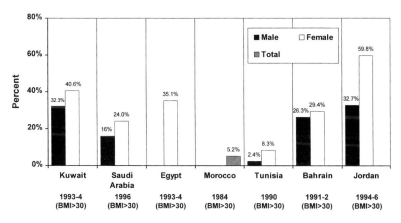

**Fig. 21.4.** Obesity patterns in North Africa and the Middle East.

### 21.3.1.5  SUB-SAHARAN AFRICA

Aside from Mauritius, there are no nationally representative surveys in sub-Saharan Africa. Data for adult women only are available for many countries and are based on the Demographic Health Surveys [6]. The scattered data from South Africa, Mali, and the Congo indicate high levels of obesity in urban sub-Saharan Africa (Fig. 21.5). Data are available from rural areas from the Demographic Health Surveys, showing that in much of rural Africa, overweight in women is still minimal. Exceptions are Nigeria, Zimbabwe, and South Africa, with greater than 20% overweight in rural areas in Nigeria and Zimbabwe and as high as 55% in South Africa. These results confirm previous studies on Africans, particularly women, indicating high levels of obesity in rural as well as urban areas [23].

### 21.3.2  *Obesity Trends in Lower- and Middle-Income Countries*

We have excellent data on trends in body composition for a small number of lower- and middle-income countries. Where we have data (Brazil in Latin America; China,

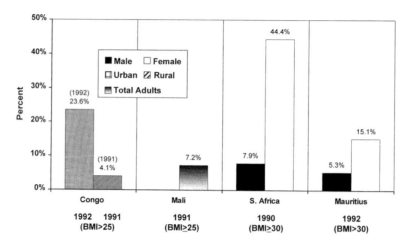

**Fig. 21.5.** Obesity patterns in sub-Saharan Africa.

**Table 21.2**
Obesity trends among adults in lower- and middle-income countries

| Country | Year | Sample (n) | Obesity criteria (BMI) | Percent obese | | |
|---|---|---|---|---|---|---|
| | | | | Males | Females | Total |
| **South America** | | | | | | |
| Brazil [14] | 1975 | 88,625 | ≥25 | 15.7 | 24,0 | 20.0 |
| | 1989 | 13,350 | ≥25 | 25.7 | 39,5 | 31.8 |
| | 2003 | 59,204 | ≥25 | 38.2 | 38,1 | 38.1 |
| Brazil [80] | 1974/1975 | 94,699 | 25 | 19.6 | 27.2 | 23.5 |
| | 1989 | 23,544 | 25 | 31.1 | 50.8 | 38.9 |
| | 1996 | 3,179 | 25 | – | 35.8 | – |
| Brazil [80] | 1974/1975 | 94,699 | 25–29.99 | 16.8 | 20.1 | 18.5 |
| | 1989 | 23,544 | 25–29.99 | 24.9 | 37.6 | 29.9 |
| Brazil [24] | 1974 | 94,699 | >30 | 3.1 | 8.2 | 5.7 |
| | 1989 | 23,544 | >30 | 5.9 | 13.3 | 9.6 |
| Mexico [21] | 1988 | 19,022 | 25–<27 | – | 10 | – |
| Mexico [21] | 1995 | 2,042 (U) | 25–<30 | 39.0 | 35.0 | – |
| | 1996 | 203 (R) | 25–<30 | 20.0 | 26.0 | – |
| Mexico [21] | 1988 | 19,022 | >27 | – | 15.0 | – |
| | 1995 | 2,042 (U) | >30 | 11.0 | 23.0 | – |
| | 1996 | 203 (R) | >30 | 4.0 | 19.0 | – |
| **South Pacific** | | | | | | |
| Nauru [37] | 1975/1976 | – | >30 | 63.2 | 72.4 | – |
| | 1982 | – | >30 | 70.7 | 75.8 | – |
| Nauru [37] | 1987 | – | >30 | 67.2 | 69.8 | – |
| | 1994 | 1,344 | >30 | 80.2 | 78.6 | 79.4 |
| Rural Western Samoa [37] | 1978 | 745 | >30 | 18.7 | 37.9 | 29.7 |
| | 1991 | 960 | >30 | 34.8 | 52.1 | 44.1 |
| Urban Western Samoa [37] | 1978 | 744 | >30 | 38.2 | 60.3 | 50.0 |
| | 1991 | 769 | >30 | 48.4 | 72.1 | 61.9 |

(continued)

**Table 21.2** (continued)
Obesity trends among adults in lower- and middle-income countries

| Country | Year | Sample (n) | Obesity criteria (BMI) | Percent obese | | |
|---|---|---|---|---|---|---|
| | | | | Males | Females | Total |
| Fiji [ethnic Fijian] [65] | 1958–1970 | 1,947 | ≥26 | 34.7 | 57.8 | 46.7 |
| | 1980 | | ≥25 | 32 | 64 | 49 |
| | 1993 | | ≥27 | 26.8 | 47.4 | 37.8 |
| | 1993 | | ≥25 | – | 64.4 | 46.9 |
| Fiji [ethnic Indian] [65] | 1958–1970 | 485 | ≥26 | 3.6 | 22.1 | 14.4 |
| | 1980 | 1,288 | ≥27 (≥25 M) | 11 | 38 | 26 |
| | 1993 | 1,226 | ≥27 | 9 | – | 21.4 |
| | 1993 | 1,226 | ≥25 | 18 | 33.9 | 25.9 |
| American Samoa, age 25–39 [48] | 1990 | | >25 | 98.4 | 94.4 | |
| | 1994 | | >25 | 100 | 95.7 | |
| | 1990 | | >30 | 76.6 | 78.7 | |
| | 1994 | | >30 | 80.3 | 86.1 | |
| American Samoa, age 40–58 [48] | 1990 | | >25 | 97.9 | 95.7 | |
| | 1994 | | >25 | 97.5 | 97.8 | |
| | 1990 | | >30 | 80.2 | 85.8 | |
| | 1994 | | >30 | 81 | 90 | |
| Western Samoa, age 25–39 [48, 81] | 1991 | | >25 | 88 | 87.3 | |
| | 1995 | | >25 | 84.9 | 89 | |
| | 1991 | | >30 | 32.9 | 54.9 | |
| | 1995 | | >30 | 33.3 | 55.1 | |
| Western Samoa, age 40–58 [48, 81] | 1991 | | >25 | 83.9 | 93.6 | |
| | 1995 | | >25 | 82.5 | 95.8 | |
| | 1991 | | >30 | 45.8 | 70 | |
| | 1995 | | >30 | 41.7 | 78.2 | |
| **Asia** | | | | | | |
| China [14] | 1991 | 8,680 | ≥25 | 10.3 | 15,2 | 12.9 |
| | 2000 | 9,570 | ≥25 | 22.1 | 24,6 | 23.4 |
| China [29] | 1982 | 6,459 | 25 | – | – | 6.0 |
| | 1989 | 4,965 | 25 | – | – | 8.9 |
| Urban China [30] | 1982 | 5,510 | >25 | – | – | 9.7 |
| | 1989 | 1,606 | >25 | – | – | 12.0 |
| | 1992 | 8,477 | >25 | – | – | 14.9 |
| Rural China [30] | 1982 | 7,814 | >25 | – | – | 6.1 |
| | 1989 | 3,556 | >25 | – | – | 7.5 |
| | 1992 | 20,911 | >25 | – | – | 8.4 |
| China | 1989 | 5,056 | 25–30 | 5.9 | 10.3 | 8.2 |
| | 1991 | 5,353 | 25–30 | 9.5 | 11.4 | 9.5 |
| | 1993 | 4,920 | 25–30 | 8.3 | 11.3 | 9.9 |
| | 1989 | 5,056 | >30 | 0.3 | 0.6 | 0.5 |
| | 1991 | 5,353 | >30 | 0.5 | 0.8 | 0.7 |
| | 1993 | 4,920 | >30 | 0.7 | 0.7 | 0.7 |

(continued)

**Table 21.2** (continued)
Obesity trends among adults in lower- and middle-income countries

| Country | Year | Sample (n) | Obesity criteria (BMI) | Percent obese | | |
|---|---|---|---|---|---|---|
| | | | | Males | Females | Total |
| India [61] | 1975–1979 | 6,428 | >25 | – | 3.4 | – |
| | 1988–1990 | 13,422 | >25 | – | 4.1 | – |
| | 1994 | 1,832 | >25 | – | 6.6 | – |
| Indonesia [14] | 1993 | 13,827 | ≥25 | 7.9 | 15.3 | 12.0 |
| | 2000 | 22,725 | ≥25 | 11.4 | 22.1 | 17.0 |
| Vietnam [14] | 1992 | 6,545 | ≥25 | 1.0 | 2.2 | 1.6 |
| | 1997 | 16,270 | ≥25 | 2.9 | 5.4 | 4.3 |
| | 2002 | 92,484 | ≥25 | 4.3 | 6.5 | 5.5 |
| Africa | | | | | | |
| Mauritius [32] | 1987 | 5,021 | <25–30 | 22.7 | 27.5 | 25.2 |
| | 1992 | 5,111 | <25–30 | 30.4 | 32.6 | 31.6 |
| | 1987 | 5,021 | >30 | 3.4 | 10.4 | 7.1 |
| | 1992 | 5,111 | >30 | 5.3 | 15.1 | 10.6 |
| **Europe** | | | | | | |
| Russia | *9/1992 | 7,305 | 30–45 | • 8.4 | 23.2 | – |
| | 2/1993 | 9,058 | 30–45 | 9.7 | 25.8 | – |
| | 8/1993 | 9,238 | 30–45 | 9.2 | 25.7 | – |
| | 11/1993 | 8,278 | 30–45 | 10.0 | 25.7 | – |
| | 12/1994 | 6,967 | 30–45 | 9.5 | 26.6 | – |
| | 10/1995 | 6,528 | 30–45 | 9.3 | 27.2 | – |
| | 10/1996 | 6,231 | 30–45 | 10.8 | 27.9 | – |
| | 9/1992 | 7,305 | 25–30 | 33.5 | 33.1 | – |
| | 2/1993 | 9,058 | 25–30 | 34.4 | 32.5 | – |
| | 8/1993 | 9,238 | 25–30 | 34.1 | 32.6 | – |
| | 11/1993 | 8,278 | 25–30 | 34.4 | 32.2 | – |
| | 12/1994 | 6,967 | 25–30 | 35.4 | 31.6 | – |
| | 10/1995 | 6,528 | 25–30 | 31.8 | 31.4 | – |
| | 10/1996 | 6,231 | 25–30 | 33.4 | 30.5 | – |
| | 2004 | 7,077 | ≥25 | 47.4 | 58.4 | 53.4 |

*R* rural, *U* urban, *M* male, *month/year.

Indonesia, and Vietnam in Asia; Mauritius in Africa; Nauru and Western Samoa in the South Pacific; and Russia), we find significant increases in obesity occurring (see Table 21.2 and Fig. 21.6). In Fig. 21.6, we have, for the purpose of comparison, converted all the trends into a rate representing annual percentage point increase.

### 21.3.2.1 BRAZIL

Elsewhere, we presented in detail the trends in Brazil [24, 25]. The proportion of obesity among adult males almost doubled (3.1% to 5.9%) between 1974 and 1989 for BMI above 30 [24]. A study of trends documenting trends in overweight (BMI ≥ 25)

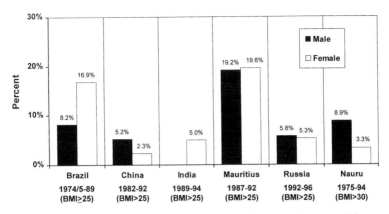

**Fig. 21.6.** Obesity trends: the percentage increase in obesity prevalence per 10-year period.

from 1975 to 2003 showed a greater rate of increase in the period from 1975 to 1989 compared to the later period (1989 to 2003). The annual rate of increase in the earlier period was nearly twice that of the later period, 0.84% per annual increase compared to 0.45% per annual increase [14]. These trends are consistent with earlier reports.

### 21.3.2.2 CHINA

The shifts in diet, physical activity, and overweight status in China are among the most rapid ever documented. Elsewhere, we showed that among school-aged children, Chinese obesity rates are rapidly reaching levels comparable with the United States, although this is not so for adults [26]. These changes are much greater among urban residents of all income backgrounds and greater still among middle- and higher-income rural residents [27–29]. In China, we have found that, although obesity prevalence is lower among the lowest-income tertile, the rate of increase among this group is the greatest. When one looks at education of women, one finds already for China that less-educated women are more overweight than women with more education [11]. The rates of obesity based on national nutrition surveys in China in 1982–1992 indicate a moderate increase; however, this obscures more rapid shifts in diet, activity, and obesity seen in the last few years [30, 31]. During the more recent period, the data in Table 21.2 show a consistent increase in obesity in urban and rural areas among adults. The increase in the prevalence of BMI of 25 or above doubled for men and nearly doubled for women between 1991and 2000.

### 21.3.2.3 INDONESIA

Data for Indonesia are based on the Indonesia Family Life Surveys (IFLS) from 1993 and 2000. The IFLS was a longitudinal survey conducted in 1993–1994 in 321 communities and 13 provinces by the Rand Corporation in collaboration with Lembaga Demografi, University of Indonesia. The survey included 7,162 households and is representative of 83% of the population. In 2000, the rate of contact from the baseline sample was 95%. The prevalence for grade I obesity and above was 12.0% overall in 1993 and 17.0% in 2000; in both surveys, the prevalence was higher for women than for men.

#### 21.3.2.4  VIETNAM

The trends data for Vietnam are based on the Vietnamese Living Standards Surveys (VLSS) conducted in 1992–1993 and 1997–1998. The surveys were nationally representative of urban and rural populations (General Statistical Office [GSO], 1994 [82]) and were conducted by the GSO. Both of the VLSS were multipurpose surveys that collected weight and height data. A third survey, conducted in 2002, was designed by the Ministry of Health and collected by the GSO in a manner similar to the VLSS. Vietnam showed among the lowest prevalences of grade I obesity and above in all survey years, with 1.6% prevalence in 1992 and 5.5% in 2002.

#### 21.3.2.5  KUWAIT

Both grade I and grade II obesity rose rapidly in Kuwait. In 1980–1981, the prevalence of grade I and above was over 50% for females and nearly as high for males. This prevalence of overweight rose to approximately 70% for both males and females by 1994, a rate of 14.5 percentage points per decade. Grade II obesity increased by a total of 12.8%, representing a per-decade percentage point increase of 9.8%.

#### 21.3.2.6  MAURITIUS

The small island republic of Mauritius has a very high prevalence of adult-onset diabetes [32]. Among males and females, a rapid increase in obesity is occurring. In particular, the increase in female grade II and above obesity was higher than that found in many high-income countries. During a 5-year period (1987–1992), there were marked increases in grades I and II obesity. It is important to note that this increase in obesity occurred despite the existence of a national health promotion campaign that successfully used the mass media, price policy, other legislative and fiscal measures, and widespread education activity in the community, workplace, and schools to change many behaviors related to coronary heart disease (CHD) and hypertension. The results were remarkable: Hypertension was reduced considerably, cigarette smoking in men and women declined, heavy alcohol use declined, mean serum cholesterol decreased, and there was increased activity [33, 34]. Of course, it is quite possible that the reduction in the extent and amount of smoking is linked partially with this weight increase [35]. However, it is also possible that the rate of increase in obesity would have been much higher without the national health promotion campaign.

#### 21.3.2.7  RUSSIA

Russia has one of the highest rates of mortality related to CHD in the world. Despite marked shifts toward a lower-fat diet in the postreform period, during which price subsidies of meat and dairy products were removed, there is evidence of an increase in adult obesity. We have collected data for seven rounds of the nationally representative RLMS and found a consistent increase in adult and elderly obesity [36]. The remarkable point to note is that the effects of the economic reform-induced dietary changes have not been linked with meaningful changes in obesity patterns. Prevalence of grade I overweight among females showed a consistent decline between 1992 and 1996, while males showed virtually no difference between the first and last rounds of the survey. The survey showed an overall increase in grade II obesity for males and females and an increase in total obesity of over 5 percentage points per 10-year period for Russia.

Despite the overall increase in obesity, year-to-year fluctuations underscore the fact that the economy is in flux, and that these changes cannot be used to predict future directions of this trend. However, based on the survey from 2004, over 50% of the adult population had grade I obesity and above.

### 21.3.2.8 WESTERN PACIFIC

A large body of literature documents the high rates of obesity, in particular grade III and above overweight status, in populations residing in the Western Pacific Islands. Modernization has been associated with a very high prevalence of obesity in the West and South Pacific islands, particularly among urban residents [37–39]. In those islands (e.g., Fiji, Kiribati, Nauru, American and Western Samoa, Vanuatu), high rates of severe obesity are seen that mirror the rates found among Native American groups in the United States [40]. The trends reported in these studies of Hodge and colleagues indicate not only that obesity levels were high but also that the prevalence of obesity continued to increase considerably in each island. In Nauru and Western Samoa, the levels of grades I and II obesity were among the highest found and were still increasing steadily.

## 21.4  IMPLICATIONS FOR PUBLIC HEALTH

The obesity epidemic is linked with rapid shifts in adult-onset diabetes and many other noncommunicable diseases [41]. Adult-onset diabetes and many other comorbidities of obesity are increasing rapidly in many lower-income countries [42, 43]. The most relevant comorbidities are hypertension, dyslipidemia, and atherosclerosis. The epidemiological prevalence data are spotty but indicate serious and high levels of these conditions, in particular adult-onset diabetes. A study from 1997 provided a strong basis for linking diet, activity, and body composition trends discussed in this chapter to increased rates of prevalence for a larger number of cancers [44].

A clear literature has shown that in terms of mechanisms and epidemiology, obesity and activity are closely linked to adult-onset diabetes. Several reviews made the case for these factors. Zimmet and his colleagues [32, 33, 42, 45, 46] have been particularly earnest in exploring these issues at the population level in lower-income and transitional societies. Some basic characteristics of adult-onset diabetes may provide a clear basis for linking key components of the nutrition transition—increases in obesity and reductions in activity—to the rapid increases in adult-onset diabetes in lower-income countries.

### 21.4.1  Obesity

It is clear that obesity and, more particularly, the upper-body regional distribution of body fat, is a key parameter in the etiology of adult-onset diabetes. A vast literature has shown significant direct obesity relationships with adult-onset diabetes, and animal studies support this relationship. The work on abdominal obesity and its effects is more recent but appears to be promising in explaining more precisely the role that body composition plays. In addition, there is a strong relationship between weight gain and risk of developing diabetes. The odds of getting diabetes are considerable with a weight gain of 5–8 kg for adults, and the strength of association is even higher as weight gain increases [47].

### 21.4.2   Physical Activity

It is understood that exercise may help to prevent adult-onset diabetes in an obese patient. Exercise may offset the hyperinsulinemia that is associated with obesity and reduces the likelihood that a person will display the signs that allow him or her to be categorized as having adult-onset diabetes, after controlling for a given level of obesity. Because exercise is associated with lower insulin levels, it may help to offset (or prevent) the hyperinsulinemia that is common among obese persons and consequentially the development of insulin resistance. Zimmet and coworkers [42, 46] reviewed these relationships and noted other critical studies on this topic.

### 21.4.3   Interactions of Obesity and Activity

Physical activity and obesity have independent effects on serum insulin, but together they interact such that the impact of physical activity differs according to the level of obesity. For example studies showed that for each level of BMI or waist–hip ratio, there is a different effect of physical activity on serum insulin level.

### 21.4.4   Genetic Component

Zimmet and others who have focused on this issue as it relates to lower-income countries have felt that the highest genetic susceptibility for adult-onset diabetes was for Pacific Islanders, American Indians, Mexican Americans and other Hispanics, and Asian Indians. Those with modest genetic susceptibility include Africans, Japanese, and Chinese. McGarvey and colleagues [48, 49] and O'Dea and colleagues [50] also have thoroughly explored the same issues among Australian Aborigines and other South Pacific groups and have provided careful documentation of this linkage of the nutrition transition with adult-onset diabetes.

## 21.5   RESEARCH AND POLICY IMPLICATIONS

It is clear that the nutrition transition as noted elsewhere in this volume is closely linked with rapid increases in obesity. It is also clear that there is great potential for serious adverse public health consequences from the nutrition transition and the resultant large increase in obesity. These trends in obesity are not limited to one region, country, or racial/ethnic grouping. The overall levels that we find in selected countries such as Mexico, Brazil, Egypt, South Africa, China, Malaysia, and most nations from both the Middle East and the Western Pacific are indicative of major public health problems. That these changes appear to be occurring across so many countries underscores the urgent need to better understand the underlying environmental causes. Focusing attention solely on genetic causes of obesity will not help to resolve, slow, or reverse the current, global, epidemic of obesity and chronic disease. International studies can help to better understand the cultural, environmental, and behavioral determinants that contribute to the universal trends toward rising overweight and obesity.

Clearly, excess body fat develops when dietary energy intake exceeds energy expenditure. Excess energy intake and insufficient physical activity are major direct determinants of energy imbalance. Diet and activity patterns have shifted in comparable ways in many countries, and as such, diet and activity may contribute to the obesity epidemic in a similar way across all populations. Other contributors, such as metabolic differences, inactivity, and macronutrient composition such as percentage energy from fat, are unknown [51]. Clearly, diet and activity do contribute to overweight and obesity as shown by longitudinal studies in lower-income countries [18, 52–54]. Although there will be large differences in the underlying socioeconomic and behavioral factors related to obesity in each country, the policies and programs that alter these patterns may be best understood by examining settings around the world.

At present, there are few examples of lower-income countries that have developed national programs and policies focused on the rapid increases in obesity and the related changes in the structure of diet and activity. There are discussions under way in several countries and smaller-scale interventions in many countries. Mauritius and Singapore are unique in following a systematic national approach. The small island republic in the Indian Ocean of Mauritius found such a high level of cardiovascular disease as part of an adult health survey conducted in 1987 that it launched a broad comprehensive health promotion program, described in this chapter. This program used the mass media, price policy, other legislative and fiscal measures, and widespread education activity in the community, workplace, and schools. The results were remarkable in terms of health effects, but overall there was no decrease in obesity [33, 34]. If diet changed in a positive manner and activity increased, there must have been some decline in the rate of increase of obesity. Singapore has also developed a national program in the schools to address child obesity. The results have not been written up, but the unpublished information suggests a very effective intervention was developed.

The challenge we face in lower-income countries is in determining how to arrest this rapid increase in obesity before the health system is overwhelmed with obesity-related problems. Effective prevention requires that obesity and chronic disease appear on the national agenda in the earliest stages. Evidence shows that obesity occurs in adults before it occurs in children, and that obesity occurs first in women compared to men. Thus, in the context of economic growth, it is important to have monitoring systems in place. To the extent that monitoring is not possible, low- and middle-income countries should emphasize economic growth in the context of ensuring a healthy food supply and an active lifestyle. While no countries have been able to reverse existing trends, there are examples of countries such as South Korea [55, 56] that have experienced a less-severe epidemic in obesity due to government programs promoting healthful, traditional, foods.

*Acknowledgments* Preparation of this chapter was supported in part by grants from the US National Institutes of Health (R01-HD30880). We thank the following staff of the Carolina Population Center, University of North Carolina at Chapel Hill: Tom Swasey for his work on the graphics and Frances Dancy for administrative assistance.

## REFERENCES

1. Omran AR. The epidemiologic transition. A theory of the epidemiology of population change. Milbank Mem Fund Q 1971;49(4):509–538.
2. McGuire AL, Barer JM, Montaner JS, Hogg RS. There and back again: the impact of adult HIV prevalence on national life expectancies. HIV Med 2005;6(2):57–58.
3. Popkin BM. The nutrition transition in the developing world. Dev Policy Rev 2003;21(5):581–597.
4. Popkin BM. An overview on the nutrition transition and its health implications: the Bellagio meeting. Public Health Nutr 2002;5(1A):93–103.
5. Popkin, BM. Global nutrition dynamics: the world is shifting rapidly toward a diet linked with noncommunicable diseases. Am J Clin Nutr 2006;84(2):289–298.

6. Mendez MA, Monteiro CA, Popkin BM. Overweight exceeds underweight among women in most developing countries. Am J Clin Nutr 2005;81(3):714–721.

7. Popkin BM, Lu B, Zhai F. Understanding the nutrition transition: measuring rapid dietary changes in transitional countries. Public Health Nutr 2002;5(6A):947–953.

8. Popkin BM, Doak CM. The obesity epidemic is a worldwide phenomenon. Nutr Rev 1998;56(4 pt 1): 106–114.

9. Popkin BM, Gordon-Larsen P. The nutrition transition: worldwide obesity dynamics and their determinants. Int J Obes Relat Metab Disord 2004;28(suppl 3):S2–S9.

10. Mendez MA, Popkin B. Globalization, urbanization and nutritional change in the developing world. Electronic J Agr Dev Econ 2005;1:220–241.

11. Monteiro CA, Conde WL, Lu B, Popkin BM. Obesity and inequities in health in the developing world. Int J Obes Relat Metab Disord 2004;28(9):1181–1186.

12. Monteiro CA, Moura EC, Conde WL, Popkin BM. Socioeconomic status and obesity in adult populations of developing countries: a review. Bull World Health Organ 2004;82(12):940–946.

13. Steyn K, Bourne L, Jooste P, Fourie JM, Rossouw K, Lombard C. Anthropometric profile of a black population of the Cape Peninsula in South Africa. East Afr Med J 1998;75(1):35–40.

14. Popkin BM, Conde W, Hou N, Monteiro C. Why the lag globally in obesity trends for children as compared to adults? Unpublished manuscript, 2005.

15. Doak CM, Adair LS, Bentley M, Monteiro C, Popkin BM. The dual burden household and the nutrition transition paradox. Int J Obes Relat Metab Disord 2005;29(1):129–136.

16. Garrett JL, Ruel MT. Stunted child-overweight mother pairs: prevalence and association with economic development and urbanization. Food Nutr Bull 2005;26(2):209–221.

17. Du S, Lu B, Zhai F, Popkin BM. A new stage of the nutrition transition in China. Public Health Nutr 2002;5(1A):169–174.

18. Jahns L, Baturin A, Popkin BM. Obesity, diet, and poverty: trends in the Russian transition to market economy. Eur J Clin Nutr 2003;57(10):1295–1302.

19. Adair LS, Popkin BM. Are child eating patterns being transformed globally? Obes Res 2005;13:1281–1299.

20. WHO Expert Committee on Physical Status. Physical Status: The use and interpretation of anthropometry. Geneva: World Health Organization, 1995. Report No.: 854.

21. Rivera JA, Barquera S, Campirano F, Campos I, Safdie M, Tovar V. Epidemiological and nutritional transition in Mexico: rapid increase of non-communicable chronic diseases and obesity. Public Health Nutr 2002;5(1A):113–122.

22. Forrester T, Wilks R, Bennet F, McFarlane-Anderson N, McGee D. Obesity in the Caribbean. In: The origins and consequences of obesity. Chadwick DJ, Cardew G, eds. Chichester, UK: Wiley, 1996.

23. Bourne LT, Lambert EV, Steyn K. Where does the black population of South Africa stand on the nutrition transition? Public Health Nutr 2002;5(1A):157–162.

24. Monteiro CA, Mondini L, de Souza AL, Popkin BM. The nutrition transition in Brazil. Eur J Clin Nutr 1995;49(2):105–113.

25. Monteiro CA, Conde WL, Popkin BM. Is obesity replacing or adding to undernutrition? Evidence from different social classes in Brazil. Public Health Nutr 2002;5(1A):105–112.

26. Popkin BM, Richards MK, Montiero CA. Stunting is associated with overweight in children of four nations that are undergoing the nutrition transition. J Nutr 1996;126(12):3009–3016.

27. Popkin BM, Paeratakul S, Zhai F, Ge K. A review of dietary and environmental correlates of obesity with emphasis on developing countries. Obes Res 1995;3(suppl 2):145s–153s.

28. Popkin BM, Paeratakul S, Zhai F, Ge K. Dietary and environmental correlates of obesity in a population study in China. Obes Res 1995;3(suppl 2):135s–143s.

29. Popkin BM, Paeratakul S, Ge K, Zhai F. Body weight patterns among the Chinese: results from the 1989 and 1991 China Health and Nutrition Surveys. Am J Public Health 1995;85(5):690–694.

30. Ge K, Zhai F, Yan H. The dietary and nutritional status of Chinese population: 1992 National Nutrition Survey. Vol. 1. Beijing: People's Medical Publishing House, 1996.

31. Ge K, Weisell R, Guo X, et al. The body mass index of Chinese adults in the 1980s. Eur J Clin Nutr 1994;48(suppl 3):S148–S154.

32. Hodge AM, Dowse GK, Gareeboo H, Tuomilehto J, Alberti KG, Zimmet PZ. Incidence, increasing prevalence, and predictors of change in obesity and fat distribution over 5 years in the rapidly developing population of Mauritius. Int J Obes Relat Metab Disord 1996;20(2):137–146.

33. Dowse GK, Gareeboo H, Alberti KG, et al. Changes in population cholesterol concentrations and other cardiovascular risk factor levels after 5 years of the non-communicable disease intervention programme in Mauritius. Mauritius Non-communicable Disease Study Group. BMJ 1995;311(7015):1255–1259.

34. Uusitalo U, Feskens EJ, Tuomilehto J, et al. Fall in total cholesterol concentration over 5 years in association with changes in fatty acid composition of cooking oil in Mauritius: cross sectional survey. BMJ 1996;313(7064):1044–1046.

35. Flegal KM, Troiano RP, Pamuk ER, Kuczmarski RJ, Campbell SM. The influence of smoking cessation on the prevalence of overweight in the United States. N Engl J Med 1995;333(18):1165–1170.

36. Popkin BM, Zohoori N, Baturin A. The nutritional status of the elderly in Russia, 1992 through 1994. Am J Public Health 1996;86(3):355–360.

37. Hodge AM, Dowse GK, Toelupe P, Collins VR, Imo T, Zimmet PZ. Dramatic increase in the prevalence of obesity in western Samoa over the 13 year period 1978–1991. Int J Obes Relat Metab Disord 1994;18(6):419–428.

38. Hodge AM, Dowse GK, Zimmet PZ, Collins VR. Prevalence and secular trends in obesity in Pacific and Indian Ocean island populations. Obes Res 1995;3(suppl 2):77s–87s.

39. Taylor R, Badcock J, King H, et al. Dietary intake, exercise, obesity and noncommunicable disease in rural and urban populations of three Pacific Island countries. J Am Coll Nutr 1992;11(3):283–293.

40. Brown PJ, Konner M. An anthropological perspective on obesity. Ann N Y Acad Sci 1987;499:29–46.

41. Beaglehole R, Yach D. Globalisation and the prevention and control of non-communicable disease: the neglected chronic diseases of adults. Lancet 2003;362(9387):903–908.

42. Zimmet PZ, McCarty DJ, de Courten MP. The global epidemiology of non-insulin-dependent diabetes mellitus and the metabolic syndrome. J Diabetes Complications 1997;11(2):60–68.

43. King H, Aubert RE, Herman WH. Global burden of diabetes, 1995–2025: prevalence, numerical estimates, and projections. Diabetes Care 1998;21(9):1414–1431.

44. World Cancer Research Fund. Food, nutrition and the prevention of causes: a global perspective. Washington, DC: World Cancer Research Fund in association with the American Institute for Cancer Research, 1997.

45. Hodge AM, Dowse GK, Toelupe P, Collins VR, Zimmet PZ. The association of modernization with dyslipidaemia and changes in lipid levels in the Polynesian population of Western Samoa. Int J Epidemiol 1997;26(2):297–306.

46. Zimmet PZ. Kelly West Lecture 1991. Challenges in diabetes epidemiology—from West to the rest. Diabetes Care 1992;15(2):232–252.

47. Ford ES, Williamson DF, Liu S. Weight change and diabetes incidence: findings from a national cohort of US adults. Am J Epidemiol 1997;146(3):214–222.

48. McGarvey ST, Quested C, Tufa J. Correlates and predictors of cross-sectional and longitudinal adiposity in adults from Samoa and American Samoa. Providence, RI: Department of Medicine, Brown University, 1998.

49. Parra E, Saha N, Soemantri AG, et al. Genetic variation at nine autosomal microsatellite loci in Asian and Pacific populations. Hum Biol 1999;71(5):757–779.

50. O'Dea K, Patel M, Kubisch D, Hopper J, Traianedes K. Obesity, diabetes, and hyperlipidemia in a central Australian aboriginal community with a long history of acculturation. Diabetes Care 1993;16(7):1004–1010.

51. Bray GA, Popkin BM. Dietary fat intake does affect obesity! Am J Clin Nutr 1998;68(6):1157–1173.

52. Paeratakul S, Popkin BM, Kohlmeier L, Hertz-Picciotto I, Guo X, Edwards LJ. Measurement error in dietary data: implications for the epidemiologic study of the diet–disease relationship. Eur J Clin Nutr 1998;52(10):722–727.

53. Paeratakul S, Popkin BM, Keyou G, Adair LS, Stevens J. Changes in diet and physical activity affect the body mass index of Chinese adults. Int J Obes Relat Metab Disord 1998;22(5):424–431.

54. Bell AC, Ge K, Popkin BM. Weight gain and its predictors in Chinese adults. Int J Obes Relat Metab Disord 2001;25(7):1079–1086.

55. Kim S, Moon S, Popkin BM. The nutrition transition in South Korea. Am J Clin Nutr 2000;71(1):44–53.

56. Lee MJ, Popkin BM, Kim S. The unique aspects of the nutrition transition in South Korea: the retention of healthful elements in their traditional diet. Public Health Nutr 2002;5(1A):197–203.

57. Dufour DLSL, Reina JC, Spurr GB. Anthropometry and secular changes in stature of urban Columbian women of different socioeconomic status. Am J Hum Biol 1994;6:749–760.

58. Shetty PS, James WP. Body mass index. A measure of chronic energy deficiency in adults. FAO Food Nutr Pap 1994;56:1–57.

59. Berdasco A. Body mass index values in the Cuban adult population. Eur J Clin Nutr 1994;48(suppl 3): S155–S163; discussion S64.

60. Dhurandhar NV, Kulkarni PR. Prevalence of obesity in Bombay. Int J Obes Relat Metab Disord 1992;16(5):367–375.

61. Sachdev H. Nutritional status of children and women in India: recent trends. Bull Nutr Found India 1997;18(3):1–2.

62. Ismail MN, Zawaih H, Chee SS, Ng KK. Prevalence of obesity and chronic energy deficiency (CED) in adult Malaysians. Malay J Nutr 1995;1(19):1–9.

63. Solon FS. Nutrition related chronic diseases in the Philippines. Nutrition Center of the Philippines Report Series, 2(1). Makati City, Philippines: Nutrition Center of the Philippines, 1997.

64. Tanphaichitr V, Kulapongse S, Pakpeakatvatana R, Leelahagul P, Tamwiwat C, Lochaya S. Prevalence of obesity and its associated risks in Urban Thais. In: Progress in obesity research 1990. Oomura Y, Tarui S, Inoue S, Shimazu T, eds. London: Libbey; 1991:649–653.

65. Saito S. National Nutrition Survey, main report. Suva, Fiji: National Food and Nutrition Committee, Republic of Fiji, 1995.

66. Federated States of Micronesia. Department of Human Resources OoHS. Technical report prepared for the government and Department of Human Resources of the Federated States of Micronesia: The 1987/88 National Nutrition Survey of the Federated States of Micronesia. Noumea, New Caledonia: South Pacific Commission, 1989.

67. Hodge AM, Dowse G, Zimmet P. Obesity in Pacific populations. Pac Health Dialog 1996;3(1):77–86.

68. Tassie JM, Papoz L, Barny S, Simon D. Nutritional status in adults in the pluri-ethnic population of New Caledonia. The CALDIA Study Group. Int J Obes Relat Metab Disord 1997;21(1):61–66.

69. Evans T, Whitehead M, Diderichsen F, Bhuiya A, Wirth M. Challenging inequities in health: from ethics to action. New York: Oxford University Press, 2001.

70. Kingdom of Tonga National Food and Nutrition Committee. The 1986 National Nutrition Survey of the Kingdom of Tonga. New Caledonia: South Pacific Commission, 1987.

71. al-Mannai A, Dickerson JW, Morgan JB, Khalfan H. Obesity in Bahraini adults. J R Soc Health 1996;116(1):30–32, 37–40.

72. Khorshid A, Galal OM. Development of food consumption monitoring system for Egypt. National Agricultural Research Project. Final Report. Submitted to the U.S. Department of Agriculture and the Egyptian Ministry of Agriculture, 1995.

73. Ajlouni K, Jaddou H, Batieha A. Obesity in Jordan. Int J Obes Relat Metab Disord 1998;22(7):624–628.

74. al-Isa AN. Prevalence of obesity among adult Kuwaitis: a cross-sectional study. Int J Obes Relat Metab Disord 1995;19(6):431–433.

75. Kingdom of Morocco Dirreccion de la Statisque. Consommation et dispueses des menages 1984/85. Vol. 6, Situation nutritionelle de la population du Maroc. Rabat, Morocco: Ministere de Affaire Economique et Sociale, 1992.

76. al-Nuaim AR, al-Rubeaan K, al-Mazrou Y, al-Attas O, al-Daghari N, Khoja T. High prevalence of overweight and obesity in Saudi Arabia. Int J Obes Relat Metab Disord 1996;20(6):547–552.

77. Delpeuch F, Cornu A, Massamba JP, Traissac P, Maire B. Is body mass index sensitively related to socio-economic status and to economic adjustment? A case study from the Congo. Eur J Clin Nutr 1994;48(suppl 3):S141–S147.

78. Jooste PL, Steenkamp HJ, Benade AJ, Rossouw JE. Prevalence of overweight and obesity and its relation to coronary heart disease in the CORIS study. S Afr Med J 1988;74(3):101–104.

79. Steyn K, Fourie J, Rossouw JE, Langenhoven ML, Joubert G, Chalton DO. Anthropometric profile of the coloured population of the Cape Peninsula. S Afr Med J 1990;78(2):68–72.

80. Monteiro CA, MH DAB, Conde WL, Popkin BM. Shifting obesity trends in Brazil. Eur J Clin Nutr 2000;54(4):342–346.

81. Ezeamama AE, Viali S, Tuitele J, McGarvey ST. The influence of socioeconomic factors on cardiovascular disease risk factors in the context of economic development in the Samoan archipelago. Soc Sci Med 2006 Nov;63(10):2533–2545.

82. General Statistical Office (1994): Vietnam Living Standards Survey, 1992–1993. Hanoi. Statistical Publishing House.

# 22 Rapid Urbanization and the Challenges of Obtaining Food and Nutrition Security

*Marie T. Ruel, James L. Garrett, and Lawrence Haddad*

## 22.1 INTRODUCTION

Over the period 2000–2030, the urban population of the developing world is projected to double—from 1.97 billion to 3.93 billion—whereas the rural population is projected to increase from 2.90 billion to 2.96 billion [1]. Figure 22.1 shows that 48% of the population, some 3.04 billion people, now live in urban areas (estimates from 2003). About 77% of Latin Americans live in cities and close to 40% of Africans and Asians [1]. The urban population in developing countries is expected to grow more than three times faster (2.29% annually) than the rural population (0.06% annually) between now and 2030. Over the same period, the urban population of Africa is expected to increase from 329 million to 748 million (the rural population is projected to increase from 521 to 650 million); for Asia, the urban population will increase from 1.5 billion to 2.7 billion (the rural population is projected to decline from 2.3 to 2.2 billion); and for Latin America, the corresponding numbers show an increase in the urban population from 417 million to 602 million (and a decline of the rural population from 126 to 109 million).

For those who produce and use food policy research, these numbers raise several issues that we address in this chapter. First, while we can be sure that the number of people living in urban areas in the developing world will increase rapidly in the next 25–30 years, we do not know how many of them will be poor and undernourished. The absolute number of urban poor and undernourished will increase unless urban poverty incidence and undernutrition prevalence rates are reduced in direct proportion to the growth in urban populations. Second, will the absolute number of urban poor and undernourished increase more quickly than the rural number? In other words, will there be a shift of poverty and undernutrition from rural to urban areas? Third, for those living in urban areas, are the constraints to, and the opportunities for, the generation of income, food security, and improved nutrition status different from what

From: *Nutrition and Health: Nutrition and Health in Developing Countries, Second Edition*
Edited by: R. D. Semba & M. W. Bloem © Humana Press, Totowa, NJ

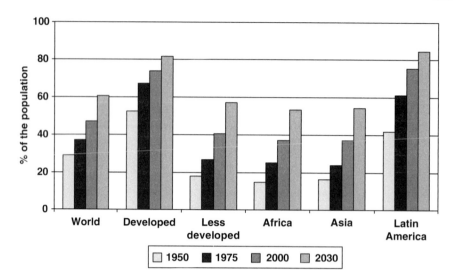

**Fig. 22.1.** Trends in percent of the population living in urban areas by region (1950–2030). Adapted with permission from ref. (1).

is faced in rural areas? Fourth, what do the answers to the first three questions imply for policy research and for policymaking?

In this chapter, we review available information on trends in urban poverty and childhood undernutrition. We also discuss the unique characteristics of urban life, which present special challenges for the achievement of food and nutrition security. These include greater dependence on cash income and hence employment for food security and livelihood; weaker informal safety nets; greater labor force participation of women and its consequences for child care; lifestyle changes, particularly those related to changes in diet and exercise patterns; greater availability of public services such as water, electricity, sewage, and health, but questionable access by poor slum dwellers; greater exposure to environmental contamination (water, food, and air); and governance by a new, possibly nonexistent, set of property rights. The implications of these special features of urban life for programs and policies are highlighted, and research priorities are suggested.

## 22.2 INCREASING URBAN POVERTY AND UNDERNUTRITION

Reliable numbers on the growth of urban poverty and undernutrition and their share in national poverty and undernutrition are generally scarce. Specifically, there is a lack of readily available data to answer the questions: (1) Are the *absolute numbers* of poor people and underweight young children living in urban areas increasing? and (2) do they represent an increasing *share* of the total poor and underweight young children?

The only information available is from a previous analysis that we conducted to examine these issues using data from the World Bank for poverty and from the World Health Organization (WHO) [2] for undernutrition [3]. A summary of the main findings is presented here.

## 22.2.1  Poverty Data

The results of the poverty data showed that for seven of the eight countries included,[1] the share of poor people in urban areas had increased over time, the exception being Indonesia. More important, the results showed that for five of eight countries (Bangladesh, China, Ghana, India, and Nigeria), both the absolute number of urban poor and the share of poor people living in urban areas had increased over time. Note that the eight countries selected account for approximately two thirds of the developing world's people. The only country for which the share of poor people in urban areas had decreased was Indonesia, but this was the country for which the interval between the two points in time was the shortest (only 3 years). The analysis also showed that for four of the countries studied (Pakistan, Colombia, Nigeria, and Ghana), the share of poor people that lived in urban areas in the 1990s was between 25% and 37% of all poor households. These data strongly support the argument that urban poverty had increased between the 1980s and the 1990s in these large countries. Unfortunately, this type of trend analysis is not available for more recent years to our knowledge.

## 22.2.2  Nutrition Data

Similar results were found for the prevalence of underweight children[2]: The share of underweight children in urban areas increased between the late 1980s/early 1990s and the mid-1990s for 11 of 14 countries[3] studied (the exceptions were Tanzania, Peru, and Zambia) [3]. Moreover, both the absolute number of underweight children in urban areas and the share of underweight children contributing to total undernutrition had increased for 9 of 14 countries. Again, this set of countries constitutes a large proportion of the developing world, given that it contains China, Bangladesh, Nigeria, Egypt, and the Philippines. Note that the share of undernourished children living in urban areas reached 30% and higher in four countries (Philippines, Peru, Mauritania, Zambia) and over 50% in Brazil.

Only China, Bangladesh, and Nigeria overlapped from the poverty and underweight children data sets, and they showed the same pattern in urban poverty as they did in urban underweight. Hence, for the majority of the countries examined, we can say that between the late 1980s/early 1990s and the mid-1990s (1) the number of urban poor increased, (2) the share of the urban poor in overall poverty increased, (3) the number of underweight preschoolers in urban areas increased, and (4) the share of urban preschoolers in overall numbers of underweight preschoolers increased. Although more recent analysis

---

[1] The countries and years of data included in the analysis were Bangladesh, 1983/1992; China 1988/1995; Colombia 1978/1992; Ghana 1987/1993; India 1977/1994; Indonesia 1990/1993; Nigeria 1985/1993; and Pakistan 1984/1991.

[2] The prevalence of underweight, as opposed to stunted, children was examined because data on height-for-age were usually not available in the data sets used. We recognize, however, the limitations of underweight data, which do not allow to differentiate between stunting (low weight-for-age) and wasting (low weight-for-height).

[3] The countries and years of data included in this analysis were the following: Bangladesh 1985/1996; Brazil 1989/1996; China 1992/1995; Egypt 1990/1995; Honduras 1987/1995; Madagascar 1992/1995; Malawi 1992/1995; Mauritania 1990/1996; Nigeria 1990/1993; Peru 1991/1996; Philippines 1987/1993; Uganda 1988/1995; Tanzania 1991/1996; Zambia 1992/1997.

of trends in poverty and undernutrition are not available, there are no reasons to believe that these trends would have been reversed since the mid-1990s.

## 22.3   CHALLENGES TO OBTAINING FOOD, NUTRITION, AND HEALTH SECURITY IN AN URBAN ENVIRONMENT

The premise of this section is that the causes of malnutrition and food insecurity in urban and rural areas are different due primarily to a number of phenomena that are unique to or are exacerbated by urban living and by the circumstances that brought the individual to the urban area in the first place. We briefly discuss the following phenomena (or "urban facts of life") and the pressure they place on the attainment of household and individual food, nutrition, and health security: (1) a greater dependence on cash income for food and nonfood purchases; (2) weaker informal safety nets; (3) greater labor force participation of women and its consequences for child care; (4) lifestyle changes, particularly those related to changes in diet and exercise patterns; (5) greater availability of public services such as water, electricity, sewage, and health but questionable access by poor slum dwellers; (6) greater exposure to environmental contamination (water, food, and air); and (7) governance by a new, possibly nonexistent, set of property rights. The main focus of the discussion is on identifying what is different about urban areas, which should help frame the program and policy responses discussed in the final section.

### 22.3.1   The Importance of Cash, Employment, Food Prices, and Agriculture for Urban Livelihood and Food Security

#### 22.3.1.1   Dependence on Cash for Food

Compared to rural consumers, who can often produce their own food, urban consumers must depend largely on food purchases. This dependence on the market is further increased by the fact that, unlike their rural counterparts, they cannot rely on exploitation of natural resources to provide for housing, energy, and water. City dwellers in metropolitan areas of countries as diverse as Egypt, Ghana, Malawi, Mozambique, Nepal, and Peru buy more than 90% of their food [4]. Even in less-urbanized countries such as Mozambique or Nepal, residents of smaller and intermediary cities commonly buy 75% or more of their food, while rural residents purchase less than half of the food they consume. Food expenditures also usually comprise a larger percentage of total outlays for urban than rural households in the developing world. A survey of the 100 largest metropolitan areas of the world showed that food costs were greater than 50% of household expenditures in 23 cities [5].

#### 22.3.1.2   Urban Marketing Systems, Supermarkets, and Food Price Policies

Clearly, food prices and the ability to earn cash income are crucial to the achievement of food security in urban areas. The cost of food for urban consumers depends on a number of factors, including (1) the efficiency of the food production and marketing system, (2) the availability and access to food subsidies or other food programs, and (3) exchange rate policies.

Urban marketing systems, especially those that serve the poor, are frequently inefficient in terms of providing adequate quantities, good quality, or competitive prices [6, 7].

Wholesale markets that connect producers and traders with retailers are often run-down and obsolete, with ineffective and often obstructive management. Urban retailers, particularly in poor areas, are small and scattered. In the absence of well-integrated markets, food prices are higher than what they could be and are particularly susceptible to seasonal fluctuations [8].

More and more, however, supermarket chains are displacing traditional retailers in many countries of Africa, Asia, and Latin America [9]. These may present a way to overcome the structural inefficiencies of traditional markets with new store placements and large purchasing and distribution networks. In Argentina, Brazil, Chile, Colombia, Costa Rica. and Mexico, for example, supermarkets now account for 45% to 75% of food retailing. In the remainder of Latin America, largely lower income and less urbanized, the share is 20% to 40% [10]. The supermarket sector in East and Southeast Asia is following a similar pattern as that of Latin America and is growing at an even faster pace [11]. In South Africa, supermarkets have about 50% to 60% of food retail sales and have a significant presence in Kenya. Multinational supermarket chains have expanded, at least nominally, into most other countries of southern and eastern Africa as well [12]. The impact of this rapid burgeoning of supermarkets on the consumption patterns of the urban poor in developing countries is unclear. It may take some time for supermarket chains to establish a significant presence in slums or ghettos; and poor urban dwellers may have to continue to purchase food in small amounts on a daily basis (because of lack of cash) at a small corner store that may also offer credit.

Macroeconomic policies can also have a significant impact on the price of urban food. For many years, "cheap food" policies, including widespread subsidies, overvalued exchange rates, and trade restrictions, deliberately kept the price of urban food low, but structural adjustment programs have reversed many of these policies. As anticipated, the urban poor have not done well in the short run [13, 14]. Demery and Squire [13] reported that even in Ghana, a country that has shown substantial commitment to economic reform and where rural poverty has decreased, poverty in the capital city of Accra has increased.

### 22.3.1.3 URBAN EMPLOYMENT

The ability of the urban poor to obtain enough food for a healthy and active life depends primarily on their ability to earn income, yet most urban dwellers work in sectors such as petty trade or construction, for which wages are low and job tenure is insecure. In the 1990s, the informal sector represented 60% to 75% of urban employment in Guatemala, El Salvador, and Honduras but only one third in Costa Rica [15]. It generated 60% of female employment in many West Africa cities [16] and was one third of the urban labor force in Nigeria [17]. Once thought to be only a coping strategy or a dead end, numerous studies have now illustrated the dynamism and heterogeneity of the informal sector. Although workers tend to earn low wages, incomes of business owners in the informal sector can be 25% or more higher than those in the formal sector [18].

Formal sector jobs (government, private sector) are also important for the urban poor. Comparing data in metropolitan areas in four countries (Egypt, Ghana, Malawi, and Peru), Garrett in 2004 [19] showed that at least as many if not a larger percentage of paid urban dwellers work in the formal compared to the informal sector. In Egypt and Malawi, for example, more than 70% of jobs paid wages or salaries, and only approximately 20% were self-employed.

#### 22.3.1.4  URBAN FOOD PRODUCTION

Agriculture, forestry, and fishing are also important to the incomes of urban dwellers, especially outside large metropolitan areas [19]. Some households improve their access to food by growing food on their own plots inside or outside the city. Urban agriculture is practiced by as much as 40% of the population in African cities and up to 50% in Latin America [20, 21]. But, even where widely practiced it is rarely the primary source of food. For example, approximately 55% of poor urban households in periurban Dar es Salaam farm, but they only rely on production from their plots for 2 or 3 months each year [22]. Still, urban agriculture can be an important coping strategy for some households and may have an important impact on nutrition, especially among poorer households [23].

### 22.3.2  Stronger Formal Safety Nets and Weaker Informal Safety Nets?

An important question for this review is whether urban populations tend to have better access to formal safety nets than rural populations. Two factors that suggest that they do would be (1) the ease of reaching urban populations in contrast with the difficult logistics of reaching the rural poor and (2) the proximity and visibility of the urban poor to those in power. Our review of World Bank Poverty Assessments from sub-Saharan Africa, however, indicated only a very weak bias toward urban areas in terms of formal safety net coverage [24]. There were 88 programs in urban areas and 76 in rural areas. Removing the programs where we were not sure regarding location resulted in 36 programs in urban areas and 31 in rural areas.[4] It would be useful to conduct this exercise for other regions to verify whether these findings hold elsewhere.

The next question is whether urban areas have weaker informal safety nets. Again, there has been very little work on this issue. Informal safety nets take on a number of forms, such as food sharing, child fostering, loans, membership in groups, the receipt and provision of remittances, the sharing of housing, the lending of land and livestock, to name only a few. These links tend to be most extensive and strong within immediate and extended family because they rely heavily on social trust and reciprocity.

Informal safety nets are mechanisms that evolve to minimize exposure to adverse shocks and to maximize the ability to cope, ex post, with shock. They are underpinned by social capital. Social capital refers to [25] "features of social organization such as networks, norms, and social trust that facilitate coordination and cooperation for mutual benefit" (p. 67).

Are stocks of social capital lower in urban areas? This is an open question. Factors associated with urban life that might be expected to diminish social capital include (1) a looser definition of community and hence less identification with it; (2) a greater incidence of violence, which rapidly diminishes the trust necessary for nonfamily collective action; and (3) the nonproximity of family members from different generations, which reduces the ability to undertake activities that do not rely on immediate reciprocity. On the other hand, information flows are better, so opportunities for col-

---

[4]Obviously, not all programs are the same size and have the same coverage. Unfortunately, expenditure figures were unavailable for most of the programs; in any case, it was not possible to verify the accuracy of these report figures.

lective action for mutual benefit will be greater. Also, nongovernmental organizations (NGOs) and community-based organizations are often active in urban areas and can serve as important catalysts for improved social cooperation. It may also be the case that access to formal safety nets diminishes the demand for social capital formation and hence the use of informal safety nets. Haddad and Zeller [26] summarized several studies that indicated that formal safety nets have partially crowded out private informal safety nets.

### 22.3.3  The Increased Labor Force Participation of Women and Its Consequences for Child Care

#### 22.3.3.1  WOMEN'S WORK PATTERNS AND CHILD CARE USE IN URBAN AND RURAL AREAS

It is thought that urban living generally implies greater female labor force participation and a more distinct separation of dwelling location and work location for both men and women. Other stylized facts suggest that the higher proportion of female-headed households and the smaller household sizes in urban areas reduce the household's supply of alternate caregivers and result in harsher tradeoffs for women between time spent in income generation (their productive role) and time spent in their reproductive, maternal, and caring roles. Employment conditions are often not flexible enough to reduce the sharpness of these tradeoffs.

We analyzed data from the Demographic Health Surveys (DHSs) from 11 countries[5] (2 in Asia, 4 in Africa, and 5 in Latin America) to verify some of these facts [24]. We compared women's patterns of employment and use of child care alternatives between rural and urban areas and looked at differences in the percentage of women-headed households. The hypothesis that urban areas host greater percentages of women-headed households was confirmed for Latin American and for two of four African countries but not for Asia. In Bangladesh and Pakistan, women-headed households represented only about 8% and 6% of households, respectively, and there are no urban/rural differences. Our second hypothesis that more women worked in urban areas, particularly away from home, was also confirmed only for Latin America (with the exception of Peru). In Asia and Africa, the percentage of women working was consistently greater in rural areas, and even the percentage of rural women working away from home was higher than that of urban women in most of the African and Asian countries studied.

In terms of child care arrangements, a smaller percentage of urban mothers took their child to work with them, probably because they tend to work in the streets, in markets, or in factories rather than in agriculture like rural women do [24]. In Latin America, a greater percentage of urban mothers used relatives as alternative child caregivers compared to rural dwellers, but no consistent pattern was found in Asia and Africa. Hired help and institutional care were consistently higher in urban areas in all three regions, although institutional care use was almost nonexistent in Asia and very

---

[5] The countries and year of survey included in this analysis were as follows: for Asia: Bangladesh 1993 and Pakistan 1991; for Africa: Ghana 1993, Tanzania 1991/1992, Senegal 1992/1993, Zambia 1992; and for Latin America: Brazil 1996, Dominican Republic 1991, Peru 1992, Colombia 1995, and Guatemala 1995.

uncommon in three of the four African countries studied. It is likely that such low reported use of institutional care is related to lack of availability of these services in the countries studied.

In sum, the DHS data indicate that more than half of the women in both urban and rural areas of Africa and Latin America are involved in income-generating activities. The greater proportion of women working outside the home in urban areas is confirmed only for Latin American countries. In Africa, more rural women work outside the home than urban women in three of the four countries studied. The main difference between rural and urban areas is in the use of hired help and institutional care, both of which are consistently higher in urban areas. Urban mothers are also less likely than rural mothers to take their child along when they go to work.

A comparative study of Accra (Ghana) and Guatemala City (Guatemala) indicated that, in both sites, women's employment and child care choices are highly influenced by the age of their youngest child [27]. Mothers with children under 3 years of age are less likely to be working, and if they do work, they are less likely to use formal child care compared to mothers with older children. In Guatemala City, another important determinant of women's decision to work is the presence of an adult woman (a potential alternative child caregiver) in the household. In Ghana, where most urban women work in the informal sector, those who have to resume work for economic reasons when their infant is still young usually take the infant along to their workplace [28]. Depending on the work environment, this may or may not be positive for the child, but at least it is likely to help preserve breast-feeding and caregiving, which should confer important nutritional and developmental benefits to the child.

These findings confirm that women do adapt their working patterns to their specific family circumstances, and that the well-being of their children is the overriding force behind their decisions to work and to use child care alternatives. These "adaptive strategies" by which mothers stop working, work fewer hours, or even take their infant to work if they have to work may be successful in protecting their infant. They may, however, seriously jeopardize the mothers' ability to generate income and to protect their household's livelihood and food security, especially if they are the sole income earner.

### 22.3.3.2 IMPACT OF MATERNAL WORK ON CHILD CARE PRACTICES

The greatest threat of maternal employment to child caring is its potential negative impact on breast-feeding practices. It is generally believed that urban mothers are less likely to initiate breast-feeding and more likely to wean earlier if they do breast-feed. Our previous analysis of DHS data from 35 countries, however, did not indicate such clear patterns [29]. We found that, although the percentage of children ever breast-fed tends to be lower in urban areas, the pattern is not fully consistent, and differences are generally of small magnitude. Urban mothers were found to initiate breast-feeding at a surprisingly high rate (greater than 90%). The median duration of breast-feeding, on the other hand, was consistently shorter in urban areas, sometimes 4–6 months shorter. Exclusive and full breast-feeding duration was much shorter than the recommended 4–6 months everywhere, but there were no urban/rural differences. Earlier studies had also shown that maternal employment was not a main determinant of breast milk substitute use in developing countries [30] or systematically related to shorter breast-feeding duration [31].

Globally, there is also little evidence that maternal employment has a negative impact on other child feeding and care practices such as complementary feeding, preventive and curative health-seeking behaviors, and psychosocial care or on children's health and nutritional status [32–34]. Our study in Accra, Ghana, documented that child feeding, hygiene, or health-seeking behaviors were not affected by maternal employment [28]. In this context, the key factor consistently associated with better caring practices was maternal schooling, which was not related to employment status.

Additional, indirect evidence that women's employment in urban areas may not necessarily have a negative impact on child care practices again comes from global urban/rural comparisons. We showed, using a set of 36 recent DHS data sets, that complementary feeding practices (timing and frequency of feeding complementary foods) and health-seeking behaviors are substantially better in urban compared to rural areas [35]. This is true even in countries where a large proportion of women are engaged in income-generating activities, often away from home.

Overall, mothers seem tremendously efficient at combining their income-generating activities and their child care responsibilities and at buffering the potentially negative impacts of their employment patterns on their children's well-being. The question is, though, at what cost—for themselves and for their household food and livelihood security? This question remains largely unanswered because whether the food security situation of poor working women is alleviated or aggravated by their participation in the labor force largely depends on the set of resources and constraints they face.

## 22.3.4   Lifestyle Changes

### 22.3.4.1   DIETARY PATTERNS

The nutrition transition,[6] which is characterized by changes from diets rich in complex carbohydrates and fiber (mainly from food staples) to more varied diets with higher proportions of saturated fat, refined sugars, and meat products as populations move from rural to urban areas, is well documented both globally and in a number of individual countries [37–41] (see also Chapter 20). The nutrition transition, however, is not simply an urban phenomenon; it is strongly associated with rapid economic growth and positive changes in household income [42, 43].

A classic study using data from 85 countries showed a positive linear relationship between gross national product (GNP) per capita and energy intake from refined sugars and from vegetable and animal fats [44]. Whereas the poorer nations derived approximately 5% of their energy from animal fat in 1962, richer countries reached 38%. A more recent similar analysis using data from 133 countries in 1990 gave an interesting twist to these findings. Drewnowski and Popkin [45] showed that the income–fat relationship has changed over time, and that total fat consumption is less strongly associated with GNP than before. Overall, richer countries have decreased their total fat intake, whereas poorer countries are now consuming diets much higher in fat than three decades ago. An independent effect of urbanization on changes in diet structure was also apparent in these data, as well as a significant interaction between GNP and urbanization, which

---

[6] Popkin [36] defined the *nutrition transition* as the shifts in dietary patterns and lifestyle that have resulted from urbanization and rapid economic development.

indicated a greater effect of urbanization on refined sugars and total fat consumption among lower-income countries compared to richer nations. These results suggest that the accelerated rates of urbanization currently found in many developing countries are likely to generate rapid and most likely negative shifts in dietary patterns over the next few years.

There are various reasons why urban diets tend to be different (and usually more diverse) than rural diets, namely, higher income, changing values and norms, and cultural diversity. Studies have also shown that the greater consumption of processed and prepared foods in urban areas is largely driven by the opportunity cost of women's time [46–48]. Bouis and Huang [49], in an analysis of data from China and Taiwan, attributed about 20% of the increases in consumption of meat, fish, and dairy products to the nonincome or structural factors associated with moving from a rural to an urban residence. Traditional staples are also often more expensive in urban areas than in rural areas, while the opposite is true for processed foods [50], which means that it is relatively less expensive to shift away from traditional staples to processed foods in urban areas.

### 22.3.4.2 ACTIVITY PATTERNS

Parallel to these changes in diet, shifts in activity patterns as populations migrate from rural to urban areas also occur. Urbanization is accompanied by trends toward less physically demanding occupations on a worldwide basis, particularly in lower-income countries [51]. This results from both an increase in the less physically demanding types of employment such as manufacturing and services and a decrease in the more labor-intensive agricultural employment as well as new technologies that have tended to reduce the physical effort involved.

The increased use of public and private transportation, of technology and paid help for domestic activities, and the shift to more passive leisure activities such as television and computer games also contribute to reductions in activity levels and affect adults and children alike [52].

### 22.3.4.3 HEALTH IMPLICATIONS

The health implications of the changes in dietary and activity patterns associated with urbanization are of much concern. Greater dietary diversity may have a positive impact on micronutrient status and malnutrition, but the higher fat and refined sugar content of diets, combined with the more sedentary lifestyle, increase the risks of obesity, cardiovascular diseases, certain forms of cancers, and other chronic diseases. Increased rates of smoking, stress, substance abuse, and the overall environmental contamination found in large cities further exacerbate these risks.

Obesity, childhood obesity in particular, has increased so rapidly worldwide in the last few decades that it has been declared a public health problem in many countries and even an epidemic in some [51, 53, 54]. The coexistence of obesity and stunting in young children as well as the coexistence of obese parents and malnourished children is also surprisingly common in many large urban areas of the developing world [42, 55, 56]. Malnutrition during critical periods of gestation and early infancy, followed by the changes in dietary patterns related to urbanization is also thought to increase the risks of chronic diseases at adulthood [57, 58].

The rapid increase in obesity worldwide and in urban areas in particular is rapidly becoming a serious public health concern even for low- and middle-income countries. Considering the unequivocal link between obesity and a large number of chronic disease risks, the obesity epidemic has to be taken seriously [54].

### 22.3.5 Increased Availability of Services, But Questionable Access by Poor Households

Health, education services, potable water, sanitation facilities, and garbage disposal are usually more available in urban rather than rural areas [59], but the rapid population growth experienced by a large number of cities in the developing world has caused a breakdown in the provision of urban services. Governments are unable to respond to these population pressures, and statistics show that one in six people in the world lack access to safe drinking water [60]. In many countries of the developing world, poor urban dwellers have to buy water at an extravagant cost [61, 62]. Poor urban dwellers are also much less likely to have access to adequate sanitation and garbage collection facilities, even in cities where wealthier households all have private bathrooms and regular garbage pickup.

The availability and use of health services are also greater in urban areas. Our review of DHS data from 35 countries confirmed that, overall, urban dwellers are more likely to use health services both for curative purposes—when children have acute respiratory infections, fever, or diarrhea—and for preventive services such as immunization [29, 62].

Simple urban/rural comparisons have limitations, however, because they mask the enormous differentials found within an area. Pockets of undercovered population are known to exist in poor shanty towns, and these populations are also those that experience the greatest risks of infectious diseases [59]. Lower education levels and greater time constraints, combined with limited knowledge and awareness of the existence and potential benefits of these services, make the urban poor less likely to use the facilities even if they are available. In addition, the lack of supplies, the unfriendly attitude of some health workers, the unsanitary conditions, and the overcrowding of the facilities as well as their inconvenient open hours may discourage poor families from using them.

### 22.3.6 Environmental Contamination

The lack of access to basic water, sanitation, drainage, and solid waste disposal services makes it almost impossible for poor urban dwellers to prevent contamination of water and food, maintain adequate levels of hygiene, or control insect vectors of disease (such as malaria). In addition, they are exposed to excessive air pollution (both outdoor and indoor). This results in high rates of infectious diseases among both adults and young children in these areas.

#### 22.3.6.1 AIR POLLUTION

Worldwide, more than 1.1 billion people live in cities with levels of air contamination in excess of the standards established by the WHO [59]. This affects both the poor and the rich alike. Poor urban dwellers, however, are likely to be more exposed to two additional sources of air pollution: indoor air pollution from poorly functioning cooking stoves and contaminants from industrial sites [59]. The latter is due to the fact that urban squatters are often established close to industries that create pollution, in sectors of the city that wealthier groups tend to avoid, and poor urban dwellers are also more likely to work in these industries and to be exposed directly to toxic chemicals.

Air pollution (both indoor and outdoor) is associated with increased acute respiratory infections, asthma, and mortality from pneumonia in children as well as chronic lung diseases and cancers in adults [63]. In Mexico City, air pollution is estimated to cause 12,500 extra deaths and 11.2 million lost workdays per year due to respiratory illnesses [64]. Exposure to lead is also thought to be responsible for the reduced intellectual performance of 140,000 children, and up to 29% of all children living in Mexico City had unhealthy blood lead levels [63].

### 22.3.6.2 WATER AND FOOD CONTAMINATION

Waterborne diarrheal diseases are known to be highly prevalent in urban areas, mainly as a result of contaminated water and food, crowding, limited access to water, and poor food and household hygiene [63]. Prevalence of diarrhea among young children in urban areas is often as high as in rural areas. Our review of DHS data from 35 countries (total of 42 data sets) showed higher prevalences of diarrhea in urban compared to rural areas in up to one third of the data sets reviewed [29]. Further analyses of 11 data sets also revealed that differences between low and high socioeconomic status (SES) quintiles within urban areas were consistently larger than differences between low and high SES groups in rural areas [64]. The prevalence of diarrhea among the urban low SES group was often greater than among the rural low SES group (in 7 of the 11 countries studied). Thus, overall diarrhea prevalence rates in urban areas rival those found in rural areas, and poor urban dwellers are often worse off than the rural poor in that regard.

Contamination of water and food, particularly of street foods, is probably largely responsible for a significant proportion of gastrointestinal infections in urban areas.

## 22.3.7 Legal Rights

How do legal rights in the areas of employment, land, residence, and water use vary between rural and urban areas? While employment rights are likely to be well defined in the urban formal sector, the extent of their enforcement is unclear. In addition, the formality and strength of land and water user rights in rural areas will vary by region, by time, and by the gender of potential owner or user [68]. Newcomers to urban areas, if not linked to well-established urban families, may find themselves literally on the periphery of the city and relying on a shaky or nonexistent set of rights in the above domains. These underdeveloped rights will likely have costly effects. We provide three examples for which legal and regulatory changes may be needed to promote food and nutrition security in urban areas: urban agriculture, street foods, and land and housing tenure.

### 22.3.7.1 URBAN AGRICULTURE

In many cities, agriculture is illegal. Frequently, urban farmers do not own the land but use public space or use vacant lots of private owners, with or without their permission. With low-tenure security and questionable legality, the farmer is not motivated either to be efficient or to care for the land. These constraints are often exacerbated by the fact that in many cities it is mostly women who are involved in urban agriculture. Legal and cultural biases against women owning or even leasing land make their attempts at urban farming even more difficult.

The uncertain legal status of urban agriculture is such that official projects or programs aimed at improving urban agriculture have been rare. In combination with a weak legal framework, the lack of awareness and of government recognition means planners often do not think about how to provide water and drainage infrastructure to handle urban farming, and governments make little provision for research and extension of urban farming techniques [21].

Success with urban agriculture does exist, however. For decades, city authorities in Lusaka, Zambia, enforced laws against crop production in the city as a health hazard. Faced with economic decline in the 1970s, however, the Lusaka city council stopped enforcing the antiurban agriculture laws. Government stores even made subsidized seeds for fruits and vegetables available. In 1977, 43% of Chawama, one of the largest slums in Lusaka, had home gardens. A decade later, 40% of households still had home plots [68]. With more knowledge of successful experiences with urban agriculture, city administrators and planners can work to remove existing political, administrative, and legal hurdles for urban agriculture.

### 22.3.7.2 INFORMAL MARKETING ACTIVITIES SUCH AS STREET FOODS

Street food vendors are ubiquitous in the developing world. Selling street foods represents an important informal sector activity. Despite wanting to stimulate microenterprises, the response of many governments is to sweep mobile sellers off the street into malls or back alleys, prohibit selling altogether, or subject selling to strict regulation. Vendors stay mobile because they cannot afford the start-up capital to establish themselves in a permanent market where they are subject to inspection and have to pay fees and taxes. Alternatively, the supply of rights or permits to permanent spaces may be severely restricted [48].

Strict regulation of mobile vendors may be detrimental. The Food and Agricultural Organization (FAO) and WHO warn that if vendors are banned only for the sake of traffic requirements or modernization plans, mobile street food vendors would simply go "underground." It would become much more difficult to reach vendors through official channels to introduce safety measures or provide key environmental infrastructures and services to reduce health hazards [48].

### 22.3.7.3 INSECURITY OF TENURE AND DEVELOPMENT ACTIVITY

The NGO and research communities are becoming more aware of the need to understand the determinants of the placement of various development interventions and projects. An improved understanding can (1) improve estimates of project impact [65], (2) identify mismatches between community need and project location, and (c) provide some insight into the political and institutional factors that drive the development process. Work undertaken by the International Food Policy Research Institute (IFPRI) and CARE indicates that one of the key determinants of NGO intervention and civic engagement may be the security of tenure of individuals in the community [67].

## 22.4 IMPLICATIONS FOR POLICY AND RESEARCH

Policy makers need to address the above issues to promote the welfare of their urban citizens and the stability of government. They need to find policy and program instruments that can (1) reduce the cost of food to urban consumers and create income-generating opportunities for them' (2) provide low-cost, efficient safety nets for those who cannot help themselves and stimulate the generation of social capital; (3) ease the tradeoffs for mothers by providing acceptable and affordable child care substitutes and ensuring the safety of prepared and processed foods sold in the streets; (4) increase resources to primary health care and nutrition in an attempt to reduce tertiary health expenditures; (5) improve water and sanitation services, which are so important to households and to food vendors; (6) reduce the general level of contamination; and (7) redefine, respect, and enforce property rights that balance the needs of consumers and producers.

Good information and analysis will shorten the process of trial and error in the design of effective policies and interventions. However, the relatively slow awakening of the policy research community to urban poverty, food insecurity, and malnutrition has left many questions unanswered.

First and most basic, we need to answer the question: What is the state of urban poverty, food security, and undernutrition? What are the absolute numbers of the poor and malnourished in urban and rural areas for countries that do not have currently available data? What are the trends over time for other countries? Will the share of poverty and undernutrition that is urban continue to increase for those countries where this pattern is already seen? To answer these questions, we need to collect more data on urban areas, and we need to do a better job in addressing some of the difficulties faced in getting accurate numbers on urban poverty and undernutrition.

Second, we need to explore the reasons for these levels and trends. Why, for example, does the share of poverty in urban areas appear to be *decreasing* in some countries? What are the main determinants of current levels and trends in urban poverty and undernutrition? What are the main constraints to urban income and nutrition generation, and how do they differ by country, city size,[7] the competence of local governance, the length of residence, the strength of property rights, the maturity of the community, the number of income sources, education levels, health status, and land access? This chapter discusses some of the challenges to income generation, food security, and nutrition that are probably exacerbated in an urban area. Many questions are raised for which there are no ready answers, but as the problems of urban poverty and undernutrition increase, so will the clamor for answers.

Third, where are the models of successful interventions in the policy and program arena? De Haan [68] noted that, compared to rural areas, there are fewer examples of successful public policies in urban environments. Whether there truly are fewer examples or whether they have simply not been recorded, best practices in local and national government need to be documented and analyzed. Examples of successful programs and policies that we can learn from are hard to find, and there have been few systematic attempts to draw out commonalities.[8]

Last but not least, a whole range of questions and problems remain unanswered and unsolved in relation to our current methods of inquiry in urban areas. First, urban populations

---

[7] This is as suggested by Brockerhoff and Brennan [69].

[8] For a selected set of examples of successful interventions, see Ruel, Haddad, and Garrett [24].

are much more spatially mobile than rural populations. This discourages local authorities from drawing up listings of households, and it makes it difficult to rely on existing listings for survey sampling. The larger number of homeless people in urban areas also makes them susceptible to underrepresentation in any survey. This mobility makes it difficult to track households and individuals over time, which is important if we want to understand the dynamics of poverty and undernutrition. The act of enumerating a questionnaire is much more complex in an environment where there is a dislocation of work and home. Mobility also makes it more difficult to control for community-level effects on household behavior and indeed even to define what we mean by a community. Mobility also affects the ease of defining a household unit. The presence of a large proportion of nonfamily household members such as tenants and seasonal residents may be more important for urban households and adds to the complexity of household definition.

Second, time is scarcer in an urban setting, because households are more likely to engage in work far away from home which makes long interviews difficult to administer. Security is also often an issue for field-workers, and nighttime interviewing, which would be the only option for finding people at home, is often not possible. Finally, in the area of income generation, the relative anonymity of the urban center is likely to make illegal income generation more widespread, and this type of income-generating activity is notoriously difficult to capture in a questionnaire. Other censured information includes that on violence and substance abuse.

## 22.5  CONCLUSIONS

The economic reforms since the 1980's have probably reduced urban bias and may have even removed it in some countries. The legacy of urban bias remains, however, and there is a greater need than ever to stimulate agricultural intensification, particularly in the poorer countries of sub-Saharan Africa and South Asia [70].

Nevertheless, as we have shown, the best available data indicate that urban poverty and undernutrition are increasing and are doing so at a faster rate than rural poverty and undernutrition. We view this closing of the rural–urban gap as a sufficient basis to call for more research on urban poverty, food, and nutrition issues; in this chapter, we indicated the areas in which we think more work is needed.

It is important to remember that there is still a poverty and undernutrition gap, and in the least-urbanized countries it is wide. Hence, it would be premature to argue for even a small reallocation of government and NGO development resources from rural to urban areas. Can those who influence development policy and programs avoid the temptation to spend more money on urban problems and instead revisit how the existing envelope of urban resources is allocated? Given political realities, this temptation will be difficult to resist, and that is why the documentation of success stories of urban governance will be so important. But, is it even reasonable to ask policy makers to respond to increased data and analysis on urban problems without drawing development resources away from rural areas? This is a question that is impossible to answer at this stage. It is our strong opinion that much more can be done with existing resources, but this, like all the other questions posed in this chapter, is a researchable issue and one that should challenge policy researchers and policy makers over the next generation.

*Acknowledgments* Many of the ideas in this chapter were developed in the context of a wider IFPRI multicountry research program on Urban Challenges to Food and Nutrition Security. In particular, we would like to thank Daniel Maxwell, Saul Morris, Carol Levin, Patrice Engle, Arne Oshaug, and Bonnie McClafferty for their insights on the issues we present and Alison Slack of IFPRI and Purnima Menon of Cornell University for their invaluable research assistance.

## REFERENCES

1. United Nations. World urbanization prospects: the 2003 revision. New York: Department of Economic and Social Affairs, Population Division, United Nations, 2004.
2. World Health Organization, Department of Nutrition for Health Development. WHO data base on child growth and malnutrition. Available at: http://www.who.int/nutgrowthdb/.
3. Haddad L, Ruel MT, Garrett JL. Are urban poverty and undernutrition growing? World Dev 1999;27:1891–1904.
4. Ruel MT, Garrett JL. Features of urban food and nutrition security and considerations for successful urban programming. eJADE 2004;1:242–271.
5. Population Crisis Committee. Cities: life in the world's 100 largest metropolitan areas. Washington, DC: Population Crisis Committee, 1990.
6. Aragrande M, Argenti O. Studying food supply and distribution systems to cities in developing countries and countries in transition. Methodological and operational guide. Rome: Food and Agriculture Organization of the United Nations, 2001.
7. Argenti O. Feeding the cities: food supply and distribution. Brief 5. In: Achieving urban food and nutrition security in the developing world, 2020 Vision Focus 3 briefs. Garrett J, Ruel M, eds. Washington, DC: International Food Policy Research Institute, 2000.
8. Food and Agriculture Organization of the United Nations. Food supply and distribution to cities. Rome: Food and Agricultural Organization, 1997.
9. Reardon T, Timmer P, Barrett C, Berdegué J. The rise of supermarkets in Africa, Asia, and Latin America. Am J Agr Econ 2003;85:1140–1146.
10. Reardon T, Berdegué J. The rapid rise of supermarkets in Latin America: challenges and opportunities for development. Dev Policy Rev 2002;20:371–388.
11. Reardon T, Timmer P, Berdegué J. The rapid rise of supermarkets in developing countries: induced organizational, institutional, and technological change in Agrifood systems. eJADE 2004;1:168–183.
12. Weatherspoon D, Reardon T. The rise of supermarkets in Africa: implications for agrifood systems and the rural poor. Dev Policy Rev 2003;21:333–355.
13. Demery L, Squire L. Macroeconomic adjustment and poverty in Africa: an emerging picture. World Bank Res Obser 1996;11(1):39–59.
14. Sahn D, Dorosh P, Younger S. Structural adjustment reconsidered. Cambridge, UK: Cambridge University Press, 1997.
15. Funkhouser E. The urban informal sector in Central America: household survey evidence. World Dev 1996;24:1737–1751.
16. Meagher K. Crisis, informalization and the urban informal sector in sub-Saharan Africa. Dev Change 1995;26:259–284.
17. Simon PB. Informal responses to crises of urban employment: an investigation into the structure and relevance of small-scale informal retailing in Kaduna, Nigeria. Reg Stud 1998;32:547–557.
18. Portes A, Blitzer S, Curtis J. The urban informal sector in Uruguay: its internal structure, characteristics and effects. World Dev 1986;14:727–741.
19. Garrett J. Living life: overlooked aspects of urban employment. Washington, DC: International Food Policy Research Institute, 2004. Food Consumption and Nutrition Division Discussion Paper 171.
20. Mougeot L. Overview—urban food self-reliance: significance and prospects. IDRC Rep 1993;21(3):2–5.
21. United Nations Development Programme. Urban agriculture: food, jobs and sustainable cities. New York: United Nations Development Programme, 1996.
22. CARE/Tanzania. Dar es Salaam urban livelihood security assessment. Summary report. June 1998. Dar es Salaam, Tanzania: CARE/Tanzania, 1998.

23. Maxwell D, Levin C, Csete J. Does urban agriculture help prevent malnutrition? Evidence from Kampala. Washington, DC: International Food Policy Research Institute, 1998. Food Consumption and Nutrition Division Discussion Paper 45.

24. Ruel MT, Haddad L, Garrett J. Some urban facts of life: implications for research and policy. World Dev 1999;11:1917–1938.

25. Putnam R. Bowling alone: America's declining social capital. J Democr 1995;6(1):65–78.

26. Haddad L, Zeller M. How can safety nets do more with less? General issues with some evidence from southern Africa. Dev Southern Africa 1997;14(2):125–153.

27. Quisumbing AR, Hallman K, Ruel MT. Maquiladoras and market mamas: Women's work and childcare in Guatemala City and Accra. Washington, DC: International Food Policy Research Institute, 2003. Food Consumption and Nutrition Division Discussion Paper 153.

28. Armar-Klemesu M, Ruel M, Maxwell D, Levin C, Morris S. Poor maternal schooling is the main constraint to good child care practices in Accra. J Nutr 2000;130:1597–1607.

29. Ruel MT, Garrett JL, Morris SS, Maxwell D, Oshaug A, Engle P, Menon P, Slack A, Haddad L. Urban challenges to nutrition security: a review of food security, health and care in the cities. Washington, DC: International Food Policy Research Institute, 1998. Food Consumption and Nutrition Division Discussion Paper 51.

30. Hight-Laukaran V, Rutstein SO, Peterson AE, Labbok MH. The use of breast milk substitutes in developing countries: the impact of women's employment. Am J Public Health 1996;86:1235–1240.

31. Winikoff B, Castle MA, Hight-Laukaran V. Feeding infants in four societies. Contributions in family studies no. 14. New York: Greenwood Press, 1988.

32. Engle PL, Menon P, Garrett J, Slack A. Urbanization and caregiving: a framework for analysis and examples from Southern and Eastern Africa. Environ Urban 1997;9(2):253–270.

33. Blau DM, Guilkey DK, Popkin BM. Infant health and the labor supply of mothers. J Human Resour 1997;31:90–139.

34. Glick P, Sahn DE. Maternal labour supply and child nutrition in West Africa. Oxford B Econ Stat 1998;60(3):325–355.

35. Smith LS, Ruel MT, Ndiaye A. Why is child malnutrition lower in urban than in rural areas? Evidence from 36 developing countries. World Dev 2005;33(8):1285–1305.

36. Popkin BM. The nutrition transition in low-income countries: an emerging crisis. Nutr Rev (1994);52(9):285–298.

37. Bertazzi Levy-Costa R, Sichieri R, dos Santos Pontes N, Monteiro CA. Household food availability in Brazil: distribution and trends (1974–2003). Rev Saúde Publica 2005;39:1–10.

38. Mendez MA, Popkin BM. Globalization, urbanization and nutritional change in the developing world. eJADE 2004;1:220–241.

39. Mendez MA, Monteiro CA, Popkin BM. Overweight exceeds underweight among women in most developing countries. J Nutr 2005;81:714–721.

40. Du S, Mroz TA, Zhai F, Popkin BM. Rapid income growth adversely affects diet quality in China—particularly for the poor! Soc Sci Med 2004;59:1505–1515.

41. Gross R. Beyond food and nutrition: how can cities be made healthy? Asia Pacific J Clin Nutr 2002;11(suppl):S763–S766.

42. Garrett J, Ruel MT. Stunted child-overweight mother pairs: an emerging policy concern. Food Nutr Bull 2005;26(2):209–221.

43. Monteiro CA, Moura EC, Conde WL, Popkin BM. Socioeconomic status and obesity in adult populations of developing countries: a review. WHO Bull 2004;82:940–946.

44. Périssé J, Sizaret F, François P. The effect of income and the structure of the diet. FAO Nutr Newsl 1969;7:1–9.

45. Drewnowski A, Popkin BM. Dietary fats and the nutrition transition: new trends in the global diet. Nutr Rev 1997;55(2):31–43.

46. Senauer B, Sahn D, Alderman H. The effect of the value of time on food consumption patterns in developing countries: from Sri Lanka. Am J Agr Econ 1986;68(4):920–927.

47. Atkinson SJ. Food for the cities: urban nutrition policy in developing countries. Urban Health Program, Health Policy Unit. London: Department of Public Health and Policy, School of Hygiene and Tropical Medicine, 1992.

48. Tinker I. Street foods: urban food and employment in developing countries. New York: Oxford University Press, 1997.

49. Bouis H, Huang J. Structural changes in the demand for food in Asia. Washington, DC: International Food Policy Research Institute, 1996. Food, Agriculture, and the Environment Discussion Paper 11. 2020 Vision.

50. Musgrove P. Basic food consumption in north-east Brazil: effects of income, price, and family size in metropolitan and rural areas. Food Nutr Bull 1988;10(1):29–37.

51. Popkin BM, Doak CM. The obesity epidemic is a worldwide phenomenon. Nutr Rev 1998;56(4): 106–114.

52. Caballero B, Rubinstein S. Environmental factors affecting nutritional status in urban areas of developing countries. Arch Latinoam Nutr 1997;47(2 suppl):3–8.

53. World Health Organization. Obesity. Preventing and managing the global epidemic. Geneva: World Health Organization, 1998.

54. Caballero B. Symposia: obesity in developing countries: biological and ecological factors. J Nutr 2001;131(3):866s–899s.

55. Popkin BM, Richards MK, Monteiro CA. Stunting is associated with overweight in children in four nations that are undergoing the nutrition transition. J Nutr 1996;126(12):3009–3016.

56. Doak CM, Adair LS, Bentley M, Monteiro C, Popkin BM. The dual burden household and the nutrition transition paradox. Int J Obes 2005;29:129–136.

57. Barker DJ. Fetal and infant origins of adult disease. Br Med J 1889;301:1111.

58. Barker DJ. Mothers, babies, and disease in later life. London: British Medical Journal Publishing Group, 1994.

59. World Resources Institute, United Nations Environmental Programme, United Nations Development Programme, World Bank. World resources 1996–97. A guide to the global environment. The urban environment. New York: Oxford University Press, 1996.

60. Third World Academy of Sciences. Safe drinking water. The need, the problem, solutions and action plan. Trieste, Italy: Third World Academy of Sciences, 2002.

61. Briscoe J. When the cup is half full: improving water and sanitation services in the developing world. Environment (1993);35(4):7–37.

62. Atkinson SJ, Cheyne J. Immunization in urban areas: issues and strategies. WHO Bull 1994;72:183–194.

63. Smith KR, Liu Y. Indoor air pollution in developing countries. In: Epidemiology of lung cancer. Samet JM, ed. New York: Dekker, 1994:154–163.

64. Bartone C, Bernstein J, Leitmann J, Eigen J. Toward environmental strategies for cities: policy considerations for urban environmental management in developing countries. Washington, DC: World Bank, 1994. Urban Management Programme Policy Paper No. 18.

65. Bradley D, Stephens C, Harpham T, Cairncross S. A review of environmental health impacts in developing country cities. Washington, DC: World Bank, 1992.

66. Menon P, Ruel MT, Morris SS. Socio-economic differentials in child stunting are consistently larger in urban than in rural areas. Food Nutr Bull 2000;21:282–289.

67. Meinzen-Dick R, Brown LR, Feldstein HS, Quisumbing AR. Gender, property rights, and natural resources. Washington, DC: International Food Policy Research Institute, 1997. Food Consumption and Nutrition Division Discussion Paper 29.

68. Pitt M, Rosenzweig M, Gibbons D. The determinants and consequences of the placement of government programs in Indonesia. In: Public spending and the poor: theory and evidence. De Walle D., Nead K, eds. Baltimore, MD: Johns Hopkins University Press for the World Bank, 1995.

69. CARE/Bangladesh. Report—urban livelihood security assessment in Bangladesh. February 1998. Dhaka, Bangladesh: CARE/Bangladesh, 1998.

70. de Haan A. Urban poverty and its alleviation. IDS Bull 1997;28(2):1–8.

71. Brockerhoff M, Brennan E. The poverty of cities in the developing world. New York: Policy Research Division, the Population Council, 1997. Working Paper 96.

72. Pinstrup-Andersen P, Pandya-Lorch R, Rosegrant M. The world food situation: recent developments, emerging issues and long term prospects. Food policy report. Washington, DC: International Food Policy Research Institute, 1997.

# 23 Impact of Parental Tobacco Use on Child Malnutrition and Survival

## Cora M. Best and Richard D. Semba

## 23.1 INTRODUCTION

Cigarette smoking causes 5 million deaths per year worldwide, and it is estimated that the annual death toll from smoking will climb to 10 million deaths by 2030, with 7 million deaths in developing countries [1, 2]. Cigarette smoke damages the lower-respiratory tract [3], increases oxidative stress, and increases the risk of bronchitis, chronic obstructive lung disease, cancer, and death [1–3]. Tobacco companies have gradually shifted their market from high-income to low-income countries, where many people are poorly informed about the health risks of tobacco use and antismoking policy is relatively weak [2]. Although much research has been focused on the relationship between smoking and adverse outcomes such as cancer, respiratory illnesses, and cardiovascular disease, the problem of smoking and its relation to malnutrition, child survival, and poverty have not been well characterized [2].

Tobacco use may have adverse consequences for nutrition, health, and household budgets, especially among families living in poverty in developing countries. Tobacco control has been relatively neglected as an issue related to child malnutrition. New evidence is emerging that tobacco use contributes to impoverishment and child malnutrition. Tobacco control should be considered a mainstream issue that is integrated with other child health strategies in developing countries. The World Health Organization (WHO) Framework Convention on Tobacco Control (FCTC) is a major public health effort to control tobacco globally and consists of specific provisions to reduce the use of tobacco in countries that become party to the FCTC. Worldwide, some countries in Southeast Asia are showing the greatest impact of parental tobacco use on the exacerbation of child malnutrition. Given the historical trends in developing countries of poor tobacco control combined with strong tobacco marketing, unless public health efforts are implemented now, much of sub-Saharan Africa will likely follow the pattern of increasing tobacco use, impoverishment, malnutrition, and increased child mortality.

From: *Nutrition and Health: Nutrition and Health in Developing Countries, Second Edition*
Edited by: R. D. Semba & M. W. Bloem © Humana Press, Totowa, NJ

## 23.2   HISTORICAL BACKGROUND

In 1981, the physician and epidemiologist Nicholas Cohen postulated in *The Lancet* that an important health risk of smoking was the exacerbation of malnutrition and decrease in survival among young children in poor households in Bangladesh [4]. He decried the rise of cigarette consumption in Bangladesh and acknowledged that although respiratory disease and cancer were the best-recognized direct health consequences of smoking, these effects probably extended to child malnutrition and child survival. Cohen suggested that smoking only five cigarettes per day in a poor household in Bangladesh would lead to a monthly dietary deficit of 8,000 calories [4]. He also noted:

> *Food shortages are unequally distributed everywhere—within families as well as over a country. Within the Bangladeshi family, the dominance of the adult male in terms of controlling income, decision making, and therefore priority for food allocation, means that the burden of decreased food intake will be borne, as far as possible, by others. … The existence of young children is already marginal. Quantitative reductions in food intake of the order estimated could thus tip the balance if their impact was, as seems most probable, largely on children under 5 years. … should these estimations be anywhere near correct, the nutrition-mediated effects of smoking, in terms of chronic undernutrition as well as survival, are likely to be far more important than the direct consequences of smoking on health.*

Cohen's seminal article was largely overlooked at the time, and much research on paternal tobacco use and its impact on child malnutrition and survival has come from the last several years.

## 23.3   EPIDEMIOLOGY OF TOBACCO USE

Worldwide, approximately 1.3 billion people (almost 1 billion men and 250 million women) currently smoke cigarettes or other products [5]. As noted, the use of tobacco products is declining in many industrialized countries, and there has been a shift of smoking from developed countries to developing countries. By 1995, there were more smokers in low- and middle-income countries (933 million) than in high-income countries (209 million) [6]. In developed countries, about 35% of men smoke, compared with 50% of men in developing countries and almost two thirds of men in China [6].

### 23.3.1   *World Health Organization Conceptual Framework for the Tobacco Epidemic*

Alan Lopez and colleagues proposed a model that has been adopted as the WHO conceptual framework for the evolving tobacco epidemic [7]. The model considers the tobacco epidemic to be a continuum that involves four stages (Fig. 23.1).

The first stage defines the beginning of the smoking epidemic in a population and is characterized by a low prevalence (less than 15–20%) of cigarette smoking, with smoking mostly limited to males [7]. Death and disease due to smoking are not yet evident, and lung cancer is relatively rare [7]. The priorities of countries in this stage are generally to reduce malnutrition and the burden of infectious diseases, and tobacco control strategies are undeveloped. Efforts are made by tobacco companies to make smoking socially acceptable. Countries in sub-Saharan Africa are generally in the first stage [6].

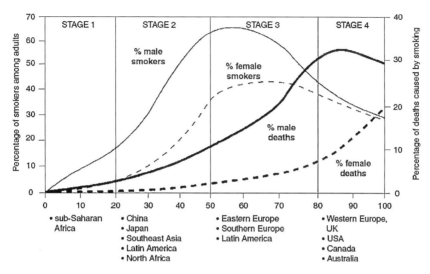

**Fig. 23.1.** World Health Organization conceptual framework for the tobacco epidemic.

The second stage is characterized by increases in the prevalence of smoking to more than 50% of men, with increases of smoking among women. Smoking is initiated at younger ages. The proportion of ex-smokers is low. Tobacco control activities are not well developed, and information about the hazards of tobacco is not organized. By the end of this phase, tobacco use is causing about 10% of male deaths, with a comparatively lower rate among women [7]. Tobacco control efforts have not been successfully implemented in part because the risks of tobacco use are not widely understood and, public and political support is not sufficiently strong [7]. China, Japan, and many countries in Southeast Asia, Latin America, and North Africa are in stage 2.

In stage 3, the prevalence of smoking among males begins to decline after having reached peaks exceeding 60% in some countries. This stage may last for about three decades, by the end of which male smoking prevalence drops to around 40%. The prevalence of smoking among females may rise, plateau, and slowly decline, and the maximum prevalence of smoking among females is about 35–45% [7]. Despite the decline in the prevalence of smoking, the burden of smoking-attributable disease and mortality continues to increase because of the lag time between smoking and chronic disease. Among males, smoking-attributable mortality rises from 10% to 25–30% of all deaths. Among females, smoking-attributable mortality rises from 5% to about 10%. Smoking accounts for 10–30% of all deaths during this stage. Many countries in eastern and southern Europe and some countries in Latin America are in this stage [6].

Stage 4 of the epidemic is characterized by a large decline in the prevalence of smoking among males and females to about 35% and 30%, respectively [7]. Again, due to the lag between exposure and disease, smoking-attributable mortality continues to rise among males to 30–35% of all deaths, as high as 40–45% of deaths in middle age [7]. Smoking-attributable mortality among females rises rapidly, with an expected peak of 20–25% of all female deaths. During this stage, there is an increased demand for smoke-free workplaces, and legislation is passed for smoke-free personal environments. Industrialized countries in northern and western Europe, the United States, United Kingdom,

Canada, and Australia are generally in this stage [6]. It should be emphasized that while the WHO model is a useful framework, not all countries fit this model for the tobacco epidemic. For example, the prevalence of smoking among females in China has remained low, and in some countries, cigarette consumption has decreased due to strict national policies that ban cigarette marketing and discourage smoking, such as in Thailand [6]. The prevalence of tobacco use is discussed in the following section, using the WHO definitions for specific regions.

### 23.3.2   The African Region

Much of the African region, which includes most of sub-Saharan Africa, is considered to be in stage 1 of the tobacco epidemic, and the prevalence of smoking, if data are available, appears to be increasing rapidly, especially among youths (Fig. 23.2) [8]. Some countries in the African region do not have any data available on the prevalence of smoking, which is consistent with the stage 1 classification. A systematic review of tobacco use in sub-Saharan Africa showed that males are more likely to smoke, but that no clear pattern regarding urban/rural or socioeconomic status was apparent [9]. Among youths aged 14–18 years in Uganda, 58.1% reported smoking cigarettes. Tobacco use in Africa commonly extends beyond cigarette smoking as pipes, snuff, and rolled tobacco leaves are also consumed [8]. The prevalence of smoking among adults in the African region varies substantially, with the prevalence higher among men than women (Fig. 23.3). In Malawi and Zambia, analyses from the Demographic Health Surveys showed that male tobacco users tend to be less educated and more likely to be from urban areas and have occupations as household or manual workers [10] Tobacco cultivation is expanding rapidly in some countries in Africa, notably Malawi, Zimbabwe, Nigeria, and Kenya. The WHO FCTC was adopted during the 56th World Health Assembly. In the African region, as of mid-2006, countries that were not signatories to the FCTC included Eritrea, Guinea Bissau, Malawi, Sierra Leone, Zambia, and Zimbabwe, while Angola, Congo, Cote d'Ivoire, Ethiopia, Gabon, Gambia, Guinea, Liberia, Mozambique, Uganda, and the United Republic of Tanzania were signatories but had not yet become parties to the FCTC.

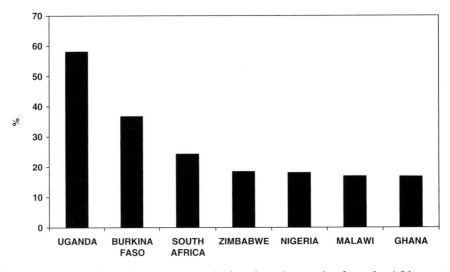

**Fig. 23.2.** Prevalence of smoking among youths in selected countries from the African region.

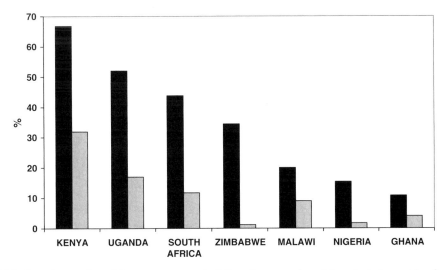

**Fig. 23.3.** Prevalence of smoking among men (solid) and women (gray) in selected countries from the African region.

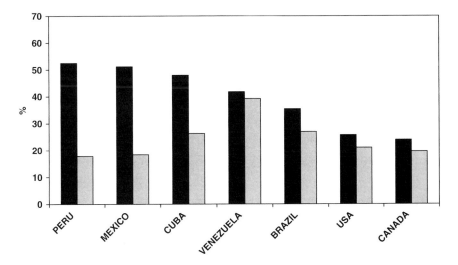

**Fig. 23.4.** Prevalence of smoking among men (solid) and women (gray) in selected countries from the region of the Americas.

### 23.3.3   The Region of the Americas

The region of the Americas consists of the countries in North and South America and the Caribbean. The prevalence of smoking among adults varies widely, from countries with a prevalence of smoking among men of 40–60% (Mexico, Peru, Cuba, Venezuela), to 30–40% (Brazil), and less than about 25% (United States, Canada) [11] (Fig. 23.4). The overall per capita consumption of tobacco appears to be declining throughout this region. By mid-2006 in the region of the Americas, Colombia and the Dominican Republic had not become signatories to the FCTC, and Argentina, Bahamas, Cost Rica, Cuba,

El Salvador, Grenada, Haiti, Nicaragua, Paraguay, Saint Kitts and Nevis, Saint Vincent and the Grenadines, Suriname, and the United States of America had not become party to the FCTC.

### 23.3.4   The Eastern Mediterranean Region

The eastern Mediterranean region includes Morocco, Egypt, Sudan, and Somalia and extends through the Middle East to Afghanistan. The prevalence of smoking reaches up to 50% of men and 10% of women [12] (Fig. 23.5). Among youths in Lebanon, the prevalence of smoking is 45.5% in males and 39.6% in females. Tobacco control laws were adopted by Pakistan, Egypt, and Qatar in 2002 [12]. As of mid-2006, countries that were not signatories to the FCTC were Bahrain and Somalia, and Afghanistan, Iraq, Morocco, Tunisia, and Yemen had not become party to the FCTC.

### 23.3.5   The European Region

The European region extends from Greenland, Iceland, and through Europe and Russia. The prevalence of smoking has generally declined in the European region over the last 30 years [13], but the prevalence of smoking varies widely, from over 60% of men in the Russian Federation to about 17% of men in Sweden (Fig. 23.6). Approximately 30% of adults are regular smokers. The death rate among women from tobacco-related causes is increasing, mostly because women were exposed to tobacco later than men. Many countries have placed bans or restrictions on smoking in public and in workplaces. As of mid-2006, Andorra, Bosnia and Herzegovina, Monaco, the Russian Federation, Tajikistan, Turkmenistan, and Uzbekistan had not become signatories to the FCTC, and Croatia, Czech Republic, Italy, Kazakhstan, Moldova, Poland, and Switzerland had not become party to the FCTC.

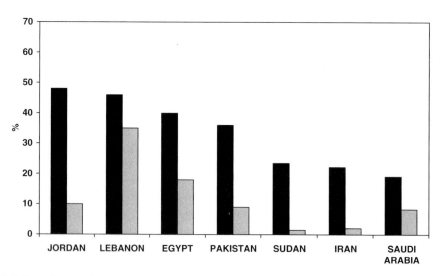

**Fig. 23.5.** Prevalence of smoking among men (solid) and women (gray) in selected countries from the eastern Mediterranean region.

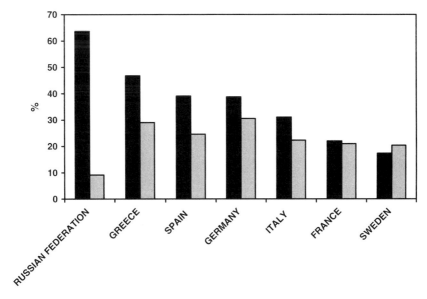

**Fig. 23.6.** Prevalence of smoking among men (solid) and women (gray) in selected countries from the European region.

### 23.3.6 The Southeast Asia Region

The Southeast Asia region includes 11 countries: Bangladesh, Bhutan, Democratic People's Republic of Korea, India, Indonesia, Maldives, Myanmar, Nepal, Sri Lanka, Thailand, and Timor Leste [14]. The prevalence of smoking varies across the region, with the highest prevalence of smoking found among men in Indonesia (Fig. 23.7). In this region, tobacco is widely used in both smoke and smokeless forms. Regular cigarettes, *kreteks* (cigarettes containing tobacco and cloves), *klobots*, cheroots, bidis, and cigars are smoked, as well as hand-rolled tobacco and tobacco smoked in a clay pipe or in *hukkas*. Chewing tobacco is consumed in India, Nepal, Bangladesh, Sri Lanka, Maldives, and Bhutan [14]. India, Indonesia, Bangladesh, and Thailand are among the top producers of tobacco worldwide. As of mid-2006, Indonesia was the only country from the Southeast Asia region that did not become signatory to the FCTC, and Nepal had not become party to the FCTC.

### 23.3.7 The Western Pacific Region

The western Pacific region includes 37 countries, from China and Mongolia to Australia and New Zealand and French Polynesia. In this region, the global death toll from tobacco has risen 14-fold, from 0.3 million deaths in 1950 to 4.2 million deaths in 2000 [15]. Overall, 60% of men and 6% of women smoke in this region. Being born male is the single greatest risk factor for tobacco use in this region [16–18]. The region has countries with some of the highest rates of smoking, with over 70% of men and women in Papua New Guinea and over 70% of men in Viet Nam reporting current smoking (Fig. 23.8). In the Philippines, smoking among adolescent boys declined from 32.6% in 2000 to 21.8% in 2003 and among adolescent girls from 12.9% in 2000 to 8.8% in 2003 [16]. By mid-2006, only the Lao People's Democratic Republic had not become a signatory to the FCTC.

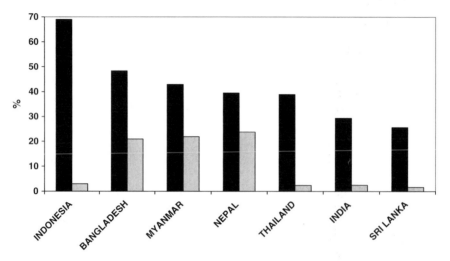

**Fig. 23.7.** Prevalence of smoking among men (solid) and women (gray) in selected countries from the Southeast Asia region.

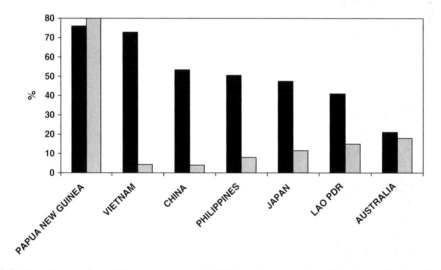

**Fig. 23.8.** Prevalence of smoking among men (solid) and women (gray) in selected countries from the western Pacific region.

## 23.4   TOBACCO USE AND CHILD MALNUTRITION

Smoking exacerbates the effects of poverty as expenditures for tobacco may divert household income from food, clothing, housing, health, and education [19, 20]. Among low-income families in the United States, children of smokers had a poorer quality diet than children of nonsmokers [21]. The amount of money spent on tobacco is especially problematic in low-income countries [19, 20]. For example, in Vietnam in 1996, smokers spent an average of US $49.05 on cigarettes per year, which was 1.5 times that spent on education, 5 times that spent on health care, and about one third that spent on food per capita in the household each year [19]. In the poorest households in Indonesia, more money was spent on tobacco than education and health care combined [22].

Child growth is internationally recognized as the best global indicator of physical well-being in children as children with wasting, underweight, or stunting are at higher risk of deficient or delayed mental development and increased infectious disease morbidity and mortality [23]. Long-term consequences of child malnutrition include poor school performance, diminished intellectual achievement, reduced adult size, and reduced work capacity [23]. Parental smoking has an adverse impact on child growth, as shown in studies conducted in Indonesia, Bangladesh, and India.

### 23.4.1 Indonesia

Indonesia is the fifth largest market for tobacco in the world, with 182 billion sticks consumed per year [24]. The absolute domestic consumption of tobacco increased by 159% between 1970 and 1980, coincident with the mechanization of the cigarette industry in Indonesia in the early 1970s [25]. In the 1990s, an estimated 50% of men and 2.6% of women smoked cigarettes in Indonesia, usually kretek, which contain about two thirds tobacco, one third cloves, and various additives and flavors [25]; at present, over 62% of Indonesian adult males smoke regularly [25]. The prevalence of smoking is also increasing among adolescents in Indonesia [26]. An analysis of 175,859 households in urban slum areas in the Indonesia Nutritional Surveillance System (1999–2003) showed that the prevalence of paternal smoking was 73.8% [27]. After adjusting for child gender and age, maternal age and education, and weekly per capita household expenditures, paternal smoking was associated with child stunting (odds ratio [OR] 1.11, 95% confidence interval [CI] 1.08–1.14; $p < .0001$), severe wasting (OR 1.17, 95% CI 1.03–1.33; $p = .018$), and severe stunting (OR 1.09, 95% CI 1.04–1.15; $p < .001$). In households in which the father was a smoker, tobacco accounted for 22% of weekly per capita household expenditures, with less money spent on food compared with households in which the father was a nonsmoker. In households with a smoker, there was a smaller per capita expenditure on animal foods, vegetables and fruits, rice and other staples, snacks and baby food, sugar and oil, and instant noodles than in households in which the father was not a smoker [27] (Figs. 23.9 and 23.10). These findings suggest that the adverse effects of tobacco use include increasing the risk of malnutrition among young children of the household as a large proportion of household income is diverted toward cigarettes with a lesser proportion spent on food.

In Indonesia, the per capita expenditure on tobacco in the lowest-income households may be increasing, from 9% of total expenditures in 1981 to 15% of total expenditures in 1996 [28]. Kretek cigarettes account for nearly 90% of the cigarettes consumed in Indonesia [29] and are available for purchase individually or in small, less-expensive packs, by which they are particularly accessible to the poor [30]. Indonesian and multinational tobacco companies advertise heavily on billboards, on television, in the cinema, and at sporting events, with tobacco ranked among the largest advertising spending categories in the country [30]. There are few restrictions on the tobacco industry conduct, advertising, and promotion in Indonesia [24], and as noted, Indonesia is the only country in Southeast Asia that has not signed the FCTC, which would require implementation of advertising limitations and the banning of tobacco sales to youths [31]. In addition,

**Fig. 23.9.** Weekly per capita expenditures for households with a smoking father. Proportion of expenditures spent on major food types and other commodities. *Other foods* were defined as ready-to-eat foods and foods not produced in the household. *Snacks* were defined as commercially packaged products made in a factory. The category *other* consisted of electricity, gasoline, telephone, soap, seasonings, and the like. (From [27]. Reproduced from *Public Health Nutrition* with permission from Cambridge University Press.)

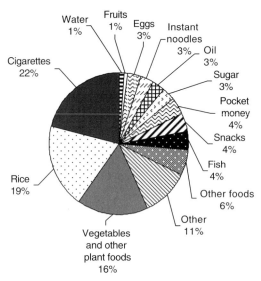

**Weekly per capita expenditures for households with smoking father**

**Fig. 23.10.** Weekly per capita expenditures for households with a nonsmoking father. Proportion of expenditures spent on major food types and other commodities. *Other foods* were defined as ready-to-eat foods and foods not produced in the household. *Snacks* were defined as commercially packaged products made in a factory. The category *other* consisted of electricity, gasoline, telephone, soap, seasonings, and the like. (From [27]. Reproduced from *Public Health Nutrition* with permission from Cambridge University Press.)

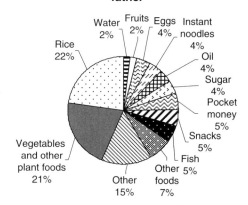

**Weekly per capita expenditures for households with non-smoking father**

relatively weak tobacco control legislation that passed in 1999 was further weakened with an amendment in 2003 to drop sanctions against the tobacco industry for violation of tobacco control regulations, such as not including health warnings [24]. The heavy advertising and marketing of cigarettes in Indonesia may be a contributing factor to the high prevalence of smoking among Indonesian men.

### 23.4.2 Bangladesh

Bangladesh is one of the poorest countries of the world, and many poor households are unable to provide for the basic essentials. In spite of this, a large proportion of men in poor families smoke, and the prevalence of smoking is highest among the poorest families [20]. Average male cigarette smokers in Bangladesh spend more than twice as much on cigarettes than the per capita expenditure on clothing, housing, health, and education combined [20]. Debra Efroymson and colleagues estimated that the typical poor smoker in Bangladesh could add over 500 calories to the diet of one or two children in the household if he spent the money on food rather than cigarettes. Overall, it was estimated that if money were spent on food rather than cigarettes, it would save the lives of 350 children in Bangladesh per day [20].

### 23.4.3   India

An analysis of data from the National Family Health Survey II, a nationally representative survey of 92,486 households in India, showed that children who came from households where at least one family member used tobacco were more likely to have severe stunting or severe underweight [32]. Regular tobacco use was associated with poverty, rural setting, and low education [33]. In Mumbai, tobacco use was common among street children and pavement dwellers, and their expenditures on tobacco were high relative to that for nutritious foods [34, 35]. In addition to cigarettes, tobacco is consumed in many different forms in India, as shown in Table 23.1.

### 23.4.4   "Going Up in Smoke": Tobacco Versus Food

Among poor families in Indonesia, Bangladesh, and India, children may be needlessly going hungry because money that could be spent on necessities like food is being diverted to cigarettes. Smoking is potentiating malnutrition among children in the

Table 23.1
**Tobacco products consumed in India**

| Name | Description |
| --- | --- |
| *bidi* | Popular form of smoked tobacco, 5–8 cm; composed of 0.25–0.5 g locally grown tobacco |
| *khaini* | Mixture of tobacco and lime prepared in the palm, formed into a ball, and placed in the mouth; placed in the groove between the cheek and the gum |
| *masheri, mishri, misheri* | Roasted or half-burnt tobacco; prepared by baking on a hot plate; made into powder and used mostly for cleaning teeth; sometimes used as alternative for chewing tobacco |
| *mava* | Mixture of raw areca nut, tobacco, and lime water; wrapped in cellophane and rubbed against the palm |
| *naswar* | Mixture of sun- and heat-dried tobacco leaves, slaked lime, tree bark ash, some flavorings, and sometimes coloring agents; water is added, and material is rolled into balls and placed in the labial groove behind the lower lip; material is expectorated after being chewed for 10–15 minutes |
| *paan* | Betel quid with tobacco; prepared by applying slaked lime and catechu to a betel leaf, to which small pieces of areca nut are added; other flavorings may be added; tobacco is the most important ingredient of paan for regular users; ingredients are folded into the betel leaf and chewed |

*Source*: Adapted from [36].

family, exacerbating poverty, and may have long-term implications for the health of future generations of children in Indonesia and other countries with poverty and widespread tobacco use.

## 23.5   OTHER ADVERSE EFFECTS OF PARENTAL SMOKING ON CHILD HEALTH

Parental smoking has an adverse effect on respiratory health of children. In addition, passive smoking lowers the levels of circulating plasma antioxidants. In poor households, the morbidity in children from passive smoking may potentiate the malnutrition that results from the diversion of household income from food to tobacco. Pregnant women who are exposed to environmental tobacco smoke have worse pregnancy outcomes, including lower birth weight among their infants.

### 23.5.1   Respiratory Health

Parental smoking is associated with an increased risk of lower respiratory illness in infants and young children [37]. A systematic review of 38 studies showed that smoking by either parent (OR 1.57, 95% CI 1.42–1.74) or maternal smoking (OR 1.72, 95% CI 1.55–1.91) increased the risk of lower-respiratory illness in infants and children [37]. Parental smoking increases the risk of respiratory symptoms and asthma in school-aged children. In a systematic review of 60 studies, smoking by either parent increased the risk for asthma (OR 1.21, 95% CI 1.10–1.34), wheezing (OR 1.24, 95% CI 1.17–1.31), coughing (OR 1.40, 95% CI 1.27–1.53), and breathlessness (OR 1.31, 95% CI 1.08–1.59) [38]. The risk of middle ear disease and adenotonsillectomy is also significantly increased in children whose parents are smokers. A systematic review of 45 studies showed that if either parent smoked, the risk of recurrent otitis media (OR 1.48, 95% CI 1.08–2.04) and middle ear effusion (OR 1.38, 95% CI 1.23–1.55) were increased [39]. Parental smoking also exacerbates the severity of disease among children with established asthma [40]. The risk of sudden infant death syndrome is doubled among infants whose mothers are smokers [41].

### 23.5.2   Low Birth Weight

Women who are exposed to environmental tobacco smoke during pregnancy have infants with significantly lower birth weight than women who are not exposed [42–44]. Environmental tobacco smoke also increases the risk of fetal mortality, preterm delivery, and retarded fetal growth [45]. A meta-analysis conducted in 1999 showed that environmental tobacco smoke exposure was associated with lower birth weight [46]. These findings suggest that parental tobacco use may have an impact on child nutritional status beginning in utero, with lower birth weight among infants born to mothers who were exposed to environmental tobacco smoke. The detrimental effects of paternal tobacco use then continue, with a large proportion of household income diverted away from food and toward tobacco, as noted in Indonesia, Bangladesh, and India. Most of studies of the relationship between environmental tobacco smoke and low birth weight have been conducted in industrialized countries. A study from India showed that nonsmoking mothers who were exposed to environmental tobacco smoke during pregnancy had a higher incidence of preterm birth, small-for-gestational-age babies, and infants with lower birth weight [47].

### 23.5.3   Circulating Antioxidants

Exposure to environmental tobacco smoke has been associated with decreased levels of circulating antioxidant nutrients in children. These effects are presumably due to the pro-oxidant load that is associated with passive smoking as antioxidants are used to quench reactive oxygen species. Children exposed to environmental tobacco smoke had significantly lower plasma ascorbate concentrations than unexposed children who consumed equivalent amounts of vitamin A [48]. In the Third National Health and Nutrition Examination Survey, a dose-response relationship was noted between levels of tobacco exposure and serum ascorbate levels in children [49]. The relationship between passive smoking and serum/plasma antioxidant levels has been more thoroughly investigated among adults, and these studies showed that exposure to environmental tobacco smoke decreases circulating levels of carotenoids and ascorbate [50, 51]. The long-term health consequences of chronic low levels of antioxidant nutrients in children exposed to environmental tobacco smoke are unclear.

### 23.5.4   Increased Health Care Utilization

As shown, exposure to environmental tobacco smoke is associated with increased respiratory disease in children. In a study of 8,327 parent–infant pairs in Hong Kong, women who were exposed to environmental tobacco smoke during pregnancy had increased clinical consultations (OR 1.26, 95% CI 1.4–1.39) and hospitalizations (OR 1.18, 95% CI 1.05–1.31) for their infants in the first 18 months of life [52]. In this birth cohort (from 1997) alone, the additional 1,581 hospitalizations attributable to environmental tobacco exposure were at a cost of over US $2.1 million [53]. If environmental tobacco smoke is causally associated with health services utilization, about 9% of the total direct medical costs in the first year of life can be attributed to passive smoking [53].

## 23.6   PARENTAL TOBACCO USE AND CHILD MORTALITY

We showed, in a study of over 300,000 families from urban slums and rural areas of Indonesia, that paternal smoking increased the risk of infant and under-5 child mortality by about 10–15% in urban slums and 30% in rural areas [54]. The prevalence of maternal

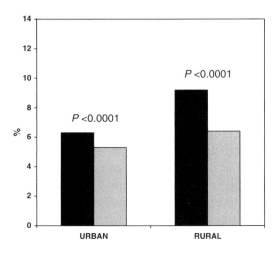

**Fig. 23.11.** Infant mortality in families with smokers (solid) versus nonsmokers (gray) among families in urban slums and rural areas of Indonesia.

**Fig. 23.12.** Under-5 child mortality in families with smokers (solid) versus nonsmokers (gray) among families in urban slums and rural areas of Indonesia.

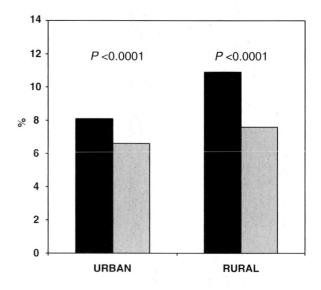

smoking was less than 1% in both urban and rural areas, but maternal smoking was also associated with a significantly increased risk of infant and under-5 child mortality [54]. The differences in infant and under-5 child mortality reported in families in which the father was a smoker or nonsmoker are shown in Figs. 23.11 and 23.12.

## 23.7   TOBACCO CONTROL

The results from the present study [54] support the growing belief that tobacco control, poverty alleviation, and child health promotion should not be looked on as mutually exclusive efforts [20, 32]. The WHO has presented three main ways by which tobacco exacerbates poverty on the household level: First, expenditure of tobacco takes over money that could otherwise be spent on basic necessities; second, smoking leads to increased health care needs, lost productivity, and premature death of wage earners; and third, those employed in tobacco-related work experience particularly low wages and high health risks [55]. While previous studies have inferred that household health is linked to household smoking expenditure and would improve if the money spent on cigarettes were instead spent on food [20, 34, 35], work from Indonesia and Bangladesh corroborated and extended these arguments by showing that paternal smoking was associated with greater child malnutrition.

The recent WHO FCTC is an important development in global tobacco control and includes measures with clear guidelines and deadlines regarding health warnings and comprehensive bans on tobacco advertising, promotion, and sponsorship. But, it lacks details regarding the control of illicit trade and cross-border advertising and the relationship of its provisions to international trade agreements. A review of the strategies employed by the tobacco industry to circumvent and undermine tobacco control activities worldwide emphasizes there is still a need for comprehensive provisions to reduce smoking and prevent tobacco-related deaths.

Since tobacco control began to take shape in the 1970s, transnational tobacco companies have employed numerous deceptive strategies as means to increase sales and profit. Tobacco industry documents revealed that these companies and their subsidiaries aggressively sought to undermine and circumvent the tobacco control efforts of WHO and a number of governments worldwide [56]. In 1999, the director-general of WHO called for an expert committee to review the once-confidential industry documents. The committee discovered tobacco companies' goals:

> Undertake a long-term initiative to counteract the WHO's aggressive global anti-smoking campaign. ... [Try] to stop the development of a third-world commitment against tobacco. [56]

The industry sought to achieve these goals with tactics such as paying WHO advisors or consultants for services, employing former WHO officials or promising employment to current officials, wielding political and financial power through contributions, using other UN agencies to resist WHO tobacco control, and influencing the WHO through surrogate companies and industry-sponsored NGOs. The industry also lobbied developing country delegates, secretly funded speakers at WHO events, held scientific symposia for pro-tobacco science while concealing industry involvement, funded counterresearch and recruited independent scientists to conduct and present findings, staged media events to detract attention from WHO tobacco control, and misrepresented scientific data to the media and regulators [56]. Other research revealed similar tactics have been used to compromise tobacco control efforts directed by governments in a number of countries. Such tactics are elaborated in the following sections and are summarized in Table 23.2.

### 23.7.1 Indirect Advertising and Trademark Diversification

Industry documents provided accounts of how transnational tobacco companies have marketed products through "brand diversification" in countries where direct advertising of tobacco products is prohibited. Brand diversification consists of creating nontobacco products that use the tobacco brand name and logo, then marketing these new products to stimulate brand recognition. Transnational tobacco companies also admit to creating surrogate companies, which utilize the same brand logo, to sponsor events such as sporting events and pop concerts [57].

### 23.7.2 Industry Programs to Counter Antitobacco Science

The 1986 US surgeon general's report on the effects of environmental (second-hand) tobacco smoke accelerated antismoking legislation and the social unacceptability of smoking in developed nations. In response, transnational tobacco companies joined forces to protect tobacco interests in the developed and developing world by creating a program to blur public and political perceptions of environmental tobacco smoke [58]. Independent industry research centers such as the Center for Indoor Air Research and the Association of Research on Indoor Air were created to study the effects of second-hand smoke. In Asia, the environmental consultants program recruited and trained scientists to form "an international network of independent scientists who can publicly and credibly address inaccurate claims on the health effects of environmental tobacco smoke" and to promote the perspective that developing countries need not waste time and funds on environmental tobacco smoke when faced with more pertinent public health issues [59].

Table 23.2

**Strategies used by the tobacco industry to promote tobacco use in developing countries**

- Target children and adolescents with cigarette advertising
- Make cigarette vending machines accessible to minors
- Target women with cigarette advertising
- Advertise cigarette smoking as a social norm among males
- Disseminate "independent research" that claims cigarettes are healthy and natural (e.g., *kretek* cigarettes in Indonesia)
- Distribute free cigarettes
- Distribute free coupons for discounts on tobacco purchases
- Make cigarette packs labeled with political party names for distribution at political rallies
- Distribute free cigarettes at discos
- Introduce smaller 10-cigarette "starter" packs
- Sell single cigarettes
- Offer cigarettes as prizes or gifts at large events
- Use cigarette name for achievement awards (e.g., "bravery awards" by Godfrey Phillips, the subsidiary of Philip Morris in India)
- Circumvent bans on cigarette advertisements by indirect advertising
- Sponsor sporting events with logo placement (e.g., car racing, soccer, badminton)
- Sponsor concerts and cultural events with logo placement (e.g., jazz concerts)
- Place cigarettes and logos in travel and vacation advertising
- Market cigarettes toward youths with emphasis on football, motorcycles, motor racing
- Construct large billboards advertising cigarettes in areas with weak tobacco control to influence tobacco sales in countries with strict tobacco control (e.g., giant "high-rise" billboards in Johor Bahru, Malaysia, facing neighboring Singapore, erected by British American Tobacco)
- Distribute nontobacco products with cigarette logos
- Promote "health conscious" brands of cigarettes
- Promote cigarettes on television in countries with weak tobacco control to influence tobacco sales in countries with strict tobacco control (i.e., Malaysian television beamed into Singapore)
- Boycott companies that sponsor antismoking activities
- Market nontobacco products with same name as new cigarette brand (e.g., Alpine wine cooler by Philip Morris in Singapore)
- Place cigarettes in movies and on television
- Offer large cash prizes that are associated with a cigarette name brand
- Make health warnings on cigarettes and advertising difficult to read
- Erode legislation and minimize penalties aimed at tobacco industry violations of tobacco control regulations (e.g., Indonesia)
- Weaken health warnings on cigarette packages and advertising
- Oppose and weaken legislation regarding the printing of tar and nicotine levels on cigarette packages
- Oppose smoking bans in public places, including religious facilities, workplaces, public transportation, etc.
- Become involved in antismoking education and in the process gather information important to the industry regarding knowledge, practice, and attitudes regarding smoking, especially among youths
- Insist that governments consult with tobacco companies in formulating tobacco control measures to buy time, delay government action, and weaken proposed measures

### 23.7.3    Offshore Strategies

Singapore was the first country to ban tobacco advertisements and today has a comprehensive ban on all tobacco advertising and promotion. Internal documents described how British American Tobacco adopted an "offshore strategy" to market tobacco to Singaporeans by advertising heavily on Malaysian television channels and sponsoring sporting events in Indonesia [60]. The desired effect was to reach consumers in Singapore via these popular mediums and thus circumvent the advertising ban.

### 23.7.4    Industry-Funded Youth Smoking Prevention Programs

Tobacco companies have created youth smoking prevention programs in a number of countries as an effort to preempt damaging tobacco control legislation and project an image of corporate responsibility. Yet, no research suggests that any industry-funded programs have been effective in preventing young people from smoking [57]. In Malaysia, the industry ran a youth smoking prevention program while simultaneously conducting market research on teenagers as young as 16. The industry claimed this research would be used to persuade current smokers to switch brands, not to market to young nonsmokers. Certain actions, such as selling starter packs and single cigarettes and sponsoring sporting and musical events that appeal primarily to the youth culture, suggest ulterior motivations [57, 61].

### 23.7.5    Appeals to International Trade Organizations and Representatives

In both Thailand and Singapore, transnational tobacco companies delayed and weakened legislation that mandated health-warning labels on cigarette packs and ingredients disclosure by claiming the regulations violated international trade agreements [61, 62]. The industry appealed to policy makers and trade representatives with the argument that such measures violated the General Agreement on Tariffs and Trade (GATT) restrictions and World Trade Organization (WTO) trade-related intellectual property rights. These lobbying efforts successfully delayed health-warning label legislation in Singapore and defeated legislation for public disclosure of ingredients in Thailand. Such scenarios indicate a real need to address the disputes between tobacco control and trade liberalization for the FCTC and tobacco control legislation to endure and protect the public's health.

## 23.8    CONCLUSIONS

In developing countries, tobacco use increases the risk of malnutrition among young children in poor families. Tobacco use exacerbates poverty by diverting household earnings toward tobacco, with less money spent on necessities such as nutritious foods, health care, and education. Environmental tobacco smoke places children at higher risk of respiratory diseases and pregnant women at higher risk of having an infant with low birth weight. Parental tobacco use, especially paternal tobacco use, increases the risk of infant and under-5 child mortality. Countries such as China, Indonesia, Bangladesh, and Vietnam have an extremely high prevalence of smoking, and the impact in terms of chronic diseases and mortality will be present for many decades.

## 23.9   RECOMMENDATIONS

- Tobacco control should be considered an integral part of strategies that are aimed at improving child health in developing countries.
- The impact of environmental tobacco smoke on birth weight needs to be examined in developing countries. This issue may be especially critical in South and Southeast Asia, the region with highest rates of both low birth weight and paternal smoking worldwide.
- The potential effects of paternal tobacco use on the nutritional status of mothers needs to be examined, especially among poor households in South and Southeast Asia.
- Tobacco control efforts need to be intensified worldwide, but particularly in the African Region, which is largely in stage 1 of the tobacco epidemic. Without implementation of stringent controls advocated by the WHO FCTC, many countries in Africa will follow the same pattern and will enter stage 2 of the tobacco epidemic. The historical record shows that crushing poverty has never been a deterrent to the tobacco industry in developing new markets for tobacco consumption.
- Further work is needed to determine whether paternal smoking adversely affects the cognitive development of children who are exposed versus not exposed.

## REFERENCES

1. Centers for Disease Control and Prevention. Use of cigarettes and other tobacco products among students aged 13–15 years—worldwide, 1999–2005. MMWR Morb Mortal Wkly Rep 2006;55:553–556.
2. de Beyer J, Brigden LW, eds. Tobacco control policy: strategies, successes, and setbacks. Washington, DC: World Bank and Research for International Tobacco Control, 2003.
3. Aubry MC, Wright JL, Myers JL. The pathology of smoking-related lung diseases. Clin Chest Med 2000;21:11–35.
4. Cohen N. Smoking, health, and survival: prospects in Bangladesh. Lancet 1981;1:1090–1093.
5. Guidon GE, Boisclair D. Past, current, and future trends in tobacco use. Washington, DC: World Bank, 2003. Economics of Tobacco Control Paper No. 6. Available at: http://www1.worldbank.org/tobacco/publications.asp. Accessed August 6, 2006.
6. Thun MJ, da Costa e Silva VL. Introduction and overview of global tobacco surveillance. In: Tobacco control country profiles. 2nd ed. Shafey O, Dolwick S, Guindon GE, eds. Atlanta, GA: American Cancer Society, World Health Organization, and International Union Against Cancer, 2003.
7. Lopez AD, Collishaw NE, Piha T. A descriptive model of the cigarette epidemic in developed countries. Tob Control 1994;3:242–247.
8. Oluwafemi A. Regional summary for the African region. In: Tobacco control country profiles. 2nd ed. Shafey O, Dolwick S, Guindon GE, eds. Atlanta, GA: American Cancer Society, World Health Organization, and International Union Against Cancer, 2003:27–31.
9. Townsend L, Flisher AJ, Gilreath T, King G. A systematic literature review of tobacco use among adults 15 years and older in sub-Saharan Africa. Drug Alcohol Depend 2006;84:14–27.
10. Pampel FC. Patterns of tobacco use in the early epidemic stages: Malawi and Zambia, 2000–2002. Am J Public Health 2005;95:1009–1015.
11. Selin H, Martin JP, Peruga A. Regional summary for the region of the Americas. In: Tobacco control country profiles. 2nd ed. Shafey O, Dolwick S, Guindon GE, eds. Atlanta, GA: American Cancer Society, World Health Organization, and International Union Against Cancer, 2003:32–33.
12. El-Awa FMS. Regional summary for the eastern Mediterranean region. In: Tobacco control country profiles. 2nd ed. Shafey O, Dolwick S, Guindon GE, eds. Atlanta, GA: American Cancer Society, World Health Organization, and International Union Against Cancer, 2003:34–35.
13. World Health Organization. Regional summary for the European region. In: Tobacco control country profiles. 2nd ed. Shafey O, Dolwick S, Guindon GE, eds. Atlanta, GA: American Cancer Society, World Health Organization, and International Union Against Cancer, 2003:36–37.

14. Rahman K. Regional summary for the South-East Asia region. In: Tobacco control country profiles. 2nd ed. Shafey O, Dolwick S, Guindon GE, eds. Atlanta, GA: American Cancer Society, World Health Organization, and International Union Against Cancer, 2003:38–40.

15. David A. Regional summary for the western Pacific region. In: Tobacco control country profiles. 2nd ed. Shafey O, Dolwick S, Guindon GE, eds. Atlanta, GA: American Cancer Society, World Health Organization, and International Union Against Cancer, 2003:41–44.

16. Morrow M, Barraclough S. Tobacco control and gender in Southeast Asia. Part I. Malaysia and the Philippines. Health Promot Int 2003;18:255–264.

17. Morrow M, Barraclough S. Tobacco control and gender in Southeast Asia. Part II. Singapore and Vietnam. Health Promot Int 2003;18:373–380.

18. Centers for Disease Control. Tobacco use among students aged 13–15 years—Philippines, 2000 and 2003. MMWR Morb Mort Wkly Rep 2005;54:94–97.

19. Jenkins CNH, Dai PX, Ngoc DH, Kinh HV, Hoang TT, Bales S, et al. Tobacco use in Vietnam: prevalence, predictors, and the role of the transnational tobacco corporations. JAMA 1997;227:1726–1731.

20. Efroymson D, Ahmed S, Townsend J, Alam SM, Dey AR, Saha R, Dhar B, Sujon AI, Ahmed KU, Rahman O. Hungry for tobacco: an analysis of the economic impact of tobacco consumption on the poor in Bangladesh. Tob Control 2001;10:212–217.

21. Johnson RK, Wang MQ, Smith MJ, Connolly G. The association between parental smoking and the diet quality of low-income children. Pediatrics 1996;97:312–317.

22. Reid A. From betel-chewing to tobacco-smoking in Indonesia. J Asian Stud 1985;45:529–547.

23. de Onis M. Child growth and development. In: Nutrition and health in developing countries. Semba RD, Bloem MW, eds. Totowa, NJ: Humana Press, 2001:71–91.

24. Achadi A, Soerojo W, Barber S. The relevance and prospects of advancing tobacco control in Indonesia. Health Policy 2005;72:333–349.

25. Barraclough S. Women and tobacco in Indonesia. Tob Control 1999;8:327–332.

26. Smet B, Maes L, de Clerq L, Haryanti K, Winarno RD. Determinants of smoking behaviour among adolescents in Semarang, Indonesia. Tob Control 1999;8:186–191.

27. Semba RD, Kalm LM, de Pee S, Ricks MO, Sari M, Bloem MW. Paternal smoking is associated with increased risk of child malnutrition among poor urban families in Indonesia. Public Health Nutr 2007;10:7–15.

28. de Beyer J, Lovelace C, Yürekli A. Poverty and tobacco. Tob Control 2001;10:210–211.

29. Lawrence S, Collin J. Competing with kreteks: transnational tobacco companies, globalization, and Indonesia. Tob Control 2004;13(suppl ii):ii96–ii103.

30. Reynolds C. Tobacco advertising in Indonesia: the defining characteristics for success. Tob Control 1999;8:86–88.

31. Shibuya K, Ciecierski C, Guindon E, Bettcher DW, Evans DB, Murray CJL. WHO Framework Convention on Tobacco Control: development of an evidence based global public health treaty. BMJ 2003;327:154–157.

32. Bonu S, Rani M, Jha P, Peters DH, Nguyen SN. Household tobacco and alcohol use, and child health: an exploratory study from India. Health Policy 2004;70:67–83.

33. Neufeld KJ, Peters DH, Rani M, Bonu S, Brooner RK. Regular use of alcohol and tobacco in India and its association with age, gender, and poverty. Drug Alcohol Depend 2005;77:283–291.

34. Shah S, Vaite S. Choosing tobacco over food: daily struggles for existence among the street children of Mumbai, India. In: Tobacco and poverty: observations from India and Bangladesh. Efroymson D, ed. Ottawa: PATH Canada, October 2002:52–60.

35. Shah S, Vaite S. Pavement dwellers in Mumbai, India: prioritizing tobacco over basic needs. In: Tobacco and poverty: observations from India and Bangladesh. Efroymson D, ed. Ottawa: PATH Canada, October 2002:63–69.

36. John S, Vaite S, Efroymson D, ed. Tobacco and poverty: observations from India and Bangladesh. Ottawa: PATH Canada, 2002.

37. Strachan DP, Cook DG. Health effects of passive smoking. 1. Parental smoking and lower respiratory illness in infancy and early childhood. Thorax 1997;52:905–914.

38. Cook DG, Strachan DP. Health effects of passive smoking. 3. Parental smoking and respiratory symptoms in schoolchildren. Thorax 1997;52:1081–1094.

39. Strachan DP, Cook DG. Health effects of passive smoking. 4. Parental smoking, middle ear disease, and adenotonsillectomy in children. Thorax 1998;53:50–56.

40. Strachan DP, Cook DG. Health effects of passive smoking. 6. Parental smoking and childhood asthma: longitudinal and case-control studies. Thorax 1998;53:204–212.

41. Anderson HR, Cook DG. Health effects of passive smoking. 2. Passive smoking and sudden infant death syndrome. Review of the epidemiological evidence. Thorax 1997;52:1003–1009.

42. Dejmek J, Solanks I, Podrazilová K, Srám RJ. The exposure of nonsmoking and smoking mothers to environmental tobacco smoke during different gestational phases and fetal growth. Environ Health Perspect 2002;110:601–606.

43. Hanke W, Sobala W, Kalinka J. Environmental tobacco smoke exposure among pregnant women: impact on fetal biometry at 20–24 weeks of gestation and newborn child's birth weight. Int Arch Occup Environ Health 2004;77:47–52.

44. Hegaard HK, Kjaergaard H, Moller LF, Wachmann H, Ottesen B. The effect of environmental tobacco smoke during pregnancy on birth weight. Act Obstet Gynecol Scand 2006;85:675–681.

45. Kharrazi M, DeLorenze GN, Kaufman FL, Eskenazi B, Bernert JT Jr, Graham S, et al. Environmental tobacco smoke and pregnancy outcome. Epidemiology 2004;15:660–670.

46. Windham GC, Eaton A, Hopkins B. Evidence for an association between environmental tobacco smoke exposure and birth weight: a meta-analysis and new data. Paediatr Perinatal Epidemiol 1999;13:35–57.

47. Goel P, Radotra A, Singh I, Aggarwal A, Dua D. Effects of passive smoking on outcomes in pregnancy. J Postgrad Med 2004;50:12–16.

48. Preston AM, Rodriguez C, Rivera CE, Sahai H. Influence of environmental tobacco smoke on vitamin C status in children. Am J Clin Nutr 2003;77:167–172.

49. Strauss RS. Environmental tobacco smoke and serum vitamin C levels in children. Pediatrics 2001;107:540–542.

50. Alberg AJ, Chen JC, Zhao H, Hoffman SC, Comstock GW, Helzlsouer KJ. Household exposure to passive cigarette smoking and serum micronutrient concentrations. Am J Clin Nutr 2000;72:1576–1582.

51. Dietrich M, Block G, Norkus EP, Hudes M, Traber MG, Cross CE, et al. Smoking and exposure to environmental tobacco smoke decrease some plasma antioxidants and increase γ-tocopherol in vivo after adjustment for dietary antioxidant intakes. Am J Clin Nutr 2003;77:160–166.

52. Lam TH, Leung GM, Ho LM. The effects of environmental tobacco smoke on health services utilization in the first 18 months of life. Pediatrics 2001;107(6):E91.

53. Leung GM, Ho LM, Lam TH. The economic burden of environmental tobacco smoke in the first year of life. Arch Dis Child 2003;88:767–771.

54. Semba RD, de Pee S, Sun K, Best CM, Sari M, Bloem MW. Paternal smoking and increased risk of infant and under-5 child mortality among families in Indonesia. Am J Public Health 2008; doi:10.2105/AJPH.2007.119289

55. World Health Organization. Tobacco increases the poverty of individuals and families. Tobacco Free Initiative. Geneva: World Health Organization, 2004. Available at: http://www.who.int/tobacco/communications/events/wntd/2004/tobaccofacts_families/en/.

56. WHO Committee of Experts on Tobacco Industry Documents. Tobacco company strategies to undermine tobacco control activities at the World Health Organization. Tobacco Control Papers. UCSF. 2000. Available at: http://repositories.cdlib.org/tc/whotcp/WHO7

57. Assunta M, Chapman S. Industry sponsored youth smoking prevention programme in Malaysia: a case study in duplicity. Tob Control 2004;13(suppl 2):ii37–ii42.

58. Assunta M, Fields N, Knight J, Chapman S. "Care and feeding": the Asian environmental tobacco smoke consultants programme. Tob Control 2004;13(suppl 2):ii4–ii12.

59. Assunta M, Chapman S. A mire of highly subjective and ineffective voluntary guidelines: tobacco industry efforts to thwart tobacco control in Malaysia. Tob Control 2004;13(suppl 2):ii43–ii50.

60. Assunta M, Chapman S. "The world's most hostile environment": how the tobacco industry circumvented Singapore's advertising ban. Tob Control 2004;13(suppl 2):ii51–ii57.

61. Assunta M, Chapman S. The tobacco industry's accounts of refining indirect tobacco advertising in Malaysia. Tob Control 2004;13(suppl 2);ii63–ii70.

62. MacKenzie R, Collin J, Sriwongcharoen K, Muggli ME. "If we can just 'stall' new unfriendly legislations, the scoreboard is already in our favour": transnational tobacco companies and ingredients disclosure in Thailand. Tob Control 2004;13(suppl 2):ii79–ii87.

# 24 Humanitarian Emergencies

## *Reinhard Kaiser and Paul B. Spiegel*

## 24.1 INTRODUCTION

Countries or regions affected by humanitarian emergencies remain challenging situations for the provision of health and nutrition services in developing countries. Major advances in recent decades have been made regarding our knowledge of the main causes of morbidity and mortality in humanitarian emergencies, the availability of standardized guidance protocols and indicators, and the development of new products, especially for severely malnourished children. The recently initiated reform of the humanitarian system is an important step forward to improve coordination, effectiveness, and quality of responses. Further areas of concern include the HIV/AIDS epidemic and changing environmental conditions that are adding to the health and nutrition burden of emergency-affected populations and the need for improving programs for displaced populations outside camp settings, especially to reduce mortality in children under 5 years of age. This chapter is primarily based on a series of review articles [1–5] with an update of the current situation and an expansion on selected topics.

### 24.1.1 *Definitions and History*

The need for an international response has been central for definitions of disasters and what is called a humanitarian or "complex" emergency, addressing the many different and connected components of many crisis situations. A *disaster* is defined as the result of a large ecological breakdown in the relation between humans and their environment, a serious and sudden event (or slow, as in a drought) on such a scale that the stricken community needs extraordinary efforts to cope with it, often with outside help or international aid [6]. The United Nations (UN) Interagency Standing Committee (IASC) defined a *humanitarian emergency* as a humanitarian crisis in a country, region, or society with total or considerable breakdown of authority resulting from internal or external conflict and requiring an international response that goes beyond the mandate or capacity of a single agency or ongoing UN country programs [7]. In a more epidemiology-oriented approach, *humanitarian* or *complex emergencies* have been redefined as situations in which mortality among the civilian population substantially increases above the population baseline, either as a result of the direct effects of war or indirectly through increased prevalence of malnutrition or transmission of communicable diseases, particularly if the latter result from deliberate political and military policies and strategies (national,

From: *Nutrition and Health: Nutrition and Health in Developing Countries, Second Edition*
Edited by: R. D. Semba & M. W. Bloem © Humana Press, Totowa, NJ

subnational, or international) [4]. This definition includes situations in which war does not play a major part (famine where government policies contribute to food insecurity) or situations in which food insecurity is not prominent (war and civil strife in developed countries); however, this definition does not include natural disasters, which are usually short term and necessitate a qualitatively different response. A *complex emergency* has been also defined as a social catastrophe marked by the destruction of the affected population's political, economic, sociocultural, and health care infrastructures [8]. Finally, to address their often long-term and always political nature, emergencies have been also called chronic or complex political emergencies [2].

A *refugee* is defined as a person who, owing to a well-founded fear of persecution for reasons of race, religion, nationality, or political opinion, is outside the country of his or her nationality and is unable or, owing to such fear, unwilling to avail himself or herself of the protection of that country [9]. The UN High Commissioner for Refugees (UNHCR) has an international mandate to protect the rights of refugees and to coordinate provision of basic services [10]. *Internally displaced persons* (IDPs), who may flee their homes for the same reasons as refugees, have not crossed internationally recognized borders, cannot invoke the same legal protections as refugees, and no specific international humanitarian agency is providing them with protection and humanitarian assistance [10]. The reason for this is primarily political. The IDPs remain inside country borders, and governments do not wish to have their autonomy challenged by international bodies with legal rights. To address the shortfall in protection and human rights of IDPs, nonbinding legal principles on internal displacement based on existing human rights law and analogous refugee law have been developed [11].

Recent reviews have discussed the changing political environment of humanitarian crises [2], in particular with the end of the cold war, and the evolving new technical fields of public health [4] and nutrition [5] in the last 30 years, when principles of public health and epidemiology started to be systematically applied to humanitarian emergencies.

Some crisis situations have been particular milestones in the way the humanitarian community has responded to emergencies. For example, with Operation Lifeline in Sudan in 1989, the international response changed from basic disaster relief to humanitarian assistance based on the norms and standards codified in international humanitarian law and human rights, and the concept of humanitarian governance evolved, a broad political and military commitment to using international laws, norms, and organizations to facilitate protection and assistance for affected populations in humanitarian emergencies [4]. This concept was in the mid-1990s replaced by a reality of limited funding and delayed responses to emergencies that were frequently characterized by high rates of malnutrition, morbidity, and mortality, especially in settings outside camps, while at the same time health specialists were confronted with a more complex working environment and rising expectations.

The crisis in Rwanda in 1994, with a massive influx of refugees into Goma, today the Democratic Republic of Congo (DRC), became known for one of the highest mortality rates ever recorded [12]. A systematic review concluded that the accountability mechanisms within the humanitarian aid system were inadequate [13]. Such shortcomings led to initial steps toward a universal code of conduct and of professional minimum standards under the Sphere project, which was started by a group of humanitarian agencies in 1998 and of which the second edition is now available [14]. Other initiatives to improve accountability and quality in humanitarian emergencies are discussed further in this chapter. The standards and indicators provided by the Sphere handbook and other technical field manuals have considerably improved the interpretation of data obtained from rapid assessments, surveys, and surveillance, allowing better planning interventions and monitoring and evaluating their impact [4]. Furthermore, guidelines and protocols for the management of specific disorders, such as cholera, meningococcal meningitis, and severe malnutrition, have led to declining case-fatality rates from these disorders [4].

The crises in the Balkans during the 1990s, characterized by relatively healthy populations with demographic characteristics and epidemiological disease profiles similar to those of other Western countries, did not fit the standard definition of an acute humanitarian emergency and the developing country paradigm. A large proportion of deaths occurred among older people as a result of war-related traumatic injury and chronic diseases [15]; there were few large-scale infectious disease epidemics. However, due to the high incidence of rape and trauma, assessments for reproductive health and psychological morbidity were needed. Older people appeared to be more at risk for undernutrition than young children [16], yet they were rarely considered a vulnerable group. The Balkan crises underscored the importance of context-specific approaches to humanitarian assessments and program implementation [15, 17, 18].

Today's humanitarian community, and the way it responds to emergencies, is characterized by a growing number of organizations, a changing political and natural environment, an increasing role of the military or quasi-state entities, the questions of neutrality and impartiality raised by working alliances, the challenge of further improving accountability and quality of work, and the question regarding how to prevent the primary causes of humanitarian emergencies.

### 24.1.2   Objective of the Chapter

The chapter has four main objectives: (1) to provide an overview of the global trends of complex emergencies and displaced persons as well as the epidemiology of the main causes of mortality and morbidity, (2) to describe the current status of programming guidance for humanitarian emergencies, (3) to address new developments and challenges for the future, and (4) to give recommendations for policy, technical, and training issues.

## 24.2   EPIDEMIOLOGY OF HUMANITARIAN EMERGENCIES

### 24.2.1   Global Trends in Number of Conflicts, Refugees, and Internally Displaced Persons

The number of conflicts globally has declined by more than 40% since the early 1990s (Fig. 24.1). Most of the world's armed conflicts now occur in sub-Saharan Africa [19]. Similarly, at the end of 2005 the number of refugees had declined from 17.8 million in 1992 to 8.2 million persons,[1] a decrease of 46% [20, 21]. This reduction is due to

---

[1] In addition, some 4.3 million Palestinian refugees fall under the responsibility of the United Nations Relief and Works Agency for Palestine Refugees in the Near East (UNRWA). These refugees are not included in UNHCR statistics.

numerous reasons, including large-scale repatriations to Rwanda, the Balkans, Angola, and Afghanistan. Currently, the largest number of refugees is in Africa (2.6 million; 31% of the total) followed by Asia (2.5 million; 29% of the total).

There are less-reliable figures for IDPs than refugees. From the second half of the 1990s, the global IDP figure increased to 25 million in 2001 and remained at that level until 2004 (Fig. 24.2). By the end of 2005, there were approximately 23.7 million IDPs, 1.6 million fewer than in 2004. Africa continued to be the continent most affected by IDPs; 12.1 million persons were displaced in approximately 20 countries in Africa by the end of 2005, more than in the rest of the world combined [22].

Besides refugees and IDPs, there are hundreds of millions of persons affected by conflict that are not displaced [1]. Furthermore, there are millions of populations that host refugees and IDPs; these populations are indirectly affected by conflict. Their interaction with displaced persons, the external aid that is brought into their areas and

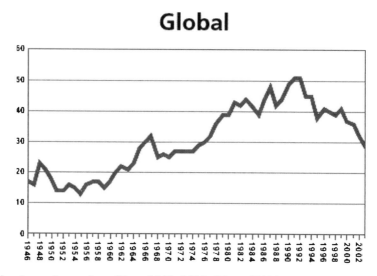

**Fig. 24.1.** Numbers of armed conflicts, 1946–2003. (From [19].)

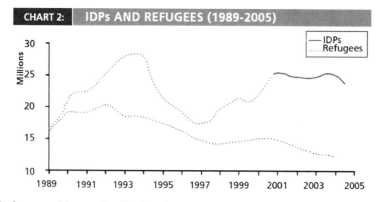

**Fig. 24.2.** Refugee and internally displaced persons population size trends, 1989 to 2005 [22].

myriad other factors greatly affect these host populations' lives. There is often insufficient information on the number and demographic characteristics of nondisplaced persons affected by conflict and surrounding host populations; however, these persons should not be forgotten and should receive aid.

Although the estimation of the total population size of persons affected by conflict and displacement (as well as surrounding host populations) is essential, it is not sufficient. The demographic characteristics of such populations are also necessary to inform program implementation [23]. However, this information is lacking in many situations. The most in-depth analysis of gender and age among refugees was made by UNHCR in 2001 [20]; such data were available for 62% of the global refugee population compared with 18% of other groups of concern to UNHCR, such as IDPs, asylum seekers, and returnees; this indicates that refugees are better registered than the other groups. In 2001, of the total population of concern to UNHCR 48.1% were female, 11.6% were under 5 years of age, 32.9% were between 5 and 17 years of age, 48.7% were between 18 and 59 years of age, and 6.9% were 60 years and over. Demographic profiles differed significantly among regions and across situations. For example, women constituted 51% of persons living in refugee camps, with women of working age constituting 53%; children younger than 5 years were 18% of the population in the East, Horn, and Great Lakes region of Africa; older persons (≥60 years) had the highest numbers in Eastern (30%) and Southeastern Europe (18%). In conclusion, gender and age composition appears to be related to the stage of the displacement process, with population who were displaced en masse reflecting a more balanced demographic structure compared with secondary refugee movements from first-asylum countries to third countries tending be more gender selective [20]. However, the demographic characteristics of conflict affected and displaced populations are region and conflict specific.

### 24.2.2  Main Causes of Morbidity and Mortality

The main causes of morbidity and mortality in conflict-affected and displaced populations are usually endemic diseases that are exacerbated due to the situation. In developing countries, these are usually communicable diseases, mainly respiratory infections, diarrhea, malaria, and measles (Fig. 24.3). Malnutrition and HIV are often exacerbating factors, whereas neonatal causes can also play a major role. In more developed countries, such as in the Balkans and Caucasus, chronic diseases may constitute the main causes of morbidity and mortality, reflecting the demographic characteristics of the population and the more developed public health systems (Fig. 24.4) [15, 24].

When refugees congregate in camps, high mortality rates may occur during the acute emergency phase but are often brought under control relatively quickly. Thereafter, in the postemergency phase, refugee populations often have lower mortality and better reproductive health outcomes than surrounding host populations [26, 27]. However, as camp situations become less common and conflict-affected and displaced persons are situated in large geographical areas or entire countries, sustained interventions to reduce mortality are more complicated and difficult to implement [4]; the long-standing crisis in the DRC is one of many examples [26]. Since access to IDPs is often limited, available data on the demographic characteristics and health status are incomplete. However, some of the highest-ever mortality rates have been recorded among IDPs during the past decade [10].

**Fig. 24.3.** Proportionate mortality of refugees in developing countries. (From [117].)

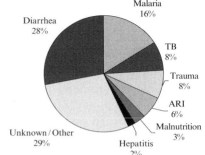

**Western Ethiopia: Fugnido Camp, 1989**

Malaria 16%
TB 8%
Trauma 8%
ARI 6%
Malnutrition 3%
Hepatitis 2%
Unknown/Other 29%
Diarrhea 28%

**Fig. 24.4.** Proportionate mortality of displaced persons in developed countries. (From [25].)

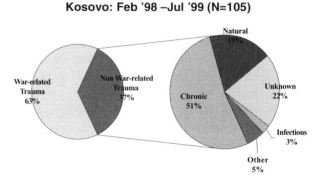

**Kosovo: Feb '98 –Jul '99 (N=105)**

War-related Trauma 63%
Non War-related Trauma 37%
Natural 19%
Unknown 22%
Chronic 51%
Infectious 3%
Other 5%

Children are at particularly high risk in conflicts; of the ten countries with the worst mortality rates for children under 5 years of age, seven are affected by humanitarian emergencies [2]. In emergencies in sub-Saharan Africa, particularly southern Africa, HIV/AIDS and increasingly tuberculosis (TB) are also important causes of morbidity and mortality.

### 24.2.3   Communicable Diseases, with Specific Focus on HIV/AIDS/STI

The combination of infection and malnutrition causes most of the preventable deaths in emergencies, especially in young children. Malnourished persons have compromised immunity and are not only more likely to contract communicable diseases, but also to suffer from more frequent, severe, and prolonged episodes of these diseases [1]. Other general risk factors for communicable diseases include movement and resettlement in temporary locations, overcrowding, economic and environmental degradation, impoverishment, scarcity of safe water, poor sanitation and waste management, absence of shelter, poor nutritional status as a result of food shortages, poor access to health care, and destruction of health services, resulting in a collapse of prevention and control programs [1]. An example for a disease-specific combination of risk factors is dry season, dust storms, overcrowding, and high rates of respiratory infections amplifying the risk of epidemic meningococcal disease. A specific example for a combination of food insecurity and a measles epidemic was documented in Gode, Ethiopia, in 2000, where a large number of deaths could have been prevented with appropriate public health interventions [28].

Prevention and control, case management, and surveillance are the three key components of humanitarian response. The essential prevention and control activities relate to site planning and shelter (e.g., adequate space between and within shelters); water and sanitation (e.g., provision of sufficient and clean water); immunization (e.g., measles immunization implemented immediately if vaccine coverage rates are < 90%); vector control (e.g., insecticide-treated nets and indoor residual spraying for malaria); and epidemic preparedness and response (e.g., establishment of simple health information and early warning systems [1]. A high standard of care and treatment using agreed-on standard treatment protocols with agreed-on first-line drugs is essential in reducing mortality. For example, poor community outreach, underuse, and poor use of oral and intravenous rehydration solutions and inadequate treatment of severe cases were the main factors in causing the very high mortality rates in the 1994 cholera outbreak in Goma, DRC [29, 30]. Accurate and timely data from health information systems are needed to provide an effective response to communicable and noncommunicable diseases in humanitarian emergencies. Types of data obtained include rapid health assessments, surveys, and surveillance [31].

There are numerous field manuals that have been developed for communicable diseases in humanitarian emergencies. These include manuals for communicable disease [32], malaria control [33, 34], cholera [35], meningococcal meningitis [36], sexually transmitted infections [37], and HIV/AIDS [38].

Recently, HIV/AIDS in humanitarian emergencies have become more of a priority in humanitarian emergencies. Previously, HIV/AIDS were seen as more of a developmental issue and thus were not adequately addressed in humanitarian emergencies [39]. However, if adequate prevention and control measures are not put in place at the beginning of an emergency and implemented throughout all of its phases, then the deaths averted from treating immediate life-saving disease may simply be postponed until the HIV infections transmitted during the crisis have time to develop into full-blown AIDS. The guidelines for HIV/AIDS interventions in emergency settings provide a matrix of interventions according to phase of emergency and sector [38], whereas the UNAIDS/UNHCR best-practice collection on HIV/AIDS in refugee settings provides policy guidelines that attempt to integrate programs and take into account the displacement cycle of refugees [40]. The importance of antiretroviral therapy (ART) in emergencies has only recently been recognized. The continuity of ART for those persons already on it in acute emergencies and the feasibility of providing ART in postemergency and chronic emergencies is not only a human right and feasible [41] but also necessary to achieve the goal of universal access.

Tuberculosis/HIV coinfection and potentially increasing resistance against anti-TB drugs in emergency-affected regions with high HIV prevalence rates [42] should be addressed by integrated TB/HIV interventions. The TB programs in humanitarian emergencies face particular challenges because of the length of treatment required and the potential to contribute to drug resistance if treatment is interrupted [43]. However, successful programs have been implemented in several emergencies [4].

### 24.2.4 Malnutrition and Food Security

This topic is more extensively described in Chapters 25, 26, and 30 [44–46]. Types of malnutrition in humanitarian emergencies include acute malnutrition (wasting);

micronutrient deficiencies (especially vitamin A, iron, and iodine; less frequently, certain vitamin B deficiencies and vitamin C); and chronic malnutrition (stunting) in prolonged or recurrent situations (e.g., Horn of Africa and Asia) [5]. The causes of malnutrition are multifactorial. Immediate causes include a reduction in caloric intake and diseases, while underlying causes include poor public health and health services, insufficient household food security, and an inadequate social and care environment [5].

The prevalence of wasting and nutritional edema among children 6–59 months of age by undertaking a cluster survey (30 clusters by 30 children) is a proxy for prevalence of the population. These data are used to prioritize aid and affected groups or areas, to plan interventions in resource-scarce environments, and to monitor program effectiveness. Despite the supposed simplicity of these nutritional surveys, numerous methodological errors have been noted [47, 48], and modifications of the standard have been suggested [49, 50] (e.g., calculating sample size instead of default size of 900 children). Unlike the measurement of acute malnutrition, the assessment of micronutrient deficiencies has not been standardized. Food security and health assessments are also essential to help to understand the underlying causes of malnutrition and to aid in program implementation. Despite increasing use of evidence-based programs, levels of acute malnutrition have remained high in many emergencies.

The major response to acute food insecurity is food provision. Depending on the groups at risk or those malnourished, food distribution may be for the whole population (general) or for subgroups (supplemental). Interventions to prevention of micronutrient deficiencies include periodic vitamin A distribution to children 5–59 months and fortification of food commodities such as oil, blended food, and salt [51]. Treatment of acute malnutrition may include targeted supplemental feeding programs (wet or dry rations) and therapeutic feeding programs. Until recently, therapeutic feeding programs were facility based. However, decentralized community and home-based treatment with ready-to-use therapeutic foods is a promising option to increase coverage and potentially reduce the risk of cross-infection [52–54]. There is a need to ensure that food-based interventions are complemented by public health interventions, and that the underlying causes of food insecurity and livelihoods are addressed. Finally, the distribution of food aid by donors, like all aspects of humanitarian emergencies, is inherently political. An inequitable distribution due to various considerations, many political in nature, had important repercussions in the past and will likely continue to have serious implications in the future.

### 24.2.5  *Reproductive Health*

The fields of reproductive and mental health (discussed in the next section) in humanitarian emergencies have developed considerably in the last decade. Some of the highest maternal mortality rates ever documented [55] and the common use of gender-based violence (GBV) [2] as an instrument of war have contributed to the increasing attention. Women in settings of armed conflict are vulnerable to extraordinary human rights violations such as rape, forced participation in the sex trade, or the need to exchange sex for food or security for themselves and their children [56, 57]. Although refugees and IDPs in post-acute-phase camps often have better reproductive health outcomes than their respective host country and country-of-origin populations [27], most emergency-affected populations still do not have access to comprehensive services [58], partly because those programs are difficult to implement in emergency situations [4]. For example, real improvement in maternal mortality needs expensive and complex programs, including safe blood transfusion and access to cesarean sections, and family planning [4].

Interventions that have been successful to increase childhood survival, such as clean delivery and antenatal steroids, require stronger health infrastructures than frequently available in emergency situations. In addition, specialized areas such as reproductive and mental health require sufficient staff with expertise and clear and feasible program strategies [4]. While basic reproductive health care, including emergency obstetric services, is the main objective in the acute phase of a humanitarian emergency, more comprehensive interventions in camp and noncamp settings are essential for the long-term survival of communities and should be implemented as early as possible. The Interagency Working Group on Reproductive Health in Refugee Situations has developed guidelines for short- and long-term interventions [59], including a minimum initial service package (MISP) that includes condoms, universal precautions, and designation of a reproductive health coordinator [60]. Postexposure prophylaxis to reduce HIV transmission is now recommended during throughout all phases of emergencies [38]. Guidelines to address GBV in emergencies and displaced settings have been developed [61, 62].

### 24.2.6  Mental Health

Humanitarian emergencies contribute to risk factors for mental health disorders that ultimately may increase the global burden of mortality and disability associated with mental illness. Apart from a direct impact on psychosocial well-being, mass violence reduces economic development, social capital, and human rights in communities and destroys health and mental health services. Population-based studies from several emergencies have found considerable post-traumatic stress disorder, depression, and where measured, nonspecific psychiatric morbidity in adults [63–65]; there are indications of long-term suffering after the crisis has ended [66]. More population-based studies are needed to determine the burden in children. A review outlined the necessary action steps to develop mental health further as a core public health area in emergencies [3]. As in general during emergencies, there is a need for immediately establishing coordination of mental health care activities. An early population-based assessment allows estimating the burden of mental health disorders, identifying vulnerable groups, mapping available mental health services and activities (including those of aid agencies), and planning appropriate interventions. Assessments can provide baseline data for continuous monitoring during the crisis to adapt interventions and measure accountability. Continuous efforts are needed to validate assessment tools in different cultural environments [67, 68].

There is now an increasing number of best practices for mental health interventions during emergencies [69–71]; however, the response to clinical treatment and psychosocial interventions needs to be systematically assessed [3], and it remains to be determined whether they are culturally effective. The IASC Task Force on Mental Health and Psychosocial Support [71] is currently under review and was published in fall 2006. The document is designed similar to the IASC Guidelines for HIV/AIDS Interventions in Emergency Settings, with a matrix on emergency preparedness, minimal response, and comprehensive response as well as action sheets for minimal response. A minimal response aims at reducing mortality and morbidity, offering population-wide psychological first aid, identifying and triaging seriously mentally ill to psychiatric treatment, and mobilizing community-based resiliency and adaptation by facilitating restoration of normal community life [3]. After the early intervention phase, a de facto mental health system of local primary health care practitioners, traditional healers, and local and international relief workers needs to be built up and financed [3]. All interventions should adopt the cultural medical worldview of the populations served and engage the local communities' participation, including decision-making processes. Capacity building in best practices among front-line responders and personnel of the mental health system is essential.

Finally, increasing attention has been directed toward prevention of negative mental health consequences in humanitarian workers. A study from Kosovo found a significant association between the number of trauma events experienced and high rates of symptoms satisfying the definition of depression [72]. Guidelines for managing stress in humanitarian workers are now available [73], addressing selection and preparation of personnel, identification and monitoring of risk factors, and self-care and mental health treatment programs.

## 24.3  PROGRAMMING

Governments, UN agencies, international organizations, and national and international nongovernmental organizations (NGOs) are key actors in humanitarian emergencies. Some organizations have accepted roles (e.g., UNHCR is the lead agency for refugee situations) and strengths in specific areas of expertise (e.g., Oxfam for water sanitation and Action Contre la Faim for nutrition). The role of the NGOs in humanitarian emergencies has grown substantially since the beginning of the 1990s, both in terms of numbers of new organizations and annual spending. The increasing number of small NGOs may make interventions potentially less bureaucratic and more cost-effective and may increase the scope and independence of the response; they may be better able to operate on a local level than traditional, large organizations. However, with increasing heterogeneity of the system and variability of experience and expertise, coordination and effectiveness of the overall response may be more difficult. The organization of agencies and other stakeholders into clusters to work in specific areas of humanitarian response, as a main objective of the humanitarian reform to improve coordination, and the changing role of the military are addressed in the section on new humanitarianism and humanitarian reform.

Today, technical field manuals are available for clinical and public health and nutrition topics in general [74, 75] as well as specific diseases, as described in the respective sections of this chapter. Interventions to improve child survival are available and need to be rigorously applied wherever feasible in humanitarian emergencies [76–80]. For interventions during the acute phase of a humanitarian emergency, the following operational priorities have been identified (commonly referred to as the *top priorities*) [75]:

1. *Rapid assessment of the health and nutrition status of a population*: The objectives of a rapid health assessment are to determine the magnitude of an acute emergency (e.g., using doubling of the baseline mortality rate as a quantitative indicator) and to determine the major health and nutrition-related needs of displaced populations [81]. Interpretation is done according to each specific context, and the assessment results in concrete recommendations for field operations. Rapid assessments are usually carried out at the start of

an intervention, together with the first operational activities (e.g., measles vaccination, water supply). They provide information on the size of the affected population and on its health and nutrition priorities and vital needs [81].

2. *Mass vaccination against measles*: If measles vaccination coverage is estimated to be less than 90%, a mass vaccination campaign for children aged 6 months to 15 years (including administration of vitamin A to children aged 6–59 months) is initiated [14]. An expanded program on immunization needs to be rapidly implemented after the acute emergency phase and in camps to maintain the achieved vaccination coverage levels.

3. *Water supply and implementation of sanitary measures*: Access must be provided to adequate facilities to collect, store, and use sufficient quantities of water (minimum of 15 L per person per day) for drinking, cooking, and personal hygiene and to ensure that drinking water remains safe until it is consumed [14]. Also, an adequate number of toilets is needed (maximum 20 persons per toilet), sufficiently close to people's dwellings, to allow them rapid, safe, and acceptable access at all times of the day and night [14].

4. *Food supply and implementation of specialized nutritional rehabilitation programs*: If there are indications for present or imminent acute malnutrition in the population, measured using weight-for-height-based indicators and interpreted using a framework to consider the context and relative importance of different causes of malnutrition [50], targeted interventions to ensure access to food in sufficient quantity (at least 2100 kcal or 8.8 MJ per person per day [14]) and quality (nutrient and micronutrient), including feeding programs, and nonfood interventions need to be implemented [5].

5. *Shelter, site planning, and nonfood items*: Interventions ensure that existing shelter and settlement solutions are prioritized, local physical planning practices and designs are used, sufficient covered space and spacing between individual shelters are provided, and adverse effects on the environment are minimized [14]. Nonfood items include clothing, bedding, and household materials to enable families to meet personal hygiene needs, prepare and eat food, provide thermal comfort, and build, maintain, or repair shelters [14].

6. *Curative care based on the use of standardized therapeutic protocols, using essential drugs*: Interventions ensure that the whole population has access to health services that are prioritized to address main causes of morbidity and mortality; well coordinated across sectors and agencies; designed to support existing health systems, structures, and providers; based on relevant primary health care principles; standardized and following accepted protocols and guidelines; and guided in design and development by the ongoing, coordinated collection, analysis, and utilization of public health data [14].

7. *Control and prevention of communicable diseases and potential epidemics*: Interventions ensure that people have access to information and services that are designed to prevent the communicable diseases that contribute most significantly to excess morbidity and mortality, including access to effective diagnosis and treatment and availability of timely and effective outbreak response capacity [14].

8. *Health information systems*: The early implementation of a basic surveillance system provides a mechanism for ongoing monitoring of morbidity and mortality after the initial rapid assessment, as well as quality, coverage, and effectiveness of interventions, and should be designed to function as an early alert system for disease outbreaks [14, 81]. Surveys are intermittent, focused assessments to gather health and nutrition data.

9. *Assessment of human resources, training, and supervision of community health workers*: Guidance is available to assess staffing levels in different levels of health facilities and the proper training and skills of health care workers [14].

10. *Coordination of different operational partners*: With the increasing number of players in humanitarian emergencies and changing operating conditions, a clear coordination structure is essential from the beginning of the response, and a reform process to better define the role of different organizations and stakeholders must be initiated [82].

During the postemergency phase of emergencies, a more community-based and comprehensive approach should be undertaken. The benefits of integrating interventions for displaced populations with those of the surrounding host community have been shown to be beneficial and cost-effective [83, 84]. Other essential interventions such as education, income-generating activities, and other programs to improve the skills of the population for when they return home are needed.

## 24.4 NEW DEVELOPMENTS AND CHALLENGES

### 24.4.1 *New Humanitarianism and Humanitarian Reform*

Humanitarian action is increasingly becoming an integral part of governments' strategies to transform conflicts, decrease violence, and set the stage for development, a change that is frequently called the *new humanitarianism*.[85] Examples are coordinated, publicized humanitarian components of military campaigns, such as in Afghanistan and Iraq. In these countries, the military goes beyond just using their logistical systems to supply key items in the acute emergency phase to becoming deliverers of aid.

Humanitarian actors have warned of an increasing convergence of aid and politics and have argued that organizations should keep their neutrality and impartiality to uphold humanitarian values and principles of universal and unrestricted aid [85–87]. The traditional goal of simply and foremost saving lives and livelihoods may also conflict with other aspects of new humanitarianism: a human rights-based approach and developmental relief or goal-oriented humanitarianism. Humanitarian values such as bearing witness, promoting human rights [88, 89], or using aid to secure peace appear to be beyond criticism. However, human rights-based approaches and goal-oriented humanitarianism may result in delaying or withholding aid in some situations, such as when aid is being scrutinized whether it contributes to human rights or long-term development. The term *developmental relief* may also support misconceptions of an implicit distinction of values between humanitarianism and development, including the concept that human rights belong to one but not the other [90]. New humanitarianism deserves credit for having raised such serious questions and having stimulated the discussion about humanitarian reform.

In 2005, the UN emergency relief coordinator, to initiate a reform process, launched an independent humanitarian response review of the humanitarian response capacities of the United Nations, NGOs, Red Cross/Red Crescent Movement, and other key humanitarian actors, including the International Organization for Migration [91]. The report called for a major strengthening of the capacity, predictability, effectiveness, and accountability of international humanitarian action, the filling of gaps, and the establishment of measures and systems to assess needs, performance, and impact. As a consequence of the report, the Office for the Coordination of Humanitarian Action (OCHA) in 2006 launched in 2006 a humanitarian response reform that has three main elements: (1) to create more predictable humanitarian finances to ensure and enable a prompt response to new or rapidly deteriorating crises, (2) to strengthen response capacity by establishing a system of cluster leads in those areas of activity where there are clearly identified gaps, and finally (3) to strengthen the humanitarian coordinator system to better support field coordination [82]. The OCHA is modernizing the existing central emergency revolving fund by adding a grant element, introducing a new financing mechanism that is expected to respond more promptly to new crises and rapidly deteriorating existing crises. To strengthen the capacity of the humanitarian response, cluster leads were introduced in nine areas of humanitarian activity (logistics; emergency telecommunications; camp coordination and management; emergency shelter; health; nutrition; early recovery; and protection). Introduction of clusters at global and country levels, with defined functions and obligations to interact with each other and with partner organizations, is expected to contribute to improved predictability, accountability, and greater effectiveness of response for the humanitarian system [92]. The country-level clusters may not necessarily replicate the global cluster arrangements. In all instances, the key principle is ensuring that country-level clusters address all identified key gaps in humanitarian response and that critical gaps are not neglected simply because they are not part of any global cluster. The cluster approach is initially being implemented in the DRC, Liberia, and Uganda based on the recommendations and feedback from interagency missions to those countries as well as to all new major emergencies with a phased and flexible implementation. The cluster leadership approach can be used in both conflict-related humanitarian emergencies and natural disasters. Although IDPs are not the main focus of the reform, improving their situation is one of the objectives after urgent calls for one international organization to be designated as the agency responsible for the protection of IDPs have not been heeded [10, 93].

The third element of the humanitarian response reform aims at strengthening the humanitarian coordination by establishing a broad and flexible selection pool of resident and humanitarian coordinators (the designated representatives of the secretary-general for development and humanitarian operations), bringing humanitarian experience to countries where there are clear humanitarian issues, and ensuring that coordinators are better prepared to respond to humanitarian crises, including natural disasters [82].

After the acute phase of a humanitarian emergency, postconflict recovery and reconstruction are vital to enable a country to heal and to ensure that it does not return to conflict. This is a very delicate phase. For example, there is some evidence that HIV transmission may be muted during conflict but increase during the recovery phase [39, 94]. To address postconflict and recovery, the United Nations established a Peacebuilding Commission to promote integrated strategies for postconflict recovery, focusing attention on reconstruction, institution building, and sustainable development, in countries emerging from conflict [95]. The commission will attempt to bring together the United Nation's broad capacities and experience in conflict prevention, mediation, peacekeeping, respect for human rights, the rule of law, humanitarian assistance, reconstruction, and long-term development.

The changing nature and focus of complex emergencies, from short-term emergencies in refugee camps to prolonged emergencies in large geographical areas, and recognized shortfalls have resulted in various other initiatives to improve accountability and quality of humanitarian action, which are addressed in the following sections. A generally changing environment bears new challenges for the international community in its response to humanitarian emergencies.

### 24.4.2    Other Initiatives for Improvement of Accountability and Quality

Reviews of emergency responses, including those in Rwanda in 1994 [13] and in Darfur in 2004 [96], resulted in criticism that humanitarian response does not always meet the basic requirements of affected populations in a timely fashion, that the response provided can vary considerably from crisis to crisis, and that accountability mechanisms within the humanitarian aid system are inadequate. Currently, a mechanism is lacking to ensure that all agencies adhere to basic standards in implementing their projects [4]; quality of assessment methods is often insufficient [48], and neither donors nor providers of humanitarian aid have a formal system for evaluations of emergency responses. As a consequence, various initiatives for quality improvement such as the Sphere project [14] have been started. The Standardized Monitoring and Assessment of Relief and Transition (SMART) program was started as another interagency initiative in 2002 to improve monitoring and evaluation of humanitarian assistance interventions (e.g., survey methods) [97]. In June 2003, donor governments met in Stockholm to discuss how donors could and should use their influence and harmonize their procedures to improve humanitarian response. The group, which has become known as the Good Humanitarian Donorship initiative, requested that implementing humanitarian organizations fully adhere to good practice and are committed to promoting accountability, efficiency, and effectiveness in implementing humanitarian action [98]. The initiative agreed on 23 principles and good practice of humanitarian donorship. As one of the consequences of the Humanitarian Response Review, the World Health Organization (WHO), as lead for the IASC Health Cluster, and the United Nations International Children's Emergency Fund (UNICEF), as lead for the IASC Nutrition Cluster, initiated a process in 2005 to develop a common Humanitarian Tracking Service for the systematic measurement of selected indicators in crisis situations. The service will draw on the best elements of current initiatives. Development of a full proposal for such a tracking service, including institutional and oversight arrangements, is in progress [99]. Since the 2004 tsunami, the evidence aid project of the Cochrane Collaboration has provided evidence summaries for interventions relevant to health care in natural disasters and other health care emergencies on its Web site [100]. Improving quality also requires adjustment of programs to introduce evidence-based approaches into capacity building and teaching practical and analytical skills to relief workers, national staff, and institutions [4].

### 24.4.3    Health, Nutrition, and Conflicts in a Changing Global Environment

Evidence is accumulating about the effect of human-made releases of greenhouse gases on global climate change [101]. Higher global temperatures and increased variability in weather patterns have been shown to affect a variety of different health outcomes, including morbidity and mortality related to changes of temperature in general [102], weather extremes [103] (e.g., heat and cold waves, floods, and storms), air pollution [104], and transmission of water- [105] and vector-borne [106] diseases. Global climate change may also aggravate scarceness of freshwater, land degradation, and desertification, contributing to loss of livelihoods and water and food insecurity and exacerbating already-existing inequalities in developing countries.

Furthermore, a global change of environmental conditions for resurging and emerging infectious diseases may be compounded by generally insufficient prevention and control programs for infectious diseases in humanitarian emergencies [1], resulting in increased risks for the affected populations as well as limitations for controlling such diseases world-wide. Major risk factors include the resurgence of old or previously controlled diseases (e.g., malaria, trypanosomiasis) and emergence of drug resistance driven by improper and incomplete use of drugs and the absence of regulatory controls (e.g., bacillary dysentery and multidrug-resistant TB) and delays in detection, characterization, and containment of resurging or emerging infectious pathogens and their widespread transmission before control measures can be implemented (e.g., monkey pox in DRC) [1].

Therefore, given that many humanitarian emergencies are in underdeveloped regions of the world, a change of global climate and environmental conditions will add an extra health and nutrition burden and increase the vulnerability of emergency-affected popu-lations. The magnitude of risks for these populations attributable to climate change has not been assessed. In 2000, WHO estimated an annual mortality of 70–120 per million population attributed to climate change in sub-Saharan countries [107], a region that has been considerably affected by conflicts, droughts, and the AIDS epidemic. Compared to health and nutrition, there is less consensus on whether global warming will become a general security issue [108] or increase conflicts due to environmental change [109, 110]. The interlinkage between global warming causing increased natural disasters and epidemics with consequent increasing ecological stress and scarceness of resources (e.g., water, food, cooking and building materials) causing increased conflict will need to be examined closely as the effects of global warming become more pronounced. However, global warming may increase the overlap between humanitarian emergencies and natural disasters because of generally deteriorating environmental conditions and higher vulner-ability to human actions that may lead to crisis situations, such as loss of purchasing power and entitlements resulting in famine [111].

## 24.5 SUMMARY RECOMMENDATIONS FOR THE WAY FORWARD

In the area of nutrition and health in developing countries, humanitarian emergencies are subject to specific technical challenges and political issues. Although the proportion of funding for humanitarian emergencies as part of the overall development assistance increased considerably during the 1980 and 1990s, obtaining funds has become more difficult because of limited resources, competing priorities, and lack of political will. Donors appear to be prepared to give more easily if the crisis is closer to the developed world [112], in case of a natural disaster that effects tourism [111], or if the situation is well covered by media. Funding may be also easier to obtain for an acute response or for certain diseases that have a higher public or political attention (e.g., HIV/AIDS vs. diarrheal diseases) than compared with other areas such as research and training. Field research has to be conducted under inherently difficult conditions and integrated into day-to-day needs of emergency work in close collaboration with humanitarian workers. For example, pressures to provide rapid assistance in acute emergency situations make it difficult to introduce new interventions and conduct intervention trials, especially in remote areas. For the same reasons, systematic monitoring and evaluation are still often lacking, limiting the lessons identified and learned. As a consequence, arguments for and against specific methods used in emergencies are often based on extrapolation of concerns regarding other methods or on theoretical considerations in different conditions rather than based on studies that occurred in emergencies. Recommendations for the next decade must call for a continuation of efforts to be proactive to secure the funding needed, move forward with various reforms in the humanitarian arena, systematically integrate research and evaluations to improve the evidence base and lessons learned, adjust to changing environments, strengthen training and education, and above all, to advocate to do more to prevent the primary causes of humanitarian emergencies.

### 24.5.1  Policy Recommendations

The IASC humanitarian reform is an important step forward to, among others, strengthen lead functions and coordination between the key players of humanitarian emergencies, consolidate initiatives to improve accountability and quality, and improve the situation of IDPs, especially in large geographical areas. Ensuring NGO participation and defining their roles and responsibilities within the cluster approach will be a major challenge in this process. Decision making should be based on universally applicable quantitative standards and, wherever possible, local baselines (e.g., for mortality) in combination with context-specific qualitative information [50]. A generally accepted methods framework and mechanism for systematic reviews of international responses to humanitarian crises is needed as part of the efforts to improve accountability and quality [113]. Finally, increased efforts are necessary to advocate for a more equitable response to humanitarian emergencies compared to natural disasters and to better address the underlying long-term causes of humanitarian emergencies [2]. This will need strong and long-term political commitment as well as better governance, meaning both less corruption and better economic policies. Long-lasting processes may be complemented by more short-term measures, such as combining humanitarian and development funding streams and promoting close collaboration between humanitarian and development agencies.

### 24.5.2  Technical Recommendations

Evidence-based interventions that have been shown to prevent morbidity and mortality in nonemergency settings (e.g., on child survival [79]) should be applied in humanitarian emergencies wherever possible. Community-based intervention trials are needed to test feasibility, coverage, and effectiveness (e.g., regarding the use of zinc [114] or point-of-use water disinfection [115] in emergencies). Especially in large, potentially insecure geographical areas, efforts have to be increased to attain high coverage and effectiveness of services, such as through community-based therapeutic feeding programs that may reduce case-fatality rates for acute malnutrition, and increase adherence because malnourished children can be mainly treated in their families [54]. Provision of sufficient numbers of qualified, local health care workers have been associated with reduced mortality [116]. Simplified drug regimens (e.g., for acute respiratory infections, TB, and typhoid fever) may also improve feasibility of interventions and adherence [1]. Rapid diagnostic tests for symptomless sexually transmitted infections (e.g., gonorrhea, Chlamydia) would allow targeted treatment while replacing the currently used syndromic management, which may facilitate antibiotic resistance [1]. Other areas in which further research is needed include new antimalaria drugs for intermittent preventive treatment and use in pregnancy; new heat-stabile, pentavalent vaccines; mapping and calculating the size of emergency-affected populations; and improving survey methods [1].

## 24.5.3 Training Recommendations

Curricula of public health and field epidemiology training programs should include modules to prepare health and nutrition professionals to work in and adjust to the changing nature of humanitarian emergencies. Programs should focus on the practical and analytical skills needed by aid workers while also familiarizing students with the roles and capabilities of the major international organizations, relevant international policies and standards [4], the need to integrate research projects and systematic monitoring and evaluation into emergency responses, and how to address mental health and strategies to sustain well-being [73]. Capacity building of national staff and institutions should be a major focus, and programs should increase their efforts to attract national staff (e.g., through international scholarships). Field exercises and carefully planned and supervised internships should be a standard component to improve field skills. An international training and education guide would be useful to help young persons who want to become health and nutrition experts in the field of humanitarian emergencies.

## REFERENCES

1. Connolly MA, Gayer M, Ryan MJ, Salama P, Spiegel P, Heymann DL. Communicable diseases in complex emergencies: impact and challenges. Lancet 2004;364:1974–1983.
2. Lautze S, Leaning J, Raven-Roberts A, Kent R, Mazurana D. Assistance, protection, and governance networks in complex emergencies. Lancet 2004;364:2134–2141.
3. Mollica RF, Lopes Cardozo B, Osofsky HJ, Raphael B, Ager A, Salama P. Mental health in complex emergencies. Lancet 2004; 364:2058–2067.
4. Salama P, Spiegel P, Talley L, Waldman R. Lessons learned from complex emergencies over past decade. Lancet 2004;364:1801–1813.
5. Young H, Borrel A, Holland D, Salama P. Public nutrition in complex emergencies. Lancet 2004;365:1899–1909.
6. Noji E. The public health consequences of disasters. New York: Oxford University Press, 1997.
7. Interagency Standing Committee. Definition for humanitarian emergency. Inter-Agency Contingency Planning Guidelins for Humanitarian Assistance. Recommendations to the IASC. November 15, 2001. http://www.humanitarianinfo.org/iasc/content/products/docs/IAContingencyPlanGuide.pdf
8. Toole MJ, Waldman RJ. The public health aspects of complex emergencies and refugee situations. Annu Rev Public Health 1997;18:283–312.
9. United Nations High Commissioner for Refugees. UN convention on refugees. Geneva: United Nations High Commissioner for Refugees, 1951.
10. Salama P, Spiegel P, Brennan R. No less vulnerable: the internally displaced in humanitarian emergencies. Lancet 2001;357:1430–1431.
11. Deng FM. Guiding principles on internal displacement. Geneva: United Nations Office for the Coordination of Humanitarian Affairs, 2006.
12. Goma Epidemiology Group. Public health impact of the Rwandan refugee crisis: what happened in Goma, Zaire, in July 1994? Lancet 1995;345:339–344.
13. The international response to conflict and genocide: lessons from the Rwanda experience. Steering Committee of the Joint Evaluation of Emergency Assistance to Rwanda. Copenhagen: Danida, 1996.
14. Sphere. The Sphere project: humanitarian charter and minimum standards in disaster response. Geneva: Sphere Project, 2004.
15. Spiegel PB, Salama P. War and mortality in Kosovo, 1998–99: an epidemiological testimony. Lancet 2000;355:2204–2209.
16. Salama P, Spiegel P, Van Dyke M, Phelps L, Wilkinson C. Mental health and nutritional status among the adult Serbian minority in Kosovo. JAMA 2000;284:615–616.
17. Spiegel PB, Salama P. Emergencies in developed countries: are aid organisations ready to adapt? Lancet 2001;357:714.
18. Toole MJ, Galson S, Brady W. Are war and public health compatible? Lancet 1993;341:1193–1196.

19. Human security report 2005: war and peace in the twenty-first century. New York: Human Security Centre, 2005.

20. United Nations High Commissioner for Refugees. Statistical yearbook 2001. Geneva: United Nations High Commissioner for Refugees, 2002.

21. United Nations High Commissioner for Refugees. Global refugee trends 2005: statistical overview. Geneva: United Nations High Commissioner for Refugees, 2006.

22. Internal displacement: global overview of trends and developments in 2005. Oslo: Norwegian Refugee Council, Internal Displacement Monitoring Centre, 2006.

23. Davis AP. Targeting the vulnerable in emergency situations: who is vulnerable? Lancet 1996;348: 868–871.

24. Spiegel P, Salama P. Emergencies in developed countries: are aid organisations ready to adapt? Lancet 2001;357:714.

25. Wei C, Gaspard C, Abigail J, Amita K, Sarah T, Michelle T. Capacity building in post-conflict. Kosovo. An Evaluation of the International Rescue Committees role in the epidemic prevention and prepared-ness program, 2005. http://www.sipa.columbia.edu/academics/concentrations/epd/2005_EPDreport_Kosovo.pdf

26. Coghlan B, Brennan RJ, Ngoy P, et al. Mortality in the Democratic Republic of Congo: a nationwide survey. Lancet 2006;367:44–51.

27. Hynes M, Sheik M, Wilson H, Spiegel P. Reproductive health indicators and outcomes among refugee and internally displaced persons in postemergency phase camps. JAMA 2002;288:595–603.

28. Salama P, Assefa F, Talley L, Spiegel P, van Der Veen A, Gotway CA. Malnutrition, measles, mortality, and the humanitarian response during a famine in Ehiopia. JAMA 2001;286:563–571.

29. Siddique A, Salam A, Islam MS, et al. Why treatment centres failed to prevent cholera deaths among Rwandan refugees in Goma, Zaire. Lancet 1995;345:359–361.

30. Swerdlow DL, Levine O, Toole MJ, Waldman RJ, Tauxe RV. Cholera control among Rwandan refu-gees in Zaire. Lancet 1994;344:1302–1303.

31. Marfin AA, Moore J, Collins C, et al. Infectious disease surveillance during emergency relief to Bhu-tanese refugees in Nepal. JAMA 1994;272:377–81.

32. World Health Organization. Communicable disease control in emergencies: a field manual. Geneva: World Health Organization, 2005.

33. World Health Organization. Malaria control in complex emergencies: an inter-agency field handbook. Geneva: World Health Organization, 2005.

34. Boland PB, Williams HA. Malaria control during mass population movements and natural disasters. Washington, DC: National Academy Press, 2003.

35. World Health Organization. Guidelines for cholera control. Geneva: World Health Organization, 1993.

36. Moore PS, Toole MJ, Nieburg P, Waldman RJ, Broome CV. Surveillance and control of meningococcal meningitis epidemics in refugee populations. Bull World Health Organ 1990;68:587–596.

37. Reproductive Health Response in Conflict. Guidelines for the care of sexually transmitted infections in conflict-affected settings. Women's Commission for Refugee Women and Children on behalf of the Reproductive Health Response in Conflict Consortium, 2004. http://www.rhrc.org/resources/index.cfm?sector=sti

38. Interagency Standing Committee. Guidelines for HIV/AIDS interventions in emergency settings. Geneva: Interagency Standing Committee, 2004.

39. Spiegel PB. HIV/AIDS among conflict-affected and displaced populations: dispelling myths and tak-ing action. Disasters 2004;28:322–339.

40. UNAIDS/United Nations High Commissioner for Refugees. UNAIDS/UNHCR best practice collec-tion on HIVAIDS in refugee settings. Geneva, 2006. http://www.unhcr.org/doclist/protect/4028b05b4.html

41. Ellman T, Culbert H, Torres-Feced V. Treatment of aids in conflict-affected settings: a failure of imagi-nation. Lancet 2005; 365:278–280.

42. World Health Organization. Tuberculosis (TB)—South Africa. Geneva: World Health Organization, 2006.

43. World Health Organization. Tuberculosis control in refugee situations: an interagency manual. Geneva: World Health Organization, 1997.

44. Webb P, Thorne-Lyman A. Tackling nutrient deficiencies and life-threatening disease: the role of food in humanitarian relief. In: Nutrition and health in developing countries. 2nd ed. Semba R, Bloem MW, eds. Totowa, NJ: Humana Press, 2007.

45. De Pee S. Multivitamin/mineral supplements for young children and considerations for programs. In: Nutrition and health in developing countries. 2nd ed. Semba R, Bloem MW, eds. Totowa, NJ: Humana Press, 2007.

46. De Pee S, Moench-Pfanner R, Bloem MW. The tsunami. In: Nutrition and health in developing countries. Semba R, Bloem MW, eds. 2nd ed. Totowa, NJ: Humana Press, 2007.

47. Boss LP, Toole MJ, Yip R. Assessments of mortality, morbidity, and nutritional status in Somalia during the 1991–1992 famine. Recommendations for standardization of methods. JAMA 1994;272: 371–376.

48. Spiegel PB, Salama P, Maloney S, van der Veen A. Quality of malnutrition assessment surveys conducted during famine in Ethiopia. JAMA 2004;292:613–618.

49. Kaiser R, Woodruff BA, Bilukha O, Spiegel P, Salama P. Using design effects from previous cluster surveys to guide sample size calculation in emergency settings. Disasters 2006;30:199–211.

50. World Food Programme. A manual: measuring and interpreting malnutrition and mortality. Rome: World Food Programme, 2005.

51. World Health Organization. The management of nutrition in major emergencies. Geneva: World Health Organization, 2000.

52. Collins S. Changing the way we address severe malnutrition during famine. Lancet 2001; 358:498–501.

53. Collins S, Sadler K. Outpatient care for severely malnourished children in emergency relief programmes: a retrospective cohort study. Lancet 2002;360:1824–1830.

54. Grobler-Tanner C, Steve Collins S. Community Therapeutic Care (CTC): a new approach to managing acute malnutrition in emergencies and beyond. Washington, DC: Food and Nutrition Technical Assistance, 2004.

55. Bartlett L, Mawji S, Whitehead S, et al. Where giving birth is a forecast of death: maternal mortality in four districts in Afghanistan, 1999–2000. Lancet 2005;365:827–828.

56. Bartlett L, Purdin S, McGinn T. Forced migrants—turning rights into reproductive health. Lancet 2004;363:76–77.

57. Purdin S, McGinn T, Miller A. Reproductive health among forced migrants—an issue of human rights. Lancet 2004; 363:76–77.

58. McGinn T, Purdin S. Editorial: reproductive health and conflict: looking back and moving ahead. Disasters 2004;28:235–238.

59. Interagency Working Group. Reproductive health in refugee situations. An Interagency Working Group on Reproductive Health in Refugee Situations, 1999. http://www.unfpa.org/emergencies/manual/

60. Reproductive Health Response in Conflict. Minimum Initial Services Package (MISP). Reproductive Health Response in Conflict Consortium, 2006. http://www.rhrc.org/rhr_basics/misp.html

61. Interagency Standing Committee. Guidelines for gender-based violence interventions in humanitarian settings. Geneva: Interagency Standing Committee, 2005.

62. United Nations High Commissioner for Refugees. Sexual violence against refugees: guidelines on prevention and response. Geneva: United Nations High Commissioner for Refugees, 1995.

63. De Jong JTVM, Komproe IH, Van Ommeren M, El Masri M. Lifetime events and posttraumatic stress disorder in four post conflict settings. JAMA 2001;286:555–562.

64. Lopes Cardozo B, Kaiser R, Gotway CA, Agani F. Mental health, social functioning, and feelings of hatred and revenge of Kosovar Albanians one year after the war in Kosovo. J Trauma Stress 2003;16:351–360.

65. Mollica RF, Donelan K, Tor S, et al. The effect of trauma and confinement on functional health and mental health status of Cambodians living in Thailand-Cambodia border camps. JAMA 1993;270: 581–586.

66. Mollica RF, Sarajlic N, Chernoff M, Lavelle J, Vukovic I, Massagli MP. Longitudinal study of psychiatric symptoms, disability, mortality and emigration among Bosnian refugees. JAMA 2001;286: 546–554.

67. Goldberg DP, Gater R, Sartorius N. The validity of two versions of the GHQ in the WHO study of mental illness in general health care. Psychol Med 1997;27:191–197.

68. Mollica RF, Caspi-Yavin Y, Bollini P, Troung T, Tor S, Lavelle J. The Harvard Trauma Questionnaire: validating a cross-cultural instrument for measuring torture, trauma, and posttraumatic stress disorder in Indochinese refugees. J Nerv Ment Dis 1992;180:111–116.

69. World Health Organization. Mental health in emergencies. Department of Mental Health and Substance Dependence, World Health Organization, Geneva 2003. http://www.who.int/mental_health/resources/emergencies/en/index.html

70. De Jong, Kas. Early psychosocial interventions for war-affected populations. Médecins sans frontières, 2003. http://www.arsenzondergrenzen.nl.usermedia/files/Earlyintervention.doc

71. Interagency Standing Committee. IASC guidance on mental health and psychosocial support in emergency settings. Geneva: Interagency Standing Committee Task Force on Mental Health and Psychosocial Support, 2006. http://www.humanitarianinfo.org/iasc/content/products/docs/Guidelines%20 IASC%20Mental%20Health%20Psychosocial.pdf

72. Lopes Cardozo B, Holtz T, Kaiser R, et al. The mental health of expatriate relief workers, Kosovo, June 2000. Disasters 2005;29:152–170.

73. Managing stress in humanitarian workers - guidelines for good practice. Antares Foundation, 2006. http://www.antaresfoundation.org/download/Managing%20Stress%20in%20Humanitarian%20Aid% 20Workers%20-%20Guidelines%20for%20Good%20Practice.pdf

74. Mears C, Chowdbury S. Health care for refugees and displaced people. London: Oxfam, 1994.

75. Médecins sans frontières. Refugee health: an approach to emergency situations. London: Macmillan Education, 1997.

76. The Bellagio Study Group on Child Survival. Knowledge into action for child survival. Lancet 2003;362:323–327.

77. Black RE, Morris SS, Bryce J. Where and why are 10 million children dying every year? Lancet 2003;361: 2226–2234.

78. Bryce J, el Arifeen S, Pariyo G, Lanata CF, Gwatkin D, Habicht JP. Reducing child mortality: can public health deliver? Lancet 2003;362:159–164.

79. Jones G, Steketee RW, Black RE, Bhutta ZA, Morris SS. How many child deaths can we prevent this year? Lancet 2003;362:65–71.

80. Victoria CG, Wagstaff A, Schellenberg JA, Gwatkin D, Claeson M, Habicht JP. Applying an equity lens to child health and mortality: more of the same is not enough. Lancet 2003;362:233–241.

81. Médecins sans frontières. Rapid health assessment of refugee or displaced populations. 3rd ed. Paris: Médecins sans frontières, 2006.

82. Office for the Coordination of Humanitarian Action. OCHA at work—humanitarian response reform, 2006. http://ochaonline.un.org/ocha2006/chap6_6.htm

83. UNAIDS/United Nations High Commissioner for Refugees. Strategies to support the HIV-related needs of refugees and host populations. UNAIDS Best Practice Collection. Geneva: Joint United Nations Programme on HIV/AIDS and the United Nations High Commissioner for Refugees, 2005.

84. Van Damme W, De Brouwere V, M B, Van Lerberghe W. Effects of a refugee-assistance programme on host population in Guinea as measured by obstetric interventions. Lancet 1998;351:1609–1613.

85. Fox F. New humanitarianism: does it provide a moral banner for the twenty-first century? Disasters 2001;25:275–289.

86. Overseas Development Institute. Politics and humanitarian aid: debates, dilemmas and dissension. London: Overseas Development Institute, 2001. http://www.odi.org.uk/HPG/papers/hpgreport10.pdf

87. Duffield M, Macrae J, Curtis D. Editorial: politics and humanitarian aid. Disasters 2001;25:269–274.

88. Leaning J. Diagnosing genocide—the case of Darfur. N Engl J Med 2004;351:735–738.

89. Woodruff BA, Kaiser R. Violence and mortality in West Darfur. Discussion. Lancet 2004;364:1290–1291.

90. Slim H. Dissolving the difference between humanitarianism and development: the mixing of a rights based solution. Dev Pract 2000;10.

91. Humanitarian response review. United Nations Emergency relief Coordinator and Under-Secretary- General for Humanitarian Affairs 2005. http://www.reliefweb.int/library/documents/2005/ocha-gen-02sep.pdf

92. Office for the Coordination of Humanitarian Affairs. Update on humanitarian reform. United Nations Office for the Coordination of Humanitarian Affairs, 2006.

93. Cohen R, Deng FM. Masses in flight: the global crisis of internal displacement. Washington, DC: Brookings Institution Press, 1998.

94. Mock NB, Duale S, Brown LF, et al. Conflict and HIV: a framework for risk assessment to prevent HIV in conflict-affected settings in Africa. Emerg Themes Epidemiol 2004;1:6.

95. United Nations. United Nations Peacebuilding Commission. Geneva: United Nations, 2006.

96. Office for the Coordination of Humanitarian Affairs. Inter-agency real-time evaluation of the humanitarian response to the Darfur crisis. UN Office for the Coordination of Humanitarian Affairs, 2005. http://www.reliefweb.int/library/documents/2005/ocha-sudan-03mar.pdf

97. Standardized Monitoring and Assessment of Relief and Transition (SMART). 2006. http://www.smart-indicators.org/

98. Good humanitarian donorship. 2006. http://www.goodhumanitariandonorship.org/

99. IASC and WHO. Tracking health performance and humanitarian outcomes. November 2005. http://www.who.int/hac/events/Finalagenda2Dec.pdf

100. The Evidence Aid project: resources for natural disasters and other healthcare emergencies. 2006.

101. Intergovernmental Panel on Climate Change. Climate change 2001: impacts, adaptation, and vulnerability. In: Contribution of Working group II to the second assessment report of the IPCC. McCarthy JJ, Canziani OF, Leary NA, Dokken DJW, KS, eds. 2001. http://www.cochrane.org/evidenceaid/project.htm

102. Braga ALF, Zanobetti A, Schwartz J. The effect of weather on respiratory and cardiovascular deaths in 12 US cities. Environ Health Perspect 2002;110:859–863.

103. Le Tertre A, Lefranc A, Eilstein D. Impact of the 2003 heatwave on all-cause mortality in nine French cities. Epidemiology 2006;17:75–79.

104. Bernard SM, Samet JM, Grambsch A, Ebi KL, Romieu I. The potential impacts of climate variability and change on air pollution-related health effects in the United States. Environ Health Perspect 2001;109(suppl 2):199–209.

105. Koelle K, Rodo X, Pascual M, Yunus M, Mostafa G. Refractory periods and climate forcing in cholera dynamics. Nature 2005;436:696–700.

106. Hopp MJ, Foley JA. Worldwide fluctuations in Dengue fever cases related to climate variability. Clim Res 2003;25:85–94.

107. Patz JA, Campbell-Lendrum D, Holloway T, Foley JA. Impact of regional climate change on human health. Nature 2005;438:310–317.

108. Abbott C, Rogers P, Sloboda J. Global responses to global threats. Sustainable security for the twenty-first century. Oxford, UK: Oxford Research Group, 2006.

109. Purvis N, Busby J. The security implications of climate change for the UN system. Environmental Change and Security Project, 2004. http://www.brookings.edu/papers/2004/05energy_purvis.aspx

110. Sondorp E, Patel P. Climate change, conflict and health. Trans R Soc Trop Med Hyg 2003;97:139–140.

111. Spiegel P. Differences in world responses to natural disasters and complex emergencies. JAMA 2005;293:1915–1918.

112. Salama P, Laurence B, Nolan ML. Health and human rights in contemporary humanitarian crises: is Kosovo more important than Sierra Leone? BMJ 1999;319:1569–1571.

113. Kaiser R. Systematic review of arrangements for humanitarian relief in emergencies. Fourteenth World Congress on Disaster and Emergency Medicine, Edinburgh, 2005.

114. World Health Organization/United Nations International Children's Emergency Fund. Clinical management of acute diarrhea. Geneva: World Health Organization, 2004.

115. Dunston C, McAfee D, Kaiser R, et al. Collaboration, cholera and cyclones: a project to improve point of use water quality in Madagascar. Am J Public Health 2001;91:1574–1576.

116. Spiegel P, Sheik M, Gotway-Crawford C, Salama P. Health programmes and policies associated with decreased mortality in displaced people in postemergency phase camps: a retrospective study. Lancet 2002;360:1927–1934.

117. Centers for Disease Control and Prevention. Famine-affected, refugees, and displaced populations: recommendations for public health issues. MMWR Morb Mortal Wkly Rep 1992;41(RR-13):9.

# 25

## Tackling Nutrient Deficiencies and Life-Threatening Disease

*The Role of Food in Humanitarian Relief*

*Patrick Webb and Andrew Thorne-Lyman*

*"Starve a fever; feed a cold".*

*Old English proverb*

## 25.1 INTRODUCTION

Communicable diseases *combined* with malnutrition represent the most prevalent public health problem in the world today [1]. According to the World Health Organization (WHO), these two problems are *jointly* responsible for an estimated 13 million preventable deaths among children younger than 5 years in developing countries each year. More than half of child deaths from infectious disease are attributable to the effects of malnutrition—leading the World Bank to argue that malnutrition is "the main contributor to the burden of disease in the developing world" [2, 3]. These links are synergistic; outbreaks of many diseases have a direct precursor in unresolved malnutrition [4], and "better nutrition can reduce the spread of contagious diseases" [2]. One condition aggravates the other, and seeking to resolve one without the other generally has limited success.

Malnutrition is not in itself a disease; the term encapsulates different symptoms, conditions, and etiologic processes, and its proximate cause involves much more than a single identifiable pathogen. Malnutrition is not a condition that only reflects a lack of food. That is, food sufficiency is not the same as good nutrition, and death during famine is not always coincident with a total lack of food [5]. Nevertheless, malnutrition is an important determinant of mortality, and food interventions play a key role in saving lives *through* their impact on the nutrition and disease status of affected populations [6]. Thus, while lack of food, malnutrition, and sickness/death are inexorably entwined, the links are nonlinear in nature.

This chapter outlines recent research findings that confirm strong links between nutrients and disease progression and outcomes; it highlights the importance of focusing on food as food, not simply regarding food as a bundle of individual nutrients or as a

From: *Nutrition and Health: Nutrition and Health in Developing Countries, Second Edition*
Edited by: R. D. Semba & M. W. Bloem © Humana Press, Totowa, NJ

social good. The implication is that analysts and planners focused on individual and public health issues should pay equal attention to related domains of nutrition and food security. The first section explores the positive and negative synergies that link food and both health and nutrition outcomes. A second section considers historical and recent evidence from the biological sciences that links nutrients with disease and health outcomes. The third section reviews how life-saving interventions during humanitarian crises are increasingly reliant on food-based delivery of nutrients that are tailored to resolve nutrient deficiency and other diseases. The final section offers conclusions.

## 25.2  FOOD AND DISEASE, CAUSE AND EFFECT

The understanding of food–nutrient–health linkages is not new, although its implications for operational programming in many ways are. In 1935, the public health commissioner of colonial India proclaimed that, "No preventive campaign against malaria, against tuberculosis, against leprosy, … [and no] child welfare activities, are likely to achieve any great success unless those responsible recognize the vital importance of defective nutrition" [7]. Similarly, but in relation to Africa, a colonial era review of major health problems across the continent noted that: "The problem of health is, indeed, in great measure the problem of [food] subsistence. Medical science must be in Africa increasingly concerned with the relations between nutrition and health, and with advising on the medical aspect of social policies bearing on the question of subsistence" [7].

These early statements on the holistic nature of human well-being were built on experiences in the previous century. Although medical science was in its infancy, it was already known that lack of nutrition contributed to ill health.[1] However, it was also known that eating *any* kind of food was not in itself sufficient to achieve good nutrition. As Rivers [9], put it: "To understand the nutritional biology of famine it must be realized that it typically consists of two superimposed phenomena; some degree of food shortage and the consumption of a strange diet. The dietary deviations of famine … are most important in dictating the pattern of nutritional disease that occurs." For example, periods of acute food shortage lead to the consumption of foods that are not part of the normal diet. During the continent-wide European famine of 1817, desperate Germans and Italians consumed sawdust baked into bread, carrion, and even dogs [10]. During famine in southern Africa in 1912, colonial officials reported that, "The majority were living entirely on … vermin and roots. These swell the stomach but do not nourish the limbs" [11, 12]. In other words, a lack of food is problematic, but so is the concomitant search for anything edible at all.

More recently, it has been noted in Ethiopia as well as India and Bangladesh that overconsumption of boiled grass pea (*Lathyrus sativus*) during periods of famine can enable consumers to survive (the grass pea is drought resistant, so it is available to eat when other grains have disappeared), but it often condemns them to a neurodegenerative disorder that leads to irreversible paralysis [13]. Similarly, in Afghanistan outbreaks of upper motor neuron symptoms (*Konzo* syndrome) were linked to dietary cyanide exposure,

---

[1] For example, a physician treating sickness in Dublin at the time of the 1840s Irish famine noted that "plenty of nourishment [was] absolutely necessary" [8].

resulting from the consumption of tartran root—toxic if not appropriately soaked, ground, fermented, and cooked [14]. The effects of consuming these toxic tubers are amplified in conditions of protein deficiency—the case in postfamine Afghanistan.

Thus, extreme hunger leads individuals to turn to what are essentially poisonous products that may kill or cripple the consumer long after the crisis has past. Part of the solution to this is making available sufficient food to those suffering deficiencies. At the same time, this food must be made available in the right way and of course be of the right kind. Available in the right way means appropriate for progressive resolution of electrolyte and nutrient imbalances and appropriate for digestion by seriously malnourished patients. As far back as the early 1800s, it was noted that while food is key to resolving acute hunger, it must not be administered ad libitum, or in the wrong form, to avoid negative side effects. One observer of famine relief in Switzerland in 1817 remarked that, "After supporting for some time a miserable existence, on scarcely anything but boiled nettles and other herbs, their organs became impaired, and when too late assisted by better food, they could not digest it … and they perished in a few days" [15]. In such cases it appears that "starvation" causes intracellular loss of electrolytes, and that a sudden shift from (self-consumed) fat to carbohydrates causes rapid secretion of insulin and a rapid uptake of phosphates, leading to profound hypophosphataemia [16]. This underlines the critical importance of understanding the relationships among nutrients, nutritional status, food intake, and disease burden to appropriately design interventions aimed at saving lives in emergencies.

## 25.3 NUTRIENT–DISEASE SYNERGIES AND NUTRIENT DEFICIENCIES

A groundbreaking monograph by Scrimshaw and colleagues in 1968 was one of the first in recent times to elucidate the synergistic, circular relationship between malnutrition and infection [17]. The dominant paradigm in the nutrition community at the time had primarily attributed "protein–calorie malnutrition" to dietary deficiencies without adequately acknowledging the linkages between infection and nutritional status that now form the basis of modern conceptual frameworks of malnutrition [18]. While many of the mechanisms through which infections worsen nutritional status were understood by 1968, little work had been done to elucidate the other half of the cycle—namely, to explain how poor nutritional status negatively affects immune status [19].

Subsequent epidemiologic studies have quantified the extent to which malnutrition elevates the risk of morbidity and mortality due to various causes. Most recently, a comparative analysis of health risks by a WHO working group found that low weight for age ($<-1$ Z-score) contributed to 44.8% of all childhood deaths due to measles, 57.3% of deaths due to malaria, 52.3% of pneumonia deaths, and 60.7% of diarrheal deaths [20]. Worldwide, malnutrition was found to be an underlying factor in more than 50% of the 10–11 million preventable deaths among children less than 5 years of age [13]. The acknowledgement of malnutrition as a *potentiating* factor for mortality from infectious diseases was a particularly important prerequisite for such an analysis as it showed that conventional methods of attributing the cause of death only by the primary documented cause had underestimated the contribution of malnutrition to mortality by eight- to tenfold [21].

The multiple mechanisms through which nutritional deficiencies impair the immune system and lead to disease are now well documented and include "interference with the production of humoral antibodies and of mucosal secretory antibodies, cell-mediated immunity, bactericidal capacity of phagocytes, complement formation, numbers of thymus-dependent T lymphocytes and T cell subsets (helper, suppressor-cytoxic, and natural killer cells), and nonspecific defense mechanisms" [22].

Micronutrient deficiencies are pervasive throughout the world and are important causes of morbidity, mortality, and disability. Diets deficient in energy are usually deficient in micronutrients; it is therefore not surprising that there is considerable overlap between underweight and micronutrient deficiencies. Indeed, the authors of the comparative risk analysis of child underweight acknowledged that:

> *The association of underweight condition with these [micronutrient] deficiencies means that some of the risk being attributed to underweight may be, in fact, due to specific micronutrient deficiencies. On the other hand, these deficiencies can occur in children who are not considered underweight, so the risk of adverse outcomes is not entirely encompassed in the subset of the children who are underweight.* [20]

As an illustration of the independent effect that micronutrients can have, vitamin A supplementation was equally effective in reducing mortality among normal weight children as it was among underweight children [23].

Of the many micronutrients required for survival and growth, research and programmatic attention has largely focused on vitamin A, iron, zinc, and iodine due to their widespread nature and public health importance in contributing to the global burden of disease. Evidence from multiple clinical trials showed that prophylactic vitamin A supplementation of children under 5 years old can reduce mortality due to infectious diseases (most notably measles, diarrhea, and malaria) by approximately 23% [24]. As a result, vitamin A capsule supplementation programs are ubiquitous alongside measles immunization campaigns in emergencies; this intervention has been adopted as a key child survival intervention with an easy mode of delivery. Significant attention has also been paid to zinc in recent years, primarily because of its important role in reducing the incidence and duration of diarrhea and respiratory infections (and possibly malarial morbidity), yet greater efforts are needed to introduce effective interventions for zinc deficiency in the field [25–27].

The relationships among iron, host, and pathogen illustrate the importance of considering both the risks as well as the potential benefits of micronutrient interventions. Iron deficiency is one of the most prevalent deficiencies worldwide, affecting an estimated 2 million people, and is an important cause of death and disability [28, 29]. Yet, while iron deficiency depresses functions in affected individuals, it also impairs the functioning of pathogens as well. As Scrimshaw and SanGiovanni described, "When individuals whose resistance to infection is compromised by iron deficiency are given parenteral iron or large[2] doses of oral iron, a disasterous exacerbation of the infection and death may occur. This happens because the agent is supplied with iron for replication before

---

[2] A subsequent review [30] suggested that a similar risk may be present even for supplementation at levels recommended for normal, healthy children.

the host immune system has had time to recover" [22]. Thus, both the quantity of iron and the mode of delivery are essential elements to consider.

It is also important to consider the setting in which micronutrient interventions are introduced and to weigh the benefits and potential harm that may result. Recent findings from a study from Pemba, Zanzibar, a setting with both high rates of anemia and high malaria transmission rates, showed children less than 3 years of age who received routine daily iron-folate supplementation were approximately 15% more likely to die than unsupplemented children [31]. Such findings differ from the findings in a parallel study undertaken in Nepal (an area of low malaria risk), which had shown no benefit or risk to survival of children as a result of the same supplements [32]. These findings have called into question the global recommendations that children less than 2 years of age in settings with high anemia rates receive routine supplementation with iron folate [28]. As noted in a commentary on these studies:

*The conclusion must be that the risks of death or severe illness of routine iron plus folic acid supplementation ... in young children exposed to high rates of malaria infection seem to outweigh any immediate benefits. In areas of no malaria risk, the absence of survival benefit or risk suggests decisions on supplementation should be made according to benefits on growth, physical performance, and probably most importantly, cognitive performance. [33] Current recommendations emphasize treating malaria as well as iron deficiency where possible.*

## 25.4   RESPONDING TO MALNUTRITION AND DISEASE THROUGH FOOD

As a result of mounting clinical evidence of nutrient–disease interactions, practitioners of many kinds are increasingly putting this knowledge into practice. The medical community is (in parts at least) acknowledging that, "regardless of whether medical complications are a direct result of the malnutrition or the disease, evidence is mounting that nutrition support ... is beneficial" [34]. In the context of HIV/AIDS treatment, Kim and Farmer [35] argued that, "consumptive diseases cannot be treated effectively without food supplementation." Similarly, the international humanitarian community argues that, "the highest nutritional priority in the post-disaster setting is the timely and adequate provision of food rations containing at least 2,100 calories and that includes sufficient protein, fat, and micronutrients" [36]. Indeed, the World Health Organization has gone so far as to state that "the cure for malnutrition is food." [37]

Food is incorporated into a range of emergency interventions that address malnutrition through general food distribution, supplementary and therapeutic feeding activities, and micronutrient fortification. It is known that (1) acute malnutrition is a strong predictor of excess mortality among young children [38]. As Brundlandt [39] put it, "death rates increase exponentially with the degree of malnutrition." (2) Even moderate malnutrition raises mortality in emergencies—partly because a larger share of the affected population is typically moderately, rather than severely, malnourished and partly because "the prevention and correction of nutrient deficiencies, even sub-clinical ones, can reduce the burden of illness and decrease mortality" [40]. (3) Micronutrient deficiencies contribute to disease-mediated mortality in emergencies [41, 42]. (4) The timely arrival of food assistance contributes to the prevention of mortality through its impact on reducing malnutrition [43, 44].

Evaluations of the effectiveness of food and nutrition programs are increasingly identifying the components and approaches needed to maximize impact [45, 46]. Food is not the only, or always the optimal, resource needed in such activities. However, where malnutrition is linked to constrained food access and where food of sufficient quality and quantity is required to meet identified needs (in combination with relevant nonfood resources), then food *is* an important element. Well-designed trials involving *food*, rather than just micronutrient supplements or medicines, in the context of development interventions (not emergencies), have documented a range of positive outcomes, including maternal weight gain, improved birth weights, and positive growth responses in children in locations as diverse as the Gambia, Indonesia, Nepal, and Ethiopia [47–50]. Indeed, in Mexico it has been shown that food supplements to children under 3 years old in poorest households had a significant impact on child growth and reduced stunting. This impact, from "nutrition supplements alone" is estimated to account for almost a 3% increase in lifetime earnings for those children through improved growth and productivity [51].

The promotion of mother and child nutrition is a complex activity. To be effective, food support should only be given when a limiting factor to child growth or maternal weight gain is inadequate food (including micronutrient intake) *and* where food can generate leverage for necessary nonfood inputs to be provided as well. In a development context, an optimal package of interventions is generally sought that revolves around a set of mutually reinforcing activities shown to reduce maternal and child malnutrition, including promotion of exclusive breast-feeding; supplementary feeding for underweight mothers and children; nutrition education (promoting good and complementary feeding practices for infants, including appropriate feeding and rehydration of sick children); health services (vaccinations, antenatal care, health referrals); vitamin/mineral supplementation (especially iron folate to pregnant women, vitamin A, and iodized salt); deworming; and disease control [2, 52]. In the context of complex humanitarian emergencies, a similar set of comprehensive services is desirable, yet often more difficult to achieve, particularly in the early phases when it is most needed. Longer-term refugee camp settings where populations depend nearly exclusively on external support for survival are some of the best examples in the world demonstrating that a simple package of basic services (including micronutrient-fortified food) can have marked effects on health and survival [53].

In acknowledging that food alone is not enough, the fundamental importance of ensuring that malnourished people have enough, high quality food to eat cannot be lost sight of.

People need food in emergencies not simply to keep alive (to prevent starvation) but also to maintain physiological (and mental) growth and to allow for recuperation of past malnutrition. The immediate cause of mortality in emergencies is disease (especially measles, cholera, diarrhea, or typhoid). However, as already noted, malnutrition, especially among children, is a major contributor to disease progression and impact—more so if the children are traumatized by conflict or displacement.

Roughly 30 million people were affected by conflicts each year of the 1990s—being displaced or having their livelihoods destroyed—in more than 60 countries; similar numbers continue to be affected in the first years of the 21st century [54]. Horrific death tolls emerged from conflicts of the past decade in the Great Lakes region, Somalia, the Balkans, and more recently in coastal West Africa and the Democratic Republic of Congo.

However, despite the increase in number and scale of disasters, excess mortality in emergencies has been falling. Reported nonviolent deaths in the context of major emergencies declined by almost 40% between 1993 and 2003 compared with the previous decade [55]. Humanitarian agencies are doing a better job than ever in saving and protecting lives, largely through more timely responses, improved mobilization of resources, and better management of both the symptoms and causes of malnutrition.

A major factor in allowing this to happen has been rapid evolution in medical and nutritional sciences during the 1990s coupled with an increasingly professional application of knowledge in the field. A wealth of applied research has accumulated that continues to inform humanitarian strategies for responding to nutritional emergencies (including medical protocols for the treatment of severe malnutrition and guidelines for effective uses of food in emergency programming).

For example, understanding how to design food rations with a view to maximizing nutritional benefits has significantly improved over time. Table 25.1 indicates the evolution of planning rations based on nutritional needs rather than on which foods were available for emergency uses. Major agencies gradually adopted a planning figure that seeks not only to protect minimal metabolic functions (at a minimalist "starvation-avoidance" level) but also to reduce mortality by correcting preexisting nutritional deficiencies and allowing for the physical activity necessary to be able to access food. Relief agencies acknowledged the danger of distributing infant formulas (the risk of substituting breast milk and of higher infant mortality linked to unclean water/bottles). Other conclusions relate to the need for diversity in food rations and food fortification to protect against micronutrient deficiencies.

Advances in the quality of distributed foods, and their more targeted uses in the field, have led to large-scale prevention of loss of life in numerous, usually difficult, and often dangerous circumstances in places like Aceh post-tsunami, Ethiopia, and North Korea [57–59]. There are three main ways in which food is delivered in emergency contexts:

1. *General food distribution* involves the distribution of a standard ration of food commodities (known as the food basket or basic ration) to every beneficiary within a crisis-affected population without distinction. The immediate aim of general food distribution is to meet food needs of people with constrained access to normal sources of food, thus trying to "protect" their nutritional situation from deteriorating.

2. *Selective feeding interventions* are targeted to specific subpopulation groups, often complementing general food distribution, and are aimed at reversing a deterioration of the nutritional status of vulnerable groups and stabilizing such gains:

   a. *Targeted supplementary feeding* seeks to prevent children suffering from moderate acute malnutrition from becoming severely malnourished and support their recuperation or channels nutrients to specified vulnerable groups (pregnant and lactating women).
   b. *Blanket supplementary feeding* is used to prevent malnutrition and related mortality when the threat is severe for subpopulations (normally children <5 years of age).
   c. *Therapeutic feeding* entails treatment of severe malnutrition with nutrient and energy-dense foods combined with medical intervention.

3. *Micronutrient interventions* involve procurement of fortified foods, local fortification, or distribution of micronutrient supplements to meet population needs or micronutrient deficiency outbreaks.

**Table 25.1**

**Milestones in the evolution of nutrition concerns in emergencies**

| | |
|---|---|
| 1960s | Food responses based on commodities available. |
| | Foods donated determined more by availability than nutritional adequacy. |
| | Limited recognition of relevance of nutritional content of rations. |
| 1970s | Focus on protein deficiency (in protein-energy malnutrition). |
| | More variety in food basket, including beans, vegetable oil. |
| | Fortified blended foods (FBFs) used only in supplementary feeding. |
| 1980s | Major agencies raise ration planning figure from 1,500 to 1,900 kcal per person per day. |
| | FBFs included in most rations for completely food aid-dependent populations. |
| | Food basket increasingly based on six core commodities: cereal, pulses, oil, sugar, salt, FBFs. |
| 1990s | Some agencies (including the World Food Programme, WFP) increase ration planning figure for fully food aid-dependent populations from 1,900 to 2,100 kcal. |
| | Advances in science led to production of F75 and F100 therapeutic mile for treating acute malnutrition. |
| | Stricter limitations on use of milk products and infant formula in crises. |
| | Development of multi-UN agency policies and guidelines on common approaches to malnutrition in emergencies. |
| | Requirement that internationally procured oil, salt, and flour be fortified. |
| | Local production of FBFs expands in some developing countries. |
| | BP5 and HEP (high energy and protein) biscuits in wide use. |
| 2000s | Greater use of local milling and fortification of cereals for relief distribution. |
| | Local (developing country) procurement of FBFs for use in third countries. |
| | Development of ready-to-use therapeutic foods (RUTFs) for "at home" treatment of acute malnutrition. |
| | More attention to links between treatment of acute malnutrition and prevention of chronic malnutrition. |

*Source*: Adapted from [54, 56].

### 25.4.1 General Food Distribution

The primary purpose of general food distribution is to prevent sustained food short-falls that would contribute to excess mortality via increased malnutrition. The general ration is tailored to meet population-wide nutritional requirements rather than individual needs. As interventions become more focused on treating specific nutritional problems among individuals, the more the nature of foods delivered changes; that is, intervention modalities themselves become more complex, and the role of public health measures becomes increasingly important.

A well-composed food basket is critical to maintaining the nutritional status of affected populations; this is especially true where beneficiaries are fully dependent on food aid or have limited coping capacities. Planning rations for emergencies is not a one-size-fits-all activity (Table 25.2). The size and composition of the food basket has to be tailored to local food preferences, the demographic profile of the population, activity levels,

**Table 25.2**
Matrix of potential strategies and commodities to provide macro and micronutrients under different emergency settings and programmatic objectives

| Intervention | Target group | Nutritional deficiencies addressed | Contexts where this strategy is appropriate | Challenges to implementing this strategy | Extent to which inter-vention has been tried in emergencies | Recent examples of use of strategy |
|---|---|---|---|---|---|---|
| **Interventions aimed at general population** | | | | | | |
| Milling and fortification of staple foods | General population | Micronutrient and macronutrient deficiencies | Contexts where a large proportion of food needs are met through food assist-ance; where capacity exists to mill and fortify this can be a very cost-effective strategy | Shelf life and local capacity to mill and fortify may be challenges although milling reduces amount of food needed as recipients do not need compensation to cover milling costs. Local milling and fortification can increase efficiency. | ***** | Nangweshi refugee camps Zambia; Southern Africa Crisis response 2001-3; Angola |
| Vitamin A and D fortified oil | General population | Micronutrient and macronutrient deficiencies | Oil is a standard com-ponent of general and supplementary food rations. Many organizations have policies that vitamin A fortification of oil is mandatory | Logistical challenges associated with packaging of oil | *** | Nearly all large emergency operations where a full food basket is provided |

(continued)

**Table 25.2**
(continued)

| Intervention | Target group | Nutritional deficiencies addressed | Contexts where this strategy is appropriate | Challenges to implementing this strategy | Extent to which intervention has been tried in emergencies | Recent examples of use of strategy |
|---|---|---|---|---|---|---|
| Iodized salt | General population | Iodine deficiency | Situations where IDD is endemic or suspected; populations fully dependent on food aid. Many organizations have mandatory iodization policies for salt. | Relatively small quantities are needed, may be challenging for logisticians | *** | Most large emergencies; Darfur |
| Diversification of ration to address overt micronutrient deficiencies (dried fish, parboiled rice, seeds for sprouting, etc) | General population | Acute outbreaks of deficiencies of B6, B12, riboflavin, B deficiencies (pellagra, beri-beri, angular stomatitis) | Situations of acute outbreaks of micronutrient deficiencies | Cost may be relatively high compared with preventative strategies | **** | Angola (pellagra); |
| Provision of fresh foods | General population | Micronutrient deficiencies | Populations completely dependent on food assistance | Transportation of fresh foods is challenging and relatively costly | **** | Many large refugee camps |
| Dietary diversification, gardening, etc. | General population | Micronutrient and macronutrient deficiencies | Contexts where emergency affected populations are non-mobile and have access to land and/or livestock | Land (and the ability to access it) is needed and can be a constraint in complex emergencies and refugee settings | ***** | Many large refugee camps |

**Interventions aimed at general population or focused on specific vulnerable population groups**

| Intervention | Population | Deficiency | When used | Notes | Rating | Examples |
| --- | --- | --- | --- | --- | --- | --- |
| Fortified blended foods | General population; also used in supplementary feeding of children, pregnant, and lactating women, and in HIV/AIDS programmes | Micronutrient and macronutrient deficiencies | For inclusion in general ration, appropriate where fortification of staples not possible. | Perception that FBF's are for children or women may limit consumption by other groups. Micronutrient content inadequate for children <2y. | *** | Most emergencies include FBF's (Darfur ) |
| Home fortification | General population or specific population groups with high micro nutrient needs | Micronutrient deficiencies | Areas where fortification of staples not possible or where staple foods not provided; | As populations are not familiar with the product, requires a BCC/communications component. | ** | Indonesia (post-Tsunami); Darfur pilot |

**Interventions targetted towards specific vulnerable groups within the population**

| Intervention | Population | Deficiency | When used | Notes | Rating | Examples |
| --- | --- | --- | --- | --- | --- | --- |
| Therapeutic feeding (RUTF's, F75, F100) | Children 6-59 months suffering from severe acute malnutrition; Adults, particularly in AIDS treatment | Macro and micronutrient deficiencies | Where prevalence of severe acute malnutrition is high; | Coverage using traditional approaches is quite low; can dramatically increase coverage using CTC approach. Cost is an issue, however local production of RUTFs reduces cost signficantly. | ***** | Most emergencies; used in treatment of AIDS in Malawi |

(continued)

**Table 25.2**
(continued)

| Intervention | Target group | Nutritional deficiencies addressed | Contexts where this strategy is appropriate | Challenges to implementing this strategy | Extent to which intervention has been tried in emergencies | Recent examples of use of strategy |
|---|---|---|---|---|---|---|
| Micronutrient supplements (vitamin A, iron-folate, etc) | Children <5, Lactating women | Micronutrient deficiencies | Vitamin A capsules are distributed in virtually every large emergency alongside immunization programmes. | Iron-folate supplementation for pregnant women often depends on availability and quality of prenatal health services. | ***** | Most emergencies |
| Multiple micronutrient tablets or foodlets | Children 6 to 59 months; Pregnant and lactating women | Micronutrient deficiencies | May be used to help meet micronutrient needs of specific groups even where fortified foods are provided | Limited experience implementing in emergency contexts but efficacy trials have been conducted | | |
| Spreads (Nutributter, etc) | Children 6 to 59 months | Micronutrient deficiencies, some macronutrients | Situations where macronutrients (staples) are available and accessible but dietary quality is a major issue | Hasn't yet been tried in emergency settings but has been piloted in development contexts | | |

climatic conditions, food preferences, an understanding of local coping capacity, and preexisting levels of malnutrition and disease load.

A typical food ration comprises five or six commodities: cereals (in grain or as milled flour), pulses, vegetable oil, fortified blended foods (FBFs), and sometimes sugar or salt. In line with recommendations endorsed by most UN relief organizations, a ration planning figure of 2,100 kcal per person per day is used as an initial reference value for calculating energy requirements among fully food aid-dependent populations [60]. Adjustments are made to this figure according to local conditions, including health conditions. For example, the southern Africa drought emergency response by the World Food Programme (WFP) used a planning figure of 2,200 kcal per person per day to adjust for high HIV/AIDS prevalence in the region (based on WHO recommendations of higher caloric and requirements for people living with HIV/AIDS). Indeed, the southern Africa crisis was the first major emergency to highlight the importance of special attention to nutrition needs in areas of high HIV/AIDS prevalence.

In some emergencies, processed foods are included in the general ration to enhance the protein, fat, and micronutrient content of the basket where such deficiencies are observed or expected. Where WFP is concerned, around 40% of emergency operations included FBFs in the general distribution in the early 2000s; FBF is a micronutrient-fortified mix of a soya-cereal flour, which is often combined with vegetable oil to increase energy density, and salt (and sometimes sugar) for taste. In Ethiopia, for instance, FBFs were delivered to 35% of beneficiaries during the 2002 drought response. In this case, it was decided to include FBF in the general food basket since acute malnutrition was a generalized problem compounded by pervasive micronutrient deficiencies.

Micronutrients can also be delivered through other foods in the general ration. Vegetable oil is typically fortified with vitamin A, and WFP requires that all salt be iodized. As a commodity needed in small amounts, salt presents logistical challenges since it can be difficult to divide, track, and distribute, yet it is often included in the food basket because of nutritional benefits. The UN High Commissioner for Refugees (UNHCR) also delivers fresh food items in refugee settings as a source of micronutrients.

### 25.4.2 *Supplementary Feeding*

Beyond the general distribution of rations to "prevent" (or at least stabilize) malnutrition and save lives, other more targeted interventions are used to correct (resolve) malnutrition among specific groups in emergencies. Supplementary feeding programs (SFPs) provide food, usually in addition to general rations, to specific vulnerable groups (typically young children and pregnant or lactating women). In some instances, SFPs were already operating prior to an emergency. For example, SFPs were already supported as part of Country Programmes in Zambia and Malawi before the southern Africa 2002/2003 drought response. In both cases, malnourished children and mothers were targeted with recuperative and preventive goals in mind, and the emergency response benefited from preestablished food pipelines and targeting mechanisms (which allowed for a rapid increase in the volume of food delivered once the large-scale relief operation got under way). In other cases, emergency SFPs serve as the basis for institution building and a focus for service delivery by nongovernmental organizations (NGOs) and government when a crisis has passed but needs remain high.

There are two main forms of SFP (Fig. 25.1). First, *blanket SFPs* provide targeted food to groups within a population who are at particular risk of malnutrition, such as young children, pregnant women, and lactating women. Blanket SFPs are typically implemented when the prevalence of child acute malnutrition exceeds 15%, which can happen when a full general ration is provided (such as parts of Sudan). One danger is that while malnutrition among young children and mothers may be contained, the status of the rest of the population could deteriorate. However, when more than 15% of children are seriously malnourished, blanket feeding may be necessary to contain an escalating public health emergency. In less-severe situations, *targeted SFPs* are implemented that specifically target malnourished children or mothers using predefined screening criteria (normally either a mid-upper arm circumference between 11.0 and 12.49 cm or a weight-for-height measurement between −3.0 and −2.01 Z-scores).

The FBFs are the main commodity distributed through SFPs, mainly because they provide a balanced source of protein, are precooked to reduce losses of micronutrients, and are relatively low as they are based on soya and corn or wheat. Often, FBFs are mixed with sugar or salt for taste or with oil to increase energy density. The composition of FBFs such as corn soya blend and wheat soya blend has remained fundamentally unchanged for decades, and while it is generally deemed to be appropriate for children 2–5 years of age, it is now acknowledged that most FBFs do not fully meet the micronutrient needs

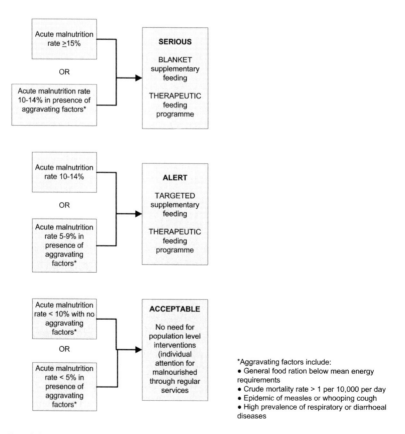

**Fig. 25.1.** Decision-making diagram of when to implement SFP and TFP in emergency situations. Derived from 'UNHCR/WFP guidelines for selective feeding programmes in emergency situations', (1999).

of certain nutritionally vulnerable subgroups, particularly those needs for iron, calcium, and zinc among children less than 12 months of age [61]. Reformulations are being explored, and more research is needed to explore issues of efficacy, cost, and programmatic feasibility of various options for different groups in emergency contexts.

### 25.4.3   *Therapeutic Feeding*

Therapeutic feeding programs are implemented with the aim of reducing mortality among populations facing severe acute malnutrition, and most often focus on children, the primary group affected by severe malnutrition. Inclusion criteria for therapeutic feeding normally include a weight-for-height ratio of 70% of the median or less or bilateral pitting edema. Generally, the proportion of children in need of therapeutic feeding is often quite low and highly dependent on the context and adequacy of other emergency intervention, such as general feeding and immunization programs. For example, in the relatively well resourced and implemented response to the crisis in Darfur, Sudan, the prevalence of severe acute malnutrition among children 6–59 months of age was 1.4% in 2005, which had fallen from 3.9% in 2004 [62].

The management of severe acute malnutrition is relatively complex and entails specific feeding protocols alongside treatment to stabilize conditions such as dehydration, hypoglycemia, hypothermia, electrolyte imbalances, and infections. The initial phase of treatment normally lasts 2–7 days depending on the return of appetite and the general state of the patient [63].

In the mid-1990s, specific products for treating severe acute malnutrition were introduced based on years of evidence-based research [64, 65]. These included high-energy therapeutic milks (called F75 or F100, which provide 75 or 100 kcal per 100 mL, respectively) as well as ReSoMal, specially designed oral rehydration salts for severely malnourished children who have greater need for potassium and less need for sodium than normal children [63]. Both types of therapeutic milk can be prepared from basic ingredients: dried skim milk, sugar, cereal flour, oil, mineral and vitamin mix (without iron), and clean water.

During the initial treatment phase, children are fed F75 in quantities individually tailored to their metabolic needs. This is important to prevent risk of heart failure caused by overfeeding severely malnourished children [63]. As children stabilize, they graduate to the recuperative phase of treatment and switch to a diet of F100, which leads to rapid weight gain and eventual discharge (often after about a month).

These products represented a major advance in the treatment of severe malnutrition—indeed, the minimum standard recovery rate for severe acute malnutrition expected in well-run centers exceeds 75% [36]. Yet, the effectiveness of therapeutic feeding centers using a center-based approach is often plagued by low coverage, high default rates (the result of keeping children and parents in the center for weeks at a time), and infections acquired at the centers [65].

Ready-to-use therapeutic foods (RUTFs) were designed in the early 1990s to replace F100 in the recuperative phase of the treatment of severe malnutrition [66]. Similar to F100 in energy density and protein and micronutrient content, RUTFs such as Plumpy nut® (Nutriset, France) are based on groundnuts, skim milk, and lactoserum and are provided in paste form. Unlike F100, which requires supervision and clean water to prepare, RUTFs can be consumed without preparation, and their lower water activity means significantly lower risk of bacterial contamination [65].

The development of RUTFs facilitated a new approach to the management of severe acute malnutrition called community therapeutic care (CTC) [66, 67]. Once a child was stabilized and treated for infections, they could return home with their families to continue their care, significantly reducing dropouts from the program. While internationally procured RUTFs can be costly (at present approximately US $3,500/ton), costs can be reduced to as little as $2,000/ton through local production, as is currently being done in Malawi and other countries [68]. That said, preliminary calculations suggested that enhanced recovery rates and reduced rates of default (fewer former patients returning for further treatment) may make such approaches better value for money in the longer run [6].

The emergence of adult malnutrition due to the HIV pandemic has drawn attention to the urgent need to develop better protocols for the assessment and management of adult malnutrition. Body mass index, the main indicator for adult malnutrition used in nutritional surveys, is challenged in its interpretation by significant variations in adult body shapes across populations, and there is increasing sentiment that the use of mid-upper arm circumference may be better for screening adults in need of feeding than BMI, although appropriate cutoffs are still needed [69, 70]. Research is also under way to test various food commodities such as RUTFs among adults in severe stages of HIV-related malnutrition [71].

### 25.4.4  Addressing Micronutrient Deficiencies

In emergency settings, the first priority of food aid programs is often to provide for the energy and protein needs of emergency-affected populations, with micronutrients considered only after ensuring the provision of these "basic" food needs [60, 72]. Yet, micronutrient deficiencies are a major contributor to mortality and morbidity in both emergency and nonemergency settings. Emergencies can exacerbate micronutrient deficiency disorders in all age groups. Thus, there are two challenges to be met: (1) how to prevent or resolve micronutrient deficiencies in emergencies and (2) how to address micronutrient deficiencies with a view to preventing deterioration in subsequent crises.

Until quite recently, serious attention to micronutrient deficiencies came only after acute outbreaks of pellagra, scurvy, or other overt micronutrient deficiencies forced agencies to respond [73, 74]. Today, serious deficiency outbreaks are becoming increasingly rare thanks to heightened awareness of the need to prevent micronutrient deficiencies from happening before outbreaks emerge. For example, a postemergency reconstruction intervention by WFP in the Russian Federation identified anemia as a serious problem in targeted regions and so requested a donation of 30,000 tons of iron-fortified wheat flour. Many agencies are also involved in setting up milling and fortification production plants within developing countries to produce fortified cereal flours or new RUTFs.

Food fortification and provision of FBFs are often the most advantageous ways of delivering micronutrients in emergencies (from both a cost perspective and in terms of ease of delivery). Yet, there are also limitations. Food is seldom fortified at levels high enough to meet the biological needs of all population subgroups, particularly for young children and pregnant and lactating women [75]. Storage and cooking lead to losses of certain vitamins (such as vitamin C) and are also limitations, and FBFs also contain antinutritional factors such as phytates, which inhibit absorption of certain micronutrients [76]. Perhaps the greatest challenge is that fortification of staples requires milling, which significantly reduces the shelf life of maize, wheat, and other commodities.

Because of these limitations, agencies are actively exploring additional ways of delivering micronutrients, particularly to groups with high nutritional needs. Recently, WHO and UNICEF developed a multimicronutrient supplement composed of 15 key micronutrients; it is recommended for daily use by pregnant and lactating women irrespective of access to micronutrient-fortified foods and for children under 5 years old on either a daily or semiweekly basis in emergency settings, depending on their access to micronutrient-fortified foods [75]. Another approach being piloted in certain emergency settings is the use of home-based fortificants that can be mixed with food at the level of the household. These approaches also carry advantages—the heightened micronutrient needs of specific individuals within the household can be met, and losses of certain micronutrients are minimized because they are not cooked [76, 77].

Of course, delivering sufficient, timely, quality foods is necessary but not sufficient in overcoming the underlying processes that cause malnutrition. The availability of nonfood resources of many kinds is essential. This is most apparent if therapeutic feeding is concerned since medicines, clean water, and skilled partners must combine with food to achieve desired results. Complementary resources are also needed to address moderate malnutrition. The more innovative nutrition interventions (which include nutrition education and fortification activities) of the WFP have tended to be linked to a large flow of grains. High tonnage is often associated with greater availability of cash resources. Ways need to be found to ensure appropriate nonfood resources focused not only on logistics or security but also equally on more effectively overcoming malnutrition.

## 25.5   CONCLUSIONS AND FUTURE DIRECTIONS

Food has long been a cornerstone of humanitarian nutrition programs, both in emergency and development settings. Under constant pressure to increase the effectiveness of humanitarian programs in reaching the objectives of saving lives and preventing/treating malnutrition, food assistance programs have evolved significantly over the past three decades. Three trends that are likely to continue in the future are (1) continued evolution of food and micronutrient products, including the development of specialized foods for treatment of various forms of malnutrition; (2) greater focus on needs assessment and the measurement and documentation of the effectiveness of nutrition and health outcomes; (3) expanded collaboration across different humanitarian sectors (particularly food, health, water, and sanitation) with the goal of improving program effectiveness.

Technological advances in the development of new food products for the treatment of severe malnutrition have significantly reduced case fatality rates of severely malnourished children enrolled in therapeutic feeding programs [66, 67]. Community therapeutic care using RUTFs offers a promising solution to the problems of low coverage and high dropout rates that have plagued center-based approaches, yet the costs of international procurement of RUTFs remain prohibitively high for use in development programs funded by resource-poor governments [71]. The cost savings achieved through local production of RUTFs using locally purchased foods (such as groundnuts, chickpeas, and sesame) may facilitate the CTC approach to spread beyond emergency contexts, enabling governments and agencies to purchase sufficient quantities of RUTFs to use for treatment of severe acute malnutrition in development contexts [6].

Advances in the treatment and prevention of moderate malnutrition have not been as rapid as those for treatment of severe malnutrition, and calls for more evidence of the effectiveness of different approaches have been made, particularly in light of the low coverage often observed in such programs [42, 78]. New models with stronger community involvement are being tested to address prevention and treatment of moderate malnutrition, drawing on the successes of CTC for severe malnutrition.

One major advance of SFPs in recent years has been the rapid expansion of local production of corn- or wheat- and soya-based FBFs to many countries throughout the world, reducing costs and increasing availability of appropriate foods for supplementary feeding [79]. However, most such products are nutritionally inadequate for young children (aged 6–24 months, the group at greatest risk of growth faltering and mortality). New products for supplementary feeding, with greater energy and micronutrient density, are greatly needed to increase the effectiveness of supplementary feeding of this younger age group [76]. When developing such products, researchers will have to bear in mind the need for data on costs, efficacy, and effectiveness to enable evidence-based policy decisions to be made.

Agencies now have a variety of response options to prevent micronutrient deficiencies in emergencies, including staple fortification, provision of FBF, multimicronutrient supplements, micronutrient sprinkles, and micronutrient spreads [75, 76]. Yet, more tools are needed for the assessment of specific micronutrient deficiencies and for estimating adequacy of micronutrient intake in emergency settings.

The growing HIV/AIDS and tuberculosis (TB) pandemics are drawing increased attention to the role of food and nutritional interventions as important components of treatment. Food and nutritional interventions provided as part of HIV/AIDS treatment and care are relatively new in developing country settings and often have multiple objectives, including (1) ensuring adequate dietary intake among extremely vulnerable populations; (2) rehabilitation of acutely malnourished adults; (3) ensuring adherence with drug regimes. While knowledge about the micronutrient needs of infected adults is unfolding through increasing numbers of research trials, more studies are needed to explore and document the impacts that can be achieved through different packages of food and nutritional support, particularly in the context of care and treatment programs.

Agencies are working toward greater harmonization of assessment tools in emergency settings, a trend that is based on recognition of (1) overlapping mandates across different sectors to prevent malnutrition and save lives, (2) the multicausal nature of nutritional status, and (3) difficulties comparing assessments done by different actors in the context of emergencies [80]. Recent assessments in Darfur and Indonesia following the tsunami have used a holistic assessment approach involving multiple agencies [57, 62]. The IASC Nutrition Cluster, a network of UN agencies, NGOs, and other agencies, is developing joint assessment tools covering nutritional status and related sectors (food security, health, caring practices, water, and sanitation), which should also help to ensure that more coordination exists across sectors in terms of implementing programs to achieve better nutritional outcomes at the population level.

## REFERENCES

1. World Health Organization. Communicable diseases and severe food shortage situations. Geneva: World Health Organization, 2005.
2. World Bank. Repositioning nutrition as central to development: a strategy for large-scale action. Washington, DC: World Bank, 2006.

3. Black R, Morris S, Bryce J. Where and why are 10 million children dying every year? Lancet 2003;361:2226–2234.

4. Gross R, Webb P. Wasting time for wasted children: severe child undernutrition must be resolved in non-emergency settings. Lancet 2006;367:1209–1211.

5. Webb P. Famine. In: Encyclopedia of international relations and global politics. Griffiths M, ed. London: Routledge, 2005:270–272.

6. Collins S, Dent N, Binns P, Bahwere P, Sadler K, Hallam A. Management of severe acute malnutrition in children. Lancet 2006;268:1992–2000.

7. Hailey L. An African survey: a study of the problems arising in Africa south of the Sahara. London: Oxford University Press, 1939:1114–1115.

8. Mokyr J, O'Grada C. Famine disease and famine mortality: lessons from the Irish experience, 1845–50. In: Famine demography. Dyson T, ed. Oxford, UK: Oxford University Press, 2002:19–43.

9. Rivers J. The nutritional biology of famine. In: Famine. Harrison G, ed. Oxford, UK: Oxford University Press, 1988:57–106.

10. Webb P. Emergency relief during Europe's famine of 1817 anticipated crisis-response mechanisms of today. J Nutr 2002;132:2092S–2095S.

11. Bazeley N. Report to superintendent of northern Victoria, August 28. 1912. Report No. A/3/18/22, folio 265.

12. Iliffe J. Famine in Zimbabwe 1890–1960. Harare, Zimbabwe: Mambo Press, 1990.

13. Getahun H, Lambein F, Vanhoorne M, Van der Stuft P. Food-aid cereals to reduce neurolathyrism related to grass-pea preparations during famine. Lancet 2003;362:1808–1810.

14. Martone G. Suspected toxic ingestion outbreak in central Afghanistan. Emergency Nutrition Network Field Exchange, August 7–11, 2004.

15. Simond L. Switzerland, or a journal of a tour and residence in that country, in the years 1817, 1818, and 1819. Boston: Well and Lilly, 1822.

16. Hearing SD. Refeeding syndrome. BMJ 2004;328:908.

17. Scrimshaw NS, Taylor C, Gordon A. Interactions of nutrition and infection. World Health Organization Monograph Series No. 57. Geneva: World Health Organization, 1968.

18. Keusch G. The history of nutrition: malnutrition, infection and immunity. J Nutr 2003;133:336S–340S.

19. Scrimshaw NS. Historical concepts of interactions, synergism and antagonism between nutrition and infection. J Nutr 2003;133:316S–321S.

20. Fishman S, Caulfield L, de Onis M, Blössner M, Hyder AA, Mullany L, et al. Childhood and maternal underweight. In: Comparative quantification of health risks. Ezzati M, Lopez A, Rodgers A, Murray C, eds. Geneva: World Health Organization, 2004:39–161.

21. Pelletier DL, Frongillo EA Jr, Habicht J-P. Epidemiologic evidence for a potentiating effect of malnutrition on child mortality. Am J Public Health 1993;83:1130–1133.

22. Scrimshaw NS, SanGiovanni JP. Synergism of nutrition, infection, and immunity: an overview. Am J Clin Nutr 1997;66:464S–477S.

23. Sommer A, Tarwotjo I, Djunaedi E, West KP Jr, Loeden AA, Tilden R, Mele L. Impact of vitamin A supplementation on childhood mortality. A randomized controlled trial. Lancet 1986;1:1169–1173.

24. Beaton G, Martorell R, Aronson K, Edmonston B. McCabe G. Ross AC, et al. Effectiveness of vitamin A supplementation in the control of young child morbidity and mortality in developing countries. Toronto: Canadian International Development Agency, 1993:120.

25. Baqui A, Black R, El Arifeen S, Yunus M, Chakraborty J, Ahmed S, et al. Effect of zinc supplementation started during diarrhoea on morbidity and mortality in Bangladeshi children: community randomised trial. BMJ 2002;325:1059.

26. Brooks W, Yunus M, Santosham M, Wahed MA, Nahar K, Yeasmin S, et al. Zinc for severe pneumonia in very young children: double-blind placebo-controlled trial. Lancet 2004;363:1683–1688.

27. Caulfield L, Black R. Zinc deficiency. In: Comparative quantification of health risks. Ezzati M, Lopez A, Rodgers A, Murray C, eds. Geneva: World Health Organization, 2004:257–258.

28. Stoltzfus RJ, Dreyfuss M. Guidelines for the use of iron supplements to prevent and treat iron deficiency anaemia. Washington, DC: ILSI Press, 1998.

29. Stoltzfus RJ, Mullany L, Black R. Iron deficiency anaemia. In: Comparative quantification of health risks. Ezzati M, Lopez A, Rodgers A, Murray C, eds. Geneva: World Health Organization, 2004: 163–210.

30. Oppenheimer SJ. Iron and its relation to immunity and infections disease. J Nutr 2001;131:6165–6168.

31. Sazawal S, Black RE, Ramsan M, Chwaya HM, Stoltzfus RJ, Dutta A, et al. Effects of routine prophylactic supplementation with iron and folic acid on admission to hospital and mortality in preschool children in a high malaria transmission setting: community-based, randomised, placebo-controlled trial. Lancet 2006;367:133–143.

32. Tielsch JM, Khatry SK, Stoltzfus RJ, Katz J, LeClerq SC, Adhikari R, et al. Effect of routine prophylactic supplementation with iron and folic acid on preschool child mortality in southern Nepal: community-based, cluster-randomised, placebo-controlled trial. Lancet 2006;367:144–152.

33. English M, Snow RW. Iron and folic acid supplementation and malaria risk. Lancet 2006;367:390.

34. Heimburger D. Adulthood. In: Shills M, Shike M, Ross AC, Caballero B, Cousins R, eds. Modern nutrition in health and disease. Baltimore, MD: Lippincott, Williams and Wilkins, 2006:830–842.

35. Kim J, Farmer P. AIDS in 2006: moving toward one world, one hope? N Engl J Med 2006;355:645–647.

36. Sphere Project. Humanitarian charter and minimum standards in disaster response. London: Oxfam, 2004.

37. World Health Organization. Emergency response manual. Guidelines for representatives and country offices in the Western Pacific Region. WHO, Bangkok, Thailand. 2003.

38. Pelletier D, Frongillo E. Changes in child survival are strongly associated with changes in malnutrition in developing countries. J Nutr 2003;133:107–119.

39. Brundtland G. Malnutrition and Mortality in Public Health. Nutr Rev 2000;58:S1–S4.

40. Poos M, Costello R, Carlson-Newberry S. Committee on Military Nutrition research activity report. Washington, DC: National Academy Press, 1999.

41. Toole M, Waldman R. The public health aspects of complex emergencies and refugee situations. Annu Rev Public Health 1997;18:283–312.

42. Young H, Borrel A, Holland D, Salama P. Public nutrition in complex emergencies. Lancet 2004;364:1899–1909.

43. Organization for Economic Cooperation and Development/WHO. Poverty and Health. Paris: Organization for Economic Cooperation and Development, 2003.

44. World Health Organization. Communicable diseases and severe food shortage situations. Geneva: World Health Organization, 2005.

45. Allen L, Gillespie S. What works? A review of the efficacy and effectiveness of nutrition interventions. Manila: Asian Development Bank and UN ACC Sub-Committee on Nutrition, 2001.

46. LoPriore C, Van Nieuwenhause C, Webb P. Best practice in using food to support mother and child nutrition interventions. Rome: World Food Programme, 2005.

47. Ceesay S, Prentice A, Cole T, Foord F, Weaver LT, Poskitt EM, et al. Effects on birth weight and perinatal mortality of maternal dietary supplements in rural Gambia: 5 year randomised controlled trial. BMJ 1997;315:786–790.

48. Ramachandran P. Maternal nutrition—effect on fetal growth and outcome of pregnancy. Nutr Rev 2002;60:S26–S34.

49. Rivera J, Habicht J. Effect of supplementary feeding on the prevention of mild-to-moderate wasting in conditions of endemic malnutrition in Guatemala. Bull World Health Organ 2002;80:926–932.

50. Yamano T, Alderman H, Christiaensen L. Child growth, shocks and child nutrition in Ethiopia. Am J Agric Econ 2005;87:273–288.

51. Behrman J, Hoddinott J. An evaluation of the impact of PROGRESA on preschool child height. FCND Discussion Paper. Washington, DC: International Food Policy Research Institute, 2001:70.

52. UN Millennium Project TFoH. Halving hunger: it can be done. London: Earthscan, 2005.

53. Spiegel P, Sheik M, Gotway-Crawford C, Salama P. Health programmes and policies associated with decreased mortality in displaced people in postemergency phase camps: a retrospective study. Lancet 2002; 360:1927–1934.

54. World Food Programme. Nutrition in emergencies: WFP experiences and challenges. Food Nutr Bull 2006;27:57–66.

55. Guha-Sapir D, van Panhuis W. The importance of conflict-related mortality in civilian populations. Lancet 2003;361:2126–2128.

56. Webb P, Thorne-Lyman A. Entitlement failure from a food luality perspective: the life and death role of vitamins and minerals in humanitarian crises. In: Basudeb E, ed. Food security. Helsinki, Finland: United Nations University/WIDER, 2007.

57. Webb P. Food and nutrition concerns in Aceh after the Tsunami. Food Nutr Bull 2005;26:393–396.

58. Yamano T, Alderman H, Christiaensen L. Child growth, shocks and child nutrition in Ethiopia. Am J Agric Econ 2005;87:273–288.

59. Proudhon C. Democratic People's Republic of Korea. Nutrition Information in Crisis Situations. 2006:15–23.

60. UN High Commissioner for Refugees/United Nations International Children's Emergency Fund/World Food Programme/World Health Organization. Food and nutrition needs in emergencies. Rome: World Food Programme, 2001.

61. Dewey KG. Nutrient composition of fortified complementary foods: should age specific micronutrient content and ration sizes be recommended? J Nutr 2003;133:2950–2952S.

62. World Food Programme/Government of Sudan/United Nations International Children's Emergency Fund/Centers for Disease Control and Prevention. Emergency food security and nutrition assessment in Darfur, Sudan 2005. Rome: World Food Programme, 2006.

63. World Health Organization. Management of severe malnutrition: a manual for physicians and other senior health workers. Geneva: World Health Organization, 1999.

64. Khanum S, Ashworth A, Huttly SRA. Controlled trial of three approaches to the treatment of severe malnutrition. Lancet 1994;344:1728–1732.

65. Collins S. Changing the way we address severe malnutrition during famine. Lancet 2001;358: 498–501.

66. Briend A, Lacsala R, Prudhorn C, Mounier B, Grellety Y, Golden MH. Ready-to-use therapeutic food for treatment of marasmus. Lancet 1999;353:1767–1768.

67. Collins S, Sadler K. Outpatient care for severely malnourished children in emergency relief programmes: a retrospective cohort study. Lancet 2002;360:1824–1830.

68. Emergency Nutrition Network. Community-based therapeutic care (CTC). ENN Special Supplement Series, No. 2. Emergency Nutrition Network, Oxford, UK, 2004.

69. Collins S. Using middle upper arm circumference to assess severe adult malnutrition during famine. JAMA 1996;276:391–395.

70. Egge K, Strasser S. Measuring the impact of targeted food assistance on HIV/AIDS related beneficiary groups, Johannesberg, South Africa: C-SAFE, 2005.

71. Emergency Nutrition Network. Operational challenges of implementing community therapeutic care: ENN report on an inter-agency workshop. Washington, DC: Emergency Nutrition Network, 2005.

72. Mason J. Lessons on nutrition of displaced people. J Nutr 2002;132:2096S–2103S.

73. Bhatia R, Thorne-Lyman A. Food aid in emergencies and public health nutrition. 17th International Congress on Nutrition; Vienna, Austria; 2001.

74. Weise Prinzo Z, de Benoist B. Meeting the challenges of micronutrient deficiencies in emergency affected populations. Proc Nutr Soc 2002;61:251–257.

75. World Health Organization/World Food Programme/ United Nations International Children's Emergency Fund. Joint statement: preventing and controlling micronutrient deficiencies in populations affected by an emergency: multiple vitamin and mineral supplements for pregnant and lactating women, and for children aged 6 to 59 months. WHO, Geneva, Switzerland 2006.

76. Herforth A, Moussa S. Food, nutrients, and child growth: the role of specific foods and nutrients in child malnutrition and implications for food assistance programs. Food Nutr Bull 2005;26:397–402.

77. Zlotkin S, Arthur P, Antwi K, Yeung G. Treatment of anemia with microencapsulated ferrous fumarate plus ascorbic acid supplied as sprinkles to complementary (weaning) foods. Am J Clin Nutr 2001;74:791–795.

78. Duffield A, Reid G, Shoham J, Walker D. Evidence base for interventions in complex emergencies. Lancet 2005;365:842–843.

79. Van den Briel T, Webb P. Fighting world hunger through micronutrient fortification programs. Food Technol 2003;57:44–47.

80. Salama P, Spiegel P, Talley L, Waldman R. Lessons learned from complex emergencies over past decade. Lancet 2004;364:1801–1813.

# 26 The Indian Ocean Tsunami of December 26, 2004

## Saskia de Pee, Regina Moench-Pfanner, and Martin W. Bloem

## 26.1 INTRODUCTION

The Indian Ocean tsunami of December 26, 2004, was a natural disaster of massive magnitude and unprecedented in the large number of countries it affected. The tsunami was caused by an earthquake with a magnitude of 9.0 on the Richter scale off the west coast of Sumatra (Indonesia), which triggered a series of devastating tsunamis that reached more than a dozen countries in Southeast Asia and Africa. The waves struck within a few hours and left massive chaos and destruction. Worst affected were the coastal areas of Indonesia, Sri Lanka, southern India, Thailand, Bangladesh, Myanmar, Maldives, Seychelles, and Somalia. Hundreds of thousands of people died or were suddenly homeless, wounded, and traumatized and without access to food and shelter. A comprehensive evaluation conducted by the Tsunami Evaluation Coalition (TEC)[1] estimated that the overall death toll was above 227,000, and some 1.7 million people were displaced [1].The "foreigner" death toll in Thailand, primarily tourists, was estimated at 1,953 people [2].

In this chapter, we largely focus on the impact of the tsunami in Indonesia, particularly on health and nutrition, and on how the experience of dealing with the tsunami has further prepared the internal community for dealing with subsequent disasters.

---

[1] The TEC was created in early 2005 and included more than 40 key aid agencies, including the United Nations (UN), donor governments, and nongovernmental organizations (NGOs); the overall TEC strategy and process has been managed by a core management group that is chaired by the evaluation department of the United Nations Office for Coordination of Humanitarian Affairs (OCHA). The TEC conducted a large-scale and most comprehensive evaluation of the tsunami relief assistance, including five thematic evaluations. It published five reports plus a synthesis report that brings together lessons learned and recommendations from the five thematic evaluations as well as over 170 additional reports.

From: *Nutrition and Health: Nutrition and Health in Developing Countries, Second Edition*
Edited by: R. D. Semba & M. W. Bloem © Humana Press, Totowa, NJ

## 26.2  LOSS AND DAMAGE CAUSED BY THE TSUNAMI

The tsunami[2] was a rapid-onset disaster, similar to earthquakes and landslides, which occur rapidly and with little warning. The Sumatra-Andaman earthquake, which caused the Indian Ocean tsunami in December 2004, was the largest earthquake in the past 40 years. It triggered waves that reached successively from within 20 minutes to more than 8 hours the coastal areas of several countries. For example, part of Indonesia (Aceh) was struck within 20 minutes, whereas Thailand was struck within 1 hour and Sri Lanka within 1.5 hours. Because it took time for the waves to travel across the Indian Ocean, a warning could have been spread if early warning systems and effective disaster preparedness strategies would have been in place. The International Tsunami Information Center (ITIC), based in Hawaii,[3] did send a few messages to alert countries in the Pacific and the Indian Ocean, but there was no system in place to respond quickly and appropriately to inform large numbers of people at the coasts. Hence, the tsunami struck thousands of people without warning.

Among the overall death toll of more than 227,000, a large proportion was children, up to one third in some regions [3]. This was not only because 39% of the total population of the eight most severely affected countries are younger than 18 years but also because children were physically less able to rescue themselves [4]. Also, the number of women who died from the tsunami was very high in comparison to male victims, in many areas three times more than men [3]. In Aceh, Indonesia, and some parts of affected regions in India and Sri Lanka, even more than 80% of the victims were female [5]. Oxfam stated that women were more likely to be at home, while men were more likely occupied with their work on the open sea or inland, thus safe from the waves. Women were also less likely able to swim due to the traditional clothes they were wearing or not knowing how to swim or climb a tree [6, 7].

The sudden destruction of major geographical areas was enormous and washed away thousands of livelihoods. The magnitude of the force of the water is clearly illustrated by the 80-ton electrical generator ship that was 3 kilometers out in the ocean from Banda Aceh when the tsunami swept it 7 kilometers inward onto the land, where it now sits 4 kilometers from the shore and generates power for the surrounding newly built houses. It was estimated that more than 3 million people were affected, of whom about 1.4 million lost their livelihoods [8]. In particular, low-income families who were living from fishing and small-scale agriculture were affected [5]. For example, for Indonesia, the Food and Agriculture Organization (FAO), United Nations Development Programme (UNDP), and the Ministry of Agriculture (MOA) estimated the most significant impact as follows: Many farmers lost their tools, equipment, and livestock; fields were leveled, water reservoirs destroyed, and irrigation and drainage facilities destroyed in an area estimated at 39,500 hectare; crops on more than 50,000 hectares of land were damaged, and some agricultural land was permanently lost because it was swallowed by the sea;

---

[2]The term *tsunami* comes from the Japanese language and means *wave* ("nami") in the harbor ("tsu") [60]. A tsunami is created when a large amount of seawater is abruptly displaced, usually by an oceanic earthquake.

[3]The ITIC is maintained by the Intergovernmental Oceanographic Commission (IOC), established in 1965 and hosted by the United States (http://www.tsunamiwave.info).

and approximately 70% of the small-scale fishing fleet was destroyed in Nanggroe Aceh Darussalam Province, where small-scale fishery was the main economic activity.

Thus, the tsunami affected primarily areas and communities of fishermen and farmers living from small-scale business or on a subsistence basis who were already poor before the catastrophe and were now confronted with increased poverty due to the loss of livelihoods. For some countries, such as Sri Lanka and the Maldives, the national economy was expected to suffer because tourism, one of their main sources of income, would be reduced. In other countries, such as Indonesia, the overall economy was not expected to be greatly affected by the tsunami, but the impact on local poverty levels was likely to be substantial. The Asian Development Bank (ADB) estimated that more than 1 million people in Aceh and North Sumatra would be pushed into poverty [9].

The impact of a rapid-onset disaster, such as floods and earthquakes, on the health infrastructure is also large, both in terms of the scope of destruction of buildings and infrastructure and the loss of human resources. In Indonesia, 30 health clinics were destroyed and 77 severely and 30 slightly damaged [5]. Of the 497 provincial health office staff, 57 died and 59 were reported missing [10]. Many of those who stayed alive had to cope with the loss of loved ones and rebuild livelihoods. These losses substantially reduced the capacity to respond and came on top of the fact that local health systems were not prepared to deliver health services in disaster situations and were already weak before the tsunami [11]. This greatly affected the ability of the health system to deal with the needs of the population affected by the tsunami.

## 26.3  RESPONSE TO THE TSUNAMI

In the first 1 to 2 weeks after the tsunami, the local people from the nearby communities, including the survivors, provided most of the needed rescue, food, and medical aid [1]. This was then followed by provincial, national, and international assistance from the government, the military, the Red Cross Movement, the World Food Programme [WFP] and other UN agencies (United Nations International Children's Emergency Fund [UNICEF], FAO, World Health Organization [WHO], etc.), other international agencies, and nongovernmental organizations (NGOs).

### 26.3.1  Relief and Recovery Phase

Generally, the first phase of disaster response after a natural disaster is called the *relief* or *emergency* phase. In this phase, search, rescue, and lifesaving and live protection such as through provision of food aid, medical aid, and shelter are the priorities [12, 13]. In the immediate relief response after the tsunami, the provision of shelter for the thousands of internally displaced people (IDP) was a priority, and displacement sites were soon established. Ensuring clean drinking water and sanitation as well as food and medical aid was the other priority action taken in this first phase. This was important because sanitary conditions in displacements camps were often poor, particularly in the first months, as for example reported from Indonesia, where commonly used water sources had become undrinkable due to infiltration of seawater or because of contamination with fecal matter and debris [14].

Efforts during this first phase were challenged by the enormous destruction of infrastructure and the large scale of the geographical area that was affected, particularly in Indonesia and Sri Lanka. Initiation of national and international reactions was also slowed by the time it took to fully understand the extent of the damage [1]. The TEC described in their synthesis report several limitations and constraints found with respect to the response in the relief phase:

*Needs assessments conducted by agencies were often of poor quality, duplicative, uncoordinated; information sharing was in general insufficient, especially the affected population felt uninformed; difficult accessible areas were neglected; local capacity was underestimated and much unused; distributed goods were duplicative or inappropriate; provided aid was overlapping or suffered gaps; and problems with logistics and distribution management occurred.*

As soon as the initial emergency phase has passed, longer-term needs are addressed in the recovery phase. Lost livelihoods have to be reestablished, and whole communities, infrastructure, and services have to be rebuilt. Longer-term needs are less well understood than immediate needs, but they may be even more significant, and their restoration is a slow process [15]. Activities to rebuild livelihoods after the tsunami concentrated on construction/production of boats and fishing nets; agriculture and fishing; small and medium enterprises providing food, recreation, and tourism services; fish drying and marketing; repair and service stations for vehicles; carpentry, plumbing, computing, and electrical services [1]. Several thousand homes, schools, and health service centers were built, and many children quickly went back to school [1].

### 26.3.2   *Coordination of Response*

The enormous response of solidarity, from members of affected families, nearby communities, and the national and international community, made hundreds of volunteers and organizations flood the affected areas to offer their assistance. At one point, almost 200 NGOs were reported to be active only in Aceh, Indonesia. In this context, and due to the complete breakdown of infrastructure, the coordination and logistics among local and international aid workers and organizations was very difficult. Furthermore, the fact that in the two major affected areas of Indonesia and Sri Lanka a long-lasting civil unrest had been unfolding was also a major obstacle to allowing immediate and wide access to the most affected populations and areas.[4]

The United Nations Office for Coordination of Humanitarian Affairs (OCHA), assumed the task of international overarching coordination of international aid and was the focal point for interagency coordination. In Sri Lanka and Indonesia, humanitarian information centers were set up to support the massive information management challenge and to increase knowledge of the dimensions of the disaster and response. To improve coordination among all parties concerned, OCHA organized in Indonesia on monthly basis donor, United Nations, and NGO coordination meetings.

Besides OCHA, other UN organizations and NGOs assumed specific tasks in each affected country. For example, UNICEF has been identified to lead "nutrition" in

---

[4] It should be noted that shortly after the tsunami catastrophe, a peace accord was reached between the government of Indonesia and the separatist movement. Unfortunately, the same evolvement did not occur in Sri Lanka, and relief efforts and recovery efforts were therefore suboptimal and hampered.

emergency situations, whereas WFP leads "food," and WHO is responsible for "disease surveillance." Further details on coordination of humanitarian emergencies are provided by Kaiser and Spiegel and Webb and Thorne-Lyman in Chapters 24 and 25. Enormous logistical backstopping was provided by different governments from the region; for example, the government of Singapore was one of the earliest to send its military to the affected countries, particularly to Indonesia. This was followed by quick responses by Australia and the United States, which provided by early January 2005 the *Abraham Lincoln* vessel as a major basis for aid workers and logistical support at sea [12].

In the first half of 2005, OCHA also played a key role in establishing the TEC. The TEC explained in their synthesis report that the immense number of agencies involved in the tsunami disaster response not only increased the costs of coordination but also made coordination difficult and reduced its effectiveness. It was observed that international NGOs had less need and will for coordination since their own funding availability allowed them more flexibility and independence from common coordination structures. Actors were insufficiently engaged in coordination efforts, agencies concentrated on proliferation, official coordination meetings were not attended, and sharing of information was unsatisfactory [1].

### 26.3.3   Financial Support

The tsunami linked the countries of the whole world as the victims were from so many different countries. This triggered solidarity for aid donations at a scale that was rarely observed before. On January 6, 2005, OCHA launched a flash appeal of US $977 million to cover the needs from January to June [14]; by the end of March 2005, 80% was firmly pledged—a record response to a UN call for help. In February 2005, OCHA established a Trust Fund for Tsunami Disaster Relief to finance OCHA's coordination and relief activities as well as to provide allocations to UN agencies and NGOs engaged in tsunami disaster relief [3]. The OCHA guided donors on humanitarian priorities and channeled the pledged funds. Those reported through OCHA's Financial Tracking Service (FTS),[5] totaled US $6.8 billion with $5.8 billion from government sources and donations and $1 billion from corporate and private donations. If donations not reported through the FTS were added, an estimated total of US $14 billion were available for tsunami aid response [3].

The volume of funds exceeded the amounts that were available for other humanitarian crises manifold. It has been estimated that each person of the directly affected population (1.9 million) would receive, if funds were equally shared, US $7,100 compared, for example, to US $3 spent per capita after flooding in Bangladesh in 2004, when 36 million people were affected [1].

### 26.3.4   Lessons Learned for Next Disaster Response

First, the tsunami catastrophe highlighted the urgent need for countries to establish early warning systems and to have a national disaster preparedness plan in place. Second, the situation after the tsunami showed the importance of international standards for

---

[5]The FTS is a global database that records all reported international humanitarian aid, including that for NGOs, Red Cross/Red Crescent Movement, bilateral aid, in-kind aid, and private donations. It is managed by OCHA.

disaster relief and the need for the international aid community to adhere to these standards and to ensure that their personnel are knowledgeable on recent guidelines on effecting relief assistance and understanding international standards such as the Sphere,[6] the Good Humanitarian Donorship Initiative (GHD),[7] and the Code of Conduct of Humanitarian Assistance issued by the Red Cross Movement.[8] Unfortunately, the tsunami relief assistance witnessed many unqualified and unknowledgeable NGOs and their staff in regard to humanitarian operating guidelines due to the fact that they enjoyed a huge funding "pillow" that made them enter into activities for which they were not qualified.

Despite these challenges, aid was given, and in some places, new emergency interventions were invented and successfully implemented, such as the vitamin and mineral (V&M) response (discussed separately). Cash grants were also used more frequently than in other emergencies.

## 26.4   IMPACT OF TSUNAMI ON HEALTH AND NUTRITION: FOCUS ON INDONESIA

### 26.4.1   *Preexisting Health and Nutrition Situation*

The health and nutrition situation in the majority of the countries that were hit by the tsunami was already poor before the catastrophe. Especially, young children and women of reproductive age were suffering from malnutrition, micronutrient deficiencies, and consequent high mortality rates. Inadequate food intake and unsatisfactory water and sanitation conditions were major causes. A natural sudden-onset disaster such as the tsunami can further aggravate poor nutrition and health status, in particular when there is no immediate access to safe drinking water and not enough food of good nutritional quality.

Besides poor nutritional status, a large proportion of preschool-aged children were without complete immunization against diphtheria, pertussis, and tetanus (DPT3). For example, in Indonesia, this was the case for 30% of the children. Also, many children were not immunized against tuberculosis, measles, polio, and hepatitis B [15]. Not having received these immunizations put these children at greater risk of morbidity. One of the first-line health interventions in emergencies among populations with low immunization levels is therefore to immunize all children against measles and to provide them with a high-dose vitamin A capsule (see also Chapter 24).

---

[6] Sphere is a project launched by humanitarian NGOs in 1997. It provides overall humanitarian principles plus a set of standards/indicators for four life-saving sectors including (1) water supply/sanitation/hygiene promotion; (2) nutrition/food security/food aid; (3) shelter/settlement/nonfood items; and (4) health services.

[7] The GHD was launched in 2004 in Sweden, where 16 donor governments, the European Commission, the Organization for Economic Cooperation and Development (OECD) International Red Cross and Red Crescent Movement, NGOs, and academics developed a set of principles that should inform donors' practices.

[8] The Code of Conduct was established in 1994 with the aim to set standards in disaster response. It is comprised of principle commitments with respect to humanitarian disaster response for the International Red Cross and Red Crescent Movement and NGOs in disaster relief.

### 26.4.2   Impact on Health and Nutrition

Natural disasters have a major impact on the health of the survivors. This can be either directly through the catastrophe itself, such as injuries caused by debris, collapsing houses, and other causes, or indirectly with the situation created by the disaster implying a threat to health. Such threats include lack of access to safe drinking water, food, health care, or other circumstances that can lead to serious health and nutrition problems. The immediate health impacts caused by sudden-onset disasters such as flooding are likely to be higher compared to slow-onset disasters. These impacts may be particularly immense if the affected population was not warned prior to the disaster or could not protect themselves. A systematic literature review of epidemiological data on flood-related health impacts revealed that limited information is available, especially in relation to morbidity, epidemiologic risk factors, and effectiveness of public health interventions [16].

#### 26.4.2.1   COMMUNICABLE DISEASES

In humanitarian emergencies, there is an increased risk of outbreaks of communicable diseases, which in turn can lead to further morbidity and mortality among the affected population. Typical communicable diseases that may occur are fecal–oral diseases such as diarrhea, cholera, shigella dysentery, typhoid fever; vector-borne diseases like malaria, dengue fever, Japanese encephalitis, yellow fever; and communicable diseases such as measles, tuberculosis, acute respiratory infection (ARI), conjunctivitis, diphtheria, hepatitis, and HIV [17]. Communicable diseases such as ARI and measles can lead to mortality among populations under stress, particularly among children younger than 5 years who are, for example, living in large refugee camps [18]. Usually, it is not the disaster that causes an outbreak of communicable diseases, but the artificial, crowded groups of people that are created as a result of the disaster [13]. Those displacement centers are often characterized by high population density and limited access to safe water, lack of hygiene and sanitation, and inadequate shelter; a limited supply of enough and good-quality food is also often the case; all of these are risk factors for contracting and increased duration and severity of communicable diseases.

In flooding disasters, the large amounts of water create conditions that are favorable for the development of communicable diseases. Fecal–oral disease transmission may be increased, in particular in locations without clean water and sanitation [16]. Also, the incidence of mosquito-borne diseases such as malaria and dengue may increase if flooding creates large breeding sites for mosquitoes due to stagnating water [19]. A rise in nonspecific infections such as conjunctivitis as well as infections of the ear, nose, and throat can also be observed [20]. However, large-scale floods are not always followed by epidemics of communicable diseases [13]. After flooding and other natural disasters of the past 30 years, epidemics of waterborne diseases such as cholera and shigella dysentery were uncommon. Yet, large population displacement and compromised water sources increase the risk of waterborne diseases after floods [20].

After the tsunami, outbreaks of communicable diseases such as diarrhea, cholera, and malaria were expected because the risk was increased due to the large numbers of displaced persons, crowded conditions, flooding, and a vulnerable population with poor health and nutrition statistics [10]. In addition, infrastructure was destroyed, the drainage system affected, and drinking water sources were unusable due to seawater pollution. Providing safe drinking water to the affected population was one of the priority areas of action, and the drinking water response, including, among others, the distribution of water bottles and the use of large water tanks, was, according to a WHO study, "timely, comprehensive and effective" [21]. When in Indonesia 35 cases of measles among children were reported from displacement camps, a vaccination campaign targeting children 6 months to 15 years was implemented in camps as well as nearby communities [22]. In Indonesia, Myanmar, Sri Lanka, and India, the flooding caused favorable conditions for mosquito breeding. However, vector control measures for malaria and dengue were implemented [23]. In the first 3 months after the tsunami more than 65 outbreak alerts were investigated and immediately addressed [24]. At 3 months after the catastrophe, WHO informed that no major disease outbreak was reported, and observed cases were not exceeding the normal endemic levels [25].

### 26.4.2.2 HANDLING DEAD BODIES

The tsunami caused huge numbers of casualties in a short time and on a large geographic scale. A persistent myth, which is regularly refueled, is the concern that dead bodies can cause epidemics among the survivors of disaster [26]. As a result, hastened mass disposal of dead bodies often takes place. After the tsunami, mass disposal of dead bodies was particularly practiced in Indonesia, Sri Lanka, and India [19, 27].

A first literature review by Morgan in 2004 on the risks of infection of dead bodies after natural disasters found that there is no evidence that dead bodies imply any risk of epidemics after natural disasters [28]. Since such victims generally die from drowning, burning, or trauma, they are not more likely to have acute infections or rare diseases than the survivors. Instead, the survivors themselves are more likely the roots for disease outbreaks [28]. However, if a dead body was infected already before death, individuals who handle the dead body after the disaster may have a small risk of exposure to bloodborne viruses (such as hepatitis B, hepatitis C, HIV), gastrointestinal infections, or tuberculosis. Yet, this risk can be minimized by applying general hygienic precautions, as recommended in the Pan American Health Organization (PAHO)/WHO guidelines on how to manage dead bodies in a disaster situation [29].

The PAHO and WHO strongly discourage mass disposal not only because dead bodies do not imply a risk of epidemics but also because it impacts the mental health of the survivors as well as the already-difficult rehabilitation process [30]. The belief that mass burials or cremations can help the survivors to feel relief is another popular disaster myth [31]. Instead of hastened mass burials, dead bodies should be handled carefully and ethically. The identification and registration should be supported as well as the delivery of corpses to family members [29]. For those who lost their loved ones, it is important to be able to properly identify them and bid farewell and to pay appropriate last respect in accordance with cultural tradition and religious practices. In the management of mass facilities in disaster situations, the preservation of bodies becomes an important and challenging issue since preserving the body may be required until it can be taken to the public viewing area or finally disposed [29]. Box 26.1 highlights some disaster myths that were also encountered during the tsunami catastrophe.

### 26.4.2.3 INJURIES

Injuries among survivors of flooding are caused by near-drowning and trauma [13]. The common belief that immense flooding leaves a large number of people seriously

---

**Box 26.1**
**Selected myths and realities in disaster situations [31]**

| | |
|---|---|
| *Myth*: | Any kind of international assistance is needed, and it's needed now! |
| *Reality*: | A hasty response that is not based on an impartial evaluation only contributes to the chaos. It is better to wait until genuine needs have been assessed. |
| *Myth*: | The affected population is too shocked and helpless to take responsibility for their own survival. |
| *Reality*: | On the contrary, many find new strength during an emergency, as evidenced by the thousands of volunteers who spontaneously unite to sift through the rubble in search of victims after an earthquake. |
| *Myth*: | Foreign medical volunteers with any kind of medical background are needed. |
| *Reality*: | The local population almost always covers immediate lifesaving needs. Only medical personnel with skills that are not available in the affected country may be needed. |
| *Myth*: | Epidemics and plagues are inevitable after every disaster. |
| *Reality*: | Epidemics do not spontaneously occur after a disaster, and dead bodies will not lead to catastrophic outbreaks of exotic diseases. The key to preventing disease is to improve sanitary conditions and educate the public. |
| *Myth*: | Dead bodies pose a health risk and cadavers are responsible for epidemics in natural disasters. |
| *Reality*: | Contrary to popular belief, dead bodies pose no more risk of disease outbreak in the aftermath of a natural disaster than survivors. |
| *Myth*: | The fastest way to dispose of bodies and avoid the spread of disease is through mass burials or cremations. This can help create a sense of relief among survivors. |
| *Reality*: | Survivors will feel more at peace and manage their sense of loss better if they are allowed to follow their beliefs and religious practices and if they are able to identify and recover the remains of their loved ones. |

---

injured has been proven wrong, also in the case of the tsunami [32, 33]. Cuts and abrasion and their infection, however, are common [20, 33] and may lead to cases of tetanus. After the tsunami, around 100 cases of tetanus were reported to have occurred in the first weeks in Indonesia [22]. The ratio of deaths to injuries after the tsunami differed among the regions; for example, in Aceh there were 6 deaths per 1 injured person, whereas in Sri Lanka there were 1.53 deaths per injured person [1].

#### 26.4.2.4 MENTAL HEALTH PROBLEMS

Populations that are exposed to extreme stresses such as natural disasters and conflicts and to refugee situations are all at a risk of developing mental health and social problems [34]. Post-traumatic stress disorder (PTSD) and depressive and anxiety disorders are the mild and moderate mental disorders that are most frequently reported after disasters [35, 36]. The tsunami was an extreme stressor to the affected population. The sudden massive waves and water masses were a shock in themselves, and survivors had to cope with the loss of family members and other community members as well as with the loss of their property, often entire livelihoods. However, the effects that flooding disasters have in particular on mental health are not well investigated [16, 35].

Yet, there were several reports of increased symptoms such as anxiety, depression, and sleeplessness among tsunami survivors [16]. Unfortunately, no large-scale, formal survey on mental health problems has been conducted since the tsunami [37]. Of the tsunami-affected population, WHO roughly estimated that 20–40% fell into the group of people with mild psychological distress that resolves within a few days or weeks and does not need any specific intervention; 30–50% fell into the group with either moderate or severe psychological distress that may resolve with time or with mild distress that may remain chronic; the proportion of people with mental (mild and moderate) disorders may increase by 5–10% after a disaster; also the proportion of severe mental disorders, which is estimated to be approximately 2–3% in general, is expected to go up to 3–4% after exposure to extreme trauma/losses [36].

### 26.4.3    Interventions for Health and Nutrition

As mentioned, interventions that are timely and appropriately implemented can reduce morbidity and mortality from infectious diseases after a natural disaster. Interventions to prevent diseases transmitted via the fecal–oral route are particularly important where people live in crowded conditions with limited access to clean water and sanitation [19], and other early-phase interventions include targeted measles vaccination (when indicated, together with vitamin A supplementation) among populations with low vaccination rates; early treatment and mosquito control measures to control vector-borne diseases, such as malaria and dengue; and the early diagnosis and treatment of ARI, especially among infants and young children. Another important area of intervention is ensuring that survivors have good nutritional status so they are less susceptible to disease.

#### 26.4.3.1   DISEASE AND HEALTH AND NUTRITION SURVEILLANCE SYSTEMS

Surveillance systems are of critical importance in emergency situations, particularly after sudden-onset disasters, for the early detection of communicable diseases and for monitoring of the health and nutrition status of the affected population. The systems need to be established very quickly or, if existing, quickly put back into operation. Early detection of communicable diseases allows for immediate intervention and prevention of disease outbreaks, whereas findings from health and nutrition monitoring in the relief and later the recovery phases can provide information to channel and focus relief efforts effectively.

After the tsunami, efforts were made by local authorities and aid organizations to set up or reestablish disease surveillance as soon as possible. The Global Outbreak Alert and Response Network (GOARN) was immediately activated by WHO and sent out a large number of disease surveillance and response experts to the affected countries, provided assistance to strengthen existing disease surveillance systems, and reported that simple early warning systems to identify outbreaks of serious disease were in place in all affected areas within 2 weeks [25].

However, these were not without problems. Difficulties in counting and targeting were reported by WHO as a result of the mobility of the population in Aceh [12]. There was also a lack of accurate denominator and baseline data as well as a lack of trained personnel [38]. And, due to the civil unrest for several years in affected areas in Indonesia and Sri Lanka, some areas were not easily accessible to conduct health and nutrition surveillance. The TEC criticized in its report, "The Role of Needs Assessment in the Tsunami Response," the "gap that existed between successful monitoring of disease at field level and the use of technical information at political levels in WHO" and stated that "the risk of communicable diseases was projected by WHO/HQ and not based on technical in-house input and were not subsequently borne out in the field" [37].

A nutrition surveillance task force was established in February 2005 for assessing the health and nutritional situation among the population of tsunami-affected areas in Indonesia. Prior to that, a rapid preliminary nutrition assessment was undertaken in a convenient sample selected from 19 camps in Banda Aceh and Aceh Besar, which found a high prevalence of acute malnutrition (12.7% of children under 5 with a weight-for-height Z-score < −2 standard deviations [SD]) and very high proportions of children with diarrhea (42.6%), cough (69.7%), fever (55.9%), and vomiting (34.6%) in the preceding 2 weeks [39]. Subsequently, two rounds of surveillance were conducted, in March and in September 2005. These rounds collected data from the entire population in affected districts, which therefore also provided information about the health and nutrition situation of non-IDPs. It was found that the difference between IDPs and non-IDPs was smaller than the difference among certain districts [40].

### 26.4.3.2 IMPROVING HEALTH AND NUTRITIONAL STATUS OF THE AFFECTED POPULATION

Webb and Thorne-Lyman in Chapter 25 provide a clear overview of how the consideration of a possible link between disease and malnutrition grew into a realization, based on accumulated evidence, that malnutrition underlies more than 50% of childhood deaths because it increases vulnerability to suffer from infections and to suffer longer and more severely [41–47]. The international humanitarian community therefore now recognizes that, "The highest nutritional priority in the post-disaster setting is the timely and adequate provision of food rations containing at least 2,100 calories and that includes sufficient protein, fat, and micronutrients [48–52]".

Chapter 25 also presents a clear overview of the evolution of nutrition concerns in emergencies, including a description of the three main ways in which food is delivered in emergencies: general food distribution, selective feeding (targeted or blanket supplementary feeding and therapeutic feeding), and micronutrient interventions. All three of these were implemented in the response to the tsunami, primarily by WFP and its partners. The main food items that were distributed among the affected population in Indonesia were rice, cooking oil fortified with vitamin A, canned fish, iodized salt, fortified noodles, fortified biscuits, and corn-soy blend (CSB; a fortified blended food). The fortified foods were primarily used in selective feeding programs. With regard to micronutrient interventions, Helen Keller International (HKI) and its partners initiated a first-ever immediate and large-scale distribution of four V&M preparations to complement food aid. This intervention is described in further detail next.

### 26.4.3.3 THE NEED FOR MICRONUTRIENTS IN EMERGENCIES

As discussed more extensively in Chapters 18 and 30, vitamins and minerals (V&M) are essential for maintaining good health. In case of deficiency of V&M, people become more susceptible to infectious diseases, have reduced growth (among children), suffer impaired physical and mental development, have lower labor productivity, and are at increased risk of premature death. Malnutrition is linked to more than 50% of the 10–12 million deaths of children under the age of 5 each year [41–43] and is defined as low weight-for-age. Except for situations of acute food shortage or a disease epidemic, such as diarrhea, most of the underweight is due to stunting, which is to a large extent due to a chronically low intake of nutritious foods, rich in V&M and good sources of essential fatty acids and amino acids, and periods of morbidity. Thus, vitamin and mineral deficiencies (VMDs) are implied in many of the malnutrition-related child deaths each year.

In the case of an emergency, susceptibility to infectious disease increases due to poorer hygiene conditions (contaminated drinking water, lack of latrines), crowding (facilitating the spread of disease), and poor shelter (poor roofing, windy, cold). Therefore, good nutrition, particularly an adequate V&M intake, is very important in those circumstances. Food aid aims to protect minimal metabolic functions (at a minimalist "starvation-avoidance" level) and to reduce mortality by correcting pre-existing nutritional deficiencies and allowing for the physical activity necessary to be able to access the food [53–55]. In the case of the general food basket provided for tsunami relief, several fortified commodities were included, such as cooking oil fortified with vitamin A, fortified biscuits, fortified noodles, fortified blended foods, and iodized salt. Whereas such foods contribute a considerable amount of V&M, together with other foods consumed that are not part of the food basket, they do not provide a full recommended dietary allowance (RDA) for most V&M, particularly not for the most vulnerable groups, such as young children and pregnant and breast-feeding women. Although these vulnerable groups receive specific attention, formulating and distributing specific, acceptable foods for these groups is a challenge also because some needs are very high (e.g., for iron in pregnancy).

Therefore, WHO/WFP/UNICEF issued a joint statement in March 2006 on preventing and controlling micronutrient deficiencies in populations affected by an emergency[56]. The statement, recognizing that micronutrient deficiencies have severe and long-lasting consequences for individuals and populations and that they easily develop or are made worse during an emergency, states that it is essential to ensure that micronutrient needs of people affected by a disaster are adequately met. The statement recommends an additional intake of one RNI (recommended nutrient intake) per day for pregnant and breast-feeding women; for young children, it recommends one RNI per day when no fortified foods are distributed and two RNI per week when such foods are distributed. It is also stated that the multiple-micronutrient supplements should be given until the emergency is over and access to micronutrient-rich foods is restored. At that time, the micronutrient status of the population should be assessed to decide whether further interventions to prevent and control micronutrient deficiencies are still needed [56]. The advantages of providing V&M preparations is that they have a high impact, are not costly, require little storage space, have storage conditions that are similar to those required for storing food (i.e., not as strict conditions as for medicines), can be consumed without preparation, can easily be transported because of low bulk, and provide a gateway for provision of other services.

The distribution of V&M preparations in emergencies is not completely new, but it has not been widely practiced. The first fortified commodity in the food aid basket was iodized salt, distribution of which started in the 1980s. In the 1990s, other fortified foods became increasingly added, such as fortified oil, fortified blended foods, fortified flour, and more [53–55]. Distribution of V&M preparations was limited to the distribution of high-dose vitamin A capsules, often in combination with measles immunization. And, where the health care system remained or again became functional, iron/folic acid supplements may have been distributed to pregnant women.

The fact that V&M preparations are of low bulk is an advantage but also a challenge. Apart from the experience gained during tsunami relief (see next section), there are few examples of distribution in emergency relief of a small, very low-bulk condiment whether fortified or not. Iodized salt has been distributed by WFP; oxo cubes (for preparing stock), and maggi cubes (for flavoring a meal) were distributed by the UN High Commissioner for Refugees (UNHCR) in refugee camps in Africa, and a multimicronutrient powder called *Rahma* was distributed by the Micronutrient Initiative (MI) and partners to refugees in Darfur in 2006. Challenges described with distribution of low-bulk condiments such as salt include that due to its low volume it is difficult to divide, track, and distribute [53–55]. These challenges are shared by other low-bulk V&M preparations, and the fact that new concepts, and thus new products, require specific information when first introduced means that considerable efforts and resources need to be set aside for distributing V&M preparations in emergencies [57]. An example of a large-scale distribution of V&M preparations, in tsunami-affected areas of Indonesia, that overcame these barriers is described next. It was this experience that led to the March 2006 statement of WHO/WFP/UNICEF on preventing and controlling micronutrient deficiencies in populations affected by an emergency [56].

#### 26.4.3.4    EXAMPLE OF DISTRIBUTING VITAMIN AND MINERAL PREPARATIONS: TSUNAMI RELIEF IN INDONESIA

The tsunami was the first emergency for which V&M preparations were distributed at a large scale. Four different V&M preparations were distributed by HKI and partners to people affected by the tsunami in Aceh and Nias, Indonesia: high-dose vitamin A capsules to children, zinc tablets as adjunct treatment for diarrhea, iron-fortified sweet soy sauce for all ages, and multivitamin/mineral powder to be added to children's (6 months to 12 years) food [57, 58].

Vitamin A capsules were provided to the government and partners for their distribution programs, and children not yet reached through these distributions received a capsule on a "sweeping" visit to camps or villages by HKI and partners. Iron-fortified sweet soy sauce contributed additional iron of good bioavailability. Because the population was already familiar with both commodities, albeit that sweet soy sauce is not commonly fortified, their introduction was very easy and acceptance very high. Soy sauce distribution started separately from food aid distributions but was later included in certain geographic areas.

Zinc tablets were distributed to clinics and hospitals together with training and information for health workers on the benefits of zinc treatment for diarrhea cases, in line with the statement by WHO/UNICEF [59]. At the same time, social marketing was conducted on the benefits of zinc as an adjunct for diarrhea treatment; this was done to increase demand and encourage caretakers to seek treatment in case of diarrhea. However, evaluation data showed that overall less than 5% of recent diarrhea cases had

**Table 26.1**

Number of vitamin and mineral (V&M) preparations distributed in Aceh and Nias as part of the tsunami relief response by Helen Keller International and partners between January 2005 and April 2006 and the estimated number of beneficiaries

| V&M preparation | Number distributed | Number and kind of beneficiaries |
|---|---|---|
| Vitamin A capsules | 1,350,650 | 500,000 children 6 mo–12 yr |
| Zinc tablets | 1,556,200 | 156,000 episodes of diarrhea |
| Vitalita Sprinkles | 28,100,000 | 200,000 children 6 mo–12 yr |
| Iron-fortified soy sauce | 39,750,000 | 750,000 internally displaced persons |

received zinc (unpublished observation). The main reason appears to be that treatment for common diarrhea was usually not sought from the health center but rather, if at all, from health volunteers, who provided oral rehydration salts but who were not authorized to provide zinc tablets.

The vitamin/mineral powder that was distributed was known as *Vitalita* Sprinkles, a home fortificant that can be added to any food prepared for a child. It contains one RDA for young children (1–3 years). It was distributed to all children aged 6 months to 12 years to ensure that they would all receive a good extra amount of V&M. More than 28 million sachets were distributed to over 200,000 children, providing each with 30–210 sachets between April 2005 and April 2006. The most important lesson learned was that because the product, including its concept, was new to the population, appropriate information and training were required as well as a thorough introduction per beneficiary, particularly on proper use, to ensure acceptance. This means that when distribution of such a new V&M preparation is considered in other emergencies, adequate time, resources, and preparation time should be set aside to ensure that the preparation is well received and used by the target population. Further details of the distribution of Vitalita Sprinkles can be found in de Pee et al. [57]. Table 26.1 shows the number of V&M preparations distributed by HKI and partners for tsunami relief between January 2005 and April 2006 and the estimated number of beneficiaries.

## 26.5  CONCLUSIONS AND RECOMMENDATIONS

The tsunami catastrophe was definitely one of the most media-covered catastrophes in the last few years. The fact that "Western foreigners" were among the casualties triggered an international aid response that has rarely been seen. However, this also created unprecedented situations in terms of a large influx of organizations that had to be coordinated within and across a large number of countries, aid organizations absorbing and disbursing huge sums of money despite limits of their capacity to disburse funds in meaningful activities, and limited willingness to coordinate program activities among agencies because of the desire to proliferate agencies' own agendas. The problem of inappropriate aid that was encountered in several affected countries also underscored the importance and need for the international aid community to adhere to the existing international standards for humanitarian relief work.

The experience from the tsunami uncovered that the rehabilitation and recovery of livelihoods provide a long and complex challenge easily lasting several years.

From a health perspective, the tsunami made lots of victims and displaced people who needed assistance of a kind not included in standard relief assistance, such as trauma treatment and psychological counseling. Outbreaks of communicable disease did not occur at a large scale after the disaster. In addition, some of the wrongly assumed myths in emergencies (i.e., that dead bodies are the cause for major disease outbreaks or that victims are helpless and cannot decide for their own recovery solutions) were witnessed again during the tsunami relief assistance. The tsunami also highlighted that people living in poverty are the main victims and will stay in a rather helpless situation despite the generous international aid response. The tsunami also raised the need for population census and disease and health and nutrition surveillance systems as well as the importance of having a disaster preparedness strategy and early warning systems in place.

The tsunami emergency also provided an opportunity to examine the feasibility of implementing new intervention strategies such as the provision of V&M preparations in Aceh and Nias, Indonesia. During the early phase of an emergency, it is possible to reach a large number of people with these high-impact, low-bulk preparations. When preparations provided are new to the population, such as zinc for adjunct treatment of diarrhea and the multimicronutrient powder, their introduction and socialization require an appropriate length of time and attention per beneficiary to ensure appropriate use and hence acceptance. The low bulk is an advantage but may also present a challenge when distributing it together with more bulky items such as food. Efforts need to focus on ensuring that V&M needs of vulnerable groups in emergency situations are met and on developing effective strategies for doing so.

*Acknowledgment*  We thank Jutta Diekhans and Wiwiek Istiawati for their contributions to this chapter.

## REFERENCES

1. Telford J, Cosgrave J, Houghton R. Joint evaluation of the international response to the Indian Ocean tsunami: synthesis report. London: Tsunami Evaluation Coalition, 2006.
2. Reliefweb. Current state of affairs in tsunami-hit nations. March 24, 2005. Available at: http://www.reliefweb.int/rw/RWB.NSF/db900SID/LKAU-6ASE4F?OpenDocument. Accessed September 25, 2006.
3. Office for the Coordination of Humanitarian Action. Annual report 2005. Activities and use of extrabudgetary funds. New York: United Nations Office for the Coordination of Humanitarian Action, 2005.
4. United Nations International Children's Emergency Fund. Children in tsunami affected countries. New York: United Nations International Children's Emergency Fund, 2005.
5. International Centre for Migration and Health. The public health consequences of the tsunami: impact on displaced people (Interim Report). Geneva: International Centre for Migration and Health, 2005.
6. Oxfam. The tsunami's impact on women. Oxfam briefing note. Oxford, UK: Oxfam, 2005.
7. Federation/ICRC I. World disasters report 2005: focus on information in disasters. World disasters report. Geneva: International Federation/ICRC, 2005.
8. General Assembly Economic and Social Council. Strengthening emergency relief, rehabilitation, reconstruction, recovery and prevention in the aftermath of the Indian Ocean tsunami disaster (advance unedited draft). New York: United Nations, 2006.
9. Asian Development Bank. An initial assessment of the impact of the earthquake and tsunami of December 26, 2004 on South and Southeast Asia. Manila, Philippines: Asian Development Bank, 2005:1–12.
10. World Health Organization. Tsunami recovery process focuses on long-term health capacity development. Geneva: World Health Organization, 2005.

11. Kohl PA, O'Rourke AP, Schmidman DL, Dopkin WA, Birnbaum ML. The Sumatra-Andaman earthquake and tsunami of 2004: the hazards, events, and damage. Prehospital Disaster Med 2005;20:355–363.
12. World Health Organization. Inter-agency rapid health assessment. End of mission report, from the offshore platform—*USS Abraham Lincoln*. West Aceh, Indonesia: World Health Organization, 2005.
13. VanRooyen M, Leaning J. After the tsunami—facing the public health challenges. N Engl J Med 2005;352:435–438.
14. OCHA. Indian Ocean Earthquake –Tsunami 2005 Flash Appeal. New York, NY, USA: United Nations Office for the Coordination of Humanitarian Action, 2005.
15. United Nations International Children's Emergency Fund. The state of the world's children report 2006. New York: United Nations International Children's Emergency Fund, 2006.
16. Ahern M, Kovats RS, Wilkinson P, Few R, Matthies F. Global health impacts of floods: epidemiologic evidence. Epidemiol Rev 2005;27:36–46.
17. Connolly MW. Communicable disease control in emergencies: a field manual. Geneva: World Health Organization, 2005.
18. Connolly MA, Gayer M, Ryan MJ, Salama P, Spiegel P, Heymann DL. Communicable diseases in complex emergencies: impact and challenges. Lancet 2004;364:1974–1983.
19. Morgan O, Ahern M, Cairncross S. Revisiting the tsunami: health consequences of flooding. PLoS Med 2005;2:e184.
20. World Health Organization. Flooding and communicable disease fact sheet: risk assessment and preventative measures. Available at: http://www.who.int/hac/techguidance/ems/flood_cds/en/. Accessed April 7, 2007.
21. Clasen T, Smith L. The drinking water response to the Indian Ocean tsunami including the role of household water treatment. Geneva: World Health Organization, 2005.
22. Public Health Agency of Canada. Communicable Disease Report. Ottawa: Public Health Agency of Canada/Ministry of Health, 2005.
23. World Health Organization, South-East Asia Regional Office. Tsunami health bulletin. Geneva: World Health Organization/South-East Asia Regional Office, 2005.
24. World Health Organization. Health in action crisis. Annual report. Geneva: World Health Organization, 2005.
25. World Health Organization. Three months after the Indian Ocean earthquake-tsunami: health consequences and WHO's response. Geneva: World Health Organization, 2005.
26. de Ville de Goyet C. Stop propagating disaster myths. Lancet 2000;356:762–764.
27. Morgan O, de Ville de Goyet C. Dispelling disaster myths about dead bodies and disease: the role of scientific evidence and the media. Rev Panam Salud Publica 2005;18:33–36.
28. Morgan O. Infectious disease risks from dead bodies following natural disasters. Rev Panam Salud Publica 2004;15:307–12.
29. Pan American Health Organization. Management of dead bodies in disaster situations. Washington, DC: Pan American Health Organization, 2004.
30. de Ville de Goyet C. Epidemics caused by dead bodies: a disaster myth that does not want to die. Rev Panam Salud Publica 2004;15:297–299.
31. World Health Organization. Myths and realities in disaster situations. Geneva: World Health Organization. Available at: http://www.who.int/hac/techguidance/ems/myths/en/index.html. Accessed April 7, 2007.
32. Sondorp E, Bornemisza O. Public health, emergencies and the humanitarian impulse. Bull World Health Organ 2005;83:163.
33. Brown H. Treating the injured and burying the dead. Lancet 2005;365:204–205.
34. World Health Organization. Mental health in emergencies. Geneva: World Health Organization, 2003.
35. World Health Organization. The world health report 2001, mental health: new understanding, new hope. The world health report. Geneva: World Health Organization, 2001.
36. World Health Organization. Mental health assistance to the populations affected by the tsunami in Asia. Geneva: World Health Organization. Available at: http://www.who.int/mental_health/resources/tsunami/en/. Accessed April 7, 2007.

37. de Ville de Goyet C, Morinière L. The role of needs assessment in the tsunami response. London: Tsunami Evaluation Coalition, 2006.

38. Lee VJ, Low E, Ng YY, Teo C. Disaster relief and initial response to the earthquake and tsunami in Meulaboh, Indonesia. Ann Acad Med Singapore 2005;34:586–590.

39. Mokdad AH. Rapid nutrition assessment Banda Aceh and Aceh Besar, Sumatra, Indonesia. January 17–19, 2005. Jakarta, Indonesia: United Nations International Children's Emergency Fund /Centers for Disease Control and Prevention, January 2005.

40. Center for Research and Development in Nutrition and Food/National Institute of Health Research and Development/Southeast Asian Ministers of Education Organization, Tropical Medicine and Public Health, Regional Centre for Community Nutrition, University of Indonesia, United Nations Children's Fund. (CRDNF/NIHRD/SEAMEO-TROPMED/UNICEF). Second health and nutrition assessment in Nanggroe Aceh Darussalam Province and Nias, September 2005. Jakarta: UNICEF, 2006.

41. Pelletier DL, Frongillo EA Jr, Habicht JP. Epidemiologic evidence for a potentiating effect of malnutrition on child mortality. Am J Public Health 1993;83:1130–1133.

42. Pelletier DL, Frongillo EA Jr, Schroeder DG, Habicht JP. A methodology for estimating the contribution of malnutrition to child mortality in developing countries. J Nutr 1994;124:2106S–2122S.

43. Pelletier DL, Frongillo EA Jr, Schroeder DG, Habicht JP. The effects of malnutrition on child mortality in developing countries. Bull World Health Organ 1995;73:443–448.

44. Pelletier DL, Habicht JP. Continuing needs for food consumption data for public health policy. J Nutr 1994;124:1846S–1852S.

45. Caulfield LE, de Onis M, Blossner M, Black RE. Undernutrition as an underlying cause of child deaths associated with diarrhea, pneumonia, malaria, and measles. Am J Clin Nutr 2004;80:193–198.

46. Caulfield LE, Richard SA, Black RE. Undernutrition as an underlying cause of malaria morbidity and mortality in children less than 5 years old. Am J Trop Med Hyg 2004;71:55–63.

47. Black RE, Morris SS, Bryce J. Where and why are 10 million children dying every year? Lancet 2003;361:2226–2234.

48. Noji EK. Disasters: introduction and state of the art. Epidemiol Rev 2005;27:3–8.

49. Noji EK. Public health in the aftermath of disasters. BMJ 2005;330:1379–1381.

50. Noji EK. Estimating population size in emergencies. Bull World Health Organ 2005;83:164.

51. Noji EK. Public health issues in disasters. Crit Care Med 2005;33:S29–S33.

52. Sphere Project. The Sphere Handbook: Humanitarian Charter and Minimum Standards in Disaster Response, 2nd Revised edition. Oxfam: United Kingdom, 2003.

53. World Food Programme. Micronutrient fortification: WFP experiences and ways forward. Food Nutr Bull 2006;27:67–75.

54. World Food Programme. Nutrition in emergencies: WFP experiences and challenges. Food Nutr Bull 2006;27:57–66.

55. World Food Programme. Food for nutrition: mainstreaming nutrition in WFP. Food Nutr Bull 2006;27:47–56.

56. World Health Organization, World Food Programme, United Nations International Children's Emergency Fund. Preventing and controlling micronutrient deficiencies in populations affected by an emergency: Multiple vitamin and mineral supplements for pregnant and lactating women, and for children aged 6-59 months. Joint statement by WHO, WFP and UNICEF. Available at http://www.who.int/nutrition/publications/WHO_WFP_UNICEFstatement.pdf

57. De Pee S, Moench-Pfanner R, Martini E, Zlotkin S, Darnton-Hill I, Bloem MW. Home fortification in emergency response and transition programming: Experiences in Aceh and Nias, Indonesia. Food Nutr Bull 2007;28:189–197.

58. De Pee S, Moench-Pfanner R, Martini E, et al. Tsunami relief operations: the role of vitamins and minerals. Eighteenth International Congress of Nutrition (ICN), Durban, South Africa, 2005; in press.

59. World Health Organization, United Nations International Children's Emergency Fund. Clinical management of acute diarrhoea. Joint statement by WHO/UNICEF, 2004. Available at: http://www.who.int/child-adolescent-health/New_Publications/CHILD_HEALTH/Acute_Diarrhoea.pdf. Accessed April 7, 2007.

60. UNESCO-IOC (United Nations Educational, Scientific and Cultural organization-Intergovernmental Oceanographic Commission). Tsunami Glossary IOC Information document No. 221. Paris, UNESCO, 2006.

# 27

# The Impact of Supermarkets on Farmers, Consumers, and Food Security in Developing Countries

## C. Peter Timmer

## 27.1 INTRODUCTION

Since the 1990s, food systems in developing countries have been undergoing technological and institutional changes as vast and rapid as any in history. Three intersecting trends are reinforcing these changes. First, entire food systems are becoming more *private*, with a far larger role for market forces and a much smaller role for government-owned parastatals and cooperatives. Policy efforts to isolate domestic food economies from the world market have increasingly been unsuccessful in the face of market incentives for private traders. Second, food systems are becoming more *integrated*, with the same firm often dealing with farmers, traders, processors, and consumers. This integration is a stark change from food-marketing sectors that traditionally had been highly decentralized, very small scale and labor intensive, and usually extremely competitive, although often operating at high cost because of poor infrastructure and high commercial risks. Third, food systems are becoming more *global*, with foreign direct investment (FDI) bringing state-of-the-art management and logistical techniques as well as access to (and competition from) global markets. Globalization is more than a "buzzword" in developing countries; it is a day-to-day reality for many farmers and consumers.

The rapid spread of supermarkets is the key to understanding all three forces and how they are interacting. The rise of supermarkets and the changed role of governments in domestic food systems raise serious questions in three domains: (1) the fate of small farmers who need to diversify into higher-valued products than staple grains because "market-led diversification" now means "supermarket led"; (2) the impact on welfare of consumers (including nutritional impact) because consumers increasingly face a confusing array of new choices, not all of which are nutritious, when shopping in supermarkets; and finally, (3) who plans for a country's food security (the government or supermarkets), who should be responsible for ensuring stable supplies of staple foods (politicians or the market), and who has responsibility for improving the quality of diets.

From: *Nutrition and Health: Nutrition and Health in Developing Countries, Second Edition*
Edited by: R. D. Semba & M. W. Bloem © Humana Press, Totowa, NJ

## 27.2   THE SUPERMARKET REVOLUTION: WHAT'S HAPPENING?

Traditional food markets in developing countries are characterized by a preponderance of small shops, wetmarkets (the main retail outlets for fresh produce, meats and fish), and central markets. Although (mainly domestic) supermarket chains were present in the 1980s and even before, in most of these countries the supermarket sector was a tiny niche, at most 5–10% of national food retail, serving mainly upper-income consumers in a few large cities. However, starting in the early 1990s and accelerating markedly in the mid- and late 1990s, domestic food markets began to be transformed by a rapid rise in the role of supermarkets [1]. While there is significant variation in trends over countries in a given area such as Latin America and within individual countries over zones and between rural and urban areas, several broad patterns are observed. From earliest to latest adopter of supermarkets, there have been three waves of diffusion.

The first-wave countries include much of South America and East Asia outside China (examples include Argentina, Brazil, Chile, Korea, and Taiwan), where the share of supermarkets in food retail went from roughly 10–20% in 1990 to 50–60% on average by the early 2000s. Compared with the 70–80% share that supermarkets have in food retail in the United States, United Kingdom, or France, a process of convergence is apparent. The inflection or takeoff point was in the mid-1990s.

The second-wave countries include much of Southeast Asia and Central America, where the share went from 5–10% in 1990 to 30–50% by the early 2000s, with the inflection point in the growth curve in the late 1990s. Examples include Mexico, Colombia, Costa Rica, Guatemala, Thailand, and the Philippines.

The third-wave countries include some countries in Central and South America (such as Nicaragua and Peru), Southeast Asia (such as Vietnam and Indonesia), and China, where supermarkets were either a tiny niche or nonexistent in 1990 and have come to have 10–20% of national food retail by the early 2000s, with the inflection point in the late 1990s and early 2000s.

In general, the waves are correlated with socioeconomic characteristics of the countries. Thus, consumers' demand for supermarket services, product diversity, and quality are related to income and urbanization. These in turn are correlated with the opportunity cost of time, in particular that of women; reduction in transaction costs through improvements in roads and transport; and increasing ownership of refrigerators. These demand-side factors are necessary, but not sufficient, to explain the very rapid spread of supermarkets in the 1990s and 2000s in these countries, most of which had at least a very small supermarket sector before 1990. Thus, supply-side factors must also have been of significant importance in explaining the rapid rise of supermarkets.

The first supply-side factor was the massive influx of retail FDI (and competitive investment by local chains) that arrived in the first- and second-wave countries around the mid-1990s and the third-wave countries in the mid- to late 1990s and into the 2000s. The influx usually started at the same time as the inflection point of supermarket growth takeoff and probably caused it. The liberalization of retail FDI stimulated this influx, but such liberalization was, at the time, merely the "little brother" of trade liberalization that occurred with structural adjustment programs and the Uruguay Round trade negotiations in the late 1980s and early 1990s.

The FDI from global multinationals based in Western Europe, the United States, Japan, and regional multinationals surged into the retail sectors of the emerging markets.

The FDI was driven by push factors—in particular, saturation and intense competition in home markets—and pull factors such as much higher margins to be made by investing in developing markets. Moreover, initial competition in the receiving regions was weak, generally with little fight put up by traditional retailers and supermarkets funded by domestic capital. Further incentives to rush in were the distinct advantages to early entry, hence occupation of key retail locations.

It is likely that FDI in the food sector, via the profound changes induced in the retail and processing sectors, is having a greater effect on local agrifood economies than is trade liberalization. For example, while much attention has been focused on the boom in fruit and vegetable exports from Latin America over the past two decades, supermarket chains in Latin America now buy from local farmers 2.5 times the amount of produce that is exported from the region [2]. The ratio is already similar in China, with supermarkets in China buying at least twice the volume of produce as is exported from China [3].

The varying role of FDI helps explain some anomalies in the relationship between socioeconomic (demand-side) variables and the pace of supermarket diffusion. For example, while incomes and urbanization rates in China and Vietnam do not differ much from those of Guatemala, the former two countries figure only in the third wave of supermarketization because policy reform of FDI in the retail sector lagged that of Guatemala. As retail FDI was progressively liberalized in China, FDI poured in at an amazing rate from around the world in the late 1990s and early 2000s, making it the premier destination for retail FDI in the world, which was the same case in Russia [3, 4]. The supermarket sector in China is growing the fastest in the world. It started from nothing in 1991 and by 2003 had US$71 billion of sales and 30% of urban food retail and is growing 30–40% a year [3].

A second supply-side factor is the adoption of dramatic organizational changes in the procurement system, and these are linked to institutional changes. The organizational changes—mostly squeezing out traditional layers in the food-marketing system—were undertaken mainly in the second half of the 1990s or in the 2000s and greatly reduced the procurement costs faced by retailers in these countries. The reduction in costs, coupled with stiff competition, allowed (as well as pushed) leading retail chains to move from large cities to secondary cities and even to smaller towns and from upper-, to middle-, then to lower-income segments. The now-common image of supermarkets with cheap products aimed at the working poor or in small and medium towns contrasts sharply with the traditional image of the supermarket aimed at the small niche luxury market in big cities.

The adoption of the procurement system changes occurred first and fastest in processed foods (for which supermarkets had a clear advantage over traditional small stores because of economies of scale) and only later in fresh foods, including fresh meats, fish, and produce. A rough rule of thumb is that in the first- and second-wave countries, the share of supermarkets in sales in the overall retail food market is twice the share of supermarket sales in the produce market—consumers tend to shop at local markets for fresh fruits and vegetables until quite late in the penetration of supermarkets. For example, in Mexico, the share of supermarkets in overall food is 40%, while in produce it is only 20%. Usually, the first fresh food categories for the supermarkets to gain a majority share include "commodities" such as potatoes and sectors experiencing consolidation in first-stage processing and production: often chicken, beef, pork, and fish.

The competition between supermarkets and wetmarkets is increasingly stiff and is based on shopping experience, price, quality, freshness, and variety. In the big cities of

Mexico or China, the differences in prices between supermarkets and wetmarkets for commodity produce items are narrowing, and prices are often equal for key items. In a recent study by AC Nielsen of 15,000 consumers in the Asia-Pacific region, they found that supermarkets are eroding the share of the wetmarkets in retail by attempting to replicate the experience of the traditional wetmarket while reducing prices to compete directly [5]. In the Asia-Pacific region, supermarkets have been making significant inroads into these categories only since 2000 and usually only after cost-cutting and quality-increasing procurement system changes, which are at the heart of the supermarket revolution.

A key change has been in the use of private standards. While food retailing previously operated in the informal market, with little use for certifications and standards, the emerging trend indicates a rapid rise in the implementation of private standards in the supermarket sector (and other modern food industry sectors such as medium-/large-scale food manufacturers and food service chains). The rise of private standards for quality and safety of food products and the increasing importance of the enforcement of otherwise virtually not enforced public standards are crucial aspects of the imposition of product requirements in the procurement systems. In general, these standards function as instruments of product quality differentiation and coordination of supply chains by standardizing product requirements over suppliers, who may cover many regions or countries. Standards specify and harmonize the product and delivery attributes, thereby enhancing efficiency and lowering transaction costs.

An important element of this is the reduction of coordination costs in procurement systems that become progressively broader in geographic scope. Regional and global chains cut costs by standardizing over countries and suppliers, which induces a convergence with the standards of the toughest market in the set, including with European or US standards. This can be seen in Wal-Mart between Mexico and the United States, in the Quality Assurance Certification used by Carrefour over its global operations that include developing countries, and in the regional chains such as Central American Retail Holding Company, CARHCO [6]. In turn, the implementation of these standards depends crucially on the establishment of new procurement system organization [7].

The development implications emerging from this rapid supermarketization produce both hope and worry. There is certainly major opportunity implied by the expansion and diversification of the food market induced by the spread of supermarkets, and there is evidence that this can raise producer incomes relative to selling in traditional markets. Meeting transaction requirements implied by the organizational change in supermarket procurement systems and the product requirements implied by institutional change in the form of private standards can present clear opportunities for producers. Adopting the new practices can open the door to suppliers to sell through supermarket chains that are "growing" the market in terms of volume, value added, and diversity. A supplier can move from being a local supplier to a national, regional, or global supplier. Moreover, private process standards can increase efficiency of firm operations and raise profitability. The market scope could also increase, compensating for per-unit profit decreases arising from costs incurred to meet the standards [8].

However, meeting these nontraditional market requirements implies changes in production practices and investments, such as coordinating to aggregate volumes, reducing pesticide use, or investing in "electric eyes" in packing sheds and cooling tanks in dairies. Some of these investments are quite costly and are simply unafford-able in many small firms and farms. It is thus not surprising that the evidence from the early wave of supermarket penetration is that the changes in standards, and the implied investments, drove many small firms and farms out of business over the past 5–10 years and accelerated industry concentration. The evidence from the third-wave countries, however, especially in Asia, is not so clear. Because of the preponderance of small farms in Asia, supermarkets have found it necessary to use creative institutional arrangements to source produce from these small farms [9].Whether these arrange-ments can be used in other parts of the world to include small farmers in supermarket supply chains remains an important question.

The task will be difficult. The supermarket chains, locked in a struggle with other chains in a highly competitive industry with low margins, seek constantly to lower product and transaction costs and risk. All that points toward selecting only the most capable farmers, and in many developing countries that means mainly the upper tier of small farmers and medium and large farmers. Moreover, as supermarkets compete with each other and with the informal sector, they will not allow consumer prices to increase to "pay for" the farm-level investments needed. Who will pay for safe-water wells? Latrines and hand-washing facilities in the fields? Record-keeping systems? Clean and proper packing houses with cement floors? The supplier does and will bear the financial burden. As small farmers lack access to credit and large fixed costs are a burden for a small operation, this will be a huge challenge for small operators.

## 27.3   AN ANALYTICAL PERSPECTIVE ON THE IMPACT OF SUPERMARKETS

Who gains and who loses from the supermarket revolution? In a market economy, profits tend to accrue to the relatively scarce resource in the system under analysis and to whoever controls those resources. Thus, to answer the question, an economist asks, What are the scarce resources and who controls them because scarcity has value? This is a particularly economic view of the world, where something has a "value in exchange" that can be completely different from its "value in use." Diamonds are at one end of the spectrum and air at the other. Or, to paraphrase Oscar Wilde, economists know the price of everything and the value of nothing. There are three basic possibilities for which resource is scarcest in the food system (although these extend outside the traditional fac-tors of production of land, labor, and capital): access to farm output, access to marketing technology, and access to consumers.

First, despite concerns that population growth will outstrip growth in food supplies, the *historical* evidence is that the capacity to produce basic food commodities is not scarce on a global level. Modern agricultural technology is land saving, there is abun-dant rural labor (again, on a global level), rural finance is readily available when there is a profit to be made in lending it, and water is becoming scarce only because it is provided free in most cases. What *might* be scarce at the farm level is the *management ability* to meet high-quality standards and to deliver reliably a safe product that meets environmental requirements and is fully traceable to its point of production. There are likely to be significant economies of scale to this management ability, even if there are few scale economies in the physical production of most agricultural commodities.

It is possible that growing demand for biofuels will change this scarcity equation, but this demand growth is driven mostly by politics rather than by economics, so it is difficult to judge its future impact.

A second possibility for what is scarce is access to marketing and information technology that improves coordination. The food-marketing system is the "narrow point in the funnel" between many farmers and many consumers. Because there are relatively few of them, the "middleman" is universally subject to the charge of exploiting both ends of the food chain [10]. However, the technology for managing supply chains—in the food system and elsewhere—is changing rapidly, even in the United States. This technology is changing especially rapidly in the modern logistics area that uses information technology to manage inventories.

In general, these technologies drive down transaction costs throughout the supply chain. Further, by reducing the need to hold large inventories, these marketing and logistics technologies reduce capital costs and risks. Since inventory is basically a form of "dead capital," improved logistics and inventory management generate real capital savings as well as lower transactions costs. Both contribute to higher productivity and faster economic growth.

The important question is whether access to this technology is sufficiently restricted that it is "scarce." That is, can excess profits be earned by controlling it? The evidence suggests that it is easily duplicated as computer power becomes cheaper and local managers learn to imitate the market leaders. Intellectual property rights (IPRs) seem not to be a serious impediment to this imitation, despite supermarket chains' efforts at proprietary control. It is the *knowledge* that such techniques are feasible and available that is important, not the specific code written for a particular supermarket's computers. The parallel to the "technological treadmill" so familiar to American farmers is striking. First adopters of new technology have a temporary cost advantage, but competition leads all market players to adopt it quickly. This seems to be the story for marketing technology.

The third possibility for what is scarce is access to consumers themselves, especially to knowledge of how consumers behave—what they want and therefore how best to serve them. As concentration in food retailing rises, there seems to be an opportunity for the leading firms—Carrefour, Wal-Mart, Metro, Tesco, and so on—to *control* this access and thus to earn higher marketing margins and profits. This has been a long-standing worry in the United States, at least since the 1940s.

The evidence so far, in both rich and poor countries alike, is that access to consumers has been highly competitive. Market power is used to drive down costs, which are then passed along to consumers as lower prices. Why? Because supermarkets need to increase market share to achieve the economies of scale that permit their costs to be even lower. So far, this whole system has been highly *contestable*. Economists know that contestable markets pass nearly all the benefits of the marketplace (the sum of producer and consumer surplus, to be technical) through to consumers. Even at this late stage in the supermarket revolution in the United States, adoption of state-of-the-art marketing technology generates annual benefits equal to half the size of the entire farm economy. This is a staggering result, driven by the calculation that Wal-Mart alone, the leader in the marketing technology revolution, lowers the annual inflation rate by roughly 1% per year. Thus, the main winners in the supermarket revolution are consumers.

This analysis and the conclusions stemming from it have powerful implications for which policy recommendations make sense for dealing with the impact of the rapid spread of supermarkets. There are three key areas to consider: (1) consumers and public health; (2) the role of and impact on small farmers; and (3) food security at the local and national levels.

### 27.3.1  Consumers and Public Health

Health professionals are either pessimistic about the political reality of using economic variables to influence dietary choices or doubtful that economic incentives will actually change dietary behavior where affluence permits a wide array of choices. Consequently, there is much more focus on trying to change lifestyle through improved health knowledge and nutrition education [11].

Supermarkets are both the purveyors of the food abundance and a possible vehicle for bringing about dietary change, through improved nutrition education within stores, health warnings on particular foods that cause nutritional damage, or even regulations on what kinds of foods are available for purchase. The rapid spread of private standards on food safety and aspects of production technologies shows that public policy is not necessarily the fastest or most effective way to bring about changes in food marketing. These private standards could easily incorporate health dimensions as well, especially if lawsuits over the contributions of "fast food" to obesity begin to be won by litigants.

As consumers become more urbanized and divorced from the production of their food, the vast array of choices in modern supermarkets can, paradoxically, lead to worsened nutritional status. The "double burden" of malnutrition, with undernutrition existing side by side with obesity and diet-related problems such as heart disease and diabetes, is already facing many developing countries, as Barry Popkin's Chapters 20 and 21 in this volume demonstrate. The policy options for responding to this problem are limited, but one approach is to use the "focusing power" of supermarkets to provide nutrition education to their shoppers. Nutritional labeling is one component of this education, but supermarkets could also use their sophisticated knowledge of consumer behavior to shape their dietary patterns in healthier directions.

### 27.3.2  Small Farmers

Small farmers are obviously a major point of concern. The evidence so far from other countries, especially Latin America, is that small farmers tend to be squeezed out of supermarket supply chains fairly rapidly because of the high transactions costs of dealing with them. This is not likely to be an optimal response in the densely settled parts of Asia or parts of Africa still dependent on small farms for basic food production, and the early evidence from China and Indonesia suggests that institutional innovations—often involving cooperatives or dedicated buying agents working jointly with supermarket procurement officers and farmer representatives—offer some hope for ensuring that small farmers retain access to food supply chains in their own countries [9, 12]

Still, the important question is what policymakers can do to help small farmers without raising costs and hurting consumers. The *World Development Report, 2008: Agriculture for Development* recognized this as a critical challenge facing small farmers and offered a number of suggestions [8]. Providing useful technical assistance to farmers, serving as a "catalyst" for the formation of farmer associations, and conducting research, extension, and training activities—increasingly as joint ventures with private sector participants—seem to be promising activities.

### 27.3.3 *Food Security*

In those large, densely populated societies where half the average daily food energy still comes from staple cereals, how will food security be managed when most of these cereals are sold in supermarkets? In the past, managing food security at the national level has meant guaranteeing availability of basic grains in local markets and keeping the prices of these grains reasonably stable. Can supermarkets take over these tasks? Price stabilization has traditionally been a public sector role because there is no private market where producers and consumers can "purchase" price stability. But, if food sales become sufficiently concentrated in a few dominant supermarket chains, it is entirely possible that consumer demands for price stability of staple cereals could be "internalized" and provided by these private sector players.

From a policy perspective, much of the underlying motivation for examining the impact of modern supply chains has been a concern for rural poverty and the fear that the rapid spread of supermarkets might actually make it worse. It is very important to remember, however, that rural poverty cannot be solved by keeping all small farmers on their farms whether or not they are supplying supermarkets. To solve the problem of rural poverty, the entire economy must continue to grow rapidly, jobs must be created off the farm, and countries must find a way onto the path of structural transformation [13, 14]. Supermarkets are only a small part of this transformation, but by pushing competitive pressures from consumers downward throughout the food system, they can play a surprisingly important role in improving productivity, and consumer welfare, for the economy.

In summary, what does this analytical perspective have to say about the supermarket revolution? First, the whole process of rapid change in domestic food systems is understandable within the context of the structural transformation, the well-understood historical process by which economic growth transforms societies from poor and rural to rich and industrial (and now, postindustrial). Second, basic economics, with its stress on returns to scarce factors of production, is surprisingly helpful in understanding the inner dynamics of the process. But third, this perspective provides little guidance on how to assist small farmers as they compete for contracts from supermarket procurement officers. Assisting small farmers is turning out to be a very site-specific task, where the potential for local institutional innovation is driven by asset distributions (including human capital as well as land and financial capital), history, culture, and ecological setting. Thus, the diversity of the global food system, rather than its common themes and forces, needs to be understood in any effort to assist small farmers, a task well beyond the scope of this chapter.

## 27.4    THE DEVELOPMENT DIMENSIONS OF THE SUPERMARKET REVOLUTION

Even without discussing details of farmer interaction with supermarket procurement officers, several basic issues for development are raised by the supermarket revolution. These issues cut across the entire economy, from agricultural technology and farmer responsiveness, to concentration in processing and retailing channels, to standards for food quality and safety, to food security at both micro- and macrolevels. The focus needs to be on how to achieve and sustain rapid reductions in poverty and hunger through interventions (or ending interventions) in the food system. The supermarket revolution cuts both ways in this, offering greater consumer choice and lower prices for the retail services provided, but with a track record of consolidating supply chains to a handful of reliable producers able to meet quality, safety, and cost standards and thus excluding many small farmers from access to supermarket customers. The issue is whether policymakers have an opportunity—in the face of very serious challenges—to leverage the impact of supermarkets on consumers in ways that do not increase rural poverty. To answer that, a better understanding of the impact of supermarkets on the overall economy is needed.

### 27.4.1 Supermarkets: Complements or Substitutes for a Public Role in Marketing?

Supermarkets are increasingly playing both the coordinating role of markets and their role in price discovery and determination. How will this increasing dominance of supermarkets influence performance of the overall marketing system? First, there will be a concern for both the *efficiency* and the *equity* of price formation as more and more transactions are internalized by supermarket procurement officers. Such transactions are not open and transparent, and hence concern will grow over the shift in market power toward a few, large buyers and over the likely exclusion of many suppliers from these arrangements. Second, however, and partially offsetting the first concern, supermarkets can also internalize consumers' desires for food safety and price stability and hence can manage procurement contracts with these desires in mind. Finally, if supermarkets in developing countries are as competitive as in rich countries, fears about monopoly control and market power will turn out to be ill-founded. The market for the food consumer's dollar seems to be highly contestable, even when only a small handful of players is able to survive the cost competition. Consumers are the winners of such competition.

### 27.4.2 Macroeconomic and Growth Issues

Most effects of supermarkets in developing countries are likely to play out at the firm and sector levels, and macroeconomic effects will be modest. But, they will not be trivial, especially as lower food costs translate into greater real purchasing power for consumers. The impact will then be felt through differential responses to higher incomes—greater stimulus to manufactured goods and modern services and gradual retardation for staple foods, traditional clothing, and basic housing. Managers of supermarkets themselves are fully aware of these trends as a stroll down any aisle will demonstrate. By passing on lower costs or improving food quality and convenience, supermarkets can actually speed up the structural transformation and the agricultural transformation that is part of it [13].

There will also be significant efficiency effects. The mantra of supermarket procurement officers is to "drive costs out of the food-marketing system." Although these "costs" are also someone's income, especially of farmers and traders in the traditional agricultural marketing chain, lowering food-marketing costs not only allows lower consumer costs, with the effects noted, but also frees up productive resources that can be used in more profitable activities. This is the process by which total factor productivity improves, and this improvement, including in the food system, is the basic long-run source of economic growth [14].

A final growth effect may in the long run be the most important: the technology spillovers that result from the use by supermarket managers of imported information technology and modern management techniques honed in the fierce competition of Organization for Economic Cooperation and Development (OECD) food markets. Most of this technology arrives as part of FDI, which, as noted, has been the main vehicle for rapid penetration of supermarkets into developing countries [15, 16]. It is often proprietary, and supermarket owners go to great lengths to keep it internal to the company. But like most technologies, the knowledge that these tools and techniques exist is the key to rapid emulation as local managers trained by the first wave of foreign supermarkets leave to establish their own companies and consulting firms. Thus, the spillovers from introducing modern information technologies and management techniques can occur fairly rapidly and have widespread effects by lowering costs across the entire economy, not just in food retailing.

Supermarkets will affect not only the efficiency of the food-marketing chain, but also the distribution of benefits from the value added in the process. In general, it is very difficult to say whether these distributional changes will be positive or negative, that is, whether income distribution will improve.

There are two important offsetting effects. On the negative side, the evidence is clear that rapid supermarket penetration into traditional food-marketing systems can quickly displace "mom-and-pop" retail shops, traders in wetmarkets, and small-scale wholesalers. In most of these cases, the people displaced earn relatively low incomes and will have to make significant adjustments to find new livelihoods. The distributional effect is likely to be negative and can be substantial if these small-scale food-marketing firms are numerous and widely visible. Their imminent demise can also generate significant political resistance to the spread of supermarkets, an effect already being seen throughout Asia, but with historical antecedents in the United States, Europe, and Japan.

The impact of supermarket penetration on the farm sector is, of course, the big question. The Latin American experience suggests that small farmers rapidly lose access to supermarket supply chains and are thus cut off from the rapidly growing value-added component of the retail food basket. The suggestion is that these farmers risk falling further into poverty [2]. The African and Asian experience is more promising, and research is under way to understand the nature of the problem and any potential governmental responses. Keeping a significant number of small farmers in the supply chain of supermarkets is likely to be essential for poor countries to reap widespread social benefits from the rapid domination by supermarkets. The impact on the traditional food-marketing sector will be small relative to this impact on small farmers. But, efforts to slow the penetration of supermarkets on behalf of small farmers and traditional agents in the food-marketing chain need to keep widespread consumer benefits in the calculus.

## 27.5   PUTTING SUPERMARKETS IN A FOOD POLICY FRAMEWORK

Finally, it is useful to put supermarkets and their impact into an integrated food policy framework in an effort to move the research agenda forward. Figure 27.1 illustrates the likely components. It is organized around the familiar vertical structure of the food system, with farmers at the bottom, passing their produce up through the marketing system—now divided into traditional markets and supermarkets—with consumers at the top of the chain [17].

Food Consumers and Behavioral Change

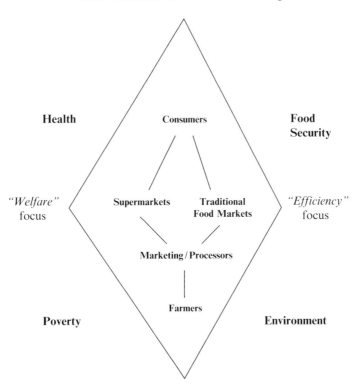

Small Farmers and the Structural Transformation

**Fig. 27.1.** Supermarkets and a food policy research agenda. (From [17].)


## 27.6 CONCLUSIONS

The four major policy issues confronting the food system are arrayed in a diamond around this vertical structure: health and poverty concerns on the welfare side and food security and environmental concerns on the efficiency side of the diamond. From below, the basic forces affecting small farmers are the structural transformation and the role of agriculture in that process. From above, the basic forces affecting food consumers are behavioral changes in the context of increasing affluence and choices available.

Within this framework, it is possible to identify the key linkages from supermarkets through the rest of the food system that policymakers will want to understand if they are concerned about food security. At the micro-, or household, level, the research question is the impact of supermarkets on poor consumers, especially the role of supermarkets in distribution and pricing of starchy staples. There has been remarkably little research on this aspect of the impact of supermarkets on food security. Can supermarkets stabilize food prices?

At the macrolevel, the issue will be the impact of supermarkets on staple food supplies, price stability, and links to global grain markets. What role are supermarkets playing in these markets at the moment? Is there any way to use supermarkets (instead of parastatals, for example) to manage "macro" food security by being the intermediary between a country's consumers and the world grain markets? Most supermarket chains have exceptionally good links to global markets and thus could prove to be very efficient links between these markets and domestic consumers.

The last issue asks whether supermarkets are a major factor in the health epidemic seen in affluent countries and among the affluent in poor countries. Are processed foods, snack foods, and fatty foods the cause of obesity, heart disease, and diabetes? Are supermarkets (partly) to blame for our rapidly rising consumption of these foods and thus for the double burden of malnutrition? Can regulations and incentives be designed to promote healthier diets, starting in the supermarket aisle?

Taken together, these questions form the core of a research agenda that is complementary to the current attention focusing on the impact of supermarkets on small farmers and research directed at finding policy or program mechanisms to help them compete successfully within the global supply chain. In combination, the consumer-oriented and the producer-oriented research will help us understand the key policy issues arising from the rapid emergence of supermarkets as the dominant players in the food-marketing arena.

## REFERENCES

1. Reardon T, Berdegue JA, Timmer CP. Supermarketization of the emerging markets of the Pacific Rim: development and trade implications. J Food Distrib Res 2005;36:3–12.
2. Reardon T, Berdegue JA. Supermarkets and agrifood systems: Latin American challenges. Theme issue. Dev Policy Rev 2002;20.
3. Hu D, Reardon T, Rozelle S, Timmer CP, Wang H. The emergence of supermarkets with Chinese characteristics: challenges and opportunities for China's agricultural development. Dev Policy Rev 2004;22:557–586.
4. Dries L, Reardon T, Swinnen J. The rapid rise of supermarkets in Central and Eastern Europe: implications for the agrifood sector and rural development. Dev Policy Rev 2004;22:525–556.
5. Retail. MMP. Consumers forsake wet markets in Asia. Daily News by M+M Planet Retail, June 7, 2004.
6. Berdegue JA, Balsevich F, Flores L, Reardon T. Central American supermarkets' private standards of quality and safety in procurement of fresh fruits and vegetables. Food Policy 2005;30:254–269.
7. Reardon T, Codron JM, Busch L, Bingen J, Harris C. Global change in agrifood grades and standards: agribusiness strategic responses in developing countries. Int Food Agribusiness Manag Rev 1999;2:421–435.
8. World Bank, 2007. World Development Report, 2008: Agriculture for Development. London: Oxford University Press for the World Bank.
9. Wang H, Dong X, Rozelle S, Huang J, Reardon T. Producing and procuring horticultural crops with Chinese characteristics: a case study in the greater Beijing area. Staff Paper 2006-05. East Lansing, MI: Department of Agricultural Economics, Michigan State University, 2006.
10. Timmer CP, Falcon WP, Pearson SR. Food policy analysis. Baltimore, MD: Johns Hopkins University Press, 1983.
11. Block SA. Nutrition knowledge, rice prices, and the micronutritional effects of Indonesia's Crisis in 1997–98. In: The International Rice Research Congress. Rice science: innovations and impact for livelihood. Mew TW, Brar DS, Teng S, Dawe D, Hardy B, eds. Beijing, China: International Rice Research Institute, Chinese Academy of Engineering, and Chinese Academy of Agricultural Sciences, 2002:789–805.
12. Natawidjaja RS, Reardon T, Perdana T, et al. The impact of the rise of supermarkets on horticulture markets and farmers in Indonesia. Jakarta, Indonesia: UNPAD/MSU report to the World Bank, 2007.

13. Timmer CP. The agricultural transformation. In: Handbook of development economics. Chenery H, Srinivasan TN, eds. Amsterdam: North-Holland, 1988:275–331.

14. Timmer CP. Agriculture and economic growth. In: The handbook of agricultural economics. Gardner B, Rausser G, eds. Amsterdam: North-Holland, 2002:1487–1546.

15. Reardon T, Timmer CT, Barrett CB, Berdegue JA. The rise of supermarkets in Africa, Asia, and Latin America. Am J Agric Econ 2003;85:1140–1146.

16. Reardon T, Timmer CP. Transformation of markets for agricultural output in developing countries since 1950: how has thinking changed? In: Handbook of agricultural economics: agricultural development: farmers, farm production and farm markets. Evenson RE, Pingali P, Schultz TP, eds. Amsterdam: North-Holland, Elsevier, 2005:2808–2285.

17. Timmer CP. Food policy in the era of supermarkets: what's different? e-JADE 2004;1:50–67.

# 28 Homestead Food Production for Improving Nutritional Status and Health

*Saskia de Pee, Aminuzzaman Talukder, and Martin W. Bloem*

## 28.1 INTRODUCTION

Human societies generally developed from foraging to horticultural to agrarian to industrial to informational [1]. While the hunter-gatherers were part of small groups, horticulturists were living in small communities and villages. The first step toward civilization was the move from hunting and horticulture to agriculture with the domestication and farming of wild crops and animals. Agricultural technology made it possible to create food surpluses, and this in turn supported population growth, specialization of labor, and the development of the first country-states [2]. The large societies began to develop ruling classes and increasing inequity emerged in both rural and urban communities. The shift from the hunter-horticultural period to the agricultural era also had consequences for the diet of large segments of the population. While the production of staple foods could provide many more people with calories, the portion of animal products in the diet declined. This resulted in an increased risk of micronutrient deficiencies, which we still see in many rural populations today, who mainly depend on staple foods for their calories. The early hunter-horticultural societies shared public-productive power equally among the men, and the role of women was more important, which was often reflected in the worship of female deities. This is in contrast with the more "masculine" societies of the agrarian era, during which men possessed a large part of the public-productive power, and the role of women was diminished to reproduction [3]. Gender discrimination is still highly prevalent in most agricultural societies, and an equal role for women was only reestablished during the industrial and information eras.

Despite the replacement of hunter-horticultural societies by agricultural societies, homestead food (horticulture) production (HFP) has been practiced through the centuries and across the globe, primarily to produce foods for consumption by the household as well as to generate income. The future of small farmers will become more and more difficult in many rural areas of the world and households will be more dependent on

From: *Nutrition and Health: Nutrition and Health in Developing Countries, Second Edition*
Edited by: R. D. Semba & M. W. Bloem © Humana Press, Totowa, NJ

**Fig. 28.1. a** A homestead cabin and its garden in the western part of the United States in the mid-19th century and **b** a homestead garden in Bangladesh in the late 20th century.

the production at household level (see Chapter 29). Figure 28.1 shows a homestead cabin and its garden in the western part of the United States in the mid-19th century and a homestead garden in Bangladesh in the late 20th century. In this chapter, *homestead food (horticulture) production* is defined as the production of largely nonstaple foods, whether vegetables, fruits, or animal source foods, on land around or close to the homestead.[1]

Homestead food production is important for nutrition and health in a number of ways:

1. It adds variety to the diet by providing foods other than staple foods. This is important both from a nutritional point of view as it increases the intake of essential nutrients (essential amino acids, vitamins, minerals) from the diet and from the point of view of improved quality of life by making the diet more enjoyable because of increased palatability and variation.

2. It generates extra money for the household either directly through the sale of some of the produce or indirectly by allowing the household to save money that would have otherwise been spent on food. The increased household spending power can then be used to add more variety to the diet, further increase food production, or be spent on other categories of expenditure, such as health care, education, housing, or clothes. Many of these expenditures add to further improving the health and nutritional status of the family members.

3. It stimulates biodiversity because it often involves growing of locally available, indigenous varieties of fruits and vegetables and keeping of locally adapted breeds of animals. Greater biodiversity is also of benefit for nutrition and health because it ensures the availability of strong and well-adapted local varieties that are able to make a good contribution to nutrition and health.

4. It adds to the empowerment of women because producing foods in the homestead has traditionally been part of the women's role, as in horticultural societies. By producing foods, the woman contributes to the household's income, which earns her respect from other household members, and it provides her with control over some of the household's resources, whether as food or as money.

In the latter part of the 20th century, when the need for combating micronutrient deficiencies became increasingly clear, HFP was counted among approaches for combating micronutrient deficiencies and their consequences, together with supplementation with high- or low-dose pharmaceutical preparations, food fortification, and public health interventions [4]. Supplementation and food fortification have a direct impact on micronutrient deficiencies because they increase the intake of one or more micronutrients, whereas public health interventions, such as immunization and improvement of hygiene conditions, have an indirect impact. Homestead food production has both a direct impact, through changing the production, preparation, and consumption of foods, as well as an indirect impact, through changing associated aspects such as income, expenditure on education and health, and empowerment of women.

The broader impact of HFP is an advantage from a development point of view but is a disadvantage when evaluating its contribution to reducing micronutrient deficiencies in comparison to supplementation and fortification. The last are well-targeted approaches that provide a considerable amount of a few specific micronutrients, whereas

---

[1] Soleri and Cleveland [76] defined *homestead gardens* as "a supplementary food production system which is under the management and control of household members. A household garden can be consumption or market oriented, but at least some produce will be consumed by the household."

HFP achieves its impact through multiple pathways that are also affected by other existing conditions, practices, and programs. Proponents of HFP note that comparative cost-effectiveness studies tend to focus on narrow achievements, such as reduction in vitamin A deficiency, and fail to account for the full array of HFP benefits. Were these benefits considered, the cost–benefit ratio of gardening projects would likely compare more favorably with alternative interventions. Moreover, in terms of alleviating food insecurity, advocates argue that food production controlled by households is more reliable and sustainable than nutrition interventions that rely on government goodwill and financial support [5–7].

This chapter focuses on the role of HFP in nutrition and health by discussing the following aspects:

1. The contribution of HFP to increasing food security.
2. Is HFP economically viable for households and communities?
3. The impact of HFP on nutrition and health—the case of vitamin A deficiency.
4. The role of HFP for development through the empowerment of women.
5. A programmatic approach to increase and improve HFP practices.

## 28.2  THE CONTRIBUTION OF HOMESTEAD FOOD PRODUCTION TO INCREASING FOOD SECURITY

The technoeconomic modes of production have changed from the beginning of humankind: foraging, horticulture, herding, maritime, agrarian, industrial, informational. Despite the fact that we live in the information era, horticulture-based family food production systems, whether known as home, mixed, backyard, kitchen, farmyard, compound, or homestead gardens, are still found in countries around the world. Traditional tropical gardens typically exhibit a wide diversity of perennial and semiperennial crops, trees, and shrubs well adapted to local microclimates and maintained with a minimum of purchased inputs. Studies of traditional mixed gardens have emphasized their ecologically sound and regenerative characteristics [8].

Field crops (i.e., staple foods) provide the bulk of energy needed by the household, while the garden supplements the diet with vitamin-rich vegetables and fruits, energy-rich vegetable staples, animal sources of protein and minerals, and herbs and condiments. Homestead food production contributes to household food security and nutrition by providing direct access to diverse foods that can be harvested, prepared, and fed to family members, often on a daily basis. Even very poor and landless people can produce food on small patches of homestead land, vacant lots, rooftops, roadsides or edges of a field, and in containers, and it may be done with virtually no economic resources using locally available planting materials, green manure, "live" fencing, and indigenous methods of pest control.

Homestead food production is also an important source of supplementary income and may become the principal source of household food and income during periods of stress. For instance, in Kampala, Uganda, after the civil war, urban agriculture substantially fed the city with noncereal foods [9]. A survey in Zambia in 1980 found that 40% of low-income households in Lusaka cultivated a home garden plot. In Kinshasa, Democratic Republic of the Congo, 70% of the women practiced urban agriculture in the early 1980s, and the practice expanded even further as a result of the economic and civil crisis in the country. In Dar es Salaam, Tanzania, the proportion of families farming grew from 18% in 1967 to 67% in 1991 in response to food shortages, inflation, and increased rural-to-urban migration [9]. Also, in the Philippines home gardening was practiced in poor urban communities [10].

Urban agriculture is growing in importance throughout the Russian Federation and to a lesser extent in other countries of Eastern Europe, both because of food shortages and because of the new freedom to engage in private production and marketing. For example, the number of families engaged in food production in Moscow increased from 20% in 1970 to 65% in 1990 [9]. Urban and periurban gardens are reliable suppliers of urban markets and a vital source of income for many households.

Homestead food production provides a diversity of fresh foods that improve the quantity and quality of nutrients available to the family. Households with gardens typically obtain from them more than 50% of their supply of vegetables and fruits (including such secondary staples as plantains, cassava, taro, and sweet potato), medicinal plants, and herbs; those households having garden systems that include animal raising also obtain their primary and often only source of animal protein from their own production [9, 11, 12]. Very small mixed vegetable gardens can provide a significant percentage of the recommended dietary allowance for protein (10–20%), iron (20%), calcium (20%), vitamin A (80%), and vitamin C (100%) [12–14].

Nonetheless, HFP is only one of the possible interventions for enhancing food security for the poor, and it should be considered in the context of a broader national food security strategy. Indeed, the complex synergies of food availability, access, consumption, and nutritional status with poverty, health, mental ability, productivity, and economic development demand an integrated approach to solving food insecurity in the long term.

It is now widely agreed that to achieve food security a population should not only be self-sufficient in terms of the production of staple foods, but also be free from malnutrition. This means that both the issue of food utilization within households and within communities or regions and the quality of food in terms of providing micronutrients (i.e., vitamins and minerals) in addition to energy have become important. For that reason, agriculturists and health and nutrition specialists need to collaborate more often in systems that integrate production of various types of food and ensure their consumption, such as food production at the homestead or in the community.

In Vietnam, the VAC system, which stands for *vuon* ("garden" or "vegetation"), *ao* ("pond" or "aquaculture"), *chuong* ("cattle shed" or "cages for animal husbandry"), was introduced in communities in the late 1980s with the aim of providing diversified agricultural products to meet the complex nutritional demands of humans. Evaluations of the system in different communities have shown that the VAC system increases the income of the people, protects the environment because it creates an ecosystem that recycles waste, and improves the health and nutrition of the people [15].

In Bangladesh, more than 900,000 households have participated in an HFP program that improved their traditional gardening practices to grow more varieties and for a longer period or throughout the year. This has sustainably improved their food production practices. These 900,000 households have been estimated to produce 20,000 metric tons of fruits and 99,000 metric tons of vegetables in the 3-month winter season [16]. Whereas daily most populations do not consume much more than 50 g of fruits and vegetables/capita, much below the daily recommended intake of 200 g/capita, the production of these households in Bangladesh completely covers their needs, which are estimated at 95,000 metric tons of fruits and vegetables for these 3 months (900,000 hh × 5.8 people × 0.2 kg/d × 91 d). In addition, it provides a surplus that can be sold or stored for leaner months. This shows that HFP can contribute substantially to the required intake of fruits and vegetables of a population.

Increasing food security through HFP has also been highlighted as an important intervention for households and communities affected by HIV/AIDS. Many households affected by HIV/AIDS experience poverty and a lack of food, which affects all household members. In addition, consuming a balanced diet with an adequate amount of vitamins and minerals is particularly important for people affected by HIV/AIDS to enhance their resistance to opportunistic infections and aid the use of antiretroviral drugs. For these reasons, production of animal source foods, vegetables, and fruits near the home is an important intervention. Anecdotal evidence suggests that producing animal source foods is particularly of interest to these households because it requires less time, and animals also have good economic value.

## 28.3   IS HOMESTEAD FOOD PRODUCTION ECONOMICALLY VIABLE FOR HOUSEHOLDS AND COMMUNITIES?

The fact that HFP has been practiced through the centuries and across the globe, primarily to produce foods for consumption as well as for generating capital, indicates its economic viability. This is not to say that it is practiced in all areas where households experience food insecurity. In some areas, such as in several parts of South Africa, the practice has ceased to exist. In some others, the existing climate and soil conditions make it difficult to establish. In other cases, pest control and fencing and obtaining good seeds are among many difficult challenges.

Nevertheless, these challenges can be overcome. When HFP initiatives successfully overcome such challenges, its economic benefits have been found to include the following:

- Returns to land and labor are often higher than those from field agriculture.
- Gardening provides dual benefits of food provision and income generation.
- Gardens provide fodder for household animals and supplies for other household needs (handicrafts, fuel, wood, furniture, baskets, etc.).
- Household processing of garden fruits and vegetables (drying, canning) increases their market value and ensures year-round supply.
- Low-input, low-cost gardening has few barriers to entry.
- Marketing of HFP produce is one of the few sources of independent income for women.

An independent evaluation of the HFP program in Bangladesh found that only 86% of control households grew some vegetables compared to 96% of households that formerly participated in the program and 100% of currently participating households. Among these categories, 15%, 50%, and 78%, respectively, practiced year-round gardening, indicating improved practices among the households that had participated in the program. Similarly, 25%, 54%, and 64%, respectively, of these households sold produce. The amount of income earned was highest among the formerly participating households, whereas the number of different varieties grown in the gardens of formerly participating households was lower compared to that of currently participating households. This indicates that the former had optimized their growing practices to be more profitable [16]. Similarly, a home gardening project in a rural area of KwaZulu-Natal in South Africa found that vitamin A intake increased both among children of project households as well as among children of nonproject households because of trade of the produce by the project households [17].

## 28.4   ASSESSING THE IMPACT OF HOMESTEAD FOOD PRODUCTION ON NUTRITION AND HEALTH: THE CASE OF VITAMIN A DEFICIENCY

The case of how HFP contributes to reducing vitamin A deficiency and its consequences is discussed to illustrate how to assess impact on (a specific aspect of) nutritional status, including how to build and use a conceptual framework.

### 28.4.1   *Conceptual Framework for Impact of Food-Based Programs on Nutritional Status and Health*

To identify ways through which food-based programs can improve nutritional status and health, International Union of Nutritional Sciences (IUNS) Committee II/8 (Food Gardening for Nutrition Improvement) modified the United Nations International Children's Emergency Fund's (UNICEF's) conceptual framework for the causes of malnutrition [18] to accommodate the effects of food-based programs, as shown in Fig. 28.2. The framework includes a wide variety of food-based programs: HFP for increasing availability and subsequently consumption of vitamin A-rich foods; social marketing for increasing the consumption of vitamin A-rich foods; and food processing to extend the period during which vitamin A-rich foods are available for consumption or reducing bulk by reducing liquid content, such as solar drying of fruits or vegetables [19, 20]. The framework shows that each program should result in an increase of the consumption or utilization of vitamin A-rich foods and subsequently in an improvement of vitamin A status and health, and that there are various pathways, direct as well as indirect, for achieving this. For example, HFP can increase food availability at community and household levels, which, together with care factors, can improve access to food and therefore directly increase dietary vitamin A intake. Indirectly, because HFP is mainly a women's activity, it can lead to empowerment of women, which may result in an increase of the household's resources that are spent on food and health care [16].

The framework also shows that there are many factors that can confound the assessment of the impact of a food-based program on nutritional status. For example, among subjects with poor health, the impact of a food-based program may seem limited because recurrent illness negatively affects nutritional status and therefore counteracts the positive impact of the increased intake of micronutrient-rich foods. Furthermore, provision of high-dose vitamin A capsules will mask any additional impact of an increased consumption of vitamin A-rich foods because of the large dose and the fact that it is given to households with and without HFP.

To design a food-based program such that it is likely to have a positive impact on nutritional status and health and to appropriately evaluate its impact, three aspects are especially important:

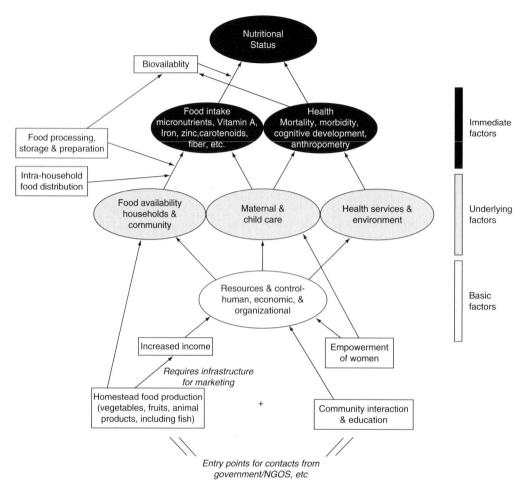

**Fig. 28.2.** Conceptual framework of causes of vitamin A deficiency showing intervention points for food-based approaches. (Reprinted from [4].)

1. Extent to which an anticipated increase of consumption of micronutrient-rich foods can improve nutritional status and/or health
2. The change of food consumption by the target population as induced by the food-based program
3. Evidence for, and magnitude of, the impact of the food-based program on nutritional status and health

Many projects for increasing intake of vitamin A-rich foods have been implemented, a number of which have been described in detail, often in project reports. Most (see overview in [21–23]) but not all [24] of the described projects were successful in increasing the production or consumption of vegetables or fruits. However, their impact on nutritional status and health has rarely been assessed. Therefore, we focus on points 1 and 3.

### 28.4.2 How Food Consumption Can Increase Vitamin A Status

For HFP to have an impact on vitamin A status, an increased consumption of vitamin A-rich foods should lead to an improvement of vitamin A status. A distinction is made between different sources of dietary vitamin A, that is, animal foods; green, leafy vegetables; red, orange, and yellow vegetables; red, orange, and yellow fruits; and fortified products. Each of these has different vitamin A activity, depending on their content of retinol or provitamin A carotenoids as well as on a variety of food- and host-related factors and their interactions, which determine bioavailability and bioconversion of (pro)vitamin A.

Vitamin A occurs in foods in two forms: as preformed vitamin A or retinol (mainly retinyl esters) and as provitamin A carotenoids, mainly β-carotene, α-carotene, and β-cryptoxanthin, which the body can convert into retinol. Preformed vitamin A is only found in foods of animal origin, such as dairy products (milk, butter, cheese), egg yolk, liver, and fatty fish and in fortified foods. Provitamin A is mainly found in plant foods (i.e., green, red, orange, or yellow vegetables and fruits; red palm oil, etc.), which contain all their vitamin A as provitamin A. In animal foods, 10–30% of total vitamin A content is in the form of provitamin A carotenoids [25]. In the 1930s, the vitamin A deficiency problem virtually disappeared from Europe when margarine became fortified with retinol. Since then, the emphasis of food-based approaches for combating vitamin A deficiency has mainly been on plant foods because they are the most affordable and available dietary source of vitamin A in developing countries.

Especially for populations that largely rely on plant foods, bioavailability and bioconversion are particularly important as they determine the amount of vitamin A that is obtained from particular foods under specific circumstances. *Bioavailability* can be defined as the fraction of an ingested nutrient that is available for utilization in normal physiological functions or for storage. In the case of vitamin A, bioavailability is the process of freeing of retinol or carotenoids from food and their absorption, distribution (to storage tissue and serum), metabolism, and excretion. The conversion of provitamin A carotenoids to retinol (preformed vitamin A), which largely occurs in the enterocytes, the cells that line the intestine, immediately after absorption of the carotenoids is called *bioconversion*. *Bioefficacy* is then defined as the combination of bioavailability and bioconversion and is best described as the efficiency with which ingested nutrients, provitamin A in this case, are absorbed and converted to the active form of the nutrient (i.e., retinol).

To calculate total vitamin A intake, preformed vitamin A and provitamin A have to be converted to the same unit, the microgram retinol equivalent (RE). Until the late 1990s, the following factors were used for this conversion [26]:

$$1 \text{ RE} = 1 \text{ μg all-}trans \text{ retinol, purified or in foods}$$

$$1 \text{ RE} = 6 \text{ μg all-}trans\text{-β-carotene from foods}$$

This assumes that the meal contains 1–4 mg β-carotene. A conversion rate of 1:4 was recommended for meals that contain less than 1 mg and of 1:10 for those containing more than 4 mg β-carotene. And, (purified) β-carotene in oil, such as in red palm oil, provides twice as many retinol equivalents as other dietary β-carotene because its bioavailability is twice as high [26].

$$1 \text{ RE} = 12 \text{ μg other provitamin A carotenoids from foods, including } cis\text{-β-carotene}$$

However, it was also stated by the Food and Agricultural Organization (FAO)/ World Health Organization (WHO) that the data on absorption of dietary carotenoids are too few and too variable to accurately predict their bioavailability.

### 28.4.2.1  STUDIES OF PLANT FOODS FOR COMBATING VITAMIN A DEFICIENCY

Since the 1950s, cross-sectional and case-control studies have studied the relationship between food consumption patterns and vitamin A deficiency or vitamin A status. In general, it was found that the higher the consumption of vitamin A-rich foods, the lower the risk of vitamin A deficiency. Associations were found for foods rich in preformed vitamin A as well as for foods rich in provitamin A [27]. While these studies suggested that vitamin A-rich foods can prevent or combat vitamin A deficiency, they did not prove causality, and they did not quantify the degree of effectiveness of the foods.

Intervention studies were conducted to assess changes of vitamin A status after feeding plant sources of vitamin A. Many of the early studies found an improvement of vitamin A status [27]. However, because many of them not only provided vitamin A-rich foods but also improved other aspects of the subjects' diet and health, it is difficult to know which portion of the improvement of vitamin A status was due to the vitamin A-rich foods and which to other factors (see conceptual framework for examples of such other factors). Also, many of the studies lacked control groups, and sample sizes were too small in relation to the variation in response. But, two important conclusions were derived from those studies:

1. Serum retinol concentration can improve when the consumption of vitamin A-rich plant foods is increased.
2. The extent to which foods rich in provitamin A carotenoids can improve vitamin A status varies widely because bioavailability and bioconversion of provitamin A carotenoids are affected by many factors.

Some of the later intervention studies in developing countries focused more on quantifying the effectiveness of different kinds of plant foods for improving vitamin A status [28–33]. Studies in developed countries, where vitamin A status is largely adequate, assessed changes in serum carotene concentrations after consumption of carotene-rich foods, such as carrots, broccoli, spinach, peas, and tomatoes [34–36]. Together, these studies confirmed that the bioavailability of plant carotenoids is a complex issue, and that it is lower than what has generally been assumed.

Because of these new findings, the US Institute of Medicine (IOM), based on research in developed countries, revised the recommended conversion factor to 12:1 for $\beta$-carotene (12 $\mu$g of $\beta$-carotene being equivalent to 1 retinol activity equivalent, RAE) and 24:1 for other provitamin A carotenoids [37]. However, as West and colleagues commented [38], one original reference was not interpreted correctly, due to which the IOM conversion factors erred toward a more optimistic value. The International Vitamin A Consultative Group (IVACG) concurred with the IOM estimate but noted that in developing countries bioefficacy may be even lower due to less-favorable health and nutritional status of many in the population. West and colleagues, who had conducted the initial studies in the 1990s that had restarted the debate on the value of fruits and vegetables for combating vitamin A deficiency [28, 29, 39], advocated for a conversion factor of 21:1 based on an estimated conversion factor for $\beta$-carotene from vegetables of 26:1 and from fruits of 12:1 and a ratio of vegetables to fruits in the diet of 4:1 [38]. This factor has also been supported by more recent studies that used stable-isotope techniques to estimate the conversion factor [30, 31, 33, 40].

The overestimation of the vitamin A content of fruits and vegetables can range from a little more than 1 to as much as 15 times. In addition to the overestimation of bioavailability and bioconversion, food composition tables that report vitamin A content based on spectrophotometric analysis of total carotene content often also overestimate vitamin A content because not all carotenoids have provitamin A activity [41]. The extent of this overestimation varies per vegetable and fruit and may be approximately 20% [28]. Thus, when estimating vitamin A intake, it is important to know which analytical method was used to assess provitamin A content and to know which conversion factors were used to estimate vitamin A content.

### 28.4.2.2 FACTORS DETERMINING BIOAVAILABILITY AND BIOCONVERSION OF CAROTENOIDS STUDIES

Factors that affect bioavailability and bioconversion can be grouped in different ways. They have, for example, been grouped into the mnemonic SLAMENGHI, which stands for species of carotenoids, linkages at molecular level, amount of carotenoid, matrix, effectors of absorption, nutrient status, genetics, other host-related factors, and interactions among factors [27, 34, 42]. Here, we group the factors based on possible entry points for intervention, which is host, food, or meal, and discuss those factors that seem to have a relatively large impact on carotene bioavailability in developing countries and could be taken into account by, or be addressed with, population-based interventions.

#### 28.4.2.2.1 Host-Related Factors.

Host-related factors include condition of the gastrointestinal tract, such as presence of parasitic infestation [43], gastric acidity [44] and malabsorption syndromes, illness, age, sex, pregnancy, nutrient status, and genetics. Whereas most of these conditions have been known to affect carotene bioavailability, the magnitude of their impact is only just emerging.

In developing countries, problems of the gastrointestinal tract may play a particularly important role. Jalal et al. showed that heavy *Ascaris* infestation has a large impact on carotene bioavailability or bioconversion [45], and it can be hypothesized that there is a differential impact depending on the food source of carotenoids, for which foods with a more complex matrix, such as leafy vegetables as compared to fruits, have lower bioavailability. In populations in which the prevalence of parasitic infestation is high, treatment of such infections should be of highest priority because they may severely limit the utilization of carotenoids from vegetables, especially among those with heavy infestations, who are usually also the poorest and most in need of vitamin A. Not only worm infections, but also protozoa infections can reduce bioavailability or bioconversion of carotenoids because they affect the health of the gastrointestinal tract.

Other host-related factors that could receive intervention are gastric acidity, malabsorption syndromes, illness, and nutrient status. With respect to gastric acidity, it seems that a low gastric pH favors the absorption of carotenoids because it facilitates the diffusion of the micelle, in which the carotenoid is incorporated, through the cell membrane of the enterocyte [44]. People with atrophic gastritis or with hypochlorhydria have a high gastric pH and hence a lower absorption of carotenoids. Hypochlorhydria is often found in elderly people and in people with chronic *Helicobacter pylori* infection, a condition that is common in developing countries. In case of illness, the body's need for vitamin A is already high, and the increased loss of vitamin A that accompanies acute infection [46] increases this even further. Meeting increased needs during illness is difficult because of reduced appetite, increased loss, and a possible negative effect of illness on bioavailability or bioconversion of provitamin A carotenoids.

With respect to nutrient status, protein status should be sufficient to enable normal metabolism and transport of retinol and carotenoids, and zinc status may play a role because it regulates the synthesis of the protein that transports vitamin A, and the enzyme that converts retinol to retinal is zinc dependent [47]. However, clear evidence of a synergy between zinc and vitamin A and its public health significance in humans is lacking at present [48].

Host-related factors that are unchangeable, such as age, sex, pregnancy, and genetics, are important for the targeting of interventions. For example, because carotene absorption is poorer among the elderly, the impact of a carotene intervention will be smaller among them than among others, and because young children appear to be less able to digest leafy vegetables than older individuals, bioavailability of dietary carotenoids is likely to be lower among them.

More research into the magnitude of the impact of different host-related factors among different population groups is necessary to be able to prioritize interventions for specific groups.

### 28.4.2.2.2  Food-Related Factors.  By *food-related factors*, we refer to the carotene-rich foods themselves. Food-related factors that affect carotene bioavailability are the matrix in which the carotenoids are incorporated, type and amount of fiber, presence of other carotenoids, species of carotenoids, and molecular linkage. Of course, before considering carotene bioavailability, the content of provitamin A carotenoids is of primary interest.

Carotene content varies between species, and within species it varies with maturity—the more mature, the higher the carotene content—and storage length and conditions, especially exposure to sunlight after harvesting reduces carotene content [41]. Furthermore, analysis of carotene content varies with methods of extraction and analysis, and results can therefore vary widely [49].

Of the food-related factors that affect carotene bioavailability, matrix has probably been studied the most. For carotenoids to become available for intestinal lumen incorporation into a micelle, which can then be taken up by the enterocyte, the carotenoids must be freed from their food matrix. The matrix is most complex in leafy vegetables, less complex in fruits, and absent in oil. Disruption of the matrix can start before ingestion of the food, by cooking or homogenizing, and is continued by chewing, low pH in the stomach, enzymatic cleavage, and so on. Van het Hof et al. showed that the type of matrix differs not only between green vegetables and red, orange, and yellow vegetables and fruits, but also between different types of green vegetables. Consumption of broccoli and green peas induced a larger plasma β-carotene response than consumption of spinach [36]. Vuong et al. found that the indigenous fruit *Momordica cochinchinensis* (gac) from Vietnam is a very good source of provitamin A because it has a very high content of β-carotene of high bioavailability [50].

Other food-related factors, such as fiber [51], especially pectin [52]; content and presence of other carotenoids; species of carotenoids, including isomers; and molecular linkage, are more difficult to influence. Options to limit their impact on bioavailability include food choice, plant breeding, or genetic engineering [53].

One other food preparation method that may be mentioned here is that of solar drying, which preserves and compacts the food and therefore allows a larger intake of carotenoids for the same volume of food. However, the amount of fruit or vegetable available for drying may be limited, and a project in Sri Lanka found that production of leaf concentrate as a community-based activity was not sustainable [20].

**28.4.2.2.3  Meal-Related Factors.** Meal-related factors that affect carotene bioavailability or bioconversion include fat content; presence of inhibitors of carotene absorption, such as fiber and other carotenoids; and total amount of carotenoids.

The most important meal-related factor, especially in some developing countries where intake is still low, is fat. Fat triggers the release of lipase from the pancreas and bile salts from the liver, which play a crucial role in the formation of micelles. Micelles consist of triglycerides that incorporate carotenoids, which can then be absorbed. Whereas 5 g fat in a meal was regarded as the minimum amount required to facilitate carotene absorption [54], 3 g might even be enough [55]. The median oil daily consumption in Indonesia is between 15 and 30 g/capita, but in Bangladesh it is only 5–10 g/capita (unpublished data from Helen Keller International [HKI]-Indonesia and HKI-Bangladesh). Thus, fat consumption may limit carotene bioavailability for a substantial portion of Bangladesh's population but is unlikely to be a problem for most of the Indonesian population.

The type of oil or fat that is consumed for increasing carotene bioavailability is also important. First, because red palm oil is naturally rich in carotenoids and therefore an excellent source of highly bioavailable vitamin A, its consumption should be promoted wherever possible [56]. Second, it has been found that long-chain triglycerides facilitate β-carotene absorption much better than medium-chain triglycerides [57]. Whether this has consequences for populations that mainly use coconut oil (chain length largely C12) instead of, for example, peanut or corn oil (largely C18) is not yet known. Third, because oil and fat, especially margarine, are good vehicles for vitamin A fortification [58], they can be an important source of vitamin A in the diet. In the Netherlands, for example, 25–30% of the vitamin A intake of adults is from fats and oils that have been fortified with vitamin A [59].

With respect to inhibitors of carotene absorption present in a meal, such as fiber and other carotenoids, not much can be done, especially not when these components are part of the carotene-rich foods themselves. Only food choice, breeding, or genetic engineering can make a difference.

### 28.4.2.3  GUIDELINES FOR MAXIMIZING VITAMIN A INTAKE FROM PLANT FOODS

Table 28.1 gives an example of the vitamin A content of different foods and the amount that should be consumed to consume 500 RAE when the previous conversion factors as well as those recommended by West et al. [38] are used. The correction that should be applied to the vitamin A content of fruits is less than half that for vegetables. However, the amount of vegetables that needs to be consumed to obtain approximately 500 RAE is generally still less than the amount of fruit that would need to be consumed because the vitamin A content of vegetables is much higher.

Guidelines for maximizing the amount of vitamin A obtained from carotene-rich foods, which may be the most feasible and possibly the most effective, are summarized in Fig. 28.3.

**Table 28.1**

Vitamin A (VA) content of different foods according to food composition analyses and corrected for carotene bioavailability

| Food | Vitamin A content (RE/100 g) | Correction factor for bio-availability[a] | Corrected vitamin A content (RE/100 g) | Amount containing 500 RE based on uncorrected VA content | Amount containing 500 RE based on corrected VA content |
|---|---|---|---|---|---|
| Chicken liver | 2,862[b] | 1 | 2,862 | 17 g | 17 g |
| Egg | 270[c] | 1 | 270 | 185 g | 185 g |
| Mango | 304[d] | 0.5 | 152 | 164 g | 329 g |
| Papaya | 148[e] | 0.5 | 74 | 338 g | 676 g |
| Carrot | 1,000[f] | 0.23 | 230 | 50 g | 217 g |
| Cassava leaves | 1,776[g] | 0.23 | 408 | 28 g | 123 g |
| Water spinach | 492[g] | 0.23 | 113 | 102 g | 442 g |

*RE* retinol equivalent.

[a] Based on [38] (1:12 for fruits, 1:26 for vegetables).

[b] From [73]. [c] From [74]. [d] Average of values for mangoes from [73].

[e] Analysis of papayas from Benin by Department of Human Nutrition, Wageningen Agricultural University, Wageningen, the Netherlands, 1995 (unpublished).

[f] Compiled from [75].

[g] From [41].

### Ways to optimize the dietary intake of vitamin A from natural sources

- **Increasing total intake of vitamin A-rich foods** by consuming more of all possible food sources. Where food insecurity is a problem, increasing availability and access to Vitamin A-rich foods, for example through homestead food production, is required.

- Giving preference to **consuming foods with a higher vitamin A content**, taking bioefficacy into account, i.e.
  - More vitamin A rich animal foods (eggs, liver, whole fish, dairy products)
  - More red, orange and yellow fruits
  - Introduce or increase intake of red palm oil
  - Producing and consuming varieties with a higher vitamin A content, e.g. orange-fleshed instead of white-fleshed sweet potatoes
  - Maximize amount of vitamin A obtained from a food group, for example
    - Consuming fruits when fully mature
    - Giving preference to fresh rather than stored vegetables or fruits
    - When storing for extending the period of availability, optimize storage conditions to minimize loss of carotenoids
    - Decrease bulk in order to increase intake, for example by solar drying of leafy vegetables to make powder rich in vitamins and minerals

- **Increasing bioavailablity of carotenoids,** by
  - Ensuring an intake of 3-5 g fat per meal and consuming carotene-rich fruit with a meal or snack that contains fat
  - Destroying the matrix when preparing vegetables, i.e. by cutting, grinding or homogenizing. Note that heat and time for preparation should be limited.
  - Deworming
  - Improving hygiene conditions

**Fig. 28.3.** Guidelines for maximizing the amount of vitamin A obtained from carotene-rich foods, which may be the most feasible and possibly also the most effective.

### 28.4.3   Health Effects of Increased Consumption of Vitamin A-Rich Foods

Until now, we have focused on the effectiveness of vitamin A-rich foods for improving vitamin A status, which is an essential part of the relationship among food consumption, nutritional status, and health as shown in the conceptual framework (Fig. 28.2). A change of vitamin A status will affect health and vice-versa. And, because vitamin A-rich foods also contain other nutrients, changes of food consumption can also result in other improvements of nutritional status, which can in turn also affect health. Foods can contribute to prevention of both deficiencies of nutrients and their consequences as well as degenerative diseases, such as cardiovascular disease, cancer, and type 2 diabetes.

#### 28.4.3.1   HOW THE CONSUMPTION OF VITAMIN A-RICH FOODS CAN AFFECT HEALTH

Vitamin A-rich foods can, depending on their content of other nutrients, also have other beneficial effects on health. Vitamin A-related health effects include improved immunity, reduced risk of morbidity and mortality, and a lower risk of anemia and xerophthalmia. Non-vitamin A-related health effects depend on the specific nutrient content of the food.

Vitamin A-rich plant foods, for example, are generally also good sources of several B vitamins, vitamin C, folic acid, non-provitamin A carotenoids, fiber, and flavonoids. Many of these have antioxidant activity and can therefore play a role in the prevention of cardiovascular disease and cancer.

Many nutritional deficiency problems are due to a lack of micronutrients, of which both plant foods and animal foods are good sources. However, the bioavailability of minerals from plant foods is relatively low. Animal source foods are usually good sources of minerals, such as iron and zinc, and the bioavailability of these minerals is much higher than when from plant foods. Minerals are especially important for health and development, and the consequences of deficiencies include anemia, reduced growth, slower psychomotor development, and reduced immunity.

Degenerative diseases are often associated with too low an intake of micronutrients and nonnutrients, such as antioxidants and flavonoids, which are mainly found in vegetables and fruits, and with too high an intake of energy or fat.

Thus, plant foods can play a rule in the prevention of nutrient deficiencies as well as of degenerative diseases, and their consumption should therefore be recommended to all populations. Consumption of animal foods, however, should be promoted among populations that suffer from micronutrient deficiencies, while among populations with a relatively high prevalence of degenerative diseases, moderation of their consumption, especially of meat and full-fat dairy products but less of fish, eggs, and lean dairy products, is warranted. The same holds for fat consumption, which is essential for carotene absorption, but should be moderate among affluent populations.

#### 28.4.3.2   EVIDENCE OF IMPACT OF VITAMIN A-RICH FOODS ON HEALTH IN DEVELOPING COUNTRIES BEYOND A VITAMIN A EFFECT

Little evidence is available for additional benefits of vitamin A-rich foods for health, other than those associated with vitamin A, iron and zinc among the poor in developing countries.

It has been found that the risk of diarrhea among women in Bangladesh was lower when they had a higher vitamin A intake from plant foods [14]. This reduction of risk was larger for vitamin A intake from plant foods than for total vitamin A intake. Therefore, it is most likely that the larger reduction of risk was related to the intake of multiple (micro)nutrients from plant foods. A similar explanation may apply to the finding from a study among children in Sudan, where a higher vitamin A intake was associated with a lower risk of mortality and where plant foods were the main source of vitamin A [60]. The hypothesis that plant foods rich in vitamin A also have health effects other than those related to vitamin A is also supported by findings from Nepal. Maternal mortality was reduced by 49% by a weekly dose of 42 mg of β-carotene and by 40% by a weekly dose of 7,000 RE of retinol [61]. Although the vitamin A activity of the β-carotene supplement was theoretically equivalent to that of the retinol supplement, it induced a smaller change of serum retinol concentration and a larger reduction of maternal mortality. This may indicate that part of the reduction of maternal mortality in the β-carotene group was due to its antioxidant function, which is additional to its vitamin A-related effect.

### 28.4.3.3 SUMMARY OF ROLE OF FOODS FOR HEALTH

Because people consume foods, not nutrients, and because the focus of this book is on populations in developing countries, the focus here is on the role of foods for combating nutritional deficiencies, in particular vitamin A deficiency.

Animal foods, including breast milk, are the best source of vitamin A and of minerals such as iron and zinc because of their high content of these nutrients as well as their relatively high bioavailability. However, the disadvantage of animal foods, except breast milk, is that they are difficult to afford for a large part of the population in developing countries, and that promoting their increased consumption, especially of meat, is contraindicated for those at risk of degenerative diseases.

The people who are most in need of vitamin A are the poorest, and the most affordable dietary source of vitamin A for them is plant foods, mainly vegetables. However, several factors, including some that are more prevalent or severe among the poor, such as gastrointestinal problems, are likely to limit the extent to which they can benefit from nutrients of plant foods. Not only will the improvement of vitamin A status be small, the utilization of other nutrients is also likely to be relatively poor. Therefore, there is a need for additional sources of vitamin A, such as supplements, fortified foods, animal foods, and red, yellow, or orange fruits. Of these, supplements may as yet be the most realistic, but only individuals who belong to the specified target groups are eligible for receiving them and will hence benefit.

Ways for maximizing the amount of vitamin A that is obtained from leafy vegetables and fruits are shown in Fig. 28.3.

### 28.4.4 Impact of Homestead Food Production on Nutritional Status and Health

The main purposes of HFP are to increase food security, to improve the diet and income, and through improvement of the diet to have an impact on nutritional status and health. In the previous sections, we discussed how consumption of particular foods can affect nutritional status and health. We now focus on the broader picture, detecting an impact of HFP on food consumption, nutritional status, and health.

Many projects for increasing the intake of vitamin A-rich foods have been implemented, ranging from nutrition education, solar drying for preservation of vitamin

A-rich foods, to large-scale HFP programs. A number of reviews have been written that, together, reviewed the projects and studies conducted until 2000 [11, 23, 62–64]. Before the 1990s, the emphasis of home gardening projects was on promoting food production and particular agricultural strategies, while little to no attention was paid to nutrition education and communication. Not surprisingly, evaluations of those projects failed to show an impact on vitamin A intake or status [23]. From the early 1990s, there was greater emphasis on nutrition education and behavior change to increase consumption, especially of vitamin A-rich foods. The reviews of studies of well-designed promotional activities using nutrition education, social marketing, and mass media campaigns (with or without home gardening) found that the consumption of micronutrient-rich foods, in particular those rich in vitamin A, increased significantly [23, 65]

Then, by the mid-1990s, as reviewed in this chapter, the first findings on a lower bio-availability of vitamin A from vegetables and fruits emerged, which triggered heated discussions on the potential contribution of home gardening to combating vitamin A deficiency. These discussions were complicated by the fact that very few data were available on the impact of home gardening on vitamin A status. As stated by Ruel in 2001:

> It is striking, however, to realize, that 5 years after Gillespie and Mason's review, with an addition of more than a dozen new, apparently successful studies, we still do not have sufficient information to understand the real potential of these interventions to control vitamin A deficiency [23, 64]. Weak evaluation designs will continue to slow down progress in understanding the real potential of production and education interventions to control vitamin A deficiency.

There are a number of reasons for these weak evaluation designs and a variety of ways to assess impact despite these limitations. Evaluations of individual HFP programs often focus on program implementation, and when outcome is monitored, it is usually limited to changes of food production or food consumption. Changes of nutritional status or health are rarely monitored because, first, only a relatively small part of a program's budget is usually allocated to its evaluation, which thus limits the scope of the evaluation. Second, demonstrating an impact on food production or consumption is often regarded as sufficient evidence for program impact. Third, the population targeted by a program may be too small to allow for an evaluation of a change of the prevalence of disease or of clinical signs of nutritional deficiencies as their prevalence is relatively low.

However, not addressing the question whether the program has an impact on nutritional status or health leaves the following questions unanswered:

1. Does the change of food consumption as induced by the program result in a change of nutritional status or health? If yes, to what extent? If not, why not?
2. What is the relative importance of the food-based program compared to other strategies, such as the distribution of high-dose vitamin A capsules?

A small-scale project in South Africa established home gardens among one third of the households in a particular village (n = 126) and found, after 20 months, a higher consumption of vitamin A among children of the project village as compared to children of the control village and higher serum retinol levels among the project children [66]. Whereas this compares specific villages where no home gardening had previously been implemented, evaluating larger-scale implementation of the practice requires a different approach for assessing its impact. We discuss an example of such an evaluation of the impact of the existing traditional practice of HFP in Bangladesh and draw some general conclusions about the contribution of HFP to improving vitamin A status and health.

### 28.4.4.1. EXAMPLE OF IMPACT OF HOMESTEAD FOOD PRODUCTION ON NUTRITIONAL STATUS OR HEALTH

To answer the question of whether HFP reduces the risk of vitamin A deficiency, data from Bangladesh' national vitamin A survey, conducted in 1997, were analyzed. The national vitamin A survey collected data from mothers and underfive children in over 24,000 households. The indicators of vitamin A deficiency included xerophthalmia, night blindness, and serum retinol concentration for mothers and children of 5% of the households. Table 28.2 shows the prevalence of night blindness among underfive children (12–59 mo) that received or did not receive a vitamin A capsule in the preceding distribution round. The children that did not receive a vitamin A capsule were twice as likely to be night blind compared to those that received it. Multiple logistic regression analysis among children that had not received a vitamin A capsule found that those of households without a home garden were 2.1 times (95% CI: 1.1-4.2, n = 4057) more likely to suffer from night blindness compared to those of households with a home garden. This indicates that those of households with a home garden were more

**Table 28.2**
Prevalence of night blindness among children aged 12–59 months by receipt of a vitamin A capsule in the preceding six months

| Vitamin A capsule receipt | Prevalence of night blindness, % [95% CI] | (n) |
|---|---|---|
| Yes | 0.53 [0.43-0.64] | (19,163) |
| No | 1.04 [0.77-1.41] | (4,229) |

**Table 28.3**
Risk of being night blind among children aged 12–59 months, from a house with or without a home garden, for those that received a vitamin A capsule in the preceding six months compared to those that did not[a]

| Home garden | Odds Ratio for night blindness among vitamin A capsule recipients [95% CI] | (n) |
|---|---|---|
| Yes | 0.7 [0.4-1.1] | (17,610) |
| No | 0.2 [0.1-0.5] | (4,100) |

[a]Controlled for socioeconomic status, anthropometry, morbidity, breast feeding status.

protected against vitamin A deficiency. Among children that had received a capsule, having a home garden did not reduce the risk of night blindness further. Analyses were also conducted for children of households with and for children of households without a home garden (Table 28.3). It was found that among children of households without a home garden, the risk of suffering from night blindness was reduced more by receipt of a vitamin A capsule, than among children of households with a home garden. This indicates that children of households without a home garden were most in need of the capsule. The underlying explanation for this would be that children of households with a home garden had a higher vitamin A status, probably because of a higher intake and/or because of less morbidity and therefore a lower requirement for vitamin A [67].

These data show that among children in rural Bangladesh, both receiving a vitamin A capsule as well as home gardening contributed to reducing the risk of vitamin A deficiency. It should be noted that home gardening as identified in this survey referred to the locally prevailing practice of growing a few vegetables near the home, and only in a few cases happened to be a garden established or improved as part of an HFP program.

**28.4.4.1.1 Impact of Homestead Food Production Is Subgroup and Situation Specific.** The above data from Bangladesh show that it is important to distinguish different subgroups in the population, such as breast-fed infants, older children under 5, and lactating women, because for each group other strategies may be the most feasible and effective for reducing vitamin A deficiency. The *life-cycle approach* guides the selection of the most appropriate mix of strategies for combating a nutritional problem among a particular group of the population, based on the fact that biological needs and processes are different during every phase of life.

The impact of a strategy depends not only on the target group but also on local circumstances. Whereas the impact of vitamin A capsules mainly varies with the need for vitamin A, the impact of food-based approaches is very different between regions because it depends very much on the particular approach as well as on the circumstances in which it is implemented. It is, for example, possible that in rural Bangladesh, where there is a large gap between the need for vitamin A and its intake, home gardening has an impact on vitamin A status, while in other places, where the difference between need and intake is smaller, impact is less.

**28.4.4.2    APPROACHES FOR ASSESSING IMPACT OF HFP ON NUTRITIONAL STATUS OR HEALTH**

The example described about the reduced risk of vitamin A deficiency associated with HFP in Bangladesh shows that HFP can contribute to reducing vitamin A deficiency. Next, we discuss different types of analyses that can be used for such an assessment (see also [40, 68]).

**28.4.4.2.1    Assessing Changes Before and After the Start of a Program.** The most straightforward way for showing an impact of HFP is by assessing changes in the intervention population between the start of the program and after 12–24 months of conducting the program and comparing them to changes in a nonintervention community. Another option is to use data of a nutrition and health surveillance system to assess changes in the different components of the conceptual framework. Simultaneous changes and the relationship among them indicates that a program had been effective in, for example, increasing vitamin A intake and vitamin A status [69].

**28.4.4.2.2 Cross-Sectional Comparison of Intervention and Nonintervention Communities or Subjects.** The strategy chosen for assessing the impact of HFP in Bangladesh was a comparison of the risk of vitamin A deficiency among subjects of households that did and did not conduct HFP, while controlling for confounding factors. Controlling for confounding factors is especially important in this type of analysis because such factors may obscure, reduce, or increase the apparent risk associated with the food-based activity. Also, among children, it was important not only to include vitamin A capsules as a confounder in the analysis of the impact of home gardening but also to analyze the impact of vitamin A capsules separately for children of households with and without a home garden and the impact of home gardening separately for children who did and did not receive a vitamin A capsule.

For the HFP practices that traditionally exist in Bangladesh, collecting and analyzing cross-sectional data was probably the best way for assessing its impact on reducing the risk of vitamin A deficiency for the following reasons. First, because HFP is a common practice, finding good control communities where no HFP was conducted would be difficult. Second, because night blindness has a relatively low prevalence (0.3–5%), a large number of households would have to be included in an evaluation. A large survey also allows for conclusions about the risk of night blindness among subjects of households without HFP.

**28.4.4.2.3 Can Food-Based Approaches Make Vitamin A Capsules Redundant?** To assess whether food-based approaches, including food fortification, are effective enough for preventing vitamin A deficiency and distribution of vitamin A capsules could be discontinued, it is not necessary to assess the impact of all food-based approaches separately. An indirect way of addressing this question is by assessing the prevalence of vitamin A deficiency (indicated by night blindness or low serum retinol concentrations) as well as the effectiveness of vitamin A capsules for reducing the risk of vitamin A deficiency.

When the prevalence of vitamin A deficiency is around or above WHO cutoff values for a problem of public health significance, the combination of strategies for its prevention is clearly not yet effective enough. In that case, all strategies should be continued, not in the least the distribution of high-dose vitamin A capsules. When the prevalence of vitamin A deficiency is below the cutoff for a public health problem, the risk of vitamin A deficiency among those who did not receive the capsule, compared to those who received it, should be assessed while controlling for other factors. When the risk of vitamin A deficiency is higher among those who did not receive the capsule, there is apparently still a need for the capsule, whichever other strategies are being implemented. To assess which strategies make an important contribution to lowering the risk of vitamin A deficiency, the effectiveness of the vitamin A capsule can be compared among the subgroup of the population with access to the specific intervention or strategy and the subgroup without it. The comparison of the effectiveness of vitamin A capsules among subjects with and without HFP in Bangladesh is a good example.

When the vitamin A capsule is not effective (i.e., does not seem to reduce the risk of vitamin A deficiency), there are two possible explanations: Either the population does not need the capsule because it receives enough vitamin A from other sources to meet the needs (in developed countries, for example, we would not expect to see an impact of vitamin A capsules) or the need for vitamin A is so high that the capsule does not supply enough to meet the needs. If the latter is the case, the capsule might appear effective when data are collected within less than 3 months after its distribution but might not appear effective when data are collected much later. In that case, the interval between providing the capsules should be shortened.

## 28.5 HOMESTEAD FOOD PRODUCTION CONTRIBUTES TO DEVELOPMENT THROUGH EMPOWERMENT OF WOMEN

Although it is often assumed that women are the primary caretakers of HFP activities, the role of women in gardening varies by region and culture. Gardening is typically a family activity involving women, men, children, and the elderly, with some tasks carried out separately and others jointly. Men generally participate in the heavier tasks (bed establishment, fence building, well digging, and tree harvesting), while women manage the day-to-day maintenance tasks. Women and children typically care for small livestock. The elderly have a special role in passing down traditional gardening knowledge to the next generation, especially their understanding of the care and use of indigenous plants. In parts of Africa, there is evidence that as gardens become more profitable, men intervene to take over the management and marketing functions.

Marketing of garden produce can be an important source of independent income for women. This aspect is particularly critical in female-headed households, where men migrate for long periods, or in cultures where women traditionally feed the family through their own work. Where women cannot leave the home to sell in markets, garden produce can be sold from the garden or by male children in the markets.

The aforementioned independent evaluation of the Bangladesh HFP program, which was implemented by HKI and partners, also evaluated the change of social status of women in households previously, currently, or never enrolled in the program. Whereas 85% of women who had enrolled in the HFP believed that their contribution to the household had increased, only 52% of the control women thought so, and the same pattern was found for women who had full or partial decision-making power in the household [16].

## 28.6 A PROGRAMMATIC APPROACH TO INCREASE AND IMPROVE HOMESTEAD FOOD PRODUCTION PRACTICES

The many benefits of HFP have led to numerous gardening projects sponsored by nongovernmental organizations (NGOs), governments, and UN agencies. Nevertheless, the results of the promotion of gardening as a nutrition or community development strategy have been mixed. Many believe that the disappointing results of gardening projects so far stem from a failure to understand the existing garden system in a particular area in the context of changing household objectives. Understanding the traditional gardening system is vital. Even in communities that have not traditionally gardened, exploration of nearby communities that garden can give a more thorough understanding of the constraints that have inhibited gardening in the past.

A good HFP model builds on local practices; involves existing structures and organizations; provides access to required inputs, including seeds, seedlings, chicks, and the like, as well as technical advice; and is sustainable because it is of benefit to the population. Also, it is flexible with respect to choice of species and cropping patterns, encouraging diversity and use of locally adapted varieties; it encourages reliance on local materials for soil, water, and pest management and on household or community seed production. Also very important, women are involved as the primary caretakers of the garden and make final decisions on the distribution of garden harvests and income generated.

With regard to time required, home gardens are more sustainable if input and labor requirements are low and somewhat flexible. A few days to set up the garden and an hour a day for maintenance are reasonable. More time and money will be invested if the gardens produce a regular marketable surplus. Projects cannot take for granted abundant family labor or a low or zero opportunity cost of family labor.

An example of a good model is the program of HKI in the Asia Pacific region, which was started in the early 1990s in Bangladesh. Fifteen years later, it has been expanded to Cambodia, Nepal, and the Philippines and has reached more than 1 million households or over 5 million people. A good description of the setup of the program can be found in an article by Talukder et al. [70]. The most important characteristics of the program are that it expands on an existing local practice; it is implemented by local NGOs, which are also conducting other programs in the communities; HKI provides technical advice; financial investments are made together by HKI, the partner NGOs, and the households themselves; village model gardens show by example and are profitable to the owners; and women's groups are formed to be trained and share ideas and experiences. Through the partner NGO, HKI support to the program lasts for 3 years, after which the NGO provides further assistance for another 1–3 years, before the beneficiaries and the model farmers continue on their own. The gardening handbook that was first prepared by HKI in Bangladesh [71] has been used very widely by many agencies and has been adapted for use in other countries with other prevailing circumstances.

The aforementioned external evaluation found that HKI's HFP program was highly sustainable, with 50% of the households that had completed the program practicing year-round gardening compared to 15% of control households. Household vegetable consumption was 70 kg in 3 months among completed households, 85 kg among currently participating households, and 38 kg among control households. Incomes from selling produce were also higher among completed households compared to active households [16].

In the late 1990s, because of the findings of lower bioefficacy of provitamin A carotenoids from plant foods, the HFP program of HKI was expanded also to include the production of one or more animal source foods, such as chickens and eggs, fish, milking cows, or goats. For chickens and eggs, an improved breed was introduced that lays more eggs but also requires caging and more care in terms of immunization and good feed. The technical assistance required for this was made available locally through the establishment of village model poultry farms, which were often combined with the village model garden. For fish, a new variety was introduced that inhabits the fish ponds at a layer not used by the other fish. For cows, a strategy of deworming combined with growing and feeding of more nutritious grass (instead of dry hay) was implemented. A first evaluation of the pilot on animal husbandry that was added to the HFP program found that production, consumption, and sales of animal source foods increased, and that the sales of the foods increased expenditure on food, productive assets, clothes, education, and savings Helen Keller International (HKI) [77]. It was also found that nutrition education on the importance of consuming some of the animal source foods was very important to prevent households from selling most of their produce as these foods have considerable monetary value. Preliminary results indicated that this optimized HFP system, including production of animal source foods, contributes to reducing anemia [72], which is regarded as an indicator of micronutrient status.

When designing a food-based program, a conceptual framework should be developed to identify where the program should intervene; to assess whether facilitating or confounding factors could also be addressed by the program (a program's infrastructure could, for example, be used for distributing deworming medication); and to decide what factors should be included in the monitoring of the program's progress and evaluation of its impact, including indicators of nutritional status or health. This brings us to the last, very important, aspect of monitoring and evaluation. Project monitoring is conducted for regular feedback and fine-tuning of project implementation, training, and response to other, surfacing, needs. Project evaluation is conducted to assess whether the project meets its objectives and desired outcomes and if not, what its causes could be and how those could be addressed.

## 28.7   CONCLUSIONS AND RECOMMENDATIONS

For centuries, HFP has been practiced in many communities. The primary goals were adding food to the family diet (i.e., preventing food insecurity) and increasing the palatability of the diet and the joy of eating as well as for earning extra income. Programs for HFP were mostly conducted to improve nutritional status, in particular vitamin A status. Only when these programs also started from the early 1990s to include a focus on nutrition education besides their agricultural orientation were they shown to increase vitamin A intake. The programs were most successful and sustainable where they built on existing, traditional, practices of home gardening and keeping livestock using local community structures and locally available varieties and breeds and required investments from all parties involved, including the household.

This chapter reviewed the evidence and confirmed that HFP, whether as a traditional practice or improved through an HFP program, can do the following:

- Make a major contribution to increased dietary diversity because of the fruits, vegetables, herbs, and animal source foods produced; this is important from a health and nutrition point of view as well as from the point of view of improving quality of life.
- Increase income, from the sale of surplus produce as well as from reducing expenditures on foods that would have otherwise been bought.
- Stimulate biodiversity because of the cultivation of locally adapted varieties of plants and animals.
- Empower women, which increases their control over resources and raises their role in society.
- Make a valuable contribution to combating vitamin A deficiency, especially where dietary diversity is low, when animal husbandry is included, and when nutrition education emphasizes good food choices and preparation methods.
- Have an increased impact on nutritional status and health when the infrastructure of an

HFP program is used to introduce micronutrient-rich cultivars and improved breeds and to add other interventions, such as deworming, micronutrient supplements, and the like.

The HFP programs should be adapted based on new knowledge and challenges as they emerge. To gain more insight and evidence on the impact of HFP on nutritional status and health, evaluation methods need to be developed that implement a plausibility approach and present a conceptual framework for impact assessment. Further research should focus on the importance of biodiversity for health and nutrition, on development of HFP models that can effectively be used by households and communities affected by HIV/AIDS, on the extent to which HFP can add to combating nutritional anemia, and on quantifying the impact of factors that affect carotene bioavailability and conversion, especially those eligible for population-based adoption. Because fruit and vegetable consumption is also recommended to protect against degenerative diseases, their impact on morbidity and mortality also needs to be assessed.

## REFERENCES

1. Wilber K. A theory of everything. Boston: Shambhala, 2001.
2. Diamond J, Diamond JM. Guns, germs, and steel: the fates of human societies. New York: Norton, 1999.
3. Wilber K. Sex, ecology, spirituality: the spirit of evolution. 2nd ed. Boston: Shambhala, 2000.
4. Bloem MW, De Pee S, Darnton-Hill I. New issues in developing effective approaches for the prevention and control of vitamin A deficiency. Food Nutr Bull 1998:19:137–148.
5. Niñez VK. Household gardens: theoretical considerations on an old survival strategy. Lima, Peru: International Potato Center, 1984.
6. Von Braun J, McComb J, Fred-Mensah BK, Pandya-Lorch R. Urban food insecurity and malnutrition in developing countries: trends, policies and research implications. Washington, DC: International Food Policy Research Institute, 1993.
7. Moskow AL. The contributions of urban agriculture in Havana, Cuba to individual control and community enhancement. Davis: University of California, 1996.
8. Sommers P. Home gardens handbook: for people promoting mixed gardening in the humid tropics. New York: United Nations International Children's Emergency Fund, 1982.
9. Urban agriculture: food, jobs and sustainable cities. New York: United Nations Development Program (UNDP), 1996.
10. Miura S, Kunii O, Wakai S. Home gardening in urban poor communities of the Philippines. Int J Food Sci Nutr 2003;54:77–88.
11. Soleri D, Cleveland DA, Frankenberger TR. Gardens and vitamin A: a review of recent literature. Vitamin A Field Support Project (VITAL). Arlington, VA: International Science Technology Institute, 1991.
12. Marsh R, Talukder A. Production and consumption effects of the introduction of home gardening on target, interaction and control groups: a case study from Bangladesh. International Symposium on Systems-Oriented Research. Montpellier, France: Association for Farming Systems Research/Extension, 1994.
13. Asian Vegetable Research and Development Center. 1983–1989. Annual progress report. Shanhua, Taiwan Province of China: Asian Vegetable Research and Development Center, 1990.
14. Bloem MW, Huq N, Gorstein J, et al. Production of fruits and vegetables at the homestead is an important source of vitamin A among women in rural Bangladesh. Eur J Clin Nutr 1996;50(suppl 3):S62–S67.
15. Hop le T. Programs to improve production and consumption of animal source foods and malnutrition in Vietnam. J Nutr 2003;133:4006S–4009S.
16. Bushamuka VN, de Pee S, Talukder A, et al. Impact of a homestead gardening program on household food security and empowerment of women in Bangladesh. Food Nutr Bull 2005;26:17–25.
17. Faber M, Venter SL, Benade AJ. Increased vitamin A intake in children aged 2–5 years through targeted home-gardens in a rural South African community. Public Health Nutr 2002;5:11–16.

18. Johnsson U. Towards an improved strategy for nutrition surveillance. Food Nutr Bull 1995;16:102–111.

19. Solomons NW, Bulux J. Identification and production of local carotene-rich foods to combat vitamin A malnutrition. Eur J Clin Nutr 1997;51(suppl 4):S39–S45.

20. Cox DN, Rajusuriya SV, Soysa PE, Gladwin J, Ashworth A. Problems encountered in the community-based production of leaf concentrate as a supplement for pre-school children in Sri Lanka. Int J Food Sci Nutr 1993;44:123–132.

21. Leemon M, Samman S. A food-based systems approach to improve the nutritional status of Australian Aborigines: a focus on zinc. Ecol Food Nutr 1999;37:523–555.

22. Smitasiri S. Nutri-action analysis. Going beyond good people and adequate resources. Bangkok, Thailand: Amarin, 1994.

23. Ruel MT. Can food-based strategies help reduce vitamin A and iron deficiencies? A review of recent evidence. Washington, DC: International Food Policy Research Institute, 2001.

24. Brun T, Reynaud J, Chevassus-Agnes S. Food and nutritional impact of one home garden project in Senegal. Ecol Food Nutr 1989;23:91–108.

25. Leung WW, Busson F. Jardin C. Food composition table for use in Africa. 1968 US Department of Health, Education and Welfare and FAO, Bethesda and Rome.

26. Requirements of vitamin A, iron, folate and vitamin B12. Report of a joint FAO/WHO expert consultation. FAO/WHO Food Nutrition Series No. 23. Rome: Food and Agriculture Organization, World Health Organization, 1988.

27. de Pee S, West CE. Dietary carotenoids and their role in combating vitamin A deficiency: a review of the literature. Eur J Clin Nutr 1996;50(suppl 3):S38–S53.

28. de Pee S, West CE, Permaesih D, Martuti S, Muhilal, Hautvast JG. Orange fruit is more effective than are dark-green, leafy vegetables in increasing serum concentrations of retinol and β-carotene in schoolchildren in Indonesia. Am J Clin Nutr 1998;68:1058–1067.

29. Khan NC, West CE, de Pee S, et al. The contribution of plant foods to the vitamin A supply of lactating women in Vietnam: a randomized controlled trial. Am J Clin Nutr 2007;85:1112–1120.

30. Tang G, Gu X, Hu S, et al. Green and yellow vegetables can maintain body stores of vitamin A in Chinese children. Am J Clin Nutr 1999;70:1069–1076.

31. Tang G, Qin J, Dolnikowski GG, Russell RM, Grusak MA. Spinach or carrots can supply significant amounts of vitamin A as assessed by feeding with intrinsically deuterated vegetables. Am J Clin Nutr 2005;82:821–828.

32. van Lieshout M, West CE, Muhilal, et al. Bioefficacy of β-carotene dissolved in oil studied in children in Indonesia. Am J Clin Nutr 2001;73:949–958.

33. Haskell MJ, Jamil KM, Hassan F, et al. Daily consumption of Indian spinach (*Basella alba*) or sweet potatoes has a positive effect on total-body vitamin A stores in Bangladeshi men. Am J Clin Nutr 2004;80:705–714.

34. Castenmiller JJ, West CE. Bioavailability and bioconversion of carotenoids. Annu Rev Nutr 1998;18:19–38.

35. Castenmiller JJ, West CE, Linssen JP, van het Hof KH, Voragen AG. The food matrix of spinach is a limiting factor in determining the bioavailability of β-carotene and to a lesser extent of lutein in humans. J Nutr 1999;129:349–355.

36. van het Hof KH, West CE, Weststrate JA, Hautvast J. Dietary factors that affect the bioavailability of carotenoids 1. Am J Clin Nutr 1999;70:261–268.

37. Dietary reference intakes for vitamin A, vitamin K, arsenic, boron, chromium, copper, iodine, iron, manganese, molybdenum, nickel, silicon, vanadium, and zinc. Washington, DC: US Institute of Medicine, Food and Nutrition Board, Standing Committee on the Scientific Evaluation of Dietary Reference Intakes, National Academy, 2000.

38. West CE, Eilander A, van Lieshout M. Consequences of revised estimates of carotenoid bioefficacy for dietary control of vitamin A deficiency in developing countries. J Nutr 2002;132:2920S–2926S.

39. de Pee S, West CE, Muhilal, Karyadi D, Hautvast JG. Lack of improvement in vitamin A status with increased consumption of dark-green leafy vegetables. Lancet 1995;346:75–81.

40. de Pee S, Bloem MW. The bioavailability of (pro)vitamin A carotenoids and maximizing the contribution of homestead food production to combating vitamin A deficiency. Int J Vit Nut Res 2007;77:182–192.

41. Hulshof PJM, Xu C, van de Bovenkamp P, Muhilal, West CE. Application of a validated method for the determination of provitamin A carotenoids in Indonesian foods of different maturity and origin. J Agric Food Chem 1997;45:1174–1179.

42. West CE, Castenmiller JJ. Quantification of the "SLAMENGHI" factors for carotenoid bioavailability and bioconversion. Int J Vitam Nutr Res 1998;68:371–377.

43. Solomons NW. Pathways to the impairment of human nutritional status by gastrointestinal pathogens. Parasitology 1993;107(suppl):S19–S35.

44. Tang G, Serfaty-Lacrosniere C, Camilo ME, Russell RM. Gastric acidity influences the blood response to a β-carotene dose in humans. Am J Clin Nutr 1996;64:622–626.

45. Jalal F, Nesheim MC, Agus Z, Sanjur D, Habicht JP. Serum retinol concentrations in children are affected by food sources of β-carotene, fat intake, and anthelmintic drug treatment. Am J Clin Nutr 1998;68:623–629.

46. Stephensen CB, Alvarez JO, Kohatsu J, Hardmeier R, Kennedy JI Jr, Gammon RB Jr. Vitamin A is excreted in the urine during acute infection. Am J Clin Nutr 1994;60:388–392.

47. Dijkhuizen MA, Wieringa FT, West CE, Muhilal. Zinc plus β-carotene supplementation of pregnant women is superior to β-carotene supplementation alone in improving vitamin A status in both mothers and infants. Am J Clin Nutr 2004;80:1299–1307.

48. Christian P, West KP Jr. Interactions between zinc and vitamin A: an update. Am J Clin Nutr 1998;68:435S–441S.

49. Rodriguez-Amaya DB. Carotenoids and food preparation: the retention of provitamin A carotenoids in prepared, processed and stored foods. OMNI technical report series. Washington, DC: John Snow International, 1997.

50. Vuong le T, Dueker SR, Murphy SP. Plasma β-carotene and retinol concentrations of children increase after a 30-day supplementation with the fruit *Momordica cochinchinensis* (gac). Am J Clin Nutr 2002;75:872–879.

51. Riedl J, Linseisen J, Hoffmann J, Wolfram G. Some dietary fibers reduce the absorption of carotenoids in women. J Nutr 1999;129:2170–2176.

52. Rock CL, Swendseid ME. Plasma β-carotene response in humans after meals supplemented with dietary pectin. Am J Clin Nutr 1992;55:96–99.

53. Bouis H. Enrichment of food staples through plant breeding: a new strategy for fighting micronutrient malnutrition. Nutr Rev 1996;54:131–137.

54. Jayarajan P, Reddy V, Mohanram M. Effect of dietary fat on absorption of β-carotene from green leafy vegetables in children. Indian J Med Res 1980;71:53–56.

55. Roodenburg AJ, Leenen R, van het Hof KH, Weststrate JA, Tijburg LB. Amount of fat in the diet affects bioavailability of lutein esters but not of α-carotene, β-carotene, and vitamin E in humans. Am J Clin Nutr 2000;71:1187–1193.

56. Solomons NW. Plant sources of vitamin A and human nutrition: red palm oil does the job. Nutr Rev 1998;56:309–311.

57. Borel P, Tyssandier V, Mekki N, et al. Chylomicron β-carotene and retinyl palmitate responses are dramatically diminished when men ingest β-carotene with medium-chain rather than long-chain triglycerides. J Nutr 1998;128:1361–1367.

58. Beare-Rogers J, Ghafoorunissa, Korver O, Rocquelin G, Sundram K, Uauy R. Dietary fat in developing countries. Food Nutr Bull 1998;19:251–267.

59. Goldbohm RA, Brants HA, Hulshof KF, van den Brandt PA. The contribution of various foods to intake of vitamin A and carotenoids in the Netherlands. Int J Vitam Nutr Res 1998;68:378–383.

60. Fawzi WW, Herrera MG, Willett WC, et al. Dietary vitamin A intake and the risk of mortality among children. Am J Clin Nutr 1994;59:401–408.

61. West KP Jr, Katz J, Khatry SK, et al. Double blind, cluster randomised trial of low dose supplementation with vitamin A or β-carotene on mortality related to pregnancy in Nepal. The NNIPS-2 Study Group. BMJ 1999;318:570–575.

62. Soleri D, Cleveland DA, Wood A. Vitamin A nutrition and gardens bibliography. Vitamin A Field Support Project (VITAL). Arlington, VA: International Science Technology Institute, 1991.

63. Peduzzi C. Home and community gardens assessment program implementation experience: the tip of the iceberg. Vitamin A Field Support Project (VITAL). Washington, DC: International Life Sciences Institute, 1990.

64. Gillespie S, Mason J. Controlling vitamin A deficiency. ACC/SCN state-of-the-art series. Geneva: United Nations Administrative Committee on Coordination—Subcommittee on Nutrition, 1994.

65. Jones KM, Specio SE, Shrestha P, Brown KH, Allen LH. Nutrition knowledge and practices, and consumption of vitamin A—rich plants by rural Nepali participants and nonparticipants in a kitchen-garden program. Food Nutr Bull 2005;26:198–208.

66. Faber M, Phungula MA, Venter SL, Dhansay MA, Benade AJ. Home gardens focusing on the production of yellow and dark-green leafy vegetables increase the serum retinol concentrations of 2–5-year-old children in South Africa. Am J Clin Nutr 2002;76:1048–1054.

67. Kiess L, Bloem MW, de Pee S, et al. Bangladesh: xerophthalmia free. The result of an effective vitamin A capsule program and homestead gardening. American Public Health Association 126th annual meeting report. Washington, DC: American Public Health Association, 1998.

68. De Pee S, Bloem MW, Kiess L. Evaluating food-based programmes for their reduction of vitamin A deficiency and its consequences. Food Nutr Bull 2000;21:232–238.

69. Habicht JP, Victora CG, Vaughan JP. Evaluation designs for adequacy, plausibility and probability of public health programme performance and impact. Int J Epidemiol 1999;28:10–18.

70. Talukder A, Kiess L, Huq N, de Pee S, Darnton-Hill I, Bloem MW. Increasing the production and consumption of vitamin A-rich fruits and vegetables: lessons learned in taking the Bangladesh homestead gardening programme to a national scale. Food Nutr Bull 2000;21:165–72.

71. Talukder A, Islam N, Klemm R, Bloem M. Home gardening in South Asia, the complete handbook. Dhaka, Bangladesh: Helen Keller International, 1993.

72. Talukder A, Stallkamp G, Karim R, et al. Homestead food production reduces the prevalence of anemia among non-pregnant women and children in Asia (Bangladesh, Nepal and Cambodia). Istanbul: Micronutrient Forum, 2007.

73. MOH, Indonesia. Daftar komposisi zat gizi pangan Indonesia (Indonesian food composition table). Jakarta, Indonesia: Department of Health, Republic of Indonesia, 1995.

74. Hardinsyah DB. Penilaian dan perencanaan konsumsi pangan. Bogor, Indonesia: Jursusan GMSK, IPB, 1990.

75. West CE, Poortvliet EJ. The carotenoid content of foods with special reference to developing countries. Washington, DC: VITAL–United States Agency for International Development, 1993.

76. Soleri D, Cleveland DA, Household garden as a development strategy Hum Org 1987;46:259–270.

77. Helen Keller International Integration of animal husbandry into home gardening programs to increase vitamin A intake from Region Office Asia-Pacific, 2003. Available from http://www.hki.org/research/pdf-zip-docs/APRO%20Special%20issue%20Jan%202003.pdf.

# 29 Food Policy

## *C. Peter Timmer*

## 29.1   INTRODUCTION

The purpose of the central analytical vision of food policy, articulated over two decades ago, was to integrate farmer, trader, and consumer decision making into the open-economy, macroframework needed for rapid economic growth [1]. The explicit goal was a sharp reduction in hunger and poverty, which would be possible if market incentives stimulated productivity and income gains in agriculture while poor consumers were protected by stable food prices and rising real wages. The marketing sector was the key to connecting these two ends of the food system.

The analytical story, policy design, and program implementation were complicated, requiring analysts to integrate models of micro- and macro-decision making in a domestic economy open to world trade and commodity markets. At its best, the food policy paradigm sharply improved the development profession's understanding of the underlying structure and dynamics of poverty and the role of the food system in reducing it [2]. As part of this understanding, food security came to be seen as involving two separate analytical arenas. The first, at the "micro-household" level, required analysis of food access and entitlements. The second, at the "macro-market" level, required analysis of food price stability, market supplies, and inventory behavior.

*Food Policy Analysis* provided policymakers a comprehensive, but intuitively tractable, vision of how to connect these two arenas and improve food security for the consumers in their societies. This vision was always consumer driven. Farmers, as food producers, and middlemen in the marketing sector that transformed farm output in time, place, and form were seen as "intermediate" actors in the efficient production of consumer welfare. Thus, the food policy paradigm as articulated by Timmer, Falcon, and Pearson fit squarely within the standard framework of neoclassical economic analysis, although it was often asking rather different questions from those standard at the time [1].

## 29.2   DEFINITIONS

Over the years, there has been a wide range of challenges to this paradigm in poor countries, quite independently of the recent emergence of supermarkets—and their revolutionary impact on marketing systems. In response, Simon Maxwell and Rachel Slater edited a special issue of *Development Policy Review* under the theme "Food Policy Old

From: *Nutrition and Health: Nutrition and Health in Developing Countries, Second Edition*
Edited by: R. D. Semba & M. W. Bloem © Humana Press, Totowa, NJ

and New." Their introduction includes the following observations on the evolution of food policy: "The very term 'food policy' induces nostalgia for the 1970s and 1980s; the first meetings of the World Food Council, the establishment of the International Food Policy Research Institute, the establishment of the journal 'Food Policy' [3].

The emphasis at that time on food policy in developing countries was important. It was not just that the world food crisis of 1972–1974 had triggered new interest in the availability of and access to food, especially at global and national levels, it was also that policymakers began to appreciate the interdependence between supply- and demand-side issues and the value of applying, especially, economic analysis to the links. Timmer et al. reminded us that "where the food system is headed, of course, is the key question" [1].

It was not long before developing countries began to answer that question, stimulated, for example, by the European Union's Plan of Action to Combat Hunger in the World and by its pilot program of food strategies in Kenya, Zambia, Rwanda, and Mali.

Amartya Sen is usually credited with shifting the food strategy discourse forward from the original food strategies toward entitlement and access. Entitlement, vulnerability, and risk became the new watchwords: This was the emergent language of food security. The idea of "food security" has dominated the debate since the early 1980s [4, 5]. Donors developed an enthusiasm for national food security planning, partly as a "proxy for poverty planning" during the darkest years of structural adjustment. The International Conference on Nutrition, the World Food Summit, and WFS—Five Years Later cemented the consensus. A reduction in undernutrition even made it into the Millennium Development Goals [6].

Meanwhile, other issues began to infiltrate. They included a concern for the commercialization and industrialization of food systems; a stronger focus on the institutional actors in food trade, including supermarkets; warnings about the environmental consequences of new technologies; and issues to do with health, including problems of food safety and the growth of nutrition-related illnesses, especially heart disease and diabetes. Often, these issues were picked up outside the mainstream or mainly in developed countries. Perhaps, to those primarily concerned with famine and severe undernutrition in the very poorest countries, they seemed superfluous.

This was not so. The core message of this volume is that what we term the *new food policy* cannot be ignored. The world food system, described only a few years ago by Gaull and Goldberg as "emerging," is no longer quite the chrysalis it once was [7]. The pace of change is accelerating. The challenges are daunting. They are immediate. And they need to be on the agenda of policymakers throughout the developing world. A preoccupation with food security is no longer sufficient. It is necessary to rediscover food policy [3]."

The new food policy agenda is very broad, and many of its core topics are treated in this volume. This chapter sets the context for these discussions. There are four parts to this chapter as it starts to answer a wide variety of questions that are on the agenda. The first addresses specifically what is different between the old and the new food policy paradigms. The second part puts the entire food policy debate in historical perspective as a reminder to focus our attention on the long-term process of economic development as the basic driver of the phenomena we are observing. The new role of modern supply chains and supermarkets is addressed in this context, following on the discussion of the role of supermarkets in health and nutrition that was presented in Chapter 27. The third part of the chapter addresses sectoral dimensions of food policy. The fourth part offers some generic policy recommendations in the form of a list of "don'ts" and "do's" and proposes an integration of the old and new food policy paradigms as a framework for the research needed to make the policy recommendations more concrete.

## 29.3    FOOD POLICY: WHAT'S DIFFERENT?

It is useful to characterize the old and new food policy paradigms in relatively simple two-by-two figures that capture the key concerns of each paradigm. Both focus analytical attention on issues at the country level as well as the household level, and this provides one dimension of the comparison. The original food policy paradigm focused analysis on the links between poverty and food security. This provides the other dimension for discussion in Fig. 29.1, which fills in the four cells of the original food policy paradigm.

Alternatively, the new food policy stresses the "double burden" on societies facing substantial degrees of hunger at the same time they face rising levels of nutritional problems of affluence—obesity, heart disease, diabetes, and so on (see Chapters 20 and 21). The "development" or poverty dimension is more sharply focused on the problem of exclusion—at the national level as well as the household level. Fig. 29.2 fills in the cells for this paradigm.

### 29.3.1    *The Food and Health Dimension*

A comparison of Figs. 29.1 and 29.2 shows how starkly the two paradigms are different. At the country level, the earlier concern for keeping food prices at a level that balanced producer and consumer interests, with price stabilization around this level an important policy objective, gives way to equally important concerns for the budgetary consequences for governments (at national and local levels) of the health outcomes of dietary choices over entire societies.

At the household level, the traditional focus on access to foods (including intrahousehold access and distribution) stressed income and price variables, with a very limited role for household education and knowledge (except possibly in the derived demand for micronutrients). Much of the quantitative research in food policy since 1975 has

|                      | **Food Security**                                                                 | **Poverty**                                                                                          |
| -------------------- | --------------------------------------------------------------------------------- | ---------------------------------------------------------------------------------------------------- |
| **Country Focus**    | Market prices: Level and stability                                                | Economic growth and rising real wages                                                                |
| **Household Focus**  | Access to Food<br>--incomes<br>--prices<br>--knowledge<br>(especially for micro-nutrients) | Jobs, especially through a dynamic rural economy, migration, and labor-intensive manufacturing |

**Fig. 29.1.** The "old" food policy.

|  | The "Double Burden" of Hunger and Obesity | Exclusion |
|---|---|---|
| **Country Focus** | Government costs of health care and pensions | "Non-Globalizers" (Governance?) |
| **Household Focus** | Lifestyle and health know-ledge (are we "hard-wired" for scarcity?) | Small farmers Unskilled workers Low education |

**Fig. 29.2**. The "new" food policy.

involved a search for the behavioral regularities that linked households to these market-determined variables [8].

Again, the contrast with the new concerns is sharp. Health professionals are either pessimistic about the political reality of using economic variables to influence dietary choices (one debate is over the efficiency of taxing fats in foods, taxing fat people, or taxing the health consequences of being fat) or doubtful that economic incentives will actually change dietary behavior where affluence permits a wide array of choices. Consequently, there is a much sharper focus on trying to change lifestyle through improved health knowledge and nutrition education.

There is also an ongoing debate over whether approaches to changing lifestyles through education will work. In particular, if the dietary patterns of affluence have a significant genetic component—that is, humans are "hard-wired" for an environment of food scarcity and have few internal control mechanisms over dietary intake in an environment of permanent affluence and abundance—much more coercive efforts may be needed to change dietary behavior (and activity levels) than is implied by the education approach. On the other hand, such coercion directly contradicts consumer sovereignty and the basic principles of a democratic society.

### 29.3.2   The Poverty and Development Dimension

One of the key messages for developing countries in *Food Policy Analysis* [1] was the link between poverty and food security at both the national and household levels. In turn, poverty was considered primarily an economic problem that could only be addressed in a sustainable fashion by linking the poor—mostly in rural areas—into the process of economic growth. A dynamic agriculture as a stimulus to forward and backward linkages within the rural economy served as the "prime mover" in this process. Through improved agricultural technology, public investments in rural infrastructure, and the end of "urban bias" that distorted incentives for farmers, policymakers could have a simple and clear approach to reducing poverty and improving food security.

With success in the rural economy, migration to urban areas would be more of a "pull" process than a "push," especially if favorable macroeconomic and trade policies were stimulating rapid growth in a labor-intensive manufacturing (and construction) industry. In combination, these activities pulled up real wages and, when sustained, led to rapid reductions in poverty [9, 10] In many ways, this paradigm could be described as an "inclusion model" because of its focus on including the poor in the rural economy, including the rural economy in the national economy, and including the national economy in the global economy. Its greatest success was in East and Southeast Asia from 1960 to 1997, but the model has been under attack since then as the benefits of globalization seem not to have been as widely shared as earlier hoped, especially in other parts of the world.

The failures of globalization provide the analytical theme for the new food policy paradigm. Figure 29.2 characterizes this theme around the analytics of "exclusion." At the national level, the question is why so many countries have been "nonglobalizers." The essence of the debate is whether the global economy, in the form of rich countries and transnational corporations, has excluded these countries from participating in trade and technology flows or whether the countries themselves have been unsuccessful in the process because of domestic shortcomings in policies and governance (including corruption).

The debate has a local focus as well. Within an otherwise well-functioning and growing economy, many groups can be excluded from the benefits of this growth. Unskilled workers unable to graduate to higher technologies and uneducated youth unable to compete in a modern economy are a sizable proportion of the workforce in countries with poor manpower and training policies and resources. Globalization makes it more difficult for these countries to compete for trade and investment flows that would provide the first steps up the ladder of higher productivity.

The exclusion lens focuses especially on small farmers. Their fate was a source of policy concern well before the supermarket revolution gained speed in the early 1990s in Latin America, but there is no question that the issue is now squarely on the policy agenda in most developing countries (see Chapter 27). The debate between the relevance of the old and new food policy paradigms is primarily about which approach offers the most useful insights and policy/program guidance for assisting small farmers in their efforts to access modern food supply chains. The answer, it seems, depends on the time horizon of analysis. In the short run, finding income opportunities for small farmers is essential, but in the longer run they have other options, including migration to urban jobs.

## 29.4   FOOD POLICY IN HISTORICAL PERSPECTIVE

The "big" question in social science is whether to study diversity or central tendencies. In the context of economic development, this question translates into whether to analyze the process from the perspective of changing welfare of entire societies over long periods of time or whether to study inequality in its many dimensions during a particular epoch. The two perspectives obviously relate to each other, possibly even in causal ways, as is illustrated by the modern debate over the contribution of income inequality to economic growth and vice versa [11].

Figure 29.3 provides a framework for thinking about these issues in the context of rapid technological change in food-marketing systems. The horizontal axis depicts the long-run process of economic growth or the transformation of societies from "poor" to "rich." This is the dominant transformation that humanity has undergone in the past ten

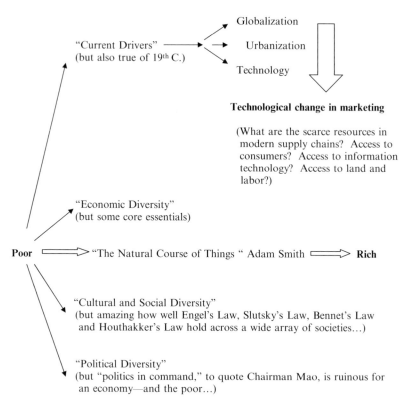

"Current Drivers"
(but also true of 19th C.)

Globalization

Urbanization

Technology

**Technological change in marketing**

(What are the scarce resources in
modern supply chains?  Access to
consumers?  Access to information
technology?  Access to land and
labor?)

"Economic Diversity"
(but some core essentials)

**Poor**          "The Natural Course of Things " Adam Smith          **Rich**

"Cultural and Social Diversity"
(but amazing how well Engel's Law, Slutsky's Law, Bennet's Law
and Houthakker's Law hold across a wide array of societies...)

"Political Diversity"
(but "politics in command," to quote Chairman Mao, is ruinous for
an economy—and the poor...)

**Fig. 29.3.** The long-run perspective.

millennia and is "the natural course of things," to quote Adam Smith's observation in the
18th century [12, 13].[1] To see the dominance of this transformation requires a very long
time horizon, more a purview of economic historians than development specialists.

The various dimensions of this process have been summarized as the "structural
transformation," wherein entire societies undergo the wrenching changes associated
with agricultural modernization, migration of labor from rural to urban areas, and the
emergence of urban industrial centers. As part of this process, as both effect and cause,
the demographic transition moves a society from equilibrium of high birth and death
rates to a "modern" equilibrium of low birth and death rates. The structural transformation has taken as long as three centuries in England and the United States (and is
still continuing) and as little as a century in Japan and its East Asian followers. The
lengthy process provides a cautionary message to those in a rush to transform their
societies [14].

At the same time that this structural transformation is unfolding, there is enormous
diversity across societies in how they organize themselves politically, define them-

---

[1] The full citation runs as follows. "Little else is requisite to carry a state to the highest degree
of opulence from the lowest barbarism than peace, easy taxes, and tolerable administration of
justice; all the rest being brought about by the natural course of things." Lecture by Adam Smith
in 1775 [12, p. 235]. The perspective here also draws heavily on [13].

selves culturally, and reward themselves economically. This is the vertical dimension that Fig. 29.3 illustrates in a crude and simple fashion. During any historical epoch, there will be a set of identifiable "drivers" that are pushing the economy to the right, from poor to rich, while at the same time structuring the diversity within societies and among them.

In the current era—post-World War II to keep things concrete—these drivers are globalization, urbanization, and technology. There is now widespread agreement that the marketing revolution itself has been driven by precisely these three drivers of overall economic change. This long-run perspective suggests that the marketing revolution is understandable within the context of the structural transformation and the long-run evolution of agriculture within that process. Further, basic economics, with its stress on returns to scarce factors of production, is surprisingly helpful in understanding the inner dynamics of the process. But finally, a historical perspective provides little guidance on how to assist small farmers as they compete for contracts in modern supply chains. For that, the diversity of the global food system, rather than its common themes and forces, needs to be understood. Still, there are some important lessons that come from combining the food policy perspective and the historical, analytical perspective. These lessons tend to play out at the sectoral—marketing—level and at the macrolevel in terms of how the overall economy is performing.

## 29.5   THE SECTORAL PERSPECTIVE

The challenges to understanding the impact of sectoral policies on health and nutrition in developing countries transcend the disparate issues dealt with by the old and new food policy paradigms. In particular, for both paradigms, the key issues remain of how to achieve and sustain rapid reductions in poverty and hunger through interventions (or ending counterproductive interventions) in the food system. Historically, the marketing sector that connects farmers to consumers has been the major focus for interventions.

The marketing sector serves two primary functions in a market economy: It generates signals between consumers' desires and farmers' costs through price formation, and it performs the physical functions of marketing—transforming raw commodities at the farm in time, space, and form and delivering them to consumers' tables. These are inherently "coordination" tasks, and they require an adroit combination of public and private investments if they are to be carried out efficiently. Historically, these investments have been made very gradually as farmers evolved from subsistence activities toward a more commercial orientation. Now that commercial activities are the norm, even in economies where efficient marketing networks have not had time to emerge, policymakers are actively seeking new models and approaches to speed the creation of these networks.

The growing importance of market interactions for farmers stems from at least three separate forces. First, the collapse of socialism has stimulated a rapid, if often painful, transition to a market economy. Second, increasing incomes have stimulated increased commercialization and diversification as part of an agricultural transformation. Three different processes of agricultural change are closely related and hence often confused: the agricultural transformation, agricultural commercialization, and agricultural diversification. The discussion in this section draws on the perspective in [14]. Third, this commercialization and diversification is increasingly taking place with supermarkets as the main buyer of agricultural output.

The agricultural sector as a whole is likely to become much more diversified over the course of the agricultural transformation, when compared with a representative individual farm, but significantly less diversified than food consumption patterns. Unless agroecological endowments are nearly identical throughout the country, farmers with different resources are likely to specialize in different crops. This increasing specialization of farms (*decreasing* diversification) is consistent with *greater* diversity at more aggregate levels because of the commercialization of agriculture.

Commercialization of agricultural systems leads to greater market orientation of farm production; progressive substitution out of nontraded inputs in favor of purchased inputs; and the gradual decline of integrated farming systems and their replacement by specialized enterprises for crop, livestock, poultry, and aquaculture products. The farm-level determinants of increasing commercialization are the rising opportunity costs of family labor and increased market demand for food and other agricultural products. Family labor costs rise due to increasing off-farm employment opportunities, while positive shifts in market demand are triggered by urbanization or trade liberalization [15].

Likewise, patterns of food consumption become more diversified than patterns of domestic agricultural production because of the rising significance of international trade (i.e., globalization). Bennett's law suggests that there is an inherent desire for diversity in dietary patterns among most populations of the world. Low-cost transportation systems and falling trade barriers have generally opened to consumers a market basket that draws from the entire world's bounty and diversity (see Chapter 29; [16]). Modern supply chains are increasingly the vehicle for providing this diversity, and consumers clearly support the trend by exercising their buying power in supermarkets (see Chapter 27; [17]).

The growing roles of commercialization and globalization in connecting diversity of production at the farm level with diversity of consumption at the household level spawn new problems, however. In particular, increased commercialization requires that farmers learn how to cope with a type of risk that is of little concern to subsistence farmers: the risk of fluctuating prices. At the same time, specialization in crop production increases their risk from yield fluctuations. Mechanisms for coping with risk, including contractual arrangements with supermarkets, thus play a crucial role in understanding the commercialization of agriculture and the government's role in it. The interplay among price fluctuations, increasing reliance on international trade, specialization of farmers in production for the market in response to profitable new technology, and continued failure of market-based mechanisms for risk management in rural areas accounts for much of the policy interest of governments in the process of rural diversification. A key task of a new food policy paradigm will be to improve the policy choices governments make as they respond to this interplay of forces with interventions into the diversification process, especially efforts to regulate the emergence and behavior of modern supply chains.

One intervention in nearly all countries is to make public investments that stimulate market development and efficiency. Efficient development of entire commodity systems, from input production and marketing to downstream processing and consumption of the final product, requires the formation of extensive backward and forward linkages from the producer level. These linkages can be both technological, depending on engineering relationships and quality requirements, for example, and financial, depending on investment patterns from profits generated by commodity production and consumption patterns from the incomes earned in the sector. Many of these linkages exhibit economies of scale and can be developed to efficient levels only if the commodity is produced in a relatively cohesive spatial pattern. This process of market deepening is a natural result of regional specialization and one of the major forces that gradually but persistently produces such specialization.

Most countries want to speed up this gradual process but have found that government investments alone are inadequate. Well-developed, low-cost marketing systems require sufficient supplies of the specific commodities marketed to justify the full investments needed to capture any economies of scale to the system. Achieving this balance is a simultaneous process, which historically has meant the gradual evolution of both the supply and demand sides of the market. The interesting question now is whether super-markets are internalizing this coordination process and speeding the rate of specialization. If so, as specialized production grows in a region, the marketing system will expand to serve it in a coordinated (but closed, to outside parties) way. The lower costs generated by specialization can confer very significant competitive advantages to regions that are both low-cost producers of a commodity and have an efficient marketing system that has adequate volume to capture the economies of scale implicit in the forward and backward linkages [18].

Regional specialization in a range of agricultural products would thus seem to be the answer to the problem of too much diversification at the farm level. Such specialization permits the cost economies of scale (and learning) to be captured while still diversifying the country's agricultural output. A problem remains, however. Although the country may be well diversified, individual farmers and regions are not. Significant price insta-bility, whether generated strictly in domestic markets or transmitted from international markets, would have substantial income distribution consequences for the farmers and regions concerned—unless their output is sufficiently negatively correlated with prices that net revenue is stabilized by unstable prices. When large regions depend heavily on a single crop for their economic base, the vulnerability from specialization is similar to that at the national level when cultivation of a staple food crop is widespread. When rubber producers, coffee growers, or maize farmers specialize in production, each can face problems of income stabilization in the face of unstable prices or yields.

The consequences for income distribution of crop specialization at the farm or regional level are straightforward. With domestic price stability, small farmers can specialize in single crops, and regional diversification can keep surpluses from developing. But, this strategy depends on price stabilization. Otherwise, individual farmers must diversify to spread risks from price fluctuations. Such diversification is likely to incur high costs because of forgone effects of "learning by doing" and the scale economies inherent in marketing systems. Compared with national specialization in a single commodity, the macroeconomic consequences of regional vulnerability are not as great—unless all prices and yields move together. But, the individual and regional problems should also receive the attention of policymakers. Especially in countries with diverse regional interests, appearing to ignore the economic plight of distressed regions can have devastating consequences for the political stability of the country as a whole.

## 29.6   LESSONS FOR FOOD POLICY

As with much policy advice, the most important recommendations start with the word "don't." But, there are positive steps as well, although all the recommendations listed here lack specificity to local situations. To address these, further research within a clear, policy-oriented framework will be needed. This chapter is a very preliminary effort to outline the main components of that framework.

### 29.6.1   *Three Things Not to Do*

1. *Do no harm.* Especially with respect to the broader agenda under debate in food policy circles, many suggestions can only be described as "social engineering." It is important to remember that the great political and economic experiments over the past two centuries, most of them done in the name of improving the welfare of the poor, have turned out to be catastrophic for the citizenry.

2. *Do not miss the forest for the trees.* It is important to keep our eye on the real objective of economic policy, which is to improve the welfare of as many people as possible, with special attention to the absolute poor. The objective is *not* to improve the lives of small farmers unless that is a means to our end. In many circumstances, agriculture can be the engine of pro-poor growth, and small farmers can participate in that growth directly. But, they might also participate, perhaps more effectively, indirectly by getting jobs in rural nonfarm activities or by migrating to urban jobs.

3. *Do not throw the baby out with the bathwater.* The debate between the old food policy and the new food policy, especially over how to analyze and intervene to offset the damaging health consequences of the double burden of malnutrition, is sharper than it needs to be. The basic question is whether economic analysis of the food system remains useful in the context of the broader, interdisciplinary problems now manifested in that food system. Just as *Food Policy Analysis* [1] pushed economists to extend the range of interests considered relevant to economic methodologies, so does the new food policy call for incorporating health and environmental dimensions, for example, into this analysis. Economics is not unique in having methodologies for addressing these broader dimensions of decisions by food producers, marketers, and consumers. But, no interventions to solve these problems will be sustainable unless the economics make sense.

### 29.6.2   *Three Things to Do*

1. *Do incorporate the new food policy issues into the analysis.* It is much better to solve real and relevant problems than "pretend" problems that have neat analytical solutions (despite the intellectual appeal of the latter kind of problem, especially to academics). But, incorporating these issues into the analysis requires getting the facts straight. Emotions, prejudices, and anecdotes run rampant in this arena, and as a field, development studies in particular are prone to follow fads. There are immediate implications for how we do research and how we train scholars and policy analysts to work in this field. The research will require long-term panel data to carry out the sophisticated analyses that can disentangle subtle health and environmental effects from other, often more powerful, trends driven by short-run economic, ecological, or weather phenomena. Training will require a breadth of interdisciplinary perspectives on top of, not in place of, deep disciplinary skills.

2. *Do design, lobby for, and implement social safety nets.* In doing so, however, it is important to realize that social safety nets are most efficient in helping families cope with transition problems and short-run crises, not with chronic poverty. To solve the problem of chronic poverty, especially as experienced by small farmers, there is no alternative to economic growth, sustained over decades. There are opportunities to make this growth more pro-poor than it might be if left to market forces, but getting the growth process going in the first place will be critical to reducing poverty [19].

3. *Do try to make corporations more socially responsive.* But, be careful what you wish for: R. J. Reynolds now advertises itself as a "health company," with information on its Web site on how to keep children from smoking and how to help adults quit. Wal-Mart's "associates" (workers, in any other company) believe in community action and actively volunteer their time for local causes, according to their advertising campaign. The multinational banks (including the World Bank) can afford to "love us to death" with NGO advisory panels and local participation in their development projects.

As an economist, I put a lot more of my trust in competition and market forces to bring about higher standards of living than I do in unregulated corporate efforts to do good works. In particular, individual corporate efforts to "internalize" environmental, health, and social (distributional) costs that are currently external to market prices bring no guarantee that they will actually improve overall social welfare. If societies genuinely want these costs internalized, then the democratic process and consumer sovereignty offer mechanisms to do so.

*Acknowledgment* Parts of this chapter were originally prepared for a Food and Agriculture Organization (FAO) scientific workshop, "Globalization, Urbanization and the Food Systems of Developing Countries: Assessing the Impacts on Poverty, Food and Nutrition Security," held October 8–10, 2003, at FAO headquarters in Rome, Italy.

## REFERENCES

1. Timmer CP, Falcon WP, Pearson SR. Food policy analysis. Baltimore, MD: Johns Hopkins University Press, 1983.
2. Eicher CK, Staatz JM. International agricultural development. Baltimore, MD: Johns Hopkins University Press, 1998.
3. Maxwell S, Slater R. Food policy old and new. Oxford, UK: Blackwell, 2004.
4. Sen AK. Poverty and famines: an essay on entitlement and deprivation. New York: Oxford University Press, 1983.
5. Drèze J, Sen AK. Public action for social security: foundations and strategy: Development Economics Research Programme, London School of Economics and Politics, London, UK, 1989.
6. United Nations. UN millennium development goals. New York: United Nations, 2000.
7. Gaull GE, Goldberg RA. The emerging global food system: public and private sector issues. New York: Wiley, 1993.
8. Timmer CP. Is there "curvature" in the Slutsky matrix? Review of Economic and Statistics, Vol 62, No. 31981:395–402.
9. Timmer CP. Agriculture and economic growth. In: The handbook of agricultural economics. Gardner B, Rausser G, eds. Amsterdam: North-Holland, 2002:1487–1546.
10. Timmer CP. Agriculture and pro-poor growth: an Asian perspective. Washington, DC: Center for Global Development, 2005. Working Paper No. 63.
11. Easterly W. Inequality does retard economic growth. Washington, DC: Center for Global Development, 2002. Working Paper No. 1.

12. Jones EL. The European miracle: environments, economics and geopolitics in the history of Europe and Asia. Cambridge, UK: Cambridge University Press, 1981.
13. Jones EL. Growth recurring: economic change in world history. Oxford, UK: Clarendon, 1988.
14. Timmer CP. Farmers an markets: the political economy of new paradigms. American Journal of Agricultural Economics, Vol 79, No.2 1997:621–627.
15. Pingali PL, Rosegrant MW. Agricultural commercialization and diversification: processes and policies. Food Policy 1995;20:171–185.
16. Chaudhri, Rajiv, Timmer CP. The impact of changing affluence on diets and demand patterns for agricultural commodities. Washington, DC: World Bank, 1985. Staff Working Paper No. 785.
17. Reardon T, Timmer CP. Transformation of markets for agricultural output in developing countries since 1950: how has thinking changed? In: Handbook of agricultural economics: agricultural development: farmers, farm production and farm markets. Evenson RE, Pingali P, Schultz TP, eds. Amsterdam: North-Holland, Elsevier, 2005.
18. Krugman P. Geography and trade. New York: Norton, 1993.
19. Project on "Pro-Poor Strategies for Economic Growth." Implemented by Development Alternatives, Inc. (DAI) and Boston Institute for Development Economics (BIDE). Bethesda, MD: United States Agency for International Development, 2003.

# 30 Need, Efficacy, and Effectiveness of Multiple Vitamin/Mineral Supplements for Young Children and Considerations for Programs

*Saskia de Pee*

## 30.1 INTRODUCTION

Undernutrition contributes to the deaths of approximately 5.6 million children under 5 years of age in low- and middle-income countries per year [1] because more than 50% of young children's deaths from infectious diseases such as malaria, pneumonia, diarrhea, and measles have undernutrition as an underlying cause [2, 3]. In addition, due to undernutrition, many more children suffer from stunted growth and reduced mental capacity and are likely to live a life of poverty and ignorance.

In 2000, the eight Millenium Development Goals (MDGs) were endorsed by 189 countries. The first MDG is to halve the proportion of the world's poor (target 1) and hungry (target 2) by 2015. Bringing an end to child hunger and undernutrition also contributes to achieving five of the other seven MDGs: MDG-2 on universal primary education, MDG-3 on gender equality, MDG-4 on reducing child mortality, MDG-5 on improving maternal health, and MDG-6 on combating HIV/AIDS, malaria, and other diseases. With regard to progress toward achieving the MDGs, between 1990 and 2000, the number of underweight children younger than 5 years decreased by approximately 1.7% per year. Although the decline is positive, it needs to be accelerated, and there is considerable variation among regions and countries. South Asia has the highest rates of malnutrition, 46%, and the largest numbers, whereas malnutrition in sub-Saharan Africa, which stands at 28%, is on the rise. These trends mean that the world is not making adequate progress toward the MDGs. Persistent malnutrition means that MDG-1 is not being achieved but also seriously hampers progress toward the other goals in maternal and child health, HIV/AIDS, education, and gender equity.

The causes of child hunger are predictable and preventable and can be addressed through affordable means. Investment in nutrition reduces poverty, increases educational outcomes, and boosts productivity throughout the life cycle and across generations. And, *not* addressing child hunger and undernutrition costs US $20 billion to $30 billion

From: *Nutrition and Health: Nutrition and Health in Developing Countries, Second Edition*
Edited by: R. D. Semba & M. W. Bloem © Humana Press, Totowa, NJ

per year [4]. The new growth standards released by the World Health Organization (WHO) in 2006 demonstrated that children born in different regions of the world can and should grow equally well, and that gender and ethnicity are minor determinants of growth in comparison with adequate nutrition, environment, and health [5]. These new standards thus enable tracking progress toward the MDGs and evaluation of the impact of interventions across different countries.

The slow progress toward achieving the MDGs while effective interventions are known and tracking of progress is relatively straightforward has led to a number of initiatives, including advocacy for *Repositioning Nutrition as Central to Development* [6], the *Lancet* series on maternal and child undernutrition, and the Ending Child Hunger and Undernutrition Initiative (ECHUI) [4].

*Repositioning Nutrition as Central to Development: A Strategy for Large-Scale Action*, published by the World Bank, makes the case that development partners and developing countries must increase investment in nutrition programs because the scale of the problem is very large, and nutrition interventions are essential for speeding poverty reduction, have high benefit–cost ratios, and can improve nutrition much faster than reliance on economic growth alone [6]. Moreover, improved nutrition can drive economic growth. The report stated that control of micronutrient deficiencies has a very high benefit–cost ratio and is essential to making progress.

The *Lancet* series was launched in January 2008 and provides an important new focus for discussions on how to improve maternal and child nutrition through working together better at all levels and places nutrition-related interventions within a broader context of different policies and programs. Five articles look at, among other things, what works in the way of nutrition interventions and programs; what needs to be done at the national level; and which effective actions are needed at the international level to accelerate progress. Strategies to promote intake of micronutrients, through dietary diversification and strategic micronutrient supplementation and fortification programs, are discussed as very cost-effective means to combat child undernutrition.

To increase progress toward achieving MDG-1, in 2006 the United Nations International Children's Emergency Fund (UNICEF) and World Food Programme (WFP) initiated ECHUI now known as REACH (renewing efforts against child hunger) [4]. Realizing that many of the world's undernourished children are grouped together, REACH goal is to end child hunger and undernutrition within a generation through acceleration and focusing efforts on what works and implementing that well where the needs are highest. In this regard, it should be noted that three quarters of the world's 146 million children younger than 5 years that are underweight live in just 10 countries [7]. Micronutrients are part of the "essential package" of health and nutrition interventions promoted by REACH because they are among the interventions that are most effective in reducing the immediate causes of under-5 mortality, play an important role in enhancing development and growth, and are therefore an important means to combat child undernutrition.

Micronutrients, or vitamins and minerals (V&M), can be supplied in several ways and in multiple combinations and dosages. This chapter reviews the evidence about the benefits of supplying multiple micronutrients to young children and ways of how this could be done programmatically.

## 30.2  EXISTENCE AND CONSEQUENCES OF MULTIPLE VITAMIN AND MINERAL DEFICIENCIES

The main cause of multiple vitamin and mineral deficiencies (VMDs) is a poor-quality diet, often due to an inadequate intake of animal source foods (ASFs), especially in developing countries. Also, in wealthier regions of the world, women who avoid meat or milk are at higher risk of micronutrient depletion during pregnancy and lactation. In diets that are high in unrefined grains and legumes, the amount of nutrients consumed may be adequate, but dietary constituents, such as phytates and polyphenols, limit their absorption [8]. In addition to poor dietary quality, nonnutritional factors such as parasitic infections, genetic hemoglobinopathies, malaria, and infectious diseases also impair nutritional status and health as well as alter the metabolism of multiple micronutrients [9, 10].

The adverse effects of VMD in children as well as adults include both functional and health outcomes involving growth and development, mental and neuromotor performance, immunocompetence, physical working capacity, morbidity, mortality, overall reproductive performance, and increased risk of maternal death [11–13]. In terms of proportion of the global population affected and its impact, the ranking of the 26 major risk factors of the global burden of disease ranked iron deficiency 9th, zinc deficiency 11th, and vitamin A deficiency 13th [14]. In addition, the Copenhagen Consensus listed providing micronutrients as second highest on the priority list of solutions to the world's great challenges; the list was based on a cost–benefit analysis of where money would be well spent for achieving measurable, much-needed, and lasting change [15].

### 30.2.1  *Vitamin and Mineral Deficiencies in Infants and Young Children*

Infants and young children are particularly at risk of VMDs. It starts with the fact that VMDs are present throughout the life cycle, and an infant born to a mother with VMDs will have lower stores of some nutrients at birth (e.g., iron), even when born at term and without low birth weight (thus, > 2500 g) [16]. Then, the presence of maternal micronutrient deficiencies during lactation can cause a major reduction in the concentration of some of these nutrients in breast milk, with subsequent infant depletion [17]. Priority nutrients for supplementing lactating women include thiamin, riboflavin, vitamin $B_6$, vitamin $B_{12}$, vitamin A, and iodine; this priority is based on the fact that low maternal intake or low store reduces the amount of these nutrients in breast milk by about 50%, and maternal supplementation can reverse this problem [17]. Maternal supplementation with iron, however, does not change the iron content of breast milk; therefore, infants suspected of low iron stores need to be supplemented directly.

From the age of 6 months, the nutrient needs of infants need to be met by breast milk and complementary foods. Therefore, Gibson et al. [18] assessed the nutrient content of a wide array of common home-prepared complementary foods and compared it with infant requirements. Even when possible modifications of the recipes were considered, such as adding extra ASFs and reductions of absorption-inhibiting components such as phytate, the array would be unlikely to meet requirements for zinc, iron, and calcium. Allen also stated that ASFs are an essential component of the diet for both micronutrients and growth, but that ASF alone, even with a feasible, moderate, extra intake, may not provide enough V&M for young children [19].

Thus, multiple micronutrients are very likely to be limited in the diets of young children between ages 6 and 23 months old in developing countries, and often their status is already compromised before then. Therefore, extra V&M need to be added to the diets of young children to improve development and growth and reduce morbidity and mortality. This can be in the form of supplements, fortification of complementary foods (note that fortification of staples does not increase the intake of young children enough because of their lower intake), or home fortification of any foods provided.

### 30.2.2   Why Supply a Combination of Vitamins and Minerals?

Because poor dietary quality is the main cause of VMDs, these deficiencies do not occur in isolation but rather concurrently, and the underlying reason for a particular condition (e.g., anemia) may be a deficiency of several V&M rather than of just one [13]. Thus, latent deficiencies of other V&M can suppress the effect of a single micronutrient. This and the fact that VMDs often occur together are strong arguments for supplementation with multiple V&M.

Furthermore, in addition to the independent effects of various micronutrients, the existence of interactions between micronutrients is a second argument for supplementing with multiple instead of single micronutrients. For example, vitamin C increases the absorption of iron [20]; vitamin A deficiency can limit the body's response to iron supplementation [21, 22] and to iodine supplementation [23]; copper deficiency may lead to IDA (iron deficiency anemia) [9, 24, 25]; zinc is involved in the conversion of β-carotene to vitamin A [26]; and riboflavin depletion impairs absorption and increases the rate of gastrointestinal loss of endogenous iron and possibly other minerals [27]. Also, micronutrients compete, for example, for absorption (iron vs. zinc, zinc vs. copper, and calcium vs. iron), which is another reason not to supply just a few micronutrients in isolation.

A fourth argument is that VMDs, through increased risk of infection and hence reduced appetite as well as poorer absorption, increased needs, and increased losses of V&M, sustain and aggravate themselves. Thus, multimicronutrient supplementation may also affect nutritional status indirectly by reducing losses through preventing infection. For example, zinc and vitamin A supplementation may reduce malaria morbidity [28, 29]; zinc and iron supplementation may result in a lower helminth reinfection rate or intensity [30, 31]; and reducing severity and duration of diarrhea with zinc reduces the duration of malabsorption of other V&M.

### 30.2.3   Need for Vitamins and Minerals is Particularly High in Emergencies

In the case of an emergency in a developing country, the need for increasing the intake of V&M is even higher and occurs among a larger age range [32, 33]. The needs are so high because livelihoods and food crops are lost; food supplies are interrupted; diarrheal diseases may break out; and infectious diseases suppress the appetite while increasing the need for micronutrients to help fight illness. Recognizing this, WHO/WFP/UNICEF issued a statement in 2006 regarding prevention and control of the problem in emergencies [34]. Because of this, the need for a good review of the evidence of impact of V&M preparations and suggestions on how to implement distribution of V&M is essential.

Evidence for an impact of V&M on improved nutritional status, better growth, and less morbidity and mortality are reviewed next.

## 30.3   METHODS USED FOR REVIEWING IMPACT OF INCREASED INTAKE OF VITAMINS AND MINERALS BY CHILDREN

Studies to assess the impact of an increased intake of V&M by children have used different ways to increase intake, including (1) dietary modification for increasing V&M content and reduction of inhibitors; (2) home fortification using sprinkles, foodlets, or spreads; and (3) fortification of complementary foods.

For a study to be reviewed here, it had to have used multimicronutrients (at least five V&M) and been conducted among young children (<5 years of age). Table 30.1 shows for each included study the age group studied, duration of the intervention, number of subjects and treatment for each group, and categories of outcome assessed. Tables 30.2a and 30.2b give the composition of the supplements used, which is discussed in detail in Section 30.4. Most of the studies were very different regarding composition of supplement, duration of intervention, primary outcome of interest, and age and nutritional status of the subjects.

First, the composition of supplements is reviewed in comparison with the recommended intake of V&M for young children. Then, the outcomes of the studies are reviewed by category of outcome, including micronutrient status, growth and development, and morbidity and mortality.

While ascertainment of consumption of supplements or foods varied among the studies reported, all but one of the studies were conducted under carefully controlled circumstances with ensured access to the supplement or food and visits to check on compliance. Only one report was available of an effectiveness study [35]. Therefore, there are specific recommendations for assessing effectiveness of V&M interventions. This is particularly relevant for when the need is high, and withholding supplements would not be ethical or feasible.

## 30.4   VITAMIN AND MINERAL SUPPLEMENTS, RECOMMENDED INTAKE, AND COMPOSITION OF SUPPLEMENTS USED

Deciding on the composition of a supplement may seem simple and straightforward, for example, by choosing one recommended dietary allowance (RDA). However, several issues make this less easy, including (1) the supplement or fortification comes in addition to an existing intake of other foods and often breast milk, (2) existing VMDs may benefit more from a composition that specifically addresses these particular VMDs by having a higher content than one RDA for some V&M and lower for others, and (3) RDAs or AIs (adequate intakes) are formulated for narrower age ranges than the age range of the target groups that are usually chosen.

Table 30.3 presents the recommended intake, according to different references, for young children [36–40]. Because of the revision of the dietary reference intakes (DRIs) by the Institute of Medicine (IOM) in 2004 [36] and the publication of the WHO/FAO (Food and Agricultural Organization) guidelines in 2002 [37], older formulations have a different composition compared to the more recent recommendations. In addition, International Zinc Nutrition Consultative Group (IZiNCG) has just published its reference intakes for zinc, which are largely based on the IOM DRIs, namely, 5 mg/day for 6- to 11-month-old children (unless the diet is more refined and contains substantial animal foods, in which case it is 4 mg/day); 3 mg/day for 1- to 3-year-olds; and 5 mg/day for

**Table 30.1**
Studies included in the review

| Reference: Country | Age at baseline | Duration | Treatments and notes | Micro-nutrient status | Reported impact on Growth | Morbidity indicators |
|---|---|---|---|---|---|---|
| IRIS Study Group [56]: Peru, South Africa, Vietnam, Indonesia, pooled | 6–12 mo | 6 mo | Daily V&M at 1 RDA daily multi micronutrients (DMM); weekly V&M at 2 RDA weekly multi micronutrients (WMM); daily iron at 1 RDA daily iron (DI); placebo All in the form of a dispersible tablet | X | X | X (except Vietnam, and no pooled analysis) |
| Thu et al. [57]: Vietnam | 6–24 mo | 3 mo | Daily V&M at 1 RDA (DMM); weekly V&M at 1-5 times the RDA (WMM); placebo All in the form of a syrup (1 mL) | X | X | |
| Rivera et al. [68]: Mexico | 8–14 mo | 12.2 mo | Daily V&M at 1–3 times RDA (DMM); placebo All in the form of a beverage (30 mL, 30 kcal) | | X | |
| Penny et al. [59]: Peru | 6–35 mo | 6 mo | Daily V&M at 1 RDA (DMM); daily zinc; placebo All in the form of a beverage Note: Enrollment criteria: suffered from a persistent diarrhea episode before study start | X | X | X |
| Sharieff et al. [50]: Pakistan | 6–12 mo | 2 mo | Daily V&M at 1 RDA (DMM); daily V&M at 1 RDA + heat-treated probiotics; placebo All in the form of sprinkles Note: Enrollment criteria: had diarrhea in preceding 2 wk | (X)[a] | | X |
| Sprinkles Global Health Initiative [51]: Bangladesh | 6–24 mo | 2, 3, or 4 mo | V&M at 1 RDA in the form of sprinkles | X | | |

| Study / Location | Age | Duration | Intervention | | | |
|---|---|---|---|---|---|---|
| | | | Three groups all received 60 sachets but had to finish in 2, 3, or 4 mo; no control group included | | X | X |
| Martini et al. [61]: Jakarta slums, Indonesia | 6–30 mo | 6 mo | Daily V&M at 1 RDA (DMM); control group no intervention V&M provided in the form of sprinkles (Vitalita) | X | X | X |
| Martini et al. [58]: rural West Java, Indonesia | 6–30 mo | 6 mo | Daily V&M at 1 RDA (DMM); control group no intervention V&M provided in the form of sprinkles | X | X | Not available yet |
| Lopriore et al. [60]: Saharawi refugees, Algeria | 3–6 yr | 6 mo | Daily V&M fortified spread at 3–5 times RDA (DMM); unfortified spread (only the 319 kcal/d), both with or without deworming (thus 4 groups total); control group no intervention Note: enrollment criteria: Height-for-Age Z-score (HAZ) < −2 SD | X | X | X |
| Menon et al. [35]: Haiti | 6–20 mo | 2 mo | Daily V&M + fortified wheat-soy blend (WSB); fortified WSB V&M provided in the form of sprinkles; no control group | X | | |
| Adu-Afarwuah et al. [62]: Ghana | 6 mo | 6 mo | Daily V&M as sprinkles, dispersible tablet, or spread (108 kcal); control group no intervention. | X | X | |
| Baqui et al. [52]: Bangladesh | 6 mo | 6 mo | Weekly supplements, all groups 1 mg riboflavin, in addition 20 mg iron; 20 mg zinc; 20 mg iron and 20 mg zinc; 20 mg iron, 20 mg zinc, and multi V&M; control (1 mg riboflavin only) | X | | X |

IRIS International Research on Infant Supplementation, RDA recommended dietary allowance, V&M vitamins and minerals.
[a]n for micronutrient status is 12–13 per group out of 21–25 per group (primary outcome was morbidity).

**Table 30.2a**

Composition of vitamin and mineral (V&M) preparations provided in different studies (or recommended in UNICEF/WHO/WFP 2005 statement)

| | IRIS Study Group [56], as foodlet | Penny et al. [59], as beverage | Thu et al. [57], as syrup, daily/weekly | Rivera et al. [68], as beverage[a] | WHO/WFP/UNICEF emergency guideline, 2006 [34], form not specified |
|---|---|---|---|---|---|
| Vit A (µg) | 375 | 450 | 333/1,700 | RDA × 1.2 | 400 |
| Vit D (IU, 10 IU = 1 µg) | 50 | 64 | | RDA × 1 | 50 |
| Vit E (mg/IU) | 6 | 8.5 | | v | 5 |
| Vit B$_1$ (mg), Thiamin | 0.5 | 1.75 | | v | 0.5 |
| Vit B$_2$ (mg), riboflavin | 0.5 | 1.45 | | RDA × 1.5 | 0.5 |
| Niacin (mg) | 6 | 11.5 | | v | 6 |
| Vit B$_6$ (mg) | 0.5 | | | v | 0.5 |
| Vit B$_{12}$ (µg) | 0.9 | 6.5 | | RDA × 1.5 | 0.9 |
| Vit C (mg) | 35 | 50 | 20/20 | RDA × 1.5 | 30 |
| Zn (mg) | 10 | 10 | 5/17 | RDA × 1.5 | 4.1 |
| Iron (mg) | 10 | 10 | 8/20 | RDA × 1.5 | 10.0 |
| Calcium (mg) | | | | | |
| Folic acid (µg) | 150 | 283 | | v | 150 |
| Pantothenic acid (mg) | | | | v | |
| Iodine (µg) | 59 | | | v | 90 |
| Copper (mg) | 0.8 | 0.65 | | v | 0.56 |
| Selenium (µg) | | 23 | | v | 17 |
| Sodium (mg) | | | | | |
| Phosphorus (mg) | | | | | |
| Potassium (mg) | | | | | |
| Magnesium (mg) | | 50 | | | |
| Vit K (µg) | | | | v | |
| Biotin (µg) | | | | v | |
| Manganese | | | | v | |
| Pyridoxine | | 1.55 | | | |

*IRIS* International Research on Infant Supplementation, *RDA* recommended dietary allowance, *UNICEF* United Nations International Children's Emergency Fund, *Vit* vitamin, *WFP* World Food Programme, *WHO* World Health Organization.

[a]RDA of NRC 1989 and 1999 for 1–3 years.

## Table 30.2b
Composition of vitamin and mineral (V&M) preparations provided in different studies (and plumpy'nut for comparison)

| | Vitalita sprinkles, Indonesia [58, 61] | Sharieff et al. [50]: sprinkles, Pakistan | SGHI [51]: sprinkles, Bangladesh | Menon et al. [35]: sprinkles, Haiti | Adu-Afarwuah et al. [62]: sprinkles, Ghana | Adu-Afarwuah et al. [62]: Nutritab, Ghana | Adu-Afarwuah et al. [62]: 20-g spread (108 kcal), Ghana | Lopriore et al. [60]: 50-g spread (319 kcal), Algeria | Plumpy'nut© sachet of 92 g (500 kcal) | Baqui et al. [52]: multimicronutrient weekly, Pakistan |
|---|---|---|---|---|---|---|---|---|---|---|
| Vit A (µg) | 375 | 300 | 300 | 400 | 300 | 400 (β-carotene) | 400 | 1,000 | 837 | |
| Vit D (IU, 10 IU = 1 µg) | 50 | 75 | | | 75 | – | – | 250 | 147 | 200 |
| Vit E (mg/IU) | 6 | | | | | | | 10 | 18.4 | 8 |
| Vit B$_1$ (mg), thiamin | 0.5 | | | | | 0.3 | 0.3 | 2 | 0.55 | 0.8 |
| Vit B$_2$ (mg), riboflavin | 0.5 | | | | | 0.4 | 0.4 | 2 | 1.66 | 1.0 |
| Niacin (mg) | 6 | | | | | 4 | 4 | 25 | 4.9 | 12 |
| Vit B$_6$ (mg) | 0.5 | | | | | 0.3 | 0.3 | 2 | 0.55 | |
| Vit B$_{12}$ (µg) | 0.9 | | | | | 0.5 | 0.5 | 2 | 0.49 | |
| Vit C (mg) | 35 | 50 | 50 | 30 | 50 | 30 | 30 | 63 | 13 | 70 |
| Zn (mg) | 5 | 5 | 5 | 5 | 5 | 4 | 4 | 20.5 | | 20 |
| Iron (mg) | 10 | 30 | 12.5 | 12.5 | 12.5 | 9 | 9 | 21 | 10.6 | 20 |
| Calcium (mg) | | | | | | 100 | 100 | 500 | 294 | |
| Folic acid (µg) | 150 | 150 | 160 | 160 | 150 | 80 | 80 | 250 | 193 | 70 |
| Vit B$_5$ (mg), pantothenic acid | | | | | | 1.8 | 1.8 | 12.5 | 2.85 | 6 |
| Iodine (µg) | 50 | | | | | 90 | 90 | | 101 | 100 |
| Copper (mg) | 0.6 | | | | | 0.2 | 0.2 | 1 | 1.64 | 1.2 |
| Selenium (µg) | | | | | | 10 | 10 | | 28 | 30 |
| Sodium (mg) | | | | | | | | | 174 | |
| Phosphorus (mg) | | | | | | | 82.13 | 318 | 362 | |
| Potassium (mg) | | | | | | 152 | 152 | 567 | 1,022 | |

(continued)

**Table 30.2b** (continued)

Composition of vitamin and mineral (V&M) preparations provided in different studies (and plumpy'nut for comparison)

| | Vitalita sprinkles, Indonesia [58, 61] | Sharieff et al. [50]: sprinkles, Pakistan | SGHI [51]: sprinkles, Bangladesh | Menon et al. [35]: sprinkles, Haiti | Adu-Afarwuah et al. [62]: sprinkles, Ghana | Adu-Afarwuah et al. [62]: Nutritab, Ghana | Adu-Afarwuah et al. [62]: 20-g spread (108 kcal), Ghana | Lopriore et al. [60]: 50-g spread (319 kcal), Algeria | Plumpy' nut© sachet of 92 g (500 kcal) | Baqui et al. [52]: multimicronutrient weekly, Pakistan |
|---|---|---|---|---|---|---|---|---|---|---|
| Magnesium (mg) | | | | | | | 16 | 78 | 85 | |
| Vit K (µg) | | | | | | | | | 19.3 | |
| Biotin (µg) | | | | | | | | | 59.8 | |
| Manganese | | | | | | | 0.08 | | | 1.6 |
| Pyridoxine | | | | | | | | | | 1.2 |

*SGHI* Sprinkles Global Health Initiative, *Vit* vitamin.

**Table 30.3**

Recommended daily intake of selected vitamins and minerals (V&M), according to different references, and upper limit of intake

| Nutrients | Priority and optimum nutrients to include in complementary foods and supplements [104] | RDA 6–11 mo, US/Canada '99 & '98 [38–40] | RDA 1–3 yr; US/Canada '99 & '98 [38–40] | FAO/WHO, 6–11 mo [37] | FAO/WHO, 1–3 yr [37] | IOM DRI, 6–11 mo [36] | IOM DRI. 12–24 mo [36] | Lutter & Dewey [43], filling the gap of RDA & intake, 6–24 mo | Upper limit according to IOM [34, 45] |
|---|---|---|---|---|---|---|---|---|---|
| Vit A (µg) | Priority | 375 | 400 | 400 | 400 | 500 | 300 | 250 | 600 |
| Vit D (IU, 10 IU = 1 µg) | Priority (rs) | 200 | 200 | 50 | 50 | 50 | 50 | 10–20 | 25–50 |
| Vit E (mg/IU) | Priority | 4 | 6 | na | na | 5 | 6 | na | 200 |
| Vit B$_1$ (mg), thiamin | Priority (esp. where rice is main staple) | 0.3 | 0.5 | 0.3 | 0.5 | 0.3 | 0.5 | 0.18 | na |
| Vit B$_2$ (mg), riboflavin | Priority | 0.3 | 0.5 | 0.4 | 0.5 | 0.4 | 0.5 | 0.18 | na |
| Niacin (mg) | Priority (esp. where corn is main staple) | 4 | 6 | 4 | 6 | 4 | 6 | 3.3 | 10 |
| Vit B$_6$ (mg) | | 0.1 | 0.5 | 0.3 | 0.5 | 0.3 | 0.5 | 0.22 | 30 |
| Vit B$_{12}$ (µg) | Priority (rs) | 0.5 | 0.9 | 0.5 | 0.9 | 0.5 | 0.9 | 0.26 | na |
| Vit C (mg) | Priority (rs) | 35 | 40 | 30 | 30 | 50 | 15 | 70–140 | 400 |
| Zn (mg) | Priority | 5 | 10 | 8.4 | 8.3 | 3 | 3 | 4–5 | 5–7 |
| Iron (mg) | Priority | 10 | 10 | 18.6 (9.3) | 11.6 (5.8) | 11 | 7 | 7–11 | 40 |
| Calcium (mg) | Optimum | 270 | 500 | | | | | | |
| Folic acid (µg) | Optimum | 80 | 150 | 80 | 160 | 80 | 150 | 41.5 | 300 |
| Pantothenic acid | | 1.8 | 2 | | | | | | |
| Iodine (µg) | Priority (rs) | 50 | 70 | na | 90 | 130 | 90 | 90 | 200 |
| Copper (mg) | Priority (rs) | 0.6–0.7 | 0.7–1.0 | na | na | 0.22 | 0.34 | 0.2–0.4 | 1 |
| Selenium | | | | | | | | | |
| Vit K | | | | | | | | | |
| Biotin | | | | | | | | | |
| Manganese | | | | | | | | | |

*DRI* dietary reference intake, *FAO* Food and Agricultural Organization, *IOM* Institute of Medicine, *RDA* recommended dietary allowance, *rs* region specific, *Vit* vitamin, *WHO* World Health Organization na not available.

4- to 8-year-olds (4 mg/day for refined diet) [41]. The AI levels are, in the absence of adequate data, used as a surrogate for the RDA in infants or for the average daily intake that is considered sufficient to meet the requirements of 97% to 98% of the population [38, 39]. The WHO consultation on feeding the non-breast-fed child aged 6–23 months resolved that the RDI for V&M would be that of the IOM or the FAO/WHO, whichever is lowest [42].

When the preferred approach is that the V&M preparation should meet the gap between recommended and existing intake, the intake from breast milk and common, home-prepared, complementary foods needs to be estimated. This has been done by Lutter and Dewey [43] (see Table 30.3), has been advocated by Zlotkin et al. [44], and was presented in the article by Nestel et al. [45] on the Boussingault meeting on complementary food supplements (CFSs). The last article stated that the concentrations of micronutrients in CFSs should result in a total daily intake of one to two recommended nutrient intakes (RNIs) for all children aged 6–23 months after the amounts already present in breast milk and complementary food are taken into account. In that approach, for each nutrient, the probability of deficiency in a population must be consider. Nutrients with moderate probability of deficiency can be included provided their tolerable upper intake level (see Table 30.3, based on IOM report, as well as Table 30.3 in the article by Nestel et al., based on WHO recommendations) is considerably higher than the usual intake. An important advantage of CFS that was mentioned by Nestel et al., which also applies to V&M preparations, is that they can provide an appropriate amount of nutrients for each child regardless of how much complementary food is consumed. This is important because intakes of processed complementary foods range tenfold depending on age and breast milk intake, in which case it is difficult to determine an appropriate fortification level for a complementary food.

The recent WHO/WFP/UNICEF statement on V&M in emergencies [34] recommends supplementing one RNI per day where no fortified foods are provided and two RNI per week if fortified foods are distributed. The basis for the choice of one RNI in the absence of fortified foods is that it is inherently safe and will fill any gap that may exist without reaching the upper tolerable intake level. It appears from Tables 30.2a and 30.2b that there is a minimum set of V&M in a multiple V&M preparation that includes at least iron, zinc, vitamin A, vitamin C, and folic acid, and that there is a common set that also includes, in addition to those five, the B vitamins, vitamins D and E, niacin, iodine, and copper.

The choice for one RDA was also made for the composition of the IRIS (International Research on Infant Supplementation) supplement [46]. In fact, the IRIS study had one group who received a daily V&M supplement containing one RDA and another group who received a weekly multimicronutrient supplement containing two RDAs (in addition to a daily iron group and a placebo group). The best results were found in the group who received one RDA daily (see next section), and therefore a daily supplement appears best. The same conclusion of the need for daily supplementation of children under 5 years was reached by Beaton and McGabe [47] in their review of studies of weekly versus daily iron supplementation among different target groups.

Once a choice for fortification levels has been made, the kind of compound or fortificant needs to be considered as well. This is especially important for iron. Specific publications should be consulted on this matter (see, e.g., [48, 49]).

## 30.5 EFFICACY OF MULTIMICRONUTRIENT SUPPLEMENTS FOR CHILDREN

The reason for giving V&M preparations to children is to avoid the negative consequences of VMDs, including reduced or impaired growth and development, mental and neuromotor performance, immunocompetence, and physical working capacity and increased morbidity and mortality. In an emergency setting, reducing the increased risk of morbidity and mortality is the immediate goal, followed by limiting the impact of VMDs on mental development and growth.

Here, guided by the availability of data and the focus on health and nutrition, the evidence for an impact on micronutrient status, morbidity, and growth is evaluated.

An important initiative studying the impact of multiple V&M preparations was formed in 1999 under the name IRIS (International Research on Infant Supplementation) because "although the potential benefit of multiple micronutrient supplement interventions is hypothetically strong, there is no concrete evidence of this in practice" [46]. The three convictions of IRIS were the following: (1) VMDs rarely occur as single-nutrient problems and should therefore be addressed concurrently; (2) combination of micronutrients to provide an average of one RDA or less is inherently safe; and (3) a convenient, novel, and perhaps intrinsically sustainable approach to public health delivery of multiple micronutrients to an infant population would be in the form of an edible food substance.

The results of the individual IRIS studies, conducted in Peru, South Africa, Indonesia, and Vietnam, are included here, as well as the pooled analysis, which has been considered a separate study.

### 30.5.1 Micronutrient Status

An improvement in micronutrient status is linked to improved performance, such as improved health, increased resistance to infection, increased developmental outcome, increased appetite, and so on. Indicators of micronutrient status include hemoglobin (Hb), serum zinc, serum ferritin and other iron status indicators, and serum concentrations of riboflavin, tocopherol, homocysteine, and so on. The impact on different indicators is discussed next.

#### 30.5.1.1 Hemoglobin and Anemia

Fifteen studies assessed the impact of multiple V&M on hemoglobin and anemia (see Tables 30.4 and 30.5, respectively). However, for one it was a secondary outcome, and the sample size was actually too small (12–13 per group; [50]) to allow a valid assessment, two studies did not have a negative control group [35, 51], and one study provided supplements on a weekly basis [52]. Of the other 11 studies, 8 found a significant impact on Hb [53–60], 2 an almost-significant impact [61, 62], and 1 of the 2 studies without a negative control group found an impact in the wheat-soy blend (WSB) plus sprinkles group compared to the WSB-only group [35], suggesting that sprinkles increased Hb. The study with the weekly supplement [52] and the IRIS study in Indonesia [63] found no impact on Hb. Of the 15 studies, 10 reported changes of anemia prevalence; in all cases, a reduction was documented (see Table 30.5).

In terms of magnitude of change, Hb improved less in the studies in Indonesia [58, 61, 63], South Africa [54], Haiti [35], Ghana [64], and Kenya [60] than in Vietnam [53, 57] and Peru [55, 59]. Similarly, it was noted by several investigators that the reduction of anemia was not

**Table 30.4**

Change of hemoglobin concentration (Hb, g/L) in the treatment groups of different studies[a]

| Reference: country | DMM | DI | WMM | Placebo | Impact of DMM |
|---|---|---|---|---|---|
| Hop & Berger [53]: Vietnam | 16.4 (12.4–20.4)[b] | 12.9 (8.4–17.3) | 15.0 (11.5–18.5) | 8.6 (5.0–12.2)[a] | Yes, higher than daily iron |
| Smuts et al. [54]: South Africa | 6.31 ± 1.75[b] | 2.47 ± 1.49 | 2.61 ± 1.33 | −0.56 ± 1.81[a] | Yes, higher than DI |
| López de Romana et al. [55]: Peru | 15 ± 4[b] | 16 ± 4[b] | 12 ± 4[b] | 4 ± 3[a] | Yes |
| Untoro et al. [63]: Indonesia | 6.4 ± 2.4 | 5.6 ± 2.6 | 2.5 ± 2.8 | 1.5 ± 1.8 | No |
| IRIS Study Group [56]: pooled | 11.0 (8.9–13.2)[b] | 9.6 (7.3–11.8)[b] | 8.4 (6.2–10.5)[b] | 3.3 (1.5–5.1)[a] | Yes |
| Thu et al. [57]: Vietnam | 15.5 ± 13.4[b] | | 13.2 ± 12.1[b] | −0.5 ± 8.8[a] | Yes |
| Martini et al. [61]: Jakarta, Indonesia[c] | 0.0 | | | −3.8 | Nearly, $p = .06$ |
| Martini et al. [58]: West Java, Indonesia | 8.6[a] | | | 3.3[b] | Yes |
| Penny et al. [59]: Peru | 15.3 ± 13.4[b] | Zinc only (10mg): 3.3 ± 1.4a | | 8.3 ± 13.2[a] | Yes |
| Sharieff et al. [50]: Pakistan[c] | 103 | Same V&M + probiotic: 102 | | 99 | n too small to determine |
| SGHI [51]: Bangladesh | 10.6 ± 18 (2mo) / 13.4 ± 15 (3mo) / 16.6 ± 16 (4mo) | | | Not included | Most likely yes, but control group lacking; Same dosage spread out over longer time had larger impact |

| Study | | | | |
|---|---|---|---|---|
| Lopriore et al. [60]: Algeria | 37[b] (fortified spread) | 19[a] (unfortified spread) | 16[a] | Yes; note that iron dose was 21 mg/d and other V&M levels at 1–5 times RDA |
| Menon et al. [35]: Haiti | 5[b] (sprinkles + WSB) | −2[a] (WSB only) | Not included | Yes, but only compared to fortified WSB; no control group included |
| Adu-Afarwuah et al. [62]: Ghana[b] | Sprinkles: 110 ± 14[ab]; Nutritab (crushable tablet): 112 ± 14[b]; Nutributter (20 g peanut spread + V&M): 114 ± 14[b] | | 106 ± 14[a] | Yes, but only significant for tablet and spread (16 and 19 V&M, respectively, compared to 6 V&M for sprinkles) |
| Baqui et al. [52]: Bangladesh | MM −0.6; Iron 1.6; Zinc −3.9; Iron + zinc −1.8 | | −1.6 | No; note that this was weekly supplementation with 20 mg iron, thus < 3 mg/d |

*RDA* recommended dietary allowance, *V&M* vitamins and minerals, *WSB* wheat-soy blend, *DMM* daily multi micronutrients, *WMM* weekly multi micronutrients, *DI* daily iron, *MM* multi micronutrients.

[a]Groups in the same row with a different letter are significantly different from each other.
[b]$p = .06$.
[c]Hb at end line (g/L).

**Table 30.5**

Change of anemia prevalence (Hb < 110 g/L) in the treatment groups of different studies

| | DMM | DI | WMM | P | Impact of DMM |
|---|---|---|---|---|---|
| Hop & Berger [53]: Vietnam | 93.4[a]<br>23.1[a] | 90.7<br>36.4 | 93.5<br>38.2 | 84.9<br>51.8[b] | Yes |
| López de Romana et al. [55]: Peru | 70.7<br>15.5[b] | 69.6<br>23.2[b] | 73.0<br>41.3[a] | 57.4<br>44.1[a] | Yes, same as daily iron |
| Untoro et al. [63]: Indonesia | 59.1<br>33.3[a] | 58.0<br>36.2 | 61.7<br>43.3 | 53.9<br>52.3[b] | Yes |
| IRIS Study Group [56]: pooled, including South Africa[b] | 67.1 | 64.9 | 67.4 | 58.6 | Yes |
| Thu et al. [57]: Vietnam[c] | 23.1<br>~50<br>~5 | 29.8 | 37.5<br>~48<br>~8 | 48.5<br>~38<br>~45 | Yes |
| Martini et al. [61]: Jakarta, Indonesia | 27.9 | | | 32.4 | Yes |
| Martini et al. [58]: West Java, Indonesia | 15.8[a]<br>33.7[a] | | | 42.6[b]<br>41.9[b] | Yes, difference at EL larger than at BL (14.1% at p < .001 vs. 8.2% at p < .05) |
| SGHI [51]: Bangladesh % of those nonanemic after intervention who were still nonanemic 6 mo later | 16.2[a] (p < .001)<br>75.9<br>45.4 (2 mo)<br>52.5 | 82.5<br>40.4 (3 mo)<br>79.6 | 72.4<br>30.2 (4 mo)<br>82.4 | 30.3[b] (p < .01)<br>Not included<br>(p < .05)<br>(p = .003) | Yes, although control group lacking; same dosage spread out over longer time had larger impact |
| Lopriore et al. [60]: Algeria | 78 (fortified spread)<br>9.8 | 82.8 (unfortified spread)<br>48.4 | | 80.0<br>60.0 | Yes, but no p value provided |
| Menon et al. [35]: Haiti | 53[b] (WSB + sprinkles)<br>29[a] | 37[a] (WSB)<br>45[b] | | Not included | Yes, but only compared to fortified WSB; no control group included |

BL baseline, EL end line, IRIS international research on infant supplementation, SGHI sprinkles global health initiative, WSB wheat-soy blend, DMM Daily Multi Micronutrients, WMM Weekly Multi Micronutrients, DI Daily Iron, P Placebo.

[a] First value in a column is prevalence at baseline; second value is prevalence at end line.

[b] Only tested for significance of change within group, not between groups.

[c] Findings presented in a figure, estimated from there.

complete. Between 5% [57] and 45% [51] were still anemic after the 2–6 months of intervention. There can be several reasons for this, including that higher dosage or longer duration of supplementation may be needed, that infection may have inhibited proper utilization of available iron [64], that the cutoff for Hb may be too high (should be 100 g/L at 9 months instead of 110 g/L [65]), or that the anemia was due not only to the V&M that were included in the supplement but also to other reasons.

The studies that compared V&M supplements to iron-only supplements (such as the IRIS studies) found that anemia tended to be reduced more in the case of V&M supplements, which supports the fact that anemia is due not only to iron deficiency but also to other simultaneously existing VMDs [10, 66].

### 30.5.1.2 FERRITIN AND IRON DEFICIENCY

Eight of the nine studies that assessed changes of serum ferritin concentration and all five that reported changes of prevalence of iron deficiency (see Tables 30.6 and 30.7, respectively) found a positive impact of the V&M supplement. For some, the impact was the same as for daily iron. For the Indonesian IRIS study, the impact of V&M was somewhat lower than for daily iron alone. Also, the magnitude of change of serum ferritin concentration or change of iron deficiency prevalence showed a dose-responsive relation with the amount of iron provided (daily vs. weekly supplements). The study with weekly supplements only found an impact only on ferritin of the iron, zinc, riboflavin supplement, but not of the multiple V&M supplement. The authors reported that the latter supplement was poorly tolerated.

### 30.5.1.3 SERUM RETINOL, VITAMIN A DEFICIENCY

Of the six studies that assessed whether the V&M supplement had an impact on serum retinol concentration, only one found an impact (see Table 30.8). The reason appears to be that that study started 4 months after the nationwide vitamin A capsule (VAC) distribution and then postponed the distribution of the next capsule to the study participants, which was due 6 months later, until after the end of the 3 months of the intervention [57]. In that case, the serum retinol concentration at baseline may not have been related to the previously received capsule anymore, and the impact of the vitamin A from the V&M supplement was therefore detectable. For the other studies, the normal VAC distribution programs were conducted as usual and likely to have masked any additional impact on serum retinol from the V&M supplements.

The fact that there was an impact in the one study in which VAC distribution was postponed, that the amount of vitamin A in the supplements was just one RDA, and that coverage of neither the capsules nor the V&M supplements would be 100% means that the V&M supplement should contain vitamin A, that they can be distributed where a VAC program is conducted, and that VAC programs should be continued where interventions with V&M supplements are planned.

### 30.5.1.4 SERUM ZINC AND ZINC DEFICIENCY

The results of studies on impact of V&M supplements on zinc status are mixed (see Table 30.9). Three of the eight studies found an impact, four found no impact, and one found an impact when compared to provision of iron only (which caused a deterioration of zinc status) but not when compared to placebo. One of the studies that compared V&M to zinc-only supplements found a larger impact when zinc only was given (same amount of zinc), but the zinc-only supplement had less impact on anemia than the V&M

**Table 30.6**

Change of serum ferritin concentration in the treatment groups of different studies

| Country | DMM | DI | WMM | P | Impact of DMM |
|---|---|---|---|---|---|
| Hop & Berger [53]: Vietnam (geometric mean) | 12.1[b] | 9.5[b] | −9.7[a] | −14.7[a] | Yes, same as daily iron |
| Smuts et al. [54]: South Africa (log) | 0.16 ± 0.26[b] | 0.14 ± 0.35[b] | −0.30 ± 0.29 | −0.84 ± 0.31[a] | Yes, same as daily iron |
| López de Romana et al. [55]: Peru (log) | 0.03 ± 0.33[a] | −0.16 ± 0.22[a] | −0.54 ± 0.20[b] | −0.71 ± 0.20[b] | Yes, same as daily iron |
| Untoro et al. [63]: Indonesia (median, range) | 12.0 (−249.3; 102.5)[c] | 22.3 (−102.2; 200.3)[d] | 1.0 (−121.2; 46.9)[b] | −4.5 (−250.0; 29.5)[a] | Yes, but higher in daily iron |
| IRIS Study Group [56]: pooled (log) | 0.28 (0.14–0.43)[c] | 0.30 (0.17–0.43)[c] | −0.28 (−0.41;−0.15)[b] | −0.68 (−0.81; −0.56)[a] | Yes, same as daily iron |
| Penny et al. [59]: Peru | 16.4 ± 24.2[b] | Zinc only: 8.1 ± 47.0[a,b] | | −0.5 ± 15.3[a] | Yes |
| Martini et al. [61]: Jakarta, Indonesia (mean change) | 6.1[a] | | | −3.2[b] | Yes |
| Adu-Afarwuah et al. [62]: Ghana | Sprinkles, Nutritab (crushable tablet), and Nutributter (20 g peanut spread + V&M) all improved ferritin and TfR compared to the non-intervention group (no detailed data in abstract) | | | | Yes |
| Baqui et al. [52]: Bangladesh | MM −18.4<br>Iron −18.0<br>Zinc −15.3<br>Iron + zinc −13.7 b | | | −21.7[a] | No, only the combination of iron, zinc, and riboflavin; note that this was weekly supplementation |

*IRIS* International Research on Infant Supplementation, *V&M* vitamins and minerals , *DMM* daily multi micronutrients, *WMM* weekly multi micronutrients, *DI* daily iron, *P* placebo, Tfr transferrin receptor.

**Table 30.7**
Change of iron-deficiency prevalence (serum ferritin < 12 μg/L) in the treatment groups of different studies

| | DMM | DI | WMM | P | Impact of DMM |
|---|---|---|---|---|---|
| Hop & Berger [53]: Vietnam | 6.7[a] | 5.9 | 15.2 | 9.1 | Yes, same as daily iron |
| | 0.0[a] | 0.0[a] | 28.9 | 50.0b | |
| Lopez de Romana et al. [55]: Peru | 52.8 | 50.9 | 75.0 | 62.7 | Yes, better than daily iron |
| | 49.1[b] | 69.5 | 90.4[a] | 88.1[a] | |
| Untoro et al. [63]: Indonesia | 36.4 | 31.9 | 31.0 | 39.3 | Yes, same as daily iron |
| | 4.5[a] | 4.5[a] | 34.3[b] | 56.7[c] | |
| IRIS Study Group [56]: pooled, including South Africa[b] | 43.9 | 44.5 | 51.0 | 48.0 | Yes, same as daily iron |
| | 26.3 | 30.8 | 60.3 | 75.2 | |
| Martini et al. [61]: Jakarta, Indonesia | 57.1 | | | 58.2 | Yes |
| | 38.6[a] | | | 59.6[b] | |

IRIS International Research on Infant Supplementation, DMM daily multi micronutrients, DI daily iron, WMM weekly multi micronutrients, P placebo.

[a] First value in a column is prevalence at baseline; second value is prevalence at end line.
[b] Only tested for significance of change within group, not between groups.

**Table 30.8**
Change of vitamin A deficiency prevalence (serum retinol < 0.70 μmol/L) in the treatment groups of different studies

| | DMM | DI | WMM | P | Impact of DMM |
|---|---|---|---|---|---|
| Hop & Berger [53]: Vietnam | 26.7[1] | 17.6 | 21.7 | 15.9 | No |
| | 4.4 | 7.8 | 2.2 | 6.8 | |
| López de Romana et al. [55]: Peru | 5.7 | 10.2 | 9.6 | 3.4 | No |
| | 9.4 | 6.8 | 5.8 | 5.1 | |
| Untoro et al. [63]: Indonesia | 20.6 | 16.9 | 29.8 | 31.9 | No |
| | 7.9 | 15.4 | 12.3 | 10.3 | |
| IRIS Study Group [56]: pooled, including South Africa[b] | 19.4 | 14.3 | 20.2 | 14.4 | No |
| | 8.7 | 10.0 | 8.8 | 8.7 | |
| Thu et al. [57]: Vietnam[c] | ~60 | | ~35 | ~38 | Yes |
| | ~8 | | ~8 | ~38 | |
| Martini et al. [61]: Jakarta, Indonesia | 26.4 | | | 51.5 | No |
| | 20.7 | | | 39.7 | |

IRIS International Research on Infant Supplementation, DMM daily multi micronutrients, DI daily iron, WMM weekly multi micronutrients, P placebo.

[a] First value in a column is prevalence at baseline; second value is prevalence at end line.
[b] Only tested for significance of change within group, not between groups.
[c] Findings presented in a figure, estimated from there.

**Table 30.9**

Change of zinc-deficiency prevalence (<10.7 μmol/L) in the treatment groups of different studies

| | DMM | DI | WMM | P | Impact of DMM |
|---|---|---|---|---|---|
| Hop & Berger [53]: Vietnam | 29.5[a] | 15.7 | 17.8 | 26.2 | No |
| | 17.8 | 25.7 | 26.7 | 31.8 | |
| López de Romana et al. [55]: Peru | 43.4 | 40.7 | 32.7 | 40.7 | Yes, compared to iron, not compared to placebo |
| | 20.8[b] | 39.0a | 17.3[b] | 33.9 | |
| Untoro et al. [63]: Indonesia | 9.1 | 15.6 | 5.2 | 11.7 | Yes, and worsening in iron-only group |
| | 1.6a | 32.8c | 10.3[b] | 15.0[b] | |
| IRIS Study Group [56]: pooled, including South Africa[b] | 33.6 | 28.6 | 22.3 | 28.6 | No |
| | 17.1 | 36.7 | 20.2 | 29.1 | |
| Thu et al. [57] –Vietnam[c] | ~45 | | ~30 | ~30 | Yes |
| | ~6 | | ~2 | ~22 | |
| Penny et al. [59]: Peru, change (μg/dL) | 16.2 ± 29.8[b] | Zinc only: 27.3 ± 33.7[c] | | 6.1 ± 23.0[a] | Yes, and zinc only had highest impact |
| Martini et al. [61]: Jakarta, Indonesia | 55.0 | | | 60.3 | No |
| | 39.3 | | | 42.6 | |
| Baqui et al. [52]: Bangladesh[d] | WMM 0.07 | | | 0.05[a] | No, only of weekly iron, zinc, and riboflavin; note that this was weekly supplementation |
| | Iron, weekly 0.05 Zinc, weekly 0.08 Iron + zinc, weekly 0.07[b] | | | | |

*IRIS* International Research on Infant Supplementation, *DMM* daily multi micronutrients, *WMM* weekly multi micronutrients, *DI* daily iron, *P* placebo.

[a]First value in a column is prevalence at baseline; second value is prevalence at end line.

[b]Only tested for significance of change within group, not between groups.

[c]Findings presented in a figure, estimated from there.

[d]Change between baseline and 6 mo is shown.

supplement. The study with weekly supplements found a comparable impact of iron plus zinc, zinc, and multiple V&M compared to placebo and less impact of iron compared to placebo.

Thus, while it appears that iron-only supplements have a negative impact on zinc status, the addition of zinc did not reduce zinc deficiency in all studies. In the study in Peru, for example, zinc deficiency was still present in 50% of children at the end of the intervention. The reasons for this are not clear. One constraint may be that, while serum zinc is used as the best available and feasible indicator of changes of zinc status, it is not a great indicator of zinc status per se [41] and may therefore in fact not be very sensitive for detecting changes.

The main benefit of adding zinc actually is in reducing morbidity. Therefore, assessment of this functional outcome is very important to really assess the impact of the zinc in V&M preparations.

### 30.5.1.5 IRON AND ZINC INTERACTION

Another issue with regard to V&M supplementation is the possible interaction between iron and zinc. A review of the issue found that supplementation with zinc alone did not have a negative impact on Hb or iron status among young children in six studies and had a positive effect in two studies [67]. In the ten reviewed studies among infants and one among young children (18–36 months) that provided iron supplements, no effect on serum zinc was observed, except for the IRIS studies, in which the pooled analysis as well as the study done in Indonesia observed a negative effect on zinc status [63]. Of the studies, or arms of studies, among young children that provided iron and zinc together, which would be the case when using a multiple V&M preparation, results were various, with a tendency to have less impact on iron status as compared to giving iron alone. However, the benefits of adding zinc may well outweigh the smaller, but still positive, impact of iron on iron status. The benefits of combining zinc with iron, as compared to giving iron alone, are most likely a reduction of morbidity due to the zinc, but data to confirm this are provided by only one study because only two of the studies reviewed by Walker et al. considered morbidity outcomes.

### 30.5.1.6 OTHER MICRONUTRIENTS

Only the IRIS studies assessed impact on other micronutrients, namely, riboflavin, tocopherol, and homocysteine (see Table 30.10). The studies in South Africa [54] and

**Table 30.10**

Changes of serum concentrations of riboflavin, tocopherol, and homocysteine in different IRIS studies, assessed or not (yes/no)

|  | Riboflavin (increase) | Tocopherol (increase) | Homocysteine (reduction) |
|---|---|---|---|
| Hop & Berger [53]: Vietnam | No | Yes | No |
| López de Romaña et al. [55]: Peru | No | No | No |
| Untoro et al. [63]: Indonesia | Yes | Yes | Yes |
| Smuts et al. [54]: South Africa | Yes | Yes | Yes |
| IRIS Study Group [56]: pooled[a] | Yes | Yes | Yes |

*IRIS* International Research on Infant Supplementation.

Indonesia [63] and the pooled analysis [56] found an impact on all three compounds, while the study in Peru found no impact on any of them, and the study in Vietnam only documented an impact on tocopherol. This may indicate that the deficiency of these compounds (note that folate is meant to reduce homocysteine levels) may not be equally present in all locations. However, information about tolerable upper intake levels shows that the likelihood of overdosing on these compounds is very small. Because of that, an approach in which one formulation, of one RDA, is chosen for all locations is unlikely to be a problem.

### 30.5.2   Growth

Impact of V&M on growth has been assessed by several studies, with various results (see Table 30.11). Most often, no impact was found on linear growth. Slightly more often, but still uncommon, some impact was found on weight gain. It appears that the studies that found an impact studied a selective subgroup of the population who were worse off and hence had more potential for catch-up growth, for example, those who were stunted [57, 60] or infants born with low birth weight [53, 68]. It should also be noted that when an impact was found, its magnitude was limited. None of the studies found a reversal of growth faltering; only reduced faltering was reported.

Other studies, using different interventions such as zinc supplementation or various kinds of complementary foods, have also found that achieving an impact on growth is not easy [69–71]. Several hypotheses have been brought forward to explain this, including that growth may be constrained by frequent infections as well as prenatal conditions, and that having an impact on growth is dependent on dosage of micronutrients, inclusion of all the particular micronutrients, macrominerals and essential fatty acids [62] that constrain growth, age, nutritional status, breast-feeding status, and potential for catch-up growth.

On the other hand, stunting and underweight may not be the best indicators of an impact on body composition as a study by Yeudall et al. [72] found an increase of lean body mass but no impact on weight or height. Such alterations in the relative proportions of fat to lean tissue have been related to changes in zinc status in earlier studies of severely malnourished children [73, 74] and of stunted rural African children [75–77]. Another indicator that may be more sensitive to changes of growth is knee height [78].

While it can be hypothesized that fortified complementary foods can improve growth better than V&M supplements because they also provide more energy, macronutrients, macrominerals and essential amino acids as well as fatty acids, results have not been uniform. Several studies with fortified complementary foods did not improve linear growth. This may be due to their composition, bioavailability of the V&M [79], the fact that it replaces part of the normal diet and hence the net increase of V&M intake is smaller, or the target group and duration chosen were not optimal. However, some studies did report an impact, including the study that provided a V&M-fortified peanut spread as a CFS. That study compared sprinkles containing 6 V&M, a crushable tablet containing 16 V&M, and a 20-g spread containing 19 V&M (for each vitamin or mineral that was included in one or more of the preparations, the amount provided was the same) and found only an impact on growth in the group who received the spread [62]. This may be due to the extra macronutrients it provided, including the omega-3 fatty acids, in addition to the V&M. This study was conducted among infants from the age of 6 months until 12 months.

**Table 30.11**

Impact on growth of treatment provided in different studies

| Study | Age group (baseline), duration | Treatment of compared groups | Impact on growth | Impact on length/height | Impact on weight |
|---|---|---|---|---|---|
| Hop & Berger [53]: Vietnam | 6–12 mo, for 6 mo | DMM vs. DI, WMM, placebo | LAZ decreased less in DMM (−0.32 vs. −0.49 for P and −0.51 for WMM); stunting increased in DMM from 11% to 19%, while for P it increased from 5.5% to 23.3% | Yes | No |
| López de Romana et al. [55]: Peru | 6–12 mo, for 6 mo | DMM vs. DI, WMM, placebo | No impact on length or weight, growth faltering occurred in all groups; however, more overweight than underweight and LBW infants were excluded (in all IRIS studies) | No | No |
| Untoro et al. [63]: Indonesia | 6–12 mo, for 6 mo | DMM vs. DI, WMM, placebo | No impact on length or weight, growth faltering occurred in all groups | No | No |
| Smuts et al. [54]: South Africa | 6–12 mo, for 6 mo | DMM vs. DI, WMM, placebo | No impact on length or weight, but trend for less weight faltering in DMM | No | No, but + trend |
| IRIS Study Group [56]: pooled | 6–12 mo, for 6 mo | DMM vs. DI, WMM, placebo | Height gain no difference | | |
| | | | Weight gain higher in DMM (207 g/mo vs. 192 for WMM and 186 for DI and P), but growth faltered in all groups | No | Yes |
| Thu et al. [57]: Vietnam | 6–24 mo, 3 mo | DMM, WMM, placebo | HAZ increased among stunted by 0.48 (DMM) and 0.37 (WMM), no difference among nonstunted | Yes, among stunted only | No |
| Rivera et al. [68]: Mexico | 8–14 mo, 12.2 mo | DMM vs. placebo | Children < 12 mo grew 8.3 mm more over 12-mo period than growth among placebo and older children (total length gain in those two groups: 10.3 cm). The 8.3 mm ~ 0.30 LAZ score | Yes, among < 12 mo only | No |

(continued)

**Table 30.11** (continued)

Impact on growth of treatment provided in different studies

| Study | Age group (baseline), duration | Treatment of compared groups | Impact on growth | Impact on length/height | Impact on weight |
|---|---|---|---|---|---|
| Martini et al. [61]: Jakarta, Indonesia | 6–30 mo | DMM vs. control | No impact on length or weight | No | No |
| Martini et al. [58]: West Java, Indonesia | 6–30 mo | DMM vs. control | No impact on length or weight | No | No |
| Penny et al. [59]: Peru | 6–35 mo, 6 mo (previously suffered diarrhea) | MM + zinc, zinc alone, placebo | No impact on growth (weight, length, MUAC, sum of 4 skinfolds) | No | No |
| Lopriore et al. [60]: Algeria | 3–6 y, 6 mo (HAZ score <−2) | Spread with MM (fortified spread, FS), (unfortified spread US), both with or without metronidazole, control | 30% faster linear growth among FS compared to US and control groups (gained 4.2 cm vs. 3.5 and 3.5 cm, respectively); HAZ at end line −2.68 vs. −2.84 and −3.00, respectively | Yes, note that all children were stunted, and that dosage was 1–5 times RDA | Yes |
| Adu-Afarwuah et al. [62]: Ghana | 6 mo, 6 mo | Sprinkles (6 V&M), Nutritab (16 V&M), Nutributter (20 g peanut spread + 19 V&M), and control | Nutributter group had significantly higher weight-for-age and length-for-age than other three groups (effect size ~ 0.3) | No for sprinkles and tablet, yes for fortified spread (20 g) | No for sprinkles and tablet, yes for fortified spread (20 g) |

*IRIS* International Research on Infant Supplementation, *LBW* low birth weight, *MUAC* mid-upper arm circumference, *RDA* recommended dietary allowance, *V&M* vitamins and minerals, *LAZ* Length-for-Age Z-score, *DMM* Daily Multi Micronutrients, *DI* Daily Iron, *WMM* Weekly Multi Micronutrients, *MM* Multi-Micronutrients.

In summary, interventions addressing growth are most likely to be effective among young children (< about 12 months) who are already stunted, and the intervention should be implemented for a relatively long period of time [70].

### 30.5.3 Morbidity and Mortality

The main micronutrients that are known to have an impact on morbidity and mortality are zinc and vitamin A [80–82]. Because of the reduction of child mortality due to vitamin A supplementation, VAC distribution programs are now implemented in many developing countries; food aid includes foods, especially oil, fortified with vitamin A; and VAC distribution is often included in an emergency response. Zinc has recently been recommended as adjunct for diarrhea treatment by WHO and UNICEF because it reduces the duration and severity of the episode as well as reduces the risk of another episode in the next few months [82]. The extent to which V&M preparations, which contain not only vitamin A and zinc in moderate amounts but also other micronutrients (including iron), can reduce morbidity due to infectious diseases has been the subject of a few, but not many, studies.

The main illnesses that are often considered are malaria, diarrhea, ARI (acute respiratory infection), fever, and pneumonia, while common biochemical indicators of infection include C-reactive protein (CRP), $\alpha$1-acid glycoprotein (AGP), and total white blood cell count. However, for ARI, results need to be interpreted with caution because an increase of coughing may indicate a response of the body in an attempt to prevent a more severe respiratory tract infection.

#### 30.5.3.1 EVIDENCE FROM REVIEWED STUDIES

Among the studies reviewed, the pooled analysis of the IRIS studies found no impact on CRP or AGP (biochemical indicators of infection) [56]; the results were the same for the Vitalita study conducted in Jakarta [61], which suggests that there was no effect of the interventions on infection rates or response to infections, or that the studies did not have enough subjects to detect such an impact. No pooled analysis was conducted for the IRIS studies for symptoms of morbidity (cough, diarrhea, fever) because each of the studies collected and reported such information in a different way or not at all [53]. Of the three studies that assessed morbidity symptoms [54, 55, 63], none reported an impact. Diarrhea prevalence in South Africa was 20.7% during the previous week, and in Peru children had diarrhea on 20–40% of the days per month. Lopriore et al., who provided a fortified and nonfortified spread to different groups, with or without deworming, found no impact on diarrhea, fever, or cough [60].

Penny et al., who compared three treatments among Peruvian infants, found higher morbidity in the zinc with V&M group compared to the zinc-only group [59]. Treatments were provided in the form of a drink. Particular symptoms that were higher in the zinc with V&M group compared to the zinc-only group were severe diarrhea (2.34 episodes/100 days vs. 1.63 in zinc [$p < .05$] and 1.97 [ns] in the placebo group); days with cough (54.7% of observed days vs. 42% [$p < .01$] and 51% [ns], respectively); and days with fever (7.3% of observed days vs. 5.6% [$p = .06$] and 6.6% [ns], respectively). The authors hypothesized that the lower plasma zinc concentration observed in the zinc with V&M group compared to the zinc-only group was due to the iron (10 mg/day) included in the V&M mix. Another study by Baqui and colleagues in Bangladesh [52] found that a multimicronutrient supplement provided once a week had no added benefit on morbidity compared to just supplying iron and zinc (20 mg each per week, also in the multimicronutrient supplement) and actually increased the risk of diarrhea by 15–22%.

However, the study by Sharieff et al. in Pakistan [50], which provided sprinkles containing 5 mg zinc, 30 mg iron, 50 mg vitamin C, 300 µg vitamin A, and 150 µg folic acid for 2 months (most subjects took 30–40 doses) to 6- to 11-month-old children who had suffered diarrhea in the 2 weeks before the trial, found a lower longitudinal prevalence of diarrhea compared to placebo as well as to the same V&M supplement with added heat-treated probiotics (15% vs. 26% and 26%, respectively) [50]. Febrile days were also reduced in the V&M group but not in the other two groups. As a 5% increase in longitudinal prevalence of diarrhea is associated with a 17% increased risk of mortality, these findings are very important. This study, which provided an even higher amount of iron than used in the studies by Penny et al. [59] and Baqui et al. [52], contradicts the findings of the other studies. One reason may be that the study by Sharieff et al. provided the V&M in the form of sprinkles and hence as (home) fortified food rather than in aqueous solution or tablet.

### 30.5.3.2  COULD VITAMIN AND MINERAL SUPPLEMENTATION INCREASE MORBIDITY?

The studies by Penny et al. [59] and Baqui et al. [52] are not the only ones that raise concerns about the possibility that iron supplementation of infants and young children, with or without other V&M, could increase the risk of infections. For example, non-anemic infants who were supplemented with iron in either Sweden or Honduras had significantly more diarrheal events than a placebo group [83]. However, a rigorous meta-analysis by Gera and Sachdev [84] that included 28 trials from a variety of environments found no more infection among the iron-supplemented compared to the placebo children, with an exception for diarrhea. However, the finding that iron-supplemented children suffered 0.05 episodes more per year is of very limited clinical significance. And, Oppenheimer, based on a review of iron and its relation to immunity and infectious disease [85], concluded that there is no evidence that parenteral iron and oral iron supplementation, given after the neonatal period and in nonmalarious areas, increase the risk of infection in any age group.

Explanations for the observed increase of diarrhea, albeit small, in response to iron supplementation is that it could create a local iron-rich environment that would enhance bacterial proliferation because it is known that many pathogens require iron [86] or impair mucosal immune function, possibly in response to iron-induced cytokine secretion [87]. And, as also stated by Oppenheimer [85], newborn infants should not receive iron because their erythropoietic response to iron may be immature [65], they may be especially sensitive to free-radical formation and oxidative stress induced by iron supplements, and they may not be as able as adults to downregulate their iron absorption according to their needs [88].

The issue of iron supplementation in malarious areas has been frequently investigated and reviewed [84, 85] and remains controversial because of the various angles from which it is being looked at, for instance, from the point of view that not addressing iron deficiency anemia has severe consequences for mental and physical performance of individuals and society as a whole at present and into the future or the point of view that iron supplementation may increase severe morbidity and mortality among non-iron-deficient individuals who suffer from malaria. The latter was the reason to halt the "Pemba trial" in 2004 as it was found that the risk of severe illness and death was increased on iron supplementation in a highly malaria-endemic area [89]. However, it should be noted that the increased risk was small, that no increased risk was observed in a substudy in an area where malaria transmission was controlled using treated bed nets and treatment of suspected cases, and that malaria was very highly endemic in the area [90]. Also, the concurrent study in Nepal reported no increase of morbidity among children receiving iron supplements [91]. Morbidity in the Pemba trial appeared to result from increased clinical severity of malarial episodes and associated infections rather than increased prevalence. Also, the risk associated with iron supplementation appeared to be restricted to children who had adequate functional iron reserves as judged by normal zinc protoporphyrin ($\mu$mol)/heme (mol) (ZPP/H) levels.

Based on the Pemba trial as well as other findings on malaria and iron (see, e.g., the review by Oppenheimer [85]) and on the consequences of withholding iron to iron-deficient populations, experts have recommended the following [93]: In highly malaria-endemic areas, malaria control measures should be implemented, and iron supplements should only be given to iron-deficient individuals. However, screening for iron deficiency is as yet not easy because of the lack of an easy field test for serum transferrin receptor (serum ferritin is increased in the case of infection and therefore does not adequately reflect iron status). Therefore, the prevalence of iron-deficiency anemia in a population should be used as a proxy for the chance that an individual child living in the area suffers from iron deficiency and therefore receive additional iron. To be on the safe side, particularly in the absence of a possibility to screen individuals for iron deficiency, it was stated that foods fortified with iron can be provided to anyone. The summary of the WHO consultation also states "The safety of iron preparations administered through home fortification of complementary foods for infants and young children (i.e., powders, crushable tablets, and fat-based spreads) is uncertain in malaria-endemic areas. Although there is reason to believe that those preparations may be safer than iron supplements, they cannot be recommended until this has been demonstrated [92].

In summary, current knowledge supports supplementation with a number of V&M, in particular concurrent supplementation of iron and zinc, together with iodine, vitamin A, vitamin C, and possibly other V&M as well, such as B vitamins, folic acid, vitamins D and E, niacin, and copper. In malaria-endemic areas, prevalence and causes of anemia, including iron deficiency, seasonal malaria endemicity, protective hemoglobinopathies, and age-specific immunity, need to be taken into account in planning an intervention. Such an intervention should include malaria control measures (insecticide-treated bed nets, availability and good access to malaria detection and treatment, etc.) in conjunction with measures to control iron-deficiency anemia, whether through a blanket or target approach. The choice of approach will also determine the best choice of sources of iron, with fortified foods preferred over home fortificants and supplements.

### 30.5.3.3  OTHER WAYS TO REDUCE MORBIDITY

It should also be noted that it is not just iron that can reduce anemia among severely anemic children, especially when infection is highly prevalent. For example, treatment of severely anemic children with vitamin A in a setting with severe malnutrition and where malaria is holoendemic was associated with rapid changes indicative of reduced inflammation, iron mobilization, and stimulated erythropoiesis [94].

In other situations, other measures are more likely to reduce morbidity than increasing the intake of V&M. For example, Ciliberto et al. [95] compared RUTF (ready-to-use therapeutic food) to standard inpatient treatment (F100) followed by home treatment (corn-soy blend, CSB), both of which were fortified with vitamins and minerals, among children with severe malnutrition (<–3 SD Weight-for-Height Z-score (WHZ), as well as other criteria commonly used in Malawi). The lower prevalence (~50% less) of fever, cough, and diarrhea among the children on RUTF was ascribed to the reduced length or absence of a stay in a nutrition rehabilitation unit, which markedly reduced the risk of getting infected due to crowding of sick people.

### 30.5.4   Development (Cognitive, Learning Ability)

As mentioned, none of the studies included in the review assessed the impact on cognitive and psychomotor development or learning ability. However, as several studies of iron supplementation have shown, improvement of iron status improves cognitive development [96, 97]. Therefore, supplements that improve iron nutriture are likely to have an impact on cognitive development in the future. Similarly, starting treatment of iron deficiency later in childhood, for example, at age 18 months, appears to already result in irreversible damage [98]. This is another effect of untreated iron deficiency that needs to be weighed against a possible negative impact of iron supplementation on morbidity.

## 30.6   EFFECTIVENESS OF MULTIVITAMIN AND MINERAL SUPPLEMENTS FOR CHILDREN

Very few programs have assessed the impact of providing multiple V&M under programmatic circumstances. The studies with Vitalita sprinkles in Indonesia [58, 61] were efficacy studies because the "sprinkles" were provided through weekly home visits during which the importance of consuming all sachets was emphasized, and the mother was asked about how much had been consumed by the child the previous week. The study by the Sprinkles Global Health Initiative (SGHI) in Bangladesh [51] in which mothers were provided with 60 sachets and instructed to feed them within 2, 3, or 4 months was programmatic in the sense that it did not observe consumption and left some freedom regarding when the sprinkles were provided, but it was not a program context, and impact was not compared against a control group. The study by Menon et al. in Haiti [35] provided sprinkles in the context of a WSB distribution program and was in that sense an effectiveness study, but the groups studied were small (254 for WSB plus sprinkles and 161 for WSB alone); because the comparison group received fortified WSB, no conclusions can be drawn about the impact compared to no intervention.

With partners, HKI implemented a tsunami relief program in Aceh and North Sumatra, Indonesia [33, 99], between January 2005 and the end of April 2006, during which more than 200,000 children were provided with a total of 28 million sachets of Vitalita sprinkles, which is 30–210 per child. Because withholding supplements to affected children was not ethical and the phasing in of the distribution meant that those most in need were often reached somewhat later, the monitoring and evaluation

(M&E) of that program was not well suited for assessment of impact and has indeed not found a relationship between the duration of the intervention or the number of sachets received and anemia prevalence (unpublished observation). However, the Center for Research and Development in Nutrition and Food (CRDNF)/National Institute of Health Research and Development (NIHRD)/Southeast Asian Ministers of Education Organization, Tropical Medicine and Public Health, Regional Centre for Community Nutrition, University of Indonesia (SEAMEO-TropMed, RCCN, UI)/UNICEF survey conducted in September 2005 found that internally displaced person (IDP) children who had received Vitalita had a lower prevalence of anemia than non-IDP children [100].

As Rosenberg stated with regard to how public health measures that are implemented at a large scale need to be monitored, it is obligatory to assess effectiveness of health promotion, disease prevention, and safety [101]. The same applies to implementation of V&M distribution programs. A strong M&E component is essential to ascertain that the primary goals of improvement of nutritional status and health and reduction of morbidity and mortality are reached. Indicators that need to be included in such M&E include morbidity (diarrhea, cough, fever, and others such as malaria, pneumonia, measles, etc., depending on the local circumstances), mortality, anemia, and anthropometry. Where the situation allows, it would be good also to include biochemical indicators of iron status, zinc status, and infection.

## 30.7   ISSUES TO BE CONSIDERED FOR PROGRAMS THAT PROVIDE VITAMINS AND MINERALS

The design of programs for distribution of V&M need to take a number of issues into consideration, discussed next.

### 30.7.1   Dosage and Kind of Preparation

For the selection of V&M and the dosage to be provided, a minimum, average, and maximum composition can be selected from the tables on supplement composition (see Tables 30.2a, 30.2b, 30.3) or be chosen to be in line with the recommendations for V&M distribution in emergencies and transition programming by WHO/WFP/UNICEF [34].

For the spreads, it should be noted that they are generally targeted to truly malnourished subjects, either as take-home treatment for treating severe acutely malnourished children who do not require (further) hospitalization [95] or stunted subjects [60]. For treatment of severe-acutely malnourished children, 10-15 kg of RUTF should be consumed by the child in a period of 6-8 weeks [105]. Only the study in Ghana used a spread in the form of a CFS (20 g, 108 kcal per day) and gave it to any breast-fed child from the age of 6 to 12 months, irrespective of nutritional status [62]. The potential benefits of such a form (the study in Ghana found an impact on growth in the spread but not the sprinkles or tablet groups) need to be compared with the costs, logistics, acceptability of the spread among the target population, and benefits associated with alternatives.

Providing V&M in the form of home fortificants appears to be very suitable because it is perceived as a food-based instead of a medical approach. Such an approach appears the most suitable for increasing the intake of V&M, on a daily and continued basis, when many people have not identified, or realized, that their needs are not adequately met [102].

### 30.7.2 Duration and Frequency of Distribution

Very few studies have assessed the duration of impact of V&M supplements on how long an intervention needs to be conducted, when it should be repeated, or how frequently supplements need to be provided. Almost all studies that were conducted to reduce anemia concluded with an assessment of the extent of reduction at the end of the treatment period and did not assess the recurrence of anemia after returning to the usual diet.

The few studies that have been done [51, 103] reported that, among those who were treated for anemia (55–70% of those who were initially anemic), the recurrence after 6 months was less than 50%. Part of the nonrecurrence is likely to be related to lower requirements for iron with increasing age, and another is most likely due to the loading of the iron stores that occurred during supplementation. However, it should also be noted that a considerable proportion of the population was not treated for anemia, and a proportion had become anemic again before follow-up.

Also, while iron can be stored, other V&M are not stored in the body and should therefore be supplied continuously [66]. And, it would be inappropriate from an ethical point of view to acknowledge on one hand that daily intake should be at the level of one RDA but on the other hand only ensure an adequate intake for a limited period of time.

### 30.7.3 Supplementation in the Case of Infectious Diseases, Including Malaria

In the case of rehabilitation of severely malnourished children, V&M supplements should be withheld until infections have been brought under control and the child's condition has been stabilized (see appropriate handbooks). For nonmalarious areas, the available evidence indicates that the only form of morbidity that may be increased on V&M supplementation is diarrhea, but the severity of this increase is limited. It is likely that this risk can be further minimized by providing the V&M in the form of fortified food or home fortificants. For highly malaria-endemic areas, foods fortified with V&M, including iron, can be provided without problem. For the time being, all other forms, including home fortificants that contain iron, are best provided only to individuals who suffer from iron deficiency, and implementation of malaria control measures is imperative. Meanwhile, research is being conducted to assess the extent to which different forms of iron increase postprandial serum concentrations of non-transferrin-bound iron which is suspected to cause the increase of malaria.

Very few studies have been done to assess the impact of V&M supplements on particular kinds of morbidity, especially in young children. The study by Sharieff among children who had suffered chronic diarrhea and used sprinkles (see discussion in Section 30.5.3.1) is an exception [50].

### 30.7.4   Concurrent Supplementation with Other Vitamin and Mineral Supplements or Fortified Foods

When supplying V&M at the level of one RDA, the question may arise whether other V&M preparations should still be provided, such as high-dose VACs, zinc tablets as adjunct for diarrhea treatment, and iron-folate tablets for pregnant women. High-dose VACs have been recommended for two or three times yearly, for prevention of vitamin A deficiency, and should as such be continued as long as the daily intake does not provide enough vitamin A to prevent deficiency in the population. When V&M supplements provide vitamin A, it is only at the level of one RDA per day and for a limited period of time and should therefore not be a reason to discontinue VAC distribution (see also Section 30.5.1.3 above).

A similar argument applies to zinc distribution as adjunct treatment for diarrhea, which is recommended to last for 10–14 days (20 mg/day from the age of 6 months and 10 mg/day for younger infants), while the RDA is 5 mg/day for a much longer time. However, whereas the adjunct treatment with zinc has been officially recommended by WHO/UNICEF [104], few programs are yet implementing the guideline. The largest programs may be the tsunami relief by HKI and partners in Aceh and North Sumatra, Indonesia [33], and the recently started program in Bangladesh that also involves in-country production of dispersible zinc tablets.

For fortified foods, the statement on V&M in emergencies is as follows [34]:

*One way to meet the RDA of micronutrients is to provide foods fortified with micronutrients. Fortified foods, such as corn-soya blend, biscuits, vegetable oil enriched with vitamin A, and iodized salt, are usually provided as part of food rations during emergencies. The aim is to avert micronutrient deficiencies or prevent them from getting worse among the affected population. … However, foods fortified with micronutrients may not meet fully the needs of certain nutritionally vulnerable subgroups such as pregnant and lactating women, or young children.*

For this reason, supplementing one RNI per day to pregnant and breast-feeding women, whether or not fortified foods are distributed, and one RNI per day for children when no fortified foods are provided and two RNI per week when such foods are provided is recommended. Note that V&M content of fortified foods should guide final composition of a V&M preparation. It is also stated that iron-folate supplementation of pregnant women should be continued and so should VAC distribution to young children; optimal breast-feeding practices should be promoted as well. In addition, it is important also to assess the micronutrient needs and intakes of other members of the population beyond the traditional at-risk groups.

## 30.8   CONCLUSIONS AND RECOMMENDATIONS

Considering that children have mothers with VMDs, and therefore lower stores at birth, lower V&M content of breast milk, and complementary foods that cannot meet the gap between needs on one hand and stores and intake on the other hand, many children suffer from VMDs and their consequences. Therefore, these children need extra V&M to improve development and growth and reduce morbidity and mortality. Because poor dietary quality is the main cause of VMDs, these deficiencies do not occur in isolation but rather concurrently, and the underlying reason for a particular condition (e.g., anemia) may be a deficiency of several V&M. Furthermore, because of an interaction between several V&M, their deficiencies need to be corrected concurrently. Also, VMDs increase the risk of infection, hence reducing appetite, leading to poorer absorption, increasing needs and losses of V&M, and thus sustaining and aggravating themselves.

With regard to composition of a supplement to be provided, a dosage of one RDA of 10–15 key V&M appears to be a good choice because it will fill any gap that may exist and will not provide too much of individual V&M. Meanwhile, it is important to consider the nutrient content of the diet.

Studies reviewed used supplements with at least five V&M and were conducted among young children. Almost all studies reported an increase of Hb and iron status. Impact on vitamin A status was masked by VAC distribution (one study that postponed VAC distribution reported an impact). Zinc status was improved in some but not in other studies. The few (IRIS) studies that assessed impact on other micronutrients (riboflavin, tocopherol, homocysteine) mostly reported an impact as well. With regard to the interaction of zinc and iron, studies reviewed here as well as by others found a tendency for supplements that contained both iron and zinc to have less impact on iron status compared to giving iron alone. However, the benefits of adding zinc (reducing morbidity) may well outweigh the somewhat smaller impact on iron status. Furthermore, it appears that for an impact on growth, interventions need to be conducted among young stunted children (< about 12 months) for a relatively long period of time.

Only a few of the studies assessed impact on morbidity, and most found no evidence of impact. Whereas this was blamed on iron, reviews of iron and infection concluded that there is only a very small increase of diarrhea, in nonmalarious areas, which could be further minimized by providing V&M in the form of fortified foods or home fortificants. Also, diarrhea (or gastroenteritis) is a major cause of mortality in developing countries, prevention of which requires multiple strategies, including safe water, reduction of crowding levels, improved sanitation, health care, promotion of breast-feeding, and improvement of nutritional status. For highly malaria-endemic areas, prevalence and causes of anemia, including iron deficiency, seasonal malaria endemicity, protective hemoglobinopathies, and age-specific immunity, need to be taken into account. Interventions should include malaria control measures (insecticide-treated bed nets, availability and good access to malaria detection and treatment, etc.) in conjunction with measures to control iron-deficiency anemia, whether through a blanket or targeted approach. The choice of approach will also determine the best choice of sources of iron, with fortified foods preferred over home fortificants and supplements.

There appears to be a clear role for micronutrients, in particular vitamin A and zinc, in disease prevention and in emergencies. Because other micronutrients, such as iron, iodine, and B vitamins, are needed for other reasons, such as reducing anemia and enhancing cognitive development, and for enabling the utilization of other micronutrients, the provision of multiple V&M preparations, in any form, appears the most appropriate way to provide micronutrients for improving child nutrition and health. This review also confirms the role of V&M supplementation for improving child nutrition and hence achieving MDG-1, target 2 of reducing child hunger and undernutrition, including its contribution to achieving other MDGs. Thorough M&E needs to be conducted to assess precise impact on morbidity as well as mortality.

Considering the discussion in this chapter, the following next steps are recommended:

• Assess the extent that home fortificants and different forms of iron given with food or as a supplement increase the concentration of free iron in the intestine as well as in the blood (of relevance for evaluating impact on gastrointestinal and malaria morbidity).

• Develop a strategy for M&E that can be applied to programs that distribute V&M preparations to assess impact on one or more of the following indicators: morbidity and mortality, nutritional status, and growth. This is relevant for the particular population as well as to broaden the knowledge of the programmatic use and accompanying effectiveness of V&M preparations.

## REFERENCES

1. United Nations International Children's Emergency Fund. Progress for children: a report card on nutrition (No. 4). New York: United Nations International Children's Emergency Fund, 2006.
2. Pelletier DG, Frongillo EA, Habicht JP. Epidemiologic evidence for a potentiating effect of malnutrition on child mortality. Am J Public Health 1993;83:1130–1133.
3. Caulfield LE, de Onis M, Blössner M, Black RE. Undernutrition as an underlying cause of child deaths associated with diarrhea, pneumonia, malaria, and measles. Am J Clin Nutr 2004;80:193–198.
4. World Food Programme, United Nations International Children's Emergency Fund. Ending Child Hunger and Undernutrition Initiative (ECHUI). Global Framework for Action. Rome: World Food Programme/United Nations International Children's Emergency Fund, 2006.
5. World Health Organization. WHO child growth standards. Geneva: World Health Organization, 2006. Available at: http://www.who.int/nutrition.
6. World Bank. Repositioning nutrition as central to development. Washington, DC: World Bank, 2006.
7. United Nations International Children's Emergency Fund. The state of the world's children 2006. New York: United Nations International Children's Emergency Fund, 2006.
8. Gibson RS. Strategies for preventing micronutrient deficiencies in developing countries. Asia Pac J Clin Nutr 2004;13:S23.
9. Allen LH. Iron–ascorbic acid and iron–calcium interactions and their relevance in complementary feeding. In: Micronutrient interactions: impact on child health and nutrition. Washington, DC: International Life Sciences Institute, 1998:11–20.
10. Allen LH, Shrimpton R. The international research on infant supplementation study: implications for programs and further research. J Nutr 2005;135:666S–669S.
11. Shankar AH. Nutritional modulation of immunity and infection. In: Present knowledge in nutrition. 8th ed. Bowman BA, Russell RM, eds. Washington, DC: ILSI, 2001.
12. Viteri FE, Gonzalez H. Adverse outcomes of poor micronutrient status in childhood and adolescence. Nutr Rev 2002;60:S77–S83.
13. Ramakrishnan U, Huffman SI. Multiple micronutrient malnutrition. In: Nutrition and health in developing countries. Semba RD, Bloem MW, eds. Totowa, NJ: Humana, 2001.
14. World Health Organization. Global burden of disease project. Available at: http://www.who.int/healthinfo/bodproject/en/index.html.
15. Copenhagen Consensus: the results. Available at: http://www.copenhagenconsensus.com.
16. De Pee S, Bloem MW, Sari M, Kiess L, Yip R, Kosen S. High prevalence of low hemoglobin concentration among Indonesian infants aged 3–5 months is related to maternal anemia. J Nutr 2002;132:2215–2221.
17. Allen LH. Multiple micronutrients in pregnancy and lactation: an overview. Am J Clin Nutr 2005;81:1206S–1212S.
18. Gibson RS, Ferguson EL, Lehrfeld J. Complementary food for infant feeding in developing countries: their nutrient adequacy and improvement. Eur J Clin Nutr 1998;52:764–770.
19. Allen LH. Causes of nutrition-related public health problems of preschool children: available diet. J Pediatr Gastroenterol Nutr 2006;43:S8–S12.

20. Lynch S, Stoltzfus RJ. Iron and ascorbic acid: proposed fortification levels and recommended iron compounds. J Nutr 2003;233:2978S–84S.

21. Suharno D, West CE, Muhilal, Karyadi D, Hautvast JGAJ. Supplementation with vitamin A and iron for nutritional anaemia in pregnant women in West Java, Indonesia. Lancet 1993;342:1325–1328.

22. Bloem MW, Wedel M, van Agtmaal EJ, Speek AJ, Saowakontha S, Schreurs WH. Vitamin A intervention: short-term effects of a single, oral, massive dose on iron metabolism. Am J Clin Nutr 1990;51:76–79.

23. Zimmermann MB, Wegmuller R, Zeder C, Chaouki N, Torresani T. The effects of vitamin A deficiency and vitamin A supplementation on thyroid function in goitrous children. J Clin Endocrinol Metab 2004;89:5441–5447.

24. International Life Sciences Institute. Micronutrient interactions. Impact on child health and nutrition. Washington, DC: International Life Sciences Institute, 1998:85.

25. Lönnerdal B. Iron-zinc-copper interactions. In: Micronutrient interactions: impact on child health and nutrition. Washington, DC: International Life Sciences Institute, 1998:3–10.

26. Dijkhuizen MA, Wieringa FT, West CE, Muhilal. Zinc plus β-carotene supplementation of pregnant women is superior to β-carotene supplementation alone in improving vitamin A status in both mothers and infants. Am J Clin Nutr 2004;80:1299–1307.

27. Powers HJ. Effects of riboflavin deficiency on the handling of iron. In: Micronutrient interactions. Impact on child health and nutrition. Washington, DC: International Life Sciences Institute, 1998.

28. Shankar AH, Genton B, Semba RD, Baisor M, Paino J, et al. Effect of vitamin A supplementation on morbidity due to *Plasmodium falciparum* in young children in Papua New Guinea: a randomized trial. Lancet 1999;354:203–209.

29. Shankar AH, Genton B, Baisor M, Paino J, Tamja S, Adiguma T, et al. The influence of zinc supplementation on morbidity due to *Plasmodium falciparum*: a randomized trial in preschool children in Papua New Guinea. Am J Trop Med Hyg 2000;62:663–669.

30. Friis H, Ndhlovu P, Mduluza T, Kaondera K, Sandström B, Michaelsen KF, et al. The impact of zinc supplementation on *Schistosoma mansoni* reinfection rate and intensities: a randomized, controlled trial among rural Zimbabwean schoolchildren. Eur J Clin Nutr 1997;51:33–37.

31. Olson A, Nawiri J, Friis H. The impact of iron supplementation on reinfection with intestinal helminthes and *Schistosoma mansoni* in western Kenya. Trans R Soc Trop Med Hyg 2000;94:493–499.

32. Webb P. Food and nutrition concerns in Aceh after the tsunami. Food Nutr Bull 2005;26:392–395.

33. De Pee S, Moench-Pfanner R, Martini E, Halati S, Graciano F, Webb P, et al. Tsunami relief operations, the role of vitamins and minerals. Proceedings of International Conference of Nutrition, Durban, September 2005.

34. World Health Organization/World Food Programme/United Nations International Children's Emergency Fund. Preventing and controlling micronutrient deficiencies in populations affected by an emergency: Multiple vitamin and mineral supplements for pregnant and lactating women, and for children aged 6–59 months. 2006. Available at: http://www.who.int/nutrition/publications/WHO_WFP_UNICEFstatement.pdf WHO/UNICEF/WFP. Statement on vitamins and minerals for emergencies.

35. Menon P, Ruel MT, Habicht J-P, Loechl CU, Arimond M, Pelto G, et al. Micronutrient sprinkles reduce anemia among 9- to 24-month-old children when delivered through an integrated health and nutrition program in rural Haiti. J Nutr 2007;137:1023–1030.

36. Food and Nutrition Board, Institute of Medicine. Dietary reference intakes for vitamin A, vitamin K, arsenic, boron, chromium, copper, iodine, iron, manganese, molybdenum, nickel, silicon, vanadium and zinc. Washington, DC: National Academy, 2002. Available at: www.nap.edu/books/0309072794/html.

37. World Health Organization/Food and Agricultural Organization. Human vitamin and mineral requirements: report of a joint FAO/WHO expert consultation. Rome: Food and Agricultural Organization, 2002. Available at: www.fao.org/documents.

38. Food and Nutrition Board, Institute of Medicine. Dietary reference intakes: calcium, phosphorus, magnesium, vitamin D and fluoride. Washington, DC: National Academy, 1999.

39. Food and Nutrition Board, Institute of Medicine. Dietary Reference intakes: thiamin, riboflavin, niacin, vitamin $B_6$, panthothenic acid, biotin and choline. Washington, DC: National Academy, 1999.

40. National Academy of Sciences/National Research Council. Recommended dietary allowances. 10th ed. Washington, DC: National Academy, 1989.

41. Brown KH, Rivera JA, Bhutta Z, et al. International Zinc Nutrition Consultative Group (IZiNCG). Technical document #1. Assessment of the risk of zinc deficiency in populations and options for its control. Food Nutr Bull 2004;25(1 suppl 2):S99–S203.

42. World Health Organization. Feeding the non-breastfed child 6–24 months of age. Geneva: World Health Organization, 2004.

43. Lutter CK, Dewey KG. Proposed nutrient composition of fortified complementary foods. J Nutr 2003;133:3011S–3020S.

44. Zlotkin SH, Schauer C, Christofides A, Sharieff W, Tondeur MC, Hyder SMZ. Micronutrient sprinkles to control childhood anaemia. A simple powdered sachet may be the key to addressing a global problem. PLoS Medicine 2005;2:e10. Available at: www.plosmedicine.org.

45. Nestel P, Briend A, de Benoist B, Decker E, Ferguson E, Fontaine O, et al. Complementary food supplements to achieve micronutrient adequacy for infants and young children. J Pediatr Gastroenter Nutr 2003;36:316–328.

46. Gross R, Benade S, Lopez G. The international research on infant supplementation initiative. J Nutr 2005;135:628S–630S.

47. Beaton GH, McGabe GP. Efficacy of intermittent iron supplementation in the control of iron deficiency anaemia in developing countries. Ottawa: Micronutrient Initiative, 1999.

48. Hurrell RH. How to ensure adequate iron absorption from an iron fortified food. Nutr Rev 2002;60: S7–S15.

49. World Health Organization/Food and Agricultural Organization. Allen L, de Benoist B, Dary O, Hurrell R, eds. Guidelines on food fortification with micronutrients. Geneva: World Health Organization, 2006.

50. Sharieff W, Bhutta Z, Schauer C, Tomlinson G, Zlotkin S. Micronutrients (including zinc) reduce diarrhoea in children: the Pakistan Sprinkles Diarrhoea Study. Arch Dis Child 2006;91:573–579.

51. Ip H, Hyder SMZ, Haseen F, Rahman M, Zlotkin SH. Improved adherence and anemia cure rates with flexible administration of micronutrient Sprinkles: a new public health approach to anaemia control. Eur J Clin Nutr advance online publication, 26 September 2007; doi: 10.1038/sj.ejcn.1602917.

52. Baqui AH, Zaman K, Persson LA, Arifeen SE, Yunus M, Begum N, Black RE. Simultaneous weekly supplementation of iron and zinc is associated with lower morbidity due to diarrhea and acute lower respiratory infection in Bangladeshi infants. J Nutr 2003;133:4150–4157.

53. Hop LT, Berger J. Multiple micronutrient supplementation improves anemia, micronutrient nutrient status, and growth of Vietnamese infants: double-blind, randomized, placebo-controlled trial. J Nutr 2005;135:660S–665S.

54. Smuts CM, Dhansay MA, Faber M, van Stuijvenberg ME, Swanevelder S, Gross R, et al. Efficacy of multiple micronutrient supplementation for improving anemia, micronutrient status, and growth in South African infants. J Nutr 2005;135:653S–659S.

55. López de Romana G, Cusirramos S, López de Romana D, Gross R. Efficacy of multiple micronutrient supplementation for improving anemia, micronutrient status, growth, and morbidity of Peruvian infants. J Nutr 2005;135:646S–652S.

56. IRIS Study Group. Efficacy of a foodlet-based multiple micronutrient supplement for preventing growth faltering, anemia, and micronutrient deficiency of infants: the four country IRIS trial pooled data analysis. J Nutr 2005;135:631S–638S.

57. Thu BD, Schultink W, Dillon D, Gross R, Leswara ND, Khoi HH. Effect of daily and weekly micronutrient supplementation on micronutrient deficiencies and growth in young Vietnamese children. Am J Clin Nutr 1999;69:80–86.

58. Martini E, de Pee S, Sumarno I, van Hees J, Halati S, Moench-Pfanner R, et al. Efficacy of "sprinkles" home fortification to reduce anemia and micronutrient deficiencies in young children in rural Indonesia. Poster presentation at the UNICEF Child Survival Conference, London, England, December 13–14, 2005.

59. Penny ME, Marin RM, Duran A, Peerson JM, Lanata CF, Lönnerdal B, et al. Randomized controlled trial of the effect of daily supplementation with zinc or multiple micronutrients on morbidity, growth, and micronutrient status of young Peruvian children. Am J Clin Nutr 2004;79:457–465.

60. Lopriore C, Guidoum Y, Briend A, Branca F. Spread fortified with vitamins and minerals induces catch-up growth and eradicates severe anemia in stunted refugee children aged 3–6 years. Am J Clin Nutr 2004;80:973–981.

61. Martini E, Foote D, de Pee S, van Hees J, Halati S, Moench-Pfanner R, et al. Efficacy of "sprinkles" home fortification to reduce anemia and micronutrient deficiencies in young children in Indonesia [abstract]. International Nutritional Anemia Consultative Group Meeting, Lima, Peru, November 18, 2004.

62. Adu-Afarwuah S, Lartey A, Brown KH, Zlotkin S, Briend A, Dewey KG. Randomized comparison of 3 types of micronutrient supplements for home fortification of complementary foods in Ghana: effects on growth and motor development. Am J Clin Nutr 2007;86:412–420.

63. Untoro J, Karyadi E, Wibowo L, Erhardt MW, Gross R. Multiple micronutrient supplements improve micronutrient status and anemia but not growth and morbidity in Indonesian infants: a randomized, double-blind, placebo-controlled trial. J Nutr 2005;135:639S–645S.

64. Stoltzfus RJ, Chway HM, Montresor A, Tielsch JM, Jape JK, Albonico M, et al. Low dose daily iron supplementation improves iron status and appetite but not anemia, whereas quarterly anthelminthic treatment improves growth, appetite and anemia in Zanzibari preschool children. J Nutr 2004;134:348–356.

65. Domellöf M, Dewey KG, Lönnerdal B, Cohen RJ, Hernell O. The diagnostic criteria for iron deficiency in infants should be reevaluated. J Nutr 2002;132:3680–3686.

66. Allen LH. Zinc and micronutrient supplements for children. Am J Clin Nutr 1998;68:495S–498S.

67. Walker CF, Kordas K, Stoltzfus RJ, Black RE. Interactive effect of iron and zinc on biochemical and functional outcomes in supplementation trials. Am J Clin Nutr 2005;82:5–12.

68. Rivera JA, González-Cossío T, Flores M, Romera M, Rivera M, Téllez-Rojo MM, et al. Multiple micronutrient supplementation increases the growth of Mexican infants. Am J Clin Nutr 2001;74:657–663.

69. Shrimpton R, Victora CG, de Onis M, Lima RC, Blössner, Glugston G. Worldwide timing of growth faltering: implications for nutritional interventions. Pediatrics 2001;107:e75. Available at: www.pediatrics.org/cgi/content/full/107/5/e75.

70. Schroeder DG, Pachón H, Dearden KA, Ha TH, Lang TT, Marsh DR. An integrated child nutrition intervention improved growth of younger, more malnourished children in northern Vietnam. Food Nutr Bull 2002;23:50–58.

71. Bhandari N, Bahl R, Nayyar B, Khokhar P, Rohde JE, Bhan MK. Food supplementation with encouragement to feed it to infants from 4 to 12 months of age has a small impact on weight gain. J Nutr 2001;131:1946–1951.

72. Yeudall F, Gibson RS, Kayira C, Umar E. Efficacy of a multi-micronutrient dietary intervention based on haemoglobin, hair zinc concentrations, and selected functional outcomes in rural Malawian children. Eur J Clin Nutr 2002;56:1176–1185.

73. Golden BE, Golden MH. Plasma zinc, rate of weight gain, and energy cost of tissue deposition in children recovering from severe malnutrition on a cow's milk or soya protein based diet. Am J Clin Nutr 1981;34:892–899.

74. Golden BE, Golden MH. Effect of zinc on lean tissue synthesis during recovery from malnutrition. Eur J Clin Nutr 1992;46:697–706.

75. Bates C, Evans P, Dardenne M, Prentice A, Lunn PG, Northrop-Clewes CA, et al. A trial of zinc supplementation in young rural Gambian children. Br J Nutr 1993;69:243–255.

76. Friis H, Ndhlovu P, Mduluza T, Kaondera K, Sandström B, Michaelsen KF, et al. The impact of zinc supplementation on growth and body composition: a randomized controlled trial among rural Zimbabwean school children. Eur J Clin Nutr 1997;51:38–45.

77. Kikafunda JK, Walker AF, Allan EF, Tumwine JK. Effect of zinc supplementation on growth and body composition of Ugandan preschool children: a randomized, controlled, intervention trial. Am J Clin Nutr 1998;68:1261–1266.

78. Penland JG, Sandstead HH, Alcock NW, Dayal HH, Chen XC, Li JS, Zgao F, Yang JJ. A preliminary report: effects of zinc and micronutrient repletion on growth and neuropsychological function of urban Chinese children. J Am Coll Nutr 1997;16:268–272.

79. De Pee S, Sari M, Martini E, Halati S, Kosen S, Bloem MW. Consumption of micronutrient-rich complementary food for 6 months by 6–11 month old Indonesian infants does not improve Hb or linear growth. Submitted.

80. Beaton GH, Martorell R, Aronson KJ, et al. Effectiveness of vitamin A supplementation in the control of young child morbidity and mortality in developing countries. ACC/SCN State of the Art Series. Geneva: United Nations, 1993. Nutrition Policy Discussion Paper No. 13.

81. Walker CF, Black RE. Zinc and the risk for infectious disease. Annu Rev Nutr 2004;24:255–275.

82. Bhutta ZA, Bird SM, Black RE, Brown KH, Gardner JM, Hidayat A, et al. Therapeutic effects of oral zinc in acute and persistent diarrhea in children in developing countries: pooled analysis of randomized controlled trials. Am J Clin Nutr 2000;72:1516–1522.

83. Dewey KG, Domellöf M, Cohen RJ, Rivera LL, Hernell O, Lönnerdal B. Iron supplementation affects growth and morbidity of breast-fed infants: results of a randomized trial in Sweden and Honduras. J Nutr 2002;132:3249–3255.

84. Gera T, Sachdev HPS. Effect of iron supplementation on incidence of infectious illness in children: systematic review. BMJ 2002;325:1142–1151.

85. Oppenheimer SJ. Iron and its relation to immunity and infectious disease. J Nutr 2001;131:616S–635S.

86. Keusch GT. Micronutrients and susceptibility to infection. Ann N Y Acad Sci 1990;587:181–188.

87. Srigiridhar K, Nair KM. Iron deficient intestine is more susceptible to peroxidative damage during iron supplementation in rats. Free Radic Biol Med 1998;25:660–665.

88. Hallberg L, Hultén L, Gramatkovski E. Iron absorption from the whole diet in men: how effective is the regulation of iron absorption? Am J Clin Nutr 1997;66:347–356.

89. Sazawal S, Black RE, Ramsan M, et al. Effects of routine prophylactic supplementation with iron and folic acid on admission to hospital and mortality in preschool children in a high malaria transmission setting: community-based, randomized, placebo-controlled trial. Lancet 2006;367:133–143.

90. English M, Snow RW. Editorial. Iron and folic acid supplementation and malaria risk. Lancet 2006;367:90–91.

91. Tielsch JM, Khatry SK, Stoltzfus RJ, Katz J, LeClerq SC, Adhikari R, et al. Effect of routine prophylactic supplementation with iron and folic acid on preschool child mortality in southern Nepal: community-based, cluster-randomised, placebo-controlled trial. Lancet. 2006;367:144–152.

92. de Benoist B, Fontaine O. (2007) Summary of the conclusions of the WHO consultation. Prevention and control of iron deficiency in infants and young children in malaria-endemic areas. Lyon, France, 12–14 June 2006. Available from http: //www.sightandlife.org/MAG/m307SalMag 307cores.pdf and in press in the Food Nutr Bull.

93. World Health Organization/UNICEF. Iron supplementation of young children in regions where malaria transmission is intense and infectious disease highly prevalent. 2006. Available at: http://www.who. int/nutrition/publications/WHOStatement_%20iron%20suppl.pdf.

94. Cusick SE, Tielsch JM, Ramsan M, Jape JK, Sazawal S, Black RE, et al. Short-term effects of vitamin A and antimalarial treatment on erythropoiesis in severely anemic Zanzibari preschool children. Am J Clin Nutr 2005;82:406–412.

95. Ciliberto MA, Sandige H, Ndekha MJ, Ashorn P, Briend A, Ciliberto H, et al. Comparison of home-based therapy with ready-to-use therapeutic food with standard therapy in the treatment of malnourished Malawian children: a controlled, clinical effectiveness trial. Am J Clin Nutr 2005;81:864–870.

96. Kretchmer N, Beard JL, Carlson, S. The role of nutrition in the development of normal cognition. Am J Clin Nutr 1996;63:997S–1001S.

97. Lozoff B, Jimenez E, Wolf AW. Long-term developmental outcome of infants with iron deficiency. N Engl J Med 1991;325:687–695.

98. Lozoff B, Jimenez E, Smith JB. Double burden of iron deficiency in infancy and low socioeconomic status: a longitudinal analysis of cognitive test scores to age 19 years. Arch Pediatr Adolesc Med 2006;160:1108–1113.

99. De Pee S, Moench-Pfanner R, Martini E, Zlotkin S, Darnton-Hill I, Bloem MW. Home fortification in emergency response and transition programming: experiences in Aceh and Nias, Indonesia. Food Nutr Bull 2007;28:189–197.

100. Center for Research and Development in Nutrition and Food/National Institute of Health Research and Development/Southeast Asian Ministers of Education Organization, Tropical Medicine and Public Health, Regional Centre for Community Nutrition, University of Indonesia/United Nations International Children's Emergency Fund. Second health and nutrition assessment in Nanggroe Aceh Darussalam Province and Nias, September 2005. Jakarta, Indonesia: United Nations International Children's Emergency Fund, 2006.

101. Rosenberg IH. Science-based micronutrient fortification: which nutrients, how much, and how to know. Am J Clin Nutr 2005;82:279–280.

102. De Pee S, Bloem MW, Moench-Pfanner R, Semba RD. Making programs for controlling anaemia more successful. In: Nutritional anemia. Kraemer K, Zimmermann MB, eds. Basel: Sight and Life, 2007:257–267.

103. Zlotkin S, Antwi KY, Schauer C, Yeung G. Use of microencapsulated iron (II) fumarate sprinkles to prevent recurrence of anaemia in infants and young children at high risk. Bull World Health Organ 2003;81:108–115.

104. World Health Organization/United Nations International Children's Emergency Fund. Clinical management of acute diarrhoea. WHO/UNICEF Joint Statement, 2004. Available at: http://www.who.int/child-adolescent-health/publications/CHILD_HEALTH/JS_Diarrhoea.htm.

105. International Life Sciences Institute. Micronutrient interactions. Impact on child health and nutrition. Washington, DC: International Life Sciences Institute, 1998.

# 31 How Much Do Data Influence Programs for Health and Nutrition?

*Experience from Health and Nutrition Surveillance Systems*

*Martin W. Bloem, Saskia de Pee, and Richard D. Semba*

## 31.1  INTRODUCTION

In 2000, world leaders signed a global declaration that outlined the eight Millennium Development Goals (MDGs). At the core of the MDGs was the vision of making the world a better place for all people [1]. The improvement of health and nutritional status are directly or indirectly part of almost all the MDGs. These goals are not just another empty promise to the world's population. All signatory countries have developed national development plans based on them, and the strategic planning processes of United Nations (UN) agencies are based on supporting these plans.

Each MDG sets specific targets; the first MDG is to reduce childhood underweight by 50% of the 1990 level by the year 2015. However, it was only in 2005 that the first serious attempt was made to develop comprehensive strategies to reach this target, with the World Food Programme (WFP) and the United Nations International Children's Emergency Fund (UNICEF) taking the initiative to develop a strategy for ending child hunger. At the same time, the World Bank published a report declaring that investing in nutrition was economically viable and would result in much greater returns than the investments that were required. Furthermore, the Johns Hopkins Bloomberg School of Public Health and the London School of Hygiene and Tropical Medicine coordinated the preparation of a nutrition series for the medical journal *The Lancet* that presented all the current evidence on the most appropriate and effective interventions to improve child survival and reduce malnutrition [2].

These exercises were very useful, but what became clear very quickly was that there is an enormous lack of data on the effectiveness of many proposed strategies. This is due to the way the thinking about public health/nutrition has evolved over the years, which resulted in less funding for the collection of relevant data and their analysis.

From: *Nutrition and Health: Nutrition and Health in Developing Countries, Second Edition*
Edited by: R. D. Semba & M. W. Bloem © Humana Press, Totowa, NJ

### 31.1.1   Paradigm Shifts in the Field of Public Health/Nutrition

Before discussing the data for public health/nutrition programs, we start with an analysis of the underlying philosophical paradigms of these programs. The reason for this is to gain better insight into the problems we will face in coming decades in making our public health/nutrition programs more effective. This topic needs more than a few pages and this chapter could thus be the beginning of more extensive literary exchanges on it.

In a speech he gave at the World Economic Forum in Davos in 2006, former US President Bill Clinton referred to a contemporary American philosopher, Ken Wilber (b. 1949). Wilber's integral theory [3] identifies human development as a progressive, emergent process characterized by a hierarchical series of stages through which perceptions of internal, external, singular, and plural environments are constantly mediated. Postmodernists have been critical of the hierarchical model of this theory; nonetheless, the theory is useful for analyzing paradigmatic changes in public health/nutrition thinking and actions [4].

While the history of medicine goes back to ancient times, the era of modern medicine only began in the 19th century. This was in the context of the founding of positivism, a philosophy influenced by Hume's empiricism [5], that upholds scientific knowledge as the only authentic form of knowledge, which can only come from the positive affirmation of theories through strict scientific methodology [6] (see also Chapter 1, this volume). In 1922, Moritz Schlick (1882–1936) started the so-called Vienna Circle, a group of academics who shared a positivist philosophy characterized by two main beliefs: first, that experience is the only source of knowledge; and second, that logical analysis performed with the help of symbolic logic is the preferred method for solving philosophical problems (logical positivism) [7]. The logical positivists were influenced by the work of Ludwig Wittgenstein (1889–1951) [8] and rejected the possibility of justifying knowledge claims that could not be proven by science. The logical positivists dismiss metaphysical arguments and claims made in theology and ethics on the basis that they cannot be empirically verified.

Many of the Vienna Circle's members emigrated or frequently traveled to Britain and the United States before the Second World War, which led to the strong influence of logical positivism on Anglo-American analytical philosophy, which greatly influenced the philosophy of language and represented the dominant philosophy of science, including medical science, until the end of the cold war [9]. The development of antibiotics during the Second World War, the eradication of smallpox, the vitamin A capsule (VAC) program in the 1990s, the expanded program on immunization (EPI), and universal salt iodization are good examples of the successes of the positivistic approach. However, other public health campaigns, such as the eradication of malaria and iron distribution to pregnant women, failed because of a lack of understanding of the cultural/environmental issues involved.

In the 1970s, under the influence of postmodernism, the conceptual thinking within the field of public health/nutrition changed. Although the criticism of positivism had already started with Karl Popper (1902–1994) in the early 1940s [7], Thomas Kuhn (1922–1996) widely diffused the view that science not only progresses through a linear accumulation of new knowledge but also undergoes periodic revolutions that he called *paradigm shifts* [7, 10]. Although it is difficult to exactly define *postmodernism*, it is characterized by the rejection of universal knowledge and a strong emphasis on cultural relativism [11]. Despite his denial of being a postmodernist, Michel Foucault's (1926–1984) work can be seen as a postmodern critique of modern clinical medicine, given his rejection of claims to universal truth [12, 13]. For Foucault, there is no universal understanding that is beyond history and society, and he was more interested in the "how" than in the "why" [12, 13]. He argued that the alleged scientific neutrality of modern medicine is in fact a cover for controlling challenges to the conventional, bourgeois sense of morality. In the 1960s, Ivan Illich (1926–2002) further questioned the role of medicine in improving health care in another influential book on the subject [14].

The work of Foucault, Illich, and other postmodernists influenced the characteristics of modern health care, particularly in developed countries. Muir Gray identified the following characteristics: a concern with health as well as health care; the evaluation of services not only with respect to effectiveness but also with respect to appropriateness and necessity; public involvement in health and health care policy making; concern with patients' satisfaction and experience of care; a commitment to continuous quality assurance; and an emphasis on accountability [11]. Postmodernism also influenced public health programming in less-developed countries. For example, this is reflected in the Alma Ata declaration (1979), which recognized the importance of the community in its new primary health care approach [15].

What was the influence of postmodernism in the field of nutrition, particularly in perceiving problems in less-developed countries? In the second half of the 20th century, most nutritionists were medically trained, but universities began developing special courses on nutrition, and more "real" nutritionists were entering the development arena. In the 1990s, UNICEF developed a conceptual framework (see Fig. 31.1) that emphasized several levels of causality for malnutrition. This was quite a revolution from the positivist medical model and the beginning of broader analysis of direct, underlying, and basic causes of nutrition and health problems. Although the scientific/technological elements of health programs remained part of these programs (tuberculosis control, vaccination programs, etc.), nutrition programs focused mainly on tackling the anthropological/cultural aspects ("caring practices"). The research field also changed from more quantitative research to qualitative and participatory research, which focused more on the belief systems of health problems than on the health problems themselves. Good examples are positive deviance and traditional growth-monitoring programs, which do not introduce particular health-promoting interventions, be it medicine, micronutrients, or food, but rather focus on promoting particular behaviors within a particular, largely unchanged, context.

While we have learned a lot since the 1980's about how to implement programs at the community level, the lack of attention to the scientific component of the interventions also led to failures. For example, many of the complementary feeding programs were doomed to fail from the start because more attention was given to the importance of having a product that was cheap, locally produced, and part of the regular diet of the target population instead of ensuring that the composition was correct from a scientific and commercial point of view. The recent experience with community therapeutic care (CTC) programs is a good example of a more integral approach. Since 2000, ready-to-use therapeutic foods (RUTFs) have increasingly been used to treat severely malnourished children. The development of these products was based on the work of Michael Golden in the 1990s and took into account all the physiological changes in severe acutely malnourished children and their nutritional needs [70]. After the efficacy trials, the effectiveness

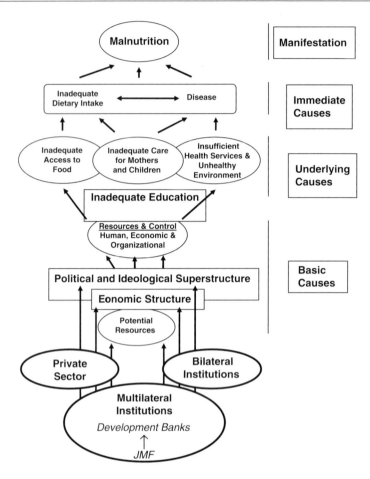

**Fig. 31.1.** United Nations International Children's Emergency Fund (UNICEF) conceptual framework for the causes of malnutrition. (Modified by Bloem et al. [22].)

of RUTFs was tested under field circumstances and then introduced in CTC programs. Community therapeutic care basically means that severe acutely malnourished children who have not developed clinical complications are treated at home, which is very sustainable because it is a much more suitable environment than a clinic, which requires the mother or caretaker to spend considerable time away from home. Thus, the reason for success has two parts; one part is the food, which is fully tailored to the physiological needs of these children, and the other part is that it is well adapted to the cultural settings and conditions of use (i.e., the community or home) [16].

### 31.1.2 Data to Inform Public Health/Nutrition Programming

Postmodernism also had an influence on the field of nutrition and health surveillance. A publication in the early 1980s [17] emphasized the importance of simple, low-cost systems focusing on a few indicators, which could be used and interpreted at the local level. The emphasis was on the usefulness of these programs at the community level. This overlooked the need for data at national and global levels to assess the effectiveness of certain policies and programs compared to others [17].

Since the declaration and adoption of the MDGs, many countries have not made enough progress in reducing malnutrition. The goals of the MDGs are quantitative and measurable, which has implications for countries to be more critical about their interventions. However, because the UNICEF conceptual framework is all-inclusive, no relative weight has been assigned to the different interventions, which makes it very difficult for decision makers to choose the most cost-effective interventions. It is now realized that integral approaches will be most effective to achieve the MDGs, which has led to renewed interest in private sector involvement and evidence-based management (EBM). This is in contrast to the distrust among health/nutrition professionals toward the industry and quantitative science in the 1980s.

From the 1990s until the mid-2000s, we operated surveillance systems in Bangladesh and Indonesia that were good examples of how technically sound surveillance systems can be used to monitor programs and influence macrolevel changes to design policies and programs to achieve the MDGs. An important factor we leveraged when implementing the surveillance systems was the advent of new technologies that allow for the processing and management of comprehensive and large data sets. With the software and hardware available today, the statistical analysis of large and complex data sets can be performed more easily than ever before. This is different from the more postmodern idea of two decades ago, when it was advocated that nutrition surveillance systems should be simple and produce small data sets for quick analysis and to achieve a rapid turnaround of data [17]. The latter can now also be achieved with large data sets, and these allow for the required comprehensive analyses.

This chapter discusses the design of the two surveillance systems, in Indonesia and Bangladesh; their implementation; and the important programmatic questions that were answered with these systems.

## 31.2  DESIGN AND IMPLEMENTATION OF A SURVEILLANCE SYSTEM

The setup of the health and nutrition surveillance system in Indonesia, the NSS, is discussed as an example of a surveillance system. The system was developed based on the experience with the Nutrition Surveillance Project (NSP) in Bangladesh, which started in 1990 and ran for 15 years [18]. First, a surveillance system was set up in the province of Central Java in December 1995 to monitor a province-wide program for vitamin A deficiency control, including a social marketing campaign [19, 20]. This system ran for the duration of the program, until early 1997. As an economic crisis hit Asia, also affecting Indonesia by late 1997, data were collected again in Central Java in June 1998, based on which the NSS was established to monitor the impact of the economic crisis on about 70% of the rural population by collecting data from the seven most densely populated provinces and on the urban poor of four of the largest cities and to be able to prioritize interventions [21–24]. Figure 31.2 shows the dates of data collection periods as well as the provinces and cities where data were collected.

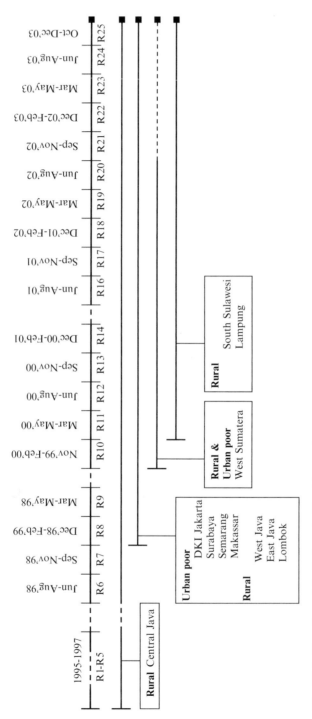

**Fig. 31.2.** Timeline of the Indonesia Nutrition and Health Surveillance System (NSS).

The NSS consisted of several components: design and sampling strategy, questionnaire development, field preparation and training, data collection, data entry, validation and editing, data processing and analysis, and information sharing for advocacy for modifying or developing programs. Figure 31.3 shows how the system went through this cycle every time a new data collection round began. The specific components of the NSS are described in greater detail next [25].

### 31.2.1 Conceptual Model, Indicators, and Questionnaire

The choice of data to be collected by the NSS was designed based on the UNICEF conceptual framework (see Fig. 31.1) [26]. Thus, data were collected on many different factors and situations affecting nutritional status, such as the impact of a specific nutrition project in a particular province or the impact of the economic crisis on the urban poor and the rural population. For the different components of the conceptual framework, different indicators were collected, as listed in Box 31.1. By 2003, the NSS questionnaire contained sections on demographic and socioeconomic status, environmental sanitation, media exposure/vitamin A campaign, agriculture and home gardening, farming and fishery, food prices and food expenditure, household food consumption, vitamin A intake of mothers and children under 5 years old, use of family planning methods, access to *posyandu* ("integrated health post") and other health services, breast-feeding and complementary feeding practices, soy sauce consumption pattern, knowledge of anemia, health, recent morbidity, anthropometry, and anemia.

Depending on the specific aims of a surveillance system or particular programs or policies that are implemented, specific indicators can be collected. For example, when the surveillance system was set up in Central Java in 1995 for monitoring and evaluating the impact of a social marketing campaign that promoted the consumption of dark-green leafy vegetables and eggs, specific questions related to the project's implementation were added, such as whether the target population had seen the campaign's materials and remembered its messages [20]. Then, when the NSS was started in 1998, the

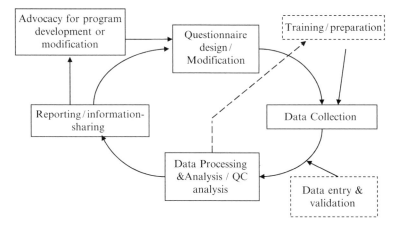

**Fig. 31.3.** The process of nutrition surveillance. *QC* quality control.

**Box 31.1.**
**Indicators collected for different factors of the conceptual framework**

Nutrition and health outcome indicators

Anthropometry indices

a. Stunting (height for age z-score <-2SD) among under-fives
b. Wasting (weight for height z-score <-2SD) among under-fives
c. Underweight (weight for age z-score <-2SD) among under-fives
d. Thinness (low body mass index, i.e. BMI<18.5kgm2) among non-pregnant women
e. Low mid-upper arm circumference (MUAC) among women and under-fives
   Anemia among non-pregnant and pregnant women, under-fives, and fathers
   Vitamin A status (night-blindness) during pregnancy among women that were pregnant within the previous three years and under-fives

**Immediate factors**

Food intake

a. Amount of rice or other staple food prepared at household level
b. Amount of cooking oil prepared at household level
c. Amount of eggs prepared at household level
d. Vitamin A intake among women and under-fives

Health

f. Diarrhea among women and under-fives
g. Acute respiratory infection among under-fives
h. Fever among women and under-fives

**Underlying factors**

Access to food

e. Ownership of paddy field
f. Access to home garden
g. Food expenditure
h. Food prices
i. Use of iodized salt

Caring practices

a. Breastfeeding practices
b. Complementary feeding practices

Environment sanitation and access to health services

c. Source of drinking water
d. Type of latrine used by the household
e. Garbage disposal
f. Vitamin A capsule coverage among children aged 6-59 months and post-partum women
g. Immunization coverage
h. Iron tablets received by pregnant women
i. Family Planning participation
j. Integrated health post participation

Basic factors

a. Household demographic
b. Level of education
c. Occupation
d. Participation in social programs

questionnaire used in Central Java was modified to include "crisis-related" questions such as the condition of the family and food prices before and after the onset of the crisis, participation of the households in relief programs, type of aid received by the households, and so on. With regard to data on expenditures, which were collected as a more reliable proxy for socioeconomic status than income, foods obtained through own production or received in-kind, often rice, were converted to their cash value and coded as expenditures.

Most of the questions were closed ended with precoded answers. By including a category "other" answers that were not anticipated were also captured. Together with the questionnaire, a guideline with detailed explanations about all questions and answers was provided to enumerators. Furthermore, to obtain reliable information, it is important to realize that an interview is a process of interaction and communication and as such is affected by the interviewer, the respondent, the topic and length of the interview, and the setting where the interview is conducted. It is very important that interviewers master a good interviewing technique and are thus well prepared before conducting the interview. The interviewers should, for example, be taught how to probe without leading the answers, how to behave, and how to manage the interview. Also, at the end of their first training, enumerators were tested for their understanding of the NSS and ability to conduct interviews and conduct anthropometric measurements. Those who had at least 80% correct answers passed the training and could collect data. Furthermore, all respondents were asked for informed consent and understood that they could withdraw from the interview at any time.

### 31.2.2 Sampling

The NSS conducted four cross-sectional surveys, each of 10 weeks of data collection, every year. For comparison, the NSP in Bangladesh collected data every 2 months, thus six times per year. The 3-monthly data collection by the NSS allowed for an assessment of situational information, capturing of seasonality, and a quick response where and when required. For each round of data collection, a new sample of households was selected. One province consists of three to six administrative zones, and each zone consists of several (1–15) districts. From each zone, 1,200 households were selected to provide a good estimate of the prevalence of the main outcome indicators (wasting, night blindness among women during their last pregnancy, maternal thinness).

The 1,200 households were selected from 30 villages, 40 households each. These 30 villages were selected by probability proportional to size (PPS) sampling, as follows. All villages in the zone were listed, with their population size. The total population of the zone was divided by 40 to derive the sampling interval. Thus, in the case of a population size of 1 million, the sampling interval would be 25,000. A random number between 1 and 25,000 would be selected as the starting point; that is, the village on the list that happened to have the 10,000th inhabitant, for example, would be the first, the one with the 35,000th would be the second, and so on. The selection of households per village would be done in a similar way based on a listing of all eligible households of the village, in this case those with one or more children under 5 years old. This is referred to as *interval sampling*. For example, if 1,000 households with children under 5 years old were listed, every 25th household (1,000/40 = 25) on the list was selected, and the first household was randomly selected from the first 25. Selected households would then, for example, be numbers 2, 27, 52, 77, 102, and so on. From each zone, 20% of the clusters, thus 6 villages, were randomly selected for hemoglobin assessment of all selected households.

In urban poor areas, a different sampling frame was applied. The urban sample included only households residing in a slum or shantytown. Two slightly different sampling frames were used, depending on the size of the city. In Jakarta and Surabaya, *kelurahan* ("villages") with slum areas were listed and selected using simple random sampling (SRS) techniques. Then, within each kelurahan, two or three *Rukun Warga* (RW; "hamlet/subvillage") with slums were selected for a total of 80–120 RWs, or clusters, per site. In Semarang and Makassar, 80 RWs with slums were randomly selected. The listing of kelurahans and RWs that were considered poor was obtained from Bureau of Statistics (BPS) and National Family Planning Coordination Board (BKKBN) and was confirmed through observations in the field. Within each RW, 30 poor households with at least one child under 5 were then randomly, but purposively, selected to participate in the survey round. For this selection, Helen Keller International (HKI) set its own criteria: (1) location (i.e., along railway, river/gutter/swamp, underneath toll road/highway, near "waste station/damp areas," around small alley, or near the beach); and (2) housing condition (i.e., "box house," zinc house, house with soil/uncemented floor, hardwood house, house attached to other houses, bamboo house, or house with wooden floor).

### 31.2.3   Quality Control

Requirements for collecting good quality data are a questionnaire that is easy to understand and easy to code, well-prepared and dedicated enumerators, well-organized supervision, and good quality control of data collection.

Within NSS, supervision was organized at different levels. Four enumerators, collecting data from 1,200 households in a zone during 8–10 weeks, were supervised by one supervisor who arranged logistics in the field, received and cross-checked all questionnaires, answered questions from villagers and enumerators, and participated in data collection where necessary. A field coordinator coordinated the activities in all (three to six) zones of a province, including day-to-day scheduling; making first contact with the communities involved; managing tools, equipment, and money; and collecting the questionnaires and supervised the quality control team. Box 31.2 shows the number of different kinds of staff involved in the NSS in 2003.

After the data were collected, a first check was conducted by the enumerators before they gave their questionnaires to their supervisor. The supervisors then checked for completeness and validity of answers and gave the answers to the coordinators on a weekly basis. In this way, it was still possible to return to an interviewed household for clarification when necessary.

For cross-checking the data collection itself, a special quality control team revisited, within a few days of the first visit, 10% of the households that had already been interviewed and administered a selected part of the questionnaire. Obviously, enumerators did not know which households would be revisited. The quality control teams were chosen from the best fieldworkers. While having a special quality control team may seem a relatively

---

**Box 31.2.**
**Manpower involved in conducting the Health and Nutrition Surveillance System in Indonesia (NSS) 2003.**

| | |
|---|---|
| 251 | Interviewers |
| 42 | Field Supervisors |
| 37 | Quality Control Team members |
| 12 | Field Coordinators |
| 5 | Field Activity Coordinators |
| 2 | Documentation Officers |
| 2 | Logistics and Administration Officers |
| 13 | Provincial Coordinators |
| 17 | Data Management officers |
| 2 | Data Entry Operators |
| 1 | Data management managers |
| 2 | Field operations manager |
| 1 | Field operation and data management director |
| 1 | Program director |
| 2 | Program consultant and advisor |
| 12 | People providing technical oversight, from Helen Keller International (HKI) and Government of Indonesia |

---

large investment, it is worth it. Enumerators may make mistakes, wrong judgments, or even fake answers. The data collected by the quality control team were compared to those of the enumerators, and the differences were discussed in the refreshment training that took place before the next round of data collection.

Furthermore, quality of anthropometry data collected by enumerators was also checked by calculating the standard deviation (SD) of the Z-scores for stunting, wasting, and underweight of the subjects on whom the specific enumerator had performed anthropometric measurements. This standard deviation should be within limits of 0.8–1.3 [27]. Depending on their standard deviations, enumerators were promoted to the quality control team, retrained, or dismissed.

### 31.2.4   Data Entry, Data Cleaning, and Data Analysis

To prepare the data for analysis, they have to be entered into a computerized database. The most user-friendly programs are those that allow for a screen design that is the same as the questionnaire, perform range checks for each variable, and can skip when certain questions do not apply (i.e. questions on home garden when the respondent does not have one will automatically be filled with "not applicable"). For the NSS and NSP, SPSS Data Entry builder was used. Another good program for this that is available at low cost is Epi-Info. Variable names, which are usually limited to eight positions, should be easy to understand and be the same across data sets. The last is particularly required when many data sets are available within an organization, such as in the case of NSP in Bangladesh and NSS in Indonesia.

The control of data entry went through different stages. After each questionnaire, data entered were compared to the questionnaire's data by the data entry typists themselves. The supervisor then did a similar check for a selection of the questionnaires. A very rigorous and objective way to ensure that data are entered correctly is a repeat-entry system that queries all second entries that are different from the first entry. By now, some surveys equip enumerators with personal digital assistant (PDA) devices to record respondents' answers, which are then transmitted by mobile phone. In this way, data entry no longer requires data entry clerks.

For converting food consumption data into nutrient intake, food composition tables are needed. In principle, local or national tables are preferred, but when certain foods or nutrients are not included, additional or other tables may be selected (see [28] for a further discussion of this issue).

After entering and checking the data, they were cleaned. Data that had an unusually low or high value were probably entered incorrectly, which was checked on the questionnaire, or had been recorded wrongly. In the latter case, there are a few possibilities: going back to the household where this value was recorded, keeping the value, or deleting the value. Whether the value could be real has to be judged by the investigators, but data should not be excluded too easily. Clear guidelines on how to clean anthropometry data have been provided, and some specific programs flag unusual Z-scores. The final step before starting data analysis is making sure that the codebook is complete. Once data analysis has started, good administration should be kept of any changes made to the data set.

## 31.3   COMMUNICATING THE RESULTS

For the formulation and communication of findings, different audiences may be distinguished: At the local level, the audience includes the population surveyed and the local government and organizations working with them; at a national level, it includes government bodies, such as the Ministry of Health and the National Planning Board, UN organizations, and nongovernmental organizations; and at an international level, it includes donor agencies, international organizations (e.g., those of the United Nations and development organizations), governments of other countries, and the scientific community. Emphasis and presentation of findings should be tailored to the specific interests of these different audiences.

For example, findings from the NSS about the impact of Indonesia's political and economic crisis on health and nutrition were communicated to the National Planning Board in the form of slide shows that identified the emerging problems, the subpopulations who were most seriously affected, and proposed effective interventions. Among a wider, national and international, audience, Crisis Bulletins were distributed (available from www.hki.org) that discussed special themes such as maternal wasting, increasing prevalence of micronutrient deficiencies, successful maintenance of high coverage of VACs, and the like. And, for an even wider, not specifically addressed, audience, scientific articles are written. In Bangladesh, results were also shared through Nutrition Surveillance Bulletins (see www.hki.org), among others; the NSP data informed the formulation of the Poverty Reduction Strategy Paper (PRSP) and of the Health and Nutrition Population Sector Program (HNPSP).

Also, the data sets of NSP and NSS have been made available in the public domain through the sharing of data sets on CD-ROMs [29, 30], and the data are being prepared for access through the Internet.

The next sections review how the analyses of the NSS and NSP data have contributed to policies, programs, and conceptual models for assessing the role of various factors of the conceptual framework to malnutrition.

## 31.4  IDENTIFYING PRIORITIES FOR AND MONITORING OF PROGRAMS: USE OF SURVEILLANCE DATA

The NSS and NSP gathered information on a wide range of topics, including those that were relevant for monitoring and evaluating health and nutrition programs, for example, VAC receipt; antenatal care and iron tablets received during pregnancy; attendance at local health posts for preventive health and nutrition services; immunization coverage; family planning practices; consumption of fortified food products, including iodized salt; and so on. Here, we summarize some findings in this regard that were obtained in recent years.

### 31.4.1  Vitamin A Capsule Distribution

In Indonesia, VAC distribution was started in the 1970s, and since the mid-1980s, VACs are distributed twice a year, in the months of February and August, at the local subvillage health post (posyandu). In 1999, the eligible age group was expanded to include infants aged 6–11 months in addition to children aged 12–59 months. To ensure that health workers knew of this age group, to raise awareness about the addition of this age group among the general public, and to increase VAC coverage among all children under 5 years, an intensive nationwide vitamin A campaign was implemented from August 2001 to February 2004 [31]. The NSS assessed both whether the campaigns materials and messages reached the population and whether VAC coverage increased.

In 2003, exposure to the campaign messages was widespread among women living in both rural and urban poor areas. Women's knowledge about vitamin A and VAC coverage rates among their preschool age children were both positively associated with exposure to the campaign. The VAC coverage in rural areas of the seven provinces where NSS collected data, which represents 70% of Indonesia's rural population, increased between August 1999 and February 2003 from 42% to 80% among children 6–11 months old and from 66% to 81% among children 12–59 months old. In urban poor areas, coverage increased from 30% to 81% and from 49% to 84%, respectively (see Fig. 31.4). These data show that the campaign was very successful, and that the national target of 80% coverage was reached.

However, the next question is whether children reached by the campaign are those with the greatest need for the extra vitamin A. A more in-depth analysis of the NSS data collected between 1999 and 2003 found that children who did not receive a VAC were more underweight, stunted, wasted, and anemic; suffered more from diarrhea and fever; were less likely to have received all childhood immunizations; and belonged to families with higher infant and under-5 mortality compared to children who had received a VAC [32]. This means that the about 20% of children

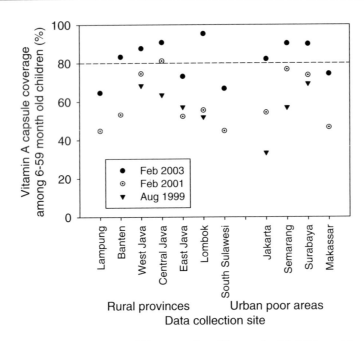

**Fig. 31.4.** Vitamin A capsule coverage (%) among 6- to 59-month-old children at baseline (August 1999), at the end of the urban-focused phase of promotion activities (February 2001), and after four cycles of an intensive national-level promotion campaign (August 2001 through February 2003) by province and urban poor population of four cities.

not reached by the VAC distribution were even more in need of receiving it than the ones who received it.

Similar findings have been obtained for Bangladesh, where the children 6–11 months old receive the VAC with their 9-month measles immunization, and the children 12–59 months old receive the VAC when the national campaign is held [33–35]. Coverage in Bangladesh was relatively low in the early 1990s but has been high since the introduction of the EPI+ approach [36]. However, continuous monitoring and attention to specific hard-to-reach populations or areas are required, and here the more vulnerable children were found to be at greater risk of not receiving the VAC [33, 37].

A large advantage of coverage data obtained through household surveys is that the denominator is known, which greatly increases reliability of the estimate. Coverage that is estimated using service-based data usually uses tally sheets of the number of capsules distributed, which is then compared to the estimated size of the eligible population. Reliable estimates of the eligible population are, however, difficult to obtain in developing countries, especially in mobile populations or in areas that border areas that have less-well-performing health services so that the population of neighboring communities also attend the VAC distribution [33, 37].

### 31.4.2 Vaccination Programs

The national micronutrient survey in Cambodia in 2000 was conducted by HKI in collaboration with the Royal Government of Cambodia, and its tools, including the questionnaire, were based on the NSP and NSS [38–40]. At the time of the survey, VACs were distributed together with immunization outreach, but VAC coverage was very low, varying from 10% to 50% per province. By overlaying, at province and commune level, coverage of measles immunization among children aged 12–23 months (measles is the last of a series of childhood immunizations and should be given at 9 months of age) with VAC coverage, it was possible to determine where they were doing equally well or poor on both distributions and where they were doing well with immunizations but not with VAC distribution [41].

For Indonesia, a similar analysis of the characteristics of children reached or not reached by VAC was done for the children not reached by immunizations. Complete, partial, and no childhood immunizations had been received by 73.9%, 16.8%, and 9.3% of children aged 12–59 months who were interviewed between 2000 and 2003 [42]. It was found that the prevalence of severe underweight (Z-score NCHS [National Center for Health Statistics] $< -3$) among these groups was 5.4%, 9.9%, and 12.6% ($p < .001$), respectively, prevalence of current diarrhea was 3.8, 7.3 and 8.6%, respectively ($p < 0.001$), history of infant mortality in the family was 6.4%, 11.4%, and 16.5% ($p < .001$), respectively, and of under-5 mortality 7.3%, 13.4%, and 19.2% ($p < .001$), respectively [42]. This leads to the conclusion that coverage of the immunization program needs to be expanded because the children who are missed are at a higher risk of morbidity and mortality.

### 31.4.3 Food Fortification

To fortify foods that are consumed by most of the population who are at risk of micronutrient deficiencies, their food consumption pattern needs to be known. For this reason, the NSS included questions about consumption frequency, by mothers and children under 5 years, of common, industrially processed, foods such as sugar, salt, monosodium glutamate, sweet soy sauce (kecap manis), noodles, and so on. An analysis of data from urban South Kalimantan and rural South Sulawesi found that salt and monosodium glutamate were the most widely consumed foods, and that whereas noodles were widely consumed, the consumption of fortified noodles was higher among households of higher socioeconomic status [43]. This example also shows that whereas food fortification can be mandatory, foods are also voluntarily fortified, such as dried milk powder, margarine, certain brands of noodles, and so on.

The method for estimating vitamin A intake that was used by the NSS and NSP was the 24 Vitamin A semi-quantitative (VASQ) method, which was developed by HKI in Asia. It distinguishes vitamin A intake from four different food groups: fortified foods, vegetables, fruits, and animal products. The fortified foods that contributed vitamin A were all voluntarily fortified, and it was found that these primarily contributed to the vitamin A intake of children, particularly among the urban poor population [43, 44].

At a national level, using a mandatory system, salt is iodized, and wheat flour is fortified with iron. The NSS asked the respondent whether the household used iodized salt and then asked for a teaspoon of salt for testing. The test involved adding a drop of test solution to the salt and comparing the resulting color to a standard to assess whether the iodine level was below or above the cutoff for adequacy (30 ppm). Analysis of the NSS data showed that 67% of households in urban poor as well as rural areas of Indonesia used adequately iodized salt, and that there were considerable differences between regions [44, 45]. It was also found that families who were not using adequately iodized salt were more likely to have children who were stunted, underweight, and wasted. In multivariate analyses, after adjusting for maternal age, paternal education, and weekly household per capita expenditures, low maternal education was the strongest risk factor for not utilizing iodized salt [44].

This example shows that the NSS data were used to assess coverage at a national as well as at provincial and district levels, and that factors related to nonutilization as well as characteristics of families who were not using iodized salt could be identified. This in-depth understanding of program implementation and impact enables fine-tuning and adjustment of programs. The same was shown for the VAC distribution program.

### 31.4.4  Assessing a Program's Impact Under Real-Life Circumstances

Public health programs usually implement measures that have been proven efficacious under carefully controlled circumstances, such as in the case of VAC distribution, which was shown in double-blind, placebo-controlled studies to reduce mortality among children under 5 years old by an average of 23% (see Chapter 13; [46]). However, how effective a program is that implements these measures under real-life conditions is rarely known. This is even truer for nutrition programs aiming at changing dietary habits to improve nutritional status and health. Usually, dietary advice, or nutrition education, is based on the knowledge that certain nutrients or components in food, such as vitamin A, are good for health, and that specific foods contain higher amounts of these nutrients than others. Whether promoting consumption of specific foods then leads to an overall improvement of nutritional status is rarely assessed, particularly in developing countries, for several reasons (see Chapter 28). First, most programs that promote dietary change are usually just evaluated for reach of the messages among the target population and for change of food consumption patterns. Second, many other factors affect the final outcome of nutritional status or health, and it is therefore difficult to assess to what extent the change of diet has contributed to an improvement or halting a deterioration if that was the underlying trend.

Data collected by a surveillance system enables an assessment of the implementation of a campaign for dietary change as well as of the relationship between a dietary pattern and specific health or nutrition indicators and an assessment of whether changes of the latter could be related to changes of the diet as promoted by the campaign. A good example is the evaluation of the social marketing campaign that was implemented in Central Java in 1996, which promoted increased consumption of dark-green leafy vegetables and eggs; the evaluation used the surveillance data collected between December 1995 and January 1997 in Central Java [20]. The following were found: First, the campaign's messages were well noticed. Second, consumption of eggs and dark-green leafy vegetables increased. Initially, 80% of mothers consumed eggs in the last week; later, this increased to 92%, and among children 12–36 months old, it increased from 78% to 92%. Egg consumption was independent of ownership of chickens and increased in all socioeconomic groups, albeit at lower levels in groups of lower status. The daily quantity of vegetables prepared in the household increased from 93 to 111 g/person. And, vitamin A intake increased from 335 to 371 retinol equivalents (RE) per day among mothers and from 130 to 160 RE/day among children 12–36 months old. Third, serum retinol levels increased among mothers as well as children and were related to consumption of eggs and vitamin A intake. Among children who received a VAC, serum retinol concentration was also still related to egg consumption. Based on these findings, and because the respondents were not aware of a connection between the province-wide social marketing campaign and the interview by the surveillance system, it was concluded that the social marketing campaign for dietary change, involving increased consumption of specific vitamin A-rich foods, was successful for improving vitamin A status.

This example also shows that to evaluate the impact of a program, it is necessary to monitor the implementation of the program (noticing campaign messages); whether the promoted changes happen (change of food consumption); whether other factors that affect the main outcome are changing (VAC distribution, intake of other main sources of vitamin A); and whether the main outcome indicators are changing (vitamin A status). Where possible, the inclusion of a control group is recommended to control for other changes that occur at the same time when a program is implemented and either positively or negatively affect the main outcome. The plausibility approach, of which that presented on impact of one social marketing campaign is a good example, is a very useful way of evaluating programs taking into consideration all other factors that could affect the outcome [47, 48].

## 31.5   UNDERSTANDING CAUSES OF MALNUTRITION: SURVEILLANCE FINDINGS

The conceptual framework for causes of malnutrition shows the different immediate, underlying, and basic factors that affect health and has been used to assess the contribution of different factors under specific circumstances and to determine what relationship exists between various macrolevel changes and health and nutrition outcomes (see Fig. 31.1). Results are described next.

### 31.5.1   Factors Related to Child Malnutrition in Bangladesh

The prevalence of stunting among children under 5 years old has decreased dramatically in Bangladesh, from 70% in 1990 to 39% in 2005 [49]. However, it is still very high, and there are substantial differences within the country. In 2003, among the poorest 20% of households (first quintile of households ranked by expenditure per capita) stunting prevalence was 49.8%, and among the wealthiest (fifth quintile) was 33.1%. A comprehensive analysis of NSP data was conducted to assess which factors were most strongly related to child stunting and hence which programs and policies should be prioritized for further reductions of child malnutrition [50]. The term *wealthiest* appeared to be relative because in fact these households, which represented the 20% wealthiest in the rural areas, were still relatively poor. They spent 47% of their income on food (all households spent on average 60% on food), had limited access to agriculture land and homestead plot for food production, and had poor access to a healthy environment (i.e., they shared the same unhygienic environment with the rest of the population). A nutrition sufficiency ratio was created that compared the amount of money spent on food to the costs of an adequate diet for an average family in terms of macro- and micronutrient intake. Thus, a ratio of 1 or above meant that the amount of money spent on food was sufficient to obtain food with an adequate macro- and micronutrient content. Only 4% of all households were found to spend enough money on food to be able to obtain a nutritionally adequate diet. In other words, 96% of households were not able to afford a nutritious diet. Because diet is one of the two immediate causes as well as routes to combat malnutrition, the inability of the vast majority of the population to access an adequate diet is a major problem that needs to be addressed urgently.

Multivariate logistic regression analysis on determinant factors of stunting confirmed that the higher the nutrition sufficiency ratio, the lower the risk of being stunted. A more frequent consumption of eggs by the mother, another indicator of dietary quality, was also related to a lower risk of stunting. Access to food and consuming a diverse diet, indicated by ownership of agriculture land and size of homestead garden, and involvement of the woman in income-generating activity involving animal husbandry, were also determinant factors of stunting. This confirmed that of the three underlying causes, access to food, caring practices, and hygiene/health care, access to food was very strongly related to malnutrition. With regard to morbidity, which is greatly affected by hygiene and health care, diarrhea and respiratory tract infections affected children in all quintiles of expenditure equally as much, which indicates that all children shared the same relatively unhealthy environment. Access to health care services was greater among the wealthier, but this had a limited impact on differences in nutritional status. It was also clear that with such great limitations of access to food for all of the population and with such small differences between poor and wealthy households with regard to access to an hygienic environment, caring practices could not contribute much to improve either of the two immediate causes of malnutrition (i.e., diet or disease). Basically, variation of the basic conditions (access to food and hygienic environment) was too limited to make a substantial difference with optimizing their use through improved caring practices.

Based on these findings, it was recommended to increase the availability and access to food and improve hygiene and environment. Furthermore, nutrition programs should include both a homestead food production as well as a poverty reduction component for households and communities to increase their resources and hence access to foods of better nutritional quality. And, because it was also found that children of households headed by women had better nutritional status than of those headed by males [51], when controlling for other factors, the need to empower women was also emphasized.

### 31.5.2   Effectiveness of Homestead Food Production

The NSP data, including the data of the national vitamin A survey that was conducted in 1997 in the place of two rounds of NSP data collection, have also provided further insights into the benefits of homestead food production (HFP) for reducing the risk of vitamin A deficiency (see Chapter 28). Because of the large sample size of the survey, it was possible to create subgroups, such as of children who had not received a VAC (coverage was close to 90%) and lived in households that did not grow any foods on their homestead (25% of households), and compare those to other groups of children regarding the prevalence of indicators that are relatively rare, such as night blindness (<5% for different subgroups).

Furthermore, the recommendation mentioned in the previous section for nutrition programs to include a homestead food production component was also based on findings regarding the increased dietary diversity, income generation, and empowerment of women that are enhanced by such programs [52–54]. These findings were also driven by the NSP.

### 31.5.3   Macroeconomic Policies and Malnutrition

As discussed, access to food is the main driver, and thus also the primary limiting factor, of improvements of nutritional status in Bangladesh. An analysis of NSP data collected between 1992 and 2000 showed a very clear relationship between changes of the price of staple food, rice, and nutritional status and how this was not related to the consumption of the staple food itself, which remained unchanged, but rather to the concurrent, fluctuating, expenditure on nonstaple foods [55, 56]. Figure 31.5 shows how the changes of proportion of underweight children between 1992 and 2000 very closely followed the fluctuation in expenditures on rice. A decrease in the price of rice meant that less money had to be spent to consume the same amount of rice, and therefore more money was available for buying other food items. As shown in Fig. 31.6, when nonrice food expenditure increased, as a consequence of a lower expenditure on rice, the prevalence of underweight decreased.

Thus, changes of the rice price in Bangladesh between 1992 and 2000 directly affected underweight among children younger than 5 years. This is a good example of a way to increase access to food. It also shows that lowering of the price of rice did not lead to more consumption of rice but rather to increased consumption of other, nutritious, foods, which is exactly what is needed to reduce malnutrition. At the same time, the availability of other foods, of plant as well as of animal origin, and fortified foods needs to be ensured so that the extra money becoming available for food can be well spent on nutritious foods.

### 31.5.4   Indicators for Impact of Crises on Health and Nutrition

We have seen that the role of access to food is very large in Bangladesh. The Asian economic crisis of 1997 was hypothesized to affect access to food because of the drop in real income, due to the increased prices of several commodities, and due to increased unemployment. Particularly in urban areas, affordable prices of food and the ability to earn cash income are crucial to achieve food security [57]. Because of the economic crisis, prices of food items in Indonesia increased two to three times, and the urban poor hardly

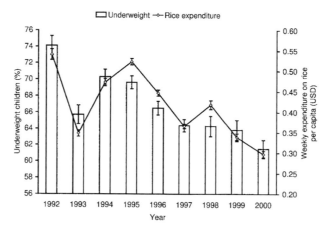

**Fig. 31.5.** The percentage of underweight children (Z-score weight-for-age less than −2 SD) aged 6–59 mo and the weekly expenditure on rice per capita in US$ (USD) in rural Bangladesh during the month of June, 1999–2000. Values for underweight are percentage ±95% CI ($r=0.91$, $P=0.001$, $n=9$). (reprinted with permission from [55].)

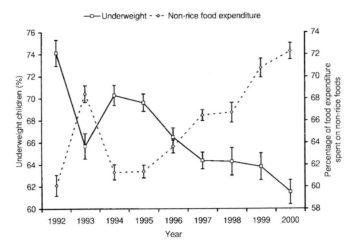

**Fig. 31.6.** The percentage of underweight children (Z-score weight-for-age $<-2$ SD) aged 6–59 mo and the percentage of food expenditure spent on nonrice foods in rural Bangladesh during the month of June, 1999–2000. Values for underweight are percentage $\pm 95\%$ CI and values for expenditure on nonrice foods are means $\pm 95\%$ CI ($r=-0.91$, $P=0.001$, $n=9$). (reprinted with permission from [55].)

had any coping mechanisms for acquiring food in another way than purchasing using cash. Furthermore, the safety net programs of the Indonesian government mainly focused on the rural areas. Therefore, the impact of the crisis on access to food was larger among the urban than the rural population and largest among the urban poor. The NSS data of the urban areas were collected from households in the poorest neighborhoods and slums. Most of the people living in these areas earned an income in the construction industry, which was one of the first sectors that collapsed as a result of the economic crisis.

The NSS documented that the first health impact of the Indonesian economic crisis was on food intake, with a decrease of the consumption of animal products to maintain the consumption of the main staple, rice. This resulted in a dramatic increase in the prevalence of childhood anemia in both urban and rural parts of Indonesia [22]. Iron-deficiency anemia among children in areas with neither extensive iron fortification nor iron supplementation programs was thus found to be a very sensitive indicator for measuring the change and impact of structural adjustment programs or of economic crises similar to that in Indonesia in the late 1990s on health and nutritional status.

Furthermore, a reduced caloric (dietary energy) intake can result in weight loss among any members of the population. The data collected in Central Java found no difference in the prevalence of underweight among children under 5 years between 1996 and 1998, and similar results were reported by the World Bank using the Indonesian Family Life Survey data. But, the same data from Central Java showed an increase in maternal thinness from 14.9% to 17.7% and a reduction of body mass index (BMI) of 0.46 kg/m$^2$ [23]. This decrease was almost equivalent to the increase of BMI of 0.50 kg/m$^2$ that had occurred in South and Southeast Asia between 1960 and 1990 [58]. Data collected among adolescents in East Java showed similar results. While the BMI of adolescents had increased in the year before the crisis (0.27 and 0.22 kg/m$^2$ among boys and girls, respectively), it remained unchanged in the school year after its start [23]. Thus, the NSS data showed that maternal BMI was reduced, but that children's underweight did not change. The underlying mechanism appears to be that mothers are more likely to reduce their own food intake before that of their children or husbands, and that children's weight is also affected by other factors, including morbidity and care factors as well as crisis relief programs. Thus, it was concluded that maternal thinness was a more sensitive indicator for reduced access to food as a result of an economic crisis than children's underweight.

A comparison of the findings from Indonesia, where child underweight was not a very sensitive indicator for the impact of the economic crisis on nutritional status, and from Bangladesh, where child underweight was a good indicator for the impact of macroeconomic policy (rice price) on nutritional status, shows that indicator performance depends on the specific circumstances. In Bangladesh, the prevalence of underweight was much higher than in Indonesia (60–75% vs. 15–25%) and was therefore more likely to be responsive because a small change of body weight among children who are underweight (a weight-for-age Z-score below –2) can get them above the cutoff level for underweight and hence reduce the prevalence of underweight. In Indonesia, a much larger proportion was already well above the cutoff and would need to lose quite some weight before they would be below the cutoff, reducing the chance for the prevalence of underweight to increase in that population. Also, dietary intake in Bangladesh was much less varied, with even oil intake increasing when rice prices are reduced; thus, not only dietary quality, which is less likely to affect body weight, but also dietary quantity, which directly affects body weight, changes more quickly. And, children will share immediately in an improvement of a family's diet but are less likely to be the first to have a lower caloric intake when a family has to reduce the quantity of its diet.

Thus, where quantity of the diet is much less a problem than its quality, a gradual deterioration of food consumption and nutritional status is well indicated by an increase of anemia among young children and a decrease of BMI among mothers. Where dietary quantity is also a problem, in addition to quality, child underweight, especially when its prevalence is substantial, is a good indicator of changes of food consumption affecting nutritional status. Where an increase of maternal thinness goes hand-in-hand with an increase of child wasting or underweight, the population suffers food insecurity of an acute and serious nature. This has, for example, recently been observed in West Timor, Indonesia, an area that has suffered serious drought and poverty over the past couple of years, where 60% of the children under 5 years old are underweight, child wasting increased from 6% to 12% within 5 months (October 2006 to February 2007), and maternal thinness increased from 32% to 39% between April 2006 and March 2007 [59].

The lessons learned from the economic crisis with regard to the impact of the deterioration of the diet on micronutrient deficiencies was also the background for the tsunami response of HKI and partners in Aceh and Nias, Indonesia, of distributing vitamin/mineral preparations to prevent morbidity and further loss of life in the aftermath of the tsunami and under conditions of crowding and a relatively monotonous diet (see Chapter 26; [60]).

### 31.5.5  *Dual Burden of Overweight and Obesity*

Based on the findings that maternal BMI was reduced before child underweight was affected when access to food was reduced due to the economic crisis in Indonesia and that child underweight was reduced when rice prices became lower in Bangladesh, one can question whether an increase of maternal BMI to levels indicating overweight or obesity also means that child underweight will be reduced.

In Bangladesh, maternal thinness is still the predominant problem, with a prevalence of 38.8% among rural and 29.7% among urban poor women in 2000–2004. However, the prevalence of overweight/obesity is growing, with 4.1% of rural and 9.1% of urban poor women with a BMI above $25.0\,kg/m^2$ in 2000–2004. It was found that the women at greatest risk of being overweight/obese were those who were older and of higher socioeconomic status [61].

In Indonesia, the risk for a family to have an underweight child and an overweight/ obese mother (i.e., to have a dual burden of both under- and overnutrition in the same household) as compared to a family in which the child was not underweight and the mother had a normal BMI was higher when the mother and father had received less education, the mother was older, and the household's weekly expenditure per capita was higher [R.D. Semba, unpublished]. This indicates two things. First, also in households with an overweight or obese mother, a child may be malnourished. Second, the fact that the mother is overweight/obese is due to a high quantity, but not necessarily quality, of her diet. In this case, households with a higher expenditure per capita but low parental education may be spending extra money on foods that have a high caloric content, resulting in overweight, whereas underweight, which is also related to dietary quality, of their children persists.

### 31.5.6  Effects of Parental Smoking on Malnutrition and Childhood Mortality

We have seen how access to food is determined by affordability and hence poverty. Smoking is thought to exacerbate poverty in developing countries and hence have an impact on a household's access to food. For example, Efroymson and colleagues estimated that the typical poor smoker in Bangladesh could add over 500 calories to the diet of one or two children in the household if the money was spent on food rather than cigarettes. However, until recently, the relationship between parental smoking and child malnutrition was not well characterized [62, 63] (see Chapter 23).

Analysis of the NSS data, both from urban poor as well as from rural areas, showed that paternal smoking is an independent risk factor for underweight and stunting and severe underweight and severe stunting among children from families in Indonesia. In households where the father was a smoker, less money was spent on animal foods, fruits, vegetables, and other foods compared to households where the father was a nonsmoker [64, 65]. These findings imply that tobacco control measures would not only reduce the impact of environmental tobacco smoke, but also contribute to reducing child malnutrition through reducing poverty, increasing access to food, and improving dietary quality and hence contribute to achieving the MDGs.

Given the very high prevalence of smoking among men in Southeast Asian countries (Vietnam 72.8%, Bangladesh 70.3%, Cambodia 65% in urban areas, Malaysia 49.2%, and the Philippines 54.0%) reducing the proportion of the population that smokes and reducing the number of cigarettes smoked can make a substantial contribution to achieving the MDGs [62, 66–68].

### 31.5.7  Parental Education: Every Year Counts

The promotion of higher levels of formal education for both women and men is part of the second MDG to achieve universal primary education. From the conceptual framework, it is clear that promotion of higher levels of education of women and men should increase income; through better informed caregiving practices, reduce child stunting; and over the long term, reduce the risk of child mortality. Because education also helps to promote gender equality and empowers women, this further enforces income-generating potential and better decision making with regard to health and nutrition-related care. Thus, achieving higher levels of education also relates to three other MDGs: eradicating extreme poverty and hunger, promoting gender equality and empowering women, and reducing child undernutrition and mortality.

A comprehensive analysis of the NSS and NSP data has found that every additional year of formal education that the individual parents received resulted in a further reduction (by 3–5%) of the risk of stunting among their children [69]. Because the analyses were controlled for socioeconomic status of the households, these findings mean that, independent of the ability to earn a higher income, education of children results in better health and nutritional status of their children once they themselves have become parents, and that every extra year of education counts. This is important information for future planning and provides good reasons for emphasizing efforts to achieve universal school enrollment and higher levels of formal education.

## 31.6  CONCLUSIONS AND RECOMMENDATIONS

This chapter has shown how two elaborate health and nutrition surveillance systems, in Bangladesh and Indonesia, enabled the monitoring of health and nutrition programs for implementation as well as impact and allowed an assessment of what the most important factors limiting further reductions of malnutrition were. It is clear that the breadth of the two systems allowed a close and simultaneous look at the immediate, underlying, and basic causes of malnutrition and how policies, programs, and macrolevel changes such as an economic crisis affected these different factors and hence malnutrition. This understanding of the major pathways to malnutrition under particular circumstances in specific countries is necessary for identifying appropriate strategies and target groups for reducing malnutrition and achieving the MDGs. One size does not fit all, and the success of specific interventions does not stand alone but is influenced by other factors.

The experience of these two surveillance programs underscores the need to address the shortcomings identified at the first Public Nutrition Meeting in Montreal in 1997 of a lack of high-quality evaluations of programs, scientific models for these kinds of evaluations, quality of data collections systems that enable such evaluations, and interest from scientific journals to publish papers on these topics. When good data and a sound analysis based on which clear recommendations can be made are lacking, decisions tend to be made for political, religious, or cultural reasons. While all these aspects are important as well, successful development programs need to take into account, at the same time, scientific/technological components, economic/sociologic/political/commercial elements, anthropological/cultural elements, and religious/psychological elements and be informed by how these interact to eventually affect malnutrition and health, as can be assessed using the conceptual framework. For example, when too much emphasis is put on promoting good caring practices without ensuring that the enabling factors of access to food of appropriate nutritional quality and a healthy environment and public health measures are in place, only limited impact can be expected.

Keys to developing a successful surveillance program are that it collects indicators for all factors affecting health and nutrition, that it monitors relevant programs and policies, and that the quality of data collection is taken very seriously. With regard to the last, the changes of leadership of the NSP during its 15 years of implementation had a negative impact on the ease with which the data can be analyzed due to sudden, relatively uninformed, changes of the questionnaire and data-coding strategy. The NSS lasted for a shorter period and did not experience this discontinuity of leadership. Also, approaches for analyzing series of cross-sectional data and further development and experience with the plausibility approach are required to make optimal use of such data. Although a surveillance system may seem elaborate and relatively expensive, it can be modified to also collect data on new or additional programs, and because it allows a good assessment of what needs to be done, it also reduces wasting money on ineffective programs.

## REFERENCES

1. United Nations Development Programme. Human development 2003: Millennium Goals: a compact among nations to end human poverty. New York: Oxford University Press, 2003.
2. Shekar M, Heaver R, Lee YK. Repositioning nutrition as central to development: a strategy for large-scale action. Washington, DC: World Bank, 2006.
3. Wilber K. A brief history of everything. Boston: Shambhala, 1996.
4. Wilber K. Sex, ecology, spirituality: the spirit of evolution. Boston: Shambhala, 1995.
5. Hume D. A treatise of human nature. Oxford, UK: Oxford University Press, 1967.
6. Comte A, Martineau H. The positive philosophy. New York: AMS, 1974.
7. Edmonds D, Eidinow J. Wittgenstein's poker: the story of a ten-minute argument between two great philosophers. New York: Faber, 2002.
8. Wittgenstein L. Tractatus logico-philosophicus. Pears DF, McGuiness BF, trans. London: Routledge and Kegan Paul, 1961.
9. Ayer AJ. Language, truth, and logic. New York: Dover, 1952.
10. Kuhn TS. The structure of scientific revolutions. Chicago: University of Chicago Press, 1962.
11. Muir Gray JA. Postmodern medicine. Lancet 1999;354:1550–1553.
12. Foucault M. The history of sexuality: an introduction. New York: Penguin, 1979.
13. Foucault M. The birth of the clinic. London: Routledge, 2003.
14. Illich ID. Medical nemesis: the expropiation of health. New York: Bantam, 1977.
15. Hall JJ, Taylor R. Health for all beyond 2000: the demise of the Alma-Ata Declaration and primary health care in developing countries. Med J Aust 2003;178:17–20.
16. Collins S, Dent N, Binns P, Bahwere P, Sadler K, Hallam A. Management of severe acute malnutrition in children. Lancet 2006;368:1992–2000.
17. Mason JB, Habicht JP, Tabatabia H, Valverde V. Nutritional surveillance. Geneva: World Health Organization, 1984.
18. Bloem MW, Moench-Pfanner R, Panagides D (eds.). Health and nutritional surveillance for development. Singapore: Helen Keller International, Asia Pacific Regional Office, 2003.
19. de Pee S, Bloem MW, Gorstein J, et al. Reappraisal of the role of vegetables in the vitamin A status of mothers in Central Java, Indonesia. Am J Clin Nutr 1998;68:1068–1074.
20. de Pee S, Bloem MW, Satoto, et al. Impact of a social marketing campaign promoting dark-green leafy vegetables and eggs in central Java, Indonesia. Int J Vitam Nutr Res 1998;68:389–398.

21. Block SA, Kiess L, Webb P, et al. Macro shocks and micro outcomes: child nutrition during Indonesia's crisis. Econ Hum Biol 2004;2:21–44.

22. Bloem MW, de Pee S, Darnton-Hill I. Micronutrient deficiencies and maternal thinness. First chain in the sequence of nutritional and health events in economic crisis. In: Primary and secondary preventive nutrition. Bendich A, Deckelbaum RJ, eds. Totowa, NJ: Humana, 2005.

23. De Pee S, Bloem M, Sari M, et al. Indonesia's crisis causes considerable weight loss among mothers and adolescents. Malaysian J Nutr 2000;6:203–214.

24. Kiess L, Moench-Pfanner R, Bloem M, de Pee S, Sari M, Kosen S. New conceptual thinking about surveillance: using micronutrient status to assess the impact of economic crises on health and nutrition. Malaysian J Nutr 2000;6:223–232.

25. Helen Keller International. Nutrition surveillance: how does it work? HKI Technical Programs Series. Jakarta, Indonesia: Helen Keller International/Indonesia, 2000.

26. Johnsson U. Towards an improved strategy for nutrition surveillance. Food Nutr Bull 1995;16:389–398.

27. World Health Organization Expert Committee on Physical Status. Physical status: the use and interpretation of anthropometry. Geneva: World Health Organization, 1995.

28. West CE, van Staveren WA. Food consumption, nutrient intake, and the use of food composition tables. In: Design concepts in nutritional epidemiology. Margetts BM, Nelson M, eds. New York: Oxford University Press, 1997:107–122.

29. Helen Keller International and Institute of Public Health Nutrition. Bangladesh in facts and figures—2005 annual report of the Nutritional Surveillance Project. Dhaka, Bangladesh: Helen Keller International and Institute of Public Health Nutrition, 2006.

30. Helen Keller International and Institute of Public Health Nutrition. Bangladesh in facts and figures—2004 annual report of the Nutritional Surveillance Project. Dhaka, Bangladesh: Helen Keller International and Institute of Public Health Nutrition, 2005.

31. Helen Keller International. Promoting the national vitamin A supplementation program for children in August 2001. Indonesia Crisis Bulletin Year 3. Issue 2. Jakarta, Indonesia: Helen Keller International/Indonesia, 2001.

32. Berger SG, de Pee S, Bloem MW, Halati S, Semba RD. Malnutrition and morbidity are higher in children who are missed by periodic vitamin A capsule distribution for child survival in rural Indonesia. J Nutr 2007;137:1328–1333.

33. Akhter N, Stallkamp G, Witten C, Anderson V, de Pee S. Vitamin A capsule distribution program among children aged 12–59 mo in Bangladesh: who are missed? Poster presented at Micronutrient Forum, Istanbul, Turkey, ILSI, 2007.

34. Helen Keller International. Vitamin A capsule distribution among 6–11 month old infants: more than 25% not covered. Dhaka, Bangladesh: Helen Keller International/Bangladesh, 2004. Nutrition Surveillance Project Bulletin No. 15.

35. Helen Keller International. National vitamin A supplementation coverage. Dhaka, Bangladesh: Helen Keller International/Bangladesh, 2006. Nutrition Surveillance Project Bulletin No. 18.

36. Bloem MW, Hye A, Wijnroks M, Ralte A, West KP Jr, Sommer A. The role of universal distribution of vitamin A capsules in combatting vitamin A deficiency in Bangladesh. Am J Epidemiol 1995;142:843–855.

37. Dalmiya N, Baker S, Darnton-Hill I, Goodman T, Harvey P, Laviolette L. Improving national vitamin A supplementation programme monitoring: conclusions of an informal consultation of the global vitamin A alliance, New York, 19–20 July 2006. Poster presented at Micronutrient Forum, Istanbul, Turkey, ILSI, 2007.

38. Helen Keller International. Conducting the first Cambodia National Micronutrient Survey. Phnom Penh, Cambodia: Helen Keller International/Cambodia, 2000. Cambodia Nutrition Bulletin Vol. 2, Issue 1.

39. Semba RD, de Pee S, Panagides D, Poly O, Bloem MW. Risk factors for nightblindness among women of childbearing age in Cambodia. Eur J Clin Nutr 2003;57:1627–1632.

40. Semba RD, de Pee S, Panagides D, Poly O, Bloem MW. Risk factors for xerophthalmia among mothers and their children and for mother–child pairs with xerophthalmia in Cambodia. Arch Ophthalmol 2004;122:517–523.

41. Helen Keller International. Routine immunization outreach is a good strategy for delivering vitamin A capsules to Cambodian children. Phnom Penh, Cambodia: Helen Keller International/Cambodia, 2000. Cambodia Nutrition Bulletin Vol. 2, Issue 2.

42. Semba RD, de Pee S, Berger SG, Martini E, Ricks MO, Bloem MW. Malnutrition and infectious disease morbidity among children missed by the childhood immunization program in Indonesia. Southeast Asian J Trop Med Public Health 2007;38:189–198.

43. Melse-Boonstra A, Pee S, Martini E, et al. The potential of various foods to serve as a carrier for micronutrient fortification, data from remote areas in Indonesia. Eur J Clin Nutr 2000;54:822–827.

44. De Pee S, Martini E, Moench-Pfanner R, et al. Nutrition and health trends in Indonesia 1999–2003. Nutrition and Health Surveillance System annual report 2003. Jakarta, Indonesia: Helen Keller International, 2004.

45. Semba RD, de Pee S, Hess SY, Sun K, Sari M, Bloem MW. Child malnutrition and mortality among families not using adequately iodized salt in Indonesia. Am J Clin Nutr 2008;87:438–444.

46. Beaton GH, Martorell R, Aronson KJ, Edmonston AB, McCabe G, Ross AC. Effectiveness of vitamin A supplementation in the control of young child mortality in developing countries. Geneva, Switzerland: ACC/SCN, 1993. Nutrition Policy Discussion Paper No. 13.

47. Habicht JP, Victora CG, Vaughan JP. Evaluation designs for adequacy, plausibility and probability of public health programme performance and impact. Int J Epidemiol 1999;28:10–18.

48. Victora CG, Habicht JP, Bryce J. Evidence-based public health: moving beyond randomized trials. Am J Public Health 2004;94:400–405.

49. Helen Keller International. Trends in child malnutrition, 1990 to 2005: Declining rates at national level mask inter-regional and socioeconomic differences. Dhaka, Bangladesh: Helen Keller International/Bangladesh, 2006. Nutrition Surveillance Project Bulletin No. 19.

50. Helen Keller International. Household and community level determinants of malnutrition in Bangladesh. Dhaka, Bangladesh: Helen Keller International/Bangladesh, 2006. Nutrition Surveillance Project Bulletin No. 17.

51. Helen Keller International. Female decision-making power and nutritional status within Bangladesh' socio-economic context. Dhaka, Bangladesh: Helen Keller International/Bangladesh, 2006. Nutrition Surveillance Project Bulletin No. 20.

52. Bushamuka VN, de Pee S, Talukder A, et al. Impact of a homestead gardening program on household food security and empowerment of women in Bangladesh. Food Nutr Bull 2005;26:17–25.

53. Helen Keller International. Eggs are rarely eaten in rural Bangladesh: why and how to improve their availability. Dhaka, Bangladesh: Helen Keller International/Bangladesh, 2002. Nutrition Surveillance Project Bulletin No. 11.

54. Bloem MW, Huq N, Gorstein J, et al. Production of fruits and vegetables at the homestead is an important source of vitamin A among women in rural Bangladesh. Eur J Clin Nutr 1996;50(suppl 3): S62–S67.

55. Torlesse H, Kiess L, Bloem MW. Association of household rice expenditure with child nutritional status indicates a role for macroeconomic food policy in combating malnutrition. J Nutr 2003;133: 1320–1325.

56. Bloem MW, Hye A, Gorstein J, et al. Nutritional surveillance in Bangladesh: a useful tool for policy planning at the local and national level. Food Nutr Bull 1995:131–138.

57. Hadded L, Ruel MT, Garrett JL. Are urban poverty and undernutrition growing? Some newly assembled evidence. Washington, DC: Food Consumption and Nutrition Division of the International Food Policy Research Institute, 1999. IFPRI Discussion Paper 63 (Discussion Paper Brief).

58. Pelletier DL, Rahn M. Trends in body mass index in developing countries. Food Nutr Bull 1998;19:223–229.

59. Church World Service. West Timur situation 2007; need for immediate action. CWS fact sheet. Jakarta, Indonesia: Church World Service, 2007.

60. De Pee S, Martini E, Moench-Pfanner R, Zlotkin S, Darnton-Hill I, Bloem MW. Home fortification in emergency response and transition programming: Experiences in Aceh and Nias, Indonesia. Food Nutr Bull 2007;28:189–197.

61. Shafique S, Akhter N, Stallkamp G, Pee SD, Panagides D, Bloem MW. Trends of under- and over-weight among rural and urban poor women indicate the double burden of malnutrition in Bangladesh. Int J Epidemiol January 22, 2007; E-pub ahead of print.

62. Efroymson D, Ahmed S, Townsend J, et al. Hungry for tobacco: an analysis of the economic impact of tobacco consumption on the poor in Bangladesh. Tob Control 2001;10:212–217.

63. Best CM, Sun K, de Pee S, Bloem MW, Stallkamp G, Semba RD. Parental tobacco use is associated with increased risk of child malnutrition in Bangladesh. Nutrition 2007;23:731–738.

64. Best C, De Pee S, Sari M, Bloem MW, Semba RD. Paternal smoking increases the risk of child malnutrition among families in rural Indonesia. Tob Control (in press).

65. Semba RD, Kalm LM, de Pee S, Ricks MO, Sari M, Bloem MW. Paternal smoking is associated with increased risk of child malnutrition among poor urban families in Indonesia. Public Health Nutr 2007;10:7–15.

66. Morrow M, Barrowclough S. Tobacco control and gender in Southeast Asia. Part I. Malaysia and the Philippines. Health Promot Int 2003;18:255–264.

67. Jenkins CNH, Dai PX, Ngoc DH, et al. Tobacco use in Vietnam: prevalence, predictors, and the role of the transnational tobacco corporations. JAMA 1997;227:1726–1731.

68. Smith M, Umenai T, Radford C. Prevalence of smoking in Cambodia. J Epidemiol 1998:85–89.

69. Semba RD, de Pee S, Sun K, Sari M, Ahkter N, Bloem MW. Effect of parental formal education on risk of child stunting in Indonesia and Bangladesh a cross sectional study. The Lancet 2008;371:322–328.

70. Golden MHN. Severe Malnutrition. In: Weatherall DJ, Ledington JGG, Warrell DA (eds). The Oxford textbook of Medicine, 3rd ed. Oxford: Oxford University Press; 1996:1278–1296.

# 32 The Economics of Nutritional Interventions

## Susan Horton

## 32.1 INTRODUCTION

Nutrition is a basic need and as such one of the desired outcomes of economic development. There are compelling reasons for investing in nutrition other than its economic benefits. Nevertheless, quantifying these economic benefits can be useful for advocating increased resources for nutrition programs. Economic analysis can also help to make informed decisions about the type of nutrition interventions to fund.

Undernutrition involves heavy human costs. Estimates suggest that underweight is the cause of 3.75 million deaths annually worldwide, with more than 0.75 million caused by each of iron deficiency, vitamin A deficiency, and zinc deficiency (see discussion in Section 32.1). We do not know the degree of overlap; hence, annual deaths from all nutritional deficiencies are somewhere between 3.75 million and 6 million annually worldwide.

Economic losses associated with undernutrition can also be large. Productivity losses related to underweight, iodine deficiency, and iron deficiency (due to both physical and cognitive impairments) can be 0.5–2% of the gross domestic product (GDP) (or even more) in highly affected countries for each of the three causes (discussed in Section 32.1). The total GDP loss from all nutritional causes is likely to be higher, although it is not clear by how much due to overlap between the conditions.

Costs of programs focused on improving nutritional status via increasing nutrient intake can be quite reasonable (Section 32.2). Micronutrient interventions and educational efforts such as breast-feeding promotion have very modest costs per capita; intensive community nutrition programs and programs involving food tend to be more costly. Cost-effectiveness results (Section 32.3) suggest that micronutrient interventions and breast-feeding promotion rank with some of the highest-priority primary health interventions. Economic analysis can provide implications for policy and help identify priority areas for future research (Section 32.4). Program priorities vary somewhat by region. The human costs related to overweight already exceed those of underweight in three of the World Health Organization (WHO) regions (more work is needed on economic costs), and this is an issue of growing importance.

From: *Nutrition and Health: Nutrition and Health in Developing Countries, Second Edition*
Edited by: R. D. Semba & M. W. Bloem © Humana Press, Totowa, NJ

## 32.2   THE COSTS OF UNDERNUTRITION

The focus here is on four aspects of undernutrition, namely, protein-energy malnutrition (PEM) and deficiencies of three important micronutrients: iodine, iron, and vitamin A, with some remarks on zinc where there are increasing numbers of studies. Deficiencies of other micronutrients such as calcium are not addressed despite their importance in developing countries since less work has been done in this area. The chapter focuses on undernutrition. It is clear that overnutrition (and associated issues such as obesity, high blood pressure, etc.) is increasing in developing countries and likewise requires policy attention. Space does not permit a full treatment here; see, for example chapters 20 and 21, and other work of Popkin et al. [1].

Undernutrition imposes several costs. These include the human costs of premature death (which also imply economic costs), the economic costs due to lost productivity and output, and the costs of treating ill health associated with undernutrition (costs both to the health service and to households). These costs are examined in turn, and some estimates of the magnitude of the first two sets of costs are provided.

Undernutrition is an important underlying cause of premature death in developing countries. There is a dose-dependent relationship between the severity of malnutrition and the relative risk of mortality. The relative risk of premature mortality, as compared to normally nourished children, has been estimated at 2.5 for children who are 70–79% of the median in weight for age, 4.6 for children who are 60–69% of the median, and 8.4 for children who are less than 60% of the median, between ages 6 and 59 months [2].

Undernutrition accounts for a large proportion of child deaths in regions of the world where undernutrition is widespread. Underweight is associated with 3.75 million deaths worldwide as estimated by WHO [3] and summarized in Table 32.1. The overwhelming majority of these are infants and children. This compares to just under 11 million infant and child deaths annually worldwide according to the United Nations International Children's Emergency Fund (UNICEF) [4]. Preventable deaths are concentrated in South

**Table 32.1**

**Regional estimates of mortality risk attributable to nutrition-related causes (millions), World Health Organization (WHO) regions, 2000**

| Region | Underweight | Iron deficiency | Vitamin A deficiency | Zinc deficiency | Overweight |
|---|---|---|---|---|---|
| Sub-Saharan Africa | 1.77 | 0.27 | 0.47 | 0.39 | 0.09 |
| Eastern Mediterranean | 0.47 | 0.09 | 0.08 | 0.09 | 0.19 |
| Southeast Asia | 1.26 | 0.36 | 0.19 | 0.28 | 0.25 |
| Western Pacific | 0.19 | 0.07 | 0.02 | 0.01 | 0.39 |
| Americas | 0.05 | 0.03 | 0.01 | 0.01 | 0.57 |
| Europe | 0.02 | 0.02 | 0.00 | 0.00 | 1.11 |
| Total | 3.75 | 0.84 | 0.78 | 0.79 | 2.59 |

Note that combined effects of any group of risk factors will often be less than the sum of their separate effects. Note also that the WHO Southeast Asia region includes South Asia.

*Source*: Compiled by author using data from WHO [3].

Asia, Southeast Asia, and sub-Saharan Africa, where undernutrition is highest. Worryingly, the rates are rising in sub-Saharan Africa, although falling slowly elsewhere.

Iodine deficiency is associated with higher rates of perinatal mortality. However, the magnitude of the relative risks involved is not well known. The introduction of iodized salt has had a very rapid effect on reducing the population at risk for iodine deficiency; nevertheless, it remains an important problem in Eastern Europe, the Eastern Mediterranean, sub-Saharan Africa, and (due to the large populations in these countries) South and Southeast Asia. See the work of de Benoist et al. [5] for data on prevalence of inadequate iodine intake by region as evidenced by urinary iodine.

Iron-deficiency anemia is associated with higher rates of maternal and perinatal mortality. Stolzfus et al. [6] estimated that a 1 g/dL increase in hemoglobin is associated with an odds ratio for perinatal mortality of 0.72 and for maternal mortality of 0.75. Given that the infant mortality rate (IMR) is of the order of 20–50 times that of the maternal mortality rate (MMR) (and the highest IMR rate is in the first week of life), the large majority of the 0.84 million deaths attributable to iron deficiency represent perinatal deaths. The greatest number of deaths attributable to iron deficiency are in the WHO Southeast Asia region (0.36 million), followed by sub-Saharan Africa (0.27 million).

The importance of vitamin A in combating infection has been appreciated recently. One estimate is that the relative risk of mortality for children with subclinical vitamin A deficiency is 1.75 that for nondeficient children [7]. Table 32.1 shows that of the 0.78 million deaths attributable to vitamin A deficiency, 0.47 million are in Sub-Saharan Africa and 0.19 million are in Southeast Asia, with the overwhelming majority of these in infants and children.

Work on zinc deficiency is at an early stage given the particular difficulty in measuring zinc status. Zinc deficiency increases the odds ratio for mortality associated with diarrhea and acute respiratory infection (ARI), as well as being linked with stunting. Large-scale mortality trials are currently under way; one existing study of full-term, small-for-gestational age infants in north India found a mortality reduction of 67% for daily zinc supplementation (1–5 mg/day, from 15 to 30 days of age, followed by 5 mg/day continued from 20 to 269 days of age; Sazawal et al. 2001, cited in [8]). Table 32.1 estimates that 0.79 million deaths annually worldwide are attributable to zinc deficiency, with the majority in sub-Saharan Africa (0.39 million), followed by Southeast Asia (0.28 million).

It is not straightforward to estimate total numbers of deaths due to undernutrition of different types. We cannot simply add the numbers of deaths attributed to different types of undernutrition since this does not take into account possible synergies between different nutrient deficiencies or the extent of overlap and multiple deficiencies in one individual. Nevertheless, it is clear that undernutrition is an important cause of premature death.

Deaths related to overweight worldwide (via increased risk of cardiovascular disease) are lower than those related to underweight (2.59 million as compared to 3.75 million). However, in three of the WHO regions (Western Pacific, Americas, and Europe) mortality attributable to overweight already exceeds that attributable to underweight and micronutrient deficiency (Table 32.1).

Premature death involves economic as well as human costs. We do not attempt to quantify these. Putting a dollar value on human life is very difficult. The economic cost of death of the mother may not seem large in market terms in some countries where women's labor market participation is very low, but the disruption to the family and the social costs may be very large. The economic cost of child deaths is also difficult to calculate.

Undernutrition also entails economic costs due to lower productivity. Some of these costs are felt immediately; currently, anemic adults have been shown to be less productive in manual labor, and there are almost immediate productivity gains from iron supplementation [9]. There are similar studies of productivity effects of calorie supplementation in manual labor [10]. Other effects take longer to manifest themselves. Some studies of wages of adults in manual labor suggest that stunted adults (holding other factors constant) earn less, implying lower productivity. Stunting in adulthood is in turn related to undernutrition suffered in early childhood. There are also effects of nutrition on cognition that take time to manifest themselves. Protein-energy malnutrition and iron deficiency in early childhood can be linked to lower cognitive scores in adults (by inference from studies; there are as yet no panel data for individuals from developing countries for a long enough duration to show this for iron). Maternal iodine deficiency is associated with mental retardation in children. We know from many studies from developing countries that wages are related to cognitive ability, both directly and indirectly via the effects of higher cognitive scores on schooling attainment. The effects of undernutrition on cognitive ability and hence adult productivity are more subtle than the effects on physical size and strength but may if anything be larger and more pervasive. After all, use of physical labor tends to decline in the course of development, while cognitive skills become increasingly important.

Table 32.2 presents estimates of the size of these productivity effects. Studies suggest that iron-deficiency anemia is associated with a 17% loss of productivity in heavy manual labor and 5% in light blue-collar work, based on supplementation studies (see Table 3 in [11] for references). A 1% deficit in adult height was found to be associated with a 1.38% reduction in agricultural wages in the Philippines [12] and with a 0.3% decrease in rural wages in Pakistan [13]. This would infer that adults who were moderately malnourished as children would be 2–6% less productive and those who were severely malnourished 2–9% less productive than their nonmalnourished counterparts. There are no estimated effects on physical productivity for iodine and vitamin A.

**Table 32.2**
**Summary of productivity losses associated with malnutrition**

| Deficiency | Losses in manual labor | Cognitive losses based on childhood malnutrition |
|---|---|---|
| Protein-energy | 2–6% (modified stunting) 2–9% (severe stunting) | 10% |
| Iron | 17% (heavy labor) 5% (blue collar) | 4% |
| Iodine | – | 10% |
| Vitamin A | – | – |

*Sources*: See text for references.

The losses due to cognitive impairments in childhood are more indirect. Estimates suggest that PEM in childhood is associated with a 15-point decrease in IQ, which in turn is associated with a 10% drop in earnings and hence productivity in adulthood, according to one early study by Selowsky and Taylor [14]. Intervention studies aimed at stunted children between 9 and 24 months old [15] found that supplementation combined with psychosocial stimulation can permit these children to catch up in development levels with nonstunted controls. Childhood anemia is associated with a decrease in score on cognitive tests of about one half of 1 standard deviation, which in turn is associated with a 4% decrease in hourly earnings based on carefully controlled studies of adult wages (see studies cited in [11].

Cognitive impairments associated with maternal iodine deficiency are very large. The average productivity loss per child born to a mother with goiter is estimated at 10% (according to [16], based on a 3.4% chance that the child is a cretin with zero economic productivity, a 10.2% chance that the child has a severe cognitive impairment, associated with a 25% loss of productivity, and an 86.4% chance of mild cognitive impairment with a 5% loss of productivity). The United Nations (UN) Administrative Council on Coordination, Subcommittee on Nutrition (ACC/SCN) [17, p. 25] added: "Even in populations known to be at risk of IDD [iodine-deficiency disease] where there is no evident cretinism, there is a downward shift in the frequency distribution of IQ in schoolchildren" and provided several references for Spain, Italy, and Indonesia, implying that there are effects of milder maternal iodine deficiency without apparent signs of goiter.

Translating productivity effects from small-scale interventions and sample surveys into economy-wide effects is a little difficult. One problem is that the effects that are easiest to measure are those in market work. It is more difficult to estimate the costs involved in nonmarket work, causing a bias that works against women, although these nonmarket costs are real. Another problem is that there is overlap between nutrient deficiencies. Children who were deficient in iron and hence suffered cognitive impairments may grow up to be adults who are also anemic and hence less productive in physical labor; the effects may be additive or partially offsetting. Children who are iron deficient may also be underweight as well as born of mothers who were iodine deficient, all of which have effects on cognitive development. A final problem is the issue regarding how important productivity losses are in economies that are labor surplus, although this objection applies perhaps more to physical labor and less to work affected by cognitive impairments.

There is also the issue of discounting. When examining nutrition interventions, some benefits occur immediately or almost immediately (iron supplementation of adults, iodine supplementation for women of childbearing age), whereas others occur only with a lag (interventions that reduce PEM in childhood, iron supplementation of young children). The usual practice is to use a long-term social discount rate, with appropriate sensitivity analysis.

The economic productivity losses associated with undernutrition may be substantial. Table 32.3 (based on [11]) presents figures for the productivity losses due to anemia for an illustrative group of countries, including both cognitive losses and losses in manual labor. These represent the present value of losses associated with maintaining the current anemia level for 1 year. Cognitive losses become relatively more important as countries

**Table 32.3**
Sources of productivity loss due to iron-deficiency anemia, selected countries

| Country | Cognitive loss ($/capita, PV) | Physical loss ($/capita, PV) | Total loss ($/capita, PV) | Total loss (% of GDP, PV) |
|---|---|---|---|---|
| Bangladesh | 12.98 | 3.23 | 16.21 | 7.9 |
| India* | 15.50 | 3.78 | 19.28 | 6.0 |
| Pakistan* | 19.44 | 2.97 | 22.41 | 5.2 |
| Mali | 6.98 | 1.92 | 8.90 | 4.2 |
| Tanzania | 3.17 | 0.62 | 3.79 | 2.7 |
| Nicaragua | 10.33 | 2.56 | 12.89 | 3.8 |

For countries denoted by asterisk (*), data on anemia in men were not available, and anemia in adult males is assumed to be zero (although rates are likely to be higher); hence, figures are an underestimate. The estimates represent present value (PV) of the costs of the current level of anemia persisting for one additional year.

GDP, gross domestic product.

*Source*: Compiled by author using data from [11].

become richer and dominate losses in manual labor in middle-income countries. The present value of losses associated with iron deficiency are on the order of 2–8% of GDP for this group of poor countries with high levels of anemia. The GDP losses are highest in the poorer countries in South Asia, where anemia rates are highest and heavy manual labor is a large share of all work.

Estimates for economic losses due to PEM and iodine deficiency do not exist for all countries. However, one can make estimates of the possible order of magnitude. In South Asia, where 50% of children are underweight [18], a 10% productivity loss associated with lower cognitive achievement could amount to a loss of 2% of GDP (if the share of wages in GDP were around 40%); corresponding losses in sub-Saharan Africa would be 1.2–1.3% based on a prevalence of underweight of 30%. There are likely to be additional losses of physical productivity due to stunting, but we do not have data to estimate this.

The cognitive losses due to iodine deficiency can be estimated as follows: In the early 1990s (before salt iodization was intensified), 12% of the global population was affected by goiter. If we assume that rate had been similar for the last generation and if the cognitive loss per birth to a mother with goiter is 10%, then the loss (again assuming wages are 40% of GDP) would be 0.48% of global GDP. This loss would vary depending on the level of goiter in the population and has been going down as salt iodization has spread. However, the losses could still be as high as 0.9% of GDP in countries where goiter remains high (Bangladesh, where 22% of adult women suffered from goiter in 1999; Sri Lanka, where the rate was 24.5% in 2000–2001; and Pakistan, where the rate was 21.1% in 2001 according to data from WHO [19]).

The last component of costs identified at the beginning of this section was costs imposed on the health sector related to undernutrition. This includes costs of nutritional rehabilitation of severely malnourished children (where this is done); costs of the treating the additional morbidity attributable to undernutrition (due to increased incidence of illness, longer duration, or greater severity); and costs associated with difficulties in childbirth and prematurity/low birth weight due to maternal undernutrition. Unfortunately, it is not possible with present data to estimate either the costs to the health system or the costs to households themselves in lost time, travel, and purchase of drugs.

This section discussed some of the serious costs that undernutrition imposes. These include the human costs of additional deaths, economic costs of lower productivity, and costs imposed on the health system. As we discuss in the next section, nutrition interventions can be relatively inexpensive and (as the third section describes) cost-effective and with attractive benefit:cost ratios.

## 32.3   THE COSTS OF NUTRITION INTERVENTIONS

Information about costs of nutrition interventions in isolation is not that useful. What matters ultimately is cost-effectiveness or the benefit:cost ratio. Nevertheless, cost per participant and per capita are important to know from the perspective of replicability at the national level. Given that undernutrition is so pervasive in low-income countries, only interventions that are of modest cost can be replicated nationally. Interventions that are more costly can only be implemented if highly targeted, which in itself is a factor further increasing costs. Note that estimates given throughout this section and the next are all in US dollars.

It is also useful to have in mind some benchmark costs for health interventions. Current government spending on health is on average about $6 per capita in low-income countries and about $60 per capita in middle-income ones (data for 1999, calculated by the World Bank [20]). The World Bank [21] suggested that in 1993 a desirable health package for developing countries would cost about $21 per capita, of which $5 per capita would consist of public health measures (the costs would be somewhat higher now).

In this section, we therefore explore additional program components that are affordable and that could have important effects on nutrition. Table 32.4 summarizes approximate unit costs of several nutrition interventions. Micronutrient fortification costs are very modest—$0.05 to $0.25 per person per year—for fortificant costs for each micronutrient. These costs can ultimately be passed on to the consumer, at least in middle-income countries (as is the practice in developed countries). These minimal costs do not include the costs of social marketing of fortificants, of technical assistance in identifying appropriate vehicles, of the equipment needed to add the fortificant to the vehicle, or of the monitoring and surveillance costs necessary to ensure compliance. These one-time costs can be fairly substantial in large countries. In Pakistan, for example, introducing salt iodization was estimated as costing $4.5 million, including $0.5 million in technical assistance, $0.5 million in monitoring, $1.5 million in social marketing, and $2 million for initial subsidy of fortificant [22], which works out to $0.03 per capita (one-time cost).

Micronutrient supplementation is more costly, although this is often necessary if a suitable vehicle cannot be found for fortification for a particular population or if the needs (especially for pregnant women) exceed what can safely be provided by fortification. The costs are still modest ($0.20 to $1.70 per person per year, depending on the nutrient involved and the target population).

Breast-feeding promotion costs $2–$3 per birth for hospitals that have already eliminated formula ($0.30–$0.40 per birth for those that have not) [23]. Other mass-media nutrition education programs cost between $0.20 and $2.50 per person per year, but very few have impact data.

Community-based nutrition programs also have a strong educational component as well as activities such as growth monitoring, targeted feeding, providing micronutrient supplements, and so on. Less-intensive programs cost $2–$5 per child (e.g., Integrated

**Table 32.4**

**Approximate unit costs of interventions with effects on malnutrition**

| Intervention | Cost/beneficiary/year (US $) |
|---|---|
| *Micronutrient fortification* | |
| Iodine | 0.05 |
| Iron | 0.09 |
| Vitamin A | 0.05–0.15 |
| Zinc | 0.06–0.24 |
| | |
| *Micronutrient supplementation* | |
| Iodine | 0.50 |
| Iron (per pregnancy) | 1.70 |
| Vitamin A | 0.20 |
| | |
| *Education interventions* | |
| Mass-media education programs | 0.20–2.00 |
| Breastfeeding promotion | 2.00–3.00 |
| Education programs (home gardening, growth monitoring, etc) | 5.00–10.00 |
| | |
| *Community-based nutrition programs* | |
| Less intensive | 2.00–5.00 |
| More intensive | 5.00–10.00 and up |
| | |
| *Food/income transfer programs* | |
| Feeding programs (per 1,000 cal/day) | 70.00–100.00 |
| Food subsidy programs (per 1,000 cal/day) | 36.00–170.00 |
| Targeted income transfers (per 1,000 cal/day) | $110 and up |

Estimates are in US dollars (1990).

*Sources*: Community-based programs [18], breast-feeding promotion [23], other programs except targeted income transfers [29]. Author's estimates for zinc fortification; lower estimate represents zinc oxide (less bioavailable) and higher estimate zinc sulfate (more bioavailable). Author's estimates for targeted income transfers, based on [30].

Child Development Services (ICDS) in India, Barangay Integrated Development Approach for Nutrition Improvement (BIDANI) in Bangladesh), and more intensive programs cost $5–$15 per child, even more if food is provided. Mason et al. [18] concluded that the less-intensive programs are not generally effective, and that intervention has to be provided at a more-intensive level to have significant effect.

Unit cost data suggest that feeding and food subsidy programs without a strong educational component represent resources that would be better reallocated on nutritional grounds. The leakages away from the most vulnerable populations are usually considerable. Feeding programs are very costly: $70–$100 per thousand calories per person per day for a year. Food subsidies have a wider range but similar median costs.

There have been successes with targeted income transfers (e.g., PROGRESA, now Oportunidades, in Mexico, Red de Protección Social (RPS) in Nicaragua, and Food-for-Education in Bangladesh). These typically cost more per calorie transferred than feeding programs Programa de Educación Salud y Alimentación (PROGRESA might cost around $110 annually, per thousand calories per person per day) but have other desirable outcomes, such as improved school attendance and improved participation in preventive health programs. The higher cost per calorie (due to leakage to nonfood expenditures) is partially offset by lower program delivery costs in well-designed programs well targeted to the poor.

There are exceptional circumstances for which food-based programs have immediate and dramatic mortality effects, such as for refugees and in HIV/AIDS programs. Provision of ready-to-use therapeutic foods (typically higher cost per calorie than school feeding programs) may be important in selected populations, such as children with severe acute malnutrition. However, costs are likely to restrict these interventions to special populations.

These unit costs suggest that nutrition interventions are well within the affordable range for "add-ons" to primary health care. Even the most expensive community programs can be afforded if well targeted to particular regions and focused on children below 2 or 3 years old, as long as food is not a component. Food-based programs are valuable for some special populations.

## 32.4 COST-EFFECTIVENESS AND BENEFIT: COST OF NUTRITION INTERVENTIONS

Cost-effectiveness data are relatively scarce for nutrition interventions, largely because there are few program impact data. Caulfield et al. [24] provided a survey. They summarized the literature for a range of nutrition interventions as part of a larger project also surveying many health interventions. This evaluation was based on program data (if available) as well as extrapolations/estimates (if program data were not available). Program estimates are preferable to those from small-scale clinical trials; efficacy in small-scale trials does not always translate into effectiveness in larger-scale programs. The results represent cost-effectiveness in "best-practice" interventions rather than the average experience.

The cost-effectiveness of nutrition interventions was very favorable. The lowest-cost range (<$25 per disability-adjusted life-year [DALY] saved) included breast-feeding promotion, vitamin A capsule distribution, and growth monitoring (the last based on one project in Honduras); health interventions in this same cost category were mainly high-priority public health initiatives. The next category ($25 to < $75 per DALY saved) included iron and iodine fortification, zinc supplementation as a complement to oral rehydration therapy (ORT), as well as child survival programs with nutrition components. This same category included some public health measures and some clinical interventions. Many clinical interventions fell into the DALY range of cost-effectiveness at more than $75. Caulfield et al. [24] did not include any nutrition interventions in this category, but most likely interventions involving food supplementation would fall in this range.

Another similar source of data was compiled by the WHO, through their Choosing Interventions that are Cost-Effective (CHOICE) project [25]. In this database, micronutrient interventions are a very high priority among a range of health interventions examined, based again on cost-effectiveness, as measured by cost per DALY saved. There is variation across the WHO regions and subregions regarding where the highest priority lies, depending on regional variations in prevalence and intervention costs.

Nutrition interventions have impacts on economic productivity as well as on health. These impacts are typically assessed by cost:benefit analysis. Estimates exist for iron and iodine and for interventions targeting underweight/stunting, relying on the estimates of productivity losses (both in manual labor and via cognitive impairments) similar to those summarized in Table 32.3.

Estimated benefit:cost ratios for iron fortification are around 6:1 for physical productivity effects alone (median, for a group of countries with high levels of anemia), 36:1 including cognitive impacts [11]. Very rough estimates for iodine prior to salt iodization are on the order of 70:1 [26]. Behrman et al. [27] estimated the benefit:cost ratio for breast-feeding promotion as around 4:1 and the range of benefit:cost ratios for plant breeding programs aimed at higher micronutrient content as around 19:1 (for iron and zinc) and between 14:1 and 79:1 (for vitamin A breeding for rice), depending on whether one employs more pessimistic or more optimistic assumptions.

Benefit:cost estimates permit nutrition interventions to be compared to other development interventions (whereas cost-effectiveness estimates restrict the comparison usually to health interventions since the outcome assessed is deaths averted or DALYs saved). One (somewhat subjective) compilation undertaken by a Delphi Group including prominent economists was the Copenhagen Consensus [28]. This compilation compared the development priority of 4 nutrition-related interventions (drawing on Behrman et al.'s [27] benefit:cost estimates), with 13 other development interventions ranging from interventions targeting health, the environment, trade, migration, and so on. Micronutrient interventions were rated among the top four "very good" priorities, new agricultural technologies to improve nutrition among the five "good" ones, and interventions designed to decrease the prevalence of low birth weight and to improve infant/child nutrition among the four "fair" priorities. No nutrition interventions fell among the four "poor" priorities.

## 32.5   CONCLUSIONS

This chapter has shown that the costs of undernutrition are very high, both in terms of child (and maternal) deaths and in terms of lost economic productivity. Undernutrition is a risk associated with 3.7 million deaths annually, primarily of infants and children, about one third of such deaths in developing countries. Southeast (including South) Asia and sub-Saharan Africa are the most affected. Iron-deficiency anemia may account for 0.8 million annual deaths, largely perinatal with some maternal, primarily in Southeast (including South) Asia and sub-Saharan Africa. Subclinical vitamin A deficiency accounts for 0.78 million child deaths annually, almost two thirds of these in sub-Saharan Africa. Zinc deficiency accounts for almost the same, with most in sub-Saharan Africa followed by Southeast (including South) Asia. Economic productivity losses can add up to 1–2% of GDP even for an individual nutrient deficiency, with iron, iodine, and underweight each important.

Well-designed nutrition interventions can be affordable. Micronutrient fortification and supplementation are an urgent priority in terms of their very low unit cost and very high cost-effectiveness. Integrating micronutrient supplementation into immunization programs make sense. Micronutrient fortification is the long-run solution of choice for the majority of the population and may require outside technical and financial assistance with the initial setup costs. Iron fortification is a particular priority since there has been the least progress on this. For some countries, there exist ready fortification vehicles, and the obstacles are the setup costs for equipment and monitoring capability (countries where wheat and maize flour are the main staple and where there is centralized processing have advantages in fortification). For other countries, there are more formidable barriers due to lack of an obvious vehicle (this is often the case where rice is the staple food). Plant breeding programs for enhanced micronutrient content are a promising alternative, especially for rice.

Supplementation programs have an important role, even if they are less cost-effective than fortification. Supplementation may be vital for harder-to-reach populations (in more remote areas, where centrally processed food is not available), for poorer households who do not purchase processed foods, and for population groups with particularly high needs (particularly pregnant women and weaning age children).

Breast-feeding promotion is highly cost-effective, particularly if the starting point is where hospitals have not yet adopted "baby-friendly" policies and still use formula.

Mass-media education interventions appear to be low in cost, but there are no cost-effectiveness data. Mass-media programs may be important if there are ways to improve diet without requiring households to buy more expensive food. They may also be useful to complement other interventions, for example, increasing awareness of and demand for fortified foods.

Community-based nutrition programs are effective if well designed and are an attractive investment for countries that already have in place expanded programs of immunization and basic public health/primary health care interventions in the lowest cost per DALY group.

From a nutritional standpoint, feeding programs (without substantial education) and food subsidies represent resources that could be better applied to more direct nutrition interventions. Using food in programs may be appropriate in programs with nonnutritional goals (e.g., as an incentive to girls to participate in education programs) and for special populations (refugees, those affected by HIV/AIDS). Targeted income transfers may have valuable nutrition outcomes but are typically affordable in middle- but not low-income countries.

There are regional differences in priorities for nutrition interventions. In South and Southeast Asia, density of population and depth and extent of undernutrition make community-based projects cost-effective. Likewise, patterns of food purchase make fortification feasible. As antenatal care coverage is extended, prenatal supplementation with a range of micronutrients should become more widespread.

In Latin America, levels of undernutrition are lower, and community-based activities (at least from the one example in the Dominican Republic) have higher unit costs (this would be expected given the higher salary levels than in South Asia). Since formula feeding is fairly widespread (Mexico is a particularly negative example), and diarrheal morbidity rates are high, breast-feeding promotion would be a cost-effective intervention, both in hospitals and in the community.

In sub-Saharan Africa, interventions are more problematic. Low population densities are likely to raise the costs of community-based interventions (although there have been isolated successful projects). Moreover, decentralized food processing (and the great variety of staples) makes fortification more difficult. Fortification also needs to be done on a regional (rather than individual country) basis due to the large volume of trade among African countries. Possibly one of the most urgent priorities is work on refugee nutrition. The outbreak of micronutrient deficiency diseases such as pellagra and scurvy in refugee camps and the worsening of rates of PEM in some camps are nothing short of scandalous.

In the region the WHO terms the Eastern Mediterranean, despite higher levels of income and lower protein-energy undernutrition, rates of iodine deficiency and anemia remain surprisingly high. Micronutrient fortification would seem to be a particular priority here, particularly since there are many wheat-consuming households for whom iron fortification would be possible.

As countries become richer, problems of overnutrition emerge (adult chronic disease, heart health). These issues, which are already facing urban elites even in relatively poor countries, are also an issue in Eastern Europe and the former Soviet Union. The present chapter has not addressed the economics of health promotion in the area of overnutrition, but this is another topic worthy of further research.

## REFERENCES

1. Popkin BM, Horton S, Kim S. The nutrition transition and prevention of diet-related diseases in Asia and the Pacific. Food Nutr Bull 2001;22(suppl):1–58.
2. Pelletier DL, Frongillo EA Jr, Schroeder DG, Habicht JP. A methodology for estimating the contribution of malnutrition to child mortality in developing countries. J Nutr 1994;124:2106S–2122S.
3. World Health Organization. The world health report 2002. Geneva: World Health Organization, 2002.
4. United Nations International Children's Emergency Fund. The state of the world's children, 2003. Available at: http://www.unicef.org/sowc03. Accessed September 25, 2005.
5. de Benoist B, Andersson M, Egli I, Takkouche B, Allen H. Global database on iodine deficiency. Geneva: World Health Organization, 2004.
6. Stoltzfus RM, Mullaney L, Black RE. Iron deficiency anemia. In: Comparative quantification of health risks. Ezzati M, Lopez AD, Rodgers A, Murray CJL, eds. Geneva: World Health Organization, 2004.
7. Humphrey JH, West KP, Sommer A. Vitamin A deficiency and attributable mortality among under-5-year-olds. Bull World Health Organ 1992;70:225–232.
8. International Zinc Nutrition Consultative Group. Assessment of the risk of zinc deficiency in populations and options for its control. Available at: http://www.izincg.ucdavis.edu/publications/default.html. Accessed September 23, 2005.
9. Basta S, Soekirman S, Karyadi D, Scrimshaw NS. Iron deficiency anemia and the productivity of adult males in Indonesia. Am J Clin Nutr 1979;32:916–925.
10. Imminck MDC, Viteri FE. Body composition of Guatemalan sugarcane cutters, working productivity, and different settings and conditions. Human Biol 1987;59:827–836.
11. Horton S, Ross J. The economics of iron deficiency. Food Policy 2003;28:51–75.
12. Haddad LJ, Bouis HE. The impact of nutritional status on agricultural productivity: wage evidence from the Philippines. Oxford Bull Econ Stat 1991;53:45–68.
13. Alderman H, Behrman JR, Ross DR, Sabot R. The returns to endogenous human capital in Pakistan's rural wage labour market. Oxford Bull Econ Stat 1996;58:29–55.
14. Selowsky M, Taylor L. The economics of malnourished children: an example of disinvestment in human capital. Econ Dev Cult Change 1973;22(1):17–30.
15. Grantham-McGregor S, Walker SP, Chang SM, Powell CA. Effects of early childhood supplementation with and without stimulation on later development in stunted Jamaican children. Am J Clin Nutr 1997;66:247–253.
16. Ross J. PROFILES guidelines: calculating the effects of malnutrition on economic productivity and survival [mimeo]. Washington, DC: Academy for Educational Development, 1997.
17. UN Administrative Council on Coordination, Subcommittee on Nutrition. Third report on the world nutrition situation. Geneva: World Health Organization Administrative Council on Coordination, Subcommittee on Nutrition, 1997.
18. Mason J, Hunt J, Parker D, Jonsson U. Investing in child nutrition in Asia. Asian Dev Rev 1999;17:1–32.
19. World Health Organization. Global database on iodine deficiency. Available at: http://www3.who.int/whosis/micronutrient. Accessed September 23, 2005.

20. World Bank. World development report 2000/2001. Washington, DC: World Bank, 2001.

21. World Bank. World development report 1993. Washington, DC: World Bank, 1993.

22. Applied Economic Research Centre. Final report on RETA-5671 Pakistan country strategy [mimeo]. Karachi: Applied Economic Research Centre, 1998.

23. Horton S, Sanghvi T, Philipps M, Fiedler J, Perez-Escamilla R, Lutter C, Rivera A, Segall-Correa AM. Breastfeeding promotion and priority setting in health. Health Policy Plan 1996;11(2):156–168.

24. Caulfield LE, Richard SA, Rivera JA, Musgrove P, Black RE. Stunting, wasting, and micronutrient deficiency disorders. In: Disease control priorities in developing countries. 2nd ed. Jamison DR, Alleyne G, Breman J, Evans DB, Jha P, Measham AR, Mills A, Musgrove PR, eds. Washington, DC: World Bank/Oxford University Press, 2006:551–567.

25. World Health Organization. Choosing interventions which are cost-effective. Available at: http://www3. who.int/whosis. Accessed September 27, 2005.

26. Horton, S. The economic impact of micronutrient deficiencies. In: Micronutrient deficiencies during the weaning period and the first years of life. Pettifor JM, Zlotkin S, eds. Nestle Nutrition Workshop Series Pediatric Program, Vol. 54. Basel: Karger, 2004:187–197.

27. Behrman JR, Alderman H, Hoddinott J. Hunger and malnutrition. In: Global crises, global solutions. Lomborg B, ed. Cambridge, UK: Cambridge University Press, 2004.

28. Lomborg B. Global crises, global solutions. Cambridge, UK: Cambridge University Press, 2004.

29. Horton S. Unit costs, cost-effectiveness and financing of nutrition interventions. Washington, DC: World Bank, 1992. World Bank PHN Working Papers WPS 952.

30. Hoddinott J, Skoufias E. The impact of PROGRESA on food consumption. Washington, DC: International Food Policy Research Institute, Food Consumption and Nutrition Division. 2003. Discussion Paper No. 150.

# 33 Ethics in Public Health Research

*Tanya Doherty and Mickey Chopra*

## 33.1 INTRODUCTION

Scientific research has produced substantial social benefits. It has also posed some troubling ethical questions. During the last century, there have been a number of notorious cases in which participants have been harmed as a consequence of unethical clinical research. Public attention was drawn to these issues by reported abuses of human subjects in biomedical experiments, especially during the Second World War. During the Nuremberg war crime trials, the Nuremberg Code [1] was drafted as a set of standards for judging physicians and scientists who had conducted biomedical experiments on concentration camp prisoners. The central feature of the Nuremberg Code was the protection of the integrity of the person participating in research. The Nuremberg Code was endorsed by the World Medical Association (WMA), which published the Declaration of Helsinki [2] in 1964. The declaration, which has been revised five times, sets out the principles to be observed in research on human participants and has become the cornerstone of research related to health care. The principles in the Declaration of Helsinki have been incorporated into many of the forms of guidance that have subsequently been drawn up to govern the conduct of research related to health care.

The objective of ethical guidance is to provide an ethical framework, a set of principles that allows us to evaluate the actions and policies of individuals and bodies such as international organizations, academic institutions, and government agencies. These principles seek to identify the considerations that should apply to individuals and agencies when making decisions or adopting policies. They constitute a framework for articulating the duties, obligations, claims, and expectations of those involved in research related to health care.

In recent years, there has been a significant increase in the number of international collaborative health research studies involving first-world sponsors and scientists and developing-country institutions and subjects. The inherent inequality of the relationship between these two groups of actors has drawn attention to the ethics of research sponsored (or conducted) by groups in industrialized countries but carried out in developing countries. A major question that has arisen concerns whether it is appropriate to apply the same set of ethical standards and procedures that are used for studies in industrialized countries to studies conducted in developing countries, where the cultural and social context may be different.

From: *Nutrition and Health: Nutrition and Health in Developing Countries, Second Edition*
Edited by: R. D. Semba & M. W. Bloem © Humana Press, Totowa, NJ

In light of the increase in collaborative research, some institutions have developed ethical guidelines that are aimed specifically at international collaborative research. The Council for International Organisations of Medical Sciences (CIOMS), in collaboration with the World Health Organization (WHO), recognized the special circumstances that arise when applying the declaration of Helsinki to research undertaken in developing countries and proposed guidelines to address them in 1982 [3]. These guidelines sought to direct the conduct of research involving human participants in a way that would recognize the social, economic, legal, regulatory, and administrative arrangements that exist in developing nations. In the United States, the ethical issues that arise when clinical research sponsored by the United States is undertaken in developing countries were given detailed consideration in the US National Bioethics Advisory Commissions (NBAC) report, *Ethical and Policy Issues in International Research: Clinical Trials in Developing Countries* [4]. The NBAC report emphasized the ethical and logistical problems that arise when research related to health care in developing countries is externally sponsored.

It is clear that the development of an adequate system of ethical review and oversight is a necessary condition of a defensible practice of international collaborative research in the decades ahead. Ethical review in many developing countries, however, is perceived as inadequate (a problem shared with many richer countries) and is an increasingly important obstacle to collaborative research.

The aim of this chapter is to generate awareness and openness of discussion that may engage researchers from developed and developing countries in an effort to increase understanding and promote guidelines that acknowledge both similarities and differences. The topics covered represent a wide range of ethical issues in public health research.

## 33.2   BASIC ETHICAL PRINCIPLES

The expression *basic ethical principles* refers to those general judgments that serve as a basic justification for the many particular ethical prescriptions and evaluations of human actions. Three basic principles are particularly relevant to the ethics of research involving human participants: the principles of respect of persons, beneficence, and justice.

### 33.2.1   *Respect for Persons*

Respect for persons incorporates at least two ethical convictions: first, that individuals should be treated as autonomous agents, and second, that persons with diminished autonomy are entitled to protection.

An autonomous person is an individual capable of deliberation about personal goals and of acting under the direction of such deliberation. To respect autonomy is to take other people's interests into account, to support a sense of self-respect and self-worth, and to encourage individuals to develop and express their capacities. To show lack of respect for an autonomous agent is to use individuals as a means either to our own ends or to the welfare of others, to increase risk of illness or death, or to misinform.

However, not every human being is capable of self-determination. The capacity for self-determination matures during an individual's life, and some individuals lose this capacity wholly or in part because of illness, mental disability, or circumstances that severely restrict liberty. Respect for the immature and the incapacitated may require protecting them as they mature or while they are incapacitated.

Some persons are in need of extensive protection, even to the point of excluding them from activities that may harm them; other persons require little protection beyond making sure they undertake activities freely and with awareness of possible adverse consequences. The extent of protection afforded should depend on the risk of harm and the likelihood of benefit. The judgment that any individual lacks autonomy should be periodically reevaluated and will vary in different situations.

In most cases of research involving human participants, respect for persons demands that individuals enter into research voluntarily and with adequate information. In some situations, however, application of the principle is not obvious. The involvement of prisoners as subjects of research provides an important example. On the one hand, it would seem that the principle of respect for persons requires that prisoners not be deprived of the opportunity to volunteer for research. On the other hand, under prison conditions they may be subtly coerced or unduly influenced to engage in research activities for which they would not otherwise volunteer. Respect for persons would then dictate that prisoners be protected. Whether to allow prisoners to "volunteer" or to "protect" them presents a dilemma. Respecting persons is often a matter of balancing competing claims urged by the principle of respect itself.

### 33.2.2   Beneficence

Persons are treated in an ethical manner not only by respecting their decisions and protecting them from harm, but also by making efforts to secure their well-being. The term *beneficence* is often understood to cover acts of kindness or charity that go beyond strict obligation. In this context, beneficence is understood in a stronger sense, as an obligation. Two general rules have been formulated as complementary expressions of beneficent actions in this sense: (1) do not harm and (2) maximize possible benefits and minimize possible harms. The problem posed by these imperatives is to decide when it is justifiable to seek certain benefits despite the risks involved and when the benefits should be forgone because of the risks.

The obligations of beneficence affect both individual investigators and society at large because they extend both to particular research projects and to the entire enterprise of research. In the case of particular projects, investigators and members of their institutions are obliged to give forethought to the maximization of benefits and the reduction of risk that might occur from the research investigation. In the case of scientific research in general, members of the larger society are obliged to recognize the longer-term benefits and risks that may result from the improvement of knowledge and from the development of novel medical, psychotherapeutic, and social procedures.

### 33.2.3   Justice

Who ought to receive the benefits of research and bear its burdens? This is a question of *justice*, in the sense of "fairness in distribution" or "what is deserved." An *injustice* occurs when some benefit to which a person is entitled is denied without good reason or when some burden is imposed unduly.

During the 19th and early 20th centuries, the burdens of serving as research participants fell largely on poor ward patients, while the benefits of improved medical care flowed primarily to private patients. Subsequently, the exploitation of unwilling prisoners as research subjects in Nazi concentration camps was condemned as a particularly blatant injustice. In the United States in the 1940s, the Tuskegee syphilis study [5] used disadvantaged, rural black men to study the untreated course of a disease that was by no means confined to that population. These subjects were deprived of demonstrably effective treatment in order not to interrupt the study long after such treatment became generally available.

Against this historical background, it can be seen how conceptions of justice are relevant to research involving human participants. For example, the selection of research participants needs to be scrutinized to determine whether some classes (e.g., welfare patients, particular racial and ethnic minorities, or persons confined to institutions) are systematically selected simply because of their easy availability, their compromised position, or their manipulability rather than for reasons directly related to the problem studied. Finally, whenever research leads to the development of therapeutic devices and procedures, justice demands both that these not provide advantages only to those who can afford them and that such research should not unduly involve persons from groups unlikely to be among the beneficiaries of subsequent applications of the research.

## 33.3  APPLICATION OF ETHICAL PRINCIPLES

The basic ethical principles described should not be thought of as rules to be applied mechanistically. By their nature, they call for interpretation and exercise of judgment. Most important, they need to be applied within research settings. This leads to consideration of the following requirements: informed consent, confidentiality, standards of care, and responsibility to the study community.

These requirements, however also need to take into consideration the special circumstances of research undertaken in developing countries and sponsored by developed countries. Developing countries often have little or no relevant national guidance which leads to a danger that the conduct of the research may fail to reflect the social and cultural values of those from the developing countries who participate.

The basic bioethical principles may have different meanings in different settings and foreign investigators and funders need to be sensitive to these different perspectives. Given the urgency of research on conditions such as HIV/AIDS, careful examination of both the interpretation of existing principles and the evolution of new guidelines is critical. This poses a challenge to researchers and ethicists from both donor and recipient organizations. The remainder of the chapter will focus on the ethical requirements for research with a focus on the challenges key areas of uncertainty.

### 33.3.1  *Informed Consent*

Respect for persons has been described as a basic ethical principle. In research, this duty requires that we do not act against a person's wishes. His or her consent to participate in research must thus be obtained. When externally sponsored research is undertaken in developing countries, a range of issues arise in seeking consent to take part in research. With regard to informing potential participants, concepts that are common in research, such as use of placebos or the idea of randomization, may be unfamiliar to the culture in which the research is conducted. With regard to the voluntary nature of consent, it may be common in a particular context for a spouse or senior member of the family to make decisions regarding health care (and by extension, to research) for the whole family or household. In addition, access to better health care and other benefits that might be made available through participation in research may act as powerful inducements hampering the true voluntary nature of a participant's consent.

Informed consent implies that the researcher and participant have entered into a voluntary agreement without any element of coercion, and that the participant is fully knowledgeable of the implications of participation. Consent, however, is only effective if a meaningful exchange of information takes place. If the obtaining of consent is largely ceremonial or if the researcher merely pays lip-service to the concept, then the autonomy of subjects is disregarded, and the process does not offer adequate protection. Given that participation is the key to informed consent, it is necessary to ensure a proper climate for the communication process.

Communicating information about a choice and its implications can be difficult and time consuming, but it allows valid, informed decisions. Widespread illiteracy is not a barrier to comprehension, especially since informed consent is more an interactive process than one that depends on reading. When appropriate, oral or pictorial depiction of concepts such as randomization could be used to improve understanding.

Ideally, each potential research subject should comprehend the nature of the investigation before providing valid informed consent. This information should be communicated and interpreted at an appropriate level of understanding so that it does not become overwhelming and senseless. The prerecruitment counseling for research conducted on patients seeking medical care should include information explicitly emphasizing that nonparticipation in the research project will in no way compromise the care provided at the institution.

We should not rely solely on individual informed consent to educate people about studies, especially community trials. Baseline knowledge in the community should be enhanced by more open discussions of the topic in places like community meetings because the more people understand the subject, the less anxious they are when given individual information as part of their invitation to participate. Moreover, the importance of community structures within many African societies should be acknowledged, and a process of dual consent may give more legitimacy to a study than individual consent alone.

The following case study provides examples of how a process of community information can be combined with innovative methods of individual consent. The case is based on an article by Preziosi et al. [6].

## CASE STUDY 33.1

In the process of this study that aimed to evaluate a new pertussis vaccine in a rural community in Senegal, the researchers wanted to assess the incorporation of clear procedures for obtaining individual informed consent from parents. In this part of Senegal, consent for all previous research with human subjects had been obtained from community leaders on behalf of all eligible members of the community. Individuals could subsequently decline to participate.

At the start of the study, meetings were held by the field staff and physicians in each village to provide information and obtain consensus. All residents were invited. Presentations were given simultaneously in Sereer and French. Each presentation included a review of the activity of the research organization in the study area, information about vaccination, and a description of the study. To illustrate the principle of randomization and the possibility that one of the vaccines might fail, the presenters used a familiar agricultural example: the evaluation of fertilizers or seed varieties on randomized plots, a procedure familiar to farmers in the area. After these meetings, the researchers began to inform the mothers further and to give them a distinct opportunity to refuse to participate. During one vaccination session, a pilot evaluation of the feasibility of obtaining individual oral informed consent was conducted. Subsequently, a physician fluent in Sereer routinely presented the information at each monthly vaccination session and recorded the mother's answers as witnessed by the vaccination nurse. From that point until the last vaccination in the study, the mother of each child eligible for inclusion in the vaccine study was asked whether she had been informed about it and if so how. If she had not, the study was explained to her, and she could then decide whether to participate. Throughout the study, whole-cell diphtheria and tetanus toxoids and pertussis (DTP)-poliovirus vaccine was available for the infants of mothers who declined to be included in the study or to have subsequent doses administered. The interventions were evaluated at the end of the study to determine the feasibility and validity of seeking individual informed consent.

Results of this evaluation showed that mothers were generally in agreement with vaccination and to the participation of their children in the study. Certain questions raised indicated their difficulty in understanding the concept of a double-blind study: They wanted to choose one of the vaccines for their children or at least to know which vaccine was given to be able to make their own judgments about both vaccines. In general, the results of this study indicated that the parents understood the study sufficiently to make informed choices. During the meetings, comments by community residents emphasized their understanding of the principles of the vaccine study after these principles were illustrated with better-known examples drawn from agriculture. The increased acceptance of vaccination overall suggested a positive effect of the information sessions held by the researchers.

The consent process described in the case provided each mother with an opportunity to make an individual choice for her child within the context of community consensus, which is consistent with the social organization of the community. To rely solely on communal consent for research is not widely accepted in ethical guidelines [3], and the use (or abuse) of cultural relativism to obviate the need for eliciting informed consent from individuals has been severely criticized [7]. In this situation, given the nature of the intervention (vaccination), individual informed consent was appropriate as a means to ensure autonomy and prevent exploitation of this society. The NBAC report [4] (recommendation 3.6) provides some guidelines regarding the role of others in the consent process. It states:

> *Where culture or custom requires that permission of a community representative be granted before researchers may approach potential research participants, researchers should be sensitive to such local requirements. However, in no case may permission from a community representative or council replace the requirement of a competent individual's voluntary informed consent.*

In this setting, obtaining individual informed consent with community consensus was appropriate and served many benefits beyond the autonomy that it gave to the participants. The community discussions indicated a common concern about health problems and a perception of research as an element of progress and of social benefit to which people wished to have access.

### 33.3.2 Confidentiality

Researchers are required to ensure that the information that they gather from participants is protected to prevent undue harm or negative consequences from participation in the research. This relates to the basic ethical principle of beneficence. This is particularly important when research is being carried out with vulnerable or identifiable population groups such as individuals with HIV/AIDS. Breaking of confidentiality is a risk to subjects that can cause people to become social outcasts, be stigmatized, and endure various other adverse social consequences. These risks are different depending on the subject under study and feelings surrounding this in the particular culture or society.

Maintaining the confidentiality of information obtained from health research poses unique challenges to researchers, especially if they may uncover practices during the conduct of fieldwork that may be substandard or even place patients at risk. The following case raises issues regarding the maintenance of confidentiality in a research study involving a vulnerable participant group.

#### CASE STUDY 33.2

**Background.** To determine the level of vertical HIV transmission, a local nongovernmental research group in Uganda designs a study that uses a prospective cohort study design to follow HIV-positive women from late pregnancy until their infants reach 1 year. The study will cover ten villages in an area where government Prevention of Mother to Child Transmission of HIV (PMTCT) services are provided through the district hospital, some rural hospitals, and a few primary health care centers.

**Recruitment Methods.** The study team proposes to set up a recruitment system that will use two main sources to find HIV-positive pregnant women: (1) community-based health workers and women's groups and (2) health workers who are providing PMTCT services.

All health providers who provide PMTCT services and who agree to be part of the recruitment process will be given an instruction sheet explaining the purpose and methods of the study. They will discuss the study with women who test HIV positive during antenatal Voluntary Counselling and Testing (VCT) and obtain their consent to be interviewed at home by the research team. Health providers will give the researchers the names of those who agree to participate but will not provide a list of those who refuse to be interviewed. Information sources within the community will be asked to serve as intermediaries to schedule an interview between the researchers and the consenting women.

As some of the women may have changed their mind about being interviewed after their original consent, a second layer of protection from unwanted attention is afforded the women by adopting the following measures: (1) During the interview, attention will be focused on the pregnancy and the health of the infant rather than issues related to HIV; (2) artificial privacy will be created during the interview by using a "team" of interviewers, with one person conducting the actual interview while the other members of the team engage family members in dummy interviews. Women will be free to discontinue the interview at any time without prejudice.

**Deliberations of the Ethical Review Committee.** The study is presented to the ethical review committee of the international funder following its approval by the local ethical review board. All but one member of the ethical review committee, an anthropologist who has worked extensively in Uganda, approve of the study. She is concerned that there is some chance that the confidentiality of the women may be compromised and wants assurances that the records that identify the research subject will be kept confidential. The study group responds that all records will be kept under lock and key in the main offices of the nongovernmental organization (NGO), which is nowhere near the study site.

In this case, the researchers used a variety of individuals to recruit participants into the study, including health care workers and community workers. This may have threatened the confidentiality of the participants because it is not clear whether the community workers were aware of the aims of the research or the HIV status of the women. The Declaration of Helsinki [2] addressed the issue of confidentiality in the following recommendation:

> *The right of research subjects to safeguard their integrity must always be respected. Every precaution should be taken to respect the privacy of the subject, the confidentiality of the patient's information and to minimize the impact of the study on the subject's physical and mental integrity and on the personality of the subject.*

There are many dilemmas that confront researchers in their attempts to uphold confidentiality. Public health research in particular often involves observational data collection within facilities. If during data collection a researcher uncovers a situation in a clinic by which bad practice places patients at risks, the researcher faces a dilemma. The researcher knows what he or she is seeing is wrong, yet there is an ethical obligation to protect the confidentiality of the health care workers and the health center. Researches often face role confusion between observing/reporting and implementing/taking action. In participatory/social science research, this role can be particularly unclear as researchers work closely with participants in a collaborative relationship. The main obligation of the researcher is to maintain the confidentiality of the participants/study sites, yet to what extent should this be upheld? Are there times when it would be appropriate to disclose information, and how is that decision made? In all cases, the need to protect confidentiality must be balanced against the risk to individual patients.

Disclosing the names of health centers that have been involved in research, especially where poor practices/care has been observed, may have serious implications for the health workers who staff these centers. Their jobs may be threatened, and they may face criticism from the management. Yet, without knowledge of the "problem" health centers, would it be possible for the management to make the necessary changes to improve the quality of care? This is a complex dilemma, but one that researchers will increasingly face as health systems research grows and the realities of service provision are brought to light.

### 33.3.3 Standards of Care

The standard of care to provide to participants in research has become an increasingly debated topic as more research is being conducted in developing country settings. Should participants receive the best current treatment available anywhere in the world or treatment based on an alternative standard of care that takes local circumstances into account? Where the best current treatment is inexpensive and simple to deliver, the answer is clear [8]. However, for most diseases and conditions, such a standard of care is routinely available to only a small proportion of the world's population and may be difficult to provide in developing countries.

This raises the question of when a placebo control group is appropriate in a randomized controlled trial. If an established treatment exists for a condition, is there ever any justification to test a new treatment against a control group? The following case highlights this dilemma.

## CASE STUDY 33.3

Since the early 1990s, several randomized controlled trials evaluated the efficacy of perinatal antiretroviral (ARV) prophylaxis regimens for the prevention of mother-to-child transmission (MTCT) of HIV. The first of these, the PACTG 076 trial conducted in the United States and France, evaluated the efficacy of antenatal and intrapartum zidovudine to the mother and 6 weeks of postnatal zidovudine to infants versus placebo. All mothers fed their infants formula milk. At 18 months, transmission was 7.6% in the zidovudine group and 22.6% in the placebo group. This was the first randomized controlled trial to prove the efficacy of an intervention to reduce the incidence of HIV infection in infants.

When the results of the PACTG 076 trial became available, a number of randomized, placebo-controlled trials of ARVs to reduce MTCT were already under way in Africa and Thailand. In September 1997, an article by Lurie and Wolfe [9] and an editorial by Angell [10] in the *New England Journal of Medicine* criticized placebo-controlled trials of short-course zidovudine given to HIV-infected pregnant women to prevent MTCT of HIV. The trials were designed to determine whether relatively affordable and more feasible shorter courses of zidovudine given to pregnant women in developing countries would reduce the risk of MTCT. They were conducted in countries where conventional local antenatal care did not include ARV treatment. The trial designs had been approved by ethics committees in the countries where the trials were conducted [11–14]. Research in which the control group would be provided with a placebo would be deemed unethical in developed countries where ARV treatment is available and the long-course zidovudine as assessed in PACTG 076 would be considered the standard of care.

The critics of the trials of a short course of treatment argued that it was unethical to give the control group a placebo when it had already been demonstrated that the longer courses reduced transmission of the virus. The Centers for Disease Control and Prevention (CDC), National Institutes of Health (NIH), the United Nations Joint Programme on HIV/AIDS (UNAIDS), and a wide range of individuals rejected this view for several reasons [11–14]. First, the 076 regimen was a complex, expensive, three-phase regimen that would be difficult to implement in resource-poor settings; second, the 076 trial was undertaken in a non-breast-feeding population, which is very different from the situation in African contexts, where the majority of women breast-feed and other risk factors such as micronutrient deficiencies and sexually transmitted infections are more frequently present.

When deciding on an appropriate standard of care for a control group in a randomized trial, the context in which the research is to be conducted needs to be carefully evaluated. A suitable standard of care can only be defined in consultation with individuals working in the country and must be justified to local research ethics committees.

The NBAC report [4] referred to the provision of treatment for control groups:

*Researchers and sponsors should design clinical trials that provide members of any control group with an established effective treatment, whether or not such treatment is available in the host country. Any study that would not provide the control group with an established, effective treatment should include a justification for using an alternative design. Ethics review committees must assess the justification provided, including the risks to participants, and the overall ethical acceptability of the research design.*

The issue of standards of care also arises regarding preventive interventions, such as participants in a vaccine trial who become infected with the disease during the course of the research. This issue has been considered extensively for HIV vaccine trials. If an HIV vaccine trial were to be conducted in a developed country, the standard treatment for individuals who seroconvert during the trial would include ARV therapy, yet in other contexts, such as countries in sub-Saharan Africa where ARV therapy may not be widely available, the standard of care for HIV-positive individuals would be purely symptomatic treatment. Would it be unethical to conduct an HIV vaccine trial in a developing country and not provide participants with the best universally available standard of care? Furthermore, would it be unethical to offer state-of-the-art care to seroconverters even if the care was not available in their country and was unlikely to be available within the near future except to the very wealthy?

These are complex questions that researchers have to face. The important principle to keep in mind when considering these issues is not to exploit those who are vulnerable. This can be achieved by providing the universal standard of care where possible, or at least the care that is available in the national public health system, and by attempting to improve standards of care through the research process.

### 33.3.4   *Responsibility to the Study Community After Completion of Research*

Not all research will have results that can be translated directly into practice. However, research related to health care is usually designed to obtain results that will lead to an improvement in the prevention, diagnosis, or treatment of a disease. One issue that arises when considering whether it is acceptable to undertake research in a developing country setting is if the intervention studied is likely to be affordable in that country if shown to be effective. Researchers also need to consider whether it is appropriate to conduct research if the benefits of that research will not be made available to the community in which the research was undertaken.

The next case addresses the issue of researchers' responsibilities to study communities. Central questions to keep in mind while reading the case are as follows: Which benefits should be provided to the research participants, and by whom, after their participation in the trial has ended? What, if anything, should be made available to others in the host community or country?

## CASE STUDY 33.4

**Background Information.** Vaccination against *Plasmodium falciparum* is the intervention with the greatest potential to reduce malaria-associated severe morbidity and mortality in areas with the most intense transmission. Infants and young children at risk for *P. falciparum* in Africa and nonimmune travelers to areas endemic for *P. falciparum* and *Plasmodium vivax* represent the extremes of target groups for whom malaria vaccines would be useful.

So far, only one vaccine, a multistage synthetic peptide, has shown any evidence of protection. Phase I studies of this candidate vaccine in the United States have been encouraging: Immunization of human subjects showed evidence of a strong immune response. No safety studies have been performed in children under 6 months. Furthermore, no synthetic peptide vaccine has previously been given to this age group.

To progress in the critical path of vaccine development and testing toward the implementation of a new vaccine in malaria control programs, a multinational pharmaceutical company is in the process of designing a randomized, double-blind, placebo-controlled efficacy trial of the vaccine when given alongside the expanded program on immunization (EPI) scheme.

A country in East Africa where malaria is endemic has expressed interest in participating in the vaccine research effort, and their scientists and the pharmaceutical company investigators are collaborating on a study protocol to see if the vaccine is effective in reducing deaths due to malaria in the population under 5 years old.

**Site Selection and Recruitment.** This study will be conducted in a town in the south of the country where there is intense year-round malaria transmission. The incidence of clinical malaria rises steeply after the first month of life, and the incidence in infants attending local health facilities for malaria and severe anaemia, a common manifestation of malaria, are 0.7 and 0.6 episodes per child year, respectively. In this town, a district hospital provides curative health services and an active mother and child clinic (MCH) delivers routine childhood immunizations and offers a monthly weighing clinic. Malaria control efforts are based on prompt diagnosis and chloroquine treatment, although 60% of parasite strains in the area are resistant to this chloroquine.

The researchers will recruit participants at the MCH clinic. Researchers will explain the trial to mothers when they bring their children for their first immunization. After receiving written informed consent from the mother, a child will receive a first dose of SPf66 or placebo (aluminum hydroxide) when they present for the first EPI immunization at around 1 month of age. Second and third doses will be given at 2 and 7 months of age, respectively.

Parents will be advised to attend the clinic if their child experiences any health problems (such as fever or diarrhea). Children who develop malaria (as determined by both clinical findings and microscopy) will be treated in the district hospital according to national guidelines (chloroquine therapy). The study will look at cases of malaria as the main study endpoint.

A few months prior to the proposed start of the trial, the pharmaceutical company investigators visit the host country to meet with representatives from the Department of Health to finalize the research protocol. The representatives from the Department of Health request that if the vaccine is effective, all children in this country should benefit from the results of the study by receiving free doses of the vaccine for 5 years following the completion of the trial.

The researchers find this an extreme request. They explain that they have a limited budget for their research, and they cannot afford to pay for the cost of vaccination coverage of the whole population of 45 million. They emphasize that they are currently conducting trials for other treatments aimed at the developing country market, and it would be unfair to provide free treatment to one country and not to another.

The issue of benefits to study subjects on completion of a trial has become a complex debate among international researchers. A plan for the routine provision of a successful new intervention to participants after a trial is one way to ensure that the study is responsive to the health needs of the host country.

If the vaccine company is unable to provide the Department of Health with the vaccine free of charge on completion of the trial, are there other benefits they could provide, such as upgrading of the district hospital to deal more effectively with malaria cases or assisting with other control measures such as provision of bed nets?

The NBAC report [4] referred to the issue of posttrial benefits and recommended (recommendation 4.1) that:

*Researchers and sponsors in clinical trials should make reasonable, good faith efforts before the initiation of a trial to secure, at its conclusion, continued access for all participants to needed experimental interventions that have been proven effective for the participants. Although the details of the arrangements will depend on a number of factors (including but not limited to the results of a trial), research protocols should typically describe the duration, extent, and financing of such continued access. When no arrangements have been negotiated, the researcher should justify to the ethics review committee why this is the case.*

The Declaration of Helsinki [2] offered a similar guideline. It stated that: "At the conclusion of a study, every patient entered into the study should be assured of access to the best proven prophylactic, diagnostic and therapeutic methods identified by the study."

It can be seen from these guidelines that the ethical obligation to provide the intervention to others in the community who might benefit from it is considerably less strong, but a plan to do so would help reduce the risk of exploitation. The NBAC report [4] made the following recommendation regarding posttrial benefits (recommendation 4.2):

*Research proposals submitted to ethics review committees should include an explanation of how new interventions that are proven to be effective from the research will become available to some or all of the host country population beyond the research participants themselves. Where applicable, the investigator should describe any pre-research negotiations among sponsors, host country officials, and other appropriate parties aimed at making such interventions available. In cases in which investigators do not believe that successful interventions will become available to the host country population, they should explain to the relevant ethics review committee(s) why the research is nonetheless responsive to the health needs of the country and presents a reasonable risk/benefit ratio.*

The fundamental goal of public health research is to improve the health and quality of care provided to individuals and communities. Researchers should therefore discuss and develop plans prior to the undertaking of studies regarding the long-term benefit to participants and the wider community. Raising the quality of health care available to those in developing countries, given current inequities, cannot be achieved in the short term. However, through the conduct of research that is responsive to the needs of developing countries together with attempts to make these interventions affordable and accessible, we could move closer to this goal.

## 33.4   ETHICAL REVIEW PROCESSES

An effective system for the review of the ethics of research is a crucial safeguard for participants in research. The accepted method of ensuring that unethical research is prevented is through the establishment of a system in which research ethics committees undertake independent review of scientific protocols. It is important for ethics committees to be independent of government and sponsors of research. Furthermore, international collaborative research should be subject to review in both the country hosting and the country sponsoring the research. The reality, however, is that ethics committees are often absent, underresourced, or ineffective in many countries.

There are three levels of assessment that should be considered for all research proposals:

- Relevance to priorities in health care within the country where the research is proposed to be conducted
- Scientific validity
- Ethical acceptability

Although ethics committees are not constituted to make policy decisions on, for example, whether the findings of a research project could be implemented in the country, they should determine if the implications of the research have been considered, including the possibility of introducing to the wider community treatment shown to be effective. In addition, they should request justification for research that does not include provisions for the development of expertise in research within the country where it is undertaken.

There is also a role for ethics committees to assess the scientific rigor of research. Research that is not appropriately designed will fail to provide answers to questions posed by the research and thus have limited or no benefit to participants or the wider community.

An ethics committee's primary task is to assess the ethical acceptability of research proposals with particular attention paid to the following: the predictable risks involved to participants, the anticipated benefits to participants, the provisions within the design relating to the care and protection of participants, the procedures for recruitment and selection, the processes for obtaining informed consent and provision for refusing consent and or withdrawing it during research, and provisions for protecting the security and confidentiality of data about patients.

The mere presence of an ethics committee is not enough to ensure that research will be adequately reviewed. Committees may be ineffective for a variety of reasons, including a lack of financial and human resources or a lack of training in and experience with reviewing the ethics of research. Furthermore, if a committee has limited independence and no clear framework of guidance, there is a danger that they make ad hoc rather than principled decisions.

For research ethics committees to function effectively, committee members must receive adequate training. As ethics committees often have a high turnover of staff, regular training programs are needed. A number of programs are being established to develop expertise in the field of medical ethics from organizations such as the NIH in the United States, WHO, and the Wellcome Trust. International organizations need to continue to expand their programs for establishing, training, and monitoring the development of research ethics committees.

Careful reflection by Western scientists about the ethics of conducting research in developing countries is essential, but it must go hand in hand with the establishment of systems of review by researchers in the host countries. To encourage the development of ethical theory and practice in medical research in developing countries, local experts, medical and nonmedical, must become more actively involved in screening research proposals and in studying examples in which ethical dilemmas and conflicts are highlighted to draw on important lessons and to improve research practice.

## 33.5   CONCLUSIONS

Researchers, sponsors, and others who are involved in research related to health care are often faced with diverse and sometimes conflicting guidance. It is important to consider all ethical questions in the context of an ethical framework that can provide a guide to use when determining how to apply guidelines. A major priority is the development of national ethical guidance and the strengthening of the process of ethical review of research, which will provide a further layer of protection to participants in research.

## REFERENCES

1.  The Nuremberg Code: trials of war criminals before the Nuremberg military tribunals under Control Council Law No. 10. Washington: US Government Printing Office, 1949:181–182.
2.  World Medical Association. Declaration of Helsinki: ethical principles for medical research involving human subjects. Adopted 18th WMA General Assembly, Helsinki, Finland, June 1964. Amended 52nd WMA General Assembly, Edinburgh, Scotland, October 2000. Ferney-Voltaire, France: World Medical Association 2000.
3.  Council for International Organizations of Medical Sciences. International guidelines for ethical review of epidemiological studies. Geneva: Council for International Organisations of Medical Sciences, 1991.
4.  National Bioethics Advisory Commission. Ethical and policy issues in international research: clinical trials in developing countries. Bethesda, MD: National Bioethics Advisory Commissions, 2001.
5.  Brandt AM. Racism and research: the case of the Tuskegee Syphilis Study. Hastings Center Rep 1978;8(6):174–183.
6.  Preziosi MP, Yam A, Ndiaye M, Simaga A, Simondon F, Wassilak SG. Practical experiences in obtaining informed consent for a vaccine trial in rural Africa. N Engl J Med 1997;336:370–373.
7.  Lurie P, Bishaw M, Chesney MA, et al. Ethical, behavioral, and social aspects of HIV vaccine trials in developing countries. JAMA 1994;271:295–301.
8.  Nuffield Council on Bioethics. The ethics of research related to healthcare in developing countries. London: Nuffield Council on Bioethics, 2002.
9.  Lurie P, Wolfe SM. Unethical trials of interventions to reduce perinatal transmission of the human immunodeficiency virus in developing countries. N Engl J Med 1997;337:853–856.
10. Angell M. The ethics of clinical research in the Third World. N Engl J Med 1997;337:847–849.
11. DeCock K, Shaffer N, Wiktor S, Simonds RS, Rogers M. Ethics of HIV trials. Lancet 1997;350:1546–1547.
12. Merson MH. Ethics of placebo-controlled trials of zidovudine to prevent perinatal transmission of HIV in the Third World. N Engl J Med 1998;338:836.
13. Perinatal HIV Intervention Research in Developing Countries Workshop participants. Science, ethics, and the future of research into maternal-infant transmission of HIV-1. Lancet 1999;353:832–835.
14. Varmus H, Satcher D. Ethical complexities of conducting research in developing countries. N Engl J Med 1997;337:1003–1005.

# 34  Beyond Partial Analysis

## David Pelletier

## 34.1  INTRODUCTION

A striking feature of this volume is that its unified title, *Nutrition and Health in Developing Countries,* belies an almost overwhelming breadth and depth of scientific perspective and detail concerning these topics. Although the various chapters do not fit neatly into a single typology, five of the most obvious analytical foci or frames for organizing the material are as follows:

1. Disease focus (diarrhea, respiratory, measles, tuberculosis, HIV, obesity)
2. Nutrient focus (vitamin A, zinc, iron, iodine, multiple micronutrients, undernutrition)
3. Special population groups (maternal, intrauterine, perinatal, child, elderly)
4. Special contexts (refugee, urbanization, socioeconomic transitions)
5. Planning and policy development (economics of interventions, food policy analysis, ethics)

These five frames represent the most common ways in which health and nutrition problems are viewed, defined, and analyzed within our professions and institutions. This diversity is necessary and useful for generating knowledge (i.e., research) related to *individual* diseases, nutrients, population groups, and development contexts. However, it may lead to fragmentation of effort in the development and implementation of health and nutrition policy and misallocation of scarce resources. This possibility arises because the optimal focus for organizing research (by disease, nutrient, or population group) may not be the optimal focus for setting priorities and organizing interventions. This is revealed by reflecting on a typology of potential actions to improve health and nutrition, one version of which is as follows:

1. Public health system
   a. service delivery (including food and nutrient supplements and various curative and preventive health services)
   b. environmental health (including water, sanitation, malaria eradication)

2. Food- and nutrient-based approaches
   a. fortification (single or multiple nutrients)
   b. nutrient supplementation (commercially and via actions outside the public health system)

From: *Nutrition and Health: Nutrition and Health in Developing Countries, Second Edition*
Edited by: R. D. Semba & M. W. Bloem © Humana Press, Totowa, NJ

    c. commercial or home-produced complementary foods

    d. home gardening

    e. home processing, preservation, and storage

3. Health and nutrition education, promotion, and social marketing (directed toward specific diseases, nutrients, foods, dietary patterns, risk factors, or behaviors)
4. Integrated community-based approaches
5. Food and income transfer policies, programs, and projects
6. Harmonizing nutrition goals within food and agricultural policy, programs, and projects
7. Harmonizing nutrition goals within rural and urban development policies, programs, and projects

These categories of actions are familiar to the international nutrition community and widely used throughout the world. However, as diverse as they are, they only begin to reveal the actual complexity of the choices facing health and nutrition planners and policy analysts. In part, this is because the scientific and practitioner knowledge base is still fragmentary regarding many issues, including when to use each strategy or combination of strategies, how to predict the likely effects in different contexts, the requirements for effective implementation, and how to most effectively promote, manage, and evaluate them at the policy level. These uncertainties are further compounded by diversity (and at times rivalry) among problem foci, disciplinary traditions, professional orientations, and institutions in the international nutrition and health field, all of which means we do not yet have an agreed-on framework for thinking about nutrition policy and guiding policy decisions.

The particular analytical frames we employ for guiding policy decisions in international health and nutrition are heavily influenced by the *research* traditions within our diverse disciplines and subdisciplines, which evolved primarily as tools for discovery rather than tools for aiding policy development. These research traditions do generate some of the knowledge required for designing individual interventions. However, there are some distinctive analytical and information requirements in the development of public policy that are not adequately addressed by these traditions or in the current training and practice of health and nutrition professionals. As a result, we tend to employ a variety of *partial* approaches to policy analysis and recommendation, a characteristic shared with many other fields [1–3].

The use of partial approaches to policy analysis, and the lack of a larger framework for thinking about scientific research, public policy, and the relationship between the two, has several undesirable consequences. Specifically, it compromises our ability to incorporate or translate our findings into policy formulation, fails to provide guidance regarding the most fruitful areas for future policy-relevant research, and compromises the appropriateness and effectiveness of policies and programs. In addition, it contributes to disagreement and controversy within our field because of the failure to distinguish scientific debates from public policy debates, which involve distinctive logics and procedures for evidence, argumentation, and decision making [4–7].

This chapter outlines a broader conception of policy analysis based on an evolving body of theory and experience in the policy sciences and explores the implications for health and nutrition. The next section describes the nature of public policy analysis, with a particular focus on how it differs from most research in international health and nutrition, followed by a discussion of the implications for research, training, and policy.

## 34.2    PUBLIC POLICY ANALYSIS

The diverse disciplines, scholars, and studies concerned with public policy tend to fall into one of three categories: (1) those that develop, use, or promote particular technical methods for policy-relevant research and policy analysis; (2) those that study the social and political processes that affect and are affected by policy formation, choice, implementation, and outcomes in various settings; and (3) those that study the relationship between the first two categories, that is, the tension that exists between technical analysis and the larger process by which changes take place or ought to take place in policy and society. For reasons given in this chapter, and following the policy sciences tradition established over half a century ago [3], the chapter adopts the perspective that "sound public policy analysis" explicitly should take account of all three bodies of knowledge.

Table 34.1 identifies seven analytical frames that underlie public policy analysis and disagreements, although these seldom are recognized and distinguished as such (these are adapted and expanded from Dunn [1]). This table provides the basis for the claim that policy development in international health and nutrition (as in most policy domains)

**Table 34.1**
**Analytical frames underlying public policy**

| *Frame* | *Key focus* | *Illustrative concepts/elements* |
|---|---|---|
| Technical | Causal analysis | Cause–effect relationships and mechanisms, dose–response, exposure, objectivity, uncertainty, methodology |
|  | Intervention analysis | Efficacy, effectiveness, coverage, targeting, quality, technical efficiency, unintended consequences |
| Economic | Allocative efficiency | Opportunity costs, incentives, self-interest, social welfare, consumer sovereignty, marginality, public and private goods, net social costs/benefits, externalities, information failures, market failures, government failures |
| Social/ normative | Equity Ethics Democracy | Fairness, distributive justice, rights, duties, obligations, autonomy, beneficence, non-maleficence, participation, consent, legitimacy, accountability, sovereignty |
| Political | Social allocation, freedom, power | Sovereignty, participation, resources, groups, identities, alliances, interests, values, compromise and reciprocity, ideologies, rules, norms, institutions |

(continued)

**Table 34.1** (continued)
Analytical frames underlying public policy

| Frame | Key focus | Illustrative concepts/elements |
|---|---|---|
| Administrative/ organizational | Performance Risk avoidance Survival Expansion Control Reputation | Routines, rules, authority, jurisdiction, discretion, professionalism, expertise, planning, management, political pressures, timing, opportunism, coping, negotiation, context, interests, beliefs, culture |
| Legal | Conformity | Laws, rules, precedents, rights, enforcement, contestation, due process |
| Multiple/ integrative | Effective Appropriate | Wisdom, judgment, justice, dignity, fairness and competence in analysis, deliberation and participation, legitimate representation of public values and interests |

is based on partial approaches. Without suggesting that all policy decisions should be based on a consideration of all analytical frames (a clearly impractical scenario), this table does provide a point of departure for identifying the gaps in our approaches so that future research, training, and practice might address some of the gaps considered most relevant to our set of concerns. This table provides the overall framework for this section.

## 34.2.1   The Technical Frame

Technical methods of policy-relevant research and policy analysis include a wide range of activities designed to study the prevalence of various problems, their causes and consequences, and the potential solutions. They also include methods for quantifying the costs and impacts of various solutions, as seen in cost-effectiveness analysis, and for studying certain aspects of the implementation process. Thus, in the case of international health and nutrition, the major task under this frame is to study the objective reality of diseases, nutrient or nutritional deficiencies, their consequences, and the effectiveness and costs of various solutions to support recommendations concerning what should be done to address these problems. Most of the chapters in this volume fall into this category.

### 34.2.1.1   CAUSAL ANALYSIS

*Causal analysis* refers to a wide range of activities, including human and animal experimental research and clinical or epidemiologic research in field settings. One way to organize our thinking about this wide range of scientific activity in relation to policy decisions is to borrow a framework from the field of risk assessment in developed countries. In this framework, four types of information are sought to help prioritize health and safety problems in these countries. Note that the terminology has been slightly altered here to conform to concepts in international health and nutrition. The example of child mortality is used here to illustrate the method [8, 9], but this method has been extended and applied more broadly in the global burden of disease analyses [10].

1. *Causal identification*: This step involves identifying the causes of a problem based on experimental, clinical, or epidemiologic research. Taking the example of child mortality in a particular setting, these might include diarrhea, respiratory infection, malaria, and undernutrition.

2. *Dose-response analysis*: This step involves estimating the relationship between the burden of a given cause (measured in terms of prevalence, incidence, duration, severity, distance to health services, or other measures appropriate to the problem) and the risk of the adverse outcome. In the child malnutrition–mortality example, the dose-response was quantified as the relative risk, that is, 2.5 for mild forms, 4.6 for moderate forms, and 8.4 for severe forms;

3. *Exposure analysis*: This involves estimating the distribution of exposure to a given cause within a particular population. For instance, in 1992, of Ethiopian children, 4.6% had severe undernutrition, 14.9% had moderate undernutrition, and 32% had mild undernutrition.

4. *Integrative measures:* These involve combining the information from the previous three steps in a policy-appropriate way, which can vary depending on the case and the nature of the information generated in the other steps. In the child mortality case, the population-attributable risk was used, indicating that in Ethiopia 56% of all child deaths were associated with the synergistic effects of malnutrition and disease, of which 76% were associated with mild-to-moderate malnutrition and 24% with severe malnutrition. These figures are close to the global estimates of 56% and 83%, respectively, that proved to be useful summary statistics for policy development at the international level.

This example is instructive for two reasons. First, it reveals that much of the research and analysis in international health and development is at the level of steps 1 and 2 (identifying or confirming causes and the strength of the relationships), but there is no systematic tradition, set of methods, or expectation in our field for combining it with exposure data and assembling it into policy-relevant, integrative measures such as step 4. This is illustrated by the fact that the information needed for doing so in the child mortality example was in existence for roughly 10 years prior to the publications by the Cornell team, and the policy implications from step 2 studies had been extensively debated [11–13], but this critical integration of the relevant information had not occurred. Such integration of information has become more common in recent years through the global burden of disease project and other initiatives and is playing a major role in policy development. It also has the potential to help distinguish higher-priority from lower-priority topics for research and basic data collection at the international level and in specific countries or contexts.

Despite its advantages, the risk assessment (and comparative risk assessment, as in the global burden of disease project) has a number of important limitations. The approach does integrate information from steps 1–3 in a policy-relevant way; however, it still represents a "partial approach" to policy analysis. This is illustrated by the US experience, in which this four-step procedure has been used for more than two decades and shown itself to be inadequate by itself for supporting the key policy decisions. Four reasons stand out [14, 15]:

1. The method is best equipped to deal with single exposures rather than multiple exposures, especially when the exposures are correlated among themselves in complex ways. This is well illustrated by the diarrhea, respiratory, malaria, undernutrition example given as well as by the work by Victora and colleagues [16].

2. The method can lead to a ranking of various problems or exposures, but under many circumstances constrained public resources should be targeted based on potential marginal improvements in health using "best-available practices" rather than on the absolute level of risk. The US experience has revealed that the rankings based on the prevalence (or population-attributable risks) of problems and exposures can deviate significantly from the rankings based on potential improvements, leading to substantial misallocation of resources [14]. As indicated in many of the chapters in this volume, individual researchers and practitioners in international health and nutrition often claim priority status for particular diseases or nutritional deficiencies based on prevalences or seriousness of consequences as opposed to the realistic prospects for improvement through currently available interventions.

3. The method requires a common metric (e.g., lives lost or disability-adjusted life years [DALYs] lost), which may not be available or may not reflect the other values that the public and society place on each outcome (e.g., in the United States some hazards are intrinsically more dreaded by the public, even if their numerical risk is low).

4. Responsibility for health and safety in the United States (as with health and nutrition in developing countries) is dispersed across a wide array of public and private institutions; thus, acting on the priority rankings (as a basis for policy priorities) would require an unusual level of coordination and cooperation in policy development and implementation. In other words, the ability to use the results of comparative risk assessments is adversely affected by interagency and interest group politics and legislative behavior. This last consideration raises a host of administrative and political complications, which underscores the need to broaden the scope of policy analysis beyond that permitted under a technical frame model alone (see Table 34.1).

### 34.2.1.2 ANALYSIS OF INTERVENTIONS

The above discussion underscores the importance of intervention analysis (Table 34.1). As distinct from causal analysis, activity in this category generates information on the efficacy and effectiveness of alternative approaches for addressing health and nutrition problems. Such information is essential not only for deciding which actions to use for a given health/nutrition problem, but also for guiding resource allocations *across* various problems based on the potential for improvement rather than the prevalence of the problem. Many of the chapters in this volume contain partial information in this category, and attempts to integrate this information are reflected in Chapter 32 of this volume and in other works [17, 18].

One of the weaknesses of our collective effort with regard to intervention analysis is that the efficacy trials and the program evaluations to establish effectiveness typically are undertaken without considering the types of information needed at the integration and policymaking phase. Thus, critically needed information may not be available or may not be comparable across settings, related to coverage, targeting, quality of services or program inputs, costs, and a host of contextual factors that affect efficacy and effectiveness.

Another way in which intervention analysis could be improved is through a more systematic consideration of unanticipated consequences at the planning stage and during evaluation. Drawing again from the experience in developed countries, the need for considering this is increasingly revealed in the risk assessment literature that has begun to conceptualize the analysis of risk–risk tradeoffs as an important class of analytical

**Table 34.2**
**Typology of risk-risk tradeoffs**

| | | *Compared to the target risk, the countervailing risk is:* | |
| | | *Same type* | *Different type* |
|---|---|---|---|
| Compared to the target risk, the countervailing risk affects: | Same population | Pesticides: Cancer<br>Butter, margarine: CHD<br>Weight cycling: CHD | Breast-feeding/HIV<br>Fish/cancer/ CHD<br>Height/breast cancer<br>Iron/zinc interactions |
| | Different population | β-Carotene supplements and lung cancer | Folate fortification<br>Iron deficiency/overload<br>Water fluoridation<br>"Functional foods"<br>Gestational weight gain |

*Source:* Adapted from [19].
*CHD* coronary heart disease

activity. Table 34.2 provides examples from developed countries in which actions taken to reduce one risk or one problem (the *target risk*) have created or have the potential to create problems in other domains (the *countervailing risk*) [19]. As shown in the table, some of the countervailing risks may be of the same type and affect the same individuals/populations, or they may be of a different type and affect different individuals/ populations. The four possibilities suggested by this table have important implications for how they are handled in public policy (e.g., as issues requiring information and education to support individual choice or as externalities that might warrant other forms of government intervention). A variety of examples may exist in international health and nutrition, including the HIV/ breast-feeding decision, single versus multiple-micronutrient supplements, supplement versus diet-based approaches, weekly versus daily iron supplementation, iron supplementation in malarial environments, and a host of others. However, the main point to be drawn from this table is that the narrow analytical frames and research designs commonly used in our field tend to focus on individual diseases, nutrients, and population groups and a limited number of outcomes (i.e., with little systematic interest in potential countervailing risks).

## 34.2.2 The Economic Frame

The economics-based version of policy analysis (hereafter called *economic frame*) is another major analytical frame in use. The economic frame explicitly or implicitly incorporates the cause–effect information from technical analysis as described, but extends on it in significant ways that lead to policy recommendations often quite different from those of health and nutrition researchers. Specifically, in this perspective the interest lies not only in knowing the prevalence of various problems and the effectiveness and cost-effectiveness of various interventions, but also in considering concepts such as opportunity costs (i.e., benefits forgone) that are associated with deploying one intervention as opposed to another or in addressing one problem as opposed to a different problem.

Although the technique of cost–benefit analysis often used for this purpose is commonly criticized because it requires a great deal of quantitative information or questionable assumptions, the underlying logic of considering opportunity costs and related concepts is compelling, widely applied in daily decisions in private and public life, and should be part of sound public policy analysis. Remarkably, it often is not evident in the recommendations in international health and nutrition because of the tendency for researchers and analysts to focus on one type of nutrition problem or intervention at a time.

Some of the strengths (and weaknesses) of this logic can be illustrated with the data shown in Table 34.3 that compares the estimated cost of averting a lost DALY by deploying selected health and nutrition interventions. The table shows that the cost-effectiveness of *nutrition* interventions shown here ranged from US $5 to US $82 per DALY. The lowest costs are associated with micronutrient interventions, and the higher costs are associated with integrated community-based programs directed at promoting child growth. The most obvious conclusion from these figures is that some interventions

**Table 34.3**
Cost-effectiveness estimates for selected health and nutrition problems in developing countries

| Cause | Intervention | Cost per DALY averted ($) | DALYs saved per $1,000 | Source |
|---|---|---|---|---|
| Vitamin A | Fortification | 34 | 29 | 1 |
| | Supplements, children | 6–12 | 111 | 1 |
| Iron deficiency | Fortification | 68 | 15 | 1 |
| | Supplements, pregnancy | 13 | 77 | 2 |
| Iodine deficiency | Fortification | 35 | 29 | 1 |
| | Supplements, pregnancy | 20 | 50 | |
| Zinc deficiency | Supplements with ORS | 73 | 14 | 1 |
| PEM | Food supplements, pregnancy | 25 | 40 | 2 |
| | Food supplements, children | 70 | 14 | 2 |
| | Growth monitoring and counseling | 8–11 | 105 | 1 |
| | Breast-feeding promotion | 8–11 | 105 | 1 |
| | Nutrition in child survival programs | 42 | 24 | 1 |
| | Iringa/Tanzania | 82 | 12 | 1 |
| ARI | Screening and referral | 20–50 | 20–50 | 2 |
| | Behavior change | 50 | 20 | 2 |
| Diarrhea | Breast-feeding promotion | 30 | 33 | 2 |
| | Improved weaning | 30 | 33 | 2 |
| | Behavior change | 170 | 6 | 2 |
| Cardiovascular disease | Screening/referral/ education | 150[a] | 7 | 2 |

*Source*: Adapted from [17, 18].
*ORS* oral rehydration salts, *PEM* protein-energy malnutrition
[a]Plus $2,000–5,000/ disability-adjusted life year (DALY) for treatment of referred cases.

are more expensive than others, but many in the international health and nutrition community feel the advantages of the more expensive options like integrated community-based programs (e.g., Iringa) are worth the extra cost and would be inclined to advocate for making these investments.

By contrast, the economic frame takes the analysis a step further by converting these into estimates of the number of DALYs potentially saved through each intervention. (The following discussion assumes, for the moment, that these data represent marginal effects.) The second column reveals in more striking terms the "price" we would pay (in human terms) for favoring the more expensive interventions, assuming a fixed set of resources for improving health. Specifically, we would forgo about 160 DALYs (200 – 40 = 160) for each $1,000 invested in a supplementary feeding program for women (compared to a vitamin A or iron fortification program), and we would forgo an additional 28 DALYs (40 – 12 = 28) to invest that $1,000 in an Iringa-style program instead of a supplementary feeding program. Moreover, if an advocate of Iringa-style programs did manage to raise $1,000 in "new funds" for improving health (rather than accepting the resource constraint imposed), economic reasoning would dictate that even that money would be better spent on fortification programs than on the more expensive options (if the only interest is in DALYs).

This example reveals that even the most rudimentary concepts in the economic rationality can lay bare the consequences of alternative actions and lead to decisions or policy preferences quite different from those suggested by cause–effect analyses described. To be very explicit about this difference, consider a nutrition researcher or practitioner operating under technical rationality (which focuses only on *effectiveness*). This nutrition researcher might demonstrate a significant impact of a program on child health, nutrition, or mortality and might be inclined to conclude that more programs of this type should be implemented, and that new funds should be allocated for this purpose if necessary. This is especially the case when there are organizational, professional, or personal incentives for drawing this conclusion. By contrast, a policy analyst employing the economic analytical frame (and assuming no perverse incentives) would be inclined to compare the cost-effectiveness of such a program to other options for improving the same outcomes or to actions that could improve even more highly valued outcomes associated with different problems. An especially important lesson from this example is that the nutrition researcher and economic policy analyst may differ in their conclusions *not* because the economist is concerned with limiting the budgetary outlay and the nutrition researcher is concerned with minimizing human suffering; to the contrary, both may share the same goal of maximizing human benefits, but their competing logics lead them to different conclusions.

While the example reveals the basic logic underlying opportunity costs, this is only one of the important concepts in the economic framework [20]. A more thorough analysis would take into account such factors as the following:

1. The difference between average cost-effectiveness of an intervention and the marginal cost-effectiveness (with the latter the more meaningful value in most analyses and holding the potential to reverse the choice between competing intervention options).
2. Costs and benefits beyond those captured in outcome indicators like DALYs; in the present case, for instance, many features of the Iringa-style program would generate social and

economic benefits beyond those reflected in DALYs. These include increased productivity associated with piped water systems, cooperative child care arrangements, and access to better health care; spillover effects from the capacity-building activities into other development activities; improved village leadership; and so on. These considerations also hold the potential for reversing the choice among competing options, and even when they cannot be quantified, they serve the useful purpose of focusing attention and debate on the most valued goals and objectives of the program (and thus the inputs/activities required to reach the priority goals).[1]

3. The possibility that positive or negative externalities might occur (unpriced effects on third parties, such as soil erosion or water contamination associated with agricultural or livestock practices).

4. The distribution of costs and benefits across different social groups (exacerbating problems of equity and power imbalances).

5. Features of the local context that may affect the actual costs or effects of various intervention types.

6. The most appropriate institutional arrangements for addressing the problem (e.g., the right mix of market, community, and government inputs).

7. Longer-run expectations regarding costs, effectiveness, equity, and externalities.

Due to limitations in the availability of quantitative data on these issues in particular settings, many of them cannot be incorporated directly into an applied economic model in a particular setting. However, they can and should be considered as important components of a sound analysis. For this reason, and because many of these issues involve perspectives, assumptions and logic distinct from the core economic frame, they are discussed as distinct forms of rationality.

### 34.2.3  The Social/Normative Frame

At their core, the technical and economic analytical frames strive to shed light on the likely or potential consequences of alternative actions. These consequences can vary from the health, well-being, and survival and women and children, to the levels and distribution of wealth and income, to the impacts on the social or natural environment. In this key respect, their core logic and methods are identical to technical and economic analyses of nonhuman systems, such as predicting the consequences of alternative manufacturing technologies on overall productivity, average product quality, variability in productivity and quality, and so on. In other words, there is nothing *inherent* to these analytical frames to indicate how much value should be placed on the various consequences. For instance, causal and intervention analysis related to child mortality takes as a given the proposition that child survival is a highly valued outcome, but it does not explicitly weigh the value of that outcome against others (e.g., the life of the mother or a younger sibling). Similarly, economic analysis can predict the consequences of a targeted food subsidy on food consumption of the poor, the national budget, and the

---

[1] The term *technical efficiency* is used in the economic framework to refer to the most efficient way to achieve a given objective, like maximizing DALYs, for which cost-effectiveness analysis is an appropriate tool. The term *social efficiency* refers to analyses involving a wider range of social costs and benefits, for which cost–benefit analysis is used and requires that dollar values or some other common metric be attached to all costs and all benefits.

economy but cannot by itself indicate the value to be attached to each of these outcomes. Despite the paramount importance or value placed on the efficiency criterion in many economic analyses, arguments, and policy prescriptions, the theory underlying the economic frame acknowledges that the value attached to various outcomes *is and should be* a socially defined construct [20–22].[2]

The social/normative frame is fundamentally concerned with the implications of public policy for human dignity and the social norms and procedures that respect, protect, and fulfill it. Thus, in contrast to the cause–effect focus of technical and economic frames, the central foci of social/ normative frame are equity, ethics, and democracy (Table 34.1). In this context, *equity* involves notions of fairness and distributive justice as important criteria in evaluating policy options; *ethics* involves a consideration of the rights, duties, and obligations that bind the state, nonstate institutions, and citizens in a just society; and *democracy* is concerned with the legitimacy and performance of social and political institutions (including norms and procedures) vis-à-vis the pursuit and fulfillment of ethical goals and outcomes. It is relevant to note that social/normative considerations receive much greater attention within the legal realm (notably within judicial and constitutional processes), and these aspects are addressed separately in another section. The present discussion addresses the social/normative considerations within sectoral policy as it pertains to health and nutrition, while recognizing that these are dependent on the legal frameworks in important ways.

Consideration of the social/normative dimensions of *mainstream* public policy (including health and nutrition) has proven difficult in recent decades for several reasons. First, the health and nutrition field has come to be dominated by a generation of practitioners whose training and professional socialization has emphasized the technical and economic analytical frames. In this "technified" version of public policy or development work, the social/normative questions and considerations have been either overshadowed by demanding requirements for the technical analysis, viewed as "unscientific" or "subjective," or taken for granted by the practitioners (e.g., when each assumes there is intrinsically high social or moral value associated with the problems they are researching or analyzing without a thoughtful consideration of the legitimacy of competing priorities). Second, there has been an institutional endorsement of this technified approach on the part of academia, government institutions, donor agencies, other development institutions, and society at large. This has permitted and reinforced the notion that technically derived solutions can provide an adequate basis for public policy and development work [23, 24]. Third, although allocative efficiency is an important and useful consideration in public policy (as noted), the extent to which it has been uncritically applied across the policy spectrum, often foreclosing serious consideration of social/normative issues, has become problematic [25–27].

Finally, it should be acknowledged that even if there were full agreement on the need for serious analysis of social/ normative issues as part of sound policy analysis, the analysis of these issues and the tradeoffs among them inherently is more ambiguous, contestable, and problematic than technical analysis. For this reason, ethical analysis

---

[2] Note that cost–benefit analyses and other economic methods may employ various techniques for assigning weights, values, or discounts to various outcomes, but all of these are (or should be) socially defined.

often is considered either a platform for advocacy or a "quagmire/morass" from which there is no clear escape and for which there certainly is no professional reward in the technical fields.

Although the levels of certainty and agreement attributed to technical analysis often are more apparent than real [5, 24, 28, 29], technical analysis has the advantage of being supported by some criteria for evidence, inference, and confirmability that generally are well established, understood, and accepted by its practitioners. By contrast, universal standards for making social/normative judgments do not have the same level of consensus among scholars in the relevant fields and do not appear possible because these judgments are so heavily dependent on the social and situational context. For this reason, the social/normative frame includes democracy as one of its key concerns, reflecting a desire for the analysis and deliberation of equity and ethics to be grounded in legitimate and authentic democratic values and processes *in the relevant context*. This highlights the fact that the scientific (or technical) components and the social/normative components of public policy analysis *should* proceed according to different sets of assumptions, logics, and procedures for deliberation and judgment [5, 30, 31], even though "public policy analysis" often is equated and conducted with technical and economic frames alone.

While this discussion may explain why social/ normative analysis has been marginalized from technically oriented policy analysis in the past, there is a renewed interest in restoring a more systematic and appropriate balance between these two inputs into public policy as revealed in recent literature, innovative forms of practice, and societal trends reveal. The academic literature is evolving from a mere social/normative critique of technocratic approaches to the development and testing of alternative approaches at community, national, and international levels [5, 32, 33]; the expanding interest in community-based development, civic engagement, and democratic renewal is an expression of the same phenomenon [34–36]. In addition, research continues on the development of econometric approaches explicitly weighted to account for equity and social justice considerations in ways that are founded on, rather than undermined by, intersubjective utility [37, 38]. The development and testing of such approaches specific to health and nutrition represent an important topic for future research, although it has yet to be conceptualized as such and rewarded within the international health and nutrition community. Such research could serve the dual purpose of rescuing social/normative considerations from its current "quagmire" or advocacy status, while fusing normative and technical considerations in appropriate ways, both of which would enhance the *public* character and legitimacy of health and nutrition policy.

The preceding sections, which describe technical, economic, and social/normative frames, all deal with the *what* question in public policy: *What should be done* to have an effective and appropriate policy? These three analytical frames are based on a consideration of cause–effect relationships, the desire to allocate resources to produce the greatest net benefit, and the desire to preserve human dignity in the distribution of social benefits and costs. The next three sections each deal with the two *how* questions: *How are* decisions made, implemented, and enforced? and *How should* the health/nutrition community proceed in the pursuit of effective and appropriate policies? Although there is temptation to consider the *what* questions separately from the *how* questions, these sections reveal the codependent nature of these questions.

### 34.2.4 The Political Frame

*Politics* is the processes through which values are allocated in society, also known as the processes that determine who gets what, when, and how. According to one scholar, Harold Lasswell, all the relevant values can be grouped into eight categories (power, wealth, well-being, skill, enlightenment, respect, rectitude, and affection), although their relative importance may vary across time, culture, and situation, and numerous alternative classifications have been proposed.[3] In the ideal of representative democracy (in the US case), elected officials would faithfully weigh the conflicting values and interests of their constituents in a deliberative process without regard to their own electoral or personal interests, resulting in well-considered public policies. The electoral process would ensure the integrity and accountability of this representation, the executive branch would discharge the will of the legislative body in a value-neutral fashion, and the judicial branch would resolve disputes and uphold constitutional rights and principles.

Although this utopic description does not fit any known political systems, it is included here to help distinguish the way politics *is* from the way it *ought* to be. It is only by specifying a normative model of politics that one can judge the appropriateness of current politics and public policy as well as the appropriateness of one's own actions and recommendations. Note the emphasis here on *appropriateness*, which is a broader, more inclusive criterion than the *effectiveness* that is central to the technical frame.

Figure 34.1 is an abstract version of the political process that permits an analysis of actual and desirable processes in many settings.[4] In this model, the evolution of public policy (viewed as the cumulative result of many individual policies or a single policy)

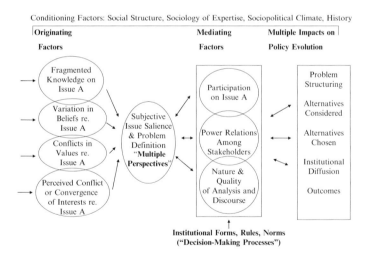

**Fig. 34.1.** Conceptual framework for the evolution of issues within policy communities.

---

[3]It is useful to think of values in terms of the goals pursued by people and organizations, the incentives they respond to, and the assets or resources available to them for pursuing their goals.

[4]Figure 34.1 is a *conceptual* model analogous to the United Nations International Children's Emergency Fund (UNICEF) conceptual framework for the causes of malnutrition (see [65]). Specifically, it does not specify the relative importance of various factors or processes in a universal sense or in a given setting, but rather identifies the range of possibilities that should be considered in each setting.

is a function of the patterns of participation (who, in what alliances, when, how); their relative power (including wealth, social standing, and alliances); and the nature and quality of analysis and discourse about the policy issues (including partial policy analyses and distorted communications about the problem and potential solutions). These factors in turn affect and are affected by the way in which the policy issue is structured and understood and thus acted on. Problem structuring and salience in turn are a reflection of the fragmented knowledge (including professional and institutional specialization) and the diversity in values, interests, and beliefs of the key participants. As shown, all of these interactions are affected by a series of conditioning factors and the prevailing decision-making processes. With respect to decision-making processes, it is important to note that politics and political frame apply to the decisions, behavior, and interactions of legislatures, agencies, and a variety of nongovernmental groups, typically operating within a coalition or policy subsystem context.

This model can be used both to analyze the way politics *is* being conducted (e.g., through selective and inequitable participation or through distorted communications concerning the nature of the health/nutrition problem and potential solutions) and to identify appropriate corrective measures (e.g., by taking steps to correct distorted communications about the problem and potential solutions, by strengthening strategic alliances and participatory processes, and by ensuring that one's own policy recommendations are consistent with the relevant *public* values rather than personal, professional, or organizational values and interests).

Although "bad politics" often is attributed to politicians and bureaucrats, it is noteworthy that professionals and their institutions also are part of the larger political context [24, 39, 40]. For instance, many of the issues in international health and nutrition have been debated and decided based on a limited subset of professional and organizational knowledge, values, and interests (ostensibly on behalf of the affected parties), with little direct input or empirical confirmation that these are in line with the values, needs, and interests of the affected publics (e.g., micronutrient supplementation vs. home gardening; cash crops vs. food crops; agricultural intensification, selective health care vs. integrated community programs, ethical targeting of food aid). There is ample evidence that professional views often depart in important ways from those of "the community" [5, 32, 41] and may lead to misallocation of scarce resources (e.g., comparative risk assessment), raising the question of whether they truly represent the public interest in a broad sense or the special interests and narrowly defined problems of concern to professionals and their institutions. In this respect, professionals are engaging in politics whenever they make policy recommendations based on a partial analysis, although they typically perceive themselves otherwise. Such practices raise normative concerns (e.g., regarding legitimacy and accountability) and increase the likelihood of ineffective or misguided policies. The latter is because relevant information may not be brought to light concerning the context of the problem or the consequences of the proposed solution and because it lessens the likelihood of cooperation, compliance, or sustained support [5].

Apart from assisting in the assessment of political processes, the literature on which Fig. 34.1 is based provides a perspective on political frame that may improve the effectiveness of policy formation efforts related to health and nutrition. This wide-ranging literature includes descriptions of the forms and strategies of policy coalitions and communities, the political processes that govern and are affected by problem structuring, issue salience and policy/program sustainability, individual and organizational deci-sion-making styles, and the strategies and tactics of policy entrepreneurs [2, 42–47]. A central message from this literature is that decisions concerning the most appropriate and effective *content* of a policy must take account of the political processes associated with its initiation, acceptance, promotion, implementation, and sustainability. This often involves uncomfortable compromises for professionals. For example, under technical frame (with a concern for maximizing benefits to the needy and maintaining cost-effectiveness), professional norms and standards would dictate that food assist-ance should be strictly targeted to the poor. However, from the perspective of political frame, in some settings attempts to strictly exclude the middle class from receiving some benefits might jeopardize political support for the entire program [44]. Such examples highlight the fact that some of the prescriptions emerging from political frame may be at odds with the professional standards and the technical frame of practitioners in the health and nutrition community. Such dilemmas represent another case in which ethical analysis (social/normative frame) is needed to help resolve the complex and conflicting demands of public policy. Such conflicting demands are a fundamental feature of public policy even under the best of circumstances but are made even more complex when ideal political conditions do not prevail.

### 34.2.5   *The Administrative/Organizational Frame*

As noted, individual organizations typically are part of larger networks or policy subsystems, and as such some of their decisions and behavior are affected or con-strained by that external political environment. However, organizations also have some distinctive internal dynamics that affect the formation, implementation, and outcomes of policy, such that these must be understood on their own terms. Contrary to the "machine view" of the policy process (in which policies are decided at one level and the only role of organizations is to implement them effectively and efficiently), there is now broad recognition in the policy sciences that a reasoned choice of "the most effective and appropriate policy" in a given situation cannot be made in the abstract. Rather, it is highly contingent on the characteristics, capabilities, and tendencies of the implement-ing organization, including its formal and informal structure; the internal and external pressures and incentives on executives, analysts, managers, and staff; the nature of the tasks to be performed; and a variety of "intangibles," such as senses of cohesion or mis-sion, personal and professional beliefs, informal culture, and recent or distant political relationships within or between various subunits [48].

Whether the goal is simply to understand organizational behavior or to develop effec-tive management strategies, it is useful to think of organizations simultaneously from a top-down, bottom-up, inside-inside, and inside-outside perspective [49, 50]. That is, to recognize that many important features of organizations, such as goals, tasks, incen-tives, politics, beliefs, and culture, exist and are shaped from each of these directions, thereby significantly complicating the task of management and control. Moreover, organizations may differ from one another along many of these dimensions (e.g., the nature of external politics and the professional beliefs of staff). The effectiveness of many of the well-recognized management tools (incentives, supervision, training, structural reorganization) depends vitally on understanding the organizational characteristics. The weakness of many "fads" in the field of organizational change and management (e.g., total quality management and results-based management) is the attempt to apply a single set of management principles to a highly diverse set of organizational forms. Some of the most important distinctions for present purposes are [49] type of politics, type of organization, task/goal ambiguity, beliefs, and culture.

*Type of Politics*: A major influence on executives, analysts, managers, and staff relates to the nature of the interest-based politics that surround the organization. Four basic types are (1) client politics, in which a policy or program relates directly to the interests of one dominant interest group, such that the benefits are concentrated but the costs are widely dispersed (e.g., an agricultural credit program may be dominated by farmers or a rural water project may be dominated by pressure from a specific locality); (2) entrepreneurial politics, in which the costs of a policy or program are highly concentrated and the benefits are widely dispersed (e.g., regulation of pharmaceutical prices or the cost of health care); (3) interest group politics, in which the policy or program creates both high costs and high benefits to many groups, thereby creating diverse and opposing pressures on the agency (e.g., the distribution of food aid commodities in rural areas that compete with locally produced commodities); and (4) majoritarian politics, in which the policy or program creates only low cost and low benefits such that there is little incentive for groups to organize (e.g., many health and nutrition interventions such as nutrition education, growth monitoring, oral rehydration, etc.). It is important to note that the politics surrounding a program or policy can affect field staff as well as higher-level staff, as illustrated by the "coalition of indifference" to the needs of the rural poor in many agricultural extension programs [51].

*Type of Organization*: Whereas the type of politics is a powerful external influence on organizational behavior, the ability to exert managerial control is influenced by a variety of internal characteristics, including the nature of the organization's production processes and the degree to which they can be observed reliably by managers and other overseers. Wilson [49] identified four types: (1) production organizations, in which both activities (work) and results (outcomes) can be observed reliably (e.g., clinic-based immunization programs); (2) procedural organizations in which only activities can be observed reliably (e.g., clinic-based nutrition education programs); (3) craft organizations, in which only results can be observed reliably (e.g., community-based education regarding use of oral rehydration or early referral for acute respiratory infection); and (4) coping organizations, in which neither activities nor results can be observed reliably (e.g., many community health worker programs).

The health and nutrition examples provided illustrate that "organization type" is a function of what is *supposed* to be accomplished and the quality of supervision, training, and reporting. Thus, a growth-monitoring program lends itself to observing activities (weighing sessions, implementation of education, and other interventions) and observing outcomes (reductions in malnutrition), but only if supervision, training, and reporting all are functioning adequately. This means a clinic-based growth and promotion (GMP) program might behave as a production organization if the organizational infrastructure is strong, but a community-based GMP program might behave as a procedural or coping organization if the infrastructure is weak. Thus, the utility of the classification is in facilitating an appropriate match among program type, program infrastructure, and reward systems and anticipating some of the positive and negative effects. Many programmatic failures in health and nutrition can be traced to a mismatch among these characteristics.

While these four types of organizations and the four types of politics described may each provide useful insights into organizational tendencies and capacities, a moment's reflection reveals that even greater insights can come from considering these two factors together. For instance, the distribution of food aid in remote areas may represent a combination of a coping organization (where neither the staff activities nor the results can be observed reliably) working in the face of client politics (in which one particular group stands to reap the benefits). Such situations should be considered a priori to be particularly vulnerable to misuse. Other combinations of organization type and politics type may lead to useful, although less obvious, predictions.

*Task/Goal Ambiguity*: When the goals of a program or organization are overly broad, ambiguous, or too many in number, analysts, managers, and staff will tend to respond to the "situational imperatives" to define their own tasks and routines in ways that may depart significantly from official goals. In other words, in situations like this, the *effective* policy is made "on the ground" rather than at the central level. Contrasting examples in health and nutrition include immunization and universal vitamin A supplementation (for which a high level of clarity of purpose and technology exists) versus an integrated health and nutrition program designed to deliver a variety of services based on local needs and situations (in which a high level of ambiguity and discretion is involved). The latter approach has very high requirements for staff training, supervision, administrative responsiveness, and monitoring of targeting and coverage. However, even with these strong top-down managerial features or strong levels of community participation, high-ambiguity/high-discretion programs are inherently vulnerable to interest-based pressures from within and outside the organization. It is relevant to note that individual analysts and staff working in ambiguous situations do not necessarily resolve their dilemmas on their own; in many cases, peer expectations play an important role in shaping the response, which can create outcomes closer to or even further from the official or desirable goals of the program [49].

*Beliefs*: Personal and professional beliefs or predispositions are another factor that influences the task definition and performance of analysts, managers, and staff. This is especially so in ambiguous situations and when supervisory and reward systems cannot be well tied to observed performance. These predispositions are based on prior experiences (in the organization and elsewhere), degree of adherence to professional standards, political ideology, and personality characteristics. This factor is of particular relevance for health and nutrition professionals because task definition in this arena can be strongly influenced by professional training and personal ideology. Some examples are the concern for equity, the desire to help, "above all do no harm," acting to alleviate human suffering with inadequate attention to opportunity costs or unintended consequences, belief in food-based approaches, and a generalized mistrust of industry, to name a few. These professional and personal beliefs, together with limited experience with and understanding of alternative analytical frames, tend to compromise the effectiveness of health and nutrition professionals (analysts, managers, and staff) at several stages in the policy process, from policy recommendation through implementation and evaluation.

*Culture*: The combination of factors discussed (type of politics, production processes, ambiguity of goals/tasks and situational imperatives, and personal/professional beliefs and rewards) creates a distinctive view of the world and response to it on the part of managers, analysts, and staff within an organization. In many cases, a single organization may possess several subcultures with conflicts and rivalries among them, greatly complicating the task of effective management and implementation. This is evident in the health sector in general (e.g., each major disease category may have its own subculture), but it is even more of a concern for nutrition because of its distinctiveness from dominant professions in health and medicine, agriculture, economics, and others. While nutrition practitioners are well aware of this phenomenon based on experience, a systematic consideration of these factors (among others) would enhance our ability to identify the key features of organizational cultures and subcultures in a given setting and take them into account in both the policy design and implementation phases.

Unlike some of the analytical frames discussed (e.g., economic), this discussion reveals that there is no single way of thinking that can be termed *organizational frame*. Rather, each organization or subunit within an organization possess some distinctive characteristics with a large bearing on its response to policy initiatives and subsequent policy outcomes. Because these organizational characteristics can be so variable, can have such strong effects, and can be far more resistant to change than previously assumed, it is the responsibility of policy analysts, planners, advisors, and others to take explicit account of these characteristics as an integral part of the analytical process. In other words, the choice of a "best policy option" cannot be specified without a clear understanding of organizational characteristics, capacities, and tendencies. There is growing interest in developing and applying methods for institutional analysis [52] precisely to deal more effectively with these issues, but these methods do not offer unambiguous answers to organizational questions, and they have yet to be systematically applied within nutrition.

### 34.2.6   The Legal Frame

National and international laws are recognized as important policy instruments for international health and nutrition in such areas as ethics (e.g., rights to food, health care), food fortification, maternity leave, and enabling legislation for a variety of specific policies and programs (e.g., food labeling, public health programs, food safety, etc.). The salient characteristics of the legal frame are its emphasis on compliance or consistency with established rules and precedents and, in some political systems, the openness of the legislative process to societal input. These characteristics sometimes generate conflict with the goals of effectiveness, efficiency, equity, or feasibility that are central to other analytical frames, thereby justifying the separate label of legal frame.

As discussed for other policy instruments, there is an important distinction to be made between the existence of a law and the ability to implement or enforce it. The clearest example of this is the right to food as articulated in the Universal Declaration of Human Rights at the international level, which is not legally enforceable at the country level [53]. Given the weak enforcement capacity for many types of laws in developing countries, legal instruments may be viewed as "sometimes useful but not sufficient conditions" for improving health and nutrition. Nonetheless, the existence of laws such as those noted provides a critically important foundation for ongoing national and international advocacy on issues of great importance to health and nutrition.

In addition, a growing body of international laws and treaties related to international trade, property rights, environmental protection, and other domains will affect developing countries in profound ways, with a variety of direct and indirect effects on health and nutrition.

### 34.2.7 Multiple/Integrative Frames

The preceding sections describe six distinctive analytical frames that are evident in various phases of the policy cycle, from problem identification and agenda-setting through implementation and evaluation. The mix of frames and their relative importance vary across different phases of the policy cycle, in different sectors and problem domains, and across different policy issues. The high levels of disagreement, confusion, and dissatisfaction associated with the process and the outcomes of public policy are traceable to (1) the existence of these distinct analytical frames in use; (2) the fact that they typically lead to quite different conclusions about which actions should be taken in a given situation; and (3) the fact that most participants or observers of the policy process are not aware that these distinctive logics, criteria, and norms are "in play" in a given situation. The resulting mix of science, economics, ethics, politics, administration, and law has been termed a "tower of babble" in large part because most participants are not fully aware that their differences reflect separate language, logics, and norms. Such collective confusion or chaos is ironic considering that each of these professions places great value on reason and enlightenment as an important basis for public policy.

The perspective reflected in the recent policy sciences literature is that sound public policy should be both effective and appropriate (Table 34.1). *Effective* refers to the notion that a given public policy should be capable of achieving its stated goal (in light of current or foreseeable political, administrative, and legal conditions). *Appropriate* is the notion that doing so is consistent with the other criteria contained in the various analytical frames (e.g., efficient, ethical, democratic). These dual criteria acknowledge that competing goals and tradeoffs do exist, that competing outcomes are valued differently in society, and that there are enormous complexities and uncertainties associated with social, political, and technological change (i.e., policy change). Accordingly, in an ideal situation the development of such policies is based on wisdom, as opposed to partial knowledge or incomplete analysis, and it places a high value on social justice and human dignity. Since these characteristics are dependent on social context, this literature emphasizes the need to integrate technical analysis (to project the likely consequences of alternative actions) with social deliberation (to reflect on and resolve value conflicts). In contrast to current professional and political practice, the integration of technical knowledge and social values should be conducted through authentic representation of social values as well as fair and competent deliberative processes. The development and evaluation of models based on citizen juries, panels and advisory groups, planning cells, negotiated rule making, and policy roundtables are becoming active areas of research for this purpose [5, 32].

In contrast to the experimental models noted, it is important to note that there is a variety of ways in which incremental improvements in practice can be achieved by employing multiple analytical frames. These are discussed in the final section.

## 34.3    IMPLICATIONS FOR TRULY "PUBLIC" HEALTH
##          AND NUTRITION[5]

This chapter began by noting great diversity in the analytical frames used in the international health and nutrition community: disease focus, nutrient focus, special populations, and so on. It also noted diversity in intervention possibilities, ranging from capsule distribution to rural development, and highlighted the uncertainties in our field regarding the conditions under which each of these might be most effective. Most often, a final chapter of a book such as this would recommend expanded research and program evaluation on the effectiveness, cost-effectiveness, and determinants of cost-effectiveness of these interventions in various settings. Indeed, such research and evaluation work is one of the priorities for our field and already is well recognized as such, and some specific avenues for investigation are identified in the individual chapters. Such work falls squarely within the realm of technical frame that has guided most health and nutrition professionals in the past and will continue to do so for the foreseeable future.

Rather than simply reiterating those recommendations and remaining within the technical frame, this chapter describes a much larger and complex view of public policy. According to this view, (1) knowledge emerging from our current research programs is a necessary but not sufficient basis for sound public policy, and even more importantly, (2) we, along with other policy analysts operating within only one form of frame, may actually contribute to poor public policy by making and implementing recommendations based on partial policy analysis.

It may be comforting or discomforting to learn that this last statement describes most policy analysts across all sectors [3, 4, 54–56]. Such a claim is based on the major rethinking (since the 1980s) of the most appropriate roles of markets, governments, and civil society in the process of social change [20, 24, 25]. An emphasis on governments characterized most of the century, followed by an embrace of markets beginning in the 1980s and a resurgent interest in community and civil society in the 1990s. The current view of governments, therefore, is that their primary role should be to *facilitate* the functioning of markets and civil society (rather than trying to solve problems themselves) and to maintain appropriate balance and tension between them. While most health and nutrition practitioners have experienced this rethinking at a community level (e.g., interest in community participation), analogous changes are under way in diverse academic fields and practice settings concerned with public policy at higher levels.

The larger view of public policy described here maintains that effective and appropriate public policy should be capable of achieving its stated goal (in light of current or foreseeable political, administrative, and legal conditions) *and* should be consistent with or justified in relation to other criteria (efficiency, equity, ethics, democracy). These requirements for truly public health and nutrition probably exceed the breadth and expertise of all practitioners and graduate training programs in health and nutrition.

---

[5] The term *public health* or *public nutrition* is often used to refer to activities that seek to improve conditions at the population rather than the individual level or activities undertaken by the public (government) sector. This chapter argues that truly *public* health or *public* nutrition also should embrace a broad view of the public interest and the combination of government, market, and civil society processes required to fulfill it (i.e., a concern for effective *and* appropriate actions).

This reflects the recent history of our professions and training institutions but does not invalidate these as criteria for sound public policy and for guiding incremental improvements in work. As described next, the reframing of our goals in terms of effectiveness and appropriateness has immediate and longer-term implications for practice, research, and training.

### 34.3.1  Implications for Practice

The multiple analytical frames described here have several immediate effects on or implications for practitioners. Some illustrative examples are provided next, from the perspective of practitioners involved with policy/program analysis or policy research in national and international agencies and applied research institutes and academic settings.

1. Each analytical frame provides a distinct "lens" for reexamining a specific policy situation and revealing features overlooked by other forms. For instance, the concept of opportunity cost or marginalism in economic frame could reverse the policy preferences formed under technical frame alone; consideration of political frame in the policy (re)design phase could dramatically improve the prospects for continued funding of a program; and consideration of organizational frame at the (re)design phase could dramatically improve program effectiveness and efficiency. Thus, familiarity with multiple analytical frames could be an asset for those who make policy decisions, those who advise policymakers, and those who manage programs.

2. Each analytical frame represents a distinctive language, logic, and set of norms and assumptions used by other professionals. In many practice settings, the technical (or ethical) frame of health and nutrition professionals is the "minority viewpoint." After a certain point, persistence in pressing that viewpoint can lead to conflict and the marginalization of individuals and their agendas. Success in promoting the health and nutrition agenda within or outside one's organization often may depend on the ability to reframe the issues in terms better understood and accepted by those with greater access to power and resources (e.g., economics or politics) and the ability to form strategic alliances with them. This requires familiarity with the dominant frames, which is far less demanding to acquire than the level of expertise required for detailed analytical work within that frame.

3. In many settings, practitioners are in a position to evaluate or respond to proposals, situation assessments, or evaluations produced by practitioners in the same or different institutions. In most cases, the work of others will employ limited analytical frames or selective elements within a given form. For instance, it may emphasize technical or economic frame but reflect little or no organizational or political frame, or it may include certain elements of technical frame but omit others (e.g., by emphasizing a high regression coefficient but overlooking the low prevalence or population-attributable risk). Familiarity with multiple analytical frames will permit practitioners to "make sense" of the partial analyses conducted by others (i.e., systematically decipher and analyze the implicit logic, identify gaps, etc.) and provide constructive feedback or critique as appropriate.

4. On many occasions, practitioners confront ethical dilemmas in policy/program design and implementation. Beyond being familiar with social/normative frame, a proper analysis of many ethical situations requires "inputs" from other analytical frames. For instance, weighing the principle of "do no harm" against the principle of "provide humanitarian assistance when needed" in a refugee situation requires some type of prediction concerning the degree of harm and the numbers harmed from a proposed intervention (in various ways)

as well as a projection of the numbers in need and the degree to which they may benefit. It may also require anticipating the behavior of program staff, local elites, and various population groups under different implementation scenarios. These examples illustrate that even when there is a concern for a single policy outcome (providing humanitarian assistance), the ethical/normative analysis might require familiarity with or inputs from multiple analytical frames.

The examples illustrate that familiarity with multiple analytical frames can facilitate a variety of incremental improvements in practice. Often, these improvements do not require a thorough consideration of all six forms or always require high levels of expertise in each. They do require familiarity with applying the various analytical frames to specific cases. In addition, they require that practitioners operating in this mode acquire certain skills, dispositions, or working styles, including the ability to recognize that one's own view of "the problem" and what "ought to be done" is shaped by one's own professional development, values, and beliefs combined with the ability to entertain alternative views of the problem and potential solutions; the ability to decide which forms of analysis are needed in a given situation; the ability to acquire and maintain working relationships with those who can assist with various forms of analysis; and recognition of the limits of one's own ability in conducting various forms of analysis. These last skills are particularly important in institutional settings where disciplinary or topical expertise is sharply delineated and defended.

Apart from these skills, practitioners operating in this mode often will face severe difficulties acquiring or accessing the relevant information required by different analytical frames. This may be because information is highly fragmented across different institutions (e.g., academic departments or government units), it is not in the form required (e.g., statistical information), there is little incentive or support to produce it in the form required, or it does not exist at all. It may be comforting to note that this situation is the rule rather than the exception in most high-level policymaking situations (e.g., expert committees) but does not invalidate the need to consider the issue from multiple perspectives. It does highlight the need for more explicit linkages between research and the informational needs for policymaking. Some suggestions are provided in the next section.

### 34.3.2  *Implications for Research*

The recognition that six analytical frames are relevant to the development and implementation of health and nutrition policy has broad implications for future applied research. In many cases, the relevant perspectives, theories, and methods already exist in other disciplines (e.g., economics, policy sciences, organizational behavior, ethics, anthropology, sociology), and the challenge is to apply them to the types of situations most commonly encountered in international health and nutrition. Without attempting to be exhaustive, some examples follow:

1. *Technical frame:* For reasons provided, the information most urgently needed in policymaking relates to comparative risk assessment (knowledge of causes, dose–response relations, exposures, and integrative measures), comparative effectiveness and costs, and unintended consequences (to support analysis of risk-risk tradeoffs). This requires continued research in specialized areas (e.g., specific diseases, nutrients, special subpopulations, and with various intervention types) but using methods explicitly designed

to permit comparative analyses at a later date. Given the importance of context (social, ecological, institutional), much of this work would need to be conducted in multiple and contrasting settings.

2. *Economic frame:* The use of economic frame in health and nutrition policy analysis would be facilitated by three types of research. The first involves the application of existing economic methods to health and nutrition concerns, for instance, to estimate marginal propensities of various subpopulations to "consume" foods, nutrients, and health/education services. These estimates are fundamental to many types of policy analyses. A second type involves the application of existing methods to the evaluation of the impacts of policies and programs in diverse sectors (health, agriculture, food, economic and trade policy, decentralization). This type of research is highly relevant to all countries because of the combined influence of changes in international trade, domestic policies, and forms of governance. The third, and arguably most important type, is to use health and nutrition concerns as empirical cases for developing methods for the explicit integration of equity and other social/normative considerations into economics-based policy analysis. Ideally, this would take place as part of the first two types of research noted and would build on the clear and growing concern for the externalities (environmental, labor, human rights, and other social concerns) associated with trade liberalization.

3. *Social/normative:* In addition to the integration of social/normative considerations with economic analysis noted, the ability to incorporate normative concerns into policy discussions and analysis could be greatly enhanced by the development and application of methods for (1) documenting and making visible the "normative sentiments" of various stakeholders in specific policy situations (including, among others, analysts, managers, policymakers, the affected populations, and the public at large); (2) incorporating these into policy discussions and analyses; and (3) evaluating the effects of these methods on the views and decision propensities of various stakeholders as well as on policy decisions themselves.

4. *Political:* As noted in the sole volume on the subject [44], there has been little systematic study of the role of political strategies and processes on policy decisions and outcomes with respect to food and nutrition in developing countries. The subject has received somewhat more attention in developed countries in recent years [57–61] and has been extensively studied in other policy domains, such as agriculture, environment, economics, and planning. Given the nascent stage of this research in developing countries, two types of applied research might be most useful: The first is a systematic and comparative analysis of purposely chosen cases for retrospective analysis. Second is the initiation of prospective studies of the policy process in "real time" using methods and approaches from the action research tradition that involve regular interviews, analysis, and reflection by and with various practitioners and policy participants. The latter approach is most likely to provide practical and useful insights, especially if conducted in tandem with purposeful and innovative methods for improving the policy process.

5. *Organizational:* Similar to the situation with political frame, organizational issues have received surprisingly little systematic study in health and nutrition considering the pervasiveness of these concerns in everyday practice. A combination of retrospective and prospective studies appears warranted, as noted for the political frame. The present case has the added advantage that many features of health and nutrition programs may be under the more direct control of program staff (e.g., training, supervision, communications, incentives) and thus more amenable to experimental study.

6. *Legal:* Two types of studies might be particularly useful in the legal realm. The first is retrospective study of how and why some countries have adopted particular laws related to health and nutrition (e.g., maternity leave, food fortification). These studies may provide guidance for practitioners in other countries concerning strategy as well as choice of issues. The second type is retrospective or prospective study of the consequences of laws once adopted. Laws, as with other policy instruments, not only may vary in their effectiveness with respect to stated goals but also may create a variety of unintended consequences. For instance, laws mandating maternity leave may have little effect if they are not enforced and may have the unintended effect of inducing discriminatory hiring against women (depending on the existence and enforcement of laws against that practice). There is a tendency, particularly pronounced in the legal realm, to declare victory with the passage of seemingly positive laws without actually conducting follow-up studies.

7. *Multiple/integrative:* The existence of several analytical frames and the goal of applying multiple forms to improve the effectiveness and appropriateness of policy raise several issues for research. First would be documentation of the analytical frames actually applied by current health and nutrition practitioners in various settings and the quality with which they are applied. This would serve to confirm or disconfirm the notion that "partial policy analyses" are the norm, and that the blind spots are a significant concern. Second would be the development and evaluation of methods and procedures for applying multiple forms in specific policy situations. Some of these may involve methods for use by individual analysts, while others might involve the interaction of diverse stakeholders as part of analysis or deliberation. Some examples have been noted in relation to specific analytical frames, but a much larger set of methods could be developed and evaluated. Third, in addition to "process evaluation" of these methods, it would be desirable to study the effects of these methods on effectiveness and appropriateness to assess whether the results are worth the added effort.

Even without being exhaustive, the above examples highlight the diverse nature of the research required to support "effective and appropriate" policy as defined here and its distinctiveness from the current research topics in international health and nutrition. Two of the preconditions for this to occur are that funding agencies would value and fund these types of research, and health and nutrition researchers will collaborate with specialists in other analytical frames in conducting the research. Some positive signs that this can occur are provided by the fact that the World Bank and the United Nations International Children's Emergency Fund (UNICEF) initiated an assessment of the progress these agencies have made in promoting nutrition policy in selected countries and have employed theories and methods from outside the health and nutrition fields in doing so [62].

### 34.3.3 *Implications for Training*

The recognition of multiple analytical frames as relevant to health and nutrition policy may, at first glance, appear to require sweeping and unrealistic changes in the training of researchers and practitioners. In reality, the use of the following strategies may be effective and feasible in improving research and practice. Additional suggestions for training have been published elsewhere [63, 64].

1. *Create, broaden, and apply policy subspecialities in health and nutrition:* The recognition of multiple analytical frames does not require sweeping revisions in the training of

all health and nutrition professionals. Rather, it could be accomplished by ensuring that opportunities for specialized training in health and nutrition policy exist at appropriate institutions, that the curriculum cover a breadth of theoretical and methodological perspectives, and that the training includes opportunities to integrate multiple analytical frames in specific case studies. At present, a health and nutrition "policy specialization" is available at relatively few sites and often is not designed with the notion of multiple frames and integration in mind.

2. *Distinguish familiarity, competence, and expertise:* A pyramid based on these three levels of mastery (with expertise at the top) is a valuable asset in curriculum planning. In the present context, it can guide decisions concerning those areas in which health/nutrition policy specialists should obtain a high level of expertise (e.g., technical aspects of health or nutrition) and those in which they may need competence (e.g., economics and organizational behavior) or familiarity (e.g., other analytical frames and subject matter). This pyramid also can be used to ensure that health and nutrition specialists *not* in the policy track do receive some familiarity-level exposure to other analytical frames and an appreciation of their role in future research and practice.

3. *Lifelong learning:* The goal of integrating multiple forms of frame should anticipate the need and opportunity for lifelong learning to occur, such that knowledge and skills in integration will be improved during one's career and need not be a "finished product" at graduation.

4. *Plan to collaborate:* If the expectation is that researchers and practitioners will seek out and collaborate with specialists in other disciplines, then principles 2 and 3 are more easily justified. By the same token, development of a broad-based specialty in health and nutrition policy is more feasible if undertaken as a collaborative effort with faculty from diverse disciplines at the training institutions.

5. *Develop and share case study materials, research sites, and internships:* Successful training of integrative policy specialists requires repeated experiences in applying different analytical frames to case studies as part of classroom instruction, as part of thesis research, and as part of postgraduate internships. At present, the case study materials do not exist and, given the effort required to develop them, should be shared among institutions. Research sites should be chosen based on the availability of appropriate project or institutional opportunities, but an organized network of internships and training institutions would facilitate practical training.

## 34.4   CONCLUSIONS

This chapter described a broader view of health and nutrition policy than that prevalent in our field at present. The justification for doing so is based on three considerations: First, the development and implementation of sound public policy requires a concern for multiple and often competing goals and consideration of far more than the technical frame emphasized in our training. Extensive bodies of theory and experience exist in other fields to assist in broadening our perspectives and approaches. Second, the use of relatively narrow research foci (based on individual diseases, nutrients, and population groups) does not foster sound public policy analysis related to health and nutrition and fails to generate the data most needed for sound policy analysis. Third, the use of relatively narrow research foci and technical frame, while consistent with disciplinary specialization and "discovery research," often detracts from the goals of health and nutrition policy by diffusing and fragmenting political resources within the health and nutrition community and interfering with the ability to form alliances with other policy communities. Some of the actions described in this chapter may help achieve the goals of public health and public nutrition.

## REFERENCES

1. Dunn WN. Public policy analysis: an introduction. Englewood Cliffs, NJ: Prentice-Hall, 1994.
2. Parsons W. Public policy: an introduction to the theory and practice of policy analysis. Northampton, MA: Elgar, 1995.
3. Clark T. The policy process: a practical guide for natural resource professionals. New Haven, CT: Yale University Press, 2002.
4. Majone G. Evidence, argument and persuasion in the policy process. New Haven, CT: Yale University Press, 1989.
5. National Research Council. Understanding risk: informing decisions in a democratic society. Washington, DC: National Academy, 1996.
6. Rogers JM. The impact of policy analysis. Pittsburgh: University of Pittsburgh Press, 1998.
7. Stone D. Policy paradox: the art of political decision making. New York: Norton, 2002.
8. Pelletier DL, Frongillo EA, Schroeder DG, Habicht JP. A methodology for estimating the contribution of malnutrition to child mortality in developing countries. J Nutr 1994;124(suppl):2106–2122.
9. Pelletier DL, Frongillo EA, Schroeder DG, Habicht JP. The effects of malnutrition on child mortality in developing countries. Bull World Health Organ 1995;73:443–448.
10. World Health Organization. Burden of Disease Project. Available at: http://www.who.int/ healthinfo/ bodproject/en/index.html.
11. Chen L, Chowdhury A, Huffman SL. Anthropometric assessment of energy-protein malnutrition and subsequent risk of mortality among preschool-aged children. Am J Clin Nutr 1980;33:1836–1845.
12. Bairagi R. On validity of some anthropometric indicators as predictors of mortality. Am J Clin Nutr 1981;34:2592–2594.
13. Trowbridge FL, Sommer A. Nutritional anthropometry and mortality risk. Am J Clin Nutr 1981;34: 2591–2592.
14. Breyer S. Breaking the vicious cycle: toward effective risk regulation. Cambridge, MA: Harvard University Press, 1993.
15. Davies JC. Comparing environmental risks: tools for setting government priorities. Washington, DC: Resources for the Future, 1996.
16. Victora CG, Kirkwood BR, Black RE, Rogers S, Sazawal S, Campbell H, Grove S. Potential interventions for the prevention of childhood pneumonia in developing countries: improving nutrition. Am J Clin Nutr 1999;70:309–320.
17. Jamison DT, Measham AR, Alleyne G, Claeson M, Evans DB, Jha P, Mills A, Musgrove P, eds. Disease control priorities in developing countries. 2nd ed. New York: Oxford University Press, 2006.
18. Caulfield LE, Richard SA, Rivera JA, Musgrove P, Black RE. Stunting, wasting, and micronutrient deficiency disorders. In: Disease control priorities in developing countries. 2nd ed. Jamison DT, Measham AR, Alleyne G, Claeson M, Evans DB, Jha P, Mills A, Musgrove P, eds. New York: Oxford University Press, 2006.
19. Graham JD, Wiener JB, eds. Risk versus risk: tradeoffs in protecting health and the environment. Cambridge, MA: Harvard University Press, 1995.
20. Rhoads SE. The economist's view of the world: government, markets and public policy. Cambridge, UK: Cambridge University Press, 1985.
21. Cohen DR, Henderson JB. Health, prevention and economics. Oxford, UK: Oxford University Press, 1988.
22. Boardman AE, Greenberg DH, Vining AR, Weimer DL. Cost–benefit analysis: concepts and practice. Upper Saddle River, NJ: Prentice-Hall, 1996.
23. Jonsson U. The global embarrassment of malnutrition and the role of nutrition engineers. Am J Clin Nutr 1993;58:579–580.

24. Fischer F. Technocracy and the politics of expertise. Newbury Park, CA: Sage, 1990.
25. Kuttner R. Everything for sale: the virtues and limits of markets. Chicago: University of Chicago Press, 1999.
26. Gillroy JM, Wade M, eds. The moral dimensions of public policy choice. Pittsburgh: University of Pittsburgh Press, 1992.
27. Reder MW. Economics: The culture of a controversial science. Chicago: University of Chicago Press, 1999.
28. Kuhn T. The structure of scientific revolutions. Chicago: University of Chicago Press, 1962.
29. Hammond KR. Human judgment and social policy: incredible uncertainty, Inevitable error, unavoidable injustice. New York: Oxford University Press, 1996.
30. Burns TR, Flam H. The shaping of social organization: social rule system theory with applications. Newbury Park, CA: Sage, 1987.
31. De Leon P. Democracy and the policy sciences. Albany: State University of New York Press, 1997.
32. Renn O, Webler T, Wiedemann P. Fairness and competence in citizen participation: evaluating models for environmental discourse. Dordrecht: Kluwer Academic, 1995.
33. Chambers R. Challenging the professions. Frontiers for rural development. London: Intermediate Technology, 1994.
34. Walzer N, ed. Community strategic visioning programs. Westport, CT: Praeger, 1996.
35. Skocpol T, Fiorina MP. Civic engagement in American democracy. Washington, DC: Brookings Institution, 1999.
36. Etzioni A. The spirit of community: the reinvention of American society. New York: Simon and Schuster, 1993.
37. Zajac EE. Political economy of fairness. Cambridge, MA: MIT Press, 1996.
38. Ellis RD. Just results: ethical foundations for policy analysis. Washington, DC: Georgetown University Press, 1998.
39. Jasanoff S. The fifth branch: science advisers as policymakers. Cambridge, MA: Harvard University Press, 1990.
40. Barker A, Peters BG, eds. The politics of expert advice: creating, using and manipulating scientific knowledge for public policy. Pittsburgh: University of Pittsburgh Press, 1993.
41. Chambers R. Whose reality counts?: Putting the first last. London: Intermediate Technology, 1997.
42. Kingdom JW. Agendas, alternatives, and public policies. New York: Harper Collins College, 1995.
43. Howlett M, Ramesh M. Studying public policy: policy cycles and policy subsystems. Toronto: Oxford University Press, 1995.
44. Pinstrup-Andersen P, ed. The political economy of food and nutrition policy. Baltimore, MD: Johns Hopkins University Press, 1993.
45. Roberts NC, King PJ. Transforming public policy: dynamics of policy entrepreneurship and innovation. San Francisco: Jossey-Bass, 1996.
46. Rochefort DA, Cobb RW, eds. The politics of problem definition: shaping the policy agenda. Lawrence: University Press of Kansas, 1994.
47. Cobb RW, Ross MH, eds. Cultural strategies of agenda denial: avoidance, attack, and redefinition. Lawrence: University Press of Kansas, 1997.
48. Palumbo DJ, Calista DJ. Implementation and the policy process: opening the black box. Westport, CT: Greenwood, 1990.
49. Wilson JQ. Bureaucracy: what government agencies do and why they do it. New York: Basic (Perseus Books Group), 1989.
50. Haass RN. The bureaucratic entrepreneur: how to be effective in any unruly organization. Washington, DC: Brookings Institution Press, 1999.
51. Heaver R. Bureaucratic politics and incentives in the management of rural development. Washington, DC: World Bank, 1982. World Bank Staff Working Papers, No. 537.
52. World Bank. Tools for institutional, political and social analysis of policy reform. Washington, DC: World Bank, 2007.
53. Eide A, Oshaug A, Eide WB. Food security and the right to food in international law and development. Transnatl Law Contemp Probl 1991;1(2):416–467.
54. Brewer GD, De Leon P. The foundations of policy analysis. Chicago: Dorsey, 1983.

55. Forester J. Critical theory, public policy, and planning practice: toward a critical pragmatism. Albany: State University of New York Press, 1993.

56. Schneider AL, Ingram H. Policy design for democracy. Lawrence: University Press of Kansas, 1997.

57. Milio N. Nutrition policy for food-rich countries: a strategic analysis. Baltimore, MD: Johns Hopkins University Press, 1990.

58. Sims L. The politics of fat: food and nutrition policy in America. Armonk, NY: Sharpe, 1998.

59. Mills M. The politics of dietary change. Brookfield, VT: Dartmouth, 1992.

60. Burnett J, Oddy DJ, eds. The origins and development of food policies in Europe. London: Leicester University Press, 1994.

61. Kjaerenes U, Holm L, Ekstrom M, Furst EL, Prattala R, eds. Regulating markets, regulating people: on food and nutrition policy. Oslo: Novus, 1993.

62. Gillespie S, McLachlan M, Shrimpton R, eds. Combating malnutrition: time to act. Washington, DC: World Bank, Health, Nutrition and Population Series, Human Development Network, 2003.

63. Scrimshaw N, ed. Special issue on institution building for research and advanced training. Food Nutr Bull 1997;18:103–178.

64. Scrimshaw N, ed. Special issue on public nutrition. Food Nutr Bull 1999;30:279–343.

65. United Nations International Children's Emergency Fund. Strategy for improved nutrition of children and women in developing countries. A UNICEF policy review. New York: United Nations International Children's Emergency Fund, 1990.

# Index

# About the Editors

Dr. Richard D. Semba is the W. Richard Green Professor of Ophthalmology at the Johns Hopkins University School of Medicine. He received his BS in Biology from Yale University, MA in Latin American Studies, and MD from Stanford University, and an MPH degree from the Johns Hopkins University. Dr. Semba has been a faculty member at Johns Hopkins since 1987. Since the 1980s, Dr. Semba has been involved in nutrition research in collaboration with colleagues in South Asia, Southeast Asia, and sub-Saharan Africa. He has been Principal Investigator of eight different investigator-initiated (R01) grants from the National Institutes of Health. Dr. Semba is author of *Handbook of Nutrition and Ophthalmology* (Humana Press, 2007) and is author or coauthor on more than 200 peer-reviewed scientific publications and more than 70 review papers and book chapters. He is currently preparing a book on the history of vitamin A.

Dr. Martin W. Bloem is Chief for Nutrition and HIV/AIDS Policy, United Nations World Food Programme, in Rome, Italy. He holds a medical degree from the University of Utrecht and a doctorate from the University of Maastricht and has joint faculty appointments at both Johns Hopkins University and Tufts University. Dr. Bloem has had more than two decades of experience in nutrition research and policy. He was the Senior Vice President Chief Medical Officer of Helen Keller International prior to his appointment at the World Food Programme. Dr. Bloem has devoted his career to improving the effectiveness of public health and nutrition programs through applied research. Dr. Bloem has participated in task forces convened by many organizations, including international nongovernmental organizations, the UN Standing Committee on Nutrition (SCN), the United Nations International Children's Emergency Fund (UNICEF), the United States Agency for International Development (USAID), and the World Health Organization (WHO).

# About the Series Editor

 Dr. Adrianne Bendich is Clinical Director of Calcium Research at GlaxoSmithKline Consumer Healthcare, where she is responsible for leading the innovation and medical programs in support of several leading consumer brands including TUMS and Os-Cal. Dr. Bendich has primary responsibility for the coordination of GSK's support for the Women's Health Initiative (WHI) intervention study. Prior to joining GlaxoSmithKline, Dr. Bendich was at Roche Vitamins Inc., and was involved with the groundbreaking clinical studies proving that folic acid-containing multivitamins significantly reduce major classes of birth defects. Dr. Bendich has co-authored more than 100 major clinical research studies in the area of preventive nutrition. Dr. Bendich is recognized as a leading authority on antioxidants, nutrition and bone health, immunity, and pregnancy outcomes, vitamin safety, and the cost-effectiveness of vitamin/mineral supplementation.

In addition to serving as Series Editor for Humana Press and initiating the development of the 20 currently published books in the *Nutrition and Health*™ series, Dr. Bendich is the editor of 11 books, including *Preventive Nutrition: The Comprehensive Guide for Health Professionals.* She also serves as Associate Editor for *Nutrition: The International Journal of Applied and Basic Nutritional Sciences,* and Dr. Bendich is on the Editorial Board of the *Journal of Women's Health and Gender-Based Medicine,* as well as a past member of the Board of Directors of the American College of Nutrition. Dr. Bendich also serves on the Program Advisory Committee for Helen Keller International.

Dr. Bendich was the recipient of the Roche Research Award, was a Tribute to Women and Industry Awardee, and a recipient of the Burroughs Wellcome Visiting Professorship in Basic Medical Sciences, 2000–2001. Dr. Bendich holds academic appointments as Adjunct Professor in the Department of Preventive Medicine and Community Health at UMDNJ, Institute of Nutrition, Columbia University P&S, and Adjunct Research Professor, Rutgers University, Newark Campus. She is listed in *Who's Who in American Women.*